ALSO BY DEIRDRE BAIR

SAMUEL BECKETT: A Biography

Simone
de Beauvoir

A BIOGRAPHY

DEIRDRE BAIR

SUMMIT BOOKS
NEW YORK · LONDON · TORONTO · SYDNEY · TOKYO · SINGAPORE

SUMMIT BOOKS
Simon & Schuster Building
Rockefeller Center
1230 Avenue of the Americas
New York, New York 10020

Designed by Edith Fowler
Manufactured in the United States of America

10 9 8 7 6 5 4 3 2 1

Library of Congress Cataloging in Publication Data
Bair, Deirdre.
    Simone de Beauvoir : a biography / by Deirdre
Bair.
        p. cm.
    Includes bibliographical references.
    1. Beauvoir, Simone de, 1908–   —Biography.
2. Authors, French—20th century—Biography.
3. Feminists—France—Biography.   I. Title.
PQ2603.E362Z59   1990
848'.91409—dc20
[B]   89-22029
                                              CIP
ISBN 0-671-60681-6

Contents

	Acknowledgments	7
	Introduction	11
1	The Family Bertrand de Beauvoir	21
2	My Sister, My Accomplice	33
3	When the Trouble Really Started	46
4	The Girl with a Man's Brain	57
5	The Young Writer	64
6	ZaZa	72
7	Eighteen, and in Love with Love	88
8	"A High-minded Little Bourgeois"	102
9	The Young Girl Who Worked Too Much	121
10	Castor	136
11	On Her Paris Honeymoon	154
12	Learning to Be Alone Again	168
13	Rouen	179
14	Paris	197
15	What Will Happen Tomorrow?	212
16	When Life Goes Slightly Adrift	224
17	To Stay and Try to Survive	233
18	Socialism and Liberty	245
19	The Promise of the Future	262
20	How to Make a Living	277
21	Flinging Oneself on the Future	289
22	Always Something to Say	297
23	Moving in Some Sort of Blur	313
24	The Most Exotic Thing	327
25	A Beautiful, Corny Love Story	342
26	The High Priestess of Existentialism	355
27	The Crocodile Is the Frog's Destiny	365

28	A Book About Women	379
29	All the Right Enemies	396
30	"Not Exactly Our Story, but . . ."	412
31	A $10 Book by an Unknown Frenchwoman	429
32	When "The Dream I Dreamed" Came True	440
33	"The Place That Goncourt Bought"	451
34	"My Life . . . This Curious Object"	459
35	Politics and Feminism	471
36	November Was a Long Sad Month	483
37	The Friendships of Women	497
38	"Something's Going to Happen"	514
39	"We Have Lived Through Some Exhilarating Times"	530
40	Women's Battles	543
41	Between Dread and Hope	558
42	The Last of the 1968 Demonstrations	574
43	Cleaning Up Loose Ends	591
44	"Women, You Owe Everything to Her!"	605
	Notes	619
	Index	681

Acknowledgments

WHEN A BOOK takes as long to write as this one has taken, an author incurs debts of gratitude to many people. One of the most pleasant aspects in preparing the manuscript for publication is the opportunity to thank them all within its pages.

Without Simone de Beauvoir, there would have been no book: I salute her memory. She and her family, friends and professional associates offered hospitality and shared both memories and private archives. I wish to thank all those who granted me interviews and made their papers available to me, but especially Sylvie le Bon de Beauvoir, Hélène de Beauvoir and Lionel de Roulet, Magdeleine Mantis de Bisschop, Count Raoul and Countess Agnès de Lavalette and their daughter Isabel, Etienne and Jeanne de Beauvoir Dauriac and Brigitte and Xavier Lavaud. Also, Colette Audry, Olga and Jacques-Laurent Bost, Claude Courchay, Robert Gallimard, John and Stépha Gerassi, Nan Graham, Mary Guggenheim, Colette and Francis Jeanson, Claude Lanzmann, Ivan Moffatt, Geraldine Pardo, J.-B. Pontalis, Jean Pouillon, William Targ and Peter and Helen P. Wenck.

Many scholars contributed to my understanding of Simone de Beauvoir's life and work, and I wish particularly to thank Hazel Barnes, Elsa Parshley Brown, Richard Centing, Blanche Weisen Cook, Michelle Coquillat, Isabelle de Courtivron, Carmen Diana Deere, Lauren Pringle Delavars, Françoise D'Eaubonne, Bettina Drew, Virginia Fichera, Geneviève Fraisse, Judith Friedlander, Françoise Gaill, Carolyn Grassi, Trudier Harris, Graciela Hierro, Serge Julienne-Caffié, Dorothy Kaufmann, Leonie Kramer, Betty Jean Lifton, Nancy MacKnight, Marcelle Marini, Elaine Marks, Karen Offen, Irène Pagès, Françoise Pasquier, Marie-Claire Pasquier, Yolanda Astarita Patterson, Oreste Pucciani, Yvette Roudy, Peggy Reeves Sanday, Margaret A. Simons, Catharine R. Stimpson, Robert V. Stone, Susan R. Suleiman, Robert Tibbets, Dilys Winegrad, Stanley Weintraub and Ewa Zadrzynska.

Portions of this book were written while I was a fellow of the Mary Ingraham Bunting Foundation of Radcliffe College, the John Simon

Guggenheim Memorial Foundation, and the Rockefeller Foundation Humanities Fellowship Program. I thank them all for their support of my scholarship. I also wish to thank Dr. Eliot Stellar and the faculty research group that supported a portion of the research, and Dr. Gerald J. Porter for his friendship and technical assistance with the IBM-Threshold project.

I owe much to Aileen Ward, for inviting me to participate in the Biography Seminar first at New York Institute for the Humanities and then at New York University, and also for her friendship and professional generosity. The members of the Biography Seminar listened to my ideas throughout the long process of gestation, read portions of the manuscript as they appeared, and gave me stringent criticism, inciteful commentary and enthusiastic support. Mary Perot Nichols has always been this book's staunchest advocate, and I thank her for her professional assistance at several key instances and her unflagging supportive friendship. Vartan A. Gregorian believed in this book from the beginning and I have benefited from his wise counsel. I thank Carl D. Brandt for introducing me to Richard P. McDonough, to whom I owe that electric moment when Simone de Beauvoir's name was pronounced. Judith Rossner was a great friend to this book at a crucial time in its development; if a book can have a godmother, she is it.

My friends sustained me, and I thank Mali Bé-Lé, Laura Burns, Lawrence Coan, Diana Cavallo and Carl Hagedorn, Betty Starr Cummin, Pamela F. Emory, Ellen Golub, Criswell C. Gonzales, Ingalil and Norman Hjelm, Winifred S. Pasternack, and Robin and James Walter. Also, Rose Marie Piccolo and the Bagettes: Myra Chanin, Sara Jordan, Carolyn Moody and Carol Rauch, who all helped me face the music and dance. Elaine Markson and her associates, Geri Thoma, Sally Wofford, Lilly Kosovic, Lisa Callamaro and C. J. Hall, were unfailing in their enthusiasm and support. This book has benefited much from James Silberman's astuteness and Ileene Smith's editorial expertise; they have truly been its better makers. Ileene and I are both grateful for Nathaniel Jacob Sobel's good-natured cooperation throughout the long process of turning manuscript into book. We were all ably aided by Alane Mason, whom I thank especially, and Vera Schneider, who copyedited it with infinite patience and care. Early research assistance, the best that one can have, came from Juliette Campbell, Mary Lou Decossaux, Dominic di Bernardi, Marie-Noelle Domke and Scott Turner.

I have thought about where and how best, in this list of acknowledgments, to thank the people who lived with this book on a daily basis, but everything seems inadequate to describe how much they have helped. So I shall simply thank my husband Von, my children, Vonn Scott and Katney, and B., M., M., and R., and beg them to know how much I cherish all they have given me. Others in my family contributed much, and I thank Linda and John Rankin, Niko Courtelis, Catherine Montecarlo, Armand Bartolotta, Helen Bartolotta and Judith and Vincent J. Bartolotta, Jr. And, for a lifetime of support and affection, I thank the late Eugene L. Barto-lotta, who started everything when he taught me to spell Constantinople.

One of the worst fears for a writer is that the name of someone who has been generous with assistance during the writing of a book will inadvertently be omitted from mention within its pages. I am sure there are some whom I have not listed here, and to them I apologize and beg them to believe that I did—do—value their contribution.

D.B.B.

Introduction

THE FIRST TIME I thought of Simone de Beauvoir as someone other than the woman who wrote *The Second Sex* was in 1974. I was sitting in a Paris café with a friend who was working on a book with Jean-Paul Sartre. "You should have lunch with us today," he said. "Simone de Beauvoir will be there and she likes to talk to American women."

The idea was appealing, but I was then writing about Samuel Beckett, with whom I had an appointment that day. "No, thanks," I said regretfully, "I must see Beckett at two, he's a stickler for punctuality, and I don't dare to be late."

So I did not meet Simone de Beauvoir then, and in the next few years, as I wrote the biography of Beckett, she remained only the woman who wrote *The Second Sex* and was therefore largely responsible (in my mind at least) for many of the opportunities that were available to women of my generation. Maybe that was why I bought her other books and studied them so intently whenever I was in Paris to do research about Beckett (my ostensible reason was to improve my French), perhaps that was why much of her writing made so deep an impression that I actually inserted some of it into the Beckett book and used it frequently in my academic articles and essays.

Still, it did not occur to me that she was someone I wanted to write about, until 1980, when I found myself telling an editor who was interested in my work how I, who had never wanted to write biography in the first place, now wanted very much to write another one. I told him of the curious things that had happened since the Beckett book was published, of the persons who volunteered themselves as my next subject and of the megalomaniacal fantasies of some of them, with their peremptory pronouncements that they would dictate their own version of their lives and all I would have to do was simply write it all down. I told him about the literary executor who announced his intention "to anoint" me to write "a latter-day saint's life" of the despicable character he represented.

We laughed at these stories which made such amusing lunchtime chatter, but the conversation grew serious when I told him I had just declined to write the biography of a recently dead woman writer because I found her work so uninteresting that I had no interest in the life that produced it. In declining to write that book, however, I had come to an important realization: namely, that I wanted to write a biography of a woman, but one whose professional life was intellectually stimulating to me and whose personal life was satisfying to her—if such a rare creature existed. I suppose I was searching for a woman to write about who had made a success of both life and work, since I and so many of my friends were having difficulty integrating satisfying work into our relationships. I wanted to know whether there might be a contemporary woman whose life would be of interest to both men and women in this last part of our century, when the only thing that seems at all certain is that goals, needs and roles for both are undefined and in flux.

The editor and I talked about my ideas at length, and then we began to toss out names, playfully at first until, suddenly, one of us (to this day we are not sure who) pronounced the name of Simone de Beauvoir. For me, it was something like those comic-strip characters who suddenly have light bulbs flashing as the word "Eureka!" explodes above their heads.

That was June 1980. I was supposed to write something else that summer, but instead I spent it rereading Beauvoir's novels and memoirs, reading her only play, educating myself in her philosophy, and enjoying her travel writings for the first time. By September, I knew that I wanted to write her biography, but still the idea seemed presumptuous. Would I end up simply rehashing her own version of her life? Were there any surprises or secrets she had not told that I might not want to tell, either, should I discover them through my research? If so, what would this do to my concept of objective biography as a form of scholarship in literary and intellectual history? My agreement with Samuel Beckett had been, in his words, that he would "neither help nor hinder" me. By this he meant that I could use any materials my research led to, that his relatives and friends were free to cooperate with me or not as they wished, and that he would grant interviews in which he would respond to my queries but would not necessarily volunteer information. He agreed not to influence the content or direction of my writing and, most important, to do nothing to interfere with or impede publication. It was the ideal situation, but, as it was my first biography, I did not know it at the time.

Now, as I considered writing about Simone de Beauvoir, I wondered whether she, who had written her own four volumes of autobiographical memoir, would even consent to talk to me, or would she refuse to have anything to do with the proposed book? Would she tell me to go my own way and write whatever I wanted, as one of my friends had recently been told by someone he wanted very much to write about? Or, as another friend had just been told, would she warn me not to write a word about her unless I wished to face legal consequences?

Despite these real and imagined concerns, Simone de Beauvoir fascinated me. How could that well-brought-up little Catholic girl have found the courage to become the fearless, free-spirited adult, who gave as good as she got in the often vicious arena of Paris intellectualism? And as for *The Second Sex*, from what place within her creative consciousness had that book come? These were my two most immediate questions; the list I made then is one it took me more than seven years to answer.

In late October 1980, I wrote a letter to Simone de Beauvoir, sending with it a copy of the French translation of my Beckett biography. "It is dangerous, I know, to send the last book to the next subject," I wrote, "but you had better see at once the kind of work I propose to do before you even agree to meet me."

Her reply was swift. She had already read the book on the recommendation of her friend Olga Bost, who admired Beckett's plays. Simone de Beauvoir said she would welcome the chance to talk about her life, because no one before me had proposed to write about *all* her work. Nowadays, she continued, only women wanted to write about her, and they were interested only in her feminism. This was very important to her, of course, but she did so want people to remember her as a writer of many different genres.

I went to Paris in January 1981 to meet her for the first time. I phoned on her seventy-third birthday, January 9, expecting that she would offer an appointment sometime in the next few days. Instead, she asked me to come that afternoon at four. This presented a quandary: should I give her birthday greetings or pretend it was just another day? Should I bring a small token present? I worried all day long because I thought my spoken French was inadequate for serious conversation; I had already stammered when we spoke on the telephone, and she had seemed brusque and unsympathetic as I searched for words and phrases. Later I realized that this was her normal speaking voice, but at the time it was enough to induce panic. I solved the problem by buying several bunches of yellow tulips and acacia at the Métro station, bundling them hastily together and thrusting them at her when she opened the door. This was the start of a custom I followed at each of our first meetings throughout the next five years.

That first meeting followed a ritualized pattern which characterized every subsequent one. We always met at 4 P.M., and, since she told me that she expected promptness, I was always punctual. Each time she opened the door, I was struck by how short she was, because her photos gave the impression of a much taller woman. Sartre died before I ever began to write about Beauvoir, and I had never seen them together when he was alive, so each time I saw her I realized how tiny he must have been to be the shorter of the two.

After pleasantries, each time saying four o'clock was a good hour to relax, she offered a drink, happy that we both took a little scotch without water or ice. Slowly and carefully, she would measure exactly one ounce into a battered pewter jigger, then pour it with equal care into a large Mexican glass tumbler. That done, we chatted a bit. She would ask what I had written or whom I had interviewed since we last met. I would ask what she had done. Then she would take out her calendar to arrange our subsequent meetings for the duration of my stay in Paris. We tried at first to make these appointments as we went along, but soon discovered that her calendar filled up too fast. I never understood those writers who wrote that since Sartre's death in 1980 Beauvoir seemed at loose ends with nothing to do, because anyone who saw her daily calendar would know how untrue such statements were.

When the scotch had been drunk (there was never the offer of a second drink until the interview was over), we would "get to work," her phrase to describe an activity she relished. The first time I met her, I had assumed it would simply be a get-acquainted session, so I arrived at her flat without notes, questions or tape recorder, and with only a small pocket diary in which to write. She, on the other hand, was ready "to work," because she had already decided that I was the one with whom she would cooperate on her biography. As far as she was concerned, January 9 was as good a day to start as any.

I had been conditioned by my interviews with Samuel Beckett, who refused to let me tape-record and would not even let me take notes in his presence, because he said he often had "conversations" with scholars but never gave "interviews." Without thinking about it, I simply assumed it would be the same with Simone de Beauvoir. Fortunately it was not. She welcomed, indeed insisted upon, the representation of "work." She seemed surprised when I asked to tape-record our conversations, and said yes— "You will need the record of what we say." These sessions did not begin in earnest until a year later, in January 1982, when I had a sabbatical leave. They usually lasted about two hours, but at one of the earliest I asked so many questions that we talked for more than three, and I saw that she was exhausted by the effort. So I learned to judge how much we could discuss in a single session and wrote each question on a single index card. I put the pile of cards on the table in front of us so that she could watch how one pile grew as the other diminished. This way, we both paced ourselves. On the rare occasion I went past the two-hour mark, she would not stop until all of the questions were asked despite my insistence that they could well wait until the next session.

My questions ranged from the intellectual to the introspective to the impertinent. I wanted detailed explications of her political theory, her philosophical perspective and the genesis of her writings. I asked for her definition of the meaning of love, and whether it changed with each of the three men with whom she was publicly involved. Taking to heart the dictum that we must interpret the facts and events of women's lives in new and different ways, I asked how menstruation and menopause affected her writing life. I am grateful that she considered all these questions with equal seriousness and answered them carefully.

Arranging their order before an interview was very serious business for me, and friends who visited my apartment often found me with the cards spread out in what one of them dubbed "intellectual solitaire." I

ordered and reordered them, often getting up in the middle of the night
to change a particular arrangement, waking again to change it back to
what it had been originally. Sometimes in mid-session, when I saw that a
particular order of questioning upset her, made her angry or otherwise
irritated her, I would try inconspicuously to shuffle the cards containing
the remaining questions into the "asked" pile without actually voicing
them.

"What's that you're doing?" she would demand sharply. "You haven't
asked those yet."

"They don't need to be asked—they are only different versions of
some you have already answered."

"Well, ask them anyway. I want to hear them."

I offer this exchange to show several aspects of my working relationship with Simone de Beauvoir. First, her curiosity was so great that even
if she didn't like the direction my questions were heading toward, she
still wanted to know what they were. Second, she was unflinching in her
self-scrutiny and her willingness to subject herself to the scrutiny of others.
If she even suspected that I was trying to spare her in any way, she grew
especially agitated, insisted on facing the issue and would not rest until
she had done so.

At the end of these sessions I was usually the exhausted one, my head
spinning with thoughts and further questions I wanted to commit at once
to paper. She generally leaned back against the brilliantly colored pillows
on her sofa, the Giacometti lamp throwing a rosy glow on her cheeks
flushed pink, most of the time with satisfaction at work well done, occasionally glowing darker because she was angry that I could not be brought
to view a particular idea or characterization as she did. Always, she offered
another scotch, which I accepted only if she did not seem too tired to be
hospitable.

These were the times I remember most, and, frankly, the ones I liked
best. In all honesty, I can't say that these conversations were personal,
because once she determined my marital and maternal status, my educational and professional background, she seldom asked about me. Mostly
we talked about books we had recently read or movies we had seen and
liked.

There were moments that sometimes presented a serious professional
quandary for me. For example, a random remark about the beautiful silver
ring she always wore elicited a long, detailed account of her relationship
with Nelson Algren. It was so poignant that I sat there mesmerized, unwilling to break the mood by asking if I might turn the tape recorder back
on, almost unable to respond to her as a woman and a friend because the
scholarly half of me was mentally taking notes to write down later. I solved
part of my dilemma by always asking her, either at the end of these conversations or at the beginning of the next, if I could use what we had just
said in the book, and she always said yes, certainly, and why hadn't I simply turned the tape recorder back on at the time? But I never did, fearful

of breaking her concentration, of disturbing the emotional intensity of the moment.

I was often in her apartment when the afternoon mail came, and I was usually the one to groan at its bulk—piles of finished books dedicated to her, bound galleys sent in hope of a preface or at least a blurb, American scholars wanting letters of recommendation for promotion and tenure, letters from admirers who wanted her to know how she had influenced their lives, and occasional letters from people who resented her life and work. She had no secretary and answered everything herself. I saw the manuscripts and page proofs of articles for *Les Temps Modernes* over which she pored with meticulous concentration. Sometimes when I spent part of our sessions studying manuscripts or letters too fragile to photocopy, I raised my head to see her totally engrossed in her work, almost oblivious of my presence across from her. Occasionally she would look up and see me, give a reassuring smile and a brisk nod, as if to say, "Isn't this good, isn't it pleasant to be here working on a day like this?"

I remember especially our last afternoon together, March 7, 1986. The sun was out for the first time in many days and it streamed through the windows of the Rue Schoelcher studio. I had been in Paris since early February, summoned by Beauvoir because she was upset with a recently published book about her and was anxious to point out what she believed were errors in it. I had very few questions of my own for her during these twice-weekly sessions because I was deep into the writing of this book and felt that my research was finished. So we talked at some length about the other book, and in quite a few instances I found myself defending some of the statements and interpretations in it. I told Beauvoir that I had coined the term "reconstructed life" to denote what I considered to be her adult reflection on things that had happened to her at an earlier age. I found our discussion of this so fascinating that I said something I had never thought to hear myself say.

I suddenly blurted out that I wanted her to read this book before it was published even though our agreement was that she would have no influence over its final content (she had willingly accepted the same agreement that I had had with Samuel Beckett). I thought it would mark a new kind of biography if we had, within the pages of my book, the autobiographer Beauvoir commenting on the biographer Bair's work, with the biographer sometimes arguing against the autobiographer's memory and interpretation, and with each explaining and defending her particular version of the life. Together we arrived at the same conclusion at the same time: we would have a sort of biographical Hall of Mirrors, an infinity of reflection, an elusive truth in all its varieties. We were so caught up in the excitement of this newly formed and very different kind of collaboration, so buoyed by the conversation and pleased with our decision, that when it was time for me to leave she did something so uncharacteristic we were both taken aback by it. In all our other meetings, we always ended with her walking me to the door and shaking my hand warmly, sometimes putting it between both of hers. This time, tiny woman that she was, she reached out and half embraced me, tall woman that I am, by placing her hands around my upper arms and giving me a brisk shake.

I thought about that embrace a lot in the weeks that followed. I worried about the objectivity I might lose because of this gesture and because of the new shape we had agreed the book should take. I wondered if whether, in the pursuit of new textual form and content, I might have surrendered some of the book's integrity. These worries were short-lived, however, for within the week she entered the hospital for what became her terminal illness, and the textual problem that resulted after her death was quite another matter.

There was, to begin with, the simple task of changing all the verbs to the past tense in the two-thirds of the book then written. It turned out to be much more complicated than that. What had been a living, breathing, feisty argument about life had to be rewritten to correspond to the latter third of the book, a final document punctuated by illness and concluded by death. As I did all this, I could not help but think how she would have enjoyed an abstract and philosophical discussion about the actuality of her life and the eventuality of her death. "My life, this curious object," she called it in her own memoir. Now it was up to me to present it as a coherent, cohesive unity.

However, I tried to write this book without holding prior theory or thesis, and to allow the written life to unfold as she lived it, with all the seeming contradictions and confusions in her thought and expression. My intention is to offer both explanation and definition of her writing life by explaining the historical circumstances of her earliest years, the Belle Epoque, *haut-bourgeois* society into which she was born. Much of this material is foreign to a non-French audience, and, surprisingly, much of it is unknown or unclear to French citizens several generations younger than Beauvoir. All of it is crucial to trace the evolution of her thought, because much of her intellectual identity was formed through the social class into which she was born. I have tried to write a feminist biography and have benefited greatly from the excellent feminist scholarship in many disciplines which I hope my own writing reflects.

I have used Simone de Beauvoir's memoirs as the source of many of the questions I asked her, her family and her friends, but at all times I questioned her chronology and content. I do not accept them flatly, in some cases I correct them, and in every case I use them interpretively. They have freed me from the necessity of following strict biographical chronology, and have allowed me to write instead what I believe is a book of synthesis and analysis. I have chosen to heed critic Peter Conrad's admonition in reviewing Grevel Lindop's biography of Thomas de Quincy:

The subject has made himself a secret, meddlesome sharer in any biography of him. He was a compulsive and confessional autobiographer. . . . Offering to tell the truth, he cautiously avoided telling all of it. . . . He has invented in advance a version of his life which it's his biographer's task not to concur with but to dispute.

In this case, it is not so much a case of disputation as it is of elaboration (filling in some details of important issues she skirts), explanation (how she arrived at personal and intellectual decisions) and occasional correction (she relied only on occasional newspapers and odd jottings in notebooks for many public events; too frequently scholars accept her opinions as statements of fact).

I have had a "secret sharer" of another sort loom large in this biography: Jean-Paul Sartre. I can explain by describing a panel discussion during a conference at Harvard when I and Annie Cohen-Solal, one of Sartre's biographers, spoke about our work. She speaks briefly and succinctly of Beauvoir in her book, whereas in mine I found it impossible to write about Beauvoir without referring to Sartre on almost every page from the time they met until her death in 1986 (not his in 1980). At the conclusion of the question-and-answer period that followed our talks, I could not help but comment to my distinguished audience that every question asked about Sartre concerned his work while all those asked about Beauvoir concerned her personal life. I must admit I was disappointed.

However, there is much intimate personal material in this book which I believe is central rather than gratuitous. I believe that the biography of women should include such information when it contributes to an understanding of the subject's decisions, her choices, and, in the case of a creative woman, her work.

I made one other decision about the form of this book, and that was to keep myself out of it. I came late into Simone de Beauvoir's life and had no role in it other than to have had the extraordinary good fortune to spend a great part of each of six years in conversation with her. I am grateful to have had her support and friendship as well as that of her sister, other family members, friends, and professional colleagues. I have tried to confine my personal observations to the notes, which also contain much information that would impede the flow of the narrative but which I think will be useful to scholars.

We live now in a time when biography is of increasing interest both to the general public and to the scholarly community, when the genre itself provokes as much commentary as the subjects of such inquiry and the books that are written about them. The biographer's methodology is discussed as much as is the life being written. In this book, I have tried to use a methodology that crosses a number of disciplinary boundaries and tries to encompass all of them: it falls somewhere between literary biography (because I discuss each of her works as it appears within the chronology of her life), intellectual history (because hers was a life involved with many of the important political and cultural events of modern France), feminist theory (because of her commitment to the feminist movement during the last twenty years of her life) and oral history (because I have collected the testimonies of Simone de Beauvoir and many persons who knew her during her life).

I want to make one personal observation. I can't count the times that I and others who have written a life are asked, "Do you/did you *like* X?" The next question is usually "Did you identify with X?" or some other variant of "Did you find psychological identity?" or "bonding" or "self-knowledge" or . . . ; you can substitute your own catchphrase here. The question that is never asked, however, is the one that reflects my reason for writing biography, that it is one of my preferred forms of critical inquiry, and that is: how did X's life and work illuminate our cultural and intellectual history; how did X influence the way we think about ourselves and interpret our society; and finally, what can we learn from X's life and work that will be of use to us once we have read his/her biography?

My aim here has been to consider all the disparate aspects of Simone de Beauvoir's life and work which separately make splendid sense but which together are sometimes contradictory and conflicting, what I have called elsewhere a kaleidoscope of image and reality, opinion and fact. I don't believe future societies will be able to ignore Simone de Beauvoir, but the real question will be how to assess her contribution and what use to make of it. I hope this book will be useful in that task.

DEIRDRE BAIR

July 11, 1989
Easton, Connecticut

The Family
Bertrand de Beauvoir

H ER EARLIEST MEMORIES were so closely linked to the color black that, throughout her life, whenever something of her childhood came to mind unbidden she often had the sensation of being smothered in blackness.[1] The first memory, linking black with frustration, was of the barricade created by the stiff fabric of her mother's dress as she attempted to embrace her. The afternoon gloom seemed black in the high-ceilinged rooms where other somberly garbed adults spoke in hushed voices and all the children sat in silence, not daring to call attention to themselves by so much as a whisper. Black was even the color of the hoop she rolled in the Luxembourg Gardens in an isolated dignity far beyond her years, for Simone de Beauvoir was not allowed to speak to other children, let alone play with them, unless they were of the proper social class and her mother had first paid a formal call on theirs. And when she went to the exclusive private school the Cours Désir, she was not allowed to speak to the little girls who were enrolled with her unless this strict formal etiquette had first been followed.

In a society where every child of three was expected to have a personal calling card, Simone de Beauvoir had hers, lavishly engraved on thick white stock with heavy black ink. Before she was four, she knew how to reach into the little black velvet bag she carried in imitation of her mother and to present it as adroitly as any adult when the silver salver was placed before her. This moment offered the only glow in all the blackness, for she did it with such aplomb that she was always praised as a very well-mannered young lady. She learned when very young that precocious behavior brought attention far beyond the ordinary, but she was too young to understand where the boundary between good manners and showing off lay. In a society where excess in any form was frowned upon, she sometimes mortified her mother, while her aunts clucked their disapproval.

This was La France Bourgeoise, into which Simone de Beauvoir was born in Paris on January 9, 1908. It was a world of propriety and "culti-vated distinction";[2] an artificial politeness and taste that regulated every aspect of her family's lives and set them apart from the great body of French society. Rules of conduct and behavior were rigid and inflexible: moderation, conservatism and understatement in all things guided—indeed, dominated—their behavior, both within the family enclave and in the larger social and political world. Membership in this class was determined by criteria such as the way families had initially acquired their wealth, how and where they lived, how they spent their money, how they educated their children, and, most important, how they arranged marriages to per-petuate themselves and their way of life.

Once one was admitted to this rarefied social realm, only the most egregious behavior could cause ostracism or banishment, for families might punish errant members privately, but publicly they saved face. The family Bertrand de Beauvoir (to give the full patronymic) was hard pressed to deal with Simone de Beauvoir's father, who lost his money and thus lost status; in her case, it was impossible to ignore or explain away behavior they considered scandalous, so many simply pretended she was a stranger and not related at all. After her death in 1986, a cousin several generations younger was embarrassed to admit to friends and neighbors in her small village that she was even distantly related to such a shameless flaunter of social convention, the most public sinner in all of France. The family Ber-trand de Beauvoir had been in existence since the twelfth century and did not easily countenance those who broke its almost eight-hundred-year-old code of behavior.

Although Simone de Beauvoir's parents were of the same social class, they were not Parisian but came from families long entrenched in regions at the opposite ends of France: her father, Georges Bertrand de Beauvoir (1878–1941) came from a landowning family in the Limousin region of southwest France; her mother was born Françoise Brasseur to a family with many branches dispersed throughout several of the northeast départe-ments, all engaged in government service and banking. They had been in-troduced to each other at Houlgate, a modest resort on the Normandy coast where well-to-do Catholic families who did not flaunt their wealth and position took their holidays, not only in search of the company of oth-ers like themselves but also to seek prospects for suitable marriage partners for their children.

The family Bertrand de Beauvoir is descended from an illustrious line considered "one of the oldest and most renowned" in the history of France.[3] In modern times, they consider themselves to be "of minor no-bility."[4] Their lineage can be traced to Guillaume de Champeaux, first mentioned in 1100 as a member of the clergy who "deserved to be con-sidered as the luminary of the Latin Church,"[5] was one of the founders of the University of Paris, and was a principal disciple of the abbots Anselm and Abélard.

The many branches of the family Champeaux spread throughout the regions of Champagne and Burgundy, uniting when Marie-Elisabeth de Champeaux (January 21, 1770–?) married her cousin Narcisse Bertrand de Beauvoir (1795–1872).[6] The paternal line of Simone de Beauvoir's immediate family began with their fourth child, Ernest-Narcisse Bertrand de Beauvoir (b. December 7, 1837),[7] who married Léontine Aglaë-Mathilde Wartelle (?–1891), of Arras, Pas-de-Calais, from an equally prosperous northern family. Léontine Wartelle brought to this arranged marriage a dowry that significantly enhanced her husband's inheritance, thus forming the foundation of the modern Beauvoir family's income and social standing.

Simone's father was the second son and third child of Ernest-Narcisse Bertrand de Beauvoir (1837–1929), the ancestor the family credits with the striking cornflower-blue eyes so prominent among them. Ernest-Narcisse could have lived very well on the considerable income amassed by his father, Narcisse Bertrand de Beauvoir, who was collector of taxes at Argenton-sur-Creuse, a well-paid position which carried great status in the community, but he was an active man who could tolerate neither a life of indolence nor the secondary role he played to his autocratic father.

Narcisse Bertrand de Beauvoir (as the family was still known) bought the large white country house called Meyrignac, on the outskirts of Uzerche, shortly after his marriage, following many other minor nineteenth-century nobility who bought land and estates in an effort to adopt aristocratic attitudes.[8] As the eldest son, Ernest-Narcisse was to inherit Meyrignac, but, rather than live there until his father died, he chose to move to Paris, where he held a low-level bureaucratic position in the Town Hall until, like his father, he retired after long service. Before that, he lived at Meyrignac only on holidays, and it was there that his and Léontine's three children, Gaston (b. March 15, 1874), Hélène (b. September 28, 1876),[9] and Georges (b. June 25, 1878), spent their own childhood summers and where they returned for many years after they were married with families of their own.

Simone de Beauvoir remembers her grandfather Ernest-Narcisse as a contented man who hummed to himself all day long as he puttered around his beloved garden. He sported bushy white side whiskers and a black peaked country cap and always wore the rosette of the Legion of Honor no matter how informal his clothing.[10] He was a man who took great pleasure in the company of his grandchildren and taught them the names of all the local wildlife and vegetation. Even when they were small children, their botanical knowledge was extensive and Latin names tripped easily throughout their conversation. He led them in exploring the vast five-hundred-acre grounds, landscaped with such "oddities" as an "English" river with artificial waterfalls, Japanese dwarf trees, white peacocks and all sorts of child-delighting things not usually found in a French country garden.

Ernest-Narcisse and Léontine were esteemed in the community, so the marriage of their only daughter, Hélène, was arranged to a pillar of the local gentry who owned an estate called La Grillère some fifteen miles away. She was the only child to live year round near her parents in the same timeless perpetuation of their tranquil life, following the duties and responsibilities dictated by the seasons, the family and the Catholic Church.

Gaston, the eldest child and first son of Ernest-Narcisse and Léontine, lived in Paris, having also made a good marriage to a woman whom Simone de Beauvoir knew as "Tante Marguerite." Like his father before him, Gaston was a "gentleman," but unlike Ernest-Narcisse he had no occupation and did not want one. As the eldest, he inherited Meyrignac, deeply distressing Simone (who was twenty-one at the time). She had great affection for the property and little respect for her uncle, in whose satisfaction at not having to work she found nothing to admire.

Her own father, Georges Bertrand de Beauvoir (for he used the full patronymic until he was an adult), was a slight, timid and somewhat sickly child whose greatest pleasure was to lose himself reading adventure stories. As is often the case with younger children, he was the one whom his mother cosseted, and so he grew up mostly in her company, for she did not trust this last and dearest child to any of her servants. His dual ambition in his youngest years was to please his mother and evade the taunts and cruelties of his elder brother.

Léontine was a dour woman whose background was austere despite its substantial wealth. Hers was a family who believed that money was never to be used for immediate pleasure, but rather to be saved and passed on to future generations, who were expected to continue this tradition in perpetuity. Léontine often told her children how her family responded to the death of their unfortunate ancestor "a Monsieur Wartelle de Simoncourt, who had his head cut off in 1790 just because he bragged about being a member of the nobility."[11] The family Wartelle continued to amass money, power and position, but quietly, without display or ostentation, and Léontine was a model daughter, the guardian of her family's moral well-being as well as its money. She responded to what she had been taught in her mother's house by viewing the ritualistic keeping of a thrifty and religious household as an extension of her Christian duty and fiscal responsibility. She made Georges the main focus of her attention and the child upon whom she depended to reflect her own moral precepts.

Léontine lived long enough to see him become an outstanding pupil at the Collège Stanislas, an excellent secondary school in Paris, where he generally stood at the top of his class and won all the prizes. Curiously, this timid boy who spent most of his time hiding from his larger older brother became quite the showoff at school. Very early, his penchant for scholarship was matched by his love of performance. Family photos show him as a child conducting classes for the peasant children of the estate during his summer holidays at Meyrignac. In these, a maid is often seen standing in the background, holding a tray filled with glasses of orange juice, the reward given to the uncomprehending and generally uncaring children for listening to Georges's pontifications.[12]

At Meyrignac, Léontine kept herself busy ordering the large uniformed staff about the house. Her only contact with the surroundings came when it was time to oversee the vegetable harvest or preserve the many fruits that grew in the orchards. In Paris, she supervised several servants in a large and luxurious apartment at 110 Boulevard Saint-Germain, a dwelling opulently furnished to her husband's taste and in marked contrast to her own austere presence within it; for Ernest-Narcisse liked to be surrounded by the trappings of success, which to him meant velvet, brocade, tapestry and heavy dark furniture. He liked things and she liked rituals, and the combination suited them both. They led a quiet life, dictated by the observance of church obligations, family holidays and celebrations, and Léontine's prescribed calls upon a select group of women whose family backgrounds and husbands' positions paralleled her own.

Just when the two older children were approaching the ages at which their future was to be decided, and when Georges was thirteen, Léontine suddenly and unexpectedly died. Sanitation in the last years of the nineteenth century was still primitive even in opulent Parisian households, and she had contracted typhoid fever. She was actually recovering when the two nuns who supervised her sickroom decided that they wanted to attend Mass together and left their patient to the care of a chambermaid, who decided she needed fresh air and opened all the windows to the frigid cold. Within the week, Léontine succumbed to pneumonia. Ernest-Narcisse did not follow custom and remarry, so the household was left to his distanced direction and a retinue of faithful servants (which did not include the two nuns, who were banished forever to a cloister).

Ernest-Narcisse loved his children with an absent-minded paternalism. He insured that the older two married well and that the youngest continued his education. Having done this, he was satisfied to try to make life in the home continue as before Léontine's death, which meant that the usually austere apartment became even colder and more silent. He was a man who disliked any form of argument or disagreement, so, while everything seemed serene on the surface, the still rooms really masked a total lack of communication between father and son, who saw each other only at dinner and then spoke of little besides food and the weather.

Everything seemed the same, but in truth all was different, especially Georges, who no longer stood at the top of his classes and who stopped trying to win prizes except in subjects he liked, such as Latin and literature. Because Ernest-Narcisse had the typical Frenchman's attitude toward religion, that of the skeptical believer who left the actual observances to his wife, Georges learned to disregard Catholicism as a young man and later became a cynical and vocal nonbeliever. Thus the basic structures of his life—home, school, religion—remained the same, but once the driving force of the mother who shaped his attitude toward them disappeared, everything changed for him.

His father inhabited a world "half-way between the aristocracy and the bourgeoisie, between the landed gentry and the office worker, respecting but not practising the Catholic religion, neither completely integrated with society nor burdened with any serious responsibilities."[13] In the eyes of most of his countrymen, Ernest-Narcisse's was the life desired, aimed for and aspired to; because he had no intellectual pretentions or perceptions, he accepted the tragedy of his wife's early death and never questioned what he considered to be his fortunate circumstance in everything else.

It was different for Georges, who became a skeptic. For the first thirteen years of his life, he had been rigorously instructed by his mother, whose strict adherence to hard work, thrift and discipline were in stark contrast to her husband's primary allegiance to comfort and good taste. Thus, in Georges de Beauvoir's adolescent years, his father's example contradicted his mother's earlier one. Ernest-Narcisse praised hard work and urged Georges to find a suitable profession, but he himself had gone to work only because idleness bored him. He never became anything more than a minor functionary ritualistically following a daily schedule set by others, a fact that Georges noted and scorned throughout his own undistinguished working life. Ernest-Narcisse had fulfilled his ideal, which was to live mainly off his income and to divide his time between his elegant Paris apartment and his large country estate, just as the higher aristocracy, the class whose life he aspired to, did.

As the younger son, Georges did not receive an inheritance sufficient for him to live as well and as independently as his father and brother. Thus, his father's urgent imprecations that he decide upon a profession because he needed to work were contradicted by the affluent life he lived in his father's home. His name, with the particule "de," reflected the aristocracy, and he identified entirely with the aristocratic way of life. He had become a handsome and articulate man who moved elegantly and gracefully in the better drawing rooms of Paris. He was a naturally bright student who passed examinations without much study, so he became contemptuous of the qualities of hard work and serious effort his mother had taught him to admire. Instead, he spent his time in theaters, at racetracks and in cafés.

He really wanted to be an actor, but there was no question of it because this scandalous profession would have ostracized him from his social class. Instead, he shaved his beard in defiance of the custom of the time, took elocution lessons, learned how to use stage makeup, and contented himself with constant attendance at all the theaters in Paris. He also took part in whatever amateur theatrical events were staged in the homes of his friends; this was his one way of gaining access to families higher in the social order than his own, where he was otherwise not entirely welcomed by vigilant parents guarding their impressionable daughters from this handsome, charming and, relatively speaking, poor playboy.

His love of acting led him to the law, the most respectable profession for a would-be performer. He exhibited his talents for rhetoric and declamation in the courtroom and limited his actual stage appearances to sev-

eral weeks each summer, when he took part in amateur theatricals at socially proper resorts. He was never seriously attracted to the law and seems
to have had no desire to excel in the profession. He passed his examinations easily, but cared so little for success that he did not bother to complete
the formalities of thesis presentation. Instead, he simply registered himself
as qualified to practice in the Court of Appeals and began his professional
life not as a lawyer, but as secretary to one.

Despite the elevated status suggested by his name, his genuine ability
to charm and entertain, and now his qualification for a lucrative profession, he was still not welcomed in the best circles. Even though the idea of
the dowry was under assault in almost every social class by the time
Georges de Beauvoir came of age,[14] it was still so powerfully ingrained
in the bourgeois class that the best families were careful to guard their marriageable daughters from charming men whose financial standing was not
at least equal to theirs. Personal charm, elegant clothing and brilliant conversation were often enough to gain entry for Georges de Beauvoir into
their drawing rooms, but were not enough to keep him there as a welcome
guest. He was sensitive and intelligent, and in his own way modestly successful, and it rankled.

So he left his secretarial job to become a practicing lawyer. But while
he practiced his profession, he did only the necessary minimum to get by
in it. For the seven or eight years that followed, he went dutifully to his
law office during the day, but at night decked himself out as the dandy he
preferred to be in music halls and drawing rooms.

When Georges was almost thirty, Ernest-Narcisse woke up to his
presence in the apartment and decided it was time for him to marry. He
was spurred on to this decision by his sister as well as by the many relatives
of his dead wife, who all adored their charming nephew. Through the unofficial but nevertheless powerful marriage-broking networks which continually absorbed so much of the attention of these families, they found
a young woman from a northern family whose circumstances and fortune
matched Georges's, and whose dowry would therefore be of the proper size
and scope to permit a suitable marriage. Actually, Françoise Brasseur's family was richer and more successful than the family Beauvoir, but, unlike
them, had chosen not to ape the aristocracy but to hold more strongly to
the traditional values, beliefs and behavior of the bourgeoisie.

Françoise's grandfather Aimé-Fidèle-Constant Brasseur was one of the
first representatives to be elected to the Chambre des Députés of Luxembourg.[15] Her father, Gustave Brasseur, was a powerful banker in Verdun,
whose rigidity was attributed to his strict Jesuit education and his lifelong
admiration for the teachings of the order. He founded the Bank of the
Meuse and enjoyed boasting of how he used modern methods, such as advertising in regional newspapers, to best his competition. Everything he
did in life had a business connection: he lived in a house opulently furnished because such a display inspired trust in potential investors; he broke
with social convention by entertaining them lavishly at home because it

disarmed them enough to open their purses even wider. He wielded power through the controlled display of his wealth, so that those who sought both power and status vied for his favors and those who received them remembered and rewarded his largesse.

He married Lucie Moret, from Châteauvillain, Haute-Marne, a plain and unassuming woman cannily selected by his parents because her wealth surpassed his and because her lack of beauty made it unlikely that someone from her own class would want her. Lucie Moret came from a family with many branches, but little is known of her except that she had been sent by a mother who rejected her to live in a convent at an early age and spent most of her early life there until she married. Her personality matched her husband's well, and the reverence for order and authority instilled in her at the convent equaled his. It was as if she were determined to be everything that this man, who had in effect rescued her from the sterile and limited life of the convent, would ever want or need. When they married, the emotionally deprived girl attached herself to her husband with such intensity that she had little affection left for her children.

Françoise, born in 1887, was the eldest child of this union. Her parents were disappointed to have a daughter as their firstborn, and all her life she knew it. The second child was a son, Hubert, who insured the succession of the family and was accorded all the respectful attention due the family heir. Marie-Thérèse, the third and last child, was the coddled favorite of both her parents.

Françoise was a bright young woman whose mother shipped her off to a convent as well, but only as a day boarder to be educated locally at the Couvent des Oiseaux in Verdun. She was an intelligent little girl, eager to please the nuns who gave her the only real affection she knew as a child. It was highly unusual for the mother superior, known as Mother Bertrand, to take an interest in a single pupil, but Françoise did so well in her studies that when she completed primary classes Mother Bertrand supervised her in a special advanced program.[16] During Françoise's years in the convent, Mother Bertrand became the one adult whom she really loved and who loved her in return. Because she loved learning as well, Françoise once timidly suggested to her mother that perhaps she too might become a teaching nun. Lucie Brasseur rudely dismissed the idea; Françoise's destiny was to marry well and increase the family's wealth and standing. There was to be no more talk of becoming a nun, especially one who read books. Thus Françoise learned what her future was to be; now all she had to do was wait for it to happen.

Françoise grew up to be beautiful, but didn't know it because no one ever told her. She had a luminous complexion, deep-brown eyes and thick auburn hair. But the constant rebuffs of her parents, the distant rapport with her siblings, and the rigid propriety of her life at home all combined to make her a sad-faced and somewhat sullen young woman; her insecurity made her awkward and timid. She was now almost twenty and well into the age when she should have been married, but as her parents took little interest in her and she had few friends and even fewer opportunities to socialize with appropriate young men, there did not seem to be a suitable mate in the offing.

It was not until Gustave Brasseur began to have business difficulties that he was suddenly eager to marry off at least one daughter as quickly as possible. When a friend of both families suggested that an alliance would be mutually beneficial, Georges de Beauvoir suddenly became an eligible candidate for Françoise Brasseur's hand in marriage. Georges was perceived by the Brasseurs as being socially higher and having a promising career even though his family clearly did not have the same financial standing as theirs. When both the families Brasseur and Beauvoir agreed to a meeting between their children on the neutral territory of the Houlgate resort in the summer of 1906, Françoise went only because she had no choice. Georges went because it was time for him to marry and he wanted a rich girl from the provinces who was young enough to insure that her virtue was intact and who was also devoutly religious—all of which he thought would guarantee that she would be a docile and devoted wife and he would never be a cuckolded husband.[17] Also, and equally as important to him, this young woman came with an impressive dowry.

Their parents arranged for his first sight of her to be in the company of some of her classmates from the convent (for she had no real friends). It was the custom for the prospective bridal candidate to be placed in the midst of a graceful tableau, such as an afternoon tea where she could preside with elegance while demonstrating her social skills. Françoise, uncomfortable with artifice, was both nervous about meeting Georges and indifferent to the impression she made. She spent the entire time hunched over her knitting, pretending to be engrossed in a shapeless mass of ratty brown yarn. Whether he saw how genuinely beautiful and interesting she was, or only the appropriate connection a marriage to her offered, within a few weeks of their first meeting Georges de Beauvoir asked Françoise Brasseur to marry him and she accepted.

During their courtship, everything that had been subdued in her personality came to the fore. As she made preparations for her marriage and subsequent move to Paris, where they would live, her happiness could not be contained. She had fallen in love with the dashing blue-eyed suitor who had charmed her, and theirs was a marriage of love despite all the financial bargaining that led up to it.

They were married on December 21, 1906, and shortly thereafter they moved to their first home, a large and gracious apartment at 103 Boulevard du Montparnasse, just above the café La Rotonde.[18] Françoise brought the linens and household items she had been collecting throughout her life for her marriage and a few pieces of personal furniture such as her armoire, a rocking chair and some linen chests. Her father had not yet paid the dowry money, but she and Georges were sure it would come eventually, and besides, there was no immediate need for it. A shy young girl from Meyrignac, Louise Sermadira, was sent by Ernest-Narcisse to be their servant, and Françoise busied herself learning to be a Parisian housewife.

The end of the honeymoon and the beginning of daily life in Paris produced a shock of enormous proportion: suddenly, she was expected to become the manager of her household and carry out the distaff responsibilities which would make her home the proper reflection of her husband's status and position, and to do it in what was essentially an alien society. She had only her husband to guide her, but once they were married the differences in their upbringing and attitudes toward society surfaced. Georges did not consider them to be all that serious, but to Françoise they were enormous, and they hit her with an impact that colored her behavior for the rest of her life.

She did not understand why, if he went off to work so dutifully every day, they did not grow rich and successful and why certain Parisian drawing rooms remained closed to them. She did not understand why he chided her for her small economies and insisted that she emulate those whose ways were obviously too grand for them if they were never invited to call. He insisted that she become cultured and instructed her in literature and the theater. He taught her what he considered was good taste and how to be stylish in her dress and correct in the decoration of their home. She had a quick intelligence and enjoyed his tutoring, but all this cost money. And when it came to the decoration of the apartment, her dowry still had not been paid and expenses were heavy.

There was much about her marriage that bewildered Françoise, but she loved her husband and wanted to please him. Despite her convent upbringing, at the beginning theirs was an intensely passionate physical relationship, and it remained so for many years, even after the conventional structure of their marriage had disintegrated.[19] So she tried to figure out what it was he expected of her, and then to behave accordingly. Both her mother and the nuns who taught her had instilled the belief that above all a wife was subservient to her husband, and that it was he who should set the tenor of the household and be the primary influence upon their life. Yet she had seen how women, "though their official position [in marriage] was subordinate, their influence in it [was] preponderant."[20]

All this was confusing to her, but not so much that it changed her role within her household. Françoise deferred to her husband throughout their marriage, and for her entire life she tried to hide any disagreement she may have had with him from everyone except her maid Louise and her children. This deference cost her much emotionally, making her prone to sudden and violent fits of temper. Her children dreaded her "black looks" and sudden tantrums.

During her engagement she had become relaxed and outgoing, discovering that she liked to laugh and doing so easily, without embarrassment or regard for propriety. All her perceptions were heightened, as color, humor and music took on new meaning and gave her extraordinary pleasure. She discovered something that gave her, for the first time, genuine pride in herself: that hers was a strong personality, and that her tastes were quickly formed and very definite.

When she married, she seemed to become to many who knew her willful and imperious, a woman of strong opinion and withering glare whose favorite comment, "That's ridiculous," could cower everyone but her husband.[21] Throughout her life, accusations that she was dictatorial and overbearing followed her, but much of this behavior was a carry-over from her bridal days when she was terrified that she would betray her humble and provincial background.

However, she had an integrity that was probably formed in her convent years and that was constantly reinforced by her steadfast devotion to her Church, so she never wavered from what she thought was morally or ethically correct even if it seemed to go against accepted social behavior. Although her perception of what was morally right may have caused her social insult or humiliation, it made her oblivious to what others thought of her. It also made her seem alienated and cold, lacking in warmth and human compassion, and to her daughters this seeming coldness and detachment became her most prominent characteristic as she grew older.

At the time of her marriage, Françoise was young, inexperienced and bewildered by the complexity of Parisian society. The young bride was confused when her husband greeted with sardonic amusement her attempts to recreate on the Boulevard Raspail her mother's thrifty and prudent Verdun household. She was fastidious about obligations and duties, and, since there was an elaborate ritual connected with even the most simple family visit in Paris, she needed someone to teach her these customs, but Georges was of little help. He either mocked these conventions or was relaxed about them, for he had always counted on his blue eyes and natural charm to carry him through. He wanted her to be as relaxed as he was; instead, she compensated for her feelings of inferiority with a coldness that was interpreted as disdainful superiority—quite the opposite of what she intended.

What Georges de Beauvoir did not know and probably did not ever realize was that, in effect, he had married his mother, for Françoise was exactly like Léontine in so many exterior ways. Despite her passionate love for her husband, Françoise would have been content with an austere household, to bury herself in prayer and devote herself entirely to her children. But Georges, like his father before him, wanted an exquisite setting, all plush, brocade, silk and velvet. The furniture he had decided they should buy was heavy and dark, most of it black pearwood, and the carpets were deep red and richly patterned in black. It was as opulent as Ernest-Narcisse's apartment on the Boulevard Saint-Germain, and as stylish as any in Belle Epoque Paris. And, of course, there was Georges's continuing love of the theater and literature, the first of which took him away from the home, and the second of which filled it with books. Georges was also a "modern" husband, seeing his wife's education as his duty to make her his true companion in life, and to give her the opportunity to understand his interests so that she could share them. Françoise welcomed this aspect of her husband's personality and quickly came to like these intellectual pursuits for their own sake as well as for the closeness they created between them. But part of her was always holding back: there was the possibility that the books and the plays might not be approved by the Church. Also, for a "good wife," supervising the household was supposed to take all her time and the pursuit of intellectual endeavors carried the aura of forbidden pleasure.

Thus, this twenty-year-old girl was thrown into the confusions and contradictions of her married life and given no time to come to terms with any of it, for shortly after her first wedding anniversary she gave birth to her first child, and her duties and responsibilities pulled her in still another direction.

TWO

My Sister, My Accomplice

FOR A FIRST BIRTH, the labor was brief. Late in the evening Françoise took to her bed, and shortly thereafter the family doctor was summoned. Louise assisted him, Georges was present throughout, and by 4 A.M. January 9, 1908, Françoise de Beauvoir had delivered a daughter. She weighed "probably about seven pounds"[1] and had a full head of reddish-brown hair and the brilliant blue eyes of all the Beauvoirs, which were dazzling from the moment of birth. She was a lusty, healthy baby of decided temperament who set about the business of living with a concentration that was unnerving in one so tiny.

If there was any disappointment that she was not a boy it was never expressed by either parent, especially Françoise, who had suffered all her life from the misfortune of being firstborn and female. The baby was named Simone (a break with family tradition of naming daughters after their grandmothers) because Georges liked this then chic name very much. He relented only partially for her other names: refusing to allow the baby to be named Léontine after his mother, he compromised with Ernestine (for Ernest-Narcisse), Lucie (for Madame Brasseur, surprisingly at Françoise's insistence), and Marie (for the Virgin Mary). She was baptized in the Catholic faith when six weeks old as Simone-Ernestine-Lucie-Marie Bertrand de Beauvoir, but was taught as an infant to give her name simply as Simone de Beauvoir.

A nursery was created for the new baby in what had formerly been the maid's room. In contrast to the opulent darkness of the rest of the apartment, it was all white, with a simple enameled cot set close to Louise's bed, for she was responsible for the infant's routine physical care. In addition to her other household chores, Louise had to bathe and feed the baby, then take her to the park for the daily airing in the cumbersome wicker pram. Françoise fretted over the latest advice to young mothers about the proper foods for a baby and often helped Louise to mash and crush whatever was deemed suitable for the developing child to eat, but most of the time she was busy with the social obligations of a young matron and the elaborate preparations for her husband's homecoming each evening.

Georges went off each morning to the Courts of Appeal and came home at night more often than not carrying a small bunch of Parma violets, Françoise's favorites. They amused themselves by playing with their beautiful baby before Louise took her off to bed,[2] then dined when Louise returned to serve the dinner she had cooked. Afterward, while Louise cleaned up, Françoise sat contentedly over her needlepoint as Georges read to her from some text chosen to enlighten and educate her. Françoise felt slightly guilty about receiving all these masculine ideas, so she compromised by keeping her hands busy with "feminine" needlepoint, declaring her intention to cover every space in the apartment with an example of her beautiful handiwork.[3] It was a glorious time in their marriage: their income was small but secure; they lived in an apartment that Françoise, with Georges's supervision, had furnished and decorated in what constituted good taste at the time; they had a beautiful baby; and now, besides Georges's brother Gaston's family and a multitude of Beauvoir relatives, Françoise had her own family in Paris.

Gustave Brasseur had fled Verdun in disgrace. He had lost not only his own money but also most of the funds invested by depositors in his bank. On July 28, 1909, the courts ordered the Bank of the Meuse into liquidation and everything was seized to be sold, including all the personal possessions of the Brasseur family. There was a run on the bank, Gustave Brasseur's wife and their two other children were unceremoniously escorted out of town, and he was sent to jail. He remained there for thirteen months before he was tried and sentenced to fifteen months in prison, but the political clout he had wielded during his days of power and influence still held and he was released at once.

Brasseur caused a scandal, known throughout Verdun but rarely spoken of in the family and then in hushed tones as "the financial disaster."[4] Françoise could not speak of it to anyone, including her children, for the rest of her life without bursting into tears.[5] Simone de Beauvoir remembered being intimidated by a grandfather who "was in prison because he was a fraudulent banker and went bankrupt. When he came out he was very boring, very quiet, but still egotistical. Only the women were ashamed. My mother only found out about all this when they lost their house and had to move to Paris. Creditors were always ringing his doorbell. It was humiliating for her.[6]

Since his wife adored him and his spinster daughter depended on him completely, Brasseur came to Paris uncowed. He continued to believe in his financial acumen and spent the rest of his life trying to persuade everyone with whom he came into contact to invest in one harebrained scheme after another. Once he even tried to persuade Georges to invest in an alchemical process that was supposed to turn base metal into gold. Time after time, Gustave Brasseur introduced relatives and friends to outlandish plots which he fervently believed would "make millionaires of us all." It became one of those private expressions that Françoise and Georges first repeated as a joke, but that then made him bitter and her embarrassed:

Gustave Brasseur had never paid her dowry, and now they had to face the fact that he never would.

He, his wife and their favorite child, Marie-Thérèse (their son Hubert broke with custom to marry a poor woman without a dowry in a non-arranged union and remained in the north), took an apartment near the Lion de Belfort, within walking distance of Françoise, Georges and the adored first grandchild. Gustave managed to keep his past secret enough to find a succession of managerial positions, but was soon dismissed from each because he spent most of his time scheming on his own behalf.

The reversal in her parents' fortune brought a new confidence to Françoise. As a young matron and head of her own household, with her husband to reinforce her autonomy, she felt brave enough to behave as their adult equal, and at times a fussy and disapproving one. She scolded her father for his continuous succession of financial schemes and day-dreams, and even insisted with uncharacteristic harshness that he let Madame Brasseur manage his occasional meager earnings. Madame Brasseur ignored her because she did not agree with Françoise's "modern" notion of marriage, where women were consulted by their husbands and sometimes gave advice on economic matters. Françoise's imprecations did not faze her father, who bragged of never having listened to a woman, let alone to have taken the advice of one.

One of Georges's favorite remarks was "The wife is what the husband makes of her: it's up to him to make her someone."[7] It never failed to elicit a shudder from Madame Brasseur as she hastily made the sign of the cross simultaneously. To keep a semblance of peace between them, Françoise grew skilled at telling her mother only what she wanted her to know, and so Madame Brasseur often resorted to stratagems such as questioning the toddler Simone about her mother's activities. In this she was also frustrated, because Simone adored her mother and told her grandmother nothing.

The one festering reminder of Gustave's disgrace within the Brasseur home was the unmarried Marie-Thérèse. He had not succeeded in arranging her marriage before fleeing to Paris, and now she lived at home, a sour and disappointed presence who had long since passed the age of marriage-ability. She spent most of her time weeping and moping, and even though social custom had changed to the point where certain kinds of work were now permitted for women of her class, she refused even to consider the idea because it would have meant "loss of face." Work, for her, was still equated with family dishonor.[8] Finally she agreed to attend classes at the Institut Catholique, where she met a man whom she soon after married. She was the first woman in the family to enter into a nonarranged marriage—a break with social convention which did not upset her at all, but which shamed her mother and, interestingly, shocked Françoise. Needless to say, no dowry was paid.

The only result of Gustave Brasseur's bankruptcy to affect Françoise and Georges's life directly was the certainty that her dowry would not be paid. It did not seem cause for serious alarm, because she and Georges were in love, they had his small income, and his modest inheritance had been invested—wisely, so they thought then.

And so most of the attention in both households centered upon the baby Simone. Georges, who had instructed Françoise in literature, the theater, and the proper political attitudes and opinions he wanted her to have, had no interest in psychology. Thus Françoise became passionately devoted to learning by reading, especially about the best methods of raising children. She reasoned that anything she learned in a book would enhance her in her husband's eyes, especially if the baby continued to be bright, alert and eager to please all the adults.

Although there was not at that time a French equivalent of the American Dr. Spock to guide young mothers, there were many "guides" published by the Catholic Church.[9] Françoise, convent-educated, was instructed in their contents and knew what was expected of her as a Catholic mother.

With her devotion to the spiritual and her belief in the wisdom of the Church, Françoise contrasted markedly with Georges, who viewed the entire world with the detachment of a nonbeliever.[10] Reflecting upon this as an adult, Simone de Beauvoir said, "The consequence was that I grew accustomed to the idea that my intellectual life—embodied by my father—and my spiritual life—expressed by my mother—were two radically heterogeneous fields of experience which had absolutely nothing in common." Her father's "individualism and pagan ethical standards" were the direct opposite of her mother's "rigidly moral conventionalism." The division in their outlook while she was growing up made her life at home "a kind of endless disputation."[11] Yet, when she tried to reconstruct the role each parent played in her early life, her mother's role is the more complex of the two. Her father sang songs, played games and made a fuss over her, but "he didn't play any well-defined role in my life."[12]

Françoise trained herself to be an arbiter of education and etiquette from the earliest years of Simone's life. She took her to church before she could walk and began her instruction in the faith before she was a year old by telling stories about the paintings and statues on the walls of Notre-Dame-des-Champs, the family parish church on the Boulevard du Montparnasse.

Françoise read the fairy tales of Madame de Ségur and Perrault alone at first to determine which were suitable for Simone. She continued this sort of literary censorship for many years, carrying it so far that when Simone began to learn Latin and English, Françoise taught herself these languages so that she could supervise the content of her daughter's reading, even in foreign tongues.

Every Thursday afternoon, Françoise took Simone to lunch with the grandparents Brasseur in their apartment on the Place Denfert-Rochereau. Simone loved to eat there because her grandmother was a much better and more adventurous cook than either Louise, who boiled everything, or

Françoise, who relied on a monotonous repertoire of heavy northern provincial dishes. It was a grown-up occasion when Simone was expected to behave like a miniature adult. After lunch, when Grandfather Brasseur had settled into his chair for a nap, Simone, from the age of two, was expected to do as the women of the family did: sit quietly, speaking only in an occasional hushed whisper until he awoke. Playing, except for a quiet turning of a deck of cards (the only diversion she was allowed), was strictly forbidden; and only those movements absolutely necessary to keep muscles from cramping were permitted.[13]

Simone was treated so much like a little adult that she even went on holidays without her parents. Aunt Marie-Thérèse took her to visit the great-aunts who were her grandmother's ancient sisters in Châteauvillain. Louise took her to visit her father's cousins, the family Florence, who lived outside Lyon.[14] With her parents, Simone spent holidays at coastal resorts in Normandy or mountain resorts like Divonne-les-Bains.

She loved being petted, cosseted, fussed over and even deferred to by her parents and their friends. Her striking coloring—thick reddish-brown hair now worn in long curls, her blue eyes enormous in her small round face—often caught the admiring attention of strangers, and within the family the list of adoring relatives was long. She grew used to having her way and, if not given it at once, learned very young which tricks and tirades worked. She held her breath until her face turned red, screamed and cried and, if all else failed, could make herself vomit from the intensity of her desire. She did not care where her outbursts took place and was as obstreperous in the park and on the street as she was at home. During one particularly violent tantrum in the Luxembourg Gardens, she even kicked a well-meaning matron who tried to make her stop crying. Her behavior soon became favorite family gossip because it so vividly demonstrated how "lax" Georges and Françoise had become.

One of the earliest memories of Simone's cousin Magdeleine Mantis de Bisschop, who was several years older than she, dated from a summer holiday at La Grillère: she remembered hearing her parents talk about how "the spoiled brat Simone" would "hold her breath until her face turned black as a thundercloud" if she was not given whatever she desired. The child Magdeleine watched in fascination one night at the dinner table as Georges, provoked beyond reason by Simone's behavior, turned suddenly and slapped her lightly. As the shocked child began to bellow, Magdeleine was "disappointed that she only turned red, actually a light shade of pink." But the lasting memory for Madame de Bisschop was not of her misbehaving cousin, but rather of the way both Georges and Françoise moved to comfort their child, apologizing to the two-year-old for the wrongness of their action: "She was a spoiled, spoiled, spoiled brat, and to her parents she could do no wrong. We were all very conscious in our family that there was the rest of us—all the cousins—and then there was Simone. She was different. She was special."[15]

Considering the rigid standards for children's deportment in the early years of this century, Georges and Françoise were incredibly relaxed and casual with their first child, because they found her so engaging. They joked about her temperamental eruptions and devilish obstinacy to relatives and friends, who all disapproved, of course, blaming Georges's artistic temperament and Françoise's newfangled notions, ill-gotten from reading books.

An elderly "Great-Aunt Titite," Thérèse Champigneulle, who wrote maxims and fables for a popular children's magazine called *La Poupée Modèle*, used Simone's outbursts in the hope that it would not only instruct other children but also embarrass her parents into disciplining their willful child. One popular story was about an unsuccessful shepherd named "Louise" who tried to modify a bad little sheep's behavior. Simone was taught by her parents to share their "almost religious reverence for print,"[16] so to see herself written about puffed up her self-importance more than ever. However, the analogy of little children as sheep left her puzzled, showing at a very early age her literal bent of mind.

Simone learned to read when she was four years old by associating the sounds made by letters with pictorial representations in a popular French children's primer. She had already learned the alphabet from her wooden blocks, and putting letters and sounds together came easily to her. From that time on, she liked to pretend that she was a teacher of reading, and tried to instruct everyone from her grandmother to Louise. She had a voracious appetite for books, and Françoise, busy now with her second child, was happy when Georges provided them. He was delighted with the pretty elder daughter who showed signs of precocious intelligence, and he praised her lavishly for each new book she read.

Henriette-Hélène Bertrand de Beauvoir[17] was born on June 9, 1910, when Simone was two and a half. She was a smaller baby than Simone, with the same brilliant blue eyes but with golden-blond hair. An air of disappointment surrounded this birth, for Françoise and Georges made no secret of their longing this time for a son and they did nothing to conceal it from Hélène. Gustave Brasseur sent a tactless letter saying how happy he was to hear of the "birth of a son." Then he added a postscript: "I have just learned it was the birth of a girl. Let God's will be done."

Tiny and doll-like, Hélène was immediately nicknamed Poupette, a name which lasted well into her adulthood and which reflected how the family perceived her. It soon became a family joke that in every photograph of the baby Poupette she was crying.[18] She herself remembers going through much of her childhood in a sort of bewilderment, always wondering what she had done to displease or disappoint those around her. Unlike the independent Simone, who threw tantrums with total disregard for others, Hélène clung to her mother and cried for special attention. This irritated Françoise and made her naturally quick temper even shorter, so that both little girls never knew when verbal reprimands would become more severe physical punishment, especially the sting of sharp slaps.

Mostly Hélène later remembered being swept along by her older sister's vitality, and because she was such a malleable child theirs was a harmonious relationship. Simone's earliest memory of Hélène was joy at having someone to teach, and Hélène's was of being taught by Simone. Neither sister remembered what they called "simple play," but only games which had an instructive quality, generally requiring pencils, paper and a schoolroom setting. Hélène did not have the bookish intellectual curiosity of her sister, but was more taken with colors and objects. She would have been content to daydream with dolls and toys, mostly snippets of cloth, baubles, and buttons. Simone, however, would not stand for undirected play, and so Hélène was typically forced to be learning something. Simone always invented the games and was always the teacher.

Although there were now two small children in the family, Simone continued to be the dominant force around which most of the activity revolved. Books were carefully chosen to be suitable for a child her age and not Hélène's; excursions were planned, toys bought, all with her in mind. Hélène, the younger child who had had the bad grace not to be born a son, was never really considered as an individual by her parents but only as the follower in her sister's footsteps. Hand-me-downs were her lot for many years, but they never caused the sort of problem that might have occurred between sisters who were not as close as they. Instead, there was the camaraderie of a shared resentment between the sisters, which became directed toward the parents, more particularly, as time went on, toward their mother.

Each sister became an extension of the other, probably because there were so few children for them to play with until they went to school. They were surrounded by little girls when they played each day in the Luxembourg Gardens, but they were forbidden to speak to any of them, even the ones with uniformed nurses and expensive clothes and toys, because Françoise could not be sure "their families were not vulgar."[19] In many ways, they were lonely children, constrained by social convention to be on perpetual guard against unsuitable contacts and to be suspicious of friendship too easily offered. For many years after they entered school, even though social customs had become somewhat more relaxed in France during and just after World War I, they carefully observed the formality of not talking to their classmates until after Françoise paid her formal call upon their mothers. And these classmates were children in a select private school whose families were generally socially and financially superior to Georges and Françoise de Beauvoir.

The times may have changed in France, but there were many families like the Beauvoirs who were oblivious to all but the old ways. Theirs was a world both full and constrained at the same time. Life had a rhythm for Simone and her sister, of Sunday Mass and twice-daily prayers and devotions supervised by their mother. There were grand Sunday dinners after Mass, polite Thursday lunches with their grandparents Brasseur, and a continuing round of family celebrations with Georges's many aunts, uncles and cousins, who all lived in Paris. Less frequent were the visits to and from Aunt Marie-Thérèse and her growing family, and they never saw Uncle Hubert—who continued to live in the north—except when Françoise wanted to visit Mother Bertrand in the Couvent des Oiseaux. So their family identification was with the paternal side, and in time they would play the role of the disgraced Brasseurs within it.

But, for the moment, life was good. Several times each month Françoise, in a swishing taffeta dress glittering with jet beads, kissed them good night before going into the drawing room to join her husband and their guests in an evening of music and laughter. At various holidays during the year they visited Georges's relatives throughout the south, and there were the glorious summers at Meyrignac when the train was met by servants with horse and carriage. The ladies in their voluminous dresses and large bonnets descended with their maids amidst a welter of luggage, while the two little girls looked anxiously along the platform for the cousins from La Grillère, Robert and Magdeleine, who were their favorite playmates. If theirs was not a world of opulence, it was certainly a world of privilege and comfort. The young family of Georges and Françoise de Beauvoir in these Belle Epoque years of the Third Republic stood both publicly and privately for "the triumph of the bourgeois ideal."[20]

In the Paris apartment, perched on the balcony just above the treetops looking down on the considerable foot traffic at the intersection of the Boulevard Raspail and the Boulevard du Montparnasse, Simone spent long hours daydreaming about the lives of the people who passed below her, inventing mythical realities based on the religious and secular stories Françoise read to her. She had graduated from the white-enameled cot to an ornately carved bed in the Louis XVI style,[21] but she still shared the tiny maid's room with Louise. Hélène now slept on the cot, but because the bedroom was so small it was placed outside in a dim hallway, with all the family armoires to shield it from view and create a sort of antechamber. This room was next to the kitchen, and part of the spartan, private side. At the other end of the hallway which connected the two separated parts of the apartment, a large room served as Georges's study, so designated and furnished because men of his education and profession always had a private retreat. The parental bedroom was next to it, and beyond that the water closet and then the bathroom. There were also dining and living rooms, public spaces overdecorated in what then represented good taste. Of course there was a piano, because pianos, along with books and the father's study, demonstrated that this was a family that had "a surplus of wealth, dedicated to cultured living, beyond the basic necessities."[22] In short, the apartment, from its layout to its furnishings, to the way in which daily life was lived there, could have been the home of any other prosperous family of the haute bourgeoisie. There was little besides the family portraits to distinguish it from all others like it, for the ideal in home décor was not to be individual, but to be the same as everyone else. One did not call attention to one's situation, but allowed objects and furnishings to proclaim it instead.

This contrast within the two sections of the apartment, of the spartan and private in sharp opposition to the opulent and public, characterized everything about their life, including the two children themselves. They had very limited clothing and at times were reduced to tears by the clumsy shoes they had to wear—gifts from Grandfather Brasseur, who had managed to find a job as director of a factory that made cheap shoes—but each little girl also had a pretty gold locket hanging from a fine gold chain around her neck. Books were plentiful in the household, mostly filling the shelves in Georges's study, but were doled out to the children parsimoniously and then only after the parents had taken their time and given much thought to determining their suitability. Good toys were few, but the girls had several dolls that were splendid, beautiful and expensive. Françoise kept them locked in the dining-room cupboard, and they were taken out only on special occasions or when company came to visit. As an adult, Hélène remembered how much she liked to play with dolls, and how Simone always pretended not to like them even though she too would become engrossed in games on the rare occasion when Françoise took them down from their perch in the closet. They had so few toys they were allowed to play with regularly that when someone gave them a new one they sometimes did not know what to do with it.[23]

Mainly, the sisters had each other for company, and so they came to depend upon themselves in ways characteristic of children who have been deprived of what is now considered ordinary parental affection. Georges and Françoise always did "the proper thing" for their daughters, but generally, by the time the girls started to attend school, any attention came in the form of correction or command and never as casual verbal praise or physical affection. Simone and Hélène invented a private language in which words and phrases had meaning only to themselves; a glance or a gesture was enough to provide instant communication and understanding, a strategem they resorted to because they wanted to escape their mother's prying presence. Their games, lacking costume or prop, became dreamlike and symbolic, as they invented fantasy worlds in which they played exotic and heroic roles, for "games were our adventures."[24] All these games had some basis in their reading at the time: grisly tales of Catholic saints prepared with the intention of instructing and ennobling young French children. Simone invented these games, in which she was usually a saint but always the martyr. Hélène's role was "the very nasty and mean person who martyrized her." She remembered feeling a great deal of satisfaction in her role as the wicked dispenser of evil punishment:

"I always knew that my parents were proud of their eldest daughter and that, as the second-born girl, I was not really a welcome child. But Simone valorized me even though she could have crushed me by siding with our parents, and that's why I remained attached to her. She was always nice, always defending me against them. In our games when she liked to play the saint, I think it must have given me [unconscious] pleasure to martyrize her even though she was so kind. I remember one day reaching the summit of cruelty: she took the role of a young and beautiful girl whom I, as an evil ruler, was keeping prisoner in a tower. I had the inspiration that my most serious punishment for her would be to tear up her prayer book so she could not pray—a symbolic prayer book, of course, because I would not have dared to harm a real one. But Simone always had the last word in these games. With symbolic glue, she put the prayer book back together. So because of her sainthood, her virtue and especially her determination, she always overcame and she always won."[25]

They explored themselves and their world with such an intimacy that the age difference between them seemed to have disappeared and they were twinlike extensions of each other. All of this was difficult because, except for summers in Meyrignac, they had no private place to call their own. There was always the watchful eye and ear of their mother during every waking moment. Both children still adored Françoise and confided in her about such things as school, lessons or questions of religion. But at the same time there was an as-yet-undefined and unexplainable feeling gradually dawning—upon Simone especially—that some things were best kept from adults, especially one's mother. This increased the bond between the sisters.

The first fracture to the sisters' symbiotic accord happened when Simone was five and a half and ready to go to school. There was never any question but that she would attend a private school, for although the lycée, or public school, was highly regarded by many bourgeois parents, Georges de Beauvoir refused to send his daughters there because it was all too possible that family standards might be compromised, perhaps even contaminated by girls of a lower class. Georges's ideas of propriety were somewhat grander than his income, a holdover from his bachelor associations with families wealthier than his. He believed that the quality of the education he gave to his daughters was among his most important responsibilities, second only to the dowry he expected to provide for them. He had had an education both excellent and fashionable at the Collège Stanislas; Françoise, since marrying Georges and being educated by him, now knew how inferior her own convent education had been, and so she did not insist upon a Catholic school sponsored directly by the Church. Besides—and probably more to the point—convent schools in Paris required expensive uniforms completed by a fresh pair of white gloves every day, and all students were required to stay for elaborate lunches. These represented expenses much larger than Georges and Françoise could afford.[26]

Together they decided upon a prestigious private school called the Cours Adeline Désir, named after the aristocratic Catholic laywoman who had established it with the intention of making it a true educational institution and not just a finishing school for daughters of the upper classes.

Unfortunately, she did not succeed: the quality of teaching and the content of the courses guaranteed the pupils little more than a junior-high-school education, even though they attended for ten to twelve years.[27] For Françoise, it was the closest she could get to a convent school; for Georges, it represented a guarantee of morality. Best of all, it was close by on the quiet Rue Jacob in "a curious hodgepodge of what must once have been private houses [with] walls knocked out, and all the rooms led into each other like a rabbit warren."[28] A modest-sized courtyard used as a play area by the little girls led to an interior of tiny, dark wood-paneled classrooms. There was even a minuscule private chapel within the school: a young diocesan priest was assigned to give the little girls their catechism instruction on the premises because it simply would not do for girls from the Cours Désir to take these lessons in ordinary parish churches in the company of children who might have been unsuitable.

The Cours Désir was the epitome of the curious contradiction that marked French private education for women throughout the nineteenth century and until World War II: it was rigorous and intellectual, but at the same time heavily policed by educators who were constantly mindful of the attitudes of the Catholic Church toward the role that women were expected to play in life. The two alternatives were either marriage and motherhood or religious vows and the convent. There was nothing else.

Simone fit into the Cours Désir perfectly. She loved the regularity of learning, and the weighty book satchel that all French schoolchildren carry had the same meaning for her as a treasure chest of rare toys. She loved pencils, paper, and lesson books, and she kept them with a neatness and precision that did not carry over to her dress and deportment. In her haste to begin each day of learning she threw on her clothes, so that she was constantly being scolded for her sloppiness, her undone sashes, falling stockings, and unkempt hair with disheveled bows. Twice each week ceremonies were held in recognition of the students' good behavior as well as good grades. These delighted Simone, and she worked hard to collect the trophies that were given.

The ceremonies took place in front of an audience of mothers who participated in judging their daughters, because all mothers were expected to attend classes as much as possible, sitting in rows of chairs behind their daughters' school table, busying themselves with handiwork while they listened intently to all that was said, on the alert for any infraction of Catholic dogma.[29] Françoise coveted the prizes as zealously as Simone and became a willing accomplice in helping to garner them. Even though she scolded and slapped her daughter at home for her sloppiness, Françoise always testified otherwise at school and gave her the highest marks for deportment. It would not have done to expose private family life before strangers; propriety and familial well-being had to be stressed, no matter what underlying tensions were generated at home because of Simone's disorderly conduct. Only on rare occasion would she publicly reprimand her daughters, and when this happened they were deeply ashamed, especially when the humiliation took place in the presence of a teacher whom they both despised.[30]

From the day Simone started school, Françoise took both daughters to early-morning Mass every day, and every evening when the homework was finished she led them in long devotions. Georges usually sat nearby while they were in progress, now and again interjecting such comments as "You know all those crippled people who crawl to Lourdes to pray to the Virgin? Well, if she is so all-powerful, how is it that she doesn't make new legs and arms grow for them?"[31] At first, before they began to think about these remarks, the little girls were shocked and buried their heads over their rosaries, as if prayer would keep his sacrilege from reaching their ears, but it was not long before his cynicism began to erode their childish faith.

Georges spoke to Simone as if she were his educational equal and a miniature adult. He selected books for her to read and then expected her to discuss them with him. Rather than the moralizing religious tales Françoise brought home when Simone was seven years old, Georges pulled copies of Rudyard Kipling, Jules Verne and James Fenimore Cooper (in French translations) off the shelves of his study and expected Simone to read them, which she did. The quickness of her mind delighted him, and both she and her sister remembered later how seriously they took these discussions with their father, when he would solicit their opinions and treat them with the greatest courtesy and respect. It made them feel important in the family scheme of things and brought Georges into their lives more directly, particularly into Simone's because he took her more seriously than he did Hélène. He played games with Simone in which she copied out passages from books and he corrected her handwriting, or he pronounced difficult words and asked her to spell them. For a few short years after she started school, he even took an interest in her appearance, urging her to sit up straight, tie her ribbons or comb her hair, but this soon became secondary to the interest he took in her education. To him, she became "simply a mind,"[32] but this was perfectly fine with her because she adored him and any attention was better than none.

It was up to Françoise to supervise the children's lessons on a daily basis. She was the parent who read every word of every book required at school; she saw to it that both girls, but especially Simone, selected proper reading materials from the Bibliothèque Cardinale, the lending library where Simone was given her own subscription when she was barely four years old.[33] The only way for someone whose education had been as spotty as Françoise's to police her daughters' education was to read everything herself, and when English lessons began at the Cours Désir, in the French equivalent of the third grade, Françoise learned English along with Simone so that she could pass judgment on everything the little girl read.

At a time when men in France had beards and mustaches, Georges remained clean-shaven all his life, and it gave him a youthful appearance that his sometimes playful disposition matched. When he felt like it, he would entertain the children with singing and dancing, but mostly his charm was reserved for the frequent visits of family and friends. He and Françoise had fallen very quickly after their marriage into roles that they played throughout the rest of their lives. She was "duty, always duty, and virtue incarnate,"[34] and he was "a very frivolous man who, before the war, played the comedy of the world—a lawyer who didn't work much, a man who liked to enjoy himself, a true *boulevardier*."[35]

So to her father Simone was "a mind," and to her mother a little girl who needed supervision, advice, discipline, and was only occasionally given affection. As adults, both Simone and Hélène believed that their mother was harder on herself than she was on them, and that her strictness was often compensation for her insecurity in Parisian society. But in the two little girls of whom so much was expected, Françoise's withholding of warmth and affection and the severity of her demeanor resulted in confusion and a certain amount of anxiety.

Françoise was proud of Simone, often at the expense of Hélène. When Simone stood first in her class, she was praised effusively, but when Hélène also came in first Françoise remarked testily, "Oh, well, it was easier for you because you have your sister as example and helper."[36] Within the family, Simone's early role as the focus of attention intensified as time went on, and the complexity of the relationship between mother and daughter heightened as well. Hélène offers this perspective on their relationship during Simone's primary-school days: "There is no question in my mind now that our mother had enormous admiration for Simone, that she identified with her in those early years. She was proud of Simone's intelligence, her quick mind, but at the same time I think she must have been anxious that Simone was not fitting into the pattern of behavior that was expected of her within her station in society. Perhaps our mother felt responsible for this."

Hélène's memories of her childhood, as perhaps happens to the younger child when the older is given such special status, are much more intense and more clearly detailed than Simone's were. Hélène's is a memory of incident, behavior, feeling, a much more visual memory perhaps because she is a painter and has had a long career exploring the inner nature of the world around her. Simone spoke of her role within the family brusquely and was prone to dismissive generalities. For example, her description of her life as a child, made when she was seventy-five: "I was a very happy child until I was eleven years old, and the happiest year of my childhood was probably my first year at the Cours Désir."

After that, as far as she was concerned, there was only misery and unhappiness, and most of it had to do with her father.

When the Trouble Really Started

T HE FAMILY HAPPINESS began to erode with the onset of World War I. Simone and Hélène were at Meyrignac in August while Georges and Françoise spent three weeks as they did each year in Divonne-les-Bains. One of the couple's friends was the director of the Grand Hotel, and he gave them and others in their circle free lodgings in exchange for nightly performances of amateur theatricals in the hotel and casino.

As soon as news of the declaration of war reached them, they fled to their children. All over France, people were in a frenzy, cutting short their August holiday, jamming trains in frantic haste to return home. After a harried forty-eight-hour journey, Françoise and Georges arrived at Meyrignac to find the household in considerable agitation. The men returned each day from the village square to closet themselves behind closed doors and discuss what to do in low voices. The women veered between preparations to hoard foodstuffs and tearful outbursts about imagined rape, pillage and plunder. Simone, Hélène and their cousins hid under windows and at keyholes, thrilled by words like "occupation" and "requisition" which they overheard the adults speaking in hushed tones. Soon Simone was directing the other children in war games she invented. She always took the role of the President of the Third Republic, Raymond Poincaré, because her grandfather Beauvoir considered him the most powerful player in the unfolding world drama. Naturally, with Simone directing the action, France always won.[1]

There was a general fear of occupation among the adults, who all decided not to return to Paris until they could determine what would happen to the capital. Gaston and his family stayed on at Meyrignac, Georges and his went to La Grillère to stay with his sister Hélène and her family, but all supported the war effort with a vengeance. There was a frenzy of canning and preserving, both for the winter ahead and for the eventuality of a long siege, and in the evenings the women sewed and knitted for their families and the soldiers with equal enthusiasm. Simone learned to knit—"the only time in my life I did those sorts of feminine occupations with any pleasure"[2]—and went along with her mother to distribute food to convoys of soldiers at the railway station in Uzerche.

Georges had been discharged from the Army Reserve because of a weakened heart in 1913, when the first rumbling efforts toward mobilization had shaken France. He had had what was probably a form of rheumatic fever when he was a child, and during an army physical examination it was discovered that he had suffered permanent damage. From then on it was known in the family as "Georges's heart trouble."[3] Whatever it may have been, it was not serious enough to keep him from being called for active service in the Zouaves once the war began, and by October he was at the front. Within weeks, Georges suffered a serious enough heart attack that he was discharged from active service and sent to a military hospital to recover. All the relatives were organized to care for the children as Françoise spent all the time she was allowed at his bedside. Early in 1915, he left the hospital for Paris and the offices of the Ministry of War. He spent the rest of the war years on duty there, out of uniform but still in military service.

In inflation-riddled Paris he tried to support his family in their usual way of life on his corporal's pay. It was tantamount to the lowliest enlisted man taking on the financial obligation of supporting a general's household. What little capital he had was soon gone, and so began a wary watch on his few investments, all of which paid ever-diminishing returns.

The war made life in Paris much more difficult than in the country, where there was easier access to food. Françoise did her part to protect the family resources, and frugality became her all-consuming passion. She grew skilled in using every last scrap, whether it was food, clothing or household objects. She sewed, patched, embroidered, no matter where she was or whom she was with, and used the daily Métro trips to and from the Cours Désir to crochet miles of decorative lace border for undergarments. She kept a household ledger, and every evening she entered her household expenditures, accounting for everything down to the last centime. She even grew adept at finagling free meals, and all invitations to dine elsewhere were eagerly accepted.

Of the two children, Hélène was the more likely to join her mother in creative feminine pursuits, but that was because her own interests were visual and tactile and at that age, such things as cooking and sewing gave her pleasure. She described herself later as having "the more pacific disposition, more conciliatory, malleable. Perhaps I thought I was protecting Simone from their disappointment and disapproval by being so." It worked against her when Françoise imposed most of the domestic chores on Hélène because Simone was opposed to doing them.

Simone's personality was just the opposite of Hélène's. She liked order and discipline, thrived on these concepts as preached at the Cours Désir, and relished the opportunity to measure everything carefully, account for everything in the house and find a use for the most unlikely object. However, she preferred directing to actually doing these things: regularity, economy and duty pleased her and, as she admitted much later in life, "probably made me a little prig."

As the war continued, physical changes occurred in both children. Hélène grew prettier as she grew older, so the name "Poupette" became more apt with every passing year. Simone was just the opposite, changing from a robustly healthy child into a somewhat sickly, plain little girl. Her appetite had always been quirky, and before the war she had been catered to by her mother and Louise, who fed her whatever she wanted to eat, mostly puddings, sweets and starches. With the war and the strained financial situation, Simone had to eat whatever Françoise was able to put together for the family meal; consequently, she ate very little and then only what she wanted. When she was eight, a scoliotic condition of the spine was diagnosed, and she was sent to special gymnastic classes in the hope of correcting it.

In these classes, and in the games and exercises at school, she discovered that she was totally lacking in grace and athletic ability. This discovery led to one of the earliest manifestations of the self-protecting behavior that she used throughout her life: what she could neither conquer nor change she taught herself to disregard entirely and to find something else in compensation. In this instance, she ignored all sports, physical contests and exercise, claiming they bored her. Since she was not popular with her classmates, whom she irritated with her know-it-all attitude, and since there was no other outlet for her compulsion for order and perfection, she became obsessed with excelling in classwork.

Simone had readily embraced the excessive order at home that war and family finances dictated, expressing her patriotism through excessive rigidity. She behaved so compulsively that her teachers had to ask Françoise to insist that the child relax her fixation on spending every moment productively. Françoise was bewildered by the teachers' entreaty, because she found it commendable that her daughter covered every scrap with minuscule writing in order to save paper, or that she programmed every waking moment with elaborate schedules for reading, study and prayer. The only aspect of Simone's compulsive behavior that Françoise did not approve of was the hysterical tantrums when something happened to disrupt the girl's self-imposed schedule.

Simone's behavior became most compulsive just when the situation in Paris became the most serious and chaotic. Guns could be heard night after night, booming in the distance, and even the words "la Grosse Berthe" (Big Bertha) filled people with palpable fear, especially when shells began to land nearby on the Boulevard Saint-Michel.[4] Fire and air-raid wardens patrolled the streets demanding that lights be extinguished, and citizens were warned to take shelter in basements as soon as alarms sounded. But the Beauvoir family slept in their own beds because Georges refused to spend his nights in the cellar, and after one or two attempts to take the children down by herself Françoise gave up and followed his example. Because of blackouts and curfew, their parties were sometimes forced to go on all night, especially when they played bridge (a new passion for both) and forgot to keep track of the time. The children sometimes woke up in the morning to find guests dozing in chairs and on the sofa.

At first, this social disorder was interpreted by the methodical Simone as the necessary excitement that war generated, and since she was a passionate little patriot, she embraced it as another example of how a good French citizen coped. She tried to find a way to turn disorder into harmonious duty and was the member of the family who made it all ritualistic: if there was to be a blackout each night, then she would shut the curtains with military efficiency; if people were coming to visit, she would prepare blankets on the off chance that they would have to stay the night. She added these rituals to her other daily chores and was pleased that, like her mother, she was not wasting a minute of her waking time.

"I needed to be confined within a framework whose rigidity would justify my existence," is how she defined herself during this time. "I realized this, because I was afraid of changes."[5]

But the changes mounted anyway, and as Françoise grew more harried from all the demands made upon her, Simone too grew uneasy amidst the increasing instability of the people around them. Grandfather Brasseur was terrified of the nightly alerts, and he became increasingly manic and developed irrational fears about what would happen when the Germans destroyed Paris, which he was sure would happen at any moment.[6] Madame Brasseur grew disoriented and suffered a breakdown. Since there was no money to send her to a rest home in the country, Françoise installed her for the duration of the war in the room shared by Louise and Simone. It caused a major disruption in the household, as maid and child had to camp out on cots set up in the living room each evening and taken down early in the morning (Hélène continued to sleep on her cot in the hallway). Françoise and Georges had to make do with the dining room for their private moments and their entertaining. His study remained his sacrosanct preserve, even though he seldom used it.

All this was an enormous burden for Françoise, who frequently lost her temper and fought with everyone. The scenes between her and Louise frightened the children, but even worse were the nightly arguments when they lay awake in their beds listening to their parents shouting at each other in the next room. During the day, they learned to find quiet corners where they would be out of reach of Françoise's scathing outbursts and the hasty strike of her fist or foot. Simone sat for hours under her father's desk in her own private dream world. The fixtures on the desk, which she was forbidden to touch, caught her imagination, so that letter opener, blotter, scissors and ink pot took on mythic status in her eyes. Just staring at these wonderful objects made her forget the household tensions and disorder.

School was no better: most of the pupils from the Cours Désir had been evacuated to the country, but Simone and Hélène attended regularly, no matter how serious the alerts. It was eerie, arriving one day as they usually did for classes, escorted by Françoise (who made six trips back and forth each day), to find the courtyard and all the classrooms deserted. While they were on the Métro an alert had sounded, and the few pupils still attending the school had been hidden by their teachers in the cellar. In her class, only Simone and one other girl had not been evacuated to the country. With her ability to turn even the most oppressive situation into a positive experience, and her need to be the center of attention no matter how small the group, Simone monopolized her teacher and turned the lessons into private tutoring sessions.

Still, it was lonely, and the fixed points on the compass of her life were no longer steadfast. Her mother was harried, frustrated and erratic; even in the twice-daily prayer sessions where she had always been so calm and loving, Françoise was distracted. She had no time for the soothing tranquility of prayer and reflection, but needed to rush through the recitation as quickly as possible so that she could move on to the next in the seemingly endless round of necessary chores. The two little girls, who had loved these ritualistic sessions, learned to pray quietly and to let Françoise end them quickly without triggering an outburst.

Simone was ten years old in 1918. She had learned to maneuver around Françoise's temper, but she had not yet learned how to deal with the unfocused anxiety instilled in her by her usually exuberant father's uncharacteristically subdued behavior. Sleeping in the living room, she could overhear conversations about money, Françoise berating Georges for not wanting to return to the legal profession, Georges retaliating with scathing remarks about her unpaid dowry. The atmosphere in the home was so pessimistic, so straitened, that the mood enveloped the children as well.

Georges had decided not to return to the practice of law, saying he could no longer afford to do so. He formed his economic and political opinions from reading Catholic journals and conservative newspapers, and in this particular instance from a more personal involvement as well. The word "Bolshevik" had recently come into his vocabulary, not only because of the political situation in Russia, but also because almost all of his inheritance was invested in prerevolutionary stocks in Russian railroads and mining and mineral concessions. Now these were worthless, and even though it was not directly Georges's fault (for his father had made the investments), he felt the shame of the loss. Thus it was all the more difficult to think about practicing law again when there was no money to pay for the office rental and furnishings and nothing to live on until the practice began to pay for itself. Also, at the age of forty, Georges de Beauvoir had already suffered two heart attacks. His health had not returned to its prewar robustness and was unlikely ever to do so.

Gustave Brasseur came to his son-in-law's rescue. The indomitable old speculator had landed on his feet once again, and spent the last two years of the war as a director of a factory that made boots and shoes. Brasseur had secured lucrative military contracts, so the factory was highly profitable, and he offered Georges a position as co-director. It was a shabby comedown socially as well as professionally, but, feeling he had no other alternative, Georges accepted. He joked that he had become "newly poor" and went off to work with good humor but not with regularity. He used his protected position as Brasseur's son-in-law to do only what he could not avoid.

It was not long before the false prosperity of the military contracts came to an end, an eventuality no one in the firm was prepared to face. This time it was one of Georges's rich cousins, co-director of the Banque de Paris in Holland, who came to his rescue, with a position as a newspaper advertising salesman. Simone de Beauvoir described it: "My father had to go out and find businessmen who wanted to put shares on the market and then ask if they were willing to pay for the newspapers he represented to speak well of their enterprise. It meant that if they didn't pay they would be written up badly. It was almost a sort of blackmail. This was humiliating work, because it wasn't very honest. Worst of all, it didn't pay well."

Charming and personable as he was, Georges de Beauvoir was not a salesman and was soon dismissed. For the rest of his life he drifted from one paper to another, sometimes as an advertising salesman, sometimes as a minor functionary for the financial pages of one of the lesser journals. Each position usually ended when his superiors realized that his personal charm did not produce sufficient revenue to pay his modest salary. He was dismissed more than once when his daily schedule came to the attention of his editors: he rose around ten, arrived at the Stock Exchange around eleven to be seen before lunch, after which he paid a brief visit to the offices before going off to play bridge all afternoon until it was time to go to a café and drink until dinner.[7]

For a full year after the Armistice of November 11, 1918, life on the Boulevard du Montparnasse went on much as it had during the war. Madame Brasseur recovered and returned to her home on the Rue Denfert-Rochereau, and Louise and the children had their room and hallway to themselves again. But that was the only real change. Françoise continued to scrimp and save. The two girls wore their tight, ill-fitting clothing until modesty decreed that it had to be replaced with larger sizes. Even then, Françoise converted the worn-out fabric into something useful elsewhere in the house. The outings to the theater, the summer walks through the Luxembourg Gardens, the occasional treats of candy or books were all gone now, and everyone's energy except Georges's was directed toward saving to maintain appearances. The children were old enough now to resent that keeping up this facade was the reason there were no treats for them. They had some friends at school whose families were ostensibly poorer than their own, but these children were dressed better and had more toys. The two girls resented their mother's "day" and the calling cards she religiously sent out to ladies she did not even care for, announcing that "Madame Georges de Beauvoir receives the first Friday of every month." They begrudged the expense of tea, cookies and other treats they had to serve but could not eat until the guests had had their fill.[8] Françoise continued to "pay visits" (to her friends and relatives) and "make calls" (more formal and ceremonial) and even gave an occasional "grand dinner" for which an outside maid was recruited to help Louise. She continued to keep the drawing room as pristine as possible, which meant, of course, that no one in the family could use it except on special occasions. She worked diligently to maintain "a very bourgeois house and an image of bourgeois life," but her daughters remembered a succession of people richer than they sitting uncomfortably in the drawing room. Besides the apartment, only the children's enrollment in the Cours Désir attested to their social position. Somehow, despite Georges's ravings that they would be better off in the lycée, Françoise always found the money to pay the tuition.

However, by the summer of 1919 when Simone was eleven and a half and Hélène was nine, all her economies were not enough, and a drastic measure was needed to stave off financial disaster. They had to move, but all they could afford was an apartment in a middle-class building at 71 Rue de Rennes, on the fifth floor without an elevator, the cheapest in the building because the only rooms above it were the tiny warrens where the maids who were employed throughout the building slept. Simone's sense of adventure had developed enough for her to be excited by the move, but when she discovered how high up they would be, and that there was no balcony, as there had been on the Boulevard Raspail, she pouted that she would be cut off from watching the life on the street, a source of her most vivid imaginings.

When she saw the apartment, pouting gave way to sadness. Françoise and Georges had left their daughters at La Grillère while they made the move in early autumn, so when the girls returned from the glorious summer in the grand old shabby-genteel house, so full of light and space and secret, private places, their old life was gone and they had not even said farewell to it. They were led up the narrow staircase of the new building to what Simone de Beauvoir always described as "a cramped apartment, dark and gloomy,"[9] probably because the heavy black wooden furniture which had fit so nicely into the old apartment now overwhelmed the small rooms of the new one. It was, however, light and airy, so high up that there were clear views on one side of the Eiffel Tower and on the other of the Panthéon. The darkness and gloom she felt were more likely due to the family's shame and unhappiness at having to live in such reduced circumstances.

This apartment had living and dining rooms opening onto each other, but they were small. Georges still had a study, actually a large storage room or closet opening onto his and Françoise's bedroom. Louise moved temporarily into one of the maids' chambers above them, and Simone and Hélène shared a bedroom now, still a small room next to the kitchen, so tiny they could barely stand in the space between the beds and then only one at a time. There was no room for anything else, not even a small dresser. It was all the space they had as long as they lived in their parents' home. The few friends whom they brought to visit as they were growing up still remember how shocked they were to see the sad little room. If any of these friends suggested that Georges ought to give up his study to his daughters, Simone was indignant. She thought it entirely appropriate that her father should have a room all his own to sit in when he wanted to be alone. Except for the blow that confinement in the small quarters dealt to her spirit, she believed the distribution of private space was as equitable as it could be under the circumstances.[10]

There was no longer even a corridor for games, because the apartment had only a tiny entrance foyer. There was a water closet but no toilet, only a chamber pot beside a small washstand. The only running water came from an erratic kitchen tap. Georges and Françoise shared the occasional burden of carrying water up the five flights, but Georges emptied the slop jar each morning. Simone and Hélène carried the daily household rubbish and peelings down to the common refuse bins at the end of the evening meal. There was no central heating, and they all carried up the wood and the coal. Georges no longer joked about being "newly poor," for the daily life of the household was an unrelenting grind and no one could find anything to laugh about.

Françoise's life changed even more drastically shortly after the move to the Rue de Rennes. Louise, who had been sleeping in one of the top-floor maids' rooms, married and left the Beauvoirs' employ. Several young girls were imported from Meyrignac to take her place, but each lasted only a few weeks, either from homesickness or because Françoise found some fault in their character. To her friends, Françoise complained of "the difficulty of finding and keeping good help,"[11] but it was really a convenient excuse for a needed further economy. From then on, Françoise had no daily domestic help, which was probably the most visibly shameful indicator of their changed social status: the *haute bourgeoisie* always had at least one live-in servant, the middle class never did.[12] Everything in the household—shopping, cooking, heavy cleaning, transporting the children to and from school—fell to her. This thirty-one-year-old woman who had been raised in comfort and expected to be well provided for in marriage, now had the last of her expectations shattered forever. For the rest of her life, she maintained an armored facade of bourgeois gentility and breeding that very few people ever saw behind. From then on, no one but family and one or two very close friends was invited to the Beauvoir apartment— they simply could not afford it—so only those few knew the true daily circumstances of Françoise's life.

As for Georges, publicly he maintained a mask of resigned good humor that never ceased to amaze anyone who realized how far he had fallen socially, professionally and financially. His wife and children, however, were "witness to his personal failure"; silence and withdrawal characterized his behavior to them.[13]

Georges's implacability was in strong contrast to Françoise's shrillness and anger. Now not only could the children hear the arguments which woke them late at night when Georges finally came home, usually drunk; they were also witness to the sharp remarks and bitter retorts during the day, when Georges prowled the house in his dressing gown drinking coffee and smoking cigarettes while Françoise did her chores around him. Still, the bond between them was strong, as much, their daughters believed, because of sexual passion as because each was so deeply imbued with the idea of the duties and responsibilities of the partners in a marriage and the necessity, if not to fulfill them, at least to give the appearance of doing so. Their one true unity remained the disciplining of their daughters.

One summer at Meyrignac, Georges decided the girls should have bicycles, an expenditure Françoise vetoed at once. He talked about it for several weeks, hinting, pleading, trying to change her mind, but she continued to berate him for "an extravagance that they can only use for one or two months each year," and finally he dropped the matter. The children were crushed, but they knew it was useless to argue with their mother.[14]

Curiously, despite the terrible fall the family had suffered, moving house eased finances enough to permit occasional outings whenever Georges's job was going well or an influential client presented him with what might be called today either patronage or a bribe, depending on how severely one wishes to judge it. He came home with expensive tickets to theaters, music halls and Punch-and-Judy shows, where the children were treated to chocolates and ices. Somehow, there was always transportation money for the glorious summers at Meyrignac and the frequent gatherings at the homes of the many cousins, aunts and uncles who lived in and around Paris. Rather than envying their richer cousins, both Simone and Hélène often felt only relief to be back in their own home after a celebration in a wealthy apartment where the rich food, the fancy clothing and the elaborate furnishings were often too excessive for their modest appetites.

During the girls' childhood years, Françoise and Georges shared the same attitude toward their daughters: since both were female, the second amounted to little more than an unnecessary appendage, especially when the first was high-spirited, independent, precocious, and demanding to be the center of attention, as Simone was. Their attitude solidified when Hélène, although prettier, grew shy, cried a lot, clung to her mother, and appeared to be generally bewildered by her whirlwind of a sister. When she became Simone's faithful follower, it simply made the circumstances much easier for Georges and Françoise to meet Simone's needs, leaving

Hélène to follow behind as best she could. Fortunately Simone adored Hélène, who in turn was grateful for her sister's attention and affection, for such "valorization."[15]

This difference in the parents' attitude toward the daughters proved to be the basis of an exceptionally difficult adolescence for Simone and a somewhat easier one for Hélène. Simone, accustomed to breezing through every situation fully expecting her wishes to be satisfied, found it difficult to accept the changing attitudes of her parents as she matured, while Hélène, who had spent her childhood expecting to be disappointed by them, learned quickly how to deflect the literal and metaphorical blows of family life by waiting to take her cue from Simone.

Recalling the onset of adolescence was painful for both sisters. Hélène spoke of it simply, directly, and with a curious sort of dispassion. Her descriptions were brief, as if she hoped to get the memory of it over as quickly as possible. Simone, who wrote about it eloquently and fully in the first volume of her memoirs, seemed to need to discuss it until she died, as if going over the territory one more time would have made it less alien, more familiar. The little girl who believed hers was the perfect childhood had an adolescence so wretched that its unhappiness takes on a classicity of form, and if there were not so many witnesses to attest to the veracity of her own representation of it in her memoirs, one might accuse her of consciously shaping it as a literary device.

"I loved my mother a lot until I was twelve or thirteen, and then I began to love her much less," Simone de Beauvoir said. "She was very hostile toward me, really unbearable, during my entire adolescence. My relationship with her, from the time I was about ten or eleven, was one of conflict. After that, we began to have a good relationship again, but it was very distant because we could not get along at all. Gradually I came to understand that my mother held dear all those bourgeois, Catholic, pious, well-thinking ideas which I was learning to detest. She absolutely did not like my ideas. I could not speak to her about anything that mattered to me. She disapproved of everything. And, of course, our earlier relationship had done nothing to make our adult relationship any easier. My mother was so much nicer [to Hélène] than she ever was with me. Still, I know that my sister suffered and that she had much the same kind of conflict that I had. She just knew how to hide it better."

Hélène de Beauvoir took a more distanced view: "I think our mother was very proud of her daughters once we were adults, even though it hurt her to accept what we had become, which was so different from herself and what she would have wished for us. The problem with our relationship dates from much earlier: she wanted to live through us, but she also wanted us to live for her. And we wouldn't do that."

When they were asked to assess the importance of each parent in their lives, Hélène replied with equanimity, moving in her description from one to the other, giving each a different importance at different times. Simone was quick to assert that her father "was the most important parent, the one who had the most influence, who meant the most to me." Yet there is no description of her father in her writings to match the intensity of the one of her mother, and both in interviews and in her own works it is her own real mother and a succession of fictional ones who are the dominant parent.[16] There are very few fathers in her fiction, and in her own memoirs Georges de Beauvoir becomes an increasingly shadowy figure.

There are so many contradictions in her portrait of her father, perhaps because, as she told it: "There were so many contradictions on my father's part toward me. It was through him I found a taste for the intellectual life, even though his tastes were so different from mine almost from the very beginning. He was very proud to have a daughter who was so successful in her studies, but at the same time he did not like intellectuals, whom he called 'free thinkers.' He liked it that I was brilliant intellectually, but at the same time he wanted me to be pretty, and to be 'the nice girl who serves tea at home' and all that. But I took only what suited me from all that he wanted me to be, and that was where the trouble really started."

FOUR

The Girl with a Man's Brain

IN LATER LIFE she thought she was ten or eleven the first time she heard her father solemnly intone the remark that became the dirge of her adolescent years: "You girls will never marry, because you will have no dowry." She remembers how her mother sat with grimly pursed lips not looking at anyone but staring intently at the ever present handwork over which her needle flew.[1] The scene, etched in Simone de Beauvoir's mind, was always the living room in the Rue de Rennes even though the words were repeated over the years in varying settings—at Meyrignac, on a train, a café terrace, an evening walk—until she and Hélène were graduated from the Cours Désir and both were training for a profession. Even then, Georges made this pronouncement with a mixture of resignation and disbelief, as if he could not accept that the reality of his words had actually come to pass.

In and of themselves, the words, indeed the concepts of marriage and the dowry, meant little or nothing to the young Simone except that they were both something grown-ups desired. As she grew older and developed more understanding of what her father's statement really meant about the determination of her future, she was puzzled by the sadness it always induced in him, for she certainly did not share his chagrin.

It is tempting to suggest that this was only another of the negative or unfortunate situations throughout her life which, if she could not change them, she would find a way to view in a positive, even optimistic light, and perhaps there is more than a little of this attitude here. More likely, however, her rejection of Georges's resignation and embarrassment in favor of her own optimism can be traced to her zest for learning and the enthusiasm with which she embraced the other part of the paternal dirge: "You girls must study hard to prepare yourselves to work all your lives, and so you must train for a profession."[2]

"Things went wrong in lots of ways" is the succinct description she gave many years later,[3] blaming her father's lifetime of low earnings in menial positions and the humiliation that came with his recurring dismissals as the cause of her family's problems and her own unhappy adolescence. In a subsequent conversation, she became sarcastically apologetic about her father, saying he did not try to recoup his lost fortunes because "perhaps he was afraid he might fatally injure his heart." Her sister disagreed that any charity should be shown toward him, because "all the men in the Beauvoir family were lazy and did not like to work; the women are the strong ones who did it all and saved face for the men."

Georges de Beauvoir was a man who had few close friends and was not inclined to share confidences with anyone. To his father and brother he exhibited an air of hale and hearty well-being. To his wife his attitude was one of benevolent paternalism, while hers to him was one of ostensible obedience.[4] Her role in their life was to uphold his dignity and authority to the children and all outsiders, and the internal conflict this behavior induced took a harsh toll. What had been pride in her elder daughter's eager mind was now a combination of resentment that Françoise herself had no time for these pleasures and anger that Simone's need for study time meant that at first she could not and then later would not assume a larger share of responsibility for the household chores. As time went on and Simone's studies became both more demanding and engrossing, Françoise tried to relieve her of some household responsibility by shunting some of it onto Hélène or else doing it herself. Reflecting on this later brought conflicting emotions to Simone de Beauvoir: "I was ashamed; perhaps [I felt] 'guilt' as the word is used now, that I let my mother do those never-ending chores while I sat and read. But I had to get my education first because I wanted it so much, then because I had to support myself." And so Françoise's verbal lashings, black tempers and negative attitudes grew more pronounced as Simone continued to grow into the kind of woman she simply did not understand.

Françoise worked hard to convey an air of gaiety that embarrassed her daughters as they grew old enough to understand the truth of the family's circumstances.[5] Perhaps this was why Georges began to go out almost every night after dinner to one of several neighborhood bars "of the better sort,"[6] meaning ones which shared his political views. Françoise never questioned his absences, so neither did the children: if she accepted it as his right, they were too young to question or dispute it.

When Georges was at home, his mood alternated between charm and silence. When charming, he treated the children to such intense gaiety that it sometimes made Simone manic with joy, as Georges the would-be actor sang songs, played games, made faces and otherwise amused them. His silence was one of withdrawal rather than anger. He listened abstractedly to their report of the school day, but when he shut the door to his study it was the signal for quiet, and the two girls would sit at the dining-room table sadly doing their lessons while Françoise peeked over their shoulders as she fussed about the apartment.

Direct supervision fell to her. Although she was deferential to her husband in matters affecting the family's status and position, hers was the strength that formed the family backbone. All consistency in daily life came from Françoise. She had to be the strong parent, in charge as she was of morals, discipline, manners and behavior; in consequence, she became rigid and dour. With her, there was never any deviation from duty, so prayers, lessons and household chores were all done in their proper order and on schedule. Her husband had in a sense abandoned her to her own devices, and so she fell back upon the teachings of her childhood to see her through what was a difficult and isolated time in her life. As Simone and Hélène grew up, Françoise's old-fashioned ideas embarrassed and her religious piety infuriated them.

Georges sometimes supervised—with distance and detachment—both his daughters' schoolwork, but because Simone was the more insistent he paid the most attention to her studies. This consisted mostly of giving cursory approval to her neat exercise books, and an even briefer nod toward the succession of pious tomes and ladylike exercises that composed her curriculum. He decided that Simone, especially, needed stronger fare and supervised her extracurricular reading. He compiled poems and stories by many popular writers whose work was considered suitable for an adolescent girl, also by some of the Parnassians like Coppée, whose poems stressed fervent Catholicism; Banville, who wrote poems of fantasy and wit; and Hégésippe Moreau, the poet of poor people and country life.[7] Because he still loved the theater, he read to them from his favorite theatrical journal, *Comoedia* (to which he still kept a subscription despite his reduced circumstances, arguing that books and periodicals were a necessity of life and Françoise would have to economize elsewhere), or from plays like Rostand's *Cyrano de Bergerac* or one of Labiche's comedies. Very early in their lives, possibly the second grade, he began to impress upon his daughters the great heritage that they, as French children, had in literature. Starting with Lanson's *Histoire de la littérature française*, he read aloud to them over the years from an increasingly sophisticated series of histories of French literature. His opinions, being Catholic, royalist and, by extension, conservative, were greeted with increasing skepticism as Simone's intellect developed and she formed her own opinions about what constituted good literature.

Simone's opinion of Françoise's abdication and Georges's direction of their cultural life was predictable. She herself, in a 1966 conversation, called it "classic." Until she was ten or eleven she had been "fixated" on her mother as the one perfect being in her life, and in her adolescence she transferred these affections to her father. Indeed, her feeling for her father, especially after he took such a commanding presence in the one area of her life that meant the most to her, the selection of what she should read, became one of such adoration that almost fifty years later she called it an "Oedipus complex." Then Beauvoir agreed that since there was nothing physical in her regard for her father, only intellectual, "in reality it was truly a love affair of the head."[8]

"I don't remember ever sitting on my father's knee," Beauvoir recalled. "I may have reached up occasionally and kissed him on the cheek, but it never went further than that. I don't think he ever embraced me. He never, as far as I can remember, had any physical contact with us at all except for the occasional peck he allowed us. He took care of our education, but that was all. There was no moral or physical rapport with him. No, one could say there was no human rapport with him. All this was entirely the responsibility of my mother."[9]

Since her father was associated with the life of the mind, she elevated him to monumental status, while her mother, who was responsible for everything mundane, became associated with the daily drudgery of making ends meet and keeping up appearances. It was easy for Simone to identify with her father, because her only contact with him was educational. But it was also her preferred form of fun, amusing tasks created especially for her by the beloved Papa who doled out the occasional sweet, entertainment, or prize. She was always ready to show off her latest achievement and usually did so to his satisfaction; then after her little performance he sent her off, happy to prepare herself for another educational triumph while he secluded himself in his study from the hard work and difficult circumstances of the rest of the family. He thus contributed, albeit unconsciously, to Simone's increasing inability to identify herself with Françoise.

"Simone thinks like a man!" Georges would say, and for years she preened herself whenever she heard these words, considering them the highest compliment he could pay her.[10] No wonder she preferred this praise to Françoise's strident scolding because she could not or would not learn to sew, mend, or prepare food and took no pride in her appearance. She identified herself with her father, not as a man, not wanting to be a man or regretting that she had not been born one, but as a superior woman, and much more deserving to be her father's partner than her mother, who never had time anymore to sit quietly by her husband's side while he read from Taine or other writers whom he deemed suitable for her ears.

Simone and Hélène began to daydream about the men they would marry. Simone's ideal was always "someone like Papa," which horrified Hélène,[11] whose hero was always tall, blond, athletic and the antithesis of her father. But Simone's was different. "What I want is an intelligent man," she would say, describing how in her daydreams she and he spent their time reading and learning together. She seldom, if ever, gave her hero a physical description, describing him instead in terms of the books they would read together and, sometimes, of those they would write together. Her ideal situation was a sun-filled room with two desks side by side where the two of them would sit contentedly working—an eerily prescient description of the life she shared with Jean-Paul Sartre for many years.[12]

If Simone had only remained the pretty, plump little blue-eyed baby who delighted all her relatives with her precocious songs and poems, all might have been well in her relationship with her father. Instead, she became a gangly, skinny, awkward little girl before metamorphosing into a lumpy, awkward, blotchy-faced teenager with an alarming and uncontrollable facial tic. Of her father she said:

"I did everything he told me to do at first. He took pride in my mind, so I embraced learning, I prepared myself for a profession from the moment he told me that was what I had to do. And then, after all that blind obedience on my part, it was he who rejected me. How shall I describe it? I suppose I should call it my 'awkward years': I was an ugly, graceless adolescent, and he preferred my prettier sister because at heart he detested intellectuals. It was very curious, and I don't think I really understood it until I was preparing for the university: he loved to read, but he detested intellectuals and I was becoming one. There was terrible conflict over that all the while I lived at home. It was never expressed in words, and we were always polite with each other, but whatever had been between us was completely broken off. Sometime around my eleventh year, from then on, we didn't get along at all."

Hélène was just the opposite of her sister, one of the fortunate few who grew from adorable babyhood to beautiful childhood and graceful womanhood. Georges, a connoisseur of feminine beauty, transferred his attentions to her. He enjoyed being seen with his pretty daughter on his arm, and began to encourage her toward a stage career by taking her to musical comedies and performances by the Comédie-Française. Hélène had a lovely clear singing voice, and at Meyrignac she often played the piano and sang with her Grandfather Beauvoir, who taught her all of Offenbach's songs and called her his "Belle Hélène." Encouraged by Hélène's success in family musical evenings, Georges secured roles for her in amateur theatricals. She hated it, could not bear to stand in front of an audience, and considered herself fortunate that although her voice was pleasant it was a small thin one, incapable of the range and projection necessary for a stage career. When he realized this, Georges lost interest in guiding her toward the stage.[13]

When Simone was twelve, Georges told her, one would hope jokingly, that she was ugly. The word cut her in ways that caused emotional pain more than sixty years later. In her memoirs and in many interviews in which she discussed her parents and her childhood, Beauvoir included the blunt statement that her father pronounced her "laide." The flat, emotionless tone with which she repeated this remark surely covered a deep and continuing pain.[14]

While Georges squired Hélène about Paris, Simone hid her disappointment and her face in a continuing succession of books. His attentions, rather than causing a rift between the sisters, served only to increase the bond between them: young as they were, they seemed to know instinctively that Georges could withdraw affection as quickly as he bestowed it. When, for example, Hélène proved unsuitable for the stage, Georges began to berate both daughters by holding up his brother's daughter, Jeanne de Beauvoir, as the ideal of what a young girl should be. Jeanne, who later inherited Meyrignac and lived there with her lawyer husband and their eleven children, was also left a considerable fortune by her mother and was therefore destined for a good marriage. She always had a sweet and agreeable disposition, but Georges probably held her in such high esteem because of her advantageous prospects.[15]

One area in which Georges's influence on Simone had important consequences was religion. He was "an atheist until he died, even then refusing to see a priest,"[16] content to leave the practice of Catholicism to Françoise, whose zeal never faltered. The young Simone who thought "like a man" had no trouble rejecting her mother's "womanly" attitude. Like her father, she became an unbeliever, but, unlike him, she had no authority or freedom to say so in the home. Simone's rejection of Catholicism caused many bitter arguments between her and Françoise, especially when sometime before her fourteenth year she declared her refusal to attend mass anymore. This honest and forthright declaration marked the first of many times when the still-dependent daughter refused to obey her mother. It shows how differently the two sisters responded to their loss of faith: Hélène pretended to go to Mass but went to the Louvre instead. Françoise, who soon caught on to the ruse, nevertheless maintained discreet silence, and there was no open argument between her and Hélène.[17]

The sisters agreed in retrospect that Simone's declaration of disbelief did seem to mark a turning or breaking point in her relationship with their mother. For Simone, Françoise's rejection ranked on a par with Georges's remark that she was ugly: the only way she could deal with it throughout her life was to dismiss it with a shrug.

As her daughters grew to young womanhood, Françoise became an even more intrusive presence in their lives. Her work, as she perceived it, became even more time-consuming and demanding. The never-ending household routine was compounded by all the new things they were exposed to in their daily travels to and from school, as well as by what they learned there. Françoise became militantly alert to make sure they were not corrupted. Now, if characters in a book were in love but unmarried, she banned the book; if there were parts she disapproved of, she clipped those pages together and her daughters were not allowed to read them. She made the three daily trips to school on the Métro or the bus until they cried that they were too big for such supervision, but she continued to watch them like the proverbial hawk everywhere they went outside the apartment long after she could do nothing to control their movements or companions. They even caught her far too often listening outside their bedroom door on the infrequent occasions they had time to idle away in daydreams and conversation. She was ubiquitous and, in consequence, an irritant.

In retrospect, what seems remarkable about Simone de Beauvoir is how indomitable was her disposition. Her life at home was emotionally barren, and in her first three or four years at school she had no friends. She had to depend on Hélène for companionship, and Hélène was not only two years younger but also popular with many friends her own age who looked askance at the unwanted tag-along older sister. There were other humiliations for Simone as well: she was the last chosen for any game or athletic contest, and her efforts to join any of the playground groups were usually greeted with hooting laughter. With the innocent cruelty of children, she was scorned by her schoolmates as much for her ill-fitting clothes and general untidiness as for her self-important pronouncements. She was a gawky chatterbox, entirely friendless. There really was no model, no influence, no one and nothing at all in her life to help her develop any social or societal graces. Her ideas were formed and her role models came almost entirely from the books she read. Hers was the closed world of a tightly knit social class, a family constrained by Belle Epoque definitions of right conduct and proper behavior, and the reading material that came to her was severely restricted. Still, she had the courage to mount a continuing procession of rebellions in the face of such constraint well into her adult life, determined to continue no matter what the humiliation.

"Of course it bothered me that I was not popular," she admitted. "But when I compared all that to the satisfaction of reading and learning, everything else was unimportant. Those slights meant very little, and soon I didn't even think about it."

There is an element of rationalization here, of course, but everything else had become truly secondary to learning by the time she was little more than eight years old. She was so good at it, in fact, that by the time she entered her teens there was no one better. If she concentrated hard enough on that fact, she believed, nothing else could hurt her.

The Young Writer

THE INSTITUT ADELINE DÉSIR, generally known as the Cours Désir, was a curiously contradictory school, a snobbish institution priding itself on the notion that its graduates would automatically exemplify the bourgeois ideal of womanhood. Prizes given at the end of the school year were not for academic excellence but for piety, devotion to duty, and deportment. In 1914, the year Simone de Beauvoir entered, one of the most important courses was known by the euphemism "general culture," and in it the young ladies were taught how to curtsy, how to preside at tea parties, and how to address respectfully everyone from the President of France to the parish priest. Handwork, such as painting pastels, knitting and crochet, was an important part of the curriculum.

In the elementary and intermediate programs, academic courses were given in half-hour increments twice each week and consisted of grammar, arithmetic, a smattering of history, natural science, and geography. Children were expected to show musical talent and were encouraged to begin lessons as early as possible. For Simone, this meant years of piano lessons, after which she could play with brio but not with any degree of accuracy or sensitivity.

At the same time, elective courses such as English language and foreign literatures began as early as the second grade, and Latin was added in the fourth or fifth. These were supplemented by readings in the history of the Roman Catholic Church, with sermons on theology, religion and ethics given by a succession of priests attached to the school. The teachers, laywomen who had adopted the strict code of the Jesuit order and adapted it for their own teaching purposes, gave the catechism lessons. Hélène described the teachers' personality and appearance: "fanatical devout women, spinsters in the old sense of the term, which does not mean unmarried but, rather, sour bitter women. The most important lesson as far as they were concerned was that we should never cross our legs.

"In the years when women started cutting their hair and wearing shorter skirts, our teachers clung to the clothing of 1900. They wore big hats, puffy coiffures, balloon sleeves, tight waists and very long skirts, so we laughed at them. It didn't help that at home Daddy would laugh and say, 'They are stupid, stupid.' Mother would have had us in the convent taught by nuns, who she said were kinder, but our father said we had to keep some standards, and so we went to this private school which was as close to the convent as Mother could put us."

Simone remembered their teaching ability: "As for instruction, they made us say our lessons. None was really capable of teaching, so they made us memorize everything on the printed page. If a Cours Désir girl ever took the *baccalauréat*, she generally did well if she had a good memory. We had no respect for any of our teachers—one in particular took the *bac* at least three years in a row that we knew of, and she failed it every time."

By the time the children were to make their First Communion, the teachers expected them to have read, digested and memorized as much as possible of *The Imitation of Christ*.[1] Afterward they were expected to receive the sacrament of the Eucharist a minimum of three times each week, and to prepare themselves for it by reading at least one chapter of the book beforehand, as well as a succession of other spiritually uplifting tracts. As they advanced in age and grade, their edition of *Imitatio Christi*, as they called *De Imitatione Christi* whether or not they knew Latin, also became more advanced, from child's primer to facsimile of the original, for they were expected to pay particular attention to the sections on the preparation for prayer and the reception of the Eucharist almost as if they were preparing for holy orders.

Simone embraced these readings with such fervor that her piety was praised by the teachers and the priests. They did not know, however, that her devotion to Christ was a personal one, formed by her perception of him as lover rather than as religious savior. She managed, despite Françoise's constant surveillance, to get her hands on an enormous collection of very bad novels, some from the other girls at school, most from her cousin Magdeleine during the summers at Meyrignac. In many of them, Christ was depicted as a hero of swashbuckling proportions in retellings of the Gospels with little basis in fact beyond the barest outline of his life. These books had copious illustrations, showing a slim Christ, dark, bearded and with a pencil-thin mustache, the image of a handsome Frenchman of the time. In reality, the radiant, visionary behavior that made Simone so popular with the teachers and the priests was only prepubescent attraction to a fictional hero.

From her infancy, the strongest influence in her life after her parents was what she read. They had taught her this reverence for books, and from the beginning she equated reading with happiness. Her earliest happy memories were of Georges reading aloud to Françoise while Simone and Hélène sat nearby, generally looking at the pictures and quietly turning the pages of their own picture books while his mellifluous voice spoke words they were not yet yet old enough to understand. Happiest of all were the times when he read stories like "Le Voyage de Monsieur Perrichon," intended primarily for them.

Their reading had been strictly supervised, selected to instruct, uplift, and provide moral exemplars. Françoise read to them from the *Contes de la Mère l'Oie* of Perrault (Tales of Mother Goose),[2] and *La Poupée Modèle*, a periodical created especially for young children. There were other such publications, especially the more popular *Le Petit Français illustré*, in comic-book format, but Françoise forbade it because she believed it would create an overdependence upon pictures and she wanted them to concentrate on the beauty of words.

Their next level of reading material consisted of books in the *Bibliothèque Rose* series—so named because of the rosy-pink color of the book covers—begun in the nineteenth century by the august publishing house of Larousse, with every story guaranteed safe for the minds of children. By the time of Simone de Beauvoir's childhood, these books had sold in the hundreds of thousands and were the most popular children's books in France. Françoise approved of them, and so Simone had a collection on a shelf above her bed, giving much-needed color to the shabby little room as well as happiness to both children, who enjoyed simply looking at them as much as reading them.

For a child with a voracious reading appetite, these books soon paled, so when Simone was seven or eight Georges began to give her books intended for much older children. During her childhood, some of the most popular reading for children in France was translated from the English, a carryover from the nineteenth century, when the tradition of literature written especially for children was richer in English-speaking cultures than in French. There were also translations of books which had not been written primarily for children, but which had become popular with them, such as *Gulliver's Travels*, *Robinson Crusoe*, the novels of James Fenimore Cooper and the stories of Washington Irving.

Georges had read these books in his own dreamy childhood, and so, when it was obvious that the quick-minded Simone needed something more, he introduced them to her. Thus her childhood was filled with dramatic adventure stories by Jules Verne, Daniel Defoe and especially Rudyard Kipling, whose popularity in France was unsurpassed. Most of these she read in the small brown crushed-leather Tauchnitz editions that Georges had collected when he was a boy, and which were very important to him. She relished this special honor.

Françoise gave her a French translation of the fairy tales of Hans Christian Andersen, which were usually considered too depressing for younger children. It was one of the rare times when Françoise erred in her criteria of suitability, for the tale of the Little Mermaid so affected Simone that she was tearful and dejected and had bad dreams for some time afterward, imagining herself caught in nets, trapped and bereft.

Georges and Françoise had not counted on books making such a lasting impression. Françoise was now very busy pinning pages together and censoring chapters not only for their moral content but also because of the emotional effect she thought they might have. Simone obeyed the strictures for a while, until curiosity got the better of obedience and she read everything even if she could not understand it. Increasingly, there were other books Françoise could not police, especially during the summers at Meyrignac. Cousin Magdeleine, whose reading was entirely unsupervised by her much more liberal and casual mother, loaned Simone every romance and potboiler then popular in France, for she spent her days in indolence, reading badly written novels and dreaming of passionate lovers.

This combination of elevated religious tracts, proper adventure stories, fantasies deemed suitable for children and popular trash was what Simone educated herself with when she was young. It was no wonder that when she began to write her own stories they all had a heroine who was fearless in the face of adversity. The plot was always a great adventure, the ending as triumphant as the heroine was chaste and good. But before then the heroine had generally saved a nation, or at least her family's reputation and fortune.

Even so, in these earliest extant stories, written when Simone was seven and eight,[3] there are intimations of the literary concerns that would shape her mature, published work. Her first attempt to write a book, "The Misfortunes of Marguerite," about a little girl from Alsace who wanted to take her brood of siblings out of harm's way—in this case the German Army in World War I—was abandoned because the children had to cross the Rhine to enter France, and Simone discovered from looking at her atlas (one of her favorite entertainments) that the river did not flow where she had set the scene of the fictional crossing. She had begun with fantasy, but verisimilitude was present and most powerful at her first moment of creation.

For a child, Simone showed remarkable knowledge of the formal requirements of fiction as well as an evident talent for telling a good story. The book is divided into eighteen chapters, each with a title. From the first, "The Death of the Father," to the last, "Perfect Happiness," there is enough action, adventure and pathos to satisfy even the most demanding young reader.

"In a poor house there lived an honest laborer and his wife," the story begins. "They have five children, the eldest is sixteen and they call her Marguerite." By the third chapter they are in dire straits: Marguerite and her four sisters (Marie, Madeleine, Hélène and Lucie, who are not named until Chapter Fifteen) are in an orphanage and are victims of all sorts of cruelties and injustices. These last until Chapter Nine, when war begins: "I forgot to tell you," says the child writer Simone, "Marguerite lived in Alsace. . . ." Chapter Ten is entirely given to the horrors of war, in this case "The Fire—The Courage of Marguerite." By Chapter Fourteen, entitled "Disappeared," everyone has done just that—but not to worry, because all are reunited in Chapter Fifteen, "Recovered." At this point, as if the author has grown tired of her characters, the form changes suddenly from novel to play, and the rest of the text becomes dramatic dialogue. Chapter Eighteen consists entirely of the sentences "Marguerite, after all her unhappiness, is finally happy. The happiness she received made her happy for a very long time."

The second story, "La Famille Cornichon" (The Gherkin Family), was based on a popular French story called "La Famille Fenouillard" (The Fennel Family). It was an adventure story about a mother, a father and two daughters, an idealized version of her own family, and sadly paralleled her own family's economic history.

Again, all the chapters have titles, and in the first, "The Family Cornichon," "They live in a pretty and happy little house situated in a pretty country, filled with green fields and pretty forests and filled with birds of all kinds." Detailed descriptions of the house, the surroundings, the family itself and all the characters follow. The father has a beard and is big and powerful, the mother is pretty and slim, elegant and charming. The children are good and sweet, dutiful and intelligent. She concludes the chapter with "You have now made the acquaintance of the Family Cornichon."

Terrible things happen to this family as well. Brave Papa loses his job and then their house. By Chapter Four they have moved to a new one, there is war, and they must move away. By Chapter Six they are on a boat which is simply "broken" (she does not specify whether or not in shipwreck). Chapter Seventeen is given entirely to the Maid, a loving representation of Louise. This is followed by a "Conclusion," in which the bowed but still-unbroken family takes charge of its life:

> One day Madame Cornichon told her husband that she had always wanted to visit faraway countries. "Where do you want to go," he asks after first telling her she is crazy. "To America," she replies. "Well let's go then" he agrees. "In fifteen days," she says. The fifteen days which preceded their departure were very busy. They had to move house from top to bottom. Finally! They left and so we don't need to say anything more of this honorable family.

Grandfather Brasseur was so taken with Simone's precociousness that he did something quite uncharacteristic for him: he bought special yellow paper and appointed Aunt Marie-Thérèse to copy the texts because her handwriting was so beautiful. At Simone's insistence, she folded the paper like the pages of a book, and so it came to be called "Simone's book," and was regarded by all the relatives with the same admiration as if it were a printed volume. Unfortunately, for many years no other stories followed these two, and the yellow "book" languished with many of its pages unfilled. At this point Simone was still not sure whether it would be better to write books or sell them when she grew up. For the time being, she was content to read them and dream.[4]

By the time Simone was ten, she had read *Little Women*, the first of two novels which made an indelible impression on her mind and gave form to her childhood. Everything about the March sisters seemed an Anglo-Saxon variant of her own life. They were poor and plainly dressed, just as she was. Like her, they were taught that the life of the mind was of much higher value than rich food, dress and decoration. They were close to each other, just as she and Hélène were. Mrs. March had given them *The Pilgrim's Progress*, just as Françoise had given her daughters *Imitation of Christ*. This fact had special importance for Simone because at the time she read *Little Women* her feelings about Catholicism were changing from unquestioning belief to the consideration of it as an ethical system in which the individual was obligated to make decisions concerning personal morality.[5] When she found out what *The Pilgrim's Progress* was about (she did not actually read it until many years later), she was pleased that she had worked out this change all by herself and at such an early age and felt that it brought her even closer to the March sisters.

It is not surprising that of the four March sisters, Jo was the one who seemed to Simone most like herself. *Little Women* made such an impression on her that she could not stop talking about it and would not rest until Hélène read it as well. Then she invented games based upon the book, she herself always taking the role of Jo. Hélène was pretty and blond and liked to draw, so Simone declared that she must always be Amy, even though Hélène despised Amy as frivolous and silly. Simone felt the usual dismay that little girls who identify with Jo feel when Laurie marries Amy. The childish anger she felt toward Louisa May Alcott for not giving this superior sister the man as well as the brains had everything to do with her own unpopularity, but she was able to personalize her feeling about Jo into a very early definition of herself. Some sixty years later she reflected, "Yes, in my *Memoirs* I did say that reading this novel gave me an exalted sense of myself. It helped me to identify with that young girl and to find comfort in myself when I read it. I felt such esteem for Jo that I was able to tell myself that I too was like her, and therefore it did not matter if society was cruel, because I too would be superior and find my place."[6]

Little Women was Louisa May Alcott's rewriting of her own autobiography, a fictionalized group portrait of a family "conflicted but not divided," the "tug of war, sometimes loving, sometimes fierce, between each March girl's right to independence and her allegiance to the cohesion of the family."[7] The dilemma which Alcott creates around Jo concerns her development as an artist. Her creativity gives her life richness and meaning, but makes her different from the others in her family and therefore sets her apart from them. Jo wrote in order to validate her place within the family; Simone had temporarily stopped writing (no new stories were added to the beautiful yellow book), but she had never stopped using words as the means of controlling and dominating the family members closest to her, namely Hélène and Magdeleine.

Over the years, *Little Women* resonated in several striking ways in Simone de Beauvoir's life: "I saw the dilemma Jo suffered over the thought of marriage, and I think it was from this book that the idea first came to me that marriage was not necessary for me, even though, of course, Jo does get married. I saw that all the March girls hated housework because it kept them from what really interested them, the writing and drawing and music and so on. And I think that somehow, even when very young, I must have perceived that Jo was always making choices and sometimes they were neither well reasoned nor good. The idea of choice must have frightened me a little, but it was exhilarating as well."

The other novel that had lifelong importance for her was George Eliot's *The Mill on the Floss*, which she read between the ages of eleven and twelve. In this book, it was the question of relationships that first perplexed, then intrigued her, and then became, in a very real sense, the central concern of all of her writing and much of her personal life. She was fascinated by Maggie Tulliver, torn between her own happiness and what she perceived as her duty to others. Love, friendship, the inner life, devotion to the self, the perception of social duty, and finally the real isolation that precedes Maggie's tragic end—all these moved the young Simone de Beauvoir to tears. She was at the age where she was beginning to realize that her own isolation (within the family and friendless at school), and the feeling that no one understood her, was true. Although there was a certain amount of adolescent angst coloring this impression, there was also an unfocused fear within her because of the terrifying truthfulness of it. To control the sense of alienation she felt, of being alone in her busy, crowded and highly regimented little world, she fell into a typical and continuing pattern: from adolescence until she was almost thirty she had only her reading to assist her emotional development.

Hindsight makes it easy to see the pattern that began to emerge in her life then, a pattern of emotional deprivation so severe that even such a spirited child as she needed the refuge offered by books in order to cope with it. Personal warmth and affection were sadly diminished between her parents by this time. They yelled rather than spoke to each other now, and generally transferred their unhappiness over all that had gone wrong in their lives to their daughters. Occasionally, while lying in their beds at night, Simone and Hélène could hear the sounds coming from their parents' room of what seemed to them to be violent lovemaking. It filled them with embarrassment and confusion. At the end of her life, Beauvoir seemed repulsed by the memory of how her parents—then in their forties—"still fucked each other," as if they had been too old to make love, and as if strong emotions such as love and anger had to be mutually exclusive of each other. Both sisters recalled this period by using the same phrase, "a growing sense of isolation, of comfort only in ourselves," to describe how they felt.

In the face of such exclusion, there is no wonder that Simone identified so completely with fictional heroines like Jo March and Maggie Tulliver to help her transcend her own life. They taught her how to be strong, to overcome the slights of others, the disappointment in her developing physical self, and how to plot and plan for a different kind of adulthood than her mother's and that of all the other women in her family.

In 1984, more than sixty years after she had first read *The Mill on the Floss*, Beauvoir reread it with the intention of using it as the vehicle for a television program about George Eliot.[8] As preparation, she began to write, more or less free-associating upon ideas and themes that struck her as important to include in the film. Among the first were love and duty, the individual's responsibility to self and society, and the problems that result when these conflict. Her way of approaching these issues was to begin with Eliot's biography, especially her unfortunate physical appearance, her early feeling of being both unloved and unlovable, and her reliance on literature as the means with which she could transcend her life.

Beauvoir's desire to examine these issues after so many years offers still another example of how her isolation as a child resonated recurringly throughout her life and colored her adult attitudes and behavior in many different ways. Even more poignantly, these earliest identifications with literary figures show not only the ideas and concepts which formed her adult character, but also what she thought of herself at that time—that, like George Eliot, she too was ugly and unlovable.

Simone de Beauvoir came to view Maggie Tulliver as a young woman of intelligence and sound emotion, at odds with the rigidity of her society, hemmed in unconscionably by its demands. The question that continued to puzzle her years later, and for which she scoured George Eliot's life for clues, was why Eliot allowed society to triumph over a woman such as this by requiring her to die within the novel: "I know Tom Tulliver dies as well, and they are clasped in each other's arms as they drown, so one could say in a sense that both society and the individual are punished, but I still question the wisdom of such an ending." This is a point worth noting, for much of Beauvoir's own fiction pits the individual against social convention in similar ways, but with totally different outcomes. Maggie Tulliver's death troubled her because she, Simone, was a child of rigid character, obsessed by routine and order. Adolescence was difficult for her because life refused to flow through the streams of artificial perfection she required. Everything kept changing, nothing was as it had been, nor would it ever be, no matter how hard she tried to impose her own standards upon it. It was somehow comforting to read and reread that Maggie Tulliver had no control over the circumstances of her life and her tragic death. It helped Simone de Beauvoir to deal with her own adolescence and to accept how little control she had over it.

ZaZa

THE FOUR OR FIVE YEARS following the move to the Rue de Rennes, from about 1919 to 1924, were intense and emotionally conflicting as Simone de Beauvoir passed through puberty and adolescence. Despite the downward slide of the family's status, theirs was now, according to the astute young Hélène, "a poverty of degree rather than of an absolute. Our financial condition was worse than it had been, but we still observed as many of the customs and conventions as we could; perhaps not in the style we would have liked, but certainly in the manner of families of our birth and bearing."[1] Françoise's "afternoons" were now simple cups of tea with cookies; her daughters were still invited to the elaborate teas and birthday parties given by their cousins and some of their wealthier classmates, but it was understood they could not reciprocate. Simone, in her awkwardness, blundered through these occasions, enduring rather than enjoying them; Hélène, with her more sophisticated social presence, overheard all too many remarks about "those poor girls" and "their tragic mother," which made her ashamed of their circumstances and bitter toward their father. Naturally she told her sister, and Simone was embarrassed, too.

All this, coupled with the ordinary physical changes of a child's growth and maturation, preoccupied the sensitive Simone as an adolescent and resonated strongly throughout her lifetime. In her adult writing she recreated the concepts of love, death, friendship and religion with freshness and vitality, making them the important events of her autobiography and major facets of much of her fiction. As a developing child, she was preoccupied by physical changes to such an extent that whenever she was not memorizing lessons she tried to interpret everything she read in order to relate these grand concepts to what was happening to her body, and thus, by extension, to explain the circumstances of her life.

Books became Simone's substitute for her mother, because Françoise, who had always been a fountain of knowledge before, was now uncharacteristically reserved. No doubt Françoise was preoccupied with all the changes in her household, but there was also the fact that Simone's questions were no longer those of a child. It was one of those moments when Georges's idea of "modern" education for women probably conflicted most dramatically with Françoise's convent upbringing: whether to provide the answers Simone sought or to evade her difficult or embarrassing questions. She chose the latter.

Simone was determined to find these answers somewhere, so books became her tools for introspection and self-absorption. Every nuance of character or plot was gravely pondered in terms of how she could relate her own experience to it. However, she also learned from books how to keep her own counsel, so her dialogues with Françoise became more cautious, reserved and infrequent. Sadly, during adolescence, when Simone most needed closeness and communication, Françoise's idea of proper conduct for mother and daughter conspired to keep them from talking to each other. A pattern developed then and lasted until Simone no longer lived at home: Françoise nagged and scolded Simone for her secrecy and unapproved reading, while Simone simply ignored her. At first Françoise raged, but eventually silence and evasion were practiced by everyone.

Since her daughters had reached a level in their studies where she had difficulty keeping up, Françoise was forced to relax her vigilance and either trust to the values she hoped she had inculcated in them or else turn away from what she might not want to see and relinquish all but the most important attempts to control their minds. And because they were quick and bright, her daughters learned to hide their natural questing intelligence behind a facade of discreet silence, thus avoiding argument and passion, for harmony, whether real or false, was desired by all.

Then Louise's little boy died; "a sad little thing, weak and puny, a wizened little man who had never been a child."[2] After she married, Louise and her husband shared one of the tiny maids' rooms crammed under the eaves of the Beauvoirs' building.[3] They lived there still when the child was born, three people crowded together in a space not big enough for one. The little boy developed bronchial pneumonia which swiftly killed him, a death that terrified Simone because it happened so abruptly and was the first she had ever known.

Then the concierge's son became ill with tuberculosis complicated by severe meningitis. His was a lingering death and the talk of the building because everyone who went in or out had to pass where the sick child lay. Each morning when Georges carried down the night slop jars, he brought back a report of the child's steadily worsening condition. Françoise, whose living quarters were now far removed from the luxury of her first married apartment, hurried her children past the concierge's tiny hutlike chamber next to the loggia containing the garbage cans, because the combined stench of it and the sick child's room was overwhelming. When Simone passed it, she dawdled, fascinated by what she imagined took place in the concierge's hut.

In the girls' room at night, Simone, solemnly intoning that soon it would be their turn to die, huddled next to Hélène, who did not share her morose views. In Simone's little world, no adults close to her had yet died (indeed, all the Brasseurs and Beauvoirs enjoyed robust good health and longevity); only children, and then after brutal suffering. Françoise was a woman of strong social conscience who railed against the economic and social conditions that caused such deaths and supported reforms, but to Simone the only logic seemed that a progression of children who lived in their building would die, and in her mind she and Hélène were the next most likely candidates.

She dramatized death to the extent of fantasizing her own, picturing herself lying on a bier, perhaps with a veil similar to those worn by little girls at their First Communion, her hands clasped in prayer, a crucifix draped around her fingers. A more chilling version (and consequently the one she preferred) was to be stricken on a street where no one would know who she was. In this reverie, anonymous mourners gave her a beautiful funeral, grieving for the loss of one so young and beautiful before burying her in a pauper's grave. Perhaps because of the growing distance between them, Simone imagined her mother crying profusely, but that her sister would be the one truly devastated by her death. But this version was too cruel and caused too much suffering to her family, so she next envisioned herself awakening from delirium just long enough to embrace her mother and sister, who had been miraculously found. This allowed her to picture a funeral where everyone wept at losing her, a fairly perverse way of convincing herself that she was loved by all. All these were self-dramatizing adolescent fantasies; morbidly satisfying as they were, they paled before the very real finality of death. The fact was that Louise's son and the concierge's child were dead and she would never see them again. Why a supposedly beneficent deity would separate mothers and their children forever became one of the facts she questioned most intently when she began to disbelieve in God and the Catholic Church.

Puberty caused crises of a different sort. Cousin Magdeleine, whose love of animals Simone did not share, was an expert on reproduction from having observed the mating rituals of her beloved dogs and cats. She read long passages of passionate prose to Simone,[4] whose literal bent made her wonder whether such marvels were true, that men were nourished with real milk if they pressed their lips to all the heaving bosoms in those torrid novels.

Magdeleine's descriptions of human sexuality, explanations inspired by firsthand observation of animals mating, took on new meaning for Simone now that they were living in the close quarters of the Rue de Rennes and she could lie in bed at night and hear her parents through the thin walls. Sometimes she caught a glimpse of them in their nightgowns of heavy white cotton, so clinging and revealing in contrast to their starched and corseted daytime clothing. The thought of them lying so close to each other made her slightly uncomfortable in a way she could not define.

Simone had not yet begun to conceal her pubescent thoughts from Françoise, and so she began, as children often do, to ask questions by first making statements: Magdeleine told her that men have the same appendages as dogs, or that soon after women marry, babies swell up in their stomachs before coming out through their navels; could either of these preposterous remarks be true? To Simone, phrases such as "ties of blood" or "blood relationships" meant that husband and wife literally cut their veins and transfused their blood on their wedding day, after which something happened to make babies grow. The relationship between cause and effect continued to puzzle her. Would Françoise enlighten her? Magdeleine also told her that each month "the whites" would cause her to bleed and she would have to wear thick bandages for several days. Hélène worried that it would be awkward, but Simone was more concerned with language: shouldn't it be called "the reds" if it resulted in bleeding?[5]

Their cousin's superior knowledge of physical functions led the two sisters to fantasize extravagantly and openly before Magdeleine's mother, their Aunt Hélène, who was always so distracted and otherworldly that she neither answered their questions nor rebuked them for their audacity. Thus thwarted, Simone began to make direct statements to Françoise, and when these failed to elicit a response she turned them into peremptory questions: Did babies really come from women's navels? Françoise cut her inquiries short, saying Simone was silly to ask when "you know everything already." Simone de Beauvoir remembered this instance as the only time she ever tried to discuss puberty and maturity with her mother. When menstruation did begin, Françoise explained that it would happen every month and showed her how to dress herself properly, but gave neither of her daughters any explanation of why it happened or what it meant.

"It is not proper," was one of Françoise's most frequent remarks, and she expanded the concept of propriety to include everything pertaining to the body. She taught her daughters that modesty demanded they keep as much of their bodies covered as possible, equating indecency not only with nakedness but also with bodily functions, insisting that "the body as a whole was vulgar and offensive: it must be concealed." As she dabbed furtively at her half-clad body in the washing area, Simone accepted this dictum even as she questioned what Françoise considered other forms of impropriety or improper behavior to be. For Françoise, marriage was the key to understanding, and until then she was content to let her daughters drift in a confused welter of half-truths and false knowledge. Above all, propriety and "proper" behavior had to be observed.

Imagine, then, when Simone was almost eleven and made her first real friend at school, how shocked she was to see the little girl tease her mother playfully, stick out her tongue and say things that she and Hélène would never have dreamed of saying to each other or anyone else, but especially to their mother. Many years later, when asked to think about what first attracted her to this little girl, Simone de Beauvoir replied without a second's hesitation, "ZaZa was a cynic. I had never heard anyone speak with such openness and force. There was no such thing as propriety, and no subject was sacred. Even at such a young age, I had learned to guard my remarks, but not she. She would say anything."

Elisabeth Le Coin was called by her given name by everyone, including Simone de Beauvoir. Years later, when she was writing her memoirs, Beauvoir decided to protect the privacy of many of her friends and invented the nickname "ZaZa." It stuck, and after *Memoirs of a Dutiful Daughter* was published most of the people who had known Elisabeth adopted it when speaking of her.

ZaZa was the third of nine children born to a youngish mother and her older husband. They were truly *haute bourgeoisie*, owners of a luxurious apartment in Paris and large estates in the "wind-blown dunes" and "monotonous pine forests"[6] of the Landes region of southwest France. ZaZa's father, Maurice Le Coin, had been educated at one of the *grandes écoles*, the Ecole Polytechnique, which prepared young men to be leaders in science and industry. He was an engineer by training and had been a director of railroads in Orléans before becoming director of works for an automobile manufacturer.

Unlike Georges de Beauvoir, Maurice Le Coin was politically liberal and a practicing Catholic, and his wife applied his relaxed liberalism to the education of their children. Unlike Françoise, Madame Le Coin permitted her children to read, think and express themselves very much as they wished. While her children squabbled, tumbled and shouted at each other in the drawing room, Madame Le Coin sat tranquilly in their midst sewing or reading, a sharp contrast to the Beauvoir household, where the two girls were expected to sit quietly or move in a careful, ordered manner. When Simone first began to visit ZaZa, she was so shocked by the children's behavior that she brought Hélène several times on the pretext of having her play with ZaZa's younger sisters but really because Hélène would not otherwise have believed the tales of what went on there.[7]

There were many other things about ZaZa that shocked Simone, beginning with the reason she had not come to the Cours Désir until she was ten years old. ZaZa was to have been educated at home by private tutors, like her elder sister before her, but at the age of eight she was severely burned over the lower half of her body when her dress caught fire at a potato roast on their country estate. For almost two years she was confined to bed, and when she was ten her parents decided she had been alone too long so they sent her to school. As ZaZa grew to adulthood, she became fashion conscious, bobbing her hair and using face powder, but she kept her skirts unfashionably long to hide her thighs and legs, which were horribly and permanently disfigured by the fire. As an elderly woman, Simone de Beauvoir believed that ZaZa's physical mutilation had much to do with her erratic behavior during their all too brief friendship, and she believed it was a great part of the reason they had gravitated to each other with an intensity that surprised them both, even as children.

Simone only had friends in her first four years at the Cours Désir when their mothers encouraged them rather than from genuine camaraderie. Two in particular, Marguerite Boulanger and Marie-Louise Levesque, became Simone's so-called "closest" friends because Françoise admired and respected their mothers and encouraged her to play with them. Françoise so admired Madame Levesque that Simone was even allowed to spend some of her vacations visiting Marie-Louise at her summer home.

Françoise nagged her daughters to play with cousin Jeanne de Beauvoir, whose family lived in Paris during the winter (Magdeleine lived year-round at La Grillère) and who was also a student at the Cours Désir. Jeanne accepted Simone's presence with her characteristic equanimity, but even before Simone could understand why, Jeanne irritated her. As an adult, she explained that she had "nothing in common" with a cousin who was "always so self-possessed, as if conscious of her role as future chatelaine of Meyrignac." After a moment's pause she added, "I suppose I am being unfair to a woman who wanted only to become everything she had been brought up to believe she should be." Jeanne and her friends still "played house," which Simone hated, preferring to "play school" with Hélène, but Hélène wanted to play with the many close friends she had made in her own class, relying on Simone only at home. It meant that Simone was frequently without anyone to play with at school.

Now, suddenly, there was ZaZa. Hélène, relegated to a lesser role in Simone's life, was miffed: "She was very caustic. She liked to make fun of everybody, and I suffered a lot from it. I remember how disappointed I was the first time I saw this great friend who had been described so magically by Simone. She was not pretty. She had beautiful dark eyes, but was little and thin, more or less in rags. We wore very bad clothes ourselves, but she was not any better dressed than we and she was so much richer.[8] She had a big scar on her leg, which, indeed, was the only thing about her at first that impressed me."

Hélène's description should be interpreted in the light of the little sister whose place was usurped in the adored older sister's affections, for the magic that Simone saw in ZaZa was seen by other classmates as well. Simone de la Chaume La Coste's description is typical: "ZaZa was really attractive; brilliant too, and much more amusing, much gayer, than Simone, full of fun and humor. They were both the two brilliant scholars of the class, but [we all] much preferred Elisabeth, whose mind was more interesting, more outgoing and stimulating." Madame La Coste remembered Simone de Beauvoir as "a brilliant pupil, but not very attractive or personable. She had masses of hair which we wondered if she had bothered to wash that week or the last. She was altogether very dour and very badly dressed."

Simone de Beauvoir's classmates and friends all agreed upon one characteristic as her most striking when she was at the Cours Désir: her lack of a sense of humor. "School seemed to mean everything to her. She was an incredibly disciplined worker, [who] never joked about it. . . . She and ZaZa were competitors because they were the two best in the class, but it was fun for ZaZa and always very serious for Simone. . . . ZaZa laughed and shrugged and still excelled, which made Simone relentless in pursuit of her, sometimes getting sick to her stomach from the intensity of the competition."[9]

Simone and ZaZa shared everything and were soon dubbed "the Inseparables" by teachers and students alike. Their competitive studiousness was approved of by both families, and at first so was their friendship. Both fathers were of the same social class; the only difference was that Maurice Le Coin was financially successful and Georges de Beauvoir was not. Madame Le Coin, the elder of the two mothers, endeared herself to Françoise by telling her she was much too young to have a daughter Simone's age. Of course, the Le Coins would have been shocked to know how shabby the Beauvoir residence was, and the Beauvoirs would have been equally shocked had they known of the Le Coin household's informality, but everyone was happy in the beginning except Hélène, and no one paid much attention to her.

In school, the teachers were pleased with the way Simone and ZaZa competed for top honors and encouraged by what they saw as an amiable rivalry. Both girls excelled in Latin, but while Simone learned English, ZaZa preferred German. Each subsequently introduced the other to books and authors in these languages, thus enhancing their knowledge of life outside France at a relatively young age. When Simone La Coste entered the school speaking impeccable British English, Simone de Beauvoir was entranced by her accent but preferred to spend her time racing through English-language books, reading voraciously and doing nothing to improve her always execrable accent. To her, speaking the language was less important than understanding the ideas contained in it.[10]

Simone usually took first place in academic subjects, but ZaZa always beat her in athletics and recitals because she had musical talent and physical dexterity, both of which Simone lacked. As the two girls matured physically, ZaZa kept her pretty complexion and graceful movements, while Simone's face grew blotchy, her body lumpy and awkward, and she bit her fingernails to the quick. All this changed around her seventeenth year, when her complexion cleared, she became slim, and she developed her mature beauty.

Still, they remained friends, and what united them was a common interest in ideas. With ZaZa, Simone could talk about subjects that bewildered others her age, who were more interested in aping the behavior of their mothers. True, Hélène had always listened to Simone and treated her with repect, but ZaZa was her own age, reading the same books and studying the same subjects. ZaZa was especially important when it came to books, because she often introduced Simone to an author or a subject after seeing her older brother and sister reading them first. However, many of these were ponderous religious tomes or histories of France which Simone dutifully plowed through only because ZaZa had already read them, and their competition with each other extended even to the quantity and kind of books they could parade before each other.

There is no question that ZaZa enhanced Simone's life enormously throughout their adolescent years, and that her friendship served many different needs, especially that of companionship. Without ZaZa, Simone would have gone through a lonely, virtually friendless adolescence. It was one thing to instruct one's younger sister, as she did with Hélène, but quite another to have someone her own age to talk to and argue with who had the same fierce intelligence and desire for knowledge as she. Still, the closeness that she hungered for eluded her. Many years later, Simone de Beauvoir described it by saying, "ZaZa and I were the children of very different households, and this difference made itself strongly felt in our friendship."

From the day she was born, Simone was the center of attention within her family. She was brought up to believe that even when very young she was a person of some importance, an opinion she held even during her difficult teenage years. Her natural propensity for learning led to her unquestioning acceptance of the work she had to do in order to be a first-class student; her interests extended through all her subjects in school to the books she found in her home and the conversations of her parents and their friends. She hardly understood politics, but she listened intently as Georges expounded his ideas; she even listened to Françoise's frequent laments about the rising prices in the shops and tried to make connections between economic reality and political opinion. Nothing was outside her sphere of interest.

ZaZa, the third of nine children and the second daughter, had a very different family situation. Her father was both mathematician and engineer, and her elder brother followed him professionally, while her elder sister, also enamored of order and precision, brought these same traits to the thrifty management of her household once she was married. These two children resembled their father physically as well, which resulted in a certain amount of coldness toward them from their mother. Monsieur and Madame Le Coin were first cousins, and he had pursued her for years while she routinely rejected him, apparently because she preferred to spend her time reading and thinking and was not interested in marriage until, when she was twenty-five, her parents arranged one to this much older and wealthier cousin. Once married, Madame Le Coin concentrated all her intelligence and energy on becoming a model wife and raising her nine children. Simone de Beauvoir believed that her only confidante was ZaZa, the daughter who most resembled her in looks and intelligence. In a rare personal conversation, ZaZa told Simone that Madame Le Coin had described "the horror" of her wedding night, that she continued to be disgusted by sexual relations throughout her marriage, and that none of her nine children had been conceived with any passion on her part. She gave ZaZa a great deal of responsibility within the family, often making her act as surrogate and charging her to look after the younger siblings as if she were their second mother. ZaZa was caught in a pivotal position within her family, had to play many different roles, and consequently hated her father, adored her mother and resented all her brothers and sisters.

Unlike Simone, the only time ZaZa felt special was when she behaved in a manner that pleased her mother. Madame Le Coin came from a provincial family, just as Françoise de Beauvoir did, but she was snug in the security of her husband's wealth and position and had never felt the need for more than an elementary education, either for herself or for her daughters. Good grades were fine, but it was more important to Madame Le Coin that ZaZa carry out family responsibilities and activities in preparation for her future married life. Madame Le Coin was fixated on this daughter as an extension and continuation of herself, and her most fervent hope was that ZaZa would be the child to make the most brilliant marriage in the family.

Imagine, then, Simone's shock when she visited the Le Coin estate in the Landes during the summer holiday and found ZaZa confined to the sofa with a severe gash in her leg. When they were alone, ZaZa confessed that she had become so desperate for time to read and reflect that she performed an act of self-mutilation, wounding herself with an ax because it was the only way she could think of to be freed from the constant round of family parties, visits, and supervision of the younger children. Simone was horrified by this irrational aspect of her friend's character.[11]

ZaZa's behavior was at best paradoxical, at worst unstable, and most of it perplexed Simone. ZaZa initiated conversations with everyone she encountered or joined any game that looked interesting. Such audacity disturbed Simone, whose friendships were still severely monitored by Françoise. Even more humiliating for Simone, who yearned to be close to ZaZa, was the way she spoke to all others her age with the familiar *tu*, teasing Simone with the formal *vous*. Yet, at the same time, ZaZa held views that Simone considered both conservative and outmoded; her sharp eye caught every nuance of behavior that was not morally or ethically correct, and her even sharper tongue spared no one as she denounced conduct that did not meet her rigid, repressive standards. Also, ZaZa believed fervently in the Catholic faith which Simone already doubted, and her uncompromising inflexibility was so frightening that Simone had to learn to temper her comments in order not to arouse ZaZa's almost irrational anger.

Simone wanted closeness in all things, but ZaZa was especially restrained when it came to personal matters. The account of her mother's marriage was one of the very few times throughout the ten years of their friendship when ZaZa ever told Simone something of her personal history. ZaZa considred most things pertaining to sex and sexuality "not proper," and recoiled from discussing them. Simone, who had grown up with the splendid luxury of having a sister in whom she confided everything, wanted to continue this happy tradition with her best friend, but ZaZa was too busy with her family, her piano lessons and the social duties her mother imposed on her. As she was expected to observe all the rituals of a young girl approaching marriageable age, Simone had to be content with being her friend at school, but one who entered ZaZa's busy life whenever there was time and space. The sad fact was that ZaZa meant more to Simone than she did to ZaZa, so Simone was the one who always feared incurring displeasure or banishment.

Just how delicate this friendship really was became apparent after a disastrous episode in which Simone persuaded Françoise to let her buy some luxurious fabric to sew into a little purse for ZaZa's birthday present. Giving on such a scale was outside the bounds of proper etiquette in the Le Coin family, and ZaZa voiced her displeasure when Simone presented the gift. Madame Le Coin attempted to smooth it over by instructing ZaZa to thank Françoise for the purse, as if to make Simone's imprudence less egregious. Simone, unwilling to see anything unpleasant in her friend's behavior, diverted her embarrassment and confusion toward Madame Le Coin, whom she hated silently for the rest of her life.

The sad truth was that ZaZa had a secretive side, perhaps a necessary defense because of the many roles she played within her family. Madame Le Coin was a skillful manipulator of ZaZa's emotions and knew how to withhold affection in order to gain the behavior she wanted. She saw her daughter's intellectual interests only as enhancements toward her eventual marriage, and so she did not encourage this bent. The grubby, hardworking little Beauvoir girl who always had a new book to share or a new idea to discuss was a very real threat to the security of Madame Le Coin's hold over ZaZa. As the girls became young women, Madame Le Coin's politeness to Simone became stringently correct, but she permitted far fewer meetings between them.

Hélène had by this time formed her own close friendships with girls her own age, which forced Simone to be alone at home as well, but literally it was never lonely in the Beauvoir household. There were still the ritualistic meals with the grandparents Brasseur, Magdeleine came to stay for extended visits, and Jeanne and her family wintered in Paris. Aunt Marie-Thérèse lived there as well, so there were invitations to family birthdays, First Communions, confirmations, recitals and graduations. Although Françoise and Georges no longer entertained friends regularly, they were always ready for unexpected visitors, so that Françoise, always so concerned about the shabbiness of her household in contrast to the other relatives', kept herself and her daughters in a perpetual state of readiness.

All the little cousins were growing up to be pretty girls, and all of them, even the romantic Magdeleine, seemed serene as they contemplated futures very much like those of their own mothers. The sisters Beauvoir knew they were different. Simone was a phenomenon, always questing, never accepting without first demanding to know how and why, irritating to some of her teachers and incomprehensible to most of her relatives. Gradually, when she was old enough to understand and make the connection, it dawned on her that their stares and whispers had as much to do with her father's lack of money and status as it did with her academic prowess. So what if she could not marry because Georges could not give her a dowry—she was delighted with the thought of being able to spend her life reading and teaching others, just as she had always taught Hélène, who wanted nothing more than to be like the older sister she admired so much. Simone was skilled in the use of words, but Hélène was skilled with her hands. Together they decided that Simone would write and teach, and Hélène would draw; this seemed an ideal solution even to Georges—as long as they practiced these vocations through the respectable profession of teaching.

There were other little signs that they were different from their cousins which embarrassed them during their teen years. Françoise told them little about the physical changes taking place in their bodies and did less to ease their perceptions of themselves as the changes occurred. There were a number of embarrassing incidents like the one at a cousin's wedding, when Françoise looked at Simone in her hand-me-down dress and saw her developing breasts bursting through the bodice. Instead of anticipating that Simone might have developed physically to the point where the seldom-worn party frock was too small, she had ignored the possibility and waited until the day of the wedding, when nothing could be done about it. Quickly, she bound Simone's chest tightly with cloths, flattening it sufficiently for her to get through the day with a semblance of propriety, conveniently ignoring her daughter's feeling that she had unwittingly done something wrong by growing.

Although Françoise was an excellent embroiderer and knitter, she was a barely adequate seamstress. Thus her daughters' dresses were often ill-fitting and always unflattering. She selected fabrics for durability, and colors and textures were usually heavy and dark, overwhelming their fair hair and delicate complexions. When one of their cousins became a postulant in a religious order, all of her wardrobe was passed on to Simone, who on the one hand was pleased to have it, on the other ashamed to be singled out as the cousin who most needed it.

One of the easiest ways to mitigate embarrassment over their appearance was to feign indifference, so Simone became careless and sloppy. Because Madame Le Coin was often preoccupied with civic and social responsibilities, ZaZa was often as badly dressed. Still, when Simone visited the Le Coins at their country home, even ZaZa was aware of the shabby clothing she brought with her, and tried to invent polite lies as to why Simone should borrow one of her own pretty frocks when the family gathered. Simone knew ZaZa's real reason for offering the dress, but it was better to take it than to embarrass her friend by wearing her own clothes.[12]

When the Beauvoir and Brasseur aunts, uncles and cousins gathered, Simone could see just how different she was from Jeanne, Magdeleine and the rest. Rather than compensate for her appearance by sitting quietly and not calling attention to herself, she flaunted her knowledge and achievements, thinking to parade her intelligence and turn her physical liability into what she imagined (wrongly) would impress them all. Now in her teens, she proclaimed loudly that she was preparing for a university career and that studying was very important to her, thus by extension telling her relatives how little she cared about her appearance when her mind required all her time and attention. Still she could not entirely mask her sadness: she said of herself, "Everywhere I went I dragged behind me the crippling shadow of the first-class pupil."[13]

There was, however, one relative who actually admired the Beauvoir sisters as they were. Jacques Champigneulle was an independent and fearless young man who enjoyed shocking the aunts with tales of the bohemian life he observed firsthand in their rapidly changing quarter of Montparnasse, or with detailed descriptions of the contemporary poetry that he devoured and that they found utterly incomprehensible. Jacques's paternal grandfather, Ernest Champigneulle, married "Aunt Alice," the author of children's stories and the sister of Simone's Grandmother Brasseur. His father, Charles, was briefly considered as a suitor for Françoise, but although she had "quite a little crush on him,"[14] the matter was never taken seriously by either family. Jacques was in his teens when his father was killed in an automobile accident and his mother remarried, moving to the country with her new husband and leaving Jacques and his younger sister, Thérèse (always called "Titite"), in the care of an old family retainer. These three lived on the Boulevard du Montparnasse in a large apartment above what had been Jacques's father's stained-glass-manufacturing plant. The housekeeper was so charmed by Jacques that she allowed him to do almost anything he wanted, and so he enjoyed unprecedented freedom to come and go as he pleased. He was an excellent student at the Collège Stanislas and had a decided artistic bent; his ambition was to reopen the stained-glass factory and become known as a world-famous artist, designer and businessman. Unfortunately, he was lazy and much better at imagining his future than he was at working to make it happen.

Jacques was a frequent visitor to the Beauvoir household, because Georges always treated him as an adult, listening politely to everything he had to say, no matter how shocking or outlandish. Françoise adored him because he bowed low over her hand and treated her with his most elegant manners.

Georges no longer found interest or amusement in Simone's ideas, so Jacques provided him with conversations that Simone's increasingly unattractive adolescence lost for her. Her mind was finer than Jacques's, but her developing figure bore increasing witness to the fact that she was growing up, and a man of Georges's background and temperament seldom discussed issues and ideas with women. At first Simone was puzzled when she was forced to sit quietly while the two men talked; soon she resented the physical separation of two spheres within the same drawing room. Her father and Jacques sat somewhat apart from Françoise and Hélène, who quietly sewed and sketched, while Simone usually sat at the table bent over a book, pretending not to listen. Worst of all were the times when Georges clapped Jacques on the shoulder and took him into the study for private conversation, leaving the women to their own devices.

At first, Jacques was careful to defer to Georges, but gradually, as he became more politically liberal, more enchanted by Surrealism and more enraptured by avant-garde painting and writing, he could not hide his disdain for his uncle's stubborn conservatism. Georges, who had become addicted to bridge, no longer delayed leaving for his nightly game because of Jacques's presence, but waved him toward the company of his daughters as he left. The gesture backfired: Georges's intended insult toward the young man who had once revered him gave pleasure to all three cousins.

"Jacques was the only young man we saw in such an informal manner," Hélène remembered. "We saw no young men during those years except our cousins, and Jacques was the only one to come to our house in the evenings when we were alone as a family, to sit with us and talk as if we were his equals. He had an aura of culture and independence which was very exciting, and we listened attentively to everything he said.

Actually, Hélène listened attentively as she sat shyly sketching; Simone gave as good as she got, exchanging information and ideas. Soon Jacques began to tell her about books and writers whose names were new to her but which offered promise of the worlds of thought and ideas she wanted so much to enter. Jacques's attentiveness made her realize that she could be attractive to a man, not for her looks but for her mind. "This was knowledge I carried with me from that time forward," Simone de Beauvoir remembered. "It comforted me to know that men were intrigued by what I thought, and it compensated for other things [such as physical appearance]."

In the extended family there was social change as well. All the aunts were shocked by Magdeleine's defiance when she began to use face powder, and were scandalized by Titite's open demonstration of physical affection for her fiancé. Although Titite would bring a modest dowry to her marriage, hers was a love match that had been arranged because she insisted on it.

Uncle Gaston, Magdeleine's father, died after a long bout with stomach cancer. As soon as the mourning period was over, the heavy silence at La Grillère ended, and Magdeleine and Robert filled the house with friends each summer for parties that lasted well into the early-morning hours. Simone danced, talked, took walks with young men in the moonlit garden and felt uneasy about the bodily sensations she could not define.

During her last years at the Cours Désir, when they were about sixteen, Simone, ZaZa and many of their classmates were sent to dancing classes. While their mothers sat on the sidelines watching, the young men and women groped their way around the floor, with the more daring couples actually dancing close enough to touch chests and cheeks. ZaZa's cynicism was in full flower during these times, teasing everyone but especially Simone, who had little idea of what her sophisticated friend was talking about: "I thought she must be connecting the pleasure of dancing with something I had only the vaguest notion of—flirting."

Open displays of affection puzzled Simone, as when classmates came to school and announced proudly that they were engaged to be married as soon as school ended. The idea of girls her own age lying in bed, in some instances, with husbands old enough to be their fathers disgusted her. Titite's open sexuality was the only example that Simone thought natural, mostly because Titite and her fiancé were in love and the same age.

She herself had been so sheltered from any and all aspects of physicality that she admitted, "Sexuality frightened me."[15] As a child in a gymnastics class, she had experienced pleasurable sensations while straddling a bar horse, but when she tried to describe it to Françoise she was greeted with such stony silence that she knew instinctively it was "not proper" to talk about it. Nudity and indecency were one and the same to Simone, who had never been to a public beach or pool and was not permitted to ride a bicycle, and whose gymnastic experiences were cut short after this conversation with her mother.

Her innocence was so immense that she actually stood passively during a play in a theater, unwilling to call attention to herself by crying out or moving, while a man behind her ran his hands over her breasts and buttocks throughout the performance. She followed unquestioningly when a young clerk in a religious-artifacts store beckoned her into dark corner and exposed himself. It took her quite a while to comprehend what she had seen, and she suffered from guilt, believing herself responsible when such things happened.

There was no one but Hélène to whom she could confide her feelings, but Hélène was more at ease with herself and did not understand them. "Am I ugly?" the Simone who had "the mind of a man" implored her younger sister. "Will any man ever want me?" These questions confused pretty blond Hélène, whose own friendships and encounters with boys were freer of her older sister's extensive self-analysis. Simone thus developed a prudery closely related to disgust whenever she tried to envision physical contact. Because she could not control what happened to her body whenever she saw her cousin Jacques, or when a dancing partner held her close, or when she thought about what men and women did in the privacy of their bedrooms, it was especially difficult for her to hear her mother and father through the separating wall: "When I lived at home, my sister and I had a room right next to theirs, and we heard them from time to time. They must have been about forty, forty-two then, and they were still fucking."[16]

In school, she used her bent for logic to interpret her family's rigid code of conduct and define everything about herself in terms of moral absolutes. She concluded that harmless flirtation and casual affection were not for her, but instead that she must have absolute commitment and lasting attachment. "If I loved a man," she wrote many years later in her *Memoirs*, analyzing herself as she was at age seventeen, "it would be forever, and I would surrender myself to him entirely, body and soul, heart and head, past, present and future." She was fifty years old when she wrote this, which is perhaps why she added wryly, "To tell the truth, I had no opportunity to test the firmness of these principles, because no seducer came along to try to get round them."[17]

In her adolescent mind, logic demanded that men should be subject to the same laws of behavior as women: if women were expected to be virginal until they married, she saw no rational reason for men to "sow wild oats," as Georges laughingly called it when Jacques's mother complained to him and Françoise about her son's escapades. Simone overheard these remarks, and in one of her rare moments of confiding in Françoise she denounced the double standard. When Françoise told Georges of the radical theory Simone had just propounded, he laughed again, dismissing the girl's seriousness as something she would "get over."

But the more Simone thought about it, the more she was convinced of its rightness: if she was to save her affections for her partner, then he should follow suit. If she was to commit herself to him before, during and after marriage, then he must do the same. She saw no reason to be excluded from liberties that he was permitted to enjoy, and she believed that both partners in a relationship should have an equal vote in deciding how it would develop. At age seventeen, she believed sexual conduct was "in its very essence a serious affair"[18] and not to be thought of in any other light. To analyze it more would have confused her, so she simply refused to consider any further ramifications. This insistence upon an arbitrary conclusion to any argument or situation she did not wish to pursue further was another strategy she developed in adolescence that she used for the rest of her life whenever she wanted a neat and tidy conclusion to an argument.

Except for Hélène, who agreed with her, there was no one who would even listen to her. ZaZa was her only friend, and her cynicism was more pronounced than usual when it came to discussing their futures. Theirs was a lopsided relationship during these years: ZaZa determined almost everything about it, while Simone's main intention was to keep her friendship at all costs. Simone feared the caustic darts of ZaZa's comments, aimed at her for being "such a ninny" to hold opinions which elicited knowing hoots of derision, especially in the rare conversations when they imagined one or two of the men and boys they knew as possible husbands. ZaZa could reduce both Simone and the poor fellow in question to comic or grotesque proportions in one or two pithy sentences. All Simone wanted was to be with her friend on any terms, and their time together was more and more limited as Madame Le Coin insisted more strenuously that ZaZa ornament her drawing room or accompany her on courtesy calls to mothers of marriageable sons. Since there was nothing of the sort in Simone's life, both girls carefully avoided discussing this aspect of ZaZa's. They saw each other mostly at school, and then the conversation always concerned their current studies or their plans for the future. It seemed to be enough for ZaZa, whose life was crowded with other things, but Simone had so little else that any time at all with ZaZa assumed tremendous proportions and loomed very large in her emotional life. She became fixated on this friendship, and keeping it meant everything to her.

Thus, Simone's relationship with Jacques developed and her friendship with ZaZa changed with the possibility of impending suitors. Brought up as she had been, Simone saw only one possible outcome for herself: marriage.

"I was there," Hélène remembered, "and I saw how Jacques played the coquette with her. In our circles, this kind of conversation had only one meaning: 'We'll get married.' She didn't know any other man then, she had no experience at all, and when Jacques told her all these stories, well, she was dreaming, in a trance really. It was only because she never saw any other young men that he came to assume so much importance in her life. It was a narrow escape, because he simply was not worthy of her."

But the fact is that Jacques Champigneulle was important to Simone, so much so that the only other aspect of her life which she cared deeply about, her education, became for a brief moment secondary to the life she imagined she would have with him. In later years, Simone de Beauvoir believed that she transferred her affections to Jacques as the natural thing to do to keep up with ZaZa and the events of her life. As the Le Coins were identifying suitors for ZaZa, and as Simone's family was not in a position to seek them for her, she decided to select one on her own because, in this as well as in everything else, she deemed it important to keep in step with ZaZa. Perhaps there is truth in her rationalization, but there is also a great deal of hindsight, for her sister and her cousins believe that she cared deeply for Jacques and for several years wanted very much to marry him. Fortunately for her, the relationship began during her last year at the Cours Désir and did not blossom until she had graduated and made all the important decisions about her educational and professional future. After that, Jacques played a role in her life, but not the most important one.

SEVEN

Eighteen,
and in Love with Love

Simone de Beauvoir's graduation from the Cours Désir in 1924 co-incided with the sweeping educational reforms in France that gave women equal access to the all-important *baccalauréat* examination.[1] Until the end of World War I, education for French women had been dominated by the view that they should have just enough to make them good companions for their husbands and mothers capable of instructing children (especially sons) in the verities of proper conduct and moral behavior. This view prevailed even though disquieting trends began to emerge sometime around 1890 that made analysts argue for social and educational change. France had not yet recovered from the drastic economic decline of the 1880s, the birthrate began to drop dramatically, and there was a trend toward far fewer marriages. By the end of World War I these statistics had provoked a concerted outcry from specialists and much concern within individual families.

The troubling question for the parents of daughters like Simone de Beauvoir was, quite simply, what would happen to bourgeois girls who could not or would not marry? What were they to do with their lives? A male teacher at the girls' lycée in Versailles described the dilemma they faced:

> The majority of girls I have had or now have as pupils have had or now have the intention of continuing their studies to prepare themselves for some profession. . . . As is natural, nearly all desire love in marriage and motherhood. But they know that in our unjust society, dominated by the cult of gold, not every girl will be able to realize the motherly life that ought to be the norm for every woman. . . . They understand that instruction will open careers for them, which will enable them if need be to support themselves without masculine aid. They are preparing themselves to make a virtue of necessity.[2]

Written in 1914, this view attests to the continuing power of the dowry in determining which women among the bourgeoisie would be married. Ten years later, in 1924, when the war had changed the fabric of French society irrevocably and Simone de Beauvoir was graduated from the Cours Désir, this situation had become modified by necessity in many families, but Georges de Beauvoir remained as intractably conservative as ever: for his daughters, marriage without the dowry was simply unthinkable. His main concern for Simone was how best to finish educating her so that she could work while still adhering to the prevailing standards of her social class. The irony is that all the while he was exhorting her to prepare herself to work, he was setting obstacles in her way.

In July 1924, at age sixteen (which had just been decreed the official age for leaving school), Simone received her *premier baccalauréat*, or school-leaving certificate, with *mention bien*, or distinction.[3] Previously, private-school education for girls ended at age fifteen, or even earlier if a marriage was arranged or for other reasons, such as the common argument that a girl with too much education would never attract a husband. For several years prior to 1924, the Cours Désir had been in the vanguard, advocating the six-year program, but most girls still left after five, many before receiving their certificate of completion.[4]

If a girl did stay for five years, she received little more than hard-core propaganda via uplifting religious tracts and formal courses in moral behavior stressing that the best future she could hope for was marriage, which was glowingly described as the "career" of *mère-éducatrice*, or mother-teacher. She was instructed in how to make her home a husband's sanctuary and how to instill patriotism and Christian (meaning "Catholic") attitudes in their children. Hers was to be a life of happy sacrifice sequestered in the home, which she was to keep free of any unsettling intrusion from the outside world. The underlying message was that if she wanted to keep her husband home at night, away from the contaminating influences of cafés and other women, she should be docile, placid and agreeable at all times.

For the young woman who found herself so unfortunate in society's eyes as not to marry, the only approved work was either the convent or teaching little girls in the primary schools, but even this was coming to depend more and more on the sixth year of study, the *baccalauréat* which until December 1923 had been reserved only for male graduates of lycées, or secondary schools. It was the scholastic rite of passage which permitted men to attend universities and thus to qualify for professional employment of any sort; technically it had been open to girls before then, but in actuality the courses in classical languages and philosophy that were required before one could even take the examination were not available to most young women.

The Cours Désir was one of a select group of private schools chosen to offer these courses in an additional year,[5] which allowed gifted students like Simone de Beauvoir to take the second *baccalauréat* in philosophy and science that qualified them to teach in schools similar to the ones they had attended. The main reason for this program was to insure that although their status in life was lesser than their married classmates, it was still high enough to keep them on the fringes of the petty bourgeois class of their birth and education.[6] For Georges de Beauvoir, this was the best to which his daughter could aspire.

Simone sailed through the first *baccalauréat* examinations in a blissful haze of self-confidence induced in part by recently handed-down clothing from a cousin. The clothes and the newly granted privilege of taking her books into the Luxembourg Gardens to study alone in the afternoons made her feel remarkably grown-up. There she read texts Françoise approved of, such as Emile Faguet's superficial French history, Ferdinand Brunetière's theories of the necessity of moral purpose in art, or Jules Lemaître's mannered and sanitized fictions. She soon grew bored with these and spent her time walking up and down the Rue de l'Odéon, standing for long hours in front of the book bins, reading books her mother would not approve of, such as the fictions of Anatole France, the brothers Goncourt and especially Colette, whose works thrilled her with a sense of an unknown adult world she found herself poised to enter.[7]

Another new privilege was being allowed to stay up late in the evenings to study after Georges had gone to the Café Versailles to play bridge. Hélène, now fifteen, was still governed by Françoise's rules, and when her mother went to bed she was obliged to do the same. This left Simone alone to daydream and indulge in what was to become a lifelong passion, voyeurism: she used Georges's opera glasses to look into the windows of other buildings. She liked watching people when they didn't know she was looking, no matter how trivial their actions, how mundane their existences. She equated watching others with real life, thinking the people observed were really living while she was still poised, waiting to begin.

All these new freedoms made her smugly confident as she soared through the first examinations to pass with distinction. "Have you come to pick up a few more diplomas?" one examiner asked her, with so much acid in his greeting that she remembered it many years later.[8] Her family was delighted with her success, which enhanced her feeling of being adult, but it still did not stop Françoise from reading the letters of congratulations from relatives before Simone was allowed to read them herself.

The second examinations one year later, in 1925, were quite another matter. The Cours Désir headmistress kept a sharp eye on the latest developments in the public lycées and changed her program accordingly, all in the hope of keeping her own enrollments high, so philosophy was added to the curriculum, taught by the priest attached to the school, as very few women had studied the subject at the time and none was available to teach it there. The outward form and structure was thus the same as the lycée course, but the content was woefully inadequate in comparison.

The old abbé taught his dozen or so pupils seated around him at a massive wooden table that dominated the small classroom. Their mothers and governesses sat on rows of chairs behind the table, hands busy with needlework as they listened to the student recitations. The abbé's method of teaching was to read an enlightening text aloud, then dictate passages from it, or else to have the students copy essays from the text into their notebooks, which he then corrected for spelling and penmanship rather than content. Everything began with piety and ended with "the truth according to Saint Thomas Aquinas."[9]

Despite the inadequacy of the teaching, Simone was captivated by the subject and was "by far the most brilliant student in the class. ZaZa generally came next, but it was clear to the rest of us that we were quite ordinary in comparison. I think the teaching we received was very serious and good, but probably not [good enough] for someone as brilliant as Simone de Beauvoir. In her memoirs, she said our teachers knew nothing, and she was far too severe on the old priest who tried very hard to do his best for us. But she was at the height of her thirst for knowledge, and she was very good and very serious, and therefore, I am sure, very impatient."[10]

The inadequacy of the teaching showed when she took the examinations: she barely passed philosophy, but her grades in mathematics were respectable. Although she did not receive distinction with this degree, merely passing it was enough to satisfy Georges, who took her to the theater in celebration.

He was not exactly showing the same interest in her mind as he had shown when she was a child, but he was taking more notice of her. Granted, she had begun to look better now that she was slimming down and the blotches on her face had almost disappeared. She was even trying to take care of her hair, washing it more or less regularly, braiding it and wrapping it around her head. It was too fine and straight to hold a shape when cut into a stylish bob like ZaZa's, but she cut it anyway once or twice before letting it grow into braids, which conveyed an aura of individuality on a seventeen-year-old while requiring very little care and no attention. If she made them tight enough, she could go two or three days without having to take it down and do it up again. In the end, saving time came to mean more than keeping up with fashion, and she wore it this way for the rest of her life.

Her father's renewed interest was not because of her better appearance but of a more practical nature: there was still the question of settling her future, and as far as he was concerned it was not to be philosophy, which he considered "so much jibberish." Françoise had her reasons as well: "You will become immoral and lose your faith."[11]

Simone thought she found a way around their opposition when she read an article about the elite training school at Sèvres, established to educate women as teachers for public secondary *lycées* and *collèges*. Françoise would not even consider Sèvres. She had heard too many stories about the freethinkers spawned within its spartan and cloistered atmosphere. She had heard tales of violent exercise regimens (actually calisthenics), no attention to dress and deportment (meaning no required classes in moral well-being), and no time for daily religious observances. Also, students boarded there, which meant that Simone would be removed from her mother's constant supervision. As far as Françoise was concerned, the excesses of life at Sèvres far outweighed the future security that attendance would guarantee her daughter.[12] Françoise refused even to visit Sèvres and would not allow Simone to apply there.

As for Georges, though he disapproved of the study of philosophy for its own sake, he thought it would provide a good foundation for the study of law, which since the war had become open to a few determined women. He reasoned that Simone could qualify for a civil-service position and be guaranteed lifelong financial security from her first day of work. She read the Napoleonic Code just once before she vetoed that idea. Françoise thought being a librarian would be all right: even though Simone would be near possibly unacceptable books all day long, she could still maintain the genteel facade that she was not really working for her living. Françoise had a friend who worked in one of the scholarly collections of the Sorbonne and she took Simone to visit, hoping to impress her with the setting. Simone found it "Dead. Too dead. Nothing was alive there."

She thwarted her parents' every suggestion because she was determined to study philosophy, but they were equally determined and stubbornly refused all her entreaties. Drastic measures were called for, so she decided on a campaign of what she called "grown-up temper tantrums," a different version of her childhood ploy of holding her breath until she turned blue and frightened her parents into giving her what she wanted; now, instead of holding her breath, she simply kept silent whenever they tried to discuss her future. Time passed, and the situation was becoming critical in a way which threatened to shame them publicly, but in a far more humiliating manner than her childhood outbursts. If a compromise was not reached soon, it would be autumn and the great lump of a daughter was determined to be sitting at home doing nothing unless it was what she wanted to do. Georges and Françoise could not afford to save face by "launching" her into adult society with any sort of reception or party, and it would not have been appropriate anyway, because they had nothing to give her afterward that would make her marriageable, which was the main intention of such rituals.

The climate at home grew heated, and there was much shouting. Still Simone remained intractable. It was she who found a way out of the impasse when she leafed by chance through the pages of an illustrated magazine to read of a woman who had been one of the first to take a university degree in philosophy and who was now successfully teaching the subject. It seemed the ideal solution, especially since she had been considering a teaching career ever since reading the article about Sèvres. The photo accompanying the article enticed her even further: it showed a mature woman, the philosopher, seated at her desk surrounded by books and papers, while her "niece," whom she had adopted and of whom she was very fond, hovered nearby. The idea of financial and professional independence combined with interesting work and pleasant companionship seemed to represent the highest aspiration for a woman unlikely to be married. As far as Simone was concerned, her future was settled: she would become a teacher of philosophy.

Such a career represented Georges and Françoise's final, most humiliating capitulation: they had spent all these years scrimping to pay for private Catholic education, only to see their daughter determined to become a functionary in the public school system. Simone's will had always been strong, but until now it was untested because she had never wanted anything so much and so had not needed to demonstrate how stubborn she could be. The reasons why her parents capitulated are complex, but mostly they centered around Georges's position within his family and how he and they regarded each other.

His elderly father lived year round in Meyrignac, increasingly feeble and distanced from the everyday life of his children. Georges had long been estranged from his elder brother, Gaston, who was rich because of successful investments and his marriage to an heiress. Since their brother-in-law Maurice's death their sister Hélène had been comfortably situated, but when she needed help or advice she turned to Gaston as the head of the family and never consulted Georges. Thus Georges played no authoritative or consultative role within his family, which made it easy to abdicate responsibility within his own home because no one except his wife and daughters was there to see it, and Françoise cared more to salve his ego in public than to destroy it. To maintain even the facade of power within his home required a commitment of energy which Georges preferred to spend on his occasional mistresses and at the nightly bridge tables. It was easier to fail at what his father and brother would have considered his masculine responsibilities, especially since they were not there to see his humiliation and would have cared only that he did not bring public disgrace upon them. What mattered, finally, was to settle Simone someplace where she could be seen by Georges's family as preparing to support herself in a socially acceptable manner without any of them knowing what internal conflict was taking place within his home.

Nevertheless, Georges and Françoise were determined to keep Simone away from the unsettling influence and perceived dangers of the university for as long as possible. They were able to do so because the Cours Désir was classified as a primary school and she needed to study in a secondary school before she could enroll in a university. Georges willingly abdicated all further responsibility for both of his daughters' education, and Françoise became the parent who investigated possibilities. Buoyed by her victory in eliminating Sèvres, she set out to learn as much as she could about other institutions. She studied the programs of various day schools bearing among their titles terms such as "Institut Normal" or "Ecole Normale," a sure indication that although they were complying with education-reform laws, they were still committed to creating a secure Catholic environment for their students and following Catholic doctrine in their curriculum.

One of the most highly regarded of these schools was the Institut Sainte-Marie in Neuilly, the fashionable suburb on the western border of Paris. The school, founded in 1907, occupied the buildings of a former convent, thus reinforcing its evident dedication to a religious and political orientation favored by rich Catholic aristocrats of the most conservative thinking, who were its staunchest patrons. The school quickly became Françoise's first choice because Monsieur Le Coin had decided to allow ZaZa to take a few courses there until her older sister was safely married off and she became the family's next eligible candidate. Françoise was greatly pleased with herself for placing her own daughter in such a socially acceptable institution.

The school day was divided into half-day sessions because the success of such schools depended on enrolling as many tuition-paying pupils as possible, and as private schools they were not obliged to follow the program leading to the *baccalauréat* as strictly as state schools. The school justified the two sessions by emphasizing that the daughters of wealthy families needed "free time for other activities such as sport, promenades, and philanthropic activities,"[13] all euphemisms for the interminable round of festivities where they could be displayed to eligible men. This too pleased Françoise, because it meant that the conditions for controlling Simone remained the same, or so she thought.

There was no real reason for Françoise to know how well indeed she had placed her daughter. Simone would be under the tutelage of Madame Charles Daniélou, a pioneer who held more degrees than any other woman in France at that time and who believed fervently in the power of education as liberation. Unlike other "directresses" of private secondary schools, usually unmarried daughters of wealthy families who chose not to enter convents, Madame Daniélou was married, to a member of the French parliament who strongly supported her ideas, and she was the mother of two children. She insisted upon the highest standards of instruction to prepare her students for the *baccalauréat*, which was assumed unquestionably to be the logical outcome of attendance at her school. Hers was a dedicated staff of intelligent women, so her school and her program are remembered today as examples of the finest French educational experience for women in the early years of this century. She appealed especially to women like Françoise who had learned just enough in the cloistered settings of their own educational institutions to be enticed by the possibilities offered by the Institut Sainte-Marie for their daughters.

Daily life was somewhat easier for Françoise now that Simone and Hélène were adult students and Georges was absent so much from home. She had more time to read and learn, which she did by trying again to follow Simone's studies. Because Françoise was intelligent, Madame Daniélou and her curriculum became objects of admiration rather than possible dangers which might remove her daughter once and for all from her control. She even considered the possibility that Simone, by observing the "Christian example" of Madame Daniélou and her staff, would be moved to regain her lost faith.[14] All in all, everything seemed propitious.

Françoise seldom spoke about herself, but when she did, it was usually to Hélène. When she did speak of her own childhood, a recurring theme was the sadness she felt about her mother's coldness and alienation toward her, and how much she wanted to be close to her own daughters. Hélène's memory is of a mother who "would say so poignantly how she wanted us to be friends, not mother and daughters, but good friends who could talk to each other and have pleasant conversations."

Simone's recollection was tinged with bitterness: "She said she wanted to be my friend, but she treated me like a specimen under a microscope. She probed into everything I did, from reading my books to reading my letters. Sometimes, when I was studying at night, I would catch her staring at me with a long face, and when I asked what was the matter she only sighed. I knew what to expect next: she would ask if there was a chance I was feeling some stirring of religious feeling. When I always said no, well, that was the end of it. No other conversation followed."

They began to communicate in a manner unfortunate for both, with ramifications for many of Simone de Beauvoir's future relationships with women. Simone thought of her mother as a spy who wanted to know all her thoughts, control all her movements and pry into her friendships. Her natural inclination toward privacy and reticence grew even more pronounced and became manifested in ways both large and small. Her handwriting, for example, always tiny and careful, now became so minute that anyone but she required a magnifying glass to read it. She wrote on minuscule shreds of paper and in miniature notebooks that she carried everywhere for fear that Françoise would find and read them.

Françoise was much more relaxed with Hélène, even able to create intimacy out of embarrassment by laughing about such things as handed-down clothing and making a game of Hélène standing on a chair striking funny poses as Françoise adjusted seams and hems or changed a trimming here or there. With Simone, quite the reverse was true. If Françoise fussed over her or touched her in any way at all, she was so irritated that she usually stalked off to her room, leaving her mother crying and screaming at her coldness. She bathed and dressed furtively, fascinated by her body but embarrassed to look at it herself for fear Françoise's spying eye might catch her nude. When she began to use face powder, she made sure she was never in Françoise's line of vision before she rushed out of the apartment. Thus their relationship became thoroughly grounded in

Simone's secrecy and evasion and Françoise's reproach and resentment. As time passed and Simone's independence grew, silence replaced argument, and an uneasy truce began that lasted throughout the next several decades.

From time to time, Françoise tried to break through to her daughter, such as with the brand-new tartan-plaid dress she had a seamstress make for Simone to wear to the Institut Sainte-Marie. These attempts, as in this instance, usually came to little. Simone seized the dress as her due, thought herself "simply stunning," and hardly bothered to thank her mother for what had been a considerable financial sacrifice.[15] Françoise was indeed an overbearing personality, but Simone was also frequently insensitive to her mother's overtures. Perhaps by then they were simply too late.

Simone's association with women her own age was somewhat more complex. Beginning with her first friend, Hélène, Simone was always the leader, the teacher, the one who made all the decisions. This extended to her next friends, the cousins Jeanne and Magdeleine, who submitted to her bossiness only as long as it suited them, until they were bored or tired of her game and drifted off. The girls at the Cours Désir who allowed themselves to be befriended by Simone (for this generally was how it happened) were usually docile and unattractive, delighted to have such a strong personality as she make their decisions. With the single exception of ZaZa, this was the kind of girl who became her friend.

ZaZa was a baffling commodity because she would neither adapt nor submit to Simone's will, she had many more activities and interests outside school, and she played many more roles within her immediate and extended family. The four Beauvoirs had one static, assigned role among themselves and with their relatives: Georges was the failure, Françoise the eccentric, Hélène the sweet girl victimized by circumstances, and Simone the odd one tolerated by some, liked very much by others, and always a bit of an embarrassment to everyone.

For Simone, sensitive to rebuffs whether or not they were actually there, this meant an even further withdrawal from any possibility of informal friendship with women and more intense concentration on her studies than ever. In fact, the studies were so demanding that she hardly had time to brood over her friendship with ZaZa. The Institut Sainte-Marie was noted for the rigor of its curriculum, and Simone realized at once how poorly prepared she had been at the Cours Désir. But she quickly caught up with the better-prepared students, and by the winter of 1926 she had time to realize that she was lonely, so lonely that she actually returned several times to the Cours Désir to participate in the philosophy discussion group sponsored by the abbé. She found these meetings to be "exercises in mediocrity and hypocrisy" and soon stopped going. Then Françoise consented to let her spend the afternoons in various libraries throughout Paris. At last she was free to read what she liked, and she ranged far and wide in her largely self-directed study. But she could not read all the time, and she found herself staring at other readers and inventing excuses to talk to anyone she thought might be interesting, intrusions that generally came to nothing.

"I soon had to admit that this year was not bringing me all I had banked on getting," she wrote years later in her memoirs. "Up to now, I had made the best of living in a cage, for I knew that one day—and each day brought it nearer—the door of the cage would open; now I had got out of the cage and I was still inside. What a let-down!"[16]

With her general tendency toward introspection exaggerated by loneliness, she found herself turning to Hélène for companionship for the first time since she had found ZaZa. Although Hélène had her own circle and was popular and happy at the Cours Désir, Simone had always been her dearest friend and she was happy to have her sister's affection and attention back again. Without Hélène, life at home would have been unrelieved misery for Simone.

As far as Georges was concerned, when Simone had insisted on becoming a teacher she had (as she put it later) "gone over to the enemy, become a traitor to my class and station and stripped myself of the responsibilities and privileges of my sex." Georges equated her studies with

> the dangerous sect . . . the intellectuals . . . blinded by their book-learning, taking a stubborn pride in abstract knowledge and in their futile aspirations to universalism . . . sacrificing the concrete realities of race, country, class, family and nationality to those crackpot notions that would be the death of France and of civilization: the Rights of Man, pacifism, internationalism, and socialism.[17]

An observation about the effect of literature upon the bourgeoisie accurately describes Georges de Beauvoir as well: "The public's idea of a great writer was largely determined by what they had read as children."[18] Georges proclaimed time and again that "only the idols of his youth . . . had any talent; only intellectual snobbery could explain the success of modern French and foreign authors." When a fellow amateur actor insisted that Ibsen was a genius, Georges replied, "You won't get *me* bowing to him!" He detested anything foreign, and anyone who didn't agree with him was "un-French and unpatriotic."[19] When he saw his daughter reading Gide, "he exploded. And when I began to read Cocteau, Barrès, Radiguet, Alain-Fournier, well . . . !"[20]

Since Georges concentrated on Simone's mind for his favorite form of attack, Françoise concentrated on the tarnished state of her soul. Under siege, Simone turned to her sister for solace. Hélène was content to serve as Simone's sounding board, and also to participate in small but soon-to-become-major rebellions. On the rare nights their parents were out together, the sisters sneaked past the concierge's watchful eye to walk through the neighborhood streets, staring into ground-floor-apartment windows or watching the people in cafés. Everything seemed so cheerful and happy that after they rushed breathless up the many flights of stairs and settled themselves in their tiny bedroom, they lay there creating fantasies about what they had seen.

Simone was eighteen and Hélène sixteen; it was only natural that these forays soon led to discussions of sex and experimentation upon their own bodies. Neither sister had ever had what in the parlance of the time might be called a "pash" or a crush upon another girl or even a teacher, and, with the exception of Simone's uncertain feeling for Jacques, they had felt nothing for a boy either. In their own way, they were as sheltered and innocent as their cousin Jeanne, who was greatly admired by Georges for still believing that babies were found in the cabbage patch.

With her innocence of life and her thirst for abstract knowledge, Simone turned to philosophy for answers to questions about love and sex. When Jacques came into her life again, the situation was ripe for disastrous consequences.

He had bought a sporty little car, a daring thing for a young unmarried man to do in those days. After having stayed away for almost a year, he came to the Rue de Rennes to show it off. Jacques was, as always, eager to have an audience; inherent in this was the pleasure he took in provocation and shock. Georges, who had found him amusing when he was younger, now ridiculed everything, so Jacques quickly learned to keep serious conversation to himself unless he was alone with his cousins in their living room.

Simone discovered modern literature through Jacques, and for that she "owed him lifelong gratitude." In her memoirs she wrote of the profound effect he had upon her: "In those days I preferred to wonder about things rather than to understand them, so I didn't try to 'place' Jacques or to explain him. It is only now that I find I can tell his story without too much incoherence."[21]

Jacques was always careful to appear deferential and respectful to Georges, but he, Simone and Hélène knew that, by leaving the room, Georges had in effect admitted defeat before the barrage of contemporary ideas with which Jacques politely teased him.

Jacques dazzled Simone with the names of writers whose works she dutifully read, and astonished her with gossip about the artists and writers who lived in Montparnasse but of whom she knew nothing and had never seen. Hélène quickly discerned the attraction Jacques had for Simone, and her sister's quick blush was enough to let her know that the feeling was reciprocated. The first time Jacques suggested an outing, Françoise, to their astonishment, gave them permission to go. Hélène resented being left behind, but was privy to her mother's "ecstasy." Françoise was "filled with joy" because she hoped Jacques meant to marry Simone whether she had a dowry or not. It brought back memories of her own flirtation with Charles Champigneulle, Jacques's father, and she confided the details to Hélène: "He was her cousin as well, and he charmed her, beguiled her, when she was sixteen or seventeen. I think it must have been a very romantic affair, like in a novel, but I don't know very much about it. My aunts all said he was supposed to have broken my mother's heart by marrying my Aunt Germaine, who was also another one of her cousins, but I think for my mother it was only a highly romanticized little flirtation. I think my aunts exaggerated it because they all knew Jacques would never marry Simone and they just wanted to create another ill-fated romance to parallel the first one."

Simone de Beauvoir agreed: "When my other aunts thought Jacques was interested in me, Hélène and I sometimes caught snatches of their whispered conversation about my mother and Uncle Charles. Either they were afraid Jacques and I would end badly or they wanted it to happen—who knows?"

Despite the qualms of others where Jacques was concerned, Françoise was so jubilant that she relaxed every standard she had cherished all her life. She allowed Simone to go out with him unchaperoned and to dine at his home with only the housekeeper present. She did not even object when Simone began to spend afternoons and evenings there, dropping in without invitation. Whenever his mother and sister were in Paris, Françoise made sure to invite them to dinner at the Rue de Rennes so that the invitation would have to be reciprocated.

In her memoirs and subsequent conversations, Simone de Beauvoir's father during this time is notable more for his absence, distance and silence than for his interest in her future. One might argue that Georges was protecting himself so that if the romance soured for any reason whatsoever, but especially because Simone had no dowry, he would not have to play the outraged father and everything would quietly subside without gossip or innuendo. Still, if he feared that this might happen, he could have asked Jacques to declare his intentions at once or else remove himself from consideration. Georges did neither, but as he refused to concern himself, Françoise grew more and more agitated and thus more indiscreet.

In the presence of both families, Françoise threw one of her famous tantrums after a dinner given by Jacques's mother which she presumed was supposed to be the prelude to Jacques's proposal. But when the dinner ended, there was only pleasant but innocuous conversation. When the Beauvoirs returned home, Françoise was enraged, Hélène embarrassed, Simone sullen, and Georges escaped to a bridge game. He took no part in these discussions, neither encouraging nor discouraging his wife's hopes; he was so neutral that neither of his daughters had any idea what he thought of the purported romance.

As for Simone, she was swept away by what was the only traditional semblance of a courtship that she ever had in her entire lifetime. She loved driving in the little car, walking in the Bois de Bologne, whiling away long afternoons curled up on a sofa with a book while Jacques played at designing stained glass. He took her to art galleries in Saint-Germain-des-Prés and taught her how to look at paintings. He gave her the poetry of Mallarmé, Rimbaud, Baudelaire and Max Jacob, who became a particular favorite.

He recommended films and plays for Françoise to take her to, because suddenly Françoise would no longer permit them to go out alone in the evenings. This was a new tack, taken not because she feared that her daughter would become compromised if unchaperoned, but, as Beauvoir recalled, "more probably because she hoped that by refusing him my company she would goad him into declaring his intentions." Also, it was because Jacques's behavior had begun to arouse his aunt's suspicions. Simone had staggered into the apartment several times in the early-morning hours with the smell of liquor and tobacco heavy on her clothing, for Jacques had introduced her to nightclubs and cafés and she liked them very much.

With one fell swoop, Simone overcame years of repressive behavior instilled by her mother's obsession with morality. She thought smoking made her glamorous, and she puffed away every time anyone offered her a cigarette (for she had no money to buy her own nor anyplace to secrete them from her mother's prying eye). She liked the taste of liquor and the exotic names and colorful mixtures of cocktails, and, because she had a strong digestive system, she was able to drink them in great quantities. Simone was indifferent to manners, morals and discretion as she willingly followed Jacques through "the real Paris" while Françoise stayed at home in uncustomary paralysis, waiting and hoping for his proposal, afraid to do anything that might interfere with it.

And so the romance, such as it was, limped along, fueled by Jacques's vanity as he played Pygmalion to Simone's Galatea. The school year ended and she passed the examinations with high enough marks that her philosophy instructor urged her to take a second year of instruction at the Institut Sainte-Marie and to spend as much time as possible attending lectures at the Sorbonne. Georges had no objection, Françoise acquiesced, and Simone was pleased with herself for having finished so well after such a shaky beginning. When she told all this to Jacques, he admitted offhandedly that he had just failed his law examinations and would have to repeat the year's work. Simone was more upset with the news than he was. He blamed the failure on his zest for life, which he said was so "intense and so filled with enthusiasm for so many different things" that he could not bring himself to concentrate on his courses.

"The truth of the matter was quite different from what he told me," said Simone de Beauvoir many years later. "He was one of those people who is intelligent but also very lazy. He liked to talk about all the great things he was going to do, and I must admit, his ideas were sometimes brilliant and extraordinary. But that was all he liked to do—talk. Also, he was starting to drink a lot, and this grew steadily worse as time passed. I think I knew very well what his character was like, but I refused to see it. I was trying to convince myself to be in love with him; no, with *the idea* of him. I was too naive and immature to see him as he really was. I was eighteen years old, I wanted to be in love, and there was no one else around. I was in love with love, but I had no idea what it really meant. I was saved, probably from myself, because the school year ended and we both went away from Paris."

EIGHT

"A High-minded
Little Bourgeois"

J ACQUES CHAMPIGNEULLE played many roles in the life of Simone de Beauvoir during their brief "relationship,"[1] but the most important and lasting was that of intellectual mentor. He began when she was eight by selecting books from the massive glass-fronted case on their Great-Aunt Alice's first-floor landing: he gave her *Gulliver's Travels* ("fantasy, suitable for girls") and kept *Popular Astronomy* for himself.[2] He was more generous when he introduced her to contemporary literature, inviting her when she was nineteen to help herself from the piles of books heaped throughout his apartment.

"Oh yes, I helped myself to his books, I gorged," in a feast of eye and ear on "volumes bound in paper covers whose colours were as sharp and fresh as those of boiled sweets: pistachio green Montherlant, a strawberry red Cocteau, lemon yellow Barrès, Claudel and Valéry in snowy white with scarlet letterpress."[3]

She read Gide, Radiguet, Larbaud, Proust, and an almost endless list of poetry and fiction which infuriated Françoise, who divided books into two categories: serious works and novels.[4] Her mother's open animosity toward anything that was not spiritually uplifting or morally instructive made Simone even more dependent upon Jacques, not only because he guided her reading but also because he allowed her to talk to him about what she read. Her thoughts poured out in torrents of emotion because the books he loaned her were so different from everything she had been permitted to read before.

In her late seventies, she still remembered the thrill of opening a book of modern fiction, finding that the words were "words I already knew," but arranged so that "everything took on new meaning": "There were concepts, relationships, attitudes which had had no place in my well ordered world before then, and which would certainly never be received in my parents' home, nor by the people I knew, and really not even by ZaZa, who had been the person I talked to before this about literature and ideas. I was completely bowled over by these books he gave me to read."

Of them all, the book which had the strongest hold on her imagination for many years afterward, and which was her guide in the murky, constantly shifting emotional territories through which Jacques led her, was Alain-Fournier's *Le Grand Meaulnes.*

Jacques was moody, subject to careening emotional zigzags, frequent unexplained absences and long periods of silence followed by bursts of unfocused conversation. As soon as Simone read his favorite novel, she was sure he had asked her to read it for a specific purpose—as the key to understanding his mind and his moods. She was convinced he regarded the novel as the explanation for his erratic behavior, and whenever she thought of Jacques it was with much the same perplexity as Yvonne, the character with which she identified, feels for Meaulnes, whom Simone was sure Jacques considered his counterpart. Yvonne asks, "Who are you? How do you happen to be here? I don't know you. . . . And yet I do seem to know you,"[5] which was what Simone thought about Jacques.

For days and weeks, Jacques seemed to be always waiting at the Rue de Rennes for Simone to come home from school or else making appointments to meet her and driving her all over Paris. Then he would suddenly disappear for equally long periods, leaving her to pace up and down the Boulevard Montparnasse across the street from his house, hoping to see him, then in desperation ringing the bell, which no one answered, before sitting on the stoop and waiting for him to come home. When he did, he was often cold to her, as if his mind were far away in another time and place. She went home feeling stupid and clumsy, hurt but trying to understand what she could have done to make him treat her this way. This self-analysis was always directed toward her own perceived faults and led her to create programs and plans for change that would make her smarter, better, prettier and in every sense more pleasing to him. It never occurred to her that she should try to talk to him about his moods or to make him change in any way, for to her he was perfection incarnate.

Yet though all outward appearances made it seem that they were sweethearts, theirs was a curiously dispassionate relationship. Simone de Beauvoir swears that he never kissed her, never put his arm around her, never really touched her except to guide her in or out of a car or a building. None of this bothered her, because she thought of him as the real-life equivalent of the perfection-seeking Meaulnes, and of herself as a living version of the idealized, ethereal Yvonne. But there were other characters in the book who were important to her as well, and she saw aspects of herself and Jacques in them.

François Seurel, the narrator who recounts the tenderness and despair of his friendship with Meaulnes in clear-eyed prose, had a lifelong effect upon Simone de Beauvoir. At that time, she used Seurel's analysis of Meaulnes for a model as she groped toward an understanding of Jacques's shifting moods. Of all the characters in the book, she identified herself most closely with Seurel, because "he went straight to essentials," which was her own preferred way of thinking. She used this phrase in her memoirs when she wrote that she was initially attracted to philosophy because it *"went straight to essentials."*[6]

It is not unusual that she identified herself with the masculine voice of reason and responsibility within this novel. From the first time she heard her father say that hers was "the mind of a man," she considered it something to be proud of and concentrated all her intellectual energies in that direction, especially as her education had been one which exhorted women students to "cultivate the man" or "the soul of a man" within them.[7]

It was not until much later that she recognized Georges's statement as a cutting remark, which rankled for years afterward, probably as he had intended. But she did as she was told and trained her "mind of a man," putting it to good use in her studies and reading, using it to capture prizes and gain high standings in her classes. When she realized that her economic future depended on it, she honed it even sharper. As the equally logical François Seurel strove to understand his friend Meaulnes, who was so like Jacques, she studied the novel as her guide to doing the same.

When Simone thought of herself in the feminine sense it was through the placid character of Yvonne after she had become the young wife of Meaulnes, and of whom Seurel wrote: ". . . what grave responsibilities she had assumed . . . a crushing one in linking her destiny with that of an adventurous spirit."[8] But passivity was difficult for Simone, almost as impossible as it had been from her very earliest years when she would not play unless she could be the leader in every game. The fictional Yvonne was content to sit patiently at home waiting for Meaulnes, but the real Simone paced up and down the sidewalk outside Jacques's house. She bit her fingernails to the quick when he went off on one of his increasingly frequent absences, and she sobbed loudly, tears pouring down her face as she careened wildly through the streets of Paris.

In these instances, it was easier to identify with Valentine, the mysterious young woman who rejected Yvonne's brother Frantz (another Meaulnes-like character) for a life of independence and vaguely hinted-at sexual license. Since Valentine cast a brief spell upon Meaulnes as well, Simone found it easier to imagine herself as the strong woman, the fearless rejector who lived independently and cared little for what the future might bring. She found Valentine's vitality, even though negatively portrayed by Alain-Fournier, much more appealing than Yvonne's languid passivity.

For Simone, Jacques had become, like Meaulnes for Seurel, "a stranger, like a man who has failed to find what he sought and for whom nothing else held any interest," and, like Seurel, Simone asked,

"Why, then, this present emptiness, this aloofness, this inability to be happy?"[9]

This "inability to be happy" characterized her summer, all of it caused by the uncertainty of her status with Jacques. She visited relatives at Cauterets, was shocked by the religious excesses of pilgrimages at Lourdes, suffered severe unfocused nighttime anxiety at La Grillère, and tried unsuccessfully to turn it all into fiction at Meyrignac. When she returned to Paris in September, everything at home seemed so constricting and confining that she thought she would suffocate.[10] Her first impulse was to seek Jacques, but Françoise forbade her to go to his house.

At that time, she attributed Françoise's action to mean-spiritedness; in later life she understood it for the ploy it was meant to be: Françoise wanted Jacques to declare his intentions and she hoped that keeping them separated would spur him to do so. Unfortunately, she chose to put it into effect during a time when Jacques was absent anyway. Then, in late October, Françoise changed her tactics once again: she instructed Simone to spend as much of her time as she could comforting Jacques, who had become lethargic and depressed now that he had failed his law examinations for the final time. Françoise may have thought throwing them together would speed things along, but Jacques's family seems to have viewed Simone more as the object or plaything needed by their darling dilettante at that moment in his life than as a serious contender for marriage. The danger signs were already there, but Françoise chose to ignore them and Simone was too inexperienced to see them. Jacques's income was small, and now that he had no obvious career there was growing concern in the family about his future. It seems Françoise was the last to know that Jacques would have to marry a woman with a sizable dowry now that his own future was so vague.

In the meantime, for almost two years he practiced an evasive sort of honesty with Simone: "It seems I will have to marry someday soon," or words to that effect,[11] but to her eager mind it meant that he was hinting of their mutual future. It brought back another attack of the previous summer's anxieties. As she lay alone in bed at La Grillère and Meyrignac, the final outcome in every tearfully imagined scenario had been that marriage would "provide the ideal solution for all my difficulties. . . . His mother and sister would lavish their affection upon me and my parents would be kinder to me: I should become once more a person universally loved and I would take my place again in that society from which I had felt myself exiled forever."[12] In other words, she explained many years later, "through marriage, the odd duck would become a swan, but at what price?"

At the age of nineteen, thinking of marriage as the solution to all her problems, she proved herself no different from countless other women in many diverse societies and cultures. She had not yet considered rejecting it, but as she thought of marriage to Jacques and contrasted it with what she was now calling "a life of freedom" (even though she had not yet defined what exactly she meant by this term), she was frightened by what the choice entailed. Either she continued to try to persuade a man, in this instance Jacques, to be responsible for her or else she had to be prepared to take responsibility for herself and her future well-being. When she finally decided never to marry, one point that might have made the decision easier was that the men she had known were not exactly models of what then stood for admirable masculine behavior. Her Grandfather Beauvoir was the sole man who gave her unequivocal love, but she saw him only in the summers at Meyrignac; her Grandfather Brasseur was someone she feared as a child and scorned as a young woman. Her father's brother and brother-in-law were quiet men who took good care of their respective families, had little interest in other relatives and also died when Simone was still fairly young. And, of course, her own father had not been someone she could count upon for very much in the way of understanding, affection or support.

Simone kept secret "journals" ever since her teens, when students at the Cours Désir were required to record their thoughts and activities in "theme books," a written counterpart of the Catholic practice of confession. Her private journals were tiny notebooks filled with small, cramped handwriting which she somehow managed to keep secret from her mother. Some entries were anguished thoughts about religion and death, but many others were pro/con lists of activities, attitudes and behavior. One such was

a long inventory of the things that separated us [herself and Jacques]: "He is content to enjoy beautiful things, he accepts luxury and easy living; he likes being happy. But I want my life to be an all-consuming passion. I need to act, to give freely of myself, to bring plans to fruition: I need an object in life, I want to overcome difficulties and succeed in writing a book. I'm not made for a life of luxury. I could never be satisfied with the things that satisfy him."

Then she added: ". . . what I was really rejecting, and what I reproached Jacques with accepting, was the bourgeois status."[13]

She was perceptive enough to realize that, for her, marriage to him was not the beginning of anything except the process by which she would become exactly like her mother, her married aunts, her cousins and all other women in her social class. She described many years later what she believed would have happened to her: "Whenever I saw the jewelry that has flies preserved in Baltic amber, I always thought of myself and Jacques. But that, of course, was much later. Then I was too much in the midst of the situation and didn't see anything at all."

The inventory of her feelings for Jacques was only one of many lists made during this unhappy time in her life. There were, of course, the ubiquitous lists of books read and to be read, divided now into categories resembling her mother's: "books for Cagne"[14] and "books to read." There were lists of good deeds to do, and there were lists of personal admonitions that included everything from being a more agreeable daughter to making some new friendships with women and being kinder to her sister. All of these, when read with hindsight, show a young woman desperately groping toward some way out of what she thought had become "an impossible life."

Once again, a book provided temporary enlightenment and became a source of comfort and inspiration. This time it was François Mauriac's *Farewell to Adolescence*, a collection of alexandrine verses about his "too happy childhood." The poems describe the wonderful old house of his grandparents, where he spent idyllic summer vacations that differed from Simone de Beauvoir's only in location, his being Bordeaux and the Atlantic scrub pines and coastal dunes. She believed that these poems of "languorous romanticism," in which "the head has not yet come to the rescue of a heart sensitive and unsatisfied,"[15] filled all her needs of the moment and described her condition exactly.

The summer and early fall of 1927 were the first and in many ways the most serious of her "dark nights of the soul,"[16] depressive periods that recurred from time to time throughout her life. This was also the first time she turned to writing about herself, as if through self-analysis she could cut through the morass of her daily life. At Meyrignac that summer she tried to write fiction, thinking that a novel based upon her unhappy situation with Jacques would be both cathartic and self-illuminating.

Simone de Beauvoir tried to use Mauriac's novels, that is, those he wrote before the 1930s, as her early fictional models because he placed his characters solidly in well-ordered, respectable middle-class situations while making them struggle with religious doubt, sexual conflict and the problems arising when they challenged boundaries of social class. Ultimately, however, novels that began as psychological family dramas always ended with the triumph of his own fervent Roman Catholicism, and so they disappointed her. In her earliest writings, she tried to follow Mauriac's plot structure without copying his religious fervor, but her prose was clinically detached and clumsy, while her attempts at character and dialogue were effusive with overblown emotion. Years later she described these early attempts at fiction as "more like an awkward imitation of *Le Grand Meaulnes*."

She struggled with her few beginning pages for most of the month in the country, but abandoned it when she returned to Paris. Just before her classes began, she tried another version, this time in the form of pure philosophical dialogue. She called both attempts "little more than crude, confused blunderings" and destroyed everything soon after she wrote it.[17] It took her more than two years to learn how to transpose her life into fiction in the stories collected as *When Things of the Spirit Come First*, and then only after momentous changes had set her firmly and finally on the path from which her adult life never deviated.

In the meantime, life at home continued to be difficult. "Our mother was the hen who had given birth to ducks," Hélène remembered. "She was very proud of her daughters; she wanted to live through us, but she also wanted us to live for her, and we wouldn't do that."[18]

Hélène was graduated from the Cours Désir in the spring of 1927, but unlike Simone, who had been directed since childhood toward a career accessible only through rigid formal education, Hélène was left more or less to her own devices. Georges never really thought about his younger daughter other than as "pretty, charming and likely to catch the eye of a rich husband even without a dowry." Hélène's own description of her role in the household was that her parents were "too busy fighting with Simone to have much time and energy left over for me." The truth is, they seriously underestimated her.

The two sisters had grown somewhat apart during Simone's involvement with Jacques, their only closeness imposed by the lack of space in their tiny bedroom and by their common resentment of their parents. Even this was muted, because Simone mistakenly perceived that Hélène enjoyed being Françoise's confidante, and Hélène believed Simone had abandoned her for ZaZa. Rather then confiding in each other as they had done when they lay so close in their separate beds that their fingers could touch, Simone had fallen into the habit of entrusting her most private thoughts to the little notebooks she carried always.

All this changed the summer after Hélène's graduation, when Françoise's vituperation toward Simone was so shrill that the entire household felt it. She had begun to lash out again, as she had done when the children were small; she threw things, shouted, cried and became increasingly obsessed with their every movement and activity, even to irrational demands to know their thoughts. Françoise was frustrated by the impasse and lack of resolution in Simone's relationship with Jacques, but rigid codes of conduct and behavior prohibited her from addressing the situation directly. This powerlessness infuriated her, but she was ashamed to tell anyone the reason for her anger. Instead, she directed all her sarcasm and scorn upon Simone, perhaps thinking it might goad her into action concerning Jacques. All it did, however, was to make the girl even more passive and, for a very brief moment, the docile one in the family. Suddenly the roles were reversed, and Hélène became the argumentative, questioning and, indeed, feisty daughter.

Her first rebellion was so bold that it even shocked her sister. "Listen," she told Simone one morning after she had been handed a letter from a friend that had been opened by Françoise, "I am seventeen and you are almost twenty and there is no reason in the world why we have to put up with this any longer. I am going straight to Mama and tell her that I forbid her to open my letters, and I suggest you go with me, too."

Simone's reply was curious: "You're right, you should tell Mother not to read *your* [emphasis added] letters anymore." She said nothing about her own, and when they were before their mother she stood uncharacteristically silent. Hélène, with flushed, tear-stained face, stamped her foot and presented her demands: "It doesn't give me any pleasure to read a letter when someone has read it before me." Françoise never opened their letters again. This domestic rebellion renewed and strengthened the sisters' deep and lasting friendship.

Now that Hélène was finished with her schooling, something had to be found for her to do. She wanted to be an artist, but no one in their milieu had any idea of what constituted serious artistic education. Again Françoise investigated, and this time she found a school of decoration, in which girls from the highest society spent their time learning to paint designs on household objects while they waited for someone to marry them. Even better than the school's social status was the scholarship Hélène was given, a charity maintained by the school for the daughter of a family "of the right sort"[19] down on its financial luck.

For Hélène, the school was "like entering the convent all over again." The thought of spending four years there depressed her so much that she cried every night for three months until Georges could no longer stand to see her swollen face and listen to her sobbing, and he let her withdraw. Her stubborn determination solidified Simone's admiration and respect, and marked the beginning of their "conspiracy of true friendship."

The previous spring, hoping to gain Jacques's respect and also "to make myself feel good that I was contributing something to society," Simone agreed to do volunteer work with Professor Robert Garric's Equipe Social, a social-service institute with a strong Catholic orientation founded by the young philosopher-professor to aid the working classes in the northeastern districts of Paris. Garric enlisted his pupils to serve as instructors and role models, and Simone was assigned to teach literature to young women, a task she began in a combination of idealism for the work and idealization of the aesthetic (and, to her, handsome) Garric. She soon found out that the motive for her pupils' attendance was based on a harsh realism: they were mostly factory girls who went there to escape from their families' crowded apartments and to meet men they might marry. To a great extent, Simone went there herself to escape from her own parents, so there was a degree of sympathy between teacher and pupils from the very beginning, even though she soon grew bored talking about subjects and ideas to an indifferent and uncomprehending audience. Nevertheless, she was stubborn and persevered for several years, trying to force them in what was probably an insistent and didactic manner to appreciate literature and culture. She never practiced self-delusion, and knew almost from the outset how unsuccessful her efforts were, but the freedom of being out alone at night was something she did not want to give up. Many evenings when she told Françoise she was off to teach, she simply walked instead along the city's colorful northern boulevards and indulged in her favorite pastime of watching people. More frequently she went to the "Cinémathèque" to watch Hélène paint, for her sister had introduced her to a milieu that until this time she hardly knew existed.

Hélène had persuaded Georges and Françoise that she could not waste the entire semester without learning something worthwhile, so although each morning she dutifully painted flowers on china teacups, in the afternoon she went to an inexpensive studio school in Montparnasse to learn engraving, and several evenings each week she attended a drawing school, the "Cinémathèque on the Rue de Fleurus,"[20] where anyone who could pay a few francs admission could take drawing classes.

Hers was a schizophrenic day: in the morning, Hélène was surrounded by pupils who spoke of "tennis, horseback riding, parties and possible husbands." In the afternoon, she was with earnest young French people, mostly men, whose families had sacrificed so that they could learn the prosperous trade of engraving. At night, she was surrounded by a spectrum that ranged from foreigners to peasants. She adored the evening classes and told Simone, who shared her enthusiasm for anything different from their daily life. They joked together about Georges's almost pathological dismissal of anything foreign: "Before this, we never even saw a foreigner, man or woman. They did not exist for us. Nothing of the world existed for our father but France. It was claustrophobic, so that Simone and I would often repeat one of his favorite remarks to each other: 'Why travel? France is the most beautiful country in the world.' It sent us into wild laughter when we imagined how he would react if he could see the people we had come to know and value."[21]

Neither of them had ever before been in such proximity to so many different kinds of people, and each reacted in characteristic fashion: Simone studied their mannerisms, watched them with unabashed curiosity and fantasized about their lives outside the classes; Hélène soon became a pet to some and, with her easygoing nature, a good friend to others.

Casual friendships never came easily to Simone, then or throughout the rest of her life. For her, friendship and intimacy were always intertwined, and unless persons had similar interests, intelligence or respect for work, she was seldom interested in knowing them better. There were few other women students in her classes at the Sorbonne, and with the exception of ZaZa she found them timid and boring. Despite the fact that she had many cousins and was often forced into their company by the relentless round of family occasions, she had never learned the art of casual conversation or small talk. The closest she came in this regard was when Magdeleine de Bisschop came to Paris for holidays and she and Simone sneaked off to a movie or wandered through department stores looking at clothing and makeup. Still, these occasions were characterized mostly by Simone studying Magdeleine as she applied forbidden face powder, not to learn how to do it to herself, but to watch Magdeleine transform herself into another, brighter, prettier and "less authentic" being.[22] For Simone, everything had to be purposeful, and even her nightly bedtime conversations with her sister were usually constructive, directed toward plans for the future, when they would be "free" of their parents.

Now during her evenings out she suddenly found herself in two different settings where other young women talked openly about their hopes and intentions, not only to each other but to men who were present as well. At the Equipe, she listened to her erstwhile pupils talk about everything from the timeliness of their menstrual periods to their dreams for furnishing modest apartments of their own when they married. She heard them giggle about the proclivities and peccadillos of the shabbily dressed young men who hung about shyly, avoiding Simone's steady gaze as they waited to walk the girls they liked best down the longest and darkest streets to their homes. At the Cinémathèque, she heard curses based on women's anatomy hurled by both men and women artists disappointed with their paintings, and ribald remarks about the models' private anatomies. She saw nude men and women and very often watched slaps, tickles and intimate fondlings exchanged casually and without pruriency. She had never seen anything like it before.

Even at the Equipe she witnessed behavior which called her standards into question. There was one other teacher, "Suzanne Boigue," whom Simone tried to befriend but whom she soon found wanting, a robust woman of twenty-five who directed her considerable energies to "indiscriminate doing good." Simone considered "action . . . a deceptive solution: by pretending to devote oneself to the welfare of others one was providing oneself with too easy a way out."[23] Even more unpardonable, "Boigue" was a devout Catholic who had recently broken off her engagement because she and her fiancé were "too passionate," which to Simone was "hypocrisy of the worst sort," a curious comment in the light of her own "dispassionate" relationship with Jacques. She wanted a woman confidante and friend very much, but was unwilling to overlook anything that seemed "a contradiction in behavior, character, conduct." At the age of nineteen, she wanted everything having to do with human relationships to be clearly defined, and she cut anyone who deviated from what she considered "right conduct" out of her life without hesitating. This attitude carried over to her own behavior.

Jacques had introduced her to cocktails, but now she formed the habit of dropping into bars alone and ordering her own drinks. During the time she went to Garric's, she often went into cheap bars, stood at the counter and ordered a whiskey or a glass of wine. Curiously, she had never gone by herself to a café before this and had no idea what one was supposed to do there. In those she could see into from the street, the people sitting at tables reading newspapers or watching the passing scene seemed to her the epitome of indolence, and she had no desire to join them.

Still, her first moment of "true liberty" came in a café, the Rotonde, when she and Hélène played hookey to drink a café-crème. At ages nineteen and seventeen respectively, they felt "incredibly grown-up," and enjoyed themselves so much that before long they stopped going to art classes and spent the hours between eight and ten-thirty entirely in bars and cafés. They got away with it by lying to Françoise: "When someone demands to be told everything, well, then, you naturally wind up lying to her."[24]

Simone had money to pay for these evenings because she had a job as a teaching assistant at the Institut Sainte-Marie. The pay was not much, but the few francs more than covered her travel expenses to and from the school, her books, her supplies, and the occasional sandwich or cup of coffee on the days when she stayed late at the library. The unusual fact about this money is that she was allowed to keep it.[25]

Simone simply assumed that her wages were her own and never offered them to the family; Georges was too proud to ask, and Françoise's silence was entirely in keeping with the way in which money was handled not only within her family but also throughout the Beauvoir family's social class. As husband and provider, Georges made all the financial decisions; thus, if he did not ask Simone to contribute, it was not up to Françoise to do so. He gave his wife a fixed sum to run the household (often even for that she had to hope that he had not spent it on his evenings out) and did what he wanted with the rest of his income. If she wanted something, she had either to save for it from her allowance or else to do without. Simone was "suffused with shame" to see her mother "reduced to a child, begging for a pittance," so it became a matter of principle as well as a contest of will and stubborn pride between her and her father when it came to the disposition of her earnings.[26] It was one of the many rebellions which culminated finally in her overthrow of parental authority and, more surprisingly, in their abdication of it.

In the meantime, life at the Rue de Rennes was far from tranquil. Georges had settled into his last job, the one which he held until his death and which might best be described as an advertising space salesman for the right-wing periodical *La Revue Française*. The position was secure and on the fringe of respectability, but the salary was barely adequate, given his propensity for café life. Georges often stayed out all night with his "mistresses,"[27] and Françoise usually spent these nights pacing the apartment, slamming doors and throwing things. Just before daybreak, when he came home to change before going to work, she went to bed and pretended to be asleep. More than once, Hélène confronted him, demanding to know where he had been and whether he was aware of the pain he was causing his wife. He always laughed and said that he had been playing bridge, and that she shouldn't take life so seriously. Simone never confronted him, but stayed quietly in her room.

Since Georges did not respond to Françoise's angry goading, she turned it toward her daughters, mostly Simone. It seemed as if she needed to create confrontational situations as a way of validating her very existence. Throughout her marriage she had always done what was expected of her, all to no avail. She had supported her husband through disgrace and failure, but he still turned to other women and amusements. Her daughters sought every opportunity to escape her unremitting scrutiny and, worst of all, rejected everything she stood for and all that she believed. She was an intuitive and perceptive woman who realized that she had not only lost control of her family but also had no authority and, worst of all, no value. No one needed her anymore; she simply didn't matter.

The unresolved situation with Jacques continued to frustrate her. Shortly after New Year's 1927, Françoise decided that Simone should commemorate her nineteenth birthday with a formal portrait photograph—primarily so she could give it to Jacques. Photographs were often taken to commemorate birthdays, but the type Françoise commissioned, of a young girl whose discreetly lowered eyes were supposed to be focused on the flowers she cradled in the hand that bore her fiancé's ring, was always taken when a young girl announced her engagement. Jacques accepted the framed photograph graciously, but nothing else happened, and Françoise fumed.

Françoise's behavior toward Simone was erratic and confusing in other ways as well. While appearing to give her the freedom to look and behave like an adult, Françoise was neither pleasant nor gracious about it. She had to be coerced into almost every permission or agreement, and then she gave it so grudgingly that she ended by spoiling every opportunity for the closeness and friendship she wanted so much. After six months of Simone's pleading to cut her hair short like ZaZa's, Françoise finally agreed. The fashionable bob was a disaster, unmanageable because Simone's hair was so fine and straight. Françoise refused to let her get a permanent wave to disguise the damage, yelling that she had wasted enough money on foolishness. To hide the mess, Simone began to tie a scarf around her head in a turbanlike fashion, a style she affected for the rest of her life.

Françoise frequently caused humiliation in matters she herself cared deeply about, such as the evening she grew so angry when Jacques's mother and sister invited Simone to dinner and she stayed too late at the Champigneulle apartment. After several hours of pacing, Françoise screamed that she was going to rescue her daughter from disgrace, grabbed her coat and ran down the stairs. For once Georges was at home; already in bed, he decided to stay there. Hélène had been asleep, but, awakened by her mother's shouting, she threw on her clothes and ran after her all the way to the Boulevard du Montparnasse, futilely trying to calm her. When they arrived in front of the Champigneulle residence, Françoise planted herself on the sidewalk and shrieked for the entire neighborhood to hear, "Give me back my daughter, Germaine, give me back my daughter!" Simone hurried down to the street, and she and Hélène raced home behind the still-screaming Françoise, so ashamed they could not look at each other, nor did they speak when in their room undressing for bed.[28]

Simone's response to her mother's irrationality was very much like her father's: she ignored it, as if by doing so she could pretend it had never happened. Beyond a cursory response to her sister when outbursts such as the one in front of the Champigneulle house occurred, it was not in her character to dwell upon them. Instead, she compensated by directing all her energies where she had always put them, in her studies, but she also began to direct them outward toward personal relationships, especially her friendships with women.

ZaZa had written her several impassioned letters before the fall term began, confiding details of her personal life that she had never discussed before. For the first time, the two young women began to talk about men in a personal way, Simone about Jacques, and ZaZa about a young cousin of hers with whom she also believed herself to be in love. Now at last Simone had the truly honest friendship she had always believed possible, and, joy of all joys, it was with ZaZa. They began to see each other on a fairly regular basis again, walking, visiting museums, playing tennis, exchanging books and discussing their studies, especially their common interest, philosophy.

Their friendship was one of the very few things Françoise continued to approve of, but not so Madame Le Coin, who wanted ZaZa to concentrate on getting married, not getting educated. It seemed as if it would have to end when Madame Le Coin publicly humiliated the already emotionally bruised Françoise by snubbing her in front of a group of women. After that, Simone and ZaZa lied to their mothers and kept their meetings secret.

To Simone, ZaZa represented "the Platonic ideal of the possibilities in true friendship"; to ZaZa, Simone represented the only link with the life of the mind that was fast slipping away from her. She was "a young woman truly desperate to use her mind," which is why, after almost a decade of so-called "friendship," she breached all her own self-imposed boundaries and confided in Simone.[29] The new closeness with ZaZa, combined with the discovery of how much she valued her sister's friendship, had a softening effect upon Simone's personality and helped her to tolerate differences of opinion and behavior in others which only a short time before she would not have tolerated for a moment.

ZaZa invited Simone for another visit to the Le Coin summer home. Despite Madame Le Coin's rudeness, Françoise had always been in awe of this somewhat older woman who had achieved through marriage everything that she had not. When the invitation came, it was as if Madame Le Coin had personally summoned Simone, and Françoise was in a flurry to have a new dress made and to see that Simone was suitably equipped for the journey. Her good mood resulted in an unprecedented permission: Simone had spent much of the summer reading Mauriac's novels, and Françoise was so relieved to learn that she was still enthralled by his old-fashioned Catholic fiction that she allowed her to take an early train and spend the better part of the day by herself in Bordeaux to see the Old Quarter where he had set so much of his fiction. The journey passed auspiciously, with Simone almost deliriously happy at the prospect of spending three weeks in her best friend's company. They were even allowed to share the same bedroom, although another house guest, a young woman they both despised, was to sleep there as well.[30]

The household was in its usual state of activity and confusion, engendered by nine children, uncounted relatives, numerous house guests and a swarm of servants, all living on an enormous property without electricity, but with two automobiles, one donkey, several carriages and a farmyard full of animals. Among them was a young woman, new this summer, known as "Mademoiselle La Polonaise," or the Polish governess; actually, she was Ukrainian. She was hired to take care of the younger children, speak German to ZaZa, and entertain the family after dinner with her piano playing, singing and stories. This was Estepha Awdykovicz, the "Stépha" of Beauvoir's memoirs, and her lifelong friend.[31]

To Simone, Stépha was a "beautiful fair blond girl with enormous blue eyes, free-spirited, irreverent, independent," of whom she was in awe because "her widowed mother gave her an allowance to go all the way from the Ukraine to study in Paris. Stépha was a spendthrift, easy come and go, who had spent all her money even before the summer and now she had to get a job. She spoke many languages, was very intelligent and came from a well-to-do family whose fortunes were all lost in those little wars of territory that happened all over Eastern Europe. She was four years older than I, she was very sophisticated and knew much more about life than I did. I could never understand how she came to be in the Le Coin household."

To Stépha, it was "very simple": "I didn't really need the money as permanent income, but yes, I had spent all my summer money, and since I wanted to go to the beach, I applied for this job and got it. I pretended to be very pious and docile and I was able to fool the sharp eye of Madame Le Coin because I wanted to penetrate this particular Parisian society—the very wealthy—and the Le Coin family was just that: *very* wealthy (each of the five daughters had a dowry of more than 250,000 old francs, and remember, there were nine children!), *very* conservative (I rolled my eyes and made faces when Monsieur Le Coin talked politics), *very* Catholic (in every generation from the beginning of time, a Le Coin had entered the priesthood), and they were also *very* stingy! So I penetrated this society for the summer, and believe me, when it was over I was happy to leave it."

In her own words, Stépha was "devilish, very gay, always playing practical jokes, and liking a good time." Soon she became friendly "with the black sheep, Elisabeth. The rest of the Le Coins thought ZaZa very strange because she preferred to go to the Sorbonne instead of marrying to get her quarter-of-a-million dowry."

The other Le Coin children described Simone to Stépha as ZaZa's "unsuitable" friend, and most of them resented that she was coming to visit. They called her "ZaZa's charity, a pathetic impoverished girl whose silly father had lost all his money and property. Now they were poor, and Simone had to study as fast as possible to get her degree and go to work." But, "worst of all to them, she was a nonbeliever." When Simone arrived, Stépha found her to be "a little bit provincial, rather awkward and unsure of herself, most likely to barge into a room, interrupt a conversation and talk too loud, but that was due to her insecurity. No one had ever taught her how to behave. She didn't look very nice to me, although I am sure she thought she did because she told me she had a new dress— awful, as I remember, very ill-fitting and hideous color. Her skin was still not nice, her hair was sort of greasy-looking and in that up-thing [turban] she always wore to hide it. She looked to me as if she had been neglected all her life, and somehow she showed her poverty in a way that embarrassed me. I knew many poor people among my student friends in Paris, and their poverty did not touch me as Simone's did. I think I was embarrassed for her because from the very first I liked her so much."

The friendship flourished despite the vigilant eye of Madame Le Coin, who disapproved of "Mademoiselle" and regretted hiring her almost as much as she regretted allowing ZaZa to invite Simone. However, at the end of summer the Le Coin family would move back to the sumptuous apartment on the Rue de Berri where Monsieur Le Coin's everimproving financial acumen had taken them, and Stépha would be dismissed and out of their lives forever. With Simone, it was quite another situation altogether.

When they returned to Paris, Simone saw Stépha almost every day because Stépha lived in a hotel on the Place Saint-Sulpice near the Rue de Rennes. Besides studying literature at the Sorbonne, Stépha was working for the Ministry of Foreign Affairs translating bulletins and advisories intended to help the many Ukrainian refugees who had settled in northeastern Paris. This gave her the equivalent of twenty dollars a week, a sizable amount in 1928, and she spent it freely on her friends. She and Simone met every day at lunchtime, and because Simone could afford only coffee and bread Stépha bought her little pastries filled with pâté and urged her to eat as much as she wanted.[32]

Hélène brought another lasting friendship into Simone's life that fall. She was now enrolled in the Academy of Montparnasse, a design school popularly known as "Art and Publicity," which specialized in preparing students for careers in advertising illustration. There she met Geraldine Pardo, whom she and Simone affectionately dubbed "GéGé," and who became one of their lifelong friends. GéGé was a rapid-fire chatterer, a vivacious working-class girl who liked to draw and design so much that she intended to work whether or not she found a husband to support her, which Simone found unorthodox.

GéGé had so much zest for her work that it was impossible for Simone to resist her enthusiasm. She had a keen eye for objects, and from her Simone learned how to see beyond their actuality and into their conception. She taught Simone that "a vase was not just a container, but design, form, color and, even more basically, someone's idea of what a container should be."[33] She expressed herself with wit and eloquence and communicated her ideas to Simone, whose observation of anything in the world around her not directly related to herself had hitherto been vague at best.

GéGé made Simone understand that social class did not necessarily determine human character and behavior. Simone contrasted GéGé, who loved her work for its own sake, with the teacher at Garric's Equipe Social who relished her work because she liked the idea of doing good, and with her own pupils, who used what should have been pleasurable work in their classes to evade the sad realities of their lives. All three came from the same working-class background but had sharply differing attitudes toward work, which had always been the most important part of Simone's life. She began to consider concepts such as authenticity, integrity and honesty at this time, and she looked to the study of philosophy to help her understand how a common attitude could eliminate seemingly insurmountable social barriers. There was still much that was inflexible in her personality, that kept her on the sidelines of her life, observing, and passing judgment. But now another side of her personality was developing, and this was the part that made her participate for the first time, at the age of twenty, in what she thought were innocent games and pranks but which were really incidents of extreme and excessive behavior.

Most of these incidents were potentially dangerous because of the underlying sexual aspect of her conduct. The idea of sex was something she had not really thought about since the onset of menstruation, when she learned that it meant she could become pregnant, but as she was not interested in having a baby she gave it no further thought beyond the fact that it was a monthly inconvenience. Although she had often envisioned marriage to Jacques, her daydreams had never gone beyond a cozy vision of domestic drama in which the two of them sat side by side in comfortable chairs—reading. Many years later, when asked if she had never once felt a physical urge when in his presence or daydreamed of the two of them in an intimate situation, such as unclothed and in bed, her response was a withering glance followed by a frosty comment: "Obviously to ask such a question means you do not fully understand the situation and circumstances of a young girl born into that society."

She remained adamant that even though she had already read enough modern fiction to know of sexual practices that ran the gamut from sado-masochism to bestiality, her most erotic thoughts were of herself and Jacques in some companionable setting. As an elderly woman, she insisted that all her thoughts of him were those "of a good girl."

Simone's "adventures" began when she and Stépha went out together at night. Using the excuse that Simone had to stay late at the

Bibliothèque Nationale, they went to bars and cheap nightclubs. Often they allowed men to buy them drinks and, when they were slightly drunk, allowed strangers to drive them around Paris, parking in areas frequented by prostitutes, where some frenetic tussles ensued. Sometimes they were dumped unceremoniously, at other times they acted with what they called "bravery" but was really the foolish risk of being seen by neighbors or relatives when they allowed these men to drive them to the general vicinity of their homes.

Stépha quickly tired of these games, so Simone told Hélène and GéGé about them, and soon the three of them began to take even greater risks at night. Simone and Hélène played a game in which one of them would enter a bar and the other would come in later, pretending to be an enemy. They staged mock fights, battering each other with their purses, pulling at hair and clothing, sometimes being tossed out bodily when the proprietor was no longer amused by the spectacle of two little bourgeois girls playing at being bad. When she was alone, Simone started to let herself be picked up by strangers and more than once had to walk home late at night after the last bus had gone. She went into bars so disreputable that she became a favorite of men who openly fondled partially clothed women or flashed their sexual organs just to laugh at her as she pretended she was too sophisticated to be embarrassed.

She and GéGé allowed two "foreigners" whom they called "Gold Helmet" (because of his red hair), and "Dark Austrian" (because he seemed to speak some kind of Germanic dialect) to get them drunk enough that they agreed to go to Gold Helmet's apartment. "You take the blonde," GéGé remembers Gold Helmet saying before each man took a tipsy girl into a separate bedroom. "They were slightly drunk, too, which was fortunate, because it got very unpleasant for us both and if they had not been drinking I doubt that we could have controlled them. They wouldn't let us off the beds, and we were so terrified we started to scream each other's name and to cry out, 'What's going to happen to us?' We were attacked, so we had to defend ourselves. I suppose Dark Austrian was nicer than the other one, but I think we eventually bored them, because they both got tired of our fighting and let us go. We must not have been too terrified, because we stole some beautiful books from their living room on our way out. We thought this childish behavior was a very daring game, but really we were very stupid to do these things. However, this experience did not stop us from continuing these adventures."

But what about Georges and Françoise, who could hear Simone come in late, sometimes even smell the odors of whiskey and tobacco that clung to her clothing after a night out? Were they always asleep—did they never hear her stumble around late at night? Didn't the concierge gossip to the other tenants in the building? As elderly women, both sisters remembered "many painful confrontations." They also remembered that "Father no longer cared and Mother was powerless to stop us."[34] The adventures continued.

Despite her participation in earlier pranks, when Stépha learned of the Gold Helmet adventure she was furious and demanded that Simone stop playing such dangerous games. Several nights later, Simone saw Stépha at a movie theater with one of her many suitors casually draping his arm across the back of her chair. The next day when they met for lunch an angry Simone confronted her, demanding to know how she could be so disapproving when she herself sat shamefully in public with a man's arm around her. Simone's reaction was so strong that Stépha asked whether she could possibly believe the two incidents to be equivalent. She was shocked when Simone said yes, that to her way of thinking each was as bad as the other. To Simone, every action or gesture that took place between a man and a woman had equal importance and meaning; no single thing was more or less intimate, good, or bad.

Now that she had a brief view of how men and women behaved toward each other outside her family and their circle, she seemed to think that anything she felt like doing was within the bounds of permissible behavior. This was a curious time in her life, of public misbehavior that shocked even her most worldly friends (Stépha, for example) and of private prudery that astonished them. So, too, did her innocence.

Simone confided in Stépha that she was "almost betrothed" to Jacques, and told her they would probably marry soon. Stépha pressed her for what exactly that meant. Simone said Jacques had told her "we will always do interesting things together, we will always help each other." Stépha was appalled: "Listen, my girl, I may be naive, but you are cuckoo! That one little sentence doesn't mean anything!" Simone was undaunted: "He is my flame. It is understood by our families, there is no need for words between us." Stépha was very worried about her friend.

Before coming to Paris, Stépha had studied for a time in Berlin and there had met the young Spanish painter whom she would soon marry, Fernando Gerassi. He was now in Paris, living in a room in the same hotel as Stépha. When Simone visited, she was shocked to find Fernando sometimes sprawled on the bed drawing with the door shut and no chaperone present, and she loudly berated Stépha for endangering her reputation. Fernando painted Stépha in the nude, but even the thought that she might have posed induced, in Stépha's words, such "shocked hysteria" in Simone that she would either refuse to look at the painting or try to cover it up. To calm her, Stépha lied and said a woman in one of Fernando's art classes had been his model. When GéGé told Simone about people they both knew who became pregnant and had to marry or who had abortions, she was so shocked that she clapped her hands over her ears and refused to listen. She actually took pride in her excessive prudery. With considerable pomposity she told both women that their behavior and opinions were all due to the laxity of their upbringing, and that she herself had been raised with much higher standards of conduct.

Stépha only laughed at her and took great delight in puncturing Simone's inflated pontifications by hugging her or kissing her on both cheeks, which drove her wild. Simone had seldom been touched by anyone in her family: Georges jumped as if scalded whenever there was any accidental contact, and Françoise had not hugged her since Hélène was born and she became "the big girl," so she had grown up in an atmosphere where physical contact was almost nonexistent. Because she hated it when Stépha hugged, kissed and tickled her, she soon learned to keep her opinions to herself. GéGé was hurt by any aspersion cast upon her hardworking widowed mother, but was so genuinely good-natured that she too soon learned to poke fun at Simone's "silliness."

Simone was very lucky to have two such friends who tolerated her immaturity and liked her in spite of it. But even though these two women were the ones with whom she had the best times, the most fun, and with whom she could truly relax, she still considered her "best" friend to be ZaZa, who was really a replica of herself in so many ways.

Simone believed that friendship should be uplifting, so she looked to her fellow students at the Sorbonne to be models for the kind of friend she thought she should have. José [sic] Le Core, a young Breton woman whom she first met at the Institut Sainte-Marie, soon disappointed her because she was "too pious." Georgette Lévy, one of the first Jews she ever spoke to, was disappointing for "her close-minded arrogance and the incorrectness of her thought."[35] One day at the Sorbonne Simone tried to strike up a conversation with Simone Weil, who was also studying for the entrance examinations to the Ecole Normale Supérieure, but she found herself dismissed quickly as "a high-minded little bourgeois." "This annoyed me," Beauvoir wrote in her memoirs, but in 1983 she said she was embarrassed to have done so: "Simone Weil was right to dismiss me like that. It took me many years to free myself from what I called in my memoirs 'the bonds of my class.' I know that even today there are many who accuse me of behavior instilled by the 'bonds of class,' especially some feminist women. Perhaps they are right, and one never overcomes the class into which one is born. I don't know."

So she drifted, uncertain of direction or goal, constrained by "the bonds of class" and desperate for "personal autonomy." She wanted friendship, affection and love, but was confused about what they should be and could neither interpret nor understand those she already had. She read books to find models for how she should live her life but some were too indefinite, others too didactic, and none complete enough to satisfy. The only thing over which she had control was her own mind, so she decided to concentrate on using it to extricate herself from "the maze and the morass" that was her life.

NINE

The Young Girl
Who Worked Too Much

D URING THE WINTER of 1928, a harassed Simone de Beauvoir decided that she was "confined to home and library" like "a rat on a treadmill" and had to do something to break free of the demoralizing circumstances of her life.[1] Everything seemed beyond her control; she chafed at the arbitrary rules and requirements of institutions, the capriciousness of people in authority, and the whims of polite society from which she found herself increasingly alienated. She felt powerless to change anything, and that in turn made her hopeless. Economic independence, and thus the kinds of freedom she valued, would come with her university degree, but that was almost four years hence, and to the unhappy twenty-year-old she was then it seemed an eternity. She was impatient with her progress and set to work with a greater zeal than ever, deciding that the only way off the treadmill was to shorten her program by one full year—an astonishing feat if she could do it, and almost unheard of in French universities at that time.

At Meyrignac the previous summer, she had studied the titles of the books in the large wooden case, then selected the one which offered the most serious intellectual exercise, a massive Latin edition of *Plutarch's Lives* printed in one of the earliest and most difficult-to-read typefaces. Every morning after breakfast she took it off into the fields, lunching there on bread and fruit[2] in order not to waste time, reading all day long until dinner, then announcing proudly that she had translated and memorized "a good twenty pages today." She finished the book in little more than two weeks, to the astonishment of the entire family.[3]

Plutarch's Lives thus became her first self-imposed test of the possibility of taking her degree in three years instead of four. Unfortunately, she naively equated the particular achievement of having read the book so swiftly in the pastoral setting of Meyrignac, where there was nothing to distract her and she had no other responsibilities, with her entire program of study.

□

That summer was one of intense emotionalism for her, filled with incidents that upset the extended family and provided their summer's gossip. It started with her bizarre behavior in Paris when she accompanied her father to the train that was to take him to Meyrignac. At the last moment, without ticket or toothbrush, she jumped into his carriage and announced that she was going with him. She spent the journey staring out the window and sobbing loudly for she knew not what, while he spent most of it staring aghast at her, humiliated when he had to explain to the conductor why she had no ticket. At Meyrignac, she walked the several miles along the country lanes all the way into Uzerche, pacing along the riverbanks muttering to herself, and careening up and down the torturously hilly streets. Back at the house, she sat for long hours under the catalpa tree at the white metal table and chair that the family called "Simone's place," alternately staring into space and scribbling furiously. At night, in her tiny closet of a room, she moaned and sobbed by her windowsill, so that the sound carried in the still air, disturbing the rest of the family.

This was the watershed summer for her, when she decided that everything that had been before must now change and that only she could make it happen, but for the family it was only another instance of Simone's self-absorption, and her nervous, quirky behavior struck them as "an exaggeration of how she had always been—in her own world and somehow different from the rest of us."[4]

Yet despite all the erratic behavior and emotionalism, her decision to accelerate her degree seemed all the more realistic after the March 1928 examinations, when she passed the philosophy section with excellent marks. In June, she was ecstatic to learn that she stood second in her class in the two required courses, moral science and psychology, with only the brilliant Simone Weil higher. Her new friend Maurice Merleau-Ponty[5] stood third.

Georges de Beauvoir treated the news of his daughter's standings as a matter of course and thus not deserving of special comment or recognition. Instead of praising her, he took the opportunity to berate her for not pursuing a specialization (i.e., the minor) in philology to complement philosophy (the major). His criticism "marked the first blissful moment when what he wanted suddenly ceased to matter." If she had continued to study philology, which she "hated with passion," it would have given her two areas of specialization when she needed only one, but Georges's concern was more personal than professional: he still thought her so unattractive that overpreparation seemed the best way to guarantee that no school would reject her despite her "unfeminine attitude and demeanor."[6] To her, however, giving up philology meant that she could cut at least half a year from her required program.

She reverted to the obsessive behavior, begun years before at the Cours Désir, of assigning a task or a project to every moment of her day, compulsively checking off items on lists that contained headings such as "Books to

Be Read," further separated into two columns entitled "Duty" and "Pleasure," with an annotation after each title as to whether it had been worthwhile or a waste of time. She made extensive timetables, dividing the day
into segments allowing shorter or longer periods for travel, depending on
whether she had the money to go by Métro or bus or whether she had to
walk. In either case, she listed projects she could recite from memory or
read during the time she was in transit.

She went to see Jacques and proudly mapped out her elaborate strategy for his approval, arguing pompously that "one had to consecrate one's
life to a search for its meaning. . . . He heard me out with good grace but
shook his head: 'No one could ever live like that.' "[7]

But she did, filled with manic joy and energy, despite the fact that
both family and friends worried about the strain of such a compulsive existence. She pursued her studies so avidly that a less regimented person
would have been left with no time for anything else, but she was "bursting
with health and youthful vigour"[8] and became a dynamo of movement and
activity as she raced to keep up with scholarly obligations while still leaving
time to see one or more of her friends on an almost daily basis.

The idea of seeing several friends at once or introducing each to another made her uncomfortable. Among her three closest, Stépha and GéGé
never met, and when she encountered Stépha accidentally while she and
GéGé were out walking, Simone spirited GéGé away in what Stépha took as
a "mean snub."[9] Simone was always reasonably at ease when it came to introducing men to women or vice versa, but it took many years before she
overcame the feeling that if her women friends were to meet they would
like each other better than they liked her.

Her professional friendships began from a different impetus. She had a
keen, instinctive sense that guided her toward students who were her intellectual equals, and she tried to position herself where they would notice
her. All too frequently, however, she was indifferent to the conventional
niceties, and, in her clunky shoes, with her loud and strident voice, she
would literally stumble upon them, blurting into situations and interrupting conversations. Her awkwardness made her seem "silly" and "perhaps
an aggressive drone who had very little intellectually to contribute."

Stépha, appalled by her appearance, had begun to instruct her on how
to dress, fix her hair and wear makeup, but Simone was a difficult pupil.
Her idea of social success was to be at the center of whatever was intellectually excellent, whether it meant being welcomed by a group of the most
brilliant students, taking the most challenging courses offered by the most
distinguished professors, or even such a small matter as sitting in what the
students thought was the best seat in the library. In every instance, success
in her terms meant being part of the "most authentic," no matter what
that might be. Still, she did try to follow Stépha's advice, but, with other
things on her mind, she "could not see the stripes from the plaids, but at
least she began to wash her hair and even started to wear a little face
powder."[10]

Now that she was a university student, Simone decided to seek a new

way of defining her views, through an affinity with certain "serious writers," mostly "nineteenth-century French philosophers totally disregarded
today," thinking that their work would serve as a shortcut to defining and
explaining herself and what she stood for. Or, as her new friend Maurice
Merleau-Ponty said, such readings would help "in the refloating of intellectuals marooned on the rocks of perdition."[11]

She found Merleau-Ponty "a thin aesthete, not physically attractive,"
but he seemed to be someone who shared her taste in literature, and soon
they were passing books back and forth. He sought her out because he
wanted to meet "the girl who beat him in the examinations, by which he
meant the Catholic bourgeois Simone de Beauvoir, not the Jewish Simone
Weil, who was outside the possible realm of intellectual friendship because of her religion." Simone was thrilled with this new friendship because at first glance they seemed to have so much in common. Merleau-
Ponty had also been raised in a devoutly Catholic home, but he told her
he now thought of himself as a quiet unbeliever. To Simone he seemed
interested in having a good time, but, also like her, he rejected most of the
raucous collegiate antics and crude language of fellow students at the Ecole
Normale Supérieure. She felt a great kinship with this young man who
shared her own fascination with what they called "low-life" while still cher-
ishing self-righteous prudery. Their friendship soon became one of self-
congratulation at the similarity of their beliefs.

Their first disagreement arose when it became apparent that Merleau-
Ponty was not the unbeliever he professed to be, saying it was necessary to
seek truth within the social and religious boundaries of their upbringing,
while she was ready to reject them entirely if she thought it necessary.
Other intellectual disagreements followed, and soon she branded him "un-
complicated, unmysterious, a well-behaved scholar,"[12] but continued to see
him because he was the most interesting person she knew at school. It was
more than a little embarrassing to know that he, her "best friend" so far,
was a member of the "Holy Willies," the group at Ecole Normale Supérieure mocked by the more worldly students for their excessive piety and respect for priests.[13]

She still had no female friends at school. There were only two with
whom she might have developed intellectual as well as personal friendships, but Simone Weil wanted nothing to do with her, and Georgette
Lévy was Jewish. Georgette's wealthy family lived in the fashionable Sixteenth Arrondissement, and Simone used the difference in their social
background as a convenient excuse to end what might have been an interesting friendship. She complained that there were "too many elaborate
teas" at the Lévy home and that Georgette "flaunted her family's money
at the same time as she was very rigid in her thinking." Many years later
Simone de Beauvoir insisted that she had never been anti-Semitic in her
life, but when asked whether her attitude toward Georgette Lévy might
have been influenced in some way by the harsh antipathy of her father toward Jews, she said curtly, "Probably."

And so Simone drifted back to Merleau-Ponty and several other male students with whom she was more comfortable, among them the Catholic Michel Pontremoli,[14] son of the successful painter, who held regular "evenings" in his parents' well-appointed home, also in the Sixteenth Arrondissement. Simone was soon given a standing invitation and was so proud of often being the only woman present that she bragged about it.[15] There she met Jean Miquel,[16] like her preparing a thesis under the noted scholar Jean Baruzi, who with his brother Joseph, an esoteric and little-read novelist, also attended Pontremoli's parties. She liked the attention both gave her, even though they treated her "like an amusing curiosity, a woman who could think and argue." But she soon grew tired of Pontremoli's parties, detesting the phony intellectualism and false aestheticism.

The Holy Willies still seemed to offer the most legitimate intellectual friendship. Maurice de Gandillac,[17] a short, dark, intense young man, was a friend of Merleau-Ponty's who almost managed to convince her that she had been mistaken about Catholic theology, until she reread Saint Thomas Aquinas and decided she had been right in the first place to reject his teachings. What she especially liked about Gandillac was that he always told her how brilliant she was and how she would succeed in everything she did for the rest of her life.

"I already told her that, but what was I, only her good girlfriend, so she didn't listen to me," Stépha Gerassi recalled. "She needed to hear that kind of thing from a man."[18]

Soon Gandillac was invited, along with Merleau-Ponty, to play tennis with her and ZaZa every Sunday morning. He may have been a Holy Willie, but he was amusing as well as flattering, and Simone gossiped gleefully with him about things that horrified her when Stépha said them, as in one telling instance: "Simone told me how he broke up with his girlfriend because she kissed him on the lips with her mouth open, but if I told her some guy tried to get fresh with me—and in those days that didn't mean very much—she would shut her eyes and put her hands over her ears and tell me she didn't want to hear it, she wouldn't listen. Sometimes I used to make it up just to tease her, because I didn't understand how this guy could tell her all these things and it was okay, and here I was, her good girlfriend, and we couldn't talk about anything. If he said it, it was an intellectual situation; if I said it, it was just sexy dirty talk." Whatever the reason, Simone de Beauvoir was more at ease in the company of men, and with few exceptions they were more likely to become her friends, closer and more quickly.

She remained close to Merleau-Ponty despite his insistence that anything socially acceptable had to be based on strict Catholic doctrine, a view he adopted after he and ZaZa became friends. He was the first intellectual whom ZaZa had ever met, and she was strongly attracted to a man of ideas who also claimed to be deeply attached to his mother and the Catholic Church. Seeing the two of them together made Simone happy, because she saw in Merleau-Ponty a man who would let ZaZa fulfill her mother's charge to marry someone socially acceptable, but without having to give up the life of the mind she also needed.

Also, her own mother adored this polite young man, which did much to make life in the Rue de Rennes less strained. Françoise met them accidentally one day as Merleau-Ponty walked Simone home after class, and was so charmed that she impulsively invited him to tea. Merleau-Ponty came frequently after that, often bringing Gandillac, and these two did much to ease the tension between Simone and her mother. Both became indirectly responsible for Simone's being granted much more freedom in her social life. When invitations came for her to visit the homes of students whom Françoise had not met, she gave permission eagerly because she associated all male students with the two she already knew. Georges also liked them, because he found their Catholic-royalist politics almost on a par with his own ultraconservative thinking. He enjoyed teatime conversations with the two men, but Hélène loathed them because she found Gandillac pompous and overbearing, especially when he alternated between lecturing her on morality and trying to get her to go out with him, all at the same time.[19]

Françoise especially approved of the books they loaned Simone, but the exchange with Gandillac was a brief one because Simone thought his taste too pious and devout, designed to lure her back to strict Thomistic belief. It was different with Merleau-Ponty, who revered Mauriac as she did, and promised to go with her the next time she made a pilgrimage to Bordeaux. Claudel was one of his favorites, but Simone had her doubts about the excessive religiosity of his writing. Merleau-Ponty did not like Proust, but neither at that time did she: "Proust was an acquired taste for me because it took me a little while to become accustomed to the labyrinths of his language. After I read Faulkner, which I began to do very early after I had taken my degree, then and only then I loved Proust."

A work which satisfied all her criteria to an extraordinary degree was the curious compendium of notes, aphorisms, confessions, dialogues and drawings that Jean Cocteau, insisting he had written a novel, called *Le Potomak*. Jacques had given her the book to read a year earlier.

One of the many descriptions which Cocteau himself gave to the book was of "occult characters [who] represent the graph of the deep confusions that accompany the moultings of the intelligence."[20] Now that Simone de Beauvoir was a university student searching for a personal system of belief, she found this and many of the aphorisms sprinkled throughout the text urging the reader to throw off received values and opinions especially meaningful. "I explore the void," Cocteau announced, creating a work in which the artist searches for himself in secret: "there one sinks into one's self, toward the diamond, toward the fire-damp."[21]

Mostly, however, the text and the drawings are about two warring clans who can be reduced to simplistic examples of stuffy bourgeois behavior (the Eugènes) and anarchic artistic conduct (the Mortimers). The "either/or" representation is what finally appealed the most to Simone.

She attributed to the Eugènes everything she hated, the sole exception being the university, and to the Mortimers the brash, questioning irreverence she found in herself and her friends there. Her embrace of all that she thought the Mortimers stood for resulted in the cementing of the most important friendship she made at the Sorbonne, the one which determined the outcome of the rest of her life.

Of all the students at the Sorbonne, Beauvoir wrote in her memoirs, "only Sartre's little band, which included Nizan and Herbaud, remained closed to me." She described them with an accurate but succinct understatement: "they had a bad reputation."[22] Jean-Paul Sartre, Paul Nizan and René Maheu (Herbaud) attended lectures only if they liked the professor; otherwise they boycotted their classes. They spoke only to one another and then in a kind of code with private nicknames. They ogled and teased women students and made fun of the men, especially the Holy Willies. Two of them, Nizan and Maheu, were worldy sophisticates who were already married, and Sartre was a figure of some awe for the numerous affairs student gossip reputed to him. Worst of all—again, so went the student gossip—Sartre, the ringleader, the most sarcastic, most brilliant of them all, was a heavy drinker! While the other students went out of their way to avoid this little band and the likelihood of its derision, Simone plotted how to make them notice her so that she could become a part of it.

"Don't look for a Mortimer except in yourself," Cocteau directed,[23] and for her, Sartre and his friends were Mortimers out to shock the world (in this case other students) by living with a fundamental truthfulness and honesty no matter how offensive it seemed to others. In the past she had been content to remain a voyeur, but now, fascinated by the bravery of their indifference to convention, she wanted to be a part of their clique because it was the most authentic behavior she had ever seen.

The student body at the Sorbonne was not exceptionally large, and each student at least knew the others by name if not personally. Sartre, Maheu and Nizan knew who she was—the youngest student in their group, quite possibly the brightest even though she was a woman, and, now that she had accelerated her program, the brilliant phenomenon who was breaking every record for high marks with such dispatch. They also knew her as "the badly dressed one with the beautiful blue eyes" and mistook her awkward shyness for a coolly sophisticated superiority which was certainly not the case.[24] So it was a situation in which she and they watched one another surreptitiously, but as the acknowledged rulers of the student society they were not about to make the first move toward the suppliant subject who yearned to be included, and so a standoff of a sort ensued.

Gandillac was a kind of weak link between Beauvoir and Sartre's band, a Holy Willie tolerated by the three young gods because they found him amusing. "I met Simone through Merleau-Ponty," he told one of Sartre's biographers, and to Simone de Beauvoir this much was correct. "She met Maheu through me," he continued, "and finally got closer to Sartre and

Nizan via Maheu."[25] This second statement was one she insisted vehemently was entirely wrong and based on his misreading of her memoirs:

"It is correct for him to say that we did all know the other members of our class, that much is true. But he misreads me when he says I wrote *Memoirs of a Dutiful Daughter* as if everything led to the great moment, the romantic thunderclap when suddenly *along came Sartre* [her emphasis]. If he had read my book carefully, he would have noticed how I told the story as it really happened. I didn't want *Sartre* [here her emphasis implied that she did not want Sartre the man in any physical sense], I wanted to be part of his *group*"—again, her emphasis. She paused for a long moment and then added, "I suppose if I wanted anybody *that way* [again her emphasis, meant to connote the physical and sensual] it was Maheu, even though I knew he was happily married. And besides, that feeling didn't last very long on my part."

She was "very conscious of the charm of [Maheu's] mocking voice, and of the ironical twist he gave to his mouth." Though he dressed elegantly, she still found "something of the country boy about him."[26] Simone knew that he lived in a Paris suburb with his wife, whom she once saw clinging to his arm as they passed her on the street. She often saw him studying in the library, but the only exchange that took place was a brief smile if their eyes met when they happened to look up from their work at the same time. Sometimes, if she passed him in the hallways when he was away from Sartre and Nizan, he said hello, which made her think he might be "fairly accessible," so she began to plot ways to engage him in a conversation that she hoped would bring subsequent introductions to his friends. She knew that he often ate lunch at the school restaurant, and she saved her money until she had enough to eat a full meal rather than her usual coffee and a sandwich. When she stood beside his table, "he invited me to sit down as if he had been saving the place, and we began to talk of Kant and Hume as if we already enjoyed a long and easy friendship."

He began to attend the lectures given by Professor Léon Brunschweig, who was supervising her last two years of study and for whom she wrote a paper on the philosophy of Leibniz.[27] Maheu was there "probably because I was, because he had not attended before that time, and Sartre and Nizan rejected [Brunschweig] and never came." He "dropped in, casually, late," usually after Brunschweig had begun, as if to demonstrate his disdain for the professor or his subject. She always saved a seat next to hers, and as if to flaunt how little he cared for the lecture Maheu spent the time doodling his own version of Cocteau's drawings of the Eugènes and the Mortimers. Their friendship flourished on the strength of this shared devotion. Cocteau became their secret code, and they often greeted each other with an aphorism: "Our favorite, the one which made us laugh loudly, was the one about the man who gave his chameleon a nervous breakdown by putting it on a piece of scotch tartan."[28]

Maheu went to great lengths to convince other students that he was a dilettante who cared little whether he passed or failed. To Simone, it seemed an incredible act of courage to flaunt academic authority, the only

one she respected. She tried earnestly to persuade Maheu to take his studies seriously, saying that his intelligence would be wasted on teaching in a
grade school somewhere in the provinces—work he joked that he could always get.

The only concrete result of her continuing entreaties for Maheu to
concentrate on his studies and do some hard work to pass them was the
nickname he gave her because of her own prodigious work habits, which
became the name she preferred and by which she was known to close
friends for the rest of her life. One day he drew a little squiggle meant to
be an animal and put a face on it meant to be hers. " 'You're a little Beaver,' he told me, 'always fussing and working,' or something like that. At
first I didn't know if I should be insulted or not, but Maheu was never
sarcastic with me, only to others, and so I liked it because it was something
private and personal that at first only he and I shared." In French, "beaver" is le castor, and she soon became "Castor" not only to Maheu but to
other students as well.[29]

Her nickname caught on among the other students, but his name was
in constant use by her, for she could not begin a sentence unless it was thus
prefaced by what he thought about the subject. Her parents were worried and asked her to invite him to tea so that they could judge this para-
gon for themselves. They insisted he come with several other male students, as if to disguise his special friendship with their daughter. Hélène
didn't give much thought to her sister's friendships, busy as she was with
her own, but Stépha wondered "what she [Simone] was doing, an innocent
like she was then, with this married man all the time."[30] To the end of her
life, Beauvoir insisted that it never entered her mind at that time that her
friendship with Maheu was anything but intellectual.

"Why should the fact that he was a married man have anything to do
with our camaraderie at school?" she countered when asked in 1982 whether
she had taken his marital status into consideration. "When two people are
friends, they are friends, and that's all."

Several years later, the question of her relationship with René Maheu
was posed again, this time more directly because her closest friends and acquaintances contended that he had been her first lover. The question provoked a thunderclap of anger: "That is absolutely not true [her emphasis,
as she slapped her hand hard on the sofa where she sat]. I never even kissed
a man on the mouth then, never, never, never! I repeat, I never even kissed
a man on the mouth. There was Merleau-Ponty, but that was really a rapport between two intellectuals. He would never even have thought to
touch me! Sure, Maheu appealed to me physically, but he was married
and he was as much of a prude as I was. Maybe he would have liked to,
but never, never, never did he try to seduce me. Never did he touch me,
and that was because he was married, and neither of us wanted any complications. I was truly the little well-brought-up young lady, the dutiful
daughter, entirely so, and I tell you I never even kissed a man full on the
mouth before Sartre, and that's the absolute truth!"[31]

All of Sartre's group at the Ecole Normale Supérieure during the years

1928–31 had an aura of romantic license which enhanced their attractive-
ness to women students and made them the envy of many of their male
peers. Part of this was due to the fact that several were already married, but
the Nizans were vociferous advocates of sexual freedom within marriage
and were happy to proclaim their views to anyone who cared to listen, and
Maheu and Castor were inseparable during the day even though he went
home at night to his wife.

Castor, as she must now be called, was still on the fringe of this group,
but the one who intrigued her most was the one she knew least, Sartre. She
remembered him then as "always surrounded by men who seemed to have
the greatest admiration for him, because they appeared to hang on his every word. They dwarfed him in their midst, and I doubt that he could even
see me beyond them. Of course he would not have spoken to me then, especially if he had to be the one to speak first."

Sartre was an unlikely looking figure to command so much respect and
attention. He was tiny, just under five feet tall, his round face disfigured by
strabismis in his right eye. He had a lumpy complexion and already thinning hair, and his teeth and fingers were stained and yellowed by tobacco,
for he was a chain smoker. His voice, however, was melodious and his intellect unsurpassed. When Sartre spoke, everyone stopped to listen; what
he spoke about dazzled them all. At the age of twenty-two, he was already reputed to be a brilliant writer and was known to have written at
least one novel. Sartre's prowess with women was already legendary, and
when Paul and Henriette Nizan both declared that marriage should be
"modern, open, entirely honest,"[32] it made a profound impression on
him. He was so taken with the idea of being part of a couple and having
a woman to look after all his needs that he became briefly engaged to
the cousin of another *normalien*, Alfred Péron. To Castor, then, he was
another of the group unavailable for anything but scholarly friendship.

Everyone she knew seemed to be involved to some degree in a relationship, and so she spent much more time than she should have—"valuable time lost to study"—thinking about herself and her own lack of
involvement. Most of these relationships upset her (Stépha had begun
to live with the Spanish painter, Fernando Gerassi, but tried to hide it
from her), some (like the Nizans) openly disgusted her for their casual
attitude toward fidelity. The only one that pleased her was the chaste
and innocent friendship between ZaZa and Merleau-Ponty. However, their
romance was not developing fast enough to suit her. It started to falter
when Madame Le Coin decided not to allow ZaZa to return to the Sorbonne that fall because the eldest Le Coin daughter had been married
and now it was ZaZa's turn. Madame Le Coin decided to keep her on
in the Landes for an extended summer holiday to prepare for a round
of presentations to eligible men that winter.

Castor was not invited for a long holiday that year, but was told
she could spend several days, possibly a week, during the month of July.
As Merleau-Ponty's family had originally come from Bordeaux, she and

he decided to meet there and make the Mauriac pilgrimage they had often talked about, before she continued farther south to see ZaZa. Both knew it would give them something to tell their friend, which might help to keep the romance in flame. When Simone arrived, ZaZa was in an agony of indecision, feeling what she was sure was love for Merleau-Ponty but still deeply committed to obeying her mother.

No one, least of all ZaZa, could understand Madame Le Coin's attitude. On the one hand, she was so loving toward her daughter and filled with plans for her future; on the other hand, there was never any mention of Merleau-Ponty—never a harsh word or a criticism, but always the relentless smile as Madame Le Coin turned the conversation to another subject. She treated Castor the same way, instantly deflating with coldly feigned cordiality what little poise and self-assurance Castor had gained during her year at the Sorbonne. The visit was such an unnerving experience that Castor returned to Meyrignac and tried to write fiction as a way of understanding what had happened.[33]

The visit to ZaZa prefigured the rest of the summer and most of the fall, when nothing seemed to provide any sense of resolution. She completed nothing she wrote, no readings satisfied her, none of her cousins had anything of interest to offer, and her sister was in the same unsettled mood as she. Time hung heavily, even after they returned to Paris and the new academic year began. The manic high of the previous year had given way to a depressive low, and even though she knew she had to keep up the brutal schedule she had set for herself to accelerate her degree, she felt little sense of purpose. Instead of reading philosophy each day in the library, she spent her time trying to write, but what was supposed to become fiction turned instead into harsh diatribes against the power of organized religion to subvert individuality, and the helplessness of youth to overcome social pressures inculcated in them by parents who had become the living manifestation of Cocteau's smug Eugènes. Quickly realizing that all this writing was awful, she destroyed most of it as soon as she wrote it.

Needing an emotional outlet that she could not find in French fiction, she turned to English instead, working her way through the novels of George Meredith, especially three which she reread several times: *Diana of the Crossways*, *The Egoist* and *The Ordeal of Richard Feverel*. Meredith's nineteenth-century-country-house intrigues, featuring star-crossed lovers and the power of their society to keep them apart, were ideas she transposed with ease to her own contemporaries. She studied Meredith's tragic life and was pleased to learn that he had earned part of his living as a journalist, since she admired the form of the intellectual essay and hoped to write her own someday. Most of all, she studied Meredith's novels to try to determine how he conveyed emotion and character, because she wanted to learn how to imitate him in her own writing. She soon abandoned this because she found another English novelist who suited all her needs much better.

Rosamond Lehmann's *Dusty Answer*, about a young woman whose emotional awakening occurred during her years at Cambridge, was as close as Castor had yet come to the fictional equivalent of her own life. She had to buy the novel, because there was such a demand for it at Adrienne Monnier's lending library that she could never keep it out long enough at any single borrowing; she reread her own copy until the pages were badly worn.[34]

ZaZa returned to Paris in November and told Castor that she was being sent to Berlin, ostensibly to perfect her German, in reality to make her forget Merleau-Ponty. To Castor's bewilderment and ZaZa's anguish, the Le Coins continued their opposition to his courtship. Merleau-Ponty said little besides preferring to trust in prayer and the kindness of a just god. Every time he expressed his faith, Castor grew more bitter, because she knew Madame Le Coin better than he did and had come to hate this woman for the way in which she manipulated her children by feigning cheerful sympathy while exercising rigid control. She was convinced that Madame Le Coin was dangerous, but Merleau-Ponty saw her only as a mother who loved her daughter dearly and wanted her happiness. He trusted time to remove her objections; Simone was sure that trouble lay ahead and trusted nobody, not even ZaZa, to behave honestly when the moment came for resolution of the seemingly ill-fated romance.

Before ZaZa left for Berlin, Castor overcame her fear of introducing one of her friends to another, and took her to meet Stépha, who had lived there before coming to Paris. It was truly a revelation to see how well her friends got on with each other, but even more how their warmth toward her increased because she had brought them together. Nevertheless she was cautious, and although she was delighted to have Stépha on hand to share her excitement when she received letters from ZaZa, she still kept her other friendships separate.

Stépha had given ZaZa the names of some of her friends in Berlin, and ZaZa liked them, especially one young German who came to Paris on a visit and thought it his duty to call upon her parents. When he met Castor afterward, he told her how shocked he had been to meet them, so cold and politely formal, so different from their daughter. She was somewhat encouraged by ZaZa's German experience, since she had just received a letter telling her, "The very respectable formalism which governs the lives of most of the people in 'our class' I now find quite unendurable." Madame Le Coin's reason for sending ZaZa to Berlin, to make her more docile at home, would seem to have had an ironic consequence, as the letter continued, ". . . All the more so when I recall the not-so-distant past when, without realizing it, I was still impregnated by it."[35]

When she returned to Paris in the winter of 1929, everyone said "how marvelous ZaZa looked, that she had gained some weight and was not nearly as nervous and twitchy as she had been before she went to

Germany." Stépha too noticed the change: "She was always so hyper-active, high-strung, as if on the verge of a nervous breakdown. [After Berlin] she was calm, serene, mostly stable, not like she would fly out of control, which was the way she usually looked." Hélène, who as an adult had grown to like ZaZa, described her as "very high-strung, like a sleek and elegant racehorse ready to bolt out of control. She often made other people very nervous, but my sister was always a calming influence on her."

ZaZa and Simone resumed their friendship on a much warmer and more intimate basis than they had had before her Berlin sojourn. Through-out the winter term, when Simone was not with her new friends at the Sorbonne she tried to be with ZaZa, despite the obstacles Madame Le Coin continued to strew in their path. Suddenly there were innumerable social occasions for which only ZaZa could provide the support Madame Le Coin needed, and one excuse followed another, such as the cousin in the south of France whom only ZaZa could nurse during a month-long con-valescence. ZaZa broke engagements to play tennis, to walk in the park or even to sit in a café and talk; they met only when she came running into the Bibliothèque flushed and breathless to spirit Castor away for a brief cup of coffee and a chat. These visits capped the relatively happy days Castor spent that winter in pursuit of knowledge and of Sartre's little band, but they were interrupted by a serious illness, the first of a succession of such that formed a recurring pattern throughout her life.

The winter of 1929–30 was one of those which Parisians claim to re-member as being more severely cold than usual, with heavy snow followed by day after day of freezing rain. It seemed as if everyone had the flu, and Castor, already weakened by the frenetic schedule she kept, caught it more severely than most. Throughout the month of February she lay in bed too weak to do more than think about herself. As usual, whenever circum-stances forced her into sustained introspection, a depression followed. Her method of trying to understand it was to write about it, and this time she kept a journal which she filled not with fiction, as she had done the previ-ous summer, but with comments and questions about herself.[36] She was awash in self-pity, convinced that she was the only person in the world who was miserable.

Hélène was pleased with her art classes and the friends she made there, and even content with the round of parties she was invited to by friends of Françoise's. She came home from these occasions and raised Simone's spirits with tales of eager young men and anxious young women. There was no laughter, however, the night she returned with an enraged Françoise who had been snubbed by Madame Le Coin. Meeting her at a party, Françoise told Madame Le Coin that Stépha had decided to marry Fernando Gerassi and she and her daughters wanted to give her a wedding present. Madame Le Coin replied coldly that she didn't know "a Stépha," only a "Mademoiselle Awdykovicz," implying that Françoise was lacking in social status if she associated so closely with someone who was really only a servant. She then berated Françoise publicly for the leniency with which she brought up her daughters, and after a lengthy harangue about Simone's undue influence upon ZaZa she concluded with "Fortunately, ZaZa loves me very much." All three Beauvoir women were furious with this public humiliation, but even more with Madame Le Coin's implacable smugness.[37] It brought a rare, fleeting moment of unity to the household, but it worried Simone.

ZaZa came to visit her once while she was still in her sickbed, and although no mention was made of Madame Le Coin it was clear that she had opposed the visit. ZaZa spoke instead of Merleau-Ponty: with the new confidence instilled by her Berlin visit, she felt sure that she could bring her mother to regard him with the same affection she felt; affection, she confided, which had grown stronger during her absence. He too saw the change in ZaZa, and their friendship blossomed into courtship.

The world, it seemed, was dividing itself into couples. Jeanne and Magdeleine were both engaged, Stépha was almost married, GéGé had a succession of admirers who wanted to marry her, Françoise alternated between muttering about and hinting at a possible dowryless engagement for Hélène (who continued to keep her own counsel and ignored her mother), and now even ZaZa and Merleau-Ponty had all but declared their intentions. Maurice de Gandillac was no comfort at all, because he insisted that even Castor would soon get over her fixation on the degree as the most important event in her life and would "go out and find [herself] a husband."[38]

Sometimes at night, when she and Hélène had gone to bed, they lay there as they had done when children, imagining what fate had in store. Quite often they recited the song they had written with their cousins two summers before, when all four had felt themselves on the brink of entering the mysterious world of adulthood, where everything would magically transform itself. As they crooned the words softly, they felt a slight shiver of apprehension to think that so much of what they had written and sung in summer fun was turning out to be true.

All four had collaborated on the song they called "L'Air connu" (The Old Familiar Melody),[39] each analyzing herself as well as the other three with an uncanny accuracy. It began with an introductory stanza in which four young girls wearing beige lace dresses walk along, chatting and laughing. But it is August, and winter's snows are not far behind. "We have to go out at once and look for happiness," they all four say together. "We have to get out into the world to look for the grown-ups, for they have the interesting lives." A refrain follows in which all four are crying because "youth doesn't last forever, and for this we cry." Each girl is then the subject of a separate stanza.

Magdeleine is first, "a beautiful blond shepherdess with dreamy blue eyes," who lives at La Grillère and sits in her big wing chair "dreaming such dreams." She thinks about meeting new people, but "she knows about people, she knows the pain they bring, how it burns, how it hurts. She stays with her animals."

Jeanne is "a young girl of rare virtue who rushes and jumps about saying, "You must do your duty and make everyone's life beautiful." The other three reply cynically that "not everyone is like her."

Hélène "can only be spoken of with lowered eyes," a euphemism for being ashamed of her: "she hasn't a shred of seriousness and responsibility. She's the Purple Shrimp, excited, spoiled . . . people shake their heads and say, 'This one will end up in Saint-Lazare.' "[40]

Simone's description was accurate to a fault: "At the Bibliothèque Nationale, very often you met a young girl who worked too much, who buried her head in dusty old books and crammed her head so full of philosophies that she had to drink too many martinis to save her frazzled brain and restore her to life." The song ends with the four young girls gathering beside the radiator on a "sad December night, in their nightclothes, without any sign of hope in their hearts." Realizing that "soon it is we who will be the grown-ups," they conclude, "with pain in their eyes," that the time has actually come, "and look at us—we will never find happiness."

And so Castor, the Beaver, lay in her sickbed, poised on the verge of adulthood with no satisfactory answers. Her formal education would end in a few short months, and she had to make all sorts of decisions about her future life. How tempting it was to think of suddenly finding herself the other half of a couple, with someone who would take care of her and see to all her physical needs.

Despite the pessimism of the song, she was an optimist, and she drifted off, convinced that something magical was bound to happen, maybe even the next day. . . .

Castor

I N JANUARY 1929, Simone de Beauvoir reported to the Lycée Janson de Sailly for her supervised practice teaching. Two other students were assigned with her: Merleau-Ponty, who "took it all so seriously, as if it were a holy and religious experience to fill his pupils' empty heads with knowledge," and Claude Lévi-Strauss, "whom I liked from the first," but whose "impassivity rather intimidated me, . . . I thought it very funny when, in his detached voice and deadpan face, he expounded to our audience the folly of the passions."[1]

She taught philosophy to "forty boys who obviously couldn't care less about it," but at the same time "it was thrilling to be there."[2] She had often walked past her father's school, the equally prestigious Collège Stanislas, on the way to and from her courses at the Institut Sainte-Marie, and had glanced enviously at the boys who lounged about, taking their right to be educated so much for granted. Now it was she, a woman whose own education until the university had been inferior, who stood before them in a classroom. The realization that she had been successful enough in her own studies to compete on a par with men buoyed her almost as much as the occasional glimmer of intelligence in an interested pupil's eye.

"I felt there was nothing in the world I couldn't attain now," Beauvoir wrote, trying in the mid-1950s to analyze why she felt so confident when nothing in her life had prepared her to think that way.[3] Her society had taught her to think of herself as sexually inferior to men, in some way handicapped and doomed to fail when she tried to compete with them. But she had not failed; she had succeeded brilliantly in every educational setting, especially the coeducational university. There, her male colleagues were not threatened by her ability, but instead treated her "without condescension, and even with a special kindness, for they did not look upon me as a rival; girls were judged in the contest by the same standards as the boys, but they were accepted as supernumeraries, and there was no struggle for the first places between the sexes."[4] Then she boasted of the praise male students lavished upon her lectures and of her pride in gaining their esteem: "Their friendliness prevented me from ever taking up that 'challenging' attitude which later was to cause me so much dismay when I encountered it in American women: from the start, men were my comrades, not my enemies. Far from envying them, I felt that my own position, from the very fact that it was an unusual one, was one of privilege."

In 1960, a dozen years after she wrote this, she told an interviewer that during her student days, "For a man to be my equal, he had to be a little bit superior to me."[5]

It was not until twenty-two years later, in 1982, that she said she could see her "attitude in regard to men in all honesty: I was a 'token' woman for so many years. At home I was taught that girls were inferior to men even while I was told to behave like one; I went to schools where girls were given textbooks exhorting them to think like a man. My father praised me for having the brain of a man. I had a privileged situation with Sartre. And then there I was in 1956–57, writing my memoirs and praising myself for combining 'a woman's heart and a man's brain,' believing at the same time I was not renouncing my 'femininity.' No wonder I had to spend so much time thinking and writing about myself, who and what I was."

No matter how confusing her relationships were, she discovered that she liked the sound of her own voice as she stood before her students, and liked "to think on my feet, to leap from argument to argument." She took her mission to educate them seriously: "I was very careful because I did not believe in bullying people and I believed that I had to know and understand each one of my pupils personally. In class, for example, I never attacked religion. It was up to the pupils to see if they wanted to reconcile it with the philosophy I taught them. In ethics and moral philosophy, however, I often tried to relate my subject to social questions . . . to teach them how to think, then how to think for themselves, and *never* what they should think."[6]

Teaching provided her only real stability during the dour winter months of 1929; when her flu developed into a severe bronchial infection in February and she was forced to curtail it, she did so with sadness. Teaching had had the effect, however, of making her certain that she really did want to be a professor, and for a brief time she put aside her attempts to write fiction and concentrated on developing ideas for essays on ethics, but nothing substantial resulted. By the end of March her health had stabilized, and she returned to her studies with a vengeance. Maheu was her constant companion during long daytime sessions in the library; surprisingly, her mother was often her companion at night.

Both she and Françoise developed a passion for the movies and went to the cinema together as often as they could afford it. Their relationship had quietly moved onto a different plane during that winter, without either of them noticing. It was as if Françoise had given up trying to control either daughter's life. She no longer pried into Castor's comings and goings, her friendship and her activities. Much of this was because of her great pride in Castor's high marks in the previous year's examinations and more recently in her successful teaching. Françoise began to do little things in order to give her daughter time and opportunity to concentrate on her work. Quietly and without comment, she brought an occasional cup of tea, mended a skirt, or threw a shawl around Castor's cold shoulders late at night when she was engrossed in her studies. And Françoise pretended not to notice even when she came in late at night, sometimes smelling of liquor and cigarettes after an evening in a bar. Castor was so often lost in her own frenetic mental world that she did not at first realize what was happening between her mother and herself, and when she finally did she made no comment about it because she simply did not know how to express her emotions openly. So the truce between them continued, and rather than show any affection to each other, they demonstrated their emotion at the movies, for the life on the screen.

There was an unspoken truce between Georges and Castor as well: neither would comment on the other's political opinions, and each would take as much care as possible not to express theirs in the other's presence. They had given up discussing literature many years before, but now, with the frequent presence of Merleau-Ponty, Gandillac and occasionally Maheu at their table, Georges was able to pontificate freely because Castor, as a dutiful daughter, was trained not to contradict or argue with her father in front of guests, especially men. Still, while he addressed the men who were present, his comments were actually intended for her ears. It was a kind of preening, a way of claiming a place of some priority in her life now that she was an adult, even though he had abandoned her and relinquished his claim on her affections so harshly many years before.

"What a shame that he could never let her know how very proud of her he was, that he had to tell others of his pride in her instead," Magdeleine de Bisschop recalled. "I suppose it was too late, after he had abandoned her as a teenager, to regain the old intimacy and camaraderie and the primary position he had held in her affection."

Nevertheless, the temporary tranquility in the household was a great improvement over the previous tension, hostility and argument, and the climate for studying was decidedly improved. The family unity was strengthened further in May when Ernest-Narcisse Bertrand de Beauvoir died in Meyrignac at the age of ninety-one and they all attended his funeral, grieving together for the kind old man everyone had loved so much. With his brother dead as well, Georges became the eldest male in his family, technically responsible for his sister and sister-in-law, but they were independent women of financial acumen who had little need of his comfort or advice. The death of his father did little, if anything, to change him personally or to change his circumstances.

Mourning dress was still customary in 1929, and so Castor returned to her classes in a black dress and a hat swathed in black tulle which made her feel very mysterious and dramatic. Whether because of her appearance, the general knowledge of her brilliance and previous high marks, or the honors everyone expected her to take in the next round of examinations, she suddenly came to the attention of Sartre and his student band.[7]

On her first day back, she encountered Sartre, Maheu and Pierre Guille lounging in a hallway, forming a trinitylike tableau with Sartre seated above the other two on a windowsill.[8] She had been missed while she was absent for her grandfather's funeral, Maheu told her as he left the others and came to greet her. Later that day, when they were in class together, he languidly handed over a present from Sartre: a drawing of a man intended to be Leibniz, the subject of her thesis, with representations of the monads[9] as bathing beauties. More than fifty years later she remembered how it made her blush.

However, although she and Sartre had exchanged greetings once or twice in passing, they had never engaged in conversation. She never saw him in the library, for example, or in the student restaurant, so there had never been an occasion when they might have gotten to know each other. Once she had come upon him walking with Maheu in the Bois de Bou-logne, but even though Maheu recognized her, he did not speak, a fact which still smarted years later when she wrote her memoirs: "How mislead-ing private diaries can be! I made no mention of this incident which never-theless had made me sick at heart."[10] After Maheu gave her Sartre's draw-ing, she frequently saw the two of them together, but even though Maheu sometimes spoke to her, she and Sartre still never talked. She had thanked him for the drawing through Maheu, who conveyed her message orally. At that time, the gift of such a personal drawing, so clearly created to win her good graces, meant little more than a casual gesture of acceptance by one brilliant student toward another.

For her, Sartre was still the genius at the center of the group in which she longed to be accepted intellectually, but whose antics continually dis-mayed her. Sartre and Guille, who had most recently dropped water bombs off the roofs of the Ecole Normale onto unsuspecting heads while shout-ing, "Thus pissed Zarathustra," were now enraptured by a rich Argentinian woman whose son they were supposedly tutoring for his *baccalauréat* ex-aminations. Their presumed relationship with this woman, Madame Morel, was a favorite subject of student gossip, which shocked Castor, but she was too preoccupied with her curious relationship with Maheu and her coming examinations to be overly concerned with Sartre.

She wrote on the subject of "liberty and contingency" and passed the first round of examinations brilliantly at the end of May. A round of celebrations followed. Everyone wanted to congratulate her, including her father, who took her for a night on the town and supper at Brasserie Lipp, a festive evening such as they had not had together since she was a child. Her relatives sent gifts and gave dinners, where Françoise accepted homage as if the triumph had been her own. Afterward, she surrendered all at-tempts to regulate Castor's life, and at last Castor's personal autonomy was complete.

She, Hélène, Gandillac, ZaZa and Merleau-Ponty formed the nucleus of a group they called "the Gang from the Bois de Boulogne" because they went there frequently for boating and picnics. She and Hélène continued their nighttime forays, but these were quite different from their earlier, reckless and dangerous searches for adventure. Now the sisters were more likely to spend a quiet evening in a café followed by a walk along the Seine discussing what they hoped to do with the rest of their lives.

Castor had not applied for a teaching position that fall because she was unwilling to leave Paris, and, since all beginning teachers were posted to the least attractive positions, it was likely that she would have been sent far from home. She planned instead to offer private lessons as a way to secure a meager income, perhaps supplementing it by part-time teaching in a Paris lycée, but her primary intention was to devote as much of her time as possible to writing. She thought she would give fiction another try, but would concentrate on philosophical essays about ethical behavior. She intended to slant them toward a general audience, hoping their broader appeal would make publication more likely in some of the many journals that proliferated in Paris in the late twenties and early thirties.

She decided to move away from home as soon as her last examination was finished and her academic life officially ended. For a young unmarried woman of her social class even to envision living apart from her family was likely to cause a scandal, but she thought of a way around it by proposing to move to the apartment of her Grandmother Brasseur, who had been renting rooms for much-needed income since her husband's death. Castor wisely calculated that such a move would satisfy everybody: it would give her independence and freedom from parental prying while at the same time giving Françoise peace of mind to think that her daughter and her mother were in the same household, ostensibly looking after each other: "My mother probably thought she could keep her eye on me while I became a second nursemaid and companion to my grandmother. I did not disavow her of this idea, especially when my father agreed to pay for the furnishings in my room."

With that settled, all that stood between her and more personal freedom than she had ever known was the written competitive examination and, if she passed it, the final oral, given at the end of June. Even though the written examinations were the more extensive, the oral was the most dramatic of all her academic trials. These examinations are public spectacles in France,[11] and in the case of a candidate who is known to fellow students for anything from intelligence (as in her case) to unorthodox behavior (as in Sartre's), the performance attracts an overflowing audience. After finishing four years' work in three, Simone was exhilarated but also mentally exhausted, and she still had to prepare for these grueling tests.

She was working diligently on her own when, one day in early June, Maheu told her that Sartre had asked to meet her: "A simple statement, nothing very special. A remark unconnected to anything such as studying together or that he found me attractive and wanted to take me out. Just that Sartre had asked to be introduced to me."

Actually this was very special indeed for Sartre, as he and his friends were known for their ill-mannered behavior, especially to women. After so long a time of surreptitiously watching Simone de Beauvoir, so many opportunities to have been introduced to her or to have struck up a conversation on his own, for Sartre to ask Maheu to introduce him formally carried a great deal of meaning. However, her own relationship with Maheu was undergoing so many fluctuations of mood and intensity that the actual introduction to Sartre was postponed for several weeks.

From her memoirs,[12] it would seem that she and Maheu were two good friends who probably would have fallen in love, especially if they both had been free. He was irritated by any intrusion upon their time together and berated her even for talking to others, so it was very much in character that when Sartre asked him for an introduction, Maheu asked her to agree not to meet him during the next few weeks, when he had to be away from Paris to visit his family. Maheu said bluntly that he feared Sartre would monopolize her and thus alter their special relationship, if he did not change it entirely. And because Maheu mattered so much to her, she agreed to his demand.

Sartre asked her to spend an evening with him, inviting her first to a movie, then to supper and the fun fair at the Porte d'Orléans, where there were games of chance, pinball machines and a shooting gallery. She sent her sister instead, claiming "an unexpected engagement arranged by my mother, a headache—I don't remember. I only know that I told Poupette [Hélène] how amusing Sartre was and what great fun she would have if she took my place. I also told her he was very ugly, but that she should not let it bother her, because he could be very charming."

Hélène came home confused by the evening she had just spent with "such a quiet, boring fellow. He certainly was not the brilliant and amusing person everyone had described to me. I think he was probably disappointed to find me in my sister's place and as anxious to be free of me as I was of him."

Several weeks later, the formal introduction took place in the most ordinary of situations: after Maheu returned to Paris the comrades decided to begin organized, day-long study sessions in preparation for the oral examinations. "The Beaver," Castor, was cordially directed to present herself the following Monday morning in Sartre's room to tell all that she knew about Leibniz. The event marked the true end of "Simone" and the beginning of her life as "Castor."

Sartre had failed the examination the year before because he had tried so hard to be original, brilliant and creative that he had not really answered any of the questions. Because he failed, he was not allowed to live at the Ecole Normale and had a room in Cité Universitaire, the collection of dormitory buildings along the Boulevard Jourdan which housed foreign students and French citizens who were not from Paris.

Sartre had shocked quite a few of his classmates when he announced with all sincerity that his ambition was to become the man who knew the most about everything in the world that could be known, which was his excuse for the condition of his room. It was a shambles: overflowing ashtrays tottered on precariously balanced stacks of books that littered the floor. The bed was lumpy and unmade, the sheets were filthy, the one chair sagged and was torn, the desk was a sea of papers, and the walls were plastered with Sartre's satirical drawings.

Castor took all this in with a quick glance, and it made her even more nervous than she had been since Maheu had issued the invitation. "I was over the moon,"[13] she said, using slang of the day to describe how she felt when he invited her. Years later she added, "I was so nervous I don't think I slept at all the night before. I know that I prepared for the first study session as if I were going to take the examination itself. I was terrified they would not find me brilliant but only a silly girl who knew very little and could not think."

Of the three, it was Nizan who frightened her the most. She had seen him peer at her intently through his tiny round glasses when she passed through the hallways of the Sorbonne, his forehead wrinkled in a frown caused by the ubiquitous cigarette dangling from the side of his mouth. In her nervousness, she mistook this expression for cynical disapproval of both her intelligence and her presence. She knew that he and Sartre had been friends since they were young students at the Lycée Henri-Quatre, that their friendship was one of complicity that extended to a shared private vocabulary and a similar opinion on almost every subject. "It is pleasant," was a favorite remark, which puzzled many people because the true meaning of the phrase and their intention in uttering it was often one of deep sarcasm or disapproval and listeners never knew which.[14]

Castor knew all this about them, so she wrestled with a double fear from the moment Maheu told her they had invited her to study. On the one hand, her yearning to be accepted by this group was so intense that she had plotted how to be a part of it ever since the day she plunked herself down squarely in front of Maheu in the library; on the other, there was the knowledge that Sartre, Nizan and Maheu formed a closed society based on many years of shared experiences. She feared that, as a woman, she could never hope to be accepted within their group.

Curiously, she seems not to have considered that she might have been invited to join them because she was a woman, especially since her friendship with Maheu was so colored by latent sexual overtones whether she would admit it to herself or not. And when compared with other women students in their *promotion*, or class, she was one of the most attractive. The ubiquitous turban concealed her unruly hair, and her striking eyes and exquisite skin more than compensated for her shabby student dress. She would be remembered later by Paul Nizan's widow, Henriette, who had taken philosophy classes at the Sorbonne with Castor, as "a very pretty girl [with] ravishing eyes, a pretty little nose. She was extremely pretty, and even that voice, the same voice she has now, rather curious and a little broken, somewhat harsh—that voice added to her attractivenes. I don't think I ever saw her then dressed in anything but black, probably because hers was a distinguished family and in those families someone was always dying and they wore mourning all the time. As I said, she was a very serious girl, very intellectual, and these qualities and the black dress actually enhanced her glamor, her unselfconscious beauty."

When they began to study together, Castor's interest in Sartre was still purely intellectual, judging by her description of the initial impression he made on her: "I think he was the dirtiest, the most poorly dressed, and I think also the ugliest [of the three]. I remember seeing him once in the hallways of the Sorbonne: he was wearing an oversized hat and flirting outrageously with some students—he was always flirting with some female philosopher or other . . . he was really turning on the charm. And I laughed derisively when I saw him, as all of us who thought of ourselves as idealists used to do in those days."[15]

When she arrived at his rooms in the Cité Universitaire, she found the others already gathered. Sartre was in "an open-necked shirt, more or less clean, and wearing slippers of one kind or another."[16] He escorted her with great courtesy to the only chair, and at once they began to work. She described this first session succinctly: "All day long, petrified with fear, I annotated the 'metaphysical treatise,' and in the evening [Maheu] took me back home."[17]

They soon dispelled her nervousness. She had no sooner begun to expound Leibniz's theory than they all decided they knew enough and pronounced him boring, which put an abrupt end to her ostensible reason for being there; nevertheless, no one suggested she leave, and Sartre went out of his way to make her feel welcome. He began to perform, punning and singing philosophical parodies to Offenbach's melodies before changing the subject again to Rousseau's *The Social Contract*, at which point they all grew serious and discussed the work with great intensity. "He is a marvelous trainer of intellects," she noted in her diary and again later in her memoirs,[18] where she described her attempts to argue with him and ferret out the weak points of his theories. She claimed that she could never best him, that his thinking was always the most persuasive and his view the one the group always accepted. Of them all, she decided that it was Sartre who knew the most about their subject and therefore had the least to gain from the group study sessions. "I was intelligent, certainly, but Sartre was a genius."[19]

This recognition of genius, the feeling of privilege at being in its presence, is something that all those who knew Sartre at that time recalled and that they later tried to express. Simone de Beauvoir declared repeatedly for the rest of her life that Sartre's intellect was superior to her own, and her remarks have caused consternation and anger in equal parts among those who study her life and work. This is probably because she frequently describes herself in ways which would make it seem that she never had a thought or idea that was not first given to her by Sartre. He himself expressed it better:

I have been able to formulate ideas to Simone de Beauvoir before they were really concrete. . . . I have presented all my ideas to her when they were in the process of being formed. . . . [S]he was the only one at my level of knowledge of myself, of what I wanted to do. For this reason, she was the perfect person to talk to, the kind one rarely has. . . . What is unique between Simone de Beauvoir and me is the equality of our relationship.[20]

The lifelong intellectual rapport they shared began during these study sessions, and throughout their more than fifty years together each was often asked to describe it. Her favored explanation:

. . . We began to work together [when] Sartre was twenty-three and I was twenty-one. Sartre was philosophically more creative than I, and it is in this respect that he had a great influence on me, because I didn't have a personal philosophy. I was interested in philosophical ideas and Sartre was creative and I quickly fell under the sway of his philosophy. . . . So philosophically I only had the role of a disciple, of someone who understood him well.[21]

Her place in Sartre's life very quickly became privileged, usurping Nizan's in ways that upset him and, more than fifty years later, still bothered his widow: "Personally . . . she should have helped me butter the toast while the two pals [Sartre and Nizan] were together, because their friendship was deeper, more complete and older than the one she had with Sartre. But there was never a chance of that because I was the wife with the baby daughter and she made it clear how she detested all that. She was very much the brilliant *agrégée*, the future teacher preparing for her splendid career, oriented only toward that. She was there, she participated in the conversation between Sartre and Nizan, but they could very well have done without her, because they had been used to speaking to each other for more than fifteen years in ways that no one who had not shared their youth together could ever understand. They had their own language and she tried to adopt their tics, their expressions, their vocabulary. She entered their world instead of leaving them in their private domain, their intimate domain, their secret garden.[22]

What Madame Nizan did not understand was that Castor merely gravitated toward the most brilliant, amusing and even mesmerizing of the group, the person from whom she felt she could learn the most.

As examination day drew closer, the studying became more concentrated and the arguments more heated as each tried to demolish the other's thesis with hypothetical questions. All Castor's energies were focused on the examination, all her time was spent preparing for it. She and Sartre dominated the group, their minds leaping and darting through philosophical treatises as if they were the targets in the shooting gallery at the Porte d'Orléans, where the entire group went to relax in the afternoons after their tense morning sessions.

By now, she and Sartre were developing a private language of their own, and Maheu was jealous. "I'm delighted that you should be getting on so well with the comrades," he told her, at the same time claiming special privileges for himself. Whenever the group decided to spend an evening together, Maheu announced that he was "taking Mademoiselle de Beauvoir to the cinema" or to some other private engagement, and the others withdrew, as if he had the unquestioned right to her companionship (his wife was curiously absent from all these occasions, unlike Henriette Nizan, who was almost always present). On the Fourteenth of July, he grudgingly allowed Sartre to be Castor's escort on a wildly boozy evening, but still vied for her attention. "I thought Sartre was even more amusing than [Maheu]; nevertheless we all agreed that [Maheu] should have first place in my affections."[23] However, anything that might have developed between Castor and Maheu ended abruptly when he failed the examination and the others all passed.

In later years, Simone de Beauvoir reflected on his failure, saying he was "a very complex personality, a young boy from the provinces, an impeccably dressed dandy of high-bourgeois pretentions who had married a charming woman when he was still very young; intelligent enough to succeed at whatever he put his hand to but unsure in his youth of what it was exactly that he wanted out of life. His association with the most brilliant, sophisticated and jaded students of his generation probably contributed to his feelings of inadequacy and displacement."[24]

Maheu left Paris without saying goodbye the day the examination results were posted. "Give the Beaver my best wishes for her happiness," he wrote in a letter to Sartre.[25] A week later he came back to Paris for an afternoon. "I don't *know* *why* he returned," Beauvoir said, exasperated by the question, before adding more quietly, "He didn't seem to have anything else to do besides seeing me."[26]

Castor and Sartre had not merely passed the *agrégation*, they had done so with brilliance. He took first place over all and she took second. Maurice de Gandillac, who later became an eminent professor of philosophy, described Sartre as having spoken during the examination with an extraordinary self-possession: "The entire jury, particularly the president, Lalande, were captivated." He remembered Simone de Beauvoir as

> rigorous, demanding, precise, very technical. . . . [S]he was the youngest in the *promotion*. Only twenty-one, three years younger than Sartre. . . . As two members of the jury, Davy and Wahl, told me later, it had not been easy to decide whether to give the first place to Sartre or to her. If Sartre already showed great intelligence and a solid, if at times inexact, culture, everybody agreed that, of the two, she was the real philosopher.[27]

In a 1987 conversation with Hélène de Beauvoir de Roulet, Professor de Gandillac described again how close the decision was and how long it took the committee to make up its mind to give Sartre first place "The examiners were so impressed by the precision of her philosophical expression that they wanted to give her the first place. Finally, they decided it had to be given to Sartre, because he was the *normalien* and, besides, he was taking it for the second time."[28]

But while Castor continued to think of Sartre as a brilliant mentor who was also amusing and fun to be with, the persons still alive who knew them well then remember that Sartre was so uncharacteristically discreet about her that the most accurate way to describe his feelings is to say that he was obviously smitten with her.

"I think he must have thought she was someone wonderful and magical, because he was so courteous and kind to me," Hélène remembered. GéGé and Stépha echoed her sentiment, each citing instances of Sartre's kindness to them, all of which they linked to his interest in Castor.

After the *agrégation* she and Sartre continued to see each other every day whenever possible, but she was committed to spending the last part of the summer at Meyrignac and La Grillère with her family, and he faced his year of compulsory military service that fall, so they began to feel a certain sense of anguish over the impending separation. They had become "necessary to each other," and just as earlier she could not wait to tell Maheu her thoughts, now she felt the same about Sartre.

Part of the reason for her dependency on him was that all her women friends had moved on to a different phase in their lives and she no longer had their companionship whenever she wanted it. Stépha had married Fernando Gerassi and was moving with him to Madrid, news Castor greeted with great relief because it meant that Stépha would become "an honest woman."[29] ZaZa had been flitting in and out of her life for increasingly brief moments and, when they met, berated herself for her unwillingness to surrender to her mother's wishes and how guilty she felt about it. GéGé and Hélène were finishing their art training and busily looking for commissions that would lead to jobs. Among the few women Castor knew at the Sorbonne well enough to chat with during an occasional meal or break between classes, only José Le Core remained, and she, now that she had squeaked through the *agrégation,* was planning to take a teaching job as far from France as possible, preferably in Indochina.

Le Core had fallen in love with Merleau-Ponty, who was in love with ZaZa, who had in turn fallen in love with him, but Castor had no sympathy for Le Core, "the kind of woman who did not seize what she wanted, but who sat around yearning for someone she did not deserve to have." As she described Le Core in her memoirs and later recalled her in conversations, Simone de Beauvoir admitted to a kind of self-absorption which precluded any genuine sympathy or understanding of the needs of others, not only of a casual friend such as Le Core but of closer friends as well. People interested her then only insofar as they contributed to what she expected of herself or wanted from them. Her sister, GéGé and Stépha all stayed within the boundaries of the space she had assigned them in her life, and so they never required any kind of emotional engagement from her other than what she directed and controlled.

□

ZaZa was a different matter, an anomaly among Castor's woman friends, the one over whose life she had little influence and no control. In July ZaZa went with her family as usual to their summer home. Before she left, she confided that she and Merleau-Ponty had agreed to become secretly betrothed until he finished his military service. They would not press their case for marriage with her parents until at least a year, if not two, had passed. Castor was astonished that they could even consider suppressing their affection and more important, their sexual desires for such a long time: "I can still see her face, how shocked she was, when I said this," Beauvoir recalled years later. "I was sure she thought that I had truly become Sartre's fallen woman, but of course this was not yet so."

ZaZa's letters grew increasingly perplexing: "Mama has told me something astonishing which I cannot explain to you now," she began before drifting off into a confused account of daily life in the country. Another letter arrived in the next mail, asking, "Can children bear the sin of their parents? Are they guilty of it? Can they ever be absolved? Do others near them suffer from it?"[30] It was all very disturbing, since ZaZa did not explain further or elaborate upon her questions. Castor decided to try to sort them out by incorporating them into the story she had begun two years earlier at Meyrignac, but instead it became a separate but unfinished episode.[31]

In this version, her hero acquires a sister to whom he is very close in age and emotional ties, just as Merleau-Ponty was with his, while the ZaZa character, here called Jeanne, wrestles with the same problems of morality and obedience. Jeanne has a brief conversation with "Mammie" (her mother) after which the unnamed narrator asks rhetorically, "To what end?" Jeanne exhorts herself to try to understand Mammie's position, but the narrator interjects that she "understand[s] too well. There is nothing; her moral system crumbles. . . ." There are several jottings that seem more like notes written by Castor to herself than fiction, after which there is one last phrase that seems to belong to the story: "The further development of her love." She stopped writing about ZaZa because "it was too perplexing" to create a story based on friends when she had no idea what was happening to them.

The manuscript seems to take up an entirely new subject on the next page. Beauvoir's notes to herself state: "Write about the conflict of a young man who does not live for the earth. Of a young girl who lives for the earth. Have them meet in Limousin and . . ." There is a long space, as if she could not decide what to write, but at the end of the same line she continued: "far away in the country." A separate sentence concludes the writing on this page: "He suffers from his too fervent love of the world and wet leaves."

She might have been writing about Sartre here, because in the few weeks before she left for Meyrignac, and especially after Maheu left Paris, their relationship had changed to one of highly charged sexuality. "*Then*—not when we were students together, but that summer—it struck like a bolt of lightning. For me it became 'love at first sight' and everything romantic that phrase is supposed to mean." They had not yet made love, but, in her words, "The American slang describes it best—'heavy petting.' Yes, everything but sex itself."

This all happened in his room at the Cité, as she did not move into her grandmother's apartment until she returned from Meyrignac that fall. She could have moved as soon as the examinations were over, but another tenant was planning to leave late in the summer and his room was the farthest from her grandmother's bedchamber; if she waited until he left she could have it. Even before their relationship had grown physical, she was already planning where she and Sartre could make love without being detected. Her grandmother was an old woman who went to bed early and slept soundly. If Castor wanted to stay out all night, she could, and if she wanted to spend the night reading in bed and sleeping all the next day, she could do that as well.

The month in Meyrignac loomed like an abyss between them, and for the first time she was reluctant to go to the place she loved so much. However, she knew that everything was different now that her grandfather was dead and her own life as an adult wage earner was about to begin, so she decided to spend what she knew would probably be her last holiday there.

The visit began propitiously, with beautiful weather and everyone in the two houses engaging in more courtesy and concern for one another than ever before, as they all sorted through their feelings this first summer without Grandfather Beauvoir's beloved presence. Many more friends of the young cousins visited than was usual, among them Gandillac, who came to visit from nearby Brive-la-Gaillarde, an hour's train ride away. On the spur of the moment, he invited the Beauvoir sisters to return there with him to spend the afternoon in the gracious home of the elderly woman with whom he lodged. But the Limousin region was not Paris, and Françoise forbade them to go for the old familiar reason: it was "not proper." Gandillac suggested a compromise, that they accompany him on the little local train as far as Tulle (less than half an hour away). Hélène recalled their embarrassment many years later: "Our mother only allowed us to go on the condition that she accompany us as our chaperone. This when Simone was almost twenty-two years old and had just passed the *agrégation*, and Gandillac was a Catholic man of great character and virtue of whom our mother highly approved!"[32]

As far as the local Limousin morality was concerned, the worst was yet to come. One morning after breakfast, when Castor was uncharacteristically dawdling over the last crumbs of bread and her bowl of coffee, Magdeleine rushed into the kitchen at La Grillère and whispered that a man was waiting for her in the fields beyond the tower, which had once been a dovecote and was now unused. It was Sartre, who had arrived from Paris late the night before, unexpected and unannounced. Walking across the fields from the village of Saint-Germain-les-Belles, he had seen Magdeleine, introduced himself and asked her to go and fetch her cousin. Castor ran to him at once, and they spent the morning together in the farthest field, lying in the tall grass, hidden from the eyes of everyone in the house. At lunchtime she returned to the house alone, thinking that her parents would invite Sartre to join them. No invitation was issued; indeed, no comment was made at all except for Françoise's indirect reference to Castor's "friend," who had surely "only stopped as he was passing through on his way to another destination."[33]

One of Castor's traits which irked her mother, sister and cousins the most was her refusal to take part in preparing, serving or removing the meal. On this day she jumped up after the first course and followed Magdeleine into the kitchen, where she whispered that Sartre was outside waiting by the tower for something to eat. She could not suddenly begin to assist with the meal because everyone would suspect her intentions, so Magdeleine became the go-between who brought Sartre his lunch. For Magdeleine, it was all just like one of her flaming romance novels come to life, and she and Sartre soon became comrades in crime, their friendship cemented for life.

Soon, alas, she was discovered by the thrifty Françoise, who missed a particularly nice cutlet that was meant for the evening meal, so Hélène took over and tried to steal thick slices of bread and cheese for his lunch. (He ate his evening meal and spent his nights in the village hotel.) But soon Castor stopped going to lunch altogether. Boldly she packed bread, cheese and fruit and went into the fields early in the morning to spend the entire day with him.

There Castor and Sartre (as they called each other for the rest of their lives) made love for the first time. She told her parents they were continuing their study sessions so that they could write a philosophical treatise which they hoped to publish when they returned to Paris, but no one believed her. After several mornings of her disobeying her parents to go into the fields with Sartre, Georges decided to put an end to the situation.

Castor and Sartre looked up from their books one morning to see him walking over the field, with Françoise peeking out from behind his shoulder in uncharacteristic timidity. Georges launched into what must have been a prepared speech, which Castor remembered many years later: Surely this young man realized that his daughter's reputation was being compromised by these daily meetings; there were two young girl cousins in the family who were expecting to announce their betrothals in the very near future; their dowries had already been arranged, the families involved had already settled the many and complex arrangements such unions entailed. Surely the young man from Paris would see reason and move along somewhere else to spend the rest of his holiday. Georges, of course, could understand that two colleagues from the university, future teachers, after all, might need to meet to discuss their work, but this was the provinces, and things were quite different here. Young women in this setting were expected to marry, not to follow careers. The entire situation was most unsettling, most distressing, and if the young man would only please show some respect for the local customs . . .[34]

Castor was furious: "Alternately red-faced with embarrassment and white with anger, I said, How did he dare to do this to me? My mother, silent until this moment, began to scream. It was awful, terrible."

Suddenly, Sartre began to speak in a voice both soothing and calm. Ignoring Françoise, he addressed his remarks to Georges, saying that Monsieur de Beauvoir surely understood the very deep bond that existed between himself and Monsieur de Beauvoir's very charming and intelligent daughter, and as they were planning to resume their very close relationship once they were in Paris, and as they were in some haste to complete their philosophical inquiry as quickly as possible so that they could get on with the writing, it was necessary for him to remain in Saint-Germain-les-Belles. Alas, Monsieur de Beauvoir would have to explain to his family the serious necessity for Monsieur Sartre to continue his daily visits to La Grillère.

Georges turned away without speaking, all color drained from his face, and did not meet his daughter's triumphant eyes. Françoise, soundless as well, followed him back to the house.

That night Castor returned to the house as if nothing unusual had happened that day. "No one said anything. My father ignored me. My mother had spent most of the day crying in her room. My cousin Magdeleine thought it was wonderful, so romantic. I felt relieved. The air had been cleared. My father and mother no longer controlled my life. I was truly responsible for myself now. I could do as I pleased, and there was nothing they could say or do to stop me."[35]

Sartre did not end the confrontation there. He returned that evening and every other for the rest of his stay to walk with all four cousins through the spacious grounds around La Grillère. Once, particularly emboldened, he suggested that he would take turns spending the next four evenings with one cousin at a time (thus compromising Jeanne's and Magdeleine's betrothals as well as both Beauvoir sisters), but, as Magdeleine recalled, "Simone was furious and said it was bad enough she had to have us along and that no one would be alone with him but her."[36] She decided they had both made their intended points—hers to defy her parents, and Sartre's to stay on as long as he wished—and so she asked her cousin Robert to drive him to Uzerche that very night. Sartre returned to Paris, Castor followed, and shortly afterward she moved into her grandmother's apartment. Then she invited her friends to visit what she hoped would become a salon where they could relax and share their ideas.

She especially wanted ZaZa to see her new life firsthand, but ZaZa was still in the Landes, where her mother intended to keep her until she could be shipped off in October for a second year in Berlin. The letters ZaZa wrote all attest to her desperation to please her mother, fulfill her familial and social duties and still maintain some semblance of intellectual independence. But once more Castor demonstrated her inability to comprehend the realities of someone else's life. With her typical brusqueness she announced that the solution to ZaZa's problem was perfectly clear and simple: Merleau-Ponty had only to demand ZaZa's hand in marriage and the Le Coins would stop interfering. He was, after all, a wellborn and wellbred young man with a good future ahead of him. She wrote this to ZaZa, whose reply was evasive, so Castor went to see Merleau-Ponty to ask him straight out why he did not confront Monsieur Le Coin to demand ZaZa's hand in marriage. He too equivocated, telling her that his eldest brother was about to accept a position in Africa and his sister was about to be married; this meant that his widowed mother had only him to depend upon, and therefore he could not marry for at least a year after his upcoming military service.

Castor blamed his unsatisfying reply on his fervent Catholicism, his exaggerated sense of duty toward his mother, and—from the vantage point of her relationship with Sartre—his sexual immaturity. She cared about Merleau-Ponty only insofar as he could make ZaZa happy and free her, even if only slightly, from her oppressive family life.

Throughout September and most of October, a stream of erratic letters arrived from ZaZa. One day she was possessed by dark "phantoms" of a life she wanted but thought she could not have, the next she was ecstatically contemplating a life of perfect obedience to her mother's desires for her, in which all such phantoms were exorcised.

ZaZa returned to Paris for what was supposed to be a brief visit before setting off for Berlin. Though Madame Le Coin forbade her to see Castor, she appeared at the apartment unannounced at odd moments, often without a hat or gloves (a serious breach of etiquette for a young woman of her background). Castor was shocked by her appearance: thin to the point of emaciation, her skin sallow, her eyes ringed by black shadows. Her mouth twitched and she bit her fingernails until they bled; she cried or burst into hysterical laughter for no apparent reason. Castor tried to calm her by talking about herself and her summer with Sartre and what she hoped her life would be now that she was back in Paris. She tried to talk to Merleau-Ponty about ZaZa, but "he responded with Catholic pieties, about self-denial and honoring the wishes of others, and a great many other remarks that made no sense at all to me."

Shortly after, Castor received the last letter ZaZa ever wrote to her, a frenzied rush of conflicting emotions in which she announced her imminent departure for Berlin and the happiness she expected to find there. A few days later there was another letter, this one from Madame Le Coin saying that ZaZa had been admitted to a suburban hospital, where she was lying in a coma brought on by excessively high fever. There was little hope that she would recover, and, indeed, several days later she died at the age of twenty-one of what was variously described as encephalitis, meningitis, embolism or aneurysm.

It is interesting that when Simone de Beauvoir wrote the first volume of her memoirs, *Memoirs of a Dutiful Daughter*, she chose to end it with the tragic fact of ZaZa's death rather than the optimism of her own new life with Sartre, especially since she had no intention at that time of writing further volumes. Her given reason for this was to commemorate their friendship: "We had fought together against the revolting fate that had lain ahead of us, and for a long time I believed that I had paid for my own freedom with her death."[37]

When the book was published and Hélène and the friends who had been close to Beauvoir during ZaZa's life read this sentence, they were surprised, if not shocked. Hélène remarked, "I had not realized ZaZa meant so much to her, or that my sister continued to think of ZaZa for so many years after her death. We knew she was upset at the time, but we all assumed it was due to her exaggerated fear of death and not specifically of the death of ZaZa.

Sometime after *Memoirs of a Dutiful Daughter* was published (1958), Simone de Beauvoir learned the truth about her friend's death from one of ZaZa's younger sisters, who read the book and decided that the family had an obligation to tell her what had happened. Beauvoir learned that Merleau-Ponty had not been reluctant to marry ZaZa, but wanted very much to do so. Knowing how stubborn ZaZa could be when she wanted something, Monsieur Le Coin took the first step toward letting the marriage take place: he hired a detective and had Merleau-Ponty's family investigated. The report, according to Beauvoir, contained information that "his mother, whom Merleau-Ponty adored, had not lived in a very moral or Catholic manner." Her husband, "who had been the father of the first son in the family, was in the Navy and often far from home. And for years in La Rochelle, Madame Merleau-Ponty had supposedly been the mistress of a very well-known, highly respected professor who was also married. Sartre's mother, who had also lived in La Rochelle, told me when I asked her that everyone there knew about it, and that it was a public scandal to see this man seated at dinner parties with his wife on one side and his mistress on the other. It was he who was the father of the other two children, Maurice Merleau-Ponty and his sister, Monique. It was an extremely serious liaison which lasted for years and years, and this gentleman took care of his two children, even though for their mother's protection they took the name of her husband."

Merleau-Ponty had no knowledge of his true parentage until Monsieur Le Coin told him. Le Coin then told his daughter, "who had all the prejudices of a devout Catholic girl," and any plan for her marriage to Merleau-Ponty ended abruptly. It was just after this that Castor received the puzzling letters about "children who bear the sins of their parents." ZaZa eventually gave up any thought of marrying Merleau-Ponty when Monsieur Le Coin insisted that he intended to make the information public if she persisted. As Merleau-Ponty revered his mother, he too was unwilling to risk exposure and public censure. As for Castor, "I didn't know anything at all about this. How old was I then—nineteen, twenty? Well, I thought it was all Merleau-Ponty's fault and I was angry with him for years afterward. Actually, he had told ZaZa the truth, but neither of them trusted me enough to tell me—maybe they were too embarrassed, we were all so naïve then—and so I spent years estranged from him because I blamed him for ZaZa's death. I kept that bitterness against Merleau-Ponty until I was already forty, when I wrote the memoir, despite the fact that when we were young I liked him a lot. But no one told me the truth about ZaZa's death, and so I used her letters and her history *as I thought I knew it* in my book as a way of punishing everyone whom I blamed for it."

There was no time for grief, however, especially with Sartre, who didn't want to hear about the death of anyone whose life had been so short and sad. Besides, the "true new year" was starting, which was how Castor always thought of autumn and the beginning of the academic calendar.[38] This year, the life she had hitherto only dreamed of was about to begin, and the future loomed so large and exciting that there was no time to dwell in the past.

She and Sartre wrote to each other frequently in those days when neither had a telephone. Usually they were short notes, giving the times and places of meetings, sometimes requests for favors or services. Their letters to each other date from 1929, but when they were published by Simone de Beauvoir in a heavily edited version in 1983, she wrote that she selected only those of his which protected the privacy of persons still living. Her letters to him, she said, had all been lost.[39]

She chose only one of his letters to represent 1929. In the first of two brief paragraphs, he asked: "Will you be good enough to give my laundry (lower drawer in the armoire) to the washerwoman this morning. I left the key in the door." In the second he wrote: "I love you tenderly, my love. Your little head was so cute when you said 'ah, you looked at me, you looked at me,' and when I think of it my heart is full of tenderness. Goodbye, my little Bond."

Why she chose to reprint this letter was known only to Simone de Beauvoir, but it is an uncanny prefiguration of the duality of her life to come with Jean-Paul Sartre.

ELEVEN

On Her Paris Honeymoon

Words. It seemed as if there were not enough hours in a day to contain the rush of ideas they wanted—actually, needed—to share with each other.

Sartre gave Simone de Beauvoir something no one, not even her sister, had ever given her before—his undivided attention. This resulted in "talk about all kinds of things, but especially about a subject which interested me above all others: myself."[1] Until Sartre, others had always grown restless when subjected to Beauvoir's relentless self-absorption, an exhausting barrage that had often irritated friends such as Stépha: "She used to talk, talk, talk—always *me, me, me*. It was usually okay, because when I saw she was in one of those moods I only half listened. But sometimes I wanted to talk about something that was bothering me, and she would get that far-away look on her face and she'd start twitching and soon she'd get up and leave. I used to get so mad. Sometimes I would plead, 'Castor, listen to me!' but she didn't know how to listen to what other people had to say."

Happily for Beauvoir, Sartre was different: "Whenever other people made attempts to analyze me, they did so from the standpoint of their own little worlds . . . Sartre always tried to see me as part of my own scheme of things, to understand me in the light of my own set of values and attitudes."[2] Sartre's description of himself supports hers: "I didn't interest myself at all. I was curious about ideas and the world and other people's hearts."[3]

It seems, then, that each defined the source of the creative impulse that would guide their life's work—hers primarily self-reflexive and introspective, his wide-ranging and outer-directed—from the very beginning of their relationship.

Also, equally—and perhaps even more importantly—from the beginning their passion was primarily verbal. "Perhaps," Simone de Beauvoir mused in 1986 only weeks before her death, "that was why it lasted so long."

It was a strange union of two opposites: she, who for most of her early life could not wait to grow up, join the adult world and be on her own, now found herself linked symbiotically to someone who never wanted to grow up, but remained locked in perpetual adolescence for the rest of his life. "We were like elves," is how she described herself and Sartre. "Our life, like that of all petits bourgeois intellectuals, was in fact mainly characterized by its lack of reality . . . like every bourgeois, we were sheltered from want; like every civil servant, we were guaranteed against insecurity. Furthermore, we had no children, no families, no responsibilities."[4]

The freedom was exhilarating. Her friends came and went, and her Grandmother Brasseur saw or spoke to them only if she admitted them when they arrived. When Françoise discovered that her mother was not a reliable ally in reporting Castor's activities, she began to make frequent, unannounced visits. After several heated arguments when the door was slammed in her face, Françoise limited her calls to prearranged invitations such as Sunday luncheon. Usually Castor managed not to be there.

Her family's attitude toward her relationship with Sartre was puzzling, even to her. Everyone knew they had become lovers, but only the two sisters spoke openly about it, in the privacy of Castor's room. Whenever "we four" (as Françoise liked to speak of her family[5]) were together, everything was governed by propriety and courtesy. Georges and Françoise treated her cautiously, as if she might explode at the least provocation. They had not spanked her as an infant for fear of her terrible temper tantrums; now that she was adult, they dared not incite wrath of a different sort. Gradually the occasions when they were all together grew so infrequent that they stopped counting on her for all but the most ceremonial, and that soon ended when she celebrated Christmas Eve with Sartre and some of his friends.[6]

Everyone took their "illegitimate relationship" so much for granted that "it was regarded almost as respectfully as though it were a marriage." Defying "conventions with impunity" only enhanced their "feeling of personal freedom,"[7] and no one dared question them. Together they formed a phalanx which no person, custom or idea could influence or change, and it all happened in the space of one month, October 1929. In the short time between her return from Meyrignac and his departure for military service, they had become a public entity, and people either accepted it or were banished.

In Sartre's *War Diaries*, part of the entry for December 1, 1939, deals with his concept of freedom as it concerned his relationships with women. He makes the cryptic comment of Beauvoir, "On one occasion I was hoist with my own petard. The Beaver accepted that freedom and kept it. It was in 1929. I was foolish enough to be upset by it: instead of understanding the extraordinary luck I'd had, I fell into a certain melancholy."[8] In 1984 Simone de Beauvoir explained, "Oh, he felt he had to propose to me after my father accosted us at La Grillère. I told him not to be silly and of course I rejected marriage."

Sartre first hinted at marriage shortly after the *agrégation*, but the hint was so vague and she was so flustered by whether or not she had heard it correctly that she was too embarrassed to reply. In the several days they spent together after Georges confronted them, Sartre spoke seriously of marriage as a philosophical concept and its continuing validity in a modern world, then as an economic construct. Some of his reasons had to do with her decision to live in Paris for at least a year or two without seeking full-time teaching employment, which would probably have taken her to one of the distant provinces, and the increased pay he would receive if he were to marry during his military service. The ostensible argument for marriage was financial, but the real reason was that both were swept away by the intensity of their need for each other—and it must be stressed that the need was as much intellectual as sexual. As intellectuals they felt the obligation to analyze their dilemma rather than to turn "naturally" to any obvious solution.

"Later," Beauvoir recalled, "after we had decided what our relationship was to be, we were both embarrassed that we had even briefly considered the most bourgeois of institutions, marriage, to be the answer."

Still, it was strange that a young woman from her background should refuse the proposal of a man she so adored that she was willing to risk her family's ostracism to be with him. If they spent all their waking moments plotting how and where they could be together, marriage did seem the obvious answer. Despite all the conventions she had flaunted so fearlessly, she was still cowed by the most important tenet of her social class. Toward the end of her life she explained patiently, but with residual bitterness, "Marriage was impossible. I had no dowry."

And so they paraded their unconventional relationship in public. They strode through Paris confidently: Castor, flushed and happy to be with "the genius who opened the world to me"; the tiny, ugly Sartre, pleased with the robust beauty at his side. They invented scenarios and constructed private fantasy lives, sometimes pretending they were "Mr. and Mrs. Morgan Hattick, the American millionaire and his wife," or "Monsieur and Madame M. Organitique," when they played their game slightly closer to their real French identity.[9] Interestingly, all depended on the idea of themselves as an imaginary married couple.

Paul and Henriette Nizan were among the first to accept their new status and were also among the few friends with whom they socialized that October. The Nizans now lived in the suburb of Saint-Germain-en-Laye, in an ultramodern glass house built by Henriette's parents which became the setting for some of the most exciting weekends Castor and Sartre spent in their first year together. Once or twice each week, the Nizans came to Paris and the two couples went to the movies together. It gave Castor a particular kind of pleasure to be with Sartre in their company even though she and Henriette had never had anything in common and she still behaved clumsily when Paul fixed his steely gaze on her. Her best explanation was that Nizan and Sartre "had been so close for so many years that it gave me pleasure to see the two of them together and to hear the ease of their conversation."[10]

For Castor, the relationship was a complex one which colored hers with Sartre. Henriette Nizan was a devoted wife, comfortable in a social situation where her husband and another man engaged in intellectual conversation. Beauvoir agreed that on these occasions both she and Henriette "took pride in listening to the men," but at the same time she denied that she had "ever, even remotely, played a spousal role." In her mind, she and Sartre "never assumed traditional postures," and her willingness to converse with Henriette and her deference to the two men was only her way of respecting their long friendship.

Beauvoir and Sartre defined the roles each would play for the other throughout their more than fifty-year-long relationship after one of these outings with the Nizans. She described the moment vividly in her memoirs:

> One afternoon we had been with the Nizans to a cinema on the Champs Elysées. . . . After leaving them we walked down as far as the Carrousel Gardens, and sat down on a stone bench beneath one wing of the Louvre. There was a kind of balustrade which served as a back-rest, a little way out from the wall; and in the cagelike space behind it a cat was miaowing. The poor thing was too big to get out; how had it ever got in? Evening was drawing on; a woman came up to the bench, a paper in one hand, and produced some scraps of meat. These she fed to the cat, stroking it tenderly the while. It was at this moment that Sartre said: "Let's sign a two-year lease."[11]

In the several months before Sartre blurted out this idea, they had talked about themselves constantly, trying to decide the best way to live. Individually, their situations were exactly opposite: she was happy to have taken full responsibility for her life, and he was not. Now that his student days were over, he was threatened first by the regimentation of military service and, following that, by the rigidity of the academic calendar when he became a professor. In their society, everyone was expected to follow conventions: as a man, he was expected to earn a living; as a woman, even though an educated one, she would never have been faulted had she married or returned home to be supported by her family. Of the two, it was he who would have preferred this "female" status, mostly because he had always been his family's pampered darling and he liked it.[12] Both had begun life as the center of attention within their respective families, but she had been rudely jolted into the adult knowledge that she had to assume responsibility for herself when her father lost his money; he was adored and coddled all his life, and only the fact that there was not enough money within the family to support him kept Sartre from being financially sheltered by his mother. However, first a small inheritance and then money earned from his writings allowed him to be as financially free as an adolescent for the rest of his life.

There were also certain other freedoms he was determined not to give up:

Sartre was not inclined to be monogamous by nature; he took pleasure in the company of women, finding them less comic than men. He had no intention, at twenty-three, of renouncing their tempting variety.

He explained the matter to me in his favorite terminology. "What we have," he said, "is an *essential* love; but it is a good idea for us also to experience *contingent* love affairs." We were two of a kind, and our relationship would endure as long as we did; but it could not make up entirely for the fleeting riches to be had from encounters with different people. How could we deliberately forgo that gamut of emotions—astonishment, regret, pleasure, nostalgia—which we were as capable of sustaining as anyone else?

But during their "two-year lease" there was to be

no question of our actually taking advantage . . . of those "freedoms" which in theory we had the right to enjoy. We intended to give ourselves wholeheartedly and without reservation to this new relationship of ours. We made another pact between us: not only would we never lie to one another, but neither of us would conceal anything from the other.[13]

These remarks are from her memoirs, the official written version of the beginning of her "contingent" life with Sartre. But within the same few pages there are a number of disquieting others in which she assesses herself and Sartre and what might possibly lie in their future. They are worth noting here:

At every level we failed to face the weight of reality, priding ourselves on what we called our "radical freedom." . . . Our way of life was so exactly what we wanted that it was as though *it* had chosen *us*; we regarded this as an omen of its regular submission to our future plans. . . . In a sense we both lacked a real family and we had elevated this contingency into a principle. . . . All through our youth, and even later, whenever we had to face a difficult or disagreeable situation we would work it out first as a private *ad hoc* drama. We turned it upside down, exaggerated it, caricatured it and explored it in every direction; this helped us a good deal in getting it under control.[14]

Of herself, she wrote:

Only those things within my reach . . . had any true weight of reality for me. I gave myself up so completely to present desires and pleasures that I had no energy to waste on mere wishful thinking. . . . By releasing the pressure of reality upon our lives, fantasy convinced us that life itself had no hold upon us. . . . Our truth lay elsewhere.[15]

Still, the realities of the "lease" in the years that lay ahead "caused me some qualms; but it lay well in the future, and I had made it a rule never to worry about anything prematurely. Despite this I did feel a flicker of fear, though I regarded it as mere weakness and made myself subdue it." She decided to regard the "lease" as a contractual agreement, recognizing that "there is no timeless formula which guarantees . . . a perfect state of understanding." What mattered finally was "the thought that Sartre was now an open book to me, as easily read as my own mind." She wrote this line after more than thirty years of contingency, which is why she added, "Later I learned better."[16]

"Telling all" had its uses, but also carried the possibility of wounding abuse: "Sometimes speech is no more than a device for saying nothing—and a neater one than silence." She then writes of the near-impossibility of achieving total understanding with another person and how she seized upon Sartre when he offered her "the sort of absolute unfailing security that I had once had from my parents, or from God." A few lines later, in a slightly different but still-related context, she concludes that "happiness is a rarer vocation than people suppose."[17]

When Beauvoir was asked about the hint of underlying tension throughout that description of their pact, she agreed that there was a sense of duality in her language. Wanting to express happiness, she had "permitted fear, uncertainty, pessimism and sadness to be expressed also." Since meeting Sartre, "so much happened to me in such a short time that it seemed my life had turned upside down, inside out." No single book, nor all the books she had read before meeting him, had instructed or prepared her for any of it: "It was as if I were someone else standing by, watching these things happen to another girl."

Hélène remembered, "When anyone asked our father what Simone was doing after her brilliant career at the university, he became very embarrassed and so he tried to cover it with sarcasm. 'Oh, she's on her Parisian honeymoon,' he would say, and then he'd try to make her life sound more important than it was by speaking of her lycée teaching."

However, the chronological events of her life from November 1929 to October 1932 were few and simple. Sartre began his military service, and she stayed in Paris and continued to live in her grandmother's apartment. She saw her few old friends and made no new ones of lasting importance. She visited Sartre when he had weekend passes, first from Saint-Cyr and then from Saint-Symphorien, near Tours, where he was transferred in January 1930. She gave a few private lessons to older students who were preparing for the baccalauréat, and she taught Latin formally at the Lycée Victor Duruy to one class of ten-year-old girls. With these two jobs and the occasional few francs some of Stépha's foreign journalist friends gave her to help them put their assignments into good French, she earned enough money to keep herself. Occasionally she thought about writing something of her own, but did little about it.

Castor's life may have seemed licentious in the eyes of her society, but she was still "largely governed by prudishness." She discovered how much so when Sartre introduced her to Madame Morel, about whom she had heard all sorts of rumors when they were still students. Sartre met Madame Morel through his classmate Pierre Guille,[18] who had been hired to tutor her son, Albert, nicknamed "the Tapir" for his course of study: one "tapired" in preparation for the exam. When Albert passed, Sartre helped him prepare for his *baccalauréat*. Soon he became a regular among the group that frequented the Morels' grand apartment on the Boulevard Raspail, and he brought Nizan and Maheu with him.

Madame Morel had been born in Argentina of French parents, and she and her sister grew up in a wild cowgirl existence on the Pampas. When they were of marriageable age, both were sent to Paris, where they were only slightly subdued by the rarefied conventions of Parisian high society. Madame Morel married a physician much older than she who devoted himself to laboratory research until World War I, when he went off to the trenches. He returned a hypochondriac who took to his bed in a sound- and draft-proof room, which he left only when his wife transported him each summer to her villa at Juan-les-Pins or to his own ancestral home, La Pouèze, near Angers in the Loire Valley. Besides Albert, they had a daughter, Jacqueline, who married young and was seldom at home.

When Castor met the fashionable, smooth-skinned little woman, "plump as a pearly pigeon, very charming, certainly very intelligent and well read," she was "shocked to find that someone I thought so old could still be so vital and alive." At the time, Madame Morel was forty. For many years Simone de Beauvoir had an unrealistic conception of sexuality, believing that women lost interest in their thirties and at forty were far too old to be sexually active. She was greatly relieved to discover that Madame Morel supported her preconceptions.

Madame Morel exclaimed frequently that she had no interest in the actuality of sex, but said she was fascinated instead by all its romantic implications. She maintained the outward appearance of a celibate, and even though she and Guille had formed a liaison in which they were constantly together, she insisted that theirs was an intellectual rapport of "unusual subtlety, and far more valuable than an ordinary liaison." It pleased Castor that Madame Morel "remained a respectable woman. . . . I had not emancipated myself from all sexual taboos, and promiscuity in a woman still shocked me."[19] So, whatever the truth of the relationships between Madame Morel and Guille and Madame Morel and Sartre, they were all careful to keep it hidden from Castor.

Prudery even characterized Castor's love affair with Sartre. He was stationed now in Tours, near enough for her to visit every weekend. Even though she always rented a hotel room, they spent most of the daylight hours walking the streets awaiting darkness, or, when their passions grew unmanageable, finding some hidden place along country roads where they could have sex. Going to bed with a man in the daytime, especially in a hotel, was out of the question. "Good girls," she said in 1982, "did not engage in such behavior."

Unfortunately for her, sexual passion unleashed torrents of agony that all but incapacitated her when she was away from Sartre. Masturbation was unthinkable, and any thought of finding satisfaction with another man was even more horrifying. There were men, friends of hers and Sartre's, who suggested their availability, but she rejected them rudely. She and Sartre had made their pact, and even though he had not hidden past liaisons from her and continued to write or tell her of the women who had flirted with him or (in her word) "worse," she kept her side of the bargain and took no other lovers. All her life she had been able to reject or discard anything she could not control, but now it was her very own body that refused to obey her.

It was about this time that she began to take a real interest in her appearance. When she moved into her grandmother's apartment she bought herself a new outfit, chosen without any sort of guidance or knowledge of fashion. She was still in mourning for her grandfather and her uncle, so bright colors were forbidden. Instead of black she chose an outfit in gray silk. The dress fabric was sleazy and the style was frivolous, more suitable for parties than for everyday wear. She bought cheap shoes in the same color which soon wore out, completing the tacky, shabby picture of herself which she remembered as "both comical and hideous." To keep from repeating this expensive mistake, she began to read fashion magazines avidly, especially *Marie-Claire*, a woman's magazine whose content lay somewhere between the present-day *Cosmopolitan* and *The Ladies' Home Journal*. It became her fashion bible for the next decade.[20] From it she learned how to drape handkerchiefs over light bulbs and lampshades as an inexpensive decorating trick, how to rouge her face to enhance her cheekbones, and where to buy inexpensive copies of scarves and jewelry.

She thought her hips were too big, even though she was very thin at the time, and to disguise them she began to wear full dirndl skirts and loose overblouses. She discovered that this style was comfortable, and even after she had outgrown her interest in "fashion" she chose to wear it. However, the total effect was never quite what she wanted. Too often the colors clashed. She wore her clothes until they were dirty or stained; she lost buttons, and her hemlines unraveled. She began a lifelong affection for espadrilles and other low-heeled, unflattering shoes, which she wore until they were in tatters. She cared about clothes and wanted "to look nice," but had no interest in maintaining them and no ability to do so. Because she could not afford to replace things easily, her reputation as a woman who cared little for her appearance was launched, a reputation she was unable to overcome until she was much older and richer.

Her body preoccupied her, but her mind distressed her in ways that made her physically sick. For the first time in her adult life, she experienced jealousy and had no understanding of how to deal with it. In her memoirs, she wrote long descriptive passages about two women who were important in Sartre's life, and to whom he introduced her in 1930, Madame Morel and Simone Jollivet.[21] Both passages are ambiguous, ostensibly describing women with whom Beauvoir became friendly despite having little in common with each, but, like so much of what seems at first reading to be straightforward description of personality and situation, they have a darker side as well.

Beauvoir begins in an anecdotal manner, describing the looks, personality, habits and attitudes of each woman, especially her relationship to Sartre. Each of these accounts ends with Beauvoir placing herself in direct contrast with them, analyzing her doubts, fears, insecurities and what she thinks are her own physical and mental deficiencies. Not once does she list any of her presumed strengths. Above all, there is always a strong underlying current of fear which can be traced to her insecurity about her relationship with Sartre. It is as if she has tried to understand these women only as the means of developing and strengthening her importance as the central figure in his life; as if understanding and assimilating their true inner being would enable her to remain the one fixed, constant woman in his world.[22]

Sartre's flirtation with Madame Morel (for Castor forced herself to believe and insisted to everyone that that was the extent of it) only confused her further. In her years in Paris, Madame Morel learned so well how to camouflage the innate cunning she learned on the Argentine Pampas into the delicate refinement of the Parisian upper classes that she made Castor's social inadequacies glaringly apparent. Within Madame Morel's circle, everyone passed languid afternoons in Paris sipping English tea from delicate china cups and engaging in the most spirited social as well as intellectual repartee. In the country, she expected her guests to participate in shooting parties in which she took the lead and *normaliens* half her age had difficulty keeping up. She assumed that everyone would dress appropriately for various occasions—except Sartre, whose idiosyncrasies she not only tolerated but expected and encouraged.

Into this elegantly discreet atmosphere burst Castor, more clumsy than she had ever been at the Sorbonne. Her voice was too loud, her clothing improper, she spilled her tea and hated all blood sports. She knew that the others smiled at one another behind her back, and when alone she tortured herself by inventing conversations in which she imagined they mocked her. But even though she was objective enough to realize her many social gaffes, she had no intention whatsoever of changing her behavior to fit in more smoothly with this group. In typical fashion, she decided they would have to accept her as she was. She took a kind of stubborn pride in her lack of social graces, and consciously refused to accommodate to the niceties of polite society, which she saw as pandering to her bourgeois upbringing and a betrayal of her newly found life of freedom.

When Simone Jollivet came to Paris, Castor's jealousy grew in tandem with her insecurity. Sartre had met Jollivet in Toulouse several years earlier and immediately begun a passionate affair, climbing across rooftops into her bedroom each night after her parents were asleep. He told Castor all about Jollivet, and together they nicknamed her "Toulouse" because everyone had a nickname in their private language.

Since they were "telling each other everything," nothing was too private to be shared. Castor listened in amazement as Sartre described Jollivet's many reckless affairs, and how she "worked" and what else she did in various bordellos. He found her easy attitude toward sexuality amusing, but Castor was both shocked and fascinated by Jollivet's promiscuity. What worried her most was Sartre's laughing description of how, when he fell asleep in sexual exhaustion, Toulouse stayed up all night to read Nietzsche, for Castor knew that an intelligent woman was a more formidable threat than one who was simply beautiful. Sartre could spend hours waxing lyrical over the perfection of Jollivet's wrists and ankles and the joys he had known in her bed, but he was also enchanted by the outrageous opinions she formed from her constant reading. Jollivet adored Emily Brontë, but she also loved Flaubert and fashioned herself after an Emma Bovary so maudlin and melodramatic that Sartre could not stop laughing. However, he spent hours discussing and explaining "the real Emma" to her, and in light of his own fascination with Flaubert so many years later the temptation is to point to these occasions as the possible awakening of his interest in the subject.[23]

Jollivet had come to Paris to be an actress, and Sartre sent a note from his military station in Tours telling Castor to meet and welcome her and see if there was anything she needed. Her response was curious, but characteristic: she learned that Jollivet was having an affair with Charles Dullin, the great French actor and producer, and that he had cast her in one of his productions, so she bought tickets for performances several days in a row. In a variation of her penchant for voyeurism, she saw the play repeatedly, as if by staring at the creature on stage she could somehow get the measure of her rival in real life. The problem was that three actresses whose characters' names were unlisted on the program were all on stage together throughout the play, and Castor could not determine which was Jollivet. When she learned that she had spent the first few productions staring at the wrong woman, she reacted angrily because the version of reality she created did not correspond to the facts: "I muttered furiously to myself that [Jollivet] ought to have matched up to *my* version, that her head simply didn't belong to her."[24]

She did not attempt to meet Jollivet until Sartre ordered her to go to Jollivet's house at her convenience. She went, because in those days she never disobeyed Sartre. It was far from successful, as Jollivet was her most outlandish and Castor her most prudish: "I found it perplexingly awkward to form an opinion about her. The casual way she used her body shocked me; but was it her emancipation or my puritan upbringing that should be blamed for this?"[25] Afterward, she walked for hours trying to sort out her feelings, "suffering from a bad attack of the most unpleasant emotion that had ever laid hold on me, and which, I believe, is most often described as jealousy."[26] Beauvoir described Jollivet in her memoirs as so filled with narcissistic self-absorption that "nothing but a really rousing counterblast of egocentricity could have restored the balance. [S]he had annexed me into *her* world, and relegated me to a very humble niche in it. . . . I couldn't get my mind off her; whereas she had forgotten me already."

Her jealousy seems not the classic sort, in which one fears and competes with a rival for the affection and attention of a third person. Instead, all her anxieties and animosities, everything she felt toward Simone Jollivet, seem to have stemmed from her inability to accept the woman in the same romantic light as Sartre: where he saw a free spirit, she saw only a prostitute. He thought Jollivet exquisitely beautiful, and she thought her overdressed and affected; Sartre found Jollivet's self-absorption charming, and Castor resented it because it kept her from controlling Jollivet's contact with Sartre. Privately, Castor could not understand how Sartre could ever have been smitten by this woman,[27] but publicly she did not dare tell him or anyone else. Castor felt she had to keep her steely-eyed appraisal of Jollivet a secret even though she and Sartre had promised to reveal everything to each other, because telling the truth would have meant that she questioned his judgment and she feared how he would respond to such serious disagreement so early in their relationship. It frightened her because the possibility of a rift in their unity was one she could not allow.

There were many times during the course of Simone de Beauvoir's life when she doubted herself or was unsure of how to remove herself from a difficult situation. In almost every instance, she turned to books to help her sort things out, but this time without success. She went sporadically to the bookshops of Sylvia Beach and Adrienne Monnier, but nothing she read there seemed to make much impression. James Joyce, whom she saw once or twice, was only "the name of a somewhat eccentric Irishman." She did not read any of Hemingway's fiction until "much later, after Dos Passos, whom I admired greatly." Faulkner "did not impress me until another ten years had passed." Someone ("probably Nizan, because he told me about Synge, Stephens and other Irish writers, and I think he was reading American fiction then as well") gave her a copy of *Soldier's Pay*, but she found it "incomprehensible" and looked for a French translation "because I was afraid I did not understand Faulkner's ideas perhaps because I did not understand his [idiomatic] English."

All her friends from the university were living and working far from Paris, and since she had broken off all contact with her cousins and other relatives, she never saw any of them. She had never had many friends and now had almost none that she saw with any degree of regularity. GéGé was married and trying to balance marriage with her work as a busy and successful advertising artist. Stépha was in Madrid and somewhat estranged from Castor because a relationship had developed between Hélène and Fernando, who had become a sort of mentor to her painting. Even Hèléne was too busy with her own work to have much time for the older sister who now had all the free time in the world. Being alone had never stopped Castor before from going to cafés and bars, but she lacked the energy even to do that. In the past she had always found ways to fill solitary time, but now there was too much time and nothing seemed worth the effort.

Her life after she met Sartre was even more frenetic than it had been as a student, and the pace continued until he left for military service. Then, of necessity, it was confined to weekends, when they often stayed awake talking several nights in succession and her only sleep was an hour or two on the late train back to Paris, where she doused her face in cold water before heading off to early classes at the Lycée Duruy. But the days between weekends were long and lonely, and even worse were the weekends when he was not free and she stayed alone in Paris. This was when the emptiness of her life overwhelmed her. She had invested everything in him, and when he wasn't with her she felt herself less than nothing.

There are many examples of persons who have had to concentrate intensely for long periods of time on a task or situation so that, once it is finished, they are too exhausted to concentrate on anything at all. It is especially common among students who have various hurdles to surmount; frequently when they succeed in attaining one goal they find themselves unable to summon their usual energy to continue at anything like their previous pace toward the next. Women often refer to this as the "postpartum blues" even when the situation has nothing at all to do with pregnancy and birth. Sometimes it is accompanied by varying degrees of depression, and tears and lethargy are often common. Simone de Beauvoir had spent the first twenty-one years of her life in nonstop intellectual activity, and even before it ended, her life with Sartre had begun, so there was no pause between the end of one and the beginning of the other, no time to sort out what she had been from what she wanted to be.

It is difficult to describe all that Sartre had become in the first two years of their relationship. He was her mentor, guiding her intellectual life by sending lists of books he wanted her to read so that they could discuss them together. He was her lover, and, whatever the actuality of their physical relationship, this romantic attachment had become the primary obsession of her life. He was also a role model, the first and most important she ever had, the one after whom she tried to pattern herself for years to come. That he was male only increased her confusion about herself.

"Elflike" indeed, she had followed him on one merry prank after another, breaking off from her family, scorning their customs and values, ignoring the confusion and humiliation her unorthodox behavior caused them. But at the age of twenty-two, seeing him on occasional weekends and having him tell her the details of his attraction to other women, all she felt was increasing anxiety over having sacrificed every form of personal security to be with him or do what he wanted.

He told her she had to do it in order to realize her potential. This was all very well, but the nagging question she could no longer ignore was, what potential? Teaching ten-year-old girls to conjugate Latin verbs several times a week was hardly a rewarding career for the youngest and most brilliant *agrégée* in the history of French education for women. He had told her that he loved her and that she would always be first in his heart and mind, but it was difficult to accept his voracious appetite for other women and the willing complicity he expected of her in what were truly emotionally painful situations.

He told her she must become a writer, and so she tried that too, but unsuccessfully. "I read the account of your first chapter," he wrote in reply to her letter describing what she intended to write, "if the writing is as direct [and forceful] as it is in your letter, it [can't help but be] excellent."[28] She became paralyzed with uncertainty and never finished the first page, let alone the first chapter. By this time, Sartre had no desire to marry Simone de Beauvoir, but he expected her to adopt every aspect of his thinking, to comment upon all his ideas and interests and the details of every possible intimacy, even those he had with other women. He took it for granted that she would express her identity through total identification with him, which she interpreted to mean that they would present an image to the world so intricately conjoined that no one would be able to tell where one of them ended and the other began. It was unquestionably a lopsided relationship, but she was insecure and willing to let him lead her.

All the same, his dependency on her was just as deep and all-encompassing. He tried to explain it in a letter he wrote while on military service:

> I want to tell you that when I want to write and can't, I'm going to find my pleasure in writing letters to you. Because it's only to you that I can say what I think, what I want to write, and only you can understand [the frequent mood swings in] my daily state, the constant smoke and fire of ideas. Only you know when my sentiments come from Spinoza or come from me. And when you receive letters filled with obscure prose and arid phrasings that may not interest my beloved Castor, I know that you are still the only one who can understand me because you are also Mademoiselle Simone Bertrand de Beauvoir, the brilliant university graduate.[29]

So Sartre was the prince she had always dreamed of, who had awakened her, the sleeping beauty. Still, life in the palace somehow eluded her. In fairy tales, princesses were not expected to conquer the world but to marry the prince and live happily ever after. In real life, the prince was itching for new adventure and growing impatient with the princess, who only wanted to get inside the castle and stay there.

Sartre decided to apply for an annual lectureship in Japan sponsored by the French government, which he hoped to begin in the fall of 1931 after his military service ended. Beauvoir was unwilling to contemplate being left behind in Paris, so she thought briefly of going to Budapest because a young Hungarian journalist friend of Stépha's, Heveshi Bandi, persuaded her that she could survive by giving French and English lessons (conveniently ignoring the fact that she had no patience to teach French and spoke English with an appalling accent). In the winter of 1930, Sartre was refused the Japan appointment and was asked to substitute for the philosophy professor at Le Havre for one semester; if all went well, he would be invited to spend the following year teaching there. Beauvoir no longer had the excuse that she was waiting to see whether he would be offered the job in Japan, which carried with it her unexpected desire that he would find a way to take her with him because two years apart would be impossible for them both. As her temporary position at the lycée was ending as well, she swallowed her considerable pride and asked her father to help her find a job in Paris in journalism or advertising—anything to keep her within weekend distance of Le Havre. Georges introduced her to editors and publishers, but only one showed any interest, and that was in her person rather than her ability. She had no choice left but to apply for a teaching position and hope that it would be close enough for their weekend rendezvous to continue. In the spring, her letter came from the Ministry of Education, telling her she had been assigned to teach in Marseille, about as far from Le Havre as one could go and still be in France.

TWELVE

Learning to Be Alone Again

NOW THAT SHE KNEW for certain the "Paris honeymoon" was ending, Castor went to bed each night expecting to awaken with rejuvenated energy for future projects; instead, every morning she woke up exhausted, with a vague sense of anxiety that incapacitated her as the day progressed. Less than five months remained before she had to report to Marseille, but instead of viewing her new career optimistically, she could think only of the vast physical distance that would separate her from Sartre. He was uneasy when he saw the woman she had become, so sluggish, negative and dejected. She, so sensitive to all his nuances of mood, could not manage to disguise her unhappiness. As their remaining days together passed in relentless succession, her depression deepened.

Sartre's maternal grandmother had recently died, leaving him an inheritance equivalent to several thousand dollars. Money meant little to him then and for the rest of his life except as something useful in bringing pleasure to himself and others. "We owe ourselves happiness and pleasure," he had told Castor in the fields at La Grillère when they became lovers.[1] He repeated it frequently, gently chiding her to relax and enjoy the present, to try to overcome the rigid strictures she imposed on herself that often resulted in physical problems. One of the most painful was toothache and sore jaws caused by nighttime gnashing and grinding, and, to a lesser degree, intense headaches and back spasms. But she insisted that ignoring ailments would make them end, and each day she slumped through the streets of Montparnasse as if nothing hurt, counting on coffee, cigarettes and wine to distract her from pain.

Sartre was uneasy for other reasons as well. He had been writing steadily throughout his national service, from poetry and drama to fiction and philosophy. Now he was almost finished with a treatise called "The Legend of Truth" (La Légende de la vérité), which he hoped to publish. He needed the sharp critical eye Castor had always focused on his work, but he could not get her to concentrate on the manuscript. Her inattention to his text finally worried him enough to take action.

Convinced that she needed to get out of Paris, he began a series of trips, using some of his grandmother's bequest. They took weekend outings to the countryside near Tours or to places where neither had ever been, once as far as the Atlantic coast near Nantes and Saint-Nazaire. Castor temporarily brightened, and it seemed as if being in the country, which he detested and she loved, would snap her out of the lethargy that so concerned him. She was invigorated during the day, but at night, when they sat over cigarettes and wine in smoky cafés, she lapsed into uncustomary silence or frightening outbursts of tears.

Throughout her life, Simone de Beauvoir kept her emotions under constant, rigid control until the strain became so great that some release was necessary.[2] Despite her quiet, almost solitary existence during the past year or so, these episodes usually occurred in a public place, generally a café. She would drink silently and steadily, consuming remarkable quantities of liquor which seemed to have little effect on her sobriety until she started to cry, silent tears at first, then audible sobs that grew in strength and volume until they racked her body. Suddenly, as if some inner safety valve warned her that she had vented quite enough for the moment, everything stopped. She would dry her tears, powder her face, straighten her clothes and rejoin the conversation as if nothing had happened.

The first time Sartre witnessed one of her outbursts, her only form of behavior over which he had no control, he reacted in panic with what became his usual response during the next few years—a proposal of marriage, "the universal soporific he depended upon when Castor became too hysterical and he needed to bring her back in line."[3] Sartre liked to think of himself as genuinely sensitive and attuned to all her emotional needs, but he was thinking of his own as well. He wanted his "pal" back, and also his alter ego, the one who understood his thoughts and ideas so well that her ideas, suggestions and revisions were often more clearly expressed than his own could have been. Only she shared the wicked jokes they made about their friends; the outrageous descriptions which filled their letters. No one could better zero in on someone's pomposity than Beauvoir and Sartre, as they conspired in creating verbal caricatures that sent them both into rollicking laughter. All this was missing now. Her letters were mostly short notes, dull factual accounts with none of the vitality and humor he relished. Worse were the fearful self-pitying paragraphs worrying how she would survive in the alien reaches of Marseille.[4] So he proposed marriage as the only logical solution to their impending separation, because married couples were always posted to the same location.

Marriage did not seem to be that much of a sacrifice anymore. His own life had not been going so well since his release from national service. The enforced exile from Paris had lessened his influence over his friends from the Ecole Normale, who no longer automatically accorded him intellectual leadership and homage. If anything, authority seemed to reside now with Nizan, who had already published his first book, *Aden-Arabie*, with great success and was now moving up through the literary and publishing hierarchy in Paris.

Also, Sartre had to enter the "grown-up world"[5] when he joined the faculty at Le Havre, which required such bourgeois activity as buying a suit, some shirts and ties, and even a decent pair of shoes. The act of buying and wearing such clothes necessitated the further investment of time and money to keep them in wearable condition, which in turn meant submitting to a certain amount of housekeeping. Living alone so far from friends meant frequent trips to Paris, and thus the need to consult timetables, buy tickets and keep to the schedules of public transportation, all things he was now taking for granted Castor would do for him. Nothing was simple anymore, and all his freedoms were constrained. Marriage seemed one possible solution to part of the problem.

He proposed, citing the budgetary advantages of being posted to the same city and living in the same quarters. She declined, refusing to give in to bourgeois standards imposed by circumstances. He said principles were all very well but to martyr oneself for them was stupid. She said marriage would end his life of freedom (never mentioning hers). He countered that, on the contrary, it would insure the continuation of his life of freedom but would not end hers as long as she "was on her guard." What he meant by that was unspecified. He insisted that the only thing about their daily life marriage would change was that their relationship would be legal before the state—unless she wanted two things to change, in which case he would buy her a wedding ring so that she could make her status public.

Despite his joke about a wedding ring, this was one of the more serious conversations they had about marriage, and it was the one and only time they spoke seriously about children. "He asked me if I would feel deprived in later years if I did not have a child. I didn't tell him everything I felt, I just said no. But I wrote in my memoirs about how children never held any attraction for me. Babies filled me with horror. The sight of a mother with a child sucking the life from her breast, or women changing soiled diapers—it all filled me with disgust. I had no desire to be drained, to be the slave to such a creature. No, all I said to Sartre was that I had no desire to recreate myself and since I had him I had no need of a miniature or substitute."

In 1977 Sartre offered a similar explanation for not having had a child,

> though acknowledging that "a great writer could have children," since obviously a goodly number of men writers have had them. He could conceivably have had a child and write (unlike the unmentioned Beauvoir, its mother), but, he insisted, he would not have been able to accord it the attention it would have needed (the classical role, of course, of the great writer's wife). And if he had had a child, Sartre was asked, what would he have preferred? "A daughter, certainly," he replied. "Undoubtedly because of the slightly incestuous feeling a father always has for his daughters."[6]

Apart from their being together, there was little to make marriage tempting within the terms Sartre defined. As Castor weighed the benefits against the disadvantages in the remaining time before she went to Marseille, what finally made her reject marriage was the simple yet profound realization she expressed succinctly in her memoirs: "Marriage doubles one's domestic responsibilities, and indeed, all one's social chores."[7]

There was one proposal that could set her mind somewhat at ease, and, to her relief, Sartre made it. They would renew their pact, he said, at least until they turned thirty—an age so unspeakable that it did not bear consideration. It made her think they would be together forever, and it truly eased her mind.

It had been a long, roundabout and exhausting process to bring her thinking to this point, but in typical fashion, once she realized that she could do nothing to change her situation, she accepted it. She had made long, complicated lists to help ease herself over various hurdles when she was a student; now she began to analyze how she would cope with life in Marseille through more lists and by writing in a little notebook that became a sporadic sort of journal.

She forced herself to think back to her life before Sartre, when solitude meant welcome time for constructive projects, not the agony of loneliness. "I would like to learn how to be alone again. It is so long since I have been alone," she confided to the notebook before adding: "These yearnings only happened intermittently; truthfully, I dreaded solitude more than I aspired to it."[8]

To revert to herself as she was before meeting Sartre was no longer a simple matter. Before, she had always been able to sublimate her will to her thinking, but that was before she became sexually active. When she and Sartre vowed they would hide nothing from each other, called it transparency and made it the central tenet of their pact, she had no idea of the degree to which it would involve her in his affairs with other women. When he wrote in exhausting detail of the women with whom he dallied in Tours, she pretended not to care, that the encounters meant nothing to her personally. He liked to describe them graphically, in "disgusting physical detail," as she put it.[9] He expected her return letter to address all aspects of his amours, from how she reacted to his descriptions of the women to how she felt about his affairs with them, to analyze her feelings and emotions in minute detail. When she tried to comply with his wishes, he wrote back to congratulate her on the honest examination of her innermost thoughts and feelings, because it was a tribute to their pact of transparency.

At the same time, she was so dissatisfied sexually that she could not read a romantic novel or see a movie that was a love story without becoming highly aroused. Whenever a man brushed against her on the Métro or the bus, the mere touch suffused her with violent physical urges. Once she actually got down from a bus before her stop and retched into the gutter along the Boulevard Saint-Michel. She described these feelings as akin to disease:

A shameful disease, too. I had emancipated myself just far enough from my puritanical upbringing to be able to take unconstrained pleasure in my own body, but not so far that I could allow it to cause me any inconvenience. Starved of its sustenance . . . I found it repulsive. I was forced to admit a truth that I had been doing my best to conceal ever since adolescence: my physical appetites were greater than I wanted them to be.[10]

In 1986, only weeks before her death, she was asked where this attitude toward sexuality had its genesis. She had known from an early age of her mother's uninhibited pleasure in sex. Could it be that hearing her parents during coitus as a child colored her own adult behavior? She agreed that two remarks in her memoirs best described her feelings. The first seems directly related to her need for control in every aspect of her life: "The notion that I partook of a condition common to all mankind gave me no consolation at all. It wounded my pride to find myself condemned to a subordinate rather than a commanding role where the private movements of my blood were concerned." The second has more to do with manners and social class: "The norms of credibility current in my former environment were no longer applicable, and I had not bothered to replace them."[11]

So for a time she tried to sublimate her emotions by pretending they were raging enemies that her willpower could bring under control. As far as she was concerned, it was not a question of understanding and accepting her hormones, it was only a matter of subjugating them.

Then, in February 1931, when Sartre's discharge from military service was being temporarily delayed while his superiors tried to persuade him to become an Army Reserve officer, Pierre Guille, whose own discharge had just come through and who wanted to take a holiday in celebration, asked her to take an auto trip around France with him in Madame Morel's car. Castor accepted at once because she liked Guille and found him, of all Sartre's friends, the one with whom she felt the most comfortable.

The day before their departure, Maheu arrived in Paris from Coutances, where he had been teaching school. He knew of her liaison with Sartre because he had corresponded with both of them since leaving Paris. He asked her to stay in Paris with him, but she preferred to honor her prior commitment to Guille. She was "so crazy about traveling" that she could not resist the opportunity to see new parts of France. As for intimacy with Maheu, it was out of the question then: "He represented something for me—an ideal, perhaps. He was married, and at that time I took someone's marriage vows very seriously whether they did or not."

So she went with Guille, and they were intimate. She did not tell Sartre, because "I didn't have to. He knew." But unlike him, she did not discuss it, nor did she confide the details to a letter. It soon became forgotten history because "it didn't happen again and we didn't talk about it."[12] For the next several years, Sartre was her only lover.

Curious though it may seem, the rupture with Maheu and the trip with Guille were both beneficial in restoring her determination to live within her self-enforced sexual constraints. She rejected them and other male friends as well for possible sexual partners, but since she had centered her entire agenda around Sartre's, her opportunities to meet new men were severely limited. She had stopped going to cafés almost entirely except on rare occasions with someone she already knew. If these friends tried to introduce her to someone new, she resented it and rushed out rudely and unceremoniously, claiming that her rendezvous had been only with them, not with strangers.[13] Her friends were astonished to see how uncharacteristically hermetic and solitary she had become.

She began to think seriously about writing for the first time in months, not because she had an idea for fiction or a thesis that she wanted to commit to paper, but mostly because Sartre was chiding her for doing nothing and she thought it might help to take her mind off their impending separation.

"You used to be full of little ideas, Castor," Sartre told her, warning that she was becoming like one of George Meredith's heroines who battle for their independence up to a point and then lapse into placidity, content to be only the domestic companion of a man. She resented this statement because she feared it was true, certainly, but more because he did not share her love of Meredith's novels and was using them to mock what he thought she had become.[14]

He especially disliked her favorite, *Diana of the Crossways*, which provoked a brief disagreement between them. She, as usual, stopped whatever she was doing when he needed her opinion of his writing or wanted her to read something he had already read so that they could discuss it together. He assumed an almost professorial air when he presented her with these reading assignments, even going so far at times as to instruct her on how she was to approach a particular text and what parts of it he most wanted her to direct her attention toward. But the situation was one way, and the disagreement over Meredith's fiction made that very clear to her.

She wanted to talk to him about the strong women whom Meredith made his heroines, and of the long and sometimes convoluted and painful self-examination they put themselves through before reaching the decisions which generally affected the rest of their lives. Sartre did not read English, so she tried to read various passages aloud to him, translating mentally into French as she went along. With *Diana of the Crossways* she thought she found a more mature heroine who better corresponded to her present self, replacing the heroine she most identified with still, the eighteen-year-old Judith Earle of Rosamund Lehmann's *Dusty Answer*. She was especially pleased to learn that Lehmann had been influenced by Meredith when she wrote her novel, and she wanted to tell all this to Sartre, but "he laughed and dismissed Diana Merion's complicated relationships as sexually silly and politically impossible."

So a pattern was established: she asked him to read a book only if she was sure it was something that would interest him. She began to make two lists, one for herself of books to read and think about privately and use as a guide to personal behavior, the other for him in the hope that he would share her enthusiasm and discuss them with her. She continued, however, to put her own reading aside immediately and without question when he wanted her literary assistance. In later years, when she began to write and publish consistently and was often under the pressure of deadlines, she still included as part of her daily work reading and commenting upon his. He did not read hers on the same regular basis, but would read only brief passages that troubled her and then only when she specifically sought his advice. This, however, was always at his convenience, generally in the evening when he had finished his daily stint of writing and they were relaxing over drinks. He was always willing to talk to her about her work once his was done for the day, but he never read hers in its entirety, or with the same critical editorial eye. She explained this by saying, "His work was more important than mine. I discovered that he was far more creative than I. Naturally I bowed to this and put it before my own. I would have been very silly not to."

She claimed she felt no anger when he did not give her the attention she might have wanted and needed throughout her own writing career: "We had a relationship based on total equality, reciprocity, a complete relationship. For one thing, I admired Sartre a great deal and I still do. But this does not mean I consider myself second-rate or that he considered me that way, either. So why did I concern myself with his work before mine? I could indeed have busied myself with my own, but if his came before mine, so be it."

But in 1931 he insisted, "You must begin to write," and then went on to remind her of how glorious she had seemed to him only a short year or so ago. He told her they must recapture that time and could do so only if she played the intellectual part he had assigned her when they made their pact.

However, she had no new ideas and did not know where to find any. Her reading this past year had consisted mostly of Sartre's castoff detective stories, to which she was indifferent even though he adored them. She loved to go to the movies, but had no interest in the medium of film except as a passive spectator who wished to be amused. She never went to the theater, because "I could never convince myself to enter the make-believe world on the stage. I hated it when I could see the actors' spit silhouetted in the light as they declaimed their speeches." So there was nothing in her life to produce any idea of interest or substance that she might write about.

His prodding continued, and she grew as anxious as a student before an exam. She cast around wildly for something to write about and produced three chapters about a young girl coming of age at the Sorbonne and finding her one true love. "I brought Diana Merion and Judith Earle to France and I copied shamelessly from Meredith and Lehmann. When I could make neither sense nor fiction of that, I gave them a hero from Alain-Fournier to fight over. I was desperate to create a novel, but I had nothing at all to write. It was so silly." She never showed it to Sartre.

However, now that she had renewed their pact and she believed their relationship was on surer footing, something she thought she had sublimated suddenly came to the forefront of her consciousness and refused to go away. This was ZaZa, whom she had not properly mourned because her death occurred just at the time she became involved with Sartre, when she preferred to concentrate on her happiness rather than on the loss of her friend. Now that she had empty stretches of time to fill, thoughts of ZaZa began to haunt her. By May 1931, when the trees were in blossom and young lovers filled the parks and gardens of Paris, Simone de Beauvoir paced among them, going over and over the tragedy of ZaZa's death.

She became obsessed with trying to understand what had happened, constructing various scenarios in her mind, listing things she might have done to help her friend and also listing what she called "sins and crimes against ZaZa by her family and others." For a month or so she struggled to write what she called "the biography of ZaZa, beginning with her earliest years." As always when she wanted to understand events in her life, she tried to turn it into fiction. Her role in this story was as her heroine's "friend and the observer of her life." She renamed ZaZa, calling her Anne, and thought that the reason she called herself Lucy was "in some clumsy attempt at symbolism: Lucy, the one who sheds the light."

From the beginning she had problems with narrative voice, or "how to distinguish the observer from the one she observes." But the one insurmountable problem was of organization and structure, of not knowing how to tell an anecdote succinctly or how to arrange transitions such as the passage of time and the movement of a character from one place to another. "The mechanics of fiction totally eluded me. It was very frustrating."

She was not ready to give up on converting ZaZa's life into fiction, but something happened to divert her temporarily from writing. Fernando Gerassi suggested that she and Sartre use what little remained of his inheritance to spend their summer holiday in Madrid. Castor was so happy with the thought of what would be her first trip outside France, she completely forgot that Marseille loomed ahead of her in two short months' time. She read guidebooks, consulted railroad timetables, plotted distances and made lists of all the things they must see. Sartre, as usual, left all the details up to her. When the day of departure arrived, he merely threw his few things into a knapsack and met her at the station at the time she appointed. It became their customary procedure for as long as they traveled together.

They traveled as they lived, absorbed in themselves. In her memoirs, Beauvoir wrote of her reactions to their first stop, Barcelona: "The city swarmed around us, indifferent to our existence; we could not understand its language, so what means could we devise to draw it into our lives? The challenge of this problem at once put me on my mettle."[15]

From Madrid, they made short trips to several other cities, among them Segovia and Toledo, Beauvoir rushing to see what sight lay around the corner or over the hill, Sartre following at a more leisurely pace, puffing contentedly on his pipe, happier still when she left him sitting in a café to think and write. "Sartre had all my natural curiosity," she wrote, "but was not so gluttonous for experience . . . I had made it my aim to explore the whole world, and my time was limited, so I didn't want to waste a single instant."[16]

These two months passed in a blur of happiness because of her desire to embrace everything Spanish. For the first time in her life, she lost all sense of time and lived only for the moment. She believed that she had succeeded in forgetting who she was, where she came from, and what she had to do in October.

Still, it came soon enough. They crossed the Spanish border at Hendaye, then took the Paris train together as far as Bayonne. He stayed on, continuing to Paris and Le Havre; she got off and waited in the fading light of an early-autumn evening for the train coming from Bordeaux that would take her to Marseille.

More than fifty years after she left Marseille, she still considered this "the unhappiest year of my life." She explained: "I did not want to leave Sartre, because I loved him then, passionately as well as intellectually, and I wanted to be with him. He was very sweet and very innocent and he often felt so sorry for the girls with whom he had other relationships. I think I was afraid that his natural sentimentality might make him a fool for some stupid girl's sobbing. It sounds as if I did not trust Sartre, but I did not trust myself as well, so I projected my worst fears onto what he might do or what might happen to him."

She coped with these fears by making her life deliberately simple. It was easy not to clutter her time with people, because she knew no one at all in Marseille, and as soon as she met the other teachers she decided they were "all very provincial, nonintellectual. I saw at once we had nothing in common, so I wasted no time on them." As for clothing, she bought two dark skirts and several shirtwaists whose severity she enhanced with plain men's neckties in dark solid colors, and she wrapped her hair in braids around her head. That done, she had no need to think further about her appearance. She moved first into a cheap hotel near the station, "to be as close as I could to Paris," and then into a comfortably bourgeois room in a house owned by another teacher in the school "who had lesbian attractions for me, but I was too naive to know it until much later when she made a pass at me which I rebuffed."

The students in the school were "bright enough. Fat little girls whose families wanted them to acquire a little polish before they got married to dumb boys from good families just like their own. The idea of such people joining in unions to perpetuate themselves for all eternity was so depressing that I tried not to think about it."

She taught them Gide, "because I had just finished reading Gide, and his writings were fresh in my mind. I had no real interest in teaching these girls and no desire to waste my time by preparing lessons they would not understand anyway, so I read Gide with them. That caused my only real problem: the parents complained to the school officials and I was frequently reprimanded, but I didn't care, so I did nothing to change."

As soon as she had neatly categorized everything external and established a daily routine, she realized there would be much solitary time to fill. Because she had never been in the south of France, and because she had so little money, she decided to spend her free half days on Thursday and all day on Sunday walking in the countryside. Hiking was popular among the other teachers in the school, and they dressed for it as solemnly as if it were an important social occasion. Because she scorned these people, she also scorned their dress, so she took her hikes in the same clothes she wore to teach and whatever shoes she happened to have, usually espadrilles. She disregarded everything about her colleagues, including their warning that a solitary woman walking along rugged mountain passes was inviting everything from accidental death to rape, and, although she never told them, she had at least one if not several of those frightening experiences on her outings.

She had reverted to the same kinds of dangerous behavior she favored when she first started to go out alone at night in Paris, hitchhiking as a matter of course because "I wanted to see a lot more of the countryside than I could cover on foot and I had no money for buses or cars." Years later, she volunteered that "those few incidents I wrote in my memoirs, about men who tried to rape me and things like that—I only described the least dangerous. My mother was still alive when I wrote that book [*Prime of Life*] and I didn't want to frighten her." She did not write about "fighting off a large man in a truck who believes he has the right to rape you, then beats you up before he throws you out into a gravel ditch because you kicked him where he hurts. Things like that," she concluded nonchalantly.

All these encounters took place on the road, never in a bar or a café as many had a few years previously when she was in Paris. "Oh, I was very careful about what bars I frequented in Marseille. That's a very dangerous city, you know. I was a teacher and I had to be careful of my reputation. In Marseille, they did not spend their free time in bars."

Her new reputation as a schoolteacher also brought a reconciliation of sorts within the family. Sartre loaned Hélène some of his inheritance money to visit her sister, and shortly afterward Françoise persuaded Georges to take a week's holiday in Marseille. She had become most impressed with her elder daughter, whom she saw as a woman with a stable profession and a good income. For a brief time she even persuaded herself of the possibility that Castor might revert to the respectable life of a spinster. When she arrived in Marseille and saw all the evidence of the continuing relationship with Sartre, she was disappointed. As for Georges, his outward behavior was gruff and noncommittal, but he did insist on taking his wife and daughter to dine in the best restaurants, as if he had plenty of money to spend. Unfortunately, his generosity was lost on Castor, who could not wait to put them both on the train for Paris so that she could resume her relentless walking.

After the Christmas holidays, which she spent in Paris with Sartre, she snapped out of this mood—at least she modified it—because he presented her with notebooks filled with writing and she had none for him: "The look on his face, so disappointed, jarred me from my obsession with my-self. I realized I had better get to work before I lost him."

Because of her earlier difficulties with narrative technique, she decided to begin by setting exercises for herself to describe people, rooms and out-door landscapes. She soon tired of this and tried again with the ZaZa material, only to encounter the same problems as before in transposing her friend's life into fiction.[17] She believed that whenever she departed from literal truth the fiction suffered, so now the task was to discern the inner truth within the events of her life and convey them to the reader. "I be-lieved I had only to determine these truths and they would somehow orga-nize themselves miraculously into a logical and comprehensive unity which would also be touching and moving and of great interest to my presumed readers. I had much to learn about writing fiction in those days."

But in the meantime, Christmas with Sartre had calmed her, and she returned to Marseille in a relatively happy frame of mind. She spent the late spring of 1932 walking in safer places, mostly within the city, compos-ing fictions in her head and writing them out in respectable cafés. In late March, a letter arrived telling her that her request for a transfer to the north of France had been granted and she would teach the next year at the Lycée Jeanne d'Arc in Rouen, half an hour by train from Sartre in Le Havre.

It made her happy, but she was happiest to think that she had passed her self-imposed test: she had been in exile, and she had survived. She hoped she would never again be separated from Sartre, but if it were or-dained, she knew she had the inner resources to sustain herself.

THIRTEEN

Rouen

W HEN SUMMER CAME, she packed her bags and sent them across the bay from Marseille to Narbonne, where she was to meet Sartre, then enduring his annual so-called holiday with his mother and stepfather, Monsieur and Madame Mancy. For the next two weeks she walked, hitchhiked or clambered aboard local buses and trains that meandered into the mountains along the southeastern edge of the Massif Central before edging back along the flat and fertile Mediterranean coast.

She was bursting with vitality and high spirits, partly because she had survived Marseille, partly because she and Sartre would be separated only by a short train ride when she moved to Rouen in the fall, but mostly because they were to go on a driving holiday through southern Spain and northern Africa with Madame Morel and Guille. They were able to afford the trip because Madame Morel paid for all the automobile expenses and because Castor had actually managed to save a little money during her year in Marseille. Sartre had almost nothing left from his grandmother's legacy, so it was the first time she paid for all their expenses.

This was not unusual, because from the beginning of their relationship Sartre insisted that any money each had must be considered as common and shared. She demurred, insisting that an important principle of their pact was for her to be independent in every way, especially financially, but he overruled her, saying that who supplied it was unimportant, what mattered was for both to have enough. Up to now, he was generally the one who had it, and he gave freely to anyone who needed or asked for it, without expecting to be repaid. His generosity became legendary, especially with the surprise presents he liked to give women. On one occasion he insisted that Hélène help him choose a new purse for Castor, walking her from store to store until she was satisfied that an expensive alligator handbag was exactly the right size and shape. When she assured him that it was the very one she would want for herself, he bowed ceremoniously and said, "Then it's yours, my little Rabbit," telling her the gift had been intended for her from the beginning.[1]

At first Castor had trouble with Sartre's casual attitude toward money, but when she saw how her fussing irritated him she soon learned to keep her worries to herself. Still, the question of money—whose, how much, and how it was spent—bothered Castor on this trip, and, indeed, it remained the one issue they squabbled over from time to time throughout their long life together.

Castor had never been introduced to Monsieur and Madame Mancy, and that did not change on this trip, since she and Sartre set off for Spain immediately after meeting at Narbonne. She did not know whether Sartre had even mentioned her to his mother, and she was too shy to ask, fearing he would interpret her question as a relic of her bourgeois upbringing[2] and tease her about it.

For Castor, the two months of travel in Madame Morel's car were blissful despite searing heat, numerous breakdowns, Guille's refusal to let anyone help with the driving and Sartre's indifference to the daily life of a tourist. It was Castor's first trip outside Europe, and North Africa was a fairy tale come true; while everyone else wilted from heat, indigestion and bad temper, she bloomed like a desert rose.

By the time she arrived in Rouen in October 1932 to teach literature and philosophy to the advanced students at the Lycée Jeanne d'Arc, she was almost giddy with happiness. She was now thinking of the year in Marseille as only a necessary hurdle she had had to surmount before she could be happy, almost managing to forget how she had frittered time away with no finished project to show for it. Never mind that she had written nothing complete, that her teaching had been slapdash, ill-prepared and thoughtless, that she had not grown intellectually, had made no new friends and had brought nothing new to her relationship with Sartre. She had spent the year virtually in stagnation of every possible kind, and it didn't seem to matter very much at all anymore.

Her way of thinking—what she called her "approach to life"—underwent a major change during the year in Marseille which would stand her in good stead from this time on, especially in regard to Sartre. Until this year, she had been unable to view her life with any sort of objectivity, so that she was constantly dredging up every past event, action or relationship, reconsidering what she might have done, what could have been and so on. If the year in Marseille had been good for anything, it was because there she learned to stop dwelling in the past, to admit that once something was done, finished or gone, it was truly over, and the best way to deal with such unwelcome psychic baggage was to dump it as quickly as possible. She had been entirely responsible for herself in her year alone, or, as she put it, "I had to make my own happiness, or at least my satisfaction." That meant living in the present, which for her was a truly astonishing change in her personality. All she really knew was that she was very happy because now she could see Sartre every half holiday during the week and they could spend every weekend together in Paris whenever they could collect enough money for the train.

This mindless bliss soon gave way to a more realistic appraisal of the situation. Sartre had never stopped thinking and writing, even scribbling steadily in a little pocket notebook as they bounced along Spanish roads, excusing himself from sightseeing to write in a café when one could be found, or on the running board of the car when one could not. She was able to ignore his abstraction while they were on holiday, and she could avoid his quizzical stares as long as she was running from one site to another, but once she was in Rouen it was impossible to evade the truth about herself. From the beginning of their pact, she had told him she wanted to live first and after that to express life through writing. He had told her that for him writing was life. Now it seemed that proximity to him would subject her to the most intense scrutiny she had thus far experienced.

Like all lovers who live together for the first time, they were discovering that each had quirks and habits the other disliked. Granted, their "living together" did not mean living in the same house, let alone the same town, but the nearness of their teaching posts and the isolation both felt because of the distance from Paris and the life they had known there forced them to rely on each other in a closeness of contact they had hitherto not had. "We had very few friends, and hardly any relations," Beauvoir wrote in her memoirs. There was one teacher at the lycée she considered worthwhile, and Sartre had several students whom he liked enough to call his disciples. But at first their few friends in Paris were all they had in common, and, as she noted, these were "our main topic of conversation."[3]

Still, each had some traits that the other found difficult to deal with, and this caused a certain number of misunderstandings, tiffs and miffed feelings, but neither he nor she wanted to risk any large rupture and so both stopped short before the possibility of an overt quarrel or an outright disagreement. She discovered that he was finicky about a great many things that had not seemed to matter before. He had become almost obsessively neat about his person, taking great care to see that his one suit was brushed and carefully hung to keep in the creases (in lieu of dry cleaning, which he could seldom afford), and he even tried to match his few shirts and neckties. She was still careless about her dress and person, taking a perverse pride in the squalor of her surroundings: having refused to lodge in a beautiful old house where the room was filled with charming country furniture and the French doors opened directly onto a garden,[4] she moved into a miserably furnished room in the cheap Hotel La Rochefoucauld where the only bathroom was on the floor below hers and was so filthy that she used it as seldom as possible.[5] For teaching, she continued to wear her Marseille outfits, which were nearly threadbare after a year of constant use. The rest of the time, she usually threw on what was nearest to hand, oblivious of its color or condition. On several occasions Sartre actually refused to take her out because her clothing was dirty or her stockings torn, but his rejection of her slovenliness bothered her less than when he turned away from the sloppiness of her mind.

However, she was attuned to his nuances of expression and sensitive enough to be embarrassed when he turned away from something she did that was particularly gauche. In many ways, she gave the impression of being large, booming and somewhat out of control. She barged stridently into public places, interrupted conversations thoughtlessly, and acted as if she were deliberately trying to disavow every remaining trace of politeness instilled by her upbringing. She was larger-boned than he, and when she stood straight (which was seldom, because in the early years of their relationship she slumped so that they would seem the same height) she was several inches taller. Sartre was a somewhat nervous man whose expressive hands moved constantly to caress a pipe, smooth his hair or adjust his glasses. He had a nervous tic which made him shrug his shoulders and duck his head in comical circular movements, but his voice, a mellifluous deep baritone which he often used to dramatic advantage, was normally as soft and tender as hers was strident.

Despite these superficial differences, as they began to develop a bond of common experiences and mutual acquaintances the little things they disliked about each other gradually became unimportant. What mattered, finally, was that they thought alike and, independently or together, came to the same opinions and conclusions about everything. More and more, they were becoming "we two," allied in ironic mockery of the world before them. Their pact became a sacred contract, founded "on truth, not on passion," as she told Colette Audry, her only friend at the lycée, before adding grimly, "and that's not an easy pact to live."[6]

She was told to meet Colette Audry by Nizan, who said, "The one person worth knowing in the entire town is the Communist Audry."[7] Nizan had joined the Communist Party and spent much of his time in meetings where he met Audry, who was not yet an active party member.

Audry first saw Beauvoir when "a brash girl burst into the teachers' room at school. She took a quick look at those of us who were sitting there reading or chatting quietly, and, without even a hello, said something like 'Which of you is Colette Audry?' I thought she looked like the perfect image of all the bourgeois things that I disliked. And as she was so clumsy and impolite, I didn't think there was much substance to her. Frankly, I had no desire to see her outside school. She was the one who persisted to seek my company, who insisted that we take lunch together, and gradually I began to see that this girl was someone interesting. Then she said to me, 'I have to introduce you to Sartre,' and that's how it began. I didn't realize until much later that an introduction to Sartre meant that I had passed the test they put people to, and that I was someone worth knowing. From that time on, especially the first two years she was in Rouen, from the end of 1932 to 1935, we saw each other all the time."

Audry was making a serious study of Marx's theory before committing herself to the Communist Party, trying to relate Marxism to interpretations of French politics and society, "and so to meet Sartre and to find that I could talk about these things with him and Castor was both exhilarating and liberating. There had been few people before this who could talk to me about these things, and we three took such pleasure in these conversations."

In one of the rare instances of her life when she confided to another woman, Castor talked to Audry about the changes her year in Marseille had made in her. "She told me that she had been living before this time as if she were in the midst of a permanent self-analysis and (this surprised me) on a quest for the personally spiritual—indeed, didn't she call her first book *Quand prime le spirituel?*—and he changed all that. It's true, Sartre swept all that away. He had a corrosive power on that sort of ideology which she found absolutely liberating, maybe even a little blasphemous at that stage. Sometimes when we were talking, I had the impression that some of the things he said shocked what remained of her bourgeois mentality and she didn't want him to know it. But soon the three of us were exchanging ideas so fast it sometimes made my head spin."

Audry also observed their relationship: "One more thing I must stress: one must not forget that her influence on him was just as great as his on her; that a boy like Sartre (because he *was* just a boy then) who had such analytic power, both destructive and polemical, within himself was all the same taken by this girl—devoted, enraptured, tied, bound to her; that he, and I know it was he, insisted not only on establishing, but then also keeping her in, this famous contract with him. Theirs was a new kind of relationship, and I had never seen anything like it. I cannot describe what it was like to be present when those two were together. It was so intense that sometimes it made others who saw it sad not to have it."

Audry was responsible for one of Castor's periodic bouts of interest in her appearance and surroundings. Audry described her own room as furnished "like an early hippie's, really," but to Castor it seemed magical with its scarves draped over bare light bulbs, Russian political posters on the walls, inexpensive rugs scattered about, and incense burning. There were always plants or flowers and a succession of little birds in a pretty cage. Audry also took care of herself, favoring tailored trousers and loose shirts in bright colors when not in school, thus creating her own personal style while still giving a vague nod in the direction of current fashion.

Because of her, Castor began to read fashion magazines again and actually bought a few new clothes, this time selecting ones that became her. She had a long, loose stride, so she shunned the straight skirts of the period and continued to favor dirndls that gathered comfortably at the waist and flowed loosely around her legs. As always, her blouses were loose and her shoes flat—partly because Sartre was shorter than she, mostly because she wanted comfort. She lost weight because she either ate simply or forgot to eat at mealtimes, and with all her walking her figure had become taut and lithe. She had become a beautiful woman, unconscious of her sensuality and unaware of the effect she had on people. She was an anomaly, a curious contradiction: so beautiful yet so clumsy, so intelligent yet so naive.

□

Her life, as she approached age twenty-five, was a curious contradiction as well. She decided she would write a novel, based on a new version of the ZaZa/Anne story. Using Stendhal's literary style as her model, she set it in Uzerche, around 1920.[8] She worked on it for two years until it became one of the few early attempts at writing that she actually finished. However, it was such an unsatisfying work that she resolved one day to cull the best parts for still another try at writing ZaZa's story. The only thing she claimed later to remember from this attempt to write fiction had nothing at all to do with it: while reading newspapers in search of local color and background material, she discovered that the owners' political orientation colored their reportage. Reading back issues of *L'Illustration* and *L'Humanité* made her aware of the reality of political positions in ways that her education and her conversations with such friends as Nizan and Audry had not done before.

Despite their proximity to politically committed friends, she and Sartre had no interest in political action. In a period during which the French government was buffeted by numerous ministerial crises, when the Stavisky Affair consumed the country much as the Watergate crisis did the United States forty years later, and when France was forced by the worldwide Depression to respond to events beyond its own economic boundaries, Sartre and Beauvoir whiled away long hours discussing the color of a new nail polish, the sexual proclivities of their friends, and all the lurid details of whatever sordid crime was reported in that week's equivalent of *The Police Gazette* or *The National Enquirer*. Also, Sartre had become devoted to the current craze, the yo-yo, and practiced tricks until he drove everyone crazy.

Describing herself in the decade 1929–39, Beauvoir wrote: "I was riddled with bourgeois idealism and aestheticism, blinded to political realities. But this blindness was not peculiar to me; it was a characteristic and almost universal failing of the period." Later, in a similar vein, she wrote: "Today it astounds me to think how we could have stood by and watched all this [events in Germany in 1933] so calmly. . . . [P]olitical articles bored me to tears: I sank under their weight."[9]

In fact, what consumed her most during the Rouen years was the avoidance of politics or political realities. All she wanted was the continuation of her own tranquil personal situation, for she had never been happier. Even her teaching, which began with a certain amount of friction between her, the headmistress and several of the senior teachers, had settled down once they discovered she was a brilliant young woman with a natural flair for her subject and once she discovered that here, unlike in Marseille, there were some very intelligent girls in her classes with whom she could exchange ideas.

The only worry was the world political situation, but it was vague and distant, and, like most of her compatriots, she tried assiduously to ignore it. She invented a personal philosophy of "the solitary man," which she believed excused her from "the futile contingencies of daily life." However, "the position I had adopted suited me somewhat ill. . . . I was really indulging in escapism, putting myself into blinkers so as to safeguard my peace of mind."[10]

So daily life continued smoothly. She went to school, ate lunch with Colette Audry, spoke occasionally to the one or two teachers whom she found tolerable, even accepted dinner invitations from the parents of a few of her pupils. For exercise and diversion, she walked among the streets of the old quarter of Rouen, or along the riverbank where the city's slums were clustered.

GéGé often made the trip from Paris, either alone during the week or on the weekend with Hélène. They and Castor spent long hours cloistered in her room, brewing endless cups of tea over an illegal gas ring, discussing their male friends and exchanging bottles of nail polish, which had become Castor's new obsession. Once she stopped biting her nails, she realized she had pretty hands, and for the rest of her life she kept her nails carefully manicured beneath a blanket of purple, scarlet or crimson laquer. When Sartre was there, he paid as much attention to every detail of the manicuring process as she did, because he was as fascinated by her hands as she was by his.[11]

On weekends she and Sartre were together, either in Paris or alternately in Rouen or Le Havre, always with a small but constant circle of friends, old and new. A French Algerian whom they knew from Sartre's days at the Cité Universitaire, Marc Zuore,[12] was teaching in Amiens, and they saw him often, especially after he was transferred to Rouen. Two of Sartre's students, Jacques-Laurent Bost and Lionel de Roulet, became his "premier disciples" and were invited more and more frequently to spend time with them.[13] In Paris there was never enough time to see the Nizans, Madame Morel and Guille, and their small band of friends from the university.

They often had just enough money to get to Paris and back and depended on friends to put them up and feed them. Sometimes, when no one could help them, they stayed up all night and stumbled off the train on Monday morning exhausted, dirty and famished, and went to teach their classes in that condition. This only increased the already strong opposition of parents and other teachers, who considered it scandalous to have two such disreputable persons in positions of influence and authority over impressionable students.

Neither would even consider staying with their families in Paris. Sartre frequently could not escape from boring Sunday-afternoon luncheons and still took a summer holiday with his mother and stepfather, but Castor avoided her parents as much as possible, inventing a million reasons why she could not dine with them but could stop only long enough for coffee or something equally brief. Georges and Françoise never visited

Rouen as they had Marseille. They were aware of how their daughter was regarded by others in her community and were frankly unwilling to face the possibility that they might be judged in the same light as she.

Thus the world Sartre and Beauvoir created for themselves remained inviolate. They saw themselves, in their own words, as "the center of a small universe," and their friends called them "the two major planets around whom the smaller suns and moons radiated."[14] They pored endlessly over the smallest details of their and their friends' lives, convinced that only they were capable of validating the reality of existence, that no others existed except as creations within their privileged world. The "elves," as Beauvoir had earlier described herself and Sartre, had managed to remain childlike, free from all the constraints of adult life despite having to earn their living within an adult world.

Everything was fine for the first year or so they were posted to Rouen and Le Havre, but then they themselves changed their game. However, they forgot to change the rules, and it turned into a free-for-all. They agreed to enlarge their couple into "the trio," and the resulting complications were so many and varied that it preoccupied them for several years to come.

One of Simone de Beauvoir's students was a White Russian, a young girl of seventeen named Olga Kosakievicz,[15] daughter of a French woman who had gone to Russia as governess to a wealthy family and married one of the sons. Olga, the first of their two daughters, was born in Russia shortly before the 1917 Revolution, and their second daughter, Wanda, was born in France, which they considered exile. The Kosakievicz family lived in Beuzeville, a tiny village north of Rouen near the Channel coast, and in this austere setting the two daughters were educated at home in an avant-garde manner during their formative years before being sent off to a succession of restrictive convent boarding schools. Olga went to the Lycée Jeanne d'Arc for her philosophy baccalauréat, after which her parents had already decided she would attend medical school.

Olga felt that she had been educated at cross-purposes all her life: first having been taught to be a freethinking individualist, then being directed to channel all this learning into socially accepted ways of thinking and behaving. She found an ally in her teacher, Simone de Beauvoir, who was always ready to champion any rebellion she associated with shocking the bourgeoisie. Olga's confusion was exacerbated by her inherent shyness coupled with her feeling that she was an outsider in French society. She was a thin pale blonde of dreamy demeanor who spoke fluent English and Russian as well as French, and who sometimes puzzled herself by thinking and speaking in several languages at once.

Castor had decided in Marseille that the best way to cope with a teaching situation she disliked was to ignore all her students except those who forced her to recognize them. She treated her students in Rouen the same way, so at first Olga, who sat in the back of the classroom, who never opened her mouth and who usually wrote mediocre essays and examination papers, was merely a pupil upon whom she did not have to expend time and energy. The surprise came toward the end of the first year, when this timid girl, who later admitted she had not understood the question, wrote a highly provocative essay on the philosophy of Kant, marked by "originality, daring and flights of fancy." After this, it was difficult for Beauvoir to ignore the wispy creature who either filled her essay books with astonishing intelligence or else unapologetically turned in blank pages.

Beauvoir and Olga agreed later that it was Olga who sought the company of her teacher. In a film made when Beauvoir was seventy and Olga sixty-one, Olga recalled her first sight of Beauvoir by describing the severe old woman she replaced, so that "when we saw Castor, it was incredible. She was beautiful, young, wore makeup and was alive!"[16] It didn't take Olga and the other students long to discover that this colorful creature lived in a hotel near the train station, spent much of her time in Paris and was the lover of a man who openly spent weekends in her hotel room.

From the moment Beauvoir announced to the class that "to my great surprise, the best composition was written by Mademoiselle Kosakievicz," the schoolgirl's crush began. Olga began to stay after class, to wait in a café until she could walk the teacher home, and, soon, to spend idle hours in Beauvoir's hotel room chatting and gossiping. It wasn't long before the teacher introduced her favorite pupil to her lover.

Sartre thought Olga a charming girl, and was actually pleased that Castor was acquiring her own disciples in Rouen. Given Sartre's proclivities, it was probably inevitable that his attraction to Olga should become sexual, but the affair did not actually begin until 1934 when he returned from a year in Berlin.

On one of their weekends in Paris, they met Sartre's fellow *normalien* and friend Raymond Aron for drinks, in what has since come to be considered an encounter of epic, if not mythic, proportions. Aron was home on holiday from the year he was spending at the French Institute in Berlin, where he had a scholarship to study philosophy and write a thesis. In her memoirs Beauvoir remembered an apricot cocktail, the specialty of the house; in his, Aron recalled a simple glass of beer. However they reconstructed life in their memoirs, while they were actually imbibing the drink Aron said the liquor reflected Husserl's remark that a phenomenologist could create philosophy from anything in life. From then on, Sartre regarded that casual comment as the moment when he began to formulate his own Existential system. He also decided that he too wanted the same exposure to German philosophy as Aron and applied for the scholarship to succeed him the following year. Sartre received it, and he and Aron exchanged places, with Aron taking over as philosophy professor in Le Havre.

The year in Berlin was a godsend for Sartre. He had always hated teaching, calling it "a hard blow,"[17] within a life that was "growing narrower and narrower." Nothing seemed to correspond to the life he had envisioned as a student: at age thirty-two, he recalled a diary entry he wrote when twenty-two, the Swiss philosopher Rodolphe Töpffer's dictum that "whoever is not famous at twenty-eight must renounce glory forever." Sartre believed it, thinking himself mired in an unrewarding profession, unable to write anything publishable and feeling trapped in a "constructed" relationship. He and Beauvoir lived in "total sincerity and complete mutual devotion," sacrificing "impulses, and any confusion there might be in us, to that permanent *directed* love we had constructed." His view of what they both yearned for was "a life of disorder . . . a way of being drowned in ourselves, and of feeling without knowing that we were feeling. . . . We needed immoderation, having for too long been moderate." He appraised himself before his year in Berlin: "In short, I took the transition to manhood as badly as possible." But nothing really changed: "I had a year's holiday in Berlin, rediscovered the irrresponsibility of youth there, and then, on my return, I was recaptured by Le Havre and my life as a teacher—perhaps even more bitterly."

So he was ripe for "that strange, black mood which turned to madness around March of that year," 1935.

Beauvoir's situation before he went to Berlin could not have been more different from his: granted, her novel had not gone well, and teaching was something she did haphazardly at best, but still she was content because he was so close at hand and each of them was still the center of the other's life. His role in hers was paramount, and she rationalized her mediocre academic career by telling herself that he was more important to her than anything else. Time after time, in her memoirs, in interviews and in conversations, she spoke of how hard she worked to bend her will to his, to accept his view of a person or situation as the correct one, to contain her thinking within the parameters he prescribed for their "constructed" accord. But he was a will-'o-the-wisp: just as she was about to understand what he thought or wanted, he darted off in quite another direction. Now, because he bemoaned the direction of their life, with their friendships seemingly formed, their careers laid out before them, their writings basically defined if still not written, she did, too, but hers was a lament of complaisance rather than an individual cry from the heart. What mattered most for her was to be in agreement with him.

Even though she was sad to think of him so far away, even farther from her than when she was in Marseille, "he wanted to go to Berlin so badly that naturally I wanted it for him as well." However, it had not occurred to her to apply to study there, because she was "only a teacher," whereas "he was a philosopher." As for the possibility of her going with him in another capacity, perhaps as a translator or even a teacher, "we never considered it, because we were good little bureaucrats and I had to keep my job."

Thus their relationship fell into the pattern which continued throughout their life together, one defined mainly by his needs and desires. Once again she coped by creating some patterns of behavior which in their own way were as obsessive as those of her year in Marseille. This time she substituted reading for walking, making detailed lists of books about the history of France and then dutifully plowing through them one after the other in chronological order, claiming a strong desire and serious need to understand her country. She wrote nothing at all in this period and blamed her stagnation on three things: Sartre's absence, her recognition that the ZaZa/Anne novel was a failure and the depressing atmosphere of Rouen. Much as she loved France, the Normandy countryside was too well manicured for her taste, and Rouen "the most bourgeois and complacent part of it." At school, she watched in fascination as Colette Audry immersed herself in politics and wondered why she herself could find no outlet but Sartre on which to concentrate her attention.

"What were we, really?" she asked herself rhetorically. "No husband, no children, no home, [no] social polish, and twenty-six years old: when you reach this age you want to feel your feet on the ground."[18]

She allowed herself to become involved in all sorts of backbiting mischief with Sartre's former neighbor at the Cité Universitaire, Marc Zuore, who was still teaching in Amiens. A bisexual, he dangled tantalizing hints of his homosexuality before her while dallying with a succession of women (including a teacher at her school) to assuage any doubt among his superiors about his sexual orientation. Zuore brought out disagreeable negative qualities that she had not known she had, and even though she resented her own behavior she found it impossible to stay aloof from his manipulation. It was as if they were in competition to see who could spread the most damaging gossip about the other teachers. She also became involved once again in a "dalliance" with Guille, who was temporarily estranged from Madame Morel.

Meanwhile, in Berlin, Sartre was having a listless affair with the wife of a fellow student at the French Institute whom he and Beauvoir agreed to nickname "the Moon Woman" because of her round face and dreamy disposition.[19] Of all his affairs, this was one of the few that Beauvoir accepted with equanimity, because Sartre's strongest emotion throughout was the thrill of cuckolding the woman's husband. Sartre's letters were filled with lurid details of the affair and the gossip of the French Institute; Beauvoir responded with the intrigues she fell into among the teachers in Rouen or with their friends in Paris.

The best that can be said about her conduct and activity was that she marked time and it passed. Olga's friendship was the only bright spot in a year clouded by malaise, pettiness and gossip. They cemented a relationship in which Olga gave unqualified devotion to her teacher and Castor was delighted that the young woman wanted to be her disciple. It was the first of a succession of intense friendships Simone de Beauvoir formed with her students, all of whom subsequently acquiesced to sexual liaisons with Sartre.[20]

In the biographical account he wrote in his 1939 notebooks (collected as the *War Diaries*), Sartre described the two-year period from March 1935 to March 1937 as "the nadir at the time of my madness and my passion for O."[21] In retrospect, he thought the madness "beneficial" because it caused him to abandon "bourgeois optimism" for "a world that was blacker, but less insipid." His passion for Olga "burned away my workaday impurities. . . . I grew thin as a rake, and distraught: farewell to all my comforts!" Olga was "precisely everything we desired and who made this quite clear to us." He continued:

> And then we fell, Castor and I, beneath the intoxicating spell of naked, instant consciousness, which seemed only to feel, with violence and purity. I placed her [Olga] so high then that, for the first time in my life, I felt myself humble and disarmed before someone, felt that I wanted to learn.

In all Sartre's known comments and writings about Simone de Beauvoir, the "necessary love" of his life, he never once used language of this intensity.

Sartre wrote of Olga with unbridled passion, but Beauvoir's account of the trio is curiously distanced. It unfolds gradually, beginning with the remark, "This friendship of ours must have rested on solid foundations, for me as well as for her, since today, twenty-five years later, she still occupies a specially privileged place in my life."[22] That said, Beauvoir sets the scene with external details: telling of how Olga failed twice to pass the medical qualifying examinations; of how she persuaded Olga's parents to let her tutor the girl privately; of how she and Olga conspired to get her moved into a room at the same hotel.

Both Sartre and Beauvoir threw themselves enthusiastically into their "Pygmalian and Galatea" relationship with Olga. She was their "tabula rasa," and they were sure that their projected curriculum would change her from a "noble savage" into the living representation of their philosophy. What they did not bargain for was Olga's desperate fear of failure: having failed the same examination twice, she preferred to do nothing rather than risk another failure, to pass the time instead in languid idleness while living on the monthly allowance sent by her parents so that she would not have to work while she studied.

Ironically, Olga managed to reverse everyone's role by being passive. Her absolute refusal to do anything intellectually or personally constructive provided Sartre and Beauvoir with the perfect excuse to wring their hands in mock-anguished helplessness while merrily following her prankish adolescent behavior. Olga provided the excuse they needed to push the reality of their lives, ages and professional responsibilities into some remote corner of their minds.

All her life, Simone de Beauvoir worried about growing old. Indeed, many of her attitudes, such as thinking herself too old to be sexually active or attractive before she was even forty, might be laughable were they not so sad. Now, at the age of twenty-six, she envisioned herself as being on the brink of old age but saved from it for a little while by her friendship with the childlike Olga, aged seventeen. As they grew older, Sartre was amused by Beauvoir's obsession with age and death and frequently chided her, but at this time he was even more obsessive about it than she. One day Beauvoir casually mentioned that his hairline was receding, and for the next year he agonized over growing bald (his hair thinned, but he was never completely bald). He had eaten too well in Berlin and gained weight on the heavy German cooking, so now he annoyed everyone with his constant futile attempts to diet and his extreme posturing to make himself look taller and thinner. He was a hypochondriac of sorts, and every time Beauvoir saw him he had imagined a new near-fatal malady, symptoms of which he recounted endlessly. The manner in which he expressed his obsessions was laughable, but his consternation was serious. He told all this to Beauvoir, looking for her sympathy certainly, but more for her denial that any of this was happening to him. He needed her to confirm that he was still young, dynamic and vital, charged with sexual energy. But though he desperately needed her reassurance, now he hardly ever demonstrated his virility or expressed his passion toward her. He made her his constant confidante, but only rarely his sexual partner. She had to find other outlets for her sexuality: "usually brief encounters with people I knew then—their names don't matter now. Mostly I just dealt with it, got it over with. After a while it stopped being important. I didn't need it as much."

Although nothing sexual had yet occurred between Sartre and Olga, there were strains in the fragile tension among the three of them. The first happened after Sartre experimented with mescaline in February 1935. Dr. Daniel Lagache, one of his colleagues at the Ecole Normale, had become a medical doctor specializing in psychiatric disorders at the Hôpital Sainte-Anne in Paris, where he conducted research in drug therapy. Sartre's general dissatisfaction with his life had resulted in what Beauvoir thought then was "just a little unhappiness," but what she later came to believe was "probably a serious depression." But as she also said on many occasions, "Psychology was not my strong suit, and I was especially determined not to use it on Sartre."[23] Her response was to be excessively cheerful and urge him to think positively, which only depressed him further and exacerbated the increasing distance between them. Philosophy in the abstract was the only subject they could talk about without considerable awkwardness. Even the scrupulous critiques of his writing usually ended with her scolding, urging him to forget his life and get on with his work.

So when his old friend Lagache described the visual hallucinations sometimes induced by his experiments with mescaline, Sartre decided to take the drug because he was then working on a study of the imagination and he thought mescaline would heighten the visual sensations he wanted to write about. Beauvoir went with him to Paris and waited while he checked himself into the hospital for the afternoon, then went off to wait for him at Madame Morel's. They expected that at most the drug would cause several days of hallucinations, but the residual effects were so powerful that Sartre spent varying periods of time during the next several years imagining himself at the mercy of giant crabs, dung beetles, vultures and lobsters.

"Doctors have told me that the mescaline could not possibly have provoked this attack," Beauvoir wrote.

> All that his session at Sainte-Anne's did for Sartre was to furnish him with certain hallucinatory patterns. It was, beyond any doubt, the fatigue and tension engendered by his philosophical research work that brought his fears to the surface again. We afterwards concluded that they were the physical expression of a deep emotional malaise: Sartre could not resign himself to going on to "the age of reason," to full manhood.[24]

So she collected him from the hospital, spent the weekend soothing his delusions, and took him back to Le Havre, entrusting his care to Bost and some of his other students. That done, she returned to Rouen and began another round of squabbling and gossip with Olga and Marc Zuore, who was temporarily infatuated with her.

Sartre came to visit as usual on weekends and holidays. At first Beauvoir devoted herself to soothing his hallucinations, but his continuing depression irritated her in ways she could not understand. She was uneasy in the face of Sartre's inability to get well or, more likely, his unwillingness to cure himself. Her own illnesses had all been physical, either colds or flu, sometimes in severe forms, but with every one of them she knew it was just a matter of time until she got better. She had neither tolerance nor patience for the illness of others, "*especially* for the illness of Sartre."[25] Rather than let him see her petulance, she found it easier to invent other duties and obligations. She, who had devoted herself to Sartre for the past few years, suddenly burned with the desire to do such things as attend literary conferences in Paris; she, who had scorned any contact with the teachers in her school, suddenly discovered that no one else could solve their personal problems. She even began to write again, claiming that she "suddenly found the way into the 'ZaZa' story" that would let her finish it. This was the only part of the elaborate facade of excuses she had constructed between herself and Sartre that came true, for she did indeed finish the story "Lisa" that spring. But because she had created all these reasons why she could not take care of Sartre, she also had to delegate a surrogate nursemaid, and that, of course, was Olga.

In her account of the situation—largely chronological—in her memoirs, Beauvoir implies that Olga and Sartre were still only friends at this point, not yet lovers: "they liked being together, and neither of them made demands on the other."[26]

The other event which shifted the emotional weight of the trio came about because of Zuore, who was especially sensitive to sexual nuances. When he saw that Olga and Sartre were attracted to each other, he could not resist the thrill of competition and plied Olga with his most charming behavior until she became infatuated with him. His behavior fluctuated between competing with Sartre as a rival for Olga's attentions and flirting with Sartre for his. Zuore preened and strutted, enjoying the game itself more than either prize he might win. For Sartre, it was the chase itself that counted, because actual sexuality meant increasingly less and less. To him, Zuore was simply competition to be bested on an intellectual level, as Beauvoir was well aware: "Sartre insisted on exclusive rights, no one should mean as much to Olga as he did."[27]

"Would he have asserted himself thus if Olga had shown no interest in Marco?" she asked herself in the memoirs before giving the sad but honest answer: "I suppose the answer is yes, and that Marco was only an excuse."

Once again Sartre required her complicity in his affairs and she had to rationalize her response: "We spent hours thrashing out such problems. I did not mind this; I much preferred the idea of Sartre angling for Olga's emotional favors to his slow collapse from some hallucinatory psychosis."

What was disquieting, however, was the way in which Sartre elevated Olga to the pinnacle of importance in his life. Her slightest whim took precedence over all else, and on the brief occasions he was alone with Beauvoir he spent all his time demanding that she accede to Olga's wishes. Slowly it dawned on her that her place had been usurped in his affections by someone she had put there. Her response was curiously evasive: "For my own part, the book on which I was now working absorbed all my interest. Yet during these two years I had only gone on writing out of loyalty to my past, and because Sartre pushed me into it. . . . I therefore determined not to allow Olga too important a place in my own life, since I could not cope with the disorder she would have sown there." She rationalized further: "Little by little, however, I began to compromise: my need to agree with Sartre on all subjects outweighed the desire to see Olga through other eyes than his."

So the deadly game began in earnest, with all power concentrated for the moment in Olga, who toyed with both of them. She teased her former mentor by abruptly demanding that Sartre go off alone with her, and sheepishly he went, preening himself before Zuore. When he returned, he told Beauvoir all the details of what they had done, like a little boy expecting his mother's blessing. If she was slow to give it, he chastised her for being selfish or jealous, saying, "That's not like you, Castor," until he forced words of approval from her reluctant mouth. Then, even more abruptly, Olga would turn on Sartre, telling him to go away so that she could be alone with Castor, and would beg her forgiveness, scolding or crying until the older woman cradled the younger in her arms and assured her that they were the same as they had always been. Worst of all was when Olga would run off with Zuore, skipping out of the café in Rouen in front of the cathedral where they all four liked to sit in the window and mock the passersby. As they ran across the square and down the crooked street under the clock tower out of sight, holding hands and laughing, Beauvoir was left behind to comfort Sartre. She felt sorry for the disrespectful way Olga had treated him, but sorrier still for the two of them, left behind like two useless and worn-out objects. These were the moments when her twenty-six years weighed heavily on her, but what weighed even more heavily was the problem of how to mollify Sartre, for whom Olga's temporary abandonment mattered so much more.

So the dynamics of the trio changed constantly, according to Olga's shifting moods, Sartre's steadfast determination to dominate her, and Beauvoir's reluctant complicity.

> Caught by the magic . . . each of us felt himself playing a double role—enchanter and enchanted at once. At such moments the "trio" seemed a dazzling success, and yet cracks began to appear in the splendid edifice almost immediately. The edifice as such was Sartre's work, though he had not . . . so much built it as called it into being, simply by virtue of his attachment to Olga. For my own part, though I vainly tried to achieve satisfaction from the relationship, I never felt at ease with it. . . . [W]henever I thought of the trio as a long-term project, stretching ahead for years, I was frankly terrified.

What the couple had not realized was that Olga's passivity was the screen behind which she kept her stubborn independence hidden. She was as aware of her position within the trio as Beauvoir was:

> Though we valued her youth more highly than our own experience, her role was, nevertheless, that of a child—a child up against an adult couple united by unfailing emotional bonds. However devotedly we consulted her interests, it was we who controlled the actual destiny of the trio. We had not established any real equality in our relationship with her, but had rather annexed her to ourselves. . . . This idea infuriated her, because she was far fonder of me than she was of him; and her anger with him was, in a sense, directed against me, too.

Colette Audry confirmed Beauvoir's supposition: "Quite honestly, I did not witness everything that went on with them, but I saw enough to know that it was an awful experience for Olga. They made her the invited one, the third party in their relationship, and she had to spend most of her time defending herself. The major complicity was between them, and they required that she bend to their wishes. The poor girl was too young to know how to defend herself really."

Nevertheless, Olga was able to convert the weakness of her position in the trio into one of power because of her reluctance to become Sartre's sexual partner. She liked his quick wit and the amusing aspects of his personality, but was repelled by his body and confused and embarrassed that she felt this way toward the mesmerizing genius before whom everyone succumbed as "he seduced and conquered young girls by explaining their souls to them."[28] Sartre was as awkward and ungainly as Olga was nimble and quick; she made him feel young, but he made her feel old and weighed down by his ugliness. She resented his sexual attentions and resented even more Beauvoir's taking it for granted that whatever Sartre wanted, Olga should consider it her honor and duty to provide. A great deal of her seemingly irrational behavior was actually her rational attempt to shake Beauvoir's implacable acquiescence to Sartre, who became more and more "like a greedy child; always 'I want, I want,' and she falling all over herself to say, 'Yes, yes, precious spoiled darling, you shall have it, I shall get it for you.' "[29]

Olga began to act out her anger through irrational behavior, such as disappearing for long stretches of time without explaining her whereabouts. She took to solitary drinking in the middle of the day until she fell down drunk, often in the middle of the Hotel La Rochefoucauld lobby, where guests simply stepped over her or the proprietor kicked her awake. Once, in Paris, where they took her to meet Sartre's former lover Simone Jollivet, now living with the producer-director Charles Dullin, she burned a cigarette into her hand while they all stared in horror.[30]

Olga forced Beauvoir not only to recognize the girl's independence but also to face the fact that for a long time she herself had not shared Sartre's view of what their life together should be. She had to admit that "when I said, 'We are one person,' I was dodging the issue." However, Beauvoir's ultimate need remained to be in agreement with him, which resulted in the constant denial of her true feelings. What hurt most was that with Olga "Sartre . . . let himself go, to the great detriment of his emotional stability, and experienced feelings of alarm, frenzy and ecstasy such as he had never known with me. The agony which this produced in me went far beyond mere jealousy: at times I asked myself whether the whole of my happiness did not rest upon a gigantic lie."

However, lying to herself kept crippling bouts of jealousy at bay and gave her the willpower to concentrate on her writing. The ZaZa/Anne story had grown into three separate finished ones: "Lisa," "Marcelle" and "Chantal," and she was now deep into the revision of "Anne." She was thinking of moving parts of it into another, separate story with another girl's name (it would become "Marguerite"). She planned to find some connecting theme with which to unify them and then offer it to publishers as a book sometime in the coming year.

It was all she thought she had to look forward to, as she had resigned herself to another year in Rouen. Both she and Sartre had applied to teach in Paris, but she thought it unlikely that such a plum would come her way. She knew that evaluations of her teaching at the Lycée Jeanne d'Arc had been mediocre at best, and she feared that her antics outside the classroom might result in disciplinary action, though that never happened. So it was a great surprise to open her annual assignment letter in the spring and learn that she had been transferred to the Lycée Molière in Paris. Although she had no proof, she believed that an influential parent in Rouen had brought the transfer about. "I wasn't actually dismissed from

Rouen, but no one tried to convince me to stay. I wasn't invited back, and no one was sorry to see me go."[31]

Sartre also received a transfer, to Laon—about an hour northeast of Paris, from where he planned to commute to his classes. He took it for granted that Beauvoir would persuade Olga's parents to let her go with them. Secretly,[32] she veered between hoping that the Kosakieviczes would force Olga to return home and wanting to take her "little satellite" to Paris. Olga used all her considerable powers of persuasion to assure her parents that she had spent a brilliant year. Whether or not they believed her, they gave her permission to go to Paris.

Sartre and Beauvoir sent Olga home to her parents for the summer while they went off to Rome alone—thus guaranteeing that their life in Paris would begin with her spite at being abandoned. But for the moment all that mattered was that they had once again escaped the confinement of the provinces and the constraints of adult life. Sartre was deliriously happy that the trio would continue; Beauvoir concentrated her happiness on the summer in Rome.

FOURTEEN

Paris

EVERYONE, IT SEEMED, came back to Paris in the fall of 1936. Even though Sartre was teaching in Laon, frequent fast trains made it seem like a distant suburb of the capital, and every weekend and twice during the week Beauvoir met his train at the Gare du Nord. She moved into a shabby hotel in Montparnasse which horrified her mother, who refused to set foot in it for fear of contamination, and who evaded questions about her daughter by saying only that she was teaching at the Lycée Molière.

Sartre was still not welcome in the Beauvoir household, and Beauvoir had not yet been introduced to his family. She had accepted—having no alternative—his ritualistic Sunday lunches with his mother and stepfather and the annual vacations he took with them, but she did not follow his example. The few times when she did go to her parents' apartment, Georges usually launched into political diatribes, goading her into arguments which led to bitter remarks about her personal situation. "You are a dried-up old prune," he shouted, "you are too old to think anymore, never mind to write a decent book. You'll never amount to more than the Worm's whore."[1] She had no rebuttal for remarks like these, so absence seemed the most prudent action.

Understandably, her reliance on friends increased. She began to call them her "real family," and later "the Family." Sartre too adopted this term, and they often congratulated themselves for having invented a new social order in which one rejected the relatives of birth and chose others to be the true members of one's family. The unchanging core of this new Family consisted of Beauvoir and Sartre, Olga and Bost, and Olga's sister, Wanda.[2]

Olga had a smaller, cheaper room in the same hotel as Beauvoir, and Bost had transferred to the Sorbonne and was living in the attic of his novelist brother Pierre's apartment. Now that they were all in Paris, the group began to call him "Little Bost" to distinguish him from his brothers, for he was the youngest son in a large and distinguished Protestant Parisian family. "Little Bost," like Sartre and Beauvoir, never invited any of his friends to visit him, because his family was as distressed at his bohemian way of life as theirs. Of them all, only Sartre was on good terms with his mother, as he was still "little Poulou," her adored and pampered darling.

For a time, besides Beauvoir, Sartre, Olga, Wanda and Bost, the Family included Zuore (also transferred to a Parisian lycée), who lived one street away in a slightly better hotel than Beauvoir's. Fernando and Stépha had been in Paris for almost a year with their infant son, John, living a hand-to-mouth existence because his paintings did not sell, and depending on Stépha's odd jobs such as translations and typing. Hélène ostensibly still lived at home, but was there only to sleep in the coldest weather, preferring her unheated studio in all but the most extreme conditions. GéGé had married unhappily and seized any excuse to leave her fractious domestic situation to be with her friends. Guille married his cousin, so Beauvoir and Sartre seldom saw him anymore, but they still dropped in casually and frequently at Madame Morel's or went driving with her on weekend excursions. They treated Guille's domesticity with the same mocking disrespect as they did the Nizans'. However, Sartre needed Nizan, who was fairly prominent in the publishing world, so their remarks about him and his wife were reserved for their private gossip sessions.

Most of their friends from their university days—Aron, Merleau-Ponty, La Gache and Gandillac among them—either had married or were about to marry, and had settled down into traditional patterns of adult life. In their gossip sessions, Sartre and Beauvoir often mocked Aron and Merleau-Ponty and their insistence on "facing reality" or "taking an adult stance" toward some political or social issue. It was not the position they mocked, merely their friends' language and insistence upon "grown-up" or "adult" behavior.

Beauvoir and Sartre were content to invent behavior as they went along, confident that their "open approach to life" and their "honest reception of all experience and encounters" would "bring the most satisfaction, the most happiness." They were encouraged in this by the matter-of-fact way their unorthodox liaison was accepted by everyone from the director of the Ministry of Education to most of the people they were meeting in the literary world on their increasingly frequent forays into Saint-Germain-des-Prés.

The two entered café life with a vengeance, making the Dôme and other Left Bank cafés frequented by international expatriates their headquarters. Although Sartre was constantly rushing around Paris promoting his writing to various editors and publishers, until 1938 he and Beauvoir still had not met any of the "newly important" French writers, artists or other intellectuals; Queneau, Leiris and Giacometti, for example, all three later to become good friends, were only names to them. Beauvoir and Sartre had no interest in anyone old, already established or foreign. She thought it was James Joyce whom she saw at Sylvia Beach's Shakespeare and Company Bookstore, "an old man in a too-large overcoat slouched in a chair at the back, holding a magnifying glass under his nose," but as it was the period of her greatest interest in Faulkner and Dos Passos, she "paid no attention at all to the man who might have been Joyce."[3]

She and Sartre were interested in young people who were likely to influence the direction of contemporary French intellectual thought, so they were thrown back upon the old friends from the university and the new ones from their provincial teaching for companionship. Within this small group, new liaisons formed and disbanded with what Beauvoir later called "sometimes painful coupling and uncoupling but usually fairly boring regularity and predictability." The first part of her remark was truer than the last, and most of the pain radiated out from one fairly constant center—Olga.

Twice each week Beauvoir went patiently to the Gare du Nord to wait for Sartre because it was sometimes her only chance to be alone with him while he was in Paris. Their late-night gossip sessions had all but ended, and she considered herself lucky when he took time for a hasty cup of coffee in the station buffet. Usually he needed to rush off to an appointment, and then their only time alone together was on the Métro. He always greeted her affectionately, but as soon as the formalities were over he quizzed her about Olga, putting her in the awkward position of having to reassure him that he was the most important person in Olga's life. It was especially disconcerting because Olga spent most of the time Sartre was in Paris trying to avoid him, if not actually hiding from him, and Beauvoir knew it.

Olga and Bost had discovered each other. At first theirs was a conspiracy of childish delight to hide from Zuore, who had transferred his affections from Olga to Bost and now pursued him with comical ardor. Olga confided this to Beauvoir, and thus Beauvoir became the unwilling accomplice in Olga's deception of Sartre. Also, Beauvoir had long been enchanted by the quicksilver personality of Bost and got a vicarious satisfaction of sorts fom Olga's accounts of their lovers' games and quarrels. Zuore, thwarted by everyone, spread gossip thickly, and soon it seemed that everyone was angry with everyone else.

Olga's friendship with Beauvoir had deepened since they moved to Paris and were free from Sartre's presence during the week while he taught in Laon. Olga shared Beauvoir's voyeuristic inclinations, and they vied to amuse each other with the bizarre, the weird and the antisocial, usually finding them all in some cheap Latin Quarter dive or strip show. Beauvoir quickly realized that she was spending almost all her free time with Olga, and also that the difference in their ages had ceased to matter. Theirs had become a friendship of equals because Olga's fascination with society's underside gave her a more sophisticated, if jaded, knowledge of humanity that Beauvoir, despite her travels, had not yet encountered. Nothing shocked Olga, no behavior was too grotesque, no relationship too pornographic. She soon discovered how much fun it was to shock Beauvoir, whose prudery made it all too easy to do.

They often went dancing together, something they both enjoyed at a time when it was not unusual to see two women in close embrace on the dance floor. They liked to sit in the lesbian bars and make fun of the various couples, and they were not beyond posing as lesbians themselves if they felt that the occasion warranted it. Theirs was indeed a close physical relationship, but both women insisted it was never sexual.[4] In fact, Olga was the first woman with whom Simone de Beauvoir felt relaxed enough to touch, let alone to hug or kiss. Her sister and all her old friends were astonished to see their easy physical intimacy. When they mentioned it, she pretended she did not know what they were talking about and insisted that she had always been casually affectionate with women. But of all the women she knew throughout her lifetime, the ones to whom she gave physical affection most easily were those who had been her students or who had had an unequal footing at the beginning of the friendship, such as older to younger. Some would describe these friendships to Beauvoir as "mother to chosen daughter," which would make her furious. "Why must people insist that when two women of unequal age have a friendship it must be interpreted as mother with daughter?"[5]

Olga was the first of the women with whom Beauvoir enjoyed warm physical friendships, and the one of whom Sartre was most jealous. Olga and all the other young women students loved her deeply, much more than they loved (perhaps even liked) Sartre, and he could not stand it. He needed to make them love him, as Beauvoir said, to put him first, to make him the center of their lives. Thus Sartre created a competition between himself and Beauvoir in which he needed to best her and she not only had to allow it, she had to help him do so. Sartre grew wild when Olga kissed Beauvoir long and full on the mouth and offered him only the hasty brush of her cheek. Beauvoir was then put into the position of urging Olga to be nicer to Sartre, which generally resulted in Olga's flouncing off angrily with Bost, not to return until Sartre left for Laon in a frenzy of unrequited passion.

And so it continued: all of them devoting the greater part of their energies to games of passion which no one enjoyed playing, especially the two twenty-year-old lovers, who were beginning to care deeply for each other and to resent the way "the kingly couple"[6] had decided all four lives should be played out, but who did not dare to challenge or thwart them. Everyone, it seemed, was as Olga described them: "We were all like snakes, mesmerized. We did what they wanted because no matter what, we were so thrilled by their attention, so privileged to have it."[7]

Another duo was beginning a friendship that led to an enduring marriage. Hélène de Beauvoir first saw Lionel de Roulet on the Sunday-evening train to Rouen when he and another of Sartre's students took seats in the same carriage as she and her sister. All four were returning from a weekend in Paris (the train continued on to Le Havre), and the two young men, "aware of their dazzling female presence, began to talk about philosophy, hoping to impress them."[8] The two women were far from being impressed: instead they took down "an enormous suitcase in which there were only a few clothes, a huge sack of walnuts and a large iron. Then they sat on the floor, used the iron to crack the walnuts, and ate all the way to Rouen."[9] A week later, when Sartre teased him by repeating snatches of his train conversation, Lionel learned that he had shared the carriage with the sisters Beauvoir. Lionel had heard stories from other students of Sartre's liaison with "the woman philosopher with the ferocious intellect,"[10] and was terrified when Sartre told him she wanted to discuss his ideas and had invited him to lunch. "I went," Lionel de Roulet remembered. "Hélène was still in Rouen, and we all three spent a pleasant day. In the evening they took me back to the station and gave me a chocolate bar to eat on the train. When Sartre asked how did it go, I told him I was humiliated that they thought me so much a child they had to give me a candy bar. But after that we all became good friends and Castor tutored me and helped me to prepare for the examinations."

Lionel de Roulet was a Protestant of Swiss extraction. His mother divorced his father when he was a very young child and took him to live in the north of France, which was how he came to be Sartre's student in Le Havre. Now his mother had moved to Paris, and Lionel was living there as well, in an apartment that was certainly the most comfortable, if not the most luxurious, of all their friends'. He was spending a great deal of time with Hélène, and by 1938 they had fallen in love and become the most constant of all the "couples" within the Family. The two of them were a calming influence on Sartre because he considered Lionel his "disciple"[11] and he and Hélène had always had an affectionate relationship. Now they had a working relationship as well, because Hélène typed Sartre's manuscripts to earn extra money when he had it to give or as a favor when he did not. Lionel was also one of Sartre's sparring partners (both men loved to box), and it helped that he was in awe of his teacher's charismatic personality.

"There was something in both of them, but especially in Sartre, which was enormously seducing," Lionel recalled. "It was their way of having interpersonal relationships with their entourage. They had a very intelligent and astute way of speaking of the events of the daily life of all of us. They saw each other constantly and tried to see all of us as well, so that they shared their daily experiences, which was what they wanted to talk about all the time. It was obvious that theirs were intellectual gymnastics acquired only through shared time and constant use. We were outsiders to this, we tried to do it as well, to be like them, but we just didn't have the same skill. Sometimes, I actually confused the one for the other, even though they had very different personalities, because through their constant talking, the way they shared everything, they reflected each other so closely that one just could not separate them."

They did come to be separated, however, physically as well as emotionally, and Olga was indirectly responsible when she introduced her sister and squared their romantic triangle. A friend persuaded Olga to go with her to an audition for one of Charles Dullin's productions, and, as has happened elsewhere in the theater, Olga got the part her friend wanted. For a brief time she was consumed by the idea of becoming a famous actress, but, as with everything else that temporarily caught her fancy, she gave it up soon after. Her younger sister, Wanda, wanted not only a career in the theater but also to live in Paris, and by early 1937 she was spending as much time there as she was at home in Beuzeville. When Sartre first saw Wanda, in the winter of 1936, a younger (and some would say prettier) version of Olga but one "who flirted back in a teasing manner that promised danger and darkness,"[12] he was transfixed. From that time on he pestered Olga as much for news of her sister as he did for her own attentions.

It was soon apparent to Beauvoir that Wanda and Sartre would become sexually involved. He had become voracious, devouring nearly every woman with whom he had any contact at all. Everyone was fair game, including the unhappily married GéGé, which hurt Beauvoir although she pretended it did not matter. He sometimes saw the woman with whom he had been involved in Berlin, Marie Ville, back in Paris with her husband, drifting in and out of Montparnasse. He also had liaisons with several of Beauvoir's students from the Lycée Molière, a pattern he continued for the rest of her teaching career.

His only taboo when it came to women was no liaison with any of the American girls who frequented the same cafés, or with any other foreigner; only French women appealed to him. Sartre needed to be in charge of his encounters with women, and since he was in control only of French, Beauvoir thought he might have hesitated to be with any woman whom he could not "seduce with his wonderful voice and his language of honey and flowers." The names or pseudonyms of many of these women appear from time to time in the various writings the couple produced throughout their lifetime, and although the list seems long, it is only the proverbial tip of the iceberg.

In the two volumes of Sartre's letters which Beauvoir edited after his death in 1980, she published some of his letters to some of these women, using as her guideline whether or not she had already mentioned them in her own memoirs. After her own death, it was discovered how vast was the correspondence she withheld and how heavily she had censored those she published. Generally, the unpublished letters to Beauvoir herself were those in which Sartre described the women he slept with in vivid detail, recounting their physical attributes in the most lurid manner, how he was either attracted or repelled by their bodies, and his emotions and sensations during his participation in the encounter. These letters usually ended with expressions of a superior love for Beauvoir before urging her to respond with her own feelings in comparable detail. Frequently, he chides her in his next letter for ignoring his instructions.

Her method of coping was to overload her life with activity and sensation. There were outings with Olga and the other members of the Family and meetings outside the classroom with some of the student-disciples who tried to follow her everywhere. There was also the teaching, of course, but she still devoted as little time to it as possible. More and more frequently, she came to class unprepared and spent the period speaking extemporaneously about Gide or American fiction and films.

When she was not frenetically active, she was ensconced in one of the back booths at the Dôme meticulously annotating Sartre's manuscripts. The inequality of their editing responsibilities to each other was particularly noticeable at this time. Sartre was revising and rewriting his first novel, then called "Melancholia" but published as Nausea, and he followed her textual suggestions and editing instructions to the letter. Typically, one of his first gestures of greeting was to shove a new handful of pages into her arms and urge her to read it as quickly as possible; often he practically pushed her into one of the booths at the Dôme or the Rotonde, fussing until she had her coffee, her bottle of ink, and the pile of papers neatly shuffled and ready for editing, and then he hurried off to a meeting in Saint-Germain followed by his liaison with Olga, Wanda or whoever else it might have been that day. Sometimes he left Beauvoir with little more than a hastily scrawled text and the peremptory demand to "deal with this."[13]

Beauvoir claimed to have thrown these pages away; thus her true role in the shaping and perhaps even the creation of some of Sartre's writing may be known only when and if she inadvertently overlooked something. He told everyone, however, that Nausea became publishable only after her intensive work on it.

She rarely had the opportunity to work on her own stories, and then she was generally too tired to write. She worked all day and played all night, trying to keep up with everyone who wanted her company, unable to refuse anything because she was "afraid to be excluded from life, from living." It soon affected her health.

In February 1937, a doctor warned her that she was suffering from "a bad cold and exhaustion," but instead of resting she drove herself even harder. Three weeks later she fainted in Madame Morel's apartment and was taken to a hospital in an ambulance. One of her lungs had collapsed and the other was on the verge. She was so ill that she missed the entire spring term, almost five months, and then had to convalesce both in Paris and in the south of France for another several months, during which she was still so weak that she could hardly walk from her bed to a chair.

Everyone fussed over her while she convalesced, even her mother. Françoise came to the hotel (which she had sworn never to enter) and actually indulged in pleasant conversation with Olga, but drew the line at Zuore and Bost, to whom she was polite but frosty. Her visits never coincided with Sartre's, "probably by deliberation," according to Beauvoir.

Sartre was at his sweetest and most attentive. "My charming Castor," he wrote to her from Laon, "I'm delighted to be writing to you again because it gives me the opportunity to address you this way once more . . . ," and then he went on to recall the beginning of their relationship in 1929 when they exchanged letters during her holiday at La Grillère. "I'm happy to think of you getting this letter with your breakfast tomorrow," he continued before fussily instructing her to take the only exercise of which she was capable, "your little walk around your armchair, and when you have made the circle, sit yourself down," concluding with "I love you."[14] It is certainly not a profound declaration of love, but, rather, the characteristic sort of message that Sartre wrote to Beauvoir, showing the charm and courtesy of which he was capable. This sort of tenderness was the metaphorical glue that bound her to him and reinforced her feeling of good luck in finding someone "who so valorized me." She had convinced herself that this sort of esteem far outweighed the physical dissatisfaction she felt in their relationship. However, between instructing her to take care of herself and saying that he loved her, his letter included a paragraph meticulously detailing his activities for the coming day, most of which centered around "La Toute Petite," or "T.P.," which was their nickname for Wanda (Olga was "La Petite").

The convalescence thus became another like the one in the winter of 1929, when she was an overburdened university student with a bad case of flu and exhaustion. Introspection at such times is only natural, but hers bordered on morbidity, resulting in a depressing picture of herself: "thirty years old, adrift professionally." She found an escape through writing, which for a long time was the only activity available to her, and then only for brief periods because of her continuing weakness. She revised the first four and wrote the last of the five stories which became *When Things of the Spirit Come First*.[15]

The titles of the five stories are women's names, each representing a different approach toward the discovery of the same personal truths, namely, learning how to deal with the excessive religiosity such as that which dominated Beauvoir's own girlhood. Each story shows how sensitive young women suffer from the constriction and limitation imposed by rigid belief, especially upon their marital and educational opportunities. In the preface she wrote more than forty years after the stories themselves, Beauvoir described "the dangerous influence of that kind of spiritual life" and spoke of a double desire to "tell their stories and also to deal with my own conversion to the real world."[16]

These are young women in the process of defining themselves, all of them daring, in ways large or small, meaningful or silly, to flaunt social convention. The stories deal with the undefinable feelings that presage the first youthful discovery of femininity and concurrent passion. There are role models who no longer serve, friends who disappoint, and men who behave quite simply as themselves, to the perplexity and dismay of the women.

The stories are accurate reflections of the bourgeois French society in which she grew up. The suffocating insularity which required great courage for poorly educated women of her class to rebel against and the emotional toll it takes are eloquently portrayed here. All have a realistic cast that makes the situations of the five women almost tangible. One can almost smell the garbage spilling out of the too-small pail that it is Marguerite's duty to carry down five flights each night after dinner; one lurches along in the overcrowded Métro with Marcelle, who sometimes feels so claustrophobic that she has to get out and finish her journey on foot.

The book begins and ends with interesting, spirited women, as Marcelle and Marguerite (who are sisters) possess by far the most intelligence and vitality. Marcelle is an "extraordinarily sensitive" young woman who yearns "to live with a man of genius" and be "his companion," for "in the company of these intellectuals she felt rich with a mysterious femininity." Instead, she insists upon making a disastrous marriage, which leads her to conclude that "life always fell short of dreams." Just as willfully, she insists that solitude and suffering form a higher calling than happiness. "I am a woman of genius," she proclaims with such conviction that most readers believe her.

Beauvoir called "Marguerite" a "satire on my youth." It is the most openly autobiographical of the stories, with its "little bourgeoise trying to act the bohemian," and it explains how she came to question everything: ". . . and sometimes it was disconcerting—furthermore, not everything is clear even now." Still, "in the end her eyes are opened; she tosses mysteries, mirages and myths overboard and looks the world in the face."

With "Chantal" and "Anne," Beauvoir takes deliberate stylistic risks that for the most part succeed. "Chantal" begins splendidly with the diary of a provincial teacher who romanticizes her dull life, but it falters when Beauvoir seems unable to decide whose point of view the narrator should adopt. Two books which she read during the time she wrote this story "may have had something to do with my own experiments." These were the writings of Jules Renard, which she read in the *Oeuvres complètes*,[17] and Céline's *Voyage au bout de la nuit*. "I found in these often sad, brutally honest writings of Renard so much that was common to my own life. From Céline I took the courage to experiment with narrative voice."

"Anne" begins with a long dramatic monologue in which Anne's mother prays at Sunday Mass while her mind wanders through bursts of pride, self-abasement, self-evasion, willfulness and vengeance. There is a smooth transition to scenes of a French family on summer holiday, but the story drifts into jargon once Anne reaches the point of making important decisions about her life. Although true to the facts of ZaZa's death, the final outcome seems contrived, as if by turning it into fiction Beauvoir has somehow trivialized the tragedy that she renders so movingly in her memoirs.

"Lisa," the most predictable of the stories, is virtually hidden in the midst of the others. "This book is a beginner's piece of work," Beauvoir wrote in the preface, with "obvious faults," and "Lisa" comes closest to fitting this judgment.

Although the book demonstrates how early Simone de Beauvoir recognized the ideas that would figure throughout her writing, particularly the

forces that determine women's lives, its importance at the time she wrote
it is almost incalculable. It was the first writing she had completed since
her university examinations almost ten years earlier, but besides merely
completing it she had done so to her enormous satisfaction and also to
Sartre's. He thought the stories were "remarkable documents which conveyed the reality of woman's situation with starkness, bleakness, passion
and conviction." He had high praise for "Castor's ability to show the world
what it is really like to be a woman."[18]

Such praise had a powerful restorative effect on her mental and physical well-being. She attacked everything with a freshness and zeal she had
not felt since she was a student completing four years of study in three.
She was so confident of their worth that she allowed Sartre to take the
manuscript to Brice Parain, then in charge of submissions at his publisher's, and she told her parents and friends that Gallimard would probably
be publishing the book very soon.[19] Everyone believed her, and many im-
promptu celebrations were held in anticipation of its acceptance. Françoise
lost no time telling all the relatives of Simone's expected success, but
Georges was skeptical.

He had become a sour and disappointed old man, but nothing he said
dampened his daughter's spirits. Her response was to retort that she had already begun another book and it was going very well. She was writing the
story of a woman very like herself, whom she called Françoise Miquel,[20] in
the form of a fictionalized autobiography. Beauvoir had begun with Françoise Miquel's infancy, childhood and adolescence, which were intended to
parallel her own; then her plan was to have Françoise meet a "man of genius" and become "his companion." The main thrust of the book was to
be the analysis of their unorthodox relationship and a celebration of its correctness in the modern world.

Sartre gave her the idea, telling her that she was "so much more interesting and complex and exciting than the pallid little heroines [of the sto-
ries]." The idea of writing about herself frightened her at first because "the
idea of confronting myself was very unsettling." Sitting at the Dôme one
day, they discussed her timidity:

> "I'd never dare do that," I said. To put my raw, undigested self
> into a book, to lose perspective, compromise myself—no, I couldn't
> do it. "Screw up your courage," Sartre told me, and kept pressing
> the point. . . . As happened whenever he put himself behind a
> plan, his words conjured up a host of possibilities and hopes.[21]

Beauvoir decided to begin, so to speak, at her own beginning, by re-
creating some of her childhood adventures at Meyrignac and La Grillère.
The first chapter has six-year-old Françoise standing on the first-floor landing of her grandmother's house all alone while everyone else is outside in
the garden. It is the child's first experience of herself as separate from the
protective entity of the family. Françoise sees her jacket hanging over a
chair:

It was old and worn but it could not complain as Françoise complained when she was hurt; it had no soul, it could not say to itself, "I'm an old worn jacket." . . . There was something disturbing, a little frightening, in all of this. What was the use of its existing if it couldn't be aware of its existence?[22]

Beauvoir had been thinking about existence and rational awareness for at least two or three years—"mostly when I helped Sartre with his writings, for I had not yet summoned the courage to deal with it in mine." Now she thought that fictionalizing her own childhood could enable her to confront what Sartre believed were her many fascinating and complex qualities. She hoped that by starting with her own vivid childhood memories, she could slide obliquely into situations and concerns of her adult life, "in a sense finding out about myself by taking myself off guard, catching myself unawares. If I started with things that had made a deep and lasting impression on me, and I could write about them with the intensity of experience tempered by the objectivity of time, of years, then perhaps I could find and keep the courage to write about myself as I was at the age of thirty."

She started with two ideas: self-awareness and the fear of death that had troubled her from a very early age. Her initial conclusion was that all rational people possess an awareness of themselves and that all of the others' were different from hers: "they exist, think, act and have desires separate from my own, often working in strong opposition to mine." The problem was how to link the idea of the separate existence with the concept of death. As she phrased it in her memoirs, she found what she wanted when, "absurdly enough, [I realized,] the one could complement the other."[23]

In the years since L'Invitée was published, anyone familiar with Beauvoir and Sartre's personal life explained the ending, in which Françoise Miquel acquiesces in the death of her rival, Xavière, as Beauvoir's way of dealing with Olga's role in the trio. Certainly Olga had much to do with the final outcome of the plot, but, as is often the case, true life—that is, what actually took place among the three—was infinitely more complex than the intricate and sophisticated fiction Beauvoir published.

It seemed that Beauvoir had no sooner made her brazen announcement to her father about her imminent success with publication than Sartre returned from Gallimard with her rejected manuscript of the stories under his arm. "Sartre told me that [Brice Parain said] it really had nothing to do with me or the quality of my writing, but that the house of Gallimard did not understand books written by women which were about the lives of women of my generation and background; that modern France and French publishing were not yet ready to deal with what women thought and felt and wanted; that to publish such a book would brand them a subversive publishing house and they couldn't risk offending all sorts of patrons and critics. Sartre told me not to worry, there were other houses less interested in maintaining such reputations, houses which were much more imaginative and contemporary, and we would try them next. And he told me not to say anything negative about Gallimard, because they were so powerful and he needed them and perhaps with my next novel I would, too. So I kept my mouth shut and swallowed the hurt and told everyone the book was poorly written and because it dealt with silly girls it would probably not have sold anyway."

Sartre took the book to Grasset's, and Beauvoir took to her bed. She had been warned by her doctor to husband her strength, but the anticipation of Gallimard's acceptance had so buoyed her that she fell into her old habits of staying up all night, drinking too much and being available for whatever adventure came along. When the book was rejected, she grew despondent and lay in bed creating vivid scenarios of her own personal and professional failures, contrasting them with Sartre's successes.

His situation had improved dramatically. He was beginning to be talked about as a writer, the young genius who had published *Nausea* to critical acclaim. He was writing articles on Dos Passos, Faulkner and Nizan, composing an enormous manuscript on phenomenological psychology, lecturing and writing on the theories of Gabriel Marcel, and blocking out a new novel which would become *The Roads to Freedom*. He had also finished the last part of another novel, *The Wall*, and there was every reason to expect that it would receive even greater acclaim than *Nausea*. More and more, he moved in the literary circles of Saint-Germain-des-Près, and would come back flushed with success and bursting to tell her the amusing anecdotes he heard there. He generally found her waiting for him alone in the Dôme, quietly but steadily drinking cheap wine, chain-smoking rough cigarettes.

Now that Bost and Olga were always together, she also waited alone for him to return from his assignations with Wanda, with the other women who amounted to little more than one-night stands, or with several of her students. He had begun an affair that lasted off and on for years with a young Jewish girl named Bianca Bienenfeld, whom he had met when she attached herself to Beauvoir as another in the continuing succession of adoring pupils. Compared to Olga and Wanda, who were exotically beautiful, Bienenfeld was plain, but she was high-strung, brilliant, erratic, and desperate to break out of her comfortable, bourgeois background—all qualities guaranteed to fascinate and entice Sartre.

Beauvoir had all but negated her own sexual needs, except for sporadic but deeply affectionate encounters with Bost. They became lovers in 1937 on a hiking trip in the south of France, and from then on they occasionally allowed their deep friendship to be expressed sexually. Olga knew this, and she also knew that for the rest of Beauvoir's life Bost remained one of her most devoted friends and occasional lovers. But in 1938 Bost had been posted to Amiens for his year of military service, and even his conversation was denied to Beauvoir. Olga was seldom around to keep her company, because she was busy plotting how to get the money to be with Bost on weekends. Olga called on Beauvoir only when she needed her to ask Sartre for money, seeing him herself only when there was no other recourse. The Gerassis were deeply involved in both action and protest over the Spanish

Civil War and had all but stopped seeing Sartre (and thus by association Beauvoir) because they were angry that he refused to become politically involved. GéGé had managed a temporary stasis in her marriage and was unwilling to jeopardize it by associating with Beauvoir, so that friendship was also denied her. Hélène's life grew increasingly frantic as she tried to balance her illustrating jobs with her own painting, the odd jobs such as typing for Sartre and Beauvoir that she needed to live on, and Lionel de Roulet, who was seriously ill. The original diagnosis was "renal tuberculosis," and he had spent several months in the same Saint-Cloud sanatorium as Beauvoir, but the disease spread after his discharge, and he was transported to a sanatorium in Berck, a remote village in the far north of France. All Hélène's energies were concentrated on getting enough money to visit Lionel, so they too were unavailable to Beauvoir. All in all, the return to Paris from the provinces had not turned out to be what she expected. Instead of the successful publication of her writings and the companionship of friends, she was continuously ill, usually alone and always besieged by Sartre's emotional maelstroms.

Every negative feeling and impulse was reinforced when Grasset also rejected *When Things of the Spirit Come First*. Henry Muller, Grasset's reader, believed the book contained "good qualities: intelligence [and] the ability to observe and to analyze." His main criticism was that it lacked "any originality at a deeper level." The story had been told, he wrote, "countless times already over the past twenty years," and his final criticism was that Beauvoir was "content to describe a disintegrating world" before abandoning her readers "on the very threshold of the new order, without giving any very precise indication of what its benefits will be."[24]

The rejection stung, so much that she refused all Sartre's entreaties to allow him to submit it to another publisher. In 1982, shortly before the English-language publication of the stories, Beauvoir described her feelings: "Two rejections were enough insult, enough humiliation. I was so naive then! If I had only known how many great writers are hurt by repeated rejection of their work, then I might have had the courage to try again with another publisher, but at the time I only believed that my work was inferior, undeserving of public attention. I saw myself as a failure and for a long time viewed myself as unworthy."

For self-preservation she had to find a way to deal with this rejection, the most wounding of all that she had endured since coming back to Paris. She did so through a combination of evasion and purgation: she refused to think about it and took up walking on long, strenuous hikes.

Her still-fragile health slowed her down temporarily, and she spent several days in bed at the beginning of the Easter holiday. As soon as she felt well enough, she and Sartre left for a short holiday in the French Basque region near Bayonne. They had intended to go to Africa, but there was not enough time.[25] The trip helped, especially because she was alone with him and he was so deeply involved in his writing that "he never spoke of his women problems." For her, it was a much-needed respite.

Nevertheless, that trip was not enough, and during her first free weekend ("when he had to devote himself to Wanda and her problems") she was off again, to the Auvergne region for the same relentless walking that had characterized her year in Marseille. Sartre "felt guilty" for sending her off alone, and suggested that the two of them take another weekend by themselves to visit Lionel in Berck and return to Paris by way of Le Havre and Rouen. He thought it would do them both good to show their former colleagues how well life in Paris was treating them, but when they took the trip Beauvoir saw only that nothing had changed in the provinces, nor was it ever likely to, and her only feeling was relief not to be living there.

Nothing gave her very much pleasure anymore, because she was demoralized by his continuing parade of women, the intimate details of each seduction that he took such pleasure in writing to her, and the bickering that now characterized most of her meetings with Olga because of Wanda. Although Olga was grateful to her sister for relieving her of Sartre's insistent attentions, their attitude toward Beauvoir was very different. Olga saw Beauvoir more as an ally than as a rival, whereas Wanda's primary emotional response to her was always competitive, mostly destructive, jealousy. Wanda defined all sorts of boundaries, rules and credos for her relationship with Sartre, insisting that he not tell Beauvoir anything about it, all of which Sartre agreed to cheerfully and dishonestly. He had finally persuaded Wanda to surrender her virginity to him, and almost as soon as the act was over he rushed to convey the news by both letter and conversation to Beauvoir, insisting that she share his pride in the accomplishment. When Wanda found out, she was furious, not at him but at Beauvoir. Her attempts at spiteful retaliation knew no bounds, and Beauvoir bore them all in shamed silence, as if she were somehow responsible.

She was tired of the role of confidante and sounding board he had forced her into and confused by what he expected their relationship to be. Everything had changed since 1929, when they left the university and made their pact of physical-intimacy-with-freedom. She had tried to be everything he wanted, but her situation had changed so long ago from its original simplicity and clarity that she was unable to understand it. In the eleven years that had passed since their original pact, there had been repeated renewals. Each had had contingent others and they had briefly been a trio. But now all Sartre's physical relationships were with other women, some of whom she knew—and many of these did not hesitate to inflict pain on her by telling her themselves of all Sartre's sexual peccadillos. There were too many evenings when, while she was sitting in a café waiting for someone, one of Sartre's conquests plunked down beside her and launched into yet another elaborate version of the encounter. She loved to hear such gossipy details when they were about others, but she had no voyeuristic inclinations at all where Sartre was concerned. Her way of coping with gossip about Sartre was simple:

"I reverted right back to my bourgeois background and found myself imitating my mother or any one of my aunts and cousins, composing myself and closing my face to any display of unseemly emotion. One thing that class of women [i.e., her mother and aunts] knew how to do, and to do well, was to keep what they felt about their men to themselves. I had no trouble at all discussing these situations with Sartre, because of course we were as one, but it was unthinkable that I should enter into any sort of discussion with these women."

She was ashamed, saddened and bewildered by her unwanted complicity in what had come to be his sexual life with others and almost never with her. Her role as the one intellectual confidante he could not live without remained constant, and she made this her rationale for accepting the larger role he forced her to play, the reluctant observer and unwilling commentator, the third person in his bed.

There was still another role which he expanded into many other aspects of his life with her willing complicity, that of "the heavy." Whenever he grew tired of a person or bored with a situation, it was always "Castor" who "would not allow" or "did not want" or "refused to permit" him to do something. Sartre knew he could not say no to anyone, so he made Beauvoir do it for him. Years later she was asked if she had ever resented how this made her seem in the eyes of others. "Sartre had to be protected from himself," she replied. "He would never have written had I not accepted to be his screen before the world." Throughout their years together, Simone de Beauvoir insisted that the one aspect of her life which had never disappointed her was her relationship with Sartre, and she unleashed her fury on anyone who dared to question it. However, in this particular instance she was really incredulous that such a question could be asked about the years after they came back to Paris. To her, the late 1930s had been happy years in which they proved the viability of their pact. She scarcely remembered anything else.

FIFTEEN

What Will Happen
Tomorrow?

I N THE SUMMER OF 1938, while Sartre danced the annual attendance on his mother, Simone de Beauvoir went off to the Alps alone for more obsessive walking. She met him in Marseille at the end of July, when they set out on their previously postponed trip to Morocco. As soon as they returned, she went off again, this time with Olga, following the Route Napoléon through the Basses-Alpes. Halfway through, at Gap, she found a telegram from Sartre commanding them to return to Paris at once. The Munich crisis was unfolding, Czechoslovakia was about to be dismembered, and the world political situation was something Simone de Beauvoir could no longer evade.

"This time war really did seem inevitable. I faced this prospect with furious incredulity; so lunatic a catastrophe could not possibly happen to *me*."[1] She wrote this in her memoirs in 1958, but in 1985 she added: "If truth be told, I'm not proud of what I was then—thirty years old and still centered on myself. I'm sorry to say that it took the war to make me learn that I lived in the world, not apart from it."

When the crisis was seemingly allayed with Chamberlain's "Peace in our time," Beauvoir was literally delirious with joy because "anything, even the cruelest injustice, was better than war."[2] Some of her friends were amused by her naivete, and others were "embarrassed by her monumental self-centeredness."[3] Even Sartre tried to prepare her "gently, for the ugliness of war," but she refused to hear him because "I preferred instead to dwell on peace, as long as someone else paid for it and not I."[4]

Nevertheless, the temporary peace was the catalyst she needed to break her depression. She worked steadily at the "Françoise and Pierre novel," her working title for *L'Invitée*. Even Brice Parain's rejection of the first third of the book—more than 150 pages dealing with Françoise's childhood, adolescence, education and sexual maturity—hardly slowed her down. She was now confident that the mere act of writing this material was enough; it gave her the necessary resolve to begin the novel with her main character already an adult who reflects back on her earlier life. She could cull this material from the rejected chapters as needed and insert it where appropriate into the history of the adult Françoise.

According to Beauvoir, Parain found the chapters Sartre gave him to read "not the sort of writing one expects from a woman. He was disturbed by Françoise's concerns for her own sexual needs as well as by her wanting a relationship of true equals. Women in France before the war were not supposed to be concerned with such things. They were supposed to measure themselves in terms of how they satisfied their men, not of how they themselves desired to be satisfied."

Parain's criticisms did not disturb her, nor was she concerned about how the public would receive the novel, because "from the beginning I believed in the value of this book." This newfound confidence was linked to the temporary political stasis. She remembered "a terrible sense of urgency during the time from Chamberlain's peace to the outbreak of war. I was filled with euphoria because I took the reprieve personally. I thought I had triumphed, that my willpower had somehow settled things in Europe. That Hitler would continue to menace Germany and probably the Balkan countries too, but that we in France were safe and no longer had to worry about his territorial ambitions. It gave me such confidence that I truly believed everything would finally come to pass in exactly the manner I wanted. Still, I must have known it was only wishful thinking." Nevertheless, she remembered enjoying herself throughout the year 1939: "There was always the nagging worry about what might happen, but I had a very good time."

In her memoirs, she describes herself buying new clothes, taking a renewed interest in her appearance, frequenting the Café de Flore and gradually moving into the social world of Saint-Germain-des-Prés. She liked looking at celebrities but decided she did not want to become one, she went to movies and the theater and later met the actors and the directors in cafés, she read all the latest novels and, whenever possible, traveled to different regions of France to hike or ski. She gave as little time as possible to her teaching: "The old faithful Gide continued to serve me well. I had entire classes who graduated from my teaching with only an imperfect pastiche of knowledge about his writing."

Still, her students adored her. The bolder ones waited at the Métro to walk her to school. The shy ones spent the time between classes admiring her dress or reading her copy of *Marie-Claire*. They all waited to learn whom she would choose to walk her back to the Métro at the end of the day, often stopping along the way for coffee. Some of the more adventurous made forays into Saint-Germain-des-Prés or Montparnasse, where they sat for hours in cafés hoping to see her.

The Lycée Molière was located in the southern section of the Sixteenth Arrondissement, where many well-off refugees from Eastern Europe had settled, mostly White Russians and Jews. Perhaps because of her earlier friendship with Olga, Beauvoir was attracted to these young women, especially the Polish Jew Bianca Bienenfeld, and the White Russian Nathalie Sorokine, whom she and Sartre always called Natasha.[5] Both were born into families where class distinctions were paramount; Natasha professed to despise such pretentions, but nevertheless flaunted them over the fearful Bianca, whose family had already experienced brutal Nazi beatings that led them to flee from Germany, and to whom being Jewish held far more serious connotations than social inferiority.

Bianca quickly became entranced by Sartre, who seduced her into a brief affair during the summer of 1939 but ended it almost as soon as it began because he was frightened by her skittishness. He used Beauvoir—not for the first and certainly not for the last time—as his shield between himself and Bianca as well as his excuse for curtailing their intimacy. Nevertheless, he continued to play a game he enjoyed very much for the next several years: writing letters professing his undying love for the girl while always being careful to state that both he and Castor shared the sentiment. Bianca's moods careened even more erratically, as she competed for Sartre's favors all the while crying for Beauvoir's affection and approval. She became, or, more accurately, wanted desperately to become, what they had desired Olga to be during their years in Rouen: the completion of their trio. But whether the couple had tired of such games or had been too badly burned by their experience with Olga to try to create the trio a second time, they were united in not wanting to place Bianca in such a privileged position within their lives.

Natasha was another matter entirely, as the American GI she later married described her, "seemingly quiet and shy but fiercely aggressive—farouche, the French would say."[6] She adored Beauvoir and only tolerated Sartre with affectionate disdain. He nicknamed her "La Sarbacane," which in French is either a weapon (a blowpipe) or a toy (a peashooter), and for him she was a combination of both. The two young women were quickly annexed to the Family, Bianca as "an object of pity and amusement" and Natasha "as an equal, as one of us, a friend."[7]

As for Beauvoir, she believed that it was after Sartre met Bianca and Natasha that he unconsciously fell into the habit of using her to maintain his hold on the young women. To an oft-made charge that her role in their relationship had become more one of a domineering older sister than an equal partner in a loving relationship—that she served as his "nanny," or that he made her "run interference," or, even more harshly, that "she pimped for him" in his many affairs[8]—she responded, "He found it convenient to avoid any unpleasantness or anything he did not want to do by saying, 'Castor would not like it' or 'I have to consider Castor's feelings,' when all the while he was using my name to insure that he got exactly what he wanted. He was very sensitive, he wanted everyone to love him always, and that sort of thing never mattered much to me. I didn't mind being rude to get what I wanted, but it pained him, so I did it for him. Also—and I think this is very important—when couples have been together for a long time they play roles and take on responsibilities for each other within the relationship. It's not all one way, there is give-and-take. You don't mind playing these roles to make things easier for the person you love."

So, with Bianca, Beauvoir did "run interference" for Sartre, but because she liked the girl herself it was usually a pleasure to spend time comforting her while Sartre was off on some other amorous escapade. With Natasha, Beauvoir's role was altogether different. Natasha had no qualms about refusing Sartre's attentions loudly and publicly, and Beauvoir had to be alert for any sign that she was about to strike.

"One time we were all sitting around, I don't remember where," Beauvoir recalled, "and Sartre was teasing her playfully about going to bed with him, which I knew was a prelude to a more insistent attack, and she said something like 'Oh, go away, you silly little man—you are so boring,' or something like that. Well, he was so puzzled by this, so hurt, and he sat there not knowing what to do—chatting on as if nothing had happened when it was quite clear to me alone that he was devastated by her thoughtlessness. And I felt so terrible. I made up my mind that no one would hurt him this way again. But I liked her, you see, and things were different with the three of us than they had been with Olga and us, so my role became not one in which I had to encourage Natasha to receive his attentions but I had to make sure that if she refused, it was in a way that did not hurt his ego. My role became to reassure him, and I could always do that with total honesty."

Their own sexual intimacy was now reduced to "the most occasional encounter," but their need for each other attained a new dimension, according to Beauvoir, "probably because of those two girls." In later years, when a woman rebuffed Sartre, "we often said to each other, 'Now, what did we do in such a situation with Bianca, or with Natasha?'"

In the summer of 1939, however, Sartre reassured her for the last time that she would never again need to question her status with him: "Every October, Sartre and I used to drink a glass of wine in salute to our first pact. But that summer at Madame Morel's villa, we were sitting in the dark one evening, just the two of us alone, and he turned to me and said, 'You know, Castor, we don't need any more temporary agreements. I believe we will be—we must always be—together, because no one could understand us as we do each other.' I don't remember what I said except that I was stunned to hear him say this, so out of the blue. Yes, of course, he often wrote such things in letters, but he wrote so many letters each day to so many people that I sometimes thought he made these statements more by rote than by real emotion. I think I just sat there. Then after a while I said, 'Yes.' I was so happy."

Even though the last few weeks of the summer of 1939 had been peaceful for her, she could no longer ignore the pressure of political reality: "History took hold of me, and never let go thereafter."[9] Her introduction to what life would be like in time of war came when she and Sartre agreed they needed a break from the many guests in Madame Morel's villa at Juan-les-Pins on the Riviera and decided to visit the fortified medieval city of Carcassonne before returning to Paris. The train was packed with troops hastily recalled from leave who shoved them aside angrily and usurped their reserved seats. This treatment prefigured the rest of their journey back to Paris, when trains were rerouted, delayed or canceled and they had to fight huge crowds as determined as they to get aboard and get a seat as well.

All Paris was shuttered and quiet, even more than usual because this year very few tourists had come to replace those Parisians who made the annual holiday exodus despite the political instability. Sartre and Beauvoir found themselves isolated in what seemed a deserted city. None of their friends was there, his mother was still in the country, and her mother, father and sister were at La Grillère. They spent all day desultorily traipsing through the forlorn streets in search of the latest newspapers. In the evenings they took refuge by seeing every American movie then in Paris several times, as if fearing that their access to such films would soon come to an end. John Ford's *Stagecoach*, starring John Wayne, was a favorite: "We saw it every night for a week. We loved that big American, and sometimes, to cheer up Sartre because he was subject to angry moods and bad temper, I tried to imitate the way John Wayne walked and spoke. Sometimes I could make Sartre laugh."

But generally nothing helped for very long:

As we fell asleep each night our last question would be, "What will happen tomorrow?" And when we awoke it was to the same mood of agonized anxiety. Why had we been landed in this position? We were scarcely over thirty, our lives were beginning to take shape, and now, brutally, this existence was snatched from us.[10]

She never forgot where she was and what she was doing when she learned that Hitler had invaded Poland: "Sartre had gone to Gallimard, and I went to the Dôme to work on some sections about Elisabeth [in *L'Invitée*] that were troubling me. I had just ordered my coffee when I heard the most curious sound, like a wave moaning, if such a sound were possible. I looked around and saw a waiter surrounded by people, who suddenly got up from their tables and rushed into the streets. I realized they were going to buy newspapers when the waiter looked at me and said, 'He's done it—Hitler has gone into Poland. Now we are in for it.' I nodded without speaking, threw down some money, gathered up my things and ran out, back to my hotel."

On the way, she stopped to telephone the offices of Gallimard so that Sartre would know she was waiting at the hotel for him. He returned, verified the rumor that mobilization had begun, and said he had to leave for the front as soon as he could find out where to go. They went down to the cellar and searched his few boxes until they found his old uniform. "Another time it might have been funny to see him crammed into that tight little jacket, but we had no laughter when we saw the gas mask and realized that this was serious."

Together they took the Métro to Passy to see his mother and stepfather. She waited in a café until he finished saying farewell, because although she had by now been introduced to Madame Mancy and had occasionally been invited to join her and Sartre for an afternoon drink in a café, Monsieur Mancy refused to permit her ("fallen woman, whore, that I was") to enter their home. Then they went to an assembly point at the opposite end of Paris, where Sartre learned that he was to report to Nancy in eastern France on a train that was to leave "sometime between midnight and six o'clock the next morning."

They went to the Café de Flore, but not even the flamboyant prostitutes whom they had befriended could cheer Sartre up. When they left, everything was eerily quiet in Saint-Germain-des-Prés. The moon lit up the cobblestones in front of the church as if it were in a lonely country village. Usually such scenes brought her incredible happiness, but not this night: Beauvoir had a migraine headache and went to the toilet several times to vomit. Sartre was as dispirited as she, and they went back to the hotel early. Instead of going to their separate rooms, they went to hers and stumbled around in the dark, unwilling to pull the curtains and forbidden to turn on the light because of the blackout. They fell onto her bed in exhaustion and spent the next few hours alternately holding each other silently and tossing and turning. At 3 A.M., when the alarm clock shrieked, she was "almost glad the moment had come. The tension of waiting to say farewell seemed worse than the actual moment." They took a taxi back to the assembly point at the Place Hébert. Two harried policemen thought Sartre was crazy for showing up there and ordered him off to the Gare de l'Est, where an official embarkation center had been established. He caught the early-morning train, and Beauvoir decided to walk back to Montparnasse. She made it as far as the Boulevard Haussmann, where she spent the day at the movies, watching *Stagecoach* over and over.

That night, unable to bear the thought of being alone, she called on the only friend who was then in Paris, Fernando Gerassi. They went to dinner in a little neighborhood restaurant, and she was so grateful for his company that she listened as if in agreement to his political arguments, "which in truth I did not understand, nor did I care about them." When dinner was over, she still could not face her hotel without Sartre, so she spent the night on Gerassi's sofa. Despite her exhaustion, it took hours before she fell into a fitful sleep.

The next morning, September 3, she began her first day without Sartre by reading Gide, the author who had never failed her before. Sometime in the past few days she had shoved a volume of his *Journals* into her pocket, and now she lay on Gerassi's sofa reading, particularly those sections dealing with the 1914–18 war. On her way home that afternoon, she bought the newest issue of *Marie-Claire*, thinking that such repetitions of her habits would ease the resumption of daily life. There was a message at her hotel from GéGé, back in Paris and now Madame Pardo (her first marriage had been annulled), inviting her to lunch. She joined GéGé and her husband, along with an English friend of Pardo's. The two men amused themselves by trying to persuade the women, who drank too much wine, that the past few days had all been a bad joke and peace would be declared at any moment. The midafternoon edition of *Paris-Soir* ended the game: the headlines announced the British declaration of war, and France's was to follow later that same day.

She and GéGé tried to elude reality a little longer by going to the Flore to keep on drinking. They stumbled upon a bizarre situation. The crowd was confused and angry, and people who knew each other well were hurling accusations of being foreign agents. Policemen were rude and traded blows and insults with those they thought did not obey their orders fast enough. Waiters stood in corners talking to each other rather than serving customers, and the two women were uneasy sitting among so many men in mismatched old uniforms getting surly drunk before reporting to embarkation centers. The occasional prostitutes who prowled among them without any takers were not happy to see them there, either.

GéGé persuaded Beauvoir to sleep in her new apartment that night, and she agreed because both women were uneasy about walking home alone through deserted, blacked-out streets, suddenly so threatening. The Métros ran sporadically and many lines had interrupted service, so the two finally arrived at GéGé's apartment well after midnight after a circuitous ride and an even longer walk. Pardo was shocked by Beauvoir's haggard face and unfocused chatter and insisted she take a sleeping pill. It was her first full night's sleep in weeks.

The next day brought her introduction to the restrictions of civilian life in wartime. They were seemingly little things, such as having to show an identity card before using public telephones, or reporting to the Lycée Molière to have her gas mask fitted. Usually she did the newspaper crossword puzzles on the Métro to kill time, but she no longer had that diversion because they had been banned for fear they might contain secret codes. The imposition of these changes upon her former easy and independent life in Paris was both irritating and frustrating. To make matters worse, taxis were impossible to come by, Métro service was further curtailed, and, worst of all, cafés, supposed to close for only one day, stayed shut for several.

By September 5, she began to receive letters from Sartre, who was a private in the meteorological section of an artillery group which moved throughout the easternmost provinces of Alsace and Lorraine. He had assured her before he left that his was probably one of the safest jobs in the Army, and his first few letters helped to reassure her that it was. He described his daily life, his military duties and companions; he told her of the changes and mixups in movements and orders; he described the people in the villages where the unit was quartered, and he concluded his letters with tender statements of his love for her.

In his first, dated September 2, he wrote: "In my mind I have a clear picture of your daily routine—the Dôme, the telephone calls, the movies. I live your day hour by hour throughout my own." He concluded his letter of September 3 with the loving language one uses to a child, telling her to behave herself, read all the newspapers, take a subscription at Sylvia Beach's lending library, and keep up with the world's literature. "Don't be bored, don't be sad. And please be ready to send me some books as soon as I know where I'll be. I wish I could give you the address now."[11]

From the beginning, he was struck by the absurdity of his situation, invoking Kafka's name frequently as a shorthand description of his daily life and military work. He recalled it in a 1974 conversation with Beauvoir:

> I launched balloons and watched them with binoculars. . . . All at once I found myself part of a mass of men in which I had been given an exact and stupid part to play, a part I was playing against opposite other men, dressed as I was in military clothes, whose part was to thwart what we were doing and finally to attack.[12]

He took refuge in writing, and spent every free waking moment filling more than fifteen beautiful little leather and canvas notebooks in his cramped, spidery hand.[13] Somehow he managed to spend more than twelve hours each day keeping his journal, as well as writing long daily letters to Beauvoir, his mother, Olga, Wanda and Bianca, and occasional letters to a host of other friends and conquests. "I asked Pierre [a fellow soldier] to let me stand guard in his stead this evening so I could write a little more," he wrote to Beauvoir.[14]

If he was writing, then she too must write. She had kept diaries sporadically in the past, but not since she had been a university student and then not in anything like the extraordinarily detailed and introspective manner of the one he now kept, which, typically, he insisted she read and comment upon. Since he was keeping a journal of wartime life, she began to do the same sometime in mid-September. Although she bought for him, at some expense, beautiful little leather notebooks for his diary, she kept hers in cheap dime-store children's exercise books or on whatever paper she had at hand.

She started by trying to reconstruct what she had done since September 1, but while writing a diary may have been his lifesaver, all her attempts to analyze herself and her situation served only to depress her even more. On September 17, she began her report with:

> Awake feeling depressed. Bright cheerful light is streaming through my little green-curtained window, and I feel horribly depressed. In the old days the worst part of my depression used to be the astonishment it caused me, the scandalized way in which I fought against it. Nowadays . . . I accept it cheerfully enough, like an old familiar friend.[15]

Despite the frequent references to her state of mind, she continued the diary, the only writing she did during the months of September and October. Olga came back to Paris from her parents in Beuzeville, and together they moved into GéGé's flat while GéGé and Pardo went away for several weeks. Bost wrote from his military camp, saying that he was well, and there was a flurry of letters from Françoise, stranded since August at La Grillère, imploring Beauvoir to convince her Grandmother Brasseur to quit Paris for the country. The old woman refused to leave her flat, fearing it would be both looted and confiscated, so after one or two dutiful visits Beauvoir ignored the rest of her mother's entreaties. Happily the Flore reopened and she caught up with friends, among them Colette Audry. She took short trips, even visiting Dullin and Simone Jollivet at their country homes in the north. Dullin upset her by saying that the Russians would surely invade Poland, which would guarantee that the war would "go on three, five, maybe even six or seven years." She had "a lot of faith in Dullin's intelligence," so she was shaken deeply by his remark and noted it in her diary, where she wrote, "I had never envisaged the possibility of a *long* war."[16]

She went back to Paris briefly, then was off to Quimper in Brittany to visit Bianca. Dullin's remark continued to haunt her, and when she found a note from Madame Morel inviting her to the house at La Pouèze near Angers, she accepted at once because the isolation and bad weather in Brittany were having an adverse effect on her mental health. She knew that the great number of servants and guests who were always in residence with Madame Morel would keep her from too much unwanted introspection, and also the house had a large library she could use to try to understand the war.

To date, her only information had come from newspaper accounts, BBC radio broadcasts, and conversations with Fernando Gerassi. She could grasp only the essential elements of the first two, mostly geographical facts about troop movements and battles. What she wanted was historical knowledge about Germany, such as internal politics, previous alliances and ententes, historical friendships and enmities, and the economic situation since the end of the First World War. Fernando told her some of this, but his political opinions were extreme and his interpretations of current events seemed violently skewed. She trusted Colette Audry's judgment better, and after several conversations she decided not to listen to Fernando anymore.

Typically, she depended again on books to help her understand what was "probably the true beginning of my political self-education." She began by trying "to understand the recent past history of my country." In the diary, she writes of sitting in front of a fire on a rainy day, listening to the occasional tapping of Jacqueline Morel's typewriter and reading "bound numbers of *Crapouillot* covering the period of the 1914–18 war, . . . a book by Rathenau, and one by Kautsky. . . . [Also] volumes of Pierrefeu." Her conclusion was not unexpected:

"This is a weird moment in history: No one can accept Hitler's peace proposals; but what sort of a war will there be instead? . . . A month ago, when all the papers printed it boldly
across their headlines, it meant a shapeless horror, something
undefined but very real. Now it lacks all substance and identity."[17]

She felt "vaguely deflated; I'm waiting for something, I know not
what." It seemed that the only thing definite she could count on was the
passage of time. For a woman to whom action was always the response to
uncertainty, waiting for some unknown thing to happen was "the same
as a living death." So she identified a choice: she could keep up her aim-
less forays from friend to friend, with occasional trips back to her hotel
room in Paris, keeping as the only fixed points of her day the letter she
wrote to Sartre and the one she hoped to receive from him. Or she could
curtail these wanderings even before her classes were scheduled to start,
when her movements would be involuntarily restricted. "Up to now," she
wrote on October 4, "I've been on holiday. Now I am about to adapt
myself to a 'wartime existence,' and it seems ominous to me." She found
herself seized by "an almost panicky urge to get away from all this tranquility, to come to grips with something again."

The first order of business was to find out where Sartre was, and to
see him. Her need to be with him was overwhelming, and she was still
puzzled by it many years later as she tried to explain it: "I was like those
Norwegian animals [lemmings] that have an uncontrollable urge to jump
into the sea and drown. I had been separated from him before for long
periods: there was, after all, Marseille." She paused for a long time as if
trying to fit language to the exact representation of her mood and sentiment and then said, "I think I felt that if only I could see him and touch
him, my waiting would end and I would learn what I should have to do in
order to resume my normal life."

She was back in Paris on the morning of October 5. School began on
the sixteenth, so she had eleven days in which to secure the necessary
permits and make her clandestine visit. Before anything, she had to find
out where he was, which was difficult because his letters arrived routinely
with large sections removed by the censors. He managed, however, to
sneak one past them in which a certain agreed-upon letter in each paragraph spelled out his location. Her first action after receiving it was to
walk boldly into the police station in her quarter and ask for a travel permit to the east to visit her fiancé, as if this were the most ordinary request
anyone could make. It astonished the official on duty, who lectured her on
the maze of restrictions forbidding such visits, emphasizing that if she did
manage to see Sartre he, not she, would be severely punished. This gave
her only momentary pause, and she decided to try another police station.
This time, instead of bluntly announcing her intention, she invented a
dying sister in a small village in Lorraine, sufficiently far from the front not

to arouse immediate suspicion, but close enough to Sartre's camp that she could walk if necessary. But before she received the travel vouchers she had to secure a residence permit, not only to prove her identity but to insure that she would return, and the only way to get one was to be domiciled in something other than a hotel. GéGé's concierge signed the document in exchange for a bribe of fifty francs.

Just when Beauvoir thought she had everything in order, a letter from Sartre arrived on October 17, saying he was being posted to an unknown destination, and it seemed that all her trouble had been for naught.

On October 18, two strokes of good fortune occurred on the same day: Hélène returned from La Grillère with some extra money, and Sartre sent a coded letter telling her he was at Brumath—a village northwest of Strasbourg. She went to still another police station, because now that school had started she needed to be excused from teaching. She secured the necessary passes, faked an illness, and found a doctor willing to authorize her absence from teaching for five days. All this took another week, and as civilian travel was restricted, it was not until October 31 that she caught the same train from the Gare de l'Est that Sartre had taken two months earlier. The police pass allowed her to travel as far as Nancy, and once there she had to queue up again in still another line to swear to local officials that she needed urgently to get to Brumath to see a dying sister. Somehow she convinced them.

The section of the diary that deals with this visit to Sartre contains some of her most emotionally vivid writing.[18] She conveys with such force her determination to see him that the tension bursts with sudden impact when she describes how she spotted a shabby, bearded, pipe-smoking Sartre walking down the little village street. Her frustration is tangible when she describes the proper burghers who won't rent a room to an unmarried couple, and how when she finally gets one she is told to vacate it because a married woman needs a few hours alone with her lawful husband. The visit winds down and Beauvoir has to face the lonely journey back to Paris. She describes her leavetaking in such wrenching language that her pain is palpable.

Sartre walked with her "as far as the station yard, under a great starry sky; then he vanish[ed] into the night." She was exhausted from the visit, having "spent nearly all our time talking. We had more need of conversation than we did of sexual intimacy." She slept all the way to Paris, arriving in the early-morning hours of November 5.

While with him, she read his manuscripts and diaries and offered suggestions and corrections. She showed him her diary, which intrigued him. He told her to expand her analysis of herself, because now that she was almost thirty-two and, to a large extent, "set into a well-defined mold," she should ask herself, "What *sort* of woman? . . . Generally speaking, what do I ask of life today, what expectations do I have of my intellect, where do I stand with regard to the world at large?"[19] She made a notation that, time permitting, she would address such questions in her diary, but several days later she wrote to him that she had decided not to undertake any intensive self-analysis, because she wanted to finish her novel. She felt instead "the urge to live actively, not sit down and take stock of myself."[20] His advice was:

> . . . not to forget about myself. Not to become so immersed in fictional characters that I would forget the most interesting character of all—myself. He told me once again what I already knew, that he found the character and personality of women far more fascinating than almost anything else in the world, and that he hoped someday to write entire philosophies about them. He said he was counting on me to write about myself so that he would have a responsible document to rely upon when he began his own work. We joked a little about this, but I could tell he was serious, and I was a little [serious] also.

Now that she had seen him, her emotions were on a much more even keel. She had things to do in Paris, especially to finish what then amounted to little more than the first half of a rough draft of the novel. He had given her instructions about books and papers to send him, about letters to give to Olga, money to Wanda, wedding greetings to GéGé, verbal wishes to Bianca, "a hug for Poupette," even "a kiss to be given to Madame Mancy." She had to find out whether her parents had made it back from the country, to resume her teaching, to see how her friends were coping, and, most important, to write.

The war would have to progress for a while without her concern. Sartre was as well off as he could be under the circumstances, and she had to finish her novel.

SIXTEEN

When Life Goes
Slightly Adrift

The "Phony War"[1] dragged on for nine long months after France declared war on Germany. French troops waited in boredom for the German Army to strike on the western front while civilians were deluged with a monotonous, never-ending stream of government propaganda about changes in daily life; but other than the onslaught of paper, nothing really happened. Simone de Beauvoir came to the unhappy conclusion that it might be not only a long war but also one of "unremitting, unrelenting, crushing boredom."

She could barely drag herself to teach her classes, which had been merged with those of the Lycée Camille Sée by the Ministry of Education in an economy move in which female teachers were exhorted to take pride in the fact that they were freeing male counterparts for military service. "The good people of Paris still had to educate their children, and, now that all the men were called to fight, women were expected to do their patriotic duty and fill men's jobs without any extra compensation at all. I remember thinking how unfair it was that I had so many extra students and not one extra franc to show for it." Her cynicism carried over to other things, as she openly ridiculed the optimistic propaganda blitz of "monumentally false energy and proportion." It had exactly the opposite effect on her than was intended: she was lethargic and depressed, sarcastic in the extreme, and numbed by the frenzied behavior and unfocused fear she saw everywhere around her. To her, it all seemed a "surrealistic propaganda nightmare, professing a vitality and offering a happiness that was simply a grotesque parody of daily life."

She found it difficult to conduct her own affairs with any semblance of normality, but, with Sartre absent from Paris, everyone in the Family looked to her, and she became "the one responsible for us all." Instruction and encouragement flowed freely through Sartre's letters, however, as he urged her to do all sorts of things from writing to Bost (with the Army in

Morzine) and Bianca (hiding out in a family home near Quimper) to looking after Olga and GéGé (who were in Paris) and Hélène (who was back and forth between La Grillère and Paris). He even urged her to placate the truculent Wanda, who was sulking at Laigle. Wanda was enraged that Beauvoir had succeeded in visiting Sartre and was determined to try as well, making him fear the punishment he would receive if she did. Her anger increased when she learned that he invented a secret code to foil the censors with Beauvoir and not with her, so only Beauvoir would be able to tell the Family where he was stationed. In his letters he gave Beauvoir detailed instructions on everything: how to deal with Wanda, how to dispense money when any was available, how he expected to divide his time among her, Wanda, Bianca and his mother when he came to Paris on leave.

Sartre's absence had brought an extra but surprisingly pleasant obligation into Beauvoir's life—Madame Mancy: now that she could not have her son with her, the clever little mother turned to the one who was closest to him. Madame Mancy began at first to telephone Beauvoir several times each week, then daily. The calls always originated with her, because Monsieur Mancy still forbade his wife to see "the fallen woman."[2] Soon the two women were meeting in cafés near the Mancy apartment to share their letters over coffee. As time passed, Madame Mancy became bolder, frequently leaving her husband's luncheon to the care of their maid while she ate her meal with Beauvoir. Beauvoir liked the tiny, plump woman, then almost sixty and still imbued with the ideas and manners of a bygone generation. Madame Mancy had an air of otherworldly innocence about her that, coupled with her tart-tongued observations of daily life, made Beauvoir laugh, something she did not often do those days. They grew to be good friends during what became a time of common trial, and their respect and affection for each other continued for the rest of Madame Mancy's life. But once Sartre was back in Paris, it was his mother's idea for her and Beauvoir to resume their old polite formality, which they did.

The Family was growing rapidly as friends and relatives of the core group came to Paris in need of food and the documents to obtain it, work and work permits, and lodging. To Beauvoir, it seemed as if each day brought new requirements for personal identity papers which all were required to carry. In the evenings, those friends who were in Paris congregated in Beauvoir's room to try to make sense of the day's news. She had moved to a hotel in the Rue Vavin, just a few short steps from the apartment where she had been born. "Sometimes at night, when I pulled the heavy red curtains shut before the curfew, I thought about that other apartment where the draperies had also been red, and about all that had happened to me in the years since I lived there. Sometimes it made me sad; more frequently it made me angry or scared."

Everyone, even those who had not been particularly close or even fond of Beauvoir, came to her to solve their problems. They had willingly surrendered authority to her and Sartre for the way they lived their lives in peacetime; now that he was absent in war, they looked to her as their natural leader. Natasha Sorokine needed proof of nationality before she could get the necessary admission certificate for the Sorbonne, but, as her parents' citizenship was in question, she was afraid to go directly to the authorities. Could Beauvoir intercede? Simone Jollivet was drinking heavily and decided that only Beauvoir could provide her with the reassurance she needed. Dullin phoned frequently, either asking Beauvoir to come to the country to stay with Jollivet or pleading with her to telephone back. All this cost money, and she had very little, so she began what became another frequent practice during the next few years: she borrowed from Madame Mancy, who had to invent all sorts of extra wartime expenses to get the money from her parsimonious husband. And what Beauvoir considered her primary responsibility, satisfying Sartre's needs, continued unabated. She had to find money for ink, pens, notebooks, reading materials, pipe tobacco—no matter what he wanted, she found a way to oblige him.

At the same time, she refused to stint herself. In December, for example, fed up with "the pressure of everyone wanting something" from her, she decided she "might as well ski." No one in the Family could afford to go with her, so when Bianca told her that Jean Kanapa, one of Sartre's former pupils, was going to Mégève, she went with him. When she wrote to tell Sartre she was going with Kanapa, he wished her a good time, cheerfully envisioning the slopes and regretting that he could not be with her. In another letter, he said he liked to amuse himself by trying to imagine what sort of interesting living arrangements they were keeping.[3] Sartre laughed when she told him that she and Kanapa kept each other company on the slopes but spent the rest of their time in solitary pursuits, he reading and she spinning the dials on the radio in the ski lodge.

Her parents were upset that she chose to spend the holidays away from home. The war had brought out Françoise's protective instincts, and she sought both her daughters' companionship and conversation in ways she had not done for many years. Her anxious fussing annoyed Beauvoir, who ignored all invitations or tried to end telephone conversations as quickly as possible. She avoided her father, whose sour and defeatist political attitudes infuriated her.

Hélène could not work in her freezing studio, so she moved to La Grillère to be near Lionel, who was living with his mother in the village of Saint-Germain-les-Belles. The French government was forcibly relocating people from Alsace and Lorraine to Corrèze and Haut-Vienne, and local citizens deeply resented outsiders. As Hélène's identity papers gave her Paris address, staying on was difficult despite her family connections. Lionel's mother then decided to marry a Portuguese national, and she wanted Lionel to move to Portugal with them because his health was still perilous, and Hélène wanted to go, too. Beauvoir felt the obligation to help her sister financially, but she also worried that she would soon have to help her parents. Now that even bread was rationed, she worried about the extra pressures her mother faced. She was willing to help with money, but "that was all. I had to be careful not to let them involve me in their lives again. I could not be held responsible for all their needs." So money became a constant, pressing worry, but what was hers was also his and theirs, so anyone in the Family (but mostly Beauvoir and Sartre) who had it gave it to anyone who needed it.

By February 1940, Sartre thought he could get a few days' leave, but several potential problems loomed. His mother wanted him to live in her apartment while he was in Paris, and she insisted that he let her buy him all new clothes, especially trousers, which she had become curiously fixated upon. He countered by insisting that he would take a room at the Hotel Mistral (discreetly omitting that Beauvoir lived there) but would first collect his old civilian clothes from her flat because he could not permit her to spend money on new ones in such uncertain times. He told Beauvoir, "Naturally she offers to pay for the pants, but I want the poor old lady to keep her money. Naturally also my remarks [in his letters to her] must be shrouded in mystery because of my step-father."[4]

They had to resort to subterfuge with Monsieur Mancy, who did not share his wife's devotion to her son. When he surprised her packing Sartre's clothes into a bundle she hoped to sneak out in her shopping basket, she lied quickly and said she was putting them into storage, although she was really taking them to Beauvoir. No matter when Sartre arrived, even if in the middle of the night, his mother did not want him to spend one embarrassing moment in his ill-fitting uniform. When Sartre showed up at the apartment a few days later in his civilian clothes, "the jig was up for the old woman and me," Beauvoir recalled. "But Madame Mancy was a tough little lady, and I think the old man knew better than to fight with her whenever her son was concerned."

Sartre's leave in February 1940 was a happy one for both of them, because he had not told anyone his actual arrival date and they managed to keep his presence secret from the others for almost a week. Since her visit the previous November, their relationship had been stable. Separated from Wanda, he grew less fond of her, and in letter after letter he told Beauvoir how little Wanda now meant to him. He had become impatient with the petulant tone of her letters, her unceasing demands for declarations of love and undying passion. Such superficial writing bored him because he needed to express his thoughts and ideas and discuss his writing, as he could do only with Beauvoir. Now that he was separated from all his women, the perfect companion of his mind became the ideal object of his love and the focus of his written attention.

What made her uneasy, however, was the frenzy of his writing and his constant references to it. He was finishing an important scene in his novel La Mur (The Wall), or he was finishing the novel itself. He was writing the last page, he had written "The end" at the bottom of a paragraph; no, he was rewriting an important scene between two leading characters, or he was incorporating new dialogue based on his philosophical reading and theorizing. He was working steadily in his notebooks—could she send paper, ink, more notebooks, more books he needed to read as background material before he could write further? Where was the Shakespeare? Was it lost in the mail? He needed it at once. The ink ran out too fast. She should send a different kind. He needed more paper, this time specifying exactly what kind he wanted, never mind the shortage nowadays. When he came to Paris he would have three filled notebooks for her to read. No, he would have five, maybe more. She must read his novel at once. He can't wait to hear what she thinks of it. But he has also sent some of it to Wanda, and he is terrified for its safety. Beauvoir must get it back. He then decides he truly cannot wait to come to Paris so that she can read what he has written: he tells her about it in his letter before sending the manuscript itself. Her opinion is of paramount importance to him. Her suggestions and revisions are vital, they are both dreaded and honored. He will accept them all. "Did you get back [from Wanda] my novel? Hurry and read it and write to me, my sweet little one. I'm trembling [awaiting her response]. Oh, my tiny little Judge . . . I have such confidence in you."[5]

Only once does he ask if she has continued to write. Only once does he ask whether she has managed to finish her novel, but apparently once was enough. She set to work with a vengeance so that she would have something to show him when he came to Paris.

"Literature is born when something in life goes slightly adrift,"[6] Simone de Beauvoir said, describing how she came to write *L'Invitée* (*She Came to Stay*).

"I began . . . in October, 1938, and ended it in the late spring of 1941," she wrote; to an interviewer she confided, "It took me three years to write this first novel, even though it wasn't very long."[7] Actually, by February 1940 she had written what would later amount to less than fifty pages of the printed text, nor did she fully conceptualize it until Sartre's first leave, in that month. She always remembered that she began the concentrated writing during the first German invasions of Western Europe, in May 1940, and finished the novel a little over a year later, in June 1941.

The parts of the earliest draft of *L'Invitée* that Beauvoir wanted Sartre to read during his leave did not concern her main character, Françoise, but rather were about Elisabeth, who had undergone several significant changes since the novel's inception. This Elisabeth had no connection with the girl of the same name in *When Things of the Spirit Come First*, nor was she based upon ZaZa. Beauvoir just liked the name, and since she had already decided that the main character, to be based on herself, would bear her own mother's name, she settled on Elisabeth "not wanting to waste time dreaming up names but writing about what they represent instead." This fictional Elisabeth was originally created to be the sister of Pierre Labrousse, the theatrical impresario who is Françoise's lover in the published work, and—in the most reductive description—the fictional equivalent of Sartre within the novel's fictional triangle. Beauvoir's original intention had been to create such closeness between brother and sister that when Françoise and Pierre became lovers, Elisabeth's intense attachment to Pierre would lead to her initial hatred of Françoise. The creation of the triangle and the resulting complications of the plot were to occur when Elisabeth realizes that she not only is fascinated by Françoise but also values her friendship. The friendship of two women thus reflected one of Beauvoir's earliest fictional concerns, that of a genuinely affectionate, noncompetitive relationship between two women of similar age.

Beauvoir put this version of the triangle, comprising some of the earliest pages she wrote, aside toward the end of 1938 when Sartre accused her of "inventing falsifications instead of real people"[8] and turned instead to writing of herself through the vehicle of her main character, Françoise. Four writers—none of them French—influenced the creation of the early versions: John Dos Passos, D. H. Lawrence, William Faulkner and Ernest Hemingway.

From Dos Passos she took a number of techniques, most notably his "camera eye," which she interpreted as "permitting the author to make the reader accept what he wants the reader to think of a character, all the while directing and ordering what it is the reader should think and know." She also liked the way Dos Passos "told the story of several characters separately within the same novel. Each is then developed independently of the others, but all are integrated into the same story."

From Lawrence she took the idea of "roots,"[9] by which she meant "giving her [Françoise] a family, a history, a heritage. I gave her my childhood at Meyrignac to enrich the adult woman. Inventing a past for Françoise made her the sympathetic woman she became. Yes, yes, what Virginia Woolf's friend [E. M. Forster] called the 'round' character."

Faulkner, whose writings had now fascinated her for more than a decade, "continued to amaze me with his ability to manipulate time." In her memoirs, she wrote of how Faulkner "contrived to play tag with . . . time," but said she differed from him because "his technique was designed for a novel constructed on a fatalistic basis, whereas I was concerned with free and unpredictable decisions."[10]

Hemingway's influence came through dialogue:

> He taught us a certain simplicity in dialogue, and this interest carried over to the little things of life. I studied the way he described ordinary things, objects and actions. I never had any tendency toward flowery prose anyway, so I felt encouraged by the simplicity of his style to adopt it as my own.[11]

By the time of Sartre's February leave, she was no further along with the novel than the initial conception and the development of the two women characters. Françoise was secure in her open and honest relationship with Pierre, and Elisabeth was a bundle of insecurities, a pathetic woman who invested her identity in the situation of her current lover. Beauvoir had incorporated Pierre Labrousse into plausible places within the text, but she had not actually written any passages in which his character was central.

In conversation, Beauvoir tried to explain what she had meant his character to represent: "I thought of him as the constant, fixed presence around whom the other two women revolved. I meant him to be very secure in his thinking—by this I meant his ideology, his beliefs. I meant Françoise to be a character equally as attractive and sympathetic as he. There were problems with this situation. Should Françoise be the only one to recognize the independent existence of others and to be troubled by such realization? If he were to be firm and fixed at the beginning, what possibility could there be for him to change—as he must—if he were to remain the ideal mate for Françoise?"

In her memoirs, she explained more fully what had stopped her "from looking at the story through Pierre's eyes":

> What I *do* regret is failing to give [Pierre] that three-dimensional quality which was the main thing that drew Françoise to him. I had put too much of myself into Françoise to link her with a man who would have been a stranger to me; my imagination balked at this switch of partners. But equally, I was loath to offer the public a portrait of Sartre as I knew him. In the end I compromised . . . I could neither create an original character nor draw an accurate portrait. The upshot was that Pierre . . . since Françoise's choice of action . . . is always made with reference to him—possesses less depth or truthful characterization than any of the novel's other protagonists.[12]

As always, analyzing Sartre or her relationship with him was, as she had described it earlier, "not my strong suit." So she still needed a way to link the luminiscent passages describing Françoise's childhood and early life, the interesting tension created among the three independent characters, and the accurate and lively background scenes about backstage life in the theater.

Sartre didn't like the new pages about Elisabeth, finding her a "disagreeable, tense character who diminishes [the novel's] scope."[13] Beauvoir was puzzled by the violence of his dislike, but unable to decide what she should do. She had invested much of herself "in this alter ego, this other side of Françoise," and did not want to eliminate her entirely. "Elisabeth was not merely a convenient device: I attached far too much importance to her character as such."[14]

But she felt she had to respond to Sartre's criticisms because, when it came to her writing, he seldom expressed them this strongly. It seemed that the only thing to do was to invent another character to become Pierre's other love object and the third angle of the triangle. Elisabeth could then remain Françoise's friend, and at the same time an object of pity and scorn for the way in which she conducts her own life, particularly her love affairs.

Beauvoir reflected upon the decisions that led to the inclusion of the real-life Olga Kosakievicz into the novel as the character of Xavière Pagès: "I tried to write about what had happened to the three of us without writing about Olga, who became very dear to me after we moved to Paris. As the war went on, we came to depend on each other in so many different ways that I felt I was violating her by inventing a version of what she had been just to satisfy my fictional needs. It was very difficult for me to recreate her as Xavière because I had given Xavière so many nasty, brutish qualities that were entirely absent from Olga. But I needed a Xavière, and too many people mistook the fictional girl for the real woman. They entirely overlooked the fact that the most unpleasant aspects of Xavière came from my prickly relationship with Wanda. Only the good things were based on Olga and my true feelings for her."

Once she decided to create Xavière, the necessary characters were almost complete, but "sentimentality was pressing" upon her: "Having decided to include a version of Olga, I felt that I must include a version of Bost." This became Gerbert, the attractive young assistant to Pierre whom Françoise scrutinizes as a possible love object, but whom, for philosophical reasons, she initially renounces. Beauvoir worked "by one rule which both Sartre and I regarded as fundamental. . . . In each successive chapter I identified myself with one of my characters, and excluded any knowledge or notion beyond what he or she would have had."[15]

She had no trouble with the setting, which was the Rouen they had all known and Paris, particularly Montparnasse. She gave her main characters occupations in the theater and acquired veracity through watching Dullin at work.

What still eluded her, however, was the crux upon which her plot should turn. Just having a triangle was not enough, because "I was not out to write popular novels for rich ladies who read books only in order to have an excuse to eat chocolates. To me, fiction had to be informed by an idea, a philosophy, or it was not successful."

"I have thought of a nice little theory about freedom and nothingness," Sartre mentioned casually in a letter of December 19, 1939. Not until she read it did she have what she needed to finish the novel. In the next few months he enlarged upon his initial thinking in letters, and during his leave he spent long hours explaining it.

Sartre began his notebook entry for Thursday, December 7, 1939, with the declaration "I must begin to set my ideas about morality in order."[16] The first question he asked was toward what end human reality should be directed. He had only one answer: "to its own end," arguing that human reality always has only one real aim, "itself," concluding that, to use his phrase, "human reality" need answer only to itself. "Its freedom," he posits,

is that it is never anything without motivating itself to be it. Nothing can ever happen to it *from outside*. This comes from the

fact that human reality is first of all consciousness; in other words,
it's nothing that isn't consciousness of being. . . . It only *discovers* the world . . . on the occasion of its own reactions.

These ideas had an "exhilarating, liberating effect"[17] upon Simone de
Beauvoir's thinking, especially in connection with Françoise's ultimate action. Sartre's conclusion, that an individual must "assume forever that terrible responsibility" of freedom, was exactly the note upon which she
wanted to end the novel. Beauvoir particularly liked two of his concluding
sentences: "I am only willing what is. . . . I am responsible for it . . . I
self-motivate myself to discover it." These were the ones she remembered,
repeating them to herself in the dismal winter of 1941 as she struggled to
find a successful way out of the fictional impasse she had created. She had
so buffeted her fictional triangle that its edges had rounded into a circle
and, like a wheel set in motion, revolved without stop. The middle part of
L'Invitée came fairly quickly to her, but the conclusion, "beyond any
doubt the weakest aspect of the book,"[18] took longer. She ground it out
during some of the darkest days of her life.

SEVENTEEN

To Stay and Try to Survive

T HROUGHOUT MARCH 1940, rumors buzzed around the Carrefour Vavin, Beauvoir's neighborhood, that the Germans were about to launch an offensive at any time. She paid scant attention, because Sartre's letters were still filled with how he passed his days writing and playing endless games of chess and the probable leave he looked forward to having in April. She wondered how attack could be imminent if all was so peaceful at the front, but she learned to keep her thoughts to herself because such sentiments were not popular with the nervous inhabitants of her quarter.

Her mood had been stable since Sartre's first leave because his letters continued to assert her preeminent importance in his life. She taught her classes and occasionally saw some of her friends, but most of her energy was devoted to his needs. She worked over the manuscript of Sartre's novel, sending long and thoughtful critiques which he studied carefully and incorporated into his text. She supervised her sister, who was typing the manuscript to earn money to visit Lionel in Portugal. When Beauvoir sent the typed pages to Sartre (which she edited first and then had retyped to incorporate her revisions), he replied by telling her how much he valued her suggestions, calling her his "little Judge." Later, he wrote that she would have unlimited authority over the manuscript, and that he would follow all her suggestions for revision before the novel was published.[1] He ended every letter with profuse declarations of love, which on the one hand made her feel secure, but on the other made her "pine for Sartre; my heart was empty and loneliness weighed heavily."[2]

This second leave, in April, passed as quickly and as pleasantly as the the first. By now, he had developed his "little theory" to the point where he was steadily writing what would become *Being and Nothingness*. She listened attentively to everything he said, pointing out inconsistencies and rebutting some of his views, but generally finding his theory worth pondering at great length after he returned to his unit.

Without telling him, she decided to put her novel aside and go each day to the Bibliothèque Nationale to read Heidegger and Hegel, "because I wanted to understand their theories for my own satisfaction, but most of all because I needed to become expert in order to help Sartre with his new [philosophical] system." She did so "without the slightest pang" at putting aside her own novel, because "his theory was worth so much more than any novel I could have written then. Who knew what would happen with the war? It was important that Sartre's writing be encouraged first so that he could finish. I had an obligation to help him."

Imagine, then, her surprise at his letter of May 12. He told her that Wanda had written, saying she was alone, ill, and had a "little lesion." She wanted him to come to her at once, and the only way he could do so without deserting would be to marry her, because then he would be eligible for a three-day pass. He told Beauvoir that marriage to Wanda would "not be too bad," but strove to assure her that it would be "purely symbolic," although he would of course do everything possible to fulfill the marital responsibilities of keeping Wanda comfortably situated. Naturally the marriage would have to be a secret from his mother and stepfather, for Wanda "was not a suitable daughter-in-law for the former Anne-Marie Schweitzer and her proper husband, Monsieur Mancy." He did realize that it would cause a certain amount of embarrassment for Beauvoir; under such circumstances, perhaps she would prefer to be away from Paris visiting Madame Morel at La Pouèze. Or, better yet, he would lie and tell Wanda that since the German invasion of Holland (on May 10) he could get only a two-day pass, and this way he could spend the extra day with Beauvoir!

All this from the man who routinely signed his letters to her as "your little husband," and who only a few short months ago had assured her that he was over Wanda, that she meant nothing to him anymore. And who ended the letter in which he told her he planned to marry Wanda with "Goodbye my sweet little one. Until tomorrow, or maybe until later tonight, because I'll write to you tonight. I love you with all my heart, my dear Castor, my love."[3]

His suggestion of marriage to Wanda shocked her even more than an earlier betrayal that happened on his February leave. He and Beauvoir hid from Wanda and she found out about it. Sartre's way of pacifying the jealous girl was to say that he would gladly trample anyone in the world to be with her, "even Castor." Proud of his cleverness, he then bragged about it to Beauvoir, giving her all the details of what he had written about her to Wanda.[4] But then he apologized to Beauvoir for the messiness of his sexual life and swore that, although he would continue to deceive Wanda (this time by telling her his leave was five days shorter than it actually was so that he and Beauvoir could be alone together), he would never deceive "my little one, my charming Castor." He begged her to believe him: "I swear to you I'm absolutely honest with you. If I weren't there'd be nothing left in the world before which I am not a liar." As Beauvoir wanted to believe him, he had no trouble convincing her that he would need no other women besides Wanda, who would be quite sufficient to satisfy his needs for "conjugal seduction" when the war was over.[5] Still, she did not for a moment imagine that he meant the word "conjugal" literally. In 1984 she insisted that she was not upset by the letter because she knew how to interpret it, and that from the beginning he had no intention of marrying Wanda:

"You have to understand what I had to do for Sartre when it was a question of other women: he was a very timid man who had an extremely sensitive ego and he could not say no to anyone. If a woman wanted something from him, he would promise her the moon. Then he would come to me. It would start out with 'Wanda—or [other women with whom he was associated in his lifetime]—wants . . .' Then he would tell me he was going to do exactly what they wanted, which I never took seriously because immediately he would say, 'Castor, find out about . . .' whatever the problem happened to be. What he really meant was, 'Here is what I *really* want you to do . . . *get me out of this mess.*' And because I was tough, and I didn't care what these women thought about me, I was the one who had to put them straight. I played the villain. They all blamed me for everything, and he would go and wring his hands with them and say what could he do, it was all Castor's fault, and he was so sorry about everything. But truly, he was happy to have me get him out of trouble."

In Sartre's brief autobiography, *The Words*, he described himself as a beautiful baby with long golden curls who, when they were shorn, became an ugly little boy. "Sartre suffered so much because of his ugliness," Hélène de Beauvoir wrote in her memoirs, "I think that his quest for beautiful women, his collection of them, was a sort of revenge. It was a way of overcoming his physical appearance."[6] Beauvoir agreed with her sister: "I was probably willing to assume such a thankless role for him because I would do anything to keep him from having to confront the painful reality, or, more accurately, how hideously ugly he believed himself to be. He was so much more—so, so, so much more—than what he looked like. And everyone who knew him loved him so much for his many wonderful qualities that I think unconsciously we may have forgiven him many excesses to keep him from thinking about himself. Perhaps we did him a disservice by letting him live in perpetual childhood, granting him every wish. But he was so charming and generous, and he never hurt anyone. It was impossible to deny him anything, because really he asked very little for himself."

On May 12, two days after the actual event, the residents of the Carrefour Vavin congratulated themselves on their perspicacity when radios blared news of the German invasion of Belgium, the Netherlands and Luxembourg. There was pandemonium throughout the quarter when news came that the Germans had broken through French lines in the Ardennes. Sartre was at Morsbronn-les-Bains, at the beginning of what became six weeks of shuffling back and forth between Alsatian villages with his unit, sometimes engaging Germans in battle, mostly sending up meteorological balloons, playing chess and writing *Being and Nothingness*. He continued to write his daily and sometimes twice-daily letters to Beauvoir, and the post office delivered them punctually. On May 19, he wrote to insist that she leave Paris and take refuge with Madame Morel a La Pouèze, instructing her first to send both Olga and Wanda to their parents, now at Laigle. At the end of his letter he told her to "take Sorokine [with her to La Pouèze] if you don't want to leave her behind."[7]

Nathalie Sorokine, her pupil, had invaded Beauvoir's life with an insistence she was unable to resist. For some time Natasha (as they called her) had been arriving uninvited at Beauvoir's hotel, often forcing Beauvoir to let her spend the night by dallying until the curfew began, talking endlessly of how little her parents understood her, all of which Beauvoir duly related to Sartre in her letters, and which he commented upon by return mail.

The Sorokines were highborn Russians who continued their own rigid social traditions even though they had also adopted the social conventions of the French *haute bourgeoisie*.[8] Porfiry, Natasha's father, had been a minor customs official in Russia and now made a good living as a rare-book dealer. He was a dandy, as Georges de Beauvoir had been, and always wore a homburg hat, pearl-gray gloves and impeccably tailored suits. His wife, also called Nathalie, was a dour woman who, according to her daughter's first husband, Ivan Moffatt, "would see a snake under the bed whenever she could. She was a paranoid who had the sort of prejudices [that included] anti-Semitism. She was a very gloomy, distrusting person." The Sorokines had a large, well-appointed apartment in the White Russian colony, an exclusive section of the Sixteenth Arrondissement. In their circle, only Russian was spoken at home; tea was served formally from exquisite samovars brought from Russia, sometimes at great peril, icons were favored decorative objects, and Orthodox priests were revered guests at every formal occasion. It was, however, as Moffatt described it, a world where "objects mattered most and anything intellectual was very remote, indeed uncongenial." Discipline for adolescents and young adults was more rigid than Beauvoir had known within her family. Activities for every age group were highly formalized and regulated, and even though many of these young people had been born in France they were taught that their primary identity was Russian. And so Beauvoir's natural sympathies were with the girl: for every indignity Natasha related, Beauvoir had a similar one to recount as she relived the bitter memories of battles with her own parents.

Beauvoir tried to help Natasha collect the necessary documentation for the Sorbonne, but the bureaucracy considered only the requests of parents or guardians who were French citizens. The Sorokines were naturalized, but their innate distrust of government agencies made them afraid to call attention to themselves and so they refused to help their daughter. When she heard this, Beauvoir lost interest, but Natasha was not to be denied. She became moody and threw tantrums, then clung like a barnacle, which at first Beauvoir found flattering, just as she had with Olga and Bianca. She now felt responsible for Natasha and worried about leaving her behind with her repressive parents if evacuation became necessary.

There was another facet to this relationship, according to Ivan Moffatt, who had a strong friendship with Beauvoir throughout his marriage to

Natasha: "My personal opinion is that it was a relationship of lesbian un-dertones. How far it actually went I don't know, and if I did I'm not sure that I would say. Quite aside from that, and had that existed or not existed, there's a far more important emotional and intellectual attachment. A sort of relationship between teacher and pupil. And certainly Natasha had a crush on Simone de Beauvoir. It was conceivably to mute this crush that [their] time [together] was so rationed [by Beauvoir]."

Moffatt's perception of Beauvoir's need to distance herself from the ferocity of the younger woman's attentions was confirmed by Beauvoir her-self: "Natasha was so charged with emotion that one had to be careful with her. One had to be on guard, because she had a tendency to consume people. She was like violent, destructive weather: beautiful to look at if you were not subject to it, leaving horrible destruction and desolation in its wake. Still, I liked her very much. She was a very good friend to me. I just had to be careful to keep our friendship under my control.

From 1940 until she left France as a war bride in 1945, Natasha Sorokine was an important player in Simone de Beauvoir's life and fiction. Much of Natasha's wartime behavior inspired that of the character Hélène in Beauvoir's second published novel, *The Blood of Others,* and that of Nadine in *The Mandarins.* Beauvoir also gave "many things about her, grand and little things, . . . to many other characters" in her fiction. "I used her actions, mannerisms, movements. One could not pin this girl down in any certain manner. She was a fascinating, elusive creature. I have very strong and loving memories of her."

By June 4, when bombs fell outside Paris and Hitler's boast that he would be in Paris by June 15 seemed a likely prophecy, most of the Family had scattered, and only Natasha and Beauvoir remained in Paris. The Kosakievicz sisters returned with their parents to Beuzeville, Bost had been wounded and was evacuated from the front, the Gerassis had gone south hoping to enter Spain as their point of departure for somewhere in the Americas, and Bianca was about to leave for a small village in Brittany where she hoped to hide for the duration from anti-Semitic persecution. But the most difficult loss of all for Beauvoir was her sister, who had finally collected enough money to visit Lionel, now recovered and working in Portugal, where both were stranded for the duration of the war. "Lionel said to me, 'Well, we might as well get married, since we are going to be stuck here together,' and since I rather liked the idea of marrying him, I was quick to agree."[9]

With all Beauvoir's good friends gone, Nathalie Sorokine became in-dispensable. Nevertheless, on June 10, when a decree temporarily sus-pended all education throughout Paris and the *baccalauréat* examinations were postponed indefinitely, Beauvoir left the city without telling anyone but the landlady at her hotel. She joined "L'Exode"—the road-clogging flight of civilians in panic who went south to escape the Germans—with Bianca in a car driven by Bianca's father, eventually ending up at Madame

Morel's. In her memoirs, Beauvoir said she took "only the essentials—including all of Sartre's letters: I have no idea where or when they were lost."[10]

The journey to La Pouèze was a nightmare.[11] By the end of June she was back in Paris, because it was obvious that she could not stay indefinitely in a household to which she could not contribute financially. But her main reason for returning so soon was that she had had no news of Sartre since leaving Paris. She went back to her hotel, to find that everything she left behind had been either thrown away or stolen, but since it was mostly old clothing she shrugged off her loss.

She met her father by chance in a café, and sat for the first time at a table surrounded by German soldiers. Georges was angry that she had left Paris without informing her parents. She accused him of trying to get even with her by telling unsettling stories about the atrocities being inflicted on French prisoners of war. When he saw how well he had succeeded, he tried to calm her by saying that "life in Paris wasn't too bad yet. The Germans were all very polite to the citizens and seemed to mind their own business."

The only problem was food, for shortages had already begun.[12] Georges "complained about how much he was suffering from lack of good food, but it was my mother who stood in the queues all day long trying to find enough for him to eat, shorting herself to give him more." Beauvoir had no sympathy for his predicament, as she too was hungry. She decided to pay a visit to her mother, thinking they might pool their resources. When she arrived, she found Françoise in extreme agitation: just as during the 1914–18 war, Madame Brasseur had abandoned her apartment and come to live with her daughter. Once again Françoise found herself burdened with responsibility for her mother as well as for her husband and herself.

Beauvoir was upset by her mother's appearance, but there was nothing she could do to help without money, and as the fabric of daily life in France unraveled in June 1940, she could not even help herself. She was unsure of how she would exist now that her lycée had been evacuated to Nantes. The only immediate help she could give her family was to move into her grandmother's apartment to set the old woman's mind at ease, because no one else could occupy it as long as a family member was there.

It solved Beauvoir's problem of where to sleep that night, but it was an "eerie sort of homecoming." The furniture her sister had painted a cheerful orange and white was "still there but strangely yellowed and faded; like me, like all of us, I remember thinking."

The next day she went to the education offices, where an inspector spotted her as she was filling out papers to collect her salary. She hoped to be paid whether she worked or not, but he sent her off at once to become a philosophy teacher at the Lycée Duruy. Most Parisians who had fled earlier were now back, and schools were among the first government institutions to resume functioning. Her classes met only for eight hours each week, but she drew a full salary with benefits and other privileges. "It might be worse," she wrote in her diary.[13]

☐

Natasha Sorokine found out where Beauvoir was living the day she returned to Paris, coyly declining to tell her how. Every time they met, Natasha was on a different bicycle, later admitting that she stole them, repainted and sold them for enormous profit, hinting at all sorts of "connections" with "people who were not going to take a German occupation sitting on their hands." When she had saved enough money, she moved out of her parents' apartment and followed Beauvoir through the succession of hotels she lived in for the rest of the war after her grandmother's death.

She had had no word from Sartre since his letter of June 9, and was worried that her association with Natasha would jeopardize his situation, admitting years later that this was "indeed irrational, but at the time very little that I did was rational." These irrational acts included accepting a splendid bicycle—but first she had to learn to ride it, for she had never been on one before.

The bicycle Natasha Sorokine gave her, like those of most Parisians, became her most treasured possession throughout the war. She was delighted to see how swiftly she learned to keep her balance, and, like skiing, cycling soon became a passion. Soon she was taking off on her own, at first only to pedal cautiously round and round the Cimetière Montparnasse, then making longer forays in and around Paris. In peacetime, she had vented her frustrations by walking; in wartime, she rode her bicycle and waited for Sartre.

France surrendered to Germany on June 22, but Beauvoir had no news from Sartre until mid-July. It was in a penciled note dated July 2, in writing she hardly recognized, and franked twice by different censors, so she could not determine where it came from:

> . . . I am a prisoner and very well treated, I can work a little and I'm not having too bad a time of it and I think that in a little while I'm going to see you again. Listen—you can write to me: Soldier Jean-Paul Sartre 20th Army Service Corps—Prison Camp, Passage Number 1—Baccarat. . . .[14]

He had sent the letter to her hotel on the Rue Vavin (the landlady had sent it on to her grandmother's apartment), and a duplicate to Madame Morel's. In both, he advised her to wait for him in Paris because he was sure he would be sent home quickly. It gave her hope, until her father told her that one of the German conditions of the surrender was that all French prisoners would be interred in Germany for the duration of the war.

By the eighth of July, she had more definite news: that Sartre had been taken prisoner on his birthday, June 21, that he was in good health and spirits, and that prison camp was quite a bit like camping out and not bad at all. By July 23, mail had begun to arrive regularly but Sartre was cross because, of the four thousand letters that had been delivered to Baccarat, "only *seven* were from you to me."[15] By mid-August, her worst fear was realized: Sartre was transferred to a prisoner-of-war camp called Stalag XII-D at Trier and it seemed as if their separation would continue indefinitely. He was not nearly as upset as she, however, for he had completed seventy-six pages of *Being and Nothingness* and was content enough as long as he could write. As usual, his writing galvanized her into action. Every day from two until five, she went to the Bibliothèque Nationale and read Hegel. Every morning and evening, she wrote a few pages of her novel. In between, she wrote to him and worried.

In September 1940 the weather turned unseasonably cold, and by the end of the month Parisians knew they were in for a long winter. That year and the next, record low temperatures and high snowfalls were recorded, further punishing an already strained population and a straitened economy. Rationing was instituted in September 1940, and long queues formed at the town hall of each *arrondissement* as residents lined up for their cards. Adults between the ages of twenty-one and seventy were entitled to "tickets" which gave them 350 grams of bread each day and the same number of grams of meat each week.[16] They were allowed monthly consumption of 500 grams of sugar, 300 grams of coffee and 140 grams of cheese. Rice, noodles, soap and fats were rationed shortly after. Inadequate from the beginning, these were routinely cut even further throughout the rest of the war. For example, the Parisian who on the average had consumed 111 grams of meat in 1939 averaged 28 grams in 1941 and 20 grams in 1942. By October 1941, newspapers were regularly carrying notices warning "cat eaters" that though they might have persuaded themselves that cats were an acceptable substitute for rabbit, they risked grave danger by eating an animal which existed on rats and vermin.

Black bread, the infamous *pain noir* made mostly of chaff, was the norm and then in minuscule quantities. The average diet consisted of "little bread, no meat and when fruits are in season no sugar. No jams or jellies, and at Christmas no chocolate."[17] The public could not understand how quickly all the necessities of daily life had disappeared. Shop windows, which one day were filled with beautifully packaged enticements, overnight became empty. *"Ils nous prennent tout*—They are swiping everything," quickly became the first topic of conversation once Parisians exchanged greetings.[18]

Like everyone else, Simone de Beauvoir became obsessed with food. She developed the habit of averting her eyes from empty shop windows when she walked along the streets. Also like many other Parisians, she frequented the black market whenever she had money enough to buy. "I looked for the biggest quantity I could get for my money, and that was usually potatoes or bad bread. I didn't realize what a healthy appetite I had or how much food I consumed each day until rationing, when I couldn't get enough."[19]

Since her salary barely covered inflationary prices and she had nothing else to trade, she depended on Natasha and what has since come to be called *le système D*—the French version of the English expression "Do it yourself." Whole bicycles commanded the highest exchange, but any spare part was a tradeable commodity. Natasha's "business" expanded, and she even commissioned others to help her steal.

Bicycles "became better than gold" when the Germans began to requisition cars, and buses and Métros ran on restricted schedules. As bicycles became the only means of transportation other than one's feet, some enterprising persons attached boxes with benches onto bicycles and "vélotaxis" were born. Ancient horses and carriages were a common sight on the streets, and when shoe leather was rationed as well, wooden soles were fashioned. Beauvoir remembers wearing down "at least two pairs."

By January 1941, there was so much snow that skiing contests were held on the hilly streets at the Porte Saint-Cloud. Beauvoir, who loved skiing, did not go. "I was too tired all the time because I was so hungry. I had no energy to spare." Most private dwellings had no heat, because they used oil and none was available. Coal stoves came back into use, but coal too was difficult to find and expensive to buy, prohibitive on the black market. Kerosene was used for cooking, often with tragic results. Even public buildings were unheated, and newspapers advised people to stay at home and spend their weekends in bed if possible, to save their energy for the work week. The novelist Colette advised: "Go to bed. Get the Saturday, or Sunday, meal over and done with, and the household chores finished, and go to bed with a hot-water bottle for your feet. . . .[20] Most cafés lacked heat as well, but the few favored by the Germans, including the Flore, the Dôme, the Rotonde and Coupole, always had some form of warmth. From October 1940 until January 1941, Beauvoir usually spent her mornings in the Dôme, and there she finally finished *She Came to Stay*.

But one afternoon in mid-January she walked by the Café de Flore on the way back from the Bibliothèque Nationale and was so tired that she decided to stop for a cup of coffee. She had been in the Flore only once or twice since the occupation began, but was uncomfortable because the German propaganda staff had all but taken it over, and (as rumor had it) all the intelligence officers and their spies and flunkies met there as well.[21] But as she drank her coffee she realized several things: the Germans were not interested in making trouble for the few French who continued to frequent the café, and, best of all, by then current standards of warmth it was positively overheated. She quickly noted that two tables in particular were almost touching the stove, and decided that from now on she would hurry over to the Flore as early as possible in the morning, claiming the table closest to the stove as her own. There she would write until it was time to go to the Bibliothèque each afternoon. Thus, from the desire to keep warm and write without interruption, both rumor and reality about Beauvoir were born.

The reality was quite simply that throughout the war she wrote two philosophical essays, another novel and a play, mostly in the Café de Flore.

The rumor which plagued her for the rest of her life was, in its kindest form, that she had not been averse to frequenting the favored hangout of the German propaganda staff in Paris and had not been averse to their company. In its unkindest form, the rumor stops just short of accusing her (and later Sartre) of allowing themselves to be enticed into a quiet but very real sort of intellectual collaboration.

She answered the charges in 1982: "People who were not there cannot understand how all-pervasive the Germans were. They were *everywhere*. It was very difficult to find anyplace where they had not congregated. There may have been one or two little *zincs* [bars] on the outskirts, but I had never gone to those places, they were difficult to get to even if one could find them, and why would I put myself to so much trouble when I was tired and hungry most of the time? No, I continued to live my life as I had always lived it, and this meant in the Dôme, the Rotonde and, yes, the Flore. Who can fault me for wanting to be warm while I worked? Germans were there, yes, and after Sartre came back and we had our plays put on, we had to go through the censorship, so we became acquainted with many Germans, but that doesn't mean that we enjoyed their company or that we had anything more than the most routine sort of dealing with them. We did what we had to do to live, and that was all."

However, life during the war was infinitely more complex than such a statement explains, and as the war dragged on some of her actions clouded its easy acceptance.

Things were not well in the Beauvoir household that fall: Grandmother Brasseur was gravely ill but indomitable; Françoise wore herself to a frazzle trying to make her mother's last days comfortable. Georges had lost a frightening amount of weight and his spirit as well. The only topic that animated him was the establishment of several agencies which he hoped would finally rid France of the Jews, whom he held responsible for the ills that had befallen the country. Beauvoir was forced to listen to him rave twice each week when she dined with her parents, for she and they pooled ration supplements to make them go further. The atmosphere within their apartment became worse still in October, when every teacher in France was required to sign a statement under oath that he or she was neither Jewish nor a Freemason. Georges praised the recent decrees restricting the movement and freedom of Jews in France,[22] and even congratulated his daughter for signing the required oath. She was mortified to think that when her father finally approved of something she did, it was something she was ashamed of: "I signed it because I had to. My only income came from my teaching; my ration cards depended on it, my identity papers—everything. There simply was no other choice available to me. I hated it, but I did it for purely practical reasons. Who was I? A nobody, that's who. What good would it have done if some unknown teacher refused to sign a statement that had no meaning, no value, and certainly no influence or impact on anything? Refusing to sign such a statement would have had only one significance: that I no longer had a profession or an income. Who, in wartime, in my circumstances, would have been so foolish as to risk such a thing?"

At one of these family dinners in October, after they had eaten the "miserable Jerusalem artichokes and some of the other messes we had endured in my childhood during the first war," Françoise told her she would have to move out of Madame Brasseur's apartment because there was no chance the weakened old woman would ever return to it. Even in wartime, a buyer had been found. Beauvoir moved her few things back to the Carrefour Vavin, this time to the Hotel du Danemark. She left the faded orange-and-white furniture for Françoise to dispose of as she wished.

Her loneliness was somewhat assuaged because many of the friends who had stayed in France were now returning to Paris. Natasha's movements were always shrouded in mystery, so it was good to have Olga and even Wanda back. They had fled their parents' bombed village and moved into a hotel near Beauvoir's, living there until the war ended. Bost had been discharged, and he moved in, too. Occasionally she saw other friends whom she had known at the university, among them Guille and Gandillac, but for the most part she found herself depending on the Kosakievicz sisters and rejoicing in the company of Bost: "After so many months exclusively in female company, it was wonderful to pick up a friendship with a man again."[23] Others to whom she had been close before the war were now widely scattered. Raymond Aron had taken his family to London, word reached her that the Gerassis were in New York, and Colette Audry settled in Grenoble. Henriette Nizan had taken her children to Hollywood, where she was now working at one of the film studios. Beauvoir learned this from Brice Parain, who told her that Paul Nizan had died the previous May in battle against the Germans. He also told her that the French Communist Party had launched a campaign to discredit Nizan because he had resigned from it in disgust immediately after the Nazi–Soviet Pact.

The news of Nizan's death made Beauvoir physically ill. She left Parain's office, went into the bathroom of a café on the Rue du Bac and vomited. As she walked back to her hotel, she worried about how Sartre would take the news and whether or not to tell him by letter. Despite the fact that her friends were back, she felt very much alone because she had "no one wise about politics and history" with whom to discuss the sudden smear campaign against Nizan. For a brief moment she envied Rirette Nizan, wishing that she too were safe in Rirette's "American wonderland," but almost at once, she was both confused and ashamed by such feelings. She told herself she was a French woman, born into an old and "formerly distinguished" family, with the "obligation to stay in France and try to survive."

Others around her may have been plotting action against the German occupiers, but Simone de Beauvoir insists that she was unaware of them at the time. She considered herself, "without Sartre to lead me, ignorant of what I could do or what could be done. And there was no one else, really. All the persons who gave me intellectual guidance had fled because they were Jews or they wanted political asylum or, as in the case of Sartre and Bost and Nizan, were taken prisoner or were dead. I had nothing to do with the teachers at the school; they were all little scared rabbits who only wanted to be paid on time. I had not yet published and no one thought of me then as anything more than 'Sartre's girlfriend.' The people who had given me intellectual direction were gone from my life. If anyone was engaged in some sort of resistance, I didn't know about it; I only had my friends, and all they did was bicker and complain, like every other French citizen."

It turned out that her women friends did not like one another and all of them hated Natasha, who was especially jealous of Olga. Bianca Bienenfeld returned to Paris, and Beauvoir actually began to seek her companionship because, of all her younger women friends, she was the most placid and refused to participate in their shifting vendettas. Whenever Beauvoir wanted companionship without confrontation, she went somewhere with Bianca.

Like Sartre, whose adjustment to life as a war prisoner was a matter of accommodating to self-imposed routine and daily structure, Beauvoir adjusted to life in a defeated, occupied city. She spent her days teaching, reading in the library, writing in the Flore or the Dôme. She divided her evenings between her parents, with whom she now took only one meal each week, and her friends. Generally, because they all lacked money and ration tickets, they gathered in her hotel room, huddled against one another on her bed trying to keep warm. They talked and squabbled, listened to the radio or to records on an old gramophone which Olga had been carrying around with her for years. When someone (generally Natasha) brought a bottle of wine or a bit of sausage and bread, they all shared it.

Beauvoir had had one or two emotional moments concerning Sartre's incarceration, the first when a letter came bearing the return address of a prison hospital. Her fears were calmed when the wife of one of his fellow prisoners told her that hospital duty was eagerly sought because it was the easiest and warmest in the entire camp. Then Beauvoir heard that prisoners from various camps were beginning to escape and wondered whether he might be among them. He was not, and apart from a brief flurry of hope she settled into the routine of writing to him as often as possible and resigning herself with equanimity to what appeared to be a long separation. His letters continued to proclaim his need for her, and this did much to keep her as calm as she could be under the circumstances.

Then, in March 1941, Sartre appeared in Paris, unexpected and unannounced, and everything changed. "Sartre completely baffled me," she wrote in her memoirs. "He had emerged from a world of which I had no more real idea than he did of *my* life during the past few months; we both felt that the other was speaking in a completely different language."[24] Instead of finding her life "reintegrated by the mere fact of his presence, the superiority of his intellect, and the power of his ability to make sense of the political situation," she found herself "disoriented," and was "to stay that way for years to come."

EIGHTEEN

Socialism and Liberty

B EAUVOIR WAS TAKING her weekly dinner with her parents the night of Sartre's reappearance. She was always anxious to get away from their sorry state and all their problems; on this night, for no special reason, she went back to her hotel especially early. There she found a note in her mailbox: "I am at the Café des Trois Mousquetaires."

She recognized Sartre's writing and sprinted all the way to the café. Out of breath, she collapsed onto the nearest seat, but when she looked around, the café was empty. She thought the power of her desire to see Sartre had probably caused her to imagine the note, until a waiter who knew her shuffled over and handed her a second one: after waiting for two hours, Sartre wrote, he had gone out to take a walk and calm his nerves. She was terrified that he might have a chance encounter with someone he knew, which might distract him from coming back for her. She spent several nervous minutes wondering whether she should run through the streets looking for him or should force herself to sit still and wait. Fortunately, she had not long to worry.

When Sartre opened the door, Beauvoir was "as if paralyzed . . . unable to stand. He saw me but made no sign, no special greeting, just walked with purpose to my table, walked around it actually, then slid into the banquette beside me. I was choked with emotion. He leaned toward me, kissed me on the cheek because at first I could not turn my face to him. Then we embraced, I cried a little. It was very strange, because he hardly talked at all, and I—mostly I tried to keep from sobbing."

He had hinted since December in the private code they used in letters that their friend "Poulou" (his mother's pet name for him) would soon be coming back to Paris, but the rest of what he wrote about his daily life made her think him an unlikely candidate to try to escape, so she did not take these casual remarks seriously. As it was, his release came through a more ordinary means. They went to her hotel, where he told her that the Germans had invented a convenient excuse to rid themselves of the problem of feeding and housing unwanted men who would not be a security threat if freed. These included civilians who had been unjustly rounded up after the French surrender because they had been mistaken for soldiers, and the wounded, injured or otherwise handicapped. Such men were invited to go before a medical tribunal, which Sartre did, claiming that his blind eye made him suffer from dizzy spells and other disorientation; one of the prisoners who forged documents gave him a phony medical certificate attesting to this condition. He was thus officially medically discharged.

Beauvoir sobbed with rage when she learned that he had been in Paris for two weeks, sent with a convoy of discharged prisoners. The group had been isolated in the guards' barracks at Drancy, then thrown into close confinement with hundreds of other former prisoners and nothing to do.[1] One afternoon Sartre's name was called, he was herded onto a train, and suddenly he found himself free for the first time in almost a year, smack in the midst of rush-hour confusion in the Gare de l'Est. He was so overwhelmed by the crowds that he went into the station buffet to calm himself. He described the experience in an essay he wrote in 1954 about the paintings of Alberto Giacometti, saying it helped him to arrive at an understanding of the concept of distance:

> I had spent two months in a prison camp, which is like saying, in a sardine can, where I had experienced absolute proximity. My skin was the boundary of my living space. On my first night of freedom . . . in my native city . . . I pushed open the door of a café. Suddenly, I experienced a feeling of fear—or something close to it. . . . I was lost; the few drinkers seemed more distant than the stars. . . . I had rejoined bourgeois society, where I would have to learn to live once again 'at a respectful distance.' This sudden agoraphobia betrayed my vague feeling of regret for the collective life from which I had been forever severed.[2]

After almost two years of army life and nine months in prison camp, Sartre was disoriented. He had actually liked camp life, finding both camaraderie and freedom such as he had not had since the Ecole Normale Supérieure. He was relieved of the hated teaching and of all financial worries, food was adequate, and he had enough tobacco, paper, ink and reading materials. As soon as his daily chores were finished, his time was his own and he had nothing to do but write, think and discuss his ideas with other prisoners, a number of whom gave him the intelligent conversation he craved. He had grown accustomed to the routine, and because his writing gave him enormous satisfaction he thought he lacked for nothing. The absence of women was a detriment, but only to a certain extent: he did not miss physical sexuality, and Beauvoir's letters satisfied all his other needs. His months in prison camp were probably the only time when Sartre, who was always uncomfortable in the company of men and relished the companionship of women, was content to be in an all-male environment.

In the 1974 conversations with Beauvoir, Sartre talked about what had happened to cause this drastic change in 1941. He cited two things, both connected with the war.[3] The first was simply being in the Army:

. . . The fact is that from '39 I no longer belonged to myself
. . . life was entirely conditioned by [Hitler's armies]. . . . So
there I was, in military clothes that fitted me badly, surrounded
by other men . . . connected by a bond that was neither of family nor of friendship but that was nevertheless very important.
We had parts to play, and these parts were given to us from
outside.

It was then that he began to reflect upon what it meant "to be historical, to be part of a piece of history that was continually being decided
by collective occurrences." Prison camp marked the change:

I had been reshaped, one might say, by the prison camp.
So I came back to France with the idea that other Frenchmen did
not realize all this—that some of them, those who came back
from the front and were liberated, realized it, but there was no
one to make them decide to resist. That's what seemed to me
the first thing to do on coming back to Paris—to create a resistance group; to try, step by step, to win over the majority to resistance and thus bring into being a violent movement that would
expel the Germans.

Beauvoir was both astonished and uneasy to hear him talk this way.
They lay in her bed his first night back talking until dawn. She could not
understand "the stringency of his moral standards" as he rebuked her for
buying on the black market and "all but denounced" her for signing the
pledge that she was neither Jew nor Freemason. He questioned her rigorously, at times almost grilling her about the degree of contact she had had
with any Germans, and what if anything she knew about "the activities"
of any of their friends who were still in Paris. He "seemed disappointed"
when she had nothing to tell him other than the usual news of the Family.
Even the news of Nizan's death failed to distract him from his line of
questioning; his attention was diverted from what she perceived as "her
failings" only by her incomplete and somewhat garbled version of how
the Communists were denouncing Nizan.
    Once again, it was as if she had failed an examination she had no idea
of taking. But how was she to know? His letters to her had been full of
himself, his only instructions to her had been to write often, send what
she could for his comfort, and do what she could for the Family. If there
had been anything else, she surely would have obeyed.
    Nevertheless, her first brief moment of self-justification gave way to
lingering feelings of failure and guilt. For the next few days, as news of
Sartre's return brought reunions with their friends, no one could understand why she was so subdued.[4] Sartre did not seem to notice, nor did he
ask why; but even if he had, she would have been unable to explain.
    In retrospect, the difference in their two situations during the first
eighteen months of the war may help to explain Sartre's sudden desire for

political action and Beauvoir's seeming indifference to it. He had been sequestered with men of some intelligence in a prison camp, far removed from anything resembling his normal prewar life. There he had discussed ideas of freedom and action on a daily basis. She, on the other hand, continued to live in the same circumstances and with much the same daily routine as she had always had. With the exception of two periods of extraordinary activity, the exodus from Paris and the subsequent occupation of the city by the Germans, life continued for her much the same as usual. She did little more than see her friends and family, fulfill her teaching duties, and try to finish a novel based on a situation which had happened almost five years previously and which had nothing to do with her current circumstances.

Perhaps because he had never experienced it himself, Sartre had difficulty accepting how the general population dealt with daily life in war. He seemed especially unable to accept Beauvoir's attitude. Since the war began, she had lived in Paris "trying to stay out of harm's way," avoiding as much as possible contact with any form of bureaucracy, hushing disgruntled friends who even hinted at anti-German sentiments, and believing, as did the vast majority of Parisians, that her primary responsibility was to keep very quiet and try to survive. As with much of the rest of the population of Paris, the passivity of her behavior was characterized by "trauma and disorientation."[5]

And now he had come back, and was accusing her of having done almost everything wrong. This accusatory Sartre was new and bewildering. In all their years together, he had never openly chastised her, disagreed with her so harshly or been so indifferent to anything she might have endured. He had come back "a zealot, with one idea only, that we must work to overthrow the Germans."

She had assumed that when (and indeed if) he returned to Paris before the end of the war, they would "wait it out together," concentrating on being together and surviving, reading, writing, and talking to each other, sharing their ideas as they had always done. She saw his return as their opportunity to work together in relative leisure and seclusion, albeit one inflicted upon them by the German occupation.

She admitted many years later that it had been "an unrealistic, highly idealized fantasy, spun in loneliness and desolation." So it was especially painful to find him ready to plunge into activity without spending a few days alone with her. Even more wounding was his almost immediate capitulation to Natasha.

Beauvoir described Sartre and Natasha's first meeting in her memoirs, concluding that Natasha "in fact became very devoted to him."[6] What she did not write was that Natasha, at their second meeting, invited Sartre to go to bed with her and he accepted. Sartre did not tell Beauvoir, but Natasha did. Even before this, Beauvoir "knew it had happened by his sheepish behavior. When he did something he was embarrassed about he could never look at me and always had a shy smile." In her memoirs, Beauvoir quoted Natasha as saying to Sartre, "I wanted to have a chat with you and find out what sort of person I was up against."[7] In a 1984 conversation, Beauvoir described in some detail what had actually happened:

"Two things about Natasha at that time: she adored me, and she was consumed by jealousy toward everybody I knew. Remember I told you how she would plot the intrigues against Olga, Wanda? Well, when Sartre came back she was jealous of him and afraid that I would ignore her. So, like a little child, after she slept with him she came cuddling to me and confessed. Perhaps she thought it would solidify her position with both of us. Perhaps she meant to gain power over him and thus over me. I don't know her reasons—no one could ever know her reasons. But I don't think she ever slept with him again. She had a horror of anything not beautiful, and Sartre was, well, he was not beautiful. She kept his friendship, but really I was the one she cared most about."

Sartre "never really spoke of this encounter directly," and Beauvoir "of course did not want to cause him any embarrassment," so nothing was said by either of them. Natasha became involved with several other men, and her relationship with Sartre and Beauvoir became one of friendship. As the war progressed, she both depended on them and aided them through her "business dealings."

"Natasha could have been the ideal completion of our trio had we let her," Beauvoir said in retrospect. "But we had been badly burned by the experience with Olga and we were not then interested in creating another such situation. Besides, Sartre had other pressing concerns."

Within days of his return, Sartre presented himself to the Education Ministry, where officials were only too delighted to reinstate his prewar position as philosophy instructor at the Lycée Pasteur. He resumed teaching after the Easter holidays, and for a time it seemed to Beauvoir that all his talk of organized resistance had been no more than the ramblings of an exhausted and disoriented ex-prisoner.

Because no room in the Hotel du Danemark suited him, they each moved into separate rooms on different floors of the Hotel Mistral and immediately fell into their prewar habits and behavior. They never breakfasted together, because Sartre "liked to be alone in the morning and could not stand anyone who talked," while she "enjoyed the conversation of the people at the bar," where she stood by preference. They seldom met until lunchtime, when they generally ate together in a neighborhood café, exchanging news of their day. Often, if teaching or appointments did not interrupt, they stayed on until evening, sometimes writing at adjacent tables, sometimes seated at opposite ends of the café in conversation with their friends. This pattern continued into early May, giving Beauvoir hope that it might last indefinitely. As far as she was concerned, "being this close to Sartre made the war seem very far away."

Then one morning he told her that he had invited their friends to a meeting in her room that night to discuss the formation of a Resistance group. Bost and Olga came, but Sartre insisted they keep it secret from Wanda because "she talked too much; not deliberately, of course, but indiscriminately."[8] Natasha was included, as was her then lover (whose name Beauvoir said she had "probably repressed. He was Jewish and they took him away.") Jean Pouillon, Sartre's pupil before the war, was also there at Bost's invitation.

Pouillon, who met Beauvoir that night for the first time, remembered the occasion as "a room full of surprisingly loud conversation for what was supposed to be a clandestine activity. Everyone was laughing and talking among themselves before Sartre addressed us, except Simone de Beauvoir, who was sitting quietly at the edge of the group smoking a cigarette in an attitude of pensive thought. I had known and admired Sartre since before the war, but this was my first meeting with her. I had heard stories that she was a formidable woman, very brusque and commanding, but that night she seemed shy, frightened, puzzled—I don't know how to describe it.

"It became a very long conversation [between Pouillon and Beauvoir]. At first we talked about the usual things—the war, the lack of food, how glad we were to see warm weather return—but then we began to talk about the philosophy of how we could act as responsible French [citizens] in such times. I remember being struck by the brilliance and persuasion of her words, and thinking that she was probably expressing something Sartre had written, because, sorry to say now, that's how we thought of her in those days. It was not until later, when I read the two [philosophical] essays she wrote during the war, that I realized I had been in conversation with an original thinker, a profound philosopher. After that, she became someone whose friendship I valued, not, as so many others thought her to be, someone one had to endure to be near Sartre."[9]

When everyone was settled, Sartre began to talk about what this group should try to do. He envisioned a two-pronged mission, but his immediate plan was unfocused and his ideas of where and how to start were vague. However, his future objective, and by this he meant when the war was over, was very clear. His description of his long-term objective gave the group its Resistance name. Beauvoir described it: "If the democracies won, it would be essential for the Left to have a new program; it was our job . . . to bring such a program into being. Its basic aims could be summed up in two words . . . which also served as a watchword for our movement: 'Socialism and Liberty.' "[10] Thus the group took for its name two words whose "reconciliation posed vast problems."

In the meantime, Sartre proposed action that would also prepare his friends for life in France if the Allied Powers were defeated, so that "if Germany won the war, our task would be to see that she lost the peace." Sartre's immediate plan was for his group to gather information which they would write up and distribute in news bulletins and pamphlets, but he was vague about what constituted suitable information. Beauvoir was puzzled at the time. "I asked him privately exactly what he meant. Were we to become spies and try to collect 'intelligence'? Were the women to infiltrate the Germans and use their 'wiles'? Would we take clandestine photographs, and of what? Collect troop movements—how could we get close enough? And finally, where would we send this information—to De Gaulle in London? (Already Sartre didn't like him.) Where would we get the radio? Who would teach us to use it? Where would we hide it? He became very angry with me, so I pretended at first that my questions were meant to amuse him.

"But then I realized that this was both dishonest and dangerous, and so I asked him to receive my questions on this matter as he so willingly received my criticisms on his written work. They were really intended to make him define precisely what we should do, just as the [criticisms of writings] were meant to make him express himself clearly. He said he didn't know, that we would have to determine what to do as we went along. This frightened me, because it was one thing to structure one's creative thought as the writing progresses, but it was quite another to play these dangerous games so cavalierly in wartime."

Sartre could not organize his own small band of friends, so he went farther afield. Merleau-Ponty, now teaching at the Ecole Normale, had recruited several of his students and was working with others at the school in a loosely organized group called Sous la Botte (Under the Boot).[11] Sartre, Beauvoir, Bost and Pouillon joined Merleau-Ponty, Jean-Toussaint and Dominique Desanti (then students of philosophy and history respectively) and (among others) the philosophers Simone Debout and Jean Kanapa and historian Raoul Lévy.[12] Several weeks of meetings followed, characterized more by esoteric philosophical argument than by any actual Resistance work. They met in a sleazy hotel in the Latin Quarter, in a ground-floor room which they entered through the window, thinking themselves very clever, "[giving] us the illusion that we could escape more easily in case the police decided to arrest us. We were still innocent then."[13] The only thing they agreed on was the need to produce a manifesto before any real activity could begin. Since they represented the whole spectrum of political thought, very little writing was actually accomplished.

Meanwhile, all over Paris people they knew were disappearing into German prisons because they took action without the need for philosophical statements to govern their acts of resistance. After the war, Beauvoir defended her group's choice of action: "We were not going out just to blow up a bridge or take a microfilm photo of a weapon or a building. Anyone could do that. We were looking ahead to the peace, no matter who the victor. We were planning for our future in France after the war. When we decided what that should be, then we would begin to work to assure it." She insisted that "intellectuals had the obligation to think of these things," adding, "Anyone who wasn't there does not have the privilege of criticizing those who were."

There was some activity, however, in Socialisme et Liberté: Bost and Pouillon carried a bulky mimeo machine through the streets of Paris to Pouillon's mother's apartment; when it leaked ink all over her Persian carpet, they took it into the garden, where it was clearly visible from the street. Pouillon left a briefcase on the Métro which contained his own name and address and those of everyone they had tried to recruit, as well as a packet of ink-smeared pamphlets. They found it several days later in the lost-and-found.[14] Natasha tried at first to roll up pamphlets so that they would fit inside the hollow metal tubes of her bicycles, but she was too impatient, so she simply stuffed them into the basket and took off across Paris, throwing them into the streets in great handfuls. She liked to flirt with German soldiers while her basket was full of clandestine materials, and liked especially to pass them out to soldiers she thought could not read French. When she bragged about it to Beauvoir, "the thought of these dumb German soldiers walking away with our manifestos in their hands made my blood run cold. I told Sartre we could no longer give her anything to do. She was crazy about danger, and we would all be killed because of her recklessness."

Information proved difficult to gather and of little value. "I did it only once," said Raoul Lévy. "I was ashamed; the information I had to transmit seemed so ridiculous."[15] He had learned that a squadron of German tanks was billeted in the Rambouillet Forest; the recommendation was to ask the British Royal Air Force to drop bombs, but since they had no idea to whom this recommendation should be made, Simone de Beauvoir remembers that "we decided to save it for later, when we had other news for the British. We were sure we could find someone to pass it on."

There were many squabbles over ideology, and so, to insure that all variants of political allegiance would receive equal representation, newsletter editorials were written alternately by Marxists and non-Marxists. There was endless debate about whether to write articles encouraging the sabotage of German installations in Paris or whether instead they should try to convince soldiers of the wrongfulness of the occupation. Simone Debout remembers that Simone de Beauvoir, learning of a trainload of French writers who were going to Germany, asked, "Who should smash Brasillach's face in, me or Debout?"[16] Beauvoir said emphatically that Debout was mistaken. "I was never that foolhardy, nor was I ever that brave."

Nevertheless, she continued to attend meetings, sitting quietly on the sidelines, speaking only when there was a possibility of turning an abstract suggestion into possible concrete action, which she considered to be her main contribution to Sartre's attempts at organized resistance. "I continued to act as his trusted critic, both for his writing and for his action. My main concern was for his safety—and mine, of course—and I thought it my duty to plot all the possibilities to insure that nothing happened to either of us." Shortly after, when Sartre and Merleau-Ponty combined their members into one group under the name Socialisme et Liberté, she decided that her self-assigned duty was more literary than political.

Sartre was the unofficial yet recognized leader, but Merleau-Ponty still vied with him for command. Because they held differing political and philosophical views (Merleau-Ponty was already calling himself a Marxist and Sartre was then a staunch anti-Communist), both were chosen to write manifestos describing the group's reason for being and its plan of action. According to Beauvoir, "They were each jealous that the other would lead, and each wanted to be the one to do so, quite apart from ideology." She continued her role as Sartre's editor and critic, but found it difficult "to reconcile his philosophy with the new vocabulary of political action. I had to give it up. He said it didn't matter. He knew what he wanted to say." Merleau-Ponty's text was twenty pages, but Sartre's came to "a hundred pages of close handwriting." Ten copies were made of Sartre's "first political contribution," but all were lost. Of those who read it, "Raoul Lévy . . . despite his 'immense admiration for Sartre,' found it painfully close to a 'parody of an electoral platform.' "[17] As the summer began, Beauvoir remembered, they were still "only talking, trying to make up our minds what to do. We had nothing and no one to guide us. As far as we were concerned, we were isolated, marooned. There was no one else in France who felt [as frustrated as] we did about the occupation."

Beauvoir later characterized some of this feeling as having been due to "Sartre's new ideas, perhaps too badly expressed for political activism to follow." One of his biographers said Sartre's proposals amounted to much the same thing as "simply continuing his discussion with the priests in the stalag."[18] Another comments that Sartre "ran around a lot; lots of activity when he came back from the stalag, trying to get everyone to jump on his bandwagon. But those who were already active didn't want him around. They couldn't trust their lives to someone so visible and so indiscreet."[19] And still a third remarks that "it had not occurred to [Sartre] that a number of resistance groups might already exist."[20]

Accounts of the true beginning of organized Resistance activity in France sometimes conflict, depending upon whether the author writes from the British or French perspective, which country's official documents have been consulted, and whose testimonies are accepted as the truth from among survivors of the various reseaux, or Resistance "cells" (as these groups came to be called). June 18, 1940, is generally accepted as the start of the Resistance, this being the date of Charles de Gaulle's speech from London pledging that "the flame of French resistance must not and shall not be extinguished."[21] However, by that date Combat, one of the most famous Resistance groups, was already active in Lyon, and by October 1940 there were a number of cells in Paris and also a long list of underground newspapers, among them Libération. By the time Sartre determined to establish a reseau in the summer of 1941, these and many others were already contributing usefully to the Allied cause.

Paris, the intellectual center of the country, was the active heart of the Resistance movement. Sartre had reestablished all his prewar friendships and contacts from the moment he returned, so it is difficult to believe that in May 1941, after more than two months in Paris, he would not have known something about Resistance activity, even if only rumor or innuendo. And despite Simone de Beauvoir's contention that teachers in the lycée system wanted only to draw their pay each month, many were putting their lives at risk on an almost daily basis.

One such was Alfred Péron, an instructor at the Lycée Buffon who had been a distant friend of Sartré's at the Ecole Normale.[22] Sartre had been briefly engaged to Péron's cousin and had spent part of one summer with both of them at their grandparents' country estate. There he and Péron formed a solid friendship but one which neither of them sought to maintain when they returned to Paris, because they lived such different personal and professional lives.

Alfred Péron returned to teach at the Lycée Buffon as soon as he was detached from his military unit. He worked briefly with a loosely structured group called the Groupe du Musée de l'Homme (Museum of Man Group). Soon after, by November 1940, he founded an offshoot cell known openly and casually as the Groupe du Lycée Buffon. At the beginning, these cells engaged in "Boy Scout stuff," as one *résistant* described it,[23] but this was soon replaced with the secrecy of code names, false credentials and serious spying. Péron's group went underground and become known as Etoile; one of the earliest and most effective *reseaux*, it was active from the fall of 1940 to August 1942, when it was betrayed by a defrocked priest who pretended to be a resistant while actually working as a German agent. Its membership was composed almost entirely of artists, writers and other intellectuals, both French and English; among them were the widow and daughter of the painter Francis Picabia, and the Irish writer Samuel Beckett.

Etoile figured briefly in Sartre's attempts at resistance when he contacted Péron in the summer of 1941, hoping to enlist him for Socialisme et Liberté. Péron declined, saying he had family to think about and could not engage in such dangerous activity. Clearly, he did not want Sartre to know the truth about his role in the Resistance, nor did he want to recruit him for Etoile. Péron's widow believed her husband thought Sartre "would probably seem an unlikely candidate for espionage because he was such an undisciplined person, his behavior so scandalously public."[24] This view was shared by a number of others who were active in Etoile. Madame Gabrielle Picabia and her daughter, Jeannine, remembered that "celebrities were to be avoided at all cost; especially those, like Sartre, for example, who hung about in the best cafés, where all the Germans congregated." Samuel Beckett, who had visited his good friend Péron at the same time as Sartre that summer, said, "There were always those whom no one took seriously, neither the *résistants* nor the Gestapo. Sartre seemed to many people to be among these."

So those who had any inkling of Resistance activity acknowledged Sartre's good intentions, but since he did not temper them with prudence, he became—at least to people who did not know him well—a rather comic figure. When it came to anti-German activity, he was either avoided or rejected by everyone outside his immediate circle. No new members came to swell its ranks, no spontaneous generation of new cells detached themselves from the parent; much was plotted and planned, but little was actually done. In mid-July, the members decided to recess for the summer.

To Beauvoir, this seemed the perfect opportunity for her and Sartre to take a holiday similar to their prewar travels, in a part of France they had not seen before. Though movement from the Occupied Zone to the Free Zone was severely restricted, *passeurs* had a thriving business smuggling people across the line, and Beauvoir took it for granted that she and Sartre would get through.

She was "delirious" at the thought of the holiday, and of having Sartre all to herself. While he had been writing the moribund group's manifesto, she had put the finishing touches to *L'Invitée* and was ready to start another novel. She wanted Sartre to read *L'Invitée* and knew that the only way she could make that possible was to be alone with him, away from the distractions in Paris. Her "dream" was for them to take the train to one of the easier passing points, get across and then spend several weeks walking in the countryside. But the group proposed a very different plan, and Sartre accepted. When he told Beauvoir, she was "disappointed," but "willing to make the best of it."

The "Central Committee of the 'Sartre Group,' "[25] an ironic title coined by those who followed Sartre's ideological position (as opposed to Merleau-Ponty's or the other splinter ideologies within the cell), decided to send Sartre to the Free Zone as their emissary, hoping he would convince some of the famous writers who had settled there to embrace their cause publicly.

The proposal was put to Sartre "sometime around the end of June," with the suggestion that he and Beauvoir leave as soon as possible. She was ready to go, because she "was used to throwing a toothbrush, a sweater and a change of clothes into a backpack," but Sartre took a little longer: "He had to decide which pens to take, and how much paper, and what part of his manuscript, and then his shoes might hurt, and which clothing would be more comfortable—he was infinitely fussier about such things than I was."

She made a brief visit to her parents to tell them that she was taking a holiday despite the war, and was unexpectedly faced with a crucial dilemma. Her father's health had declined seriously since early June, when he had had prostate surgery and cancer was discovered. The doctors insisted that he would recover, but her mother did not want her to leave Paris. Sartre was anxious to get started on his mission, and for several days it seemed as if she would have to choose between them. She made "the private decision, in my mind, without telling anyone, that I would go with Sartre. That my responsibility was to the living rather than to the nearly dead."

She did not have to decide, because Georges de Beauvoir died in his sleep in the early morning of July 1, 1941, at the age of sixty-three. In her memoirs, Simone de Beauvoir said his death was exacerbated by "months of undernourishment [which] had weakened him, and the defeat and the subsequent occupation had given him a grievous shock."[26] Hélène de Beauvoir said it was a death "more due to sorrow than to hunger":

> Papa had no sympathy for the German presence in his country, on the sidewalks of his city . . . All those people, those good French people . . . who followed [Marshal Henri] Pétain in a spirit of collaboration—his patriotism would not permit him to tolerate this. To see this bourgeois class into which he was born, to see his friends, nearly all of them, become Pétainistes, robbed him of all his illusions. For a man of the Extreme Right, as he had been, this was a hard and cruel awakening.[27]

Nevertheless, months of undernourishment due to a diet of "war vegetables" and whatever was being passed off as coffee weakened him. He had always been a robust man of healthy appetite, but from the beginning of rationing he forbade Françoise to shop on the black market and warned Simone that he would not tolerate any such goods she might bring into the house. To Georges this was the only "politically correct protest he could make." It gave his daughter a new respect for him, enhanced by his utter indifference to illness and the prospect of death. She sat with him throughout his last days in "a floating state, a tranquil sensation." He had resigned himself to dying, so the last days were free of the bitterness that had characterized much of his lifelong conversation.

"Do me a great favor," Georges said to Simone one sunny afternoon while she sat by his bedside, both of them dozing from time to time. "See to it that my wife does not bring a priest here." She was struck as much by the way he referred to Françoise as she was by his request. She told Françoise with trepidation, prepared for all sorts of emotional outbursts, but her mother surprised her by saying quietly, "All right."

Georges de Beauvoir was interred in the family plot at Père Lachaise Cemetery.[28] Françoise noted that his was the last name that could be carved onto the large communal tombstone, and that hers would have to be mounted on a separate plaque when she died. "Where will we put your name, and Hélène's?" she asked distractedly. Her elder daughter ignored the question; they were not sure that the younger, marooned in Portugal by the war, even knew that her father was dead. "Anyway," Beauvoir said, "I had the feeling it would not matter very much to either of us."

Françoise seemed to Simone to take her husband's death with surprising composure. For the first few weeks, Simone watched her mother carefully, waiting for she "knew not what—depression, tears, outbursts," but nothing came. Françoise announced that she was "planning to go about the business of living," and she urged her daughter and all their relatives to do the same. She was fifty-six years old and looked much

2

1. Françoise Brasseur de Beauvoir as a young bride.

2. Georges de Beauvoir as a young husband.

3. An infant Simone de Beauvoir doted on by (left to right) her father, her grandfather Ernest de Beauvoir, her aunt Marguerite, her mother, and her uncle Gaston de Beauvoir, 1908.

3

4

4. Meyrignac, Ernest de Beauvoir's estate in Uzerche, where the family spent summers. "Simone's place" is at the back of the small patio to the left; her bedroom was directly above on the second floor.

5. Hélène de Beauvoir and her adored older sister, ages 3 and 5, in the garden at Meyrignac.

6. Françoise and Georges de Beauvoir with their daughters on the balcony of their first apartment in Paris.

5

6

7

7. Simone (far left, first row) and ZaZa (far right, second row) with their classmates and two instructors at the Cours Désir.

8. Hélène and Simone as teenagers, about 1924.

9. Simone (left), ZaZa (center) and an unidentified companion, about 1926.

10. Simone (far left) with her cousin Magdeleine (far right) and two friends at Château La Grillère in Saint-Germain-les-Belles. Behind them is the tower where Sartre surreptitiously waited to be fed the summer after he met Simone.

11

11. Members of Sartre's circle during one of their ritual promenades on the roofs of the Ecole Normale Supérieure, 1927. In front: Henriette and Paul Nizan with arms crossed; behind them, Daniel Lagache (second from left), Simone de Beauvoir (partially hidden) and Sartre on the chimney.

12. Castor (wearing a hat and lace collar, center) studying at the Bibliothèque Nationale, 1929 or 1930.

12

151923

13

13. The young philosophy teacher (fourth from left in the second row) with her students and their headmistress at lycée Jeanne d'Arc in Rouen, 1932–1933. Olga Kosakievicz is in the bottom row at the far left; Wanda is in the second row, second from the right.

14. Stépha and Fernando Gerassi with their son, John, on the beach at Nice in 1937, during Fernando's leave from the Madrid front. The paper announces recent events in the Spanish Civil War.

14

15

16

17

18

15. Sartre and Castor in Paris, 1938.

16. Beauvoir and Nathalie (Natasha) Sorokine Moffatt, around 1943.

17. Beauvoir working at her habitual table in the Café de Flore, 1945.

18. Beauvoir with Richard and Ellen Wright on her first trip to New York, 1947.

19. Beauvoir with Sartre and Boris and Michelle Vian in the Café Procope, 1951.

19

20

21

22

20. Nelson Algren, revealing a vulnerability rarely seen in photographs, snapped by his Simone (with his new camera) on his first trip to Paris, 1950.

21. Olga Bost, Algren and Simone in Cabris, 1950.

22. "Frog wife" and "crocodile husband."

23. Algren's wall collage devoted to photos of Beauvoir, her letters, book jackets and reviews of her work.

23

24

24. Beauvoir with Sartre in China, 1955.

25. Beauvoir being asked to sign copies of her books (and, ironically, one of Sartre's) in São Paulo, Brazil, 1960.

25

26. Sartre and Beauvoir with Fidel Castro in Cuba; a photo reproduced around the world by both friends and enemies of all three figures.

27

28

29

27. Sartre and Beauvoir in Moscow with Nikita Khrushchev (pointing) and members of the Writers Society of Europe, 1963.

28. The writing couple at work in Sartre's apartment on the Rue Bonaparte, 1966.

29. Michelle Vian (far left), Sartre and Beauvoir (center) during a demonstration in support of the Maoist newspaper *La Cause du peuple*, June 1970.

30. A drawing of Simone de Beauvoir (with Sartre's head atop her flagstaff) which appeared on the cover of *The New York Times Magazine* in July 1971, captioned "Simone de Beauvoir on the Barricades." 30

31. At a feminist colloquium in Brussels, 1972. 31

32

32. Beauvoir with her adopted daughter, Sylvie
le Bon de Beauvoir, in the early 1970s.

33. Sartre with his adopted daughter, Arlette
Elkaïm-Sartre, at a rehearsal of one of his plays.

33

34. Claude Lanzmann with Beauvoir and Sartre at an editorial board meeting of *Les Temps Modernes*.

35. Beauvoir in her apartment on the Rue Schoelcher, decorated with objects from her many travels.

35

36

36. A meeting of the editorial board of *Les Temps Modernes* at Sartre's apartment on the Boulevard Edgar-Quinet, November 1977. Left to right: Jean Pouillon, Pierre Victor (Benny Lévy), Claire Etcherelli, François George, André Gorz, Simone de Beauvoir, Jean-Paul Sartre, Pierre Ribould. Missing: Pierre Goldmann, Claude Lanzmann, Jacques-Laurent Bost.

37. Beauvoir, Sartre and Sylvie in his apartment on the Boulevard Edgar-Quinet, 1979.

37

38

38. Beauvoir and Sartre toasting their fifty years together on his birthday, June 21, 1979, in Sylvie's apartment.

39. Beauvoir with Sylvie (left) and her sister (behind her) at Sartre's graveside during his burial, April 19, 1980.

39

40. Meeting with feminists, 1985. Left to right: Colette Audry, Kate Millett, Simone de Beauvoir, Anne Zelensky, Yvette Roudy, and Sylvie le Bon de Beauvoir.

41

41. Beauvoir at seventy-six, during a 1984 interview with the author.

younger, in sound health ("from climbing all those stairs several times each day") and full of vitality. Her daughter was surprised at the number of people at the funeral who were friends of Françoise's, people who knew her from her parish church and the library she frequented in the quarter, where her kindness and good deeds were well known. Simone was surprised by the disparity in their age, social class and financial status. There were several distinguished old ladies (whom Françoise visited regularly and with whom she sometimes shared what was available), but there were also young families (whom she often helped with their children), tradespeople (for whom she always had a sympathetic remark despite the shortages of wartime), and several girl students whom she met at the library (and whom she encouraged to study by offering her daughter's example). When they told Simone how much they liked Françoise, she saw her mother for the first time as someone other than the nagging, prying disciplinarian of her younger life.

Françoise told her daughter that she planned to move as soon as she could find a smaller apartment, but first of all she intended to find a job. She was very good with people, and she liked to help them; she was sure she could find something at the library, and if not she planned to volunteer at the Red Cross. However, she could not work without pay indefinitely: the convent-bred girl who had been a sheltered wife was now a widow who needed to earn her living. She agreed to accept financial help from her daughter, but only until she could take care of herself. In the meantime, she was going to burn all the letters she and Georges had exchanged over the years, and there would be no reason to keep those written by her daughters, or their exercise books and report cards, for that matter—she would burn those too. The furniture could be sold, she would take only what she needed.

"Go," she told her daughter. "Resume your life. Mine is just fine."[29]

The trip to the south actually took place from mid-August to the end of September.[30] Beauvoir and Sartre shipped their backpacks and bicycles (his too a gift from Natasha) to Roanne in the Free Zone and took the train to Montceau-les-Mines, where they found a *passeur* who took them across the line. They picked up their things at the Roanne station and made their way south on the bikes, sleeping most nights in sleeping bags and a tent loaned by Bost.

Sartre was looking for Resistance groups to join with his, or others simply to join, and men who would help in either instance, André Gide turned him down in Vallauris, as did André Malraux at Cap d'Ail and Daniel Mayer in their southernmost stop, Marseille. They headed north toward Grenoble to see Colette Audry, and on the way Beauvoir fell off her bicycle, cracked her front teeth, blackened her eyes and skinned her face. When she looked in a mirror that night, she thought her entire head was swollen to almost double its size.

Audry never forgot the sight of her "beautiful friend, so frightful to see." They told her how unsuccessful the trip had been and she was touched by "their childlike innocence and sadness." Audry had been active in her local Resistance from its inception, and she thought the gulf that separated her group from theirs was "beyond any bridging." She told them gently that they should go back to Paris and "try to be useful," but to concentrate on their writing and "leave espionage to those who know how to do it."[31] Beauvoir urged Sartre to listen to her, but he was determined to keep the group alive in Paris.

So they made their way home, slowed down by repeated flat tires and general exhaustion, to the west of Roanne, where they paid the *passeur* his fee and were escorted across in broad daylight with twenty or thirty other people who had done the same. "The Germans caught onto the business and cut themselves in for a share of the profits," Beauvoir later told Olga and Bost.[32]

Embarrassed and chagrined, Sartre reported back to Socialisme et Liberté of his total failure to convince even one person to join the cell. Though everyone was dispirited, they all agreed to continue. But before the year was out, personal attacks on Sartre became so frequent, concentrated and vicious that they all realized it was senseless. Socialisme et Liberté had disintegrated.

"There is one element in the Resistance coalition that requires a special note: the French Communist Party," writes the historian Peter Novick. "They were unquestionably the single most important element in the Resistance (though they were far from being a majority. . . ."[33]

The party in France had been in disarray for several years and was now seeking to take a leading role in the Resistance, partly in order to counter the loss of members since the Nazi–Soviet Pact. To keep its members from resigning in disgust, as Nizan had done, party leaders resorted to besmirching other reputations in order, so it was said, to keep members in line and to vindicate the various about-faces of Soviet international policy.

Now it was Sartre's turn to be the victim of party attack. The Communists wanted to unify all resistance in France under their aegis, as, despite his inability to organize anything political, he was someone they perceived as a threat. The two published biographies of him give interesting accounts of what happened. Cohen-Solal writes:

"Don't trust Sartre; he is a German agent," was just one of the lies that the communists had spread throughout the southern provinces to discredit the head of the group. It was "learned" that he had been freed from prison camp thanks to the direct intervention of Drieu la Rochelle, and that he was a henchman of national socialism, just like his mentor, Heidegger. . . . In other words, wallowing in their paranoia, the communists had decided to turn Sartre into their ideal scapegoat; after all, hadn't he been Nizan's childhood friend, and, as such, wasn't he also likely to be a potential spy? Given these conditions, how could Sartre have joined forces with the communists?[34]

Ronald Hayman describes Sartre's departure from the stalag as an "escape"[35] and the French Communist Party's subsequent attempt to discredit him as an allegation "that the escape had been staged." The Communists inferred that Sartre had made a bargain with the Germans and been released "because he had promised to work for them." Hayman notes further that

> one problem remains. After *Bariona* [a play Sartre wrote and staged in the stalag] they could hardly have failed to realize he was the Sartre who had written *La Nausée* [published in March 1938 with much success], and if they had wanted to recapture him in Paris after his escape, it would not have been difficult.

The Communists were ready with a response, alleging that the Germans believed it was to their greater advantage to have Sartre roaming freely in Paris: "If he was one of the intellectuals who could function freely under their régime, he would be helping to demonstrate that it was not oppressive."[36]

Whether or not these allegations were spread by the Communists remains unproven, but Sartre himself gave them ammunition when he wrote an article for the collaborationist journal *Comoedia*. Founded in 1960, it had been a respected journal dedicated entirely to reviews and articles about art, the theater and literature. By 1936 "it had become a shadow of its former self."[37] By 1941, under the direction of the distinguished journalist René Delange, it had become an important instrument of German propaganda: ". . . the collaborationist game played by *Comoedia* was indeed *subtle* . . . it was to strengthen the image of a restored cultural life. . . . Seen from this angle, [it] therefore carries great significance."

In the first issue published under German supervision, Sartre wrote a review of the French translation of Herman Melville's *Moby-Dick*, which appeared prominently on page 2, but Simone de Beauvoir dismissed the magnitude of his contribution:

> An old journalist called Delange, whom he regarded with some sympathy, offered him a regular literary column in *Comoedia*. . . . [The] old man swore it did not come under any sort of German censorship. . . . [When] the number actually appeared Sartre realized that *Comoedia* was less independent than Delange had said. All the same, Delange did manage to give his weekly a tone sharply at variance with that of the rest of the [German propaganda] press.[38]

Delange fostered Beauvoir's career and came to her financial rescue later during the war, so this explanation from her memoirs is both offhanded and disrespectful. She wrote it when his reputation had been sullied by the association with *Comoedia* and she was anxious to downplay their friendship. Literary journalist Pierre Assouline notes that throughout the war Delange remained the "benefactor" of Sartre and Beauvoir, and that "it was in *Comoedia* that [their] writings found their best reception and the promptest review."[39]

Sartre's third biographer, John Gerassi,[40] discussed whether Sartre (and, by extension, Beauvoir) had done anything that might have proven the truth of allegations of collaboration, other than having allowed their works to be published or presented onstage during the war: "I think the answer is that Sartre certainly profited. He gave his works to the censor, and when they suggested that three words be changed here and there and so forth, he did it. He didn't compromise what he wanted to say, didn't change what he was going to say . . . but he [still] played by the rules of the occupation. There's a kind of moral collaboration involved in that. On the other hand, he went to see Malraux, he tried to join the Resistance, and later he wrote for *Les Lettres Françaises* which at that time was an underground literary magazine. It's not a clean record. He lived well, as did Simone de Beauvoir. Well, they were into survival."

As the war continued, their conduct remained open to further question. Very few writers could afford not to publish; given Sartre's emotional makeup and personality, not publishing was impossible to contemplate. Beauvoir said that "the first rule on which all the intellectuals of the Resistance were agreed was: 'no writing for the Occupied Zone papers.' "[41] And Sartre did just that. When the infamous "Otto List" came out, banning the works of more than eight hundred writers deemed unfriendly to the Third Reich by the German ambassador in Paris, Otto Abetz, Sartre's name was not on it, giving renewed credence to the rumor that he had been "allowed to escape" from the stalag to further German intentions for a peaceful collaboration among the occupiers and the occupied. Both Sartre and Beauvoir published their novels with Editions Gallimard, whose owner and publisher, Gaston Gallimard, was accused (but acquitted) of collaboration in the purge that followed the end of the war. And both wrote plays that were staged with great success later in the war, the hit of their respective seasons. But: "Nobody kept firmly to the rules,"[42] said one critic with hindsight, while a more contemporary account stated flatly that "it would be fruitless to deny that during these four years of German occupation Paris continued to be a brightly lit spectacle and to spread its great artistic influence throughout the counry."[43] A third said succinctly, "It doesn't seem to matter what one did in the war; what mattered was if and when one went on trial for it afterwards."[44] Significantly, no formal or official accusation was made about either Sartre or Beauvoir.

As for Simone de Beauvoir, her "happiness" depended only on being with Sartre, and despite the war this was probably the most tranquil year of their relationship. He was still too preoccupied with unfocused ideas

for resistance to have time for any woman besides Wanda, who grudgingly accepted the fact that Beauvoir would continue to be first with him.
The two women had established a truce of sorts: Wanda was "uneasy"
about Beauvoir, but Beauvoir was "indifferent" to Wanda.

Her life during this crucial year depended almost entirely on his
thoughts, opinions, movements and activities. She had done nothing of
public merit on her own; she had not yet published, she was still only a
philosophy teacher in a lycée, and she was—in the derogatory term by
which she was best known then—"only Sartre's girlfriend."[45] Her primary
identity came through her relationship to him, and because of it she was
tainted by association. It was a mixed blessing.

NINETEEN

The Promise of the Future

I N SPITE OF EVERYTHING my heart beats, my hand is held out, new projects are born and urge me on,"[1] says the character Pyrrhus in the philosophical dialogue Simone de Beauvoir wrote during the blackest period of the war. The promise of the future is a recurring theme in her wartime writing, in part because, after more than fifteen years of trying, this was when she succeeded in becoming what she had always wanted to be—a published writer.[2]

Sartre's ego had taken a tremendous beating when his ill-conceived Resistance attempts were so decisively rejected, but, resilient as ever, he returned to his writing with the same intensity he had given it during the Phony War. Nothing could have pleased Beauvoir more. Sartre's long hours of writing gave her own life the basic structure and form she had yearned for ever since her first adolescent dream of the ideal relationship, which for her meant sitting in a room reading and writing beside an otherwise featureless man. Now, despite the grimness of their daily existence, she was finally living this dream: "I no longer experienced any feeling of security, any overwhelming sensations of elated joy; but my day-to-day mood was one of gayness, and I often reflected that, despite everything, this obstinate gaiety was still a kind of happiness.[3]

Her happiness was further enhanced by what was for Sartre a near-celibate existence: he took no new lovers during this time, and his only contingent affairs were with women he already knew. Wanda remained "the itch or the prick, but certainly not the thorn" of Beauvoir's existence because, although Sartre continued to respond to Wanda's whims and caprices, it was not at the expense of his writing—or Beauvoir's.

Teaching still provided their income, and for Beauvoir it filled between twenty and thirty hours a week, depending on her schedule each term. She also found time for a daily stint in the Bibliothèque Nationale, still reading Hegel and Heidegger so that she could edit Sartre's work with assurance. She spent "almost no time at all" preparing for her classes, preferring to read and write philosophy. Mostly, she depended on Leibniz and Descartes, trusting her memory of university studies fifteen years earlier to satisfy her students. If they seemed capable of following a more sophisticated line of inquiry, she explored questions to which she herself sought the answers in the German philosophers she was currently reading. Her classroom lectures then became "a dialogue mostly conducted with myself, mostly for my own benefit."

This period marked the beginning of her active life as a *"café habituée,"* or, in her own English translation, "café squatter," when the familiar picture of her emerges, seated alone at a table, fountain pen in one hand, cigarette in the other, a pile of manuscript pages before her, a beautiful but shabbily dressed woman, occasionally shivering in the cold but happily lost in thought.

It was also her *femme de charge* period, a term that, conscious of the irony, she preferred to translate as "housewife."[4] For the first time in her life, she lived in a hotel room with cooking facilities—a gas ring and a tiny sink. Hélène, marooned in Portugal, was no longer able to pay the rent on her studio, but, despite the shortage of housing throughout Paris, no one else had yet squatted there,[5] so Beauvoir requisitioned all her sister's pots and pans and set up housekeeping in the Hotel Mistral as "an intellectual proposition."

She and Sartre were each paid 3,500 old francs a month.[6] Together they had the equivalent of $230, more than enough for their own simple needs, but they had made themselves responsible for seven people on a full-time basis and often for one or two others temporarily in need. First there was Françoise de Beauvoir, to whom Beauvoir began to give a monthly stipend that continued until her mother's death in 1964.[7] Then there were Olga, Wanda and Natasha, who depended entirely on Sartre and Beauvoir, and usually Bost, whose family was ashamed of the way he lived and only gave him occasional money under the most grudging circumstances. Natasha had a succession of romantic liaisons, and the young men with whom she was involved shared both her room and Beauvoir's cooking from time to time. In one instance the young man was Jewish, his papers were not in order and he had no ration tickets, so Beauvoir's "intellectual engagement" at stretching the food portions was put to an even more severe test than usual.

Reverting to an old habit, she elevated necessity into fixation, turning "culinary worries into a full-blown obsession . . . for the next three years. I watched while the coupons were clipped from my ration book, and never parted with one too many. I wandered through the streets rummaging . . . for unrationed foodstuffs, a sort of treasure hunt, and I thoroughly enjoyed it." She found the "alchemy of cooking fascinating" and later, in her room writing while some concoction simmered on her makeshift stove, had "a glimpse of the housewife's joys."[8]

The Family had become a small, tightly knit band, almost entirely dependent on themselves. Sartre was thirty-seven, Beauvoir thirty-four, and the others were all eight to ten years younger. But rather than assuming the role of *in loco parentis*, they preferred to interact as if they were equals. Natasha's squabbles with her boyfriends and battles with her parents became Beauvoir's; Bost's unwillingness to look for steady work and his dabbles in journalism may have infuriated his family, but they delighted Sartre; and the antics of Olga and Wanda were savored and approved by everyone. The pairings, intrigues and alliances of some against the others were discussed by all with a seriousness none of them gave to the world political situation.

Except for the old friends, those Sartre and Beauvoir made in their youth, the persons with whom they were friendly on an intimate, daily basis were generally much younger than they, causing frequent speculation about their (but particularly Sartre's) obsession with the cult of youth. During his adulthood, he had few, if any, genuine friendships with men his own age or older, and he actively pursued much younger women sexually until the last decade of his life. Because Sartre preferred younger people, and since their company was pleasant for her as well, Beauvoir went along with it. Many of her contingent lovers "just happened to be" younger than she, but this was "simply the way it was," and not something she had actively sought. Of course, throughout her life there was the recurring pattern of intense friendship with a much younger woman.

The myth of the "Sartre-Beauvoir couple" added a dimension during the war when their critics accused them of "being like Peter Pan, always looking to stay in Never-Never-Land." She shrugged off accusations such as the one accusing them of "devouring young people": "Certainly we fed on [their] vitality. It nourished us. We preferred it to the talk of our contemporaries, with their endless descriptions of house furnishings and the intelligence of their babies and their smugness in the bureaucratic security of their work. They [critics] were jealous of our honesty, but more so of our freedom." In an undated letter written to her mother during this time, Beauvoir cited Pierre Guille specifically, saying, ". . . they are having another child. It is all he can talk about now, and gives us no common topic of conversation. I am afraid he has become very boring to us."[9]

Jacques-Laurent Bost had a ready answer as to why Beauvoir and Sartre cultivated youth and why so few of the Family ever married and none had children: "One can play at marriage, but having children means having to grow up. And none of us ever wanted that!"

The winter of 1942–43 passed with record-breaking cold, much snow and further restriction and rationing. There was also psychological disorientation because Germany put France, like all the occupied countries, onto Berlin time,[10] which meant that "it was terrible, terrible to wake up in the blackness that went on so long each day because . . . we lived on Berlin time, so we never really knew what time it was, only that it was black all the time, black."

Like most other women in Paris, Beauvoir bundled up in heavy trousers except when teaching, as women were still expected to wear dresses. She was on her second pair of wood-soled shoes and wore a turban all the time to disguise her unkempt hair. Personal hygiene was sporadic at best; there was little soap and never any hot water. She fared better than many because after her father's death she and her mother shared his unused clothing-ration tickets. She felt "only a little guilty" about using the tickets of a dead person because Georges "had become so honest before his death as his protest against the occupation and the conduct of his friends," but she made good use of them. She also refused to let Françoise give away Georges's clothes. "I gave some of his wool trousers and coats to my mother, and I took the rest. We wore them to sleep in because it was so cold. I also had a heavy suit and coat made for myself from his old overcoats." These were her only clothes, and she wore them constantly until the end of 1945.[11]

It was the winter when "the problem of food became an obsession,"[12] and in "Paris above all, people have ceased to use their reason; their digestive tube constitutes their main daily preoccupation."[13] Madame Morel sent them packets of food several times each month, and Beauvoir grew expert at scraping maggots off the meat and culling weevils from the dried beans, careful to do it when Sartre was not around. Once he seized a particularly vile-smelling rabbit and threw it into the garbage can. She retrieved it when he wasn't looking, soaked it in vinegar, boiled it in herbs and served it to him. He ate it. In 1985 she admitted that despite Sartre's proscription she sometimes bought on the black market when she was so hungry she could not resist.

They continued to vacation together in the Free Zone, crossing more openly now that Sartre had legitimate papers. In June 1942 they decided to make a loop, riding their bicycles down to the Basque country of southwest France and over to Marseille, returning through Vichy and the center of the country. Françoise, alarmed at how thin they both were, tried to discourage them, saying they could not afford to expend the energy that riding bicycles would require. But they went anyway, buoyed by Gallimard's decision to publish L'Invitée as soon as enough paper could be allocated to print it, paying for the trip with the several hundred francs Brice Parain paid as advance against royalties. Parain liked the book, but was puzzled by the ending and wanted Beauvoir to "try to write several other possibilities," but she had "come to the firm decision that the book must be published as written," and he, "reluctantly," accepted it as it was. "I wanted to put that book behind me, whether published or not," Beauvoir remembered. "I had several other projects under way at the same time and had no more time for it. I had outgrown it, if such can be said. Of course I wanted it published, but it was a book of my youth now, and I thought it unworthy of further consideration."

So the bicycle holiday began, and, as if to reassure her mother, Beauvoir wrote letters sometimes daily, usually every other day.[14] On September 11 she wrote an account which confirmed all her mother's fears.[15] They had had no luck finding food, but Bost, who had gone with them partway, had even worse luck: he tried to cross the line openly at Châlons without papers, was arrested and sentenced to ten days in prison and fined 1,500 francs. In the same letter, she also told her mother of terrible experiences between Marseille, Montpelier, Toulouse and Albi, when she and Sartre could not find anything to eat or else, when they did, could not afford to pay the price—"25 or 30 francs for a lunch without nourishment. One lousy piece of bread took all my ration tickets. And my bike kept breaking down more and more. I could hardly bring myself to pedal, and the tires were in shreds." They ran out of money because the bikes were in such bad condition and needed such expensive repair that they had to take the train from Pau to Toulouse. They were disappointed with everything, including the scenery, and were both bitter and awestruck by the "opulent restaurants, filled with gorgeous pastries, which we could not eat because we had not a sou between us." Worse still, when they arrived in Toulouse their bicycles were not in the train's baggage car, and they spent an anxious day waiting for them to arrive on a later train. They could not wire Françoise to send money, because telegrams to Paris were forbidden from that region. Without bikes and camping equipment, they decided to use their remaining pittance for a real bed in a hotel, but none was cheap enough, so they slept in a shed. The next two days they ate nothing and walked more than twenty kilometers before they found a farmer on whose mercy to throw themselves. He let them sleep in his granary and eat with his family. She exulted: ". . . soup, beans, café au lait with some sort of bread, and the next morning coffee and more bread!" There didn't seem to be any way out of the mess they were in, so they telephoned Annie Duval, a friend of Françoise's who lived nearby. She loaned them a thousand francs, enough for train fare to La Pouèze, where they hoped to borrow enough from Madame Morel to repay the loan and get themselves back to Paris.

Another day and a half passed without food. Arriving at La Pouèze, they

> drank tea, took a cold wash, ate an enormous omelette with potatoes. My stomach was such a mess I vomited everything, so it was another day without food. The next day I was better and I ate bread, honey, coffee with milk, meat, and potatoes. . . . Today I had three huge meals!

Best of all, she told her mother, "Madame Morel has found us 100 kilos of potatoes. You'll have to keep them at your place. But how this will change our winter! We are going to be rich as all get out!

"I am thin as a nail but in excellent health," she concluded, so they stayed on at La Pouèze for a month "to fatten ourselves for the coming winter."

The atmosphere there was always conducive to work. In another letter to her mother, Beauvoir said she was sitting in the garden reading T. E. Lawrence's *Seven Pillars of Wisdom*, which she found "extremely interesting." She was also writing, a work she described in some detail:

I am writing a play, which is almost finished. I hope that it's good, but I don't think they'll be able to stage it before the end of the war. There are too many characters and too much scenery. The subject is drawn from a story in a book which I read on the Middle Ages. It's a little town in Flanders that is being besieged and where everybody is dying of starvation. They decide to get rid of the children, the women and the old people, so they can hold on the whole winter and wait for rescue which will arrive in the spring. And then they realize that they can't sacrifice half the population that way. And they decide to try to get out all together in order to vanquish the enemy together, or else to die all together. When it appears in the fall, I will dedicate it to you.[16]

Now that books in general were so hard to come by in Paris and all contemporary American and English titles were unavailable, Beauvoir depended on Madame Morel to supply her with a steady stream of reading materials. The book about the Middle Ages she alluded to was one she found in Madame Morel's extensive library, *The Italian Chronicles*, by Sismondi. Beauvoir changed the setting to France and a war between the besieged city of Vaucelles in Flanders and the kingdom of Burgundy under a despotic and tyrannical king.

The idea to write a play came to her from watching Sartre, who was engrossed in writing *Les Mouches* (*The Flies*). She found their conversations about theatrical techniques to be "very simply, great fun."[17] They had never gone much to the theater, as both preferred the movies, and so both had to learn a great deal about stage necessities as the process of writing unfolded.

There are a number of correspondences between her play and his. Both began as an amusement: his provoked by Olga's casual remark that Dullin had told her all aspiring actresses needed someone to write a play as a showcase for their talents; hers, by seeing what pleasure the writing gave him. He chose the doomed house of Atreus as his setting; she took the siege of one medieval kingdom by another. He, being more protean, intended his play to carry a veiled message about free choice and the responsibility entailed by action; she, being more earthbound, wanted to convey "the decisions and choices every Frenchwoman entrusted with the welfare of others had to make every day when she struggled to put enough food on the table to feed her family."

Food, more specifically, the lack of enough to nourish a population, is the controlling metaphor of *Useless Mouths*.[18] However, it is also Beauvoir's attempt to demonstrate through dramatic action the existential ethic Sartre was then constructing in *Being and Nothingness*. In 1983 she explained, "I was trying to show how one could live the precepts Sartre espoused in his philosophy, but I could not, because of the occupation, put it into contemporary circumstances. Sismondi gave me the necessary fictional distance. Transposing history with contemporary concerns worked so well that I began a habit of many years' standing: when I was troubled about the way to present something in my own life that I wanted to write about, I often turned to history to find the proper setting."

Beauvoir said herself there were "too many characters and too much scenery," and she might have added that there is also too little dramatic action. What there is occurs when the characters confront each other to declaim their situation or, as she joked in 1983, "when the audience could fidget and cough during the long pauses necessitated by the complicated stage setting and the eight changes of scene."

The speeches are overly long and difficult to say in anything less than stentorian voice. The actors do not interact but rather follow each other in the building of a seamless philosophical argument. As most critics have noted, it is not so much a play as a dramatized philosophical statement about ethical choices. In a world where resources grow increasingly scarce, Beauvoir dramatized questions about how societies should govern them-selves: "How is power defined and established? How is power shared? How are societal values determined? Are some persons seen as having more intrinsic worth than others? On what basis? What does it mean to be useful or useless to society?"[19]

"This isn't what the theater's about! This isn't theater at all . . . ,"[20] Jean Genet declared when the play was performed, but perhaps Beauvoir's own analysis was more to the point: "My mistake was to pose a political problem in terms of abstract morality." Still, it is this solid philosophical underpinning which gives the play its significance. It is the first of her wartime writings (all gathered loosely under the heading of "existential" or "existentialist")[21] and the first to deal with the individual's capacity for moral reasoning and ethical choice in a society bent on precluding them.

Much of Beauvoir's writing centers around a series of oppositions within which there are at least two possible choices, but the play presents this idea most clearly. The most apparent examples: a small group of men make the laws which govern the entire population, thus pitting the few against the many; and all men at first stand in opposition to the women, who are denied the right to nourishment and thus to life. Individual members of each group question the right of the state to make such deci-sions, and thus add another opposition. The proposed solutions result in yet another division, this time between those who accept casuistic answers and those who seek moral and ethical absolutes.

The only manuscript of the play was destroyed, indirectly because of food: true to her word, Simone de Beauvoir not only dedicated the play to her mother, but also gave her the only manuscript as a gift, the first ever given "in genuine affection and not from a sense of duty." But this was war, and paper was difficult to come by: when a neighbor gave Françoise a basket of berries, enough to make preserves that would last the winter, she wrapped the precious jars in her daughter's carefully handwritten sheets of *Les Bouches inutiles*. As she consumed each jar, she threw away the stained paper wrappers. Neither woman considered Françoise's action anything other than a necessity of wartime.

Philosophy was much on Simone de Beauvoir's mind during the time she worked happily on her play. It became an increasingly important category of thought as she continued her accustomed role of "favored critic" for Sartre while they both pored over his manuscript of *Being and Nothingness.*

"I accepted his formulations as soon as I heard them," Beauvoir recalled. "His ideas about the nature of human freedom and the obligations carried by the concept of choice made as much sense to me as his earlier theory of contingency. It was only natural that I sought to express these ideas within literature; I am still not sure why I thought I should express them philosophically." To the end of her life, she insisted that she was "not a philosopher. Neither intelligent enough nor creative enough, nor possessing the sheer creative brilliance it takes to propound a thesis or construct a system." She explained further: "In philosophical terms, he was creative and I am not . . . I always recognized his superiority in that area. So where Sartre's philosophy is concerned, it is fair to say that I took my cue from him because I also embraced existentialism myself."[22]

However, her university classmate Maurice de Gandillac, who himself became a distinguished scholar and professor of philosophy, strongly disagreed with Beauvoir's assessment of her philosophical capabilities. After her death, he made the point of emphasizing to her sister that Beauvoir had been far too self-effacing about her intellectual abilities, and that he had always believed her capable of creating work of equal importance to Sartre's but entirely independent of him. Gandillac reminded Hélène of the Sartre and Beauvoir *agrégation*, when the examiners were divided on which of the two should be given the first place, deciding at last to give it to Sartre because "she was only a Sorbonne student and he was the *normalien* and here he was, poor fellow, having to take it for the second time."[23] Both Gandillac and Madame de Roulet further speculated that, when it came to philosophy, perhaps Simone de Beauvoir's lifelong deference to Sartre might indeed be traced back to this early ranking, when he won first place by less than one-fiftieth of a percentage point in the complex system the jury used to rank students.[24] But both admitted their perplexity and their final inability to understand why this brilliant woman, engaged with philosophical questions all her life, removed herself from the discipline she held to be "the most important and certainly the most interesting"[25] field of study and expression.

Also, when she was asked which of her works she considered the important starting point for any interpretation and evaluation of her *oeuvre,* she responded without hesitating, "The two [philosophical] essays, *Pyrrhus et Cinéas* and *Pour une morale de l'ambiguité,* and the essays collected in the volume called *Privilèges* are, I think, probably important as well. I also like that essay I wrote about Brigitte Bardot and then . . ." Only then did she suggest that her memoirs, *The Mandarins* and *The Second Sex* might be among her best writings.[26]

In her memoirs, Beauvoir credits the genesis of *Pyrrhus et Cinéas* to Jean Grenier, to whom she was introduced by Sartre in the Flore in 1943. "What about you, madame," she quotes Grenier as asking her, "are *you* an Existentialist?"[27] She described Grenier as editing an anthology to which he invited her to contribute a short essay on any subject that interested her. "Sartre encouraged me . . . telling me to at least try."

Since she was interested in "the relationship of individual experience to universal reality," and since "someone was offering me a chance to deal directly with the problem on my mind, why not take advantage of the fact?" So she began to write the essay, "spent three months on it, and it swelled into a small book."[28]

She began her initial version of *Pyrrhus et Cinéas* as an attempt to think through some of her disagreements with what eventually became Sartre's fourth section of *Being and Nothingness*, in particular the chapter dealing with questions of freedom.

Pyrrhus et Cinéas is a spare and lucid work which Beauvoir wrote to explain Existentialism for the thoughtful reader. Its style exemplifies the "intelligent, sophisticated essay" she hoped to write when she was still a student and attempting to define her life's work. As she began the essay, her primary intention was to write a companion piece to *Being and Nothingness* which would serve as an "existential working out of the ethics of freedom." Ultimately, she aimed toward "a reconciliation" between her views and his: Sartre was arguing that all freedoms are equal, an idea she could not accept entirely because, for her, "situations are different, and therefore so are freedoms."

Beauvoir divided the essay into two separate sections. The introductory first part is generally regarded as an explanation of Sartre's Existential thinking couched in her own terms; the second, as her assessment of the "indivisibility of freedom,"[29] or the idea that true freedom comes only when the individual recognizes and accepts it for others as well as for the self. She worked on the introduction and the first section in the blissful early autumn of Madame Morel's garden, which is why she dedicated the book "*à cette dame*" ("To That Lady"). It is also the reason why she decided to use Voltaire's *Candide* as an analogy for freedom and responsibility. "We must cultivate our garden," says Beauvoir, quoting Voltaire in her introduction, but then she adds, "This advice is not of any help to us. For what is my garden?"[30] A series of juxtapositions follows, beginning with "men who try to plow the entire earth, and . . . others who would find a flower pot too great." She expands further to questions about attitude and situation, such as "if I shut myself in, the other is also shut off to me. . . . No ready made attachment exists between the world and me." Reflecting further, she decided: The only reality which pertains completely to me is thus my act: a work that is fashioned from materials that are not mine escapes me in some of its aspects." This leads her to conclude:

> All I have to do to possess this fragment of the universe is truly cultivate it. . . . To know what is mine it is necessary to know what I truly do. We thus see that no dimension can be assigned to the garden where Candide wishes to enclose me. It is not designed beforehand; it is I who chooses its site and limits.

Her text unfolds as a "dialogue" in which Beauvoir roams freely through much of Western intellectual thought. She introduces arguments from (among others) Benjamin Constant, Hegel, Spinoza, Flaubert, Kafka, Kant and Maurice Blanchot, correcting, clarifying and, in most cases, rejecting them all. This steadfast determination to remain faithful to Sartre's precepts allows her also to document her own particular version of his thought. Her conclusion is strong:

> I act only when I take responsibility for this future; the risks involved are the inverse of my finitude and by assuming my finitude I am free.
>   Thus man can act, he must act: he only is in transcending himself. He acts amidst risk and failure. He must assume risk: in projecting himself towards an uncertain future, he founds with certainty his present. But failure cannot be accepted.

These last words were her original ending for the essay, but once back in Paris she decided to "give the book a roundness of form" and so ended just as she had begun it, with a dialogue between the two characters who give the essay its name. As she and Sartre prepared to leave La Pouèze in late September and join the *rentrée*, the annual return to Paris after the long August vacation, she was satisfied only with the introduction and the first section, and these were still in what she called "semifinal form."

She had begun to keep a notebook[31] in which she jotted down her questions about Sartre's work and how her own ideas differed from it. She also took notes from her readings, in particular Kant, whom she was using as what she called "a focal point or a sounding board, or the standard upon which my own arguments and the arguments of other philosophers must be judged. It was not so much that I espoused his beliefs as it was that I admired the form of his expression." As for Sartre, "He rejected my Kantian standards, fearing they would become notions within my writing and thus harmful to my expression. It irritated him to discuss this, so we did not talk much about this aspect of my thinking. Gradually, I found Kant less appealing, and so my jottings ceased to be an irritant to Sartre. Anyway, I had begun my second novel and he was always more comfortable acting as critic for my fiction than my philosophy."

Once she was back in Paris, the most pressing concern was housing. She always checked out of her hotel room during the summer and used what would have been the rent money to pay for her holiday expenses. This time she and Sartre stayed away so long that the manager of the Hotel Mistral thought something had happened to them, so he rented Beauvoir's room permanently to someone else and threw away the cardboard suitcases she had stored in the basement. Most of Hélène's kitchen utensils were lost, as were a few articles of supplemental winter clothing Beauvoir could ill afford to lose and the materials she had prepared over the years to use in her teaching.

She loaded what remained onto a wheelbarrow and trudged across Paris in her wooden-soled shoes to the Rue Dauphine and the Hotel Aubusson, "the most miserable hovel" she was ever to live in. Sartre moved in as well, and within days Wanda moved in with him, "using the excuse that there was no separate room available, and that she wanted us to save our money to use for food."

Soon after, Natasha followed with her newest lover, Bourla, a wealthy young Algerian Jew of Spanish descent who frequently provided them with luxuries stolen from his father, reputedly a dealer on the black market.[32] Beauvoir was entranced with the physical beauty of this young couple: "He was as dark as she was fair. Both were slim, supple, lithe and exotic in their appearance. Sometimes I would go down to their room when they were getting ready to sleep. I sat on the bed and we laughed and talked and I stroked their hair, and Natasha always asked me to kiss her good night. 'Me, too,' he would say. 'Tuck me in and kiss me too.'"[33]

So after Beauvoir shopped and cooked for Wanda and Sartre, Natasha and Bourla, and usually other members of the Family as well, and after she tucked "the youngsters" in for the night, and because she could not risk visiting Sartre's room for fear of Wanda's tantrums, she went back to her room alone. She remembered this period as "happy and contented as it could be, under the circumstances dictated by the war." She felt "needed, important to the well-being of the people I loved most," and thus her own sexual appetites "mattered little." She was "mostly celibate" and received "satisfaction, gratification, in other ways that mattered more. Sexual completion is not everything. There are other ways to care for people, to love and be loved."

What probably made the winter of 1943, the worst of the war, "not only bearable but sometimes pleasant," were the possibilities that lay before them, including the publication of *L'Invitée*. Sartre's play, *Les Mouches* (*The Flies*), was to be staged by Dullin in the spring, and Gallimard was to publish *Being and Nothingness* in June.

Sartre had shown her the dedication, "To Castor," suffusing her with emotion she knew better than to express openly: "He had a hard time with emotions. He was embarrassed to show them and totally awkward, almost unable to receive them. Any demonstration of affection made him blush and stumble. So we were very formal with each other, which has often been commented upon but never understood. Indeed, we said *vous* to each other, to give but one example. But behind our formalities was a ritual code of behavior, and within those rituals there was a closeness that existed only for ourselves. Only we could crack the code and interpret it correctly."

So the fact of Wanda's presence in Sartre's room meant little to Beauvoir because he and she were together in ways that mattered far more to her. They were truly now what she had always wanted them to be, a writing couple. Each day they scurried from the Rue Dauphine to the Café de Flore because it was heated and their hotel was not. She got there most often when the doors opened, at 8 A.M., because she wanted the table closest to the stove; he was not at his best in the mornings, so his arrival was usually as much as two hours later. There was nothing to eat at the café, so they trekked to their hotel for lunch, but unless they had to teach they went directly back to the Flore. There they stayed until dinnertime, when they retraced the route to their hotel, and unless it was so bitterly cold that they bundled into their separate beds to keep warm they usually went back again to the Flore until closing time. When they were accepted as regulars by the manager, he allowed them to hide out during air raids in the upstairs salon, closed for the duration of the war, while everyone else had to take shelter in the Métro Saint-Germain. Soon after, they began to go directly upstairs and claim their tables when they arrived in the mornings, a mark of privilege accorded only to a special few. There the pages of her novel, *Le Sang des autres* (*The Blood of Others*) "seemed to flow from [her] pen."

She loved this life, cloistered in the warmth of the Flore, with other members of the Family settled in at various tables around the room. She and Sartre were sometimes alone on the second floor with only the sound of a pen scratching across the paper and the smell of his pipe and her cigarette marking the other's presence. Everything, it seemed, was finally coming together as she wished it. Although French resistance and German retaliation were resulting in increasing atrocities all over the country and especially in Paris, the direction of the war seemed to be turning against the Germans, so on the infrequent occasions when she allowed herself to think about the outside world she was more often optimistic than not.

Her feelings of security lasted well into the autumn, based on the false foundation of herself and Sartre as the happy writing couple poised on the brink of success. She conveniently ignored Sartre's increasing frustration with so much inaction and indecision in his life and hoped that his appointment to the Comité National des Ecrivains (CNE, the National Writers' Committee) would change his mood. For a time he went to their meetings, but she was never invited to join: "I had not yet published a book. Why should they invite me? I was a nobody."

Actually, the galleys of *L'Invitée* had already been read by many of the members of the Writers' Committee, but even after it was published and she was an acclaimed author she still was not invited to join. She believed it was because she was still "only his mistress," but as usual she had a rationalization handy: "I didn't really want to go. It was enough that he went. He attended for both of us. He paid attention to what went on and he came home and told me everything. So I knew all about it through him and I didn't need to go myself."

On the one hand, not being a member allowed her to hold on to the routine she had finally established in her life; on the other, she seldom missed an opportunity to be seen at Sartre's side, especially when it furthered her vision of them as the happy writing couple.

Sartre's play, *The Flies*, had been presented to generally unfavorable criticism. Theater audiences were small and reviews tepid at best. After twenty-five performances, Dullin decided to close until the fall, hoping there would be enough word-of-mouth publicity to reopen it. Michel Leiris, the poet, art critic and anthropologist who later became a good friend and strong influence upon Simone de Beauvoir, was one of the few who praised it.

In June 1943, during the run of the play, *Being and Nothingness* was published, so Sartre's name was becoming better known even though his work was largely ignored. Although sales were modest, they were consistent, but critical appraisal was slower in coming.[34] In 1943 it was mentioned only once, in passing in a scholarly article; three reviews appeared in all of 1944, nine in 1945 and about fifteen in 1946.[35] Most critics seemed unsure of what to make of it, none recognized its originality, and none praised it. The book that became a kind of holy scripture for postwar generations throughout much of the world took a while to catch on.

Despite the fact that Sartre was still teaching full time, occupied with production of the play and publication of the book, and writing a solid progression of works that would be published or produced in steady succession during the coming years, he was as restless and bored with his life as Beauvoir was satisfied with hers. By the summer of 1943, the war had truly turned. Resistance activity was organized and efficient, and the results, especially sabotage, were often highly visible. So, too, was the literary Resistance. Underground newspapers and journals proliferated, and novels and poems written under pseudonyms were received by the general population with "varying degrees of sarcasm or respect, depending upon whether the habitués of the Flore knew the true identity of the author and what they thought of him before the war."

Sartre, who had played no part in any of this, yearned to be among these writers and resistants (who sometimes were both at once), while Beauvoir was just as anxious to keep him from having any contact with them. The attempts he made to join show a frustrated man who wanted to be part of what he probably perceived as a swashbuckling world of high adventure based partly on two heroes of his boyhood imagination: the Knight of Pardaillan, a popular French juvenile fiction, and Nick Carter, "America's Greatest Detective."[36]

Beauvoir was "relieved" when all Sartre's attempts to become involved were rebuffed. For whatever the reason, no one wanted to trust him enough either to recruit him or to accept his offers to help. It may have been simply that he was too public a figure, too well known as much for the bad-boy-who-thumbs-his-nose-at-society tone of his life as for the slowly but steadily increasing influence of his writing. Then, too, the old rumors of his having been released from prison camp in order to serve the Germans as an example of the freedom of French intellectual life under the occupation were still heard as late as 1943–44. Beauvoir joked in her memoirs and other members of the Family remember as well that Sartre teased the Writers' Committee by asking if they were sure they "wanted a spy in their midst."[37]

One French Resistance leader perceived Sartre as "soft, an effeminate personality who always took the easy road, who talked far too much, and, if subjected to the most ordinary questioning, was perceived—rightly or wrongly—as likely to tell all he knew rather than suffer hurt himself." A British agent saw him as "a chap who enjoyed talk; thinking language his weapon, he was quite likely to chatter indiscriminately and thus give a good deal away. Or so we thought when his name was passed round to us in '43. We simply couldn't take the risk."[38]

Sartre and Beauvoir were isolated, islands adrift on the stream of war, as untouched as it was possible to be by the daily irritations and unspeakable outrages of the occupation. They were cocooned within the Family, none of whom faced more than the ritual indignities of lack of food, heat and freedom of expression. No one from the Resistance asked them to help; the Germans left them alone to further their careers.

By 1943 they were both published writers, their names known to everyone in artistic and intellectual circles in Paris. Still, they remained bourgeois intellectuals, and for whatever reason—the simple one of shyness, the complex one of instinctual paranoia bred into them by their bourgeois backgrounds—they established superficial friendships with many but reserved their genuine intimacy as they always had, for the Family. They met everyone, from Adamov to Zadkine, but they still kept themselves for themselves, trusting few new acquaintances and forming no real friendships until or unless the newcomers consented to annexation within the Family: if they surrendered their primary allegiance to "the couple," as they were increasingly known, and if the entire Family approved, then they were incorporated. Otherwise they remained acquaintances, and intimacy of any kind, intellectual as well as personal, was withheld. Thus, while everyone could claim to "know" Beauvoir and Sartre, very few knew anything except what they themselves consented to make known.

So Sartre and Beauvoir remained (and, indeed, reigned) intellectually supreme. Their ideas, theories and writings began at this time to set the tone and measure the boundaries of intellectual discourse for several decades to come. And since no one among their intimates challenged them or questioned their authority, their thought remained curiously insular—because the arguments and criticisms of outsiders mattered so little. By the end of the war, they had become players on the worldwide stage, but rather than enlarging themselves to fit it, they made the world fit into Saint-Germain-des-Prés.

So Sartre chafed when rebuffed by the intellectual Resistance, and, as was his wont when things did not go his way, frenetic movement became his substitute for what he really wanted and could not have. His life suddenly became frenzied, and so, therefore, did Simone de Beauvoir's. In the midst of war, she was swept up into a bewildering carnival atmosphere, a kaleidoscope of parties and "fiestas," crowds of people in smoky basement clubs and bars, too much bad booze, indiscriminate sex, gossip, petty intrigue and even, to a certain extent, political drama. She thrived on it.

TWENTY

How to Make a Living

ALL THROUGH THE WINTER, Beauvoir worked contentedly on her second novel, *Le Sang des autres* (*The Blood of Others*), and by the end of May it was essentially finished. She was pleased with the first draft and thought that all the manuscript needed was "some refinement of language, minor changes here and there," which she could do before summer and the cycling holiday she and Sartre planned to take in the Massif Central. They intended to end the trip at Meyrignac, where she had not been for many years. Sartre was to spend several days on his own in Uzerche because he was not acceptable in Meyrignac to her cousin Jeanne (now Madame Dauriac), her husband and the first several of their eventual eleven children. Then they planned to put the bikes on a train and head for La Pouèze, where they would spend four to six weeks until it was time for Beauvoir's fall teaching to begin.

There had been only one recent development of note in their lives, and even that was not yet settled: Sartre had been asked by Jean Delannoy, a director at Pathé-Cinéma studios, to write a film script on a subject of his own choosing. If Delannoy accepted it, Sartre planned to resign from teaching, which paid him much less, and substitute film writing as the assured basis of his income. Beauvoir thought that she too might be able to quit teaching, which she disliked as much as he, because word had come from Gallimard that they expected *L'Invitée* to be successful and were interested in another book. Then suddenly there was catastrophe, embarrassment and humiliation. Nothing was settled financially, but everything changed.

Natasha's mother had paid a visit to the Hotel Aubusson that spring, sometime in early March. A rigid woman, impeccably dressed, ramrod stiff and icy cold, she struck Beauvoir as "a woman used to getting her way in everything." Madame Sorokine was "horrified by the condition of the hotel," but especially by Beauvoir's "filthy room." She wasted no time on pleasantries but "came at once to the point: 'Mademoiselle de Beauvoir,' she said to me, 'I know that my daughter is infatuated with you and will do whatever you tell her. Her father and I . . . would very much appreciate it if you would see to it that she ends her unfortunate liaison [with Bourla] and resumes one which will insure her future.' What she meant was that I was to tell Natasha to go back to a rich boy so the mother and father would have everything *they* wanted. Well! How could I do such a thing to Natasha!"

Beauvoir tried to end the meeting: "You can't imagine how difficult it was for me to get rid of this woman without inflaming her. She was formidable, and I was never known for my social graces with women like that! Also, she was a woman of deeply held prejudices, extremely anti-Semitic. I always had the feeling that she confused two things: the atmosphere in Paris that made it all right to condemn Jews by betrayal, which made her condemnation and betrayal of me all right as well."

Beauvoir promised Madame Sorokine that she would not tell Natasha about their meeting, but at the same time tried to convince her that whatever influence the woman imagined she held was greatly overestimated. "And that," she thought, "was that." She never saw Madame Sorokine again, and since Natasha never mentioned her mother's visit, Beauvoir presumed the matter had ended as quietly and amicably as possible.

But on the last day of the term Beauvoir was summoned to the school director's office for a private conference. There she was told that a serious complaint had been lodged against her "by a parent," and that she had been accused of "behavior leading to the corruption of a minor, a girl student placed in [her] care and trust." The charges had been under investigation for several months, and had been found true: "The girl, one Nathalie Sorokine, was living in the same hotel as her teacher, who was often seen entering the girl's room, both pupil and teacher in the company of a young man. Although the teacher was seen to leave at a later time each night, the young man stayed. The parents would press the charges unless the teacher was dismissed immediately and forbidden all contact with minor students."

Beauvoir protested her innocence vigorously but unsuccessfully. The director "was sorry—under the circumstances, the war, the girl being Russian—best I go quietly." The implied threat was that the German-controlled Ministry of Education might somehow become involved, since Madame Sorokine's complaint held allegations of unnatural sex acts, a serious charge that led to prison and sometimes deportation. At first, it was enough to frighten Beauvoir into a quiet resignation. Then she thought better of it and asked for a hearing to present her side of the story. It was scheduled for early October, but in the meantime she was relieved of all teaching duties. After twelve years of teaching, she was suddenly without a profession.[1]

The Family were all outraged by the injustice, and, with the bravado of the truly powerless, they urged her to protest the decision. Sartre knew better. He listened to her emotional retelling of the interview, then told her to accept dismissal quietly and forget about a hearing in the fall so as not to arouse German or collaborationist interest in her and, by extension, him. Then he worried aloud about how they would manage without her income. Together they decided that she must control her emotions long

enough to break the news to Françoise and persuade her that the dismissal
was the catalyst Beauvoir needed to make the decision to earn her living as
a writer. She believed that her mother "saw through the ruse, but was kind
enough to keep her disappointment to herself." The frugal Françoise had
saved much of the monthly stipend her daughter gave her, and now she
volunteered to give it back; Beauvoir refused to take it, but asked her
mother to keep the money handy in case it was needed.

Beauvoir glossed over the incident in her memoirs, describing in one
evasive paragraph how Madame Sorokine caused her dismissal and then
adding several of what she considered to be "the most unsavory moments"
of her life:

> This break with an old familiar routine did not disturb me un-
> duly. The only problem was how to make a living. I can't remem-
> ber how I managed to wangle a job as a features producer on the
> national radio network. As I remarked earlier, our unwritten code
> allowed us to work for this organization: it all depended on what
> you did there.[2]

It was Sartre who solved the problem of how she would make her
living. At his instigation, René Delange, the collaborationist editor of *Comoedia* who had many spheres of influence in the German-dominated media, found a job for Beauvoir on Radiodiffusion Nationale, the official state
station, as a *metteuse en ondes*, best described in English by the catchall
phrase "writer-producer." She worked with Pierre Bost, the elder brother of
Jacques-Laurent, selecting stories, songs and poems written during the Middle Ages, and modern ones pertaining to the period. They melded both
into a vocal montage for a segment of a program known as "Historical Music." Beauvoir's specific duty was to collect enough suitable material to fill
an hour each week, which she looked forward to doing because it would
take her to various libraries around Paris and keep her away from the controversial offices of the station. The BBC, broadcasting to the people of
France, announced repeatedly, "Radio Paris lies! Radio Paris is German!"[3]
And by 1943, no matter how the Germans tried first to prevent and then
to remove it, enterprising French resistants managed to keep boldly painting the slogan on the walls of the building. She was both "embarrassed and
a little uneasy" to think of walking by it each day.

The job began at the end of the summer holidays, and she was to be
paid in the range of 1,500 to 2,000 francs a week, a fortune compared to her
salary as a teacher. Sartre tried to paint a rosy picture of what their life
would be like now that she was guaranteed such a handsome salary and he
was beginning to make money on his writing as well. He told her they
would move themselves and the Family into a better hotel as soon as the
summer holiday was over; he hinted without being specific that they might
just as well begin to allow themselves some of the luxuries they had been
without for a long time, but said nothing about where they would come
from.

None of this cheered her up. She knew what the reputation of the

French radio was, that most people of any intelligence sneered at it and that all its journalists and announcers were considered to be "undeniably partisans of collaboration."[4] When she told her mother about the job, Françoise did not meet her eyes, but concentrated all her attention on darning a stocking. Simone de Beauvoir said in 1985 that because she "only prepared materials dealing with the Middle Ages," and "had nothing to do with the war or anything happening at the time," she considered herself "untainted" and felt "no guilt by association with German radio, because that's what it was." She explained testily, "I went to the library, collected a few songs, a few poems, put them together and someone else read them over the radio. I gave the stuff to [Pierre] Bost in the Flore. I never went near the radio station unless I had no other choice. I needed money and I was happy to take theirs. I did nothing wrong."

No matter how she explained it away, she was uneasy about this work. She glossed over it in her memoirs, always resented being questioned about it, and was furious whenever she learned of a scholar or journalist who wrote about it. She claimed that "nothing remained" of her work, that she had "no memory" of anything she selected or how it was used on any program that aired. When she was told shortly before her death that a French journalist whom she admired was writing a book in which he planned to state that she and Sartre were quite possibly "opportunists who saw passive collaboration as the way to become rich and famous,"[5] she became furious and demanded, "Can't you shut that bastard up? Will these lies never end?"[6]

Sartre shattered Beauvoir's happy summer plans when he announced that he could not go on vacation and leave Wanda behind in Paris because she was nervous about rehearsals for a play. He sent Beauvoir off alone on the bicycle trip, promising to meet her three weeks later in Uzerche as planned. This too she described obliquely in the memoirs: "The entrance examinations to Sèvres were held in June, and I found myself free from the end of that month. I wanted to get away again during the summer holidays. . . . I fixed a rendezvous with Sartre for 15 July and caught a train to Roanne.[7] In truth, she had been fired several weeks before the Sèvres examinations and did not administer them; and she was bitterly disappointed that Sartre had chosen to respond to Wanda's insecurities rather than to what she thought were her very real needs.

The Flies was staged to lukewarm reception in early June, shortly after Beauvoir learned that she had been fired. The shock and shame of dismissal were still fresh, and her self-esteem took an even greater battering when she saw what was happening to Sartre. This was the year when he was becoming a celebrity, and she was still "Sartre's girlfriend," the "shabby, badly dressed woman, the 'busy beaver' who sits in the Flore biting her fingernails as her pen scratch-scratches." Or sometimes she was the "prim spinster who towers over him [Sartre], the one who makes all the decisions about who sees him and for how long and for what purpose." Or she was "his girlfriend, someone he had taken up many years ago and had simply forgotten to discard now that he was a brilliant, exciting writer and she was still only a schoolteacher. But wait—was there not some scandal, had she not been accused, dismissed?"[8]

She was mortified by what she perceived as "all the gossip" that swirled around her, because she thought it all stemmed from her dismissal. In truth, scarcely anyone outside the Family knew about that; any curiosity directed toward her was only that of the celebrity hunters surrounding Sartre or the genuine interest of some of the literary intelligentsia who wanted to know them both better. It was only a few months before the publication of *L'Invitée*, and gossip was already rampant among those who had access to advance copies, but she was unable to believe that anything about herself could possibly be positive. As always in a situation where she felt uncomfortable, Beauvoir behaved awkwardly, internalized everything as her own social failure, and then stubbornly refused to adapt to the new situation in any way at all.

She left Paris for the summer in early July, taking the train to Roanne, where she was forced to stay longer than she planned because her bicycle was lost. As she had done the previous year, she wrote long, detailed letters to her mother, but she who was so determined to travel no matter what the circumstances seldom described what she saw except to say that it was "beautiful" or "breathtaking" or the weather was "too hot" or "positively frightful." For her, travel writing consisted of describing what she did and what happened to her; seldom does she describe a setting in detail, never does she write with any depth or insight about the place and its people.

This year the problems continued to center around the search for food, but now the difficulties of transportation were just as bad. Between RAF bombings and Resistance sabotage, rail travel throughout France was in chaos. Of the trip to Roanne, for example:

> I had a good trip because my seat was reserved, but the crowd was incredible. You couldn't use the toilets because of the people crammed in there, and along the way people couldn't board and women were crying when they saw the train pull out without them. People had to get off through the windows because the corridors were so jammed. I slept very badly. As soon as I got there, I found a room in a charming little hotel at the rear of a small square that has quite a country air. This is a sad little city and I don't want to stay here too long. Especially since the diet is so austere. It's ten times worse than Paris, and even the best hotels only serve spinach or potato croquettes. Even with ration tickets you can't get any meat. . . . My shoes were not the best for walking and by the time my bike came, I had blisters on my heels the size of walnuts.[9]

For the next three weeks she cycled alone to Thiers, Riom, through Mont-Dore and La Bourboule and then across the country to Uzerche, where Sartre met her. Her bicycle had broken down repeatedly, but she fixed it herself. Her food generally consisted of whatever she could cadge along the way and persuade a farmer to cook for her ("I found a feast of wild blueberries and I ate till my skin was blue," "A farmer sold me twenty-two eggs, and I ate till I clucked").[10] She was sunburnt and her feet were a mess, but her general outlook on life was much improved, even though her finances were depleted. "Could you send me the 2,000 francs now?" she wrote to her mother. "I'll return it immediately, as soon as I'm back in Paris."[11] She and Sartre headed back in the direction from which she had just come, into the Cantal region, she "going over the mountains and the twisting pass to the Viaduct Garabit while he took the easy road on the level,"[12] then southwest on a leisurely course through Aurillac, Entragues and Espalion, and down through the Gorge of the Tarn, which was one of her favorite sites in all France. They went as far south as Toulouse before heading north mostly by train to La Pouèze, where, since they no longer had to follow the academic calendar, they planned to stay until mid-October.

She had to interrupt her stay to return to Paris for a day, as she wrote to her mother from La Pouèze:

I had an interview with the guy who is in charge of the radio stuff—that Julian I told you about, the one who does the singing, the one you heard before. He has already accepted fourteen proposals of mine and will pay 2,000 francs for each.

Her attitude to the job—at least from the distance of La Pouèze—had changed decidedly.

"That's only the beginning," she continued.

My book was finally published [L'Invitée], and I sent it to you. . . . [T]ell me what you think about it, because I'm very eager to know. I have heard that R.F. [Revue Française] people like it very much. [Critic Marcel] Arland is going to write a good review for me in Comoedia.[13]

The next day she wrote again.

I'm sorry you didn't get my book. The concierge told me she couldn't forward it to the Free Zone. It will be waiting for you in Paris. I'm flattered that it costs 60 francs and that I see it in all the bookstores in Angers. I've already received a flattering letter from a female admirer. They are going to publish another one of my books, the N.R.F. [Nouvelle Revue Française] writes me, a little philosophical essay [Pyrrhus et Cinéas]. And it looks as though they will put on Sartre's play [The Flies] in September after all, and we'll come back to Paris for that."[14]

She wrote to her mother several times each week, sometimes even daily, when she was away from Paris, partly to make up for what she perceived as her "neglect" when she was there. On the infrequent occasions when they did meet, usually in Françoise's new studio apartment on the Rue Blomet, Beauvoir was always pleasantly surprised to see how many friends her mother had in the building, how many people greeted her in the shops.

Her letters demonstrate the change in their relationship, as she tells Françoise all sorts of things in chatty, breezy prose:

> Olga is so unhappy because no one will give her a part in a movie. She says it's because her nose is too big. I think she's going to get it fixed. . . . The Guilles's little girl is absolutely adorable. She's two and a half and chatters like a magpie. . . . The other one is a month old and I can't say that I appreciate them at that age. . . .
>
> That's all my news. When you write, make sure you tell me everything. A thousand kisses to everyone, and keep the best for yourself.[15]

Spending the month of September at Madame Morel's in La Pouèze had become a ritual that Beauvoir counted on, a way of winding down, in some cases recovering from the exertions of summer before resuming the intellectual life of the fall and winter. For her, accustomed as she was to the rhythms of the academic calendar, the new year began in October, and she looked forward, especially during the war years, to "fattening up" on Madame Morel's food and perusing her library hoping to find inspiration for writing. This year, Madame Morel gave her a room in a separate cottage just to the rear of the main house because "a spoiled old senile woman who was never to be seen" took the room Beauvoir had always used before. Sartre kept the room he had always used, one connected to Madame Morel's by large French doors, which "he went through only when invited, and then only in friendship." Beauvoir was happy in the little house because it had its own garden. After being awakened every morning promptly at nine by a servant bearing a steaming bowl of real coffee and some bread, she wrote letters, read and lolled in the sun until lunch at one ("and we dine very well here—much meat, vegetables, huge potatoes especially, and apples . . ."), then she took a walk and returned to the garden to read and write until dinner.

She was working on two novels at once: dallying with revisions of The Blood of Others, even though she knew she had little chance of getting a book about resistance published until the Germans were banished from Paris, and reading and making notes for what became All Men Are Mortal. She was encouraged about the chances for eventual publication of The Blood of Others when the BBC announced the Allied invasion of Italy and the collapse of the German–Italian entente.

After four years of uncertainty, she had one month of pure euphoria at La Pouèze in September 1943. Everyone's spirits were raised by news of the Allied advances in Italy, but hers were even higher because of the overwhelmingly positive sales and reviews of *L'Invitée*. Also, Madame Morel's huge library of esoteric European history had provided her with enough material for a half-dozen radio scripts, so she was able to pay back her mother the two thousand francs she had borrowed. And, best of all, the re-search for the radio scripts gave her historical background for *All Men Are Mortal*. Each day, she was happily torn between revising *The Blood of Others* and writing *All Men Are Mortal*. Her life seemed as full and rich as she had always dreamed it would be, and when her mother wrote to tell her that overnight she had become a literary sensation whose name was at the top of the list for the season's major literary prizes, she could only say that she was happy.

She was pleased that people liked her novel, but she had no idea of just how successful it was until she returned to Paris in October. Everyone, it seemed, wanted to meet her. Many made the pilgrimage to her table at the Flore; others, among them writers such as Cocteau and Mauriac whose work she had once praised as they were now praising hers, sent letters of congratulation; still others invited her to parties and dinners. One couple in particular, Zette and Michel Leiris, became her lifelong friends. Sartre met them first, when they came to congratulate him after a performance of *The Flies*; when Beauvoir came back to Paris in October, Zette Leiris asked them both to come to dinner. There they met the writer Raymond Que-neau and playwright Armand Salacrou and their wives, Jeanine and Lu-cienne, as well as many others whose names were listed among the "new friends" Beauvoir and Sartre made during the initial postwar years. Through the Leirises she met Picasso, Lacan and Georges Bataille, and renewed the acquaintanceship with Alberto Giacometti that became a strong friendship with him and his brother Diego as well. Beauvoir, who claimed toward the end of her life that "anyone who attempts to see the influence of the Sur-realists in my writing is completely crazy," was, however, among the few readers in early 1940 who had read Leiris's autobiographical confession *L'Age d'homme* (*Manhood*) before the onslaught of war caused it to disappear from public consciousness. After she met the author, the book became one she read again and again, especially after she began to write her own memoirs, and it was probably "as great an influence as any" upon them.

Meeting Zette and Michel Leiris made her realize how solipsistic her world had become. For the past several years its boundaries were her hotel room and Sartre's, and only the Family passed through them. Her worldly reality was composed entirely of their fractious intrigues, unsatisfied appe-tites and economic insecurities. She had had an inkling of it when well-known authors began to sit down uninvited at her table in the Flore and talk about her novel, welcoming her into their magic literary circle. But the reality of the larger world really hit when she was in other people's homes.

Suddenly she was in a world where people cared for many things she had either never thought about or else blotted out of her mind. The

Leirises, for example, continued to hide Jews in their apartment or that of their brother-in-law the art dealer Kahn-Weiler, whose gallery Zette then managed. They also supported artists who spent the war years in France, many in hiding, by buying their paintings, worrying only about where to display them to best advantage in their beautiful apartment on the Quai des Grands-Augustins overlooking the Seine. The casual way they incorporated these dangerous practices into their daily life—especially since Michel was still quietly working with the Resistance group that had started several years earlier at the Musée de l'Homme—awed Beauvoir.

Zette was a shrewd businesswoman dedicated to her career, attractive as well as artistic, expressing her aesthetic concerns in everything from her clothing to cooking. She was a strong influence upon Beauvoir in the first few years after she became a public figure. For the rest of her life, Beauvoir considered Zette Leiris "an extraordinary woman, smart, pretty and an honest good friend."

True, Beauvoir was sick of the hotel she lived in, but she would most likely have stayed there had she not been to Zette's beautiful apartment and come to the realization that one did not have to live in squalor, even in wartime. Thus she moved into the Hotel Louisiane on the Rue de Seine, to Room 50, a large round room with a kitchenette and, if one contorted oneself enough, a view of the River Seine from the large high window. Zette Leiris was a sleight-of-hand cook who always seemed to have enough for at least eight people to gather at her dinner table; Simone de Beauvoir took a renewed interest in cooking, and with Bost's help (for he had suddenly discovered that he was good at creating interesting dishes) she too served dinner frequently to eight or ten in her apartment. Albert Camus, who was often a guest on these occasions, said of her cooking, "The quality's not exactly brilliant but the quantity is just right."[16] Beauvoir enjoyed the "new experience of entertaining," but this was the only time in her life. After the war ended she never cooked again, and if she had to serve food to guests it was usually cold meats, cheese and salads that she bought already prepared.[17]

Beauvoir was especially happy about her new clothing, which she had prudently commissioned from a local seamstress the previous summer at Madame Morel's. With rumors reaching her as early as August that she would be a candidate for both prestigious literary prizes, the Goncourt and the Renaudot (she won neither), she wrote to Françoise asking for all her ration tickets. Françoise dispatched them at once, but, as mails were sporadic, they did not arrive for several weeks. "Where are the tickets?" Beauvoir demanded in her letters. "I must have the tickets—the work is already begun." The seamstress created an electric-blue dress and a matching turban in an ersatz satin material, but Beauvoir feared they were too much together, so she always wore them separately. She also had a new skirt made in what was supposed to be hardy tweed but which quickly snagged and unraveled. She wore it with a jacket cut down from an old one of her father's. The entire outfit was a sorry one she discarded as soon as the war was over. The blue dress was put to better use: she wore it to every party or dinner that winter, and although it was stained and shabby by March 1944, she wore it to the Flore on the day the Prix Goncourt was to be announced, because it was the best she had. She continued to wear it until the seams gave out.

She met "so many people" during this time that she began a habit she kept for the rest of her life: if people stopped at her table when she was not in the mood to be interrupted, she sent them away after giving them a fifteen- or twenty-minute appointment later that day or on another day entirely. Soon anyone who wanted to see her knew enough to do so at her convenience.

Every night there was a party of sorts. Liquor, usually a form of rotgut whiskey or bad wine, had suddenly become plentiful in Paris, and everyone drank excessively. Beauvoir had always liked the taste of alcohol, and now she drank as much as she could get. Her capacity was enormous: while others fell into drunken stupors, she was still strong enough to walk back to her hotel, and the next day sober enough to keep to her daily schedule.

It was a glorious winter for her. She had become a person of influence if not power, a Gallimard author who could persuade an editor to commission a hitherto unknown writer, a social arbiter who could tell a hostess that she did not want to dine with a certain person and be sure that he or she would not be invited. The change in her life since she had been called into the school director's office only that previous June was dazzling. The dismissal seemed already to belong to another time, another world, even to have happened to another person.

Now everyone in Paris knew who she was, the brilliant philosopher who had become a novelist, who dared to write a novel in which the thinly disguised heroine murdered her rival; who lived unashamedly with the other writer-philosopher everyone wanted to meet.

Her public persona both pleased and frightened her. She loved the fact that she had arrived as a novelist; she had been working toward this recognition all her life, after all. But she had never stopped to consider that the obverse of literary success was notoriety, and the curiosity about her personal life, which seemed to her excessively prurient, perplexed her.

She needed to think about this so that she could decide how to proceed, but there was no book to guide her, nor was there anyone to whom she could talk—especially not Sartre, who loved women but was incapable of understanding what he considered the concerns of women. Olga was furious with her because of the success of L'Invitée and perhaps in retaliation had suddenly decided to take her acting career seriously; Wanda had never been her confidante. Natasha was absent for longer and longer periods, and Beauvoir avoided her anyway, fearing to be told of the girl's Resistance activity and thus be presumed to be her accomplice.

Beauvoir met many successful women during this time, and of them all there was no one in whom she could confide. Zette Leiris and Jeanine

Queneau once told Beauvoir how much *L'Invitée* meant to them as a way to work through their own personal problems. Such a remark might well have inspired a similar confidence in most women, but not in her. She was deeply touched by their remark but unable to reciprocate—"too shy and embarrassed to speak of my personal life to a woman who was really little more than a stranger. I was too much the child of my upbringing. We did not confide the details of our most intimate lives to mere friends."[18]

Although she continued to tell Françoise of her literary successes and whatever Parisian gossip she thought would amuse her, "there were certain things one did not discuss with one's mother, no matter how excellent the rapport." Letters from Hélène had begun to trickle through from Faro, where she and Lionel, his health restored, were working in French cultural affairs, but they were little more than brief notes forwarded by the Red Cross saying that she was well and happy. Even GéGé was gone, confined to a sanatorium in central France for a crisis of nerves and suspected tuberculosis.[19]

There was only Sartre, and although she was with him nearly every day, he was more and more absent at night. He and his new friend Camus now spent many of their evenings chasing the starlets who frequented the Flore.[20] Sartre's sexual appetites, which had been so uncharacteristically restrained for the past several years, were aroused once again, and he was off on a succession of one-night stands.

So there she was, suddenly famous as the author of the novel purportedly telling all about the triangle he and she had created, and in her mind—at least during her bleakest moments—once more the object of unfriendly gossip as well. She tried to keep up with him, going to the Flore, to the smoky clubs and wretched little theaters where the women he chased congregated. She smiled, chatted, drank enormous quantities of rotgut liquor and then, when everyone else had drunk enough not to notice, made a quiet exit and went home alone. The next day, when they met in the corridors of the hotel or when one came into the Flore to find the other already ensconced, he and she found themselves averting their eyes and, more often than not, evading the subject entirely.

It was one of the first of several turning points in her relationship with Sartre. They had gone from being just "a couple" to a "writing couple" and were now headed toward becoming a "professional couple." But each definition of their relationship must always include every previous one, because they gave nothing up and simply added new levels of being and layers of understanding to those already formed. Frequently their public actions, no matter how seemingly rude or unkind to the other partner, were tinged with the nostalgia of a long-standing emotional commitment. Throughout their lives their relationship never hardened into a predictable pattern. Instead, each new person or event became the occasion for the newest working-out of not only what they had meant to each other but what they would continue to mean in the future.

By the beginning of 1944, all of this coalesced, and she began to direct her energies and attentions outward from the Family and slightly away from Sartre, toward herself and the writings that would soon make her known internationally. By the New Year holidays of 1944, when Sartre sent her off alone to ski, she had begun the difficult and often painful process of shedding the well-brought-up young girl and the prim and proper schoolteacher. She was learning how to wear the mantle of one of the most famous women of the twentieth century.

TWENTY-ONE

Flinging Oneself
on the Future

Beauvoir was stunned when Sartre mumbled excuses about why he could not go skiing with her during the Christmas holidays. She had been planning the trip for several months, putting money aside to pay for it, keeping abreast of the steadily worsening transportation throughout France to determine which trains had the best chance of getting through. She was hurt, but had decided to stick to her plans and go alone when Bost, who felt sorry for her, offered to take Sartre's place. She accepted at once, grateful for his support.

Sartre's ostensible reason was work—deadlines for screenplays, production details only he could attend to, book reviews, articles, all certainly requiring his attention at some point but not within the inflexible schedule he described. Sartre was never very good at lying to Beauvoir, but she was no good at all in confronting him with his lies. So each fell behind a facade of politeness, and as she said many years later, "We always contrived to let each other off the hook because we were uneasy about the ruptures that could result from embarrassment."[1]

She knew his real reason for staying behind, Wanda, but she had no idea what to do about it. It also involved Albert Camus, and Beauvoir was still trying to sort out how she felt about him. Sartre met Camus when he came to offer congratulations after a performance of *The Flies*, but their friendship really began in the autumn with a conversation in the Flore at which Beauvoir was present.

Albert Camus figured in both their lives for only a few brief years, but his importance during that time was inestimable. Nevertheless, Beauvoir devotes only one page in *The Prime of Life*[2] to this first meeting and to what she thought of him. Each subsequent time she writes of him, it is with guarded appraisal, for she wrote this and the subsequent volumes of the memoirs after the famous rupture of the Sartre-Camus "friendship." Beauvoir's memoirs have often been quoted to support what has become almost "the myth" of the beginning of that "friendship," but her version has been questioned in only one instance: Patrick McCarthy, in his critical-biographical study of Camus, cautions that "Simone de Beauvoir's memoirs are, of course, a dubious source for Camus because by the time she wrote them she cordially detested him. She and Camus never had much in common. Yet, if one remembers her prejudice, her comments are interesting."[3]

McCarthy's caution is well founded. In her account, Beauvoir described Camus as "a simple, cheerful soul" of "great charm." "What I liked most about him," she wrote, "was his capacity for detached amusement at people and things even while he was intensely occupied with his personal activities, pleasures and friendships."

What she should have written was that she found him to be someone who took great care to hide the complexities of his personality, especially from her and Sartre, behind this facade of simplicity. Camus had an ironic view of the world which he expressed so caustically that Beauvoir was frequently caught off guard by the force of his comments, and his quiet self-confidence seemed to her a mask for extreme arrogance. She saw him as Sartre's potential rival in the literary world, and was afraid that he had "such flash, such dazzle," that he would eclipse the small and ugly Sartre. Besides, she didn't like the way he looked at her when they met, only to dismiss her at once as unworthy of his attentions, let alone his politeness.

"Camus couldn't stand intelligent women," she said in 1982. "They made him uncomfortable, so he either mocked or ignored them, depending on how much they irritated him." In her case, he did both. He excluded her from his conversations with Sartre, addressing her only when she insisted on interrupting. "His usual tone of voice for me was, to say it politely, ironic mockery. That stops short of what it really was—generally insulting."

Her view of Camus was equally harsh: "Camus had a very simplistic mind, and he took extremely simplistic views in politics, ethics and philosophy. He wrote well, but he was not a profound man. The difference between him and Sartre is that Sartre was a true philosopher and Camus was a pure journalist, a journalist who was also a bit of a writer. When you put his work next to Sartre's, really, you are going to find that he didn't make any impact. Nobody in France today reads anything he wrote. It was all too facile, too obvious."

What frightened her most when they first met was how swiftly Sartre fell under Camus's sway. He talked nonstop about his friend in ways which he had only previously used for his latest female infatuation. When he was speaking of Camus his language was one of competition and conquest, which instantly alerted Beauvoir to the fact that this was no ordinary man in Sartre's life. Since Sartre had "without a doubt not one trace of homosexuality in his disposition" and was "the strongest heterosexual" Simone de Beauvoir had ever known, his "infatuation" (as she called it) puzzled her at first, then worried her very much.

Camus was dazzingly handsome, a man of rugged good looks enhanced by the cigarette that dangled from his full lips. His eyes had a hooded, brooding quality, and the turned-up collar of his ubiquitous trenchcoat added to the air of mystery surrounding him. The fact that he had come to Paris from Algeria and was rumored to be in the Resistance deepened it.[4] To Sartre, Camus was an Algerian tough guy, a working-class, badly educated child of the mysterious streets. Sartre, the bourgeois voyeur, was fascinated by his background and wanted to know everything there was to know about him.

Sartre shared Simone de Beauvoir's passion for voyeurism, and Camus became one of their favorite targets. But, to their dismay, he refused to give them sovereignty over his private self, choosing to deflect their questions by mimicking absent friends. So they had to settle for the part of Camus that he wanted them to see, which was generally the public, witty, friendly and intellectual side of himself—except for Beauvoir, whom he continually tried to ignore or exclude and to whom he was usually rude. She believed that although at first he found Sartre amusing, Camus never really liked him, and so he kept the private side of his life carefully hidden from the couple. For Sartre it was enough because Camus was "good-looking . . . [and] could dance and . . . seduce [women]."[5]

When they met him, Camus was thirty, eight years younger than Sartre. And as Sartre always sought young and handsome men ostensibly as friends but actually as satellites, he and Beauvoir simply assumed that Camus would become the latest of the bright young men whom Sartre expected to be the rising stars of French intellectual life after the war, but whom he also expected would owe their first allegiance to him as their leader.

Where they were nearly equal—if such a judgment can be made— was in the public's reception of their creative output. Both were in the process of becoming extremely well known in Paris because of their writing; their message of moral commitment was so fresh and inviting after so many years of the influence of the old Surrealists Bataille, Leiris and Queneau, and such disparate writers as Gide, Claudel, Paulhan and Malraux. But here again Camus had an edge on Sartre, because he was firmly ensconced in the publishing house of Gallimard and, even though only a junior member of the firm, was on the prestigious reading committee, the group of writers and editors who decided what books the house would publish. When a new literary prize, the Prix de la Pléiade, was established by Gallimard, Camus was responsible for Sartre's invitation to be a member of the jury. Sartre was delighted, but Beauvoir was miffed, since Sartre "was already a writer of distinction who should have been invited by someone not so unimportant [at Gallimard] as Camus."

However, as Sartre was captivated by Camus, Beauvoir felt she had no choice but to like him as well. She tried, she claimed many years later, but never quite succeeded, and she believed that he knew it. Pressed to explain why this animosity was there almost from the first, she said, "We were like two dogs circling a bone. The bone was Sartre, and we both wanted it. I cared about it more than Camus. After a while he got bored and went sniffing after other things." "The unkind Simone de Beauvoir," as Patrick McCarthy calls her,[6] both failed to recognize and then refused to admit that Camus was an independent man who had a full life quite apart from hers and Sartre's. Both knew that Camus was married and had a full-time job, but he was so reserved that neither knew how many grueling hours he spent alone at his writing, or that he was being drawn into the Resistance more and more, or that he still suffered from the tuberculosis he had had since his youth.

In the beginning, Camus was in their company nearly every day. He dropped in at the Flore, dined with them at the Leirises' and at Beauvoir's, for a time even agreed to act in one of Sartre's plays. Their ideas for cooperative ventures ranged far as they made enthusiastic plans for "after the war" (a phrase now in common usage). Camus knew that Gallimard intended to publish an encyclopedia of philosophy; he and Sartre decided that they and Beauvoir, along with Merleau-Ponty, would write the section on ethics. Sartre came up with the idea of starting a postwar magazine that would represent their collected thoughts on politics and ideology. Camus added his own views on who should be invited to serve on the governing board and what the subjects of the first articles should be. While the two soared on ideas and theories, Beauvoir worried about whether or not they could find enough paper to print it and whom they could persuade to do the typing and editing. Their replies were only of their dreams of how successful it would be, while she tried to squelch the entire undertaking as "impractical, impossible, and taking too much time from writing."

Camus became such an integral figure in their lives that his name and Sartre's were lumped together as though they were alter egos, identical literary twins whose writings represented the same philosophy, the same outlook on life. In the public's perception, they were both exponents of "Existentialism," and the name of one became an easy substitute for the other's.[7]

Camus became so popular within the Sartre/Beauvoir circle that when Michel Leiris staged a public reading of Picasso's play *Le Désir attrapé par la queue* (*Desire Caught by the Tail*), he was put in charge of the production. The play was written in the language and style of 1920s' avant-gardism, and the characters' names reflected this. Camus gave Sartre the role of "Round End." With female characters called by such names as "Fat" and "Thin Misery" and "The Tart," he cast Simone de Beauvoir as "The Cousin." Beauvoir considered this an intentional slight, but chose to concentrate instead on how good it felt to be among friends at "a noisy, frivolous party that went on for hours. Prematurely, and despite all the threats that still hung over so many of us, we were celebrating victory."[8] She had dressed up for the occasion, wearing Olga's red angora sweater and Wanda's big blue costume pearls, undaunted that all she had to wear with them was the hideously disheveled wool skirt and the tweed jacket that had once been her father's. She remembered resenting Camus's mocking appraisal of her outfit. That evening, she met Jacques Lacan, a perpetual-motion dynamo of thought and idea. She watched him surreptitiously, too bashful to engage in anything more than "an occasional liquor-induced platitude."

Camus had become so important in their lives that when he was recruited by his friend Pascal Pia to work in the Resistance cell, Combat, they followed him. Actually, Sartre followed him; Beauvoir followed Sartre. Camus worked alone with the group for several months until the late spring of 1944.

> One time, Camus himself brought a new couple to their meeting, under pseudonyms. The small man offered to do anything, including writing crime stories. And he did anything he was asked. Then Jacqueline Bernard [a member of the cell] went to see *Huis Clos (No Exit)* and discovered that her volunteer couple were Jean-Paul Sartre and Simone de Beauvoir.[9]

Simone de Beauvoir remembers it differently: she never attended another meeting of Combat, and when the genuine invitation to join the Resistance that Sartre had sometimes comically sought finally came, he was too engrossed in his own work to put it aside, preoccupied with both the production and the publication of *No Exit* and with putting the last pre-publication touches to his novel *The Reprieve*. He too never attended another meeting. Camus fell into the habit of discussing the work of Combat with Sartre and then sometimes reported his observations back to the group, so Sartre's name was much in use. Consequently, it may have seemed that he was much more active than he actually was.

Neither he nor Beauvoir did anything for Combat until the fall of 1944, when Camus asked Sartre to go out into the streets and write a series of impressionistic accounts of the Liberation of Paris to be published in the group's newspaper of the same name. Indeed they were published under the byline of Jean-Paul Sartre, but Simone de Beauvoir wrote them because "he was too busy."[10] Many years later, she defended her action as "a perfectly reasonable thing to do." She had always acted as Sartre's "most favored reader and trusted critic," and so it seemed natural that after conversations about events of recent days she should take all these events, combine them with her own observations and write the articles. She believed she was performing a service that left him free to concentrate on his own creative writing.

These articles had little impact on Simone de Beauvoir's subsequent nonfiction writing, particularly the books about her travels in the United States and China. In all her vast body of writing, she never again wrote so vividly about the absurdity of the daily life she depicted in these wartime articles. Beauvoir saw a group of Resistance fighters, and to her they looked like Chicago gangsters in an American movie. An old woman tried to do her daily shopping in the midst of fleeing German soldiers who sprayed the street with bullets. "You can't stop eating just because there's a war going on," she told Beauvoir before continuing to shop. There is an aura of surrealism in the black humor of Beauvoir's observations, but, as she said, it was "an unreal time. Perhaps observation of reality is heightened in such circumstances."

Still, she was a respected writer because of *L'Invitée*, and if Sartre had been too busy to write these articles, she was certainly an appropriate substitute. So the question remained as to why she had not signed her own name to them. Fear of German reprisals had nothing to do with it, she insisted, but she fell back on the excuse that she had not been the one asked to write them. "It was Sartre. Anyway, what did it matter whose name it was? Someone had to write them."[11]

Her view of herself until the day she died was absolutely settled upon the idea that she was part of a couple, firm, fixed and inviolate. In one sense she was, as both she and Sartre proclaimed repeatedly, in almost every interview they ever gave, that each was the most important person in the other's life, but in 1944 Simone de Beauvoir began to discover that if she wanted to continue to believe in the infallibility of their pact she would have to learn to think about herself in another way.

She found it difficult to express how she felt during the last year of the war, and it was still so years later when she wrote her memoirs: "Of all the periods in my life, I find it hardest to recollect just how things looked to me during this particular phase." She described the all-night parties they dubbed "fiestas," when everyone brought food or wine to last through the night because no one was allowed on the streets after curfew, and how they all drank to oblivion and danced till exhaustion. She tells of those who had worked surreptitiously in the Resistance coming out into the open, of friends returning from detention camps, of how she suffered when she learned how many friends were dead and would never return. Despite inherent danger now that the Germans were being openly attacked on the streets of Paris, there was an air of holiday reunion after long separation as people who had been in hiding suddenly emerged, and others who had been away returned.

She wrote of the people she met who would figure in her postwar life, such as Jean Cocteau and Jean Genet, who, unlike Camus, would allow her and Sartre to satisfy all their voyeuristic longings delving into his personality and later would allow Sartre to write a book about him.

Despite all the unusual occurrences, she and Sartre still went to La Pouèze for the Easter holidays and again for several weeks at All Saints' Day, November 1. During Easter she wrote to her mother as usual.

> I lead a king's life here. There are a lot of airplanes roaming above my head and you can hear the bombings in the distance, but the place where I am is very calm. I sleep, eat, work and read. Absolutely nothing else is happening. We have the English radio all day long. . . . I am sending you my ration tickets for bread because I don't need them here."[12]

Back in Paris, she and Sartre were warned by Camus to change addresses after the Germans arrested a member of Combat who betrayed others in the cell. They made a holiday of it, hiding at the Leiris apartment for several days before going to a hotel in the nearby suburb of Neuilly-sous-Clermont. She left first, and spent a few more days alone until Sartre joined her, bringing the Leirises for the weekend to continue the good time they had had in Paris. Then Bost came as well, on a short leave from reporting for *Combat*.[13] She wrote to her mother to tell her that she had more than enough entertainment, as everyone brought her "armloads of books."[14] She particularly enjoyed one with a lot of pictures on "the gold rush in America," where she hoped to go when the war was over. Clermont, she said, was "a charming little town with a nice view," but

> the only problem is the constant bombings all around. It's not dangerous for me, but I am a little uneasy when I know that people are on the road. But it's very rare when accidents happen. The other day more than 300 planes passed over my head, absolutely superb, all silver and shining in the sun. The cops are patrolling all the roads and sometimes they shoot so hard that I stay home because I'm afraid to get shot at out in the country. I won't go to visit [her mother's friend] because it's 30 kilometers from here and I don't want to get machine-gunned. I listen from morning to night to the BBC. It's all starting to happen. It's truly coming [to the end] now.

This letter frightened Françoise, so Beauvoir wrote a second to reassure her: "Everything is very peaceful here and I'm coming back soon."[15]

She and Sartre pedaled their bikes furiously to get back when they heard that American troops were outside Chartres moving toward Paris. On August 25, 1944, she went without Sartre to stand among the many Parisians who lined the Avenue d'Orléans (now the Avenue du Général-Leclerc) to watch the Leclerc Division march into the city. The next day, she went without him to the Champs-Elysées to see General de Gaulle march by on foot. She, Olga and the Leirises joined the celebration, which she called "not a military parade . . . so much as a magnificent, if chaotic, popular carnival show." That night they all dined with the first American Simone de Beauvoir had ever seen, let alone met, Patrick Walberg.[16]

"That was the end of it," she wrote in *The Prime of Life*, "Paris was liberated now; the world and the future had been handed back to us, and we flung ourselves upon them."[17]

The war was indeed over, but that was not the end of it for Beauvoir and Sartre. For the rest of their lives, rumor and innuendo plagued them. They were haunted by allegations that they had been less than honorable during the war years, that they had shut their eyes to the realities of the German occupation, equivocating to advance themselves whenever it suited them. There were charges that their careers profited and their literary reputations flourished while others took the more honorable path of not writing for German-controlled media and, in some few extreme cases, of not publishing at all.[18] It is a fact that Sartre's name never appeared on the infamous "Otto List"[19] of writers (mostly Jewish) whose works were either banned or destroyed. But it is also a fact that he and Beauvoir (like almost all other writers in France who published during the war) complied with the requirement to submit their works to the Propagandastaffel censorship. He wrote for *Comoedia* and she for the German-controlled radio, but both felt they had valid reasons for doing so. Their behavior withstood both the scrutiny and the punishing mechanisms of postwar judgments and tribunals, for they were never called to account for what they had done.

By the end of 1943, they were both published authors, and both fairly well known if not actually famous. Although they had sat side by side with German officers in cafés, concert halls and theaters, they still remained securely fixed within the world defined by the small and demanding circle of bourgeois intellectuals who did not fraternize. Their names were never listed among the glitterati who dined *chez* Florence Gould or Marie-Laure de Noailles.[20] The German ambassador, Otto Abetz, and his French wife, Suzanne, never fêted them even though *L'Invitée* was the sensation of the 1943 publishing season. And if their names appear in the memoirs of the society hostesses and other Parisians who were lavish in their entertainment of the German occupiers, it is usually a nonspecific reference made in passing. Most of these works were written long after the end of the war, and if they cite the memoirs of Simone de Beauvoir it is usually to give themselves an air of historical grounding and authenticity.

So, at a time when "[no one knew] just who was up to just what,"[21] the most they can be accused of is selfishness and self-centeredness, but even these charges must be tempered by the known fact of Sartre's first attempts to mount a resistance effort and the knowledge that Simone de Beauvoir, who followed his lead in everything else during these years, would certainly have followed him if his efforts had been successful.

Sartre and Beauvoir, who spent all their adult lives trying to purge themselves of their bourgeois upbringing, would no doubt have resented the charge that their behavior during the war was typical of the majority of their class: they did not openly or willingly consent to the German occupation and they did not fraternize, but neither did they take heroic or extraordinary means to resist it. At a time when "everyone experienced his own occupation,"[22] Sartre and Beauvoir did what they felt they needed to do in order to survive. If they felt better about their actions by analyzing and explaining them under a guise of philosophical or political terminology, their equivocations should probably be judged accordingly.

Their record is not scrupulously clean, but neither is it clearly soiled.

TWENTY-TWO

Always Something to Say

W HY WAS IT," Simone de Beauvoir asked, trying to recall herself as she was at the end of 1944, "that from this point on I always had 'something to say'?"[1]

By 1945, she had completed an astonishing amount of writing despite a steady stream of interruptions in Paris and elsewhere. Her only play, *Les Bouches inutiles*, was performed to generally favorable reviews; she saw *The Blood of Others* through publication, finished writing *All Men Are Mortal* and published her second book of philosophy, *Pour une morale de l'ambiguité* (*The Ethics of Ambiguity*). She also wrote several long philosophical essays and book reviews for *Les Temps Modernes* and a series of articles for other journals. In Paris she gave public lectures on contemporary fiction, and in Portugal she lectured on life during the occupation. She even wrote a profile of Sartre, "Strictly Personal," for *Harper's Bazaar*.[2]

She did all this despite the fact that it was more and more difficult to write in the Flore because of the continuous interruption. In the first flush of her public notoriety, so many people wanted to meet her that she scarcely had any time left for the old friends she herself wanted to see. They complained of having to make appointments sometimes several days in advance for fifteen minutes of public conversation, and generally that was interrupted as well.[3]

Each morning she was one of the first arrivals at the Flore despite the fact that every night she went to a different club or party, drinking heavily and staying out very late. She put the early-morning hours to good use, writing until the late arrivals began a steady stream of interruptions. She took her usual Easter and autumn holidays at La Pouèze, went on several bicycle and ski trips, and traveled to Spain and Portugal, leaving France for the first time since the war began.

She actually struck up new acquaintances with several women which looked for a time as if they would develop into real friendships, the most important among them with the writers Violette Leduc and Nathalie Sarraute. Leduc soon became "an amiable pest, sometimes a bore, a sad person, usually too pathetic to criticize," whom Beauvoir never referred to by name but always as "the ugly woman."[4] Sarraute interested her because of "the initial novelty of her writing," and because of "her unusual Russian-French background," but soon Sarraute transferred her primary intellectual allegiance to Sartre, and Beauvoir was quick to nip their budding friendship before Sarraute became a possible rival.

Beauvoir was still writing radio scripts to earn money, but spending as little time as possible doing so. She preferred to concentrate on her own work, but Sartre's needs, as always, came first. He required all her energy and attention because no sooner had he conceived the idea of a new review than he went off to the United States, leaving her to cope with the details of launching and publishing the first issue of *Les Temps Modernes*.

Despite Sartre's demands, despite the fact that her life was suddenly full of the thrilling events she had always dreamed about, of seeing her book in shop windows, her name and face in newspapers—despite all these welcome distractions, she wrote thousands of pages that year which nearly equaled Sartre's prodigious output. She wrote for a number of reasons, one of which was that she had "grown used to living inside a writer's skin"[5] and to sitting down each day and producing a certain number of pages. She wrote also because there did not seem to be any books which reflected her feelings and could thus serve as guides. But perhaps the most important reason of all for her tremendous literary output was one she evaded for the rest of her life: her world, centered for so long upon the idea of herself and Sartre as an inviolate couple, was falling apart.

"Sartre has just finished writing a manifesto for *Les Temps Modernes*. . . . So be it and God save the so-called literature of commitment!" Jean Paulhan wrote in a letter of December 10, 1944. He had just agreed to be on the editorial committee of the review, "which, by its very nature, is doomed to be boring and false. But in literature anything goes."[6]

Despite her initial reluctance and all her unflattering epithets whenever Sartre waxed eloquent about the magazine he intended to start, once Beauvoir realized that he was serious she threw herself into working to make it happen. The immediate concern was to form the editorial committee and create the magazine's manifesto. Paulhan's cooperation was vital, because he had been the editor of *Nouvelle Revue Française* for many years and was the only one of their friends who knew the nuts-and-bolts details of bringing out a monthly magazine. Leiris and Queneau were invited to take charge of poetry and literature because Sartre respected their views so much; Camus was invited because Sartre now thought of him as his best friend and someone able to attract the audience that was certain to follow him from *Combat*. Others included Merleau-Ponty because of his background in philosophy, and Raymond Aron because he had worked for *La France Libre* during the war and could also offer technical advice about printing and publishing. Beauvoir suspected Aron's reasons for joining the editorial committee, accusing him of "trusting, I think, that Sartre would not have the perseverance to find it interesting for long and that he would then take over."⁷ Albert Ollivier completed the original editorial committee, of which Beauvoir wrote that "in those days, none of these names clashed."⁸ However, before the magazine was a year old, Ollivier, like Aron, resigned because of an ideological disagreement.

With financing promised by publisher Gaston Gallimard,⁹ the first hurdle before publication was surmounted. Almost immediately, Beauvoir was faced with another: paper was still rationed, and only publications already extant were eligible for allotments. Editors and publishers who hoped to begin new journals and reviews were required to submit extensive written documentation and, in most instances, to spend days going from office to office to plead their cases. Naturally, it fell to Beauvoir to do this. Sartre gave the magazine its name, a takeoff on Charlie Chaplin's film but also a reference to the hoped-for changes in postwar society, but it was she who arranged for the clipping service that often confused the magazine with the film and sent the wrong articles and reviews. It was she also who cast the deciding vote against an original cover design by Picasso, thinking it "much too arty, distracting from the politics inside," and insisted upon the plain white cover, the black and red lettering and the block initials "TM" that the magazine has used ever since: "Camus said it was good to have catchy initials, so I just put them at the bottom of a page of printing given to us by a disgusted Gallimard designer who told me if I didn't make up my mind soon we would be forced to use ordinary letters for our cover. The others went along with me because Sartre wasn't there and I think they must have thought he had deputized me in his absence. It wasn't true, but I didn't tell them. I felt we would have to make many decisions in a great hurry, and so I just kept quiet and made them myself."

Sartre missed all the pre-publication decisions because he had finally gotten to the United States, leaving behind a disappointed Simone de Beauvoir who could find no one to sponsor her for the trip. Representing both *Combat* and *Le Figaro*, two ideologically opposite newspapers, Sartre was among the first group of French journalists invited by the State Department to spend two months in the United States observing American culture in the hope that they would then write favorable articles, thus influencing postwar French attitudes. On January 11, 1945, Sartre took his first plane ride, to New York, which made Beauvoir both angry and sad. Flying was something they were both very keen to do, and she had always assumed that their first flight would be together.

Camus was responsible for Sartre's good fortune, and it forced a change in Beauvoir's rapport with him. There was no regular postal service between France and the United States while the war was still on, and the only way she could get news of Sartre was by reading the articles he sent to Camus and whatever other messages got through with them. Camus fell into the habit of stopping at the Flore each afternoon when he had news, and then whether he had news or not. He was married, and his wife had come from Algeria to join him in Paris, but he also had a long-standing liaison with the brilliant actress Maria Casarès. Camus needed someone to talk to, and he found a sympathetic but wary ear in Beauvoir. He spoke directly of his intimate feelings for his wife and his mistress, which she, still smarting because of his shabby treatment, tried to turn into abstract philosophical propositions. These, she assured him, would provide rational answers to his untenable situation if only he worked them through to their logical conclusion. When she discovered how much Camus valued her opinion, she became more relaxed and, in her words, "truly thought we had established a solid friendship because we told each other things. It was this private friendship that I regretted losing when the time came that he disappointed Sartre and their friendship was broken."[10]

But that was still several years away; in 1945, she discovered that she was the one in need of philosophical advice, and from Camus.

In New York, Sartre met Dolores Vanetti Ehrenreich, a French woman who was married to a wealthy American doctor and was herself working for the Office of War Information. She had been an aspiring actress in France before the war, and now made radio broadcasts in French which the American agency hoped would influence a female French audience in pro-American ways. She was a vivacious woman, quite unlike all the others with whom Sartre had had romantic encounters, because she was neither young and blonde nor shapely and beautiful, merely a thin, pleasant-looking woman of average appearance. However, she was tiny, quite possibly the only woman with whom Sartre was ever involved who was shorter than he. Dolores made many friends among the French exiled during the war in New York, and she introduced Sartre to them all, so that he claimed his lasting impressions of New York came about because of her. Soon he was writing long missives to Camus, full of hints about Dolores, knowing full well that Camus would not miss the opportunity to pass them along to Beauvoir. As always, Sartre was unable to tell Beauvoir directly that he was initially "smitten" and later "in love" with Dolores. She could only infer that he had begun a new infatuation from the veiled references she found in the notes he sent to her via Camus.

Beauvoir was able to piece together very little of this at the end of February 1945, when Sartre's infatuation was reaching its highest pitch, because she had finally gotten her own assignment and she went off to Madrid and Lisbon. Since the Liberation, letters from Hélène had begun to reach Françoise, and subsequently Simone, on a regular basis. Lionel de Roulet was now working with the French Institute in Lisbon as the editor of a Franco-Portuguese review called *Affinidades*, and he arranged an invitation for Beauvoir to give lectures on the situation in France during the occupation.[11] Camus made her an official correspondent for *Combat*, which hastened the necessary government permission, and, doubly armed with imposing credentials, she left to spend several days in Madrid before going on to Portugal. Her articles "Four Days in Madrid" appeared in *Combat* April 11–15, and those about Portugal appeared a week later, some in *Combat* and the rest in *Volonté*, all under the name Daniel Secrétan, a

pseudonym she used so as not to embarrass Lionel because of her pronouncements against the Portuguese dictator Antonio Salazar.

As she was to do in so many of her foreign travels from this point on,
Beauvoir viewed society through the prism of Marxist thought, which in
the beginning was the official though unstated doctrine governing *Les
Temps Modernes*. When she arrived in Portugal as a social commentator,
she was struck for the first time by the contrast between rich and poor, excess and poverty, and her articles reflected this dichotomy in absolutes,
without shading or nuance. The prose is simplistic, but the outrage and
emotion are genuine.

Still, even though she was shocked by the disparities she saw everywhere around her, the privation of life in Paris during the war caused a reaction which later embarrassed her, but which at the time she was unable
to resist. She gave in to all the riches around her and consumed everything
voraciously and excessively. She ate or bought everything that came her
way, from chocolates and oranges to nylon stockings and a rabbit-fur coat.

She hadn't seen her sister for almost five years, but the first thing
Hélène asked when they met was, "What are those things?" as she stared
in a mixture of astonishment and disgust at Beauvoir's wooden-soled clog
shoes and the grimy socks that fell around her ankles.[12] They went shopping at once, and Beauvoir described in her memoirs what happened next:
"Never in my life had I surrendered to such a debauch; my lecture tour
was very well paid, and in one afternoon I assembled a complete wardrobe:
three pairs of shoes, a bag, stockings, lingerie, sweaters, dresses, skirts,
blouses, a white wool jacket, a fur coat."[13]

She returned to Paris loaded down with all her finery plus chocolate
bars, enormous sacks of oranges, packets of dried olives, spices, sausages,
and presents for everybody: silk scarves, shawls, sweaters, bits of native pottery, glass baubles. She dumped everything onto her bed at the Hotel
Louisiane (they were living there again) to admire the colorful profusion,
but everything paled when she heard Camus's news of Sartre.

He was staying on in New York after the departure of the other journalists and would not return to Paris until the end of May. He had bolted
the tour which was taking them around the country, had gone back to New
York and was living with Dolores. Beauvoir retaliated by embarking on a
contingent affair of her own, turning to the first man who found her attractive enough to make "a sort of pass," Michel Vitold. Vitold agreed to
direct Beauvoir's play, *Useless Mouths*, during the winter of 1945, and by
the time she heard that Sartre was staying on in New York she was ready
to admit to herself that she did indeed find Vitold a most attractive man.

Before her trip to Portugal, she had either "not recognized" or else
"refused to admit" that Vitold's interest in her was personal as well as professional. She was thirty-seven years old at the time, still missing the tooth
knocked out when she fell off her bicycle several years before. Her hair was
unkempt, usually confined under a turban because shampoo and soap were
still so hard to come by. Her clothing, except for the Portuguese finery,

which she could not wear every day, was still a shambles. None of this mattered to her except her age. Several years had passed since she and Sartre shared passion, and the occasional "fling" (her word) she had desultorily "submitted to" had "amounted to nothing." She thought of herself as "old, far beyond passion, too old to be with men," and this despite seeing many of the women she knew, all older and some much older than she, happily involved in passionate relationships. Her attitude toward age had much to do with the attitudes of the women of her social class, for whom middle age began in their midthirties. For Beauvoir personally, the fact that no man had found her sexually attractive for such a long time only strengthened her negative feelings about herself, all of which were reinforced by the early conditioning of her *haut-bourgeois* background.

Together she and Vitold set off on bicycles along the River Creuse and into the Auvergne, ostensibly to discuss the play away from the distractions of the theater, but really to conduct an affair in private. They were together frequently after that, always on the pretext that they were only friends or that they were conferring about the play, because Beauvoir took great care to hide their intimacy from the people she knew in Paris.

This was characteristic of her behavior in all her contingent liaisons, even though it seems to fly in the face of her pact with Sartre. Although he openly paraded all his other women in full public view (except for those few who insisted upon privacy), Beauvoir kept all her affairs as secret as possible because "it didn't look good for me to be with other men. People expected me to be faithful, so I pretended that I was."[14] When Sartre came back from New York, she did not tell him the truth because the way he talked about Dolores terrified her.

Dolores Vanetti Ehrenreich tried never to speak publicly about Simone de Beauvoir, whom she met only once and then briefly, and said that she never allowed Sartre to speak to her of Beauvoir: "I was very jealous and he was sensitive to know and respect this. He never discussed her with me." As for how Sartre felt about her and Beauvoir during their involvement, Mrs. Ehrenreich believed he was "troubled, unsettled, undecided," adding that all three of them "were all of these, and much worse."[15]

In 1982, Simone de Beauvoir was asked to talk about Dolores Vanetti Ehrenreich and was unable to do so without becoming agitated and emotional: "It's no longer of any great importance, but at the time I was writing [*Force of Circumstances*] I didn't want people to know anything about her, so I called her 'M.' Sartre wanted me to write about her, but I said no. He said I was being dishonest. I said they were my memoirs. He said they were about him as well. But I didn't want people to know about her, who she was. They would look her up. They would see her, and pretty soon she would be talking about me. I could not have that. I insisted that she be only 'M.' Now there isn't any mystery concerning her anymore. Did she worry me? Of course she worried me! Well, if she worried me, it was because I didn't know her at all, and I knew—rather, I think I was told, somebody must have told me—that she was hostile to me. All the other women, the important ones such as Wanda and Olga and [his other lovers in other countries], we are all friends because they knew that if they wanted to count for him they had to count for me. If they came to Paris, we dined together, and they learned to write to me, and send me birthday and New Year's greetings. And we were all friends together. As a whole, the women with whom Sartre had his relationships, they were almost all friends for me as well, even the ones who were not important, they knew to be friendly to me. But this one, Dolores, this is almost the only case where . . ." She lost her thought and paused. "I saw her, however. I saw her on the other side of the Atlantic, but we were not friends. Obviously since she would really have liked to marry Sartre, obviously I was a little . . ." She did not finish the sentence.

It was ten years after the onset of Sartre's infatuation when Beauvoir wrote about Dolores in *Force of Circumstance*, and her emotions were still confused even then. She begins by devoting several paragraphs to dispatches Sartre filed from the United States (page 26), then says, "Sartre was still in New York" (page 38), and (on page 41) "Sartre came back to Paris and told me about his trip." There is not a word about Dolores until page 60. All she wrote was:

> Sartre was . . . going back to New York. In [the previous] January he had met a young woman there, half separated from her husband and, despite her brilliant position in the world, not very satisfied with her life; they had been very attracted to each other. When told about my existence she had decided that when he went back to France they should forget each other; his feelings for her were too strong for him to accept this; he had written to her from Paris and she had replied.

By this time Beauvoir's vaguely chronological narrative is well into 1946, and she finally introduces her rival on the printed page: "After his return from America, Sartre talked to me a great deal about M" (page 77). Beauvoir then proceeds in careful, well-ordered prose, somewhat unusual in an account which to this point has jumbled time, space, her own life and the lives of others with neither accurate chronology nor textual unity. In telling about Dolores, Beauvoir writes of herself as she was then with clarity, precision, and deep feeling kept carefully under strong, distanced authorial control. It is one of the most personal, if not the single most personal, passage in all four volumes of her memoirs, and for that reason it is quoted at some length here:

> At present their attachment was mutual, and they envisaged spending two or three months together every year. So be it: separations held no terror for me. But he evoked the weeks he had spent with her in New York with such gaiety that I grew uneasy; till then I had supposed him to be attracted mainly by the romantic side of this adventure; suddenly I wondered if M. was

more important to him than I was; my heart's old armor of optimism fell away; anything could happen to me. In a relationship that has lasted for fifteen years, how much is a matter of mere habit. What concessions does it imply? I knew my answer, not Sartre's. I understood him better than I used to, and for that reason I found him more opaque; there were great differences between us; this did not disturb me, quite the contrary, but him? According to his accounts, M. shared completely all his reactions, his emotions, his irritations, his desires. . . . Perhaps this indicated a harmony between them at a depth—at the very source of life, at the wellspring where its very rhythm is established—at which Sartre and I did not meet, and perhaps that harmony was more important to him than our understanding.[16]

Her account continues as she adds that, typically, she could not control her emotions, and as "often happens . . . when a dangerous question is burning our lips, we choose a particularly unsuitable moment to ask it." They were lunching with Armand Salacrou and his wife, and Beauvoir blurted out, "Frankly, who means the most to you, M or me?"

Sartre's answer "took my breath away. I understood it to mean 'I am respecting our pact. Don't ask any more of me than that.' Such a reply," she wrote, "put the whole future in question."

Lunch proceeded, for Beauvoir "a nightmare that would never end," and she remembered with clarity almost forty years later "the white fish so filled with dangerous sharp bones" that she used it as her excuse for not being able to swallow. "That afternoon," she wrote, "Sartre explained what he had meant: we had always taken actions to be more truthful than words, and that is why, instead of launching into a long explanation, he had invoked the evidence of a simple fact. I believed him."

She believed him because she wanted to believe him. What she did not write in her memoirs was that this conversation took place in mid-May 1945, and that Sartre was already openly plotting to return to Dolores as quickly as he could arrange it. He was writing letters to French friends who had spent the war teaching at American universities, asking them to arrange lectures, and he was "playing up to anyone and everyone in Paris, in and out of government, to help him get back to New York."

She spent the first two months of summer as busy as ever, even going with Sartre to Belgium to participate in a discussion organized by the religious publishing house, Cerf. A measure of how deeply affected she was by their conversation about Dolores came in August, when she and Sartre went quietly to Madame Morel's to spend the month and she requested the room in the little house at the end of the garden, even though Madame Morel wanted her to take her usual room in the main house.

The Blood of Others was to be published in September, and the advance notices were superlatives that would ordinarily have put her "over the moon," to use one of her favorite expressions, but instead of dwelling on the happy reception that would await her in Paris, she worked steadily on her next novel, *All Men Are Mortal*, growing more serious and pensive as the vacation progressed.

While she was writing these two, *The Blood of Others* proved the more difficult "to get right," by which she meant integrating the philosophy of Existentialism within the fictional account of two lovers caught up in the Resistance. The manuscript shows evidence of how she persevered to perfect her technique: "all dog-eared and covered with cross-outs, and written on different sizes of paper with different inks and even in different scripts."[17]

Her intention was to express the paradox of freedom experienced by an individual and the ways in which others, perceived by the individual as objects, were affected by his actions and decisions. When the book was published, none of this was mentioned in the barrage of praise that was showered upon it, only that it was a "Resistance novel," the first to deal with the experience all France had just endured. Camus, who liked the book, was surprised by its success; Aron told her he found its public reception "revolting,"[18] but everyone else seemed genuinely pleased, especially Sartre and the Family, because it brought Beauvoir enough money to permit her to quit the hated radio job.

She wrote the greater part of the novel during the worst years of the war, throughout 1943 and 1944, and much of the bleakness and uncertainty of that period pervades its background. She chose a man called Jean Blomart to be the individual character against whose experiences in the Resistance all other characters will be perceived, their experiences filtered through his by first-person narration. At the beginning of the novel, he is seated at the bedside of his dying lover, Hélène Bertrand, who has been fatally wounded in a resistance encounter with the Germans. Her story is told through a distanced third-person narration, with the only grounding in time and space coming through the immediacy of the events described. Within this technique of dual narration, Blomart's story comprises the better part of the novel, but Hélène's fills in many of the details that his long interior monologues fail to provide.

During the long night's death watch, Blomart ponders his future, realizing that his every action brings with it the possibility of his own death, the death of others involved with him, and perhaps even death by reprisal for innocent people who are chosen randomly by the Germans to pay with their lives for his actions. He is sure that Hélène has not regretted her involvement, but he wonders about all the others who may not have made the decision to participate as rationally as she.

Blomart was born into a comfortable bourgeois family, received an excellent education, and was seemingly headed toward a good career and a secure future before the war, but he turned his back on it, choosing to become a worker in a printing factory. He tells his mother, "I disapprove of the system. How can you expect me to be willing to benefit from it?"[19]

"But you've already benefited from it," she replies. "It's your duty that you are refusing to do."

Blomart has an answer: "The benefits I've had up to now I had in spite of myself. I don't consider that I am under any obligation."

His friend Marcel debates this decision from an opposite viewpoint:

> "But your cultural background, your friends, your boyish, well-fed bourgeois health—you can't rid yourself of the past. . . . There'll always be a gulf between you and a working-class man, you choose freely a condition to which he submits."
>
> "That's true, said Jean, but I shall, at least, have done everything I could."[20]

This definition of Blomart's character and situation is presented early in the novel, and his recollection of life before the war is juxtaposed with his vigil at the dying girl's bedside. His personal story parallels the history of his time, as, like many others in the 1930s, he looked to Communism as the key to social change. When war broke out, he tried to use his political position as his guide to conduct in an occupied country.

On the first page of *The Blood of Others*, Blomart must decide whether or not to go ahead with a sabotage mission. As the night grinds slowly on, he agonizes over whether or not to instigate actions which will jeopardize the lives of others. He decides that he must live his life by making choices which are often painful because collective freedom depends on individuals who are willing to risk their own lives and bear the guilt of risking the lives of others. Blomart reflects as he makes the choice for further sabotage to be carried out:

> Those who will be shot tomorrow have not chosen; I am the rock that crushes them; I shall not escape the curse; forever I shall be to them . . . the blind force of fate. But if only I dedicate myself to defend that supreme good . . . which saves each man from all the others and from myself—Freedom—then my passion will not have been in vain. You [Hélène] have not given me peace, but why should I desire peace? You have given me the courage to accept forever the risk and the anguish, to bear my crimes and my guilt which will rend me eternally. There is no other way.[21]

Beauvoir's commitment to Existential freedom is expressed in terms equally as strong on almost every page of the novel, and was noted by almost every reviewer in all the languages in which it was published. When it appeared in the United States in 1948, reviewer Richard McLaughlin called her the "most Existential of all the Existentialists" and said the novel was "the fictional primer on existentialism we have all been anxiously awaiting." He said further that Beauvoir had written "the real thesis novel in an economical, sometimes flat style which conceals a remarkably sustained note of suspense and mounting excitement due to the sheer vitality and force of her ideas. This is perhaps the way a novel of ideas should be presented. . . ."[22] McLaughlin is also typical of the more perceptive reviewers who found fault with Beauvoir's thesis by doubting that any individual could possibly exist in a state of pure freedom and remain untouched and unfettered by the will of others because, according to Existential tenets, other people possess the same freedom as well: "One is forced to doubt the ultimate achievement of this liberty, since if the existentialists insist on total responsibility they also urge total involvement."[23]

Beauvoir continued to insist upon wearing the mantle of disciple and chief spokesperson for Sartre's philosophy, and thus she continued to tailor her fiction to fit his philosophical orientation. Often, the manner in which she expressed this ethical system results in fictional rigidity, making her characters behave at times as if they were only theoretical constructs. Fortunately, in this novel such subservience to her chosen system of behavior is muted, and if there are flaws within the philosophical underpinnings, her critics are correct to find them in her conceptualization of freedom. Beauvoir holds to the premise that each individual has both the ability to conceptualize freedom and the material circumstances to live his or her life accordingly.[24]

To a lesser extent in L'Invitée, to a greater one in All Men Are Mortal, but in this novel especially, were it not for the historical situation of war and resistance her characters would seem to be free-floating in a vacuum, alone in a world unpopulated by others whose individual and perhaps differing conception of freedom might interfere with theirs. In her world of individual freedom, social considerations, let alone constraints, have no meaning for or impact upon the individual. In a very real sense, hers is a bleak message of loneliness and alienation, more central to the French New Novel than to the literature of commitment, where her novels are generally classified.

She did not begin to write All Men Are Mortal with the idea of loneliness and alienation as her central concern, but as the writing progressed this theme became more prominent. Rereading the novel at the time she was writing her memoirs, she asked herself, "What was I trying to say? I was trying to say nothing more than the story I invented."[25] However, the story was a failure, ignored by the public and reviled by critics as vehemently as they had praised The Blood of Others. Some dozen years after publication, she wrote that she still felt "warmly" toward it, a deliberate understatement because, of all her novels, All Men Are Mortal was her sentimental favorite and that of many of her closest friends, all of whom consider it the finest example of her imaginative writing.[26]

Shortly before she confided her reflections of this novel to her memoirs, Anthony West wrote a harsh review for The New Yorker that was typical of most. In it he said, "It is hard to believe that this pretentious and stunningly vulgar piece of writing is a serious novel."

Again she used the technique of double narration that worked so well in *The Blood of Others*. A prologue of sixty-eight pages[27] introduces her female protagonist, Regina, a self-centered, excessively introspective and highly ambitious actress. While on a tour of the French provinces (in Rouen as the novel opens), she becomes aware of a man, Raymond Fosca, who seems to have no interests, no ambition and no personal history. Fosca's withdrawal, exactly the opposite of Regina's need to be the center of attention, evokes all her competitive instincts, and she becomes determined to revive his interest in life by seducing him. When she learns that the Raymond Fosca she meets in the France of the 1940s was born near the end of the thirteenth century in northern Italy, she is more determined than ever to make him love her as he has never loved another woman before, thus insuring that she will become immortal—not in the physical sense, but in the sense of being remembered forever, because Fosca will be unable to forget her. She also admits to herself the duality of her intention, the other part being her ambitious desire to be superior to all his other lovers so that hers will be the name associated with his throughout time, thus eclipsing any and all other women with whom he may become involved as he wends his lonely way through future centuries.

This need for superiority and pride of place is one of Regina's strongest characteristics. She dismisses another actress as "nothing but a talented child without any real genius. No woman in the world can compare with me."[28] She studies herself in her purse mirror because she loves her face. "Ah! if only there were two of me, . . . one who spoke and the other who listened, one who lived and the other who watched, how I would love myself! I'd envy no one."

Beauvoir's way of defining Regina's character and situation is through self-absorbed interior monologue: all her perceptions of others become immediate fodder for comparison and contrast with herself. Regina watches the other actress dance with her lover and thinks, "Why am I like that? When people are living, when I see them in love and happy, I feel as if someone were twisting a knife in me." And when she first sees Fosca lying on a lawn chair from dawn till dusk, immobile, his gaze never leaving the sky, she envies him because he seems to lack all desire and ambition. Immediately she compares him to herself: "I want everything, and my hands are empty."

When they finally make love, it is Regina who is the aggressor in an act of bitter copulation. "You must never leave me,"[29] she says as she throws herself against Fosca. She shudders under his hands, which "existed, and in them she felt herself an object of prey." At the moment of orgasm, "she was left without hope, rudely ripped from the burning silence, suddenly thrown back into herself—Regina, futile and betrayed." Coitus is disappointing for them both:

His voice was so full of sadness that she wanted to open her eyes, to speak to him. Was there no way out? But she remained silent, for she knew that he had already read her thoughts. There had been too many other nights for him, too many other women. She turned over and pressed her cheek against the pillow.[30]

The next day, Fosca tells Regina his history, much of it a direct parallel of Sismondi's *Chronicles*, which provided Beauvoir with both "historical background for the fiction and brief escape from the story of Dolores." Fosca begins with his life in the thirteenth century, moving to the Hapsburg empire, visiting South and Central America, crossing the North American continent to the Pacific, back to Paris, and ending after the Revolution of 1830 with a sixty-year nap, a brief confinement in a mental asylum and his meeting with Regina.

This is what particularly incensed West in his review. Fosca, he wrote, "is wrapped in the cheapest sort of egotism, the one that declares the universe is a futility if the egotist is not its center and his happiness its purpose and raison d'être. . . . The intellectual poverty of this pessimistic materialism is as striking as its lack of courage." West's conclusion mirrors those generally made in several languages and countries when the novel was translated and published: he calls Beauvoir "the Mother Hubbard of the Existentialist movement" and says she has opened a bare cupboard once again.[31]

Like many other critics, West totally missed the point of Beauvoir's intention in this novel, her most misunderstood writing of them all. Most interpretations concentrate on two issues: Beauvoir's allegiance to Existentialism as it was then both understood and misunderstood by critics and scholars throughout much of the Western world, and the immortality of her male protagonist, Fosca, which they found irritating, confusing and ridiculous, generally all at the same time.

What the novel really is about is herself and Sartre, as they were after his first meeting with Dolores and before his second journey to be with her. Beauvoir had feared any number of things during her fifteen-year pact with Sartre, but never had she faced such a formidable rival, made even more theatening by distance and secondhand testimony. Bost, for example, who had also been to the United States on a journalistic junket, came home entranced by Dolores and made the mistake of telling Beauvoir that he too was half in love with her. He stopped at once, trying to qualify his remarks, but it was too late. Beauvoir's stricken face made him realize what a terrible gaffe he had made.[32]

Dolores was thus the cause of Beauvoir's returning to her familiar way of trying to cope with personal problems by writing about them in order to understand them, just as she had done first with ZaZa's death, then with Olga and the idea of the trio.

In a 1982 conversation, she contrasted *L'Invitée* and *All Men Are Mortal* with *The Blood of Others* and *Useless Mouths*. The first two, she said, were "those which are personally concerned with me," and the others were "very exciting to write because they represented the unification of fiction with philosophical theory." She also described the first two as "wrenching" and the others as "exhilarating," saying that her mind "raced with joy each day to solve the problems posed by technique and theory."

What remained in October 1945 was to give the book structure and form. Beauvoir decided to divide Fosca's story into five "books" or chapters, framed by Regina's prologue and epilogue. She had much of Regina's prologue and all of Fosca's story in final, edited form, and although "nothing personal had been resolved" through the writing, she was satisfied with it as fiction. The historical background she used in the middle section—the very portions critics would loathe—especially pleased her. The ending eluded her for the time being, but she looked forward to writing it at Christmas, when she planned to ski again at Mégève. Sartre agreed to go with her unless he could book a passage to New York before the holidays, so, for the moment at least, all seemed as well as it could be.

Useless Mouths was to open at the Théâtre des Carrefours in late October, and everyone, especially Beauvoir, was pleased with the rehearsals. It was all very exciting, and she "grew to love this other side of the theater, the bareness and sweat and dirt, before all the makeup was put on, and the costumes and lights, and all the fancy people in the audience." Rehearsals became the place for people to see and be seen, and Beauvoir held court there, receiving all who passed through the theater each evening.

For several days in mid-October, she was uncharacteristically absent, and no one knew why except the Family, her sister Hélène (now back in Paris with her husband) and her mother. The first issue of *Les Temps Modernes* was on the newsstands, with an introductory manifesto by Sartre, the entire issue dedicated "To Dolores." It was not entirely unexpected, because Sartre had hinted to Beauvoir without being specific that "a dedication" would surprise her. Still, the sight of it in print on the very first page wounded her more deeply than anything that had ever come between them before.

None of her friends ever heard her speak of it, nor did they try to discuss it with her. J. B. Pontalis was typical of many when he said, "We were astonished at Sartre's audacity, and wondered who this Dolores could be, but as Castor said nothing, neither did we. Perhaps because we all cared for Castor and we saw how hurt she was—perhaps that was why none of us cared to gossip about her pain."

By the last week of rehearsals, Beauvoir was back in the theater again, watching the actors deliver every line as if she had nothing else on her mind. On October 13, *Le Soir* welcomed the "Young *Agrégée* of Philosophy who is Staging her First Play" with an interview in which Beauvoir talked about what happens when food is used as a weapon and various groups of people are arbitrarily selected to die of starvation. She said her aim in writing the play was "to prove that the struggle for freedom requires the unity of end with means."[33]

On opening night, October 29, she watched through a hole in the curtain as the audience filled the theater. Then, composed and radiant, she watched the play from the third-row aisle seat, going backstage to receive praise and floral bouquets with Vitold and the actors. Afterward they all gathered at GéGé's apartment for a champagne supper, and to all but the trusted few she and Sartre both appeared flushed and happy with her success and with each other.

The first reviews quickly dispelled her euphoria. Jean-Jacques Gautier, writing in *Figaro*, said she had written a

> thesis of ideas, a strong dose of hyperintellectuality . . . much less theater than idea. . . . I believe that if anyone but Mademoiselle de Beauvoir had written this play, it would have had a very short run. But we'll be able to measure from the number of performances just how effective is this school of Existentialism. Will the public swallow it?

Camus was miffed once again by Beauvoir's recognition, this time because his work was compared to hers in print. "And remember—I'm still 'only a woman' to him!" Beauvoir chortled years later, recalling that Léon Treich, the reviewer for *L'Ordre*, wrote: "Incontestably the most interesting play of the new season (I haven't seen *Caligula* yet) is *Les Bouches inutiles*. . . ." Camus was even more enraged by Gabriel Marcel's review in *Les Nouvelles Littéraires* comparing the two plays but calling Beauvoir's "construction" the superior of the two. Marcel tossed a bone to Camus by saying the acting in *Caligula* was better.

Ultimately, though, the first review carried the day. Yvon Navy, in *Cité-Soir* said: "What we have here is dramatic art confused with the professoriat. . . . This doesn't wash: the theater is quite another thing entirely."

The production shut down after fifty performances, but Beauvoir was content because she "made a little money, made my mother happy, and pleased my friends and myself." She also sponsored a benefit for the orphans of those who had been deported during the war, giving all the proceeds of a full house to the fund. André Collignon wrote of it in *Opéra*, praising her gesture as well as the play itself—"without doubt, well done!"[34]

Now, with the play closed, and the first several issues of *Les Temps Modernes* in production, plans for the ski trip were almost final when Sartre told her that he would be leaving for New York on December 15. She went to Mégève after all, alone at first, then joined by Olga, Bost, Wanda, and Pontalis and Salacrou and their wives.

It was not the happiest of holidays. In her memoirs she included a portion of a letter she wrote to Sartre:

> Six years ago I wrote to you from here and the war was on. It seems much longer ago than six years. I feel in some way out of things, as though in another life; I don't recognize either myself or the world as it was then any more. And yet there are still memories, the memories I shared with you in that first life. But they

have so little connection with the present that they have a strange, rather painful effect.[35]

In her despair, she wrote Regina's epilogue, and *All Men Are Mortal* was finished:

Let him go! she said to herself. *Let him disappear forever! . . .* He had disappeared, but she remained the same and he had made her—a blade of grass, a gnat, an ant, a bit of foam. She looked around her; perhaps there was a way out . . . it was not even a hope, and even that quickly vanished. She was too tired. She pressed her hands against her mouth, bent her head forward. She was defeated. In horror, in terror, she accepted the metamorphosis—gnat, foam, ant, until death. *And it's only the beginning,* she thought. She stood motionless, as if it were possible to play tricks with time, possible to stop it from following its course. But her hands stiffened against her quivering lips.

When the bells began to sound the hour she let out the first scream.[36]

TWENTY-THREE

Moving in Some Sort of Blur

RETURNING TO PARIS after the New Year holiday was always a let-down. In 1946, however, coming back from Mégève was especially lonely and depressing because no one was there to cushion her return. Mentally she followed Sartre's route, estimating that his ship was only just reaching New York, unable to keep herself from picturing his reunion with Dolores in every graphic detail. In similar situations in the past, she had always counted on the Family, especially Bost, who had become her confidant and comfort, to help her keep her emotions under control, but he was in Italy on assignment for *Combat*. Camus was too busy preparing for his own trip to New York to help her get information about Sartre. Olga was confined to a sanatorium outside Paris with a serious flare-up of tuberculosis, Wanda was involved in the production of a play, and even Natasha was gone, married to her American GI, Ivan Moffatt, and on her way to join him in Hollywood, where he was to be an associate producer for filmmaker George Stevens.[1]

There were plenty of people in Beauvoir's life, from those who wanted only to talk to her to the larger group of those who wanted something from her—namely, publication in *Les Temps Modernes*. She was surrounded by people, but there was no one in whom she could confide her unhappiness. She was once again in contact with some of the very old friends from her university days, but these relationships had changed. Merleau-Ponty was on the review's editorial committee, and she had to work with him on a daily basis just to get the magazine out. They disagreed so often on pub-lishing policy and political position that it was clear to Beauvoir their old camaraderie was gone. Aron was distancing himself from Sartre politically, so there was no question of Beauvoir's continuing the friendship, and their rapport became more professional than personal. René Maheu, who had introduced her to Sartre, came back to Paris briefly and she thought he might substitute for Bost as recipient of her confidences, but he spent most of his time scolding her for her weeping and moping. She was crying in her wine again, waxing lugubrious about the meaning of life, and, because none of the old friends were there to take care of her, those who were present considered her an oddity and an embarrassment.

One of the reasons she was so fond of Alberto Giacometti was that nothing she did or said upset him. No matter how outrageous her behavior, Giacometti accepted it with aplomb.[2] She fell into the habit of sitting down at his table whenever she saw him in a café and letting her thoughts and emotions spew out helter-skelter. Giacometti sat immovable, usually smoking, his eyes gazing at the farthest reaches of the room, seeing everything but recognizing nobody. When she wound down her tirade, he continued to sit silently, sometimes for a very long time, as if nothing out of the ordinary had happened. If and when he spoke, it was usually to say something "surrealistic, silly, weird—totally removed from everything" in Beauvoir's unfocused monologue. By trying not to influence her, he cheered her up and made her laugh, and she came to value his silent, distanced presence.

Others who wanted to be her friends during this time only served to annoy her. Violette Leduc was fluttering, solicitous and too eager to offer physical comfort, which irritated Beauvoir. Leduc never knew that in conversations with others Beauvoir recoiled from using her name, always calling her "the Ugly Woman" in what some considered a "deliberate, unnecessary cruelty, of which she was often quite capable."[3] Beauvoir would see Leduc only at prearranged meetings, one every other week, where she avoided having to deal with her on a personal level by interrogating her about what she had written since their last meeting.[4] Then Beauvoir would concentrate all her energies upon the manuscript before her, managing to avoid "the excess of love and devotion in Leduc's writing" by distancing herself from it, considering it "exclusively as literature."[5] Often she would not go into the Brasserie Lipp or the Flore if she spied her pathetic admirer sitting just inside the door, where she could see everyone who entered, patiently awaiting Beauvoir's arrival. Beauvoir admired Leduc's writing, but "really, it was all just too much! I wanted to help her but I could not encourage her desire for intimacy, poor thing, because she was a little bit crazy and never knew when to stop."

Despite her determination to maintain distance between herself and Leduc, Beavoir became her principal literary adviser and editor and her most stringent reader, and "along the way . . . evolved not only into Leduc's lifelong mentor, but into her muse as well."[6] This relationship lasted because Beauvoir controlled it, keeping herself detached and emotionally uninvolved, permitting Leduc into her life only when she was willing to have her there.

One thing Beauvoir learned about herself in 1946 that lasted until her commitment to feminist activity in the 1960s was that she could not tolerate women of strong intellect as close friends, especially if they were writers and, by extension, competitors. Like her character Regina in *All Men Are Mortal*, she was "a woman greedy for domination over her fellow men and in revolt against all limitations."[7] Nathalie Sarraute provides an example: Beauvoir's acquaintance with Sarraute began when the latter called upon Sartre to offer him a text for *Les Temps Modernes*. Having founded the review, he had gone on to other things and was now too busy elsewhere to do any actual work on it. Sartre sent Sarraute to Beauvoir with a warm recommendation because he had been much taken with her 1939 book, *Tropisms*, and so Beauvoir (who had not yet read it) welcomed her the same way.

It was soon very clear to both women that they had little in common. Unlike Violette Leduc, Sarraute was a strong and independent personality. A Russian Jew, she spent the war openly in Paris, calling herself Nicole Sauvage. She hid her father and a series of other resistants[8] in her attic and posed as the governess of her own children. The contrast between Sarraute's and Beauvoir's recent past extended to their fiction: Sarraute bragged that "not once does a character of mine close a window, wash her hands, put on an overcoat, pronounce the words of an introduction."[9] Beauvoir thought such writing to be "an arbitrary collection of words posing as fiction. They could be any words at all passing themselves off as a novel, withdrawn from the very real problems of life. In 1945 I believed that such fiction could no longer be valid in France." When Sartre, who remained Sarraute's friend much longer than Beauvoir, wrote the introduction to her 1948 novel *Portrait of a Man Unknown* and described her as an "anti-novelist," Beauvoir thought the term should have been expanded to include "somehow the concept of nihilism, in the sense that nothing was there, no concrete reality."

The situation between Beauvoir and Sarraute was very soon close to open warfare. "She was in love with Sartre," Beauvoir insisted unkindly; "she wanted to take my place with him. He found some of her writing to be amusing and entertaining, but we never took it seriously. She was an old woman then; there was certainly never the possibility of anything but casual acquaintance between them."[10] Sarraute believed that Beauvoir "did not mind how many beautiful young women surrounded Sartre as long as they were mindless. Whenever he seemed about to form a lasting friendship with an intelligent woman, Beauvoir moved to end it. As far as she was concerned, there was to be only one intelligent woman in his life, and she was it."[11]

In a diary Beauvoir kept during this time, she described Sarraute's "frustration with Sartre's lack of interest in her" at a "typical" meeting:

> Went down to see Sartre . . . Nathalie Sarraute was there, hair beautifully waved and wearing a lovely bright blue suit. She explained quite soberly that we act as if we were Kafka's Castle; in our records, each person has a number he doesn't know; we allow so many hours per year to one, so many hours to another, and it's impossible to get an extra hour even by throwing oneself under a bus. We manage to convince her, after endless arguing, that we like her.[12]

It was unusual for Beauvoir to form independent friendships with men whom Sartre had not met first, because she always took her cue from him: if there was even the slightest possibility that the man in question would not allow himself to be drawn into Sartre's orbit and become a willing satellite, then Beauvoir would not consider a separate friendship. But in the case of Boris Vian she was sure that he was exactly the sort of man Sartre would adore, and so when Raymond Queneau brought him to the office of *Les Temps Modernes* Beauvoir actively pursued a closer intimacy.

Boris Vian was only slightly older than twenty but already had been married for several years to Michelle L'Eglise, whom everyone called "the beautiful blonde." He had been a leader of the group of upper-class teenagers who called themselves the Zazou and who used their Paris homes for wild, destructive parties during the war while their parents, Pétainist sympathizers if not actually collaborators, were sitting it out safely in the Free Zone. Vian and his friends first affected English tweeds, plaids and fine leathers, sometimes sported monocles, and aped the manners of the English country aristocracy. When Paris became flooded with American soldiers on the GI Bill, they changed costume and country, soon sported blue jeans, black turtlenecks and lumber jackets, and became newly minted experts on serious jazz and Hemingway's fiction. The parties continued, but, as the parents had all reclaimed their large apartments on the Avenue Foch, the scene shifted to Saint-Germain-des-Prés. Parties *chez* Vian were a godsend for Beauvoir because she found them both substitutes for the Family and additions to it. By March, she and Boris had developed "a deep friendship," but she thought Michelle "beautiful but insipid, a little boring if you want the truth." When Sartre returned to Paris that spring, he congratulated Beauvoir on the "brilliant" new young couple she had brought to them; what he never actually told her, but what she knew intuitively as soon as he described them this way, was that within weeks of his return he and Michelle had become lovers, which they continued to be until he died in 1980.[13]

Arthur Koestler was another story entirely. Beauvoir met him first, again through "*Temps Modernes* business." She had "moved her court," as Bost called it, when the constant interruptions became unmanageable, from the Flore to the basement bar in the Hotel Pont-Royal, which was just around the corner from the review offices at Gallimard. It was almost impossible to write there, as the tables were then only wooden kegs, but it was quiet. Koestler went there frequently hoping to find Beauvoir, trying to "conduct his flirtation" by exposing flaws in Sartre's thinking and theorizing, hoping to convince Beauvoir of his own superiority. She "sometimes enjoyed" these debates, but usually Koestler tired and exasperated her because "he never knew when to stop. Always pushing, pushing, pushing— arguing until I agreed with anything he said, just to shut him up." Then "the inevitable" happened: "One night I got so drunk I let him come home with me. We slept together. It wasn't any good. It didn't mean anything. He was too drunk, so was I. It never happened again. Only that night was real, the rest is how I loathed him. I really detested him, that arrogant fool."[14]

There was "too much of this Koestler sort of thing" in her life while Sartre was away. The only activity that brought her out of her unhappiness was the weekly luncheon at her mother's atelier on the Rue Blomet. With all her friends away and she still lonely, she increased these visits, eating dinner there at least one night each week and sometimes on Sunday, but as soon as Sartre came back she reverted to the scheduled weekly luncheon alone. It cheered her up to dine with Françoise, because as Beauvoir walked down the street everyone greeted her respectfully, this famous daughter of their dear friend and neighbor. And at luncheon Françoise was the perfect listener, eager for gossip and inside information about all the famous names among whom her daughter now moved with such ease. When the weekly magazines *Cavalcade* and *Fontaine* both mentioned in their gossip columns that Sartre and Beauvoir had shifted their base to the Pont-Royal, Françoise was as proud as if they had been royalty. Even the unflattering appellations that hostile critics began to dub Beauvoir, "Notre Dame de Sartre" and "La Grande Sartreuse," were to Françoise only the "jealousy and spite of lesser people."[15] She never tired of reminding everyone that "the stage hit of the previous season" had been written by her brilliant daughter and dedicated to her. Forty years later, when Beauvoir recalled these luncheons she still flushed with pleasure at the memory of her mother's genuine affection and deep pride in the woman she had become.[16]

Beauvoir chafed at the way everyone else was traveling to foreign countries on official junkets, especially the steady stream of journalists invited to the United States. All she could manage was a trip at the end of January to Tunis and Algiers, sponsored by the Alliance Française.[17] In exchange, she was required to give lectures about contemporary French literature, explaining and defending Existentialism in the process.

It was her first plane flight. "*We used to say to each other: some day, when we're rich, we'll take the plane to London; but they say you're ill most of the way, and in any case you can scarcely see a thing.*"[18] This elliptical statement was her only allusion to the unhappiness she still felt at not sharing the experience with Sartre. Her gloom deepened when she returned to Paris and he was still not there. His occasional letters continued to be full of excitement and zest for life in New York, which only made her feel worse. The happy moments that winter were few and far between. When Gallimard reinstituted "le Cocktail," parties they had given before the war to promote the firm's books in the beautiful enclosed garden behind the offices and the family living quarters, Beauvoir went to them all in search of escape and got very drunk each time.

For the first time in many years she became obsessed with her health and mortality. She suffered from excruciating headaches which often made it all but impossible to work,[19] and she smoked heavily until she noticed people staring at her shaking hands. Unable to control the tremors, she gave up cigarettes unless she was alone or with trusted friends away from prying scrutiny. She forced herself to make her appointed rounds despite blurred vision, spots before her right eye, upset stomach and attacks of free-floating anxiety. She walked from the Hotel Louisiane every day, making the loop down the Rue Jacob, across the Rue de l'Université to Gallimard's offices on the Rue Sebastian Bottin, around the corner on Rue de Bac to the Pont-Royal, and home by way of the Boulevard Saint-Germain and the Flore.

She was writing again, dashing off several quick essays in response to literary and political issues for *Les Temps Modernes*.[20] They filled time, but when they were finished the emptiness was still there. She knew she needed to write something that engaged her more completely, and, because *All Men Are Mortal* had not given her the easy answers she sought about herself, she thought that a philosophical system might better suit her quest for self-knowledge. She began a long philosophical essay which she hoped would help her understand all the changes that had occurred in her life since the Liberation.

After four miserable years waiting for the glorious future, by which she meant the end of the war, now it was here and she felt worse off than ever. At least during the occupation there was the camaraderie of everyone in their little group pulling together and sharing what they had while she and Sartre planned for the leadership role they hoped to play in intellectual situations. Now they were indeed among the foremost intellectual leaders in France, in ways they had not even thought to dream about, but the larger public was not rushing to close ranks behind them. Simone de Beauvoir simply could not understand why when "Sartre's position was so obviously the only sensible one to follow!"[21] There were so many differing ideologies in everything from politics to literature in postwar France that she found herself constantly bombarded by the fragmentation of ideas, issues and positions, and, to use Beauvoir's example, "We could not even tell the Right from the Left anymore. Nothing was direct and simple, everything was confused." She herself was so naive politically that whenever she learned of someone within the broad spectrum of French political ideology whose position differed from Sartre's, she was not above publicly reproaching the person for not seeing "the correctness" of Sartre's position and falling into line behind him.

But apart from the competition of other intellectuals, they themselves were playing so many different roles besides the simple one she had envisioned in her dreams—that of the writing couple whose work influenced the society in which they lived. Now they were both perceived as philosophers, political theorists and social arbiters, whether correctly in her case or not. Probably their most important current role was as publishers, with an increasingly influential forum in which to express their ideas. Since Sartre was so often away during the first year or two of the review's existence, Beauvoir became the butt of public criticism and vilification, either for the articles the magazine published or through the anger of those writers whose works they refused.

When Sartre was in Paris, they were asked more and more to speak in public and defend their ideas. Sartre was capable of staying out all night, getting falling-down drunk, then swallowing a handful of pills the next morning and working feverishly on the speech he delivered that afternoon. His remarks may have been erratic, but they were generally brilliant. She was incapable of such behavior, first of all because she feared drugs. The idea of "surrendering control" terrified her, so that whenever she succumbed to pressures and took either a stimulant or a sedative, it made her so anxious that she decided she was better off without it. The only thing she was comfortable about ingesting was an aspirin. Also, Sartre could stand in front of a hostile group and banter until he disarmed it. Beauvoir was jittery for days in advance of a lecture, and then she perspired nervously in front of even the most friendly audience. Sartre could be informal and friendly, but she was wooden, unable to modulate her voice, booming and strident under the most relaxed conditions.

Now, with Sartre in New York, all her insecurities were cohering around a single thought: that the idea she held most important, even sacred, of herself and Sartre as the writing couple, was in a precarious state. She believed that Sartre no longer considered the union engendered by their pact inviolable. She worried that she herself, her needs, her ideas, even the magazine, had all become irritations that distracted him from his greatest and most consuming interest—French politics, political theory and idealized political action. Dolores represented another threat, but one so serious she had difficulty trying to verbalize it. Everything about Sartre seemed "like a foreign language," of which she "did not even understand the alphabet." She thought the statement he made about her in 1965 was "probably appropriate": "There's only one matter on which she completely staggers me, and that's politics. She doesn't care a damn about it. Well, it's not exactly that she doesn't care, but she just won't have anything to do with it."[22]

But she tried desperately to keep up with him in 1946. She adopted the plural pronoun "we" for all statements about political positions, thus enhancing her "solidarity" with Sartre. Some of her more simplistic remarks of that time reflect both her need to be aligned with him and her inability to comprehend any position or action that differed from his. Of the French Communist Party she said, "[T]he problem of our relationship with them is crucial for us and they won't allow us to resolve it; it's a dead end."[23] This plaintive cry, "*they* won't allow *us* to resolve it," echoed so many of her other positions vis-à-vis Sartre, because to her it was always the other person who was to blame for any disagreement. Since the end of the war, Camus had become a prime offender, leading the list with almost all he did and said. As for Merleau-Ponty, he "did not understand Sartre's thinking very well."[24] She did not forgive Aron until the end of his life for walking out of Sartre's play *The Victors* at intermission, even though his wife was visibly ill, because his departure seemed to her an affront to Sartre's ideology within the play.[25]

With Sartre in America, Beauvoir was faced every day with making decisions to defend his political positions, writing rebuttals to his opposition, and explaining his philosophy. She was doing so alone, without him there to let her think things through out loud, shaping and refining her views through their usual dialogue. When she did talk, it was to those whom she did not trust entirely: Camus, Merleau-Ponty and sometimes Maheu, so that her only consistent outlet for her views was the printed page. She expressed her ideas in the four essays she wrote for *Les Temps Modernes* and published between November and April 1946,[26] all of which attempted to explain the implications of Existentialism and its influence upon specific areas of contemporary life and thought.

During these immediate postwar years, when Sartre was writing feverishly and establishing himself as a consistent focus of political controversy, Beauvoir described herself as "moving in some sort of blur."[27] But while he, buoyed increasingly by drugs, wrote feverishly to explain his political positions in terms of his philosophy, she was turning her attention in an altogether new and different direction: toward herself, and an examination of her role and place in society. Thus, while Sartre turned from literature to social and political theory on a highly visible public level, Beauvoir became—to coin a somewhat contradictory expression—publicly introspective. One of the things that most concerned her was to understand herself within the context of Existential philosophy, whose eloquent spokeswoman she had become.

One year previously, in February 1945, she gave a lecture to a group of the Catholic philosopher Gabriel Marcel's students in which she defended Existentialism against their hostile attacks. In conclusion she said that "it was possible to base a morality on *Being and Nothingness*, if one converted the vain desire to be into an assumption of existence."[28] Marcel urged her to write an essay explaining this position, but she was too busy with other things at the time. That winter, Camus asked her to contribute to a collection of essays he was editing, and she told him about her idea but said she could not write it because she was too busy with *Useless Mouths* and *Les Temps Modernes*. She did, however, use the lecture she gave to Marcel's students as the basis for one of the articles she wrote for *Les Temps Modernes*, "Littérature et métaphysique."

This essay is her only sustained example of literary criticism, even though it reads more as a personal credo than as a theoretical appraisal. In her view, the novelist writes as a means toward self-discovery, because in the process of creating fiction certain truths about the self emerge. Therefore, one of two things must happen to resolve the plot: either the necessary action that can bring resolution becomes clear to the writer as the plot unfolds or else the writer finds that, in the process of seeking the truth, certain problems and situations have been created for which no answer can be found. Beauvoir wrote that

> If the author knows in advance the conclusion he intends, if he
> insists upon pressing a predetermined thesis upon the reader, if

he refuses to permit even the illusion of freedom, then . . . the novel has no value and dignity, which must be there if both author and reader are to discover something alive. It is this necessity that one speaks of . . . when one says that the novel must escape from its author, who must not dispose of his characters, but on the contrary must let them impose their will on him. A novel is not a manufactured object, and it is even pejorative to say that it is fabricated; without doubt it is absurd to say that heroes in the literal sense of the word are free, but in truth this freedom that one admires in the characters of Dostoevsky, for example, is that of the novelist himself who has respect for his creations, and the opacity of events which he evokes should manifest the resistance which he has met in the act of creation.[29]

Her conclusion is that the metaphysics within Existentialism offers the only system within which a writer can express freely the individual quality of experience in fiction. However, it is a conclusion which reflects Beauvoir's own view of the novel more closely than it does any organized, convincing overview of philosophy.[30]

In a far-ranging discussion about her reading and how it influenced her writing, Beauvoir said that she sought answers to her personal problems and situations through reading, and that she attempted to write fiction as a means of understanding her personal life whenever she could not find an appropriate extant work to help her do so. She included the philosophical essays of 1945–46 among those other writings that helped her to understand herself. She called these essays "the prelude to my most important work about myself, the memoirs and The Mandarins."[31]

So "Littérature et métaphysique" became one of the sources for the two long essays which were published together as Pour une morale de l'ambiguité (The Ethics of Ambiguity), first in the magazine and then as a separate book. She wrote it while Sartre was with Dolores in New York. "Of all my books," she said in her memoirs, "it is the one that irritates me the most," and at the end of her life she called it "a frivolous, insignificant thing, not worthy of attention."[32] She attributed its inadequacy to the fact that "it's neither one thing nor the other. It's supposed to be a defense of Existentialism and a definition of morality, but at the time I wrote it I was too conscious of myself to think objectively."

Most readers would probably agree, as this is one of her least popular writings and one which scholars have generally tended to ignore.[33] She chose a quotation from Montaigne as her epigraph: "Life in itself is neither good nor evil, it is the place of good and evil according to what you make it." The entire essay focuses on the question of freedom for the individual and the difficulty of attaining it unless others have the same freedom. She offers no definite answer, only the weak observation that each individual situation requires an ad-hoc solution. She seems to be saying that there is no certainty except uncertainty, but she is surprisingly optimistic:

. . . any man who has known real loves, real revolts, real desires, and real will knows quite well that he has no need of any outside guarantee to be sure of his goals; their certitude comes from his own drive. There is a very old saying which goes: "do what you must, come what may."[34]

She finished the essay in April, at the same time that Sartre returned from New York. She was stunned by the depth of his feeling for Dolores, especially when he told her that they had agreed to spend several months together each year, probably in New York where they could be alone. He told Beauvoir he had thought of teaching at Columbia University, but decided against tying himself down to such a definite commitment. His intention was to offer possibilities for Beauvoir to occupy herself while he was away, but she was disturbed when he urged her "to bury myself in my writing for the magazine and to make new friends, to go to parties and find new ways to entertain myself." When he and Bost one night at dinner regaled each other with their happy memories of Dolores, completely forgetting Beauvoir, who sat between them at the table, she was humiliated that they talked "shamelessly . . . about New York in front of me."[35] Both men recognized how embarrassed she was and tried to change the subject, but it was too late, and she ended up crying into her wine.

There was no time to brood about it, because Sartre came down with a bad case of mumps, giving Beauvoir the chance to take care of him and to control the flow of visitors who wanted to see him. He tried to joke about his possibly impaired sexual potency, wanting to assuage some of her fears about Dolores, but she was not amused. On May 5 she confided to her diary that she was having bad dreams, "which left a sort of chill around my heart."[36] Her headaches returned, worse than they had been when he was away.

It worried her to hand over her essays to the printer without first discussing them with Sartre, but he seemed uninterested in what she had to tell him about the magazine and about the French political and cultural situation in general. Like everyone else, she kept her concerns to herself rather than disturb him. His stepfather had died while he was in the United States, and his mother, rather than interfere with his pleasure or cause him to cut short his trip on her behalf, kept the news from him until he was back in Paris. Beauvoir was even more anxious about her place in Sartre's life when Madame Mancy suggested that he move into her apartment in the Sixteenth Arrondissement so that she could take care of him again. Sartre liked the idea in general, but had a better suggestion: they would sell that one, located so inconveniently for him, and buy one big enough for them both at 42 Rue Bonaparte, where he could look out the window onto the square in front of the Church of Saint-Germain-des-Prés and the café crowd that walked to the Flore and the Deux Magots. Beauvoir was horrified, not because of Madame Mancy, to whom she had become close during the war, but because she saw it as a further sign of Sartre's slipping away from her.

Bost thought she was "in a very bad way,"[37] but she perked up momentarily when the old Surrealist Philippe Soupault told her that he might be able to secure an invitation for her to visit the United States sometime in the fall or the winter. She told Sartre her good news, but he only mumbled something faint and then evaded her eyes. She thought it was because he feared she might meet Dolores, but it was actually because he had asked Soupault to try to get the invitation and didn't want her to know it.

When he recovered from the mumps, he cheered her further by suggesting she accompany him to Switzerland, where he was to meet publishers and give lectures. Lying in bed on the eve of their departure, she wrote in the diary: "Tomorrow I'll work and soon I'll be going to Switzerland. I'm very happy with things as they are." It was very far from the truth. The trip to Switzerland took place in mid-June at the behest of the publisher, Skira. She felt like an outsider, watching Sartre meet the press, give lectures, argue with audiences and defend both his politics and his philosophy. She felt even more extraneous when he went off with Wanda, who was appearing in Zurich in a production of his No Exit.

Sartre and Beauvoir were invited to Italy, but because of the unsettled political climate their Italian publisher telephoned them in Switzerland and rescinded the invitation. She kept the details of the conversation from Sartre, fearing his scruples. She was determined to have a holiday no matter what, and when they arrived unexpectedly in Italy, Sartre's commitments were rescheduled. When they were over, he returned to Paris and she went off to the Italian Dolomites to spend three weeks alone walking through the mountains. The mental equilibrium she hoped to recover eluded her, and when she returned to Paris she was "like a gray ghost," making her daily rounds, spending unusually long hours alone in her room, uncharacteristically silent.

"How wild you look!" Giacometti said to her one day when he came upon her sitting in the Deux Magots, staring off into space.[38] It was the middle of the afternoon, and she had been drinking only coffee, not wine, but she began to sob anyway. Giacometti had become "not a father," but "a kind of brother" to her, and because of his unfailing kindness she found herself able to admit emotions that she kept hidden from virtually everyone but Bost. She had grown even closer to Giacometti since the Swiss trip because he had been there at the same time and had introduced her to Annette, who would soon be his wife. She found Annette to be very much like Natasha both in looks and in personality, and told Giacometti how much she liked her. Beauvoir's admission made him very happy and served to increase his affection for her. She recalled, "He was not a demonstrative man, but I knew that he felt very kindly and protective toward me. He never showed it in what some people would think were the usual ways, but, no matter how crazy the things he said, I knew he cared about what happened to me."

This was an unusual relationship for her. Other men who knew both her and Sartre—Bost and Vian, for example—were her friends and his disciples or acolytes. But Giacometti and Sartre, for all their initial declarations of friendship, had a kind of verbally jousting relationship that made them seem more like rivals than friends, so it was an unusual act for Beauvoir to form a close personal friendship with such a man. Especially at that time of her life, it was truly a rarity.

But now Giacometti was concerned that something was very wrong with her, and her immediate response was that it was nothing personal— it was just that she had finished *The Ethics of Ambiguity* and she had nothing to write. Finishing *All Men Are Mortal* had satisfied her need to write fiction, but, because it had not given her the personal answers she sought, the aftereffect left her unwilling to go through that agonizing process again. Until she could "find a subject that had no connection" to her personal life, she decided to write no more novels. The irony is that the decision inspired even more intense probing and self-examination. It led to the works that brought her greatest fame and solidified her reputation as one of the most influential writers ("women" writers, many would argue—a term that enraged her) of her time.

One of the works that started her in this direction was Michel Leiris's memoir *L'Age d'homme* (*Manhood*). To her, the work was a series of "sacrificial essays, in which the author strips himself bare without excuses."[39] And, since both fiction and philosophy had failed to provide the self-knowledge she desperately needed, she thought autobiography might be the genre that would work for her. But the content of Leiris's memoir, especially the frank discussion of his sexuality, was something that well-brought-up women of Catholic *haut-bourgeois* background did not discuss. Her situation especially—the fact that she "lived in very public sin"—was perhaps too dangerous to discuss. Also, if she wrote about her liaison with Sartre, she would be writing his life as well because they were so inextricably bound together. What would society make of "his sexual shenanigans"? What about the Family—how would Bost's parents and his many brothers and sisters, for example, react to her friendship with their youngest son? If she wrote of her education, and what she knew would result in bitter attacks upon Catholic education for girls and harsh diatribes against the role of women in France, would anyone dare to publish what she had written? Would she simply be writing the nonfiction equivalent of "closet drama"? Women were still one year away from attaining the right to vote in France; very few, comparatively speaking, went on to higher education; even fewer were employed. Would anyone want to read her personal history, so far from the actuality of the lives of most contemporary French women? And finally, would she be able to withstand the sustained verbal abuse she was sure would be heaped upon her if she were to publish "this bizarre account of a very strange French woman"? In the late summer of

1946, with everything else in her world crashing down around her, she decided that she could not.

She tried to discuss this with Sartre, all the questions she had asked herself repeatedly, but he did not answer them directly. No doubt he realized that she was really probing into herself in order to determine his level of commitment to her and the form their future relationship would take. Instead, he couched his responses in the context of philosophical inquiry, condensing them into one large general theme with any number of related parts: "What does it mean to be a woman today? How has this situation changed, if at all? What had it meant to me personally, to have been born a woman but to have lived with most of the freedoms enjoyed by men?" She thought it was all very interesting, but could not see that it applied to her. She had never known discrimination, she had never felt inferior, she had always been able to do everything she wanted to do, and no barriers had been placed in her way.

"You are very unusual," Sartre told her. "You have had an exceptional life. Your condition is not the condition of others of your sex."[40] And then, " 'Remember back in Rouen,' he reminded me, 'how I was always arguing with Colette Audry about that book she always threatened to write?' "

"He used to make me so angry!" Colette Audry recalled. "He was always making fun of my involvement with politics, telling me it was no place for a woman and pointing out how women were powerless to make changes in society. I used to tell him that someday I was going to write a book about my experiences, and it would be a book about women, and it would cause a scandal among men!"

"Well!" Sartre told Beauvoir, "it's obvious Audry is not the one to write that book—you are!"[41]

The conversation was for Beauvoir the "Eureka!, the moment of true revelation":

> This world was a masculine world, my childhood had been nourished by myths forged by men, and I hadn't reacted to them in at all the same way I should have done if I had been a boy. I was so interested in this discovery that I abandoned my project for a personal confession in order to give all my attention to finding out about the condition of women in its broadest terms. I went to the Bibliothèque Nationale to do some reading, and what I studied were the myths of femininity.[42]

But then she had a disturbing thought:

> What if I do write this, I said to Sartre. Will I ever be able to publish it? 'Oh, that's the least of your worries,' he assured me, 'there is always *Temps modernes*.' So I started to work on it, happy to have something worthwhile to do. He was happy, too, because when I was busy, I was no bother to him.

Suddenly, she was happier than she had been in several years: Philippe Soupault had made good his promise to get her an invitation to the United States. Through his contacts in several American universities he secured invitations for her to lecture, and the French government's Office of Cultural Relations agreed to pay her plane fare. However, she would have to stay for at least four months and appear before any university audience that issued her a paid invitation to speak.

Four months was a long time, and she worried about what such a separation from Sartre might do to their shaky liaison, but the opportunity was too great to turn down. She was to arrive in New York at the end of January and begin her lecture series at the Alliance Française. In addition, all the women's colleges wanted her to speak—Vassar, Wellesley, Connecticut College, Smith, Randolph-Macon, Mills. Even Yale, Harvard and the University of Pennsylvania had extended invitations to "the High Priestess of Existentialism."[43]

The last three months of 1946 were "a period of feverish activity"[44] as she tried to lock up as many advance issues of the magazine as she could, put together a wardrobe, say goodbye to all her friends and finish what she thought might be "part one of a two-part essay on women."

"You look wonderful!" Giacometti told her one day in December when he bumped into her on the Boulevard du Montparnasse. She told him she was going to America, and he told her "to watch out. Don't let one of those big Americans steal you away from us."

"What? Me?" she answered. "You know me better than that. Who would want me? And who is there in this world I could want more than Sartre?"

The Most Exotic Thing

Y OU RAISE QUESTIONS without answering them. We answer questions without raising any,"[1] said a perplexed editor of *The New York Times Magazine* who had just encountered the force of Simone de Beauvoir's argument, the bewildering rush of her ideas and, no less important, the striking presence of "France's No. 2 Existentialist (No. 1 of course is Jean-Paul Sartre.")[2]

She flew into La Guardia Airport on January 24, 1947, and was met by a representative of the French cultural services who took her by taxi to the Hotel Lincoln at Forty-fourth Street and Eighth Avenue. As soon as she had checked into her room and assured her chaperone that she knew enough English to be left on her own, she walked to Third Avenue and Fifty-seventh Street, to the apartment of Stépha and Fernando Gerassi,[3] but they were in Philadelphia, where both held positions on the faculty of the Curtis School of Music. Beauvoir left her hotel address with their then sixteen-year-old son, John, who was at home, and spent the rest of her first day in New York all alone, walking, riding buses, "gawking in astonishment" at the noise and confusion of the city.

She ate her first meal in New York in a Times Square drugstore: a BLT club sandwich, a large glass of freshly squeezed orange juice and a cup of "white" coffee, a British expression which the waitress quickly let her know was "'regular' over here, Sweetie." She sat and stared at her sandwich for a while, waiting for the waitress to bring her a knife and a fork, hesitant to call further attention to herself by asking for them. But when no utensils arrived, she watched other diners hoisting thick clumps of meat enclosed within bread or buns to their mouths, and so she did the same. She was embarrassed to ask for anything because, although her spoken English was fluent despite her heavy accent, she could not understand—as she tried to imitate almost forty years later—"Nooo Yawk English" and decided not to risk the possibility of being drawn into conversation.

She liked the sounds and smells that enveloped her as she perched anonymously on a counter stool, and thus she began her lifelong love of drugstores and dime stores. When *The New York Times* asked her to write an article summing up her impressions of America shortly before the end of her trip, she marveled that it had taken less than two hundred years for such a vast continent to catch up to the ancient civilization of Europe. "A humanist cannot but marvel at this magnificent triumph of man," she wrote about Lexington, Concord and Valley Forge, before making what might strike most Americans as a ludicrous comparison: "For reasons somewhat akin to this, I found much poetry in the drug stores and the ten-cent stores."[4]

The next day, before she was to dine with a group of scholars from metropolitan universities, Beauvoir trekked once more to the apartment of the Gerassis, who were now back from Philadelphia. She had hardly greeted the dear friend whom she had not seen for almost six years before she demanded that Stépha, who until that moment had not known of Dolores's existence, arrange a meeting with her at once because she was scheduled to leave for France in a few days to stay with Sartre for the duration of Beauvoir's American tour. Stépha was aghast at the idea and told her to "leave well enough alone,"[5] but Beauvoir insisted and Stépha "gave up" and made the telephone call. After firmly refusing, Dolores hesitated, then agreed to meet them for a drink at the Menemsha Bar the next evening. Stépha was greatly relieved: "She probably said yes because she could feel the terror in my voice over the telephone. I was afraid of what Castor would do if Dolores said no, and maybe she could sense it."

In the meantime, Beauvoir continued to walk around Manhattan and Brooklyn for at least three hours each day. She claimed to have walked to Inwood in northernmost Manhattan, and from there south to Greenwich Village and, via Canal Street, through Chinatown, the Bowery and the Lower East Side to the Brooklyn Bridge—approximately twenty miles—in a single morning. She wanted especially to go to Canarsie, and the American intellectuals of whom she asked directions were astonished that she should want to visit this run-down section of Brooklyn. No one could give her directions, because none of them had ever been there. "I could not understand," the American philosopher William Phillips wrote, "why a French writer on a first visit had to rush out to Canarsie as soon as she got off the boat. Only later . . . did it occur to me that she probably had heard that Canarsie was a 'workers district,' in the European sense."[6]

She found her way, though, to Canarsie, Williamsburg, Sheepshead Bay and Coney Island, and almost forty years later she could still roll these names off her tongue as if they were magic. She remembered street names with great pleasure: "I loved so much about New York, especially the little things that do not make much sense if you are unaware of the city's history. Like Little West Twelfth Street, when there is already a Twelfth Street, and Great Jones Street, which is really very small."

She interrupted her marathon walking sessions only for her favorite lunch, a BLT club and fresh orange juice in other drugstores. On one occasion, only because she was due to meet a group of graduate students at Columbia University in the late afternoon, she took a series of buses and subways back to the Upper West Side. On her way, she made a detour for her first foray to Harlem, walking across 125th Street to Park Avenue and back, then up Amsterdam Avenue to Philosophy Hall. When she told her audience at Columbia, they cautioned her never to do such a foolhardy thing again. She held her tongue but smiled inwardly, having no fear of Harlem. Ellen and Richard Wright had agreed to take her to the Cotton Club, to the Reverend Adam Clayton Powell's Sunday services at the Abyssinian Baptist Church and to several private parties in the homes of their friends who lived in Harlem.[7]

On her third evening in New York, she and the three Gerassis and their friend Ira Woolfert, an editor of *Partisan Review*, were in the Menemsha Bar arguing about the influence of Stalin on the French Communist Party when a "stunningly beautiful, very tiny mulatto woman" appeared.[8] She walked to the table, introduced herself by announcing to the group at large, "I am Dolores," then sat down opposite Beauvoir without paying any specific attention to her. Conversation, if there was any, was awkward. Someone in the group ordered a glass of wine for Dolores, and Stépha began to chatter nervously about how long it had been since she was in France and how she envied Dolores her coming trip. Mrs. Gerassi remembered watching Beauvoir's face turn crimson as she stared intently into her whiskey glass, unable to raise her eyes to her rival's face. Although Dolores seemed more at ease than Beauvoir, she too had difficulty meeting the eyes of anyone at the table and seldom looked directly at anyone. Everyone was grateful for Woolfert's neutral presence, and because of him they all spoke English—all except Beauvoir, who, embarrassed by her thick accent, did not speak. Dolores drank her wine quickly, then stood up and shook hands all around, saying she had to leave to keep another engagement. She offered her hand to Beauvoir, who took it, and the two women exchanged brief pleasantries in French. Then Dolores left, as swiftly and gracefully as she had entered. This was their only meeting in New York.[9]

Stépha was fearful that one of Beauvoir's crying jags would follow, especially since she knew that Beauvoir was late and a probably restless audience would be waiting for her at the Alliance Française. But as if there had been no visitor to their table and no interruption in their conversation, Beauvoir turned to the young John Gerassi to finish their earlier political discussion. Her last comment to the assembled group came as she stood up and drained her glass before leaving: she compared Stalin and de Gaulle to each other and said they were prime examples of how dangerous such paranoid despots could be. She didn't say a word about Dolores.

"If she was worried about Dolores, she didn't show it. To tell the truth, Castor surprised me because she didn't behave like her [usual] self when they met," Mrs. Gerassi remembered. "It was as if this woman was her obsession, but then once she saw her, well, that's that and it was all over. Castor was so businesslike that at first she worried me. She was too cold and detached about someone who had worried her so much. I think it was probably good she saw Dolores in New York, because then she freed herself to have a good time in the U.S. and when she got back to Paris there was no surprise waiting for her. Sometimes she made me mad with how stubborn she was, my good girlfriend Castor, but other times I had to admit she was a smart one, she knew how to take care of herself. Maybe this was one of those times."

Her lecture tour proceeded smoothly and successfully. Sartre had paved the way for her, because in his tour the previous year he had made many friends among faculty members of the leading universities. Now these professors extended the same friendship to her and also asked their colleagues at other universities to invite her to their campuses.[10] Generally, her visits were announced without fanfare in various college calendars or newspapers such as this one in The Crimson at Harvard:

> Mme. Simone Beauvoir [sic], noted French novelist and playwright and a leader in the Existentialist Movement, will lecture in French on "La Responsibilité de L'Ecrivain" this afternoon at 4:30 o'clock in the Modern Language Center. Mme. Beauvoir's talk will be open to the public and is presented under the auspices of the Department of Romance Languages.[11]

Where she made the greatest impression was among the students at the women's colleges, such as at Smith, where her turban, long skirt, regal bearing and incisive questions about women's education remained strong memories for many women almost forty years later.[12]

She was interviewed by a writer for the "Talk of the Town" section of The New Yorker, who caught up with "the French novelist, playwright, and No. 2 Existentialist, just before she left town on a coast-to-coast lecture tour."[13] The anonymous writer knew that Beauvoir was "regarded in Paris [he should have added "and thought of in the United States"] as the female intellectual counterpart of Jean-Paul Sartre," whom he called "the Existentialist head man." Knowing all this in advance of meeting Beauvoir, the writer confided that he was "set for a grim half-hour."

"Well, surprise!" he exclaimed in print, "Mlle de B. is the prettiest Existentialist you ever saw; also eager, gentle, modest and as pleased as a Midwesterner with the two weeks she spent in New York." She told him about her long walks, how she climbed up to various rooftops for better views of the city, about the Blue Angel, Café Society Downtown, and Sammy's Bowery Follies—which she found "wonderful. It's absolutely dissolute [crapuleux]—all those old singers whom nobody wants with feathers on their heads." She told him about the movies she saw, "thrillers" which in her "rickety English" she called "thrillings."

"I used to walk in Paris," she concluded, "but I've seen everything there, so now I mostly sit."

But in the United States she was, as she remembered herself many years later, "like a whirling dervish because I was afraid I might miss something."[14] She descended upon each city armed with guidebooks and long lists of things she wanted to see or do, and her sometimes hapless hosts had to go along with her program, no matter what else they might have had planned for her entertainment.

She was quiet enough at Vassar, where the Romance Languages faculty gave her a family-style dinner in a residence hall, and at Connecticut College in New London, where she was taken to a restaurant fronting on Long Island Sound and a bib was put around her neck so that she could eat "New England Boilie": steamed lobster, quahogs (the local clams), corn on the cob and potatoes. At both colleges, she was fascinated by the students who were decked out in rolled-up blue jeans and oversized men's shirts on campus, but who dressed in a matronly garb more befitting their mothers—hats, gloves, suits and fur coats—when they took the train to New York. She left both colleges with a lasting impression that only "rich girls" attended. To the end of her life she held that the best of American education was only for the rich.[15]

A more typical visit occurred in Philadelphia, where she was the guest of the Romance Languages Department at the University of Pennsylvania. Her host was Professor George Seiver, who was then the chairman of the department. She arrived on the morning of April 24, having spent the previous night at Princeton, and because Professor Seiver did not have a car he asked his young cousin Lawrence M. Seiver to borrow his father's and go with him to the Thirtieth Street station. They recognized Simone de Beauvoir at once because "people were looking at her as if she had come from outer space: in this bastion of middle-class values, the woman was wearing a dress down to her ankles. It was the first time anybody in Philadelphia had ever seen the New Look."[16] She had no luggage other than a large accordion-style briefcase.[17]

As soon as the two men introduced themselves, she announced that she wanted to visit the Barnes Foundation to look at the vast collection of Impressionist paintings housed in a mansion just outside the city. She had done thorough research before arriving in Philadelphia, grilling Stépha and Fernando Gerassi at great length about what she should see, and then poring over maps and guidebooks to coordinate her brief time there for maximum sightseeing. Professor Seiver told her that his wife was expecting them for luncheon in the suburbs, but he thought that if they hurried they might be able to make a quick visit to the Barnes. Lawrence Seiver remembered what happened next:

> This was in the days when Dr. Barnes was in full sway, and no visitors were admitted. I knew what would happen, but she insisted, so we drove there anyway. When we rang and rang the bell, the door finally opened just a crack and a hand dropped into Miss de Beauvoir's outstretched hand a printed card advising that the Foundation existed only to teach students and was not a public museum.[18]

Simone de Beauvoir's recollection is more graphic. Shortly before her last visit to the United States, in 1983, she said, "I want to go to the museum that is never open, where all the Impressionist paintings are stacked one on top of the other. It's the one where the nasty man drops a card into your hand that says in big handwriting, 'GO AWAY.' "

Not being admitted to the Barnes Foundation was the first frustration that day. Then Lawrence Seiver's car broke down just outside the museum's gate, so they had to take two buses and a trolley to get to their suburban luncheon. Beauvoir arrived at the luncheon Edith Seiver prepared for her much the same way as she had arrived at the women's colleges: with her mind already made up on a number of issues. She wanted to talk about jazz, but her hosts were "still in the Big Band era" and knew little about "hot jazz in Greenwich Village and Harlem." Beauvoir instructed them peremptorily that she had been to Harlem and that "jazz represented an oppressed culture." She punctuated her conversation with references to *Partisan Review*, Dwight MacDonald and the magazine he edited, *Politics*, and delivered all her remarks in a polite but restrained manner. It seemed to her hosts that "conversation would have taken a more flexible mind than hers." They recognized themselves several years later when they read her scattered remarks about "how the capitalist system rewarded its scholars very poorly," but they "laughed over all this and agreed that socialist dogma will supersede observed facts every time," for their circumstances were actually very comfortable by the standards of the time.

The Seiver family's opinion of Beauvoir was shared by many of the people she had already met in New York, especially among those connected with *Partisan Review*, and they all later wrote about it. William Phillips noted that Hannah Arendt was hostile to her, scolding him for treating Beauvoir "as a thinker instead of a woman," and he himself thought that "she could not be swayed by either arguments or facts."[19] Mary McCarthy compared Beauvoir's opinions of the United States to "an inhabitant of Lilliput or Brobdingnag . . . [reading] in a foreign tongue, of his own local customs codified by an observer of a different species: Everything is at once familiar and distorted."[20] Diana Trilling viewed Beauvoir's American experience as "a four months psychological contest whose terms had been established well before [she] set foot on our shores," and called her "a woman of unusual inclination to impose herself on her environment."[21]

Not everyone regarded her with such disfavor: despite her preconceptions of American academic life, her Philadelphia hosts thought her "a charming lady" determined to get exactly what she wanted from every place she visited. They found her knowledge of the city's history and culture astonishing, especially for a foreigner who had no real need to acquire it, and they admired both her energy and her tenacity. When the luncheon was finished, she rose abruptly and told her two male hosts that it was time they left if they were to see Valley Forge before her lecture. Lawrence Seiver borrowed another car, and the three set off so that Beauvoir could see the place where George Washington and his troops spent their grim winter during the Revolutionary War. "Don't forget," Beauvoir remembered in 1984, "I thought I would never return there again, and so I had to move very quickly."

This was not the only instance in which she felt she "had to move very quickly." In the late afternoon, as she was resting in Professor Seiver's office before giving her talk, she asked for stationery so that she could send a note to Nelson Algren, a writer in Chicago who had shown her "the Real America" when she passed through his city earlier that year. "Dear Friend," she wrote, telling him that after leaving Philadelphia she was on her way to spend her last two weeks in New York before her May 10 departure for Paris. She wanted to return to Chicago, but had too many engagements. Perhaps he might join her at her hotel, the Brevoort, on Fifth Avenue near Washington Square (which, she told the "Talk of the Town" writer, was her favorite place in New York). "I will be happy to see you again," she concluded with polite formality before signing her letter with the customary signature she used for strangers and people she did not know well: "S. de Beauvoir."[22]

The signature disguised her shyness, because in the two days she had spent with him in late February Nelson Algren "turned [her] life upside down." They became lovers almost at once, and with him, she remembered, she had her "first complete orgasm" and she learned "how truly passionate love could be between men and women."

Mary Guggenheim,[23] one of Algren's previous lovers and the person responsible for introducing Beauvoir to him, was not surprised when she learned of their immediate attraction to each other: "Nelson was completely crazy . . . the most adorable and charming person in the world, but a complete lunatic . . . a totally solitary person. She [Beauvoir] gets the prize for keeping him longer than anybody, and remember, this dame wasn't all that famous then in America except for reflected glory, on account of Sartre. How could they have fallen—whamo!—so hard, so fast? Easy—each was the most exotic thing the other had ever seen."[24]

Mary Guggenheim was a friend of Pearl Kazin Bell, the staff member at *Harper's Bazaar* responsible for entertaining visiting dignitaries who wrote for the magazine. Because of Beauvoir's profile of Sartre written the previous year, Bell had been put in charge of her in New York.

"She [Bell] called me up," Guggenheim remembered, "and said, 'Listen, I've got Simone de Beauvoir in tow and I don't know anybody but you who speaks French. Can I bring her for dinner?' " The dinner, in Guggenheim's New York apartment, was "close to a fiasco," according to her. "I'm a worse cook than she [Beauvoir], so the food was lousy. All she wanted to do was ask me questions I wasn't competent to answer, about the condition of women in this country. I was deep into analysis at the time, so to turn the subject in that direction I said that I thought women everywhere were basically the same, that there were not any really heavy differences between cultures and countries. This didn't sit with her at all.

She started to talk about her pal Lévi-Strauss, and of course I had never heard of him at that time—he was unknown here then. Anyway, I think she was bored to death, so I asked where she was going, just to make conversation, and when she said, 'Chicago,' I said, 'Maybe you'd like to look up this good friend of mine who's a writer.' She took his address as if it were the only thing she had come for, then she got up and left."[25]

The next day Guggenheim had misgivings, so she sent a warning note to Algren describing in some detail "the Blue-stocking" to whom she had given his address. He replied with playful scatological references about Beauvoir's relationship with Sartre, ending the letter with "Who is this 'Simon Boo-doir' anyway???" Guggenheim took it in stride: "Nelson liked to play the role of an anti-intellectual: if you liked him anyway despite this, then you passed some sort of test and he would relax and be himself with you."

This casual introduction was, according to Guggenheim, "evidently what started this wild affair. Scratch a bum like Nelson and you will find a snob somewhere. I guess he was sort of impressed with her, and he— well, for her he was virility incarnate, and those of us who had lived and worked in Paris knew she didn't get very much of that with Sartre."

Beauvoir and Algren both described in subsequent writings how they met. Hers was in *America Day by Day*, the book about the United States which was based on a collection of articles she wrote for *Les Temps Modernes*. Written in 1948, her version is the more circumspect of the two:

> My friends in New York had given me two addresses: that of a writer and that of an old lady. If my evening was not to be wasted, one of them would have to come to my rescue. The writer seemed preferable. . . . I telephoned and asked for Mr. N.A. A sulky voice replied: "You have the wrong number." I checked it in the directory: my pronunciation was wrong. I began all over again. I had hardly opened by mouth when the voice repeated, with annoyance, "WRONG number." I hung up again. What to do? . . .
>
> I must try again. Once more I phoned the writer; but he hung up. I was furious. I asked the operator to make the connection. When she heard the phone ringing, she said with authority and in tones that inspired confidence: "Will you be so kind as to hold the line a moment. . . ."[26]

Algren described it in an article written long after they had parted— bitterly on his part, sadly on hers—and, like everything he wrote about Beauvoir after the end of their affair, it should be read with his attitude in mind:

> I hung up twice on the voice of Simone de Beauvoir when she phoned me in Chicago in 1947. She did not use a phone well and I was impatient with voices calling the wrong number. Finally the operator asked me to be good enough to hold the line for just a

moment as there was someone who wished to speak to me. The voice informed me, with a European accent, that she was at the "Little Café" in the Palmer House and would be carrying a copy of *Partisan Review*. If she were a regular subscriber, I decided, I'd be able to tell on sight and could slip away. So I waited outside the entrance on a shadowed chair. The woman carrying the magazine was not a subscriber, I perceived. In fact, she appeared attractive at first glance. I followed her into the Petit Café. She spoke volubly, intensely, emphatically, with force. I didn't understand a word she said. Later she assured me she had not understood one word of mine, either. She appeared to me to be a French schoolteacher. I had never heard her name and wasn't sure of it now. . . . A few days after she left town I read an interview in *The New Yorker* with Simone de Beauvoir. It was, obviously, my French schoolteacher.[27]

Nelson Algren Abraham (his name at birth) was a third-generation Chicagoan descended from Jewish, Swedish and German stock. He was born in Detroit on March 28, 1909, but his machinist father took his family back to Chicago when Algren was three.[28] He grew up in an ethnic, blue-collar neighborhood which made a profound impression upon him and became the subject of much of his fiction when he began to write after his graduation from the University of Illinois in 1931. For the next several years he drifted through New Orleans, Texas and Mexico, supporting himself as (among other things) hustler, hobo, service-station attendant and carnival worker. He also spent four months in a Texas jail because when he decided to become a writer he stole a typewriter in order to do so.

When he and Beauvoir met, he was already the author of two published novels, *Somebody in Boots* (1935) and *Never Come Morning* (1942)—for which the American Academy of Arts and Letters awarded him a $1,000 grant because its members believed that the book had not received the recognition it deserved. In 1947, the year he met Beauvoir, Algren was also about to publish a collection of short stories, *The Neon Wilderness*, and was in the last phase of writing what became his best-known and most successful novel, *The Man with the Golden Arm*.[29]

This was the man to whom Simone de Beauvoir wrote on April 24, inviting him to join her in New York in May. They had spent exactly thirty-six hours more or less together in February, when she was in Chicago and wanted to see it all. "I decided to show her Chicago's underside," Algren wrote.

I wanted to show her that the U.S.A. was not a nation of prosperous *bourgeois*, all driving toward ownership of a home in the suburbs and membership in a country club. I wanted to show her the people who drove, just as relentlessly, toward the penetentiary and jail. I introduced her to stickup men, pimps, baggage thieves, whores and heroin addicts. Their drive was downward, always downward. I knew many such that year. I took her on a tour of the County Jail and showed her the electric chair."[30]

She was so upset by what Algren showed her that she did not return to her hotel, as she wrote in *America Day by Day*. They went instead to his exceedingly humble apartment on Wabansia Street, where they made love for the first time, "initially because he wanted to comfort me, then because it was passion."

She chafed because she had to spend so many hours of her final day in Chicago away from him, giving a lecture and lunching with some of the French officials who sponsored her visit. They were all set to entertain her until dinner, when she was to dine with another group, but she told them she had to pay a call on a sick friend. She told them her friend's address— really Algren's—and they insisted that she could not take a taxi to such a dangerous place. They drove her there in a sleek new official car, the object of much subsequent curiosity in the neighborhood. She jumped out and pounded on the surprised Algren's door; she caught him quietly waiting for the phone call she had promised to make that night from the station. "My impetuosity thrilled him," she remembered, and they made love again. Later, as they drank whiskey together, Algren joked about her arrival in such a spectacular car, saying this "Crazy Frog" had given him just the sort of status he did not need among his neighbors, because they would now think him rich and ask to borrow money they could not repay. He was so visibly touched by her unexpected visit that she called him her "Crocodile" because of his "funny, toothy grin." Thus their pet names for each other were set for the rest of their affair. However, he "was a gentleman and did not ask about Sartre," and she never mentioned him, either.

She wrote the first of some 350 letters to Algren that night, in English, because, although he had served in the Army in France during the war, he spoke no French and from the beginning pronounced himself unwilling to learn. She later credited this correspondence with making her fluent in the written language. He found her first letter, with its errors of grammar and spelling, "charming," and usually corrected her mistakes "with loving teasing" both when they were together and sometimes also in his letters. As soon as she was settled into her berth on the train, she began to write to him:

I'll try to write in english—so, excuse my grammar, and if I do not use the words in the right meaning, try to understand. When leaving you, I went to the hotel . . . Then I had a diner with these french men and I hated them because they were hateful, and because they did not let me have a dinner with you—After phoning to you they put me in the train and I lied in my berth and I began reading your book [*Somebody in Boots*], and I read it until I slept. Today, I sat near the window . . . reading it . . . Before going to sleep I have to tell you I really liked the book very much, and I have thought I liked you very much too—I think you felt it though we spoke so little—I am not going to say thank you any more, because it does not mean much; but you have to know I was happy, being with you—I did not like to say good bye, perhaps not to see you again in my whole life. I should be pleased to come back to Chicago in april, and then I should speak about myself, and you would speak about yourself. But I don't know if I'll have enough time. And then, I ask to myself: if it was unpleasant for us to say good bye, yesterday, will it not be worse saying good bye when we shall have spent five or six days together, and surely be quite good friends? I don't know. Anyway, good bye or farewell, I'll not forget these two days in Chicago, I mean I'll not forget you.[31]

She signed the letter "S. de Beauvoir," and asked him to send a copy of *Never Come Morning* to her in care of Natasha Moffatt in Los Angeles.

Only a letter was waiting for her when she arrived on March 12, but that was enough. Natasha and Ivan Moffatt lived in Westwood, in a house which Simone de Beauvoir described as "converted from a barn" but which was really a small apartment above a garage.[32] They gave pride of place among their few furnishings to a bookshelf on which every issue of *Les Temps Modernes*, which Beauvoir sent them, was displayed. Natasha told how Ivan's mother, the British actress Iris Tree, enjoyed teasing that "the *Mauvais Temps* [Bad Times] has arrived." Beauvoir thought Iris Tree was fascinating, beautiful and intelligent, but she was not amused by her jest.[33]

Moffatt had, in a sense, rejoined his "old Army unit"[34] when he became an associate producer for Liberty Films, the company George Stevens formed with Frank Capra and William Wyler. Because he liked *All Men Are Mortal*, Moffatt asked Stevens to consider producing it. He was agreeable, so Moffatt wrote a film treatment which Beauvoir liked, and then arranged for Stevens to meet her. She immediately wrote to Algren: "My friends here in Los Angeles are selling the subject of my last novel to a producer. I'm very happy with it. I could come back for a long time and I'll manage to stay a while in Chicago."[35]

The Moffatts took her to the RKO studios to meet Stevens, but he was too busy to do more than be introduced to her. When he learned that Natasha planned to drive Beauvoir to all her California speaking engagements, and that afterward they planned to meet Ivan in Las Vegas for a brief holiday, Stevens suggested that they meet him for lunch in the little town where he grew up, Lone Pine, near Death Valley on the edge of the California–Nevada desert. All this was agreed to with a great deal of enthusiasm, which Ivan Moffatt credited to the sense of optimism in the immediate postwar years: "America was at its finest, the most pleasant place to be. The country basked, and we in turn basked, in that feeling of security, hope and strength. So it was lovely and intoxicating, and because foreigners were made to feel very welcome, Castor basked in it, too." Moffatt believed that Beauvoir impressed everyone in California with her "ardor and the vitality of her face and those marvelous blue eyes and lovely smile

and laughter. All those things, all that animation and those clear features."
They all thought she was "enormous fun, a constant source of pleasure."

But the enthusiasm of Beauvoir's RKO meeting with Stevens did not carry over to the luncheon at Lone Pine. To the others, he seemed distracted by other concerns but also awkward, as if he was suddenly overawed by Beauvoir's reputation. She was amused by his deference, but characteristically did little to put him at ease. A "naturally shy but incredibly decent man," he "wilted in her presence,"[36] took Moffatt aside when the meal was over, and announced that he would not be able to drive across Death Valley and on to Las Vegas with them as they had originally planned, but had to return to Los Angeles at once. Moffatt believed that Stevens' discomfiture in Beauvoir's presence was the reason the film was never made.

So the three of them continued on in the huge, dusty Packard to Las Vegas, where they stayed in a cheap hotel because no one had much money. What little they had, they wanted to save for gambling and scotch whiskey. Scotch had been her favorite drink ever since Moffatt had made it so freely available during the Liberation of Paris. It was still difficult to come by and expensive in France, but whenever she could, Beauvoir liked to spend her evenings sipping it surrounded by friends. She herself did not like to gamble, because "gambling is something over which one has no control," but she was so fascinated by "the gambling zombies" that the Moffatts could not persuade her to leave until the very last moment she could still keep to her tour schedule.

She crossed the country again by train, and sent Algren the letter from Philadelphia inviting him to come to New York.[37] She checked into the Brevoort Hotel, where she soon settled into the *"vie de quartier,"* pleased that she had finally become a true New Yorker by moving to Greenwich Village, because "true New Yorkers" would no more live in the Times Square district, where her previous hotel had been, "than would true Parisians live in the Champs-Elysées."[38]

What she liked especially about Greenwich Village was that Richard and Ellen Wright lived within walking distance of the Brevoort. The casual friendship that had begun the previous year when the Wrights were in Paris developed into one that was very important for Beauvoir. She liked Ellen and Richard equally, but much about their relationship puzzled her, and some of it gave her thought when she came to wirte *The Second Sex*. Mostly she was with Richard, because Ellen assumed full responsibility for the Wrights' five-year-old daughter, Julia. Beauvoir was puzzled as to why Ellen, whom she thought an intelligent woman, was content to spend all her time meeting the needs of her husband and child rather than using her considerable editorial talents in a profession of her own.[39] Significantly, she never questioned Richard's need for uninterrupted time to work. Because she herself had no prejudices, she was saddened to witness the harsh stares and cruel remarks directed toward the biracial Wrights when they were out in public. On several occasions the warm spring afternoons lengthened into dusk as Beauvoir and Richard sat in the front room of the Wrights' house sipping Scotch and discussing the situation of the black writer in America while the footsteps of passersby on the street punctuated their conversation. When they told her that they were considering moving permanently to Paris, she encouraged them because she looked forward to continuing these discussions but also because she thought French society would be more accepting of the Wrights than American.[40]

Virtually every night there was a party, and she made many new friends through the Wrights: Nancy and Dwight MacDonald, members of "the *Partisan Review* crowd," and others not connected with literature or politics who had come to hear her speak at the Alliance Française. What puzzled her was the ubiquitous dinner party. She wondered why women chose to devote so much time and energy to serving others when it was so much easier to meet in a bar for drinks and then go on to a restaurant to eat.

Many of the women she met in New York were content to sit quietly on the sidelines while she sat alone, the only woman among the men whose ideas and arguments were listened to with attention and respect. To Beauvoir, it seemed that American women were responsible for nurturing their men: in charge of the couple's entertainment in many cases, entirely burdened with the care of their children, and saddled with all the details and responsibilities of maintaining the home. She was puzzled as to why they would so willingly want to take on a role in which they gave of themselves to everyone—husband, children, parents and community—and she wondered what they could possibly find in such situations that gave them satisfaction and contentment. She credited this first trip to America with truly opening her eyes to the everyday condition of women.

Most of the women she saw on a daily basis in Paris were allied with men, it was true, but as mistresses, companions or childless wives. It was not until she was in New York that she realized how very unusual her situation was, and how different her and her friends' daily lives were from the reality of most women's existence. "I didn't think there was anything special about myself in regard to these other women except that I had more willpower and a much stronger understanding of myself than they did," she recalled. "No man had ever asked me to fetch the coffee or iron the clothes, because I had no intention of doing it for anyone, myself or others, and they probably sensed that. I believed that if women felt about themselves as I felt about myself there would be none of this caretaking that led to so many misunderstandings by men of the role of women. I've often said this, and it bears repeating, but because I had never felt discrimination among men in my life, I refused to believe that discrimination existed for other women. That view began to change, to crumble, when I was in New York and I saw how intelligent women were embarrassed or ignored when they tried to contribute to a conversation men were having. Really, American women had a very low status then. Men wanted them for sex and babies and to clean house, and that's very much what they wanted for themselves, too."

In later years, she regretted that she had so willingly joined the men in conversation and had expressed so little sympathy for the women they excluded from intellectual equality: "I am sorry to say that I ascribed it to the shortcomings of the women rather than to the churlishness of the men."

Suddenly everything changed: she who had refused all her life to play the traditional woman's role in a relationship with a man found herself doing everything she reviled and more with Nelson Algren.

"Today, I went out with N.A., *who had come to New York on business*," she wrote in *America Day by Day*.[41] He came to stay with her around the first of May, and it was clear to her as soon as they were together that the attraction she had felt for him in Chicago was greater than ever. She was supposed to return to France on the tenth, but the day after he moved into her room at the Brevoort, while he was out meeting a publisher, she went to the Pan American ticket office and postponed her flight until the seventeenth. She had corresponded infrequently with Sartre because she was moving around so much, but she later remembered sending him a telegram saying that he probably wanted a few extra days with Dolores, and, since there were still things she wanted to do in New York, that she would stay on another week. She did not tell him her real reason, nor did she even tell him about Nelson Algren until after she returned to Paris.

As soon as Algren arrived, she dropped all contact with her New York friends. She did not take him to meet the Gerassis or the Wrights, she stopped going to parties, and she ended all previous liaisons. "I had a 'couple flings' in New York in 1947," she said in 1983, uncharacteristically lapsing into English to describe how little they meant to her. "Just say I slept with 'the smartest man in America' and let them all think they were the one." Her comment was a form of aspersion on the American man as lover and/or intellectual companion, but it was also camouflage: "The one I liked best was married, and I didn't like the way he sneaked around. He should have been honest with his wife about me. As for the rest, just say the New York intellectual has a big ego."[42]

With Algren, everything was different. Now they were on her territory, the New York that she had explored on her relentless foot tramps around the city. He had passed through New York at various times but did not know the city well, so she took great pleasure in showing him what she thought corresponded to the parts of Chicago he had shown her. When they walked on the Bowery and went to clubs in Harlem, he looked and listened as attentively as she had in Chicago. Sometimes he teased her by calling himself "only a boy from the provinces" or "a Chicago man" or his favorite self-appellation, "a local youth," but most of the time they stayed in bed in the Brevoort. She spent the next two weeks fussing over him "just like all the American women I had ridiculed for the way they catered to men's needs. I was surprised by how much I enjoyed it."

She agreed that Nelson Algren was "everything that Mary Guggenheim said he was," and she used Guggenheim's words to describe Algren in her memoirs: "unstable, moody, even neurotic." But she added, "I liked being the only one who understood him." For her, Algren possessed "that rarest of all gifts, which I should call goodness if the word had not been so abused; let me say that he really cared about people."[43]

On Saturday, May 17, she wanted to say goodbye to him in their room at the Brevoort, but he insisted on putting her into a taxi. She went alone to the airport bus terminal, and because she was sobbing so loudly the taxi driver asked whether she would be away from her "husband" for a long time. It soon became one of her favorite terms for Algren, a description she never, ever, used for Sartre. Algren gave her copies of his novels and told her not to open them until the plane was aloft. When she read his loving dedications, especially the poem he inscribed in *Never Come Morning*, she began to cry again.

à Simone:

I send this book with you
That it may pass
Where you shall pass:
Down the murmurous evening light
Of storied streets
In your own France.

Simone, I send this poem there, too,
That part of me may go with you.[44]

She couldn't wait to write to him from Paris, so she mailed a letter from the first stop on her return trip, Gander, Newfoundland, and sent it to Chicago. "My own nice wonderful and beloved local youth," she called him, saying he would find her waiting for him in Chicago when he returned there, because she loved him and would never leave him. She would be, she wrote, "his loving wife." She signed the letter "your Simone."[45]

She wrote again as soon as she arrived in Paris. "My precious beloved Chicago man," she began this one. She missed him terribly and her heart was still with him. Now that she was back in Paris she was unwilling to get involved again in her life there. She truly loved him, she said, with a love that gave her as much pain as pleasure.[46]

In truth, she was so disoriented that she actually took drugs for the first and last time in her life. Sartre gave her a bottle of the Orthodrine that he popped like Life-savers, and for almost a week she drugged herself as well. Then she stopped, because Sartre's life was more out of control than hers and it was clear to her that he needed her to manage it. She decided it was time to take charge of things.

What she did is best described by her concluding sentence in *America Day by Day:* "I would have to relearn France and get back into my own skin."[47]

TWENTY-FIVE

A Beautiful, Corny Love Story

LL SHE COULD THINK OF when she returned to Paris "was when and how I would see Algren again. I was not capable of thinking ahead to my real life in Paris."

Readjustment was difficult after almost five months in another language and culture, and was not eased by the way the Family swooped down on her, "like chattering little birds, everybody nibbling away, all talking at once, demanding attention and energy" she did not have. Sartre was in the midst of a crisis, and so, therefore, were they all. It concerned Dolores.[1]

Dolores was supposed to have left Paris in late April, but when that time came she announced that she would stay, giving as her ostensible reason that Sartre needed looking-after on a daily basis. Then, shortly before Beauvoir was due back, Dolores began to press for marriage, vowing to divorce her husband and leave her life in New York behind without qualms.

This frightened Sartre. A year earlier he had written to Beauvoir: "[Dolores's] passion for me literally scares me to death, especially because I'm no expert in that area."[2] He had grown to like the idea of spending part of each year with Dolores, because she was a charming companion with whom he enjoyed cavorting both sexually and socially. He had assumed that she would be like every other woman with whom he had been involved, willing to play whatever role in his life he assigned to her. In this instance what he wanted was for her to continue to live in New York, but to make herself available several months each year at his convenience. When he first realized her unwillingness to go along with this idea, he hinted that perhaps she could keep an apartment in Paris, but that he would still see her only when it suited him. She found such a life untenable and let him know definitely and emphatically that it was one she could not accept.

It was not until Beauvoir's long absence, however, that he truly realized how important she, Beauvoir, was in his life. Beauvoir was the ideal companion for the most important part of his existence, the life of his mind. Without her, he had no sounding board for his ideas, no critic for his writings, no editor for his texts, no manager for his magazine, and no buffer between himself and the fractious world of intellectual ferment which swirled around him in ever-increasing intensity.

With Dolores, it was just the opposite: he had to be the policymaker, the event planner, the financial caretaker, and the initiator of almost every other aspect of their life together. She waited for him to make all the decisions and then to take action, expecting him to treat her as the honored presence at his side while he escorted, protected and guided her through everything he did. In short, she totally misinterpreted Sartre's personality and the role he wanted women to play in his life, which was exactly the opposite of what she wanted him to do for her. This was her first serious misjudgment. Her second one, equally serious, was to try to enlist the Family as her allies.

Although the Family were conditioned to give Sartre everything he wanted without question, they all loved Beauvoir as deeply as they loved him. The thought of helping him to cut her out of his life was so horrifying that they were grateful not to have to think very long about it. In his usual manner, through indirection and evasion, Sartre let them know that he did not want to marry Dolores, that he wanted her to go back to New York. However, he also let them know that he wanted to keep her carefully slotted into his life, to be pulled out during those times when he wanted a holiday and someone to take his mind off his work. They demonstrated their loyalty by coming to Sartre's rescue and closing ranks around him, isolating Dolores and frequently keeping him incommunicado during the last few weeks before Beauvoir's return. They succeeded so well that many years after the end of the affair, Dolores still spoke of

> "incredible cruelty" without accusing anybody; she spoke of "destruction," of "the destruction of several lives," of "thoughtless acts," all the while refusing to attribute any guilt; she spoke of "will power and implacable harshness" among the people of Sartre's circle who were hostile to their relationship.[3]

As soon as Beauvoir returned, the Family convened to apprise her of what had happened in her absence. Dolores was furious with them for taking Beauvoir's side and began to make scenes designed to draw Sartre closer to her. Instead, he sheepishly withdrew, as was his custom, asking Beauvoir to help the others keep Dolores at bay.

The world as the Family knew it, the carefully ordered universe that revolved around Sartre and Beauvoir, was in chaos, and not only because of Dolores. They were all stunned to see a Beauvoir they scarcely recognized. They expected something similar to her return from Portugal, when she had dumped presents for everyone on her bed, chattering and laughing, regaling them all with stories of the trip. Instead, she was more subdued than they had ever seen her. Even more uncharacteristic was her reaction when they spilled out all the details about Sartre and Dolores. They expected Beauvoir to forge ahead, to take charge by barking orders and directions at everyone; instead, she listened attentively, then seemed to retreat into some private sphere of her own that she was unwilling to share with them. She had always been the one who organized their lives and resolved all their difficulties, so her air of withdrawal puzzled them.

Then they saw the ring on the middle finger of her left hand—the wide, ornate silver band that extended almost to her knuckle. She stared at it, sighed over it, fussed with it constantly by turning it round and round. The big silver ring seemed to be the key to her dreamlike condition and her indifference to all their urgent entreaties. Except for an occasional inexpensive necklace or pair of earrings, she had never worn jewelry before, so this particular object baffled them. When she told them that Nelson Algren had given it to her and that she intended never to take it off because she thought of him as her "husband,"[4] they were first "astounded,"[5] then thrown into panic. Although they were very worried about what might happen to Beauvoir (and, consequently, to the Family) if Sartre did indeed marry Dolores, they had never even considered the idea that Beauvoir might willingly remove herself from their lives to be with another man.

Dolores had been an unwitting catalyst: the idea of either Sartre or Beauvoir without the other was unfathomable to the Family, but she caused the two principals to realize that it was equally unfathomable for them as well. With the excuse of wanting to become reacquainted, but actually to avoid Dolores and her outbursts, Sartre and Beauvoir left Paris for the nearby suburb of Saint-Rémy-les-Chevreuse, Seine-et-Oise, where they took a room in a picturesque little "blue-and-yellow inn"[6] for a stay that lasted almost a month.

It was during this sojourn in the countryside that the relationship between Simone de Beauvoir and Jean-Paul Sartre became cemented, to last for the rest of their lives as that of a professional couple. Because both were equally involved in contingent relationships, their bond was strengthened by knowing that they could turn to each other for comfort and, more important, for approval. And all the while that Nelson Algren and Dolores Vanetti Ehrenreich were bewildered by their lovers' seeming indifference to separation, Beauvoir and Sartre were congratulating themselves for the clarity of the vision which let them place fidelity to their pact and its importance within their lives ahead of everything and everyone else.

There was one difference between Sartre's and Beauvoir's situations, however: Dolores was only one among Sartre's many lovers, from those who lasted (like Wanda and Michelle Vian) to the more fleeting and now forgotten, for, in his own words, "passion" was "not his strong suit." It was quite the opposite with Nelson Algren, who was, in Beauvoir's words, "the only truly passionate love in my life."

While she and Sartre were in the country, Beauvoir spent every spare moment writing long, gushing love letters to Algren, filled with every detail of her life, from past love affairs to what she thought about her family and her girlhood friends, her pact with Sartre, their daily routine, their hopes and plans for the future. Again, it was just the opposite for Sartre, whose relationship with Dolores had disintegrated into one best characterized by his fear of her tantrums. He had spurned her, and she was furious. For the duration of her time in Paris, he and Beauvoir stayed in the country, sneaking into Paris when there were appointments they had to keep, returning to their hideout just as surreptitiously.

Because they were alone together more than they had been in years, they began to talk about their personal lives as much as they discussed the increasingly public and commanding position that Sartre now held in the postwar arena of politics, literature and philosophy. It had been a long time since Sartre listened to her counsel with the careful attention and thoughtful concern that he had shown in the early years of their pact. One happy result of their new closeness was that it encouraged her to tell Sartre everything she felt for Nelson Algren, and to recount the development of their relationship in the same detail that he had always used to tell her of his other women. Sartre listened attentively and congratulated her on finding someone as "suitable to [her] needs" as Algren, and because of his unstinting approval she was able to find the necessary stasis to balance her role as French intellectual and companion to Sartre with the equally important role of that exotic creature, Nelson Algren's "Frog wife."[7]

So her daily life gradually fell back into the usual pattern of writing and editing for Les Temps Modernes, of meeting friends, of dealing with Sartre's boosters and detractors, of thinking about what her own next writing project should be, and of the happy time at the end of each day when, in lieu of a diary, she confided all her thoughts and emotions to her beloved "Chicago local youth, friend, lover, and husband of one week."[8]

It helped that Sartre seemed contented also, living in the best of all possible worlds: the Family won the battle of wills with Dolores, who finally gave up and went back to New York; and Beauvoir was better than ever at sheltering him from the inordinate demands of others without making any emotional claims upon him. Wanda remained constant, content to be whatever he wanted; Michelle Vian was increasingly helpful with such things as English translations and was also affectionately docile; he had written a song for the newest entertainment sensation in the Saint-Germain nightclubs, Juliette Greco, and it helped that she was enthralled by him; and there were other women as well, from the young and nubile seeking thrills to the sophisticated and well-connected who were fascinated by his irresistible combination of power, fame and seductive ugliness. "Sartre had a rather diabolical side to him," according to Colette Audry, who remembered Simone de Beauvoir telling her at this time how he "conquered young girls by explaining their soul to them."

During the years 1946–49, Sartre was in the midst of one of the most frenzied and productive periods of his creative life. No matter what else happened, he wrote at least three hours each morning and three at night.[9]

He and Beauvoir usually worked separately in the mornings, she at her hotel and he in the apartment he shared with his mother at 42 Rue Bonaparte. They met in midafternoon to lunch together, then both returned to the apartment, and while he "played the piano, read, daydreamed and smoked" she edited texts for the magazine, wrote articles of her own and pondered what she should write next.

It was difficult to concentrate on her own work because of the pressures of putting out a monthly magazine. Sartre had taken on a former student, the writer Jean Cau, to be his secretary, but Beauvoir still worked alone.[10] First of all, there was the pile of submissions that never seemed to diminish no matter how much she read or how quickly. She tried to skim through them, but something was happening in French fiction that required close reading, and she did not have sufficient time to give to it. The term "the New Novel" was one she heard frequently, but she made no attempt to understand it, generally dismissing it as a "temporary aberration" inspired by "people wanting to forget about real life for a little while after the war." She was "confident that soon they would want to return to robust fiction that dealt with the realities of life, especially because the political situation was so interesting."[11] Many of her decisions about which literary submissions the magazine would print were based on snap judgments, and in making them she made many enemies.

A situation with Samuel Beckett was typical: she earned his lifelong enmity over a misunderstanding about a text he submitted which she thought was a complete story "because it had no beginning or end and none of it made any real sense." She made the immediate decision to publish it, "even though I did not understand it, and frankly didn't like it very much, but he was Paule Allard's friend and we were all very fond of Paule."[12] A month later, Beckett sent "the final portion"[13] of his story, "Suite," and Beauvoir, thinking it "a second submission," rejected it without reading it. Beckett, whose politeness is legendary, decided that it must have been an editorial mixup, but he was still very firm about it: he was sorry, but he wanted his entire story to be printed. Beauvoir refused, telling Beckett the second half "was simply not in keeping with what we wanted to print in the magazine,"[14] which was her standard rejection. However, her real reason was something quite different. She believed that Beckett "deliberately tricked me because he never liked Sartre and thought we were both out of touch with modern literature. It gave him pleasure to extend his dislike to me." Basically, she was "suspicious of that crowd that had started to gather around [Jerome] Lindon and his press [Les Editions de Minuit]." As she sat in the cafés, journalists and critics frequently teased her that "this New Novel" was all her and Sartre's fault, claiming that the new techniques in fiction were a logical reaction against their literature of commitment.

Beauvoir was "a little bit sensitive" about the entire subject of fiction because her last novel, *All Men Are Mortal*, had been criticized so severely. Although she thought about trying to begin another, she was reluctant because "I would have written about my love for Algren, and I was truly afraid to expose it to a harsh and jealous world." When she next wrote to Algren, she told him that she had been in a dream ever since they parted, brooding on their love story for hours, reliving it over and over again "from their first kiss in the airport" to his "last smile on the street corner." If he knew how much she loved him, she concluded, he would become "very conceited and . . . unbearably aloof."[15]

Although Beauvoir complied willingly with whatever demands were made on her time by *Les Temps Modernes*, she was still restless without a large project to occupy her creative energies. She told Algren about it, confiding that she was trying to resume "the essay on women" started some six months ago. Originally, she intended it to be a journalistic survey of the contemporary status of women in French postwar society, "a tidy little essay suitable to provoke discussion and dialogue [in *Les Temps Modernes*,]" but could not write it because she was too preoccupied with "remembering Chicago."[16] Then she decided that the topic was too vast and important to handle superficially. A number of things struck her as particularly worth discussing: she was intrigued by the many differences she had noted between French and American women when she was in the United States. Also, French women had just gained the right to vote in 1947, and she was curious about what influence this would have both on their personal lives and on political life in general. People continued to question her about the role of women within the framework of Existentialism, and she thought this too might be suitable for inclusion in a larger, more ambitious study of women. She had many ideas and possible topics, but, at the time, not enough energy and concentration to tackle the hard work necessary to make a book of them.

As the summer continued, she found herself obsessed with Algren and unable to do much more than replay his part in her American sojourn over and over again. Since she was unable to concentrate on anything else, she decided to write "a sort of memoir" about her impressions of the United States. Sartre thought it a good idea, because their separation was slowly dissipating her euphoria at being in love with Algren. She had reverted to crying jags and drunken depressions, and, as Sartre was looking forward to an August holiday in Sweden, he wanted to make sure she was in good enough shape to stick to their plan. A series of American sketches seemed the ideal way to keep her occupied until then. Also, since there was a great curiosity about the United States at that time in France, such sketches would boost the review's circulation. So she picked up the red fountain pen Algren had given her as "added insurance that I would write to him every day," and set to work.[17]

She divided her time between the "blue-and-yellow inn" and her "lousy toothpaste-pink" hotel room and tried to write. In between, she went with Sartre to watch the filming of his script of *Les Jeux sont faits* (*The Chips Are Down*), which movie director Jean Delannoy had wanted to produce since 1943; she saw many other movies, including *Le Diable au corps* (*Devil in the Flesh*), with her new favorite actor, Gérard Philippe; and she sat in the Deux Magots or the Flore working on translations of Algren's fiction for *Les Temps Modernes* or reading the books he had recommended to her.[18]

She also told him about her dinner with "the Ugly Woman," Violette Leduc, who had agreed to abide by a schedule of strictly regimented meetings if she wanted to continue to see Beauvoir: one deviation from this arrangement by Leduc, and Beauvoir said she would never consent to see her again. Leduc knew she was serious and was too frightened to cross her.

Leduc presented the manuscript of *L'Affamée* to Beauvoir, a novel in diary form about Leduc's thinly disguised passion for her. Beauvoir confessed to Algren that it was strange to read about herself as the object of such passion, but Leduc was so good a writer that she often forgot she was reading about herself. What she found even more curious was that she was able to discuss Leduc's passion so clinically, as only a fictional entity. Still and all, she dreaded these meetings, she told him, because the ending was always the same: she had to tear herself away from Leduc's clutches, and usually left her sobbing about her lonely and friendless life.[19]

In reaction against Leduc's despair and to ward off a possible depression because of being separated from Algren, Beauvoir decided "to give a coming-home party,"[20] but despite the "nice club, good records and great liquor" the party was "a failure. . . . The problem was that nearly everyone got dead drunk almost immediately, and vomited, or cried, or slept most of the night." She was surprised when, several days later, everyone "said how nice it was."

After that, she gradually fell back into the routine of life in Paris, of too many parties and too much drinking, of too many people to see and not enough time to daydream about Algren, of trying to write and having nothing exciting to write about. She finally finished the account of her first three weeks in the United States and had now reached the point where she felt she had to write about meeting Algren for the first time. "Well," she concluded, "I have to find a way of saying the truth without saying it; that is exactly what is literature after all, clever lies which secretly say the truth."[21]

Algren sent her a photograph of the two of them standing in front of the Chicago skyline, which cheered her momentarily.[22] He wrote that he always felt sad after reading one of her letters; she replied that they were always filled with love, but it is clear that distance and separation were having an adverse effect on her as well, because from mid-June until the end of July 1947 her letters are suffused with sadness.

The weather was unseasonably hot that summer, and she drifted aimlessly in the heat. She went to a cocktail party in Gallimard's garden and saw John Steinbeck, whom Algren knew and admired, but she made no attempt to meet him "in such a crowd." Jean Genet, "the homosexual burglar-poet," was the honored guest, but Beauvoir chose not to speak to him either. Leduc was there because she was a friend of Genet's. She invited Beauvoir to dine after the party with her and Jean Cocteau, "a famous poet and pansy." Beauvoir accepted because she was bored, and as "the only heterosexual among them" she felt "vaguely immoral." She should have gone home to work, because an unspecified New York magazine had offered her five hundred dollars for "a piece" of her "book about women," but instead she killed time with Madame Morel, the Guilles and Bianca.

Then the weather changed, and there was one of the worst summer storms she had ever experienced. Beauvoir invited Sartre, Madame Morel, the Guilles, Bianca and Olga to dinner in her hotel room. Everyone drank too much and, perhaps because of the miserable weather, wallowed boozily in their problems, none of them listening to anyone else. Olga still had tuberculosis and had to go away for another cure; Bianca wanted a divorce from her teacher husband, who wanted her to return with him to Algeria; Madame Guille had swallowed a safety pin and bored everyone with the graphic details of her four-day-long ordeal as she waited to pass it. Bianca and Olga fought over which of them was the most devoted to Beauvoir. "I don't care much for either of them," she wrote to Algren, "I like Madame Morel and I like my Russian friend in Los Angeles [Natasha Moffatt], who is like a daughter to me."[23]

Beauvoir's refuge from the lugubriousness of the party was to get exceedingly drunk herself, after which she "raved into the night about life and death." She told Algren about how she both hated and feared death, of how it "interferes in the end" with living life fully and how the mere thought of it keeps one from ever being completely happy. Also, she was very lonely, afraid of what the rest of the month held for her, because the dinner was intended as a last gathering before they all dispersed for the summer holiday season. Sartre had given in to Wanda, who claimed he had ignored her for months, and was going to spend a week with her in the south of France. Madame Morel and the Guilles went back to the country, Olga went to a sanatorium, and Bianca went off with her husband. All Beauvoir had, she told Algren, was his love, which sustained her.

On the spur of the moment, she decided to fly alone to Corsica, hoping to duplicate the experiences she remembered from a visit twelve years before. In three days she became "very ugly . . . sunburned, wild-haired, scratched and shabby" as she walked relentlessly through a landscape "lonely and with the smell of dried maquis everywhere."[24] She described everything to Algren, telling him that everywhere she went it was as if he were there with her as well. She punctuated her obsessive walking with bus trips to isolated villages, where she watched the people and tried to swim, which she had never learned to do—"only to float."

On Monday, July 13, she took the boat train to London with Sartre in the company of his Swiss publisher, Louis Nagel, for the London premiere of two of Sartre's plays, *Mort sans sépulture* (*Men Without Shadows*) and *La Putain respecteuse* (*The Respectful Prostitute*). Once again she shared her impressions and experiences with Algren. Neither she nor Sartre liked Nagel very much,[25] but still Beauvoir tried to convince him to publish Algren's books in French. She and Sartre eluded the serious, dignified Nagel (whom they thought humorless) and went off on a sightseeing spree around London, which saddened her because of all the rationing and shortages. She found the sight of bombed-out ruins covered with wildflowers somewhat cheering, but the sound of British English was bittersweet: she thought it strange to hear Algren's language but to be so far away from him. She told him that although it had been almost two months since they were together, her life was inextricably bound to his. His ring never left her finger, she wrote.[26]

The highlight of the trip was the great success of Sartre's plays at the shabby Hammersmith Art Theatre, brightened by the presence of actress Rita Hayworth on opening night. Sartre was honored after the performance with "a very dull dinner . . . guests isolated at little tables, Sartre alone in a corner and [Beauvoir was seated] with Rita Hayworth, who was very bored."[27] In her memoirs she commented acerbically, "With her golden shoulders and her magnificent bosom, Rita Hayworth was magnificent; but a star without a husband is a sorrier sight than an orphaned child."[28]

By July 19, she and Sartre were back in Paris. Being separated from Algren was making her so unhappy that she was reverting to all her old depressive behavior, drinking heavily and crying in public. In their letters, both she and Algren had reached the point where they were questioning each other more about their relationship than sharing news of their daily activities or work.[29] She was writing about the "pain" of missing him, imagining that they had only one heart between them which was "painfully split between two aching bodies." She wrote of her yearnings for him and described her physical sensations. She even told him her dreams, of how he came to her with "a big hat and whiskers" and how, when she tried to kiss him, he disappeared.[30] She kissed the paper she wrote on, as if she were kissing him, sometimes leaving the imprint of her lipstick. Theirs, she concluded, was "a beautiful, corny love story."

Still, there was the specter of uneasiness behind all her protestations of eternal love and undying devotion. In a long letter of July 22, she addressed their situation head on. He had written that he coped with missing her by gambling; she replied that she coped by drinking. She then compared their situation to the screenplay of Les Jeux sont faits (The Chips Are Down)[31] and synopsized the plot of the two dead persons who fall in love and are given a second chance at life on the condition that they make their love real and human. "They fail," she wrote, and then compared it to her situation with Algren. She ended the letter by asking the question that had been troubling her ever since she met him: was she being fair to him by allowing their relationship to continue and deepen, since he knew that she would never commit her whole life to him? He had never mentioned it in his letters, she continued, but because they promised never to lie to each other or to keep things hidden she felt she had to ask. She tried to soften the question by telling him how bad she felt at not being able to commit herself entirely to him, to give him "everything." She implored him to read the letter with love and understanding, without resentment, because she loved him dearly and wanted their love "to succeed."

The next day, on brilliant blue stationery, she made a sudden, spur-of-the-moment decision. "This bright paper reflects the brightness of my heart," she began the letter to "Nelson, my love."[32] She had decided to fly to Chicago on September 6 and would stay until the twentieth. Although she was reluctant to go so far for such a brief time, she wanted—actually, needed—to see him. She cautioned that they would have to live simply, because she might have as little as fifty dollars to spend, and she told him to wait for her in his apartment because "the airport is no place for a husband and wife to meet." All she needed from him was "whiskey, ham and jam," and they would spend their time "talking, working, listening to records and loving." Afraid that her letter would take too long to reach him, she sent a telegram the next day, July 29, repeating the dates of her planned visit, saying she would come if he had "no objection."[33]

She received his reply on July 31, on the eve of her departure for Scandinavia with Sartre. It was a telegram enthusiastic enough to put any rational mind at rest, and it buoyed her as she busied herself with laundry and packing.[34] She and Sartre spent five days in Copenhagen while he lectured and met with scholars and intellectuals; then they went on to Stockholm, where he did much the same for a week before they went off alone for a tour of the northernmost regions of the country, using her accumulated Swedish royalties to pay for it. She was amazed by the warmth of Sartre's reception in both Denmark and Sweden: "He is remarkably popular in Scandinavia, considering that in France people spit in his face."[35]

In her memoirs she wrote that at the beginning of the trip she and Sartre were very quiet, and she "wondered in terror if we had become strangers to each other."[36] She corrected this in a 1985 conversation, saying that her relationship with Sartre "had never been more stable—we were like devoted brother and sister, entirely solicitous of each other," and that her "terror" over the possibility of becoming "strangers" was really what she felt about Nelson Algren. Now that she had made the decision to go to him, and despite the warmth and eagerness of his telegram, she was afraid she might find that what they shared had been a wonderful brief affair but not a lasting relationship.

Still, she could not contain her eagerness to see him. "Look at the date, my beloved Nelson, my dearest husband,"[37] was how she started a letter dated exactly one month before the day she was to be with him. It did not lessen the anxiety attacks to which she was prone throughout most of the trip as she waited for him to reply to the letter in which she voiced her concerns over their long-distance relationship. She received his response in Stockholm on August 13, relieved that he had written exactly what she had hoped to read: he understood all her concerns and was well aware that not being able to spend her entire life with him did not mean that she did not love him. She wrote back at once, ending the letter by telling him of a banquet given by French and Swedes the previous night, "horrible," at which she had gotten very angry and very drunk. She had been "appeased slightly" only when some of the French admired her ring.[38]

On Thursday, September 4, she sent a telegram from Paris to tell him that she would arrive the following Sunday in Chicago. She asked him to wait at home for her call. On her scheduled day of departure, Saturday, September 6, she sent a second wire telling him the flight was postponed until Tuesday. She sent impatient kisses. She arrived finally in Chicago in the early morning of September 11, so she moved her departure date to the night of September 24 because she had allotted thirteen days to be with him and she was determined to have them no matter what commitments awaited her in Paris.

Algren's apartment at 1523 Wabansia Street consisted of two rooms— a large kitchen and a smaller bedroom. He had few amenities: in the bedroom there was a sagging double mattress in an iron frame and a makeshift table that held a reading lamp; in the kitchen a scratched Formica-and-aluminum table and three dilapidated chairs atop a cracked and chipped linoleum floor. He had a toilet, but the only sink was in the kitchen and there was no bath, so each day he went to the local YMCA to swim first and then bathe. Beauvoir joked about the apartment, saying she would be "stylish on Wabansia Avenue because it's such a stylish place."[39] They saw no one really, except for neighbors they passed in the hallway when they went out to take their daily bath or do their shopping. In the evenings they sometimes went to his favorite local bars, but usually they stayed in the apartment, content to read, write and make love.

At this stage of the relationship, it was quite unlike the one she shared with Sartre, which since the war had gradually become an exchange of theoretical ideas, the giving and seeking of advice and criticism about their works in progress, or what their ideological positions should be vis-à-vis public comment or controversy.[40] With Algren, it was more one of "getting to know you" in the sense of determining likes and dislikes in everything from whiskey (Southern Comfort) to politics (she hopes he is "not turning into Phillip Rahv," whose views she dislikes) to literature (Hans Christian Andersen is "just as much a writer for adults as . . . for children"; yes, she did read *Tender Is the Night*, but she likes *The Great Gatsby* better; *Of Time and the River* "seems a bit too hard." "Why don't Americans like Poe more?" Does he like Poe?). She also asked him to collect a set of newspapers and copies of *Time* magazine during the period of her previous stay in the United States, and together they pored over them, selecting items relating to topics they thought she should discuss in *America Day by Day*. He came to value her opinions about his work as well, and his letters to her are filled with possibilities for the titles of his novels and stories, for the names of his characters, and suggestions for ways in which they might be developed.

It was Algren with whom she first discussed her "essay on women," and it was he who initially encouraged her to think about expanding it into a book.[41] They had discussed the situation of women when they were in New York in May, sitting and smoking in the twin beds of their hotel room after they made love; he was curious about the lot of French women and how she differed from most of them, and she wanted to know what he thought of her observations about American women. He had been fascinated to learn that French women had only just received the right to vote, and as his questions became more probing they had settled on the topic of "women's status throughout the world" as the possible theme of, if not a book, then certainly a long article for Les Temps Modernes. But everything had conspired to keep her from it until she was in Sweden, when the knowledge that she was going to see him in a few short weeks, that he had written what he considered some of his best writing with an intensity and passion all due to her, and that she had written next to nothing since leaving him, all coalesced to galvanize her. She wrote to him from Sweden to say that she had stopped drinking and started working, that she had finished the long chapter on women (thinking at this time that it would simply be an article rather than a book), and that she was working steadily on her "book about America."[42]

During the two weeks in Chicago, as they talked about their plans for future writings, Beauvoir found the necessary distance and objectivity to think about what she would write when she returned to Paris. Algren verified that her views of all things American were both interesting and valid, and this gave her the necessary confidence to tackle the work. More important, this time with him had (to her way of thinking at least) resolved her doubts about their continuing relationship in the best possible manner.

Their time together had only deepened her feelings for "this crazy loner, this shy boozer, this gentle wild man." She returned to Paris buoyed by the thought that he would be there for her whenever she wanted him, first in the twice-weekly exchange of letters, then in the biannual visits they planned to make to each other. He had given her what she never dreamed would be hers: passion, devotion, affection and intellectual support. Quite simply, he thought she was "wonderful," and, unlike Sartre, he did not hesitate to show it with a quick hug and a spin around his kitchen, by staring at her with open delight on his face, or by grabbing her spontaneously and taking her into the bedroom. When she left Chicago on September 24, her sadness at parting was balanced by the anticipation of their plan to sail down the Mississippi the following spring and then spend several months in Mexico and Guatamala.

As far as she was concerned, she had the best of all possible worlds: the perfect happiness she had craved as a child was hers; granted, it was based on a very different model from the one she envisioned then. Sartre was right after all: contingency worked for them. She had everything and everyone slotted into neat little compartments, all seemingly willing to rest in suspended animation until she declared that it was time to take them out and start the movement of their lives as she wished them to be entwined with hers. But, like many other best laid plans, this too was soon to go awry. Sartre waited for her in Paris in the midst of the most intense political ferment they had thus far encountered in their life together.

TWENTY-SIX

The High Priestess
of Existentialism

THE CAB DEPOSITED HER at the Chicago airport much too early for her flight, so she went into the passenger lounge and tried to read a book to kill the time.[1] Thinking of her last sight of Algren as they said goodbye in front of his building on Wabansia made her so despondent that she almost missed hearing her name on the public-address system. When she answered the page, she found a large bouquet of flowers he had sent. She telephoned him in tears, her "heart [breaking] at the sound of his voice for the last time."

Twenty-three hours later she was in Paris and back in her toothpaste-pink hotel room. She slept for fourteen hours, waking only once "to cry bitterly" over him. The next day she passed Camus in the street and he asked if she was pregnant, because in all the years he had known her he had never seen her look "so tired and drawn." She went back to her room at once and slept another twelve hours, which made her feel a little better and ready to return to life in Paris.[2]

Camus's perception of her strain was accurate, because Algren had begun to ask the one question that eventually resulted in the final rupture of their relationship.[3] During their last few days together he had questioned her in exhaustive detail about why, if she loved him as much as she said she did, she could not continue to write while living in Chicago as his wife. Up to this point in their relationship, Algren had seen only the part of Beauvoir that "was on holiday, relaxed, always ready to play, to amuse and be amusing." He knew nothing about the frenetic pace of her life in Paris.

She told him all the details of her pact with Sartre, and he was confused by its constancy despite the absence of anything physical between them. She also told him of her presence at Sartre's side during meetings of all sorts, from editorial-board meetings at Les Temps Modernes to the ever-increasing meetings about more public, generally political matters. Algren's response was blunt and "so very American": quite simply, he wanted to know why, if she played no direct role in any of Sartre's activities, she needed to be constantly present at his side. What, he demanded, was the sense of her continuing to sacrifice the happiness that could be hers if she were living on Wabansia with him, "cooking his pot roast and maybe washing his socks in the kitchen sink!"[4]

Algren listened to Beauvoir's reasons why she had to return to Paris. They all revolved around Sartre's decision to position himself ideologically to confront General de Gaulle, who had resigned from the government the previous spring and was readying himself and his followers for a political contest later in the fall. Sartre was determined to speak out against de Gaulle and to urge the French to take an independent position between the United States and "bourgeois capitalism" on one side and the Soviet Union and "the rigidities of Communism" on the other. She tried to convince Algren how vital it was for her to be there, but he was both skeptical and unsympathetic. In the end, she managed to placate him with a promise to return early in the spring of 1948 for four months. She told him then, and in later letters, that their first farewell in New York had been "only the beginning of love," but that when they embraced on Wabansia this time it was "full love."[5] It made her nervous, she wrote, to think that she had placed herself so much in his power because she loved him so much.

In the same letter, she apologized for "rattling on" about coming back the next year to see friends in New York, give lectures, go to Canada and visit her "daughter in California" (Natasha Moffatt), when all she really wanted was to be with him. Then she made an uncharacteristic offer: to do all the housework and shopping and even to rent a room so that *he* could work alone. What she really meant was that, despite her love for Algren, four months was a very long time for *her* to live in the same apartment with someone, when she had not shared living quarters with anyone at all since she and her sister shared a room at home.

She was trying very hard to appease him, because Algren was capable of thunderous rages and prone to paranoid suspicions. He cut people out of his life forever if he suspected them of even the smallest infraction of his private code, secret rules they may not even have known they were breaking. Beauvoir alluded to this when she promised that her love would "never burden" him.

This was said in the third letter she wrote after her return, and by the time she sent it a pattern had begun to emerge. She usually began by telling him how much she loved him before launching into an apologetic explanation of why she could not live permanently with him in Chicago. Her language grew more formal and her tone more serious as she told him about "our work," which was a euphemism for Sartre's activity, as she was doing virtually nothing of her own at that time. She implored Algren to understand that it was too important to give up, and said that she would willingly forgo travel, friends and entertainment, but never "our work." Then she described it as the imperative to tell people about their (hers and Sartre's) views, opinions and values, all of which she sincerely believed were valid and true. She wrote with a sense of mission, saying, "People who can influence others for good must do so for the sake of those who are not free."[6] Then she tried to placate him by saying she was sure he understood what she meant because it was exactly the same thing he tried to do in his own writings and was the one sure reason why they understood each other so well.

A letter written two days later follows the same pattern: soothing words of love intertwined with information about her activities in Paris. Sartre's name begins to appear regularly, as in she "and Sartre" attended meetings, issued manifestos, planned radio broadcasts or—in what must surely have aroused all Algren's worst instincts—spent a beautiful fall evening sitting outside discussing Hegel, "whom we are studying together."[7]

From this point on, a certain toughness is present in her letters. The private language of love is still there, but more frequently there are long, thoughtful passages about her activities, her analyses of both people and situations, and philosophical ramblings which she invites him to share by commenting in his reply. She believed that their correspondence now proved the validity of her observation that what had been "only the beginning" was now "full love." She wrote that her impetuosity had been right after all when she dropped everything and flew to be with him in Chicago. A week after Camus told her how terrible she looked, both he and Arthur Koestler remarked that she looked young and happy. She credited Algren, who she said had given her "youth and happiness." When she wrote to him next, she told him she had never loved anyone as she loved him, "with mind and body at once."[8]

She came back from Chicago to a veritable hurricane of political activity, and Sartre was right in the eye of the storm. Much had changed in her absence, including the cancellation of their usual autumn holiday at Madame Morel's country house because of Sartre's many commitments in Paris. Alphonse Bonafé, one of his former colleagues in Le Havre, had succeeded—so Sartre was led to believe—in getting the state radio to sponsor a weekly broadcast for him and other members of the editorial board of Les Temps Modernes to express their views. Called "La Tribune des Temps Modernes," it was supposed to concentrate on Sartre's proposal for the "third option," the independent stance between the politics of the United States and the Soviet Union.[9] "We will be able to influence thousands of people with these broadcasts," Beauvoir exulted to Algren.[10]

The program was scheduled to air every Monday evening at eight-thirty. The first broadcast dealt with the third option, and Beauvoir took part, along with Sartre, Merleau-Ponty, Pontalis and Bonafé. The first two broadcasts passed without incident. Even though their opinions were far from what the majority of the French public believed, the number of supportive letters and messages they received was satisfying. Then Sartre learned that he had been the dupe of the Ramadier government, and that the only reason they were given the program was that President Ramadier himself expected them to direct a steady stream of invective and increasingly hostile attacks upon General de Gaulle and his Rassemblement du Peuple Français (RPF).[11] "Well, we are anti-Communist and anti-Gaullist, but we don't support Ramadier either," Beauvoir wrote to Algren, giving him a lesson in contemporary French politics whether he wanted one or not. When Sartre refused to do another show, the furious Ramadier ordered the radio station executives to force him and the others to speak. Initially he refused, but when it became clear within the week that the General's party was going to win the election on October 19, Sartre changed his mind and decided to go ahead with the broadcast.

On October 20 the panelists openly attacked de Gaulle, who had just won an overwhelming electoral victory. Sartre criticized everything about the General, including his looks. The public considered his remarks outrageous, and a vilification campaign directed against Sartre began, ranging from threats to his person to insults about his looks equal in kind. Paul Claudel wrote: "Mr. Sartre does not like General de Gaulle's appearance: is he happy with his own looks?"[12] When his friends reported encounters with roving gangs of thugs who were looking to beat him up, Sartre added up the hate letters and suddenly realized that he was receiving no fewer than twenty each day. He decided it would be prudent for him and Beauvoir to hide out at the Leirises' just as they had done during the last months of the occupation.[13] When both he and the program's director received death threats, they spent some of their nights and most of their afternoons hiding out in Madame Morel's Paris apartment, which she had never given up although she had lived in the country since before the war.[14]

The director of the literature and drama section of the state radio, who sympathized privately with Sartre, urged him to continue the broadcasts, but Sartre believed that their usefulness to his cause was at an end and refused.[15] "This is a dirty business," was Beauvoir's final comment on the matter to Algren.

Beauvoir's contribution to these broadcasts was minimal. In the de Gaulle broadcast, for example, her comments amount to little more than two brief interjections.[16] Earlier she had told Algren that her voice was "dreadful," and that she would try not to speak very much during the broadcasts because she hated the sound of it. She had never heard herself recorded before and was surprised by her "stridency and harshness."

Something that she had never experienced before began to happen. As Sartre's companion, she was used to receiving respectful attention when she spoke, but now she found herself in situations where no one listened to her or, if they were forced to do so, did not take her seriously. "Yesterday we met with a large group of Socialists to discuss a manifesto which will seek peace through a Socialist Europe, not through alliance with either Russia or the U.S. Since I was the only woman among fifteen men, I kept quiet."[17] This is her description of the first meeting of the Rassemblement Démocratique Révolutionnaire (RDR), a political party founded by Georges Altman and David Rousset, which Sartre had agreed to join. Soon it was known popularly as "Sartre and Rousset's party," and for the next eighteen months or so Rousset's name appears frequently in her correspondence. "We are working with Rousset on this political business," she told Algren.[18]

Rousset, a Buchenwald survivor, was emaciated when he arrived in Paris but soon ballooned up to his prewar corpulence. He had been noted before the war for his unsavory appearance, which was further heightened by the privations he had suffered. What few teeth he had remaining were decayed, and he wore a black patch to hide a missing eye. Still Beauvoir was fascinated, and all her voyeuristic tendencies were alerted whenever she saw him. "He is forbidding at first, but very direct and funny, and you can't help but like him." He was also the author of two books about his experiences in the death camps, *The Days of Our Death* and *The Other Kingdom*, both of which made a lasting impression on her and which she recommended to others for many years afterward.

However, the role she played and the way others regarded her in "Sartre and Rousset's party" is typical of how she was treated by all of Sartre's political allies and friends. Everyone took it for granted that she held no convictions of her own and that all positions she espoused were based on Sartre's. She could attend anything she wished—just so long as she was accompanying him or was sent by him. She was never invited independently to participate on any governing board or planning committee, and, although she sometimes went alone to meetings Sartre could not attend so that she could report back to him, she was never considered his official representative and was never really welcome without him. In political matters she was truly La Grande Sartreuse, with no value or respect of her own.

Still, her account of the last months of 1947 and the beginning of 1948 in her memoirs is told entirely through the filter of Sartre's work, thought and activity.[19] Every anecdote, incident and event relates his life much more fully than it does hers, as if by her telling what he did her readers would know what she did as well. In one sense this is true, as she was at his side; in another, truer sense, it is an evasion. By deciding to talk about Sartre, she effectively avoids talking about herself.

In a few brief paragraphs, she synopsizes the chaotic postwar political conditions in France, with the tripartite coalition that had been in power since 1945 in dissolution, the labor unions on frequent strikes, inflation rampant and goods in short supply. But after this capsule summation of French history, even though she uses the plural ("*We* met every week at Izard's home . . . ," "There were other points of dissention between Camus and *ourselves* . . ."), what she is really saying is that all this applies principally to Sartre and that she was merely tagging along.

The reality of her life was the daily schedule she outlined for Algren, and the pattern of her days seldom varied. She rose between 8 and 9 A.M., walked to the Deux Magots, drank coffee and read the newspapers. She stayed there to work until one, when she lunched either with her mother or with her "Russian [Olga Bost] or Jewish [Bianca Bienenfeld Lamblin] girl friends." Then she went to Madame Morel's Paris apartment to spend the afternoon incommunicado with Sartre. In the evening they followed his agenda for whatever political or social event he wanted to attend. If he had nothing scheduled, they went either to a movie or else back to her room, where they drank whiskey and listened to the radio. Sartre was becoming interested in the music of Arnold Schoenberg and Alban Berg, so she began to listen to works by these composers and other examples of modern music, even though her tastes ran more to Beethoven's late quartets.[20] Because neither of them liked to eat heavily in the evening, they often bought a few slices of ham and a loaf of bread and dined on that in her room.[21] By midnight they were usually asleep in their separate bedrooms.

Rumors have multiplied in the years since about the frenetic activity of both Beauvoir and Sartre during this time. Their pictures were plastered throughout the world on the covers of everything from tabloids to serious intellectual journals, and in almost every article about them there was mention of their predilection for smoke-filled cellar nightclubs and all-night boozing and carousing. Often there was a related photo showing younger "followers" in "Existentialist uniform"[22]—ubiquitous black turtleneck sweaters with flowing skirts and ballerina slippers for the women, and blue jeans for the men.

"We were there twice! Exactly twice in our lifetimes!" Beauvoir wailed against accusations that she and Sartre were seen every night in the Tabou, a popular nightclub. "And as for those clothes—never! We wore what clothes we had. Sartre liked turtleneck shirts, but I don't think he wore them then, not until much later." If she had any preference in clothing, it was increasingly for ethnic jewelry and fabrics from places like Morocco, Thailand or Central America, but generally she was still wearing the New Look dress and the few other things she had bought for her first trip to the United States.

This sort of gossip was nothing, however, to the deeply wounding rumors about Sartre's behavior during the war which began to circulate with increasing frequency and which grew more damning with each retelling. Some of the most hurtful concerned his lack of any solid Resistance credentials and his continuing publication and production during the occupation. He was the "High Priest of Existentialism," a philosophy variously associated with excesses of every kind by Sartre's detractors, and it became almost taken for granted among certain political and intellectual coteries in Paris that he had behaved badly during the war as well. Naturally his "High Priestess" was guilty by association.

It was primarily because of this that Beauvoir and Sartre began to hide out in Madame Morel's Paris apartment and spent so many evenings sequestered in Beauvoir's hotel room. She commented on this in 1983: "We always lived our lives in public view, so we were able to withstand much more criticism than others who had not been subjected to such scrutiny for as long as we had been. Everyone thought we lived so quietly in 1947–1948 because we were afraid of all the threats that were made after the de

Gaulle broadcast and because we were so friendly with Rousset. Granted, these concerned us, but not to the extent of making us change the way we lived. Two things really were important then. The first was that Sartre was writing, writing, always writing, and he needed to be alone to think and write. I was not yet writing *The Second Sex*, but I was thinking about it, getting ready to write it, so I too needed quiet. And of course the other, what really hurt, was—well, it hurt to know that people hated us so much that to inflict the most pain they made unfounded accusations about the war. There was nothing we could do to disprove such viciousness. So we just carried on, and, as we always did when something threatened, Sartre and I relied upon each other."[23]

It did not help their general state of affairs to find themselves quarreling with those who professed to be their friends and political allies. Arthur Koestler's name appears frequently in Beauvoir's letters to Algren in this regard. She recommended two of his books, *The Spanish Testament* and *Darkness at Noon*, but criticized Koestler's obsessive anti-Communism, which allowed him to "support the conservatives and approve Bevin's policy and *Partisan Review*."[24] She makes frequent references to drunken encounters when Koestler cornered Sartre and harangued him for differing political views. On the eve of Koestler's departure for England, he announced that he was "100 percent Gaullist" and therefore could never be Beauvoir's and Sartre's friend again. But the next time Beauvoir saw Koestler, despite the fact that he was with his wife, he "tried to begin something again." She told him firmly that she was not interested in sleeping with any other man now that she had met Algren, so Koestler shrugged and moved the conversation along into other, safer areas of discussion. Beauvoir had already told Algren about her brief encounter with Koestler, that she had spent one night with him, "uncomfortably," because he spent most of it nattering on about politics, accusing her of not being "anti-Communist enough." She was relieved when he left for England, vowing not to return to France for a very long time and never to seek her company and Sartre's again.[25]

Before he left, however, he had been a major player in several unfriendly encounters involving Camus, toward whom Beauvoir had softened somewhat: "When [Camus] is unhappy with his writing he is arrogant, but when he is happy and successful, as he is now, he is modest and friendly."[26] Camus's wife, Francine, gave several dinner parties at their apartment, which Beauvoir thought were very dull until Koestler began "arguing and quarreling with Sartre."[27] Camus also disagreed frequently and vocally with Sartre, which upset Beauvoir because she still wanted him to behave as if he were a disciple even though it had been apparent almost since the time they met that Camus was his own man and held many strongly differing views. Beauvoir reflected on these relationships in 1985:

"When I recall these times, the violent quarreling and excessive drinking, all the argument and deep disagreement on important issues, I don't see how I managed to avoid the knowledge that soon our friendship with

Camus would have to end, just as we had ended our superficial friendship with Koestler. It was different, I suppose, with Camus because both Sartre and I wanted him to remain in solidarity with us; whereas with Koestler it was different from the first because we were always on guard against his opposing views. Despite all our differences, Camus was honest and therefore trustworthy; Koestler was never politically honest, because his anti-Communism made him irrational, maybe even insane. We could find no common, peaceful accord with him in anything."

So political differences consumed more and more of Sartre's energy, leaving Beauvoir to follow in his wake or be left behind entirely. She had little else to do of her own. Extracts from *America Day by Day* were finished and ready to be published in *Les Temps Modernes* starting in January 1948. As for the magazine itself, Merleau-Ponty had taken over its day-to-day operations while Beauvoir was in America, and he kept on after her return because she was too distracted to do it again, so her only ongoing duty was to evaluate submissions. This was not an insignificant task, but still it left her with much more free time than she had had before. Nagel, Sartre's Swiss publisher, was planning to issue several of her magazine essays as a book entitled *L'Existentialisme et la sagesse des nations* (*Existentialism and the Wisdom of Nations*), so she had a brief flurry of editorial activity to get the texts ready. But, for the most part, her life at the end of 1947 and the beginning of 1948 consisted of following Sartre from meeting to meeting and keeping up their contacts with old friends and the Family.

Although this was the period in Sartre's life when he became heavily involved in political activity, it is difficult to find any overtly political commentary within Beauvoir's writing that pertains to her thoughts and opinions other than to explain his.[28] "Since [World War II], I have never ceased to be involved," is how she described herself before adding pointedly, "But I have never been militant."

She made "good use of the language of politics" throughout her life, especially in her later, feminist pronouncements, but said that until 1970 her life had been dominated "by two concerns: my commitment to Sartre and to my writing." She explained this by saying that she had allied her public expression with his as he went from being a writer with purely literary concerns to a philosopher who believed in writing as the logical and legitimate expression of political commitment. When he became a political activist, she was content to be at his side, content with the role of follower, saying, "I did not desire to play even the smallest political role, so that for me to read the same books as Sartre and to meditate upon the same themes would have been a gratuitous activity."[29] She kept her political opinions to herself, mostly because no one (and this included Sartre) asked for them. In 1949, when Sartre was a constant presence at political rallies, she noted with asperity: *"For once I gave him a piece of political advice: not to go."*[30]

She must not have been as silent as she thought. Raymond Aron was one among many who criticized her, saying she could be compared to "a blind person who would not hesitate to discuss painting; she was simply demonstrating in her writings her ignorance of politics."[31] But now that several decades of history's dust have settled, and the complex relationship of Sartre and Aron has been studied at some length, it seems likely that Aron's comment was more likely meant for Sartre than for Beauvoir. It was during the years from 1947 to 1960, when she published the works which solidified her reputation as a major thinker and writer and the myth of the professional couple became hardened fact, that an interesting dichotomy emerged. While Sartre turned from literature and wrote feverishly to espouse social causes and explain his political positions vis-à-vis his philosophy, Beauvoir's attention turned in a different direction: toward herself, and an examination of her place in society.

While political theory grew more fascinating to him, it was never quite enough to satisfy her questing mind. When he turned to political action, she ruled it out for two reasons: she realized that because she was a woman no one would take her views seriously; even more important, she was too shy and awkward to speak in public. If she was to have a role in public life at all, it would have to be in some supporting role under Sartre, but she was distressed by his lack of success in influencing the course of French politics.

Trying to sort out her feelings about Algren and the role he should play in her life caused her to think about herself and Sartre and all that had happened to them since the end of the war. She was a disheartened woman at the end of 1947 when she realized that the euphoria of the Liberation had not brought any lasting social change in France, and that the excitement of "the Year Zero," as 1945 was so hopefully dubbed, had given way to "business as usual." All around her she saw former collaborationists being rehabilitated daily. She heard anti-Semitic remarks treated as jokes. People she had formerly considered to be allied with her in their dislike of General de Gaulle were now openly supporting him. What bothered her most of all, however, was how Sartre was openly scorned, mocked and sometimes even threatened. As a writer he reached ever-increasing audiences, but his active political influence was minuscule in comparison. He kept at it, however, she told Algren, "because others expect him to be [political]—he'd be just as happy living by a blue lagoon, laughing."[32] She recalled later, "Sometimes I said [to Sartre], 'Why bother, when no one cares?,' but he continued to fight for what he believed. I believed as he did, but I had no stomach, no energy, for his fight! This was a confusing time for me, and I needed to sort some things out. I had to move away from politics and find out what they were."[33]

As always, her method of analyzing herself was to write about it. By the end of November, she was preparing to do so. She signed the contracts for her "book about America and the collection of the *Temps Modernes* articles," had overseen the translation of Algren's "Letter from Chicago," and along with Sartre had prerecorded several radio broadcasts before going to Madame Morel's country house.[34] There was nothing now that stood between her and the examination of herself.

"Can you send me a copy of [Alva] Myrdal's *Nation and Family?*" she asked Algren. He had already sent her Gunnar Myrdal's *An American Dilemma,* a book she liked and one which turned out to have a far-reaching effect on her future writing.

"I am thinking again about a book on women's situation which I started before," she told him. "I would like to write a book about women as important as [Myrdal's] is about blacks."[35]

TWENTY-SEVEN

The Crocodile
Is the Frog's Destiny

ALGREN FILLED a very important role in Beauvoir's life, that of mentor for all things American, especially the political and social history of the United States. In almost every letter, he recommended books that he particularly liked and wanted her to share. He also sent her comic books, which he adored for their humor and fantasy. As she had a limited sense of humor and no liking for nonreality, she used comic books as a source for intellectual comparisons about many things, including gender roles that Americans expected their heroes to play. She found comic books to be excellent illustrations, for example, of the concept of *dédoublement*, or "doubling": "The hero and the average man are the same—Clark Kent is also Superman."[1]

Sometimes, as with the books by the two Myrdals, Algren managed to select works which she found both interesting and directly applicable to her own writing and thinking. At other times she disagreed strongly with his recommendation and could not resist expounding on it at length in her letters. She read Mark A. Aldanov's *The Fifth Seal* because Algren reviewed it favorably for an American journal, and found it "unsatisfying, but interesting in parts." She read "some little novels by Carson McCullers" and "liked them in spite of their femininity." Algren liked Edith Wharton almost as much as he liked Henry James, and for Christmas he sent her Wharton's *Ethan Frome* in the edition with an introduction by Bernard De Voto.[2] She agreed with De Voto's opinion of the ending, but liked "the body of the book more than he does. The love between Ethan and Mattie is expressed very well in its ordinary setting." She concluded that the book reminded her of Thomas Hardy's novels, but "without Hardy's intense sympathy for his characters."

She read O. Henry's *The Four Million* ("sometimes heavy, sometimes funny, always American"); she reread Thoreau's *Walden* in French ("I do not like narrow-minded Thoreau, but I like the nature he talks about").

365

The Ox-Bow Incident "seems as good as the movie." While reading John Dos Passos's *Number One*, she became "so terribly homesick for America" that she got drunk on cider to "avoid missing scotch-and-soda."[3] She also liked the fact that they disagreed sometimes "so strongly" about books and movies, because "challenging each other" made their relationship "more exciting."

"After all," she teased, "we must consider the sex-struggle, freedom in love, and all those other progressive ideas."

"I continue to learn about my husband's culture," she wrote from Madame Morel's, "although he will not learn anything about his French frog-wife's country."[4] That, she remonstrated playfully, was all she disliked about him now that he had stopped wearing suspenders.[5] Apparently Algren was making a serious effort to change many of his habits and attitudes, because her letters often insist that she loved him as he was. She told him she felt "humiliated being such an adoring wife, finding nothing to disagree with. If it's true that men despise women who worship them, then I am on the wrong track. How come you get to be the big crocodile and I am just the little frog?"[6]

By way of reply, he sent her "Seven Good Frog Commandments," in a letter that made her "so excited by his love" that she could neither sleep nor work, but only daydream of him. She, his "faithful frog, loves her crocodile very deeply."[7]

Much of their correspondence during this time was loving and playful, but beneath the teasing lay the concerns which were coalescing in her mind and preoccupying her more and more, particularly the role of the female in a heterosexual relationship. She contrasted the two men she loved, her place in each of their lives, and the two societies in which they lived and in which she now had to function because of them. Coupled with her own firsthand observations of women in the United States and France, the idea of studying the condition of women grew slowly and steadily more appealing. All she needed was time in which to do it, but large periods of uninterrupted time were very hard to come by.

In mid-November 1947, she and Sartre hurriedly recorded five radio broadcasts so that they would not have to return to Paris during the month they planned to spend at La Pouèze. She planned to direct her reading toward a study of women, asked Algren to send a list of books he thought she should read, and went off to Brentano's to buy some others, planning to borrow the rest from Madame Morel's library. During their stay, Sartre received the news that the new government had "fired" them and that their radio broadcasts were canceled. "As Job said, God—as Ramadier—gives, and God—as Schuman—takes away," Beauvoir wrote. Sartre was both upset and disgusted, but she didn't care, thinking she would be "better off writing only for myself."[8]

The one friend who would understand what she wanted to do was Giacometti, and before they went to Madame Morel's she made a visit to "my friend [Alberto] Giacometti's atelier; he is really the only person we [she and Sartre] ever see with pleasure." She described Giacometti at length for Algren, saying she had used him as a partial model for Jean Blomart in *The Blood of Others* because she admired not only his sculpture but also "his honest patient way of working." Of Annette, the woman who became his wife, Beauvoir wrote, "His girlfriend, who left her family to be with him, has no winter coat. I like her very much."[9] Being with the Giacomettis did refresh her, although she did not actually begin to write. She continued to evade the actuality of writing, as if she still needed to prepare herself for it.

When they were settled in at La Pouèze, she wrote to Algren at length to describe the place and its people, as if by doing so she could bring him closer to her.[10] She, Sartre and Madame Morel all had rooms on the second floor of the house. Sartre's was large, so Beauvoir often took her work there and the two of them read or wrote in companionable silence. On most days, she didn't even bother to dress, but spent the day in her robe and slippers. There was no need for anyone to go downstairs, because the cook and the maid (who lived in cellar rooms off the kitchen) brought all their meals to Madame Morel's room on trays. Monsieur Morel had been a recluse for almost twenty years: "I never saw him in my life and Sartre, last time 15 years [ago]." Only Madame Morel was permitted into the room of her "sick neurotic husband." Now she was ill herself and spent most of her time in bed, so the only footsteps were the old servant's as she moved from one sickbed to the other carrying messages between the ailing couple. Occasionally, the "tiny sound of call" was heard, and Madame Morel would have to leave her bed to soothe her husband's irrational fears as he lay smothered under piles of blankets, his bed shrouded in heavy drapes, his room in total darkness. Still, Beauvoir loved La Pouèze: "What is pleasant, everybody does exactly what he likes and does not speak to others if he does not choose."

Besides writing of life at La Pouèze, she confided the embarrassing details of her family history to Algren, trying to make him understand the way of life she had chosen for herself. She told him she especially liked staying at Madame Morel's because she had never had a home of her own except when she lived with her parents and her sister in a "tiny, dirty, sad flat" which she hated. The only times she remembered with pleasure were the afternoons alone, reading "forbidden books like those of Musset and Victor Hugo." One thing she knew from a very early age was that she did not want "a housewife's life" like that of her mother, and she gave that as her reason for choosing to live in hotels since becoming a teacher. But now she felt at home in Algren's flat and she had always loved Madame Morel's house, so her days passed "comfortably eating apple pancakes and reading, writing and talking."

She spent Christmas Eve and Christmas Day "almost alone." Madame Morel, her daughter and her granddaughter went off to midnight Mass, and Sartre went to Paris to spend the holiday with his mother. He returned the next day, bringing several books Algren had suggested she read, among them poems by e. e. cummings and fiction by Katherine Anne Porter.[11] When she reread Faulkner's *Pylon* she could not help contrasting him with Algren: "Faulkner is too tragic—everything is as pathetic as the next thing—whereas [in Algren's books] one sees that life is tragic and not tragic at the same time"—which was what she liked best about them. Even so, she had to admit that "one ends up believing in [Faulkner's] tragedy."[12] Algren, knowing how much she liked Myrdal's *An American Dilemma*, sent her a collection of essays called *What the Negro Wants*, but she was "disappointed" with it, especially the introduction, so "curiously stupid and prejudiced."[13] She was also reading André Maurois's *History of the United States*, and was "irritated by his prejudice" against capitalist democracy. She also felt "smug about knowing more than he does on some topics.[14]

By January 2, 1948, *America Day by Day* was finished, as was her sojourn in the country.[15] She sent the manuscript to her typist and planned not to make any further revisions until she could read the typescript. Despite the simplicity of its reportorial style, she had already revised the book so extensively that she blamed all the rewriting for damaging the shiny red pen Algren had given her. Of his other gift, the silver ring, she told him it was fine except that her skin beneath it was turning "white and dead-looking." Although she insisted she was "happy in his love," she questioned whether the ring might symbolize "the way of love—real love is not quite healthy."

She was sorry to have to return to Paris, because it meant that "working, reading, relaxing, at [her own] pace"[16] would end, and she was anxious to keep all her attention centered on the "book about women." She had spent the first two days of the new year drawing up an outline and was "excited about this book," claiming she had never encountered difficulties with being a woman, "as so many women around me do," but was looking forward to "studying and analyzing, as I have not done since I was a student." She was so engrossed in thinking about it that in her sleep at night she even dreamed about some of the famous women she later wrote about.

She was in an introspective mood, and her letters reflect both looking forward to the book to come and looking back at her own life and what she herself had become. January 9 was her fortieth birthday, and she did not feel like celebrating. Having returned to Paris, she found the weather cold and gray, her room damp and chilly, and herself missing Algren desperately. She began her first letter by telling him that she got up early each morning and tried to sneak off to the library before anyone could engage her in something she did not want to do. This routine brought back memories of when she was twenty, studying for her last and most difficult examination. She told him how she had spent the hours from 9 A.M. to 6 P.M. studying, with only a break for bread and sausage carried from home, which she ate alone in a little park nearby, too ashamed to let other students see that she had no money for a restaurant lunch. She described herself as "a serious student who never flirted with men, poorly dressed, wearing no makeup."[17] The only brightness in her day came when her "Ukrainian girlfriend," Stépha, interrupted the dreary routine. At day's end, how she hated to go home to her parents' "ugly flat." All she wanted then was to be "free and alone."

"Today I turned forty," she wrote, "twice as old as I was in those days. I am ashamed of it, and I wish I could offer you a younger girl's love." The year before, age hadn't bothered her at all. She had stopped thinking about aging, having accepted its inevitability, but now, because of her love for him, she thought and worried about it a great deal.

For the first four months of 1948, her letters to Algren recounted the details of her daily life as fully as any diary she might have kept. She continued to regale him with accounts of the lives of people he had not yet met, as if by being made to share their histories he was sharing the fabric of her life. It worked, because his letters offered suggestions about what she might do to further her own work and how best to cope with everyone's problems. They discussed Olga, who was still very ill with tuberculosis and who Beauvoir thought might die; Bost was very discouraged and they were both depressed. Algren suggested that Beauvoir tell Olga she had no choice but to enter a sanatorium for treatment, then to help Bost find a writing commission that would keep him too busy to brood. Bianca had begun psychiatric therapy but insisted that she could get better only if Beauvoir returned her "passion" (for she had decided that her unhappiness stemmed from unresolved lesbian attraction); Beauvoir and Algren agreed on what she should do in this case: order Bianca to recover without it or go away (she recovered and stayed). Beauvoir continued to avoid any situation where Violette Leduc might find an opportunity to confess her love. This drove Leduc to new heights of emotional frustration, including a halfhearted attempt to throw herself in front of a truck. Algren was worried about her stability and told Beauvoir not to see her anymore, but Beauvoir was confident that she could handle Leduc by pretending to believe that someone else was the object of the poor woman's passion. There was a parade of visiting Americans, all writers, editors and journalists, whom she usually described in less-than-flattering terms, "pansy" and "fairy" being two of her favorites no matter what the sexuality of the person may have been.[18] Her sister and brother-in-law had come back from Belgrade and were now living near Paris. She saw them both occasionally and sometimes told Algren stories of the childhood they recollected when they were two sisters alone together, as they had so often been within the family.

And there was Koestler, back from England, more abusive than ever.[19] One night, after persuading Beauvoir, Sartre and Camus to dine with him in his favorite Russian restaurant, he got so drunk that he threw a glass at Sartre and gave Camus a black eye. Camus departed in a rage, but Koestler and Sartre fell into a gutter outside the restaurant, where they were both "robbed of a lot of money." Beauvoir was depressed by the encounter and did not cheer up until several days later, when she and Sartre took Madame Morel's fifteen-year-old granddaughter out to celebrate her birthday. Camus joined them and made Beauvoir laugh with the sunglasses he wore to hide his black eye. A week later, when she was enduring a lugubrious dinner with Leduc, Koestler interrupted rudely, baiting her with insinuations that Sartre was courting the favor of right-wing political groups. Furious, she grabbed Leduc and left. Algren was concerned that Koestler managed to upset Beauvoir each time they met, and advised her to treat him coldly from then on. The next time she saw him, she did as Algren instructed.

"He is a disgusting bit of trash," she wrote. Koestler, worried about events in Czechoslovakia, feared that he would not be safe with either the Russians or the Americans in the event of armed conflict. She described Koestler's cowardice to Richard and Ellen Wright, and Richard told her to ignore him because he could not help himself from still "thinking like a Communist. It seems Koestler is remorseful about leaving the Communists only because the Communists will win and he wants to be on the winning team." Tempering politics with affection, she told Algren that the Wrights were "more lively than French intellectuals, and if I could cook like Ellen, you would love me until we were one hundred years old."

She was much in the theater now, because Sartre was beginning rehearsals of a new play, Les Mains sales (Dirty Hands) and because he considered her "a good advisor."[20] He wrote the play for Olga, who had recovered and was, as always, impatient for it to be finished. "I could never work that way," Beauvoir said, "writing on demand for strict deadlines."[21] There were problems with this production, and Sartre had hired a new director, Jean Cocteau, "a likeable poet, pansy and movie director." Beauvoir thought it "unusual because . . . playwrights are usually so jealous they would never dream of coming to another's assistance."[22]

Algren was understandably curious about her relationship with Sartre and every now and again could not help questioning her about it. When Beauvoir told him about Sartre's trials in casting the play, Algren tried to soften his desire to know what they meant to each other by commenting that "funny things always happen to Sartre." Beauvoir agreed: "It's because he never takes anything, least of all himself, seriously. You will like him very much: he is always laughing, a good hearty man as well as a brilliantly talented one. No, I do not belong to Sartre, but we have helped each other all our lives."[23] It was probably the most accurate as well as the most tender assessment of what they had become for each other and why their relationship endured.

Her most visible commitment to Sartre at this time was centered around his continuing political involvement with David Rousset. A manifesto "they" (implying both of them but in reality only Sartre) wrote with Camus and Rousset "failed, and everything seems hopeless."[24] Beauvoir attended a meeting on March 12, with "more than a thousand people," and a second on March 16, with "more than 4,000 present . . . Sartre and Rousset spoke and garnered much support, although it may not do much good." She described herself as "completely immersed in politics, whether I like it or not, and I don't."[25]

Sartre's activities and the needs of her friends all conspired to keep her from the two things that meant the most to her during the early months of 1948: determining her itinerary for the trip she planned to take with Algren in the summer, and writing *The Second Sex*. Her letters are full of details for travel plans that constantly changed, but her comments about the book that became *The Second Sex* are offhanded and occasional. Although she worked on it during this period, it seems to have been something she tried to fit in during spare moments. It was as if, feeling that she must justify herself by writing something, she wrote sporadically on "the book about women" more as a self-imposed exercise than as a book whose message she espoused and wished to convey to the reading public, or even as an interesting research project. The passion and commitment she later felt toward this work did not begin until after she returned from her next sojourn with Algren.

They had agreed to spend at least four months together in 1948, part of the time in Chicago and the rest traveling somewhere in the Americas after taking a vintage paddlewheel steamboat down the Ohio and Mississippi Rivers from Cincinnati to New Orleans. He proposed that they celebrate the day he put the silver ring on her finger, their "first anniversary, May 10th, with a honeymoon on this boat" no matter what else they decided to do during her time in the United States. She was thrilled with the romance of it and agreed at once, then devoted herself to planning the rest of the trip. Friends who had been to Cuba told her she must go there, others touted the West Indies, and still others praised Mexico and Guatemala.[26] At first she planned to sail to New York, and Sartre thought he might make the voyage with her to spend some time with Dolores, but his schedule changed constantly and so, too, did their travel plans, so that every letter offered a different possibility.

She posted a large map of the Western Hemisphere on her bedroom wall, collected brochures from travel agents, went to the library to read guidebooks, and actually contacted a curator at the ethnographic section of the Natural History Museum in Paris for advice about what they should see. Richard Wright insisted that she go to Mexico and stop in Mérida, a village in the Yucatán he particularly liked; Maheu, who had just returned from a UNESCO conference in Latin America, urged her to take a boat to Veracruz and then a train across the mountains to Mexico City. Everyone had someplace different that she "must not miss," so her letters continued to suggest a profusion of possibilities to complement their "Mississippi honeymoon."[27]

Gradually, however, "the book about women" began to fill her thoughts as well, and Beauvoir was torn between wanting to be with Algren and wanting to keep on with her research. "Of all my books," she recalled in 1982, "that was truly the easiest to write, especially in the beginning. The material just seemed to arrange itself naturally into patterns of analysis." Although she read English well, it was still easier to work in her native language in libraries where she was familiar with the holdings. Also, despite her insistence that politics bored her, Sartre still depended on her as his primary critic and editor, and she took that responsibility seriously.

For all these reasons, she decided that she could not possibly spend May through September in the United States, but would stay only until July. To cushion Algren's disappointment, she said she would return for a second visit because Sartre and Camus had decided to present their "third option for France" as a series of American lectures starting in October and possibly lasting until the New Year. That plan also changed almost as soon as it was proposed. In the one that followed, she would go to Chicago on May 8 or 10 and two months later would meet Sartre and Camus, traveling with them as they lectured in South America (they had given up on the United States as a possible forum). She would then return to Chicago for another month before flying back to Paris in time for the New Year. It was all very complicated.

In her memoirs, written long after she and Algren parted, Beauvoir presented a slanted account of this trip.[28] By the early 1960s the myth of the couple was the dominant, paramount entity of her life, and she constructed the entire book with that in mind. In this particular instance, she omitted the fervor with which she looked forward to the trip and deliberately undermined her deliriously happy rapport with Algren to make it correspond with Sartre's uneasiness about his continuing troubles with Dolores, who had decided not to stay with him in Paris while Beauvoir was away.

Her trip with Algren was one of the happiest of both their lives.[29] They planned every detail together, from money to the itinerary. Nagel had promised that $1,000 from American royalties would be waiting for her in New York. She then worked out complicated spending formulas, based on Maheu's calculations of what he had spent on a recent trip there.

"You'll be receiving $250 for an article I wrote for a *Time-Life* magazine which was never issued, you must not fritter it away but must save it for our trip," she commanded Algren. Also, her zest for seeing all the sights, her desire to miss nothing, took over: "Find out how to get to Vera Cruz from New Orleans . . . We should split up the planning—you can plan the nights and I'll obey you, and I will plan the days and you must obey me." She usually softened her peremptory tone by assuring him that "The crocodile is the frog's destiny," and that she kept busy obeying his seven Frog Commandments.[30]

In early February she went with Sartre to Berlin for the opening of his play *The Flies*.[31] She complained to Algren of meeting "lots of stupid, wicked people . . . an elegant crowd of Allied occupation officials" who "disgusted" her. She and Sartre did not like the production of the play, and were appalled by the devastation of the city, but the visit ended happily when they pretended they were leaving several days earlier than they actually did and spent the rest of their time prowling around Berlin trying to find places they had visited before the war.

Back in Paris, she wrote to her "Darling, dearest Mexico husband," presenting to him the route they later followed, including precise details about climate and sites. From New Orleans she thought they should go to Mérida, touring the ruins in the Yucatán, then on to Guatemala, Oaxaca, Veracruz, Fortín and Mexico City. She confirmed plane reservations for early May, first to New York and then three days later to Chicago.

She needed the time in New York to consult Stépha Gerassi on a matter about which she was confused: birth control. She first broached the subject shyly to Algren:

> Honey, there is something I wanted to speak about. I am just a little afraid you'll laugh at me. Well, you are my husband we have to discuss some wife and husband matters. So I'll write it, though I don't like to do so.[32]

On their previous stay together she had told him

> not to take care of anything, and [I] did not care either. If I had caught a baby, I should have gone to some surgeon and it would have been quickly fixed up.

She was worried now because they were planning to spend several months in foreign countries and "it would be terrible if anything happened—it must not have a single chance of happening." Up until now, she told him, she had always asked the men to take "care of the thing, and as they were few of them and always reliable and friendly, they always did and there was no problem for me."

She urged Algren to tell her what to do:

> I don't like the idea of the woman rushing to the bathroom after love, but there are better ways, I heard . . . but here in this old country we don't really know your fine new ways. So maybe you could tell me what's the best to do. Who can, if not you? . . . Do you think I'm silly, Honey? . . . I don't want any chance to be trapped by a baby . . . I'll do exactly what you'll decide—just don't choose the most unpleasant [means] for you.

Algren insisted that he would be "a cautious crocodile" and offered to use either of the traditional male methods of contraception, premature withdrawal or condoms. Both were unthinkable to her, because she wanted him to be "free as free can be." She was touched, she said, but "caution has no place in our life or in our bed." She would "see what I can manage in New York."[33]

That settled, she and Sartre went off to the Riviera village of Rama-teulle, in Var, for two weeks to recuperate from the frenetic pace of their lives. For three nights in a row before they left Paris she did not go to bed, but only napped in the theater during the last rehearsals of *Dirty Hands*. When the play opened, there were several nights of nonstop festivity with "a lot of unpleasant society and theatre people bragging about themselves."

Beauvoir, in one of the few instances in her life, resorted to "benzedrine for days, to keep myself awake."[34] She had also had extensive dentistry during this time, at last replacing the tooth she knocked out during the war. She did it not because she was in pain, but because she wanted to improve her looks for Algren. She was spending long days in various libraries doing research for her book, and, as always, was handling many of the arrangements and details of Sartre's life as well as all of her own. Everything conspired to make her "depressed and anxious and aching and crying" about Algren. She was "nervous" about seeing him again.

Fifteen years before, on one of her relentless hikes when she lived in Marseille, she had found the village of Ramateulle and had vowed that she would return to spend time there. "My famous stubbornness is paying off again," she told Algren as she described the beauty and tranquility she found in the small hotel with the beautiful garden. She spent her mornings writing and, because Ramateulle is two miles inland, walked each afternoon to villages that overlooked the water.

In the evenings she read herself to sleep, sharing her thoughts with Algren, who had recommended most of the books to her. Duff Cooper's *David* was interesting, while Koestler's latest, *Thieves in the Night,* was "interesting but weak." She finished Truman Capote's *Other Voices, Other Rooms,* but did not like it as much as Algren did. Langston Hughes's *Not Without Laughter* "could not compare to Richard Wright's *Black Boy.*" She recommended George Du Maurier's *Peter Ibbetson,* saying Algren would like it, "especially the part about dreams."[35]

She sent a short note saying she would show him this beautiful village, either the next year or some year after, "since we will love each other until we die."

On May 4, she sent a telegram telling Algren she was flying to New York that night and would phone him the next morning. She sent "impatient love." Her main task in New York was soon accomplished: Stépha Gerassi took her to a woman physician who spoke fluent French, knew both Beauvoir's and Sartre's writing, and thanked Stépha profusely for bringing her such a distinguished patient. After she was fitted for the diaphragm, Beauvoir suggested a walk, and the two old friends, having started at Seventy-eighth Street, suddenly discovered they had walked in the opposite direction from the Gerassi apartment all the way to East One Hundredth Street.

"She was telling me about Algren, and what she felt for him," Mrs. Gerassi recalled. "She lost track of everything when she spoke of him, and I was so astonished to hear her talk about a man other than Sartre like this that I forgot everything, too." Beauvoir was all set to walk the fifty-some blocks back to the Gerassi apartment, but Stépha persuaded her to take a taxi despite her protestations that she had to save all her money for Mexico.

Four days later she was in Chicago. She and Algren decided to keep a diary in a cheap notebook of lined paper. On each page there is an account of the day just passed in both Algren's and Beauvoir's handwriting. She writes in spidery black ink; he wrote in pencil first, sometime later retracing his comments in blue ink. The entries are brief notations of whom they saw, where they went, what they did or what they ate or drank. Each entry is loving, teasing, sweet and charming, and entirely contradictory to Beauvoir's account of this trip in her memoirs. Throughout their travels, their passion deepened but so, too, did their commitment to each other. Reading the diary, contrasting it with her memoirs and his later, bitter denunciations, only makes this a more poignant record of their inability to reconcile their eventual differences.

On Saturday, May 8, she wrote:

Arrival in Wabansia at midnight. Greeted in the alley while trying to run away by a representant [sic] of Nelson Algren . . . the man seemed a little strange—.

He wrote:

Happened upon a strange creature, apparently of foreign extraction, running aimlessly down Wabansia Avenue—took her upstairs with intention of phoning police, but the hour was late and she obviously needed sleep and a warm meal. I am too kind for my own good!

The next day she wrote:

. . . staying home trying to find each other—rainy day—went by street car to see some cats[36]—ate some barbecued chicken with them. Back home, finally found each other. Rain did not stop.

His version describes the people they met, then says, "Everybody squared up when I introduced the little French square."

"Fed the little beast a late evening snack of scotch, sardines & bananas," he wrote several days later. They went to the Guatemalan consulate to make sure their visas were in order and stopped at a local bar called Shangri-La, which led Beauvoir (according to Algren's entry) to offer a disquisition:

. . . the beast explained how Shangri-La wasn't any Shangri-La after all—that we'd be bored to death in such a set-up. What she was trying to say was that its values would lose meaning by lack of contrast: that peace, and art, and high philosophy are meaningful only after the seeker has suffered from lack of peace, art & high philosophy.

By May 13, the day before their departure, she summed up their activities as "bank, traveller's checks, laundries . . . busy day—Fucking— and so on." He joked that

this was the day when I was vacinated [sic] for smallpox without an anesthetic. All I asked the doc for was a dime to put between my teeth. He confessed, later, he had never witnessed quite such courage. While he confessed, I pocketed the dime.

On May 14 they took the train to Cincinnati, where they stayed for two days before boarding the boat to New Orleans. He wrote that "the cab driver agreed . . . that the best thing to do in Cincinati was to get a hotel room and lock oneself in until it was time to leave town. I agreed secretly."

On board the boat, Algren commented on Beauvoir's nervous habit of crumbling bread: people they met at breakfast "were puzzled at the French touch of decorating the table, floor & chairs & wall with bread-crumbs."[37] They stopped in Louisville, Memphis and Natchez before arriving in New Orleans on May 21. One of Algren's comments reads: "This was the night we felt something wonderful and strange was going to happen. And I got drunk in anticipation. Got so I don't know whether it ever really did."

The weather was unbearably humid, especially for a European unaccustomed to such extremes. New Orleans seems to have been a disappointment that neither wanted to admit to the other.[38]

They flew to Mérida and then to Chichén Itzá, where Algren described how Beauvoir

climbed the great temple without figuring how you'd ever get down again. I was glad, to myself, that you'd brought me here. I felt like a discoverer . . . By the end of the afternoon, you were burned, sweating, swollen, tired, thirsty—and quite happy, it seemed.

Algren kept his sense of wonder throughout the Yucatán:

Finally saw the wonderful ruins of Uxmal. Didn't even take time to have a cup of coffee, we felt our time was too limited even for that.

They traveled through Mexico by bus, visiting ruins, markets and Spanish churches, keeping such a pace that Algren confided to the diary on June 8: "a hard day for poor dear me." They took a boat to Santiago de Atitlán, where she wrote: "drank oporto near the fire in the evening," and he wrote:

In the evening I told you a long story, but I forget about what. You got tight listening and looked quite lovely, naked by the fire.

At Chichicastenango he wrote: "This was the best place we stayed at." She then wrote: "Nelson *very bad*" and "I was nice." The next day he countered with "You were very bad." They appear to have followed her suggestion that she plan the days while he take care of the nights. "Nelson *very bad*" (her emphasis), she wrote several times in her account, while he commented after an evening when her stomach was upset: "You ordered hot milk and I had to drink it. By breakfast you felt better, so I didn't have *a day* [his emphasis] off after all."

On June 12 they arrived in Mexico City. "Poor me," she wrote, "awfully tired." He said: "You were very sick and altogether comical about it."

They made the Federal District their headquarters, taking excursions to the nearby pyramids at Teotihuacán and the cities of Taxco, Cuernavaca, Cholula and Puebla, where Algren wrote: "The brothels . . . were the nicest I'd ever seen. Have to go back alone someday." They stayed in Mexico City until June 28, because they were both having a very good time. They saw everything from bullfights to the Ballet Folklórico, sampled regional cooking, visited slums and tramped on foot all over the city. They even went to the movies, seeing Danny Kaye in *The Brooklyn Kid* (*El Lechero*). "Fair," Algren called it, while she, who did not appreciate comedy, said nothing.

She was supposed to return to France on July 5, but they both had too many things they wanted to do in New York, so her first stop was the Pan American ticket office, where she changed the date of her return to July 13. Now that they were back in familiar territory, they both had to face the fact that she would soon be leaving. The next few days were busy. The weather was "terribly hot" as she trekked to the dry cleaner and the hairdresser and saw people she had met the year before. He had his own agenda, including luncheons with the anthologist Martha Foley and his agent and friends, as well as getting a much needed infusion of cash from the Theatre Guild. In the evenings they went to movies, the fights or the races. "Bad luck," she wrote after a day at Monmouth, while he said: "Your suggestion we didn't bet the last two dollars. Very good thing. Dinner at the Automat. Very thin fare, 60¢ apiece." They had tickets to *A Streetcar Named Desire* that same night. "Nothing special," Algren commented for both of them.

She introduced him to Stépha and Fernando. He and Stépha "adored each other at once," but "there was to be no friendship" between the two men.[39] One evening when Algren was mellowed by drink, he took Stépha aside and sheepishly whispered his gratitude for her help in getting Beauvoir's diaphragm.

"I could see how much he loved her, Mrs. Gerassi recalled. "He was very sweet around her. He seemed very shy and bashful and tried to be a tough guy, but you could see he adored her. Castor—well, she was like she always was, you know how she always blundered right into everything and how sometimes she didn't understand jokes and was always so serious. But I never saw her with Sartre like the way she was with Algren. I got very scared after I saw them together, because I thought, What's going to happen here? What's going to happen to her and Sartre? How can an American man, a *machiste* like Algren—how can he put up with her coming and going and being with Sartre?"

One other aspect of their relationship struck Mrs. Gerassi: "We always called her 'Castor,' but he never did. He told me that was someone else's name for her, and I knew who he meant—Sartre. No, for him she was always 'Simone,' and he always said it softly, like he was embarrassed to say it. I had the feeling he never called her that in private, that in private he had another name for her, something really tender."

In the last few days, the tension of the parting-to-come caught up with them. On July 11 she wrote of a "poker game until 2 a.m.," while he said:

> You played very well for someone who doesn't know how to play, exhibiting all your weaknesses of character: obstinacy, light headedness, impulsiveness, over-confidence and naivete.

The next day was her last full day in New York:

> Get up at noon. Lunch University restaurant. Simone tour. Gerassi dinner on 3rd Ave. "The Sargent" with Laughlin. Long walk along 3rd Ave. Ratskeller place. Washington Square. Home.

He made no entry at all. On the last page, only she wrote something: "Tuesday—Going away."

This time she caught a taxi alone. He stayed behind in the hotel, hurt and bewildered that she was going back to Paris after all, despite everything they had been to each other during the last two months. She phoned him from the airport, but the call did nothing to cheer either of them.

"So Nelson," she began her first letter from Paris on July 15.

> Once more the cab drove away and I saw your face for the last time, and a little later I heard your voice for the last time, and there was grief in my heart, but in my ears, I felt love (oh darling, darling, beloved *you*, it is hard to write . . .).[40]

She tried to explain her reasons for not staying with him permanently:

> Nelson, I'll have to explain things better one day but you *have* to know that it is not for pleasure or glamour or anything of the kind that I stay. I must stay here. I just *cannot* do anything else. Believe me please, please. (I'll explain one of these days but tonight, just believe me). If by any chance I *could* stay with you, Oh God! I should. . . . The happiness you gave me may be bought by pain and anguish, it was worth it.

She urged him, despite her love, not to feel "tied up" (i.e., tied down).

> When you'll stop loving me, you'll stop, there is nothing I could do to it. When you'll choose not to see me any more, I'll have to agree. No, Nelson, I shall never want from you something important that you don't want. Just, I *hope* you'll still love me for some time, because I love you more than ever, more than I ever loved. Oh, Nelson, how much I do love you!

In the next few days she received his first letter since their parting, and he assured her of his continuing love. "Now I can live again," she replied.

TWENTY-EIGHT

A Book About Women

COLETTE AUDRY was sitting in the Flore one quiet evening in the summer of 1948 when she looked up to see Simone de Beauvoir standing hesitantly next to her table.[1] She was surprised, because although they had remained friendly toward each other their lives had gone in separate directions since they taught together in Rouen. By way of greeting, Beauvoir, "never one to waste words,"[2] said, "You know that book you were always talking about when we were in Rouen? The one about women? Well, I'm the one who's going to write it."[3]

Audry remembers her heartfelt reply: "Fine. Perfect." She said this because to her Beauvoir's statement signified that the friend who had always insisted "her life as a woman was as free and equal as any man's" had probably "encountered some serious obstacle that made her change her mind."

In their conversations in Rouen, the two women had often compared their experiences in life, both of them surprised by how differently they perceived their personal situations. Audry generally chose to interpret her opportunities, choices and responses in the light of politics, her primary interest and activity: "I realized that there were certain points of contact with people which were denied to me because I was a woman. I couldn't vote, for example, and this made me very frustrated. No matter how kindly, how equal, men treated me when I tried to participate in politics, when it came right down to it they had more rights, so they had more power than I did. I think I had been sensitive since my childhood to my lesser status."

Beauvoir chose to interpret her status in the world primarily in terms of her relationship with Sartre, which exasperated Audry, who remembered that "she didn't feel my frustration at all, precisely because she had an egalitarian relationship with a man. It was enough for her, because all Sartre's friends treated her exactly as they treated him. And then, of course, in her family she was trained from the beginning to have a career, so there too she did not suffer the frustration of many women of her class who wanted a career but were prevented from having it by that false comfort, the security of their family's money and position."

The two women spoke frequently of "the lot of women" in Rouen, which usually resulted in Audry expressing her frustration and vowing to write a book that would show women how clearly exploited they were. It was to be "one which would enrage them, inflame them, make them unite to end the injustice in their lives." Beauvoir encouraged her to write it, "probably just to shut me up and get me off my soapbox, because she certainly did not share my radical view of women's situation."

Audry began to keep notes for the book, but soon found herself so immersed in political activity that she had no time for anything else. After a while she lost interest, and it became a sort of joke between the two women on the infrequent occasions when they met. However, it was Sartre rather than Beauvoir who continued to tease Audry about it as the years went by: " 'Still writing the book about women that's going to change the world?' he would ask, and I'd always say, "Just wait, Sartre— if not by me, then surely by someone else.' "

But Beauvoir's initial conception of the book was not the full-scale examination of the sort Colette Audry had envisioned so many years earlier. In her memoirs, Beauvoir said it originated "almost by chance. Wanting to talk about myself, I became aware that to do so I should first have to describe the condition of woman in general."[4] Later she told an interviewer, "One day I wanted to explain myself to myself. I began to reflect all about myself and it struck me with a sort of surprise that the first thing I had to say was 'I am a woman.' "[5] She said she "spent two years" on the actual research and writing, but in actuality it was more like fourteen months: "It was begun in October 1946 and finished in June 1949; but I spent four months of 1947 in America, and America Day by Day kept me busy for six months."[6]

This chronology offers a convenient scaffolding upon which to mount the evolution of both the book's structure and its content, because, as the writing unfolded, the one practically dictated what the other had to be. However, getting to the point where she fully conceived what she intended the book that became The Second Sex to be was a long-drawn-out process, unfocused, and haphazard in the extreme. At various times she envisioned one long essay, then several essays, then a short critical book, then a longer, more inclusive book, and finally, when she was halfway finished with what became the first volume, she knew that, given the exigencies of French publishing, it would probably be large enough to necessitate being printed in two separate volumes.[7]

In the fall of 1946, after she had put the finishing touches to The Ethics of Ambiguity, she thought about turning her attention to a third, more personal philosophical study, a book-length essay suitable for publication in several segments in Les Temps Modernes. She thought it should be a continuation of the previous book and also a "sort of credo" of herself as both woman and Existentialist. However, she was not thinking of autobiography as a possible form; at this point, her impetus was more philosophical than biographical.

As attacks on Sartre by journalists, scholars and politicians mounted, some of the criticism and gossip was also aimed at her, with everything from vicious cartoons depicting her sex life to unflattering appelations such as "La Grande Sartreuse" and "Notre Dame de Sartre."[8] Although she cared little what critics said about her, she did want to defend herself without entering the arena of gossip and insult. She thought to do this by writing an essay in which she could define herself personally (as woman) and philosophically (as Existentialist). She intended to relate both to the system Sartre had constructed in *Being and Nothingness*, which she accepted unquestioningly as her own *raison d'être*. Her primary intention was to construct a work that would confuse and embarrass her detractors by its intelligence and dignity, and would gain converts for Sartre by the lucidity and persuasion of her argument.

Even though this was clearly reasoned, the idea of actually writing it left her with a series of confusing and rapidly shifting emotions. Her original intention was to try to define what it was that made the two of them so united in thought and purpose, but this only made their (to her) obvious differences all the more apparent. It seemed to her that Sartre recreated both himself and his philosophy each time he gave a speech or put his pen to paper, his mind leaping and dazzling as he veered from one subject or idea to the next. Nothing, it seemed, was beyond the realm of his imagination or interpretation as novels, plays, political essays and manifestos poured forth. She, however, remained fixed in her loyalty both to him and to the philosophy he had created during the war years. But since then, all his writing seemed to be designed for specific public issues and political events, some of it disavowing the earlier system, other parts of it contradicting, indicting, disclaiming or, quite the opposite, building upon earlier models. So, for Beauvoir, part of her need to write about herself and Existentialism was for self-discovery, to see whether she needed to modify her rigid adherence to his original theory, or whether she simply needed to express his overall thesis in a manner that the critical public would then better understand and be persuaded to accept.

Like all her other writing, it had a strong autobiographical basis, because in order to defend what she believed were universal pinciples she needed to start from the specific and the individual—in this case, her role within his philosophy. At first the idea made her feel "brave, emboldened." Then she "doubted" that what she might eventually write would have any larger value beyond her own immediate needs. This made her feel "embarrassed by my temerity" and "reluctant to parade myself, on a matter which was to me crucial and therefore intimate, before hostile public scrutiny." But from October 1946 to January 1947, when she left for her first trip to the United States, she got little further than thinking about these issues and making several possible outlines of how she might proceed, since most of her energies went into writings of a more general, editorial nature, usually for the review.

One idea, however, began "to emerge with some insistence, with clarity," from these musings. Whenever she tried to define herself as a French Existentialist who believed in the system proposed by Sartre and who followed his lead unquestioningly, she found herself concentrating specifically on her own role and place within his system. This brought her to "the very profound and astonishing realization" that she was different from Sartre "because he was a man, and I was only a woman." She explained what she meant by "only" in a 1982 conversation:

"I had not yet settled on the idea of woman as the other—that was to come later. I had not yet decided that the lot of woman was inferior to the allotment of men in this life. But somehow I was beginning to formulate the thesis that women had not been given equality in our society, and I must tell you that this was an extremely troubling discovery for me. This is really how I began to be serious about writing about women—when I fully realized the disparity in our lives as compared to men. But make it understood that at the time of which we speak [i.e., fall 1946–early 1947] none of this was clear to me. It was somewhere in my head. Oh, I hate to use that word 'unconscious,' because if you write it feminist women will pounce on me, but I can't think of another, better word, so it will have to do."

Reflecting further, she said that she would have been "surprised and even irritated if, when I was thirty, someone had told me that I would be concerning myself with feminine problems and that my most serious public would be made up of women." Then she added, "I don't regret that it has been so."[9]

In this frame of mind, she began her first tour of colleges and universities throughout the United States and began to think about enlarging the scope of the book further, to a comparative analysis of the situation of women in the United States and France, solidly grounded in the precepts of Existentialism, with careful attention paid "not to Marxism *per se*, but certainly to the politics of the Left."

She told an interviewer for *The New Yorker* that she was going to write "a very serious book about women."

"I've talked to a number of American women," she said, "to get their point of view. I find this differs from that of most French women, but you'll have to wait for my book to find out how, or how I think how. It can't be explained in three words."[10]

Whenever she had the opportunity to converse with women, she asked question upon question about the differences in the two cultures, but everything she asked was couched in the specifics of their individual situations rather than in themselves as representatives of class or culture. In France, she asked every woman she knew to tell the story of her life, intending to use all the case histories.[11] She wrote about it in *The Prime of Life*:

I knew very few women of my own age, and none who led normal married lives. The problems that confronted people like . . .

Colette Audry or me were, as I saw them, individual rather than generic. I began to realize how much I had gone wrong before the war, on so many points, by sticking to abstractions. I now knew that it *did* make a very great difference whether one was Jew or Aryan; but it had not yet dawned on me that such a thing as a specifically feminine "condition" existed. Now, suddenly, I met a large number of women over forty who, in differing circumstances and with various degrees of success, had all undergone one identical experience: they had lived as "dependent persons." Because I was a writer, and in a situation very different from theirs—also, I think, because I was a good listener—they told me a great deal; I began to take stock of the difficulties, deceptive advantages, traps, and manifold obstacles that most women encounter on their path. I also felt how much they were both diminished and enriched by this experience. The problem did not concern me directly, and as yet I attributed comparatively little importance to it; but my interest had been aroused.[12]

Her last comment is the most telling, even though she still insisted that the "problem" had never concerned her "directly" and was of "comparatively little importance"; nevertheless, her interest had been aroused." Initially, it was as a voyeur, in much the same way as it had been throughout her life. She herself was far removed from the concerns of most women: unmarried (but a partner in a stable intellectual relationship with Sartre, and a partner in a satisfying physical relationship with Algren); financially independent (according to her cavalier consideration of Sartre's money as her own); and professionally successful (again, partially through his agency). No wonder she felt removed from the stories people told her. No wonder also that when she compared her life to the lives of other women, she saw similarities that made her realize how much of her success and independence she owed to the fortunate situation that resulted from the choice of her first and most enduring male companion.

What is interesting is why so many people, especially women, poured out the intimate details of their lives for her critical appraisal, because, except for the few people who knew her well, Simone de Beauvoir was not usually considered a sympathetic figure. Indeed, for many who knew her but were not members of the magic, intimate circle of the Family, she was considered "formidable," "distanced," "cold," "arrogant," "superior" or, in the words of a surprising number of French women of her generation, "not like us, different."[13]

Many years later, when Francis Jeanson accused her of having written *The Second Sex* as someone who understood the feminine condition because she herself had escaped it, she agreed with him.[14] Some others were outraged that Beauvoir described women as if she were not one herself. From the first paragraph of her introduction, where she asks

One wonders if women still exist, if *they* will always exist, whether or not it is desirable that *they* should, what place *they* occupy in

this world, what *their* place should be. . . . But first *we* must
ask: what is a woman?[15]

Simone de Beauvoir infuriated readers who believed that she had separated
herself from other women through the deliberate use of third-person pronouns and verb forms. Scholarly ink in many languages and cultures has
been spent on the book, much of it on this paragraph alone and how the
entire work should be interpreted because of it. Throughout her life,
Beauvoir maintained a curious distance from *The Second Sex*, refusing to
respond to criticism or mount a separate defense. The closest she came to
responding was during a 1982 interview: "Women are wrong to accuse me
of separating myself from them. If there is blame, it should be upon language, for we speak in the language of men. It is they [men] who have
given us our verbs and pronouns, and we [women] who must do the best
we can with them."[16]

When she first came to the United States, in 1947, piqued by the
stories French women had already told her, she began to ask questions for
what she thought would become a long article about the contemporary
situation of women in the two different cultures. She asked her questions,
"from Mary Guggenheim to Mary McCarthy, to the many anonymous
Marys" who were students at such diverse women's colleges as Vassar,
Sweet Briar and Sophie Newcomb (Tulane). She wanted to know everything about their lives from career goals to contraception, but she used
most of what they told her in *America Day by Day*, not wanting to wait to
use it in "the essay on women." Some of her most outrageous observations
can be found in the prissy and sometimes false descriptions and anecdotes
that infuriated American readers, such as the one containing her comments
about the wardrobes and lifestyles of American working women. When
they read *The Second Sex*, many of the women whose life histories she
listened to so avidly were puzzled by her sympathy and understanding in
that book and the flippant way she denigrated them in the other.

But as she raced through the composition of *America Day by Day*,
her conception of *The Second Sex* changed once more, this time to be
modeled on the first book as a series of independent, purely reportorial
articles. She planned to start with a long satirical article about the typical
American college girl's extreme anti-intellectuality. She was convinced that
American women deliberately hid their intellectual abilities in order to
make themselves eligible candidates for marriage. She, who had always
sought to excel scholastically, was incredulous at the thought of women
deliberately rejecting their "superior, expensive educational training in
order to become good little housewives." But soon she lost interest, wisely
aware that she did not have patience enough to sustain her initial scandalized reaction long enough to write it.

She did no writing at all on "the essay on women I started six months
ago"[17] while she was in the United States, and for the first few weeks after
her return to Paris she was unable to begin again. Nelson Algren had upset

her rigidly ordered world; the happiness she had known with him turned into "depression" as soon as she landed in Paris and realized how long it might be before they were together again. By early June 1947, she was "feeling much better" and thinking about future projects. She had decided the order of what she wanted to write,[18] telling Algren she would postpone "the essay on women" (for she was still not thinking of it as a book) until *America Day by Day* was complete and published, both in *Les Temps Modernes* and as a separate book.

This decision actually had a far-reaching effect upon her, because as soon as she decided not to worry about the "essay" on woman, whatever mental barriers had kept her from both constructive thought and actual writing disappeared. Instead of putting it aside entirely she worked "a few minutes here or there." By the end of August, she had finished "the long chapter on women,"[19] and as she worked steadily on *America Day by Day* all her formerly haphazard ideas coalesced into the form which became her long, serious and sustained examination of the condition of women.

This was another of the recurring periods in her life—perhaps the most important to date—when she needed "to explain myself to myself."[20] Nelson Algren had disturbed her rigidly defined, self-controlled world when he showed her that passion and reason could indeed be present within a single man and offered her the opportunity to be part of the traditional male–female couple she had always scorned as an "impossible contrivance of fools who write romance." Now that she was part of a satisfying relationship with a man, it caused her to question everything about herself except for two things that were so entwined they were impossible to separate. These were her continuing commitment to Existentialism and her insistence on maintaining the successful relationship of the professional couple that she and Sartre had established.

As Sartre's fame increased, his relationships with other women proliferated with varying degrees of intensity and duration, but as long as Beauvoir remained securely enthroned as the one indispensable intellectual companion of his life, his "trusted critic and adviser," she was comfortable with everything else. The primary threat to this happy stasis came from Algren, because he wanted her to live with him permanently in Chicago as his legal wife. Her English was becoming more fluent with each letter she wrote, and he saw no reason why she could not recreate herself as an American writer. If she insisted on writing in French and publishing in France, then he saw no reason why she could not continue to do that as well, because "mails were swift and postage was cheap."

The idea was momentarily tempting because Algren was so seductive, but, even as she flirted with the possibility of life in two countries and writing in two languages, she knew almost from the beginning that it would not work for her. She was a Frenchwoman and, as such, could not leave France. She had been delighted to find that she could work in the United States—she had written parts of *America Day by Day* there—but was wise enough to know that this was a book already well defined by the culture she sought to explain in it, and that the topic practically required that she write much of it in the United States. She knew it was unlikely that future subjects would be so strongly American, and knew it would be impossible to write about France and French subjects from the enormous cultural and physical distance of Chicago.

Still, she could not bear the thought of losing Algren. She knew that he was "a *machiste* man" who would probably grow tired of waiting for the pace of her life at Sartre's side to slacken enough for her annual or semiannual escape to Chicago. Almost from the beginning of their relationship, her letters invited him to take lovers or, if need be, to marry again. But even as she made these offers, she poured out her feelings, describing what he meant to her and what they meant to each other in the same elevated terms she used throughout her memoirs to describe her relationship with Sartre. Clearly, her love for Algren held the same sanctity and pride of place as her pact of contingency with Sartre, but the very difference of the two relationships bred internal confusion in her. What "the essay on women" offered her, then, was a forum in which to analyze herself while creating a work suitable for publication. By extension, it would be suitable for a reading audience which would not know that she herself was the subject under discussion.

The French feminist writer Christine Fauré unknowingly described Beauvoir's intention nonjudgmentally: "As a woman writer, she explicitly takes her own life as a literary object. From memoirs to novels, she thus communicates the sense of her being in the world while continuing to safeguard the intimate and secret part of her experience of life."[21]

Others do not agree with Fauré that Beauvoir succeeded in combining the personal and the universal, among them the British scholar C. B. Radford, who finds her "guilty of painting women in her own colors or of directing women toward her own ideological goals" and faults her for having written "primarily a middle-class document, so distorted by autobiographical influences that the individual problems of the writer herself may assume an exaggerated importance in her discussion of femininity."[22]

She was fortunate that she had never outgrown the love of learning that characterized her student years. She put this zest for research to good use in expanding the study of herself into the study of all women in many different cultures and situations throughout time. "Sexuality and socialization" became Beauvoir's "poles of analysis and reflection"[23] as she interpreted the lost or missing history of women through biology, history, mythology, politics and gender, viewing them all through the filter of philosophy, more specifically Existentialism.

Simone de Beauvoir was conscious of her identity as a writer during these years, especially conscious that, next to Sartre's prodigious output, hers was small and (again, in comparison to his) infrequent. It was important to her that she not waste precious time writing a private document, a closet drama of value only to herself and perhaps of limited interest to some of her friends. She felt an "internal, private pressure" of competition with Sartre, strictly self-created and not in any way fostered by him, so that as far as she was concerned anything she wrote from this time on had to be written for publication. This self-induced pressure contributed to the public introspection that characterized her life and work so strongly for the rest of her writing life. It is also the basis for the autobiographical filtering, analysis and interpretation of the universal experiences of all women through her own.

She decided to divide her research into two parts, and these ultimately became two separate volumes in the French edition and Books One and Two in English translation. Book One is a historical overview of women which she called "Facts and Myths." These she divided further into three separate sections called "Destiny," "History"[24] and "Myths," and these are divided further into individual chapters. In "Destiny" she discussed the condition of women through biology, psychoanalysis and historical materialism. "History" followed women through nomadic societies, as early tillers of the soil, and from the time of the Patriarchs and classical antiquity through the Middle Ages, the Enlightenment, the French Revolution, and the granting of French suffrage in 1947. In the third section, "Myths," she spoke of dreams, fears and idols, followed by the myth of woman as portrayed by five different authors (Montherlant, D. H. Lawrence, Claudel, Breton and Stendhal),[25] concluding with a discussion of "Myth and Reality."

The second volume, or Book Two, is entitled "Women's Life Today." Both contemporary and personal, it too is divided into three parts: "The Formative Years," "Situations," "Justifications" and a conclusion, "Toward Liberation." She writes of childhood, adolescence, maturity and old age, and describes sexual initiation and various expressions of sexuality from Lesbianism to heterosexual marriage. She writes of love in its many forms, from narcissism to mysticism, and in conclusion defines both a way of being and a model for action by women in the future.

The book that resulted has been many things to many readers in the years since it was published, and perhaps the description of it by American writer Elizabeth Hardwick as "madly sensible and brilliantly confused"[26] captures most of them. Hardwick also said that

> to take on this glorious and fantastic book is not like reading at all—from the first sentence to the last one has the sensation of playing some dreadfully exciting and utterly exhausting game. Gasping, straining, remembering, trying to remember, pointing out, denying, agreeing with qualification, the reader collapses at last, still muttering, "yes, but . . ." and "where are we?" What is so unbearably whirling is that the author too goes through this mad effort to include nearly every woman and attitude that have ever existed. There is no difference of opinion, unless it be based upon a fact of which she may be ignorant, she has not thought of also. She makes her own points and all one's objections too, often

in the same sentence. The effort of this thing must have been killing . . . one imagines Simone de Beauvoir at the end may have felt like George Eliot when she said she began *Romola* as a young woman and finished it an old one.

British scholar Terry Keefe called it

> one of the most important and far-reaching books on women ever published . . . unfortunately, her detailed execution of this highly ambitious project leaves a good deal to be desired, for the book cannot be said to be very carefully composed, or even, on the whole, particularly well-written. There is little to criticise in its general structure as such, but none of the seven major parts is satisfactory in its entirety, as each is fairly seriously flawed either in organisation or by the markedly uneven quality of its individual chapters. While almost every section contains some fertile ideas and valuable insights, argument of the highest quality is rarely sustained for long.[27]

Keefe's assessment of the book, both as literature and as polemic, is a fair one; for writing *The Second Sex* gave Beauvoir the professional rejuvenation that Algren gave to her personal life. The friends who knew her well in 1948 marveled at her boundless energy and good spirits. She was a whirlwind of activity, racing to various libraries early each morning to read, writing in the afternoons, keeping up her rigid schedule of appointments until far into the night, and still finding time for intimate conversations with good friends and the Family before ending the day with long, diary-like letters to Algren. She wrote fairly long descriptions of her reading and frequently followed them with cogent criticism. He responded in kind, always ready to discuss her work with her in the fine, critical detail that she was seldom able to elicit from Sartre.

Algren was responsible for a particularly American slant to *The Second Sex*. It was he who first suggested that she conduct her study of women in the light of the experience of black Americans in a prejudicial society, and who first introduced her to the contemporary literature about black Americans, starting with the Myrdal books. Algren also introduced her to his black American friends in Chicago, where she saw for herself what the experience of segregation was like. He presented to her much of the literature of the 1920s and '30s with a strong social and political content, and their letters are full of discussions about James T. Farrell, John O'Hara, John Dos Passos, Frank Conroy, Tess Schlesinger, Meridel Le Sueur and others.

Her interest in American culture and society was further buttressed by her growing friendship with Ellen and Richard Wright. She had already seen firsthand what difficulties an interracial couple faced when she visited the Wrights in New York; when they moved to Paris, she continued her discussions with them there. The comparisons of blacks with women seemed obvious to her, especially the idea that men (more specifically, white men in the United States) had succeeded in relegating both groups to positions of *alterité*, or "otherness." As time passed and the Wrights' marriage grew increasingly troubled, Ellen came to depend on Beauvoir as a trusted sounding board for her marital distress, while Beauvoir came to depend on Ellen for further insights into the problems of women who married outside their culture and society. When Ellen Wright started her own literary agency, Beauvoir became her client, and she remained so for the rest of her life. Beauvoir finally despaired of Richard, saying that his only interest in racial problems had become "limited to his own," and she further politicized his marital situation by saying, "It's funny how all these ex-Communists [Koestler and Silone as well] made wrecks of their marriages."[28] In later years, she admitted that these had served as important models for her opinions about marriage in *The Second Sex*, the section most often faulted for erratic and bizarre observations.

Increasingly, the word "other" became an important part of her vocabulary, so that when friends asked what she was writing she said as frequently as not, "Just something about the other sex." She had no title until she was almost ready to publish it in book form, and then it came from a less-than-lofty conversation with Sartre and Bost during a night of friendly drinking and conversation. In her memoirs, she set the event in her room, but corrected this in 1984, saying they had found themselves late one evening in Montparnasse and decided to pay a sentimental visit to the Falstaff, a bar they had often gone to many years earlier. In the memoirs she wrote: "Sartre, Bost and I spent several hours trying out words. I suggested: *The Other Sex?* No. Bost changed it to *The Second Sex* and when we thought it over, that was exactly right."[29]

To Nelson Algren, she wrote that the book would be called *The Second Sex* "since pansies are called 'the third sex' and that must mean women come in second." Not content with saying it once, she repeated it several letters later in almost the exact same words, very pleased with the in joke from which she, Sartre and Bost had selected her title.[30]

Everything began to coalesce with her decision to define groups of people as "other" in relation to men. The next logical step seemed to be "the need to define what these 'others' were, then to study the historical situations which made such alterity possible in the first place, then to see what were the circumstances that made it legitimate." This was when she began to read history with a special eye to women's role in it and discovered there was none, for generally they were not mentioned at all. She found support for her views in the Frenchman Poulain de la Barre, whom she called "a little-known feminist of the seventeenth century," and who wrote: "All that has been written about women by men should be suspect, for the men are at once judge and party to the lawsuit."[31]

Beauvoir's citation of Poulain to prove her point is only one example of the scope of her research and methodology. It makes the global influence of the book all the more extraordinary when the circumstances of its cre-

ation are considered, that it was written by a Frenchwoman of a specific
social and intellectual background who had very little firsthand knowledge
of previous feminist movements, writings or ideas within France itself to
guide her initial explorations, and almost no knowledge of feminist activity outside her own country.[32] Yet she was able to go unfailingly to the
important documents, sources and writings in many fields, and to synthe-
size all this information within her self-imposed framework of Existential
philosophy.

She was inquisitive about contemporary scholarship and able to incorporate new information from developing disciplines into her own writing, both critically and creatively. Two such instances concern anthropology and psychology, where she was an early practitioner of gender theory
as she attempted to extract and define characteristics common to women
from other studies that only menioned them as the necessary figures in a
larger background. Her former teaching colleague Claude Lévi-Strauss had
just published his influential study of primitive societies, *Les Structures de
la parenté*.[33] She spent several mornings in his laboratories reading and discussing it with him, trying to extract issues, themes and ideas which would
be shared by women in Western society as well. She also went sporadically
to hear Jacques Lacan lecture. Beauvoir had known him since the days of
the wartime fiestas at Zette and Michel Leiris's, but she had never tried to
engage him in any discussion about his work because of her "instinctive
distrust of psychology as a legitimate means of explaining and understanding human conduct and behavior."[34]

Above all, her aim was to examine these and all other systems of inquiry through the philosophical overview of Existentialism. Her theory,
which later became a given in her mind and in the thinking of many writers who followed her dictum, was that all theories of human history and
human relationships were biased because women had been eliminated from
the official record since the beginning of time.

In *The Second Sex* she drew upon earlier feminist writers, among
them Virginia Woolf, to develop her perspective. She shared Woolf's
view of the relationship between economic independence and intellectual
freedom in *A Room of One's Own* (even though she had such a casual attitude about using Sartre's money).[35] She also used the documentation of
women themselves: besides the case histories of women she knew in
France and the United States, she studied, evaluated and formed theories about letters, diaries, personal psychoanalytic histories, autobiographies,
essays and novels.[36]

In one fell swoop, when this book was published in 1949, it changed
the terms in which "the official anti-feminist and feminist discourse have
been carried on in France [since] the Middle Ages":

> Her text does not defend, does not answer previous attacks. Al-
> though she recapitulates them, the center of her study is else-
> where: how does a female baby become or not become a "femi-

nine" woman? The focus of the argument is an analysis of process rather than an enumeration or realignment of categories. It took eight centuries [in France] for this shift to take place.[37]

But, for Beauvoir, "the shift" came easily after she identified her thesis. Asked to describe herself during the writing of the book, she said, "Of course I was very much interested in the topic, but once I had the thesis it was very easy to write and did not take very long. I almost felt like a scribe, knowing full well the task before me and what I must do to accomplish it. Each day I had to put so many words on such and such a subject down onto the page, and finally they all added up to the finished book. It didn't even take two years when you look at it that way. I said many things I deeply believed in, but, in a certain sense, everything I wrote seemed natural to me, obvious: I was only the one who organized and wrote it, everybody already knew it. When I finished it, it didn't seem all that important, certainly not so influential or so lasting. I was much more involved in *L'Invitée, The Mandarins* and my memoirs. I felt all those books much more emotionally than I felt *The Second Sex*."[38]

Since she had thought through so carefully all that she wanted to write about, the actual writing sometimes seemed little more than a daily exercise in which she transferred a portion of her convictions to a certain number of pages. She did feel more like a scribe than a creator. Shortly after extracts from the mythology section were published in *Les Temps Modernes*[39] in the summer of 1948, she wrote about this to Algren, estimating that she had "another year at least"[40] before it would be finished. Publishing the extracts seemed little more than routine, so she was both surprised and delighted by the many angry letters she received and the number of people, especially men, who stopped her on the streets and in cafés to berate her for "exposing . . . men's myths . . . and the phoniness of their romantic poetry about women."

She followed this comment with an unusual reference to her methodology—unusual because she seldom described *how* she approached her subject but concentrated instead on *what* it meant to her in regard to interpreting the lives of women. Here she observed, "Although my work is scientific, it seems to interest many people." When the book was published, Beauvoir's claim for scientific distance and accuracy was held up to ridicule, castigated or denounced more frequently than it was praised, and she herself was often angry whenever her "methodology" was questioned.[41] A letter of the distinguished American historian Mary Beard expresses many of these criticisms:

> I have Simone de Beauvoir's book and I consider it perfectly ridiculous. The persons from whom she quotes are theoreticians. She pretends to knowledge of primitives, to give long history as background, and says that man *made* woman till the fields! She is a most pretentious person. Not profound as the publishers and her translator claims. I can see why he falls for this book—since

she plays up man [and] his sense of the existence of himself as the *One*, and of woman as just the *other*. It's utter nonsense in view of actual long history. But no doubt it will have a big sale, I think. Folly usually does.[42]

Undoubtedly, some criticisms of her methodology and infelicities of style were the result of frequent "cycles of taking wake-up pills and never sleeping."[43] This was highly unlike her, as she was always scolding Sartre for the way he gulped pills by the handful, but it does illustrate how the actual composition of *The Second Sex* was a sheer physical job of transmitting thoughts onto paper. With some of the other books for which she felt emotional involvement—*The Mandarins*, for example—she not only stopped taking all pills (including simple aspirin) but also stopped drinking to keep her head clear for the seven or eight hours of nonstop writing that filled each day.[44] Not so with *The Second Sex*: she swallowed pills, booze and whatever else would give her the energy for another bout of writing.

She went to Algiers with Sartre for several weeks in early September on "mostly a working vacation." It interrupted her writing because she had to "work on the screenplay for *Dirty Hands* in the mornings," leaving her only "afternoons and evenings" for what she had now started to call "my book about women."[45] She was putting her work aside to help Sartre because, as always, his work came before hers, but also because he was paying her a hefty sum of money from the advance which had been given to him. Money was a serious consideration for Beauvoir at this time, because she had made very little from her last several publications and she depended on the stipend Sartre paid for her contribution to *Les Temps Modernes* and whatever other money he may have passed her way. But now that she was so deeply involved with Algren, she had some qualms about taking money from Sartre and it became increasingly important to her to "build a little nest egg" of her own. She saw *The Second Sex* as the way to do it. From the beginning, she sensed that it would be controversial and, as such, would sell well. This only increased her impatience to be finished with it.

It was dragging on, taking too much time. She was "tired of this book" and wanted to write a novel: "I have some ideas, but I still have months of work left." She apologized to Algren for being "so angry and depressed," but said she needed to confide in him because he was her "husband, friend and lover."[46] As the days passed, she found herself—and Bost too, for he had gone with them to Algiers also to help Sartre—working almost entirely on the filmscript to the neglect of her book. She told Algren she was "anxious to get back to work writing about how strange women are, as strange as men,"[47] for, despite her innate distrust of psychology, she was deep into what became the section on psychoanalysis.

The ideas for the novel which became *The Mandarins* were pressing to the forefront of her consciousness, and, although she was exhilarated that she already knew what her next project would be, she was subdued by the knowledge that it too would be "a long job." She continued to plod away, to "work on one book and dream of the next one."[48] She needed a respite because she was "sick of reading mysteries and writing this book"[49] and could not wait to get back to Paris, because "anything" was better than the grinding routine of her work.

Mystery novels were "an acquired taste" for her: Sartre loved them, and had been passing them along to her since their teaching days, when they read them on the train to and from Paris. For a long time they were "the only diversion" she allowed herself while she was writing *The Second Sex*, because "it was the only kind of writing I could trust myself to read that would not lead my thoughts to still another area about women that I would then have to put into the book!"

Once back in Paris, she decided to branch out with her reading for pleasure and went through "a lot of silly books about women,"[50] especially a systematic reading of the novels of D. H. Lawrence. She felt so strongly about them that she decided to make him one of the authors she discussed in depth in the book. She thought they were "especially tedious, telling the same story over and over again about a woman having to surrender herself to a man who looks just like Lawrence." It made her huffy enough to tell Algren that she certainly had never surrendered herself, and "we seem pretty happy." Still, she did not dismiss Lawrence entirely, because "sometimes he writes the simple truth about love." She especially liked the bullfight in *The Plumed Serpent*, but again felt obliged to make a slight disclaimer: "That's not how you or I felt about bullfights!" she wrote, admitting that she much preferred "Lawrence of Arabia to the other Lawrence, the one who commendably tried to write about sex, but unfortunately failed."[51] The best way, she concluded, "is to mention it indirectly, as Faulkner does in *The Wild Palms*."

Algren told her he thought D. H. Lawrence's novel *The Plumed Serpent* was really very good and suggested that she read several other books about Mexico, both for historical background about women and for what the contemporary situation had become. These included William H. Prescott's *The History of the Conquest of Mexico* and Graham Greene's *The Power and the Glory*. Of the first, she had no comment, probably because women (with the exception of Cortez's mistress) are missing from Prescott's account. But of Greene she wrote: "Yes, I know about [him], and I don't like him. He wrote good mysteries before he started trying to be an important writer, and *The Power and the Glory* is just ersatz Faulkner for pious old English ladies. He bores me. He is popular here among the bourgeoisie."[52]

What she did like very much, however, was *The Kinsey Report*, which Algren had sent to her ("How I wish this same work had already been done for women!"), and a "most amusing book about the Mormons, Joseph Smith and his many wives."[53]

Someone had left a copy of Stendhal's *The Charterhouse of Parma* in a café, and she picked it up and began to reread it one afternoon when her hand was cramped from several hours of writing. She liked it, and so she reread *The Red and the Black*. Both novels made her think she should include Stendhal among the male authors she intended to discuss in the book. She told Algren that he "must read" Stendhal, because she thought him "the greatest French novelist," and that by reading *The Red and the Black* he would "learn something about France." She also wondered whether "one has to be French to understand him."[54]

Suddenly, in November 1948, there were all sorts of interruptions and demands upon her time. Violette Leduc was a constant teary-eyed presence, now threatening suicide if Beauvoir did not return her love. Beauvoir did not, but managed to assuage her ardent suitor by promising to dine with her at least once each week, the first time in Leduc's home. Leduc was further pacified when Sartre arranged for Gallimard to pay her a small monthly stipend, which she thought was money owed her from book royalties but which was actually a gift from him. She thus became one of the increasingly large number of people whom Sartre supported, some without but most with the knowledge that all their income came from him.[55] Leduc too became grist for Beauvoir's ever-grinding mill: much of the section on lesbianism is based on Leduc's situation and experiences.

Sartre had become active again in the RDR because Rousset persuaded him to join in editing a newspaper and supporting (mostly financially) the weekly magazine he proposed to start. An important meeting was planned for mid-December, and, to her surprise, Beauvoir was invited to speak, as was Richard Wright.[56] It seemed to her an omen of political success for the RDF's cause, because she and Wright represented two groups of people, women and blacks, who had hitherto been excluded from such prominent and visible participation in political gatherings. Her pleasure was muted when the organizers caved in under pressure from Camus and agreed that only Wright could speak, but that Beauvoir would be allowed to interpret for him.

"Camus whined that too many people from *Temps Modernes* were going to speak," she wrote Algren.[57] "Of course that was not entirely his reason," she added in 1985. "He didn't want *me* to speak. It upset him to think of me standing on that platform talking to men. Partly because I was a woman, certainly, but also simply because I am *me*, and by that time he was detesting me. Even before he read *The Second Sex*." It is interesting that Sartre did not protest her exclusion, and that she did not expect him to do so. She continued to troop faithfully along, following Sartre throughout his political activity, especially in "the Gary Davis affair," supporting "the man who gave up his U.S. passport and told the UN he is a world citizen who wants peace."[58] However, they did not attend the protest meetings supporting Davis, because Camus was so eloquent and outspoken on his behalf. Already there were rifts in the Sartre–Camus friendship, and their final rupture was not far off, but for her the rupture "had already happened. Camus never lost a chance to belittle me, so I simply ignored the person he had become since the war's end and tried to remember the charming man he had been earlier. He did not make it easy for me."

There was yet another complication to keep her from finishing the book. Merleau-Ponty went to the United States and Mexico, and she had to take over the day-to-day running of *Les Temps Modernes*.[59] The task required all her time and attention when Gallimard, deciding to follow Malraux in siding with de Gaulle, would no longer publish the magazine, and all the files and equipment had to be removed to the premises of Editions Juillard.

By the end of January 1949, she was concentrating again on *The Second Sex*. The first volume was with the typist, and most of her day was consumed in writing Volume Two while correcting the typescript of Volume One. The massive weight of her task led her to cry out to Algren, "Oh, God! I have read every book ever written by and about women and I am sick of all of them. I want my own man!"[60] But still she went to bed "like a decent old spinster."[61]

She celebrated her forty-first birthday on January 9, an occasion which was not made easier by their separation. "Since I still love you so much I obviously have not learned anything all this year through," she wrote to him. She was immersed in *The Second Sex* and was uncompromising with her stringent self-imposed demands to get the book finished. This birthday was "sad and rainy," and "the electricity failed." She worked "so savagely" that she strained her back, but she gave herself a birthday present: the "treat" of taking Volume One to her publisher. "I can't relax now," she told Algren, "because I want the second half done before you visit."

"One day I looked at myself in the mirror," she said in 1985, referring to a time shortly before her forty-first birthday. "I looked terrible. My eyes were red with strain. I had eruptions on my face such as I had not had since my adolescence. I had permanent blue dye on my neck from the jacket Algren gave me in Guatemala. I was fat, with a huge stomach from too much drink and pills and not enough food. Well, I said to myself, this book is killing me. We had better do something about this miserable old lady before it's too late. So I moved, and then I waited for Algren to come in the spring. Poor man—he was here, you know, when all the shit hit me, when *The Second Sex* was published."[62]

TWENTY-NINE

All the Right Enemies

I N EARLY DECEMBER 1948, Nelson Algren, frustrated by his long-distance romance, told Simone de Beauvoir he was coming to Paris as soon as he could make the travel arrangements. By return mail, she told him she was "mad with love and happiness," but he should not come before May 1949, when she would be finished with *The Second Sex*.[1] How interesting that, in a relationship composed in equal parts of physical attraction and intellectual respect, she was restrained enough to place a higher priority on reason than on passion. Her reply is especially curious, since her letters are filled with effusive descriptions of her yearnings and dreams, all thinly veiled accounts of sexual longing.[2] She sent him imprints of her lips as kisses, pointed out spots on the paper as the tears she shed for him in her loneliness, and then described herself as a "nice girl . . . on the bad side of forty . . . with a number of figure flaws and bad habits, who hasn't slept with a man in Paris for two years."[3]

Beauvoir felt secure enough about Algren to ask him to postpone his trip, because of two earlier incidents that threatened to upset and possibly end their affair. Shortly after she returned from visiting him in the summer of 1948, Algren wrote a letter pouring out his anger and frustration at their continuing separation, especially her refusal to stay in Chicago—at least for the foreseeable future.[4] She had originally promised to stay four months, but returned to Paris after two on the excuse that Sartre needed her help with the barrage of work to which he had committed himself. Sartre was now supporting so many people that it took a great deal of money, and so during that period and for the next few years he agreed to write almost anything that was proposed to him as long as it paid handsomely.[5] The only way that he could get it all done was with Beauvoir's support, and sometimes with Bost's as well.[6] When he wrote and said that he could not complete a lucrative filmscript with an immediate deadline if she stayed in America the full four months, Beauvoir changed her plans at once and returned to Paris after only two. Understandably, Algren felt betrayed.

As soon as she returned, she learned that the filmscript had been temporarily postponed. It left Sartre in a quandary, without an excuse to avoid Dolores, who was furious when she discovered that all the reasons he had invented to keep her from coming to France (she came anyway) were untrue. The truth was that he needed Beauvoir's assistance and therefore could not risk putting the two women in proximity to each other. Dolores's jealous tantrums always disrupted Sartre's work, but now he was afraid that her presence might give Beauvoir just the excuse she needed to go flying back to Algren.

His fears were well founded: she sent a cable at once, telling Algren she could come back to Chicago to finish her stay, and was stunned by his reply: "No. Too much work."[7] However, the period was missing after the first word, and she thought he said "Not too much work," which meant that she should return. So she wired her departure plans. He then sent a second telegram which clarified the first, and only then did she realize the depth of emotional distress she was causing her lover: "He preferred to be without me rather than to reopen so soon the terrible deep wound I had caused when I left him the time before."

He explained his position in his next letter, which was more puzzled than angry. In hers, she agreed with him that, yes, their love had begun "like a corny movie plot," and that now "it is real life and we have to take care of it properly." He was frustrated by not knowing how she could call him her husband and swear that she loved him before jumping at Sartre's every beck and call. He needed to know what exactly Sartre meant to her before he could see her again, indeed before he could believe anything she told him. She agreed that she had probably been unfair and should have tried to describe in person (as she had occasionally done in her letters) what she and Sartre meant to each other, but said she had been unwilling to do so because her time with Algren was so short and so precious. Also, as she said many years later, "Algren was like a dream come true for me, and I did not want anything to spoil it. Yes, all right: I too was like Sartre. I wanted to avoid confrontation, I wanted everything to be nice."

In her reply to Algren, she tried again to tell him all that Sartre meant to her, and she did so by speaking first of Bost, who had "not quite forgiven" her for "breaking off our sleeping together last year." She told Algren she had given up Bost "willingly," and would give up "everything" for his sake "except my friendship with Sartre." She told Algren that no one would ever love him more than she did, but added, "I cannot leave Sartre. I am his only true friend, and I owe him a great debt for all that he has done for me for more than twenty years. I would rather die than leave Sartre."

She told Algren that she and Sartre had stopped being lovers after their first eight or ten years together because Sartre was "never enthusiastic in bed," but that their friendship had become strong and deep. She and Bost continued to sleep together on a fairly regular basis ever since they first became lovers on a prewar camping trip, and they did so "tenderly, but without real love." Besides Bost, she confessed to only "three overnight affairs with men I liked," carefully omitting all others.[8] She told Algren that when they met she thought he would be just another of the "overnight affairs," but he made her fall in love with him. She said that as long as he and she were so deeply in love, there would be no other men in her life.

This must have calmed whatever fears and doubts Algren had about the degree of her commitment to him, because he did not mention it again until the end of November, when he confessed not only that he had been sleeping with another woman, but that he wanted to marry again.[9] He told Beauvoir that he would not have an affair with the unnamed woman, but

> that doesn't change the fact that I still want what she represented for me for two or three months: a place of my own to live in, with a woman of my own and perhaps a child of my own. There's nothing extraordinary about wanting such things, in fact it's rather common, it's just that I've never felt like it before. Perhaps it's because I'm getting close to forty. It's different for you. You've got Sartre and a settled way of life, people, and a vital interest in ideas. You live in the heart of the world of French culture, and every day you draw satisfaction from your work and your life. . . . I lead a sterile existence centered exclusively on myself: and I'm not at all happy about it. I'm stuck here, as I told you . . . because my job is to write about this city, and I can only do it here. . . . But it leaves me almost no one to talk to . . . my personal life was sacrificed in all this. This girl helped me to see the truth about us more clearly; last year I would have been afraid of spoiling something by not being faithful to you. Now I know that was foolish, because no arms are warm when they're on the other side of the ocean; I know that life is too short and too cold for me to reject all warmth for so many months.[10]

Despite her halfhearted insistence that he should feel free to take other lovers, Beauvoir was not prepared to receive a letter telling her that he had done so. She told him it disturbed her, not because he was sleeping with another woman, but "for the other woman's sake."[11] She tried to console him by saying it was easier for her, "since women can stand sexual deprivation better than men can." She should have stopped while ahead: "anyway," she concluded, "there is no one in Paris I want to sleep with."

Several days later, she wrote again and said she was glad they had discussed his needs so openly. She had cried all night when she read that he had taken a lover and wanted to get married, but now she could understand and accept it. What meant the most to her was that he and she had been faithful to each other for as long as they had been: "we were not fools to have loved and sacrificed for each other."[12]

His infidelity cleared the air, however, and rather than causing a rift between them, it seems to have cemented their rapport on a newer and deeper level. Algren continued to confide in Beauvoir, telling her many intimate details of his relationships with other women—in his own way, using her as a sounding board much the same as Sartre had always done. She seems to have adapted to the role easily, without undue distress, or at least none that she would let anyone notice. Nevertheless, it was shortly after he told her of his first affair that she wrote the letter telling him not to come to Paris until the following May and he agreed to wait. The only thing she insisted upon was that he be there to celebrate their third "anniversary, the 10th of May."[13]

In the meantime, although she wanted to direct all her energies toward finishing *The Second Sex*, Sartre assumed that she would participate in his political activity according to his needs. The end of 1948 and roughly the first half of 1949 marked the height of Sartre's involvement with Rousset and the RDR. As Sartre worked with the RDR and met delegations from Indochina, North Africa and various Caribbean territories and nations, his point of view shifted, from one which stressed the need for an independent, unified Europe that would coexist with the United States and Russia, to one of sympathy for the Third World and strong identification with workers' causes (no matter what the country). This view remained important in his political thought and activity for the rest of his life. An address he gave to a group of Moroccan students demonstrates his position:

> . . . it is France who oppresses [Moroccans], not the French masses. You were told that France was the country of freedom each time you fought against a foreign nation. You were deceived. Many of you were killed for the sake of imperialism all the while you thought you were dying for freedom. You are right to accuse France. . . . We [in France] will not be free until we can say, "There is not a man on earth who is oppressed because of us."[14]

Beauvoir's natural sympathies were more in tune with Sartre's evolving interest in the Third World than with French politics *per se*, but as postwar France reeled through various governments, innumerable strikes and constantly shifting domestic alliances, Beauvoir's main concern was to buttress Sartre. Her interest was aroused only when she began to meet the individuals who represented what she called "oppressed peoples," who had come to France seeking a forum to make their positions known. In November 1948 she went with Sartre and Rousset to lunch with a delegation of "Indochinese men" to discuss the racial problem in the French colonies. Merleau-Ponty, just back from a voyage to Martinique, joined them and described the situation as "very bad, whites ostracizing whites who are friendly with blacks, and outspoken blacks mysteriously murdered." They discussed a recent rebellion in Madagascar, where 90,000 blacks perished as opposed to 150 whites who were killed.[15]

The meeting marked a turning point in her life: as she listened to impassioned firsthand testimony about injustices she was so deeply moved that she became committed to helping political refugees from the Third World in any way she could. Stateless, homeless persons found her good for everything from a few francs to a meal, a place to stay (on the floor of her hotel room, later in her apartment) and sometimes help in finding jobs or publishers for their writings, and even the resettlement of their families in Paris. If there was a particular moment when her sympathies as a Frenchwoman moved away from unquestioning sympathy for the French nation (as opposed to some of its elected governments, which she did not support) to becoming allied with its colonies, this was arguably it.[16]

Sartre left the RDR in October 1949, following a number of disagreements, among them Rousset's appeal to American intellectuals (Sidney Hook among others) and the two major unions, the American Federation of Labor and the Congress of Industrial Organizations. This seemed to him a departure from the independent intermediary position the group had been founded to assume; it also seemed to favor one superpower over the other, with potentially serious consequences to follow. Resignation seemed the only answer. More than thirty years later, in an interview with one of Sartre's biographers, Rousset described Sartre's role in the ill-fated group as having had "very few positive effects":

> . . . he always retained his almost papal dogmatism. I believe
> this is what finally hindered his participation in political action,
> because despite his lucidity, he lived in a world that was totally
> isolated from reality. . . . He was very much involved in the play
> and movement of ideas, but not so much in events . . . he was
> never terribly interested in the world. Yes, that's it, Sartre lived in
> a bubble.[17]

Sartre may have lived in a bubble, but it was one which served to educate Beauvoir to live in the world of political action and to crystallize her feminist identity. For the next few years, as Sartre moved away from organized political action but strengthened his commitment to individuals and groups whose ideology he shared and whose causes he supported, Beauvoir became increasingly committed. She found it easier to go along with Sartre on political outings because, for the first time in a long time, she shared his need to demonstrate his beliefs through public action. Her accord became another strengthening bond in their already secure relationship, or, as she described it to Algren, their "friendship."

Nelson Algren had serious difficulty in understanding what Simone de Beauvoir meant by "essential" and "contingent" love, which he said "American hookers name, more simply, chippying."[18] And despite his agreement not to question her, he was still curious about exactly what role Sartre played in her life, since "despite the fact that [Sartre] was undersized, wall-eyed, and shabbily dressed, he had no more difficulty finding women to sleep with than Cary Grant." He continued to be puzzled by the answers she gave, and when she rebuked him for his irreverence and lectured him about Sartre's importance Algren replied that Sartre gave "the impression of being a small merchant, possibly into cheap shoes, who is going under." His remarks made Beauvoir furious but amused Sartre. But what about Sartre? What did he want to know about Nelson Algren? According to Beauvoir, it was "simple: when he saw how happy I was, he was happy for me."

Beauvoir's answer seemed too pat, couched too much in history long since settled rather than on the true feeling and emotion of the moment. Was Sartre perhaps as concerned that he might lose her as Algren, in his own way, was? "Frankly, I don't think it ever occurred to Sartre that I would leave him," she said. "He was delighted that I had found a man to love, he was concerned that we found it impossible to live together. When I was distressed by the separation, when I got drunk and cried too much, Sartre, who did not know how to comfort someone and who was always embarrassed and awkward in such situations—then it was always Sartre in his sweet clumsy way who tried to make me feel better. Generally, I did, because I knew how much it upset him to see me like that. It always interrupted his thinking and his work, and I never wanted to be the cause of that. That was what the others [women] did, and I was different from them. My role was to help Sartre, and that sustained me through the pain of my love affair with Algren."

The Family greeted the news that Algren was coming to France in the spring as if one of its own were returning. They were eager to meet the exotic American whose brash, irreverent writings they had read in *Les Temps Modernes*. Two among them, Olga and Michelle Vian, were translating his tales of drifters, drug addicts and down-and-outers for publication in book form. Now that Sartre's liaison with Michelle was public knowledge, he sometimes worked on Algren's texts with her. Sartre, whose command of English was minimal, did it for his amusement, but Michelle spoke and wrote fluent English, so for her it was a serious undertaking to which she gave the same devotion that she lavished on everything connected with Sartre for the rest of his life.

The Family itself had grown in the last several years, but it is difficult to state with authority who was actually "in" and who was simply "always there."[19] Jean Cau became Sartre's secretary and privy to the details of Family life and history, but he was treated more as hired help than as friend.[20] Others connected with the magazine were welcomed, among them Bernard Frank and Robert Scipion and the woman who later became Scipion's wife, Lisa; for various reasons, the friendships were brief.[21] Old friends Jeanine and Raymond Queneau, Annette and Alberto Giacometti, and Zette and Michel Leiris were the three couples whom Sartre and Beauvoir, as another couple, saw together the most, and with whom they felt comfortable enough to relax. Other old acquaintances were quite another matter.

Violette Leduc, to whom Sartre was indifferent, tormented Beauvoir with her constant demands for affection and attention. Sartre remained entranced by Genet and could have followed and listened to him for hours on end, while Beauvoir and Genet regarded each other warily, as he considered her "a tough bitch" and she never hesitated to let him know how much she despised his "silly fairy entourage."[22] In turn, Leduc and Genet tormented each other with outrageous lies and insults about what Sartre and Beauvoir had told each about the other. They all created a circle of gossip and spite, as everyone took turns observing, explaining and denying what the others had said or were alleged to have said about the rest. After Boris and Michelle Vian divorced, each told a separate version of their marital discord to Sartre (Michelle) and Beauvoir (Boris), so that another smaller and meaner circle of gossip resulted.

These years, the end of the 1940s and the early 1950s, were the epitome of all that Saint-Germain-des-Prés has come to stand for in the contemporary social history of France. Although a brilliant future was supposed to have begun at the war's end in 1945, "the Year Zero," the beginning of Existentialism as a dominant force in French intellectual life did not really happen until the early 1950s. By that time, Paris was once again filled with refugees who had chosen to be there (not, as they had done during the war, simply gone there hoping to survive). Americans were there in droves, especially ex-soldiers studying on the GI Bill, and college girls on a year abroad looking for excitement not generally found in the parietal restrictions of the Seven Sisters colleges. For most it meant freedom, although they were hard pressed to explain its principles. The word if not the substance of Existentialism had filtered down from the arenas of intellectual debate and was now the catchword of the day. Existentialism reigned as the supreme expression of youthful revolt and hope for the future, and the dynamism of its reception extended to Sartre and Beauvoir, who were the uncrowned rulers of the neighborhood.

They all, it seemed, clutched battered copies of *Being and Nothingness* even though many of them did not read French well enough to understand it; however, whether or not one was Existentialist had suddenly become determined more by dress than by philosophical argument. The men sported berets (possibly in imitation of Sartre, who occasionally wore one in the coldest weather and then only if Beauvoir or his mother insisted), but the women preferred the ubiquitous tightly cinched flowing black skirts, turtlenecks, and ballerina slippers, although Beauvoir still wore brightly colored ethnic clothing and jewelry.

Still, while everyone wanted to see them, not everyone wanted to be seen with them. Cocteau was jealous of Sartre and disliked Beauvoir, who seldom counted gay men among her friends, so he and his entourage watched warily from a table discreetly removed from theirs in the Flore, or at the Deux Magots or the Lipp, where the café crowd in Saint-Germain-des-Prés had begun to spill over because it had grown so huge. Sartre and Beauvoir's entourage, to avoid both unwanted interruptions from people they knew and from tourists who wanted to gawk at them, had begun to frequent, at night as well as during the day, the secluded basement bar at the nearby Hotel du Pont-Royal, where they had gone originally to be able to write uninterrupted.

Truman Capote made the mistake of wandering in there one day. He disliked Beauvoir and Sartre from the first moment he saw them; she was amused by his "fussy fastidiousness" and amazed that he was "so much smaller than even Sartre." In his oversized white sweater and powder-blue velvet pants, Capote looked like "a white mushroom," she thought. When he spread the rumor around the Pont-Royal that Sartre had called him a "fairy Existentialist," Beauvoir retaliated, "He did not! He just called him a fairy!" Bartenders laughed at Capote, she told Algren, not only because of "how funny he talks French" but because of his name: in a time of strong anti-American sentiment, they all found it amusing that his first name was the surname of the current American President, Harry Truman, and that his last was a French slang expression for a condom.[23] Capote got even, however, unfortunately too late for her to read it:

> At the time the Pont-Royal had a leathery little basement bar that was the favored swill bucket of haute Boheme's fatbacks. Walleyed, pipe-sucking, pasty-hued Sartre and his spinsterish moll, de Beauvoir, were usually propped in a corner like an abandoned pair of ventriloquist's dolls.[24]

Feuds, gossip, jealousy and spite marked one kind of emotional expression; all varieties of pairings, couplings and uncouplings marked another. A dozen or so years after they had pored over the details of other people's lives in the sad little cafés of Rouen and Le Havre, Beauvoir and Sartre were doing so again from the pinnacle of their success and at what was for them the exact center of the world. It made them feel young, as if no time had passed at all; dynamic, important and, in Beauvoir's words, "necessary: as if no one could live without first giving the details of life to us." The way other people sought their attention and advice "verified who we were, what we were," made her feel "authentic." Now that she was forty and Sartre forty-five, it made them feel young because "we thought about youth a lot now that we no longer had it."

Bost's love affairs required serious attention, especially from Beauvoir, because Olga's health was precarious and she was almost always away during these years in various sanatoria taking tuberculosis cures. It was a delicate matter, because Beauvoir had to consider both Bost's needs and Olga's sensitivities. Beauvoir's curiosity was piqued when he began an affair with Marguerite Duras, because she was curious about the other woman's creative vision[25] and also about how Duras's husband coped with the situation. He was furious over his wife's involvement with Bost, and Beauvoir thought his fury excessive even though the assignations usually consisted of an hour-long meeting four times each week. What did concern Beauvoir was the irate husband's threat to take away his son as well as to make the liaison public and thus finish off Bost's ever rocky marriage.[26] Beauvoir's advice was to forget Duras and find someone less prominent, which Bost soon did.

Cau's involvements were more amusing and, because she cared little for him, less threatening. Rich women pursued him, among them the wife of a well-known industrialist rumored to be one of the richest men in France; Cau himself chased other women with varying degrees of success, providing amusement for Sartre and Beauvoir. Through him they met the poet Anne-Marie Cazalis (whom Beauvoir dubbed "the little Cassoulet") and the singer Juliette Gréco, who were (again, according to Beauvoir) at alternate times friends, rivals for Cau and others, and perhaps lovers themselves. Gréco told reporters that she was having an affair with Sartre because she needed the publicity. This infuriated Cazalis because she wanted to sleep with both of them and had not been invited to by either, which made Michelle angry because Sartre had promised to inform her before he slept with other women, which made Sartre angriest of all because "Gréco did not [actually] sleep with him before telling the world she had."[27] Wanda was surprisingly quiet throughout all this, busy with a new lover and her acting career, content with the visits she and Sartre had arranged. He divided his time according to a schedule as strict as he could manage (given his acquiescent personality where women were concerned): two hours for this one, an evening for that, a full afternoon with another. But no matter how many other women filled his list, there was always some sort of daily contact with Beauvoir. If either had other engagements during the day, they kept the hours from 5 to 8 P.M. free and met without fail.[28]

For Beauvoir, in the midst of so many people and so much activity ("and so much of it frivolous, not connected with work at all"), the first half of 1949 was one of the happiest, most serene periods of her life. Les Temps Modernes had evolved into a truly professional magazine with a paid staff, so that her responsibilities now consisted almost solely of attending meetings at which the content of future issues was planned or else evaluating submissions on her own time. The work she did for Sartre—discussing his planned projects, reading his manuscripts and providing critiques—became easily integrated into their daily sessions, and even the "endless book," The Second Sex, was coming to an end. Excerpts were scheduled for publication in the magazine in February, May and June, and the first volume was to be published by Gallimard also in June. By then she expected to finish the second, which would appear either later that year or the beginning of the next.

Her life was so tranquil and—for her—so ordered, that for the first time in her life she wanted to live in something other than a transient hotel room. She moved out of her hotel at the end of October 1948 into "a small three-room place with no bath, but a magnificent view of Notre Dame," at 11 Rue de la Bûcherie. "This will be our place," she told Algren, "no man but you will ever sleep there."[29]

She furnished it with souvenirs of their travels together, brightly colored fabrics, rugs and pottery from Central America, and the frequent presents he sent from Chicago. Almost every letter contained something, from cartoons and news cuttings to cards, valentines, bits of ribbon or whatever else he could fit into an envelope. Several times each year he sent large packages for her to share with the Family, and separate ones for her mother, a kindness which astonished Françoise. Sartre was always polite to her, but she seldom saw him and had never received a single gift from him in all the years he and Beauvoir had been together (although Beauvoir often gave her mother little things like handkerchiefs and sachets she herself had chosen and said were from Sartre). But Algren, a total stranger, sent heavy packages containing such staples as oatmeal, powdered eggs and flour (into which he managed to hide bottles of scotch for Beauvoir that, to her joy, escaped the detection of customs officers). He also sent her bottles of ink, at first because Beauvoir claimed they were in short supply in France, then because she said she liked American ink better. Aware that rationing was still in effect in France, Algren wanted to know whether he should send warm clothes, thread and wool for Françoise, but Beauvoir told him not to, as they were becoming more easily available. She told him emphatically, "Not soap. We have that here. French people wash, too." When he came in May, she told him, all he needed to bring "to the Beauvoir Hotel" was his "clothes and scotch." Did he know, she added coyly, that he would be "one of the 375,000 Americans" who would visit France that year? She reminded him again that she had not "slept with a man in Paris for two years."[30]

Algren's ship docked in Le Havre several days before the May 10 deadline she had given for his arrival so that they could be together on their "anniversary." After much equivocation about whether to meet his ship when it docked, she finally decided to wait for him in Paris and meet the train that would bring him to the Gare Saint-Lazare. She waited at the barrier until all the passengers had disembarked, but Algren was not among them. Dispirited, she went back to the Rue de la Bûcherie to wait for some form of communication from him. She heard a ruckus in the street, looked down, saw him surrounded by suitcases, boxes and brown-paper parcels that a cab driver had piled unceremoniously on the curb: Algren was bringing so many presents for her, her mother and the Family that he had not been able to get it all off the train until she had left the station. They spent the first hour of their time together in Paris racing up and down the five flights of stairs and dumping everything in the center of her flat, helped by several patrons of the café on the street level. Algren liked it:

I stayed with her there in the Rue Boucherie [sic], which was a little tenement street. It's the fifth floor . . . just a little place under the roof where, as in the good French tradition, when it rained you put buckets to catch the water. There was an Algerian café right below. You could hear the music . . . and you could see Notre Dame and that was a very good summer.[31]

The Family could hardly wait to meet Algren, and everyone congregated at the Flore. He was prepared to "circle Sartre warily, like two gladiators, jousting for position," but instead the tiny Sartre reached out to the much larger Algren, shook his hand warmly, then put his arm as far around Algren's back as it would reach, guided him into the Flore and chattered away in French, which Algren neither spoke nor understood, as if they had known each other forever. Bost and Cau were waiting with Michelle; Gréco joined them, as did the Little Cassoulet and the entertainer Mouloudji, Boris Vian, Giacometti and many others who formed an unending procession to and from the table where the big, bewildered American sat blinking through the haze of smoke, booze and incomprehensible babble.

Algren later described the general atmosphere by combining several incidents into one account:

> Unthinkingly, Madame once got me cornered against a restaurant wall among a dozen existentialists all speaking French. I recall Raymond Queneau, Merleau-Ponty, Michel Leiris—Koestler, I believe—Sartre, Madame, Michelle Vian, and Mouloudji. . . . My embarrassment was twofold: I couldn't understand French and I couldn't get out of my seat. Michelle came over, sat opposite me, and translated questions and answers. . . . She enabled me to join in the laughter and made me a member of the group. I became an existentialist, too—for an entire evening.[32]

Algren was a complex man who soon enchanted everyone in the Family with his casual attitude toward life. He moved with what Beauvoir called "his typical American slouch," a defense he adopted to cover his basic shyness in certain social situations. He was a man accustomed to being alone for long periods of time, and when he was with people this sometimes resulted in moodiness and periods of black silence. Beauvoir believed herself his kindred soul because of her solitary year in Marseille and the earlier uncertainty in her relationship with Sartre, so whenever Algren withdrew into these silences she hovered about him solicitously. He was intuitive, so when he sensed her anxiety he made a deliberate effort to be friendly and, in some instances, even charming to all those who accepted him for what he was—a socially conscious writer with strong leftist sympathies.

Bost, for example, proudly told everyone that his new American friend "voted for Henry Wallace!"—despite the fact that most French people had no idea who Henry Wallace was or what he represented. Olga, who also spoke quite good English, adored Algren, and for many years afterward she carried on a lively correspondence with him, filled with banter and gossip about all their friends. When things cooled between Algren and Beauvoir, Olga's letters became the conduit for information each wanted the other to know.[33] Algren was also fond of Michelle, whom he called "the Golden ZaZu," and he agreed with Beauvoir that she was truly the one who "cares for people."[34]

All the friends to whom Beauvoir introduced Algren were as smitten with him in their own way as Beauvoir was with him in hers, and they were all astonished to see, as Bost described her, "our no-nonsense Castor" behaving as tenderly toward him "as a schoolgirl with her first love." To entertain them, Algren invented one wild story after another about colorful, semimythical characters of Chicago folklore. His tales of gangsters and detectives fascinated Sartre, who listened enthralled for hours at a time, and his sad prostitutes with hearts of gold brought tears to Michelle's eyes. The friends, in turn, tried to introduce him to their own Parisian oddities and freaks, and he took delight in everything.

They were amused by his attitude toward Beauvoir, especially the way he teased her about her casual dress and deportment: "Friends sometimes had to remind her that it might be just as well to hang up last winter's dress, midsummer having come to France. Most Parisian of Parisians, she was the least *Parisienne*."[35]

He was ready for any adventure that the Family proposed, but he also wanted to be alone with her,[36] so she planned a trip that would take him back to some of the places where he had served during the war, as well as some of her own favorites.

He hadn't been there very long when things began to happen that made her think it would be wise if they left Paris as soon as possible. Algren had landed smack in the middle of a verbal firestorm created by excerpts from *The Second Sex* in *Les Temps Modernes*. Both rhetoric and heat intensified throughout the four months he spent in Europe and Africa, first with Simone de Beauvoir alone, and then in the company of Sartre and the rest of the Family.

The first unpleasant episode happened when Beauvoir took Algren to see a typical "Parisian crowd" on June 18, at the ceremonies when the Avenue d'Orléans was officially renamed to honor General Leclerc, the French liberator of Paris. As they walked through the gathering, a man recognized Beauvoir and, "with murder in his Gaullist eyes," spat out that she had no right to be there.[37] The outburst surprised her, but she thought he was only referring to her political stance and dismissed it. Later that same day, as she and Algren were sipping drinks in the shade outside the Flore, someone from the magazine staff walked by and told her that the June issue was selling "like hot cakes" (as, later, the July and August issues would sell). Sartre joined them and told her the happy news that in the week since the first volume had been published Gallimard could not keep copies on bookstore shelves, for more than twenty thousand copies had been sold and sales showed no sign of diminishing.[38]

She was suddenly the talk of Paris, but she was surprised to learn that her chapters were being "read, as it were, with averted eyes. . . . What a festival of obscenity on the pretext of flogging me for mine." She described what happened next:

> I received—some signed and some anonymous—epigrams, epis-
> tles, satires, admonitions, and exhortations addressed to me by,
> for example "some very active members of the First Sex." Un-
> satisfied, frigid, priapic, nymphomaniac, lesbian, a hundred times
> aborted—I was everything, even an unmarried mother. People
> offered to cure me of my frigidity or to temper my labial appe-
> tites; I was promised revelations, in the coarsest terms but in the
> name of the true, the good and the beautiful, in the name of
> health and even of poetry.

When she sat in cafés with Algren, people snickered or pointed at her in derision. She took him to dine on the outskirts of Montparnasse, where she had not gone in years, and a large family from the neighborhood stared openly and giggled loudly all through dinner. It was then that she realized how notorious she had become, because these were ordinary peo-ple, citizens of the quarter who were not likely to recognize anyone but film stars or other celebrities. "I didn't like dragging Algren into a scene," she remembered, "but as I left I gave them a piece of my mind." To Algren, Beauvoir's "decisiveness shook the arrondissement."[39]

Some years later, Algren admitted that he "worried a bit about how the human race was going to perpetuate itself once Castor took over,"[40] but in 1949, during the time he was with her in Paris, when so much outraged hostility was directed toward her, he thought her views were "preposterized in every newspaper and magazine edited by the French bourgeoisie. She was cartooned, ridiculed, sometimes made gentle fun of and, at other times, reviled with no restraint."

All this changed by his next (and last) visit to Paris, in 1960:

> There was no more laughter: she was feared. She had broken
> through the defenses of the bourgeoisie, of the church, the busi-
> nessmen, the right-wing defenders of Napoleonic glory, and the
> hired press. She was, at once, the most hated and the most loved
> woman in France. It had become plain: she *meant* it.

That was when he sent her the note saying, "You've won. You've made all the right enemies."[41]

But even in 1949, all the while that he marveled at the calm self-assured manner in which she deflected some criticisms, retaliated against others, ignored the rest, *The Second Sex* was becoming a convenient ex-cuse for the differences that increasingly arose between them. In a 1964 conversation, after their final break, Algren described their relationship as one that assumed the secondary status of the female in relation to the male . . . It had no philosophical basis. A few years later Miss de Beauvoir found a philosophical justification—but that was a literary discovery and had nothing to do with any living human being. The irony of the title *The Second Sex* is a purely literary irony. In reality there was no irony. Second is where second belongs. It is still interesting to me how a woman may accept the secondary status of the second sex in a personal relationship and [our] relationship never got off that basis. . . . I thought posterity ought to know that. . . . She understood that in the relationship between a man and a woman the man is the dominating factor specifically.[42]

Algren was a direct and forceful man whose first response to negative criticism of his friends was "to give a punch in the nose."[43] The phrase soon became the Family's catchword, as in "Send Algren to punch his nose," which made everyone laugh and helped to deflect the harshness of the situation. Then they reduced it simply to the phrase "Send Algren" and, when he had gone back to Chicago, to "Send for Algren." Sartre continued to use it for the next several years whenever he wished to bolster Beauvoir's spirits, but at one point it made her cry uncontrollably, and he never said it again.

Algren's presence helped her to withstand such criticisms as those that Janet Flanner, writing as Genêt in *The New Yorker*, described mildly as "some rough, unjust reviews."[44] Still, he must not be given all the credit for the toughness with which she deflected them, but must share it with the other men who gathered round her in solidarity: "Sartre, Bost, Merleau-Ponty, Leiris, Giacometti and the staff of *Les Temps Modernes* . . . Pouillon and Cau [flew] to my rescue. . . ."[45] Finally, her own response must be credited:

> Ever since I published *L'Invitée* I had suffered a certain degree of public criticism. In the beginning it hurt me—I would be lying to say that it did not. But by the time I published *The Second Sex*, so much ugliness had been aimed at me, both for myself and because of my association with Sartre, that I grew accustomed to shrugging it off. Certainly I felt anger and disgust at some of the most hostile of the critics, but I recognized it for what it was and soon got over it. Most of the time I could not afford the luxury of anger because I had to comfort my friends and defenders and tell them not to waste time with such foolishness.

Then she romanticized her childhood, claiming that it was "very solid, very secure," and giving credit to family background for Sartre as well as herself, "even when crises occurred, the solidity of our childhoods made us externalize these crises. . . . We were too structured to feel insecure."[46]

It actually gave her a perverse sort of pleasure to collect the most violent attacks when she was composing the third volume of her memoirs in the early 1960s, especially the remark of her former hero François Mauriac, who had written, "Your employer's vagina has no secrets from me" in a personal letter to a writer for *Les Temps Modernes*. Horrified by the remark, the recipient showed it to her, to warn her to defend herself. She and Sartre retaliated by printing it, which forced the old man to write an ill-conceived series of articles condemning pornography in general and Beauvoir's writings in particular.[47]

Algren, "who thought he knew how terrible writers could be to each other," was "shocked by the violence of French intellectual argument." That was when Beauvoir decided it was time they left Paris.[48] They flew to Rome, then toured southern Italy, from Naples to Sorrento, Amalfi and Ravello. From there they flew to Tunis, Algiers, Fez and Marrakesh. Another flight took them to Marseille, the port from which he had departed for home at the end of the war. They drove to Monte Carlo, Antibes and Cabris, where Bost and Olga had bought a vacation cottage. In mid-August they returned to a Paris emptied by the annual holiday exodus, and they spent the next month there so happily that Beauvoir, who was not especially superstitious, feared she might have to pay back some jealous spirits for it.

When Algren left in mid-September 1949, he made her swear that she would come to Chicago before the next year passed and spend at least four months with him. His wanting to be with her for such a long time cheered her, so that this parting was only "bittersweet" because she had never loved him so much or felt his love so deeply.[49] She was as elated as he when he sent a telegram to let her know that when his plane landed at Gander, he read in a magazine that *The Man with the Golden Arm* had won the National Book Award for Fiction. In his next few letters he was bursting with plans for future books. It was a contagious energy, and started her thinking about what she should do next.

As soon as Algren departed, she and Sartre left Paris for a holiday to rest up from their busy summer. This was the beginning of a routine that lasted the rest of their lives: sometimes as early as August but definitely by October they went away together for from two weeks to a month, first to the south of France, then always to Rome. On this trip, to Cagnes-sur-Mer, she rushed to finish her review of Lévi-Strauss's *Elementary Structures of Kinship*, which she had read in manuscript while writing *The Second Sex*. Sparked by Algren's enthusiasm for his future projects, she was anxious to finish all her obligations to the review so that she could get on with her own work.

"Dearest Man with the Golden Arm," she wrote to him on September 27:

You know that time on Ischia, when you were accusing me of laziness? Well, I was really meditating on my novel, thinking up characters and situations. I am going to dedicate this book to you, since I am yours and my work is yours in so many ways.

On October 8 she wrote again: "I wrote the first page of my new novel: To Nelson. Now it is so brightly begun, it will be easy to go on."[50]

"Brightly begun" at the height of her relationship with Algren, by the time it was finished, more than four years later, they had come to the first of their several sad partings. The novel became *The Mandarins,* one of her own favorite writings, one which many believe to be the finest work of all the genres in which she wrote. It was the most difficult of all her writings, the one on which she lavished the most care, the one she wrote and rewrote, revising it until the very last minute when the type was set and locked. It became the book which first earned her the respect and financial security that *The Second Sex* eventually guaranteed. It brought her the Prix Goncourt, one of France's most prestigious literary prizes, thus moving her out of Sartre's shadow for the first time in her professional life; in doing so, it started the long process of self-examination that resulted in the four volumes of memoirs and her outspoken commitment to action on behalf of women.

"And to think," she recalled with an element of genuine surprise in her voice, "that when I started to write *The Mandarins,* all I had in mind was to pay homage to Nelson Algren by writing our love story!"

THIRTY

"Not Exactly Our Story, but . . ."

Simone de Beauvoir thought about *The Mandarins* for more than a year before she began to write it in the fall of 1949. When she sat down to work on what eventually became the first long monologue of the character Anne Dubreuilh, the sight of the blank paper before her made her "feel giddy": "I wanted it to contain all of me—myself in relation to life, to death, to my times, to writing, to love, to friendship, to travel; I also wanted to depict other people, and above all to tell the feverish and disappointing story of what happened after the war."[1]

The optimism that gripped Parisian intellectuals after the Liberation was so exhilarating that it transcended the boundaries of France, giving hope to many disparate groups who were disenfranchised for reasons of race, class, gender or political status. The black American writer Ralph Ellison, for example, wrote to his friend Richard Wright, "France is in ferment. Their discussion of the artist's responsibility surpasses anything I've ever seen." He singled out Sartre as "one of the younger writers [who] would have no difficulty understanding your position in regard to the Left."[2] Wright was in complete agreement: "How rare a man is this Sartre!" he wrote in his journal following a conversation in which Sartre had compared the situation of the citizens of all colonized entities to that of the French under the occupation. He concluded, "Sartre is the only Frenchman I've met who had voluntarily made the identification of the French experience with that of mankind." Profoundly touched by his friendship with Sartre and Beauvoir, Wright also wrote, "I feel very close to [them]."[3]

But by 1950 everything that Sartre believed in and worked for seemed to have come to very little. He had split with the RDR, was in disgrace with the French Communist Party and was reviled by intellectuals of both Left and Right. From his former student Jean Kanapa to his former colleague Raymond Aron, Sartre was anathema because he refused to come down firmly on one side or the other. By that time, even Richard Wright had become disillusioned with him, which started a rift in his friendship with Beauvoir. Even the flagship *Les Temps Modernes*, launched in such high idealism only a few years before, was like a boat with slackened sails drifting on a windless lake. "Four years before we had been everyone's friends, now we were looked upon by everyone as enemies," Beauvoir noted glumly.[4]

Initial unity among the leading intellectuals in postwar France had given way to ideological fragmentation and political disorganization. Small fissures had become large fractures; charges and countercharges were hurled. Sartre was so disappointed by the failure of everything he espoused that he withdrew from the public arena to read, study, and rethink his positions, both personal and intellectual. Sartre's frustration with his inability to influence the course of French society through the organized political action of like-minded persons, especially artists and intellectuals, can be seen in some of his unpublished notes. He made several especially bitter comments in notes toward a philosophical treatise on morals, which he abandoned in what Beauvoir called "a combination of despair and disgust." There he wrote: "Ethics is a collection of idealistic tricks intended to enable us to live the life imposed on us by the poverty of our resources and the insufficiency of our techniques."[5]

His attitude had a profound effect on Beauvoir's novel-in-progress, as one of her intentions with *The Mandarins* was to try to understand why the initial political harmony had so quickly disintegrated. She looked forward to researching the history of postwar French politics, naively assuming that all she would have to do would be to visit her local public library and read post-Liberation newspapers and magazines.[6] Doing this depressed her because she discovered that "the past six years . . . seem very dead."[7] Still, she continued to read and try to reconstruct recent history, partly for her own literary purposes but also because Sartre had become so gloomy, brooding, "What went wrong? When did it start? What could I have done to keep it from happening? What should I do now? What is my role, if any, to be?"[8]

They had almost entirely stopped going to cafés and clubs, spending their evenings quietly alone together. Searching for some diversion to take Sartre's mind off politics, Beauvoir hit upon music. She enjoyed listening to it, but he was a gifted pianist with a beautiful tenor voice and an extensive knowledge of music. As she claimed to be helpless when confronting any machine, she asked Bost to find the best phonograph available in Paris and to buy it with some of her first earnings from *The Second Sex*. Then she began to amass the many records that comprised the extensive collection she cherished all her life. She soon had so many that the Family joked that "Castor would have trouble moving her belongings across Paris in a handcart now!"[9]

Still it was not enough to divert Sartre, tired of the endless argument and controversy that swirled around him despite his withdrawal from public life. His introspection extended into his personal life, as it too seemed bleak. He had made the final break with Dolores in the spring of 1950. He and she had traveled to Mexico and Guatemala together the previous summer, and it had been a disaster. At Dolores's insistence, they retraced the exact route that Beauvoir had followed with Algren, because, according to Beauvoir, "she was jealous of our happiness."

What Dolores failed to realize was that Sartre was not a good tourist. He never made any arrangements, he was incapable of making decisions, and he preferred to go at his own pace rather than adapt to anyone else's schedule. Monuments and museums bored him, nature disgusted him, and he was suspicious of most native foods. He always came down with a strange indigenous malady in almost every country he ever visited. Dolores expected, indeed demanded, that he play the traditional male role in their travels, initiating and deciding their itinerary, which Sartre was simply incapable of doing. Dolores demanded at the very least that he take equal responsibility for everything, alternately screaming or sulking as he sat in bewildered indecision. It made her furious when he merely withdrew and kept silent.

Dolores had moved to Paris before this trip, announcing that she planned to end her marriage and live permanently in an apartment that Sartre earlier, in the full flush of their romance, had agreed to provide and finance. If this action did not result in Sartre's marrying her, she expected him at least to live with her rather than with his mother (where he was most happily situated). When they returned from Central America, Sartre was so exhausted that he cloistered himself on the Rue Bonaparte under his mother's soooothing ministrations while the rest of the Family formed ranks around him to keep Dolores away. She announced angrily that she was incapable of living in the limbo to which Sartre had consigned her and was returning at once to her husband in New York. Sartre was greatly relieved.

So, too, was Beauvoir, who was afraid that he would give in to Dolores's demands of marriage simply because she was so persistent and his main concern with women was to give them what they wanted so that they would not interfere with his writing. All this came from what Algren called "Sartre's inability to say no. He was incapable of sending a woman away after he had slept with her."[10]

Thus Sartre and Beauvoir arrived at the time in their life when, night after pleasant night, they sprawled in the Rue de la Bûcherie, he on her one dilapidated armchair, she across her sagging bed, beneath the soft light thrown by her two new Giacometti lamps, listening to music and sipping scotch and water.[11] Each was comforted by the presence of the other, as only two people who have shared the most important moments of each other's lives can be: "I think it was when Dolores went back to New York that I knew for the first time that, no matter what, Sartre and I would always be together. I still had Algren, and I had no doubt that for Sartre there would always be other women. But we had become necessary to each other in a way that I don't think people ever really understood. They [critics, journalists] all said we had become like a little old married couple, and they snickered at us. I suppose they said this because they had no other referent. It's true, we knew each other so well, no one ever understood us as we understood each other. But rather than to see us as senile old people, too lazy or too tired to change, which is how most old married couples become, they should have said that all our shared experiences made us supremely at ease and comfortable with each other. In my memoirs I said that if Sartre gave me an appointment to meet him at a certain hour of a certain day and year in a strange place many miles away, I would go there in complete faith to find him waiting, because I knew I could always depend on him. Well, after so many years, this was still true. In spite of everything—no, perhaps *because* of everything we had been through together—we always depended on each other. He would never disappoint me; I would never let him down."

The Mandarins is a novel of ideas, and French politics since the Liberation is one of its several important strands, but equally important is the idea of human relationships. Beauvoir described the "central plot" as "the breaking and subsequent mending of a friendship between two men," but she also said that one of the "privileged roles" in the novel was assigned to a woman because "a great many of the things I wanted to say were directly linked to my condition as a woman."[12] However, before she wrote about those things pertaining to women in the novel, she addressed the question specifically in an almost unknown essay.

Fleur Cowles had just been made the editor of a sleek American magazine, Flair, by her media-magnate husband. Extremely chic herself, Mrs. Cowles transmitted many of her own interests and ideas onto the printed page by selecting some of the most gifted writers, artists and social commentators to contribute to her regrettably short-lived gem of a publication. For a brilliant issue focusing on all aspects of French culture since the Liberation, Beauvoir contributed an essay called "It's About Time," which dealt with what she thought relationships, in this case only heterosexual ones, should become in the future.[13]

Beauvoir dismissed her essay as "trash, written just to get $300"[14] so that she could visit Algren in Chicago during the summer of 1950. Perhaps she said this because the magazine was never taken very seriously; but more likely her diffidence was an attempt to distance herself from another easily recognizable attempt to explore and explain her relationships with Sartre and Algren through impersonal analysis.

"It's About Time" was a clarion call for women throughout the world to "put a new face on love." Her premise is that love has always been founded on an inequality which requires women to "kneel worshipfully before their master." She believed this idea to be "so deeply rooted in men's hearts that if a woman does not lie prostrate at their feet, they fear that they may themselves be forced to play the ignominious slave."

She then posed the question "Is it not possible to conceive a new kind of love in which both partners are equals—one not seeking submission to the other?" In Beauvoir's opinion, "love given and love received . . . will be the most powerful aid in bringing about this paradoxical synthesis."

She rejected the traditional view of love, of a couple bound together to the exclusion of all others until death, because it both devours them and they are "devoured in turn by inaction, immobility, boredom; they are already dead." Instead of "grimly hanging on to what is dying, or repudiating it," she argues, "would it not be better to try to help invent the future?" She adds in conclusion:

> Too many women fight off love because it evokes ancient slaveries, and too many men refuse to believe in it because they fail to know it by its ancient face. Let both men and women overcome their distrust, and they will find that it is possible to restore, in freedom and in equality, the human pair.

In 1983 she was asked whether Algren had ever commented upon the essay. "Oh, yes," she replied, amused by the memory. "He said it was bullshit. It was okay if I wrote tripe for a lot of silly women but not to bring it home to Wabansia."

Algren did read the article, and demanded to know what she meant by "all this equality between the sexes." To placate him, she replied: "No, equality is only a myth. I only said you [men] were equal with me [women] to be polite. We'll achieve our kind of equality this summer when we do the same thing at the same time."[15]

She was uneasy with his recent letters which carefully evaded her pleas that he let her return to Chicago as soon as possible. Finally he admitted that he was involved with another woman, who was partially supporting him. Beauvoir did not mind his "practicing what men do" as long as he did not marry the woman. She hinted that she too might "practice" and get her "own pimp," adding that she had been seeing William Phillips, in Paris from New York. "He looks like Koestler," she wrote, "only handsomer." To emphasize her veiled threat, she wrote sweetly that she would soon see Phillips again.[16] Several days later she took him to lunch with Ignazio Silone, who became highly indignant when she insisted on paying. "Carlo Levi would not have objected," she noted.[17]

Because nothing seemed to work with Algren, even direct requests that he let her come to Chicago, she reminded him that he had invited her to visit sometime during 1950, and now she wanted to set the date. This too failed to produce a response, so she tried another ploy: she had just sold the American rights for The Second Sex to Blanche Knopf, wife of the publisher Alfred A. Knopf, for the then handsome sum of $750 (with an equal amount going to Gallimard). The money would be waiting for her in New York, she wrote, for them to spend in Chicago.[18] Still no invitation was forthcoming. She sent an angry letter to Algren with the photo taken for the *Flair* article enclosed, calling it "proof" that she could "get money as well as the next whore." She intended it as a reproof for his situation with the unnamed other woman, who was all but supporting him.[19]

Algren chose not to answer the letter, and she grew even more anxious and confused. She tried another reproach, blaming the loss of "two months work on the manuscript" of *The Mandarins* when she left "the whole bundle" in a taxicab because she was absentmindedly thinking of him. Most of what she lost contained Anne's introspections and monologues about her love affair with the American writer Lewis Brogan, which in this early version of the text were almost exactly Beauvoir's own thoughts about Algren. Fortunately, she remembered the lost passages "almost word for word," but rewriting "from memory" frustrated her because it consumed time better spent on something new.

The lost manuscript was only one manifestation of her "new scatter-brained way of living." She who had always been so efficient now forgot appointments, lost her keys, and walked out of stores without the items she had just purchased.

She was late for her appearance in a documentary film about Saint-Germain-des-Prés which was being shot at Les Deux Magots. When she arrived flushed and breathless, a crowd of student onlookers recognized her from newspaper photos in articles that reviled *The Second Sex* and began to hoot and whistle, yelling and chanting rhythmically for her to take off her clothes and perform a strip-tease. She was flustered and deeply upset, shouted something about postponing her appearance until another time and ran back to the Rue de la Bûcherie to drink Algren's Christmas-present scotch.[20]

She recovered her equanimity ten days later, when her manuscript was recovered from the lost-and-found and she learned that *The Second Sex* was third on the French best-seller lists. Volume Two had just been published and was creating even more of a stir than the first. "I have just seen my second child," she told Algren, "it is twice as big as the first and I like it better. I'm waiting now for the insults to start."[21]

The wait was short: bookstore owners throughout the north of France decided it was indecent and agreed to ban it. Gallimard was planning to sue them, which she thought was appropriate because it would be "good for publicity." Men heckled her while she was on the air during a radio broadcast; she overheard two others arguing in a café because one of them insisted he would not permit his wife to read such trash. One of her favorite "strange" letters came from an old man who reproached her for not defending the 100,000 women killed by members of the Resistance because they slept with German soldiers during the war; they should not have been punished, he argued, because women were "innocent of the knowledge of politics and nationality." She had her supporters as well, and told Algren he was not the only "local hero" (one of his favorite names for himself), because she too was a celebrity in her quarter. She was deluged with "love letters from women and pansies," and when she went to buy a new carpet for her room the man who sold it recognized her name and wanted to give her a handsome discount (which she refused to take, so he sent her a beautiful vase as a present the next day).[22]

She was suddenly a woman of stature: the American anthropologist Margaret Mead was in Paris, and Gallimard and Blanche Knopf decided it would serve both well if the two most prominent writers of the condition of women were to meet in a forum before journalists and scholars. For Beauvoir, Mead was a "horrible American woman . . . people arranged our meeting even though neither of us had read the other's book. Mead did not understand my English, so I talked to prettier women instead."[23] The attempt to create a dialogue between her and Mead failed, and for the rest of her life, whether it was true or not, Beauvoir insisted that she had never read "one word" of Mead's writing and "would never take such a one seriously."[24] Jean Wahl, whom she called "the old Chicago Existentialist professor," attended the discussion "with his glamorous young North African wife," who attacked Beauvoir on the question of women's frigidity: "She said no women had ever been frigid until I told them they were." Beauvoir turned her back on everyone and talked about the ruins of Uxmal with a group of ethnologists.

Beauvoir resented Blanche Knopf for putting her in an adversarial situation with Margaret Mead, all for the sake of publicity for her publishing house. Mrs. Knopf continued to irritate Beauvoir by insisting on lunching or dining with her and Sartre. When they ignored her invitations, she cleverly issued them through the editors at Gallimard. Sartre, uncomfortable with "aggressive, obnoxious women,"[25] said at once that he was too busy, and so Mrs. Knopf, a formidable presence, concentrated all her attentions on Beauvoir, who had no objection to her personality but faulted her for being "violently anti-communist."[26] Beauvoir listened without comment to the impassioned pleas of Gallimard's staff, who had collectively paled before the force of Mrs. Knopf's argument, then she simply failed to show up at the appointed time and place. Mrs. Knopf was understandably furious, and her dislike of Beauvoir colored all their future dealings, including being rude as well to Beauvoir's lawyer, Maître Blum, and her new literary agent, Mrs. Jennie Bradley (for whom Ellen Wright was then working).[27] In the next several years, because of her and Mrs. Knopf's personal animus, Beauvoir cared very little to assist her American publisher and in some instances actually went out of her way to impede the translation and publication of The Second Sex in the United States.

With grim relish, she told Algren there were some "nice plane crashes in Sweden, France and Dallas." But most of all, since Blanche Knopf was returning to New York, there was the chance that "perhaps her plane will crash."[28]

She was still worried about Algren's silence. Since nothing she suggested seemed to be working, she did something most uncharacteristic for her: she couched her request in terms of what Sartre needed and wanted. This was a true measure of her desperation, since she knew very well that no matter how much Algren professed to like Sartre, he did not understand her contingent relationship.

Despite their ostensible camaraderie when Algren was in France, "Sartre remained the red flag one flung before the bull to goad him." Knowing this, she still wrote that she had "a great favor to ask," that she "rarely demands anything," but this time she "must." She "begs" him to let her come to Chicago if he "possibly can," and concludes by asking him "not to be angry" with her.[29] Then came what must have been the ultimate outrage to Algren: she asked to come as early as June, because Sartre planned to be away from Paris for at least three months, and he had asked her "only to travel when he is away."[30]

Algren made no reply at all. She then tried another tack: in her next letter she suggested that one of the reasons for his hesitancy to have her visit for such a long stretch of time was that he could not work when she was with him, and, following the success of *The Man with the Golden Arm*, she imagined he must have felt a great deal of self-imposed pressure to maintain a disciplined daily writing schedule. Beauvoir said she understood this, and said that if she came to Chicago she would live separately for at least part of the time. She pointed out that she respected his need to work, but that theirs was "not just a vacation love" and they really needed "time to let our love grow." These last arguments must have persuaded him, because several weeks later he wrote to tell her she could come for the summer and he would rent a cottage on the dunes of Lake Michigan at Miller, Indiana.

His capitulation made her realize that it was one full year since she had told him she was writing a novel that would be in part about their love affair. She planned to work nonstop until her departure for Miller, hoping to have it finished and ready to show him. She had already told Algren of her idea to create a character who would be an American writer and Anne's long-distance lover. She hinted about what she wanted to do in a letter in which she described the moment she first knew she loved him, when he stood over her as she lay on the bed, "with a sheet over his arm and a puzzled expression on his face."[31] Her intention was to write "Lewis & Anne" sections of the novel before her trip to Miller. Algren had accepted the parts of *America Day by Day* that included the "Chicago writer, N. A.," but only after his friends there persuaded him that he had nothing to be embarrassed about. He was an intensely private man who could not understand how Beauvoir and Sartre managed to carry on their lives under constant public scrutiny and, even worse, to write about themselves in such intimate detail. He needed constant reassurance from Beauvoir that she would never write anything about him again, let alone anything that might bring him undue attention or shame, so the possibility for trouble was clearly present.

However, other things intervened first: like all her plans where Sartre was concerned, this one had to be changed. Since he could not go to Egypt in the fall, he had surprised her by deciding to spend the months of May and June traveling throughout the farthest reaches of North Africa, deep in the Sahara Desert. Naturally, he expected Beauvoir to go with him. She accepted at once, even though it meant telling Algren she could not possibly get to Miller before the twenty-fifth of June or, more likely, the first of July. Algren was so angry that he did not write to her for more than a month, and then he wrote only because she was so incoherent with worry that she sent an incomprehensible telegram. "The rain always stops after you buy the umbrella," she told him when he wired back noncommittally.[32]

Algren was in Hollywood, where he had gone to work on the screenplay of *The Man with the Golden Arm*. He was seeing his former wife, Amanda Kontowicz, again, and told Beauvoir (whether seriously or in the hope of spurring her to some sort of action is not clear) that he might have made a grave mistake when they divorced. Beauvoir was worried about it, but not enough to cancel her trip with Sartre. Instead, she evaded the issue by giving Algren detailed instructions about what he was to tell and not tell Natasha Moffatt about their affair if he happened to meet her.[33] She was still apologetic about writing so often, blaming everything on the garbled telegram. When that failed to elicit a response, she wrote again, asking him to forgive her for frightening him, but she had been having nightmares that he was dead, killed in a plane crash. She pleaded with him to understand, but he did not reply. She wrote again anyway, calling him a "heartless mean jackass," hoping that he would "remember how to kiss [her] this summer."[34]

It seemed as if everything conspired to keep her from writing, from worrying about Algren to—out of the blue—the return of her cousin Jacques Champigneulle to Paris. She had not seen him for almost twenty years when she ran into him accidentally on the street. Her mother had previously told her that Jacques was a hopeless alcoholic who had lost everything. His wife had abandoned him, and now she, his daughter and his five grandchildren were all being supported by his father-in-law. Beauvoir, astonished at the derelict he had become, met him several times for lunch and gave him as much money as she had to spare. When it seemed as if he might like this arrangement enough to try to make her support permanent, she cut him off by saying she would pay only for a cure if he would sequester himself in a place of her choosing. He drifted off for a few months, but returned with one of his sons, using the excuse that he wanted Beauvoir to advise the young man about getting an education. She refused, saying the only thing the son wanted was to make a lot of money without working for it, as he was handsome enough to have many women squabbling to support him. Jacques had the good grace to leave without a fuss. She never saw him again, because he died shortly after.[35] She did not mourn the man she once thought she loved.

Then Violette Leduc grew frantic when she learned that Beauvoir planned to leave Paris, first for two months with Sartre, then for three months with Algren. She was hysterical, accosting Beauvoir publicly to declare her "sexual" love, saying she would one day love her "completely." Beauvoir "froze," and would not accept an apology from "the Ugly Woman" when she came around tearfully the next morning. Her coldness only exacerbated Leduc's irrational behavior, so that Beauvoir could not wait to get away from her and ushered her unceremoniously out of the building.[36]

She and Sartre flew to Cannes in early March. He stayed to discuss various film possibilities while she went off alone to Marseille for several days until he joined her and they flew together to Algiers. Beauvoir's only obligation in Africa was to see Bianca Bienenfeld Lamblin. It was not a pleasant reunion, because Bianca was still unhappily married and hated living in Algiers and teaching African students. Beauvoir was glad when the visit was over and she and Sartre headed south into the desert, where they traveled for the next two months.

In the meantime, Algren returned to Wabansia, but did not write despite Beauvoir's continuing stream of letters giving him the addresses of all her hotels in the hope that she would find a letter waiting at each. He broke the silence only once, to send a picture of himself in a tuxedo being kissed by Eleanor Roosevelt on March 16 at the National Book Award ceremony.[37] Unfortunately, she did not receive it until she was in Casablanca at the end of May visiting her sister and her brother-in-law, who was the cultural attaché there. In her last letter from Africa, written May 3, she told Algren that a plane like the one she and Sartre had flown in for the past two months had gone down in the Sahara, and on the flight back to Paris she worried because she was "afraid of crashing and never kissing [him] again."[38]

On their "anniversary," May 10, she sent him a soppy love letter even though he had been so cold to her in recent months. As with so many of her letters, this one was mostly apologetic: for its general messiness, for her tears and silliness and for the way she repeatedly kissed his photo, which he had previously told her made him angry and embarrassed. However, the letter had the effect she wanted, because not only did he reply, but also he sent floor plans of two cottages and asked her to pick the one she liked for their coming "honeymoon." His letters began to arrive again on a regular basis. "I like it," she wrote, "when you send such long letters!"[39]

Her departure was finally set for June 25. She would fly to New York to spend several days seeing Stépha and calling at various American publishers to collect money owed to her and Sartre, who arranged for her to have $200 from his United States royalties. With that plus a total of $800 owed her from *Flair* and Knopf, she would have more than enough for the simple life she envisioned leading with Algren at Miller.[40]

By the first of June she had given up entirely trying to write any more of *The Mandarins*, because she was so nervous about seeing him again.

His moods fluctuated, one moment romantic and happy about her visit, the next either cold or else totally silent, not writing at all. By mid-June, when two Paris-to-Saigon planes crashed in the Persian Gulf within two days of each other, she decided to book passage on a ship. On her way to the booking office she changed her mind because she did not want to waste a week at sea.

Her nervousness turned to almost paralyzing fear when the Korean War began and another world war, perhaps a nuclear conflict, seemed a real possibility. In her memoirs, she wrote that Sartre told her to go to Chicago anyway despite the panic that gripped the French economy and the fear that infused the people.[41] She modified this during a 1985 conversation, when she said that Algren's most recent letters were so puzzling by their coldness that she was determined to make the trip. "In the fear I shared with everyone in France, I did believe the Russians would invade us and then the Americans would retaliate and bomb us to oblivion. I wanted to see him, especially if it were to be for the last time ever, because I had to know what was happening to our affair."

Finally, on July 8, bolstered by tranquilizers and liquor, she left, flying first to New York and then to Chicago. Algren was waiting for her on Wabansia, where he greeted her casually and then issued all sorts of pronouncements and ground rules for her stay. He had decided that their relationship was "going nowhere," and that he no longer loved her. She wrote about it in *The Mandarins* "almost literally, almost word for word, the way we ended it," when Anne makes her last visit to Lewis Brogan during the summer they spend together at a beach cottage in "Parker," her fictional name for Miller.[42] Algren told her that he had changed, that it was too difficult for him to sustain the emotion of loving her when her long absences created such a deep void in his life. She tried to brush aside his comments, insisting that, as her feelings for him had not diminished, she would work hard to rekindle his earlier passion for her. But all her attempts to do so failed. She had succeeded in convincing him that her real life was in Paris, so she failed to persuade him that her most important emotion was loving him in Chicago. On this trip at least, she was not able to rekindle the intensity of their earlier passion. Their primary emotional response to each other was "not passion, but deep and caring friendship."

In *The Mandarins,* when Anne has come to the end of her stay in Parker and is preparing to return to Paris, Beauvoir ends the fictional recreation of her love affair with Algren with an actual conversation that happened between them:

> The night of my departure, I [Anne] said, "Lewis, I don't know if I'll ever stop loving you; but I do know that all my life you'll be in my heart."
> He held me against him. "And you in mine, all my life."[43]

In the novel, just before she boards her plane a messenger hands Anne "a cardboard box in which lay, under a shroud of silky paper, a huge orchid. When I arrived in Paris, it still hadn't faded."[44] In real life, Beauvoir flew to New York on September 30. It was understood that they would see each other again sometime, but for the first time Algren did not press her to set even an approximate date for her next visit. He took her to O'Hare Airport, but left as soon as she checked her luggage. Their farewell consisted of "a friendly hug." Her plane was delayed for more than an hour, which was fortunate, since a messenger did bring her a "purple flower with little birds." Later that night, when she was in her room at the Hotel Lincoln in New York ("I could not break my heart by staying in the Brittany," where they had stayed together in 1948), she wrote to thank him for the flower:

> I may have lost your love, but I have not lost you, and I will treasure your friendship. I love you as much as ever, with my whole heart and soul. But you must feel no obligation to me, though. You should write only when you want to, not because you feel you must. I will always consider myself your own Simone.[45]

Once back in Paris, she told him the truth: "The flower died when the plane was above the ocean, but I still keep the singing birds in my purse."[46]

Sartre was waiting for her when she arrived; he took her out to dinner in a restaurant where they were unknown, and they sat there talking far into the night. The attacks against him had continued unabated in her absence, and now, with the Korean War raging, they intensified every day. No matter where people stood on the political spectrum, they still expected Sartre to take a stand, and, when Les Temps Modernes (under Merleau-Ponty) remained silent, all accusations and denunciations were aimed directly at Sartre. Many of their friends feared that the Russians would occupy France and were considering exile. For a brief time, Sartre was among them.

She confided all this to Algren, who found their fears amusing at first. It was easy for him to scoff, Beauvoir retorted, because he was so far from the danger of Russian occupation. She had once scoffed, too, she told him, "at the fears of all my Jewish friends in 1939 and 40."

The fear of being squeezed between the two world powers, Russia and the United States, was rampant in Europe, and Beauvoir reflected the thinking of many in France when she wrote, "War certainly means that the Russians will occupy France." She believed that because of their independent stance Sartre and she would "surely be killed or sent to Siberia. We are considering moving to Brazil or Africa."[47]

Algren replied at once, offering to send them a hundred dollars, which was all he had at the time, and any other money he could raise from his agent, his publisher and his friends. He thought they should consider Mexico, because it was closer than Rio de Janeiro, but he also offered to find a place for them in Chicago or Miller, whichever they preferred.[48] She was deeply moved, but she declined:

> Politically it would be impossible for me and Sartre to move to the U.S., hating American policy as we do. Financially it would be too difficult to live there. Brazil offers us money and the benefit of a neutral country. Oh, I wish I could talk to you about these things![49]

The situation had become chaotic and irrational:

> People in Paris, the non-Communists and the wealthy—worry about where to go when the Russians come. Sartre will be killed immediately and I will be in danger. I live now expecting to leave in six months to two years.[50]

Her preoccupation with exile was shared by Richard Wright, who fanned the flames of her panic

> with the favorite topic of non-Communist intellectuals: where will we go, and when will we have to? We decided all to go to Brazil—Dick thinks we should all live in one "deeply committed" village. I disagree.[51]

Algren wrote back, telling her not to pack her bags too quickly, and by early 1951 she agreed: "we are hoping for peace and don't talk about exile any more."[52]

When she wrote her memoirs, Beauvoir eliminated the various scenarios, plans and counterproposals she and Sartre made to remove themselves from France. She wrote only that Sartre

> rejected the idea of exile to the very marrow of his bones. . . . He was convinced that by going into exile, no matter how good the reasons for doing so, one lost one's place in the world, and that one could never quite recover it again.[53]

Instead of going into exile, they made their annual winter trek to La Pouèze.

It is difficult to say with any exactitude just what *The Mandarins* should be described as: part autobiography, part social and political history, part love story and part literary credo—it eludes both category and definition. In 1982, Beauvoir spoke of the position this novel holds in her canon, what it meant to her life during the four years she wrote it, and what it continued to mean until her death:

"It is the book I wrote with the most passion. It is the book I found the most important among my novels . . . It is the novel which remains alive [to me] . . . I feel sometimes like reading it over because I loved it a lot. You can say that the tone of *The Mandarins* is the most committed of all my novels, but remember—there are three main ideas in it:

love and friendship are the most important, and then politics. Also, there are many different points of view: Anne's is not Henri's, which is not Robert's. All these points of view clash, and that's why the novel had to be constructed as it was. In my opinion, that style [of writing] has a certain aesthetic value, a literary value. And that's why I had to write and rewrite that novel for almost four years."[54]

As soon as she was settled in at La Pouèze, the first thing Beauvoir wrote was the end of Anne's affair with Lewis. By early 1951, all the sections concerning Anne were nearly complete, and she turned next to the parts about Henri's relationships with women, first Paule, then Anne's daughter Nadine. In later years, when Beauvoir talked about the composition of the novel, she said she had written "the easiest parts first," because the personal relationships were in many instances her own or a mélange of those of her friends; prominent among these were the Wrights, who were having marital problems.[55]

She wrote to Algren from Saint-Tropez—where she and Sartre went after leaving La Pouèze—because she wanted him to know that she had written about their affair, but she was unable to tell him the truthful extent to which she had done so. All she said was, "I will tell a little bit about OUR story [both capitalizing and underlining the word to make sure he knew what she meant], "because the situation is so modern and I love reminiscing, even though it makes me so sad."[56]

Having written of friendship and love by the winter of 1951, she had the hardest part, politics, still before her. The political framework unifies the novel, but, more important, it permits Beauvoir to treat under the general guise of politics many other themes which really have little to do with politics *per se*. It also makes the plot difficult to summarize because of the intricacy of its themes and the subtle complexities of both the personal and the political relationships. As she wrote these sections, it soon became apparent that she needed a foil for Anne, and so Henri became her second protagonist. She made him both journalist and creative writer to establish a potential for conflict between him and Anne's husband, Robert, who hopes to found a new political movement after the war is ended, similar to Sartre's idea of France as an independent entity between the two world powers.[57] The political (or "social," to use Beauvoir's preferred term) conflict arises when Henri, having learned of the Soviet labor camps, must decide whether or not his newspaper will publish the story. He decides to maintain his independence as a matter of principle and prints it. But rather than allowing this defection from the Communist line to isolate Henri from the politics of the Left entirely, Beauvoir makes him become valuable to the party's cause as a spokesperson because the politically nonaligned will believe what his paper prints as the truth.

Besides the question of whether to print the truth when it contradicts his larger political belief, Henri, as a journalist, must deal with several other important realities, such as how he will acquire the paper on which to print anything at all during a time of crucial shortages, and, if he does manage to find the paper, where he will get the money to pay for it. It is this sort of grounded evocation of the difficulty of everyday life in the immediate postwar years that gives *The Mandarins* so much of its fictional vitality and veracity.

Beauvoir makes Anne a psychiatrist, an unusual occupation when one considers her own lifelong suspicion of the subject. But by doing so Beauvoir is able to address what might well be called the collective mental health of an entire society and to comment upon what form and direction its healing should take. She also politicizes psychiatry by writing of classical psychoanalysis in the light of contemporary Marxist theory. One could say that Anne's role throughout the novel is one of constant rethinking of all her opinions, positions and relationships. Professionally, she must reconsider her most profound beliefs in order to determine whether people who have survived a war should be allowed to forget the past, since the future is also subject to terrible possibilities—atomic war, for example. It is not until Anne sees some of the first deportees who have returned to France that she regains any sort of equilibrium, if not faith, in her profession. Personally, she must be able to accept all sorts of changed relationships, from hers with her husband and her grown-up daughter to the end of her long-distance love affair with Lewis Brogan.[58]

Anne serves another important purpose: she is Beauvoir's first fictional representation of what critics of *The Second Sex* were now calling "*la condition féminine*," or, more accurately, of Beauvoir's burgeoning politically committed feminism. Anne has been married for twenty years to an older man who has come to fill the role of the good friend she depends upon, and she has also had a passionate love affair with another man, who allowed her to believe for a time that essential and contingent love were both possible. She is the mother of an adult daughter, Nadine, her relationship with whom is both affectionate and troubled. She is also a friend to women, and Henri's abandoned lover, Paule, lets Beauvoir put Anne in direct contrast with another example of the desperate, abandoned women who continue to figure in her later fiction, especially in the collection of stories called *A Woman Destroyed*.

There are many other contrasts as well, on many different levels. Rich Americans are balanced by pretentious French society hostesses. The settings vary from Paris to Portugal (where Henri visits) to the center of France (where Anne, Robert and Henri take a holiday) and, of course, the United States. Because the book has two protagonists, the language is rich in variety and form. These range from Anne's searching and dispassionate first-person monologues, recited in both past tense and historic present, to the slangy immediacy of Henri's speech and internal monologues. The dialogue is packed with confrontation and ideology; the plot is dense with event. In short, it is an extraordinary book which many scholars and critics believe to be one of the best and most important novels—and certainly one of the most undervalued—of the twentieth century.

□

But finishing *The Mandarins* was no easy matter. Beauvoir described this period as one of the most difficult times of her life, because she withdrew almost entirely from living in the public eye and carrying on her daily business before the world. She spent most of her time alone in her room, and even stopped drinking altogether in order to have the stamina to concentrate a minimum of six or seven hours each day on the book. When anyone interrupted her concentration, even if Sartre or Bost knocked unexpectedly, they were likely to be greeted with a string of curses and told to go away.

Algren groused that this was making her normally difficult penmanship impossible to decipher, so she even stopped writing to him. He complained angrily about it, listing all the things of which loving her had "deprived" him. She replied in the same testy tone, saying, "You should know that I gave up a few things, too, for your sake. Our affair certainly didn't improve my relationship with Sartre, I broke off my romance with Bost, and I never looked at anyone but you for all these years." Then she softened her attack, saying that even if life was "bleak" for her, having him in it made it all worthwhile.[59] By Christmas 1951, she was in a better mood and sent him greetings, saying she had worked hard all day and had not had a single drink.[60]

She also began to call it *his* book, as, for example, in early fall 1952 when she said, " 'Your' book is almost done . . ." She assured him that only one part was about him, and the rest

> about French intellectuals between '44 and '48. I put lots of things in it—travels, nights out, young and mature people, and some of Koestler, Camus, Sartre and myself. Sartre says it is the best thing I have ever written. I will give it to Gallimard within three months. I wonder if Knopf will ever translate it.[61]

It took somewhat longer: by late 1953 the book had become 1,200 typed pages, which she thought Algren would most likely never read, "since it is anti-American enough to be unpublishable in the U.S." Beauvoir planned to give the typescript to Gallimard at the end of April 1954, but added, "It doesn't have a title as yet." Since publication was scheduled for October, she had time to think about it.[62] She gave Bost credit for the title: he had said quite seriously that he, she and Sartre, because they were intellectuals, represented the only remaining nobility in France, just as the Mandarin class did in pre-Communist China. She liked the sound of *Les Mandarins*, as did Sartre, Queneau, all the rest of their friends and everyone at Gallimard.

The publication date was set for early in October, to launch the novel at exactly the most fortuitous moment to be a candidate for the prestigious Prix Goncourt. A massive publicity campaign was launched, and Beauvoir cooperated with everything her publisher asked her to do. It was reviewed favorably by both the left- and right-wing presses, each of which, she said, "interpreted it in its own light." Sartre, Olga, Bost and Michelle were convinced the prize would be hers. "They want me to win because I will make a lot of money," she told Algren offhandedly. "As for me, I don't really care." Which was not at all true, because she wanted this prize more than she ever wanted any other honor.

What she really cared most about, however, was Algren's reaction. She did win the Prix Goncourt, and in January 1955, when he and she had supposedly ended their love affair and he had married and divorced his first wife for the second time, Beauvoir was still wondering what his reaction to the book would be. "The love story is highly praised," she repeated once again, as if to convince him that he should not take um-brage at it. Again, she quibbled with the truth: "It is not exactly our story, but a story about a man a little bit like you and a woman a little bit like me. I want very much to know what you will think of it." Earlier she sent him a copy of the French edition—"even though you never learned to read French, you will recognize your name on the dedication page."[63] It carried the simple dedication "To Nelson Algren."

He did not read the novel until it was translated and published in 1956, and then it made him furious and caused the second most serious rupture in their relationship. But until then he took great pride in show-ing it off to his friends in Chicago, and if any of them bought a copy he would autograph it, writing just below the dedication: "on account of becuz he is mah ideel!" Then he would usually forge her signature.[64] He thought it funny until he read the English translation in 1956. She sent him a copy with a handwritten dedication. Under the printed "To Nelson Algren," she wrote:

> He knows why and how—
> In memory of the old never to be
> forgotten happiness, when I was
> Your own Simone[65]

He read the book, and after that she was never again his "own Simone." Everything about her was fair game for attack as far as he was concerned.

THIRTY-ONE

A $10 Book by
an Unknown Frenchwoman

THE AFFAIR WITH ALGREN lurched along in fits and starts throughout most of the 1950s. At the beginning of the decade it was temporarily sidetracked for the better part of a year while he courted Amanda Kontowicz, and then it was dormant during the first year of their two-year-long second marriage, which lasted (on paper, at least) from 1953 to 1955. In the spring of 1951, while he tried to make up his mind whether or not to marry his ex-wife again, he invited Beauvoir to make a second visit to Miller. It was as if, before embarking on another relationship, he had to bring a sense of closure to theirs, but Beauvoir had no idea of his intentions until she got there that October.[1] Although he did not say so in his letters, many years later, and with what she called "much hindsight," she believed he still hoped to persuade her to leave Sartre and her life in Paris to live permanently in Chicago, with or without marriage. As she changed her plans repeatedly to conform to Sartre's needs and whims, Algren probably realized how unrealistic this was, so that by the time of her arrival he had built a solid fortress of unspoken barriers which she was quite unprepared to scale.

In 1982 she said, "Algren made fun of what he called my insensitivity to the feelings of others. I never understood why he mocked me for this. These accusations caused me great pain, because it seemed to me that I worried more about pleasing him than any other person in my life, that I changed myself to be what he wanted me to be, and still, somehow, I never seemed to do the right thing. I suppose he felt this way because of the last time we were together in Miller, when our situation was so tense. But he was no more sensitive than I, so it was as much his fault as mine that we were not sympathetic and understanding of each other. Neither of us really knew how to say what the other wanted to hear, and we were too awkward to know what to do about it."

Algren was prone to moods of brooding silence, and these had already ruined much of her first sojourn in Miller. When he invited her for a second visit, she hoped it was because he wanted to try to make amends. She was happy, but soon there was an added cause for concern.

There was the possibility that she would not be given a visa to enter the United States. She learned this from Jean Cau (who had become her errand boy as well as Sartre's) when he returned unsuccessfully from the American Embassy to tell her that the visa would not be granted until consular officials studied *America Day by Day* and all the other supposedly anti-American articles she had written for *Les Temps Modernes*. Also, despite the fact that she had never joined a Communist organization, three years previously she had signed a petition for the French Women's League, a group with strong Communist sympathies, and this too was suspect. She was very worried, because even though she had enough money to pay for Algren's fare to Paris, she knew that his pride at this point would not permit him to accept. Unless she could get to Chicago, they would not be able to see each other.[2]

It took almost four months for the visa to be approved, and in September 1951, after a stop in New York to get money owed her and Sartre by various publishers,[3] she arrived at Algren's new apartment on Forrest Avenue early on the morning of October 15. Algren had had almost six months to brood, and as soon as she was in the apartment he announced that he wanted them to live the entire length of her visit as friends, because it was obvious to him that they could no longer be lovers. Beauvoir was shocked, but agreed to do whatever he wanted. She stayed with him until the twenty-ninth, and throughout that time they slept in separate bedrooms at the cottage and in separate beds (actually he slept on the lumpy couch) when they went into Chicago and stayed in his new flat.

On the morning of October 28, the last day of her visit, Algren came into her bedroom, where she was sprawled on the bed surrounded by newspapers and magazines, drowsing in the unseasonable heat of an Indian Summer day.[4] From the expression on his face, she thought something terrible had happened, and sat bolt upright. Suddenly "his face crumpled, he fell to his knees beside the bed, he told me he loved me." For the next few hours they were lovers, "even though we both knew it was all over between us." She flew to New York, took a room in the Hotel Lincoln overnight, and wrote to him the next day before her flight to Paris. She was still not over the shock of hearing him say he loved her after all the weeks they had lived under the strain of what was supposed to have passed for friendship.

Once again, she felt compelled to explain, in several long letters, why she behaved as she did toward him. She agreed that every accusation he had hurled at her before her departure was all too true, and she felt deeply guilty about how their affair had inhibited his life. Despite her insistence that she could never commit herself to him entirely because she could not leave either Sartre or Paris, fully aware of how unfair it was to him, she could not resist loving him. She understood that he wanted to end their affair as a means of self-preservation, but "knowing it is fair does not make it easier to accept." She told him that she had tried to be satisfied with friendship because it was better than nothing, even if it had driven her nearly crazy to be with him under such circumstances. But when he blurted out his love, she was "scared again" because it made her see how easily he could break down all her carefully constructed defenses: "I am open to being hurt again and again if you decide to stop loving me. I beg you to keep me or drop me, once and for all. Consider my feelings, too." Since she wanted him in her life no matter what the circumstances, everything was up to him: "I will accept whatever you decide and make no trouble for you." She loved him, she concluded, because he loved her in return and because they had had such sexual happiness as she had never known with another man. Even if all that ended, she vowed to continue to love him.

She blamed the emotional tension of her last few days in Chicago and New York for giving her a cold, a fever and flu. She was sick on the flight to Paris and so upset over their parting that she forgot to worry that the plane might crash. "For me, this meant I was very, very sick!" she said many years later. She could not stop crying, which was embarrassing because other passengers recognized her. "These must be the tears I have not shed for a year," she wrote on a note mailed in midflight from a stop in Gander. "I look eighty and feel as foolish as a twenty-year-old."[5]

Once they had separated, both regained their equanimity. Algren wrote, profusely apologetic for upsetting her but firm in his resolve to end their affair:

> One can still have the same feelings for someone and still not allow them to rule and disturb one's life. To love a woman who does not belong to you, who puts other things and other people before you, without there ever being any question of your taking first place, is something that just isn't acceptable. I don't regret a single one of the moments we had together. But now I want a different kind of life. . . . The disappointment I felt three years ago, when I began to realize that your life belonged to Paris and to Sartre . . . [has] become blunted by time. What I've tried to do since is to take my life back from you. My life means a lot to me, I don't like its belonging to someone so far off, someone I see only a few weeks every year. . . .[6]

In an attempt to conciliate, she replied, "Now it is over and we are friends forever, with no resentment." Awkwardly, she told him that she planned to be his "best friend" and would give her "love" to another— her new car.[7]

Gallimard loaned her the money to buy it, Genet helped her to find it, and she was now the proud owner of a new Simca Aronde.[8] She was a terrible driver and in years to come would be involved in many minor scrapes and several serious accidents, but she never lost her zest for driving and enjoyed automobile trips, no matter where or for how long, until the end of her life.

While she was with Algren that October, she spent much of her time writing the essay "Must We Burn Sade?," which was published in the review after she returned to France. She described the Marquis as a "fascinating man who for twenty years brutally loved and hated women and then spent the rest of his life in jail writing about what he couldn't do any more. . . . Next to him [Henry] Miller is a child and Genet an angel."[9]

In many crucial instances 1952–53 was a watershed year for Simone de Beauvoir. It marked, among much else, the first time she ended her relationship with Nelson Algren, the start of a period in which she set intellectual priorities separately from Sartre, and—although it did not happen in France—a publishing success that has frequently been cited as the most important of her entire literary career.

"With spring came a great satisfaction," she wrote in her memoirs: "*The Second Sex* appeared in America with a success unsoiled by any salacious comment. . . . [E]very time it has been published in another country, I have been pleased to receive fresh proof that the scandal it aroused in France was the fault of my readers and not myself."[10]

Blanche Knopf deserves credit for discerning that *The Second Sex* would be an important book worthy of translation, but not for the reason she first assumed. On one of her frequent trips to Paris, Mrs. Knopf was apprised of the book by several members of the Gallimard family, but she spoke no French and understood her interpreter to say that the book was a "modern-day sex manual, something between Kinsey and Havelock Ellis."[11] She was counting on the popularity of Existentialism among young Americans, particularly those of college age who were increasingly fascinated with romantic (and usually apocryphal) tales of Saint-Germain-des-Prés, to translate into substantial sales. Young Americans were increasingly caught up in the stories of bohemian life that found their way across the Atlantic, and the time seemed propitious to launch a book for them. So Mrs. Knopf bought a copy of Volume One and took it home to ask her husband's advice. She made no effort to meet Beauvoir at that time, preferring to wait for her husband's opinion about the book.

Alfred A. Knopf wanted an expert's judgment, and, since the book was purported to be a study of female sexuality, he asked H. M. Parshley, a professor emeritus of zoology at Smith College, to provide one. Since neither of the Knopfs had an inkling of what Beauvoir's book was about, Professor Parshley was not as unlikely a candidate to evaluate it as many critics of his translation have since complained. Howard Madison Parshley (1884–1953) began his career as an expert on insect behavior and later became an expert on problems of human reproduction and allied matters.[12] He also collaborated frequently on translations from the French of a scientific nature, was particularly well informed on contemporary scientific research in France and, above all, was someone whom the Knopfs knew personally and whose intelligence they respected. In short, they believed they had carefully selected the most trustworthy candidate to provide them with the expert judgment such a work demanded.

They sent the book to Parshley on July 11, 1949, and received his report one month later. It was because of Parshley's perceptive analysis and his strong support for it that *The Second Sex* was translated so early on in its long publishing life. Parshley called it "a thoughtful and well-written work which throws new light on an old question." He also thought:

> A book on women by an intelligent, learned, and well balanced woman is, I think, a great rarity, and this is indeed such a book. It is not feminist in any doctrinaire sense, nor is it an attack on the male sex; and it does not belong to the category of ululations about the "lost sex," etc., of which we have plenty. . . . The book is a profound and unique analysis of woman's nature and position, eminently reasonable and often witty; and it surely should be translated, as I have already said, with the second volume, if the quality is maintained. However, the first volume can stand alone, in my opinion. It is frank in places, but not as a whole sensational, and I would be surprised (and pleased) at a large sale. It should pay for itself, and in any case will be a credit to the publisher.[13]

From the beginning, Parshley knew he had to cut and condense the unwieldy book. A letter to him from Alfred Knopf gave the general consensus of all who worked on the project:

> She [Beauvoir] certainly suffers from verbal diarrhea—I have seldom read a book that seems to run in such concentric circles. Everything seems to be repeated three or four times but in different parts of the text, and I can hardly imagine the average person reading the whole book carefully. But I think it is capable of making a very wide appeal indeed and that young ladies in places like Smith who can afford the price, which will be high, will be nursing it just as students of my generation managed somehow to get hold of Havelock Ellis.[14]

Parshley worked diligently to keep as much of the text and to compose as faithful a translation as possible, but difficulties arose because many of Beauvoir's sources were French, to be found only in France, and thus unavailable to him. Also, she used many terms which had a particular meaning in Existential philosophy, and the question became not only how to translate them but also how best to explain them. Parshley read as widely as possible in Sartre's Existentialism and precursors such as Hegel and Heidegger, but he naturally felt the need to be in direct correspondence with Beauvoir to make sure that he interpreted all these others correctly

in terms of her particular thesis. One example typical of the many Parshley struggled with concerns the relatively easy word *alterité*, which he
finally decided should be translated literally as "alterity," a synonym for
"otherness" and brought into common English usage as such, but this
was minor compared to other situations.[15] Worried that Existentialism
would prove too difficult for American readers to comprehend, the publishers asked Parshley to provide a translator's preface "which . . . will—
or should—be important 'in putting the book over.' "[16] Parshley agreed
but doubted

> whether it would be advisable for me to undertake any serious
> account of existentialism, or even a formal definition of terms;
> it is a touchy business to explain a controversial philosophy and
> in any case I now believe that the serious reader gets to under-
> stand the relatively few existentialist concepts and more or less
> obscure associated phraseology as he goes along. Evidently the
> author felt the same way, for those matters would be no easier
> for French readers than for others, yet she presents them with-
> out much explanation.

Before going ahead with this, he wanted to consult the author, so he
sent a long letter to her in May 1951. He had to write in care of Mrs. Bradley's office, since, after two years into the translation process, Beauvoir
would still not allow Gallimard to release her address to anyone at Knopf.
Parshley explained his intention to reduce the book "without omission or
modification" of Beauvoir's ideas, "our purpose being in part to effect some
reduction in bulk, but primarily to make the work more attractive to English and American readers." Then he listed some of his suggestions, including, for example, a reduction of the extensive material she had quoted
from the work of Helene Deutsch, since it was "readily available here."[17]
Parshley was a gentle, tactful man who was referring as politely as possible
to an earlier request he had made to Beauvoir to supply him with a list
of the sources she used in *The Second Sex*. Months later, Beauvoir replied
through Mrs. Bradley's office:

> I am sorry, but it is impossible to recover the references to the
> English books which I consulted. There are too many of them,
> and some I had only in translation. In any case, I would not know
> how to find the passages I cited without a tremendous amount of
> work.[18]

Parshley found them himself. By this time he was well along with
Volume Two, and he sent her a complete list of all his suggestions for
cutting and abridging both it and Volume One as well, again stating his
intention to abide by her wishes. She was upset "in particular about the
History section," and thought it "extremely regretable [*sic*] to cut the detailed studies which make my writing vivid and convincing."[19] Finally she
"agreed in principle to the idea of cuts provided they were submitted to her

for her approval, and did not involve her treatment of Montherlant, which she insisted must be translated exactly as she wrote it."[20] Blanche Knopf suggested that Parshley compose yet another "tactful and very explicit letter . . . doing your best to get her to write to you that she is confident in your and our judgment . . . and thus give you an okay."

On June 21, 1951, Parshley was startled to find a letter from Beauvoir in his mailbox at Smith College:

> I found your letter when I came back from a trip and I'm apologizing for replying so tardily. I'm sure you understand that an author does not like to cut or condense a work upon which she has lavished great care. I suppose however, that you have good reason for wanting to do so. I will ask you only to state in your preface that what you are presenting has been cursorily adapted for the American public. I can't accept it if you present it as an exact translation when so much of what seems important to me will have been omitted. I want you to make a statement that discharges me of all responsibility for this; in return for which, I'll give you *carte blanche*. Agreed?[21]

Months passed, during which Parshley argued that Beauvoir's "wish to be 'relieved of all responsibility' . . . would be ridiculous, as my very minor condensations in no way change her ideas or form or style."[22] Finally, by late October 1951, he gave up and sought to compose a translator's introduction that would incorporate Beauvoir's statement while both Knopfs continued to argue against any at all. Blanche Knopf returned from a trip to Paris on October 19 and told Parshley that "La Beauvoir" (as they were all now calling her) was in New York but would give no one her address. "It seems silly for her to be sitting in New York without communicating with you or me, but there she is."[23] On October 24, she wrote again to the distraught Parshley (who had spent more time in that week trying to find Beauvoir than he had in translating the book): "There is not a thing about La Beauvoir that I can do for you. I tried my best . . . to get her address while I was in Paris but couldn't. I think you will simply have to carry on as you did." Mrs. Knopf also thought "making such a statement in the preface is ridiculous so that I would just tell her that you are not doing it and let it go at that."[24]

But when it was submitted to Knopf's lawyers to be vetted, they decided that since Beauvoir had had total control of the text written into her contract, her wish in this matter had to be honored. Parshley added the final paragraph, a statement of procedure and intention which every American edition of the book has since carried. In the letter that accompanied it, he told Mrs. Knopf that he had been "laboring for some time on it," and

> to me, it seems to express what the reader might want from me . . . it is, as you see, a personal statement and yet it gives

certain necessary information. I have not wished to undertake a more elaborate statement of the existentialist philosophy, for which I am hardly qualified; but it has seemed to me important to state Mlle. de Beauvoir's relation to it in this book. I may provide a footnote at some suitable place defining some of the existentialist terms, if you feel that this is not sufficiently well done by my occasional addition of explanatory words in the text, here and there.[25]

On November 2, 1951, Blanche Knopf read and accepted Parshley's translation, giving him high praise for what had been nonstop devotion to a book he had come to believe in and cherish. But she also said:

> The only thing that I want to point out to you is that existensialism [sic] is really a dead duck. Where you have to mention it, of course you will, but it seems of no great importance any longer in the literary world of France or anywhere else.

Parshley, who had originally undertaken the translation because the fee of $2,000 would have been just enough to allow him to purchase something he had yearned for all his life, a new Buick sedan, had by this time become Beauvoir's defender, champion of her text and strong believer in all that she had written. He could not let such a comment pass:

> I suppose you mean that it is no longer a current sensation, as you say, in the literary world; but I fancy that Sartre's novels have some permanent value, and certainly *Le Deuxième Sexe* contains enough existentialist material to require some special mention, and, further, I believe that existentialism has provided philosophy with certain new insights of permanent value.[26]

Everyone at Knopf who had been involved in the translation was satisfied with Parshley's work, and the decision was made to publish the book on February 23, 1953. "This is one of the handsomest books we have ever made," Mrs. Knopf wrote to Parshley, "and also one of the finest translations on our list."[27]

Three copies were flown to Paris, and Beauvoir replied—not to Mrs. Knopf, who also sent a personal letter filled with praise, but to Mrs. Bradley, whose only role had been to post the books on to her:

> I received the copies which you sent me; I find the book superb, the translation seems excellent to me, and I will be happy if she [Blanche Knopf] comes to Paris this year and I can tell her in person how much I appreciate Mr. Parshley's work and the appearance of my book.[28]

Four years of nonstop Herculean effort had taken its toll on Parshley, who had been hospitalized on several occasions throughout the translating process for general exhaustion and frail health. He bore much of the expense himself, as the money Knopf allocated for translation was barely

enough to pay for the new Buick,[29] but his enjoyment of the car was tempered by both conscious and unconscious rebuffs from the publishers. He
wanted his affiliation with Smith College listed after his name in the
translator's preface, but he also asked respectfully for both his name and
his affiliation to be given on the book jacket if possible; if not, at least on
the title page. Harold Strauss, the book's editor, replied that Parshley's
request seemed both "proper and useful,"[30] and Parshley rested content
that he would be credited for his work.

He first suspected that this was not to be when he saw a publicity
circular in his local bookstore, calling the book

> an exciting and enlightening study of what it means to be a
> woman in mind, in body and in spirit. Here is the definitive, all-
> inclusive, uninhibited story of modern woman and her place in
> Western culture—a book that will take its place alongside of
> Havelock Ellis's *The Psychology of Sex*.[31]

This was accompanied by a photo of a marble statue of a nude Greek
woman whose hand is strategically placed on her genital area, and the
subheading "One of the great books of our time on sex and human personality." Parshley's name was nowhere to be found. He wrote in some
alarm and Harold Strauss replied that sales circulars were entirely the
responsibility of the sales department, so he, as editor, could not be
faulted for the nonappearance of Parshley's name.

> I explain this to you so that the next fact shall not take you too
> much by surprise. . . . We [the Editorial Department] are alto-
> gether to blame for the omission of your name on the jacket. . . .
> In case you think I am being callous regarding your feelings, I
> hope you will take another look at the circular and observe that
> the name of another interested party has been omitted. Ours.[32]

The title page was reset to include Parshley's name, but his most
fervent wish, that it appear on the dust jacket, was never granted. He had
to be content with the inside of the front jacket flap, and Alfred A. Knopf,
Jr., was designated to write Parshley in an attempt to placate him:
". . . perhaps we can convince you that there is nothing funny about the
problems involved in selling a $10.00 book, written by a Frenchwoman
who is virtually unknown."[33]

Parshley had a correspondence of a different sort with Katherine Anne
Porter, who was furious to find herself referred to in the book as "His" and
her initials given as "C.A." He sent a gracious apology, but by this time
Porter was determined to have her say. It is an interesting statement, especially as it comes from a writer who, although she did not profess to be a
feminist in the contemporary sense of the word, certainly lived a feminist
life:

> Only a zoologist trained to the rigors of the scientific method
> could, I feel sure, keep his head to the end of Mlle. de Beauvoir's
> excursion into nightmare. . . . I would shake my head, and ask

myself, "but what sex *can* she be talking about?" For indeed, except in glimpses, I could recognize neither men nor women as she described them. She lives I am afraid in that strange borderland neither male nor female; a pitiable state. Her book has a kind of phosphorescent brilliance, the real night-shine of decay. The interesting thing is, she not only comes near what we may accept as truth in many things, but symbolic truth as well; and then with a twist of that disordered mind, she perverts the whole thing just enough to spoil it.[34]

Within two weeks after publication, *The Second Sex* was on the best-seller list, and well on its way to becoming one of the most written-about books of our time. Stevie Smith shared Porter's view:

Miss de Beauvoir has written an enormous book about women, and it is soon clear that she does not like them and does not like being a woman. . . . In these pages woman is seen through the eyes of misogynists, the odd-man-out who speaks in her favour being regarded as an anomaly.[35]

As did Charles J. Rollo, calling it "an encyclopedic work on 'the situation of women' dedicated to the proposition '. . . and he done her wrong.' "[36] Dwight MacDonald thought she carried "the feminist grievance too far." "Methinks the lady doth protest too much," he said of what he called an "immense and deformed work."[37] William Phillips referred to it obliquely in a review of *America Day by Day*, saying, "*The Second Sex* is now offering us . . . a compendious highbrow low-down on women."[38] Elizabeth Hardwick expressed perplexity with "this very long book . . . that . . . lacks a subject" and declared it to be "madly sensible and brilliantly confused."[39] Hardwick's general air of not knowing what to make of the book characterized much other commentary.

Believing the book's scope and thesis to be too large for review by one person, the editors of *Saturday Review of Literature* selected six, among them psychiatrist Karl A. Menninger, anthropologists Ashley Montagu and Margaret Mead, and novelist Philip Wylie, best known for his unflattering portrayal of women in *Generation of Vipers*.[40] Mead thought that the book violated "every canon of science and disinterested scholarship in its partisan selectivity," and that when read in context it gave "insight into the psychology of one woman whose society has convinced her that it is terrible to be born a woman." However, she still found "the main argument—that society has wasted women's individual gifts . . . a sound one." This symposia of reviews, treating the book with such seriousness from so many differing perspectives, had a profound effect on subsequent reviews. *Library Journal* said:

Its thesis, developed logically not emotionally, is that because woman is always considered in relation to man, she is the Other. She is pushed into a secondary, inferior position, causing severe alienation in herself and in society. . . . [Beauvoir's] conclusions will not be undisputed, but they are arresting and constructive.[41]

An anonymous reviewer in *Time* wrote:

As she sees it, the male's conquest of the earth, the sea, etc. is just an analogue of his smug conquest of the little woman. . . . By the time she has finished her biological, psychoanalytical and historical-materialist dissection of the situation of her sex, the warm aura of mystery that commonly surrounds woman has been reduced to a steely chill.[42]

Brendan Gill, who called it "probably the best manual of instruction on making love now available in English," also praised Beauvoir for asking why woman has always been considered the other, "with the clarity and passion of one who is aware that the question has never been properly put before." Of the many puzzled commentators who attempted to analyze the book in the first months after publication, Gill's has stood the test of time to become one of the most appropriate judgments: "What we are faced with is more than a work of scholarship; it is a work of art, with the salt of recklessness that makes art sting."[43]

Professor Parshley was thrilled by the public's response to the book he championed during four years of dedicated work, but he had less than three months to enjoy his success: he died suddenly and unexpectedly on May 19, 1953. Beauvoir made a callous joke of it when she wrote to thank Algren for "so doggedly" reading the book: "My translator died, probably because his life lost all meaning for him after he finished the translation."[44]

In the meantime, sacks of letters from American readers poured into Knopf's offices and were duly sent on to Mrs. Bradley, who had them all delivered to the Rue de la Bûcherie and a delighted Beauvoir.[45]

Because of the translation, she was suddenly newsworthy once again in Paris, as reports of the book's reception in the United States and England were filtered through the French press. It revived controversy, and more than one male French critic or scholar was heard to say in the years that followed, "You Americans—it is all your fault that we French must take her seriously. Without your translation, the book would have withered and died, as what she had to say had so little importance in France." The younger generation of French feminist critics had a somewhat different appraisal: "Americans made her our 'sacred monster,' and, for better or worse, we have since had to deal with her."[46]

Controversy swirled around her, but Beauvoir was unmoved by it. She was serenely content with American sales and the reading public's reception of the book. Her only regret was that she would not be able to spend her "dollars" in New York and Chicago, because Nelson Algren gave up on waiting for her and got married.

THIRTY-TWO

When "The Dream I Dreamed" Came True

NELSON ALGREN did not remarry Amanda Kontowicz until 1953, but Simone de Beauvoir suspected he would do so as early as January 9, 1952, her forty-fourth birthday. When she finally accepted his decision to end their contingent relationship, she was forced to think about what lay ahead for her. She made a temporary truce with aging by arbitrarily deciding that she was now an old woman who would never love or be loved again. Although she was in the prime of her physical and intellectual life during her forties and behaved with the zest of a young woman in her twenties, the way she described herself sounded more typical of an old woman in her seventies.

Part of this was a residual holdover from her childhood, when her mother, aunts and cousins, in their middle-aged matronhood, had all settled comfortably into a steady, downhill slide toward dowager respectability. She thought of herself and those her age whom she saw most frequently as "not like other women" but outside the mainstream of French middle-class society. These women whom she saw in the cafés of Saint-Germain-des-Prés were either unmarried and filled with uncertainty about their status or unhappily married but involved in love affairs, usually childless, and living in nontraditional situations where physical settings and decorative objects meant very little. The only elderly women she knew were her mother and Sartre's and Madame Morel, and she considered their behavior entirely consistent with what she believed her own should become through the gradual evolution of aging. Madame Morel's husband had now not left his darkened bedchamber for well over twenty years, and the formidable old woman continued to live her life entirely separate from his while still serving all his needs; the widowed Madame Mancy continued to dote on her middle-aged son as if he were a child. Without really thinking about it, Beauvoir considered them her two models for what she assumed she too would someday become. Interestingly, she did not consider her own mother as a model, although Françoise had an exciting new life and was busy and happy with her job, her friends, her new apartment and her holidays at Meyrignac.

Beauvoir and Algren still wrote frequently. His decision to remarry cleared the air between them, and they became friends in the true sense of the word, sharing much about their lives in a deeper intimacy than they had ever had as lovers. She sent him a long reflective letter on her forty-fourth birthday, saying she no longer resented becoming an old woman. Using the analogy of Horace Walpole, who visited a French friend annually well into his eightieth year, she told Algren she couldn't wait to become that old so he would visit her in the same way.[1]

Throughout this time, she worked steadily on the end of *The Mandarins* and on the essay on the Marquis de Sade. The many revisions she made to the novel caused her to spend more time than usual with the woman who had been her faithful typist for almost a decade, Lucienne Baudin. Beauvoir was aware of her typist's long struggle with breast cancer, and, despite her often ill-concealed repugnance toward illness and her fear of death, she visited Baudin regularly and took responsibility for paying many of her medical bills and partially supporting the widowed Baudin's young daughter. She did this quietly, telling no one except Sartre.

Unlike him, she was careful about money and always in control of what she had. During this time she was earning less than he and had her own separate responsibilities. For many years she had given her mother a regular stipend; frequently she helped her sister with expenses connected to her painting; for a time she paid part of Violette Leduc's stipend from Sartre, until she was able to assume total responsibility for it. Although she and Bost had no formal agreement, she found ways to give him money on a regular basis while still letting him maintain a facade of independence. Sartre's generosity was careless, but Beauvoir's was a measured and steady one. His support, especially of the women with whom he was involved, is well known; hers was a quiet support of many and has gone largely unrecognized, mostly because the people she helped on a regular basis wanted it that way.[2]

Lucienne Baudin's horrible death made Beauvoir realize that her own body might someday turn on her as well. For the first time in her life, she examined her breasts and was shocked to discover an enormous lump, an incident that reveals as much about her attitude toward her body as it does about her response to illness. It had not changed since her childhood on the Rue de Rennes, when little girls were cautioned to take great care always to keep part of their body clothed as they undressed or bathed, and never to be entirely naked because it could lead to an occasion of sin. Despite the size of the lump, she took her time consulting a physician, and from January 10 until early March she lived with the fear that it was malignant. To her great relief, it was a benign tumor, and she recovered swiftly when it was removed. She disliked touching her own body, and, despite the terror of the breast cancer scare, she conducted self-examination "seldom, sporadically" in the years that followed.[3]

When she described the episode to Algren, she said it seemed appropriate that such a thing should happen at the end of their affair, because even if he had not ended it, her aging body would have brought it to a halt.[4] Her memoirs, correspondence, and conversations with friends during the first half of 1952 are filled with descriptions of herself as aging, old or in many instances "too old for" any number of things. The discovery of the tumor, especially the possibilities it raised for disfigurement or even death, contributed to this attitude, which had begun as soon as she left Algren and decided that she was now too old for love.

As each new translation of *The Second Sex* appeared, Simone de Beauvoir's reputation grew throughout the world as the foremost authority on women and everything about them, so it is curious that she still held so many residual conceptions dating from her background as a well-brought-up young daughter of the *haute bourgeoisie*. For despite the easy sexuality of almost everyone she knew and her own relatively casual approach to her sexual companions, she retained much that she had acquired from merely being her mother's daughter and the classmate of the young ladies at the Cours Désir. Some basic part of her still believed that women of forty were, if not old, then certainly matronly and were supposed to behave accordingly.

This attitude may have been a strange one for the lifelong companion of the perennial adolescent Sartre, but hold it she did. When her friends in Paris, married women her own age, embarked on affairs, she refused to listen to them, in one instance clapping her hands against her ears and shouting, "I don't want to hear this! It is not proper!" as one woman attempted to confide the sexual details of her liaison.[5] Beauvoir's attitude might be explained as generational, because her younger friends told her about their love affairs and she often passed along all the intimate details to Algren with relish; it was the sexuality of her contemporaries or of women older than she which tended to fluster her.

So, at the age of forty-four, thinking herself too old to love anything but her car ("at last my true love and I were married—I finally got my driver's license"),[6] she began an affair with a man seventeen years her junior.

Claude Lanzmann, who is today best known for his film *Shoah*, was then a twenty-seven-year-old journalist, a friend of Bost and Cau, who had just written an article for *Les Temps Modernes* and first saw Beauvoir in Sartre's flat on the Rue Bonaparte at one of the magazine's editorial meetings. In an effort to diffuse the criticism directed at him, Sartre (along with Beauvoir and several others) had increased the membership of the editorial advisory board to a total of eleven, most of whom were young committed journalists thrilled to be in such august company. It was a deliberate effort on Sartre's part to surround himself with younger people who would keep the focus and content of the magazine vital and dynamic.

This gathering of the new editorial board was the first that Lanzmann attended, and it was the first time as well that he had ever seen Beauvoir in such close proximity. He was particularly struck by her "wonderful face, luminous, intelligent," and as the meeting progressed he noted her "honesty and straightforwardness."[7] "Okay," he added many years later, "so I was an opportunist—'on the make,' you say. But she was *beautiful!* My attraction to her was genuine."

Beauvoir was as surprised as Lanzmann by the mutual attraction. She wrote to Algren at once to tell him that an "incredible thing" had happened: "someone wants to love me, even though I thought my love life was over forever."[8] She described Lanzmann as "young . . . with blue eyes and black hair, a Jewish friend of Bost and Cau . . ." She remembered seeing him around Saint-Germain-des-Prés, but had not been introduced to him. Their first real conversation took place at a farewell party Bost and Cau gave for themselves on the eve of their departure for Brazil, to write a guidebook for the Swiss publisher Nagel's well-respected series. Beauvoir and Lanzmann chatted, but she left early because she was anxious to get back to work on *The Mandarins.*

When she met Lanzmann, she looked better than she had in years. She had gone on a strict diet in preparation for her last visit to Algren, then lost even more weight when she returned, probably because she was depressed. She recognized certain personal danger signals (such as too many and too frequent excessive crying jags), so, to keep in shape for the grueling daily task of writing *The Mandarins* for six to eight hours at a stretch, she did something extremely uncharacteristic: she stopped drinking and started to take long exercise walks around the streets of Paris. A happy consequence was that she temporarily lost the enormous stomach that had disfigured her. This was a period in which she was still wearing clothes made of ethnic fabrics bought in Mexico and Guatemala, and the bright colors and patterns flattered her clear skin and deep-blue eyes. Thus, when she met Lanzmann, she was probably in the best physical condition of her adult life, and since she always looked younger than her age, the seventeen-year difference between them was not as great as the literal figure might seem.

The morning after the party, Lanzmann telephoned to invite her to a movie. "When I hung up the phone I burst out crying as I had not done since leaving you," she told Algren. "I was crying from happiness that someone cared for me, and because it was a last good-bye to you."

Lanzmann came back to the Rue de la Bûcherie with her, and they spent the night and the next day together. He then left for a trip to Israel and she went off to Italy with Sartre. "We will start a real affair when I return from Italy in October," she told Algren. She gave him this news as a friend, she said, even though he would always be more than that to her.

She too could no longer live in the past, but she would never betray what they had had. "I am no longer your own, but I still feel tenderly toward you," she concluded.

In October, when she returned to Paris, she wrote another letter, repeating most of what she had written in several letters that he had not answered. One thing she especially wanted to impress upon him was the recurring dream she had been having since meeting Lanzmann: "I dream that I told you that I will be buried with your ring on my finger, and indeed I will."9

Lanzmann was the only man with whom Beauvoir ever lived in the same dwelling. He described it: "I moved into the Rue de la Bûcherie. It was really only one room, no matter how she described it. Cohabitation was a problem. She worked all the time, tremendously disciplined. Sartre was, too. On the first morning, I thought to lie in bed, but she got up, dressed and went to her work table. 'You work there,' she said, pointing at the bed. So I got up and sat on the edge of the bed and smoked and pretended that I was working. I don't think she said a word to me until it was time for lunch. Then she went to Sartre and they lunched; sometimes I joined them. Then in the afternoon she went to his place and they worked three, maybe four hours. Then there were meetings, rendezvous. Later we met for dinner, and almost always she and Sartre would go to sit alone and she would offer the critique of what he wrote that day. Then she and I would come back to the Rue de la Bûcherie and go to sleep. There were no parties, no receptions, no bourgeois values. We completely avoided all that. There was the presence only of essentials. It was an uncluttered kind of life, a simplicity deliberately constructed so that she could do her work."

They were together as a couple for seven years, from 1952 to 1959, although they did not live in the same residence throughout that entire time. During their relationship they took holidays together, traveled with Sartre alone or with Sartre and whatever female companion he brought along. Lanzmann described his relationship with Sartre as "very friendly, not the slightest problem . . . it was one of those things where it [meaning their life with Beauvoir] was completely shared." The distinction between himself and Sartre in her affections, Lanzmann said, was "made by Beauvoir herself." He added, "I don't know that other people can understand why this relationship worked. It was very easy for me to be a part of it because things were put very straight at the beginning and there was not the slightest question of rivalry with Sartre. . . . There were no tensions, because Sartre was the uniting factor, the catalyst, with everyone. The Family, the *Temps Modernes* Board—all of them had something in common, the relationship with Sartre, so this gave us an extra unity, a complicity, because we all had the same way of thinking."10

Throughout the seven years they were together, each took care of his or her own needs. She never ran his errands and she never asked him to run hers. It was unthinkable to both that either should perform any sort of domestic service for the other. Yet they were truly a couple in a highly visible sense. Soon their relationship was accepted by friends and strangers alike as casually as they accepted Sartre's changing parade of female companions.

Lanzmann's presence in her life temporarily lightened the negative self-absorption that had made her depressed since returning from Chicago. In her memoirs she said: "Lanzmann's presence beside me freed me from my age. Thanks to him, a thousand things were restored to me: joys, astonishments, anxieties, laughter and the freshness of the world. . . . I immured myself in the gaiety of my private life."[11]

Their life, hers and Sartre's and now Lanzmann's as well, continued to be centered around their few trusted friends. This always consisted of Olga (now recovered and back in Paris), Bost, Michelle (now divorced from Boris and publicly allied with Sartre), sometimes the prickly Wanda (who resented Michelle), and one or two of the younger members of what was now loosely called "the *Temps Modernes* group." Two new friends were the Spanish writer Juan Goytisolo and his companion (later his wife), Monique Lange. Beauvoir was especially fond of Lange, who became a good friend to her in years to come. At that time Lange was working for Gallimard, arranging publicity for visiting writers and generally overseeing their activities while they were in Paris. She invited Beauvoir to all the parties, but Beauvoir generally declined, having "lost the taste for ephemeral encounters."[12] Her days were taken up with writing *The Mandarins*, and she kept her nights for friends, going to the movies, reading widely to catch up with all that had been published in the last year or so. Everything, it seemed, was in rare harmony: ". . . there could be no question of trying to duplicate the understanding I had with Sartre. Algren belonged to another continent, Lanzmann to another generation; this too was a foreignness that kept a balance in our relationship."[13]

When Algren finally answered her letters, it was to announce combatively that he had asked Amanda to remarry him. Beauvoir thought it a good idea, because it seemed to signal an equality in their lives. She told him that since he had always wanted children very much and was now in his forties, he must hurry before time ran out for him to be the kind of father that he wanted to be. Beauvoir did not add that if each of them had someone "contingent" in residence to satisfy their needs—from the sexual in his case to the feeling of youth that being loved by a younger man gave to her—the love they felt for each other would continue to be paramount in both their lives. It was a "necessary" relationship, different from the one she had with Sartre, but equally important. Once they were no longer lovers, he became exactly what she wanted him to be: the sounding board she had always been for Sartre. Algren continued to listen attentively and make detailed comments on her thoughts, ideas and writings, whereas Sartre did so only when it suited his convenience. Algren's letters still included lists of books to read and movies to see and, perhaps in the hope of making her consider what she had lost when she gave him up, photos of himself and copies of interviews he had given.

Their correspondence flourished on an even higher intellectual level than before. He knew a great deal about contemporary American politics and literature and shared it all with her, so that she became as expert as he. Each offered suggestions when the other was stymied in writing; frequently they thanked each other for introducing an author or a subject they might have missed. All this made her very sad, she wrote, not because their love had died, but because theirs was such a tender friendship that the great distance between Chicago and Paris kept them from enjoying it fully. She told him, "I will always remember our love and will never be completely lost to you." She signed the letter "Your never-quite-lost Simone."[14] To demonstrate how friendly she felt toward him, she even invited him to bring his bride to Paris for their honeymoon, and for a brief time he thought he would.

He did not, mostly because of the hysteria in the United States over Communist witch-hunting. Algren learned that he was under surveillance by the FBI and thought it wiser to stay in the beach cottage. Beauvoir was disappointed, unsettled by what she read and heard, but not unduly alarmed. Her friend Janet Flanner had been subpoened to testify on Kay Boyle's behalf and told Beauvoir that her testimony had been "shamefully twisted against her." Everyone in Paris, Beauvoir said, was "hoping that general [Eisenhower] will not win [the 1952 election], and everyone had a good laugh over that Nixon business [the Checkers speech], which was a real comedy."[15]

Suddenly, Sartre was "deeply and reluctantly involved in politics," which meant that she was, too.[16] Much of their activity was indirectly caused by and connected with things American. Look magazine asked Sartre to give an interview explaining his political stance to American readers, but after protracted negotiations he declined because they would not promise to run his commentary without first editing it. She drafted a letter protesting the execution of Julius and Ethel Rosenberg which Sartre and others signed and sent to President Truman, and she helped journalist René Guyonnet translate articles which had appeared in The Nation for Les Temps Modernes.[17]

"The French Communists are not doing well," she told Algren gloomily, "what with the Marty-Tillon business and the Slansky trial."[18] Sartre was helping to arrange the program for the 1953 Vienna Peace Congress, and he told Beauvoir to invite Algren and ask him to organize other American leftists to participate as well. She did, adding that she knew it would be "impossible . . . for all American Leftists [to attend]."[19] Algren was following the French political situation closely and was curious about what would happen since the Communist leader, Duclos, was arrested on trumped-up conspiracy charges. The police hoped for public anti-Communist demonstrations, but "working people didn't strike because Duclos is not as popular as Thorez," Beauvoir told him. "Temps Modernes is beginning to realize that alliance with the Communists against the Right is the only way."[20] What she meant was that Sartre believed his only chance for success was to support them, and so "a flirtation led to a rapprochement with the Communist party."

Yet, despite the fact that Sartre was "consumed by politics" during the years 1951–53, Beauvoir condensed his activities into less than three pages when she wrote the third volume of her memoirs, *Force of Circumstance*.[21] It bears noting because even the most informal page count of this particular volume reveals how much more space she devoted to Sartre's life than to her own. When she writes of politics and history, the inbalance is most noticeable, for she views all the events of the immediate postwar years through the filter of his life rather than hers. Thus, when these two crucial years in Sartre's political life receive such scant commentary, it becomes all the more obvious that what was important within her own life lay elsewhere, and that she accepted Sartre's position reluctantly. Her explanation of "Sartre's new attitudes" and her own equivocation can be seen in her description of how Lanzmann viewed Sartre's involvement: Lanzmann, she wrote, was filled "with joy, for politics seemed to him more essential than literature. . . . Every step that Sartre took towards the Communists he called a step in the right direction." She was more cautious when she described herself:

> I was far from disapproving of what Sartre was doing, but he had not persuaded me to follow him because I evaluated his development by referring to his point of departure: I was afraid that his rapprochement with the Communist Party would take him too far from his own truth.

Lanzmann became Sartre's staunchest ally in persuading Beauvoir to "liquidate" her "ethical idealism and adopt Sartre's point of view" as her own. "All the same," she said, "to work with the Communists without renouncing one's own judgement was scarcely any easier . . . than in 1946." Many years later, she offered a partial explanation for her attitude: "It was not specifically the Communists, it was politics that bored me. Talk, talk, talk, that's all we did. It bored me to be with these men who wanted to change the world to suit their own purposes, little men with dangerous toys [both words and weapons]. Philosophy was one thing, very important to devote oneself to, but this kind of politics, especially after the atomic bomb, was something else indeed. I wanted Sartre to continue to write—call it political philosophy, if you will—until his message was accepted. It did not seem right to see him wasting time exchanging views—insults, really—with all these political factions. But he explained to me that words no longer sufficed, and that for him it was a time for action. Fortunately for me, I had a good excuse not to participate. I had to finish *The Mandarins*, and then there was always something to do with *The Second Sex*. I also had another good excuse in those days: I was busy with Lanzmann."

Throughout 1953–54, she did little more than work on *The Mandarins* and travel. With Lanzmann, she went to the south of France several times, and to Switzerland, Italy, Yugoslavia, Algeria and Spain among other countries. He had not traveled much, either in France or elsewhere; since she now had money, she took great delight in taking him to places she already knew and loved. They were happy, she said, "in a kind of incestuous mother–son relationship, and it will probably last our lifetimes."[22] She went to Holland several times with Sartre; alone with him to Rome and Venice, then in the company of Michelle and Lanzmann; alone with Sartre to Brittany, Alsace, Germany, Czechoslovakia, and Austria—where they were joined by Lanzmann, who then accompanied them to Italy. There was a great deal of movement and activity in her life, and throughout it all she wrote steadily toward the completion of the novel.

The only interruption came during the week or so when Sartre asked her to sequester herself and read his more-than-800-page manuscript on Genet. She stopped everything else to do it, working twelve to sixteen hours at a time to give it the same painstaking scrutiny she had always lavished on Sartre's work. "I am so frustrated," she told Algren, "bursting to get on with my own book but I cannot until I finish Sartre's first."[23] It was exactly the sort of remark that drove him crazy, but she had to vent her frustration and he was the most trustworthy confidant she had.

Beauvoir had her own particular problems with the work published as *Saint Genet*; partly because she had never really come to terms with Genet, the "bitchy queen, fairy, gossip, tormentor of The Ugly Woman," who was also "the thief, juvenile delinquent, bastard, and protégé of Sartre."[24] Sometimes she found him amusing, but not so in the situations where he entranced Sartre. She was uncomfortable when he recounted graphic depictions of homosexual encounters, uneasy when he told of robberies, extortions and beatings. Sartre was fascinated where she was repelled. As she worked her way diligently through the text, in which Sartre was clearly out to insinuate himself in every facet of Genet's work and being, she felt both "repulsion and violation."

It seemed to her that Sartre had done something with this book that signaled an entirely new direction in his writing: in what was ostensibly the critical biography of an illegitimate homosexual former convict, he had created a willful collision of two polarities by inserting himself within the text in all of his many guises, from "Pardaillon" to "Poulou" to "Normalien" to "Sartre"—this last with every connotation his name carried for others throughout his adult life. Having begun as biographical interpretation, the book veered into psychoanalysis, careened into philosophy and came to a thudding halt somewhere in the realm of social politics. Beauvoir was the first to recognize Sartre's startling convergence of autobiography, biography and philosophy.

Now it was her turn to seek new routes of expression. In January 1954 she gave the manuscript of *The Mandarins* to Gallimard. "I have to find an idea for my next project," she told Algren. "I have nothing left for a novel, so it will probably have to be an essay, although I may write some short stories." In the exhaustion of what had amounted to four years of intense concentration, she found new expression difficult to come by. So she dragged out the old psychic baggage that she had carried around for years, the story of ZaZa's death, and tried again to write of it. She showed it to Sartre, who simply held his nose to express his disgust.[25] She went back to correcting the text of *The Mandarins*, which was scheduled for publication in late October, just in time to be a contender for the Prix Goncourt.

Supposedly, she was too old for the prize, as it was generally awarded to a writer under thirty-five and she was now forty-six. But everyone who read the novel was astonished at Beauvoir's vivid recreation of all they had lived through since the Liberation of Paris. It also helped that so many aspects of each character were recognized as being based on her life and Sartre's, as well as on Camus, Koestler and many others. Everyone, it seemed, knew about the book well before it was published; galleys were passed from hand to hand because it was the mark of the chic insider to say that one had read it before publication. Soon there was talk of nothing but the scandalous *roman à clef* that Beauvoir had created: Henri was Camus, Dubreuilh was Sartre, she was Anne, and, of course, Algren was Lewis Brogan. People even remembered that Natasha Sorokine Moffatt had once been exactly like Nadine, and it did not help when some in the Family let it slip that Beauvoir had tucked her into bed at night with her lover in much the same way that Anne does to Nadine in the novel. She was distressed that people were "treating it like a puzzle, with one character Camus, one Sartre, and so on." She complained with a certain degree of bitterness that no one gave her credit for having an imagination of her own.[26] "I can do more than reconstruct reality," she said testily when she recalled this many years later. This book meant so much to her that as she awaited publication day "there were moments when my cheeks burned at the idea of indifferent or hostile eyes moving across its pages."[27]

No one was surprised when she won the Prix Goncourt, least of all Beauvoir herself. Yet, because she knew that the event was a media blitz of publicity, photo opportunities and nonstop interview sessions, she went into hiding at the home of her lawyer, Maître Blum, several days before the announcement. She had warned everyone at Gallimard that she would not participate in publicity and would not pose for photographers or talk to journalists. But the press had space to fill so it created stories, photographing her concierge and laundress ("the one who marked all your underwear with my initials," she explained to Algren). All the reporters were frustrated by how completely she managed to elude them, so the editors of *Paris-Match* retaliated by tampering with a file photo, making her look "like an old hag."[28] When photographers finally caught up with her several days later outside her mother's studio, she agreed to pose only if they would let Françoise sit or stand beside her.

Everyone was delighted with her success: her mother because it vindicated all the struggles Beauvoir had endured to establish herself as a writer; Sartre because he was truly the most altruistic of men, who wanted everyone he cared for, and especially Beauvoir, to see all their wishes granted. Olga, Bost and the others were pleased as well, certainly for her success but also because it meant she would receive a great deal of money (not from the prize but from the tremendous number of sales it guaranteed) and thus would be a steady source of funds for the needy among them. And Lanzmann was pleased because at last it meant that she could afford to buy an apartment and they could move from the dilapidation of the Rue de la Bûcherie, where the rain dripped steadily into her room and the walls rotted and peeled.

She was delighted, too, because all the reviews were amazingly good, every political faction found something in it to praise, and people everywhere sent her admiring letters. People from her past life, as far back as the Cours Désir, began to write to her; strangers sent impassioned letters telling how much the book meant to them. These were the moments when "the dream I dreamed at the age of twenty, to make myself loved through my books," came true. "Nothing," she added, "can spoil my pleasure."[29]

THIRTY-THREE

"The Place
That Goncourt Bought"

I HAVE TO FIND an idea for my next project," Beauvoir wrote to Algren at the end of 1954, but Sartre was also at loose ends, casting about for something to write. He had accepted a commission to write a play because of the sizable advance, which he spent at once, only to discover that he had no idea for a plot.[1] He veered from thinking about himself and scribbling furious notes for what he finally published in 1963 as *The Words* to another attempt at writing philosophy, which did not become *The Critique of Dialectical Reason* until 1960. But Beauvoir was truly drifting, with no idea what to write other than an unfocused desire that it be something more specifically about herself than her last two books.

The Second Sex and *The Mandarins* had been two entirely different attempts toward self-understanding, and each in its own way had been a great success. Still, there was the nagging urge to write something further about herself, and, for a brief moment, the feeling that "I would have to write Volume Three of *The Second Sex*, which would be myself explained in the light of all I had previously written. But the magnitude of such a task was immediately apparent to me, and I abandoned it even before I had expressed the possibility of writing it to Sartre. He agreed that I should let that book stand alone and find something new."[2]

Other events transpired to keep her busy, and it was more than two years before she was free enough of "politics, travel and the intensity of my relationship with Lanzmann" to return to writing about herself. She found herself caught up in Sartre's newest wave of political activism, which meant attending meetings in Paris, traveling to other countries and once again demonstrating her solidarity (an increasingly important word in her vocabulary) by writing essays to defend his positions and views. In this last, perhaps one might better say to defend *her* version of *his* views—that is, what *she honestly thought* they were.

This began as early as 1954, when Sartre threw the influence of *Les*

Temps Modernes behind such activists as Colette and Francis Jeanson, who worked for Algerian independence through the position espoused by the radical separatist group FLN (Front Libération National). The Mendès-France government drew up its own proposal for a settlement of the situation, but fell soon afterward, in part because its position on Algeria proved unpopular in France (Beauvoir called it "right-wing policy with a facelift"). When all the leftist factions began a realignment of position, she recalled in her memoirs, "it became evident to us that we would have to make distinctions between our real allies and our adversaries in this new 'Left.' "[3]

The editorial board decided to commission a series of articles to clarify the new meanings of the terms "left" and "right" in French political parlance, and Beauvoir was given the assignment of defining contemporary right-wing ideology. It resulted in the essay "The Thought of the Right Today." A year later, 1955, Merleau-Ponty published a book entitled *Adventures of the Dialectic*, with a chapter on "Sartre and Ultrabolshevism," and Beauvoir wrote another essay, this time to "re-establish the truth" of Sartre's theory.[4] The result was "Merleau-Ponty and Pseudo-Sartrism." Gallimard, anxious for another book since the success of *The Mandarins*, persuaded her to publish these two, along with the essay on the Marquis de Sade, in 1955 as a separate work, which she called *Privileges*.

In both political essays, she employs the same technique that served her so well when writing *The Second Sex*. By first "unravelling the myths," she believed she was "laying bare the practical truths." Her attack on their old friend Merleau-Ponty was really a howl of outrage that dated back to what she considered his first betrayal of Sartre, in 1952, when he left the magazine to accept the chair of philosophy at the Collège de France. Merleau-Ponty had written a farewell article called "Indirect Language and the Voices of Silence," which was printed in the June and July issues of the magazine over Beauvoir's strong objections; now, with his book, he had written a meticulous analysis of Sartre's flirtation with Communism that was a monument of understated yet clearly expressed disagreement with all Sartre's conduct and writing in the three years that had elapsed. Beauvoir believed that her essay "contradicted, point by point, the allegations Merleau-Ponty had made." Her argument is that Merleau-Ponty did not clearly understand the ontological basis of Sartre's theory, and that he had misread and misinterpreted everything else. She accuses him of "pseudo-sartrism" and attacks his "a-communism." But she does not approach the subject dispassionately and therefore does not give anything approaching an explication of Sartre's doctrine, thus making any real rebuttal of Merleau-Ponty's argument impossible. Also, in her own words, "Sartre's theory changed every time he put his pen to paper"; hers remained locked in the Existential theory he expounded in *Being and Nothingness* and refined in his formulations of the immediate postwar years. By 1955, Sartre was rethinking every philosophical and political position he had ever held; she may have thought she was following him, but in reality she was holding fast to those views he had first expressed and she had accepted a full decade or more earlier.

"The Thought of the Right Today," her first real attempt at writing political theory, begins with a compelling analysis of the contemporary situation. But all too soon she becomes polemical, and what was supposed to have been rigorous attack disintegrates into dogmatic rehashing, condescension and little more than caricatures of conservative positions.

Despite her lifelong insistence that the essays in *Privileges* remained the starting point for any explication of her political position and philosophical thought, Beauvoir still insisted, "I was not very occupied with politics or philosophy. I never wrote truly political books. I hardly committed myself to political action, and I can't say that politics took any of my time."

Yet in a 1960 interview with Madeleine Chapsal she seemed surprised to remember how much politics had occupied her and how much she had written about it during this period.[5] Reflecting on this time in her life, she said she considered herself and others of like mind to be "in a period of political powerlessness," and that more and more she found it imperative to "try to construct some sort of balance sheet" to assess what she called "the realities of her situation."[6] Again, the impetus was toward autobiographical introspection, and with it a strong movement away from pure political theory or action and toward the individual social responsibility that culminated in her advocacy of feminist issues and positions. But although the seed of the idea was there, the fruit of the actual writing was yet to come.[7]

In mid-August 1955, she was finally able to leave the crumbling ceiling and mildewed walls of the Rue de la Bûcherie and move into an artist's atelier, a large studio apartment that she bought with money earned from *The Mandarins* after the book received the Prix Goncourt. At age forty-seven, for the first time she could afford an apartment in Paris and still indulge her only two passions: to buy as many records and to travel as much as she wanted. She called it "the place that Goncourt bought." Located just two Métro stops farther south in Montparnasse than the building in which she was born, it was the corner apartment on the ground floor of an Art Deco building at 11 *bis* (11A) Rue Schoelcher, a small street that, with the adjacent Rue Victor Considérant, forms a triangle off the Boulevard Raspail. Overlooking the Cimetière Montparnasse, the large open space in the midst of Paris, the apartment had unobstructed northwestern light and gave her the feeling of being far away from the city. In later years she liked to pretend that she bought that particular apartment because both Schoelcher and Considérant were strong early advocates of feminist principles, but she did not know this when she moved there.

She described it as "large and sunny, with a little staircase, a balcony, a real kitchen and bathroom, and no neighbors across the street, just a big cemetery."[8] She decorated her new flat with all the treasures acquired on her travels, so that it became a showcase for Guatemalan textiles and Mexican folk art, souvenirs of her travels with Algren. Sartre brought back a number of tribal masks from his trip to Haiti with Dolores, and she had bought more when they were in Africa. These were hung on the walls above collections of primitive statues and, later, dolls and icons from travels in China, Russia and South America. They formed interesting contrasts to her Picasso drawing, her Léger print, and various other paintings and drawings given to her by the famous and the unknown over the years. She bought a small student's desk for an alcove in the large room and surrounded it with photos of herself, Sartre, Lanzmann, the Family, and actors in publicity stills from Sartre's various productions. There were also many photos of Algren which took pride of place. Just beyond the desk was a spindly cast-iron spiral staircase leading up to the balcony, which she used as a sleeping alcove. There she placed a single bed, a small chest and a large collage of news clippings and photos of Sartre, which many who saw it found either repellent or slightly obscene. In later years she kept a television set there and liked to watch badly dubbed American movies at night while propped up in bed and sipping scotch whiskey.[9]

Françoise gave her a set of books that had been Georges's, an elegant collection of more than thirty volumes of Tauchnitz editions of French classics, all bound uniformly in soft brown leather with gold-trimmed pages. These she installed on a high bookshelf that wrapped around two sides of the large sitting alcove. Beneath them she placed two daybeds at right angles to form a cozy sitting area and covered them in thick gold satin spreads topped with pillows in gemlike colors of amethyst, emerald and sapphire. Three small slipper chairs flanked the sofas, separated by a coffee table on which she placed a large Brazilian drum and a feathered headdress, a little tray in elegant lacquers and woods on which she kept fountain pens, and a small dish of clay masks picked up in Central America and the Far East. The chairs were covered in the same materials as the pillows, and her two Giacometti lamps lit this area softly and made the furniture glow like rare jewels. In later years, this seating area assumed a slightly comical aspect because Beauvoir, like her mother before her, exhibited the practical behavior of a frugal bourgeois housewife: to protect the gold coverlet of the one sofa where she liked best to curl up and read, she covered it with a flamboyant American Indian blanket. It was especially jarring in the midst of her one attempt at decorative elegance, since the blanket was where she kept her telephone and piled books, manuscripts, stacks of unanswered mail, wadded paper handkerchiefs, a comfortable old sweater and the other detritus of a writer's workplace.

She had special bookcases made for the far corner of the alcove, where she placed her extensive collection of long-playing records. In the middle of the room, a large round table held, as if in a place of honor, a plaster cast of Sartre's hands. She usually surrounded it with cut flowers or plants which she then forgot to take care of, so they were all clumped forlornly together in motley jars or plastic containers, either wilted, dying or dead.

In the kitchen there was a kettle to boil water for morning tea, and a few dishes and pots which she had taken from her sister's studio during the war and which were what she used for the rest of her life. When she did finally buy a refrigerator, there was no room for it in the kitchen, so she placed it beside the front door in the tiny foyer, a grotesque presence that visitors had to navigate around. The most it ever held was a drying slice of ham she forgot to eat, a few fruits, lots of ice cubes and several bottles of vodka and scotch. These she liked to serve in clunky Mexican tumblers, but she used a battered pewter jigger to measure out minuscule shots which all but disappeared into the large, thick glasses.

There were books everywhere, and as the years passed they proliferated, along with folders of papers—her own manuscripts, submissions to the magazine, piles of magazine page proofs, and scores of other printed materials sent to her by admiring or disgruntled readers. Every so often, she would drop whatever came to hand into cartons and ask the concierge to take it down to her cellar storage area.[10]

But she hardly had time to do more than dump her possessions during her first two weeks in the flat, because she and Sartre left for China on September 2, 1955, to spend two months as official guests of the Communist government. Sartre had been invited; Beauvoir was with him only as a companion and in no separate official capacity. Although she wrote a book about this trip, *The Long March*, and discussed it extensively in her memoirs, the letters she wrote to Algren are a more reliable source for the truth of what she actually saw and did in China.[11]

Algren was now divorcing Amanda Kontowicz, and once again he and Beauvoir were in frequent correspondence. He was depressed and considering a move to Havana, where the FBI would be unable to keep him under the close surveillance he endured in Chicago. Beauvoir tried to persuade him that he would be better off in Paris, but she had to do so carefully. Even before he wrote of ending his marriage, he had begun to hint about resuming their relationship. Hoping to convince him without the added pressure of their fluctuating emotional involvement, she promised to "find a Parisian student" to keep him company. As rumors had reached France that left-wing and Communist Americans were now able to secure visas to travel, she invited him to visit in time for her next birthday. She was curious about what had happened to him in the years since they last saw each other, and wanted to resume—if nothing else— at least their correspondence, which is perhaps why her letters are so friendly and chatty, full of the details of her China voyage. She knew that Algren "could be like a skittish puppy, and one had to be careful to approach him in so many instances obliquely rather than directly."[12]

She knew as soon as she returned to France that she would write a book about the trip, also that it would be "filled with lies about the things I did not see, and so I must do some heavy research." She joked that *America Day by Day* had been much easier to write because she had had help from a "local youth," but that she had met no such person on her trip to China.

Carlo Levi was a prominent figure on this trip, acting as their semi-official guide on behalf of both Russian and Chinese Communist groups. According to Beauvoir, he took his responsibilities "too seriously," and she and Sartre were "irritated by his officious personality."[13] In the two months she was there, she "often fretted about never being free to wander." Guides were omnipresent, carefully insulating them from any informal contact. Conversations were censored, she believed, in the course of translation. They spent a month in Peking and were present at the October 1, 1955, tribute to Mao Tse-tung. Sartre was introduced to Mao, but she was hemmed in by a cordon of Chinese officials and lackeys and was never sure that the interpreter told Mao who she was or why she was there. "In any case," she recalled years later in a somewhat miffed voice, "he was clearly uninterested in meeting me."

They went also to Mukden, Shanghai and Canton, and she told Algren: "What impressed me the most is the patience and stubbornness of the Chinese people, slowly and deliberately conquering poverty and ignorance and making their poor country into a great nation." She believed that the government-required labor of Chinese workers, as opposed to that of the Indians and Mayans of Guatemala and Mexico, was "sublime" because the Chinese were doing it "to better their country." Her remarks reflect what she saw and heard, which was only what Chinese Communist officials wanted her and Sartre to see and hear. Everything about the visit was "official" and therefore, as she recalled in later years, "drab and boring, nothing memorable except some of the scenery."

She started the book, *The Long March*, after the Christmas holidays and finished it by July 1956. In later years she called it "hasty journalism . . . written to get money because there was the possibility I might need it to see Algren again . . . of no value whatsoever . . . a travelogue of the worst possible sort . . . a dishonest undertaking; really—ignore it." She told Algren, "It isn't very good, but then, I didn't invest a lot in it."[14]

All the reviews agreed with her, but an exiled Nationalist Chinese scholar writing in *The Catholic World* was most succinct: "This difficult and disturbing book is an affront not only to the French tradition of scholarship but also to her countrymen's cherished fidelity to reason and justice."[15]

"I'm not ashamed of that book," she said in 1983. "Embarrassed maybe, but not ashamed. It served its purpose."

In the same week that she gave the manuscript of *The Long March* to her publisher, Sartre told Beauvoir that he had "something amusing" to tell her: an article in *L'Osservatore romano* entitled "Immoral Existentialism" announced that *The Second Sex* and *The Mandarins* had been placed upon the Index of prohibited books by the Catholic Church.[16] The Vatican's official publication defended the necessity to protect "not only our young people, who might most easily succumb to such influences, but also adults, because hers is a very subtle and hidden poison." *Le Monde* tried to explain why the decree had been issued:

> The organ of the Vatican has decreed: "The author considers the institution of marriage to be a hoax and defends free love. All [Beauvoir's] beliefs are good, she insists, when they permit woman to flee the enslavement of motherhood. She defends the emancipation of woman above all, especially from moral laws, and she accuses the Church of being opposed to this emancipation. The Church must condemn with all its energies these immoral doctrines which trample underfoot the good character and sanctitude of the family."

The Vatican decree had exactly the opposite effect intended by the Church: sales increased dramatically for both books and remained high throughout the rest of the summer.

She had a more pressing problem than the Index: Algren was so upset by the American publication of *The Mandarins* that he actually went so far as to place a transatlantic telephone call to her on the Rue Schoelcher—no easy feat in 1957, when such calls were expensive and both the caller and the person being called had to stand by, often for hours, until everything was in order to let them speak.[17] Lanzmann answered the phone and told Beauvoir it was the operator saying that the call would be put through, but Algren, perhaps because he heard Lanzmann's voice at the other end, changed his mind and canceled. It made Beauvoir exceedingly nervous as she waited for an explanatory letter that never came. She assumed that his call had something to do with *The Mandarins*, which had just appeared in the United States, so she waited until shortly before her departure for the summer holiday and then sent a long letter trying to explain what her intentions had been in the book. She began by excusing him for not completing the call, saying it would have been "too hard" to hear his voice after such a long time apart.[18] Even though she now had a "new life," she stressed that she would "always care deeply" about him. Then she told him that in the few weeks since the book appeared in English there had been many reviews and her American publishers had sent them all to her. This made her think a lot about Algren, because so many of the reviews played up their affair. "The love story is really a lot different from the truth," she insisted, in what reads like an obvious attempt to placate him. "People missed the point that the lovers go on loving even though they cannot stay together. It is their 'coming and going' affair that left neither of them happy."

The last few years had been difficult for Algren because he made many unfortunate publishing decisions, which in turn left him embittered and poor for the rest of his life. Beauvoir became the recipient of his diatribes against the world in general, and from this point on her letters are often soothing and full of uncharacteristically optimistic platitudes, all urging him to believe that better times were soon to come. In this particular instance, he was so angry with her equivocations about *The Mandarins* that he did not reply. When she returned in October from a holiday in Rome, she wrote again, with the excuse that he might not have received her previous letter. "Perhaps you think I am angry with you because you were angry with me?" she asked, concluding by telling him he would always be in her heart, signing it "your Simone."[19]

Again he did not reply, but at Christmas he sent a card with a vague note shifting the blame for his silence to her (which was also his way of trying to mend the rift), by saying he had heard that she told people he was "mean" to her. She replied with New Year's greetings on January 1, 1957, and a long letter saying, "I never told anyone you were mean to me, never even thought it—but I'm glad you heard it if it caused you to write."[20] It made her sad to see how bitter he was about his life, and so once again she trotted out all the old platitudes, urging him to believe that the hard times were behind him.

Algren was a man who hid his deep emotional tenderness beneath a facade of gruffness, so that when, in the midst of a long diatribe about how old and miserable he had become, he referred to their original meeting as a "miracle" and said that to see her again would be a second, Beauvoir was so moved that she needed two letters to respond.

"I've grown old myself," she told him. "You'll be surprised to see me when we meet again. It's been nearly ten years since we first met." In her second letter, she assured him that he need not worry about how disappointed she might be to see the old man he said he had become, because "one miracle in our lives was enough." She urged him to come to France, because "you will be forever in my heart."[21]

In those same two letters, she hinted at her next project: "I am anxious to begin a memoir of my childhood and youth, which will be interesting to write even if I do not finish it." A few weeks later, she told him she was writing "an autobiography of my childhood, and Sartre and Bost are amused by it."

THIRTY-FOUR

"My Life . . .
This Curious Object"

MY LIFE: it is both intimately known and remote: it defines me and yet I stand outside it. Just what, precisely, is this curious object?"[1] It was Simone de Beauvoir's continuing preoccupation between the years 1957 and 1972, and it resulted in not one but four hefty volumes of auto-biography: *Mémoires d'une jeune fille rangée* (*Memoirs of a Dutiful Daughter*), 1958; *La Force de l'Age* (*The Prime of Life*), 1960; *La Force des choses* (*Force of Circumstance*), 1963; and *Toute compte fait* (*All Said and Done*), 1972.[2]

In 1957, as she began to write her autobiography, she had just ended fifteen years of concentrating upon herself in her writing, but always from the distance required by the particular form of the work. Now she decided to address her situation head on, without the buffers of various conventions of genre. Four volumes of self-scrutiny later, in a summation of all that she had written, she asked herself the rhetorical question above because it had governed the entire process of intense, sometimes painful and generally scrupulously honest self-examination.

She had always been inner-directed, but it was not until she approached fifty that circumstances conspired for her to write her version of her life. At the age of forty-eight, she was securely situated as a successful writer and companion to a man whom she respected and who returned the sentiment in kind (Sartre), and she had loved passionately a man who loved her in return (Algren). Her life had indeed become what she wanted it to be, "a lovely story that became true as I told it to myself," which, as she herself wrote, she nonetheless "touched . . . up improvingly here and there in the telling."[3] Still, there is something missing from this statement: nowhere in the four volumes did she discern and then address why the urge to write about herself grew so strong she could no longer ignore it by the mid-1950s. Many years later, she felt it could best be explained if she were to divide her life during the 1950s and early 1960s into three separate categories entitled "friendships, writing and men." During the time she wrote her memoirs, the first two were as satisfying as she could have wished; the third, however, was fraught with turmoil.

Lanzmann had not moved with her to the Rue Schoelcher, and she was once again living alone.[4] It took "some difficult adjustment," not only in changing the patterns of her behavior "back from the couple to the individual," but also "because I was an old woman. I would be alone from this moment until the rest of my life."

As always, Sartre was pivotal in the circumstances that led to her autobiographical expression. Throughout the 1950s, his restlessness in so many areas, from political activism to literary expression, kept Beauvoir puzzled and exhausted as she tried to figure out what he was searching for and how she could help him find it. He was a major cause of her own anxiety, especially when his erratic behavior began to affect his health. In search of, it almost seemed he knew not what, he drove himself to the brink of exhaustion or, as some of his doctors believed, perhaps even death. He had already been hospitalized several times for hypertension and its side effects, first in the Soviet Union and then again in Paris (sometimes so quietly that no one but Beauvoir, Bost and Michelle knew of it).[5] Beauvoir's role consisted mainly of following him from place to place and meeting to meeting in the hope that he would not collapse.

To spur himself on to greater productivity, Sartre had become addicted to a deadly combination of barbiturates, amphetamines and tranquilizers—uppers and downers which he popped by the handful, all washed down with vast quantities of coffee, tea and red wine. The stimulant Corydrane was his drug of choice, and he crunched them nonstop, chewing as if they were jelly beans or popcorn as he scribbled furiously, convinced that he owed his productivity to them. He also had a rotating list of doctors from whom he obtained a steady stream of prescriptions for another drug, Orthodrine, which he went through at the rate of one bottle per day.[6] Surprisingly, his appetite for food remained prodigious, and he always ate a large midafternoon meal of high-cholesterol foods. He adored chocolates, and every meal ended with a rich dessert. His (and Beauvoir's as well) fondness for scotch had intensified over the years, and it was not unusual for them to consume a fifth or more during a quiet evening of listening to music.

"Sartre held his liquor much better than I did," Beauvoir recalled. "But me—I woke up each morning like a sick person. I could hold my liquor pretty well, but not too well, and the truth of the matter is, I had stomach problems sometimes."

Although she never took anything stronger than an aspirin during this time, she began to drink a lot because Sartre did and she wanted to keep him company. In 1982 she described her drinking habits since 1950: "I like to drink very much. Since Sartre's first illness [in the 1950s], it has become for me an element of equilibrium. I mean, I feel better when I drink something in the morning. In general, I have, let's see, one or two vodkas [she points here to a large Mexican tumbler] before lunch, and then in the afternoon I have two or three scotches during the day [holding up the glass, she measures with her fingers what approximates four to six shots per drink]. I drink very little wine because I don't like the taste anymore. I drink some when I'm having a nice meal with friends, but very little. But [vodka and scotch] in my opinion is necessary for me now. You know, I absolutely have no more desire to get drunk. That sort of thing no longer entertains me. Well, it was fun just after the war, when everyone got drunk. But I don't do that anymore. However, the drinking I do during the day and the evening—that, for me, is essential. I need that."

So night after night they sat on the gold sofas under the Giacometti lamps, sipping scotch with a pretense of water, comforted by the dissonance of Hindemith, Berg, Bartók and Schönberg. Beauvoir tried to divert Sartre's attention with the music, but he spewed forth a litany of anger and disillusion, from the Soviet invasion of Hungary to the unending succession of ruptured friendships in French political circles. He was exhausted by too much traveling, too many people clamoring for his attention, too much writing and too many squabbling women. He was ready for something—anything—to happen, and this was what worried Beauvoir.

"Sartre's method of understanding and experiencing a foreign country was to experience and try to understand its women," she commented without noticeable expression in 1982. In 1954 he visited the Soviet Union, and Lena Zonina was assigned to interpret for him. They began an affair, and after he returned to France they corresponded. Zonina remained important to Sartre for the rest of his life. She also became a good friend to Beauvoir, and on the several occasions that she was permitted to travel outside the USSR she stayed in Beauvoir's apartment on the Rue Schoelcher.[7]

Sartre's relationships with women had been relatively stable since the frenzied Saint-Germain-des-Prés years wound down, around 1952, and Michelle Vian's addition to the Family became public. By 1956, "perhaps because he was bored with his life, frustrated by his work," according to Beauvoir, things began to change. He intensified his conquest of many women and annexed some of them to the Family. That summer, an eighteen-year-old Algerian Jewish student named Arlette Elkaïm telephoned Sartre to ask him to discuss Being and Nothingness with her. He liked her, according to Beauvoir, "because she was very young, very pretty, very intelligent. And also, because she was shorter than he." What began as ego-flattering flirtation soon became an affair that later had far-reaching ramifications for Beauvoir's relationship with Sartre. But at that time Arlette was welcomed by the Family, especially Beauvoir, because they could foist upon her much of the daily intellectual scut-work that Sartre required for physical support while he concentrated on his writing.

In the beginning, Arlette's willingness to do whatever Sartre needed or wanted freed Beauvoir to carry on with her own friendships and writings. She and the Family had always counted on a continuous succession of starry-eyed young women to take care of Sartre, so there was no reason for her to suspect that Arlette would become anything more than another of his sexual playmates and runner of his errands, who would eventually grow tired of his many demands and move on to other interests. Neither Beauvoir nor the rest of the Family realized that Arlette's unabating willingness to serve Sartre's needs would eventually usurp Beauvoir's privileged position.

Also, there was Lanzmann's sister, a promising actress who used "Evelyne Ray" as her stage name. She was an extraordinarily beautiful woman of strong political passion who supported leftist causes with energy and commitment. Fascinated by Sartre, she too became his mistress.

Their liaison came as a shock to Beauvoir, because she had grown as fond of Lanzmann's sister as if she were her own. The entire affair, brief and furtive as it was, upset her. When she wrote her memoirs, Evelyne Ray received only three lines of direct commentary: "To tell the truth, of all the deaths that occurred among people I knew during these last years [i.e., 1962–72], only one really moved me very deeply, and that was Evelyne's. But I have no wish to speak of it."[8] When asked why, Beauvoir blushed deeply and spoke in a voice so soft it was difficult at times to hear what she said: "I didn't even mention Evelyne in my memoirs because at that time Sartre didn't want people to know of his liaison with her. I should have written about her because, as [she was] Lanzmann's sister, I saw her a lot and liked her very much. I owed that to her. She was a ravishing beauty, extremely intelligent as well, which is frequently rare for a woman who is that pretty. You can see how Sartre was captivated at once.

"She was a person of extraordinary kindness and generosity. She kept a place, a kind of shelter or aid station, for people who needed help, and she was often there sweeping and scrubbing and doing menial work. I suppose she was too intellectual to be simply an actress, but Sartre still wrote The Condemned of Altona for her. She didn't have the fire an actress needs to succeed, so she never got any other parts unless Sartre got them for her. Politics interested her and she wanted to take a role, but she was a woman so she could not, and of course because of Sartre and his need to keep their liaison private, she could have no role at all. I think this pained her.

"Sartre was too busy, he had too many women, too many other commitments, so he could not give her too much of himself. She suffered because of that, so she began to have these liaisons. She had a lot of men, and they all adored her, but they didn't make her happy. Little by little, she couldn't stand life anymore. She was getting old [almost thirty], and she had trouble accepting the idea of aging. But it was this very, very, great, great friendship she had for Sartre that scarred her enormously. She couldn't handle it that she could not exhibit this friendship in public because he did not want her to. And she wanted children, and of course that was out of the question. So she wrote very nice little letters to everyone, to her brothers, to me, Sartre, her friends. And then she killed herself."

Evelyne Ray must have been important to Sartre, because while she was alive Wanda decided that the younger woman was her most formidable rival for Sartre's attention. Wanda had been relatively quiet in the past few years, content with the roles that Sartre dutifully wrote into his plays for her (she acted under the stage name Marie Ollivier), but whenever she perceived any woman to be a serious rival she reverted to all her old quarrelsome behavior.

Another part of Beauvoir's unease stemmed from the fact that she and Sartre had not had much in common ideologically for the past several years. She was philosophically content with what he had written prior to 1955, but after that, she felt a tremendous obligation to go along with everything he espoused because of the public's perception of them as an intellectual couple. She believed her most important duty was to accompany and support him, to be seen at his side. With the exception of the Family, he and she no longer shared a common group of acquaintances. More important, they were forming individual friendships that reveal the subtly differing directions in which their lives were heading.

At the conclusion of her memoirs, Beauvoir stated, "My relations with others—my affections, my friendships—hold the most important place in my life. Many date from long ago." She also insisted, "Sartre's life is as closely a part of mine as ever."[9] However, writing of this same period, one of Sartre's biographers described it as the period in which "he modified his network, acquired new friends, new habits, new means of expression."[10] Both statements are relatively true.

Olga, Bost, Lanzmann, Bianca Bienenfeld, Violette Leduc were those she still saw often. "Less often, but regularly," she saw Jean Pouillon, the writer André Gorz, Ellen Wright, GéGé Pardo and a new acquaintance, Gisèle Halimi, the lawyer with whom she would be linked closely during the Algerian crisis and for a few years after because of feminist issues and causes.[11] This second group, and many other individuals whom she did not name specifically in her memoirs, all believed they shared her closest friendship, and perhaps in many ways they did. But several letters she wrote to Algren in 1960 cast a different light on the degree of intimacy she permitted in all other friendships than the Family. Algren had been in London and met Ellen Wright there, and they had had a brief affair. Wright returned to Paris and told Beauvoir all about it, entirely unaware of his and Beauvoir's "intimacy," even though she had been the agent for The Mandarins.[12] Ellen Wright confided, as did many others, the details of her private life to Beauvoir, but Beauvoir never responded in kind. Algren made no comment, even after Beauvoir teased him several times in letters in an attempt to get his version of the story.

The strangers who sought Beauvoir's company were less well known than those who pursued Sartre: instead of prominent political leaders and well-known writers, the people who asked to see her were more likely to be readers who had been moved by her work.[13] Others became more casual friends whom she saw whenever their paths crossed, such as the young French-Canadian journalist Madeleine Gobeil, who was frequently in transit between her native Canada and Paris. So while anyone of any nationality who was in Paris during 1955–65 and wanted to meet Simone de Beauvoir for any reason whatsoever could have done so relatively easily, in truth very few people knew her well. Her acquaintances became global, while her friendships remained local, and the strongest were usually those of long duration.

Most of the time, Beauvoir was at Sartre's side when he was the guest of foreign governments, and she did meet, for example, Castro and Khrushchev. She was less at ease than Sartre, but stoically endured these occasions as part of the price they had to pay for the ideology they hoped to persuade others to adopt. "I dread the swarming crowds at big exhibitions," Beauvoir wrote; "I detest cocktail parties, vernissages, boring social functions. I hate, hate, hate them!"[14]

Among writers, especially in France, she and Sartre were generally ignored by the generation that became known as the New Novelists, among them Michel Butor, Claude Simon and even Sartre's former friend Nathalie Sarraute. Structuralism was in the ascendancy now, and differing theoreticians such as Roland Barthes, Jacques Lacan and the Tel Quel group made Sartre's particular brand of literature and politics seem old, tired and out-of-date.[15]

Sartre never learned to speak English and, unlike Beauvoir, had no real interest in contemporary English or American writers, so he was almost totally unaware of recent publications in Britain or the United States unless they were by "committed" authors who came to France and introduced themselves to him. Even then, he seldom did more than glance at their books, counting on Beauvoir to read and summarize for him. She did the same with writers in many other languages as well, among them the Italians Alberto Moravia, Giuseppe Ungaretti, Guido Piovene and Ignazio Silone, the only one who tried to befriend Sartre, who was always reluctant to befriend men. Beauvoir was responsible for any semblance of friendship with the Silones and then, as she detested Ignazio, it was because of her great sympathy for Darina's unhappy marital situation. She also detested Elsa Triolet and Louis Aragon, and Triolet had never liked her, so Sartre usually saw them without her. She blamed the violence of Triolet's recent resentment toward her on her greater literary success and her indifference to direct political action.

A luncheon given by Sartre's mother to introduce him to his cousin Albert Schweitzer has been so written-about that it has since become almost apocryphal, but it did indeed take place. Naturally Madame Mancy observed the bourgeois proprieties and did not invite Beauvoir, who pretended not to care but was hurt nonetheless. Throughout the meal, journalists, who had been alerted by Jean Cau ("That opportunist!" Beauvoir sneered), did indeed pound on the door demanding to take photographs, but Sartre told Beauvoir that he and his cousin simply continued to eat quietly and listen politely to Madame Mancy's attempts at conversation because they had nothing to say to each other than occasional remarks about their common Alsatian background. As he left, pausing in the doorway to oblige the photographers, Schweitzer told Sartre, "Well, we are both looking for the same things, but in different ways."[16] They never met again.

Cau's chicanery continued, but this time Beauvoir chose to be absent from the dinner where Sartre met Charlie Chaplin and Picasso. Cau, according to Beauvoir, tricked the three men into attending by telling each that the others had accepted. He then persuaded Michelle Vian to host it in her apartment, and invited a number of others to witness what he hoped would be a stimulating event of lasting intellectual significance, one that he could write about lucratively. Sartre told Beauvoir that Chaplin was "friendly and talkative" and "everyone loved him except Picasso," who "wanted the spotlight" for himself.

"Too many egos, so I didn't go," Beauvoir recalled, saying she preferred to go to the movies with Lanzmann, who had just returned from three months in Israel.[17] This became a frequent refrain throughout the 1950s: Sartre had the retinue of women to take care of all his needs except editorial, critical and intellectual, and as long as she could continue to fulfill those functions she had no fear of leaving him to the company of others so that she could spend her time writing or with her friends.

A situation she related to Algren described how she continued to feel about famous or distinguished people. Her friend in New York the editor Bernard Wolfe went to a reception at Columbia University given for Dylan Thomas in 1950, and wrote to her of the drunken Thomas's "obscene behavior." Retelling it to Algren, Beauvoir commented that it was "a good story, because people should know what their literary heroes are really like—I wonder what people would have thought if Joyce or some others had revealed themselves in this same way."

She had all but given up attending literary occasions, and when Gallimard hosted a cocktail reception for William Faulkner and applied pressure to persuade her to be there, she still stayed away, telling Algren that "everyone was disappointed at his [Faulkner's] lack of brilliance—meaning he did not behave as Dylan Thomas did. I did not attend—one American writer [Algren] is enough for me."[18]

Despite the burgeoning interest in new forms of literature and critical inquiry, Beauvoir and Sartre were still big-enough names that "some publisher or politician was always trying to trot [us] out for some visiting big shot." She chose her occasions carefully, however, insisting, "if I were not at [Sartre's] side to protect him, he would give in and do what they wanted."

But as the 1950s ended, Sartre's attitude toward politics and literature changed again in several significant ways, and to a bewildered Beauvoir it seemed that he was rejecting all the protective measures he had simply taken for granted she would always provide. He was making decisions about whom to see and for how long, without her advice or consent. At first she was not concerned, because most of these meetings were connected with Sartre's evolving Marxist ideology, and she insisted that pure politics continued to bore her. A more disturbing matter was Sartre's uncharacteristic indifference to her role as first reader, critic and editor of his work. He wrote so fast and furiously that he was either too busy to stop and listen to her daily critique of his work in progress or else so befuddled by drugs that he was incapable of understanding what she said. They knew each other so well that their critical discussions had long ago become a kind of intellectual shorthand because of their private, personal vocabulary, but now he was introducing change into their long intimate discourse.

Sartre now believed that artistically constructed prose was a bourgeois device designed specifically to keep the true meaning of a text from its reader. His new theory was that ideas required the kind of prose which would allow them to be communicated directly to the people, who were then supposed to put them to the greatest social good. To that end, the shaping of a text and the choice of language were irrelevant. What mattered most was the direct statement of the idea.[19] This had a double-sided effect on his writing, resulting in, first, a combination of Marxism and psychoanalysis, which became The Critique of Dialectical Reason; and, second, psychoanalysis and biography, for this was also the decade of The Words, Saint Genet, Baudelaire and the beginning of his monumental obsession, Flaubert and The Family Idiot. These are among the most controversial of all Sartre's works, as they are seen either as the culmination of his long and varied career or as the beginning of the sad decline of his once powerful intelligence.

In the introduction to The Critique, Sartre called his previous views of Existentialism "a past, peripheral cultural fashion, not unlike a particular brand of soap."[20] "Philosophy must continually be destroying itself and being reborn," he said.[21] As early as 1948, he had stated that "a liberation that proposes to be total must start from a total knowledge of man by himself."[22] By 1971, he asked more directly, "What, at this point in time, can we know about a man?" He answered his own question by saying, "It seemed to me that this question could only be answered by studying a specific case."[23]

Typically, the only way for Beauvoir to understand, let alone accept, what he now proposed was to examine it in the light of her own experience. For a brief moment she thought of writing another essay, along the lines of Sartre's Critique and perhaps patterned not after Baudelaire, which she called "my least favorite of all his writings," but instead similar to Saint Genet, which she had earlier described as "a terrific thing of 850 pages in handwriting . . . a real freak as a book because he speaks about everything . . . a strong mixture of philosophy and obscenity."[24]

Several of Sartre's arguments were extremely influential in helping her define a framework for studying herself. In an extension of his earlier argument, he was now insisting that Marxism should be freed from the particular ideological demands of Stalinism, then channeled into the service of biography.[25] He now believed that psychoanalysis should become a methodological tool used, for example, "to establish how a child lives his family relations *inside a given society*."[26] More and more, the idea of class became paramount in Sartre's thinking. Sometimes he called it society or culture, but always he interpreted class in conceptual terms of the individual's behavior within it and belief about it. His only bow toward Structuralism was in accepting the anthropological definition of a "given society," and he planned to use psychoanalysis to study how the individual acts within and reacts to this "given society." The method Sartre chose was biographical introspection, in combination with his own view of Marxist history, so that in his view the individual, biographical fact defined and explained the larger historical totality. Thus, each of Sartre's biographical studies took on other, extraliterary attributes. Like the *Critique*, they consider history and philosophy in almost every methodological category, and they treat hard economic reality and the effect of social mores upon an individual's growth and development. And, above all, they contribute to Sartre's paramount aim to create an ethical anthropology.

Simone de Beauvoir watched, read, listened, and argued very little as Sartre wrote and talked about it. In many instances, she described her role as "something it had not been since we were students: I studied, so as to learn from him."

Although everything she ever wrote owed something to Sartre, from subject matter (*L'Invitée*) to topic (*The Second Sex*) to conceptualization (the memoirs in general), she still managed to create something entirely her own in each of the four volumes. Sartre began with a conception of Marxism that Beauvoir worked hard to learn and understand, and she believed that she too followed it; but a close examination of her memoirs shows that when she attempts to superimpose a political framework onto the events of her life her ideology is clumsy, ill-conceived and badly expressed.[27] Sartre defended the clumsiness of his prose, its repetitiveness and digression, saying they were trivial issues with which the writer should no longer concern himself. Form no longer mattered; intentionality was all, and his was to situate his own thought within the context of historical development. Beauvoir was unconvinced: form mattered deeply to her. Discussing the memoirs in 1982, she said, "When I write, I try very hard to choose precisely the right word, the very carefully chosen word. . . . I rewrite enormously, everything, not just the novels."[28]

Sartre broke with Lévi-Strauss, but Beauvoir maintained their long friendship because she found "much that pertained specifically to myself and my life in my former colleague's work." She shared "in principal" Sartre's statement that one must always attempt to situate his or her own individual thought within the context of historical development, but in her case this meant an analysis of her family background, social class, upbringing and education. It took all of her first volume of memoirs to do so, and it was a theme she returned to again and again. "I have already said how concerned I am at present with the problems of early child-hood," she wrote in the last volume in 1972, still analyzing her early years while sifting through the theories of others for answers.[29]

In its own way, *Memoirs of a Dutiful Daughter* became as influential a work as *The Second Sex*. It is the most moving and also the most liter-ary of her autobiographical writings. Her prose is controlled, yet passionate, as she evokes situation and event and interprets her life from her birth to ZaZa's death. When it was published, women all over France wrote to her, astonished at how she had mirrored their lives and captured the sense of their daily existence. Even classmates from the Cours Désir who had been outraged by *The Second Sex* wrote to tell her that they forgave her, and to ask, "Then what happened to you?"

She had no intention of continuing beyond what she had written. "My last book, the story of my childhood, was fun to write and is selling very well, but I don't know what to write next in these upsetting times," she told Algren in her New Year's greeting of 1959.[30] He had written a dispirited letter and she warned him that hers would not be happy either. She described the events in France since 1958, saying the country had "lapsed into fascism" and that she, Sartre and all their friends had strug-gled against it in vain, but now found themselves feeling like strangers in their own land. "The torturing of Algerians will go on," she concluded sadly.

Less than six months later, she wrote again, telling him she had decided to go on with her memoirs. There were two main reasons why she decided to continue: the first, in response to the enormous volume of letters asking her to do so; the second, to distract herself from political realities, especially certain aspects of the Algerian War in which Sartre was now involved, and so consequently, was she. Nevertheless, to continue the memoirs meant writing of Sartre and their pact, her parents' dis-approval of her conduct, the trio with Olga, the beginning of the Family, her dismissal from teaching, her and Sartre's life during the war and after. It meant telling about Algren and Lanzmann and other lovers and giving the details of her friends' lives insofar as they touched on her own.

Telling about herself carried the danger of invading the privacy of others, but she decided to write anyway, blithely deciding that all she needed to do was provide everyone she wrote about with a pseudonym. She described her criteria in a general conversation about the memoirs:

> I tried to say everything I could about myself, but I erased inci-
> dents or events that could be harmful to other people. For ex-

ample, if I had a relationship with a man who did not want it to be known, I just didn't write about it. I exercised this discretion only about other people. Sometimes this meant that I had to omit certain episodes of my life because these would have been indiscreet in regard to others, and I did not want to hurt them. But this is the only selectiveness that I imposed: everything that concerned me, I wrote about as truthfully as I could. . . . My selectivity, then, was directed at what might be called the indiscretions of others who figured in my life, rather than any attempt at protection or enhancement of myself as I was then.[31]

So she wrote about herself, intending to take the book to the present day, which was then the end of 1959. But it grew too long and she decided to divide it into two parts, ending the second volume with the Liberation of Paris and beginning the third with the events immediately after. She told her readers in Volume Two that her reason for continuing to write about herself was that her life had developed a pattern which she had previously avoided asking about, and "I must find out now or never."

But an informal, unscientific page count of both *The Prime of Life* and *Force of Circumstance* shows that she wrote as much about Sartre as about herself if not more, filtering the details of her life through his philosophy, political activity and travels. Her autobiography becomes in many instances an apologia for Sartre's life, a diatribe that scolds all those who ignored, reviled or disagreed with him. In most instances, there are only glimpses of her as she passes by in little more than a travelogue, an "I went, I saw, I did" compilation that is chronologically faithful but frequently evasive of all the threads that comprised the tightly woven fabric of her daily life.[32]

There is also the question of real life versus "reconstructed" life,[33] as seen in her description of the family home on the Rue de Rennes as "dark, gloomy, cramped and crowded." Light streamed through the windows, Hélène de Beauvoir de Roulet remembers, but to Simone de Beauvoir, who passed the most unhappy years of her adolescence there, sunlight mattered little and the apartment was always in the shadow.

In another instance, she defended Sartre when he took a crucial episode from Giacometti's life, an accident that damaged his foot on the Place des Pyramides, and, when he used it in *The Words*, made it happen across Paris on the Place d'Italie. Beauvoir thought Giacometti was wrong to be angry with Sartre, because "as an artist, he should have understood Sartre's need to shape it to his need. Giacometti simply did not understand just how important it was for Sartre's vision that this accident happen on the Place d'Italie!"

She concluded the third volume, *Force of Circumstance*, in March 1963, in extreme depression, with one of the most bitter phrases to leave her pen. At the age of fifty-six, she wrote of the young girl she had been, when her life still lay before her: "The promises have all been kept. And yet, turning an incredulous gaze towards that young and credulous girl, I realize with stupor how much I was gypped."[34]

Of all the statements she made throughout her lifetime of writing, none has been the subject of more speculation than the phrase, "I was gypped." In a 1982 interview Beauvoir said, "I am tired of explaining that. Just say that I meant what I wrote in the book, and nothing more. I went into great length about why I felt that way, and if you read the book you will understand why I said it."

However, realizing this was an unsatisfying answer that shed no new light on the question, she elaborated: "When I wrote this statement, I had just been through the most intense period of political activism of my life. I lived through the terror of hiding out in my own city from bombings and death threats. It was as if everything Sartre and I had worked for meant nothing. We had very little hope in our lives, and I expressed it in my writing."

The years she wrote about, from the Liberation of Paris in 1944 to the spring of 1963, were the years in which she saw herself gradually being replaced in Sartre's life by an eager crowd of young people who dazzled the sick and aging man with their fiery revolutionary rhetoric. She also found herself being sought after, but in her case it was by women who wanted her name, her presence, her time and money on behalf of feminist causes. All these young people made her feel old and bewildered by what the world had become, especially, as she thought at first, because it had all happened without anyone heeding her writings, and thus without her leadership. She had the feeling that everything she cared about in life was, if not disappearing entirely, then at least changing, and there was nothing she could do about it.

Much of this had to do with Algren, who did not answer her letters, and who seemed to be gone from her life for good and all. She was beginning to think that she would resign herself to a lonely old age, when, to her surprise, he came back.

THIRTY-FIVE

Politics and Feminism

So you will come to Paris in the spring," Beauvoir wrote to Algren in the fall of 1959.[1] The British firm of Neville Spearman had just published *The Man with the Golden Arm*, and Algren was going to London to promote it. Beauvoir's many chatty letters since his attack on *The Mandarins* had paid off: he asked, without comment or apology, to stay for two or three months in Paris when his London business was finished. Her next letter was carefully designed not to alarm him, as she knew he and Amanda had divorced for the second time in 1955. She did not want to give the still-skittish Algren any cause to cancel the trip and tried to assure him that she wanted nothing more than he was willing to give and would settle for friendship if that was all he offered. As a further enticement, she invited him to stay with her on the Rue Schoelcher in his "own room" (probably her sleeping balcony, as the flat was really one large open space). She added that she "felt like being a bachelor again" and that she lived "alone now."

Lanzmann was seriously involved with another woman, which caused a certain amount of tension for everyone in the Family because they believed his defection had left Beauvoir confused, on the one hand embarrassed when it became public knowledge, on the other quietly resigned to what she had always predicted would eventually happen. Many of her friends were worried by how lethargic she had become.

Algren's letter changed all that. She was eager to catch up on the several lost years of their lives when he had maintained such brutal silence in his anger over *The Mandarins*. Privately, she worried that it would still cause trouble between them once he was on the scene, but she was prepared to face it when the time came. In her letters, she kept her tone light and bantering, offering to take him for rides in her beloved car ("if you are not afraid") and to let him eat her cooking ("which really will scare you"). "We will be as happy as in the old days," she concluded. Algren replied in the same tone of seeming bravado, assuring her of his courage where her driving and cooking were concerned, and telling her to warn Sartre and Bost that he could still whip them any day of the week in boxing, which Sartre adored and which they had all done together, supposedly for exercise but in "curious strutting macho virility" on his previous visits to Paris.[2] Still, she found it difficult to disguise her true feelings for long. Her letters almost immediately became filled with remarks about her impatience to see him and the great geographical distance between them that she had so chafed under during the height of their romantic involvement.

It was almost ten years since they had seen each other, and she was quite literally terrified that Algren would be repelled by the fifty-two-year-old woman she had become. Never mind that her hair was still radiantly brown, her skin firm and her figure almost as trim; as far as she was concerned, she was too old to make love and not physically worthy of receiving it. She conveniently forgot that Algren had also aged ten years since she last saw him, but then she was used to all the men she knew, starting of course with Sartre, remaining friendly with aging lovers as they transferred their physical affections to a continuing succession of younger women. Beauvoir was also afraid that Algren would not be able to forgive her for revealing their love story in The Mandarins. She worried especially that now that she was writing her memoirs he would be incapable of relaxing in her presence, not trusting her to keep the details of his visit private. In the terror induced by imagining all that could go wrong between them, she reverted to her old habit of first drinking large quantities of wine and then sobbing uncontrollably, and for several months she actually bit her crimson-polished nails to the quick.

Algren's letters, uncharacteristically charming, disconcerted rather than soothed her. It was as if she were waiting for the second shoe to drop, but the much-awaited explosion of his anger never came. He responded to her concern about her age and the awkwardness of their reunion with more tenderness than ever. He sent all sorts of little things that could fit into an airmail letter, from a pressed leaf to funny newspaper cartoons to bits of ribbon or fabric for her mother. At Christmas he sent a huge box of books as presents for everyone. Hers were about travel, which he intended as a peace offering for the past and a source of all the places they might see together in the future. Sartre received books "about the real America," which she read in order to catch up on what she had missed in the past few years, but the one she liked best was Mark Twain's autobiography, which he sent for Michelle.[3] "France is lousy," she concluded in her usual year-end letter, "but Sartre, Bost, Olga and I are happy." The thought of seeing Algren in an otherwise gloomy time was a tremendous revivifier.

Politically, things were at a very low ebb for Sartre, and thus for Beauvoir as well. She quoted Sartre early in 1960 as having asked her "whether it's not just physical exhaustion that stops us, rather than moral fatigue."[4] To her, it was a combination of both. She was stunned by Albert Camus's violent death in a spectacular automobile crash that also killed her friend Michel Gallimard. Boris Vian's sudden death from a heart attack a few years earlier still induced a combination of panic and shock when she thought about it. "The series of deaths had begun," she intoned solemnly, thinking ultimately of her own to come "inevitably too soon, or too late." Death was a fearsome reality despite their insistence on surrounding themselves with the protective buffer of an ever-more-youthful circle of friends.

Sartre's fluctuating health continued to be Beauvoir's most pressing concern, as his consumption of stimulants and barbiturates soared and his bouts of hypertension and other ailments intensified. The drugs affected his hearing, so that as each day progressed he grew increasingly deaf. Sometimes by midafternoon he was unable to hear people speak, and such sounds as the ringing of his doorbell simply did not register. Most alarming of all was the toll on his vision, and the fear of blindness hung over Beauvoir and the Family long before it actually struck Sartre. So his worrisome illnesses and the unexpected death of friends frequently younger, coupled with the many political rebuffs he was dealt, all combined to make Sartre apathetic about all else in his life.

This malaise included the many opportunities that were now proffered for him and Beauvoir to pay official visits to countries with social revolutions actually in progress. Sartre had long been aware that foreign governments or leftist groups (in other countries as well as in France) were using him for publicity purposes, but, since he believed it his duty to cooperate, he kept his objections to himself. Now Beauvoir found herself courted as well, as Sartre's companion and his deputy on *Les Temps Modernes*, but more so as the spokesperson for women within both established and emerging socialist governments. Only a short time before, such invitations would have found them ready to leave on a moment's notice, but now they both wondered dispiritedly whether "age had blunted our curiosity," or whether their lethargy might be due to the fact that they were increasingly regarded as aging icons, sacred monsters who had progressed to the stage in life where younger intellectuals must now begin to dispossess them of their leadership. To Sartre and Beauvoir, it seemed as if the golden years of Saint-Germain had come to a screeching halt, but in reality the brakes had been applied for quite some time.

The revolution in literature and culture inspired by postwar Existentialism had been supplanted by theory of a totally different cast, and a new litany of saints had been created. Sartre was deteriorating, Camus was dead, and the new holy (or "unholy," depending on the orientation of the observer) triad of Lacan, Derrida and Barthes was in the ascendant. Sartre was puzzled by how quickly Existentialism had given way to Structuralism, Deconstruction and other rarefied systems of contemporary thought. Scholars no longer interpreted books, articles or essays, but instead analyzed what was now grouped under the impersonal, nonspecific term of "texts." Sartre grew more dependent upon the genre of biography to explain his evolving system of Marxist thought, and found himself increasingly disregarded or ignored by other intellectuals who responded to the ascetic lure of textual criticism and the concurrent belief in the death of the author. Beauvoir, lost in the self-scrutiny of her memoirs, was almost totally unaware of the changing literary landscape, so she blamed the malaise both she and Sartre felt on the most obvious scapegoat, their unhappiness with the political situation.

Curiously, as their political influence waned in France, it increased greatly in much of the rest of the world. The invitations multiplied, and the pleas for their persons became more insistent. Sartre became the one intellectual whose presence and commentary emerging governments clamored for, as if he alone could validate their revolutions. Carlos Franqui is but one example: editor of the most influential Cuban newspaper, *Revolución*, he insisted that Sartre was morally obligated to visit Cuba.

And so Sartre and Beauvoir left in late February, without any particular fanfare, to spend a month during what he called "the honeymoon of the Revolution."[5] For Beauvoir, "after Paris, the gaiety of the place exploded like a miracle under the blue sky." They were wined and dined and shown Castro's triumphs, often by Che Guevara.[6] Castro himself took them by motor launch to visit his home at Cienaga de Zapata; cigar clenched between his teeth, he towered above Sartre and Beauvoir in a photograph that was widely reproduced throughout the world. Castro introduced Sartre and Beauvoir before a televised press conference as friends of the revolution, and for the rest of their visit they were surrounded by admiring throngs whenever they went out in public.

Later in her life, Beauvoir regarded this trip as the catalyst for their peripatetic activity throughout much of the coming decade. Travel became a priority for her as much because it energized Sartre as for the way it validated them both in the eyes of the world. They loved it when crowds shouted their names, when waiters gave them the best table, when public officials sent limousines to pick them up.

Sartre responded to questions for hours on end, and Beauvoir gave separate interviews as well. As the decade progressed, she discovered with initial surprise and lasting pleasure that women everywhere cared deeply about everything that pertained to their status, and they clamored for her thoughts, beliefs and suggestions for change.[7]

For the return trip, officials arranged for Sartre and Beauvoir to fly via New York, where unknown to them the Cuban press attaché had arranged a conference in which Sartre was expected to render a further snub to the United States by praising the glories of Castro's Cuba. He did not disappoint them. When they returned to France, Sartre suggested to *France-Soir* that they publish a series of articles about his impressions of Cuba. Beauvoir helped him to organize the material, but there was so much that they called in Lanzmann, who helped them cut and edit it into sixteen articles, published in June.[8] It was the second time that year that Beauvoir put aside her memoirs to read and edit Sartre's writing; the first had been the *Critique of Dialectical Reason* (published that same year). Her own repayment to her Cuban sponsors for their hospitality came through an interview in *France-Observateur*, praising Castro as the incarnation of a tremendous emotional power and calling his leadership "not only a success but an example."[9]

These were only some of the many tasks that interrupted her visit with Algren.

He wanted to come to Paris no later than March 10, but she was not due to return from Cuba until the twentieth, so she gave her apartment keys to Bost along with detailed instructions about how to make Algren welcome. Early on the morning of the twentieth, she rang her own doorbell and Algren let her in, not recognizing who she was at first.[10] He had given up the little round glasses he had previously worn only for reading when his vision deteriorated to the point where he needed glasses all the time. Instead, he chose contact lenses, but did not discover how painful they were until he was in Europe and unable to replace them. So he went without them, peering myopically at her for several days until she insisted on buying him a new pair of glasses, which he could not afford. This was the first blow to his ego.

At first it seemed that they would be able to revert to all they had been to each other between 1949 and 1951. Both agreed that they were so nervous about their first meeting that several days passed before each was calm enough to recognize any sign of aging in the other. By then it did not matter, as they had fallen back into their former intimacy: once again she was his "Frenchy" or "Frog Wife," and he was her "Local Youth" or "Crocodile." He blushed with pleasure every time she, in mock horror over his many bad jokes and sarcastic comments, wagged the finger that wore his ring. Still, too much had happened in the intervening years to make the resumption of their affair totally untroubled.

Algren "was awakened every morning by his own anger," which "always lasted till the evening." He was angry with all those who he believed had betrayed him personally and professionally. He always had a suspicious bent to his personality, which developed into paranoia as years passed and critical and financial success, despite the National Book Award, continued to elude him. Algren cast the blame on everyone but himself for all the bad deals he had made to publish his novels or sell movie rights. Politically, he also found fault with others: left-wing intellectuals had sold out and those on the right had created a country in which he could no longer live comfortably. "Once I used to live in America," he told Beauvoir, "now I live on American-occupied territory." The litany of those who he believed had sinned against him was long and boring for her, but she listened patiently all day long to the sad man she still believed she loved. By evening he had drunk enough wine and played rhythm and blues for enough hours that he felt mellow enough to leave the flat. This was all very well for the first few weeks of his visit, because it gave her time to reestablish their relationship, but too much was happening in Sartre's life that required her presence and support. It made Algren furious and her frantic as she tried to balance the emotional needs of one man against the political support required by the other.

The situation was somewhat mitigated when Algren discovered that several Americans rented apartments in Beauvoir's building, and he struck up friendships with them. They introduced him to the American novelist James Jones, which admitted Algren into the heart of the American expatriate colony Beauvoir described as "cut off from the French, whose language they could not even speak, and from the United States which they had all left, indifferent to politics but marked by their origins." He soon drifted away from what he told Beauvoir was "their lack of any real context," preferring "his daily bouts of anger to their rootlessness."

Most of the players in her daily drama had changed since Algren's last visit to Paris. Those who had amused him, like Cazalis, Cau and Gréco, had all left the fringes of the Family, and the new younger members were as indifferent to Algren as he was to them. Michelle was preoccupied with her children and her own relationships. Everyone avoided Wanda after she expressed her opinion of Beauvoir's first volume of memoirs by slicing it up into little pieces with a large butcher knife. Beauvoir introduced Algren to Lanzmann, but neither man much liked the other. That left only Bost and Olga, and fortunately their friendship with him remained strong. They introduced him to Beauvior's friend Monique Lange, who liked him enough to give him invitations to all Gallimard's famous publishing parties. Lange's companion and later husband, the Spanish writer Juan Goytisolo, liked him as well, so this little group was often called upon to entertain Algren, which they usually did with pleasure.

Monique Lange came up with the idea of inviting Algren to Spain, where a group of international writers and publishers was meeting to establish the Prix Formentor. Beauvoir sent him off alone and spent the next ten days catching up on her own obligations before joining him in Madrid. Then they spent the next several weeks traveling throughout Spain, where they had gone together on his earlier trip to Europe.

When they returned to Paris, Algren announced that he was enjoying himself so much that he had decided to stay for at least five or six months, if not longer. Beauvoir received the news with as much chagrin as pleasure. It was clearly time for her to establish priorities. The Cuban junket had received such publicity throughout Latin America that the Brazilian government sent a second, more insistent invitation (Sartre had rejected the first) to visit for several months beginning in August. Although he was hesitant to be away from France for such a long time, Sartre felt an obligation to go.

Before that, he felt obliged to accept an invitation from the Yugoslavian Writers' Union. Two of his plays had been translated and staged in Belgrade, and Sartre was asked to discuss them. Naturally, Beauvoir was determined to go with him. Sartre was also invited to meet Marshal Tito, which she believed was important to his standing in France because of the successful attention his meeting with Castro had brought. He was also asked to lecture at Belgrade University, and it was here that she felt the most urgent need to be at his side.

Her role on these occasions had come to be a combination of bodyguard, buffer, general organizer and nurse. It was she who barked commands to official security guards to keep the crowds from pressing on Sartre, and she who decided how long the questioning that followed his lectures should last. She packed and unpacked his baggage, collected his scattered papers and manuscripts, arranged for prescriptions to be filled, and insured that he ate well and drank as little as possible. She had come to believe that he could not function on these trips without her managerial intercessions.

Algren didn't like the idea that she would leave him alone in Paris to dash off to Yugoslavia with Sartre, but she never gave him the chance to object. She simply told him, just as she had always done in the past, that Sartre needed her, so that was that. But he felt abandoned, and his emotions festered for several years before erupting in his several violent reviews of her memoirs, when he described her pact with Sartre as her "insistence upon aggrandizing a casual affection twenty years dead into a passion of classic dimension."[11]

She was forced to leave Algren almost every day to work on the *France-Soir* articles with Lanzmann at Sartre's apartment, because he interrupted them too much at hers. When Francis Jeanson asked her to help with his clandestine work on behalf of the FLN in Algeria, she accepted, mostly because she believed in his cause but also because it was a legitimate reason to be away from Algren for significant periods of time.

There was no question that the official French position in Algeria revolted her and Sartre, but until 1960 she had not been overtly political. She professed admiration for those who were actively involved in protest and demonstration, but added that "to do so demanded total commitment, and it would have been cheating to pretend that I was capable of such a thing. I am not a woman of action; my reason for living is writing."[12]

Francis Jeanson had been criticizing official French policy in Algeria since 1950, and *Les Temps Modernes* had published several of his essays on the subject. In 1955 he and his wife published a book in support of the Algerian revolution, and by 1956 he was one of the leaders of the FLN in France, both in fund-raising and in sheltering militants. Shortly thereafter he went underground, and for the next few years he carried out clandestine tasks on behalf of the rebels. At the beginning of 1955 he tried to persuade Sartre and Beauvoir to join him in some form of action, but they refused unequivocally. Jeanson always believed it was because they were frightened by the violence of the Algerian rebels. He remembered a conversation sometime in 1955 or 1956 when Sartre described the Algerians as "cruel, bloodthirsty," and said the Chinese were "much better at revolution." Sartre described a Chinese play in which a revolutionary general circled around a city rather than attack it, believing that the besieged people would eventually understand and join the rebellion. Jeanson believed it was Sartre's way of distancing himself from what he called "the Algerian Problem" even as he kept a very lively interest in "the Rights of Man," his euphemism for the issue of torture. Jeanson left them alone until 1960, believing that "they did not see the situation in Algeria as their problem." When he asked for their help then, they did not hesitate. He called their cooperation "flawless," but made a distinction between Sartre and Beauvoir, saying that by this time "it was the feminist struggle that motivated her participation in politics."[13]

Jeanson's assessment is astute. Throughout the 1960s, Beauvoir's public life reads like a political travelogue which evolved into a public declaration of support for feminist principles and goals. A brief summary of her major travels shows her and Sartre in Brazil and Cuba in 1960, the Soviet Union in 1962, '64, and '66, Japan in 1966, Israel and Egypt in 1967. Besides several visits to Yugoslavia, they were in Belgium and Holland several times each, in Czechoslovakia, and in 1966 in Stockholm to participate in the Russell Tribunal on the war in Vietnam. Throughout the decade, she gave interviews and published articles on politics (mostly about her views of what she witnessed) and feminism (mostly interviews soliciting her opinions). Because of the success of *The Second Sex*, the first critical studies of her work began to appear, so this is also the period when, for the first time, she began to look beyond the intention and completion of an individual work to the impact it would have in a much larger sense. She was now very much aware of how any current writing or statement would reflect back upon everything she had said or written in the past, and, even more important, what its impact would be upon Sartre's writing and commentary, especially the public and political. For the first time, she received requests to speak separately from Sartre, as writers and feminists invited her to address them with increasing frequency.

This is only the briefest summary of most of the high points of her public activity, but when all of it is examined in detail certain patterns do emerge. It is clear that on the occasions when Beauvoir and Sartre were the guests of governments or intellectual organizations, her official status was seldom little more than that of his intellectual consort.[14] This was certainly a visible position, but her role became important and her influence the most lasting among the women outside the ranks of the powerful who were enterprising enough to seek her out. At first they were few and often in privileged positions determined by wealth through heredity or marriage and not by individual accomplishment; but as years passed and her reputation as well as the reputation of *The Second Sex* grew, many women braved everything from ostracism to punishment to hear what Beauvoir had to say about their condition and what they should do to change it.

All this happened spontaneously, during what the German journalist Alice Schwartzer calls "the darkness of the Fifties and Sixties, before the new women's movement dawned," when *The Second Sex* was "like a secret code that we emerging women used to send messages to each other."[15]

And, as the "secret code" gathered momentum in the still-unorganized feminist underground throughout the world, Beauvoir began to speak and write more directly and more frequently on behalf of women. When all these statements, manifestos, prefaces, interviews and articles are collected, a vivid pattern emerges: almost a full decade before her open declaration of commitment to feminism, Simone de Beauvoir was pressing for all that she had advocated in *The Second Sex*. She began to practice what she had previously only preached.

Much of this activity began in the summer of 1960, and it took her away both mentally and physically from Algren, who was "as *machiste* as Sartre in so many ways." In later years, she considered this visit of Algren's to be the time when major changes occurred in her attitude toward the men in her life and in her behavior with regard to them,[16] some of which would have been unthinkable to her in the early years of those relationships. In her memoirs, she described how she did not want to spend his entire visit away from her normal routine and how she kept up her usual habits, especially spending each morning in bed to read, write, and answer her correspondence while he prowled restlessly around the apartment. She apportioned her afternoons and evenings between Algren and Sartre, keeping them separate because Sartre was too tense and overstimulated from work and drugs to have any time for boxing and drinking with Algren. He also had to see Wanda, Michelle and Evelyne regularly, and, increasingly, Arlette as well. Algren was miffed by what he considered Sartre's snub, but Beauvoir glossed over his true feelings by saying that Algren "had articles to write, he had no lack of friends, and he liked being alone; this arrangement suited him as well."[17] In 1985 she amended this by reciting a list of the activities that kept her busy throughout Algren's visit, adding, "I know he didn't like it, but there was very little I could do about it. I knew that he would soon be returning to America. I had to live in France, and as a Frenchwoman there were certain things I had to do."

She persuaded herself that she was giving precedence to public activity over her private relationship with Algren; but in reality she was choosing to be with one man instead of another, because everything she chose to do was somehow involved with Sartre's political activity. Beauvoir's deference to his needs and desires remained unchanged; as did her relationship to Algren, for just as she set the terms of their times together in the United States, she continued to do so in Paris. Algren must have recognized this, because much of his behavior seems to have been calculated to provoke a response from her. He reacted by getting very drunk in public and becoming abusive and pugilistic. Beauvoir's reaction was not what he hoped for: she enlisted two newcomers to the *Temps Modernes* staff, Serge Lafourie and Florence Malraux, to distract him when Olga and Bost were unable to do so. Lafourie and Malraux soon grew adept at keeping Algren quiet during his binges and carrying him home to bed afterward.[18]

Meanwhile, Beauvoir continued with her self-appointed tasks. Several kept her away from both men throughout much of May and June. She

480 SIMONE DE BEAUVOIR

wrote prefaces for two books by Dr. Marie-Andrée L. Weil-Hallé which dealt with contraception and family planning.[19] When Algren complained of her absence, she was angry and, "to spite him," attended a press conference in support of Dr. Weil-Hallé. Consequently, Beauvoir's actions pitted her against both Left and Right when she agreed with the slogan "For a woman, freedom begins in the womb": the Communists accused those who supported birth control of attempting to weaken the proletariat by denying it children, and conservatives argued that such methods as the diaphragm (newly introduced to France) interfered with the romance and pleasure of love.[20]

Beauvoir's support for Dr. Weil-Hallé was reported in the newspapers and came to the attention of a young activist lawyer, Gisèle Halimi, who enlisted her to help gain publicity as a means to stop the mutilation by torture of Algerian women suspected of aiding the FLN. Halimi was defending an Algerian girl accused of espionage, Djamila Boupacha, who had been "tortured and raped with a bottle by French soldiers."[21] She had also been burned with cigarettes all over her body, deprived of food and sleep and shocked by electric prods. Beauvoir was "outraged," and it shows in the way she described it in her memoirs. She is fierce on the attack and outspoken in her defense of both the girl and the cause of Algerian nationalism.

As summer heat settled on Paris, a restless Algren began to create more confrontations as a ploy for her attention. To diffuse tension on the Rue Schoelcher, she agreed to spend several weeks in July with him in Greece and Turkey and several days in Marseille, where they had been so happy on his previous visit. She went, but her mind was elsewhere, preoccupied with the growing resistance among young French men and women to the situation in Algeria.

When she returned in August, she signed the "Manifesto of the 121," a document containing the signatures of intellectuals who were against French policy in Algeria. It became one of the most significant and influential statements made during the conflict and had considerable impact upon the shift in public opinion in favor of Algerian independence. Sartre signed the manifesto as well, as did everyone else at Les Temps Modernes. Later that year, Beauvoir and Sartre both campaigned vigorously against de Gaulle's policies in the 1961 referendum on the Algerian question. She went alone for the first time in Paris to deliver speeches to various student groups, imploring them to join her in voting "No."

She credited her experiences speaking to groups in Cuba with giving her the courage to make these speeches. It took courage of another sort to bid farewell to Algren, still in residence in her apartment, stubbornly refusing to leave and doing much to impede her departure for Brazil, which she remembered as "a nightmare."

For all intents and purposes, Sartre was virtually alone on the spectrum of the political Left in France. Derided by everyone, he denounced them all in return, saying the only true men of the Left in France were the twenty-year-olds.[22] He continued to rant and rail until he came down with shingles, which threw him into a deep depression. The pain was incapacitating, and, as usual in situations where Sartre needed to be nursed for a physical ailment, all his women except Beauvoir took turns. Beauvoir, with her horror of illness and her fear of death, invented pressing intellectual concerns to distance herself from the indignity of these embarrassing tasks. As time passed, and Sartre's illnesses intensified, this distancing was to cost her dearly, but as always she was too absorbed in the tasks at hand to realize that others were usurping her place. So Beauvoir, who was trying to finish up all her editing obligations to the magazine, gather enough information about the recent political past to take with her in order to keep working on her memoirs, place the rest of her affairs in order and—most pressing of all—placate Algren, now had many of Sartre's affairs to worry about as well.

They were met in Rio by the novelist Jorge Amado, who with his wife, Zelia, became Beauvoir's good friend. Everything about Brazil struck her as different from anything she had experienced, which is why she devoted more than sixty pages of reportage to describing it in her memoirs.[23] For more than two months, she and Sartre crisscrossed its vast distances, met its people, enjoyed its variety, resources and pleasures. But no matter how busy they were, she wrote faithfully to Algren, who was still stubbornly occupying her apartment. She teased him by beginning her letters with such greetings as "Dearest wonderful thing, beautiful flower of the rue Daguerre," or "Flower of the Rue Schoelcher, Giacometti de la camera, silent beast of nowhere" and "Subversive beast of nowhere."[24] She wrote to him as she had written when he was angry with her in the past, cheerfully and continuously, ignoring the fact that he did not reply. She told him how the French government tried to prevent Sartre from lecturing for fear that he would speak out against its Algerian policy, which he did anyway, giving "a real slap in the face" to France. She told him how they had been made honorary citizens of Rio de Janeiro, which she deliberately compared to Chicago in the hope of placating him. Bahia was voodoo country, where the highest priestess called Sartre the son of a powerful god and Beauvoir the daughter of the loveliest goddess.

By September 24, she was in Brasília, "Kubitschek's crazy artificial city which I hate." There were other things she disliked as well: "Sartre has decided to add a red-head to his collection of dark-haired Arlette, fair-haired Wanda, and the fake blondes Michelle and Evelyne: he has begun an affair with a well-bred 25-year-old virgin from the north of Brazil." Even this was not enough to prod the gossip-loving Algren into writing. By mid-October she could no longer stand his silence and tried to phone him, unsuccessfully, from the city of Belém. They went on to Recife, where she became ill and was hospitalized with what was diagnosed as "Brazilian typhoid: it only lasts a few days."

"Sartre really did go crazy," she wrote later to Algren, "he drank a lot of scotches and took a lot of gardenol, which enraged me as I lay helpless in the hospital." He had quarreled with the Brazilian woman, Christina T., "because he wanted to sleep with her and virginity is so important here." Then Christina "went on a drinking binge, too, and tried to kill herself." Fortunately all the penicillin Beauvoir was given took effect. She insisted on being released from the hospital, just in time to learn that "Sartre is really thinking of marrying her [Christina] and I don't know what will happen to Arlette then!" At this point, the only thing that mattered to her was that Sartre's desires were satisfied, no matter who or what had to be sacrificed to them.

That problem was moot when Lanzmann telephoned to warn them not to return to Paris by plane because of anonymous threats made against Sartre: he "would be met at the airport and arrested or murdered" for a combination of pro-Algerian statements he had made, issued or signed in recent months. They decided to spend ten days in Cuba, where they could board a plane secretly for some destination in Spain that would let them cross the border to France surreptitiously. They had had no news of France during their stay in Brazil because no French newspapers were available. Lanzmann informed them that while they were away all those who had signed the Manifesto of the 121 were forbidden to issue any further statements or to speak on radio or television. The latest issue of *Les Temps Modernes* was seized, and a veterans' group of several thousand marched down the Champs-Elysées shouting support for de Gaulle and "Kill Sartre" by turns.

It made them fearful and was a depressing end to the trip, and she sent another letter to Algren as soon as they reached Cuba to tell him about it. She found the people to be "different, afraid of American aggression." Castro, who had just returned from New York, was "happy about his Harlem adventure," and "lively and wonderful as ever." He personally escorted them to the airport. In a subdued note she added: ". . . a lot of good work is being done to help the peasants . . . [but] the country is not as happy as it was in March."

Lanzmann sent a message advising them to fly to Barcelona, and he and Bost drove there to meet them. The trip back to Paris was uneasy, as Sartre was certain they would be charged for signing the manifesto but not taken to trial or jailed. De Gaulle supposedly ended all such talk of Sartre's arrest by proclaiming, "One does not arrest Voltaire."[25]

Beauvoir was disappointed to find nothing from Algren in her apartment but a few magazines he had left behind, some photos of Istanbul and a moldy candy bar. She also had the unhappy task of rerouting a great pile of his mail on to Chicago. It was not until the spring of 1961 that she learned how much he wanted to hurt her before he left. Bost got tipsy and let it slip that Algren had also left "rent" money. Bost found it one night when he let himself in with Algren's key to use the apartment for a tryst. He took the money and spent it.

THIRTY-SIX

November Was
a Long Sad Month

I N APRIL 1961, Sartre received a letter telling him to expect "a 'killing package': you know, you just pull the string and off you go. Now he will carefully let his mother or Arlette or the secretary, or Bost or anyone open the packages for him," Beauvoir told Algren, "I should not."[1] Shortly after "Sartre got a second anonymous letter saying he is going to die. It doesn't seem serious at all, but it scares me. People really don't like him."

The Algerian situation in France was heating up, and both Beauvoir and Sartre were receiving hate mail from ultraconservative supporters of the French government. At first, these were individuals or members of small groups without any real organization or power whom they called simply the "Ultras" and whose letters they generally disregarded. However, when the powerful and vicious Organisation de l'Armée Secrète (OAS) was formed, they took the threats more seriously. Their friends decided it was unsafe for them to return to their apartments and installed them in the luxurious flat of "somebody we don't know" who volunteered to move elsewhere.[2] The hideout depressed Beauvoir by reminding her of World War II, when people were afraid for their lives and many were in hiding. It was in the elegant Sixteenth Arrondissement, an area she had seldom been in since the war, when Sartre's mother and stepfather lived there.

Beauvoir and Sartre rattled around their hiding place, bored and lonely in the midst of so much splendor and space. Their friends were afraid to visit openly, for fear they were being followed by "over-excited ultras." The Family forbade her and Sartre to be seen in public, so they could not go into restaurants or cafés, one of the worst punishments imaginable. Once again, just as she had done during the war, Beauvoir took over the kitchen: "I *cook* for him," she told Algren proudly, "ham and sausages and a lot of cans. That is what he eats except when Bost or Claude [Lanzmann] come and cook a dinner."

Her favorite entertainment was looking out the window at the Seine or watching the activity of the other tenants in the parking lot below. She had recently met the American sociologist C. Wright Mills, so to her these people seemed prime examples of what he called "the Organization Man"; the men went off to work each morning with briefcases in hand, and a few hours later their well-dressed wives departed for a day of shopping or otherwise killing time.[3]

For a little while, it almost seemed the Ultras had forgotten about them. Sartre went to Milan, where he was awarded a substantial monetary prize from a leftist publishing group and also collected more than a million francs in donations and lecture fees, all of which he gave to the Algerian cause with great public fanfare. Beauvoir went alone several times to Belgium, where she spoke with leaders of various leftist trade unions and to "bourgeois senators and deputies" who seemed amenable to her message. She was surprised by how interested they were in what she had to say about Cuba and Brazil as well as Algeria; and when some of the students and trade-unionists asked her to visit factories and coal mines, she went.

She learned something about herself during this speaking tour: that she was uncomfortable speaking in a public, political forum, but that she had to do it because of her power to influence people. For the rest of her life she suffered from an almost irrational fear of exhibiting herself in public, but, with nervous stomach and sweating palms, she girded herself to do it whenever she thought it necessary. André Gorz, who was now closely associated with both her and Sartre, heard her speak during these years and recalled how much he was struck by her timidity: "She has a dry, scholarly way of lecturing to crowds, as though she were hiding herself behind the lectern, hiding her feelings behind her intellectuality."[4]

For much of the rest of the winter, she went throughout Paris and the surrounding towns addressing any group that invited her, urging them all to vote "No" on the referendum, but "people voted yes anyway, and now de Gaulle is still doing nothing and the war continues." She needed a rest from the tension, the activity and, for what was probably the first time, even from Sartre, or at least from his frenetic political activity. So she went alone to a hotel outside Paris, "a little castle in a park," where she slept, read, listened to records and heard a nightingale sing for the first time in her life: "in fact, I thought Shakespeare had invented them and that they did not exist at all."[5]

It had been almost six months since she tried to write anything. She thought she would write a third volume of memoirs, but all the activity surrounding the Algerian question led her to think she should reconsider this decision:

I ask myself what kind of book I am going to write. Will it not be the last part of my life? That is what I planned when you [Algren] were here and I went to the Bibliothèque and I worked [at] home, but since I came back, I hesitated. I thought of writing a novel. Now I am decided: it will be the third and last part of my memoirs. The second has just been published, the "force [Prime] of life," and I am pleased about it.[6]

As well she might have been: all the publicity surrounding her stance on the Algerian situation contributed to the 45,000 copies of the book that were sold before the official publication date. In the first week it was in bookstores, another 25,000 were sold, and Gallimard was reprinting so that more than 200,000 copies would be available. "And that means money for years!" she told Algren, adding that she would have plenty to lose at the racetrack the next time she was in Chicago. Her only regret that winter was that she had to spend so much time in hiding, because she would have enjoyed holding her head high in cafés and restaurants in celebration of her success and, in a sense, in vindication of her life.

She and Sartre decided to take their annual Easter holiday in Antibes, where they had spent so many happy vacations in Madame Morel's villa, but things would be different this year. The dear old lady, too infirm to travel, had sold the villa, and it was now a nursing home. Beauvoir and Sartre stayed nearby in a charming little hotel they had often admired on their walks. This trip was different from all the previous ones because Arlette was there, too, with her "handsome boyfriend." Increasingly these holidays came to include one or more of Sartre's women, either in the same hotel or nearby in an apartment or a villa, usually with a companion of their own during the time he was officially domiciled with Beauvoir. She was usually grateful to have them there, because Sartre continued to overdose himself with drugs and drink, and his health continued to be precarious. Arlette especially responded to Sartre's every whim, and Beauvoir took advantage of the younger woman's pliable disposition to go off by herself in her new little white car. At the beginning of this holiday, it seemed as if she would have more freedom from Sartre—both from actually caring for him and from running interference between him and all the women who squabbled over their rights with him—because "all his women seem to have new lovers now, so that makes things easier for him." Even Christina T., "the red-haired Brazilian girl," had been put into a certain perspective with time and distance: Beauvoir, who read the "nice letters" the girl wrote, sometimes even before Sartre did, said, "Sartre doesn't think he will [have to] marry her after all." But as the holiday progressed, the car became a welcome refuge. She drove to Marseille, telling Algren it was to revisit places where she had taken him the previous summer, but really it was to get away from the tension of being around Sartre.

They were in Antibes on May 4, when news came that Merleau-Ponty had died unexpectedly of a heart attack. Beauvoir was devastated by the shock of his death, but Sartre's reaction was to throw himself into a frenzy of writing that included an essay about his dead friend. His only concession to his entourage's concern for his deteriorating health was his agreeing to leave earlier than usual for the annual summer holiday in Rome.

On July 19, the morning of their departure, the Ultras made good their continuing threats. A plastic bomb exploded in the entrance hall of Sartre's building at 42 Rue Bonaparte, but it did little serious damage. Fortunately, they had taken the precaution some weeks before of settling Madame Mancy into the Hotel L'Aiglon on the Boulevard Raspail (a short walk from the Rue Schoelcher), and Sartre had since stayed either with Beauvoir or, on his usual rotating basis, with Wanda, Michelle, Evelyne, Arlette or a number of others who were important to him for one reason or another.

The summer passed uneventfully in Rome as Beauvoir worked on the third volume of her memoirs, Force of Circumstance (La Force des Choses). It seemed important to her under the specter of so much uncertainty, and especially after the bombing, to leave a record of Sartre's political activity, so she chose to slant the book along those lines. The facts and events of her life frequently become only the pretext for what might be called the unfolding of his public biography, as she painstakingly delineates his writing, thinking and political activity, relegating her own to a secondary status within the text. In many ways, this volume is little more than her apologia for his life, and she has been frequently taken to task by feminist scholars for the subservience of her own language, ideology and behavior to his. If there is one particular work in all her canon that is most infuriating, it is generally believed to be this one.

"The book is centered on me, but we have always lived in such total intimacy. I can't speak of myself without speaking of him," she told Madeleine Chapsal, who asked whether she had consulted Sartre about what she wrote. "Oh, yes, enormously," she replied, "because we have the same memories."[7] Still, a writer's memory is often grounded in both fact and imagination, and in this instance it was grounded in equivocation as well. In the introduction to this work she wrote that some of her readers had sent letters pointing out errors in the previous volume, and she apologized in advance for any she might have made in this one, insisting, "I have never intentionally distorted the truth." She probably should have added that Force of Circumstance is the one work in which she frequently ignores or evades what she does not want to discuss, usually by blurring chronology or telescoping several different events into one account. Perhaps the best description of her methodology is to say that she strove to tell the truth according to what she believed it to be, but at the same time she either blurred those facts and events that troubled her or else omitted them entirely. This may be part of the reason Beauvoir called this volume, originally intended to be her last writing about herself, "the hardest writing I have ever done."[8]

□

Life was hard, too, as France tightened the screws on the Algerian insurrection. The mysterious owner of the apartment (whom they never met) returned, so they left their "plush prison," but anonymous notes and telephone messages warned Sartre not to return to his apartment or Beauvoir's, and they were afraid to move in with any of their friends for fear of what might happen. No one would rent to them, as Sartre discovered when he tried to register in a hotel and was unceremoniously escorted to the door by the terrified manager. Sartre's new secretary, Claude Faux, finally solved the problem by renting an apartment in his own name in a building under construction on the Boulevard Saint-Germain and sneaking Sartre and Beauvoir into it under cover of darkness. The apartment was dismal, at the bottom of an interior well, with the only light coming from a bare bulb hanging from the ceiling.

They stayed for several weeks, surrounded by the rubble of workmen, until a bomb was set off early one morning. They assumed they were its targets, but it landed exactly where it was supposed to, in the shop of a Frenchman born in Algeria who refused to contribute to the OAS. Several days later, another bomb exploded at 42 Rue Bonaparte, and this time Sartre's front door was blown off. Windows were shattered, doors jarred from their hinges, and the stairwell hung precariously in the open air, in full view of the street below. Someone got into Sartre's apartment and looted it systematically; many of his unpublished manuscripts were never seen again. He and Beauvoir moved once more, this time back to the luxurious apartment of the mysterious "somebody we don't know," where they found out that two fugitive OAS killers were hiding in the apartment just below theirs. Since they had no place else to go, they stayed.

Another outcry arose and more public anger was focused on Sartre and Beauvoir when lawyer Gisèle Halimi's book sympathetic to the Algerian torture victim, *Djamila Boupacha*, was published in February 1962. Even though she only contributed the preface, Beauvoir's name appeared as co-author so that she could share in both responsibility and punishment if Halimi were in some way brought to task by French authorities. Somehow, her whereabouts and Sartre's leaked out, because there was a spate of threatening phone calls, and they had to move still another time, to a wretched hotel on an alley near the Seine, so decrepit that the manager shrugged off their presence, saying no damage could possibly make the place any worse than it already was.

Beauvoir was so nervous she could hardly function, so Lanzmann spirited her away one evening after dark to dine at a little village inn outside Paris. "Suddenly," she wrote, "hell was back on earth." He handed her a dossier containing verified accounts of torture inflicted upon Algerians by the *harkis*, whom she described in a letter to Algren. Her English, normally quite good, suffered from the intensity of her emotion:

Here in Paris it is worse and worse. We do torture and kill Algerians in the heart of the town. We have found a clean, nice way of doing it. We get some poor trecherous [sic] Algerians, payed [sic] them well and made cops of them. When an Algerian is taken by the French policemen, they give him to the "harkis"— the Algerian cops—and these ones torture the Algerian in an underground [prison] and "work" on him until they kill him or he kills himself or gets mad [insane]. And the French cop can say honestly "We don't torture nobody!" How do you like it? Isn't it shrewd?[9]

The situation worsened: police officers confessed to having tortured and killed a Moslem woman, but were released without punishment and one even returned to his student-teaching job. When his superiors dismissed him, the entire village was outraged, "saying he was such a nice man . . . and if the woman had died, so what?"[10] He was given his job back. A young boy was strangled by policemen in a Métro station in full view of other passengers. At Métro Charonne, in a district where many Africans lived, the crowd was exhorted to "charge Algerians," and many people were indiscriminately herded onto the tracks and killed. Despite the marks on their bodies, most newspapers attributed the deaths to crushing and suffocation by the stampede of the crowd. All over the city, others were rounded up and sent to a stadium, reminiscent of Jews who were detained in the Vel d'Hiver during the deportation.

There were many demonstrations, and Beauvoir avoided almost all of them. "I did not go, but the friends who went . . . had some broken bones or black eyes or were badly beaten," she told Algren, adding that the funerals "were very moving . . . , really, with all the Parisian people in the streets, peaceful, dignified, angry, friendly. It gave hope, hope something could yet happen here. But it is a false hope."

She decided to check on her apartment despite her friends' warnings to stay away, and found her concierge frantic following a midnight telephone call saying, "Watch out! Simone de Beauvoir is getting blown up tonight!" She told her friends, who sent a group of student FLN sympathizers to spend the night guarding the apartment. Unfortunately for Beauvoir, the students liked it and refused to move out. Peace was declared in March, but still they stayed, playing her records, reading her books, soiling her golden sofas with their dirty boots. Several weeks later she was still in the dingy hotel near the Seine, and she told Algren she needed a "strong American to chase them out."[11]

She decided not to worry about it and went away for the summer, first to Moscow, where she and Sartre were guests of the Soviet Writers' Union for the month of June, and then to Rome for a holiday. The Russian trip was the first of four they made together in the next several years.[12] They met most of the younger writers who were then under attack, among them Solzhenitsyn, whom she called "excellent," and who she hoped would "win this battle with the old academics and Kruschev [sic]."[13] She was not impressed with Khrushchev, who invited them to his holiday villa on the Black Sea. She found him both irrascible and intractable, and credited this visit as the beginning of her complete sympathy for the Chinese Communists in their quarrel with Moscow. They left Khrushchev as quickly as was decently possible and, with Sartre's translator and lover, Lena Zonina, as their guide, traveled throughout the Crimea, Georgia and Soviet Armenia. At Mount Ararat they were "treated" to what she referred to sarcastically as a "piece of the original ark."[14] Travel filled their lives during these years, with visits to Warsaw and other Polish cities sandwiched in on several occasions and an official visit to Czechoslovakia as guests of the Writers' Union there. In each of these years, there were short holidays at Easter, usually to the south of France, and always the long one during the summer in Rome, which came to be one of the most important activities they shared together.

It was there, "at four o'clock in the afternoon of Thursday, 24 October 1963, . . . in Rome . . . at the Hotel Minerva,"[15] the day before she was to return to Paris, that Simone de Beauvoir received a telegram from Bost telling her that her mother had had an accident and was in a hospital.

Françoise de Beauvoir had lived alone in a studio apartment on the Rue Blomet since 1942. In recent years, complications of arthritis in her hips and legs had left her almost paralyzed, but she still lived as independently as possible, making her way slowly and painfully around her neighborhood, even taking summer holidays to Meyrignac by train, where the conductor had to lift her wheelchair on board. She was seventy-seven years old, and for some time had been suffering from what her doctor described as constipation; but her heart was strong and she was otherwise in good health for a woman her age. Now she had fallen in her bathroom and fractured her hip—more accurately, the neck of the femur. It took her two painful hours to crawl to the telephone and call a friend, who in turn called police to force open the door of her apartment. Bost and Olga lived in the same building, and when they came home that night they saw Françoise about to be transported to a hospital. They assumed responsibility for the frightened old woman and phoned Beauvoir at once. She reached her mother the next day and learned that the doctors believed the break would heal without surgery. The problem, for a woman of Françoise's age, was that the several months of total immobility would certainly result in bed sores and quite possibly in pneumonia.

When Beauvoir telephoned her sister and brother-in-law she learned that Françoise had complained during a recent visit to their home in Alsace of abdominal pains so severe that Hélène and Lionel almost took her to the hospital in the middle of the night. The next morning the pains were gone and Françoise swore she was better, but Hélène still insisted on taking her mother to a radiologist, who diagnosed the problem as a fecal pocket in the intestines, gave her a prescription and told her to eat a better diet.

Françoise de Beauvoir died of cancer one month later, after complications following the broken femur and surgery to remove a tumor blocking her large intestine. Her eldest daughter wrote about it in *A Very Easy Death,* a slim volume considered by many to be her most eloquent and moving book, one she wrote in a few short weeks at the end of 1963. It was cathartic, as she asked herself the question "Why did my mother's death shake me so deeply?"[16] She discovered that, in contrast to her father's death, which she mentioned only in passing in her memoirs and then well after the fact, she needed to write a book to deal with her mother's. The book is other things as well, certainly a searing indictment of the medical profession. Most of all, it is the tragic story of a woman whose life spanned the incredible social changes and political upheavals of the twentieth century, who beheld too much sadness and disappointment and whose joys were too few and, in many cases, too late. According to her daughter's account, Françoise de Beauvoir "had a very easy death; an upperclass death,"[17] but no summary of the events leading to it can possibly capture the full import of her remark and all the anger and irony it contains. The book itself must be read.

As was her custom, Beauvoir dealt with her feelings by confiding them to paper, both in the book and to Algren, the only person not in Paris whom she trusted to share her grief. She told him some of the things she did not wish to put into the book quite so frankly:

November was a long sad month for, indeed, my mother was dying, and at last, she did it. But, as you say, how these old women cling to life. My mother fell down and broke a bone in the hip. She was taken to a clinic and there it was discovered she had a cancer and could die within a few months, or days. We did not tell her, indeed. They operated [on] her, opened her belly and all that. And then she felt much better than before and was sure she would soon recover. She had two very happy weeks, everybody taking care of her, my sister and myself spending our days and nights in her room—not from love, in my case, but from a deep and bitter compassion. She wanted so much to live! She began to feel very tired, and pains began, too, and we *ordered* the doctors to give her a lot of morphine and in fact to kill her slowly. They were obedient: no hope anyway. Then, the last three days she felt good, and slept nearly all the time . . . but she said reproachfully to my sister . . . "Today, I have not *lived*." And the day before her death when I told her it was good for her to sleep more, she said "Well, I am wasting days." What did she call life? Interesting thing was that she never wanted to see a priest. And she accepted none of her old pious friends. She wanted young faces and minds around her. She was nearest my heart during this month than she had been since my early childhood. And I had an irrational guilty feeling of cheating her, guaranteeing she would see spring and summer and long years, and knowing she would not.[18]

She had many flashes of guilt in the months following her mother's death, some genuinely sad, others almost comic. Several years earlier Algren's friend Studs Terkel had interviewed her for a radio show he hosted in Chicago, and asked what her mother thought of her memoirs. "She is very proud that I make money, but she doesn't look too close at what I do," Beauvoir replied, but added that when Françoise read *Memoirs of a Dutiful Daughter* she was upset to discover that her daughter had lied about the books she read as a child: "After forty years she could not accept that I had been a liar when I was ten."[19] Throughout the Algerian crisis, Beauvoir had not seen her mother at all. On the rare occasion when they were together in the last year or so before Françoise's death, she often caught her mother staring surreptitiously at her, as if she could not believe that her brilliant little girl had become the woman whose life inspired some of the most malicious gossip in Paris. Once, Françoise asked Beauvoir to drive her to Père Lachaise Cemetery so that she could put flowers on the family plot. Beauvoir did it, ungraciously hurrying her mother, who walked with great effort and considerable pain. When they stood before the massive family tombstone, Françoise said again, as she had at her husband's funeral in 1941, "There is only room for me. Where will you and your sister go?" Beauvoir did not tell her mother that she intended to be cremated. Françoise also made the remark Beauvoir included in the book: "Of course I should like to go to Heaven: but not all alone, not without my daughters."[20]

Beauvoir's relationship with her sister had been a complex one as well since the war, first when Hélène was interned in Portugal, and then when she married Lionel de Roulet and began a peripatetic life as the wife of a cultural attaché for the French government. She lived at different times in places that ranged from Portugal to Eastern Europe before settling in Alsace during Lionel's last posting, in Strasbourg with the Council of Europe. They bought a fifteenth-century farmhouse in a nearby village, which they restored and filled with many beautiful souvenirs of the countries where they had lived, and Hélène turned the ground-floor storage rooms and several outbuildings into studios of various kinds where she worked diligently on her art.

The two sisters had led very different lives in the thirty or so years since they shared the tiny bedroom on the Rue de Rennes. Simone's writing was recognized throughout the world, while Hélène's painting had reached only a small but devoted following in each of the countries where Lionel had been posted long enough for her to have a gallery showing. Hélène was, as she had always been, enormously proud of her big sister's success, but Simone had a more difficult time understanding the woman her sister had become.

Hélène took great pride in her home, loved to entertain friends there, and was an accomplished cook and a gracious hostess. She had no children, but adored domestic pets, particularly cats, while Simone had detested all animals ever since the days when her cousin Magdeleine's dogs copulated and gave birth at La Grillère. Hélène loved the Alsatian countryside and was content to spend her days working quietly in a village of less than two hundred people; after her mother's death, Simone lived in irrational fear that something would incapacitate her so that she would have to live away from Paris. Since Hélène was her closest legal relative, the thought of confinement in the small Alsatian village became almost a recurring nightmare.

But, most important, Simone de Beauvoir had never really understood the visual arts or the differences between writing and painting, especially between the successful writer and the less successful painter. She was impatient with the slights and rebuffs her sister experienced as she attempted to have her work accepted by galleries, and she could not understand how, in the face of continuing rejection, her sister found the courage to keep on working. For, despite her belief that writing was necessary to live, Simone de Beauvoir still believed that publication was the necessary completion of the act, and that without an audience to receive what she had written the work had no value.

Simone de Beauvoir may not have understood her sister, but she was enormously supportive of her work. Whenever possible, Beauvoir attended her sister's exhibitions, and in 1968 the sisters collaborated on an edition of Simone's collection of stories, *The Woman Destroyed*, for which Hélène provided sixteen illustrations. It was to be their only joint production.

Françoise de Beauvoir's death brought her daughters together temporarily as they dealt with details of the funeral and the closing of her apartment on the Rue Blomet, but from then on the two sisters communicated mostly by telephone or on the infrequent occasions when Hélène came to Paris. Their feelings for each other remained steadfast, but time, distance and the many differences in the way they lived gave a certain formality to their sisterly devotion.

A few days after her mother was buried, Beauvoir accompanied Sartre to a writers' congress in Czechoslovakia, to begin a year of intense travel and writing. When they returned in December, Beauvoir, unable to forget the circumstances of Françoise's demise, wrote A *Very Easy Death*. In January they made another trip to the Soviet Union, and in the summer they went to Rome. Throughout, Beauvoir wrote, mostly introductions and prefaces for the books of others. A British publisher asked her for an introduction to a translation of the *Contes de Perrault*,[21] the fairy tales she had so enjoyed when a very small child. She wrote it "for the money," but contributed a preface to Violette Leduc's *La Batarde* with much more passion because she believed that the "Ugly Woman" had finally found her true voice and was producing work that was both excellent and important.[22] She gave a series of interviews to the young French-Canadian journalist whom she had recently befriended, Madeleine Gobeil, and she collaborated on the sometimes fractious meetings where editorial decisions were hammered out for several special issues of *Les Temps Modernes*. Also, she participated in a number of meetings concerning the purpose of literature in society, most notably at the large meeting hall known as the Mutualité.[23]

Because her memoirs had been translated into several languages, she was sought after frequently by periodicals in several countries both as a writer and as the subject of features and review-interviews, ranging from *McCall's* to *The Paris Review*. For the next several years, she contributed prefaces to a variety of works ranging from Jean-Françoise Steiner's *Treblinka* to E. and P. Kronhausen's *Sexual Response in Women*. From this time until the end of her life, she was deluged with requests to write, speak, give interviews, and provide statements of support for a variety of organizations and other forms of comment intended to legitimize, bless or benefit all sorts of occasions, events or publications.

In the midst of her individual literary success, Sartre's name came to the forefront as that of the next logical candidate for the world's most prestigious literary honor, the Nobel Prize. They were in Rome the first time a journalist asked Sartre what he would do if he received the honor in 1964. Soon others began to raise the question as well, and a puzzled Sartre asked Beauvoir whether he should take it seriously. Her initial response was that the award was overdue and he should have won it even before Camus (whose prize had come seven years earlier). At first she did not think beyond that point, certainly not to the possibility that he would or even should refuse it.

But Sartre continued to mutter, nervously avoiding her eyes, talking as if to himself but at the same time speaking clearly enough for her to hear him. These evasions had characterized much of their relationship, and she knew how to interpret them. It meant that he wanted to do something contrary to what he believed her advice would be, but he needed first to plant the idea in her mind and make it seem as if his subsequent action and behavior had originated with her, or, if not, that she at least had given her blessing well before he acted. In this case, she canvassed the Family and the editorial board of the magazine, who were, for the most part, astounded that Sartre would even consider refusing the prize if it were offered. Beauvoir described the initial consternation they all shared during a 1982 interview when she said she herself felt like "a little girl in a convent school, refusing the first prize offered from the hand of the Archbishop. Could I have the courage not to take something which was supposed to be wonderful, but which I did not believe in anyway? That was how I felt, and I think some of it was shared for a little while by Sartre too." But she wanted to stress one point that she believed had "somehow been lost over the years": "In the beginning, we were all delighted for Sartre to receive the prize, because it validated all of us in the eyes of the world. It was only later, after *he* explained to us why he could not accept it and after *he* made his decision that the rest of us said at once that we agreed with him. It is dishonest for anyone to pretend otherwise."

Sartre's decision was primarily political: he did not believe he should accept a prize which had never been awarded to a nondissident Soviet writer or to a Communist or other declared leftist from a Western nation.

He chose not to believe that the Nobel Committee was breaking this un-stated tradition by awarding the prize to him, but to see it instead as an attempt by the Swedish committee to co-opt him for the side of the bour-geoisie, to claim him for the conservative Right. Once he expressed this view, none of his friends attempted to persuade him otherwise, that by giv-ing the prize to one of the most outspoken politically committed writers in the world the Nobel Committee may have been attempting to rectify what could indeed have been interpreted as a pattern of anointing only those writers whose politics it deemed correct.[24]

However, Sartre gave no indication to any of the inquiring journalists or to friends other than the Family that he would refuse the Nobel Prize, so there was no reason for the members of the committee to think he would do so. All these discussions happened during a time when Sartre's reason was often clouded by drugs, and he sometimes suffered from halluci-nations and milder forms of paranoia (which grew worse in the last fifteen years of his life). Nevertheless, Beauvoir and all the others continued to believe in him, and no one tried to persuade him to reconsider once he told them he would refuse it.

By mid-October, Sartre was convinced the rumors were correct and he would be offered the prize, so he sent a letter to the Nobel Committee ask-ing them not to give it to him. One can only speculate about what the committee would have done had his letter reached them in time, but it did not,[25] and on October 22 the announcement was made that the prize was Sartre's.

He and Beauvoir were sitting in a café around the corner from her apartment, enjoying what was for them an unusually relaxed afternoon, because they had only just returned from Rome and were not yet into the rhythms of their Paris life. At that moment, the first of the journalists spotted Sartre and told him of the prize. Beauvoir took over, herding him into a kind of asylum in the manager's office, where Sartre sat nervously smoking and muttering his incomprehension that it could have happened at all, especially after he had written such a careful letter to the committee eight days previously. She telephoned the offices of Gallimard, where Rob-ert Gallimard, who had already heard the news, was elated until Sartre told him of his decision to refuse the prize. Gallimard came for them at once in his car and took them to a meeting with a Swedish journalist, Carl-Gustav Bjurstrom, whom he had met some years before and trusted im-plicitly. Sartre wanted to make it very clear that his action was not in-tended as a slight to the Swedes, so he gave Bjurstrom the only official statement he issued on the occasion, going so far as to scrawl across his written notes that it had been "translated from the Swedish" even though he and Beauvoir had written it in French. He said he was refusing the prize for both personal and objective reasons, and that it was "not an improvised act."[26]

So, several hours after the first announcement, when Bjurstrom tele-phoned Sartre's statement to the Nobel Committee in Stockholm, they issued a second announcement: Sartre would not accept the Nobel Prize in Literature for 1964, and no award would be given that year. His only pang concerned the prize money and came after he had firmly refused the 250,000 Swedish crowns (26 million old francs). He fleetingly regretted turning down such a large amount of money, one which could have done much to support causes in which he believed.

His refusal set off a furor that resounded around the world and lasted for months in the Paris press. Beauvoir's role throughout was the one she had assumed for the first time when they were in Cuba and Brazil, placing herself as the buffer between Sartre and a demanding and sometimes hostile world. "I wonder that she does not taste the food before it is presented to him," said an official in the Brazilian government who did not welcome her constant intervention in everything from the schedule of his speeches to deciding whom he should agree to meet. Now hostile Parisians were echoing a radio commentator who said, "Of course Sartre refused the prize because he could not risk offending Simone."[27] This unfortunate jibe was to be expected as common gossip among their enemies, but, sadly, it was all too frequently expressed by people who should have known Beauvoir's deferential attitude to Sartre better, especially her lifelong insistence on placing him on a pedestal far above herself.

Sartre's Nobel Prize touched off months of chaos in Beauvoir's life, and she believed it was the first of several crucial incidents which changed her relationship not only with him, but with many other people who either were or became important in her life after that event.

She sheltered Sartre as much as she could from the continuing press of journalists who each felt he or she should be the one privileged to hear "the real reason" why he declined the prize. She was with him almost constantly as 1964 ended, keeping the nosy and inquisitive from her door on the Rue Schoelcher and from his at 222 Boulevard Raspail, where he had moved after the Rue Bonaparte was bombed. Occasionally, she took charge of moving him into the apartments of various friends when some reporters became too pressing.

All through these peregrinations, Sartre was uncharacteristically evasive. She wondered why, but blamed it on the brouhaha over the Nobel Prize and did not press him for reasons, especially since he seemed in better health than he had been in for some time and she didn't want to do anything to upset him. Even though he continued his daily ingestion of pills and liquor, he had lost a lot of weight, mostly bloat, and seemed better able to concentrate on the work at hand.[28] More and more, he wanted to do his writing at Arlette's apartment, which he claimed was most conducive to concentration and relaxation. Beauvoir was not alarmed by this departure from their usual routine, because to her Arlette seemed neither a threat nor a usurper, but only another in the continuing succession of young women eager to be a part of Sartre's life. She was happy to have the extra time to catch up with her many new friends. Beauvoir was the one who routinely drove Sartre on his appointed rounds from the home of one mistress to another's, and nothing seemed amiss to her on those occasions. This was why she was so stunned by the news a sheepish Bost gave her one night when he had first fortified himself with a great deal of liquor.

On January 25, 1965, without Simone de Beauvoir even suspecting that he was thinking of such action, Sartre applied formally to adopt Arlette Elkaïm as his legal daughter (it became final in March). Ronald Hayman, one of Sartre's three biographers, described it as "an act of aggression" by which, after "a lifetime of devotion, de Beauvoir's reward would be to see the youngest of her rivals given unchallengeable ownership of everything Sartre had written, everything he possessed."[29] His other biographer Annie Cohen-Solal, a personal friend of Arlette's, evades the complexities of Sartre's decision by saying only that through the adoption Sartre was "showing his faith in the future. He knew that, whatever might happen, she would take care of the publication of his posthumous works."[30]

Both these explanations bear a semblance of the infinitely more complex truth. The explanation of the third biographer, John Gerassi, describes the catalyst that sparked Sartre to such uncharacteristic action. Gerassi recounts an anecdote describing Sartre's abashed but nonetheless official version: "One day Sartre was walking with Arlette and invited her to go into a florist's they were passing to select a bunch of flowers. The patron asked 'Monsieur' [Sartre] what he would like to buy for his 'beautiful daughter.' Sartre looked at Arlette and said something like 'Well, I'm not so good in bed anymore and this guy makes a lot of sense. If you are my daughter, you become a French citizen and then nobody can deport you, because you won't be an Algerian Jew anymore.' "[31]

Whatever the reason, from that moment on, all the principals involved stuck to their official version of the story: that Sartre believed in the future, and he had demonstrated this belief by surrendering total control of himself and his estate to the young woman who would now be known as Arlette Elkaïm-Sartre.

The news came to Beauvoir at one of the lowest moments of her life, during a period when "literature seemed to me pointless—I had swung over towards death and the silence of death."[32] But, with her usual indomitable optimism, by March, when the adoption was final, she had not only stood as one of the sponsors (Lanzmann was the other), but was able to raise a glass of champagne to help the new father celebrate the joy of having a brand-new daughter.

THIRTY-SEVEN

The Friendships of Women

SARTRE'S ADOPTION of Arlette served as the catalyst for many changes in Beauvoir's life that had been a long time coming. All her relationships, from Algren to her more casual friends and associates, underwent a significant shift. Some of those to whom she had been close throughout her adult life suddenly became less important in her daily existence; others, brand-new acquaintances, became her closest confidants during the last twenty-one years of her life. By 1965, the only one which had not changed was the one that had always been constant, the primary facet of her identity: the Sartre-Beauvoir couple which she insisted upon presenting to the world.

The public perception of her role in Sartre's life remained largely the same because she continued to accompany him to meetings and conferences and proclaim her public support for the same causes. They kept Arlette's adoption very quiet, and for a surprisingly long time afterward only their most trusted friends knew that the rumor others in Paris whispered was true. Still, although Beauvoir's relationship with Sartre appeared on the surface to be as placid as it had ever been in recent years, there were strong undercurrents of changing allegiances.

Even though they had long been used to his unorthodox behavior and arbitrary decisions, all Sartre's other women were bewildered by what he had done in adopting Arlette. As always, it was Beauvoir who had to deal with everything, from Wanda's hysterical and destructive behavior to a sharp acceleration in Michelle's habitual heavy drinking, now a serious problem. All during her long relationship with Sartre, Michelle had maintained a more permanent liaison with another man, but he died unexpectedly just at the time Sartre adopted Arlette. Sartre wanted to distance himself from Michelle's emotional distress, which her lover's death had exacerbated. He urged Beauvoir to take care of the sweet woman who had been so devoted to him, so Beauvoir spent long hours talking to and caring for the distraught Michelle, who needed constant reassurance that nothing would change in her relationship with Sartre. Despite her own bouts of alcoholic crying, Beauvoir had a fastidious distaste for "bleary-eyed drunken bleatings," but she endured them patiently for his sake and to comfort Michelle for her long years of devoted service to the Family.

497

Bost was usually the buffer between Beauvoir and his sister-in-law, Wanda, but in this instance he was frightened by her public tirades and private rages. Angry with Sartre for adopting Arlette, Wanda trashed the contents of her apartment late one night, disturbing all her neighbors, who then threatened to call the police. Instead they called Bost, who called Beauvoir to deal with it, even though she and Wanda had carefully avoided all but minimum contact with each other for years.

Later, when Beauvoir used some of the speech and behavior of both women in her collection of stories *La Femme rompue* (*A Woman Destroyed*), Wanda was angry and Michelle hurt by what she deemed a betrayal of her most private concerns. One woman Beauvoir could not incorporate into these stories was Evelyne Ray, who was seriously depressed. Everyone knew it, but no one did much about it. Lanzmann was married now, and although he remained busy with *Les Temps Modernes* and continued to serve as Sartre's unofficial factotum, he was not as concerned as Beauvoir was about his sister, saying she would probably "snap out of it on her own."[1]

Several other women, whom Beauvoir described in 1985 as "groupies," had recently joined Sartre's entourage, and what she detested most about them was the way they fawned over her with exaggerated courtesy as if she were "an ancient relic." She was brusque to the point of rudeness with them, in many cases not even bothering to learn their names. She hated their breezy familiarity when they called her "Castor," a nickname she could not bear to hear from anyone she did not like. She put up with them for Sartre's sake.

Olga was quite another matter entirely, and suddenly a most perplexing one. Olga had known for years of Beauvoir and Bost's continuing sexual relationship, and although she professed not to like it she did nothing to interfere with or stop it. Bost had many other liaisons throughout their long and stormy marriage; Olga had fewer, mostly because of recurring problems with her health stemming from her wartime tuberculosis. Olga began to exhibit extreme hostility toward Beauvoir from this time on, which by the time of her (Olga's) death in 1983 was exacerbated to the point of irrationality. She would accuse Beauvoir of transgressions she had "most likely been guilty of" without providing any details. Beauvoir's genuine attempts to placate her friend only resulted in vague diatribes and threats to condemn her in public and to the press. Again, Bost absented himself, actually residing separately from Olga from time to time, so it was Beauvoir who bore the brunt of her anger.

Olga soon discovered the perfect method of retaliation. Beauvoir answered her telephone only between 1 and 2 P.M. As she saw her friends every day, they seldom phoned each other, so this time was reserved primarily for scholars or journalists or anyone else who wanted to reach her for professional reasons. Olga spitefully began to phone every day at 1 P.M., to harangue Beauvoir for the full hour before hanging up abruptly; Beauvoir was too concerned for her old friend to hang up on her, so for months she was unable to transact much business by telephone. It was a genuine hard-ship, but her relationship with Olga came first, and so she endured these near-daily assaults by using the time to correct manuscripts and proofs for the magazine and to answer her correspondence.

Then there was her relationship with Arlette. She had prepared herself to feel humiliated in her presence, but discovered instead that nothing had really changed in Arlette's demeanor toward her. She was still the same shy, polite young woman who was always ready to do what the younger members of "the *Temps Modernes* crowd" were now describing as "to baby-sit Sartre."[2] It was a great relief for Beauvoir to see how Arlette still gave pride of place to her, how quietly deferential she was when the three of them were in a restaurant, or how she phoned Beauvoir to check Sar-tre's weekly scheduled rotation with all the women. It was probably be-cause of Arlette's unassuming behavior that Beauvoir honored the official version of the adoption: Sartre, she said, adopted Arlette "because she was much younger than I, at least thirty years or so, and because we both thought that I could die before or just after him, or even at the same time, so it would be good to have someone a lot younger who had a good chance to survive, because of the literary inheritance. And also because of the money, because Sartre gave money like a salary or allowance to certain peo-ple and he thought—and he was right—that Arlette is very honest and she would continue to give this money, especially to the women, who had no other income. So we agreed completely on this. Now, as to why it was Arlette, well, he already knew her about ten years or so, and he found her very intelligent and sensitive, which she was, and quite dedicated to him and entirely suited to do the work she would need to do once he was dead. So we agreed completely on this adoption. It only took a bad turn for me later."[3]

So, for the time being at least, very little had changed besides the legal formality of Arlette's citizenship and surname. Beauvoir told her version of the adoption story once or twice in Sartre's presence, and he too was greatly relieved by her placid acceptance of an act that left the rest of the Family shocked, bewildered, and even a little frightened by the shifts in personal power within their once snug and secure little world. Even the petulant Wanda telephoned Beauvoir in an unusually deferential manner to ask how she should behave toward Arlette—should she address her in any new form, and did she need to do anything to remind the girl where to send her monthly stipend? When Beauvoir assured her she need do nothing differ-ent from what she had always done in the past, Wanda reverted to type and managed to slip in a few barbs before slamming down the receiver.

There were two other relationships that changed during this time. One, with Algren, came to a bitter end, while the other, with Sylvie le Bon, grew into what Beauvoir called "the strongest and most important friend-ship" of her life.

For a while, her affair with Algren seemed to have died a natural death, time and distance conspiring in its demise. Although each in many ways had enjoyed a genuine good time with the other during his 1960 visit to Paris, they were both left with the overwhelming sense that too much time had passed and they were too greatly changed ever to resume the passion they had known during the previous ten or so years. Algren saw firsthand that she would drop whatever she was doing to rush to Sartre's side on the merest hint that he needed her. He saw how impatient she became when he interrupted her work. His little quirks that once seemed so amusing, like his penchant for taking embarrassing photographs of people with his little Kodak box camera, now irritated her to the point where she could not hide it. Also, in the midst of one of his diatribes against a hostile, opportunistic world, he would suddenly accuse her of patronizing him and grow angry and curse her. It didn't help that he was broke and she was affluent, if not rich, from her writing, or that he had to depend on her for spending money much of the time he was in Paris.

Still, when he returned to Chicago she continued to write the news of her day and the gossip of the friends they had in common. Interestingly, she never once mentioned Sartre's Nobel Prize, probably knowing how much his seemingly blasé rejection of success would anger Algren, who so hungered for the barest recognition of his own literary worth. Her letters were chatty, friendly and amusing; full of tender friendship, but not of passionate love. She had not called him her "husband" for years, nor had she referred to herself as his "Frog wife." Instead of the humorous greetings, he was now simply "Dearest Nelson," and she was only "your Simone." There was no talk of love or sex, never any mention of what they would do together in the future, nor were there any but the most fleeting references to what they had done in the past. She had not referred to her ring, which she still never took off, since he left Paris in 1960. They were letters of sad nostalgia, written in memory of and with a degree of regret for a love that had not died, but simply had not grown.

They probably could have gone on like this for some time to come if it hadn't been for the English translation of *Force of Circumstance*. Algren's rage over *The Mandarins* was nothing compared to his fury over what she wrote about him in the memoirs. She freely admitted that she had dictated the time, place and duration of their meetings throughout their affair; now he believed that she had dictated what she wanted posterity to remember by writing her version of what had happened between them.

He spent the next few years castigating her in reviews and articles, and the rest of his life denouncing her to anyone who would listen. "Autobiography—shit!" he roared several weeks before his death in May 1981. "Autofiction, that's what she wrote."[4]

Incredibly, Simone de Beauvoir never understood what she had done to inspire such rage in the man who she said had been "the one true passion" in her life. "If circumstances had been different, if Algren were French, or I American, if there had been no Sartre, I think we could have married and been happy together. I think we had enough passion between us that we could have been faithful to each other. I know we had enough ideas that conversation would have been fresh and entertaining forever. We were very much alike, Algren and I, except that he wanted children and he always had those damn cats, but he could only live in Chicago and I could never leave Paris."[5]

Having said that, she was still puzzled that Algren could have felt "betrayed" by "what was essentially the truth," but when she was asked to explain the word "essentially" she declined to answer and refused to discuss Algren any further. Once or twice she waved a handful of the letters he wrote to her after the memoirs appeared in English, saying they were "bitter, cruel and terrible letters," and that she would allow "no one, *ever, ever, ever!*" to read them, because "Algren had a bad, spiteful side to his character that I would prefer not to reveal to the world. I would prefer that the world remember his goodness and kindness, how he was funny and shy and sometimes comic. He was a generous man who deserved better than what he got from life."

So their direct correspondence ended, but, despite Algren's expressed anger over the memoirs, Beauvoir still wrote several times saying that she planned to accompany Sartre to Cornell University, where he was to give lectures in 1964; if they were permitted to enter the United States, she hoped to see Algren. He did not reply, and although their correspondence ended, each kept up with what the other was doing through third parties. In response to Beauvoir's memoirs, Mary Guggenheim, who had suggested their initial meeting, now wrote a novel (untitled and never published) that purported to tell the truth about her relationship with Algren. Guggenheim's novel contained many bitter passages in which the Algren character amused the many women he seduced by telling them stories about his clumsy and stupid French lover. When Guggenheim sent her the manuscript, Beauvoir translated the sarcastic letter that accompanied it and sent it to Algren with only minimal comment.[6]

Later, when she sent the French-Canadian journalist whom she had befriended, Madeleine Gobeil, to meet and possibly interview him, Algren at once initiated an affair, even taking the young woman to the same cottage at Miller where he had lived with Beauvoir. Beauvoir believed that the detailed accounts of the affair which Gobeil sent to her were written at Algren's insistence, because he could not resist the impulse to hurt her whenever he could.[7]

Algren died of a sudden, massive heart attack on May 9, 1981, at the age of seventy-two, just when it seemed his literary luck was turning. He had recently moved to Sag Harbor, New York, where he became a beloved fixture in the literary community of eastern Long Island. Gloria Jones, widow of the novelist James Jones whom he had met in Paris in 1960, lived there, and she remained a constant friend, as did his neighbor Betty Friedan. Algren's longtime agent, Candida Donadio, asked her clients Peter Matthiesson, William Gaddis and Muriel Murphy to look after Algren, and they soon became his friends, along with Kurt Vonnegut. Several days before his death, Algren received word that he had been elected to the American Academy of Arts and Letters, the American equivalent of the French Academy. It seemed that the recognition that had eluded him all his life was about to come at last, and he decided to give himself a celebratory party on May 9. The previous day, he visited a physician in the village, Dr. Robert Semlier, complaining of chest pains. Dr. Semlier gave him a cardiogram, which did not show any specific illness or abnormality, but he still wanted Algren to check himself into the hospital in Southampton.

"Not today, Doc," Algren said. "I'm getting inducted into the American Academy of Arts and Letters and I'm having people in to celebrate."[8]

W. J. Weatherby, who interviewed Algren for *The Times* of London the day before he died, wrote that "the first guest to arrive at the cottage found his body, with the unopened bottles of liquor for the party around him."[9]

The Weatherby interview was the last Algren ever gave, and his vitriol against Beauvoir was as fresh as it had been when they parted sixteen years previously:

> "She tried [in *Prime of Life*] to make our relationship into a great international literary affair, naming me and quoting from some of my letters. She must have been awfully hard up for something to write about . . . The publisher asked my permission to quote the letters. I thought about it for a few days and then I reluctantly said okay. Hell, love letters should be private. I've been in whorehouses all over the world and the woman there always closes the door . . . but this woman flung the door open and called in the public and the Press . . . I don't have any malice against her, but I think it was an appalling thing to do."

Algren also told Weatherby that he intended to sell his letters from Beauvoir, because "If one half of a correspondence is made public, then the other half should be. They're no longer of any sentimental value to me. You can't commercialize half and keep the other half sacrosanct. Let's make it all public!"[10]

Unlike all the other papers that she had collected over the years, including most of Sartre's manuscripts, which she dumped unceremoniously into her cellar storage area, Beauvoir kept Algren's letters in her apartment, on the sleeping loft near her bed. When news of his last comments reached her, she waved a handful of them and said, "You have to make it clear that I lied [about her personal feelings for Algren] in all those letters" written to him. Then she averted her eyes and muttered, "Everything was a lie," before refusing to discuss it further, insisting that her memoirs contained the truth "of a not very important love affair."

Hélène telephoned her sister as soon as she heard the news of Algren's death. "Aren't you sorry?" she asked. "Don't you feel anything for him?"

"Why should I?" Simone de Beauvoir replied. "What did he feel for me, that he could have written those horrible things?"[11]

However, she continued to wear his ring.

The years that marked the end of Beauvoir's relationship with Algren coincided with the beginning of her friendship with Sylvie le Bon. It started casually enough in 1960, when Sylvie, as a young philosophy student preparing for the *agrégation*, wrote a letter to Beauvoir asking for a meeting to discuss her work. By September 1965, when they took a thirteen-day trip to Corsica together, it had become the most important relationship in the last two decades of Beauvoir's life.

Their first meeting was like so many others that filled Simone de Beauvoir's daily calendar during this time: any letter from a student who appeared interesting and intelligent was enough to gain at least half an hour of conversation, because Beauvoir now believed it was her duty, if not her responsibility, to talk to people (especially young women) who wanted to learn more about her work.

"I adored her even before I met her, because of her books," Sylvie recalled. "I used to say to so many people, 'There is only one person in this century who is worth anything to women, and that's Simone de Beauvoir.' "

Sylvie le Bon was then an eighteen-year-old student from Rennes, Brittany, preparing for the *agrégation* at the École Normale Supérieure, after which she planned to enter the elite teachers' training college at Sèvres.[12] Her family background and education were similar to Beauvoir's: she came from a well-to-do conservative family, was the product of a rigid Catholic secondary education and now was on the brink of a teaching career. The similarities between them also included a strained relationship between Sylvie and her mother, just as Beauvoir had had in her adolescence, but they did not discover this until sometime later.

Beauvoir invited Sylvie le Bon to a meeting which she recalled as a dinner in a restaurant on the Place Denfert-Rochereau, but which Sylvie remembers as an afternoon cup of coffee in the Café Raspail Vert on the same square. Beauvoir described Sylvie as "shy," but Sylvie described herself as "incredibly nervous, very anxious." What impressed Sylvie most at this meeting was Beauvoir's interest in her: "I was very young, eighteen, and I was very moved because we spoke of myself mainly. She questioned me about my studies. I remember how she reproached me for not taking an interest in politics, and for not reading newspapers. She had to rush to an appointment, but before she left she bought all the newspapers from the kiosk on the corner. She bundled them into my arms, laughing, and said, 'It's a shame you don't read,' and then she ran off, so vibrant and impressive. So of course I began to educate myself, because I wanted to talk to her again."

In the next year or so, Sylvie remembers, they met "only once or twice," each time ostensibly to discuss her studies; but increasingly they discussed her personal life as well. Sylvie became "less nervous," and because she is a naturally voluble person the conversations were light and amiable. Both women discovered that they liked to laugh a lot. "I frightened her less . . . she smiled and even laughed: she had an agreeable face and I liked her being there," Beauvoir wrote of these early meetings.[13] The friendship remained sporadic and casual, mostly because of Beauvoir's friendship with two other young women who had been attracted to her work, specifically *Memoirs of a Dutiful Daughter* and *The Second Sex*. All three young women, whom Beauvoir called "my three girls," claimed to see their own lives reflected in the *Memoirs*; with regard to *The Second Sex*, the other two expressed their inability to understand exactly what Beauvoir expected them to do with their lives, how she wanted them to live out the thesis she had expounded. Sylvie, the third girl (for she describes herself as little more than that at the time), was not bewildered by Beauvoir's thesis; rather, she wanted to talk about how it could be adapted to women's needs in the decade or so since the book first appeared. This was what attracted Beauvoir to Sylvie initially and what made their friendship prosper while the other two withered.

Interestingly, she told Sylvie all about the others but seldom told them about her. Beauvoir soon tired of both young women, who very quickly became "less interesting" because they had nothing to offer her beyond the original facts of their lives. One simply dropped out of her life and went her separate way. The other was, in Sylvie's words, "a fragile girl whom Beauvoir helped [financially] throughout her whole life." This woman became the first of several to whom Beauvoir paid a monthly stipend, much the same as Sartre did with his own separate dependencies. But by 1962 both had all but disappeared from Beauvoir's life (the second did not reappear until the late 1960s), and Sylvie was her only student friend. This was when Beauvoir began to ask detailed questions about Sylvie's background. "When I asked her about her relations with her parents she avoided the subject—they lived at Rennes; they had sent her to Paris . . . there was nothing to tell about them."[14]

Sylvie's family found out about her intense friendship with the notorious woman more than thirty years her senior when her mother read her diary. Beauvoir described what happened as "threatening to be a repeat of Madame Sorokine and Natasha," a reference to her dismissal from teaching for allegedly corrupting a minor. Sylvie was forcibly removed from Paris by her parents, not to return until a year later, when she attained her majority and was legally free to do as she chose. Her always strained rapport with her parents was severely ruptured, not to be repaired until the 1970s and then only superficially. Throughout Sylvie's year in Rennes, Beauvoir maintained a discreet silence and distance.

Other friendships with women waxed and waned during Sylvie's enforced absence, including the one with Violette Leduc, who was happily writing *La Batarde* (*The Bastard*) with Beauvoir's enthusiastic encouragement, submitting chapters for her to read as she wrote them. Beauvoir was so sure the book would receive either the Prix Goncourt or the Prix Fémina, if not both, that she agreed to help bolster its chances by writing a preface. This was probably the most tranquil period of their emotionally erratic friendship, and in retrospect Beauvoir was happy about it because she had always felt "slightly guilty" about her dismissal of Leduc as "the Ugly Woman." Unfortunately, despite becoming an immediate best-seller that sold more than several hundred thousand copies in its first years in print, the book, which was nominated for both prizes, did not receive either of them.[15]

Beauvoir began her friendship with Madeleine Gobeil during the years of the "three girls," but it was very different and she kept it separate from the others. Gobeil had interviewed both Sartre and Beauvoir for various publications (among them the *Paris Review* series, where Beauvoir wanted Gobeil to place an interview with Algren, which was her reason for introducing them and which subsequently led to their affair). Beauvoir particularly liked Gobeil because she was an independent woman who had overcome personal hardships to become a respected journalist. "Madeleine Gobeil always has something interesting to say," Beauvoir said.

Sylvie's description is a bit more precise: "She held Gobeil in esteem, nothing more. It was a certain kind of friendship that is based more on respect than affection. Gobeil would have liked more, but that's all Beauvoir could give her."

What neither Sylvie nor Beauvoir realized was that Gobeil could not afford to become one of the "girls" because she had to work for her living, while the others, all of whom initially had independent means, did not. There simply was not enough free time in Gobeil's life to allow her to dance a daily attendence upon Beauvoir, because her career was so all-consuming. Nevertheless, Beauvoir's esteem was lifelong, and she frequently mentioned with pride the increasingly important positions Gobeil held with UNESCO, referring to her as one of the possible models for what she meant women's lives to be when she wrote *The Second Sex*.

Not all of her friendships were with women whose lives she considered admirable, especially the erratic Natasha Sorokine Moffatt.

When she published the last of the four volumes of memoirs, *All Said and Done*, which dealt with the years 1962–72, Beauvoir included a detailed description of Natasha Sorokine's troubled life after she became Ivan Moffatt's war bride and moved to Hollywood.[16] She described Natasha's failed first marriage and her curious second one to the scientist and scholar Sidney Benson, as well as her fascination and later her friendship with the then young instructor at UCLA who became the distinguished Professor of French Oreste Pucciani (and Beauvoir and Sartre's friend as well).

Natasha died suddenly in 1967, of complications stemming from a flu-like virus infection, but both of her husbands were alive and her children (a daughter by Moffatt and a son by Benson) very young when this memoir was published in the United States in 1974. Knowing this, Beauvoir still wrote a brutally frank account of her friend's chaotic life. Natasha had become a horrible grotesque, her delicate beauty disfigured because of a combination of illnesses, operations and medications, and Beauvoir rendered all her physical ugliness with cruelly dispassionate precision. Her description of Natasha's tirades and obsessions on her last visit to Paris is cold as steel.

For a writer who was so concerned to spare the feelings of others that she cheerfully admitted to leaving out whole chunks of her life from these same memoirs, the revelations of Natasha's pathetic last years seems a betrayal of all they had been through together, especially during the war. However, her treatment of Natasha's demise is consistent with her lifelong attitude toward illness and death. It can be compared to the clinical detachment she showed when writing of her mother's fatal illness, or to *Adieux*, the memoirs of the last ten years of Sartre's life which she wrote as another attempt at catharsis. In all these writings, she faced everything with brutal honesty, accurate description and cold stoicism. It was simply her way of dealing with loss.

She learned of Natasha's death through a letter Benson sent her, she recalled. "On Monday she had gone to bed with 'flu. On Thursday [Benson] took the children for a walk. . . . When he came back he went into her room and found her dead." Beauvoir's final comment about Natasha was, "I never learnt anything more." Nor had she asked. "Why should I? I knew what there was to know—she was dead." She was deeply upset several months later when she received the Christmas fruitcake Natasha had sent by surface mail the day before she died.

Sylvie came back to Paris in the fall of 1963, during Françoise de Beauvior's final illness. Her first meeting with Beauvoir took place one dismal afternoon in the same Café Raspail Vert, but this time the conversation was different, Sylvie remembered. "We still barely knew each other when her mother died, but I remember that this day she told me virtually word for word what became the story of *A Very Easy Death*. I remember how she would stop from time to time and ask, 'What do you think? Do you think I can write that? I'd like to write that.' She needed catharsis, so I said, 'Yes, you must do it.' I suggested later that I should accompany her to the funeral, but although she was happy that I suggested it, she said no. She was right, there was no reason for me to go. At the beginning [of the renewed friendship] she was very cautious, she didn't throw herself into things. But it was her mother's death that brought us together."[17]

Sylvie had just read *Force of Circumstance*, which, like the first two volumes of memoirs, had become a target for mostly hostile letters and reviews, and she had instinctively grasped the meaning of Beauvoir's concluding phrase, ". . . I was gypped." They talked about it, and from that time on Beauvoir trusted her young friend's judgment so much that Sylvie became the first to hear of and comment upon ideas for future writing, which up to this time had been a privilege reserved exclusively for Sartre. They grew so close that by the early months of 1964 the passage with which she concluded her account of how Sylvie came into her life was an accurate description of their relationship:

> . . . we can see one another every day. She is as thoroughly inter-woven in my life as I am in hers. I have introduced her to my friends. We read the same books, we see shows together, and we go for long drives in the car. There is such an interchange be-tween us that I lose the sense of my age: she draws me forward into her future, and there are times when the present recovers a dimension that it had lost.[18]

Soon they were inseparable. Sylvie had become a teacher of philoso-phy and, after a brief stint in Rouen at the same Lycée Jeanne d'Arc where Beauvoir had taught, was teaching in a suburb outside Paris. From the beginning Beauvoir encouraged her to give up teaching in order to be free to travel at a moment's notice, saying, "I have enough money for both of us." Although she did not tell Beauvoir her reason, Sylvie was cognizant of the great difference in their ages and decided to maintain her career until or unless Beauvoir's health ever deteriorated to the point where she required constant attention.

So Sartre had Arlette and his other women, and his weekly rotation among them, and now Beauvoir had Sylvie, and they also established a schedule which they followed until Beauvoir's death. They spoke on the phone every day, Sylvie placing the call as soon as she arrived home from teaching. On Thursdays and Saturdays, Sylvie spent the night at Beauvoir's apartment. They were always together on Sunday, no matter whom Beau-voir had to see or meet on that day, and Beauvoir spent every Monday night at Sylvie's apartment. On Wednesday afternoon they spent at least several hours together, and if Beauvoir did not have another engagement they frequently dined simply together in her apartment. Shortly after they established this pattern, Beauvoir also began to dine regularly with Claude Courchay at least one or two Tuesdays each month, so her schedule left only Wednesdays and Fridays and some Tuesdays free for Sartre and the Family. She began every day by working alone on her correspondence, then she lunched with Sartre as long as he lived. After his death, she gen-erally lunched alone on something Sylvie provided for her, eating as she continued to work through the early afternoon.

Before and after Sartre's death, she tried not to arrange meetings before 4 P.M., and to save time she usually invited to her apartment those who wanted to see her. Getting rid of them was not a problem, because social courtesy was never her strong suit: when she thought they had been there long enough, she would pick up the small travel alarm clock she kept on her coffee table and tell them it was time to leave. If they kept on talking, she walked over to the door and held it open until they walked through it. A British journalist remembers how the door slammed on her heels and almost knocked her over because she did not make a fast enough exit.[19]

□

So the relationship with Sylvie very quickly dominated the pattern of Beauvoir's life. Sartre was delighted that she had Sylvie, whom he initially regarded as the counterpart to Arlette. "Bring your little friend," he would tell Beauvoir, inviting Sylvie to join them for lunch or dinner.[20]

At first they were a foursome, but animosity and competition soon arose between the two young women. Arlette was quiet, meditative and given to long periods of introspection. She liked to devote herself to an intensive study of anything that attracted her wide-ranging intelligence and would read everything written on the subject until she was an expert. She was musically inclined and took lessons on several instruments; frequently, she and Sartre spent entire afternoons playing the piano and singing together, so that music became as much of a bond for them as his evenings listening to Beauvoir's records had been. Also, Arlette had no profession or occupation, depended on Sartre for all her income and enjoyed the role of handmaiden to his muse. Sylvie was a more volatile personality, quick in her actions as well as in her comments. She had always had her own profession, her own private income, her own residence and her own interests. She had abandoned a thesis on Husserl when she realized she was not suited to the enforced solitude of scholarship, and was happy to have chosen the life of a lycée teacher of philosophy. She was vivacious and outspoken, and thoroughly enjoyed teasing Sartre with banter and repartee that Arlette worried was too exhausting for him.

The differences between the two younger women simmered, so the older couple decided it was better for all concerned if they met as a threesome: Sartre, Beauvoir, and either Arlette or Sylvie, but never both together for a social occasion in Paris. For several years all four took vacations together, usually with Arlette's male companion as well, but after some unpleasant episodes in Saint-Paul-de-Vence, Sartre and Beauvoir decided that for the next few years it would be more peaceful not to bring either woman on any holiday they took together.

At first the rest of the Family was puzzled by Beauvoir's seeming obsession with the young stranger she so suddenly deposited in their midst. She made it very clear that she had no secrets from Sylvie and that she wanted them to have none either. Initially they were hesitant, but no one had ever denied Beauvoir anything she wanted, so Sylvie soon became an integral part of their lives as well.

The relationship of the two women has been the subject of intense speculation ever since Beauvoir made it public in 1972, especially because she let it be known that she considered it, in its own way, equal to her relationship with Sartre.[21] As far as Beauvoir was concerned, it was simply a friendship and nothing more. "We are *very very very* good friends," she insisted, her face flushing with anger at the thought that anyone might consider it in any other light. However, most people who knew them did feel the need to interpret the relationship as something other than simple friendship.

Generally the speculation fell into what she herself defined as three separate categories: "mild rumors not worth listening to" (that she was only trying to imitate Sartre with his adoption of Arlette); "vicious gossip" (she had come out of the closet and accepted her always latent lesbian identity); and "what all those feminists who can't fit me into lesbian categories are determined that I will be—maternal" (she refers here to that feminist scholarship which concerns itself with images of mothers and daughters in her work, an area that came to irritate her greatly toward the end of her life).

The first is the most easily dismissible, because there were always those who refused to see Beauvoir as anything other than a pallid imitation of Sartre, a "me-too copy-cat" who took all her cues in life and work from him. From Sylvie's first public appearance at Beauvoir's side, Paris gossips snickered that because Sartre had adopted Arlette, Beauvoir had to do the same with Sylvie. In truth, she did adopt Sylvie legally, but not until after Sartre's death in 1980, and then for a more complex reason than establishing a legal literary heir.

The other two reasons proved more irritating and more difficult for Beauvoir and Sylvie to counteract, but each argued long and forcefully for what they believed their relationship was as well as what it was not. First, Simone de Beauvoir: "My own mother was quite enough for me, thank you. And as for children, I knew from my own childhood that I did not want them. I had no vocation for such things. You can explain my feeling for Sylvie by comparing it to my friendship with ZaZa. I have kept my nostalgia for that my whole life. Since she died, I have often desired to have an intense, daily, and total relationship with a woman. I have often desired a feminine friendship. It did not work with Olga, it did not work with Natasha, but now I have Sylvie, and it is an absolute relationship, because from the beginning we were both prepared to live in this way, to live entirely for each other."

Sylvie le Bon spoke at length: "Neither of us had any taste for motherhood or family ties. I loathed the mother–daughter relationship and wanted only to escape from it. With Castor, she thought as I did: there are only individuals, there are no stereotypical situations, relationships must be invented. That's the way it was. But absolutely no mother–daughter relationship. I loathe that especially. That's why I was so set against the adoption, because inevitably it brings to mind the maternal relationship, but since there was no other way to give me the legal rights, I accepted because what was at stake was too serious not to. Finally, when I accepted, it was flattering, and it didn't bother me anymore, this adoption. We joked about it and she would say, 'After all, it's like marriage, because you share my name.'"

For Sylvie it was "love between Castor and myself. What made it complicated is that neither one of us was prepared, especially me, to love someone who was a woman. But that's what it was, love, that's all." To explain what she meant by "love," she found it necessary to reflect upon the role ZaZa played in Beauvoir's life: "Ever since ZaZa, she always wanted a total and intense relationship with a woman. She said she loved ZaZa, that it was she who taught her the joy of loving. As young girls from good families, there was never anything physical, but it was love as far as the intensity of the happiness it brought her. This was what she found with me. I was ready for it, too. I had also had a friend when I was thirteen who had counted a lot for me and so I realized this desire with each other. Do not think this boastful, but Beauvoir often told me, 'My relationship with you is almost as important as mine with Sartre. I could not have had such a relationship with another man, because I have Sartre. But with a woman I have always desired it, and since ZaZa I have only found it with you.' So it is important to say that with me, she had something she always wanted, always missed, and tried to have in her life with other women but with them it never worked. In front of me one day, she said to Sartre, 'I have always desired, let us say, a feminine friendship.' Well, he said he always knew it, and then he encouraged her to have it. 'Fine, fine,' he would say, 'bring your little friend, bring her to Rome with us.' "

When asked to compare her relationship with Sylvie to that with ZaZa, Beauvoir was more succinct: "ZaZa was the idealized love of my youth; Sylvie was the ideal companion of my adult life. If I wish one thing, it is only that our ages were closer, so that we could have known each other longer, earlier in our lives."

The question of a lesbian relationship made both women angry, but each addressed it. Beauvoir was furious whenever scholars, writers and political activists urged her to proclaim a lesbian identity, not for herself but because she feared personal embarrassment and possible professional reprisal for Sylvie, who made one cryptic remark on the subject: "[Beauvoir would only say] that we were good friends because I didn't want her to say anything more, for many reasons, many bad reasons."

Alice Schwartzer noticed that when Beauvoir talked about her own sexuality, she talked only about men. Schwartzer asked bluntly whether she had ever had "a sexual relationship with a woman."

S. de B.: No. I have had some very important friendships with women, of course, some very close relationships, sometimes close in a physical sense. But they never aroused erotic passion on my part.

A.S.: Why not?

S. de B.: It is most probably the way my upbringing has conditioned me. I mean my entire education, not just what I was taught at home, but all the reading and all the influences which shaped me as a child and which pushed me in the direction of heterosexuality.

A.S.: Do you mean that you accept homosexuality on a theoretical level, for yourself as well.

S. de B.: Yes, completely and utterly. Women should not let themselves be conditioned exclusively to male desire any more.

And in any case, I think that these days every woman is a bit . . . a bit homosexual. Quite simply, because women are more desirable than men.

A.S.: How so?

S. de B.: Because they are more attractive, softer, their skin is nicer. And generally they have more charm. It is quite often the case with the usual married couple that the woman is nicer, more lively, more attractive, more amusing, even on an intellectual level.[22]

Francis Jeanson was among those who knew Sartre and Beauvoir well enough during this period to comment on her friendships with women. He saw them as "mostly disciples, girls who claim her entirely as their leader; who are quite openly under her sway." He based his perceptions of Beauvoir on his study of her writing, his extensive interviews with her, and daily observation during the years he was connected with the magazine. "I had the impression, perhaps wrongly, that she always had female friends in the sense of intimate relations. Truthfully speaking, I thought her more sexualized in that sphere than the other, because I never saw her act seductively with a man. I thought it very rare that such a beautiful woman never even flirted with men. She was actually rather sharp, sometimes cutting in her remarks, only generous to men when her comments involved the stances or causes she favored, but even then she was very dry and distant. No one dared be familiar with her: I never heard a man use *tu* to her except Lanzmann, who was irreverent to everyone. Sartre certainly, but even Bost said *vous*. All that was very different with her female friends. At every level, there was much more openness and intimacy. She was so much more relaxed with women."

If the question of age had any importance, it mattered more to Beauvoir than to Sylvie, who said, "It had absolutely no importance. There were many times when it was I who was in a position to protect her, acting the elder. At other times, she protected me and I was the younger. At times she would say, 'What can you expect of me, I am thirty years older than you,' or 'One of these days you will have to admit that I can't do such-and-such anymore,' but mostly it just didn't matter. We laughed together like two schoolgirls most of the time. We each did for the other what was needed at the time, and it was not primarily a question of age or seniority."

No doubt much scholarly ink will be expended on their own comments in an attempt to assess this friendship between two women. Other women, in other countries and cultures, have tried to explain what the friendship of a woman meant for them. One such is the English writer Vera Brittain: "From the days of Homer the friendships of men have enjoyed glory and acclamation, but the friendships of women, in spite of

Ruth and Naomi, have usually been not merely unsung, but mocked, belittled and falsely interpreted. . . ."[23]

Beauvoir was well aware of the false interpretations and even mockeries that plagued hers with Sylvie, and perhaps that was why she was always so willing to try to interpret it for sympathetic interviewers. She said in 1985 that she had elevated Sylvie to a separate plane within her life, one parallel if not equal to Sartre's.

"I am fortunate," she concluded, "to enjoy a perfect relationship with both a man and a woman." Then she was asked whether she had not unconsciously fulfilled what D. H. Lawrence was advocating in *Women in Love* when he created the character Rupert Birkin and made him yearn for "two kinds of love," an "eternal union" with both a man and a woman.[24]

She said she would have to think about it, but several days later she telephoned excitedly to say that she had reread the novel, "which I am now sorry to say I did not fully appreciate when I was with Algren and read it first." Her general opinion of Lawrence ("terrible *machiste*") had not changed, but in this one instance she said, "I now find much in the character of Rupert Birkin that suits entirely what I think about the enlightened roles men and women should play in each other's lives. It is only when Lawrence himself cannot resist intruding into his novel to preach that I am repelled."[25]

Still, all this self-analysis leaves vague the question of what the friendship of Simone de Beauvoir and Sylvie le Bon really consisted of, what use it can be to other women who seek to apply any or all of it to their own lives, and, finally, how scholars of feminism and gender should ultimately interpret it. The distinguished philosopher Hazel Barnes believes that "women are what they think they are, and in this instance, Simone de Beauvoir clearly did not think of herself as lesbian."[26] Professor Blanche Weisen Cook takes a different approach:

Women who love women, who choose women to nurture and support and to create a living environment in which to work creatively and independently, are lesbians.

It may seem elementary to state here that lesbians cannot be defined simply as women who practice certain physical rites together. Unfortunately, the heterosexist image—and sometimes even the feminist image—of the lesbian is defined by sexual behavior alone, and sexual in the most limited sense. Physical love between women is one expression of a whole range of emotions and responses to each other that involves all the mysteries of our human nature. Women-related women feel attraction, yearning, and excitement with women. Nobody and no theory has yet explained why for some women, despite cultural conditioning and societal penalties, both intellectual and emotional excitement are aroused in response to women.[27]

Elizabeth Abel moves the discussion clearly beyond the sexual when she calls the friendship of women "a vehicle of self-definition . . . clarifying identity through relation to an other who embodies and reflects an essential aspect of the self."[28] Still, Cook best sums up the question of what Abel calls the recently "trendy topic" of female friendship when she writes, "As we begin to ask different questions, we will discover new answers."

So, all the players were in their new places in Simone de Beauvoir's life at the end of 1964; all the subtle shifts of personal power were complete and in the positions they would hold until her death in 1986. If one were to select the exact moment when she and Sartre began to move out of each other's lives in the sense of becoming less important both intellectually and personally, this might be it.

"I could hardly understand what he was doing," she said of the period around 1960 when he was writing *The Search for a Method* and *The Critique of Dialectical Reason.* "He was moving into realms of philosophy that were—they were simply *not Sartre!*" Her perplexity increased throughout the 1960s, as there was much that he said, did and wrote that, to her, was "simply not Sartre." Nevertheless, they were together almost constantly in this decade, mostly for other than personal reasons: "The French war in Indochina had upset me deeply. The Algerian conflict depressed me. The Russians disappointed me. The Americans betrayed the Geneva agreements, and the fate of Vietnam was once more in question. Sartre denounced the United States, and I, for once, was in total accord. If you want to talk about my life in politics, then these are the years [1965–69] that matter, because this is when I was truly political."

Sartre's speaking engagement at Cornell University was now scheduled for February 1965. Beauvoir was planning to go with him as far as New York, where she still hoped, despite everything that had happened, to persuade Algren to spend a few weeks with her.[29]

On February 7, 1965, the United States bombed North Vietnam, and Sartre canceled his trip. When she looked back on this time, Beauvoir was surprised that she "wrote anything at all," because for the next few years "politics took over."

THIRTY-EIGHT

"Something's
Going to Happen"

I CAN'T TALK ABOUT MYSELF without speaking of Sartre," Simone de Beauvoir said or wrote about their "affinity of ideas" time and again throughout their long relationship.[1] Beauvoir's attitude has produced irritation, anger and outrage in almost equal parts among those who study her life and work, but any attempt to ask how she, "the Feminist Mother of us all,"[2] could hold such a decidedly nonfeminist opinion always upset her. The idea that by putting herself and her work second to Sartre she may have placed herself in many different ways and on many separate occasions under a lifelong disadvantage, both personally and professionally, made her furious.

The Italian scholar Anna Boschetti synthesizes these criticisms when she examines the particular role each played for the other at *Les Temps Modernes:*

> Simone de Beauvoir's trajectory is conditioned more than anyone else's by her relationship to Sartre. It reflects the traditional sexist division of labor. Sartre develops existentialism's philosophical, aesthetic, ethical, and political principles. His companion applies, disseminates, clarifies, supports, and administers them.[3]

Boschetti's view is reflected most clearly in the three volumes of Beauvoir's adult memoirs, where she filters most of the events of her life through an analysis of Sartre's, explaining what he did and denouncing anyone who dared to challenge him. But by the mid-1960s there were so many changes in their individual situations that their "affinity of ideas" was on somewhat shaky ground. Hairline cracks developed and later became serious fissures which Beauvoir either denied, evaded or equivocated about for the rest of her life. As Colette Audry, old friend and longtime observer of them both, remarked, "Their contract, founded on truth, not passion, was not an easy one to live."

To the general public, there was every reason to believe that Beauvoir and Sartre remained true to their original pact. However, for many reasons—from Sartre's failing health to his protean ideology, to new currents in French intellectual thought and political action, to Beauvoir's own changing personal relationships and her public commitment to the concerns of women—during the late sixties she and Sartre became less important to each other in the daily fabric of their lives. Even so, she was unwilling to concede that anything had changed and clung to the myth that all was exactly as it had always been.

Perhaps Beauvoir kept the myth alive through sheer stubbornness and determination to make the world accept her presentation of herself and Sartre as the successful couple with the ideal relationship; perhaps his indifference was due to failing health and his lifelong avoidance of conflict in all his dealings with women. Whatever the reason, she continued to adhere to "the Sartrian ideal"[4] by which she and the Family meant his writing and thinking before he published the *Critique of Dialectical Reason* in 1960. Yet even as they tried to nudge him back within the intellectual confines of his earlier work, Sartre was leaping and bounding just beyond their reach.

Francis Jeanson explained it: "In the last ten or so years before his death, Sartre's entourage, the Family, wanted to keep a certain image of him that was not the authentic Sartre, which was the Sartre who was constantly, all the time, in the process of becoming something new. In his last years, he said things with daring, without reserve; he risked and took chances. Time was hurrying him along: he had nothing left to lose, and he knew it. There was a lot he could not write, so he said it in interviews. Thoughts and ideas all tumbled out. Maybe they were not carefully presented, but they were interesting all the same because they showed how he was always evolving. This bothered the Family, because their need was to hold him frozen, preserved as the Sartre he had been, the one they wanted him to be. But he eluded them; he was constantly slipping away."[5]

Beauvoir was the main keeper of "the Sartrian ideal" because she was the one who had been with him the longest. She believed hers was indeed the most privileged of circumstances, that of having been in perpetual dialogue with someone remarkable. "Privilege" was a word she used in many instances to describe some aspect or other of their relationship, and one of the most important usages was in the sense of herself as Sartre's "privileged reader," the first to hear his ideas, to see his actual writing, and the final critic and editor before publication. All this had always happened without the intrusion of any problems of domestic life. This was the relationship she urged all women to aspire to, but any attempt to press her to explain how it might be possible for most of them resulted in a complete change of subject or else a return to what Sartre's intelligence meant to her own life and work.

"Anyone who lived with him, no matter how intimately, was marked by Sartre's thought," she believed. This opinion had great resonance at

Les Temps Modernes, where anyone who disagreed with Sartre or who held a different view of what the magazine should be usually made a swift exit after being frozen out by Beauvoir and those who thought as she did.

"I think Sartre was really a genius," she added, "and I don't see why I should not say it. All his male friends recognized that Sartre was superior to them, so why shouldn't I recognize it, too? It's just bad feminism to pretend otherwise, so why shouldn't I say so!"

Her view was that theirs had been something far more complex than the master–disciple relationship that so many others interpreted her many and frequent explanations as implying. As far as she was concerned, any submission on her part to his greater knowledge and authority was very different from the submission/domination she stigmatized in her books. She considered herself different because it was not "the prostitution of a woman bought, paid for and kept by a husband." Her pride came in being able to write about the domination inherent in domestic drudgery while never knowing it herself. Everything about their living arrangements gave her the secure feeling of being in spiritual and intellectual harmony with a man; if the physical aspect of their relationship troubled her, she was an expert at concealing it. What mattered most was that she had been a teacher, earned her own living, wrote books that sold well, and was honored as much for being Simone de Beauvoir as for being Sartre's companion. She believed that she was a free woman in every way but one, and that was the most important of all: she saw herself as "branded by Sartre's thought."

This feeling of "privilege" lasted, she claimed, "until the very end [of Sartre's life], even though the *Critique of Dialectical Reason* went right over my head." It was a less than honest comment, especially in light of the circumstances of his last decade.

The beginning of their differences can be traced to the 1960 publication of the *Critique.* She had strenuous objections to this work "because it was a new philosophy that contradicted *Being and Nothingness.*" To her, the earlier work represented "the Sartrian ideal" because it was basically the keystone of all her own work and she had lived all her life according to its tenets. Now, after more than thirty years together, he was telling her in effect that if he had not entirely changed his mind, he had certainly changed most of his thinking. Beauvoir was nothing if not faithful to an idea, and his declaration was very threatening. She trained all her critical energy on to the *Critique,* hoping to convince him to jettison it if he would not change it, but none of her arguments served any useful purpose, because he published it anyway just as it was.

Then he became interested in another writer's life, which she initially viewed as "his way to distract me from the *Critique,*" but she quickly realized that this opinion had no basis in reality. "He got involved in Flaubert with passion," she said, "passion for the man, more for Flaubert in general than *Madame Bovary* in particular." So she "became interested in Flaubert, but only to the extent to which I could help Sartre," because the entire undertaking puzzled her. "Sure, *Madame Bovary* is a masterpiece, but it never particularly exicted me, and in fact I don't think Sartre was all that excited by it, either. At first I didn't understand when he became obsessed by Flaubert, until I realized it had much to do with our mutual interest in autobiography. I thought that Sartre was involved in this project of writing the biography of a man by trying to understand him in any way possible, in order to understand himself better, so that was all right with me. But his interest fell upon Flaubert for a whole lot of reasons, mostly because he had a lot of documents about him, an immense correspondence, the works of his youth, et cetera. With Flaubert, he had a lot to work with. Well, at first it interested me a lot, too, but still . . . ."

Sartre explained what she could not in a 1964 interview with the journalist Jacqueline Piatier, who asked why he was writing about Flaubert. His reply was immediate and unhesitating:

> "Because he is the opposite of what I am. I need to rub against everything that puts me into question. In *The Words* I wrote, 'I have often thought against myself.' That sentence has never been understood . . . But in fact, that's exactly how one should think: one should always be questioning one's own assumptions."[6]

For Beauvoir, that was exactly the problem. She needed Sartre to be the fixed center of her universe, the still point of her turning world. A Sartre who thought against himself was confusing and difficult to accept, especially now when she found herself in complete accord with his political and social opinions. Now that she was more willing than ever to speak openly in his support, he seemed to have lost interest in telling her what he wanted her to say. All he really wanted to do was write and think about Flaubert. Based on Sartre's past history with women, it is probably fair to say that this was not a conscious action on his part but simply his usual way of avoiding conflict. Beauvoir kept her confusion to herself because she did not want to upset their equilibrium as a professional couple, but also because Sylvie was there to distract her.

"Sylvie's friendship has played an important part in my life," Beauvoir wrote in *Adieux*,[7] and from this point on Sylvie was always present. She became part of the Saturday evenings when Sartre and Beauvoir listened to music in the Rue Schoelcher flat and of their Sunday luncheons at La Coupole. Sylvie and Sartre tolerated each other with good-humored joking and teasing. There was no competition between them; indeed, he was pleased that Beauvoir had such a good friend to keep her busy and happy during the increasingly long periods of time he spent with Arlette. Beauvoir and Arlette disliked and distrusted each other, so their times together were infrequent and then characterized by each behaving with frosty politeness to the other. A pattern evolved: Arlette seldom appeared with Sartre in Beauvoir's presence, but Sylvie was omnipresent. She went to Rome and on other trips and frequently joined them at meetings or conferences. When Sartre and Beauvoir were together, the professional couple now became an entirely different entity: the family threesome.

Between 1961 and 1966, when Sartre's obsession with Flaubert was mounting, he still devoted much of his time to political activity. Beauvoir accompanied him, for example, to the Soviet Union on seven different occasions. Sartre's presence was certainly a boon for Soviet propaganda, but these visits had two equally important purposes for him. Ostensibly, they were concerned with writers' conferences, questions of human rights and the fusion of ideology, literature and public life. Also, they allowed him to see Lena Zonina, who Beauvoir began to fear would become "another Dolores." Sartre wrote long letters to Zonina that Beauvoir knew he was writing but was not invited to read; even more worrisome was the way he hid Zonina's replies. Beauvoir discovered just how close they were on one of the Moscow visits, when she heard Zonina discuss details of Arlette's adoption that she herself did not know.

Nevertheless, time and the usual pattern of Sartre's relationships with women were on Beauvoir's side: by 1967, his passion had cooled, both for the Soviet Union (whose invitations he refused from then on) and for Zonina. When his ardor was gone, he corresponded affectionately for several years with Zonina, as did Beauvoir, who began a separate exchange.[8] Zonina was allowed to travel to Paris on several occasions, and each time she stayed in Beauvoir's apartment. Usually, she saw Sartre only once each trip, a visit which amounted to little more than a duty or obligation on his part.

Throughout the 1960s, Beauvoir followed Sartre all over Europe, usually for meetings organized by writers' groups with a strongly political agenda, as official guests of governments, or as supporters of dissident factions of various kinds. Much of her final volume of memoirs, *All Said and Done*, is given over to a day-to-day account of where she went, whom she saw and what she did. She based the memoir on a travel diary she kept for every trip they took, but most of her diary entries are about inadequate hotel rooms, high prices or poor internal transportation. There are almost no remarks about people, meetings or activities, and these are only superficial notations such as "Met X and was interviewed for ½ hour" or "Went to Y, very unpleasant."[9]

However, from the few news clippings that have filtered into the West from Eastern European nations, and from the scattered notes pertaining to talks or interviews that Beauvoir kept in her files, it seems clear that her self-imposed role as Sartre's principal factotum was being challenged by another role as women everywhere sought her out. They wanted her to clarify some of her ideas as put forth in *The Second Sex* and relate them to the specific situation of their culture and society. They wanted advice on their own individual situations and fledgling movements, and concrete proposals for future action. These women wanted to know Beauvoir's opinion of many things that she had to think about for the first time, from abortion to clitoridectomy of small children, to the right of women to be educated or self-supporting. Some of these women became her personal friends, others sought her advice or support in a more formal manner, some even moved to Paris and attached themselves to her for varying periods as minions or disciples.[10] Many of them simply wanted to see her, to touch her, to be able to say that they had been in her presence. Shyly, they gave her bouquets of flowers and gifts of their own handiwork, sometimes they presented their daughters to be patted on the head or kissed—"To my horror," she said, shuddering. "What was I—the Pope?"

So while Beauvoir was traveling with Sartre as his companion, these women took up more and more of her time and attention. His initial amusement gave way to bewilderment and then to mild irritation that she was often not there when he needed her. It was probably the closest he ever came to a twinge of pique (for jealousy was an emotion Sartre truly lacked) over her popularity.

There was another moment of irritation between them when Sartre canceled his trip to Cornell. His lectures were originally scheduled for March 1965, as a protest against the February bombing of North Vietnam and the subsequent invasion of the south by U.S. Marines. "Selfishly, I had hoped against hope," Beauvoir said, "that the United States would not escalate the conflict until after we had been there and departed, because I wanted so much to return to New York. I probably expressed this wish to Sartre, who would no doubt have been disappointed to hear how I put my personal interests against the needs of the people. He was a little tentative when he told me he was not going to Cornell, but very relieved to hear me say that of course he had made the correct decision. It was good for him to know that we were in solidarity on this matter."

So even though she wanted very much to see the United States again, and although she had enough money and friends there (even without Algren) to make a pleasant private visit, going without Sartre was unthinkable. Later, when other invitations came, she said, "Sartre needed me to travel with him."

In 1966 they spent several months in Japan, which Beauvoir found "thrilling, but it was still a frightful mixture of capitalism and feudalism, even though daily life was full of charm and we were received extraordinarily well."[11] In 1967 they were official guests of the Egyptian and Israeli governments, but she spoke very little to her friends about these trips beyond what she wrote in her memoirs. She returned alone to Belgium to speak to labor groups, but her message was really Sartre's, delivered in his stead. They went together to Sweden and Denmark to participate in meetings of the Russell Tribunal, an international commission which was organized in protest against the United States presence in Vietnam, and for the next several years they were outspoken in their opposition to the war. As the conflict escalated, Beauvoir could not help but compare the position of the United States to France's unsuccessful colonial policy first in Indochina and then in Algeria.

Beauvoir originally accepted membership on the Russell Tribunal, because she thought "I would not have to do very much more than lend my name, attend occasional meetings and sign statements and manifestos." But soon she was as involved as she had been during the French–Algerian war, incensed by what she deemed "the unjustness of the American position." In December 1967 she wrote to the American Quaker Helen P. Wenck, with whom she had established a friendship-by-mail through another "affinity of ideas," to say that she had been concentrating all her energies on the Copenhagen sessions of the Tribunal, which were "particularly thrilling."[12] The following spring she wrote again, saying, "We have had here some great demonstrations against the war in Viet Nam. I hope with all my heart that something is going to change in America because I want very much to return there."[13]

In 1968, which was the last year of their ostensibly political traveling, they returned to Yugoslavia and then twice to Czechoslovakia, where Sartre appeared on television to express hope about the "Prague Spring" and support for the student rebellion. In Yugoslavia, Beauvoir imitated Sartre by rekindling briefly a relationship begun some years earlier with Vladimir Dedijer.[14] Later she joined Sartre in petitioning the Yugoslav government to allow Dedijer to leave the country to participate in sessions of the Russell Tribunal.

Beauvoir and Sartre's activities within France continued to be largely political as well, but assumed a more personal cast during this decade of frenetic traveling. Much of their activity in France reflected changes in the composition of the editorial board of Les Temps Modernes, but also the decline of the magazine's influence on a French intellectual community that had all but discarded Existentialism in favor of new ideologies.

As early as 1948, Sartre's attention drifted away from the day-to-day running of the magazine, which he left to Merleau-Ponty until the latter left the editorial board in 1953, when Beauvoir took it upon herself to act as Sartre's spokesperson.[15] Claire Etcherelli, another member of the board, took over Merleau-Ponty's role some years later, but even though Beauvoir admired her fiction and liked her as a friend she still held the reins of control tightly in her own hands. Anything that went into the review had first to pass her intense scrutiny; nothing, no matter how small or insignificant, was printed that did not meet her approval. Anyone who was late to meetings was severely chastised; if someone dared to joke or make light of an issue, she treated the poor unfortunate to a shrill tongue-lashing. So, from the original "disciples" to those who became "established and consecrated" because membership on the board of the highly respected magazine conveyed this status, to those for whom "belonging to Les Temps Modernes is the only capital they can bank on for recognition," Simone de Beauvoir was the one consistent element they could always count upon to remain true to "the tone of the review."[16]

Claude Lanzmann credited her "willpower and determination" with being "the glue to hold us together in the manner she believed Sartre would have wanted."[17] She was the one who insisted on weekly meetings of the entire board, and she decided to hold them in her apartment on the mornings after Sartre had spent the night there. It was the only way she could insure his attendance, but he did nothing to hide his boredom from her and the others.

"Sartre, *listen!*" she would command. "Sartre, pay attention, *please!*" she entreated. Those who were there remember how embarrassed they were when she scolded him as if he were a misbehaving toddler. Most of the time he smiled, apologized, offered a comment or two that might or might not have been related to the subject at hand, and then his attention wandered once more.

By the early 1960s, membership on the editorial board changed fairly regularly, but the review's content still reflected the intellectual background, training and written expression of Sartre, Beauvoir and their staunchest allies, Bost and Lanzmann, who were now considered "their earliest disciples—who recognized them before they were highly consecrated—the trusted lieutenants they need in order to maintain and defend the position they have won."[18] Suddenly,[19] Existentialism or, more specifically, philosophy became increasingly challenged in France as the one true discipline to proffer intellectual excellence. The shift toward anthropology, sociology and linguistics as the sources of intellectual power and authority was under way, Sartre's slide down the pinnacle of leadership was well advanced, and the magazine's all-powerful influence waned as well. What had once been a visionary journal on the cutting edge of culture and society had in recent years become mostly commentary or review, well written, to be sure, but usually about events that had already taken place or ideas that were already being replaced by new ones.

As for Sartre, he was remote from this newest intellectual ferment, content to delegate responsibility to an editorial board which grew ever younger and less inclined to treat him with the reverence of "the original Sartrians, all of whom [began] their careers by following the trail blazed by the master." These new board members were young men who adopted "a more easygoing, egalitarian relationship . . . to a Sartre who is having problems and needs their help." After 1968, "they stand their ground stubbornly against Sartre and try to win him over to their side."[20] To Beauvoir's consternation, he now seemed eager to surrender his power to these young men, many of whom held views of what the review should be that were quite different from hers.

Their relationship to Sartre seemed a curious juxtaposition of two things: his holding on to authority while retreating from leadership:

He [delegates] power to them as a result of their ambiguous position of dependence in independence which makes them objectively much more staff workers than allies. Their lack of [intellectual] capital of their own makes them, in spite of their apparently powerful position, actually subject to Sartre's authority.[21]

Sartre liked these "Young Turks"[22] and actually seemed to enjoy the self-righteousness with which they corrected and sometimes denounced his positions.[23] Beauvoir was shocked by their irreverence and horrified at Sartre's easy acceptance of it. They mocked her as well, but mostly behind her back, for to them she was "the stubborn old biddy" whose mannerisms they imitated for their own amusement, and whom they tried to ignore as much as possible. Bost and Lanzmann became her buffer, trying to insulate her from the indifference that greeted many of her editorial comments and decisions. In the process, Lanzmann, who originally put all his energy to work on Beauvoir's behalf, turned out to have the most staying power of all, and after the death of both Sartre and Beauvoir he became the editorial director of the magazine.

Lanzmann was married now and was more involved with film than with print journalism, but he still remained Beauvoir's champion defender. She turned to him for advice and consolation in equal parts, and he became one of her few trusted advisers (Sylvie and Bost were the others) for the rest of her life. What is interesting is that Lanzmann, in his own way, was as much a detractor of Sartre as the younger members of the board, and his comments were frequently harsher than theirs. Beauvoir either trained herself not to notice or else liked Lanzmann so much that she truly did not see his irreverence and sometimes his open antagonism. He could say just about anything to Sartre and she had no complaints. Perhaps it was a good thing, because, now that Sartre was (consciously or not) bent on slipping off the pedestal she was still determined to keep him on, she needed an ally strong enough to cushion her distress.

"It happened so fast," Beauvoir reflected in 1986. "One day we were the main attraction (not that we wanted to be in that sense, you understand) of Saint-Germain-des-Prés, and the next day there was an entirely new way of looking at the world of politics and literature." Sartre was engrossed in Flaubert, but Beauvoir was metaphorically looking over her shoulder at Structuralism and trying to outrun it. Many of her speeches and interviews included didactic pronouncements of what she believed literature should be.[24] Each contained some sort of denunciation of the New Novel or an attack upon any sort of writing that lacked commitment or did not reflect life in an attempt to give it meaning and value. In the 1965 symposium Beauvoir declared her conception of literature to be

an activity performed by men, for men, with the intention of revealing their world to them . . . Language must bear the mark of someone . . . it must be identified with someone: with the author; it is necessary that I [i.e. the reader] enter into his world and his world must become mine . . . Literature bears the responsibility of making clear to each of us what was formerly cloudy.[25]

The last sentence quoted here could well serve as the credo for her entire life as a writer.

By 1965, eleven years had passed since *The Mandarins* was published. During that time, Beauvoir claimed repeatedly that she had no more ideas for a novel and would probably not write any more fiction in her lifetime. She also thought she was finished with the autobiographical impulse, having decided that "what was happening to me now [i.e., the mid-1960s] was nothing I wanted the world to know about."[26] As more women (and some men) asked her to write prefaces and introductions to their books or to contribute essays or manifestos on behalf of specific causes, she expressed the belief that she might not ever write another book of her own because no single subject seemed important enough to hold her attention.

But then, in 1965, something happened to change her mind. In October, at the conclusion of their annual Italian holiday, she drove Sartre to Milan, where he was to see his publishers. After she dropped him off, she drove on alone to Paris, expecting to meet him there after his flight the following evening. Her first day's drive was uneventful, but on the second day she woke up to heavy fog with most of the driving still before her. She started off anyway, unwilling to wait for the fog to lift, and as the day progressed and the weather cleared she relaxed and began to daydream. As she rounded a sharp curve before a steep hill near Joigny, she saw a trailer truck bearing down on her and realized she had crossed over into its lane. "Something's going to happen," she thought, just before it struck her. When she woke up, a crowd was gathered around her, and she later remembered thinking, "I'll no doubt catch a train to get me back to Paris before seven."[27]

She resisted medical assistance, but the police insisted than an ambulance should take her and the truck driver (who was not injured) to a hospital, where she was found to have severe bruises and three broken ribs and was pronounced in shock. Her one thought was to telephone Sartre so that he could hear the news from her, but it had already been broadcast on television. Sylvie phoned from Paris to say that she was bringing Sartre and would hire a private ambulance to carry them all back to Paris together the next day.[28]

For the next three weeks she had to stay in bed to allow the ribs to knit, and, with time to fill, she began to write fiction again. Like her character Françoise Miquel in *L'Invitée*, who had so much time to think about herself while she was confined to bed, Beauvoir began to reflect upon all that had happened to her in recent years. This time, however, her thoughts did not take the form of analyzing herself and her changing relationships, but, rather, of analyzing the rapidly changing society in which she now lived. One of the reasons for this, she concluded in 1984, was that in the autumn of 1965 she was still "totally bowled over" by Sartre's adoption of

Arlette and simply could not bear "to find out if I had been wounded at all, and if so, how deep were the wounds, which writing about myself would have meant pouring salt all over." Instead, in an attempt at "amusement, diversion," she thought about how she had crisscrossed the world by plane and driven through several countries in a single day, and how she thought nothing anymore of picking up the telephone to chat with someone across an ocean. That led her to think generally about the changes in human relationships since her youth, when she was "the object of gossip, and, it would seem, the only 'fallen woman' in all of France," to the current ease with which persons of various sexes and statuses coupled and uncoupled.

The work that resulted, *Les Belles Images*, is the shortest of all her novels and was the easiest and fastest to write. Begun at the end of October, it was finished just after the start of the new year 1966 and was published the following November. It was almost universally panned by reviewers, who did not understand how the foremost spokesperson for the literature of commitment could write a novel with a heroine who worked in advertising and whose family, friends and co-workers all worried constantly about television sets, washing machines and new cars as they hopped in and out of various beds. There is not a single left-wing intellectual in the entire novel. The only way to describe what, if anything, the characters believe in is to call it conspicuous consumption and to describe them as the New Bourgeois, the contemporary version of the class into which Simone de Beauvoir had been born.

The title (untranslated in the English version) refers to pretty pictures—the advertising layouts for which the heroine, Laurence, writes catchy slogans suggested by the "motivation experts" of her firm. She carries this way of seeing things into her personal life, envisaging herself, her architect husband and their two pretty daughters in their cozy home as the perfect tableau of domestic tranquility.

If there is a plot, it is so slight as to be almost nonexistent: the story unfolds during a period of five months in Laurence's life and concerns interwoven developments in the lives of those who are closest to her. She is married to Jean-Charles, but has a demanding, full-time career as an advertising copywriter. She also has a lover, Lucien, who wants more of her time and affection than she has or wants to give him. Her elder daughter, Catherine, age ten, is beginning to question why she is so cosseted while other children experience so much misery and suffering; the child gets much of her information about injustice and inequities from a worldly friend, Brigitte, a Jewish girl whose family lives in straitened circumstances and who is slightly older and much wiser than she. Laurence's parents are separated: her father is a scholar who disdains contemporary culture and prefers to immerse himself in ancient civilizations; her mother is obsessed with aging, probably because she lives with a much younger man who is about to leave her for a nineteen-year-old girl. Of her parents, Laurence thinks: "It's my father whom I love but my mother who made me what I am."[29] She admires his voluntary withdrawal from materialism all the while she continues to follow her mother's superficial behavior.

It is a novel in which the child Catherine is sent to a psychiatrist to help her deal with her worries about the world, and where adults pop sleeping pills, tranquilizers and amphetamines as they consume too much alcohol. Women worry about face-lifts, stomach-tighteners and how to keep their men from straying, but the men stray anyway. Of all the characters, Laurence is the least able to commit to anything: she steels herself not to feel emotion, and her lover accuses her of a hardness of heart. It is not her fault, she insists, but the fault of her upbringing; her mother conditioned her to be this way. She has scant respect for her husband, accusing him of being foolish for the easy way he accepts her moods and evasions, which again she insists are not her fault but his. The only relationship that seems to give her any sustenance is with her father, but, being a modern woman, she pop-psychologizes and decides (although no one has accused her of it) that hers is not an unresolved Oedipus complex. However, when he ponders reconciliation with her mother, she develops what seems like anorexia followed by bulimia, and seeks relief in cold showers, deep breathing and frequent glasses of ice water.

In the end, Laurence finds her stability by disregarding the well-meaning but conflicting advice everyone gives her about how to cope with Catherine's increasingly irrational fears. She allows her to continue the friendship with Brigitte that everyone else has urged her to end, but cancels the child's therapy sessions and decides to take full responsibility for her education and upbringing. At first glance, it might seem that Laurence is simply substituting an obsession with her daughter for the previous one with her father (she is still unsure about the pending reconciliation of her parents), but Beauvoir paints the new fixation in a positive light. Laurence decides that "the game," meaning life, is over for her, but "Catherine will have her chance," so finally there is hope for a better future, based not on slick advertising catchphrases but on exposure to the real vicissitudes of life.

All synopses risk banality by simplification and reduction of character and plot, and all the French reviews did just that, panning the novel, stressing its sensationalism, calling Beauvoir a pallid imitation of the much younger Françoise Sagan.[30] Still, despite the almost hysterical negativity of the reviews, within months the novel sold more than 100,000 copies in France. As with *The Second Sex* before it, Beauvior had touched a nerve, this time of the complexities of modern life, and readers jumped eagerly with the shock of recognition.

This is a prescient novel, written in 1965, when there really was no feminist movement to speak of in France—where women had been allowed to vote only since 1947, few had entered professional life, and even fewer were addressing the inequities Beauvoir wrote about in *The Second Sex* with anything more than private conversation. In the United States, Betty Friedan's seminal work *The Feminine Mystique* had just been published, and the country was only beginning to gear itself up for the protests that gave rise toward the end of the decade to what we now call "The Sixties." Because of Friedan's book, American women were beginning to gather for something more than casual conversation about their lot, while in France Beauvoir had already written about the stresses of career versus marriage, responsibility (husband and children) and self-fulfillment (work and lover). She discerned the insatiable thirst for luxury goods contrasted with the altruistic need to do something for the world's suffering. She recognized substance abuse, excessive reliance on therapy, broken marriages and women who are dumped by men because they are unfortunate enough to show the effects of their age. She depicted realistically what happens to them when their economic support is gone. French critics may have missed these issues, but French readers did not, and when the book was translated into other languages Beauvoir's prescience was sometimes noted.

A. S. Byatt was among the reviewers who grasped Beauvoir's intentions, who saw "underneath the mockery of stereotyped Freudian and moral images" to her "true novelist's gifts of selecting detail and creating individuals whilst refusing to sum up situations."[31] Such thoughtful analysis was rare among critics, and Beauvoir was disappointed with what she believed was a "shortsighted refusal to see the complexities that living forces upon us today." The last thing she needed at this moment in her life, when rebuffs seemed to be coming at her from all directions, was a critical failure. To deal with it, she started a new work at once.

If she was unhappy with reviews of *Les Belles Images*, she was "extremely bitter" about the reception of the book that followed, three stories collected under the title of one of them, "La Femme rompue" ("The Woman Destroyed").

She wrote them during 1967, mostly on airplanes, in hotel rooms and during any other spare moment on the trips with Sartre to Egypt and Israel, later editing them the same way during a congress of writers in the Soviet Union and the Russell Tribunal meetings in Stockholm. Writing the stories in the midst of so much political traveling "restored me to myself."

"It is dangerous to ask the public to read between the lines, yet I did so again," is how she described her intention to continue writing "obliquely."[32] By this she meant specifically the inequities of life faced by many women, which she described through fictional archetypes. She had always been the confessional repository for women in her own circle, but after *Les Belles Images* was published she heard from women who poured out their souls to her in letters that ranged from the tragic to the irrational, all claiming that their experience was something she had written about and asking her to write more along those same lines.

She decided to write about how women deceive themselves, using three different fictional techniques. The first story, "The Age of Discretion," is narrated in a straightforward first person by a sixtyish woman scholar whose scientist husband is in crisis over his perceived inability to do original research, and whose son disappoints her by abandoning the academic career she planned for him in order to take a job working for a government administration she despises. Her latest book, which she thought daring and original, has been panned by critics who believe it to be hackneyed.

"Monologue," the second story, is a hysterical, vituperative outpouring of real and imagined insults and slights by a woman in her forties whose husband and son have abandoned her. She sits in her room on New Year's Eve and spews forth invective in an unpunctuated stream of self-pity and irrational hatred for all those who may or may not have done her wrong. Murielle, as Beauvoir calls her character, is a Molly Bloom out of control, who so upset the critic André Billy that he wrote in his review of the book: "I [won't discuss] the second story, scurrilous and slangy. It offends me. I hardly know why. I am probably a little behind the times."[33]

The last story, "The Woman Destroyed," is meant to refer collectively to all three, as each in its way treats a woman whose world has collapsed around her and whose identity is threatened or lost. In this one, Beauvoir uses the technique of a diary kept by the central character during a period of just over six months. Monique La Combe has been married to Maurice for about twenty-two years, and now that the younger of their two daughters has left home, he reveals that he has been having an affair with a well-known lawyer six years younger than his wife. Monique has always been content to stay at home and invest her entire life in husband and children, and now none of them needs or wants her anymore. She tries to find help, going to family and friends and even a psychiatrist, but nothing seems to work for her. In the last entry of her diary, which concludes the story, she writes:

> A closed door. . . . It will not open if I do not stir. . . . But I know that I shall move. The door will open slowly and I shall see what there is behind the door. It is the future. The door to the future will open. Slowly. Unrelentingly, I am on the threshold. There is only this door and what is watching behind it. I am afraid. And I cannot call to anyone for help.
> I am afraid.[34]

The stories were published in the popular woman's magazine *Elle* before they appeared in book form.[35] Serial publication gave Beauvoir a much larger initial audience than some of her books commanded, and she was deluged with letters from women who, as she said in 1982, "either believed I had listened at the keyhole outside their bedroom door or else thought I was a crazy Amazon, hater of men."

Critics in France, England and the United States were soon as divided in their judgments of this book as they had been with the previous one, and reviews were more negative than positive. Jacqueline Piatier dismissed it as "the voice of Simone and perhaps of Jean-Paul trembling in all its candor, and how can one not resist commeting on this?"[36] *London Magazine's* review was much the same: "Sartre and Mme. de Beauvoir have long been regarded as specialists in how not to be a human being, and Mme. de Beauvoir more particularly in how not to be a woman."[37]

In the years that followed, especially after the feminist movement took hold in France, many actors created dramatized situations based on different sections of the three stories, generally interpreting the parts of the women as strong, courageous and triumphant, which made Beauvoir frequently angry and always upset. She explained in 1982, "It is wrong to say that I portray women from the distance of one who is removed from them, who can neither understand nor sympathize with their condition. I am merely presenting the reality of what happens to women in our society. It is up to my readers to profit from their mistakes, to learn from their experiences and keep themselves free of situations that end the same way."

Still, hers is a depressing view of women who are only passive partners in unequal relationships, who gave all and got little in return and were then tossed aside for younger ones who will provide men with the same services until they too begin to grow old and are discarded in turn. Beauvoir puts the book's title into the passive voice, a deliberate reinforcement of her view, although one American critic believed "It is hard to think of such aggressive women as victims."[38] Most American critics also noted that all three stories have one element in common, "the subject of aging women,"[39] on which "she writes with perception, grace and intelligence."[40]

It was shortly after her sixtieth birthday in January 1968 that *La Femme rompue* was published in France. Perhaps it was the facile way critics assumed that she was writing about herself and her own disappointments in the three stories, or the way they dismissed the book as the bitter expression of an old woman whom nobody wanted anymore, either in life or in literature; perhaps it was Sartre's health, now strapped firmly into the cycles of illness, renewal and relapse that led to his death in 1980, or her lifelong habit of seeking to understand herself by writing about a subject from every point of view: whatever the reason, she suddenly found herself "working very hard [on] an essay, analogous to *The Second Sex*, on old age."[41] She confided her intentions to Helen Wenck, and a dialogue through letters ensued. On June 24, she thanked Mrs. Wenck for sharing her own experiences and observations. On November 19 she wrote again, saying, "It's fascinating, but it's also terrible, this old age." In May 20, 1969, she told her, "I've finished my book about old age. . . . [It] gave me a lot of trouble [to write], but I'm happy that I've done it. It will be published no doubt at the beginning of next year." It was published in January 1970. During the Christmas holidays she was busy correcting proofs for "this huge book, same genre as *Second Sex* and it isn't very [optimistic]. I believe that the old people are not very happy in the U.S.A., nor are they in France, where their sort is simply desolate."

With this comment, she was writing of herself as well. She had been at Sartre's side throughout the upheavals that came to be known in France as "Mai '68." Now she saw him in ill-health and increasingly under the sway of Benny Lévy, the young revolutionary whose pseudonym was Pierre Victor. The book was her refuge against facing the actuality of how old age affected Sartre. Writing it helped her deal with what was happening to him and cushioned her to withstand it. She used the excuse of research and writing as a convenient way to avoid his infirmity and get others to ministrate to him. And because of the distance this created between them, in retrospect *Old Age* came to be the one of all her works that she was "sorry to have written."

THIRTY-NINE

"We Have Lived Through Some Exhilarating Times"

Two letters express Simone de Beauvoir's sentiments about the political and personal emotional roller-coaster she rode during 1968.[1] In the first, written in June, she had just begun the descent from the highest peak:

> In Paris, we have lived through some exhilarating times. This youth that everyone believed was sleeping has been magnificent in its courage and intelligence. But now everything has returned to the way it was . . . this [protest] has only been the beginning, there will be others to follow. It has restored hope to our hearts.

By November, she was in the lowest trough: "Here, the rentrée[2] is totally dead after the magnificent outbursts of May." She was sad that all had come to naught, but not unhappy to immerse herself in her research again: "I am working very hard. It's exciting but also terrible, this old age."

Any evaluation of Simone de Beauvoir's activity during and after the May '68 uprising must include the fact that this was the period following the two works generally considered the most negative and depressing in her canon, *The Woman Destroyed* and *The Coming of Age*. Two factors were important during this time, one which she defended at length and another which she spoke of not at all. On more than one occasion Beauvoir demanded to know, "Why should I be punished for exposing what society does to women? Why should I be killed because I am the messenger who brings the bad news?"[3] The unspoken factor concerned both Sartre's health and hers, and had much to do with the tone of hopelessness and despair in her written work. In later years, when she reflected back upon this, she viewed it as an important, even if "unconscious, unexpressed factor"[4] in how both works came into existence.

Sartre's health had been relatively stable for several years, but there had been some worrisome incidents. Every so often he lost his balance and fell or forgot where he was for a few moments, or suddenly suffered from an excruciating headache or spots before the eye which left him momentarily sightless. Beauvoir had always enjoyed "embarrassingly excellent health," but now that she was sixty she sometimes found it difficult to get up in the morning because of what she referred to alternately as "arthritis or bursitis" in her right, and writing, arm. She also realized that she was no longer striding around Paris as quickly as before, and when she walked up the steps of the Métro she was frequently out of breath. She worried that her concentration wandered during intellectual tasks she had once bounded through, so she sometimes gave herself "secret mental exercises" which she was "always delighted and relieved to pass." She regarded Sartre's ill-health with fear and dread, and her own visible aging with the objectivity of a scholar, but the changes in both of them evoked her pessimism and despair much more than mere acceptance. Sometimes she sneered when referring to "life's golden years."

Curiously, this pessimism in her private life coincided with the brief period when she was the most actively and vigorously involved in politics. In retrospect, she viewed having been thrust into contact with the militants of '68 as a fortuitous circumstance, believing that it gave her the confidence for her feminist activity in the decade when she became an outspoken internationally known advocate for women everywhere.

A statement she wrote in her last volume of memoirs several years after the events of '68 reflects the pessimism she felt at the time: "I must confess that I am not one of those intellectuals who were deeply shaken by May 1968."[5]

She had not paid much attention to internal politics since the end of the Algerian War, preferring to concentrate her energies on such things as the Russell Tribunal, which kept both her and Sartre occupied until the end of 1967. They were planning to begin 1968 with another trip to Cuba when he became ill with what was diagnosed as "an inflammation of the arteries." His doctor was not particularly alarmed by the "inflammation," but he still ordered Sartre to rest quietly at home for the next few weeks. Beauvoir was relieved with him ensconsed in his flat under the ministrations of Arlette, Michelle, Wanda and his less significant others. It left her free to enjoy Sylvie's company and continue her research for a nonfiction study about the physical changes that afflict aging women.

Originally it was supposed to be fiction, which she abandoned because she could not get beyond "a Françoise Miquel [her heroine in L'Invitée] sitting in her room imagining her demise." Instead, she steeped herself in whatever library holdings she could find about old age, took careful notes about physical changes she noticed in herself and her friends, and revived a long-dormant friendship with Lévi-Strauss so that she could use the materials he and his colleagues had assembled in their laboratory of comparative anthropology. This last she did warily, because she believed that Lévi-Strauss (along with Barthes, Derrida and Lacan) was now a serious threat to Sartre's supremacy in French intellectual life. Nevertheless, she was curious about these new methodologies, and while Sartre continued, in one of her favorite expressions, "to tend his own garden, Flaubert, and mainly ignore these new challenges," she wanted to know whether they had any bearing on her own work.[6]

While she did her research, she resumed more frequent contact with the Family (of whom she had seen relatively little in the last several years). She also broadened her acquaintances slightly, seeing several young women students from nearby Nanterre who were interested in *The Second Sex* and who kept her informed about what was happening among the students there. Nanterre was one of the new campuses built to assuage student complaints about the difficulty of admissions and lack of facilities in the older French universities; but outmoded bureaucratic policies remained unchanged, and soon this new facility was as overcrowded and its administration as unresponsive to student needs as all the rest. Beauvoir was keenly interested in what the students told her about contemporary university life in France. The idea of their actually demonstrating on behalf of their grievances fascinated her, as she would never have dreamed of expressing any such displeasure in her own student days. She relayed all this information to Sartre, hoping to distract him while he was still mostly confined to his apartment, but he listened with the detached interest of an outside observer and did not show any special interest in what she told him.

Beauvoir heard the news on her car radio when violence broke out at Nanterre on March 22. After she had finished her errands, she returned to her apartment and telephoned Sartre, as she did every afternoon they did not spend together, just to make sure that he was all right. At some point in the conversation, she told him casually to watch the evening television newscast, where he might perhaps see some of her student friends. In the meantime, a young sociology student, Daniel Cohn-Bendit (later to be known as "Danny the Red") appointed himself spokesman for a demonstration that occupied the administration building, and "the Mouvement du 22 Mars (M22M) was formed by spontaneous combustion."[7]

The campus was officially closed for three days, but violence persisted. An attempted assassination of the German student leader Rudi Dutschke in West Berlin, and rumors that attacks could be expected throughout the French university system from right-wing commando groups triggered further conflict, and Nanterre remained closed. Demonstrations spread to the Sorbonne, and when police charged into the crowds to make arrests students threw rocks and were bombarded in return with truncheons.

On May 6, Cohn-Bendit was summoned to appear before the Sorbonne's disciplinary council, and the French student league demonstrated in support throughout the Latin Quarter. All day long riots raged. The police were so brutal that people who had been only passersby aligned themselves with the students, who were beaten, assaulted by tear gas and set upon by fire hoses. In retaliation, the students hurled the cobbles from the streets at police and set fire to barricades of overturned cars. As the police moved in to arrest students, spectators joined the fray until it was unclear who was beating whom. On streets such as the Rue Gay-Lussac, where the battle raged thickest, horrified residents watched from their apartment windows, sometimes throwing water or garbage down onto the conflict below.

Beauvoir worked at home that day and, to pass the time until Sylvie joined her in the early evening, she turned on the radio:

> Europe No. 1 and Radio-Luxembourg were giving a minute by minute account of the battle in the Boulevard Saint-Germain: behind the somewhat breathless voice of the reporters could be heard the roar of the crowd and the crash of explosions. Extraordinary things were happening. . . . [The] riot had turned into an insurrection.[8]

The next day, thousands of demonstrators marched from the Place Denfert-Rochereau (just down the street from Beauvoir's apartment) to the opposite end of the city at the Place de l'Etoile, all waving red flags and singing the "Internationale." Beauvoir and Sartre stayed in their respective flats, she working on Old Age, he on Flaubert. At this moment, the students stepped in and co-opted Sartre.

Speaking of those who influenced the formation of his political views, Cohn-Bendit said that he and perhaps some of the others in M22M had read "Marx, . . . Bakunin, and of the moderns, Althusser, Mao, Guevara, Lefebvre." He admitted that "nearly all of the militants of the M22M [had] read Sartre," before affirming the movement's independence by declaring that it "was not inspired by any author in particular."[9] Nevertheless, Cohn-Bendit and the others sought Sartre's approval because, of all the intellectuals in Paris, they believed he had the greatest access to the media and could best publicize their cause.

On May 8, Sartre, Beauvoir, Colette Audry and Michel Leiris (among others) signed a manifesto urging the working class to unite with intellectuals in support of the student cause. The next day they joined Henri Lefebvre and Jacques Lacan to reinforce their message with a second manifesto.[10] Sartre's next gesture of solidarity was delivered on Radio-Luxembourg on May 12, when he urged students to take to the streets until they destroyed the university system as it was then constituted. Students mimeographed his speech and gave it away throughout the Latin Quarter. Their hunch had been right: Sartre's statements gave them maximum publicity and increased the momentum of their protest; as long as they had him on their side, they were largely in control of the media in France.

When the Minister of Education ordered the barricades removed from entrances to the Sorbonne, students immediately occupied it. Beauvoir was enthralled:

> Neither in my studious youth nor even at the beginning of this year of 1968 could I ever possibly have imagined such a party. . . . I often went there with friends, and we wandered about the cor-

ridors and the courtyard. I always met people I knew. . . . Young
or old, everybody fraternized.[11]

This was a very different attitude from the bitterness she expressed
during the protests against the Algerian War and the contempt she held
for the American position in Vietnam. Above all, it shows how detached
she was from the physical battles between students and police, as well as
from the ideological debates within student factions as they grew increasingly fragmented over how best to unify workers and intellectuals and thus
overthrow the ruling party structure. Interestingly, no one asked Beauvoir
to espouse a position, lead a cause or argue a particular view; even more
telling, all these differing factions wanted Sartre to use his voice and influence on their behalf, but none wanted his leadership or his vision. Sartre
had been reduced to a figurehead; Beauvoir was simply his shadow.

On May 20, Sartre was one of a number of writers who were invited
into the Sorbonne to discuss issues with the students. Beauvoir described
the event in *All Said and Done,* estimating the crowd in the hall at seven
thousand ("It was made for four thousand"), but other members of the
audience believe it was "more like two [thousand]." Both she and Sartre's
biographers make it seem that Sartre was, if not the only speaker, then
certainly the most important one. Other writers, among them Marguerite
Duras and Claude Roy, remember it as a forum in which almost all those
invited were given varying amounts of time to speak.[12]

Despite the fact that his doctor told him his blood pressure was elevated to dangerous levels and he should neither walk nor stand unless it
was absolutely necessary, Sartre was determined to attend the meeting.
The students called all the shots, demanding answers to their questions in
hostile and peremptory tones, addressing Sartre as "Jean-Paul," which no
one, not even his mother, had ever done. He did not respond to any taunts,
but remained quiet and composed, answering all their questions patiently,
affirming his solidarity time after time. However, he did not make "any
new declarations"; he was "mostly [a] supportive presence."[13]

All this happened in Beauvoir's absence. The crowds frightened her,
the room was claustrophobic and too hot, and she was concerned about
the normally high-strung Sylvie, who was nervous and wanted to leave, so
they and several others went to a nearby café, leaving a message behind
telling Sartre where to find them. He joined them later, walking unsup-
ported, surrounded by students who continued to harangue him for "not
being sufficiently Maoist," demanding that he put aside his study of Flaubert and write something on behalf of their cause. Beauvoir, horrified to
see him thus, stepped in, ended the discussion and comandeered a ride
home for Sartre, Sylvie and herself. The students were furious with her interference.

Beauvoir took no part in the demonstrations during the days that followed, and on June 10 she went to the Sorbonne for the last time. She was
disgusted with what she saw of the students there, believing that the politi-

cal momentum had disintegrated, to be replaced by "epidemics of lice" and "beatniks, whores and tramps, . . . drug-traffickers and even abortion." However, she still refused to lend her signature for an article on "the decay of the Sorbonne" which the sociologist Georges Lapassade wanted her to send to *Le Monde*, because she believed it was sponsored by the parties of the Right, with whom she would never cooperate. Later, when "the elections were a brilliant success for the Gaullists [and] the revolution was stillborn,"[14] she accepted it as the logical outcome of a rebellion doomed to fail by its very fragmentation and lack of definition. Any ideological disappointment she felt was mitigated by the personal freedom she now had to spend the rest of the summer driving her new car through France on a holiday with Sylvie.

Sartre bought a house for Arlette in the south of France and usually went there with her for several weeks each summer while Beauvoir and Sylvie went off alone on automobile trips to various parts of France, Spain, Sweden and the Austrian Tyrol. Arlette usually stayed on with her own friends when Beauvoir and Sylvie came back to collect Sartre. Then the three went on to Rome, where Sylvie now shared their annual vacation until the school year began. Sartre and Sylvie had their differences, mostly initiated by her competition for Beauvoir's attention in the face of Sartre's polite indifference. If Beauvoir had a good friend who wanted to take care of her as she had taken care of him, then he was happy; nonetheless, Sylvie mistook his ready acceptance of her place in Beauvoir's life as his way of goading her, and it made her frequently argumentative. Beauvoir often had to soothe Sylvie, assuring the young woman of how important she was. Beauvoir described it with a curious kind of honesty: "She was not always kind to him. She would not have it that he was ill, and some aspects of his behavior irritated her, while he would blame her for what he called her 'ill temper.' But none of this affected their relations in any way," she concluded, perhaps more hopefully than honestly.[15] However, all three principals were always on their best behavior in Rome, and these vacations usually passed tranquilly for all.

Beauvoir's direct dealings with the militants of May '68 were not entirely over: more than a year later, she would take to the streets in defense of free speech and the right of the Gauche Prolétarienne (Proletarian Left) to publish and distribute its newspapers. She kept, however, one lasting impression from her observations of May and June 1968. In a far-reaching 1984 interview discussing the condition of women throughout the world, she made this observation:

I believe that militant feminism grew directly from the '68 demonstrations, that properly feminist attitudes arose when women discovered that the men of '68 did not treat them as equals. Men made the speeches, but women typed them. Men were on the soapboxes and the podiums, but women were in the kitchen making coffee. So they got fed up with this because they were intelligent women. They realized that they would have to take their fate into their own hands and separate their battles from the larger revolutionary rhetoric of the men. I agreed with them because I understood that women could not expect their emancipation to come from general revolution but would have to create their own. Men were always telling them that the needs of the revolution came first and their turn as women came later . . . and so I realized that women would have to take care of their problems in ways that were personal, direct, and immediate. They could no longer sit waiting patiently for men to change the society for them because it would never happen unless they did it themselves.[16]

In the meantime, the censorship and seizure of leftist publications and the arrest of their publishers were a catalyst that spurred Beauvoir to direct action, something no other aspect of the student uprisings had been able to do. Governmental interference with the right of free speech inflamed her. "No editor had been arrested in France since 1881," she wrote. "What could be done against a repression as shameless as this?"

La Cause du peuple was a crude, four- to eight-page publication printed on coarse beige paper with red-and-black block drawings and print. It was subtitled a "revolutionary, proletarian, communist paper," and this information was printed between a drawing of Chairman Mao and a hammer and sickle. On March 22, 1970, the anniversary of the Nanterre uprising, Jean-Pierre le Dantec, its editor in chief, was arrested. Michel Le Bris replaced him, and he too was arrested within the following week. Alain Geismar, a young radical who had been instrumental in enlisting Sartre's support the year before, went to see him once again, and a luncheon was arranged for April 15 at La Coupole to discuss how Sartre could help them. Both Beauvoir and Arlette went there with him, as his health was now a matter of serious concern to them both; among the others were Geismar and Pierre Victor, as Benny Lévy was then calling himself.

The lunch proceeded along the same lines as Sartre's speech at the Sorbonne, with the students, according to Beauvoir, "questioning him rigorously, sometimes chastising him for not doing more to help them—worst of all, accusing him of not being sufficiently committed because he did not stop all his other writing and deliver his pen to their service full time."

She was worried about Sartre and wanted to take him away; nevertheless, the luncheon did not end until the students decided it was over. They kept up their imprecations until April 28, when they persuaded Sartre to become the new editor in chief. This meant that, by French law, he was responsible for the editorial content of the publication, and if it were to be found in violation of statutes and laws he was now liable to be arrested. Beauvoir insisted on sharing the risk. On each page of every issue, his name and hers appeared.

On May 1, the editorial committee printed a statement which was supposed to have been written by Sartre, but which they themselves wrote and he did not even see until the issue was on the streets. In it, they included the sentence "By assuming the functions of editor in chief, I hereby affirm my solidarity with all those actions intended to express the revolutionary impulse that moves the masses to action. If the government wants to take me to court, my trial will be political."[17] Beauvoir was horrified when she read it, and she rushed to Sartre's apartment. She insisted that he demand, if not a retraction, at least a clarification, but he was totally uninterested.

"He said to me, 'Do what you want about this, but leave me to my work,'" Beauvoir recalled. "From then on, I had to watch everything closely to see that they did not use his name wrongly, and, oh, how they hated me for it! I was accused of interference and much, much worse."

The next issue of the paper carried the correction which she insisted they print: "Sartre's letter should not have read 'I hereby affirm my solidarity with all those actions,' but instead 'I hereby affirm my solidarity with all the articles [printed within]."[18]

Her task of guarding Sartre's supposed expression grew when he accepted the same position at two other radical publications, Tout in September 1970, and J'accuse in January 1971. All this came about in large part because Raymond Marcellin, the French Minister of the Interior, led a successful drive in the French assembly to dissolve the Gauche Prolétarienne and outlaw demonstrations by them or on their behalf. Sartre believed he had no recourse but to side with the Maoists; Beauvoir, as usual, believed she had no recourse but to follow him. She expressed her reservations in the memoir she was writing during this time: "I am not so naive as to suppose that they will accomplish the revolution in the near future, and the 'triumphalism' of some Maoists seems to me childish."[19]

Despite her less than enthusiastic endorsement of their view, she still agreed to co-chair an association of "the Friends of La Cause du peuple" with her old friend Michel Leiris. When the police refused to give them the necessary papers to organize as a legal entity, they went to court and won. The next harrassment came soon after, when the young revolutionaries who took to the streets to sell the paper were arrested and jailed. Beauvoir and her friends decided to replace them: "What we wanted was not . . . to get ourselves arrested but to put the government in a state of self-contradiction by reason of its failure to arrest us."[20] They alerted as many journalists as they could reach, and set the date for June 21, Sartre's birthday ("He joked it was his present to himself," Beauvoir recalled). Then they and several others (including Michelle Vian, who believed strongly in the Maoist cause and took an active part in several key protests) headed off toward the busy market street, the Rue Daguerre. It was early in the evening, an hour when the streets were thronged with shoppers buying their dinner. From there, the Beauvoir-Sartre contingent, which had picked up supporters from the crowd, moved onto the Avenue du Général-Leclerc and passed through the throngs, shouting, "Read La Cause *du peuple.* Support the freedom of the press!"[21] By the time they reached the Alésia Métro, they had sold all their copies.

Just walking those few short blocks was quite an experience. At one point a policeman seized the papers Sartre was carrying, grabbed him by the elbow and steered him toward the Fourteenth Arrondissement precinct house. The crowd began to shout that the young policeman, who had no idea of the identity of the old man whose arm he clutched, was arresting a Nobel Prize winner. He dropped Sartre's elbow as if it were hot coals and tried to melt back into the crowd, forgetting that he still carried the confiscated papers. Sartre and his supporters ran after him yelling, "Stop, thief!" while news photographers snapped away and the crowd laughed and clapped. After that, the flustered policeman and his embarrassed comrades hurried off, leaving Sartre and the other lawbreakers disappointed that no one was there to arrest them. They decided to stop in a café to toast their victory and plot their next action.

Five days later, they went to the Grand Boulevards in the middle of the day, when they knew they would have a large audience. After they crossed up and down the street fouling traffic and handing out their papers, several excessively polite policemen asked them to get into a van and go to a police station—not to be arrested, but to have their identity papers checked. When they arrived, all were made to go in but Sartre, who was told to leave if he wished. A comedy of errors ensued when the others were taken to the booking desk. Beauvoir related it thus:

> "Apart from Monsieur Sartre, you're none of you public figures? Bertrand de Beauvoir—that's not the writer . . ." In a chorus we replied, "We are all public figures." "I don't know a single one of you." "It's not our fault if you are ill-informed: we are all public figures." "Well then, so am I," said the exasperated cop.

Beauvoir and the others soon realized that the police had been given strict orders not to arrest Sartre under any circumstances, only his companions. Since Sartre refused to leave until they were all safely back on the street, and since Beauvoir swore that she would be the last one out of the station, the police acquiesced and set everyone free. "We were having great fun," Beauvoir wrote, so much so that when they were outside surrounded by journalists and speaking into microphones for radio and television broadcasts, she lost her shyness and gave a relaxed and cheerful interview to all those who asked her to speak.

It was her last public appearance until the following January, when she and Leiris took part in a meeting staged by the Friends of *La Cause du peuple* to boast their success in besting the police, who had given up trying to confiscate the paper. Recounting the details of her "brief and happy career as a newsboy—news carrier? news 'person'? what should I call myself?,"[22] Beauvoir made her audience laugh at her escapades. She joked as she stepped out from behind the podium to illustrate how she tormented the frustrated policemen who had no idea of what to do with her.

She said they were unprepared for (as she described herself) "a sixty-two-year-old grandmotherly woman, her head wrapped in a turban and wearing a 'housedress.'" She demonstrated how she brandished her fist at the police in the militant salute, but said she hit them hardest with sarcastic remarks for which they had no answer.

Sartre did not attend the meeting with her. He was at home, working contentedly on the Flaubert manuscript, which he hoped to finish by the end of the annual Roman holiday that summer.[23] His health had been relatively stable for a little while, and it seemed that all his contact with the young Maoists was giving him renewed energy and even, at times, the old youthful zest.

For the first time since he adopted Arlette, things seemed to be settling down into a comfortable pattern. He had his evenings with Arlette, Beauvoir had hers with Sylvie, and they had theirs together in her flat, where they drank whiskey and listened to music as tranquilly as they had ever done. Even members of the Family laughed about their resemblance to an old, long-married bourgeois couple, but they were careful never to do so in Beauvoir's hearing.

Sartre had several new women friends who perked him up and therefore earned Beauvoir's approval, at least for the time being. He lunched occasionally with Françoise Sagan (with whom he shared a birthday, a great bond between them). Liliane Sendyk Siegel, the legal editor of *J'accuse* (i.e., the one who would be arrested in case of trouble), called for him each morning at whichever woman's apartment he had slept and took him out for breakfast. There was a young Greek journalist and student of his philosophy with whom he began a passionate liaison, but, like many of his affairs, this one eventually waned.

Knowing that he was happy and well cared for, Beauvoir was free to concentrate on her political action, her friendship with Sylvie and her writing. And since writing always meant expressing her own preoccupations, it seems curious that in a time of relative personal harmony she should have written so much about abandonment and loss.

When *La Vieillesse* (Old Age[24]) was published in France in January 1970, reviewers hailed it with remarkable unanimity of praise, all the more surprising because of the near-unanimous hostility with which they had attacked the two previous fictions. Acclaim for the book spread like the proverbial wildfire to England and the United States, and even though it was not translated and published in those countries until several years later, within one month of French publication both book and author were the subjects of several magazine articles.

Beauvoir told reporter Steve Saler of *Newsweek* that she had been thinking about old age in a personal sense since she was fifty years old.[25] She told Nina Sutton in *The Guardian* that she wanted to study old age because in *Force of Circumstance* she "hinted" at her "coming old age" and discovered that women, especially, were shocked.

Why should people be so terrified by the words themselves? Yes, old age is a reality. . . . And the contrast between this very obvious fact and the silence in which people were trying to cover it up struck me. . . . I found out that old age had never been dealt with from a global point of view before. . . . [No] existing book envisages the condition of old people as I envisaged the condition of women in *The Second Sex*.[26]

Nina Sutton thought Beauvoir's conclusions were "rather pessimistic." Beauvoir countered that they were instead "revolutionary" because "old age is a problem on which all the failures of society converge. And this is why it is so carefully hidden." Sutton then asked the obvious follow-up questions, to which Beauvoir gave answers ostensibly about herself. For example:

Does [old age] revolt you?
     It did: at the end of *Force of Circumstance* I talked as a rebel. But I don't any more. . . . I just keep my revolt for things I can hope to see bettered. . . . But the almost metaphysical fact of old age and death, I no longer rebel against. Even when it is my own.

In one way or another throughout her entire life the one overwhelming torment expressed repeatedly in her fiction is the fear of losing someone dear to her. Dearest of all, she claimed, was Sartre, and in the last few years she had faced losing him, first to another woman under circumstances she could not possibly hope to best—Arlette, in her official capacity as the adopted daughter and legal heir—and now, worst of all, to his own illness, infirmity and death.

She had been obsessed with the idea of death from the time she was a child. She thought of herself as old, or "too old" for one thing or another, for almost her entire life, from her sadness at being "too old" to sit on her mother's lap to her idea of herself as "too old" for physical passion at the begining of her affair with Nelson Algren, when she was in her late thirties. It was as if from her earliest rational moments in childhood she began to prepare herself for people and things to be taken away from her—from the wonderful apartment where she was born to her father's love and attention, to the loss of ZaZa, to name only a few of those that mattered most.

Once she met Sartre, it was much the same. "There has been one undoubted success in my life: my relationship with Sartre," she declared in the epilogue of *Force of Circumstance*. Yet, as early as 1947, when she was thirty-nine and so worried about Dolores that she was almost crippled with anxiety, she fantasized about a happy old age with Sartre, but then said abruptly, "I must have been even more shaken up than I actually recall to have taken refuge in such a far-off, well-behaved dream."[27]

So her fear of old age really had several different aspects to it: she was the woman who witnessed the changes in her own body with horrified fascination, powerless to stop the inexorable biological clock; hers was also the detached, observant eye of the writer and social critic who could understand and accept what was happening to her only by putting it into an impersonal context and then speaking of it personally. "Old age," she mused;

> but they are all young, these people who suddenly find that they are old. One day I said to myself: "I'm forty!" By the time I recovered from the shock of that discovery I had reached fifty. The stupor that seized me then has not left me yet. I can't get around to believing it.[28]

The sight of her own face upset her: "I loathe my appearance now: the eyebrows slipping down towards the eyes, the bags underneath, the excessive fullness of the cheeks, and that air of sadness around the mouth that wrinkles always bring." She was fifty-one years old when she wrote this, and photos taken then show a woman whose physical appearance is the exact opposite. Her skin is taut, her face unlined; no bags, no wrinkles. Hers is an enviable youthfulness—in everyone's eyes but her own. "Death is no longer a brutal event in the far distance," she wrote at age fifty-one. "It has already begun."

But whose death was she writing about in her memoirs in 1961 and discussing with interviewers in 1970? Her health was radiant, so it could only have been Sartre's. Panic overwhelmed her at the merest hint of losing him:

> What threats [death] includes! . . . Either I shall see Sartre dead or I shall die before him. It is appalling not to be there to console someone for the pain you cause by leaving him. It is appalling that he should abandon you and then not speak to you again. . . . one of these fates is to be mine.

Once again she equates loss with abandonment, and here abandonment is coupled with "not speak[ing] to you again." She dreaded the loss of Sartre's words as much as she feared the loss of his physical being.

In this depressing climate of abandonment and loss, of illness and old age, of all systems breaking down and finally failing completely, there were several things happening to contradict Beauvoir's despair. First there was Sartre's buoyancy: physically, he bounced back after every illness and attack; mentally, writing about Flaubert produced exhilaration and satisfaction, while dialogue with the young Maoists gave him boyish zest and energy. Then there was Sylvie, with her insistence that Beauvoir enjoy herself by going to the opera, the movies, on holidays, for weekend drives in the country. Any feeling of guilt she had about leaving Sartre turned quickly to gaiety in Sylvie's company.

Also, there was the satisfaction of the job well done she gained from speaking out on issues, of standing before an audience and spreading Sartre's message through her words. It gave her enormous pleasure to see that most of the people who now sought her advice, her presence and her efforts on their behalf were women. They had read her exhortative writings, and now they wanted her help in their battles for equality. Within a short time, feminist action became the most important outlet for her intellectual energies and the dominating factor of the last fifteen years of her life.

And so the despair in her two novels of contemporary women and her disappointment in the failed politics of the 1960s gave way to the ground-breaking study of aging, which subsequent generations of readers have agreed is much more "revolutionary" than "pessimistic." The political situation in France and the mixed response to her writings, along with the uncertainties surrounding Sartre's health, all combined to become the catalyst which caused Beauvoir to focus her attention on feminist issues and causes. In retrospect they made her remarks to the *Newsweek* reporter a most appropriate summation.

"My defense is work," Beauvoir said. "Almost nothing can prevent me from working. . . . I am on the edge of old age, but many of the things I wrote about do not apply to me. I hope to live to the end of my days."

She did.

FORTY

Women's Battles

I AM A WRITER," Simone de Beauvoir insisted. "I have written novels, philosophy, social criticism, a play—and yet all people know about me is *The Second Sex*. Granted, I am pleased that that book has had such an impact, but I want people to remember that *I am a writer!* A feminist certainly, and I do not deny the importance of feminism in my life, but first of all *I am a writer!*"[1]

In 1971, when she was writing the final pages of her last volume of memoirs, *All Said and Done*, Beauvoir was already trying to put her brief alliance with feminists into some kind of perspective.[2] She began her account with a simple declarative sentence: "At the end of 1970, some members of the Mouvement de Libération des Femmes got in touch with me; they wanted me to speak on the new abortion bill that was soon to come before parliament."[3]

This was the first time any group had specifically approached her for her support as an individual rather than as one half of the Sartrian couple. Less than a year later, she was a committed feminist, already attempting to explain how and why she had so immediately allied herself with this cause and what she had done to exhort others to follow. She called these few brief pages at the end of the 1972 memoir "a deliberate addition, written in the hope of gaining publicity for the cause and converts to it."

In retrospect, what most surprises about Simone de Beauvoir's public commitment to women's issues is its brevity: she made her first public appearance on behalf of a specifically feminist issue in 1970, and from that date she made herself available for any individual or group until her death in 1986. Although all of her writings contain a strong feminist underpinning, sixteen years of public support in a life of seventy-eight is a relatively brief period. Still, it was enough to make Beauvoir known throughout the world primarily as a feminist, secondarily as a writer. It was a situation that both pleased and troubled her.[4]

She stressed, however, that she was a writer for whom commitment was the all-important concept: "I had the obligation and the responsibility, having written *The Second Sex*, having expressed my belief in the literature of commitment, to make myself available in the service of women's battles. I just wish the one did not have to make the other vanish from people's memory."

So her initial response to "women's battles" came about not only because of her strong sense of "commitment" and "obligation and responsibility," but also because of her recent political activity, which had given her genuine enthusiasm for the fight. Although speaking publicly for political causes frequently caused her much anxiety, her attitude changed when she sold *La Cause du peuple* on the streets and then spoke about it in meetings of "the Friends." She was both surprised and pleased to discover that she felt comfortable raising her voice or marching at the head of a supportive phalanx, and from that time on she accepted almost every feminist invitation or entreaty that came her way.

There was one other reason, however, and it was equally as important as, if not more important than, those above. As always, it had to do with Sartre; this time with his health, now in an erratic swing of ups and downs. His decline coincided with her rise to prominence in the women's movement. "The timing of my work with women was not conscious, nor was it deliberate," she said some years later, "but it was certainly providential in distracting me from Sartre." All her feminist activity gave her satisfaction in and of itself, but it also provided a genuine alibi for entrusting much of the nurturing and nursing that Sartre needed to his retinue of other women. It gave her the buffer that she needed to soften the realization that he had begun the long arduous process of dying which she later described so movingly as "Adieux . . . the ceremony of farewell." It helped her accept that the life she lived now would be a "life set between parentheses."[5]

In the beginning, it seemed natural for her to move from leftist politics to feminist causes, as she told John Gerassi in a 1976 interview:

> A Feminist, whether she calls herself Leftist or not, is Leftist by definition. She is struggling for total equality, for the right to be as important, as relevant, as any man. Feminists are, therefore, genuine Leftists. In fact, they are to the left of what we now traditionally call the political Left.[6]

In 1971, as she wrote *All Said and Done*, Beauvoir traced the evolution of her feminist ideology, concluding that she may have modified or changed her feminist "practice and tactics" from those she had used in politics, but that nothing significant had happened to convince her that the premises identified in *The Second Sex* (already more than twenty years in print) were different or in any way deficient from what she was now seeing and experiencing firsthand.

"All male ideologies are directed at justifying the oppression of women . . . women are so conditioned by society that they consent to this oppression," she wrote in the memoirs.[7] This, says British scholar Mary Evans, "is radical feminism with a vengeance."[8]

It is remarkable that she wrote *The Second Sex* while living in relative isolation from other women and their problems, without the context of a feminist environment, yet Simone de Beauvoir succeeded in defining the central issues which are still the focus of international feminism today.[9] The years between 1950 and 1970 found her writing about a different subject in a different genre almost every time she put her pen to paper, but, even so, each of these works shows a growing political awareness of the problems faced by women within society.

The Mandarins was a book about postwar politics, certainly, but it was also about women, the choices they made in their relationships, and how their lives were conditioned by their culture. But at the same time as she wrote the novel, she was writing Privileges, two essays important for the development of her political feminism. "The Thought of the Right Today," an essay about right-wing politics in France, ostensibly an attack on Mendès-France and his government, is also a clarification of her attitude toward the bourgeoisie both as an economic class and as a theoretical body. "Must We Burn Sade?," another essay, deals with pornography and sexuality, as does the essay "Brigitte Bardot and the Lolita Syndrome" (later published as a separate book). By the late sixties and early seventies, all this led to a frenzy of articles, editorials and manifestos mostly stemming from Sartre's involvements, written at first in his defense but then on her own, in individual support of leftist causes.[10]

In March 1971, she told Helen P. Wenck that she was eager to write for leftist journals because it gave her "the opportunity to learn about a lot of things,"[11] one of which was the continuing development of burgeoning protest movements in the United States, especially those for civil rights and black power. "Angela Davis's letters are superb: Read them!" she exhorted her friend before she personally edited a selection published in Les Temps Modernes. She no longer had the steady supply of information about the United States that Algren had provided her, but her interest in American politics and culture was as keen as ever, so she depended on the International Herald-Tribune and whatever news magazines and books she could find in the English-language bookstores of Paris. Sartre inadvertently aided her when he began "a friendship" with "a young American girl" whose father was a foreign correspondent in Paris, and she became one of Beauvoir's most dependable sources of American information.[12] She studied these books and periodicals carefully, especially those pertaining to women, and adapted much of this information to both theory and action on behalf of French women.

The development of her feminism, like The Second Sex, had a strong American cast to its scope and methodology: having begun the worldwide resurgence of feminism by writing her book in France, she now studied what uses and responses American women made of it, in order to see what she could adapt back again for French women. When American feminists visited Paris throughout the 1970s, she was always eager to meet them and hear what they had to tell her, enjoying what she sometimes called "transoceanic feminist reciprocity."

By 1971, her person and her pen were both totally committed to women's issues, but there were still many women who questioned her commitment. These criticisms surfaced as early as 1960 and intensified after the 1964 publication of Betty Friedan's *The Feminine Mystique*, which, like its predecessor, was translated almost immediately into many other languages. As readers of Friedan's book turned to Beauvoir for leadership and guidance, it seemed to many that she was still only Sartre's dutiful disciple and had no independent, feminist voice of her own. Women could not help but question the degree of Beauvoir's commitment because, in a decade when her theoretical reflections and autobiographical introspection were setting off a chain reaction of women questioning themselves and their societies throughout much of the world, she was busily following Sartre everywhere from the meetings of the Russell Tribunal to Eastern Bloc and Latin-American countries. Most of her public statements during these years had the "me-too" quality that enraged those who believed she owed it to the cause to separate herself from Sartre.

By 1966, the continuing question of her feminism or the lack thereof became too strong for Beauvoir to ignore. Francis Jeanson expressed the charge best when he accused her of understanding the feminine condition only because she had escaped from it. She denied this, claiming she had never written condescendingly of women but had only depicted their true position in society. She insisted that "the only interpretations of my feminism that are false in my eyes are those that are not *radically* feminist. One never falsifies my views in drawing me toward *absolute* feminism."[13]

Several years after this, Beauvoir decided that the utopian revolutionary thought that had characterized much of the thinking of the French Left since the early years of the century (and which certainly helped to shape her initial philosophical outlook as she rebelled against her father's conservatism) had had no lasting effect. Along with this realization came her concurrent feeling that all extant socialist models had been disappointments but were still better than what she called "the Gaullist alternative." "We didn't vote for Mitterrand in '74 because we didn't believe that he would be any different from all the rest," she explained.

> I decided to support him [in the 1980 election] because I felt that despite all the mistakes his government would probably make, it would still be better for more people than [former president Valéry] Giscard d'Estaing's. I have always believed that socialism was a more enlightened form of government than the so-called liberalism of earlier [post–World War II] French governments.[14]

She tempered this remark with pragmatism:

> I knew very well that Mitterrand would not be able to conduct a real, genuine socialist revolution because he thinks too much like a capitalist and because a real, genuine socialist revolution would

bring too much violence and nobody wants that. I didn't expect him to perform miracles, but I thought that with his election all the people in France would have to be aware of the policies of socialism whether they accepted to believe in it or not.[15]

Beauvoir believed that the sudden and violent changes that shook Paris after May 1968 started the public's awareness of socialism, but that the upheavals held more resonance for the feminism of 1970 and later. This sort of reasoning led her to throw her energies into "countercultural" demonstrations, as she put it, and from then on she began to make herself available for almost everything women asked her to do. Acting separately from Sartre in the matter of issues and causes for the first time in her life, she expressed her individuality through feminist "solidarity."

The first major cause with which she allied herself was the fight for legal abortion in France. She chose to do so because "the law here is a disgrace . . . even if a mother is carrying a monster, she has to give birth to it."[16] On April 5, 1971, a statement signed by 343 women declaring that they had all had an abortion, which was illegal in France, was published in *Le Nouvel Observateur*. The list contained the names of ordinary women of all social classes and economic conditions, from every section of the country. Their signatures were collected by leaders of the protest, famous women in the arts, letters and government. Prominent among them was Simone de Beauvoir.

"The Manifesto of the 343" created an uproar, and naturally much of the attention was focused on Beauvoir, who had been the favorite target of right-wing writers and publications for years. Now they had proof that the advocate of free love was indeed the negative role model for French women they had always said she was. What they and almost everyone else in France (with the exception of the Family and a few trusted feminist friends) did not know was that Simone de Beauvoir had never had an abortion; however, she frequently allowed illegal abortions to be performed in her apartment when women had no other choice, and she often paid for them, whether they were carried out in her apartment or somewhere else.

"I was never pregnant, so how could I have an abortion?" Beauvoir said in 1982. "By the time I signed 'The Manifesto of the 343,' I was no longer a stranger to the threat of arrest or imprisonment—*La Cause du peuple* prepared me for that. I believed that it was up to women like me to take the risk on behalf of those who could not, because we could afford to do it. We had the money and the position and we were not likely to be punished for our actions. Like Sartre, I was now a sacred cow to the authorities and no one would dare to arrest me, so don't give me too much credit for bravery because I was untouchable. Save your sympathy for the ordinary women who really suffered by their admission."

In 1976 she explained why she was so willing to take the risks involved in espousing unpopular causes:

Those who have the most to lose from taking a stand, that is, women like me who have carved out a successful sinecure or career, have to be willing to risk insecurity—be it merely ridicule—in order to gain self-respect. And they have to understand that those of their sisters who are the most exploited will be the last to join them.[17]

So from the beginning her role in French feminism was much the same as Sartre's had been in politics with the young leftists; the only difference was that the feminists described her in more generous terms than the Maoists used for Sartre. She was "the spiritual mother of the young generation,"[18] whose physical presence or written support guaranteed a forum and often brought in converts to the cause. But as far as she was concerned, her main role was to take a prominent position in protests, if not to lead causes unpopular with the establishment in order to shelter other women from possible reprisals. She wanted to contribute by helping to identify further action and provide written agendas, both theoretical and active, thus supporting historian Stanley Hoffmann's belief that an important trait of French intellectuals is "the conviction that they are the conscience of society." Beauvoir's attitude exemplified what Hoffmann calls "protest intellectualism," a holdover from the eighteenth century, when "there was an imposed separation between the world of the intellectuals who were kept quite out of touch with practical politics and the world of power, which tolerated no participation."[19]

When Beauvoir began her feminist activism, these lines were not drawn so clearly. Political battle lines, that is, the traditional notions of Right and Left, had been confused for some time in France, and within each camp there were further splinters, fractures and outright divisions. By 1970, it was no longer clear when one said "the Left" what specifically was meant. When feminists began to demonstrate, they often found themselves aligned with political groups they had not planned to join, but with whom they nevertheless felt an affinity. Beauvoir described one such felicitous encounter when she marched in a women's protest for legal abortion which chanced upon the same route as a group of antiwar protesters:

Their demonstration had been forbidden, and some of them had the idea of joining us. Upon this our procession began shouting 'No children for cannon-fodder! Debré, you swine, the women will get you!' And we all sang the Internationale. . . . We danced in a round and there were more songs: it was a happy, companionable celebration.[20]

Also, Beauvoir was one of the fortunate intellectuals who had been involved at various times both directly and indirectly, willingly or reluctantly, in the world of practical politics and had frequently collided with the barriers thrown up by the world of power, which indeed brooked no participation from her or her company. Words were her weapon, social commitment was her chosen form of expression, and her method of retaliation had always been to write something exposing inequity and injustice wherever she found it.

From 1971 until 1974, she fully intended to write a book about the contemporary situation of women in France, with perhaps a chapter or two dealing with the situation of women throughout the rest of the world. She struggled with ways to describe her intention, but never quite found the proper terminology. She knew more what it was *not* to be rather than what it should become. It was "not" an update, a sequel or a reaffirmation—some of the terms she used to discuss the proposed work for which she never wrote a single word. All she was certain of was that this new work would not have a philosophical basis for analyzing the condition of women, as Existentialism had served to do in *The Second Sex*. Instead, she contemplated an economic analysis of woman's estate because she believed money or the lack thereof, on every level from the individual to the national, was what kept women from true autonomy. She described her intention in the memoirs, stressing the conditionality of the project:

> *If* I were to write *The Second Sex* today I should provide a materialistic, not an idealistic, theoretical foundation for the opposition between the Same and the Other. I should base the rejection and oppression of the Other not on antagonistic awareness but upon the economic explanation of scarcity.[21]

This was the belief she held to the end of her life, and the sheer magnitude of the project was what finally kept her from writing the book. She had just risen early every weekday morning for the better part of a year while she wrote *Old Age*, traipsing across Paris to the Bibliothèque Nationale, rushing inside with other researchers the moment the doors opened, in search of the best seat and the quickest access to materials. She knew she would have to do this all over again to write the new book, and, although she was initially willing, there simply was not enough time in her day anymore to do it.

Now there was a seemingly endless round of meetings convened by various women's groups to plan protests, organize demonstrations or send delegations to petition various government officials. There were also several other strains of activism concurring with her feminist involvement, a social activism that had been lifelong and a new one evolving since the publication of *Old Age*. All three, she said, are "the human problems which stare us in the face," and she described them as

> the status of women; the "three million underpaid, over-worked, over-exploited immigrant workers in France"; the homeless; old people; juvenile delinquents; prison conditions; and "the dreadful conditions in hospitals, the awful asylums for the people who are considered to be 'mental cases.' . . . On all levels, the fight is for justice and humanity. That is the essential battle."[22]

Her activism throughout this decade is impressive when viewed in isolation, but when it is placed within the context of her other activity it is phenomenal.[23] Besides "The Manifesto of the 343," she was a witness at the Bobigny abortion trial and the first president of Choisir, the pro-choice organization. She was prominent at the meetings at the Mutualité, held to denounce crimes against women. For a time, she was president of the League for the Rights of Women to denounce discrimination against women in the work force. And she was generous with time and money to fund shelters for battered and abused women. She conducted an inquiry for the leftist publication J'accuse, to help women injured in a factory accident at Méru in their fight for compensation. She sat in at the CET technical college, really a home where unwed mothers were shunted until their babies were born. Beauvoir was horrified by French law which placed these unwed mothers under the jurisdiction of their parents, thus giving the latter legal authority over the lives of their infant grandchildren.

She continued to publish in Maoist journals well into the eighties. She wrote many prefaces to books and long articles of investigative journalism, and instigated a column in Les Temps Modernes called "Le Sexisme ordinaire" ("Everyday Discrimination"), which took the press, politicians, advertisers and ordinary citizens to task for discriminatory language and sexist visual depiction of women.

From 1970 until the mid-1980s, she spoke out against governments with repressive policies, on behalf of citizens unjustly persecuted for differing political views, and she denounced crimes against nations or peoples. Petitions she signed include those protesting the death sentence of Basque nationalists, appeals to the Soviet government for Jewish immigration to Israel, and many Latin-American protest petitions including one against Castro's imprisonment of the poet Huberto Padilla, whom she and Sartre had befriended. She denounced Syria's violation of the Geneva Convention with prisoners taken in the Arab–Israeli 1973 conflict, in this instance by simply calling Le Monde to publish her statement; she had long since learned to use the establishment left-centrist press to further her needs.[24] Many of these protests may appear to, and indeed some do, contradict each other, but Beauvoir had what was to her a perfectly reasonable explanation for them all: "In any case, one cannot not sign."[25]

This attitude dominated her thinking on feminist issues as well, and was the reason she was frequently at the center of disagreements among warring factions. One of the most public concerned the journal known variously throughout its history as Nouvelles Féministes, then Questions féministes, and finally Nouvelles Questions féministes. Beauvoir agreed to be the directrice de publication, meaning again that she would take full responsibility in case the magazine ran afoul of government policies. By the late seventies, the editorial board was divided between those who adhered more to a leftist political perspective and those who espoused a separatist vision. Beauvoir, along with Christine Delphy, Emmanuèle de Lesseps and Claude Hennequin, was faithful to the former:

One's hope is that history will bring within society more profound changes than have appeared thus far, changes that will truly transform the rapport between men and women . . . all the things that have remained unchanged in spite of collectivization and the nationalization of the means of production in socialist countries. That is the leftist hope.[26]

Those who supported the latter included Monique Wittig, Colette Guillaumin, Noelle Bisseret, Nicole-Claude Mathieu and Monique Plaza. Their dissent from the others on the editorial board centered around the concept of *l'écriture féminine*, which two American feminists, Margaret A. Simons and Jessica Benjamin, discussed with Beauvoir. Simons asked whether the biological difference between men and women is an *essential* difference, or, more specifically, whether the biological given is the center of a woman's existence and acculturation. Beauvoir replied:

> Well, I am against this opposition. . . . In France also, some women have taken this stance. Here, there are a certain number . . . who exalt menstruation, maternity, etc., and who believe that one can find a basis there for a different sort of writing. . . . I am absolutely against all this since it means falling once more into the masculine trap of wishing to enclose ourselves in our differences. I do not believe that we should deny these differences; neither do I believe that we should despise or ignore them. . . . But one should not make the body the center of the universe.[27]

The interviewers asked whether Beauvoir was rejecting separatism because "it takes the biological fact as the social fact." She answered:

> Yes . . . it [is] playing man's game to say that woman is essentially different from the man. There exists a biological difference, but this difference is not the foundation for the sociological difference.

So the battle lines were drawn on the editorial board, and Simone de Beauvoir sided with the leftist group against the "separatists" (called by this name here for purposes of distinguishing them from the former). In October 1980, finding themselves at an ideological impasse, the entire board agreed to dissolve the publication by a legal agreement filed at the Prefecture of Police in Paris, and all were enjoined never to use the title *Questions féministes* again. Delphy, Hennequin and Lesseps persuaded Beauvoir to support them as *directrice de publication* in a new version of the old journal which they called *Nouvelles Questions féministes*, and the separatists immediately protested the use of the old name within the new. In a letter outlining their position, the separatists said they learned of the "breach of agreement" only through an interview Beauvoir gave in *La Revue d'en face* announcing the beginning of the new journal.[28] A delegation then sent a letter and later called on her, asking that she withdraw her support, but, in their words, she "refused to see anything wrong."[29]

Her own explanation, offered in 1982, was more specific than theirs: "Christine Delphy had become a friend of mine, a woman who shared my views and who frequently in those days approached matters as I did. It was only natural that I support her. Also, what those women are not telling you is that they are not only 'separatist,' but 'lesbian separatist.' Although I support every woman's right to choose how she expresses her sexuality, I cannot support any ideology which exalts one and excludes all the others."

From her very first demonstration to her very last position paper, the one thread running through all was Beauvoir's rejection of any group or ideology which limited freedom of choice. At the beginning of the decade she worked, for example, to legalize abortion in France because contraception was illegal: "Women who must find the courage for this most drastic of measures frequently are crippled for life and many are even killed. How much more humane for everyone if the unwanted life is prevented from occurring in the first place. Feminists choose the most drastic measure to fight for because such action usually results in more moderate gains as well. When contraception was made legal and easily available, then the need for abortion diminished."

As the decade ended, she found herself embroiled in a controversy that, given the particularities of French law, could have happened only in that country. It concerned the legal registration of a freedom so basic that it shocks anyone unfamiliar with the French legal system: words and terms hitherto in the public domain, such as "women" and "Women's Liberation movement" (in French des femmes, Mouvement de Libération des Femmes, and the acronym MLF), were registered by a group calling itself "Psych et Po" (an abbreviation for Psychanalyse et Politique—Psychoanalysis and Politics). Because it was legally registered with the Paris Prefecture of Police, no one was permitted to use these terms but this group, led by a practicing psychoanalyst, an adherent of Lacanian methods named Antoinette Fouque (who preferred to be known only by her first name). At that time her foremost disciple was Hélène Cixous, whose adherence to écriture féminine set her in direct opposition not only to Beauvoir but also to any other group calling itself "feminist," which to Antoinette, Cixous and company was a pejorative no matter how these other groups interpreted the notion of "difference."[30] Their action was contested by other factions, but, through a convoluted defense which concentrated on business concerns to the exclusion of political and ethical questions, Psych et Po won the case.

Other feminists prepared a thorough documentation of the case entitled Chronicles of a Deception: From the Women's Liberation Movement to a Commercial Trademark. They enlisted Simone de Beauvoir to write a preface, and thus once again she took full legal responsibility on behalf of women whose cause she supported. The pamphlet had a limited distribution, mostly to the French media, but it had the desired effect: by

March 8, 1982, the date proclaimed "International Woman's Day" by the Mitterrand government, news stories usually carried the disclaimer that MLF did not represent the women's movement, but only this small frac-. tious group.[31]

Beauvoir's involvement with feminist groups was often personally frac- tious as well. Almost as quickly as she began to work for Choisir in con- junction with the outspoken lawyer Gisèle Halimi (with whom she had co- operated on the Djamila Boupacha case during the Algerian War), Beauvoir began to quarrel with her. Beauvoir was frank in admitting that they were both strong-willed women who each wanted her own way, and since she could not always win, she simply quit. Although she usually went along with most things that various feminist groups felt strongly about, she still felt it her privilege to scold them when they insisted upon their original ac- tion or view. Françoise Pasquier, the forceful leader of the feminist pub- lishing collective Editions Tierce, sometimes felt the brunt of Beauvoir's ire, as did Yvette Roudy, whom Mitterrand chose to lead the Cabinet-level agency known as the Ministry for the Rights of Women. But in both these cases, as in many others, Beauvoir's ultimate belief in their cause kept them always in "solidarity."

These many different kinds of fragmentation within the French wom- en's movement were a disappointment to Simone de Beauvoir, but even more so was her recognition that since 1968 French feminism had rejected her own philosophical underpinnings for a totally different anthropological and psychological foundation. She did not argue that hers was more cor- rect than others, but only that she was suspicious of some of the more radi- cal precepts, such as Psych et Po's declaration that it alone was qualified to impose specific meaning upon language.

Two particular statements, however, both written by Antoinette, par- ticularly enraged Beauvoir. In 1978, Antoinette assaulted both socialism and feminism as "pacifist, reformist and progressive or supposedly revolu- tionary—both heirs of Western humanism . . . the two most powerful pil- lars of the patriarchy in decline, the final stage, well-known in history, of Phallogocentrism." In 1980 she made a further pronouncement: "The fem- inism of non-difference—sexual, economic, political—is the master trump card of gynocide."[32]

When Beauvoir was shown these remarks she was understandably furious, because they contradicted everything she had ever espoused, but beyond restating her own beliefs she had no argument to counter An- toinette's thesis. As Beauvoir aged, her views, always strong, dogmatic, and subject to change only on rare occasion, became hardened on permissible forms of feminist expression. It was similar to her earlier reluctance to accept Sartre's evolving philosophy, which she did only after much initial hesitation and recalcitrance.

A French politician, Brigitte Gros, spoke for many when she accused

Beauvoir of closed-mindedness, of holding fast to outmoded theories and ideas: "The intransigent feminism of Mme. Simone de Beauvoir is that of a woman from another time. The feminist solidarity of the women of my generation no longer has anything in common with that of our suffragist mothers."[33]

Gros's comment underscores the sad reality that young women in French lycées and universities today hardly recognize what a commanding presence Simone de Beauvoir was in the struggle for women's rights. And as for her writings, many admit sheepishly that they "know of" *The Second Sex* but have not read it; and of the many others who admit to having read "all" or "part of" it, most find it "out of step with recent theory."[34] The term "sacred monster," first used by one writer in semijest, was suddenly the most appropriate description of Simone de Beauvoir for many others who were exasperated by her continuing presence, which loomed so large over all issues pertaining to women.[35] Perhaps a further indication of how she has been relegated to a lesser position among French feminists is the way "Le Manifeste de 85," an appeal for the equality of women, uses the following introduction to describe each of the signers: ". . . 85 women, from Catherine Deneuve to Marguerite Duras, have chosen . . . to launch an appeal in favor of women's equality in salary, career and responsibility." Simone de Beauvoir's name simply appears on the list, hidden among other signatories.[36]

But the late Jacques Ehrmann, one of the first male scholars to assess Beauvoir's contribution, offered a thoughtful observation that is important for any lasting evaluation of her role in contemporary society:

> Simone de Beauvoir enables us to realize clearly something of in-estimable importance if we would understand current French in-tellectual history. Namely, that commitment has no precise mean-ing until it is placed in its historical and political context.[37]

Simone de Beauvoir, who spent most of her life in male groups cen-tered around Sartre's political concerns, found herself more comfortable in communal situations with women in her last fifteen years. Previously, she had been only a satellite to Sartre's shining star; now she was in a leader-ship role and happy to have assumed it on her own. She felt that her voice, powerful alone, was even more powerful when it was the focal point for a larger movement. In a 1976 interview she said:

> . . . in mass action, women can have power. The more women become conscious of the need for mass action, the more progress will be achieved. And, as to the woman who can afford to seek individual liberation, the more she can influence her friends and sisters, and the more that consciousness will spread, which in turn, when frustrated by the system, will stimulate mass action. Of course, the more that consciousness spreads, the more men will be aggressive and violent. But then, the more men are aggres-

sive, the more will women need other women to fight back. That is, the need for mass action will be clear. Most workers of the class world today are aware of the class struggle whether they ever heard of Marx or not. And so it must become in the sex struggle. And it will.[38]

Her recognition that women would have to assume male language and strategy stemmed from her observations of the 1968 demonstrations:

> . . . properly feminist attitudes arose when women discovered that the men of '68 did not treat them as equals. . . . They realized that they would have to take their fate into their own hands and separate their battles from the larger revolutionary rhetoric of the men. I agreed with them because I understood that women could not expect their emancipation to come from general revolution but would have to create their own. Men were always telling them that the needs of the revolution came first and their turn as women came later . . . and so I realized that women would have to take care of their problems in ways that were personal, direct, and immediate. They could no longer sit waiting patiently for men to change the society for them because it would never happen unless they did it themselves.[39]

Beauvoir had several thoughts about how "properly feminist" women could effect social change. She did not believe elected office was the answer, for it would only result in the creation of women who would assume the attitudes of men and lose solidarity with other women:

> Look at Indira Gandhi, and especially at Margaret Thatcher—she can make war as well as any man. No, I don't believe that women as heads of state will make any significant change in society because . . . the moment a woman gets power, she loses the solidarity she had with other women. She will want to be equal in a man's world and will become ambitious for her own sake.[40]

In 1978, she declared emphatically that "no political party then constituted, either left or right, offered a suitable forum for the concerns of women."[41]

Still, she worked hard for the election of Françoise Mitterrand in 1980 because "he promised, indeed fulfilled his promise, to create a Ministry for the Rights of Women." This did not mean that she had at least modified if not changed her opinion about membership in political parties and elected office for women: "not necessarily," she insisted. Like Virginia Woolf, she measured her "political consciousness" through feminism, which was "her only true politics."[42]

In an early but important essay—important mostly for the wrongness of the argument—British scholar C. B. Radford urged Simone de Beauvoir's readers to pay very careful attention to her feminism as the central feature of her fiction and thought. He accused her of having abandoned restraint and common sense, saying, ". . . there is little doubt that neither international relationships nor feminism is likely to benefit from Simone de Beauvoir's more extreme political pronouncements."[43] This argument should have provoked widespread discussion, but it has largely gone unchallenged.

Beauvoir's pronouncements raise many questions without providing satisfyingly consistent answers. In the last years of her life, they grew increasingly radical, from the 1960 statement that "men are the enemy" to her angry rejection of Betty Friedan's "second stage," to her description of the present structure of society as "one of the great battlefronts for women today." Until the end of her life, she denounced childbearing and housework, but the only alternative she offered women was that they should refuse to do both. It is as if, having allowed her thinking to proceed logically up to a certain point, she then threw down a Lucite curtain: anyone who followed her reasoning that far could perceive clearly what lay on the other side, but she would not pass through her own barrier, nor would she continue the discussion with anyone who chose to do so. Beauvoir had no qualms about pointing out inequities—up to the point she chose—but in certain instances she felt no responsibility to provide redress or proceed to logical conclusions.

She saw the route to change happening not as Friedan would encourage, through a reconciliation of the personal with the professional, but through an initial separation in which women should change their lives radically:

> . . . women in greater numbers [should] refuse to allow themselves to be considered any longer as natural property to be controlled or dominated. Women will turn to feminism for their self-education, and the fight will begin. It will be a hard struggle because men will not easily surrender their freedom from housework and family responsibility and all the other burdens that typify women's lot today.[44]

How did she think this radical behavior should be focused? What can such radical action be if not political? This is exactly the point where she considers political action to become a necessity:

> I think that when women really begin to consider liberating themselves seriously, they will take more of an interest in politics. And since liberation is a democratic concept, they will become more democratic and thus more radical. Men must be made to understand that, in the final analysis, feminist behavior is not gratuitous but serious. Feminists are not useless and silly hysterics. They have studied and thought, and they want to make changes that will benefit all of society. Throughout the world, women are still being sold, beaten, raped, and killed, so this is a struggle that

must be in the minds of all women and be the basis of all feminist behaviour. We can no longer tolerate anti-feminist behaviour, from other women or from men.[45]

Thus, Beauvoir offers no concrete answers, no specific model or plan for action, no coherent theory upon which to build new forms of feminist behavior. When her contribution is assessed, only one thing is certain: there has been no other woman in contemporary literature so completely associated with the major events, causes and actions of her society. Language was her chosen instrument, the rhetoric of politics on behalf of social change has been one of her most intriguing uses of it. Considered separately, most if not all of her remarks make splendid sense; seen together, they create a kaleidoscope of image and reality, opinion and fact. Feminist ideology cannot ignore Simone de Beauvoir; as a historical fact, her importance should be unquestioned and undeniable. The real question will be how to assess her contribution and what use to make of it in years to come.

FORTY-ONE

Between Dread and Hope

T HROUGHOUT THE DECADE of the 1970s, when all her public activity was on behalf of women and her private time was centered around her deepening commitment to Sylvie le Bon, Beauvoir chose instead to describe her life in one succinct sentence about Sartre: "I wavered between dread and hope."[1]

The decade started well enough, with his declining health temporarily stabilized. He delivered the manuscript of *The Family Idiot* to his publisher in October 1970 and was content to bask in a subsequent period of euphoria, pleased with work he believed done well. Although he had cut down on both food and drink, he continued to smoke his usual two packs of rough Boyard cigarettes each day and to consume nearly a fifth of Johnny Walker scotch every night. He insisted that such "moderation" was not harming his health any further, convincing those close to him because they wanted to believe what he told them.

Still, there was no real cause for concern besides what was now known as the "normal" fluctuation in his health, which had been going on since 1954 when he was first hospitalized for high blood pressure during a trip to the Soviet Union. He had been diagnosed then as having arteriosclerosis, a progressive hardening and shrinkage of the arteries which inhibited the flow of blood to his heart and brain, but except for taking various medications prescribed in the years since, he had done nothing to change the way he lived. His lifelong attitude toward his physical condition was simply to ignore it and live life fully for as long as he could. At the beginning of 1971, his most obvious infirmities besides the deteriorating vision in his sighted eye were rotten teeth and a "bilious" liver, both annoying but not life-threatening. It was only when abscesses made it difficult to eat that he consented to have the worst of his dental problems treated. He was relieved when the upper plate he was fitted with did not inhibit his speech, because his greatest fear was that he would no longer be able to speak in public.

At loose ends, with no new work to consume him, Sartre became the recipient of too many earnest petitions and peremptory demands. In the past, he had always had Beauvoir to run interference for him, but now she was absent a great part of the time, preoccupied by her own interests—or, more accurately, Sylvie's. These mostly centered around weekend excursions to country inns outside Paris, or season subscriptions to the opera (which Sylvie adored), or the movies, and the longer holidays in Sylvie's academic calendar, when they left Sartre in Arlette's care and went off alone together. Added to this were the long hours Beauvoir spent in meetings organized by various feminist groups and her prodigious activity on their behalf; all of which meant that the time she had to spend with Sartre was greatly diminished, and therefore so, too, was the protective buffer she had always provided.

No matter what the request or what was his initial response, she had always known how to interpret what he really wanted and never hesitated to step in and speak for him. It made people furious and she knew it, but what they thought of her mattered far less than what Sartre wanted. His whimsical smile, the shy, apologetic shake of the shoulders, the upturned palms, all indicated to others that sweet, gentle Sartre was powerless to argue with brusque and tough Beauvoir, but it was mostly a facade, a game they both played to make sure that Sartre got to do only what he wanted.

Now that Beauvoir was busy elsewhere, Sartre no longer had this convenient excuse, so he turned instead to Arlette, whose main personality traits were docility and compliance. With Beauvoir, Sartre had always "to think, to do," but with the waiflike Arlette he had "only to be."[2] With Beauvoir there was always a manifesto to issue, a speech to make, a cause to support; with Arlette he could play piano duets, watch television or read detective stories.

But he also needed Beauvoir, or else—now that her attention was divided between him and Sylvie and, to a lesser extent, feminist activity—someone like her. Into this breech stepped Benny Lévy, with Beauvoir's blessing, Arlette's full acceptance and Sartre's delight, but this was after several frightening episodes concerning his health.

There had been several minor scares, but the first dangerous one occurred on May 18, 1971. Sartre's apartment on the Boulevard Raspail was on the tenth floor of an old building with an elevator that was frequently out of order. To keep him from walking up the ten flights of stairs several times a day, which he insisted he was well enough to do, all his women friends agreed that if he had to leave the apartment for any reason he would spend the rest of the day in Beauvoir's flat; if the elevator was still not working by nightfall, he would sleep there as well.

On this particular afternoon, it seemed to Beauvoir that he must have suffered a "slight stroke"[3] the previous night. His legs buckled under him if he tried to walk, so she installed him in her apartment on one of the sofas on the main floor because she worried that he might fall if he tried to mount the tiny spiral staircase that led to her sleeping area. At first she attributed his slurred speech to too much whiskey drunk during the afternoon, but then she noticed that his mouth was distorted and he had a severe facial tic between cheek and eye. Eating was impossible, but nevertheless he drank a great deal of whiskey, spilling as much as he consumed. At bedtime he insisted despite her protests on climbing the staircase and following his usual routine.

When Liliane Siegel came to take him to breakfast the next morning, they went instead to his doctor. Tests revealed that blood was not properly circulating through the left side of his brain, and the condition was exacerbated because Sartre had not taken his medication for more than two months. The doctor forbade him to walk at all, let alone up ten flights of stairs. Sylvie drove him back against his wishes to Beauvoir's flat, where she played one record after another in a vain attempt to divert him from wanting to return to his own apartment. He either dozed off or was indifferent to their attempts at conversation. His right arm was almost paralyzed; he tried to smoke but was unable to make his lips firm enough to grasp the cigarette, which kept falling to the floor. The elevator in his building was temporarily repaired, so they took him home. The next day, the indomitable Sartre, despite the doctor's warning against walking, got out of bed and insisted on lunching at La Coupole. His mouth was still so twisted that he could not keep the food from dribbling down his face, and Beauvoir blushed for him as friends, acquaintances, enemies and tourists all stared openly at the pathetic old man.

Eight days after his first seizure, on May 26, Sartre was so completely recovered that he could walk without aid, his face had relaxed into its normal contours, and his disposition was so much improved that he sang, laughed and entertained Sylvie, Beauvoir and Bost, who had come to visit. The only trace of the illness was his weakened right hand, but even so he could still play the piano or hold a pen for short periods of time.

In June there was another painful nuisance: cysts and abscesses on his tongue made speaking and swallowing all but impossible until oral surgery and antibiotics improved the situation. Beauvoir tried to console him by telling "Poor Sartre" that he was having a terrible year, with "troubles all the time."[4]

> Sartre replied, "Oh, it doesn't matter . . . when you're old it no longer has any importance . . . you know it won't last long."
> "You mean because one's going to die?" Beauvoir asked.
> "Yes," he said, "it's natural to come to pieces, little by little."

His tone was one of such complete detachment that, to Beauvoir, "he already seemed to be on the far side of life. . . . He was losing interest in his own fate. He was often if not sad then at least remote."

But once again he bounced back: Sylvie invited him to celebrate his sixty-sixth birthday on June 21 at a dinner in her apartment, and he and Beauvoir raised their glasses in celebration while Sylvie clicked many happy photographs. Then the two women went off alone for five weeks of driving through southern Italy, leaving Sartre to spend his usual two not-so-restful weeks with Wanda in the south of France, followed by three weeks to recover under Arlette's soothing ministrations. He and Arlette ended their holiday in Switzerland, where Arlette put him on the Rome express and wired Beauvoir when to collect him at the Termini Station.

"Before I caught sight of him he hailed me," Beauvoir wrote later. "He was wearing a light-colored suit and he had a cap on his head. His face was swollen—one of his teeth was abscessed—but he seemed in good health." Then he told her what had happened to him in her absence. On July 15 he had had an attack more serious than the one in May. His mouth was even more disfigured, and not only was his arm paralyzed, but he had also lost feeling and sensation in it.

"Arlette took him to a doctor in Berne, and Sartre utterly forbade her to let me know," Beauvoir wrote in *Adieux*; but in 1981 while she was correcting the manuscript she wondered aloud whether or not to include a sentence saying she suspected that it might well have been the other way around: that it was Arlette who refused to let her know about it.

"Sartre was indifferent to much that went on around him," she said, "but he always had enough strength, of mind as well as of body, to pay attention to the feelings of the women close to him." But, according to Beauvoir, he never regarded Arlette in this way, and after the adoption he never discussed her. Several years after this conversation, Beauvoir was asked whether Sartre's refusal to discuss Arlette elevated her to the same status within his life that she, Beauvoir, had always held. After a long silence she said flatly, "Some people thought so." Beyond that she would not elaborate.

In the first years of his final illness, Sartre was aware of how the two women bickered over him. Those who knew all the principals well recognized how careful he was not to inflame either one of them, often taking responsibility or blame to dampen flames of anger or smoldering resentments. In the last ten years of his life, Sartre found himself playing the role of mediator more than ever before, extending it from Beauvoir and Arlette to Benny Lévy and the Family as well. He played it willingly, but, more important, with detachment: he never forgot the good manners of his bourgeois upbringing, and was scrupulously polite until the end.

Being in Rome was always good for Sartre's health, and this year it was made even better because part of the terrace off their customary suite of rooms had been enclosed in glass and air-conditioned, so he could spend the hot afternoons taking his siesta in comfort. Beauvoir and Sylvie fussed over him, and, for once, he listened to them. He wore a hat to shade his balding head, took his medicines and gave up all stimulants except a single glass of wine with lunch, one beer with dinner and two late-night whiskeys. Even the abscesses responded to medication, and all seemed well except for a few traces of the earlier attacks: stiffness in his face which impeded chewing or swallowing, and occasional slurred speech. Beauvoir, who was always overly optimistic where Sartre was concerned, was "overjoyed" with his partial recovery: "Sartre is entirely recovered from the little crisis of last May and works on a third volume of his Flaubert," she wrote to Helen P. Wenck.[5]

When they returned to Paris, he thought himself so well that he joined Genet, Foucault, Claude Mauriac and others in a march to protest the murder of an Algerian boy and demanded to take his turn doing the same work as the rest of the committee. Genet was not fooled by Sartre's enthusiasm and did not mistake it for what it was not, good health. He told Beauvoir to keep Sartre at home because, while his spirit was eager to cooperate, his body was a mere husk and his mind frequently unable to grasp the most basic details of the protest.

In early December, apropos of nothing in the conversation, Sartre suddenly turned to Beauvoir and said, "I've used up my store of health, I won't live beyond seventy," and for the rest of the month he was depressed. He insisted on discussing what he wanted for his funeral and was adamant that he not be buried between his mother and his stepfather because he so detested Monsieur Mancy. Most of all, he insisted that he be cremated. The conversation "paralyzed" Beauvoir, "this time by fear."

She did what she had always done to cope with illness and death: she wrote about it. She bought a little notebook and began to fill it with the details of Sartre's fluctuating health, noting his blood pressure, bodily functions, and medications prescribed and taken or not as his whims dictated. For almost ten years she kept detailed notes about his visits to doctors, which woman attended him and when and for how long, what he said about himself and what others thought about his condition. After his death, she published it as the first part of *Adieux: A Farewell to Sartre*.

If she had plotted graphs in this notebook, it would have been filled with peaks and valleys. One of the first would have been this depression, which was followed by a surge of optimism. "Perhaps we'll live a great while yet," Sartre said in January 1972. "Now and then," Beauvoir wrote, "he would make a laughing allusion to his 'miniplegia,' but he did not think that he was in any danger."[6] He took part in demonstrations, wrote prefaces, and worked with the Maoists while she was at the height of her involvement with Choisir and often away on feminist projects. There seemed no reason not to continue their usual pattern of daily life, and so they did for several months. She went to the provinces to speak on behalf of Choisir, confident that the Maoists were keeping his mind occupied and that Arlette, Michelle, Liliane and the others were amusing him the rest of the time.

In May, returning from Grenoble, she was told that Sartre had had a setback. For more than a month he had been attending daily meetings of the Gauche Prolétarienne because *La Cause du Peuple* was failing financially and the leadership was undecided about whether to suspend publication. There were interminable meetings during which the sixty-seven-year-old Sartre was harangued for not dedicating himself to the creation of a major work on behalf of the Maoist cause. They wanted, at the very least, a rousing manifesto that would inspire converts—at the most, a new system incorporating all their beliefs into a rational combination of Marxism and philosophy. Sartre was exhausted by all this argument, probably (among other reasons) because he realized that no single work would satisfy all the differing factions. He had no intention of abandoning Flaubert for a Maoist manifesto, but his commitment to the cause was so great that he tried not to let anyone know it and gamely attended every gathering. He usually sat quietly, smiling and smoking, and let them berate him for as long as they wanted.

A new, dangerous trend began to worry Sartre's friends: he had always consumed a great deal of alcohol, but now he drank to the point of inducing stupor, secreting bottles in other people's apartments as well as his own, furtively ordering extra bottles in restaurants, sneaking into dining cars on trains or darting into cafés on streets, sometimes commissioning virtual strangers to buy liquor for him.

One evening in early summer, when Beauvoir was away working for Choisir, Arlette was out of town with a friend, and no one else was available to stay with Sartre. Arlette settled him into her apartment before she left, because she had a television set and he did not. It was one of the rare evenings in his long lifetime when he was entirely alone, and Sartre took advantage of it to get falling-down drunk. Like all the rest of the Family and the Women (as Beauvoir was now loosely calling everyone but herself), Arlette had begun to ration the amount of liquor she kept at home, but Sartre managed somehow to secrete his own bottle, and the first time he was alone he drank it all. André Puig, who was now working as Sartre's secretary, came to take him home and found him drunk on the floor, passed out. Puig managed to lead Sartre the short distance from Arlette's apartment to his own, but not before he fell, bruised his lip and bloodied his nose. His face, which had been distorted, was now disfigured as well.

Beauvoir scolded him. "Why, why did he do this! What need did he have to hasten the destruction of his body!"

"I like [whiskey]," he said evasively. "[To be drunk] is pleasant."[7]

Beauvoir and Sylvie went off alone for the month of July, and in August they met Sartre in Rome at the train station. He arrived drunk, having consumed several bottles of wine on the train, but when he sobered up his blurred speech and stumbling gait seemed worse than when they had seen him last in Paris. Then one day, as they were out for their customary afternoon ice cream, Sartre announced, "Cats have just pissed on me. I went too close to the balustrade and I was wet on."[8] Sylvie laughed and Beauvoir blushed.

Sartre was incontinent and had been for some time, but he had always had a ready excuse, such as that he had been clumsy and spilled his tea in his lap, or else he said nothing and Beauvoir tactfully did the same. "Cats pissing" was finally too much for her. "You are incontinent," Beauvoir said. "You ought to tell the doctor." She was astonished when Sartre told her he had already done so and then nonchalantly blamed his lack of control on the medication he took to lower his blood pressure. He was not embarrassed, he told her, because "when you're old you can't expect too much, your claims have to be modest."

Sartre was born with strabismus in his right eye and lost all sight in it after a serious bout of influenza when he was four years old. The vision in his left eye was always less than perfect, and he had had problems with it all his adult life. His eyes were the only part of his body to which he gave routine medical attention—an annual examination—and on May 21, 1973, he was found to have lost 40 percent of the remaining vision in his only sighted eye. For a writer, it was the worst possible tragedy. He could only read large print with the aid of a powerful magnifying glass, and then only for very short periods of time. In July, following another dizzy spell, his eyes were reexamined and the diagnosis was thrombosis in a temporal vein and triple hemorrhage at the rear of the eye.[9] Treatment with an assortment of medications resulted in about 20 percent of his vision being restored. With the false hope that he would soon regain the rest, Sartre tried to write.

Playwright Georges Michel described the pathos of the old man who kept on writing despite the fact that neither he nor anyone else could decipher pages that were "entirely illegible . . . words written one atop the other, lines that veered up and down like certain writings done by the mentally ill." What struck Michel most, however, was "the serenity with which he spoke of his misfortune." He asked Sartre whether he would be able to write again. "I won't write anymore," he replied. "I can write, but I can't read what I write."[10] He had finally given it up.

He could not see to eat either, and he depended on others to cut his food and guide his hand to glass and plate. He could no longer do much of anything for himself and was almost totally dependent upon his women friends, who parceled him out among themselves, especially during the summers.

At the end of June, Beauvoir and Sylvie went to Arlette's house in the village of Junas to take Sartre as far as Venice, where they would pass him along to Wanda and stay on for a holiday of their own. They stopped in Menton for lunch, and Sartre was so withdrawn that when he spilled a steaming bowl of fish soup all over himself "he observed the accident with an abnormal indifference, as though he no longer felt responsible for his actions or concerned by what happened to him."[11]

Once in Venice, he asked to stay in Beauvoir's hotel so that he could spend his mornings with her because he was an early riser and Wanda was not. He was a fitful sleeper and unable any longer to see the hands on his watch. Sadly, he awoke on several occasions while it was still dark, dressed himself and woke Beauvoir to go for their morning coffee, only to have her tell him that it was still the middle of the night.

Beauvoir makes a telling remark in *Adieux* directly after relating this incident: "Then one morning I left him. I did not want Sylvie to get bored with Venice, which she was beginning to know by heart." As if to justify her decision, she added that although Sartre said he would miss her, their mornings together "did put him out a little."[12]

The truth of the matter was more complicated. At the age of sixty-five, Beauvoir was in glowing health, and Sylvie's companionship gave her even more zest for life. Sylvie liked Sartre and accepted the special place he held in Beauvoir's life, but she was a young woman not yet thirty and impatient with old age and infirmity. Also, her primary allegiance was to Beauvoir, so she could not help but resent, or at least to mind the many services Beauvoir felt it her responsibility to perform for Sartre. For Beauvoir, it required a delicate balance to keep the high-strung Sylvie from blurting out cutting remarks that, despite Sartre's growing detachment from life, still hurt him and embarrassed those around him. In this instance, as in others in the next seven years, she decided that discretion lay in avoiding possible confrontation by removing Sylvie from the scene. Initially this tactic made Beauvoir feel guilty at not tending to Sartre's needs and, even worse, having such a good time traveling with Sylvie while he was being shunted like so much baggage from one woman to the other. However, Beauvoir never brooded long over things she could not change, and very soon the two women were enjoying themselves fully like two happy schoolgirls on an outing.[13]

Beauvoir always left her itinerary with Arlette when she was away with Sylvie, but Arlette and Sylvie disliked each other, and Arlette was cold to Beauvoir as well, although their animosity was not yet openly expressed. On several occasions when Sartre was taken seriously ill, she did not notify Beauvoir, who said little then, but after Sartre's death it became something she held against Arlette, saying she "resented" her for "trying to usurp my rightful place with Sartre."

In August, she and Sylvie were in Rome to meet him at the station. Beauvoir was distressed when she saw him because his eyesight had deteriorated dramatically in the few short weeks they were apart. She decided not to wait until they returned to Paris but to consult an oculist at once. There was another hemorrhage in the middle of the eye as well as incipient glaucoma, and a newly diagnosed pre-diabetic condition. Sartre was good about controlling his intake of alcohol, but insisted on ordering ice cream, pasta and sweets in huge quantities every day. He could not see the food or control his lips to make them close around it, and because of false teeth he could not chew it properly. Consequently, food rolled down his face and onto his clothing, and when Beauvoir admonished him to wipe his face or let her cut his meat, he grew as angry as a toddler in a high chair, determined to feed himself no matter what the mess. He also drooled, and when Beauvoir attempted to wipe the saliva off his face and shirt he said matter-of-factly, "Yes, I dribble," and "attached no importance to it."[14]

☐

Back in Paris in October, he was taken by Arlette to his regular oculist, who told him that because of the thrombosis he would continue to suffer hemorrhages in his eye and would never regain the degree of sight he had once had. Because his retina was damaged, he was fitted with an apparatus that was supposed to allow him to read as much as an hour a day by using lateral vision, but he was unable to use the clumsy device. He also found out that he was now seriously diabetic and had to be put on an entirely sugarless diet, which was not easy for him to follow. He had a new physician, who painted an ugly picture of his brain turning to mush if he did not stop smoking, and to placate him Sartre agreed to cut down. For a time he actually did, but soon he was back up to his usual two packs a day. He also insisted on a daily dose of whiskey, so Arlette and Sylvie both began to dilute it with water. He knew what they were doing but said nothing. Instead, he persuaded Michelle that in the condition he was in nothing could harm him much anymore; so she secretly bought him his whiskey, because she believed he had the right to decide what to do with his life and his body and resented the way both Arlette and Beauvoir made all decisions for him.

Nevertheless, they continued to do so, often without even consulting him. If reading was impossible, so, too, was living alone. Arlette decided that he had to move into a more manageable flat than the one in the dilapidated building on the Boulevard Raspail. Since someone had to be with him at all times, she decided that he must have two bedrooms, one for himself and another for whoever was on duty at night. She and Liliane Siegel found a suitable apartment in a new building on the Boulevard Edgar Quinet, just behind the Gare Montparnasse and overlooking the cemetery where his ashes are now buried. It was a plain modern box of a building with no decorative frills and two elevators, which they assumed meant that one would always be working. They were wrong.

All the women tried to make the move into a wonderful new adventure, but Sartre was depressed and showed no interest in anything they did, either with his furnishings or with his papers. When they took him to the Boulevard Edgar Quinet for the first time, the man who had spent all his life writing eight or ten hours each day said, "This is the place where I don't work anymore." Before Arlette made any decisions, Beauvoir announced that she would sleep there weeknights and that Arlette could spend the weekends. Liliane, Michelle and the others all took turns being with him during the daytime hours. He began a new affair with a Greek student and journalist, Hélène Lassithiotakis, and there was also a revolving list of young women of different nationalities who came and went with no set schedule. Most of these were students or friends of the Maoists or political hangers-on attracted to the idea of the great philosopher and writer; once they saw the unpleasant physical reality of what he had become, they usually went on to something or someone else. For Beauvoir, the important thing was that they amused and distracted him, no matter how briefly.

Despite all this feminine attention, Sartre was still depressed. One day Beauvoir found him sitting at his writing table staring blindly into space. She asked what was wrong and he said "in a heartbroken voice . . . 'I have no ideas.' "[15] He was working on an appeal for funds for *Libération*, the newspaper which he had helped to start in late 1972 and which had been operating on the proverbial shoestring ever since. Beauvoir described in *Adieux* what happened next: "I advised him to have a short sleep, and afterward we both worked on it together. He found it hard to concentrate, but even so he gave me the essential lines."[16] The subtext of this passage is that when she realized he would not be able to think of anything to say, she volunteered several possible ideas, he muttered a few phrases in response (the so-called "essential lines") and she wrote the appeal. She then read it to him, he made several suggestions, and they sent the text to the editor, Serge July, in her handwriting.

It was widely known that she had always been his most severe critic and that he had never published anything without first subjecting it to her exacting editorial scrutiny. It was less well known that sometimes, especially during the years when he was overextended and taking drugs to stimulate creativity and give him stamina to complete the many tasks he had allocated himself, she frequently studied the situation, volunteered the idea and suggested an outline or framework, and sometimes the actual language as well. Yet she never considered this to be either collaboration or deceit, and since she was careful to destroy many of the notes or working papers for these projects, the actual degree of her contribution to his writing and thinking will probably never be known.

But things were different in 1974, and what frightened her when she prepared the *Libération* appeal was that she might have to do more of this sort of thing in the future simply because he would not be able to think anymore, let alone write. The question was, should she allow Sartre's audience to see how their spokesman had deteriorated and thus risk that they might abandon him if he was no longer useful to their cause? She knew that abandonment would kill him faster than any physical infirmity. Or should she try to cover for him, to hide his true condition for as long as possible? Simone de Beauvoir was a woman who could erase certain aspects of her own life from memory if she did not want to face them, but she was also that rare bird who simply could not lie. The thought of possibly having to do so with something so important as Sartre's writing frightened her as much as did the fear that Sartre would no longer be able to write by himself.[17] She thought of these concerns and berated herself for "abandoning him to one such as Benny Lévy," but that came later, because in the beginning she thought "he was a godsend."

Her enthusiastic welcome of Benny Lévy into Sartre's life had to do with another, more immediate concern: the amount of time she spent each day with him. After spending the night, she saw to his morning routine and prepared him to go off to breakfast with Liliane or Michelle, the two who most regularly alternated this task. Beauvoir usually spent the rest of the morning reading to Sartre unless he had meetings or interviews, such as those which resulted in the later published "three-way conversations"[18] with the then revolutionary journalists Philippe Gavi and Pierre Victor (as Benny Lévy was still calling himself, and as Sartre always addressed him). Even though André Puig was now employed as Sartre's secretary and was charged with his correspondence and his appointment calendar, Beauvoir took it upon herself to keep a watchful eye on Puig, often to his annoyance. It may have seemed that Sartre did little more than visit doctors, nap and spend time with his women friends, but this was also the period during which he made a film with Alexandre Astruc and Michel Contat,[19] helped to launch *Libération*, gave frequent interviews, met sometimes daily with the Maoists and took part in demonstrations. He also appeared in a lengthy court procedure when the right-wing newspaper *Minuit* sued him, and was upset when the judge fined him an insulting one franc. He still took extensive vacations and continued to meet, especially during the Roman sojourns, with intellectuals and activists who wanted his collaboration in projects that he worked on there and after his return to Paris. It was a routine that would exhaust a healthy man, but it was the only one Sartre had ever known. Without it, Beauvoir believed, "he would have turned his face to the wall and died. It was imperative for us to keep his mind occupied."

However, the strain of all the extra care he needed was taxing her own reserves. Getting him up, shaved and dressed each morning required considerable time and strength. He was often disoriented, so it was a slow and laborious process. After that, she had her own correspondence, appointments, writings and meetings to fit in around her daily responsibilities to Sartre. Sylvie never came to the Boulevard Edgar Quinet because she did not want to see Arlette, so Beauvoir's time with her was limited to the weekends and one or two early weeknight dinners. Even Beauvoir's robust health faltered under all the extra work and unfamiliar routines and settings; she was exhausted. Into this breach stepped Benny Lévy, whom she welcomed.

He was still using the alias Pierre Victor to elude the police and the haphazard surveillance they kept on former '68 revolutionaries. A slim, slight Jewish refugee, born in Cairo but stateless, a Maoist *gauchiste*, he slunk around Paris thinking he was eluding everyone with dark glasses and a false beard while telltale strands of his thinning brown hair peeked out from under a cap to give away his disguise; once or twice he tried a wig, which called even more attention to his appearance. He looked ludicrous, but friends took him seriously because of his questing, jousting intelligence.

In the beginning, he was just one of the "Young Gauchistes" to Sartre, a loose grouping that included (among others) Alain Geismar and Philippe Gavi. "I like them," Sartre told Beauvoir frequently, with more enthusiasm than he showed for almost anything else in his restricted universe, "I like them because they make me feel *young*, that our cause is the same, that the fight goes on." Beauvoir elaborated: "Sartre was on Benny Lévy's side because of what Benny represented for his future. Since he could no longer project himself into action, he projected himself into 'Pierre Victor,' the revolutionary, militant intellectual. He influences (women especially, especially Arlette) because he loves to talk; oh, he talks so well, and remember, Sartre could only listen. Benny Lévy does not write well simply because he was not, could never be close to the equal of Sartre's intelligence. But remember, too, Sartre could no longer read and, because of the problems with oxygen not going to the brain, sometimes he could not hear or think clearly. He was deluded by his illness into thinking Benny Lévy his intellectual equal."[20]

Lévy's status in France was precarious, and each month, uncertain of what the outcome would be, he had to present himself at the local prefecture of police to renew his residence visa. His Maoist colleagues were concerned that eventually he would be deported, because all attempts to legitimize his status, even letters from the head of the École Normale Supérieure, were rebuffed. Geismar and Liliane Siegel decided to ask Sartre to help Lévy attain citizenship, thinking at first only of a letter or petition bearing his name. Then Liliane, who had worked closely with Lévy on Maoist causes and had been personally involved with him, thought of a better solution: if Sartre were to employ Lévy as his secretary and pay him a monthly salary, he could not be deported arbitrarily without government officials risking that Sartre would cause a public outcry. It guaranteed Lévy ironclad protection, and as he was otherwise unemployed and without income, he agreed that it was an excellent proposal.[21]

When she was alone with him, Liliane outlined her plan to Sartre, who was thrilled because he thought Lévy's assistance guaranteed the support he needed to finish the final volume of his study of Flaubert. It seemed a "godsend" to find a young man who was both "intellectual and militant activist" and who actually wanted to work with him.[22] Puig, who worried that there would be nothing for him to do, was told that he could continue to be Sartre's "ordinary secretary,"[23] but Lévy would be Sartre's amanuensis, alter ego and, in the most positive sense, intellectual counterpart and equal. In exchange for such companionship, Sartre would pay him the equivalent of eight hundred dollars a month, an excellent salary in France during the early seventies, and incredibly high compensation for the part-time position of reading aloud a few hours each day; never mind that Sartre, already supporting several women and a collection of itinerent hangers-on, was so badly strapped for money that he could not afford to buy himself a pair of shoes although his own were in shreds.

Sartre was not the first to tell Beauvoir of his decision: she heard it on the telephone when an ebullient Liliane called. Soon there was another call, this time from Arlette, who was furious that Lévy was hired, fearful that he would manipulate the blind old man to do his bidding. Arlette compared him to Ralph Schoenmann, Lord Russell's last secretary at the International War Crimes Tribunal, who said, "Lord Russell insists that . . ." whenever he wanted to have his own way.[24] Beauvoir, who did not know Lévy other than to greet him on a few occasions at Sartre's flat, blithely ignored Arlette's concern: "Sartre was very happy at the idea of working with Victor. And it suited me, no longer having to read aloud every morning. I had a little time to myself once again."[25]

But in 1982 she said, "My selfishness was stupid! Stupid! I sacrificed my peace of mind for the rest of Sartre's life just to have a little more time to myself, for me and Sylvie. When the American feminists told me the expression 'penny wise and pound foolish,' I said yes, that is what I was, because I had already heard the warning signals and I refused to listen."

She already knew the widely circulating accounts throughout the intellectual Left of Lévy's enigmatic place within the Gauche Prolétarienne and his role as a Maoist leader. He hid behind the pseudonym Pierre Victor because, being stateless, he feared reprisals. He seldom signed the articles he wrote, never attended meetings unless he was sure that only the most trusted intimates would be present, and thus "acquired the troubling, mysterious image of the occult and powerful Maoist leader, energetic but invisible."[26] His male colleagues viewed him along a spectrum that ranged from uneasiness to suspicion; feminists in the movement despised him for treating them as unworthy of being taken seriously for any task more important than making coffee or passing out leaflets. Because Sartre had established Liliane Siegel so firmly among his other women, many of his friends resented her relationship with and what they viewed as her total dependence on Lévy. Perhaps all those who suspected his propensity for Machiavellian machinations were correct to do so, because Arlette, his initial enemy, fell under his sway, while Beauvoir, his defender, ended by despising him.[27]

Lévy's employment began in much the same manner as that of all the other men who were Sartre's secretary at one time or another. Like them, he was not given a key to the apartment, so he rang the bell at 11 A.M. every day and waited for someone to admit him. Beauvoir often left before he arrived, which meant that he had to wait in the hallway until Sartre heard him and opened the door. She usually left Sartre ensconced in his oversized armchair, which faced away from the window so that the bright light (all he could see) would not hurt his eye. All his life, Sartre did not like to be alone, and now, without sight, the stillness and absence of sound were frightening, so Beauvoir always left the radio tuned loudly to France-Musique. Sometimes Lévy had to pound repeatedly until he penetrated Sartre's stupor long enough to be heard. In a conversation with Annie Cohen-Solal, Lévy described it:

It was a constant struggle against death. At times, I had the impression I was there to fend off sleep, lack of interest, or, more simply, torpor. . . . [At] first, what I was really involved in was a sort of resuscitation. . . . It was very hard, and strenuous for Sartre to learn to depend on others . . . I often thought of quitting . . . because I doubted he would ever succeed. And yet, despite all these difficulties, I persevered because, deep down, I was convinced that this struggle against death was his only way of feeling alive.[28]

Lévy worked hard to arouse Sartre's intellectual interests. His techniques ranged from simply modulating his voice to shouting theatrically as he read. At times he wheedled and cajoled Sartre for his attention, at others he shouted or insulted. Arlette was sometimes so alarmed that she actually confided her concern to Beauvoir, describing how she would intervene to offer refreshments or volunteer "to do anything to diffuse the tension in and on Sartre." But Sartre liked it, and told a number of his friends that he enjoyed the no-holds-barred element of confrontation in their daily jousting matches. "I like working with Victor," he said. "We have fun together. We really bawl each other out."[29]

At first they worked on the Flaubert, with Sartre speaking his thoughts and Lévy recording them, or with Lévy reading what he considered relevant texts. After the first few years of Lévy's faithful attendance, they moved on to general questions of history, mostly concerning the French Revolution. And, as Lévy became disaffected from his earlier revolutionary ardor and turned instead to an intense inner scrutiny of himself as a Jew, they worked on topics of interest initially only to him, of heresies and Gnostic texts. In the final years of Sartre's life, they dealt with what Cohen-Solal describes as "purely ontological questions," many designed to make Sartre question and affirm his own partially Jewish identity through the Schweitzer side of his family.[30] When news of this reached Beauvoir and the Family, they were terrified that Lévy had succeeded in capturing Sartre's failing mental faculties for his own personal gain. This was when they began to speak of Lévy as the "wily, manipulative Machiavellian" and to fear what Sartre might do or say.

As if to prove their suspicions correct, it was during this time that Lévy grew close to Arlette by playing on their mutual beginnings as displaced African Jews adrift in France. As Lévy grew more interested in the Talmud, he and Arlette engaged in a project of learning Hebrew and reading texts and scriptures together in that language. Often, when his daily stint of reading to Sartre was finished, he stayed on to work with Arlette while Sartre either listened or dozed, depending on the always fluctuating state of his health. Arlette began to preface all her decisions concerning what should be done for Sartre with a sentence that usually began that Lévy said or thought something or other was best and she agreed. By 1975, her trust was so great that whatever Lévy wanted was generally done.

Meanwhile, Beauvoir had very little idea of what was happening because she was at the height of her feminist and political involvement and was also trying to maintain her allegiance to causes she was sure Sartre would have supported. In November 1974 she signed and affixed Sartre's name as well to a manifesto of thirty other intellectuals (among them Raymond Aron, Eugène Ionesco and Arthur Rubenstein) accusing UNESCO of trying to exclude Israel from participation in the organization. Lévy gave her his hearty (and needed) approval. Lévy also approved her work within *Les Temps Modernes* to form a committee charged with setting up an international commission to investigate the prison death of the German revolutionary Holger Meins. She took many of the editorial duties upon herself for a special issue of the magazine entitled "Women Listen to Each Other" which was so popular that it was later issued as a separate book by Gallimard, but to this Lévy was indifferent.[31]

In 1975 she was awarded the Jerusalem Prize at the annual Paris Book Fair. In her address, she said this prize meant more to her than any other except the Goncourt, and that by accepting it she was registering a further protest against UNESCO and demonstrating anew her solidarity with Israel. She interviewed Sartre for a special issue of the magazine *L'Arc*, which was originally supposed to be only about her and her work, but which she insisted be enlarged to include "the Women's Struggle." It endeared her to many differing feminist factions and was one of the actions that drew her into a leadership role as the most prominent French feminist of the time. She also began laying the groundwork for what became the 1975 Mutualité meetings to protest discrimination against women and the imprisonment of dissenting militants, and to argue for the release of political prisoners worldwide.

Still, both she and Sartre had a feeling of only marking time, of going through the motions. "I have the feeling of perpetually living the same day over again," he told her. "I see you, I see Arlette, various doctors . . . and then it is all repeated." He spoke of the recent French elections, when Mitterrand lost to Giscard d'Estaing, saying that even that had failed to relieve his general gloominess. "I told him I had much the same impression [about working] with the feminists," Beauvoir said. "It's age," was his response.[32]

The point was that, despite her wholehearted belief in feminist issues and causes, her involvement was to some extent really a subterfuge that allowed her to evade the reality of his decline. Shortly before her death she reflected on the last decade of her life, and offered the possibility that if Sartre had been in good health she might have relaxed her lifelong militancy and commitment in favor of enjoying herself. She wanted "to put it on the record" that feminist involvement was her "godsend" during the time when she "watched Sartre die a little every day."

It was exhilarating to see how women throughout the world looked to her for leadership. She enjoyed entertaining the continuing procession of international acolytes who made their way to the Rue Schoelcher. But at the same time she also had the nagging feeling that, as with Flaubert's *Salammbô*, "the pedestal is too big for the statue."[33] To become revered after so many years of being considered a scandalous woman and writer was a little disconcerting. "Saint Simone is a hard part to play," she said in

1981. Worse was the knowledge that since the ascendancy of critical theory as expounded by Barthes, Derrida and Foucault, or—to her thinking even worse—Lévi-Strauss, intellectual theory seemed to be largely bypassing Sartre's contribution. But along about 1975 and for the next several years, there seemed to be a resurgence of interest in his work. "It seems that I'm growing famous again," he told Beauvoir, taking obvious pleasure in the fact.[34] It gave her "a great feeling of relief."

There was a temporary stasis in his condition in mid-decade, when Beauvoir thought him "transformed" and they conversed again with the same intensity as they had done before his illness. A new friend, the German feminist Alice Schwartzer, prompted some of their conversations because, after coming originally to interview Sartre, she came again periodically to interview Beauvoir.[35]

Sartre began to talk about writing the continuation of The Words, and Beauvoir suggested that it might be helpful if they tape-recorded some of their conversations which he could replay when he was either alone or with Lévy, thus triggering his memory for things he might wish to write about. They decided to do it formally, and agreed that their summer holiday in Rome was the perfect time and place to begin. "That will cope with this," he told Beauvoir, gesturing toward his eye "with a heartbreaking gesture."[36]

These became the "Conversations with Jean-Paul Sartre," an exceedingly long collection of interviews comprising the second part of Adieux, in which she asked him questions about his childhood and early life, his politics, writing, philosophy, relationships with men and other women, and much more. They are direct, personal and honest, but they are also sentimental and redundant. Beauvoir claimed to have edited them, but her personal involvement was so great, her feeling that every word Sartre uttered so important, that in 1986 she believed she should have "surrendered perhaps some little part of [her] emotional attachment to a more impersonal editorial eye." Beauvoir does prompt too much; she is peremptory in other places, instructing and correcting him as to what he really means with any number of answers to her questions; frequently, she cuts him off when she does not want to delve deeper into a subject that he appears happy to expound upon further. "Don't let's talk about me," she orders during a long dialogue about his relationships with women.[37] Still, they are spritely, unguarded and thus an honest collection of remarks by Sartre, and, in the opinion of many, the last such that he made in his lifetime.

What makes these repetitive passages worth reading is that they demonstrate the easy camaraderie, the unorthodox but stable interaction between two remarkable people long used to communicating in a kind of emotional shorthand. "The real world," he tells her in one instance, "that was what I lived in with you," as if to say that all other people and things mattered less to him.[38]

FORTY-TWO

The Last of
the 1968 Demonstrations

BENNY LÉVY was twenty-eight years old when his relationship with Sartre became what many called "the corruption of a sick old man."[1] "It was a tug-of-war, and Sartre was the rope, but we held on," Beauvoir said. "We were not giving up, and so he sneered at us and dubbed us 'the Sartrians.' It was supposed to be an insult, meaning we were old-fashioned, out-of-date. He took positions against us, always more and more hostile. There was room for us all in Sartre's life, but he wanted to be the one and only. He persuaded Arlette to take his side, and, unhappily for Sartre, she did and he won."

In March 1980, Sartre agreed to the publication of another series of conversations with Benny Lévy, but this time without Philippe Gavi. Beauvoir had openly pitted herself against Lévy long before, but now she, the Family and certain members of the *Temps Modernes* board took it upon themselves to urge Sartre, whom they thought too befuddled to hold his own, not to engage in these conversations, let alone allow them to be published. They turned Lévy's insult into a badge of honor and referred to themselves as "the Sartrians."

The Sartrians were frightened by the many instances of Lévy's "paranoia," first toward the police, then toward anyone who dared to question his judgments, opinions or actions. He was the target of hostile criticism from others as well, beginning with his former allies the Maoists, who were critical of his "verbal dogmatism." In her biography of Sartre, Cohen-Solal collected what others thought of him: "a Talmudist astray in Maoism" (Pierre Goldmann), "the least humanist of all the leftists, a monster of cynicism and mysticism" (Roland Castro), "a philosopher enthralled by the law," (François Châtelet), "a moralistic fool . . . capable of turning a whole audience around with his perfect speeches and crushing intelligence" (unnamed former Maoist comrade). Maurice Clavel's judgment was the most chilling: "a man from nowhere, and maybe because of this, a redoubtable Sartrian."[2]

But Sartre saw none of this back in 1977 when Lévy's influence first reigned supreme, nor was he aware of Beauvoir's belief that "the battle lines were drawn." What Sartre thought was probably reflected in one of the discussions with Lévy that were published periodically in *Libération:* "Either I am a doddering old fool you want to manipulate or a great man from whom you expect to get food for your thoughts. These are two possibilities. But there is a third, and the best: we could be equals."[3] By this time, all the Sartrians believed that if Lévy had his way they would be far less than equal in Sartre's life.

Everyone knew that Sartre had been bored with *Les Temps Modernes* for years and that only Simone de Beauvoir's stubborn insistence brought him to board meetings. It was Beauvoir's idea to put Lévy on the board in the hope of reviving Sartre's interest. But this was just the excuse Sartre was looking for and he no longer came to meetings at all, saying Lévy could represent him. It was Arlette's fear of "Schoenmann speaking for Lord Russell" come true. All that Beauvoir succeeded in doing by putting Lévy on the committee was to cause a severe rupture between the Sartrians and Sartre.

By 1978, Beauvoir and Lévy were in hostile but guarded conflict. Because of his interest in Hebrew, he chanced upon the writings of Emmanuel Lévinas, one of the earliest French exponents of phenomenology. This led him to a study of the Cabala, and he decided that Sartre too should study it with him. It happened at the end of a year of serious health crises, when Sartre's blood pressure was at times higher than 250. He had severe pains in his legs, was often unable to walk at all, and was told by his doctors that if he did not stop smoking he would so impair circulation that he would lose his limbs in painful stages, first his toes, then his feet and then his legs. Still he kept on drinking, and declared himself unable to sit through a session with Lévy unless he was promised whiskey at the end of it. In combination with his medications, it left him disoriented and it so affected his bodily functions that he was incontinent again. On a number of occasions, Beauvoir helped him to change his trousers and cleaned his defecation while he either pretended to be or else—worse—was truly unaware of what he had done.

He was still surrounded by women, and "with naive self-satisfaction" he told Beauvoir, "I've never been so popular with women before."[4] However, some of the most important relationships were changing. Beauvoir forbade Michelle to spend the night and limited her to supervised visits because she continued to succumb to Sartre's pleas and bring him whiskey, which they drank together in happy complicity. He decided that Hélène Lassithiotakis no longer made him feel young and zestful and banished her from the flat. Even though he was in desperate financial straits, he continued her allowance—in effect, a salary that allowed her to stay on in Paris.

Despite Sartre's deteriorating health and finances, Lévy conceived the idea that he, Sartre and Arlette should all travel to Israel for a long weekend to see firsthand the results of Anwar al-Sadat's recent visit.[5] Sartre scarcely knew where he was going, had to be lifted onto the plane in a wheelchair, and spent most of the time in his hotel room. He did meet with Israeli and Palestinian intellectuals, but by Arlette's admission his conversations were "very superficial."[6] When they returned, he told Beauvoir that Lévy saw himself as "the one to keep Sadat's mission alive," and that he, Sartre, thought this to be "an excellent objective for which Lévy was well suited." She told Sartre she was aghast at "the idea of Benny Lévy as the new Messiah—the one for whom we all wait to bring peace to the land," but immediately regretted it because Sartre flushed and shortly after changed the subject. Above all, she wanted to avoid forcing Sartre to choose between her and Lévy, and she was afraid that any further comment such as this one would cause the breach she dreaded.

Lévy wrote an account of what they had done in Israel and sent it to Le Nouvel Observateur with both his name and Sartre's as the co-authors. Jean Daniel, the editor, was appalled by its sloppiness and alerted Bost, who was then working for the magazine. Bost was "deeply upset" when he read it, and phoned Beauvoir at once to tell her that he was on his way to her apartment with something "puzzling."[7] Beauvoir read it and was "roused to indignation." Despite Bost's plea to wait until she had calmed herself, she stormed over to Sartre's apartment and confronted him with the original text in her hand. She told several different versions of what happened next.

In Adieux, which she intended to be the official version of the last ten years of Sartre's life, she described herself as passing along Bost's request that Sartre withdraw the article because "it's horribly bad. Here at the paper everyone is appalled." In this account, Sartre's reply is " 'Very well,' . . . said carelessly." She then wrote that Sartre did not tell Lévy, so she did, after which "he flew into a rage. Never had he been so insulted," but for some time afterward they still kept up the pretense of cordiality for Sartre's sake.

She gave a more detailed statement to Cohen-Solal:

> "Indeed, the piece was worthless: they had spent only four days in Israel, not nearly enough time to formulate a clear idea of the situation. Sartre would never have done anything like that on his own. The text was really much too weak: Victor, who could not write, had taken advantage of Sartre's name to try to get it published. I told Sartre what we thought of the piece, and he told me: 'Then drop it, I don't really care about it.' "[8]

In 1982, going over this same ground, she admitted to "mixed feelings" about the incident: "Yes, of course I would be less than honest if I try to deny that it gave me a certain amount of perverse satisfaction when all the world saw how Lévy could not think logically or intelligently and could not even write well enough to hide it. But I knew the shame it would cause Sartre, and the pain too, when he saw his favorite disciple unmasked in the eyes of all the people who loved him [i.e., Sartre] best.

Bost tried to tell me that I should not be the one to bring this disaster to Sartre's attention. But I said I was always the one whom Sartre trusted most and so I was the one to do it. Perhaps I did it a little too strongly, but I had never had to be tactful with Sartre before. I always spoke my mind and I thought I should do so this time as well. Especially this time. Ah, well, in light of what happened, I suppose I should have followed Bost's advice. What mattered is that Sartre listened to me, and for the moment we prevented a tragedy."

Others saw the event differently. Bost remembers being troubled that Sartre, although polite, was unusually reserved at their next meeting. Pouillon remembers that "Sartre was very angry that we had created a situation in which we were forcing him to side with us and against Benny Lévy. None of us understood then how much of himself he had invested in this strange young man."[9]

Confrontation was inevitable. Shortly after their return from Israel, the *Temps Modernes* board met, with Sartre absent as usual and Lévy there to represent him. A heated discussion about the article ensued when Beauvoir, unaware that Sartre still had not told Lévy the reason why it was not being published, began to justify the reasons why the Sartrians had acted as they did. Suddenly she realized that Lévy knew nothing about what had happened; Sartre, avoiding confrontation as usual, had not said a word about it to him. It was made even worse when Pouillon and André Gorz (then calling himself "Horst"), jumped into the dispute, both to defend Beauvoir and to attack Lévy, who was livid with rage. Lévy fell back upon Maoist techniques for dealing with unruly members and demanded that all the board examine themselves, their past lives and their written works and then "write a confession, which only he would judge." Lanzmann, Pouillon, Beauvoir and the others laughed at the "posturing demagogue" who called them all "dead bodies, putrified corpses." Lévy stormed out, never to attend another meeting. After that, neither did Sartre, and if the others insisted upon telling him later about some matter they thought it important for him to know, he became so sheepish and uncomfortable that they stopped at once. From that time on, *Les Temps Modernes* was firmly under the direction of Beauvoir and the Sartrians.

She and Lévy never spoke to each other again. Because he was now spending so much time at Sartre's flat, she spent only the nights there and tried to leave as early as possible in the morning. "Sadly, sadly, what I did not realize," she said in 1982, "was that it was all deliberate: if he stayed with Sartre, then I could not. He was determined to cut me off entirely. I don't want to blame Arlette for this, but obviously he could not have done so without her consent." Until then, she wrote in *Adieux*, "Sartre's real friends had always been mine too."[10] For the first time in their long lives together, this was no longer true. Stories reached her of how Lévy, who lived in a communal home with his wife and others who practiced Orthodox Judaism, often took Sartre and Arlette there to dine. What rankled was that Sartre was said to enjoy these outings, sitting on the floor surrounded by young people whom he could not see, eating foods native to their African origins. Beauvoir believed it was only one of a number of activities planned by Arlette and Lévy to keep Sartre occupied and further removed from the Sartrians.

It did not end there, however. All over Paris, common gossip had it that the Sartrians had ganged up against Benny Lévy—that they as Goliath were determined to crush the little David. Just as in the Biblical story, public sentiment was with the underdog, which infuriated everyone else in the Sartrian camp, and they accused Lévy of starting the rumor in the first place. Pouillon's explanation is typical of them all: "Lévy presented himself as the object of a campaign of slander originated by all those who had been with Sartre for a long time. Never, not for an instant, did we say anything about him except, of course, among ourselves. Never did any of us speak publicly to denigrate him. To speak of an organized campaign against him—which he did—is a pure lie. . . . [It] was in his interest to have people believe there was a campaign. The only reason none of us worried about it is that he does not know how to write. He does it so badly and with such pain that I for one do not know how he will succeed in getting his ramblings to be published."[11]

Still, one thing remained sacrosanct between Sartre and Beauvoir: the summers in Rome. There they were free of the tension and bickering that governed life in Paris, and even the outspoken Sylvie learned never to mention Benny Lévy's name. Sartre usually returned rested, his condition stabilized in whatever degree of health he then possessed.

When they returned to Paris in the fall of 1979, Sartre immediately resumed work on a series of tape-recorded discussions with Lévy that were meant to be the basis of a book he described as the culmination of his life's work, the ultimate statement of his political and moral theory.[12] Beauvoir was frustrated because Sartre told her nothing about it except that it was in progress. It was humiliating to learn that her role as privileged first reader had been usurped and that Lévy had been elevated or, as she believed, had elevated himself to the role of Sartre's collaborator. Whenever she asked Sartre what they talked about, he either pretended not to hear her question or else spoke in generalities. Since she did not speak to Lévy, she swallowed her pride and asked Arlette, who was equally evasive. Whenever she asked Sartre whether she could read the transcripts, he told her that "nothing was quite ready yet," or else "You must ask Arlette about that."[13] It was "humiliating" to have to ask Arlette for permission to read them, but she did. She still felt it her duty to protect Sartre even when it seemed he did not care to be protected, and she was frantic to read these transcripts because she feared another contretemps like the 1978 article. Arlette always had an excuse ready, and her subterfuge always worked.

Even after Beauvoir found out the truth, that a friend of Benny Lévy's and not Arlette was in charge of preparing the transcripts, Beauvoir still treated the subject discreetly. When she wrote *Adieux* she said: "I should very much have liked to know about these conversations directly, but they were taped, and Arlette, whose job it was to decipher and type them, worked slowly."[14] Beauvoir never read any of it until it was too late to halt publication, but she could not have done so anyway, because Sartre insisted upon it.

It was one of the last, if not *the* last public act of his life. The conversations with Lévy had gone on for three or more years, and the expected completion date was sometime in the fall of 1980. With the exigencies of publishing—i.e., the transition from manuscript to printed page—the expected publication date would then have been sometime in mid-1981. Benny Lévy explained why this timetable was not followed in an interview with Annie Cohen-Solal:

"It was important that we be ahead of all political changes, and, at the moment, the political circumstance of a new right wing was becoming very threatening. So, we removed from our reflections that whole part in which metaphysics could have been expressed in a political language. Our discussions should have been published in the fall of 1980, followed by the foundations of our reflections, mostly hinging on Sartre's revision of the concept of 'being for others.' As our work progressed we would each jokingly wonder, 'How are *they* [the Sartrians] going to react?,' insisting on a 'they' at once terribly elusive and unavoidable. In any case, we were determined to avoid the tantrums of 1978; we thought they might be shocked, but we were far from envisaging the sort of violence that ensued."[15]

Lévy was responsible for instigating the last argument between Beauvoir and Sartre, and the one with the most tragic consequences for their fifty-year-long relationship. Aware of how she and Bost had sabotaged the 1978 article, he went in person to Jean Daniel with text in hand to ask him to publish it as soon as possible. In the meantime, Sartre felt he owed it to Beauvoir to let her read the long selection he and Lévy had extracted together which they wanted *Le Nouvel Observateur* to publish. With hindsight, she thought he did so because he wanted to diffuse her anger and keep her and the other Sartrians from trying to stop it. All that it did, however, was show her that he was ready to side with Lévy at her expense, and it made her furious.

"I thought I was prepared for anything where Benny Lévy was concerned," Beauvoir said in 1982, "but I was wrong. Nothing, nothing at all, could have prepared me for the shock of what I saw before me."

Many of Sartre's statements were self-accusative: when he had written about despair, he said, it was only "nonsense" which he discussed simply "because it was fashionable"; he had used the concept of angst, but "it did not correspond to anything for me."[16] Much of it is recantation or disavowal, particularly of *Being and Nothingness*, the primary system of Simone de Beauvoir's belief. Sartre wrote: "I kept the idea that everyone's life is ultimately a failure . . . and that leads to absolute pessimism. . . . Which I did not say . . . but I am obliged to affirm now." Beauvoir was astonished to read that Sartre now affirmed a morality based on "the idea of fraternity" connecting all individuals, a humanistic solidarity that sounded suspiciously like some of the naive Maoist texts in the '68 papers and pamphlets: "I left people too independent . . . Each individual is dependent on all others."

Sartre practically apologized because he had not treated "the reality of the Jew" in any of his major works, and said, "I now see men differently," before going on to affirm an identification of himself as Jew that was almost religious. But his ultimate, most un-Sartrian comment of all, was his acceptance of the credo that Benny Lévy had put forth as Pierre Victor in 1968:

> "Revolutionaries want a society which would be humane and satisfying to men but they forget that a society of this kind is . . .
> a society in which relations between men are moral. . . . Well,
> this idea of ethics as the ultimate end of revolution—it's by a sort
> of messianism that you can truly conceive it."[17]

All she could think of when she read the passage above was her earlier bitter comment about Benny Lévy as the new messiah.

Sartre sat impassively in his armchair while Beauvoir read the text. All the while, his demeanor was expressionless. "He knew I was there, of course, but it was as if he were alone. No emotion came from him. I was beside myself. I could scarcely see the text through tears of rage, I could not concentrate on what I read, because I was so upset. But what upset me most of all was the familiarity of his [Lévy's] address." Throughout the dialogue, Benny Lévy addressed Sartre in the familiar second-person *tu*. It was not the manner in which Lévy interrupted or corrected Sartre, or how sarcastically he dismissed Sartre's past writing and thinking that Beauvoir settled on as "the most distressing shock of all," it was the way in which he "so casually placed himself on equal footing with a genius like Sartre." It was Lévy's "arrogance" that made her explode with anger. But her entreaties to stop publication fell on Sartre's (almost literally) deaf ears.

She believed she understood Sartre's reasoning: that if she felt this strongly about Lévy's role in the dialogues, then obviously he had succeeded in becoming the "equal" Sartre hoped he would be and, by extension, the intellectual heir who would carry on Sartre's work after he was dead. The specter of Benny Lévy saying, "Sartre would have written, said, wished, or done" terrified her. She was determined to stop it no matter what Sartre wanted.

Beauvoir returned to the Rue Schoelcher and telephoned Lanzmann to tell him what she had just learned. Lanzmann was now fulfilling the role of confidant, amanuensis and spokesperson that Bost had played for so many years because Bost's hearing was failing and he was secluding himself from the rest of the Sartrians; he had even stopped going to meetings of *Les Temps Modernes* after so many years of faithful attendance. Lanzmann called the others on the board to ask for their public support, but only Pouillon rallied behind Beauvoir without first wanting to read the article. André Gorz insisted on reading it himself, and the next day he went to the offices of the *Nouvel Observateur*. Afterward he told Jean Daniel he would not join the Sartrians in "defending the Temple," meaning Sartre as they chose to see him. Nevertheless, Lanzmann continued to try to change the minds of Gorz and others on the board, but it all became moot when Sartre himself phoned Daniel:

> His voice was loud and clear, and he spoke with extreme authority. "I believe you are quite troubled . . . my friends must have besieged you. Never mind them. I, Sartre, ask you to publish that manuscript and to publish it in its entirety. . . . I know my friends have gotten in touch with you, but their reasons for doing so are totally wrong: the itinerary of my thought eludes them all, including Simone de Beauvoir."[18]

So the protection for which she risked humiliation and embarrassment was for naught, and the usurpation she tried at all costs to avoid happened anyway. In reality, Benny Lévy was the second person Sartre had chosen to side with instead of Beauvoir (Arlette was the first), opting again for youth and vitality against her dedication to and respect for all that he was. For Sartre, it was as if Simone de Beauvoir represented all that he had been rather than what he still hoped to become.

All their long life together Beauvoir had treated Sartre like a monument, a statue that she was determined would dwarf the pedestal on which it sat. All he ever wanted was to be like his childhood ideal, Pardaillon, the swashbuckling comic-book hero who was always rushing about from one adventure to another, a French Peter Pan flying forever in eternal youth. All through their relationship, Beauvoir had wisely, carefully insulated Sartre from having to choose between her and someone else, knowing instinctively that if he did she might well be the loser. Other women had issued ultimata and they lost every time. Now so, too, had she, bested by a "mere boy" certainly, but bested also by Sartre's desperate refusal to be on the side of anything but youth and change.

According to Cohen-Solal, Arlette believed that the disagreement upset Sartre very much, "nor is it sure that they ever fully made up in the two months [until] the end of his life." Cohen-Solal also accepts as true Arlette's comment that Sartre often referred to Beauvoir and Sylvie as "those two austere muses" who, when he lunched with them, according to Arlette, "did not speak to me once."[19] Perhaps Sartre did confide his most intimate thoughts to Arlette, but since no one else ever heard him voice any except the most playful and harmless criticism of Beauvoir, her remark must be considered in the light of her mutually antagonistic relationship with Simone de Beauvoir.

No matter what the personal cost to herself, Beauvoir needed the idea of herself and Sartre as the successful couple, the perfect representation of the contingent relationship. After she had invested her entire adult life in this, it was unthinkable that she would have surrendered to what she saw as "such lesser competition." Indeed, a further proof of this is the tactful "shading" of reality throughout *Adieux*, because by protecting her two mortal enemies, Lévy and Arlette, Beauvoir also protected her personal version of her history with Sartre.

Francine du Plessix Gray, writing of Marguerite Duras, has described perfectly what Simone de Beauvoir made of her relationship with Jean-Paul Sartre:

> . . . her principal concern has been the interplay of fidelity, memory and obsession. . . . Her central theme is that the power of our obsessions vastly supersedes our fidelity to the remembered *object* of our obsessions.
>
> Miss Duras's women identify so totally with the male object of their obsessions that their loyalty is ultimately a form of fidelity to the self. Their fixations far transcend any erotic longing, are almost mystical in their irrationality and fervor.[20]

Both Beauvoir and Sylvie denied that they treated Sartre any differently after the disagreement over Lévy than before. If anything, both insisted that they were more affectionate and solicitous after the text was published because they wanted to reassure Sartre that no matter what professional action he took, nothing would interfere with their personal relationship. "There was an argument, yes," Beauvoir said emphatically, "but there was never, never a break."

The first article appeared on March 10, 1980, little more than a month before Sartre died. Hurt and humiliated, Beauvoir said nothing except in private to Bost, Lanzmann and the other Sartrians. Several months later, as she wrote *Adieux*, she wanted more to protect her version of her relationship with Sartre than to retaliate. But when the biographies of Sartre began to appear and when several studies of her own life were in progress, she felt the need to describe more fully what had happened from her point of view. From 1982 until her death in 1986, in interviews and conversations for this book, she spoke about the Sartre-Lévy articles and their aftermath, each time refining her comments, but never satisfied that she had expressed herself properly. This is the account which she thought the most exact:

"If you read those interviews, you see Benny Lévy constantly interrupting Sartre. He does not let him finish his sentences, he corrects him, he taunts him, he makes him contradict himself. They are shameful because they are the persecution of a sick, tired, pathetic old man. Sartre could not see, he could barely hear, he had trouble following even the most simple conversation. And here is this Benny Lévy coming at him—taunt, taunt, interrupt, jibe—how could anyone believe that Sartre was capable of doing anything more than agreeing with whatever it was that Benny Lévy put to him? If he could not follow ordinary conversation, how could he follow sophisticated philosophical argument? Of course Sartre said yes, yes, to everything—he had been doing it for years with everyone else, so why not with Lévy? Benny Lévy makes him contradict everything he ever believed in, everything he ever championed. Many writers correct their earlier beliefs and they are the stronger for it, but Benny Lévy would have Sartre disavow everything, and what he did was criminal.

"It is true that I sometimes did not choose to follow Sartre's thinking in those last years, but I should have stayed with him and allowed him to argue as we did before, when we were both young and I was his privileged reader and trusted critic. He was an old and sick man, and naturally he was powerless before the youth and zealotry of a man seized by a fanatic idea. What pained me most of all was when they [Arlette and Lévy] told me he thought I had failed him. After all our years, that they could make him believe I would refuse to follow him. They said he refused to accept that I only did so because I wanted to protect him. I can't believe he could think this."

When the first article appeared, Sartre asked Beauvoir, perhaps to learn what she thought of it, whether anyone from the *Temps Modernes* board had discussed it at their recent meeting. She lied and said no, because she was afraid that if she told the truth he would want to know what was said and it would only create further distance between him and the Sartrians.[21] His response, "as if I were a little child, who had to be told gently something she did not want to hear," choked her with emotion. She remembered that he said, "You know, Castor, I am still alive and thinking. You must allow me to continue to do so." It was the closest he came to either explanation or apology, and because she did not trust herself to comment she said nothing. She remembered sitting on in silence, after a while wondering whether the blind old man in the big chair knew that she was still there. Then she went over, squeezed his hand, put her arm around his shoulders and got him ready for lunch. This demonstration of physical affection was her way of saying that all was well between them. After that, there was no need to speak of it again.

The last night that Simone de Beauvoir slept at the Boulevard Edgar Quinet was March 19, 1980. The next morning, at the usual hour of nine, she went into Sartre's room to begin the slow ritual of getting him ready for the day and found him sitting on the edge of the bed gasping for breath. He managed to tell her that he had been like that since 5 A.M. but was unable to call out to her because he could not move. She reached for the telephone at once, but service had been disconnected because he didn't have the money to pay the bill, not, as she said ungraciously in *Adieux*, because "Puig left the bill unpaid."[22] She was about to run down the ten flights of steps when the elevator finally lumbered up to Sartre's floor. From the concierge's she phoned the nearest doctor, and he in turn called the SOS emergency ambulance. Then she did something curious. She was not permitted to ride in the ambulance, and the driver did not know to which hospital the radio dispatcher would direct him, but, rather than return to her apartment to wait for a telephone call informing her where Sartre had been taken, she set off for a luncheon date with Jean Pouillon.

She learned before lunch that Sartre had been taken to the Hôpital Broussais, but she waited until after they had eaten before asking Pouillon to go with her. Sartre was in the intensive-care unit with a pulmonary edema, his lungs filled with fluid. He was delirious at first, dreaming that he and Arlette were both dead and had been cremated, or that his doctor had driven him to eat lunch with Benny Lévy at his suburban commune. Because he could have only one visitor at a time, Arlette decided that she would spend the mornings and evenings and Beauvoir could take the long afternoon vigil. To Beauvoir, this was a deliberately perverse decision because everyone knew that she kept her afternoons free for meetings. Since she was powerless to contest Arlette's decision, she agreed. She stayed until 6 P.M. or later, when Arlette came to see to Sartre's dinner or to admit Benny Lévy.

Within a few days Sartre was recovered sufficiently to start complaining about the hospital as if it were a bad hotel. He was eager to be released in time to spend Easter with Beauvoir and Sylvie at Belle-Ile in Brittany, but Beauvoir knew by then that he would never leave the hospital alive. His liver, scarred by cirrhosis brought on by years of heavy drinking, began to malfunction. This caused a variety of other problems, including the accumulation of fluid in his abdomen as well as his lungs, jaundice, and new circulatory damage to his brain. His diabetes led to bedsores and gangrene, and the cirrhosis brought on the dreaded uremia that had caused Françoise de Beauvoir so much pain during the last month of her life. The doctors told Beauvoir that Sartre was too weak to withstand kidney surgery. Even if he could have tolerated it, circulation to his brain would have been impeded, resulting in senile decay. "The only answer was to let him die in peace," she wrote.[23] All she asked was that he not suffer, and his doctors assured her they would see to it.

He slept most of the time during his last few weeks of life. It was as if all his bodily systems had broken down, including the ones which allowed pain to register. His only concern was money, and when he was lucid he was consumed by anxiety for all those he was supporting, telling Beauvoir to "see to it" that Arlette kept up their monthly stipends. He worried that Wanda and Michelle would be destitute, and asked Beauvoir to insure that their incomes would continue after he was gone. To a lesser extent, he worried about his funeral, but Beauvoir managed to persuade him that French Social Security would take care of it, because "he knew he had not one franc [at that time] and would die of embarrassment if he thought his friends had to pay for him" (in the end, she and they did just that). It seemed to calm him. "I saw that he knew the end was near and that the knowledge did not overwhelm him," Beauvoir remembered.[24]

On April 14, he was sleeping when she arrived to take up her afternoon duties. As she stood near his bed, he reached over and managed to grasp her wrist. Without opening his eyes he said, "I love you very much, my dear Castor," and tilted his face up to be kissed. She brushed his lips with hers and rested her cheek against his. He went back to sleep and did not wake up when Arlette came to relieve her. Beauvoir went home without any indication that the end was so near. Arlette had always had general instructions to telephone if there was any serious change in his condition, but she did not call that night.

The next morning when Beauvoir made her usual telephone call to inquire how Sartre had passed the night, a nurse told her that he had not awakened since she left and the doctors had told Arlette then that he was obviously in some sort of terminal coma. But Arlette had kept the information to herself, spending the evening as if it were any other routine change of shift. So the next day Beauvoir went to the hospital as if she too were taking up her usual afternoon post. At six, Arlette returned, and, trusting her to call if there was even the slightest change in Sartre's condition, Beauvoir went back to the Rue Schoelcher to wait. Shortly after 9 P.M. on April 15, Arlette telephoned and said simply, "It's over." Beauvoir was stunned, totally unprepared because Arlette had not shared any of the doctors' reports and she had no idea Sartre's demise was so imminent.

Sylvie had been sitting with her during the death watch on the Rue Schoelcher as she drank whiskey and took Valium in an effort to lessen the impact of what she knew would happen sometime soon but had no idea would happen that night. She drove Beauvoir, already sedated from whiskey and drugs, back to the hospital. Once Beauvoir was back in Sartre's room, she learned that Arlette had not telephoned the Sartrians, so she sat down next to the bed that still bore his body and telephoned Lanzmann, Bost, Pouillon and Gorz. They all came immediately, and hospital authorities allowed them to spend one last night in the room with Sartre's body. Beauvoir asked Sylvie to go out and buy whiskey, but Pouillon did not want her to leave Beauvoir untended, so he went instead. They all spent the night drinking and reminiscing in hushed tones about the man whose life and work had so influenced theirs. Toward morning, when the orderlies indicated that it was time for everyone to leave, Beauvoir, stuperous from lack of sleep and too much whiskey, pulled back the sheet that covered Sartre and started to get into bed beside him.

"No, watch out!" a nurse shouted as an orderly grasped Beauvoir roughly and pulled her away from the bed.

"It's the gangrene, madame," he said politely. "It's very dangerous and you must not come in contact with it."

Only then did she see that most of Sartre's body was covered with gangrenous sores. Still, she smoothed out the sheet and lay down on top of it anyway. Everyone left the room and let her sleep beside him until they came to take the body away.

Lanzmann took her to his flat, which was just down the street from hers. The next morning, Sylvie took Beauvoir to her apartment on the Avenue du Maine because journalists had staked out the Rue Schoelcher and the phone rang incessantly with condolence calls from all over the world. Her sister and brother-in-law, Hélène and Lionel de Roulet, came from Alsace, so she was surrounded by people who cared for her, as she, "like a zombie,"[25] scarcely knew what was happening. All the arrangements for Sartre's cremation and burial were made by Lanzmann, Bost, Pouillon and Sylvie. Arlette went into seclusion, and to the end of her life Beauvoir really did not know how she coped or with whom during this sad time.

On the morning of the funeral, Beauvoir went to the hospital in a taxi with her sister and Sylvie. It stopped directly in front of the entrance, but she could barely walk and had to be supported by the two other women because she had doped herself up with whiskey and Valium. There was a brief viewing, during which she slumped with her hand on Sartre's double coffin (the interior one would bear him into the crematorium, the outer would contain the ashes in the cemetery). He was dressed in a maroon velour suit with white shirt and abstractly patterned tie, the last outfit he had worn in public when he went to the opera some months before with Sylvie and Beauvoir. Sylvie found them where he had left them in Beauvoir's flat, and since they were the best clothes he had, they became his last. Someone had placed a red rose next to his face, which added a touch of surrealism to the already unreal sight of him without glasses or pipe, his face powdered pink and heavily rouged. Bernard Pingaud had brought a camera to take pictures during the funeral procession, and when Beauvoir saw it she asked him to take photos of herself and the other Sartrians surrounding the casket. He was so astonished by this unusual request that he dropped the camera and sent it crashing to the concrete floor. Surprisingly, it still worked, so Beauvoir asked him again and he took the pictures. As the mourners filed past the bier, she said to each, "He did not suffer," as if it was her responsibility to comfort them. When the men came to close the casket, she leaned over and kissed Sartre firmly and fully on the lips.

The funeral was first set for Friday, April 18, but was changed to Saturday to permit more people to attend. President Giscard d'Estaing offered to pay the funeral expenses in lieu of a state occasion, which he knew Sartre would not have accepted, but all the Sartrians refused on principle. More than fifty thousand people lined up behind the bier as it was transported through the streets of Montparnasse to the cemetery which Beauvoir could see from her apartment window. Beauvoir thought to herself that it was "exactly the funeral Sartre had wanted"; Lanzmann called it "the last of the 1968 demonstrations."[26] Sartre was buried on the nineteenth, but, in accordance with French custom, several days later the body was to be disinterred and taken to Père Lachaise Cemetery to be cremated, and then returned to Montparnasse for final burial.

Beauvoir rode to the cemetery in the limousine immediately behind the hearse. Arlette, Hélène and Sylvie were with her. The crowd massed against the car, shoving and pounding the fenders, straining to see her, while photographers pushed their cameras against the windows, snapping flashbulbs blindingly into the interior. Beauvoir hardly knew what was happening, for all that long day she had been quietly opening her purse and swallowing several Valiums at a time. Because of this, she drifted unknowingly while everyone with her was frightened by the force of the crowd, which threatened to turn into a mob because of the intense emotion of the moment. A group of people, upset by the crush of curiosity-seekers and paparazzi, formed a human chain around the limousine, allowing her a modicum of privacy to express her grief. She was aware neither of the tears that streamed down her face nor that every so often Hélène or Sylvie would reach over with a tissue and dry them.

When they got to the graveside, she refused to leave the car until the casket was fully lowered into the ground. Someone produced a folding metal chair and she was put into it, sitting directly beside the grave in the raw dampness and fading light of the late afternoon, but too numbed by all the pills she had ingested to feel the cold. When the interment ceremony was over, someone (she did not remember who, but it was Georges Michel and Lanzmann) grasped her under the arms to help her stand, and her movement impelled the crowd forward, almost toppling her into the grave (someone else, a stranger to them all, actually did fall in); Beauvoir thought she would be smothered. She had no memory of how she was escorted from the cemetery to the car that carried her around the corner to the Rue Boulard and Lanzmann's apartment, but she remembered all the Sartrians staying on together for a very long time, unwilling to separate, unable to face a world without Sartre.

They decided to dine together, and Lanzmann booked a private dining room at the nearby Café Zeyer on the Rue d'Alésia. Beauvoir was in a very bad way. She could walk only if others supported her; unable to lift her legs, she shuffled between them. She kept on taking Valium and drinking whiskey, and with each swallow Sylvie could be heard scolding, "That's enough, Castor . . . be careful . . . it's too much . . . you will take an overdose. . . ." In the past, to the Sartrians' amazement, Beauvoir had always obeyed Sylvie's commands, but this time Sylvie's voice made no impression on her. Throughout the evening, she ate nothing and sat with tears rolling down her face. "She wasn't able to face the inadmissible," Georges Michel remembered, "that what she had feared for such a long time had finally happened."[27]

At midnight, she asked them to take her home. Michel described it:

With Sylvie, we tried to put her in a car. She couldn't stand on her legs. The mixture of alcohol, tranquilizers, sadness, fatigue—she had reached the limit of her reserves. I drove her home, and for the second time that day I had to put her arms around my neck and carry her the few meters into her apartment. I put her on the sofa. Sylvie took over: "I'll undress her and put her to bed." I embraced them both and left.[28]

The next day, to escape the well-wishers and the telephone, Sylvie took Beauvoir to her apartment, and she remained there for the next few days, still taking Valium and drinking heavily. On the day of the cremation, April 23, it was clear to all that she would be unable to attend, but the difficulty was in persuading her to stay at home. Surprisingly, she acquiesced, saying Sylvie would go in her place. When Sylvie and Lanzmann returned, they found Beauvoir sitting on the floor in a daze. She had fallen out of bed and was unable to get up by herself. "Ah, Sartre," she kept repeating, smiling to herself, "how strange that you should be eating such cool fruit. It must be very good. Perhaps you can share it with me."[29] She was delirious and running a high fever, so Sylvie and Lanzmann took her to the Hôpital Cochin, where she was diagnosed as having pneumonia. Silent and depressed, she stayed there for almost a month. When she was released, she insisted on returning to the Rue Schoelcher.

Throughout June and July, Sylvie stayed with Beauvoir as much as possible during the week, leaving only to meet her classes and then spelled by Lanzmann and Bost. Every weekend, whether Beauvoir wanted to go or not, Sylvie put her into the car and took her to a secluded inn or a small hotel in the countryside. They had good reason to keep someone with her all the time, because Beauvoir had always said that her life would end when Sartre's did, and they feared that in her depressed state she might try to commit suicide. One day in August, at just about the time when she always went to Rome with Sartre, she turned to Sylvie and said, "We must go away somewhere, on a long trip, because I want to live and I need to go somewhere far away to do it."

So they went to Norway and took a cruise through the fjords. Sylvie was relieved, at ease for the first time since Sartre's burial because now she knew that Beauvoir would not carry out her threat to commit suicide. "She always told me she would kill herself if he died first, so you can see why she could not be left alone after his death. Then, when she told me she wanted to go to Norway, it was as if she had put it all behind her. She talked about our relationship and said it gave her a taste for life, a reason to live. She said, 'I don't live for you, but I live thanks to you, through you.' And that was the kind of relationship we had. It gave her meaning and direction."

Three days after Sartre's cremation, Beauvoir later remembered, she was told by either Sylvie or Lanzmann (she did not remember who) that Arlette was removing everything from Sartre's apartment. This was surprising, because French law requires that the residence of a citizen who dies intestate be sealed until the contents are evaluated for tax purposes. Beauvoir asked Sylvie to go to the flat and see whether such a preposterous rumor could possibly be true. When Sylvie arrived, she found that it was indeed so: Arlette had emptied the flat. In separate conversations, Arlette told Robert Gallimard, Lanzmann, Sylvie, Bost and later Beauvoir herself that she did it because she did not have the money, approximately four hundred dollars, to pay the half month's rent until the probate was complete.[30] But as the probate was scheduled to take place within two weeks of Sartre's death, they were still puzzled by the haste of her decision. Then she said that she had emptied the apartment because she feared someone might break in and steal Sartre's papers. This was highly unlikely, since there was only one door into the flat and Beauvoir had installed armor plate some years earlier because she feared for Sartre's security.

"Everyone knew why she did it," Beauvoir said. "I was the only other person who had a key, and she was afraid of my legitimate claim to many things there."

It was a brief dispute, but still unpleasant. Lanzmann pleaded with Arlette to give some memento to Bost, who had served Sartre so long and faithfully. Arlette picked up the shabby old slippers that Sartre had worn for years, and, holding them disdainfully at arm's length, she said, "Give him these." Lanzmann took them and Bost kept them. It was his only memento.[31]

Sylvie was furious and confronted Arlette. At the very least she wanted Beauvoir's father's books back. These were a beautiful old collection of small leatherbound volumes of the repertory of the Comédie-Française. It was all Beauvoir had taken after her mother's death, preferring that her sister inherit the rest of the family's possessions. After "a battle of words," Arlette returned them.[32] Beauvoir wanted several other things, including Picasso's drawing and Riberolle's painting—both of which she felt had been given to her as well as to Sartre. "Let her ask me for them if she wants them that much," Arlette told Sylvie and Lanzmann, both of whom had asked on Beauvoir's behalf. Beauvoir chose instead to let them go and never saw them again. She also wanted Sartre's armchair, because it was originally a family chair that had come to him from the Alsatian branch of the Schweitzer family and she felt a certain entitlement to it, but she could not bring herself to ask for that either. Despite many months of concerted effort and squabbling on Sylvie's part, she got the Beauvoir family's books and that was all.

But the one thing Beauvoir did bring herself to ask for was the manuscript of the *Cahiers pour une morale.* Sartre had given Beauvoir the manuscript of *Being and Nothingness* as soon as the book was published, and of all her possessions it was the one she treasured most. Arlette knew how much Beauvoir wanted the *Cahiers,* which Sartre had announced his intention to write in the conclusion of *Being and Nothingness.* Beauvoir believed that the real reason she emptied the apartment so precipitously was to insure that Beauvoir would not get the *Cahiers.*

But she wanted it above all else. As soon as she was released from the hospital, when she was still weak and walking was difficult, she took a taxi to Arlette's apartment, where she "humbled" herself to plead for it. " 'Ah, no, I don't think so,' she said to me—not even trying to lie, to say, 'I can't find it,' or some other excuse. Just 'Ah, no, I don't think so,' and then cruelly, 'I don't want to.' "

In 1983, Arlette published it with her own introduction.[33]

Arlette took all the manuscripts, papers and personal possessions, but she gave all Sartre's furniture to Benny Lévy, who moved it into the suburban commune where he lived and arranged it exactly as it had been in the big room in Sartre's apartment on the Boulevard Edgar Quinet. Sartre's workplace thus became Lévy's study.

When she heard what Lévy had done with Sartre's things, Beauvoir was bitter. "That was when I knew that Sartre was really gone," she said. "That was when I accepted that what was real, the best part of my life, was over."

Cleaning Up Loose Ends

SIMONE DE BEAUVOIR was in the Hôpital Cochin for almost a month after Sartre died. For the first eight days, she was mostly unconscious and unaware of what was happening around her. The doctors held out little hope that she would make a full recovery and assumed she would need constant attendance for the rest of her life. It was taken for granted that her pneumonia would be cured, but because she had cirrhosis of the liver they feared that other related afflictions might result from her impaired circulation. Also, the binge of pills and liquor just after Sartre's death exacerbated the liver damage and motor-neuron activity that affected her movements.

Released in May, she was so weak she could not walk and her doctors feared she would lose ambulation permanently. On the eve of her discharge, the doctors told Beauvoir their grim predictions, warned her to stop taking drugs and eliminate alcohol entirely, to continue the massage and therapy she had already begun, and to hope for only a modicum of reasonable health. She agreed to everything but the elimination of scotch and vodka. "I need those," she said.

The doctors suggested a cure of *thalassothérapie*, a regimen of mineral baths and massage under controlled conditions in a Breton spa, where she would have no access to any substance that was not prescribed. The treatment only restored her ability to walk slowly and for several feet at a time, but she considered this such an improvement that for the rest of her life she continued to have regular massage treatments and *kinesthérapie* when she was at home in Paris.[1]

Beauvoir's treatment was complicated by the fact that her doctors could not legally discuss her condition with Sylvie. Like Sartre, Beauvoir had not made a will, and according to French law her sister Hélène, her closest blood relative, was her legal heir. In fact, Sylvie could not even drive Beauvoir to and from the Brittany spa until the doctors received Hélène's permission. It seemed as if history might repeat itself if the two women conflicted over Beauvoir as she and Arlette had done over Sartre.

The problem of who would care for her and where she would live was serious. Hélène and Lionel lived contentedly in a farmhouse with several outbuildings in a tiny village more than four hundred miles from Paris. They needed the large spaces for his many books and the various studios she had set up for her painting, and they also had gardens and animals which they enjoyed, so there was no question of their giving up their comfortable life to relocate in Paris. With her sister as heir, logic dictated that if Beauvoir were ever unable to care for herself, she would have to leave Paris and live in her sister's house. When she recovered enough to think about this possibility, she was alarmed because in her mind being away from Paris was akin to death itself. She liked Hélène's little Alsatian village and enjoyed visiting there, but her greatest fear was that despite Sylvie's faithful attendance, Hélène might someday be legally obligated to take her there to live permanently. There was only one thing to do, and despite the gossip it was sure to cause, she decided to do it: to adopt Sylvie.[2]

She was still in the hospital when she made the decision, and the first person she told was Lanzmann; the second was Bost, who happened in during the discussion. Both were in favor, because they too feared that the simple circumstances of Hélène's domicile might be valid enough reason for Beauvoir to be taken away from them against her will if she were to need permanent, full-time care in the future. Bost, especially, had become waiflike since Sartre's death, and he needed to know that Beauvoir, the true center of his Sartrian world, would remain nearby. Because they all knew from experience what problems could arise among people when their rank and status changed, they advised Beauvoir to do all that she could to make the adoption acceptable to both women. They advised her to tell Sylvie first and then Hélène, but to make it seem as if Hélène would be the first to know. The best approach, all agreed, would be to convince Hélène it would be in everyone's best interest. So when Beauvoir told Hélène, she did not mention her fear of being taken away from Paris but concentrated instead on the same grounds Sartre had used to justify his adoption of Arlette—that the woman was young and would therefore have both the longevity and the energy to act as literary executor. At first, and then only briefly, Hélène said, she felt the natural resentment of a sister whose role was being usurped, but, as a painter whose work was now beginning to be appreciated and who needed time to concentrate on it, she was quick to realize the wisdom of Beauvoir's decision.

Surprisingly, Sylvie was the only reluctant one among those whom Beauvoir entrusted with the news of her decision. She resisted at first because she "hated" anything to do with "the adoption relationship" as Arlette interpreted it. Sylvie was an independent woman of considerable means who also had a secure and rewarding professional life; Arlette had neither career nor independent means and depended entirely on Sartre for her physical well-being. Also, Sylvie claimed that she hated family relationships because hers had always been strained: "Mine with my mother was very bad and I did not need another mother at this time in my life."

The situation was exacerbated because of the proliferating scholarship that dealt with mothers and daughters in Beauvoir's writings and which was now concentrating on that aspect of her personal life. Sylvie feared "they would feast on this adoption for all the wrong reasons."

Beauvoir didn't like this sort of interpretation either, but had had a lifetime of schooling herself to be indifferent to it. She wanted Sylvie to concentrate on the fact that their friendship transcended the difference in their ages, and totally ignored the traditional roles that might seem to outsiders to be only those of mother and daughter, but Sylvie was unconvinced. Unused to being in the public eye, she did not think she could withstand the harsh criticisms sure to come her way and the unfair comparisons with Arlette. Lanzmann and Bost, however, persuaded Sylvie to get beyond this way of thinking because it was important for someone in Paris to have the legal responsibility for Beauvoir's person and property. Finally, despite her reluctance, Sylvie threw up her hands, said, "What difference does it make if I am adopted or not? Nothing will really change except our peace of mind," and, to Beauvoir's relief, accepted. Several months later, with Lanzmann as corroborating witness, the adoption was legalized and Sylvie's official new surname became le Bon de Beauvoir. She did not use it, however, until after Beauvoir's death.

There were misunderstandings between Hélène and Sylvie, mostly due to their differing personalities, but never the turf wars that erupted between Beauvoir and Arlette even after Sartre's death. The adult relationship between the sisters was largely one of affection based on the shared memories of childhood. Since Beauvoir's illness, Hélène tried to fuss over her in ways similar to those when she made herself the buffer between her sister and their mother. Hélène is a warm and engaging woman whose greatest pleasure is to offer bountiful hospitality, often putting her own work aside to do so. In this she contrasted sharply with the brusque, efficient Sylvie, whose personality mirrored Beauvoir's, and who reinforced Beauvoir's decision not to suffer fools and never to be bound by the traditional constraints of marriage, family or housework. So Hélène's generous, well-intentioned efforts to do something pleasant for her sister were frequently rebuffed, not because Beauvoir and Sylvie meant to be unkind, but simply because they were unaware of any other way to behave.

Beauvoir wanted to live, she told Sylvie in August 1980, but the next year was still a difficult one, full of long bouts of crying and periods of depression that left her completely depleted. When she did manage to speak, it was usualy a gloomy reiteration of all that had contributed to her displacement as the central figure in Sartre's life. She replayed what she should or could have done to prevent it from happening with everyone who cared enough about her to listen to these long tirades, from the Family to the board members of *Les Temps Modernes* (specifically the novelist Claire Etcherelli, who was now a member), to the many ideologically differing feminists who had become her friends, to the great variety of people throughout the world who had been influenced by her work and Sartre's and who called upon her when they were in Paris.

Still, all this talking did little to alleviate her depressions, which were serious and frequent and led her to seek refuge in tranquilizers (Valium was still the drug of choice) and liquor (Johnny Walker Red the preferred drink; she was not particular about the brand of vodka with which she began her day). When she was in one of these brooding, self-pitying moods the only person she would listen to was the forceful Sylvie, who insisted that she get over it and get on with her life. Time after time, Sylvie made her promise "to live another ten years at the very least," and finally Beauvoir agreed to try to go forward. It became their private catchphrase.[3]

To deal with memories of Sartre meant expressing emotion, which was always difficult if not impossible for Beauvoir unless she could find a way to control it at the same time. The best way for her to do this was, as always, to write about it, so she decided to write an account of his death, which became *Adieux*, and to organize the transcripts of the conversations which they had taped together in Rome during their last few summer holidays. She thought it fortunate that the tapes were already transcribed on paper, because she did not know whether she could bear to listen to his voice. Since his death, there were many things she could not do that she had always done with him, among them spending an evening listening to her extensive record collection. On the few occasions when Bost asked her to try, she always stopped whatever record was playing before it finished. But to describe the chronology of the events leading to Sartre's death was to relive the pain, and the process was deeply wrenching, at times actually making her physically ill. Persons who met her for the first time while she wrote the book were sure that she would not survive to complete it.

Despite her friends' concern for her physical well-being, instinctively she knew this was another instance when she needed to write in order to be able to accept death, just as she had done first with ZaZa and then with her mother. By writing their story in all its brutal truth, she had expended all emotion, from pain to sorrow to the acceptance of loss, and thus achieved catharsis. She may have been powerless to stop the process of dying and the inevitability of death in those she loved, but she possessed a powerful weapon that let her best it after all, which indeed made her the victor in the contest: she was a writer, and she could turn the process of grieving over loss into a living monument of words; an account of the loved one's death and her role in the process made them both immortal.

These testimonials served the further purpose of raising the protective screen she needed between herself and the actuality of death. She described what she meant by this in several conversations: "I often reread my memoirs to see what I thought about things, to remember what I felt, to relive relationships and recall places that were important to me. I also reread what I wrote about people who have died, and it lets me remember them without the sorrow of just thinking about them. I don't know why exactly, but it takes me away from feeling pain. It gives me the 'distance'—the 'necessary distance'—to remember without pain."

Once she had put the work between herself and the loss of the person, she could go on living because the memory was now stored in the part of her mind where it no longer hurt to think about it.

Adieux is sometimes referred to as Beauvoir's fifth volume of memoirs, the logical continuation of the fourth, *All Said and Done*. However, it is unlike that book, which departs from the first three volumes (mostly chronological recapitulations of her life and work) to present a more impressionistic overview of friendships, travels, people and things which were influential in the way she lived her life. In both structure and content, *Adieux* resembles the third volume, *Force of Circumstance*, much more closely, because once again she filters her activities, impressions and beliefs through Sartre's, as if to say that by writing about him she is writing about herself as well.

She based the book on the daily journal she kept during the ten years it took him to die; she added little more than minimal detail to supplement the journal entries, in some instances barely enough to provide substance or background for some of her descriptions. *Adieux* is less polished than the other memoirs, because there is little evocation or commentary, and although the anecdotes are telling, they are brief. The book departs from memoir, which ideally seeks to inform, persuade and evoke, and becomes instead a plaintive cry from the heart, her last salute to the primacy of the relationship with Sartre in her life, a ritual of catharsis. But her lifelong belief in the purpose of writing was that it should provide communication (and ultimately persuasion), and so it was only natural that she would seek to present what had happened to Sartre, and therefore to herself as well, to the public at large. It was a way of properly putting him to rest, according to her version of his last reality. And like all her other autobiographical writings, this too had to support her version of their relationship, even if it meant muting the slights and insults she had undergone in certain crucial instances, particularly from Arlette and Benny Lévy.[4]

However, she believed she was writing the book for another reason as well. The book she published just before *Adieux* was *Old Age*, a sociological overview of the status and condition of the elderly. She believed that *Adieux* was its extension, with the personal memoir expanding upon the impersonal collection of data about old people in general.

She did not count on the public's reaction. *Adieux* is intimate and personal, and so filled with graphic details of Sartre's every illness and affliction that it caused an immediate furor. Beauvoir predicted before publication that critical opinion would be harsh, and she was for the most part correct, as many were scandalized by what they termed the "indiscreet details" and accused her of trying to "get even" with a man who was safely in his grave and could not rebut her statements. Her account of his physical deterioration outraged readers the most.[5] In her own defense she said, "We have one of the most sexually liberal societies in the world here in France.

You can do anything you like with any combination of people in any bed-room in this country, but if you say someone shit in his pants because he was sick and old, oh, how you offend the national prudery!"

Still, critics were not persuaded. "Having survived him, she got the advantage of the last word," Pascal Bruckner wrote in *Le Point*, describing the book as a combination of "homage and vengeance."[6] She had her de-fenders, but they were mostly women and primarily British and American. Representative of them was Hazel Barnes, who noted, "I understand that in some feminist circles gossip paints Beauvoir as finally getting her own back, in return for having to put up with Sartre's infidelities. This is slan-der. The narrative is both factual reporting and a tribute."[7]

L'Express called it a "pathetic and mean-spirited ambush," accusing her of appropriating Sartre for her own needs "one last time by drawing a cruel picture that only she, from her privileged position, could paint . . . a Sartre crushed by the ravages of age, defeated and decayed."[8]

Even the usually sympathetic Bertrand Poirot-Delpech could not re-sist accusing Beauvoir of never going beyond the minutiae of Sartre's daily life, wondering why "she imposes on herself and on us these hideous de-tails which scarcely shed any new light on a career [Sartre's] already finished [long ago]."[9]

Commentary about the book was nearly always based on the reviewers' emotional response to the details of Sartre's protracted dying, but to look beyond that is to see a curious hybrid of genre and form. First of all, it is two books in one: memoir (*Adieux*) and dialogue (*Conversations with Sar-tre*). *Adieux* comes first, ostensibly memoir but also autobiography (hers), biography (his) and political and social history (theirs). The *Conversa-tions*, which are really "interviews," as she asks all the questions, show them at various times as equals in conversations; but, for the most part, she is director of the procedure, interlocutor, questioner, skeptic and judge. In all these instances he is the player who responds to her direction, the key figure without whom the drama could not be enacted, but also the playful little sprite who tweaks her seriousness and eludes her occasional pedantry. To read it is almost to eavesdrop on the fifty-year-long conversation that was their life together. Their cooperation here verifies her memory of what they were to each other; their dialogue enhances, corroborates and some-times corrects her version of their mutual life.

Still there are many flaws in both parts. *Adieux* is too long; the daily ups and downs of Sartre's condition become an endless medical chart de-tailed to the point of inducing fatigue if not boredom. Her reactions to his highs and lows become an emotional roller coaster, and after a while it all becomes a blur in the reader's consciousness. She does not seem to have done the sort of editing in this narrative that resulted in the gripping ac-counts of ZaZa and her mother, and it suffers from lack of the attention to form that made sections of *Memoirs of a Dutiful Daughter* and all of *A Very Easy Death* into polished works of art. She allowed everything in *Adieux* to spill out the way it happened to her, or at least the way she chose

to remember it, and, as frequently occurs, the raw stuff of life with no refinement makes for bad art.

Adieux is brief next to the exceedingly long collection of interviews,
but perhaps this is as it should be, since she meant them to be "a worthwhile approximation to the autobiography [Sartre] never wrote."[10]

Like the memoirs, these interviews ramble, and the order is sometimes
puzzling. The questions are occasionally quirky, but they are also direct,
personal and honest, important in crucial ways. First, they show the unorthodox but stable interaction between this extraordinary couple; second,
they illuminate and complement so much of Sartre's writing. As the definitive editions of his works appear posthumously, these interviews will be important statements to be read alongside them, because in many instances
they help to explain the creative force behind much of his thinking.

When the book was finished, Beauvoir was satisfied that she had accomplished what she set out to do. She was undisturbed by the negative
reviews but unprepared for Arlette's reaction. Arlette sent an "open letter"
to *Libération*, disparaging Beauvoir's relationship with Sartre and denigrat-
ing her role in his life, but most of all attacking her for the controversy surrounding the Benny Lévy dialogues.[11] Arlette took this tack in lieu of legal
action, and suddenly what they had all tried so hard to avoid during Sartre's life happened now that he was dead. It was an undignified exchange,
and both sides seemed to be picking over the bones of the dead man, fighting for bits of his remains. Beauvoir did not answer in print, saying she did
not want to dignify Arlette's attack by responding and especially did not
want to give her grounds for rebuttal, thus prolonging the dispute in print.
But she was free with her disdain in conversations, saying Arlette could
"write whatever she wants, and me, I'll say and do as I please." Some of
her friends urged her not to antagonize Arlette, because she might retaliate
by withholding or withdrawing Sartre's unpublished writings and correspondence from print, but nothing daunted Beauvoir and she continued to
make inflammatory remarks, most of which fortunately were not relayed to
Arlette.

Beauvoir was in the mood to clean up all literary loose ends, her own
and Sartre's. She had put the early stories that constitute her first and
hitherto unpublished book in order in late 1979 because, with him ill, it
was all she could concentrate upon. It was published a short time before
Adieux as *Quand prime le spirituel* (*When Things of the Spirit Come
First*). "It isn't very good but it will amuse my friends," she told Helen P.
Wenck.[12] With her cooperation, Claude Francis and Fernande Gontier
compiled the bibliography *Les Écrits de Simone de Beauvoir*. When it appeared in 1980, Beauvoir claimed she had no other unpublished manuscripts except the abandoned first section of what later became *A Woman
Destroyed* and she saw "absolutely no reason to publish this rubbish."[13]

Then she decided to turn her attention to Sartre's unpublished manu-

598 SIMONE DE BEAUVOIR

scripts still in her possession. However, as literary executor, Arlette could affirm or deny the right to publish any words he wrote, no matter who owned the paper on which he wrote them. This applied to everything in Beauvoir's possession, from personal letters to manuscripts. Because Arlette had attacked her in print, Beauvoir decided to strike back by publishing Sartre's correspondence. "After all," she reasoned, "he wrote those letters to me and they were in my possession. Why should I not publish them?"

She consulted Robert Gallimard, who in years to come would play an increasingly delicate role mediating between the two women. He recognized the value of Sartre's writing, no matter what the form, and told Beauvoir to put the manuscript in order and leave the persuading of Arlette to him. He was sure that Arlette wanted all Sartre's unpublished work made available to scholars as quickly as possible, especially while other principals were still alive and able to comment upon it. He hoped that despite the two women's open animosity toward each other, their common goal of keeping Sartre's work accessible and in print would overcome their differences.

Armed with Gallimard's support, Beauvoir began to sort and collect Sartre's letters to her and some he had written to other women which, she volunteered, "I did not steal from his house: I just got them somehow. 'Toulouse' [Simone Jollivet], for example—when she died, they were sent to my address and as he was already blind I just never got around to giving them to him. He gave Bianca's to me to read when he received them, and I just never gave them back. That's all. Nothing underhanded." Among these were letters to Olga Bost, Simone Jollivet and "Louise Védrine" (Bianca Bienenfeld).

She had not been in touch with Bianca for years, and Simone Jollivet was dead, but Olga was in Paris. For a long time, theirs had been an off-again, on-again friendship, but since about 1975 it had settled into a sort of armed truce on Olga's part, with Beauvoir generally ignoring her unless she needed something. Although the Bosts had separated and reconciled several times during these years, Beauvoir was always closer to Bost because of his connection to Sartre and *Les Temps Modernes*. Olga resented her for this but even more for their complicated sexual history and Bost's abiding fidelity to her.

Beauvoir did ask Olga whether she could reprint the letters Sartre wrote to her, and Olga ordered her not to do it. Beauvoir told Olga to be prepared because she would print them anyway and to warn her sister Wanda that they both might be upset by some of what Sartre had to say about them. Olga was outraged. Gossip had followed her for years after Beauvoir let it be known that she was the Xavière of *L'Invitée*, and Olga was determined not to suffer another public humiliation because of Beauvoir and Sartre. She warned Beauvoir again not to print any letter that contained anything about her or her sister, but Beauvoir blithely ignored her and published them. This was the last straw for Olga, who broke off all contact, saying she refused ever again to be victimized by Beauvoir. Their rupture was permanent, and Olga died several years later without a reconciliation.

Beauvoir forged on, however, determined to publish the letters as retaliation for Arlette's newspaper attack and to prove her wrong about the role she, Beauvoir, had played in Sartre's life. "Anyone who reads his letters to me will know what I meant to him," she said in the winter of 1982, when the letters were frequently spread out around her on the sofas and the coffee table as she worked contentedly almost every afternoon. By early June, putting them into order had become "a time-consuming task" complicated by the equally large amount of time she had pledged to assisting various feminist groups. She and Sartre seldom dated any letters, and so she had to study each one to determine its actual provenance.

In November 1982 she gave the manuscript to Robert Gallimard, knowing there was still "a lot of work to establish a text." In the meantime, she was keeping busy with "giving lots of lectures [to feminist groups]."[14] Next to her preoccupation with Sartre's text, her work on behalf of feminist causes had become her most important activity, and from this time on her letters usually contain references to both in tandem. The following January (1983), for example, she wrote that she had

> just put the last touch to Sartre's correspondence . . . which will appear in May. And I'm also very busy with a series of broadcasts which I must make on television about feminism. The New government [Mitterrand's] is trying to do very good work, particularly touching on the cause of women. Everything [i.e., Sartre's texts included] is going so well.[15]

That soon changed:

> Sartre's "correspondence" won't appear until the fall: two big fat volumes. But Gallimard has just published the *Cahiers pour une morale* [*Notebooks Toward a Moral System*] and *Les Carnets de la drôle de guerre* (*War Diaries: Notebooks from a Phoney War*)."[16]

Beauvoir evaded the reason for the delay in bringing out the correspondence: a publishing duel with Arlette, who deliberately set obstacles in Beauvoir's path while she solidified her own position as Sartre's legitimate heir by bringing out the two major texts mentioned above, writing a brief but intelligent introduction for each.

To promote the books, and at the same time possibly to deter Beauvoir, Arlette gave her first interview to *L'Express* and talked about the letters.

> Too-rapid publication would put the reader into the position of voyeur. The passing of [historical] time will change perspectives.

One doesn't read Proust's and Flaubert's letters today as one
would have read them immediately after their deaths.

The interviewer asked what Arlette thought of Beauvoir's announcement
that she would publish the letters, and Arlette said simply, "I would not
have taken that initiative." She agreed that letters written during the same
time as the *War Diaries* would certainly be interesting, but she feared problems that were sure to arise among those who felt their privacy invaded.
Her own letters from Sartre were

> willed to the Bibliothèque Nationale under the stipulation that
> they not be accessible . . . until after a certain length of time. I
> wish that all those who have any writings by Sartre would think
> about withholding them [from publication] and deeding them to
> the Nationale where they can become part of the Sartre collec-
> tion.[17]

Her intention was obviously to take the high road in the hope that a
shamed Beauvoir would follow.

This did not happen, so Arlette turned her attention to the letters
Beauvoir had assembled and began to quibble over what became a long
series of objections explicitly designed to delay publication. Beauvoir listed
some of them: "Wanda had to be called Tania, and she and Olga were
to be called Zazoulich instead of Kosakiewicz. Now, isn't that silly—everyone knew who they were! There were other stupid changes she wanted as
well, such as changing the names of the men in his regiment, and that
didn't matter to me, so I did it. But when she threatened to go on and on
like this, I told her to stop the game because if she continued I would call
a press conference and denounce her for impeding the publication of important letters written by Jean-Paul Sartre. She knew this would mean big
trouble, big public outcry, everyone would turn against her, and that was
why she gave in to me. It was also why she suddenly began to work with
[Michel] Contat and those others to try to get some of Sartre's manuscripts
into print before mine, and why she agreed to a [Cohen-Solal] biography.
She was determined to rewrite Sartre's history, especially where I was concerned."

So the recriminations continued on both sides, and might have gone
on till the end of Beauvoir's life except that it was a contest heavily weighted
in Arlette's favor: once Beauvoir published the letters, she had no other
unpublished manuscripts in her possession except several partially filled
notebooks that belonged to what she called "the abandoned '47 Ethics."
Since they had little value unless placed within the context of other notebooks owned by Arlette, Beauvoir overcame her personal feelings and gave
them to her, asking her to pass them on to Michel Contat and Michel
Rybalka, who she understood were preparing some of Sartre's texts for the
definitive Pléiade edition.

Curiously enough, when the letters were finally published, critical reaction was muted, as if after *Adieux* there was nothing left that could shock anyone. Almost all the reviews had one question in common: why, having chosen to publish Sartre's letters to her, did she not publish her letters to him as well? Did she not, by suppressing one half of the correspondence, give credence to Arlette and all the others who contended that her relationship with Sartre was a construct of her own determined creation?[18]

To explain why she published only his, she quoted Sartre's comment from their 1974 interviews that his letters should be published after his death because they were the autobiographical equivalent of his life. In making them available to the public, she argued, she had simply complied with his wishes. Furthermore, she decided (for a reason she never explained), the time was right to release all those addressed to her and others which were either "willed" to her (as she now viewed the Jollivet letters) or "given to me by their recipients" (the category in which she placed Olga Bost, who angrily denied ever having given her anything). Beauvoir said that she did not change "one iota" of anything within these letters concerning her relationship with Sartre, but that she had chosen to suppress some passages and to change some names, and that other changes were "desired" by "Mme. Elkaïm-Sartre." In a conversation several months after the book was published, she insisted that this explanation was inserted only to placate Arlette, who was responsible for all changes, omissions and deletions, and that she, Beauvoir, had inserted them only to force Arlette to agree to publication.

Still, the reasons for the suppression of her letters remained unclear, and throughout the three years she was asked the question her responses varied greatly. At first she said she didn't publish them because she couldn't: that her letters were lost when Sartre was in the stalag; then that they were lost more than twenty years later when the apartment on the Rue Bonaparte was bombed. At various times she mentioned having given them at Sartre's request, along with some of his manuscripts, to various people— Olga, Bost, her sister, her mother—for safekeeping, and that these people were responsible for the loss. She was infuriated and would not answer the question when asked why, if she thought it so unsafe, she had kept his papers with her while putting her own into the hands of others.[19] In interviews and conversations during September 1983, and from then on, this is what she said:

"Look, my letters just are not interesting! Sartre is the one who wrote the interesting letters. His are long and full of news and gossip, and he talks about his work and his life, about the Army, and his women, and he does go on and on about what he feels for me. Now, mine, on the other hand, are all shorter. I just tell him what he needs to know, or I write the answers to questions he asked me about his writing. Or the arrangements I have made to meet him, or to send him things, or to plan our rendezvous. I'm not the emotional one in this exchange—he is. So people don't need to know what I wrote, that's all." Her ultimate conclusion was, "It's nobody's business but my own." From 1983 until her death, this last was all she would say on the matter except to add occasionally that she had "found" another letter, "nothing of any value," and that "someday" she would publish "the few there are."[20]

With Sartre's letters published, Beauvoir concentrated on the two things that gave her the greatest pleasure in life: working on behalf of women and traveling with Sylvie.

"After I published the letters, I would have been content to enjoy myself with Sylvie," she said. "But the Socialists asked for my help, and that's how it started."

From then until Sartre's death, any public stance she took was exclusively on behalf of or in connection with a feminist cause or action, and it seemed that, with Sartre's departure from the political arena, hers, no matter how infrequent or sporadic, was ended as well.

This changed in 1980, when Mitterrand and one of his strongest supporters, Yvette Roudy (whom he appointed after his election to be minister of the first Cabinet-level agency for the rights of women), sought her support. She liked Roudy, the French translator of Betty Friedan's *The Feminine Mystique*, and she believed that Mitterrand was the best candidate of those running for office, but she was still reluctant to commit herself openly to a political candidate. She and Sylvie had been to Norway and Sweden and several holiday regions of France and were now planning her eagerly anticipated return to the United States. She knew from past experience that public political commitment took a lot of time, and at this stage of her life she did not want anything to interfere with her enjoyment of it.

Gisèle Halimi, who had been responsible for Beauvoir's earlier feminist involvement through the group Choisir, was responsible again for enlisting her support for Mitterrand. Halimi, on behalf of Choisir, invited all the candidates to address a forum entitled "Which President for Women?," and the only one who accepted was Mitterrand.[21]

This was enough to convince Beauvoir to support him publicly in 1981, and in 1983 she said, "I'd do it again, of course" because

> under Mitterrand, we have a lot more, thanks essentially to his recognition of the need for women to have not only a ministry but also a budget that enables it to get things done. I don't think Mitterrand is personally a feminist in his thinking, but he is perceptive enough to recognize that women play a key role in political elections in France, and so he supports them.[22]

Mitterrand kept his promise and charged Yvette Roudy within her ministry to better the position of women throughout French society. This, according to Beauvoir, was "wise," because Roudy had been

> a committed feminist for many years. She is a translator, a scholar, a perceptive political woman. Happily, Mitterrand has given her

enough of a budget so that, in combination with her energy and intelligence, she can effect change. She has passed a very important law which forbids antisexist exploitation of women and their bodies in the media. She works to obtain equal salaries, the opportunity for women to enter jobs and professions that have been closed to them, and of course she supports the right of women to make their own decisions about their bodies.

Beauvoir thought so highly of Yvette Roudy that there was nothing she would not do to help her ministry be successful. When Roudy founded the Commission Femme et Culture, composed of women from all professions and walks of French society, and charged with making concrete proposals for change, Beauvoir accepted the honorary chair but was from the beginning an active, committed participant. She blushed with pleasure when she spoke of the "Commission Beauvoir," as the group had taken to calling itself informally in tribute to her.

Once each month, Roudy's deputy, Michelle Coquillat, called for Beauvoir at the Rue Schoelcher and drove her to the ministry headquarters on the Avenue d'Iéna, where the commission members gathered to study the entire social construct, from legal and reproductive rights to the economic status of women in everything from business to the arts to professional sports. Beauvoir described it as carrying out

> research on various aspects of the role women play within their culture so that we can then make concrete proposals to the government. We believe that we must examine the entire culture in order to understand the feminine condition.

She explained how they went about it:

> We begin with the proposition that women are excluded from most parts of culture. They have little or no money of their own, therefore they have no real economic control. They are excluded from education or they are given inferior education or less training than men, thus fewer professions are open to them and they are generally inferior. Even in intellectual and creative pursuits like writing and painting, women must still suffer from the restrictions that require them to tend first to household and family needs before they try to fit their work into whatever free time they can manage. . . . If [a woman] does marry, even if she marries well, she finds herself responsible for all the aspects of life because the husband must be free to follow his business, his profession. The woman is overwhelmed by daily life, and there is no leisure to read or think. She does not control enough money to do any good with it, and so the endless cycle continues. . . .
> . . . The importance of this commission [is] that it was created by an official arm of the government . . . , which charges it to come up with recommendations for action. As such, it makes

legitimate the issue of woman's place within society, and it shows
that the Mitterrand government is in favor of positive change.

From then until the end of her life, Simone de Beauvoir remained
committed to the Mitterrand, or, more specifically, the Yvette Roudy,
agenda. There was a difference, however, between this involvement and
the activity of the 1970s. Then she was an active participant; now, at the
age of seventy-five, hers was a more ceremonial role. She was now more
likely, as with the honorific of the "Commission Beauvoir," to lend her
name than her presence. Privately, however, she was still free with her
purse and pen, supporting both causes and individuals. Writers who needed
a preface or an introduction for a book knew they could ask her to write it,
scholars who needed letters supporting tenure or promotion got them by
return mail, as did activists who wanted written testimonials on behalf of
causes.

She sent, for example, statements to the government of the Republic
of Ireland in support of the legalization of contraceptives and for homosexual rights. She sent letters to Polish intellectuals whose rights had been
curtailed under the Jaruzelski coup in 1983, and letters of support to
women activists in Mexico.[23] In France, she supported subsidies for feminist publishing houses like Françoise Pasquier's Editions Tierce, and she
herself gave large sums of money as anonymously as possible to fund shelters for battered and abused women.

All this activity gave her tremendous pleasure, and in the bleak years
after Sartre's death, when her own health was often troublesome, speaking
of her work on behalf of women seemed to bring zest to her voice and vitality to her countenance. These were truly her years of joyful participation in feminist affairs. In retrospect, from her vantage point in the 1980s,
all her feminist activity was rewarding, and all of it brought more satisfaction than many other activities within her long and fruitful life. However,
in reality it should be considered separately from the decade of the 1970s,
when it was first of all a way of evading Sartre's drawn-out process of dying,
and only after that a source of personal and professional pleasure.

But the best part of her feminist activity throughout the 1980s was not
having to take to the hustings or the barricades any longer. "There is something to this getting old after all," she said on the eve of her seventy-fifth
birthday in 1983. "I can say what needs to be said and demonstrate what it
is important to do, and because I am now this 'sacred relic,' younger women
will rush to do it for me."

She had made a dramatic recovery in the two years since Sartre's
death, a recovery which surprised her doctors and delighted Sylvie. The
woman who only a short time before searched for ways to give meaning to
her life now smiled like a happy schoolgirl, raised her empty glass in a
mock toast and said, "And I can do the things I want to do—like going to
America!"

FORTY-FOUR

"Women, You Owe Everything to Her!"

WHEN SHE LEARNED of Algren's death in May 1981, Beauvoir felt a strong need to return to the United States to find out what had happened there in the years since their correspondence ended. Her attitude toward the United States was always a complex one. There was much that she "adored, simply simply adored," and much else that was "simply detestable." In the first category she placed everything from literature and music to people and places; she reserved the second for politics and foreign policy, and a few individuals whom she had never liked. All in all, she was "fascinated by America," because "it did not fit into the framework of expectation she had formed from 'books written by certain American liberals.' "[1]

The idea for the American trip actually orginated with Sylvie at the beginning of 1981, as a ploy to tantalize Beauvoir back to health. "If you get better, we can go to New York next year," Sylvie would promise during Beauvoir's darkest moods, or she would cajole, "Tell me about New Orleans again—are you certain we can speak French there?"[2] But it wasn't until Algren had died on May 9 that they made serious plans to travel, planning to go in late summer. It was a little more than a year since Sartre's death, but Beauvoir's health was still fragile and she could not concentrate on itineraries and other details, which Sylvie, who had never been there, could not arrange without her cooperation. Every time Sylvie asked her to plan the itinerary, Beauvoir frittered away valuable time worrying about peripheral concerns such as how she could avoid public recognition and how she would fend off those who tried to invade her privacy. She also wasted time on fantasies, such as how to get an American Express card, a checking account in an American bank and a French passport, all under a false name.[3]

From fantasy to reality, the problems multiplied. Sylvie was terrified of airplanes, so they had to find ships that sailed during her vacation, and by the time they thought to look for one it was July and already too late. The trip was postponed until the following year, when Beauvoir was up to finding a ship with the right sailing dates. All her friends in the United States were alerted and sworn to silence. But just as they were about to get the trip under way, Sylvie fell and broke her leg. Since she had done all the driving following Sartre's death and managed all their logistics except for planning the itinerary, and since Beauvoir was still unable to walk easily, the trip was canceled a second time.

It seemed doomed never to happen when in 1983 the Mitterrand government restricted the currency a citizen could export to an amount inadequate to pay for such a long and expensive vacation.

"If I ever regretted voting for Mitterrand, this was the reason," Beauvoir joked, "but then the Danish government saved my holiday." She received the Sonning Prize for European Culture, which carried a cash award of $23,000, in her words "for my lifetime of writing."[4] She asked that the money be paid in American dollars and sent directly to a New York bank.

Beauvoir was anxious to leave as soon as possible, so she persuaded Sylvie to fly on the Concorde. "Better to risk three hours in the air and get it over with than to risk another postponement. It is worth the money if it means you only have to be afraid for a few hours instead of many."

Sylvie paid for the flight because she refused to let her phobia cost Beauvoir extra money. "We paid for it in France, in French money," Beauvoir said, "and each of us took the legal amount of francs out of the country, but I didn't intend to use mine, because I had the prize!"

The Sonning Prize had given her a boost—she who had refused so many others, including the Legion of Honor, which Mitterrand had offered the year before. The Danish recognition gave her hope that critical evaluation of her work was changing from what she perceived as a dangerous trend to view the entire corpus as feminist. She greatly appreciated her elevation to the feminist pantheon, but she hoped the reputation of this honor would enhance her status as a writer in other critical interpretations. One positive thing had already resulted: her former robust good health, which she had not had for the past three years, seemed back to stay.

So at last all was in place. On a hot July day in 1983, the seemingly frail old woman of strong will and stubborn disposition shepherded her skittish younger companion onto the Concorde for the flight to New York. The initial arrangements had been made by Nan Graham, who was then Beauvoir's American editor at Pantheon Books. She, as well as Stépha Gerassi and her son John, Beauvoir's new friend Kate Millett and one or two trusted others were in readiness to see that the trip was as private and restful as it could be.

She wanted it to be a sentimental journey to see old friends and favorite places, but also to explore parts of the country she had never seen before. She did not plan to participate in any public activity, nor did she intend to take notes or to write about it when it was over, as she had often done on earlier travels. She especially did not want to talk to the press, so that her friends, many of whom worked for news organizations, walked a metaphorical tightrope between professional responsibility and personal concern as they tried to keep her presence a secret.

"Sylvie works hard and deserves a rest," Beauvoir declared emphatically, using this as her excuse to avoid public entanglements. Because of it, they planned to stay in New York only long enough to recover from the flight and to cash the prize check before heading up to a quiet inn on the beach in Provincetown. They planned to use it as their jumping-off point for national parks and resorts in New England and New York State, ending the tour with visits to Millett's farm in Poughkeepsie, to John Gerassi in Montauk, and a side trip to Philadelphia to see "the museum that is never open" (the Barnes Foundation) and "that cracked bell" (the Liberty Bell).

They checked into the Algonquin Hotel, now her favorite place to stay in New York, and were spotted almost immediately by a writer from *The New Yorker* who telephoned the room several times, to hear Beauvoir snap, before hanging up, that she never gave telephone interviews. Surprisingly, he did not phone again, and for the next few days she and Sylvie roamed the city freely without being identified.

Three things in particular struck her about how New York had changed since her last previous visit, a stopover in 1971. "There are a lot of new skyscrapers . . . Many of the beautiful buildings I knew are torn down and I wonder why, because they seemed in good condition to me. Also, Times Square has changed a lot. There were more sex shops then. Now, sure, there are still a lot of them, but there are also new skyscrapers of beautiful aluminum and glass which, mixed in among the old, make a very beautiful skyline." The other change disappointed her: "There are very few drugstores left. Thirty years ago, I often had lunch in a drugstore. I'd go sit at a counter and order coffee and a sandwich, listen to the chatter, watch the people eat. It was all very warm and friendly. Now there are only impersonal fast-food places and it's not the same. That strange mixture that was the New York drugstore seems to be gone entirely."

She and Sylvie spent much of their time in museums—the Metropolitan, the Guggenheim, the Modern Art and Beauvoir's favorite, the Frick Collection. They went to the top of the World Trade Center, and to Elaine's restaurant because they heard it was "the thing to do in New York," but found it a "less than thrilling experience." Woody Allen and Mia Farrow were among the diners that evening, and Beauvoir was introduced to them, "but they had nothing to say to me and I had nothing to say to them. I like what Woody Allen does a lot, but he doesn't know me or who I am or anything about me. There was Elaine, who supposedly knows everything about everyone, but she didn't know who I am, either. So we ate our dinner by ourselves and then we went home." Though everyone she met gave her exactly what she said she wanted in the United

States, total freedom to come and go as she pleased, she was still a tiny bit miffed that no one made any sort of fuss over her.

Despite her eagerness to get on with the trip, everything changed when Beauvoir discovered that she could not cash the $23,000 check for two months even though it had been deposited directly into a New York branch of a Danish bank. This left her in dire straits because the only money she had at her disposal was what she and Sylvie had legally taken out of France. It was gone by the end of their first week in New York. Frantic telephone calls to Nan Graham, Kate Millett and other friends followed, and they, along with Beauvoir (who first had to produce passport, credit cards *and* other photo identification) were able to convince bank officials to clear the check within the next ten days.

Beauvoir was thriving on the fast pace of life in New York, but Sylvie was exhausted by it and wanted to leave for Provincetown. So Beauvoir, accustomed to the paternalism of French publishers, asked officials at Pantheon for an immediate loan of two thousand dollars so that they could leave the city. Nan Graham tried to explain that most American publishers are subsidiaries of giant corporations and that financial transactions are often labyrinthine and protracted. Also, the ramifications of the new French currency restrictions were complex, and it was Graham's understanding that it would be an infraction of the law if Pantheon were to consent to such a loan. But Beauvoir remained unconvinced that a sympathetic editor could not write a check without first having to go through corporate channels.

Meanwhile, she considered herself "a prisoner of the Algonquin," depending on her charge cards and her friends. Kate Millett came to the rescue with enough money to enable her to move on, but it was too late for Provincetown, as their rooms had been let to others, so Beauvoir and Sylvie drove off for "somewhere in New England" in a rented car. Eventually the prize money caught up with them.

For the next six weeks they drove through northern New England and New York State, circling from Maine's Acadia National Park to Niagara Falls and back along the seacoast. Whenever possible they stayed in tourist cabins with kitchenettes, and Sylvie amused herself by visiting American supermarkets and cooking foods not usually found in France, especially hot dogs and baked beans, pancake batter and frozen waffles. "We each gained five pounds," Beauvoir boasted proudly.

She was recognized only once, when a "pompous" Harvard student stopped her and asked for an explanation of several passages in *The Second Sex* to take back to her professor in the fall. "I told her to beat it, just like that, BEAT IT!" Beauvoir recalled, filling her voice with menace. "You should have seen her run away!"

She particularly liked the drive down along the Hudson River, because she had long enjoyed looking at paintings by artists of the Hudson River School. Clermont, the Livingston mansion, was "a spectacular favorite" where she found it "easy to imagine the countryside with the Indians and the first pioneers." Her highest accolades were for Millett's Christmas-tree farm, where a rotating group of nine or ten women calling themselves "the Pioneers" lived together every summer in a women's art colony, reclaiming decaying farmland, restoring old buildings, creating studios and planting trees. This was Beauvoir's first experience with a "feminine commune," and she was fascinated by the way they managed to work the land in such harmony.[5] When she returned to Paris, she spoke frequently of this farm, holding it up as a possible model for feminist life in France. The farm was the setting for the only professional event of her trip—a filmed discussion between her and Millett for a projected French television series on *The Second Sex*.[6]

But all this took more time than expected, and so the trip to Philadelphia was canceled, as were several visits to old friends in Connecticut. There was time only for an overnight drive to Montauk to stay with John and Chantal Gerassi. That visit was made even shorter because Sylvie kept missing the turnoff to Long Island and three times they found themselves crossing most of the Bronx and the George Washington Bridge.

They spent their last four days in the steamy late-August torpor of New York with Sylvie resting and Beauvoir rushing through museums and bookstores. Every afternoon, Beauvoir repaired to the Algonquin lobby, took one of the thronelike chairs against the wall and ordered a double martini straight up, glaring at anyone who dared to look at her, let alone recognize or attempt to speak to her. Beside her on the small table was the pile of books she had bought that day. Usually these were novels by American women, particularly Alice Walker, Toni Morrison, Maya Angelou and Gloria Naylor. She thought black American women were the most interesting contemporary writers and said she had no plans to "waste money and space" carrying recent books by male writers back to France. It was obvious that she had not kept up with American fiction since her previous visit, for many names were unfamiliar to her.

Of the feminist writers, her admiration for Millett was unqualified, even though "she should have given credit to *The Second Sex*, because that's where she gets all her theory." Some of her other views were less objective. Of Betty Friedan's *The Second Stage*, she said she rejected everything about it and "tossed that book in anger across my room." In her opinion, "Americans are not creating the best feminist theory now. That is being done by the British, women like Juliet Mitchell and Sheila Rowbotham—those are the women [whose writing] I most admire." She also mentioned Germaine Greer specifically, saying "she must be brilliant, because I don't understand a thing she writes." However, she was careful to add once again that she read "only those books which people send to me or otherwise call to my attention, and then I usually don't read them thoroughly."[7]

Loaded down with books and other souvenirs, they returned to France on the Concorde, just in time for Sylvie's *rentrée* to the classroom and for Beauvoir to become embroiled in one of the last major controversies in her life. Josée Dayan had wanted to film *The Second Sex* for a long time; Yvette Roudy thought it important to make the film, and Françoise Verny, Beauvoir's friend and at that time the *directrice littéraire* at Editions Gallimard, wanted to produce it. Originally TF 1, the first of the three state-owned television channels, agreed to sponsor the film, which was to be broadcast over six hours and sold to an American distributor in order to defray the cost. However, American companies refused to participate, citing as problematic the excessive length and the difficulty of filming. Most problematic of all was the likelihood of getting the censors both in France and in the United States to pass on certain subjects, such as the clitoridectomy of Arab girls, one of the most disturbing segments of the film. These concerns led to other arguments and disagreements: on the political orientation of the book itself and how to mute it within the movie; on which individuals or groups of women should be either included or excluded; and, the first and foremost concern, on how to condense such a massive tome into just six 55-minute segments.

In an attempt at consensus, Yvette Roudy scheduled a luncheon for all those involved, "to break bread in lieu of breaking each other's heads," as Beauvoir said. But she was furious when the negotiator for one of the three state-owned television channels (for by now all three were involved) did not send word that he would not be there and kept the sizable group that had attended waiting for him at table. Everyone who was present used his rudeness to air individual complaints to various segments of the French press, which was delighted to report on women fighting with other women as well as with men. Still, Beauvoir was determined to endure every indignity if it only meant that the film would be made. And it was: not six hours but four, in 52-minute segments, shown only on French television because no other country or distributor bought it.[8]

Beauvoir appears throughout the film as a largely ceremonial figure wearing a bright-red turban and matching lipstick, nodding, smiling, and seeming by her presence to be giving benediction to the undertaking. Some women are asked for their testimonies, writers such as Elisabeth Badinter and Susan Sontag praise the book, and the American conservative Phyllis Schlafly counters by dismissing it. The scenes of clitoridectomy are as bloody and brutal as the original male producers (replaced early on by an all-woman team) feared they would be.[9]

In other segments women leaders such as Indira Gandhi offer their views, and in still another Norman Mailer admits that he never read a single book by Simone de Beauvoir and that the first of his wives (unnamed) to read *The Second Sex* divorced him at once. Beauvoir was delighted. In another, more serious segment, Yvette Roudy talks about employment, voting and what the future holds for women in France, warning them of encroachment on their gains by the Chirac initiative, or campaign, which was heating up with the March 1986 elections then on the horizon.

The programs aired in November 1984, and, all in all, Beauvoir was pleased with the outcome and willing to grant an interview to anyone who would allow her to expand upon both book and film. She answered the usual questions about her relationship with Sartre with unusual good humor, mostly to get them out of the way so that the interviewer would go on to other subjects. Having him as her "companion," she said, changed her entire life because "though he was not particularly interested in feminism, he gave me strength and supported all my endeavors." Camus, who was "scandalized" by the book, was "Latin and predictably macho." A reporter for the Associated Press asked her whether she still thought marriage, as she had written thirty years before, was an "obscene bourgeois institution." "I still think it is," she said, "in the sense that it is often a question of financial gain. Confusing money with questions of the heart and sexuality is what's obscene." But, above all, she found one aspect of the film a cause for celebration and worth publicizing at every opportunity: the fact that a woman, Josée Dayan, directed it, and that her entire crew was composed of women. "I couldn't possibly have worked with a man director for this project," Beauvoir insisted.[10]

She was really looking forward to the holidays as her activity for the film died down, and she and Sylvie began to plan where they would spend the vacation between New Year and the resumption of school. She had been in excellent health since returning from the United States, having gained a little weight and—so everyone thought—cut down on her drinking. So it was a shock one morning in December when Sylvie found her lying on the floor beside her bed, saying she had fallen in the night when she got up to use the bathroom.

By the time Sylvie arrived, Beauvoir had been lying on the cold floor so long that pneumonia set in, and she spent her Christmas holidays and most of January in the hospital. Again, hospital officials kept the press from learning that Beauvoir was a patient. By the time she was well enough to return to the Rue Schoelcher to convalesce, it was just before the Easter holiday, when Sylvie took her to Biarritz. She tried to evade conversation about this hospitalization, and when Bost or Lanzmann tried to talk about it she cut them short. But she did complain, albeit indirectly. "Ah, old age!" she wrote to Helen P. Wenck. "It's just as you say. I don't have the most solid bones and my legs don't work very well, and the idea of a fall terrorizes me."[11]

By summer she was well enough to travel, and she and Sylvie flew to Budapest and rented a car in which they drove around Hungary and then through the Austrian Tyrol. She was struck by the unexpected prosperity and gaiety of Hungary, and was delighted that the weather was so pleasant in the Tyrol, which had long been one of her favorite vacation places.

In Paris that fall, staff disagreements at Les Temps Modernes led to her "mediating," as she called it, but actually making dogmatic pronouncements that managed to offend just about everyone. Although she was still the titular head of the publication, Lanzmann was now determining content and policy with her cooperation and approval. His personality, as strongly defined as hers, led to frequent resignations among other members of the board. They still met regularly at the Rue Schoelcher, and she still read submissions, selected articles and patiently edited proofs and galleys. She considered it a sacred obligation and frequently put all else aside to tend to it. Otherwise, she wrote to Mrs. Wenck,

> I have too many [feminist] manuscripts to read (rarely interesting, alas); and also I have to do so much feminist work in liaison with Yvette Roudy, whom I told you I respect so much. But all this is nothing overwhelming, and the weather is wonderful. We're awaiting the elections in March with a great deal of anxiety. It's certain that the Right is going to gain, but the question is how much and what's going to happen then?[12]

She persuaded herself that worry about the March 1986 election was affecting her health, but those who knew her well knew better. By the end of 1985, the years of heavy drinking had exacerbated her cirrhotic condition: her belly was so distended that she could not stand up straight. She was so jaundiced that the whites of her eyes were now yellow, turning her cornflower-blue irises into a watery green that sometimes startled people who had not seen her for a while. Even simple tasks such as walking the few steps from her sofa to the refrigerator were agony for her. Horrified guests sat glued to their chairs, wondering whether to get up and help her or pretend nothing was amiss. She behaved, however, as if nothing were wrong, and insisted on following her usual routine. The friends who came to fetch her for their regularly scheduled dinners ended up by awkwardly supporting or carrying her across the square to her favorite restaurant. "Just give me your arm," she would say during the ritual of pretending that she was walking.

Now Sylvie was doing for Beauvoir what Beauvoir had done in Sartre's final years, watering the scotch. Beauvoir adapted by simply dispensing with her pewter jigger and filling her glass to the brim with the vile watered concoction. Sylvie even tried to banish Bost, who drank with Beauvoir as Michelle had drunk with Sartre, but Beauvoir would not stand for it and Bost remained, a lugubrious attendant grieving for his dead wife, the dead Sartre and his dead youth. Sylvie tried to scold him and Beauvoir out of their moroseness when they sat in the dark, crying and drinking together, but they did not seem to hear her. More and more, Sylvie turned to Lanzmann for support.

He gave what he could, but he was about to launch the product of more than twelve years of labor, his massive nine-hour documentary about the Holocaust, *Shoah*, to which Beauvoir had contributed money.[13] As Sylvie was now frantic about Beauvoir's drinking and determined to distract her from the bottle, Lanzmann thought he had the perfect answer. He assigned Beauvoir to write the preface for the book of the *Shoah* filmscript, knowing that her support would help boost the film, and she set to the task with pleasure.[14] It did not keep her from her daily consumption of liquor, but it did occupy her, and so Sylvie thought to try again.

This time, it was the preface for *Mihloud*, the story of an American expatriate who died of AIDS in France.[15] Beauvoir's preface is little more than a summary of the book's content, and, despite the seriousness of the subject, what she wrote can best be described as a charming little story in the manner of one of Perrault's fairy tales. There is no bite, sting, social commentary or proposal for action. Nevertheless, it gave her pleasure to write it and actually made her feel that she was contributing something important on the subject. Sadly, the only lasting importance of this introduction is that it is the last thing she wrote in her life.

Amazingly, she was mentally well until the very end. Her mind was razor sharp when it came to argument or editorial criticism. She could discuss movies and, because of Sylvie's interest, operas, as if she were a professional critic; she read several newspapers each day, listened avidly to international news, and discussed world politics with enthusiasm and real knowledge. "The Americas" (North and South) became a special interest in the last six years of her life. She "despised" Ronald Reagan, saying, "His grandchildren will pay for his sins, for the way he abandoned the poor, the homeless, the underclasses. America will suffer for that." She was very knowledgeable about the Latin-American debt and worried about Reagan's "shabby treatment" of Mexico ("He should pay attention to that border"). She wondered whether she should try to write a position paper about Nicaragua (she supported the Sandinistas), but decided she should expend her energies on feminist causes instead.

But at the same time, just getting up in the morning was a trial of immense proportion. She stopped climbing the spiral staircase to her sleeping loft and slept on the sofa bed because walking was so difficult. In recent years she had become—in her own words—"quite the dandy" about her clothing, always matching her turban to her sweater or trousers.[16] Now she could not even put on her clothes most days, and shuffled about in black patent-leather bedroom slippers, a brilliant-red robe of fuzzy-looking polyester and a matching scarlet turban. Her lipstick and nail polish matched the other reds, garish against her yellowed skin. At times her stomach was so distended that the robe barely stretched across it.

Sylvie, who dismissed Beauvoir's charwoman after an innocuous quarrel, now did everything for her. After her teaching she shopped, and on weekends she cleaned. Beauvoir accepted everything without comment. Sylvie grew thin and strained; the flat became more cluttered and dusty. The refrigerator was filled with tempting little snacks Beauvoir seldom touched. The petit fours, fruits and salads were left to molder beside the three bottles of vodka and four of scotch she kept chilling at all times.

This was the situation for the first few months of 1986. Throughout it all, Beauvoir continued to see her friends, to meet with scholars and writers, to grant interviews and dispense favors—usually in the red bathrobe, now slightly the worse for constant wear. Everyone thought she would go on like this for years to come because she had no visible incapacitation except her swollen stomach and her impaired walking. The friends who saw her frequently had grown so used to her appearance they had come to accept it as just another sign of her aging.

So it was a great surprise when, on the evening of March 20, Beauvoir turned to Sylvie as they sat quietly together in the Rue Schoelcher and complained of stomach cramps.[17] She blamed it on the ham she had eaten for dinner, but when the pains did not subside Sylvie insisted on taking her to the Hôpital Cochin. The initial diagnosis was possible appendicitis, and the doctors decided to keep her there for tests and observation. After several days, when she seemed more likely to be suffering from an obstruction of the colon or possible colitis than from appendicitis, exploratory surgery was performed. It confirmed what her physicians had suspected: complications resulting from severe cirrhotic damage, retention of fluid and pulmonary edema. She had all Sartre's diseases minus the diabetes and the arterial damage.

Following the surgery, she developed pneumonia along with the edema and was moved into the intensive-care unit, where she remained for the next two weeks. Treatment with antibiotics and various drainages brought the pulmonary problems under control, and she was moved into a private room in early April. Her doctors believed she was well enough to get out of bed, and because they wanted to keep her circulation flowing they recommended daily walks and kinesthetic massage to toughen her skin against bedsores. This was prescribed for two weeks in the hope that she would recover sufficiently in that time to be released into Sylvie's custody. The masseuse brought the only levity to a sad and tense time: despite all Beauvoir's attempts to convince the woman to vote for the Socialists, she had cast her ballot for the right-wing candidate, Jean-Marie Le Pen.

During these two weeks, Beauvoir's greatest enemy was boredom. She was too weak to read, and even though visitors were permitted one hour each day, she was too exhausted to receive them. Her friends, and especially her sister, who remained at home in Alsace, depended on Sylvie's telephone calls to keep them informed. It was exhausting for Sylvie, who continued to teach while coping with all the extra demands. She, Lanzmann, Bost and Hélène all agreed that the illness should be treated with strict secrecy to prevent reporters and admirers from laying siege to the hospital staff or grounds. Somehow they succeeded in keeping Beauvoir's presence from the press and her fans.

Throughout her hospitalization, one of Beauvoir's major concerns was her sister. Hélène's paintings were being exhibited at Stanford University in conjunction with a conference held by the Center for Research on Women, but she was reluctant to go there because Lionel had just undergone ear surgery and was recuperating slowly at home. Now, with Beauvoir in the hospital, Hélène decided not to go at all. Beauvoir did not want her to miss the opening and sent a plane ticket as a good-luck gift to insure that Hélène would take the trip she had looked forward to throughout a long cold winter of hard work. Her departure date was assured when it co-incided with Beauvoir's removal from intensive care to a private room and Lionel was invited by friends to recuperate in North Africa. Hélène flew to San Francisco, with everyone relieved that life for all was continuing as normally as possible under such difficult circumstances. It was an unex-pected shock when she arrived in the Bay Area on April 11 and was greeted by a phone call from Sylvie with news of her sister's destabilization. The pulmonary congestion was not responding to treatment and Beauvoir was once again in the intensive-care unit.

For the next two days the telephone calls between the two women were "a series of ups and downs,"[18] as Beauvoir first rallied, then failed, then rallied again. By April 13, she seemed to have stabilized in a mostly unconscious state. She slept nearly all the time, but when she awoke she appeared to be lucid. Thus it was as much a shock to Sylvie, Hélène and the few devoted friends who knew of her illness as it was to the world at large when she died the next day.

On April 14, at 4 P.M. in Paris, Simone de Beauvoir died, just eight hours short of the anniversary of Sartre's April 15 death six years previ-ously. The official cause of death was "pulmonary edema."

Sylvie, now calling herself le Bon de Beauvoir, took charge of the fu-neral arrangements with the help of Lanzmann and Bost. Six years ear-lier, Lanzmann had quietly bought the space next to Sartre in the Mont-parnasse Cemetery and made arrangements for Beauvoir to be buried there rather than in the family plot at Père Lachaise. It seemed the final irony that she, who had shunned marriage for more than fifty years, was buried beside her companion, an irony compounded by the fact that they died of the same causes and almost on the same day of the year.

Simone de Beauvoir's body, wearing the red turban, the bathrobe and Nelson Algren's ring, remained in the hospital amphitheater until Saturday, April 19. A viewing was scheduled for family and close friends from 1 to 2 P.M., and they assembled in a large lounge adjacent to the room which held the coffin. They entered and filed past the bier, greeting Sylvie and Hélène, who stayed there the entire time. As if to proclaim their separate relationship with Beauvoir, Sylvie stood on the right of the coffin with Bost by her side, Hélène on the left with a friend to support her. Lionel de Roulet, still too weak to stand, was seated in the lounge. Lanzmann moved quietly among those gathered, allowing others to grieve while he attended to arrangements and details.

Those who viewed Simone de Beauvoir's body represented her living autobiography. Her cousins Jeanne and Magdeleine had come from Meyrig-nac and La Grillère; her friend GéGé was there, as were friends from the postwar glory days of Saint-Germain-des-Prés; colleagues from *Les Temps Modernes*, both past and present, filed past her bier. Four former ministers of the Mitterrand government attended: Yvette Roudy, Jack Lang, Laurent Fabius and Lionel Jospin.

At the end of the hour, the wooden inner coffin in which, like Sartre, she would later be cremated was sealed shut and placed in a hearse piled so high with flowers that they nearly doubled the height of the vehicle itself. Attached to the rear door was a wreath from *Libération*—the newspaper she and Sartre had helped to found—so tall it could be seen from the rear of the cortege. Lionel was unable to walk, so he and Hélène were driven to the cemetery, but everyone else formed behind Sylvie and Lanzmann, who walked behind the hearse close enough to touch it frequently all the way to the gravesite. Immediately outside the amphitheater, reporters and photographers swarmed with cameras, thrusting them into everyone's face in order not to miss anyone their editors might consider important. A crowd estimated at between three and five thousand people, a cross section of society so diverse in appearance and background, yet unified in grief and the desire to pay respect, jammed the courtyard and the narrow streets that fed into the Boulevard du Montparnasse.

Strangers struck up conversations and small groups spontaneously formed and reformed as the cortege proceeded slowly toward the cemetery. The thousands who marched included the famous and the unknown, among them a surprising number of young fathers bearing small children on their shoulders because they wanted them to be able to say someday that they had paid their respects to one of France's greatest women. Scholars and feminists from many countries marched, renewing friendships and making new ones. A large delegation of African women in native dress supported a cumbersome mass of flowers. There were many old people, men and women whose dress and mien were of the working classes, some with small patches of the tricolor on their lapels, most carrying single flowers that would later be strewn on her grave. Many women of Simone de Beauvoir's generation walked along supported by middle-aged women who could have been their daughters, a great number shedding real tears.

As the procession wound slowly down the Boulevard du Montparnasse, all other traffic was halted. One irate cab driver who left his car to bellow at the slowness of those who marched at the end of the procession was so chagrined when he found out whose funeral it was that he parked the taxi and joined the march. Many persons turned in silent homage as they passed by the Paris that Simone de Beauvoir loved so much: from her birthplace above the Dôme to the Coupole where she danced and drank so many nights away, to the Rue du Départ and the Boulevard Edgar Quinet, past the white apartment building that was Sartre's last home. Just as the streets were thronged, so, too, were the balconies and windows of the houses along the way.

At the cemetery, guards fearing the surge of thousands of people among the fairly fragile tombstones rushed to shut the massive iron gates. The crowd, sensing exclusion, pushed forward, many climbing over the portable barriers in an attempt to get inside. Some enterprising photographers used the barriers to climb onto the high wall, where they ran back and forth snapping shots of the people inside and out. Light rain had begun to fall, but even though the iron gates were shut no one left the procession. Those who crowded around the grave heard Claude Lanzmann read softly from the closing pages of *Force of Circumstance*, ending with the moving last paragraph in which she rails against death, refusing to go gently into the darkness which she never once in her life thought gentle. As he read, a murmur of protest, a low moan, moved throughout the assemblage, made by a number of women who were distressed that a man had been designated the graveside speaker and not a woman. Periodically the guards opened the gates and allowed more mourners to come in, but many of those already there refused to move on, so it was difficult to approach the grave itself. Cries of *"Circulez!"* and entreaties to move along in several other languages rang out, as everyone seemed to want to spend some time staring into the grave, but the crowd moved exceedingly slowly. The heartrending declaration of French writer and feminist Elisabeth Badinter, "Women, you owe everything to her!" was repeated by many who seemed unable to believe that Simone de Beauvoir was dead. Then someone complained, an oft-repeated remark ever since, that just as she had always put Sartre first in life, he was now first in death as well: his name was engraved above hers on the tombstone. It mattered not that he had died first.

For weeks after her funeral, however, it was difficult to see their mutual gravestone for the flowers that were massed high on it. After Sartre's death, there were just as likely to be objects of insult, such as the shells of lobsters and crabs (the crustaceans he so despised), as there were flowers. For Simone de Beauvoir, there was only tribute and loving homage from all over the world.

She was remembered by the Parti Socialiste, Section Montparnasse; internationally by the Féministes de Grèce; the Women's Health Center, Woman Books and Columbia University, all of New York; the international Simone de Beauvoir Society; the Campañeras du Instituto la Mujer of Madrid and the Mujeres Andaluda; the Women's Studies Programs of New South Wales and Sydney and Adelaide Universities of Australia. An African women's wreath carried the simple and touchingly misspelled sentiment "poor toi, Castor." Political realities appeared in a handmade wreath by the "Association des Ecrivains Iraniens en Escil [*sic*]."

Long after the principal mourners left the cemetary, people still clustered in groups inside and out. There seemed to be a shared sense of loss and bereavement among those who stayed on in the rain, from those who had known her well or worked with her to those who had only seen her from afar or who had not known her at all.

She had been an inspiration to many, the little girl with the mind of a man who turned the adversity of poverty into the good fortune of getting an education, becoming economically independent and taking charge of her own life. She lived that life on her own terms, prepared to defend her stances and decisions and willing to take whatever consequences came her way. All her life she valued friendship, choosing those persons she cared for most as her family. Inculcated with the views of an ultraconservative society, she nevertheless formed the most unorthodox love relationships; still, her fidelity to her personal credo never wavered and came to be accepted by many as the ideal to strive for and emulate. Much that she did confused her supporters and confounded her critics, but she was an indomitable woman, outspoken and generous with time and money for her strongly held beliefs. She was largely responsible for creating the current feminist revolution that changed the lives of half the human race in most parts of the world, and to the end of her days she was eager to challenge any nation or individual that interfered with the rights of women. She was affectionate, generous, witty and wise, but she was also quirky and opinionated, gruff and sometimes without a sense of humor. She was a beautiful woman unaware of her striking physical presence, but she was also awkward and ill-kempt. Sometimes she scolded more than she praised, and her celebrated honesty could be withering. Nevertheless, she was an inspiration, even as she refused to let herself be made into a monument, insisting that she be treated as the living, breathing, "feisty old woman" that she was. To treat her as such was difficult for many to do, and despite her wishes she did become a cultural icon. She regretted being known in France as "Our Sacred Monster," but if this dubious distinction meant that she still had influence among younger generations, she was willing to let it stand. She may have been a mass of contradictions, but she was still, in the most profoundly respectful sense of the phrase, "the mother of us all."

Notes

ABBREVIATIONS

FdB	Françoise de Beauvoir
HdB	Hélène de Beauvoir de Roulet
HPW	Helen P. Wenck
JPS	Jean-Paul Sartre
MDD	Simone de Beauvoir, *Memoirs of a Dutiful Daughter* (Cleveland: World Publishing, 1959)
NA	Nelson Algren
NA/OSU	Nelson Algren Collection, Ohio State University Library, Columbus
SdB	Simone de Beauvoir
SS	Simone de Beauvoir, *The Second Sex* (New York: Knopf, 1953)

1 | THE FAMILY
BERTRAND DE BEAUVOIR

1. This information is based on interviews with Simone de Beauvoir (hereafter SdB), her sister Hélène de Beauvoir de Roulet (hereafter HdB) and Geraldine Pardo, Jan. 21, 1982, Paris, and with Stépha Gerassi, April 12, 1982, Putney, Vt. I base my analysis of SdB's family background on extensive interviews with her and her sister; with the two cousins she writes of in her memoirs Mmes. Magdeleine de Bisschop, Oct. 18–19, 1986, and Aug. 15–18, 1987, and Jeanne de Beauvoir Dauriac, Oct. 18–19, 1986; and with other family members and their friends who will be cited where appropriate. The memories of their family and views of their society correspond strongly to Theodore Zeldin's analysis of the bourgeois family in his *France 1848–1945,* Vol. I, *Ambition and Love* (Oxford: Oxford University Press, 1979), Chap. 1, "The Pretensions of the Bourgeoisie."

2. Zeldin, *op. cit.,* p. 15.
3. M. de Saint-Allais, *Généalogie historique de la maison de Champeaux: Extrait du Tome X du Nobiliaire universel de France* (Arras: P. M. Laroche, 1892), p. 3. I am grateful to Count Raoul de Lavalette, SdB's cousin by marriage, who made this text available, and for his considerable assistance with the family genealogy.
4. SdB, HdB, Mme. Magdeleine de Bisschop and Count Raoul de Lavalette, Oct. 19, 1986, St.-Germain-les-Belles.
5. Saint-Allais, *op. cit.,* p. 3.
6. Saint-Allais gives his dates as Sept. 28, 1795–July 12, 1872; dates here are from the Beauvoir family tombstone in Père Lachaise Cemetery, Paris.
7. Saint-Allais records his birth as 1838, but the family tombstone in Père Lachaise Cemetery gives the year as 1837.
8. Zeldin, *op. cit.,* p. 17, discusses how the nobility took up agriculture after 1830 and were subsequently aped by the bourgeoisie.
9. Hélène-Elise-Marie Bertrand de Beauvoir was actually the second daughter of this union to bear the name Hélène; their first child, Hélène-Armande, was born March 3, 1871, and died Feb. 20, 1872. Hélène is a favorite name in the Beauvoir family, and at least one child in every branch bears it in each generation.
10. SdB, *Memoirs of a Dutiful Daughter* (Cleveland: World Publishing, 1958; hereafter *MDD*), pp. 23–24; SdB, HdB.
11. HdB, letter to DB, July 3, 1987. The year is disputed by others, who sometimes give it as 1797.
12. *MDD,* p. 32.
13. *MDD,* p. 32.
14. Zeldin, *op. cit.,* pp. 18–19.
15. Aimé-Fidèle-Constant Brasseur wore throughout the rest of his life the medal

619

which symbolized this office. It passed after his death to his daughter, Françoise. Just before she died, she burned all the family letters and papers in her possession but gave the medal to her sister's grandson (Brasseur's great-grandson), as she considered it an heirloom to be passed down through the males in the Brasseur family.—HdB.

16. It was probably the equivalent of an American junior-high-school education and far beyond what most convent-trained girls received as academic knowledge. Long after she was married, both SdB and HdB remembered, Françoise continued to visit and write to Mother Bertrand, entrusting the elderly nun with confidences no one else ever heard. Also, when Mother Bertrand died, Françoise mourned her much more emotionally than she mourned the death of either of her parents.

17. SdB, HdB.

18. Although the building's official address was the Boulevard du Montparnasse, the Beauvoir apartment was located on the side bordering the Boulevard Raspail. In a letter to DB, July 3, 1987, HdB described it as follows: "When you are in Paris, stand facing the Rotonde in front of the statue of Balzac and you will see on the second story [third floor], Boulevard Raspail side, the *three* windows of our apartment, each with a balcony: the dining room, living room and my parents' bedroom."

19. "When I was a very little girl, I think my parents had a very amorous relationship. My mother had been beautiful and at thirty was still very pretty. I think they were discreet—they never let me inside their bedroom. Physically, I think my mother was an ardent woman and my father knew how to make her happy sexually. They loved each other enormously and we felt it just by looking at them. . . . Gradually the relationship turned sour. . . . My mother accepted it with resignation, she screamed a lot. I think they continued to fuck for a long time. When I was home my sister and I lived in a room right next to theirs and heard them from time to time. They must have been about 42 and 49 then."—SdB. During the six years of my interviews and conversations with SdB, this was the only time she used this expletive. See also Chap. 6, Note 16.

20. Amédie de Margerie, *De la famille*, Vol. I, xxxi, p. 209. This study of the family was first published in 1860 and was subsequently so popular in France that it was reprinted in five editions. It is, as Theodore Zeldin writes (*op. cit.*, p. 300), "a strange work praising the virtues of the family but clearly uneasy that there was something wrong with it." Zeldin's chapter "Marriage and Morals" is a synthesis of the institution of marriage in modern France and has an excellent bibliography which I have used to shape my own opinions. The study by Margerie, for example, bears many correspondences to the Beauvoir family.

21. SdB, HdB. Stépha Gerassi and Geraldine Pardo both said they were very much afraid of Mme. de Beauvoir, and that her abrasive manner often made them feel awkward and inferior.

2 | MY SISTER, MY ACCOMPLICE

1. "My mother never really spoke to me of those things, and I never saw any registration documents. Louise told me the little that I have told you here. I do know that I was born in her bedroom, not in a hospital or clinic, and that my father was present along with the family doctor. I suppose everything went well, but my mother was too reserved to speak about such things, especially to her daughters."—SdB.

2. "These were some of the happiest memories I have of my earliest years— SdB. Also, *MDD*, p. 6.

3. HdB.

4. Regional newspapers wrote extensively about this scandal. Among those consulted were *Le Courrier de la Meuse*, *Le Courrier libéral*, *Le Petit Verdunois* and *L'Union verdunoise*.

5. "He had a spectacular bankruptcy. My mother couldn't talk about it because she would start crying—it was terribly traumatic for her but even worse for my aunt, because my mother was already safely married. She, my poor aunt, had to leave Verdun, her friends and all her hopes for marriage. It was quite a drama for families in those days; the literature of the 19th century talks a lot about those kinds of things, but now, of course, everything is very different."—HdB.

6. SdB. HdB has the same memory.

7. *MDD*, p. 36.

8. HdB.

9. Much of the subsequent analysis of the Beauvoir family is based on conversations with SdB and HdB. For a historical overview of the period, I have relied on

Linda L. Clark's *Schooling the Daughters of Marianne* (Albany: State University of New York Press, 1984) and my own reading of her excellent bibliography. Also, Karen M. Offen's article " 'First Wave' Feminism in France: New Work and Resources," in *Women's Studies Int. Forum*, Vol. 5 (1989), No. 6, pp. 685–89, and her book coedited with Susan Groag Bell, *Women, the Family and Freedom: The Debate in Documents*, Vol. II, 1880–1950 (Stanford: Stanford University Press, 1983).

10. Zeldin (*op. cit.*, "Children," p. 318) describes this split between parents as producing in children "conflicts resulting from the unreconciled coexistence of varying aspirations and traditions in parents." It had tremendous effect on the adult lives of both Beauvoir sisters.

11. *MDD*, p. 41.

12. *Ibid.*, p. 6.

13. SdB, HdB.

14. The Florence family was an illustrious one: Charles Florence held patents and manufactured electric-light-bulb sockets; Gabrielle Florence was a physician and professor at the Faculté de Médecin, Lyon, and was tortured and killed during World War II for her leadership of a Resistance cell. Other members of the family also included prominent physicians and manufacturers. Family history courtesy of HdB.

15. *MDD*, p. 11; also interviews with SdB, HdB, Jeanne de Beauvoir Dauriac, Magdeleine Mantis de Bisschop, and letter to DB, Dec. 3, 1986. Mme. de Bisschop is the "Magdeleine" of SdB's memoirs.

16. *MDD*, p. 11, and HdB, Aug. 30, 1984.

17. "I hated the name Henriette-Hélène. When I was little they called me 'Poupette,' so I was rarely called the hated 'Henriette.' When I exhibited [paintings] for the first time, I signed 'H. de Beauvoir.' A critic who wrote a favorable review called me 'Hélène de Beauvoir,' and I said to myself, That's a lot prettier, it has a better sound to it, so I kept that name. I think it suits me better."—HdB.

18. "Besides the tears, I was always eating, so they said."

19. SdB, HdB.

20. Zeldin, pp. 11–22. Zeldin's descriptions of the average bourgeois family are almost verbatim parallels of the family descriptions given in interviews by SdB and HdB.

21. "Simone created a scandal at home when she called it a 'false' [phony] bed in her memoirs. It was almost the only thing she wrote that outraged our mother, who kept saying, 'Your sister has created a scandal! She has disgraced the family! That bed is real, an original!' "—HdB.

22. Zeldin, p. 15.

23. HdB.

24. This phrase was used by both SdB and HdB in independent interviews.

25. HdB.

26. Information concerning their education is taken from interviews with SdB and HdB.

27. Henri Peretz, "La Création de l'enseignement secondaire libre de jeunes filles à Paris (1905–1910), in *Revue d'Histoire moderne et contemporaine*, Société d'Histoire Moderne, Paris, 1985. Peretz cites the study by F. Gibon, *L'Enseignement secondaire de jeunes filles* (Paris: S.G.E.E., 1920), which also contains informative assessments of the education of women during this period.

28. Simone de la Chaume La Coste, March 6, 1986. As Simone de la Chaume, she won the English Girls' Golf Championship at the age of 15. Her family lived in London during World War I; when they returned to Paris she entered the Cours Désir and prepared for two stages of the baccalaureate exams in the same classes as SdB and Elisabeth le Coin. She left before finishing to play in amateur golf tournaments and in 1927 was the first foreigner to win the British Ladies' Amateur Championship. Dr. Pamela Emory, golf historian, graciously provided this information. SdB describes Mme. La Coste in *MDD*, p. 155.

29. A *cours* was an educational institution that competed with boarding schools or seminaries and was the name given to a day school. Its origin dates to 1786 and *Les Cours d'éducation à l'usage des jeunes filles du monde*, a foundation of Abbé Gaultier.—Gréard, *Education et instruction, Enseignement secondaire*, Vol. I, Part III, pp. 117, 125. Frances I. Clark explains that "the *cours* differed from boarding schools particularly in this respect, that as [they] were day schools, the mothers of pupils could attend the classes and so take an active part in the education of their daughters," thus exercising constant supervision and "tightening . . . the family links." Clark provides an excellent discussion of such schools in *The Position of Women in France* (Westport, Conn.: Hyperion Press, 1981), pp. 126ff.

30. "These women who were our teachers all wore very old-fashioned clothing: very long skirts and petticoats, stiff blouses and ties—all from a much earlier era. They tried to give the impression that they came from very fine families, and indeed some of them did, but for the most part they gave an air of snobbery and superiority which they did not generally deserve. Many of them were stupid women who could teach us very little of value, and, as we did not hold to their outmoded ideals, it was often a situation of conflict as we grew older and more likely to resist or disagree with their teachings."—HdB.

31. HdB, SdB.
32. *MDD*, p. 36.
33. *MDD*, p 70; also SdB.
34. HdB.
35. SdB.
36. HdB.

3 | WHEN THE TROUBLE REALLY STARTED

1. *MDD*, p. 26; also SdB, HdB, M. de Bisschop, J. Dauriac.
2. SdB.
3. SdB, HdB, M. de Bisschop.
4. HdB. There is a plaque on the wall of the Ecole Nationale de Mines at 60 Boulevard St.-Michel, above the still-damaged walls showing where shells from Big Bertha struck the building, less than half a mile from the Beauvoir home.
5. *MDD*, p. 62.
6. "Grandfather Brasseur was such a cowardly pessimist. No matter what one said, he always had a negative response. Whereas Grandfather Beauvoir, whom we adored, was so comforting to little children. We called Grandfather Brasseur the 'Pessimist Grandfather,' and Grandfather Beauvoir was 'the Optimist.' If we said to him it was raining, he would say oh no, it was only mist, but Grandfather Brasseur saw Paris already destroyed and was pessimism incarnate."—HdB.
7. SdB, HdB.
8. HdB, interview, Aug. 30, 1984.
9. This was the phrase she used repeatedly during our six years of interviews and conversations. Despite the fact that her sister frequently corrected her, pointing out the unobstructed view of the Eiffel Tower from one row of windows and the Panthéon from the other, she refused to change her opinion. She agreed that her response "probably had much to

do with how unhappy I was living there."
10. Stépha Gerassi, Geraldine Pardo.
11. HdB.
12. I am grateful to Karen M. Offen for calling this to my attention. Also, it is important to note the distinction that the term *classe moyenne*, or middle class, at that time in France denoted a lower social order than what the American terminology usually represents. Joan W. Scott and Louise A. Tilley also write of this distinction among servants in *Women, Work and Family* (New York: Holt, Rinehart and Winston, 1978), p. 154.
13. SdB, HdB.
14. HdB.
15. This is HdB's term for her sister's attitude toward her.
16. The notable exception to this statement is probably Laurence's father in her 1966 novel *Les Belles Images*, and many critics dispute this as well.

4 | THE GIRL WITH A MAN'S BRAIN

1. SdB. HdB remembered, "Our mother's hands were always busy. Even when she read the newspapers or a book, she tried to knit or crochet, and when she took us to school on the Métro she crocheted thin strips of lace for petticoats."
2. Both SdB and HdB repeated this anecdote in every interview, which reinforces my contention that it made a powerful impression upon them from a very young age, one which lasts until the present time.
3. Remark made on *The Southbank Show*, London Weekend Thames TV network program, Jan. 8, 1983.
4. I have been greatly aided in my analysis of Françoise de Beauvoir during these years by two especially interesting studies: James F. MacMillan, *Housewife or Harlot: The Place of Women in French Society, 1870–1940* (New York: St. Martin's Press, 1981), and Bonnie G. Smith, *Ladies of the Leisure Class: The Bourgeoises of Northern France in the Nineteenth Century* (Princeton: Princeton University Press, 1981). MacMillan assesses the double standard facing both bourgeois and working-class French women as society evolved in such areas as the law, education, sexual morality and the possibilities for employment. Smith investigates the conditions among women from the northern regions of France, the area native to Françoise de Beauvoir, and con-

cerns herself especially with attempting to define what exactly a bourgeois woman is through an analysis of sexual reproduction, domestic life and religious practice and belief.

5. SdB, HdB, J. Dauriac.
6. SdB.
7. SdB, HdB, also *MDD*, pp. 36ff.
8. Francis Jeanson, *Simone de Beauvoir ou l'entreprise de vivre* (Paris: Editions du Seuil, 1966), p. 253.
9. SdB. Jeanson, *op. cit.*, p. 254, has a variant of this remark.
10. This version of her remark is from interviews with SdB. In *MDD* (p. 121) she writes: "Papa used to say with pride: 'Simone has a man's brain; she thinks like a man; she *is* a man.' And yet everyone treated me like a girl."
11. SdB: Jeanson, p. 254. HdB: interview with DB.
12. SdB, HdB.
13. HdB.
14. She made this remark in interviews with DB. Among the many printed interviews, it appears in the *Premier Entretien* with F. Jeanson, p. 254. She also repeated it to (among many others) S. Gerassi and G. Pardo. Louise J. Kaplan, Ph.D., in her book *Adolescence: The Farewell to Childhood* (Simon and Schuster, 1984), makes the following observation: "Because they were made at a time of life when we were utterly dependent on them, the love attachments of infancy have inordinate power over us, more than any other emotional investment."
15. "Jeanne was very different from us. She was nice, you could not say anything against Jeanne. She was the perfect child, the one who always obeys. If you have read Mme. de Ségur's book, you could call Jeanne her model child. We felt she had no personality of her own because she was so obedient and placid, but our father thought she was perfect."—HdB. "Jeanne was the perfect product of her upbringing. For many complex reasons, I believe my sister and I resented her even though we liked her."—SdB.
16. HdB.
17. HdB.

5 | THE YOUNG WRITER

1. "In a version translated from the German of Thomas à Kempis and abridged and simplified for French school-children."—SdB.
2. SdB wrote an introduction to a

1964 ed. called *Bluebeard and Other Fairy Tales by Charles Perrault* (London: Collier-MacMillan). "I did it simply as a literary assignment, for the money, because they asked me to write it. There was nothing sentimental about it."—Interview with DB.
3. In February 1986, Robert Gallimard, publisher of SdB and JPS, found in his firm's files, mixed in among Sartre's papers, the ms of her earliest writings; "Les Malheurs de Marguerite" bears the dates December 15–February 15, 1915, and "La Famille Cornichon" the notation "Fin" [End] October 1916. It is a browning, originally yellow packet of papers, approximately 5 by 7 inches, folded into the shape of a book and carefully wrapped now in a sheet of plastic. I am grateful to SdB for allowing me to read and quote from this ms. All translations that follow are mine.
4. "I loved the praise that came to me as the young novelist of the family, but really, I can't say that my ambition began at that time. I used to dream of owning my own bookstore, or perhaps a lending library, where people would come to me and I would help them choose their books. Mostly, I just enjoyed reading."—SdB. "I wasn't sure whether when I was grown-up I wanted to write books or sell them, but in my view they were the most precious things in the world."—*MDD*, p. 53.
5. As a university student, she turned to the American Transcendentalists, originally reading Emerson, Thoreau and Margaret Fuller, e.g., for much the same reason that she had read Alcott. In interviews, she said that she discussed American Transcendentalists with Sartre and tried unsuccessfully to persuade him to read some of their works while he was writing *Being and Nothingness*. She also insisted that they had little influence upon her own thinking and writing, but the connection is probably one philosophers should explore further.
6. SdB; *MDD*, pp. 90–91. Also, when she reflected upon the condition of women during the writing of *The Second Sex*, she found herself focusing on the four March sisters as examples of different kinds of women and she projected different adult lives upon them, all of which served as points of departure for the formation of some of her theory in that book.
7. Ann Douglas, introd. to *Little Women*, by Louisa May Alcott (New York: New American Library Signet Clas-

sic, 1983), pp. xii–xiii. Prof. Douglas' discussion of the relationships within the Alcott and March families bears an almost constant comparison to the family Beauvoir. I found her perceptive reading of this novel to be of great value and I used her remarks to formulate many of the questions I asked Simone de Beauvoir during our interviews.

8. Simone de Beauvoir wrote letters in 1984 to her American friend Helen P. Wenck, asking her to recommend and if possible send the best biographies and critical studies of George Eliot. In September 1984 conversations, she asked me to do the same. I recommended that she begin with Gordon Haight's biography and offered to prepare a list of texts I thought she should consult. In February, in a telephone conversation shortly before I was to return to Paris, she said the project was "temporarily stalled," and that I should not "waste time" on this matter. In conversation, March 1985, she said that although she continued to be interested in the project, it seemed "too daunting," and that she "could not seem to muster the necessary energies" to do it. She told me she had made "random notes," but I never saw them and do not know if they still exist and in what form. My description of her work on this project is the repetition of what she told me she had done during our March 1985 conversations.

6 | ZaZa

1. HdB; see also her description in *Souvenirs* (Paris: Librairie Séguier, 1987), pp. 74–75. "We would have been happier if our mother had not been so intent on keeping up appearances."—SdB.

2. SdB. The following is based on interviews with SdB, HdB, J. Dauriac and Mme. Yvette Sermadira Bonbolu (Louise Sermadira's daughter), Meyrignac, Oct. 19, 1986).

3. "A major development in the nineteenth century, mainly associated with the large-scale building of blocks of luxury flats under the Second Empire, was the separation of the maid from the rest of the family by having her live in a tiny room at the top of the apartment (*la chambre de bonne*). . . . In these garrets it was not always possible to find somewhere to stand up straight. The windows were often too small to admit sufficient light or air, making for excessive heat

in the summer, while it was perishingly cold in the winter. The only furniture would consist of a small iron bed, a washbasin, a table, a chair and a waterpot. Outside would be a filthy toilet. A domestic servant lacked not only the time but also the means of keeping herself clean. At a congress on tuberculosis held in Geneva in 1906, one delegate claimed that the designer of these rooms, the engineer Mansart, had done more than any other man to promote the spread of this disease."—James MacMillan, *Housewife or Harlot: The Place of Women in French Society 1870–1940* (New York: St. Martin's Press, 1981), p. 73.

4. "God, they were awful! After the first few, impressionable as I was, I still could not read them anymore. For years afterward, though, Magdeleine read them. Whenever I saw her I would scold, 'What, are you still reading that trash?' "—SdB.

5. HdB; M. de Bisschop; *MDD*, pp. 85–88; and SdB: "Well, when it did finally come, I had no trouble with my periods. They were regular, they did not traumatize or incapacitate me. They ceased the same way, so you might say that I was never much troubled by my hormones: both menstruation and menopause came and went and that was that."

6. *The Blue Guide: France*, ed. Ian Robertson (London: Ernest Benn Ltd., and New York: Norton, 1984), p. 439.

7. SdB, HdB, G. Pardo, J. Dauriac.

8. "[These] were a very 'Blvd. St.-Germain' class of people, very serious, bourgeois . . . it wasn't done to be dressed in any way sort of fashionable. I was rather spoiled, but I would never put on a smart dress to go [to the Cours Désir], always gray, a lot of beige. I wouldn't have dared to wear a nice dress there, it would have been quite out of tone."— S. La Coste.

9. J. Dauriac, S. La Coste, HdB.

10. Although she was fluent in English, SdB's accent never improved and was, at best, comprehensible throughout her life. She tried never to speak it unless absolutely necessary, claiming, "Understanding is all that counts."

11. SdB wrote a factually correct account of this incident in her friendship with ZaZa in the story "Anne," published in *When Things of the Spirit Come First* (New York: Pantheon, 1982), pp. 117–166. Her only fictional liberty was to gloss her own character, Chantal, into a much more glamorous person than she was at that time.

12. In "Anne" (*loc. cit.*, p. 134), SdB allows her character, Chantal, the triumph of having her clothing admired by Anne's sisters, "a revenge that she had promised herself with tears of rage in earlier days."

13. *MDD*, p. 118.

14. HdB.

15. *MDD*, p. 163.

16. She made this comment about her parents in 1984, when she was 76 and discussing the development of her own sexuality as a 17-year-old. As an elderly woman, she still held the view that people in their forties were too old for sex, and her view of old age was as bleak as it had always been. The uncharacteristic harshness of the sexual verb (for she seldom used profanity) was even then a facade, still her way of softening and distancing herself from physical realities she was unwilling or unable to face directly.

17. *MDD*, p. 166.

18. *MDD*, p. 167.

7 | EIGHTEEN, AND IN LOVE WITH LOVE

1. For information about the French educational system during the years Simone de Beauvoir was in attendance, I have consulted (among others) the following sources: Susan Groag Bell and Karen Offen (eds.), *Women, the Family and Freedom: The Debate in Documents* (Stanford: Stanford University Press, 1983), Vol. I, pp. 169–172; Frances I. Clark, *The Position of Women in Contemporary France* (Westport, Conn.: Hyperion Press, 1981), pp. 106–59; Linda L. Clark, "The Molding of the *Citoyenne*: The Image of the Female in French Educational Literature, 1880–1914," *TR/TR*, No. 3–4 (1977), pp. 74–104, and *Schooling the Daughters of Marianne* (Albany, State University of New York Press, 1984); Steven C. Hause with Anne R. Kenney, *Women's Suffrage and Social Politics in the French Third Republic* (Princeton: Princeton University Press, 1984); James F. MacMillan, *Housewife or Harlot: The Place of Women in French Society 1870–1940* (New York: St. Martin's Press, 1981), pp. 46–55; Henri Peretz, "La Création de l'enseignement secondaire libre de jeunes filles à Paris (1905–1920), *Revue d'histoire moderne et contemporaine*, Société d'Histoire Moderne, Paris, 1985. Karen Offen, "The Second Sex and the Baccalauréat in Republican France, 1880–1924," *French Historical Studies*, Vol. XIII, No. 2 (Fall 1983, pp. 252–286; and Theodore Zeldin, *France 1848–1945*, Vol. II, *Intellect and Pride* (New York: Oxford University Press, 1980), pp. 139–204.

2. Félicien Challaye to Amélie Gayraud, in *Les Jeunes Filles d'aujourd'hui* (Paris, 1914), pp. 281–83, quoted in Offen, "The Second Sex and the Baccalauréat," *loc. cit.*, pp. 262–63.

3. Laws enacted March 25 had extended the duration of secondary education for girls from five to six years, to conform to the same program as that which had existed independently for boys.

4. It made little difference whether a girl completed the course or not, because the Cours Désir was legally considered to be a primary school, which meant that the certificate of *diplome de fin d'études secondaires* (a "finishing certificate") had no practical value whatsoever and signified merely that a girl had attended for five years.—Peretz, *op. cit.*, p. 247, n. 23.

5. It allowed them to compete with Catholic schools which had offered Latin since the laws separating Church and State of 1905. MacMillan, *op. cit.*, p. 52, writes: ". . . by way of retaliation against these attacks [the vigorous anticlerical measures enacted in the aftermath of the Dreyfus Affair, culminating in the 1905 law separating Church and State] and of refuting republican allegations about their inferior educational standards, Catholic headmistresses seem to have decided to upstage their rivals by making provision for the teaching of Latin in their schools."

6. Joan Scott and Louise Tilley, *op. cit.*, p. 160, note that even after 1914 "teaching remained . . . a means of social improvement for daughters of peasants, artisans and factory workers"; see p. 185 for "the status of teachers in France."

7. "I still remember how emotional I felt when I read Colette's stories, and I don't know why I didn't try to communicate that feeling when I wrote my memoirs. Perhaps it was because at the time I was writing, I worried about giving too much credit to other writers, or too much emphasis to the influence they might have had on me. Probably it was because I was then in the process of becoming a well-known writer and I did not want to call too much attention to women writers other than myself."—SdB.

8. SdB recounted a version of this incident in *MDD*, p. 156. In an interview she added, "I think I knew when I was

writing this [incident] how nasty he was to me, but I didn't want to take the time there to explain it. It distracted from what I was writing."

9. *MDD*, p. 157.

10. S. La Coste.

11. SdB, HdB.

12. Françoise's opinion of life at Sèvres was perhaps based on the spartan regimen of the years between its founding and World War I. Students were permitted to take a bath only once every three weeks until showers were installed in 1888, and then they were still infrequent; unnecessary heating and lighting were prohibited, which meant none at all except for the scantest in the public rooms; and only the meanest facilities existed for such things as food and hospital care.—MacMillan, *op. cit.*, p. 52.

13. Peretz, *op. cit.*, p. 253.

14. HdB.

15. SdB described the dress in *MDD*, p. 171.

16. *MDD*, p. 175.

17. *MDD*, p. 178.

18. Theodore Zeldin, *France 1848–1945*, Vol. II, *Taste and Corruption* (New York and London: Oxford University Press, 1980), pp. 9 and 11.

19. *MDD*, p. 174.

20. SdB. In 1982, when she tried to reconstruct the period in which her father finally lost his domination and influence over her, she very quickly reached the point where even the recollection of some of the authors she had read during this time was so emotionally painful that she found it difficult to continue to list them.

21. *MDD*, p. 198.

8 | "A HIGH-MINDED LITTLE BOURGEOIS"

1. SdB's word, used in interviews and conversations about Jacques Champigneulle; in a certain sense, an accurate one.

2. SdB; *MDD*, p. 60.

3. SdB; *MDD*, p. 186.

4. *MDD*, p. 187.

5. Alain-Fournier, *Le Grand Meaulnes* (New York and England: Penguin, 1968), p. 63.

6. *MDD*, p. 158.

7. Linda L. Clark, *op. cit.*, p. 31: [women students studying to be teachers at Fontenay-aux-Roses were exhorted] "to be conscious of their responsibility to form in each student 'une âme d'homme' or 'to

cultivate the man.' A Paris *inspectrice* of schools complained openly in 1911 about the predominance of the male gender in much school literature for girls, but few others joined her."

8. Alain-Fournier, *Le Grand Meaulnes*, p. 173.

9. *Ibid.*, p. 157.

10. In every interview discussing her adolescent feelings and emotions, SdB used the word "suffocate" frequently.

11. SdB; HdB.

12. *MDD*, pp. 209–10.

13. *MDD*, p. 218.

14. Cagne, sometimes spelled Khagne, is the course followed by students who hope to gain admission to the "Grandes Ecoles" in France. Although she was not enrolled in this course until 1928, surviving lists in unpublished mss dating from 1926 contain this heading.

15. Robert Speaight, *François Mauriac: A Study of the Writer and the Man* (London: Chatto & Windus, 1976), p. 49.

16. At a loss for words one afternoon, I used this phrase to try to describe what seemed to me to be periods of depression, and she seized upon it as an apt and fitting phrase. She liked it so much that from then on, when we discussed a period or situation in her life that had troubled her, she would give a somewhat nervous laugh, wave her hand, shrug her shoulders and say, "Well, I suppose it was another dark night of my soul."

17. Not all of it was destroyed, however. A collection of loose pages dating from 1928 is now in the possession of the publisher, William Targ, who graciously made it available to me. In a letter to me postmarked June 25, 1985 (SdB never dated her letters), she wrote, "I am astonished that Mr. Targ has a manuscript of mine dated 1928. I wrote little more then than crude, confused blunderings, all of which I destroyed."

18. Both sisters frequently used the analogy of ducks to describe themselves during their adolescence, often as an "ugly duckling" or an "awkward duck."

19. HdB.

20. HdB does not remember whether this informally constituted "school" had a more formal name.

21. HdB.

22. M. de Bisschop.

23. *MDD*, pp. 224–25; SdB did not remember her real name.

24. HdB.

25. Traditionally, a daughter's earnings were given to her parents as an expected

contribution to the family income, but as the nature of work changed in the early 20th century so, too, did the idea that an unmarried daughter's total earnings belonged to her family. It had become generally accepted throughout society that, as individual wage earners, young women had the right to dispose of at least part, if not all, of their income on themselves. See Scott and Tilley, *op. cit.*, Chap. 8, "Women in the Family Consumer Economy," pp. 176–213, also pp. 176–88. Linda L. Clark, *op. cit.*, p. 43, notes how textbooks throughout the 19th century were written to underscore the social reality that women were taught to value earning money primarily as a way to contribute to the family economy. Textbooks continued to stress this message throughout the early 20th century during the years when SdB was being educated. Tilley and Scott provide documentation to demonstrate how this attitude changed after World War I. Although their research is centered primarily upon working-class families, their conclusions are appropriate for the economic realities of the Beauvoir family as well.

26. SdB; HdB.

27. This is the term used by both his daughters to refer to a series of women to whom he gave substantial sums of money, but whom he did not support entirely. They infer that these were women of whom he was genuinely fond, and that the relationships were more than sexual. They base their opinions on arguments overheard between their parents and from conversations with other family members.

28. SdB.

29. SdB, HdB.

30. "Better to leave her unnamed. She's very proper in society now and just a private citizen, wife of a rich man."—SdB, 1983.

31. Stépha Gerassi. She was Ukrainian, but the Polish spelling of her name, Estepha Awdykovicz, is given here because the Ukraine was under Polish rule at the time of her birth and on all legal documents the Polish spelling was used, and this was how she was known in Paris. However, she preferred the Ukrainian spelling of her family name, Awdykovitch, and asked that the distinction be noted here.

32. "That girl had the appetite of a horse. She ate everything, especially if it looked pretty. I found out why when she invited me to her house. Her mother was a lousy cook—everything gray and boiled.

There was enough to eat, but it was not very appealing."—S. Gerassi. HdB agreed: "My mother never learned to do more than imitate the convent cooking of her girlhood. We looked forward to visiting our grandparents and other relatives and friends because our mother was such a bad cook." SdB said, "Our mother was very frugal, and even after the '14–18 war she continued to make awful dishes."

33. G. Pardo.

34. SdB; HdB made a similar comment.

35. SdB. Lisa Quermadec and Blanchette Weiss respectively in her memoirs.

9 | THE YOUNG GIRL WHO WORKED TOO MUCH

1. SdB; *MDD*, p. 261.

2. "It was a great sacrifice for me to miss the big midday meal—I had a huge appetite in those years, and the food at Meyrignac was fresh and wonderful. But I have always hated butter and cheese, so I made do with bread and fruit."—SdB.

3. J. Dauriac, M. de Bisschop.

4. J. Dauriac, confirmed by M. de Bisschop.

5. Jean Pradelle in her memoirs.

6. SdB.

7. *MDD*, p. 259.

8. *MDD*, p. 261.

9. S. Gerassi.

10. S. Gerassi.

11. The first two comments are SdB; the third *MDD*, p. 247.

12. *MDD*, p. 247.

13. In French, *les talas*, a slang expression probably based upon a term for priest, *talapoin*. The counterpart in English would probably be the Irish expression of disdain, "one who kisses the hem of the priest's cassock."

14. Michel Reismann in her memoirs.

15. S. Gerassi.

16. Jean Mallet in her memoirs.

17. Pierre Clairaut in the memoirs.

18. Mrs. Gerassi was pleased to read in *MDD*, p. 288, that SdB finally gave her the credit for this observation, because when they were all young only Gandillac's comment had seemed to matter.

19. HdB.

20. Francis Steegmuller, *Cocteau: A Biography* (Boston: Little, Brown/Atlantic Monthly Press, 1970), p. 92.

21. Jean Cocteau, *Oeuvres complètes*, Vol. II, *Le Potomak* (1925–27), pp. 101, 115.

22. *MDD*, p. 309. Herbaud is the name she gave to René Maheu.

23. Cocteau, *op. cit.*, p. 57.

24. SdB; Henriette Nizan, May 9, 1983; Annie Cohen-Solal, in *Sartre: A Life* (New York: Pantheon, 1987), p. 74, writes that "Sartre had already commented on one philosophy candidate, tall, serious, with blue eyes: 'Charming, pretty, dresses horribly.'"

25. Cohen-Solal, p. 75.

26. *MDD*, p. 310.

27. Prof. Léon Brunschweig (1869–1944) was responsible for supervising the DES, or Diplôme d'Etudes Supérieures, which for SdB meant her last two years of study. In her memoirs, she writes that he supervised her "thesis," but no record of any such work exists in the three libraries likely to contain such documents or the record of them, the Bibliothèque Nationale, the Ste.-Geneviève or the Sorbonne. SdB remembered it as an "ambitious undertaking, very long and detailed," but the likelihood is that it took the form of an analytical term paper of approximately 100 pages or less, chosen in cooperation with her adviser and intended to satisfy him that she was capable of further advanced, independent research. She did not keep a copy of this work and did not "recall anything at all" about its content, so it would appear to be lost.

28. Francis Steegmuller translates this as "Once upon a time there was a chameleon. Its owner, to keep it warm, placed it on a piece of scotch plaid. It died of exhaustion." He also says of *Le Potomak*, "No translation has ever been made or is likely to be made. . . ." Steegmuller, *op. cit.*, pp. 90–91.

29. It is pronounced Kas-TORR, with the accent on the second syllable. One day while I was using the synonym finder of my computer program, the cursor was mistakenly on "Beauvoir" instead of on the word I wanted to change. The suggestion was "Beaver," which I found an uncanny coincidence.

30. HdB; S. Gerassi.

31. The first interview was Feb. 4, 1982; a second was March 4, 1986. In a conversation (our very last meeting) March 9, 1986, SdB returned to the subject of Maheu, saying, "Maheu was very respectful, without question. And he was especially prudent because he was very young and he had a jealous wife. He had not the least desire to involve himself in such a situation. They [people who believed she and he were physically involved] are dreaming. It's all false." However, in interviews with John Gerassi, Maheu insisted that he had been SdB's first lover. J. Gerassi, telephone conversation, Oct. 5, 1989.

32. H. Nizan.

33. Several indecipherable notes in the Targ Ms attest to this. SdB verified that they date from this time.

34. Rosamond Lehmann's fiction became a secret passion for SdB throughout the 1930s: "I had to hide it from Sartre, because he would have laughed at me wasting my time. I told Olga [Bost] about these novels, my cousin Magdeleine too, but they only read French and I'm not sure Lehmann was ever translated." She read each one as it appeared until *The Ballad and the Source* (1944), which she read after the war. "But by that time I think I had outgrown her, because I never read another and really don't recall any that were published after that."

35. *MDD*, p. 303. SdB quoted this letter without permission of the Le Coin family, and in 1983 she said they had briefly threatened to bring legal action against her when she published it, but decided not to risk the publicity.

36. Indecipherable fragments are extant in the Targ Ms, such as: "at this moment a reunion of the [unclear] of all the ethics, the work of my whole life." Several lines farther: "I am going to try to write a book in order not to lose my [unclear] and then [unclear] my [unclear] and then this love where I will also try to employ myself [unclear] and then nothing of my ethics. First the 2nd part, then the first. To be [unclear] to be someone [unclear] rather than to do something." SdB read this fragment and tried unsuccessfully to decipher it, saying, "I must have been in a very bad way, because I cannot understand the only words that would make sense of it. I wonder—did I not want to understand what I was writing?" I am grateful to her, Dominic Di Bernardi and Marie-Noëlle Domke for assistance with this translation.

37. SdB and HdB both related this incident in separate interviews. Another version occurs in *MDD*, p. 303.

38. SdB, HdB.

39. I am grateful to Mme. de Bisschop, who showed me the original and only existing copy of this song at La Grillère Oct. 18, 1986. My translation.

40. "The Purple Shrimp" was a nickname meant to connote the exotic, the foreign, the beauty and taste (in both senses of the word) lying just beneath the

hard ugly shell. St.-Lazare was a home for lost and wayward girls.

10 | CASTOR

1. The description of Merleau-Ponty and the first Lévi-Strauss quotation are from interviews with SdB. The second about Lévi-Strauss is from *MDD*, p. 294.

2. *MDD*, p. 294, and SdB.

3. *MDD*, p. 295. All quotations until noted otherwise are from this source.

4. Women students were not taken seriously because, although they may have been enrolled in the university, it was understood that if they did not marry they would not compete for the highest positions with men but would be content with inferior status and remuneration.

5. Madeleine Chapsal, *Les Ecrivains en personne* (Paris: Julliard, 1960), pp. 17–37.

6. The first and third sentences are from interviews, the second is from Chapsal, *op. cit.* A former student, Célia Bertin, described herself as "transported with admiration" by Beauvoir's teaching: "it was a masterful presentation of traditional material, but she was so fascinating that the students followed her out into the street to find out where she lived, what she did. We didn't know a single thing about her."—"Témoignages," *La Vie en rose*, No. 16 (March 1984), p. 38.

7. As students, Sartre, Nizan and Maheu were nicknamed "Les Trois Mousquetaires." After graduation, circumstances separated them, but Sartre and Guille remained friendly for a number of years, throughout which they were known by their student nickname, "Les Petits Camarades."

8. This statement, from a 1982 interview, represents her correction of the description in *MDD*, p. 321.

9. Monad: an entity conceived after the fashion of the self, and regarded as the ultimate unit of being or as a microcosm. The basis of Leibniz's philosophy.

10. *MDD*, p. 319.

11. Two to three weeks are entirely devoted to them; anyone is free to attend and watch what is certainly a rigorous, often grueling, sometimes humiliating affair.

12. *MDD*, pp. 321–38.

13. *MDD*, p. 331.

14. H. Nizan.

15. *Sartre by Himself*, trans. Richard Seaver (New York: Urizen, 1978), p. 23.

16. *Ibid.*, p. 22.

17. *MDD*, p. 335.

18. *Ibid.*

19. SdB. In a 1974 conversation, they talked together about Sartre's attitude toward himself and his novel *Nausea* (published in 1938, written shortly after his graduation), but the remarks apply as well to this earlier period. SdB: ". . . while you were arrogant you were also—the word modest doesn't suit you—but let's say reasonable and long suffering." Sartre: ". . . I still looked upon myself—though in all modesty, if I may say so—as a genius. I talked to my friends as a genius talks to his friends. Quite unpretentiously, but seen from within, it was a genius who was speaking."—SdB, *Adieux: A Farewell to Sartre* (New York: Pantheon, 1984), p. 158.

20. Sartre, *Life Situations: Essays Written and Spoken*, trans. Paul Auster and Lydia Davis (New York: Pantheon, 1977), transl. of *Situations X* (Paris: Gallimard, 1975), p. 59. The full text of this interview appeared in *Le Nouvel Observateur*, June 23 and 30 and July 7, 1985.

21. I am grateful to Prof. Dorothy Kaufmann for allowing me to quote from her unpublished interview with SdB, March 2, 1982.

22. H. Nizan. SdB responded, "She is probably correct that they resented me to some degree, but she resented me the most and you must make her personal resentment of me very clear."

23. *MDD*, pp. 337–38.

24. As an elderly woman, Beauvoir rejected the fact that his relationship with her might have influenced his performance, but her denial was so vehement that the observation must have touched a sensitive cord. Maheu left Paris, and SdB lost all contact with him until many years later when he returned as director of UNESCO and they conducted an intimate friendship.

25. *MDD*, p. 338.

26. The emphasis is mine, used here to indicate her annoyance at my repeated questioning.

27. Cohen-Solal, *Sartre*, p. 74.

28. HdB, letter to DB, April 12, 1987.

29. S. Gerassi.

30. This is from another letter SdB quoted without permission of the Le Coin family.

31. The following is from a portion of the Targ Ms, which SdB was shown in 1983 and asked to comment upon. She

was unable to do more than ascribe portions of it to 1927, 1928 and 1929, and to say that it referred to philosophical essays, a planned novel to deal with ZaZa (there is actually a dedication page for such a work, dated "1928") and a section on "Jeannine arriviste" and "a friendship of youth and childhood." There is also the section on philosophy discussed in Chapter 9. Much of this ms, written on tissue paper in minuscule handwriting, is full of inkblots and stains and is impossible to decipher. Even SdB could not read it. She did not believe it was a single piece of fiction, but rather a motley assortment of unrelated jottings that had somehow been gathered together and offered for sale by someone unknown to her.

32. HdB, letter to DB, April 12, 1987.

33. M. de Bisschop.

34. Georges de Beauvoir's remarks were reported in interviews with SdB, HdB, M. de Bisschop and J. Dauriac.

35. SdB denied that it had taken courage to stand up to her parents so decisively: "There was no courage in the sense of rational thought. Everything happened so quickly that it just happened. Sartre was the only one who showed courage, if that is how we describe his response to my father. My mother and I were only demonstrating our deep emotions on this subject."

36. M. de Bisschop, letter to DB, June 11, 1987.

37. MDD, p. 360.

38. "The opening year promised well," she wrote in September 1970, noting, "We had kept the habit of reckoning by school years."—SdB, Adieux, p. 8.

39. Lettres au Castor et à quelques autres, ed. SdB, Vol. I, 1926–1939 (Paris: Gallimard, 1983), introd., p. 7. This is one of the few times to my knowledge that SdB was not entirely honest. In our interviews she told me repeatedly that all of her letters to Sartre had been lost over the years, either "through carelessness" or "in that bombing when he lived on the Rue Bonaparte," or "someone took them and tried to sell them for a little money," or "I don't know what happened to them; perhaps someone is keeping them until I die to make some money from them." These are typical of the comments she made to my repeated requests to see her side of the correspondence, because I had seen Sartre's letters as she was working on them for the published edition. Now and again, she claimed to "find" some which were pertinent to my questions or neces-

sary for my understanding. After her death, her executor, Sylvie le Bon de Beauvoir, told me and others that SdB had recovered all the letters she wrote to Sartre, when he gave them to her as a gift toward the end of his life, but that no one would be permitted to see them until she decided what to do with them, and that it could take many years before she came to any decision. The originals of Sartre's letters which appear in the two volumes were deposited shortly after publication in the Bibliothèque Nationale in Paris with the proviso that they will not be open for inspection for an unspecified number of years.

11 | ON HER PARIS HONEYMOON

1. MDD, p. 340.

2. Ibid.

3. Jean-Paul Sartre, War Diaries: Notebooks from a Phoney War, 1939–40, ed. Arlette Elkaïm-Sartre (London: Verso Editions, 1984), p. 138. He confided this to a notebook kept while on military duty in 1939, but unlike SdB, who continued to be fascinated with the effect of events upon herself until she died, he concluded, "After the war I shall no longer keep this diary, or if I do I shall no longer speak about myself in it. I don't want to be haunted by myself till the end of my days."

4. In a 1986 interview, she said she used the singular "life" deliberately, to convey to her readers the unity she shared with Sartre. The entire quotation is from SdB, The Prime of Life (Penguin, 1962), p. 362.

5. HdB.

6. In Prime of Life, p. 53, she wrote: "I had dropped nearly all the family connections—with aunts, cousins and childhood friends—that I found boring. I quite often went for lunch with my parents." In interviews in 1982 and 1984, she admitted that she had written the second sentence hoping to placate her mother, who she knew would read this book and be hurt by the truth, which was that she had eliminated all but the most necessary and unavoidable contact with her family.

7. Prime of Life, p. 363.

8. Sartre, War Diaries, p. 75.

9. Prime of Life, pp. 19–20. The idea of a morganatic relationship is particularly irritating to feminist scholars. Mary Evans

gives an intelligent analysis of the Sartre-Beauvoir couple at the beginning of their relationship in *Simone de Beauvoir: A Feminist Mandarin* (New York: Tavistock, 1985), pp. 13–14.

10. SdB. In *Prime of Life*, p. 53, she writes of going to nightclubs alone with Henriette Nizan after Sartre left for military service, but Mme. Nizan (interview with DB) does not remember being alone with SdB on any social occasion.

11. *Prime of Life*, p. 23. In an interview, I asked SdB if she used the incident of the cat as prefiguration of their pact, to enhance and possibly dramatize it for literary effect, and, if so, could she explain any possible intention she may have had for juxtaposing and/or correlating the incident of a caged animal with the beginning of her "contingency" with Sartre. At first I thought she did not understand my question, but soon I realized she was only puzzled by it. "I told it that way because that was the way it happened," she replied. She insisted that for her the literal representation of position and situation were paramount when she wrote this passage, and any metaphorical beauty was "purely unintentional."

12. The following exchange takes place between SdB and Alice Schwartzer in *After "The Second Sex": Conversations with Simone de Beauvoir*, trans. M. Howarth (New York: Pantheon, 1984), p. 111: AS: "Jean Genet once said of the two of you that you were the man and Sartre was the woman in your relationship. What did he mean exactly?" SdB: "He was trying to say that in his view Sartre was a great deal more sensitive than me, sensitive in a way that could be described as 'feminine.' My behavior, on the other hand, was much more brusque. But that had a lot to do with Genet's relationship with women, whom he doesn't exactly like very much. . . ."

13. *Prime of Life*, p. 23.

14. *Ibid.*, pp. 16, 17, 19.

15. *Ibid.*, pp. 17, 20.

16. *Ibid.*, pp. 17, 20, 24, 25.

17. *Ibid.*, p. 27.

18. Guille was called Pagniez in the memoirs, and Mme. Morel was called Mme. Lemaire. SdB did not remember her first name but thought it might be Jeannine. "In any case, I never became that familiar with her, but always called her Madame and addressed her politely [*vous*]."

19. *Prime of Life*, p. 36.

20. Sarah Hirschman, her former student at the Lycée Molière in 1938–39, remembered how she came to class every Thursday with the new issue tucked under her arm.—Interview, Jan. 20, 1987, Princeton, N.J.

21. She is called Camille in the memoirs, sometimes Toulouse in the *Lettres au Castor* and in Sartre's *War Diaries*.

22. *Prime of Life*, pp. 34 and 66 respectively. In writing about this period of SdB's life, Carol Gilligan's "central assumption in *In a Different Voice* (Cambridge: Harvard University Press, 1982), is especially useful here: "that the way people talk about their lives is of significance, that the language they use and the connections they make reveal the world that they see and in which they act." (Introduction, p. 2). Nancy Chodorow's discussion of the differences in individuation and relationships between men and women in *The Reproduction of Mothering* (Berkeley: University of California Press, 1978), pp. 166–67, makes the important point that "women do not have 'weaker' ego boundaries than men, but have a basis for 'empathy' built into their primary definition of self in a way that boys do not. Girls emerge with a stronger basis for experiencing another's needs or feelings as one's own (or of thinking that one is so experiencing another's needs and feelings)."

23. SdB believed that "his fascination with Bovary began then."

24. *Prime of Life*, p. 73. SdB's emphasis.

25. *Ibid.*, p. 71.

26. *Ibid.*, p. 74.

27. "It is obvious that the values of women differ very often from the values which have been made by the other sex," Virginia Woolf wrote in *A Room of One's Own*, a remark Carol Gilligan (*op. cit.*, p. 16) applies to her discussion of how women defer to the values and opinions of others: "The difficulty women experience in finding or speaking publicly in their own voices emerges repeatedly in the form of qualification and self-doubt, but also in intimations of a divided judgment, a public assessment and private assessment which are fundamentally at odds."

28. *Lettres au Castor*, Vol. I, p. 41, n.d., my translation. The work is not identified; she believed it might have been a continuation of one of the unfinished ZaZa/Anne stories.

29. *Ibid.*, pp. 43–44, my translation.

12 | LEARNING TO BE ALONE
AGAIN

1. SdB.
2. These episodes were witnessed by
most of her friends, including (among
many others) HdB, G. Pardo, J. Pontalis,
C. Lanzmann, S. le Bon de Beauvoir.
3. J.-L. Bost.
4. These are among the letters SdB
claimed were "lost" (*Lettres au Castor*,
Vol. I, p. 52).
5. J.-L. Bost said that Sartre and SdB
used phrases such as "grown-ups" and
"grown-up world" deliberately to separate
themselves from the respectable bourgeoisie. These expressions connoted "freedom from the rules everybody else had to
live by."
6. Joseph Barry, *French Lovers* (New
York: Arbor House, 1977), p. 296. He
refers to Sartre's interview in *Le Nouvel
Observateur*, Feb. 7, 1977.
7. SdB, *Prime of Life*, p. 77.
8. SdB, *La Force de l'âge* (Paris: Gallimard, 1960), p. 81. My translation.
9. SdB published some of these in *Lettres au Castor*. Her literary executor is
editing others for publication sometime in
the 1990s.
10. *Prime of Life*, p. 63.
11. *Ibid.*, pp. 64 and 71.
12. SdB.
13. SdB was outraged with an account
by Claude Francis and Fernande Gontier
in *Simone de Beauvoir* (Paris: Librairie
Académique Perrin, 1985), pp. 127ff.,
that she frequented in particular the Café
des Arts, where (among others) Apolli-
naire, Tzara, Varèse, and Robert and
Sonia Delaunay congregated. "They make
it seem that I knew all these people,
whom I never met at all. Also, and more
important, I don't think I was ever in that
café for more than one or two cups of
coffee. Everything they say there is all
wrong."—Interview, Feb. 18, 1986.
14. SdB uses this remark of Sartre's in
Prime of Life, p. 61. When asked what
he meant by "little ideas," she said *petit*
was a word he used to preface almost
everything, a "grandmotherly manner of
speaking meant to convey tenderness and
caring." She said it was an expression that
carried no pejorative connotation.
15. *Prime of Life*, p. 82.
16. *Ibid.*, p. 86.
17. She gives a full account of the
stories she tried to write in *Prime of Life*,
pp. 101–5. Shortly before her death, she
believed these notebooks still existed

among her papers, but had not found
them.

13 | ROUEN

1. HdB. Sartre nicknamed her "Rabbit" because everyone in their circle was
known by an animal's name (SdB as
Beaver, Maheu as Llama, etc.).
2. SdB.
3. SdB, *Prime of Life*, pp. 129 and
124 respectively.
4. She used this room as the setting for
"Chantal," in *When Things of the Spirit
Come First*, p. 51.
5. In a rare irony, her adopted daughter, Sylvie le Bon de Beauvoir, was posted
to the same Lycée Jeanne d'Arc almost 30
years later. To emulate Simone de Beauvoir, Sylvie le Bon (as she was then) went
to the same hotel, thinking to rent a
room, but found it "so impossibly filthy
and disreputable I couldn't stay there
even one night. I never understood how
Castor could have been so indifferent to
her surroundings. She could live in filth,
surrounded by garbage, and it never bothered her at all."—Interview, Oct. 20,
1986.
6. Colette Audry, March 5, 1986.
7. SdB.
8. She gives a full account of this work
in *Prime of Life*, pp. 149ff. Parts of the
ms are extant and remain uncollected
among the many cartons of papers in the
cellar storage area of her apartment building.
9. *Prime of Life*, pp. 363, 145, 147.
10. *Ibid.*, p. 148.
11. G. Pardo, April 21, 1986: "I have
never seen two people more fascinated by
hands than those two were. For a while,
he was vain about his, until all that nico-
tine made them so ugly. But he never
stopped admiring hers and could spend
hours watching as she filed and painted
them."
12. Called both "Marco" and "Zuorro"
in her memoirs.
13. J.-L. Bost, L. de Roulet, Jan. 29,
1982.
14. SdB, HdB, L. de Roulet, J.-L. Bost,
Olga Bost, C. Audry, G. Pardo.
15. Information that follows is based
on interviews with SdB, HdB, G. Pardo,
S. Gerassi, J.-L. Bost, and telephone conversations with Olga Kosakievicz Bost,
who was too ill to be interviewed personally.

16. *Simone de Beauvoir: Un Film de Josée Dayan et Malka Ribowska* (Paris: Gallimard, 1979), pp. 40–41.

17. Quotations ascribed to Sartre are from his *War Diaries*, pp. 76–77.

18. *Prime of Life*, p. 157.

19. Marie Ville, the wife of Jean-André Ville. She is also called "Marie Girard" and "the Moon Woman" in letters and memoirs.

20. Ultimately there were four persons involved in the Beauvoir/Sartre/Olga "trio," the fourth being J.-L. Bost, Sartre's pupil at Le Havre whom Olga married several years later. Of the four, only SdB and Sartre wrote about the trio or commented for publication, which gives them privileged status because they gave the only written record of it. O. Bost declined to comment or write about it; J.-L. Bost sometimes discussed it freely but was also fond of telling interviewers that he would simply deny any attribution he did not like. Throughout the actual time of the Rouen situation, all four were isolated from close contact with those who later became their friends and witnesses to much of their lives, so the four principals are the only ones who could have spoken with authority about what might really have happened among them, and their accounts must be judged accordingly.

21. Sartre, *War Diaries*, p. 78. Only Olga's initial is used in this book. Her sister Wanda is called either "Tania" or by the initial "T." Until otherwise noted, all quotations are from this text.

22. *Prime of Life*, p. 227.

23. *Ibid.*, p. 212. In 1982 she said, "I wish I had paid more attention to psychology. That I had read more, tried to understand it better. I wonder why I was so afraid of Freud when I was young—most likely because I was afraid of what I would have to learn about myself. I think that had a lot to do with my refusal to analyze myself."

24. *Prime of Life*, p. 211.

25. SdB.

26. *Prime of Life*, p. 239.

27. *Prime of Life*; all quotations until noted otherwise are from pp. 239–57.

28. C. Audry.

29. O. Bost.

30. SdB later used this incident in *She Came to Stay*, basing the character Xavière loosely on Olga.

31. SdB.

32. "I never told this to anyone before."—SdB.

1. SdB.

2. SdB and Sartre were known by scores of people, many of whom insisted they were close friends who knew them well, and to a certain extent they are correct. However, those who really knew them were "the Family" (for others were so in awe of this group that they capitalized on it). Any attempt at honest and accurate biographical assessment of both SdB and Sartre rests largely within the testimony of this small and dedicated band.

3. SdB's library card from the Shakespeare and Co. Bookstore is now in the Sylvia Beach Collection at Princeton University.

4. O. Bost introduced this subject during a telephone conversation, saying she believed it was important to address; SdB, in a subsequent interview, said, "I am surprised that Olga feels she must say this, but she has not been well in recent years and her feelings toward me have undergone a great change." (SdB refers to their estrangement after Sartre's death, to be discussed later.)

5. SdB made this sort of remark in almost every conversation or interview we had during the years I knew her. I have selected her comment of Jan. 16, 1982, to represent them all.

6. J.-L. Bost.

7. O. Bost.

8. L. de Roulet. Also HdB and SdB.

9. HdB.

10. L. de Roulet.

11. *Ibid.*

12. SdB.

13. O. and J.-L. Bost remembered seeing what sometimes amounted to little more than a phrase or a working note, followed by a "note to Castor" asking her to "deal with this."

14. Sartre to SdB, Laon, April 1937, in *Lettres au Castor*, Vol. I, 94.

15. The title, *Quand prime le spirituel*, is an ironic pun chosen after she discovered that Jacques Maritain had already used her first choice, "Primauté du spirituel" (The Ascendancy of the Spirit). SdB decided not to publish the stories in the order she wrote them. They appear as "Marcelle" (written second, originally entitled "Renée," and "the most difficult to write and the most rewritten"); "Chantal" (third, "based on a teacher at Rouen I did not like, but based more on myself, alas"); "Lisa" (the first written, most quickly abandoned, and believed by SdB

to be "the most artificial and contrived"); "Anne" (fourth and "the most painful to write"); and "Marguerite" (last, "written during my convalescence, and my favorite, the best in the book, the most successful").

16. Comments by SdB are from a telephone conversation June 21, 1982; textual citations are from the Pantheon ed., New York, 1982. Some of this analysis appeared in slightly different form in *New York Times Book Review*, Nov. 7, 1982, p. 12.

17. Paris: Bernouard, 9 vols., 1925–27. Beauvoir especially liked *Poil de Carotte, Correspondance inédite, 1880–1910* and *Journal inédit, 1887–1910*.

18. These two remarks, in language that varied only slightly, were made by many of the persons who knew Sartre and Beauvoir well during this period. Among them are J.-L. Bost, O. Bost, G. Pardo, S. Gerassi, J.-B. Pontalis, HdB, L. de Roulet, C. Audry.

19. SdB.

20. She based the character on herself, but "I gave her my mother's name," she wrote in *Prime*, p. 317. In interviews she said she never paid much attention to names but used those she liked or "those which came to mind easiest" without worrying about repetition.

21. SdB, *Prime of Life*, p. 315.

22. A 63-page typescript is still extant. Elaine Marks quotes this passage from that text, followed by the published version in *L'Invitée* and a third, nonfiction account taken from *MDD*, in her *Simone de Beauvoir: Encounters with Death* (New Brunswick: Rutgers University Press, 1973), pp. 13–14. Prof. Marks writes: "This is the incident that, with variations, appears most frequently in the writing of Simone de Beauvoir. Its importance is enhanced because it opens one of her earliest works, the unpublished *récit* of Françoise Miquel. . . . It marks the first discovery of the self and simultaneously of other people, of the solitude of the self and of its precariousness and mortality."

23. *Prime of Life*, p. 316. She noted also "Hegel's phrase about all awareness seeking the death of the Other; I did not read it till 1940."

24. *Prime of Life*, p. 327.

25. In *Prime of Life*, pp. 326–27, SdB is vague about chronology, but makes it seem as if the rejection from Grasset came after these travels, when actually it came before. She said that the holiday in the Basque region was the only one planned before the rejection; the others were a direct result of it.

15 | WHAT WILL HAPPEN TOMORROW?

1. SdB, *Prime of Life*, p. 336.

2. *Ibid.*

3. Respectively, G. Pardo, Raymond Aron and S. Gerassi.

4. SdB.

5. Bianca Bienenfeld is called "Louise Védrine" in the *Lettres au Castor*; Nathalie Sorokine is called "Lise" in the *Memoirs* and *The Mandarins* and "La petite Sorokine" in *Lettres au Castor*. She is the subject of a memoir, "Natasha: 1921–1968," by Oreste F. Pucciani, in *Perspectives sur Sartre et Beauvoir: essais en l'honneur d'Oreste F. Pucciani*, ed. Patricia de Méo, numéro spécial de *Dalhousie French Studies* (1987), pp. 5–6. Her own story, "Nuits sans importance," is included in the volume, reprinted from *Les Temps Modernes*, I, No. 3 (Dec. 1, 1945), pp. 471–93.

6. Ivan Moffatt, April 9, 1986, Beverly Hills.

7. O. Bost.

8. The first two remarks are indicative of and similar to many others I have heard at various professional meetings and conferences dedicated to the life and work of Sartre and SdB, or that I have read in much feminist scholarship. This question of their roles within their relationship is one which continues to inspire heated discussion and controversy among scholars. The latter two remarks were made to me in a telephone conversation by Nelson Algren, April 18, 1981. Algren was not interviewed in person for this book; a meeting was arranged for May 14, 1981, but he died unexpectedly on May 8.

9. *Prime of Life*, p. 359.

10. *Ibid.*, p. 376.

11. *Lettres au Castor*, Vol. I, pp. 276, 278. My translation.

12. SdB, *Adieux*, pp. 387–88.

13. The five that survived became the posthumously published *War Diaries*.

14. Sartre to SdB, in Sartre, *Oeuvres romanesques*, ed. Michel Contat and Michel Rybalka (Paris: Gallimard, Bibliothèque de la Pléiade, 1981), p. 1895. My translation.

15. *Prime of Life*, p. 392. She reprints the diary more or less as she kept it from p. 378 to p. 442, where she writes: "At this point my account breaks off. I have given a more or less accurate description of the days that followed in *The Blood of Others*, making Hélène go through the experiences that I did."

16. *Prime of Life*, p. 393, her emphasis.

17. *Ibid.*, pp. 401, 402.
18. *Ibid.*, pp. 412–21.
19. *Ibid.*, p. 418, her emphasis.
20. *Ibid.*, p. 419.

16 | WHEN LIFE GOES
SLIGHTLY ADRIFT

1. In French, the Drôle de Guerre; this was the period from the declaration of war in September 1939 to the initial German invasion of Western Europe in May 1940. Besides the writings of SdB and Sartre, references consulted for World War II include the following: Henri Amouroux, *La Vie des français sous l'occupation* (Paris: Librairie Arthème Fayard, 1961); Raymond Aron, *The Committed Observer* (Chicago: Regnery Gateway, 1983), and *Mémoires* (Paris: Julliard, 1983); Pierre Assouline, *L'Epuration des intellectuels* (Brussels: Editions Complexe, 1985), and *Gaston Gallimard* (Paris: Balland, 1984); Richard Cobb, *French and Germans/Germans and French* (Hanover and London: University Press of New England, 1983); Milton Dank, *The French Against the French* (Philadelphia: Lippincott, 1974); Adrien Dansette, *Histoire de la Libération de Paris* (Paris: Fayard, 1946); Jacques Debû-Bridel (ed.), *La Résistance intellectuelle* (Paris: Julliard, 1970); André Gide, *Journals*, Vol. IV, 1939–49 (New York: Knopf, 1951); Françoise Giroud, *I Give You My Word* (Boston: Houghton Mifflin, 1974); Bertram M. Gordon, *Collaboration in France During the Second World War* (Ithaca: Cornell University Press, 1980); Marie Granet, *Ceux de la Résistance (1940–44)* (Paris: Éditions de Minuit, 1964); Stanley Hoffmann, *Decline or Renewal? France since 1930* (New York: Viking, 1974); Pascal Jardin, *Vichy Boyhood* (London: Faber & Faber, 1975); R. Kedward and R. Austin (eds.), *Vichy France and the Resistance: Culture & Ideology* (Totowa: Barnes & Noble, 1985); Herbert R. Lottman, *The Left Bank* (Boston: Houghton Mifflin, 1982), and *The Purge* (New York: Morrow, 1986); Hervé Le Boterf, *La Vie parisienne sous l'occupation, 1940–44* (Paris: France-Empire, 1974), Vols. I and II; André Malraux, *Antimémoires* (Paris: Gallimard, 1967); Henri Noguères, *La Vie quotidienne des résistants de l'armistice à la Libération* (Paris: Hachette, 1984), and with M. Degliamie-Fouché and J.-L. Vigier, *Histoire de la Résistance en France 1940–45*, Tomes I and II (Paris: Robert Laffont, 1969); Peter Novick, *The Resistance Ver-sus Vichy* (New York: Columbia University Press, 1968); Pascal Ory, *Les Collaborateurs 1940–1945* (Paris: Editions du Seuil, 1976); Robert O. Paxton, *Vichy France: Old Guard and New Order, 1940–41* (New York: Knopf, 1972), and, with Michael R. Marrus, *Vichy France and the Jews* (New York: Schocken, 1983); David Pryce-Jones, *Paris in the Third Reich* (New York: Holt, Rinehart and Winston, 1981); David Schoenbrun, *The Story of the French Resistance* (New York: New American Library, 1980); Gertrude Stein, "The Winner Loses: A Picture of Occupied France," in *Selected Writings of Gertrude Stein* (New York: Random House, 1946); John F. Sweets, *The Politics of Resistance in France, 1940–44* (De Kalb: Northern Illinois University Press, 1945), and *Choices in Vichy France* (New York: Oxford University Press, 1986); Herbert Tint, *France Since 1918* (New York: St. Martin's Press, 1970); James D. Wilkinson, *The Intellectual Resistance in Europe* (Cambridge: Harvard University Press, 1981); Theodore Zeldin, *France 1848–1945*, Vols. I–V (London: Oxford University Press, 1973–79).

2. Whenever she spoke of herself in connection with M. Mancy, SdB used terms such as "the fallen woman," "the whore," " 'your son's [meaning Madame Mancy's] slut' " or other equally graphic remarks. She said, "The silly old man may have hurt me once or twice at first, but he was so ridiculous—all puffed up with phony moral outrage—that we only laughed at him. We [she and Sartre] never said anything to him directly or gossiped about him, for the sake of Madame Mancy's feelings."

3. *Lettres au Castor*, Vol. I, pp. 499, 508.

4. *Ibid.*, Vol. II, p. 20.

5. These comments occur throughout his letters of November 1939–January 1940, in *Lettres au Castor*, Vols. I and II. Sartre's comments quoted here are from letters of Dec. 11 and 17, 1939, in Vol. I, pp. 476 and 492.

6. SdB, *Prime of Life*, p. 365.

7. *Ibid.*, p. 369; "Une Interview de Simone de Beauvoir par Madeleine Chapsal," *Les Ecrivains en personne* (Paris: Julliard, 1960), pp. 17–37, reprinted in Claude Francis and Fernande Gontier, *Les Ecrits de Simone de Beauvoir* (Paris: Gallimard, 1979), p. 394.

8. I base my analysis of the conception and creation of *L'Invitée* on my interviews and conversations with Simone de Beauvoir and also on several bundles of loose

handwritten pages, one small notebook and parts of a typescript of about 60 pages similar to the one Elaine Marks cites in her book. SdB was not sure what had happened to the entire work, both manuscript and typescript. Earlier, on Jan. 16, 1982, she said, "Maybe that was the one [Claude] Lanzmann's stepfather wanted to buy from me, I'm not sure. I think it was *Les Mandarins* that my mother used to cover the jelly jars during the war—no, of course not, that must have been *L'Invitée*. Or could it have been *Le Sang des autres*? [It was *Les Bouches inutiles*.] I never really kept track of what happened to most of my manuscripts. Some I gave away and others got lost."

9. *Prime of Life*, p. 317.

10. *Ibid.*, p. 317.

11. SdB interview with Madeleine Gobeil in *Paris Revue*, June 1965, reprinted in Serge Julienne-Caffié, *Simone de Beauvoir* (Paris: Gallimard, 1966), p. 212; and interview with DB, Jan. 16, 1982.

12. *Prime of Life*, pp. 342–343.

13. Sartre, *War Diaries*, p. 197.

14. *Prime of Life*, p. 341: "Elisabeth's artful deceit . . . extended to every aspect of her life; Françoise, on the other hand, tried to achieve overall consistency in her life without cheating or trickery; she was therefore led to ask herself . . . just where the dividing line is set between a true and false construction."

15. *Prime of Life*, p. 338.

16. Sartre, *War Diaries*, pp. 107ff. All quotations are from this passage until otherwise noted.

17. SdB.

18. *Prime of Life*, p. 339. She discusses her intentions and her attitude toward the ending on pp. 339–40.

17 | To Stay and Try to Survive

1. *Lettres au Castor*, Vol. II, pp. 162, 201.

2. SdB, *Prime of Life*, p. 431.

3. *Lettres au Castor*, Vol. II, p. 221.

4. Ronald Hayman, in *Sartre: A Biography* (New York: Simon and Schuster, 1987), pp. 167–68, considers that "De Beauvoir must have been astounded" by "this act of betrayal."

5. *Lettres au Castor*, Vol. II, pp. 94, 110, 111.

6. HdB, *Souvenirs*, recueillis par Marcelle Routier (Paris: Librairie Séguier, 1987), p. 91.

7. *Lettres au Castor*, Vol. II, p. 236.

8. Information about Nathalie Sorokine and her family is from an interview with her first husband, Ivan Moffatt, and from Oreste F. Pucciani, who described "Natasha Moffatt" as "unusual" and "powerful" and a presence of both "defiance and charm."—"Natasha: 1921–1968," in *Perspectives sur Sartre et Beauvoir*, p. 5.

9. HdB.

10. In 1984, when I discussed with SdB the two volumes of Sartre's letters which she had just edited and published, I asked where and how she happened to find those which supposedly had been lost. "Yes, well," she replied, "obviously I never lost them." When she would not explain, I raised the possibility that she had said they were lost because he or someone else wanted them and she may not have wanted to surrender them. She refused to comment further and insisted that this line of conversation be abandoned.

11. SdB, *Prime of Life*, pp. 437–58.

12. Food rationing was instituted in France in September 1940, but in the larger cities, especially Paris, shortages were felt even before the Germans arrived and became extreme shortly after.

13. *Prime of Life*, p. 455.

14. *Lettres au Castor*, Vol. II, p. 282.

15. *Ibid.*, p. 285.

16. Pryce-Jones points out (*op. cit.*, p. 94) that the British adopted the French word *coupons* for ration cards, while the French adopted the English word "tickets."

17. Amouroux, *op. cit.*, pp. 131 and 146.

18. Pryce-Jones, p. 94: ". . . the sentence had the force of folklore about it. How else were empty shops to be explained? And in fact between half and three-quarters of the entire French produce—from crops to cattle and wine— was siphoned off to Germany."

19. SdB. In *Prime of Life*, p. 479, she wrote, "Did I buy things on the Black market? A little tea occasionally . . ."

20. Colette, *Paris from My Window*.

21. In *Prime of Life*, p. 475, she wrote: "Most evenings I spent in the Flore, where no member of the occupation forces ever set foot." Most histories of this period contradict her statement.

22. Beginning in the fall of 1940, various commissions were established barring Jews who had recently acquired citizenship from any role in public life. On Sept. 27, Jews in the Vichy sector were forbidden to return to the Occupied Zone, special

identity cards were issued, and businesses owned by Jews were required to post a sign announcing the fact. On Sept. 28, the "Otto List" was announced, a "suggestion" by the German propaganda staff that all French publishing houses voluntarily purge their lists of Jewish writers. It is estimated that more than 800 writers were so classified. Shortly thereafter, the Germans directed that a French agency be created to take responsibility for anti-Jewish policy. It was called the Commissariat Générale aux Questions Juives, the CGQJ. In October, a second agency, the Controle des Administrations Provisoires, was created to take over Jewish businesses and factories. The lists of agencies and directives dealing with the "Jewish question" continued to proliferate. Detention camps had been functioning in France for some time; by the summer of 1941 the camp at Drancy, to the north of Paris, received prisoners in what had been a half-finished housing project, now newly surrounded by barbed-wire fences. By November, the Police aux Questions Juives, the PQJ, or anti-Jewish police, had been established, and denunciations of Jews and Jewish sympathizers were commonplace.

23. *Prime of Life*, p. 466.
24. *Ibid.*, p. 478.

18 | SOCIALISM AND LIBERTY

1. Drancy was still a collection of imposing high-rise buildings that were intended before the war to be a low-income-housing project. It was just being set up as a detention center for French Jews, which the soon-to-be-released prisoners were not meant to know about or to spread the news of among the general population.
2. Jean-Paul Sartre, "Concerning an Exhibition of Paintings by Giacometti at the Galerie Maeght," originally published in *Les Temps Modernes*, June 1954, reprinted in Sartre, *Situations* (New York: Braziller, 1965), p. 178.
3. SdB, *Adieux*, pp. 387–91.
4. J.-L. Bost, G. Pardo, J. Pouillon. SdB verified that she was "confused, and therefore I suppose not acting like my usual self."
5. Wilkinson, *Intellectual Resistance*, p. 37.
6. SdB, *Prime of Life*, pp. 480–81.
7. *Ibid.*, p. 481.
8. J.-L. Bost. Jean Pouillon, Jan. 25, 1982, confirmed the names of those present.

9. Pouillon refers to *Pyrrhus et Cinéas*, published in 1944, and *Pour une morale de l'ambiguité (The Ethics of Ambiguity)*, which was not actually published until 1947.
10. *Prime of Life*, p. 482. All quotes are from this work until otherwise noted.
11. Resistance groups, known as *reseaux*, or cells, were all identified by code names. It was sometimes very confusing, because they named themselves and often more than one group took the same name, or an individual member unwittingly took his own or another cell's.
12. SdB: "Except for Merleau-Ponty, I never saw these people much after the few weeks we spent trying to get a resistance group going. I ran into them from time to time, but was never close to any of them, especially the Desantis because Dominique never liked me, always resented me for something I never understood."
13. Dominique Desanti, "Le Sartre que je connais," *Jeune Afrique*, Nov. 8, 1964.
14. J. Pouillon.
15. Cohen-Solal, p. 168.
16. Quoted in Cohen-Solal, p. 167. Robert Brasillach was a critic for the archconservative *L'Action Française* who became a collaborator; he was tried and executed by firing squad on Feb. 6, 1945.
17. Cohen-Solal, p. 169.
18. *Ibid.*, pp. 163–64.
19. John Gerassi, Dec. 7, 1981, New York.
20. Hayman, p. 180.
21. Charles de Gaulle, *Discours de Guerre* (Fribourg, 1944–45), Vol. I, pp. 13–14.
22. Information about Alfred Péron is from 1974 interviews with his widow, Marie Péron, Jan. 9, Paris; Samuel Beckett, Jan. 8, Paris; W. S. Maguinness, Jan. 24, London; and Jeannine Picabia, Jan. 10, Paris.
23. S. Beckett.
24. Between 1971 and 1976 I conducted interviews for the biography of Samuel Beckett with many persons who had known him in the French Resistance. While doing the research for SdB's life during the war, I reread much of the literature and all of the interviews I had done for the war years in the Beckett biography. At the time I was writing that book, I had no idea that I would ever write the biography of SdB, so there was no attempt on my part to solicit information about either her or Sartre. In rereading my interviews with four separate persons, among them Mme. Péron and others who will be cited

separately in this text, I discovered several references to Sartre which all these persons had volunteered as pejorative examples of an unsuitable resistant.

25. Cohen-Solal, p. 170.

26. *Prime of Life*, p. 489.

27. HdB, *Souvenirs*, p. 153.

28. Père Lachaise Cemetery is as famous for the elaborate headstones and mausoleums as it is for the people buried there. The Beauvoir family gravestone is located at the northwest corner of the cemetery, Division 61, Line 11, Nos. 4–66.

29. Françoise de Beauvoir did burn everything but some old family photograph albums and a few letters from SdB written during the war, now in the possession of HdB. SdB saved only one thing from burning, "La Famille Cornichon," which she gave to Sartre as a belated birthday present. After his death, the ms was found among his papers and returned to her by Robert Gallimard.

30. SdB gives an account of the trip in *Prime of Life*, pp. 490–98. Cohen-Solal gives further detail in *Sartre*, pp. 170–75.

31. C. Audry.

32. J.-L. Bost.

33. Peter Novick, *The Resistance Versus Vichy*, pp. 16–17.

34. Cohen-Solal, p. 173. Pierre-Eugène Drieu La Rochelle was a well-known writer and the editor of *Nouvelle Revue Française*. He collaborated with the Germans and in 1945 committed suicide.

35. Hayman, pp. 176–78.

36. *Ibid.*, p. 178.

37. Pascal Ory, *Les Collaborateurs: 1940–1945* (Paris: Editions du Seuil, 1976), p. 205. Ory's analysis of *Comoedia* is the generally accepted one, and is found on pp. 205–8. The quotation that follows is also from this work.

38. *Prime of Life*, p. 484.

39. Pierre Assouline, *Gaston Gallimard*, p. 318. Assouline also notes: "Marcel Arland wrote the first review in praise of *L'Invitée*, and, shortly after, Jean Grenier wrote a highly favorable review of *L'Etre et le néant*." (Oct. 30 and 16 respectively, 1943).

40. John Gerassi, *Jean-Paul Sartre: Hated Conscience of His Century*, Vol. I, *Protestant or Protester?* (Chicago and London: University of Chicago Press, 1989). Gerassi was interviewed on Dec. 7, 1981.

41. *Prime of Life*, p. 484.

42. Pryce-Jones, p. 168.

43. Hervé Le Boterf, *La Vie parisienne*

sous l'occupation, 1940–44, Vol. II, p. 202.

44. Patrick McCarthy, telephone conversation, June 2, 1986.

45. This expression was used by SdB, HdB, members of the Family and so many others that I single no one specifically for attribution.

19 | THE PROMISE OF THE FUTURE

1. SdB, *Pyrrhus et Cinéas* (Paris: Gallimard, 1944), p. 11. My translation.

2. The novels include *L'Invitée* (*She Came to Stay*), published in August 1943; *Le Sang des autres* (*The Blood of Others*), 1945, and *Tous les hommes sont mortels* (*All Men Are Mortal*), 1946; the philosophical essay *Pyrrhus et Cinéas* was published in September 1944 and *Pour une morale de l'ambiguité* (*The Ethics of Ambiguity*) in 1947; *Les Bouches inutiles* (*Useless Mouths*) was staged in 1945.

3. SdB, *Prime of Life*, pp. 501–2.

4. *Femme de charge* is usually translated as "household manager."

5. "It was my beloved studio, but who would have willingly chosen such a hovel?"—HdB.

6. About $115 at the 1988 exchange rate. Amoroux, p. 8, has a table showing the declining value of the franc during the war years. In 1942, ten old francs was worth 5.68 at the 1979 rate, which was approximately 5 francs per dollar.

7. "My sister's quiet generosity was legendary among those who knew her well, and it should be stressed in her biography. To our mother especially, her devotion and her financial support were unwavering."—HdB.

8. *Prime of Life*, p. 503.

9. SdB to FdB; in possession of HdB.

10. I am grateful to Prof. Stanley Weintraub for calling this to my attention.

11. SdB; SdB to FdB, in the possession of HdB.

12. Stanley Hoffmann, review of *Vichy France and the Jews*, by Michael R. Marrus and Robert O. Paxton, *New York Times Book Review*, Nov. 1, 1981, p. 30.

13. Pierre Nicolle, *Cinquante Mois d'armistice*, quoted in Pryce-Jones, p. 116.

14. HdB found these letters crammed into a small disintegrating cardboard box among FdB's possessions after her death. She either did not choose to burn them or else missed them when she destroyed

everything else after her husband's death. There are 28 letters and 6 postcards, written on various holidays taken by SdB during the war. Most are undated, and, as no envelopes remain, dating depends on internal evidence. SdB did not remember whether she reread these letters when writing her memoirs, but a number of them closely parallel what she wrote. All the letters deal primarily with accounts of her travels, but especially with what she found to eat, usually listing every food eaten at every meal. They are very affectionate letters, beginning with *"Ma chère Maman"* and concluding with genuinely fond sentiments. I am grateful to Mme. de Roulet, who most graciously made them available to me.

15. This letter corresponds to the account in *Prime*, pp. 519ff.

16. Undated letter headed *"Lundi"* (Monday). Since she mentions in her memoirs that she read Lawrence's book on this trip, the likelihood is that she wrote the play, *Les Bouches inutiles (Useless Mouths)*, this early even though it was not produced until 1944 or published until 1945.

17. "I can't speak for Sartre, because he wrote more plays than I did," SdB said in 1983, "but, for me, writing a play was a diversion from what I consider to be my serious work, and that, of course was the prose—whether novel, essay or memoir."

18. Virginia M. Fichera, in one of the most perceptive feminist readings to date, also considers it "a major work exploring the relationship between gender and power predating *The Second Sex* by about four years."—"Simone de Beauvoir and 'The Woman Question': *Les Bouches inutiles*," *Yale French Studies*, No. 72 (1987), p. 51.

19. *Ibid.*, pp. 51–52.

20. SdB, *Force of Circumstance* (New York: Putnam, 1965), p. 59.

21. Mary Evans' term in *Simone de Beauvoir: A Feminist Mandarin* (London and New York: Tavistock Publications, 1985), p. 37.

22. SdB; Alice Schwartzer, *After "The Second Sex": Conversations with Simone de Beauvoir*, p. 109.

23. HdB, letter to DB, April 12, 1987.

24. Françoise D'Eaubonne, Oct. 7, 1986; see also her *Une Femme nommée Castor: mon amie Simone de Beauvoir* (Paris: Encre, 1986).

25. SdB.

26. It is curious that she dismissed her intellect and ability as a philosopher but thought that any key to understanding her creative life must begin with her few and brief philosophical writings. However, she did not consider herself only a "disciple of Sartre," so the question of how to interpret her essays remains. Sonia Kruks is among the feminist philosophers who argue that SdB's "submission" to Sartre's concept of freedom (a central issue in *Pyrrhus et Cinéas*) was "token": "Although she was never willing to challenge Sartre's conception of freedom head-on, she was quietly to subvert it—both in her ethical essays and above all, in *The Second Sex* . . .—her tenacious pursuit of her own agenda led her, perhaps in spite of herself, to some most un-Sartrean conclusions."—"Simone de Beauvoir and the Limits to Freedom," *Social Text*, Fall 1987, p. 111.

27. *Prime of Life*, p. 547. All quotes are from this until otherwise noted.

28. In 1984 she corrected this chronology, remembering that she actually began to formulate the ideas for the essay "in the early fall of 1942, probably in September, in Madame Morel's garden" a month or so before she thought about trying to write a second novel.

29. Robert V. Stone, "Simone de Beauvoir and Existential Ethics," in *Simone de Beauvoir Studies*, Spring 1968.

30. I have used the original French text in the 1960 reprinting of the original 1944 text, published in Paris by Gallimard. The English translation given here is by Jay Miskowiec in *Social Text*, Fall 1987, pp. 135ff. As of 1989, no translation of the complete text has been made.

31. Although she was sure that she still had the notebook and the rough drafts of the essay in her possession, she had not found them before her death.

32. SdB called him "Bourla" in her memoirs and could not remember his true name in later years.

33. The comment above is from an interview, March 4, 1986. In *Prime of Life*, p. 528, she describes him as a Spanish Jew, but in the interview she changed it to the description given here. On p. 529 her written description of the incident above appears. She also used a variant in *The Mandarins* (Cleveland: World Publishing, 1956), p. 33.

34. Hervé Le Boterf *op. cit.*, Vol. II, pp. 266–67, disagrees with Beauvoir, who states in *Prime*, p. 555, that the book did not sell well at first, a contention echoed by two of Sartre's biographers, Cohen-

Solal and Hayman. Le Boterf asks how it can be explained that, despite the restrictions upon paper throughout the war, this large book of 725 pages should have been chosen for reprinting the following year if the first printing had not been sold out. He cites the popularity of several other philosophical studies published around the same time and concludes that the interest in philosophy during the war carried Sartre's work along on the same current.

35. Full citations are in *The Writings of Jean-Paul Sartre: A Bibliographical Life*, compiled and ed. by Michel Contat and Michel Rybalka, trans. Richard C. McCleary (Evanston: Northwestern University Press, 1974).

36. This observation is based upon interviews with (among many others) SdB, J.-L. Bost, J. Gerassi and Michel Contat, Jan. 26, 1982, and J. Pouillon, J.-B. Pontalis and Francis Jeanson, March 1, 1986; and on conversations with Michel Rybalka, Feb. 27, 1987, André Gorz, Jan. 13, 1982, and O. Bost. It is shared by Cohen-Solal and Hayman. Prof. Dorothy Kaufmann noted the importance of Sartre's attachment to Pardaillan in a paper read at the Sartre/Beauvoir Conference at Harvard, Feb. 28, 1987. I wish to acknowledge her observations here.

37. *Prime of Life*, p. 500, and J.-L. Bost.

38. The first comment was made in correspondence, the second in an interview, both to DB in connection with the biography of Samuel Beckett. Both sources requested anonymity at that time; one has since died and the other has instructed me to honor his original request.

20 | How to Make a Living

1. No documentation at the Bureau of National Education could be found concerning this matter, which is not especially unusual since any complaint concerning the morality and behavior of a teacher was considered private and confidential. Also, since SdB's name was cleared and restored to the teaching rolls after the Liberation, it is quite likely that any file pertaining to her dismissal was destroyed. No public judgment (*droit pénal*) was rendered in this case. Interviews were conducted with several women who were SdB's students during her last year of teaching, and none of them knew anything of her dismissal until they read about it in her memoirs (*Prime*, p. 540).

When they returned to school the following autumn, they remember, they were told that the philosophy instructor had resigned to devote herself to her writing. They believed this because *L'Invitée* had just been published.

2. SdB, *Prime of Life*, p. 540.

3. Le Boterf, *op. cit.*, Vol. II, p. 323. See also Ory, *Les Collaborateurs*, pp. 78–84. In Louis Malle's film *Au Revoir, les Enfants*, the schoolboys sing the popular ditty "Radio Paris ment" ("Radio Paris Lies") to the tune of "La Cucaracha" ("The Cockroach").

4. Le Boterf, *op. cit.*, Vol. II, p. 325.

5. This is a direct quote from his ms, which his publisher made him withdraw, so he withdrew all references to Sartre and SdB. He has asked not to be cited by name here.

6. I told her that scholars and writers were routinely denied access to INA, the national radio archives, and to whatever wartime materials existed, so there was no way to respond to any charges until or unless actual documentation was made public. I asked her to go to the officials there and request that any materials pertaining to her wartime radio work be released, but she refused. We never spoke of it again, as I left Paris shortly after and she died within the month. My subsequent attempts to gain admission to INA were unsuccessful, as were those of Marjorie Van Halteren, producer of the radio documentary about SdB on WNYC, the New York City National Public Radio station. Ms. Van Halteren was told only that materials pertaining to SdB were "*interdit*" (forbidden).

7. *Prime of Life*, p. 551.

8. The first statement was made by J.-L. Bost, Feb. 3, 1982, as he tried to describe what others thought of her then. The second statement was made by Mary McCarthy in telephone conversation Jan. 12, 1982, Paris. Ms. McCarthy attributed this remark to Nathalie Sarraute, saying that although she did not meet SdB and Sartre until after the war she herself would describe them as "precious" at that time. Mme. Sarraute, in telephone conversation Jan. 14, 1982, confirmed the statement attributed to her, adding, "She [SdB] played that role then and for many years afterward. She was most unpleasant to many people." The third statement was made by SdB in a bitter tone of voice during conversation March 8, 1985, as she spoke about her feelings after the firing.

9. SdB, "*samedi*" (Saturday), undated

letter to her mother which is exactly the same as the portion of the letter she quotes in *Prime*, p. 551. The account of the meal she gives there in what she says is a letter she wrote to Sartre is also in the letter to her mother. The content of the several letters she wrote to her mother during this trip, even though they are undated, are so similar to the account she gives in her memoirs (pp. 551–53) that either she used them as a source or her memory of the trip was so strong that she recreated it almost verbatim more than 15 years later.

10. SdB, undated letters to FdB, *"jeudi"* (Thursday) and *"samedi."*

11. SdB to FdB, Wednesday, Aug. 4, 1943.

12. *Ibid.*, n.d., *"Jeudi."*

13. *Ibid.*, n.d. (Friday, Aug. 27). In *Prime of Life*, p. 556, she said of Arland's review, "No article had ever pleased me so much."

14. SdB to FdB, n.d., *"vendredi"* (Friday).

15. *Ibid.*, *"samedi."*

16. *Prime of Life*, p. 562.

17. This information from, among others, SdB and S. le Bon de Beauvoir.

18. SdB; *Prime of Life*, p. 563.

19. During the three weeks she cycled alone the previous summer, Beauvoir visited her friend and wrote about it in letters to her mother. It was a visit she greatly enjoyed because the invalids were given copious amounts of food and their visitors were invited to share it.

20. P. McCarthy, *op. cit.*, p. 183. Verified by SdB, who discussed it independently on Jan. 16, 1982 (shortly before McCarthy's book was published).

21 | FLINGING ONESELF ON THE FUTURE

1. SdB. In *Prime of Life*, p. 565, she wrote only: "I went off early in January for a short skiing holiday. Sartre did not come with me, but Bost did."

2. *Prime of Life*, pp. 562–63.

3. Patrick McCarthy, *Camus*, p. 183. McCarthy faults Beauvoir for writing her memoirs from a "retrospectively marxist viewpoint . . . which superimposes on her experience and her period a framework which they did not possess at the time." He is correct to state that she has superimposed a framework upon her memoirs, but to describe it as "retrospectively marxist" is not entirely accurate.

4. SdB wrote in *Prime of Life*, p. 561, that Camus "had important and responsible duties in the Combat movement. Both his biographers, Herbert Lottman and Patrick McCarthy, present convincing proof that Camus did not become involved in Combat until sometime in 1944. Asked in 1983 if she knew this, SdB said she did. Asked why she wrote an incorrect account, she said, "I was in a hurry and it wasn't important anyway."

5. P. McCarthy, *Camus*, p. 184.

6. *Ibid.*, p. 177.

7. P. McCarthy, p. 183, writes that this "infuriated Camus. *Sisyphe* had stated that there could be no metaphysical system; Existentialism was a philosophy, a statement about the entire universe and hence an affirmation of man's ability to understand it. Moreover, Camus disagreed with the primacy awarded to existence. Already he wondered whether lucidity and courage might not be values that predated the state of 'being in the world.' "

8. *Prime of Life*, p. 569.

9. Lottman, *Camus*, p. 302.

10. SdB. In *The Writings of Jean-Paul Sartre: A Bibliographical Life*, p. 12, eds. Contat and Rybalka give two contradictory accounts of Sartre's work with *Combat*. Under "1943" they write: "[Sartre] is one of the people collaborating with the clandestine *Combat*, although he does not do any writing for it." Under "1944": "Articles on the days of the liberation in *Combat*, with the help of Simone de Beauvoir." For this account, I have consulted the complete set of *Combat* in the Bibliothèque de l'Arsenal, Paris.

11. This conversation raised the question of whether or not she ever repeated the action of writing in his stead but signing his name, and again she gave an evasive reply: "Maybe sometimes. I forget."

12. SdB to FdB, *"jeudi."*

13. She refers to the newspaper. SdB asked Camus to give Bost a job, and for the past few months he had been roaming throughout France on assignment.

14. SdB to FdB, *"vendredi."* All quotations from this letter until noted otherwise.

15. SdB to FdB, *"jeudi."*

16. *Prime of Life*, pp. 597–98. There she calls him Patrice Valberg. She remembered his name but nothing else about him.

17. *Prime of Life*, p. 598.

18. Le Boterf, Vol. II, pp. 195–96, writes: "One can count on the fingers of

both hands the writers who put their pens into a drawer until the Allies arrived . . . on French territory, who refused categorically to submit [their] manuscripts to the scrutiny of the Propagandastaffel. Practically no one."

19. Otto Abetz was the German ambassador in Paris. On Sept. 28, 1940, a 26-page "list" was circulated containing the names of 842 authors and more than 2,000 prohibited books. These were the works of writers who were either Jewish or whose writings portrayed Jews in sympathetic light. A second list was prepared in 1942 and a third on May 10, 1943, and a total of more than 900 authors eventually found their works included. For further information, see Le Boterf, Vol. II, pp. 202ff.

20. They were two of the most prominent society hostesses during the war, known for their lavish entertainment of the German occupiers. The only mention of anyone in this society is on p. 584 of *Prime of Life*, where SdB writes that Marie-Zaure [*sic*] de Noailles attended a performance of *No Exit*.

21. Steegmuller, *Cocteau*, p. 445.

22. Françoise Giroud, *I Give You My Word*, p. 80.

22 | ALWAYS SOMETHING TO SAY

1. SdB, *Prime of Life*, p. 606.

2. SdB, "Jean-Paul Sartre: Strictly Personal," trans. Malcolm Cowley, *Harper's Bazaar*, Jan. 1946, p. 113.

3. O. Bost, I. Moffatt and J.-B. Pontalis were among many who noted this.

4. The first remark is from an interview with SdB; the second is how she referred to Leduc throughout her correspondence with Nelson Algren (now at Ohio State University Library), and in conversation with the Family.

5. SdB, *Force of Circumstance*, p. 54.

6. Unpublished letter from the Paulhan archives, quoted in Cohen-Solal, p. 220. Jean Paulhan (1884–1986) was a critic, essayist and editor of the *Nouvelle Revue Française* from 1925 to 1940 and the *Nouvelle Nouvelle Revue Française* from 1953.

7. *Force of Circumstance*, p. 55. SdB wrote this after 1960, long after Sartre and Aron had had an ideological break and were no longer friends. Anyone who became Sartre's enemy remained hers long

after the fact: she could not resist her own attack on Aron, adding here: "Excellent as an analyst, he was pathetic as a prophet. . . ."

8. *Force of Circumstance*, p. 22.

9. Immediately after the Liberation of Paris, the CNE began to debate the question of purge and punishment for proven or suspected collaborators within its ranks. Gaston Gallimard was one among several publishers whose record was considered murky. Cohen-Solal, p. 219, describes Sartre's position on the CNE succinctly: "The publishers will be spared. . . . As for Sartre, he has been lukewarm on this question; he is elaborating a theory on individual involvement and individual responsibilities, and incidentally, Gallimard has just agreed to finance his projected review, *Les Temps Modernes*." See also Pierre Assouline, *Gaston Gallimard* (Paris: Balland, 1984), pp. 365–98, and *L'Epuration des intellectuels* (Brussels: Editions Complexe, 1985), pp. 95–100.

10. It is important to note here how careful she was to vindicate Sartre and assign blame to Camus.

11. She describes the journey in *Force of Circumstance*, pp. 30–36.

12. HdB, interview, Jan. 29, 1982.

13. *Force of Circumstance*, p. 34.

14. As in so many other instances where Sartre was concerned, whether in life, art or philosophy, SdB was willing to entertain discussion of her actions—*up to a point*. Beyond that, foreseeing a discussion which would bring her actions, writing or theories into question, or—as she especially feared in the last ten or so years of her life—into rigorous scrutiny by women who viewed them in the light of feminist scholarship and attitudes positing acceptable behavior for women, she stopped cold. Her questioners often found themselves on the other side of a glass wall, urging her to move beyond her often incomplete rationale by seeing through, but she never did. On the subject of Sartre she remained adamant until the day she died, and, like Flaubert describing Salammbo (*Correspondence*, Vol. 5, p. 69), would become furious should anyone suggest that her pedestal might be too big for his statue. If her answers and actions disappointed others, she had a simple yet abrasive answer for them: "Well, I just don't give a damn. It's my life and I lived it the way I wanted. I'm sorry to disappoint all the feminists, but you can say that it's too bad so many of them live only in theory instead of in real life. It's very

messy in the real world, and maybe they should learn that."

15. D. V. Ehrenreich, telephone conversations, New York, April 23, 1982, and March 25, 1987. Cohen-Solal presents Mrs. Erhenreich's version of the affair on pp. 236–38. Mrs. Ehrenreich disagreed with Cohen-Solal's statement on p. 270 that she "fell in love with him during his second stay," with the cryptic remark "I don't believe it was like that."

16. *Force of Circumstance*, pp. 77–78. All quotations are from this text until noted otherwise.

17. *Ibid.*, p. 92. There she also wrote that she gave the ms to the playwright Adamov, who was organizing a benefit auction to pay the expenses of Antonin Artaud, then confined to a mental hospital. The ms has since disappeared from public view and may no longer be extant.

18. *Ibid.*, p. 45.

19. SdB, *The Blood of Others* (New York: Penguin, 1964), p. 24.

20. *Ibid.*, p. 27.

21. *Ibid.*, p. 240.

22. Richard McLaughlin, "Mouthing Basic Existentialism," *Saturday Review of Literature*, July 17, 1948, p. 13.

23. *Ibid.*, p. 13.

24. SdB's concept of freedom has been similarly discussed but at greater length by Anne Whitmarsh in *Simone de Beauvoir and the Limits of Commitment* (Cambridge: Cambridge University Press, 1981), pp. 61ff.; and Mary Evans in *Simone de Beauvoir, A Feminist Mandarin*, pp. 49–51. For a sensitive reading of this novel (and many of her other writings as well), see Terry Keefe, *Simone de Beauvoir: A Study of her Writings* (Totowa, N.J.: Barnes & Noble, 1983), pp. 161–68.

25. *Force of Circumstance*, p. 75.

26. SdB, S. le Bon de Beauvoir, Robert Gallimard (in interviews with DB and Marjorie Van Halteren), André Gorz (telephone conversation Jan. 13, 1982) and J.-B. Pontalis.

27. This is in the English-language edition; in the French it is 86 pages.

28. SdB, *All Men Are Mortal* (New York: World Publishing, 1955), p. 5. All citations are from this edition.

29. *Ibid.*, pp. 65–66. All quotes are from these pages until noted otherwise.

30. When asked to comment on these and other passages in the novel dealing with Regina's inability to reach Fosca in ways that would satisfy her, SdB made

the cryptic remark "Most of it happened that way."

31. Anthony West in *The New Yorker*, Feb. 5, 1955, pp. 101–4.

32. J.-L. Bost and Mrs. Ehrenreich remained friends and visited each other in Paris and New York. Bost tried not to speak of her with SdB except in generalities, but sometimes it was difficult because SdB pressed for specific details. After she met Nelson Algren, her inquiries were less insistent.

33. "Jeune Agrégée de Philosophie Simone de Beauvoir va presenter sa première pièce," *Le Soir*, Oct. 13, 1945, p. 2. This clipping and all other quotations regarding the first production of *Les Bouches inutiles* are contained in a single scrapbook entitled "*Les Bouches inutiles*: Pièce en deux actes représentée pour le 1er fois au théâtre des Carrefours, le 29 Octobre, 1944" (*sic*) in the Bibliothèque Arsenal, Paris. There are approximately 68 newspaper clippings which include interviews with Beauvoir and reviews of the play. In every instance, the handwritten date affixed to the article is wrongly given as 1944. Also, the month of the first performance, "*Novembre*," in the printed text, published by Gallimard, is in error.

34. *Opéra*, Oct. 31, 1945.

35. *Force of Circumstance*, p. 61.

36. *All Men Are Mortal*, pp. 344–45. Emphasis is in the text.

23 | MOVING IN SOME SORT OF BLUR

1. Nathalie Sorokine and Ivan Moffatt were married Sept. 12, 1945, in a small ceremony with only her parents present, and they did not invite SdB. Natasha Moffatt had hoped to sail on the same ship as Sartre, but was not given passage until early March 1946. "One of the ludicrous aspects of that immediate postwar autumn was that war brides were taken on Liberty Ships across the Atlantic. When Natasha's train from Paris arrived at Le Havre, they were met by a band composed of former German prisoners of war who played 'Here Comes the Bride'— one of those Preston Sturges–like absurdities"—I. Moffatt.

2. In one of the rare instances during six years of interviews and conversations when SdB lapsed into English, she said she liked Giacometti because he was so "imperturbable [using the French pro-

nunciation]—'unflappable,' as kids say in America!"

3. Nelson Algren, telephone conversation, April 18, 1981.

4. Information about Violette Leduc and Nathalie Sarraute which follows is from interviews with SdB.

5. Isabelle de Courtivron, "From Bastard to Pilgrim: Rites and Writing for Madame," *Yale French Studies*, No. 72 (1986), pp. 147–48. See also Courtivron's *Violette Leduc* (Boston: G. K. Hall, TWAS 757, 1985).

6. Courtivron, "From Bastard to Pilgrim," *loc. cit.*, p. 135. She also writes that SdB's support "reached every aspect of Leduc's existence. She assisted . . . financially by arranging a small monthly stipend ostensibly paid by Gallimard during the years of extreme poverty. She also introduced Leduc to her network of friends, in the hope of alleviating her protégée's acute isolation." In interviews between 1982 and 1985, SdB verified that she "continued to help Leduc in many different ways" until Leduc's death in 1973.

7. SdB, *Force of Circumstance*, p. 74.

8. Among them the Irish writer and Nobel Prize winner Samuel Beckett.

9. Ruth Z. Temple, *Nathalie Sarraute* (New York and London: Columbia University Press, 1968), p. 31.

10. Sarraute was approximately 47, Sartre 40.

11. Nathalie Sarraute, telephone conversation, Paris, Jan. 13, 1982. Sarraute's friend the American novelist Mary McCarthy gave the same account of the SdB–Sarraute antagonism in a telephone conversation Jan. 12, 1982.

12. Entry for May 11, 1946. Portions of this diary are still extant in SdB's archives. Extracts (including this one) are reprinted in *Force*, p. 88. In the telephone conversation of Jan. 13, 1982, Sarraute questioned SdB's reliability as "a historian of her time," saying, "Every time she mentioned me in her memoirs she made some comment about my 'blue' hat or dress or suit. She knew very well that I seldom if ever wore blue, always green." I questioned SdB about this, and she said unhesitatingly, "But I always *think* of her as blue." At another date, SdB defended Sartre's transposition of Giacometti's accident from the Place des Pyramides to the Place d'Italie, saying, "Sartre *needed* it to take place there. It was important *for his vision* of Giacometti." Emphasis mine in both instances.

13. Cohen-Solal, p. 323, dates Sartre's involvement with Michelle L'Eglise Vian from 1950, after her separation from Boris Vian. SdB disputed this: "Everyone knew that Michelle succumbed to Sartre shortly after they met, even while he was still involved with Dolores. None of us said anything, pretending not to know, because why not, if that's the way she [Michelle] wanted it."

14. "Yes, I did use him in *The Mandarins*, but you give him too much credit, too much authority, when you say that he is the only model for [the character] Scriasine."—SdB.

15. SdB; HdB made a similar remark.

16. "I wish I had written more about the good years of my relationship with my mother, but there never seemed to be the appropriate place within my memoirs to do so. That's why I had to write the book when she died." SdB refers here to *A Very Easy Death*, the book she wrote when her mother died in 1963.

17. She discussed this trip in *Force*, pp. 60–68.

18. *Ibid.*, p. 62. SdB's emphasis.

19. In the diary, published in *Force of Circumstance*, pp. 78–90, there are many references to headaches, anxiety and tension. She included these deliberately because "I wanted to convey my condition without directly calling attention to it."—SdB.

20. "Oeil pour oeil" (February 1946) and "Littérature et métaphysique" (April 1946).

21. SdB discussed her political thinking of 1946 during an interview of Sept. 4, 1984. This particular remark was delivered in an ironic tone of voice because she was describing herself at that time as "impossibly naive in politics." The interview was part of a larger discussion, "Women's Rights in Today's World," published in the 1984 *Britannica Book of the Year*, pp. 24ff.

22. Madeleine Gobeil, interview with Jean-Paul Sartre, *Vogue*, American ed., July 1965; reprinted in Serge Julienne-Caffié, *Simone de Beauvoir*, pp. 38–43.

23. *Force of Circumstance*, p. 87.

24. *Ibid.*, p. 70.

25. In *Force of Circumstance* she mentions the incident. Dominique Aron Schnapper said in an interview March 3, 1986, Paris, that SdB refused to accept the real reason her parents left the theater: Mme. Aron was so upset by the staged torture that she became ill. SdB (separate conversation, March 3, 1986),

insisted that Aron should have sent his wife home in a taxi and remained until the performance was over because no matter what the reason, his action seemed a deliberate insult to Sartre.

26. "Idéalisme moral et réalisme politique" (November 1945), "L'Existentialisme et la sagesse des nations" December 1945), "Oeil pour oeil" (February 1946) and "Littérature et métaphysique" (April 1946).

27. SdB, *All Said and Done* (New York: Putnam, 1974), p. 33.

28. *Force of Circumstance*, p. 75.

29. "Littérature et métaphysique," *Les Temps Modernes*, April 1, 1946, p. 1156. My translation.

30. If it represents any system, it is the personal, unformulated one which she followed throughout her entire writing life, but which she claimed never to have envisioned or consciously expressed until she was asked about it in interviews and conversations for this book from 1981 to 1986.

31. When she was asked if she wanted to include *The Second Sex*, she said, "No. Anyone could have written that book. Only I could have written the others." This comment was made during our last conversation, March 7, 1986.

32. *Force of Circumstance*, p. 75; SdB, conversation.

3. Terry Keefe, one of the few who has studied it in some detail, writes in *Simone de Beauvoir: A Study of Her Writings* of the "merciless probing of conduct and motives and the ferreting out of all forms of self-deception" (p. 87), but also notes how little care she has taken over the material and "the uneven quality" of much of the writing (p. 85).

34. SdB, *The Ethics of Ambiguity*, trans. Bernard Frechtman (Secaucus, N.J.: Citadel Press, 1948), p. 159.

35. *Force of Circumstance*, p. 94.

36. *Ibid.*, p. 84.

37. J.-L. Bost.

38. She writes of this incident in *Force*, p. 103. We discussed it in a conversation of May 5, 1983. Unless otherwise cited, her remarks are from our conversation.

39. *Force of Circumstance*, p. 103.

40. SdB. She repeated this remark with only slightly different wording in many other instances throughout the interviews and conversations for this book.

41. SdB.

42. *Force of Circumstance*, p. 103.

43. This is the appellation used independently by graduates and former faculty members of Smith, Yale and the University of Pennsylvania who attended Beauvoir's lectures.

44. *Force of Circumstance*, p. 114.

24 | THE MOST EXOTIC THING

1. SdB, "An Existentialist Looks at Americans," *New York Times Magazine*, May 25, 1947, pp. 13, 51–54. In this article she attributed the remark to "an American journalist, but in her book *America Day by Day*, trans. Patrick Dudley (New York: Grove Press, 1953), p. 43, SdB says it was made by "the chief editor"; on p. 44 she gives this comment as "In France you ask questions, but you do not answer them. But we do not ask them, we answer them." She corrected herself in 1983, saying she had never met "the chief editors of the newspaper itself."

2. This is the *New York Times* copyeditor's description of SdB in the article cited above.

3. The following information is from interviews and conversations with SdB, S. Gerassi and J. Gerassi; from telephone conversations with N. Algren and D. Vanetti Ehrenreich, and from the original French edition of *America Day by Day*, *L'Amérique au jour le jour* (Paris: Gallimard, 1947). Portions of this book also appeared in *Les Temps Modernes* in December 1947 and January through April 1948.

4. SdB, "An Existentialist Looks at Americans," *loc. cit.*, p. 13.

5. S. Gerassi.

6. William Phillips, "A French Lady on the Dark Continent: Simone de Beauvoir's Impressions of America," *Commentary*, July 1953, p. 26.

7. See photo 19.

8. J. Gerassi.

9. They were in each other's company infrequently in France during the next few years, but later both D. Ehrenreich and SdB did not remember ever meeting again in New York. Each thought there "might have been a phone call or two," but neither wanted to see the other.

10. In this way, during the two separate visits she made to the U.S. in 1947 and a third in 1948, she gave lectures at Columbia, Yale, Harvard, Rochester, Vassar, Smith, Wellesley, Connecticut College, Princeton and the U. of Pennsylvania. She went south to George Washington, Randolph-Macon Women's College, Sweet

Briar and Hood; then across the continent from Oberlin and Denison to the U. of Chicago and several Midwestern colleges before Tulane, Rice, UCLA and the University of Southern California, and then up the coast to Mills College and Berkeley. This is only a partial listing, both addition and correction to the chronology offered by Claude Francis and Fernande Gontier, *Les Ecrits de Simone de Beauvoir*, p. 52. No official record was kept by the French government, and SdB did not keep a complete listing. She remembered that she spoke in almost every city in which she stopped for more than a few hours, often to local cultural groups (such as in Omaha) and women's clubs (in either Kansas or Oklahoma, she did not remember which—"perhaps it was both"), as well as at universities and colleges. It is important to note, however, that the chronology contained in *America Day by Day* is not an accurate one, but rather a pastiche of the several journeys, melded, condensed and otherwise heightened and changed to make it more accessible to and readable by the French audience for whom it was intended. The book was first published serially in *Les Temps Modernes*, so much of the political commentary was deliberately inserted into the text to make it more appropriate for the journal's readers. She thought briefly about changing or deleting much of it when she gathered the articles for the book, but decided not to do so because she was so involved with *The Second Sex* and the portion of her memoirs which became the first volume, *Memoirs of a Dutiful Daughter*. As far as she was concerned, *America Day by Day* was a book "written to fill space [in *Les Temps Modernes*] and to make me some money so I could keep on returning to see Algren." (Interview, Feb. 4, 1982.)

11. *The Crimson*, April 18, 1947, p. 1.

12. Nancy W. Bauer was a student at Smith College then. I am grateful for her impressions of SdB.

13. *New Yorker*, Vol. XXIII, No. 1 (Feb. 22, 1947), pp. 19–20.

14. SdB, interview, Sept. 11, 1984.

15. In a conversation shortly before the election of Pres. Ronald Reagan to a second term, she asked me to explain the "trickle-down" theory. As I stumbled through the economics of it, she said, "That's the best that can be said for your university education: toss a few scholarships to women and minorities to quiet their opposition. Trickle down of the worst sort. I believe that's how Reagan's

policies are constituted, another form of 'bread and circuses.' It strikes me as not having changed very much since I saw it for myself at Vassar and that place in Connecticut."

16. Lawrence M. Seiver, interview, June 11, 1984, Philadelphia.

17. In an interview Sept. 11, 1984, SdB spoke of this trip as follows: "I didn't have any clothes to speak of. I had a couple blouses, a skirt, a pair of pants I think were left from the war, and this dress. Listen, it cost me plenty to buy this dress! It was the latest fashion, and I counted on it to knock out the eyes of America. I wore it everywhere, so very soon it didn't look like very much, but it was all I had, so it was all I wore. That's why all the photographs from that trip show me in it. I think it was maroon top, with plaid skirt—no, maybe it was navy blue. I forget. I got sick of it by the end of the trip, but when I got back to Paris I kept on wearing it because I had no time to buy clothes, I had to work. Remember, in those days you went to the dressmaker and she made you something to wear. We didn't have all these shops for poor people and middle class to go into and just buy something." Ivan Moffatt recalls her clothing on this trip as well: "When she came to California, she had only a very small bag containing her things. She was wearing a dress that must have been heavy wool and deucedly uncomfortable, and I must say—well, Castor's personal hygiene frequently left much to be desired. Anyway, I think Natasha got her out of the thing, and we put her into shirts and pants and things while she stayed with us. But she put the bloody dress back on when she left." J.-L. Bost said, "Pity you didn't talk to Algren, because even to us he used to say, 'We always know when it's summer—we tell Simone (he never called her 'Castor' as we did) to take off the navy-blue wool dress and put on the cotton one; and in the winter we have to do just the opposite and tell her to take off the cotton and put on the wool!'" SdB discussed American vs. European clothing in *America Day by Day*, pp. 51–52, concluding arbitrarily that "even the clothes worn by those American women who defend their independence on every occasion and whose attitude to men so readily becomes aggressive are not clothes designed for comfort; they dress for men. Those heels which paralyze the foot, those fragile plumes, those flowers with wintry hearts and all

those furbelows are clearly dazzling effects designed to stress femininity and attract men's looks. European women's clothes are certainly less servile."

18. Lawrence M. Seiver, letter to DB, May 14, 1984.

19. William Phillips, *A Partisan View: Five Decades of the Literary Life* (New York: Stein and Day, 1983), pp. 126 and 128.

20. Mary McCarthy, "Mlle. Gulliver en Amérique," *The Reporter*, Jan. 22, 1952, p. 34.

21. Diana Trilling, "Simone de Beauvoir's America," p. 208.

22. SdB to Nelson Algren (hereafter NA), n.d. [April 24, 1947?], letterhead of the University of Pennsylvania, Department of Romance Languages and Literatures. The letters SdB wrote to NA are among the correspondence and papers which he sold shortly before his death to the Ohio State University Libraries. I am grateful to Mr. Robert Tibbetts and his staff, who generously gave their time and assistance as I read them in 1982; to Richard Centing, who called them to my attention initially; and to Lauren Pringle Delavars for her many years of responding to my queries and for permitting me to use her unpublished doctoral dissertation "An Annotated and Indexed Calendar and Abstract of the Ohio State University Collection of Simone de Beauvoir's Letters to Nelson Algren," Ohio State University, 1985. SdB never dated her letters, so in future references to the Algren collection I shall give the dating information which Delavars based on internal evidence and cited throughout her dissertation, and will refer to the letters' provenance as "NA/OSU."

23. Called "D.V." in *America Day by Day*, p. 287, and "Nelly Benson" in *Force of Circumstance*, p. 134.

24. Mary Guggenheim, interview, May 8, 1983, Paris.

25. Guggenheim was right about the dinner. SdB: "Neither was married. For the first time in my life, a meal for women seemed like a meal 'without men'; despite the martinis, despite all the good cheer, we were surrounded by a bitter air of absence. . . . I felt that both women were obsessed by the lack of a wedding ring."—*America Day by Day*, p. 287. SdB speculates about the situation and condition of women throughout this book. It deserves a close reading, because it served as her initial forum for *The Second Sex*.

26. *America Day by Day*, pp. 104–5.

27. NA, "Last Rounds in Small Cafés: Remembrances of Jean-Paul Sartre and Simone de Beauvoir," *Chicago*, December 1980, p. 213. He makes no mention of Guggenheim or of the letter she wrote about SdB.

28. The biographical information about NA is from his obituary, *New York Times*, May 10, 1981, p. 32.

29. The *New York Times* obituary describes it as follows: "The novel, published in 1949, was a best seller and won a National Book Award. It was also made into a successful motion picture by Otto Preminger, ending a long-time ban on the depiction of narcotics in the movies. Mr. Algren, who thought his plot had been turned into a sentimental vehicle for Frank Sinatra, received only $15,000 for his rights. He sued, but withdrew for lack of funds."

30. NA, "Last Rounds," *loc. cit.*, p. 213.

31. Sunday Evening [Feb. 23, 1947], NA/OSU.

32. *America Day by Day*, p. 118. She also said they were able "through the installment plan, [to] buy a car," but Ivan Moffatt said they were still driving the bright-red 1938 Packard he had owned before the war. The "small yellow car" she mentions on p. 119 was actually purchased more than a year later. This is only one small example of how SdB distorted the sequence of time in this book.

33. Ivan Moffatt, April 9, 1986; SdB, Sept. 11, 1984. She calls Iris Tree "E" in *America Day by Day* and describes her visit to her Ojai, Calif., ranch beginning on p. 137.

34. Stevens had led the official film crew that photographed the liberation of Europe from the D-Day landing to the Allied occupation of Berlin.

35. 12 March [1947], NA/OSU.

36. I. Moffatt.

37. In *Force of Circumstance*, she wrote that she telephoned him from New York, then went to Chicago for three days, after which he returned with her to New York. In 1983 she said this was a fictionalized account of their second meeting, "written to throw nosey people off my track."

38. *America Day by Day*, pp. 276–77.

39. Ellen Wright, telephone conversation, Paris, Jan. 12, 1982.

40. Because of these conversations, Wright arranged for her to contribute two essays to the periodical *Twice a Year*. The essays, both of which had been pre-

viously published in *Les Temps Modernes*, were slightly refined and rewritten from the original French. Their English titles are "Literature and Metaphysics" and "Freedom and Liberation." They appeared in the 1948 "anniversary issue." She worked on the translations with Ralph Manheim, whom she called "R.C." in *America Day by Day*, p. 276.

41. *America Day by Day*, p. 280, my emphasis.

42. She describes it somewhat differently in *Force of Circumstance*, p. 135.

43. *Force of Circumstance*, p. 135.

44. Richard Elman, who graciously made the poem available to me, found this book in a $2-used-book bin in Selden, N.Y., in 1988. SdB allowed Michelle L'Eglise Vian to use it in the 1950s as her working copy when she translated several of Algren's stories for *Les Temps Modernes*, and her handwriting appears throughout. J.-L. Bost believed that Algren, on his last visit to Paris, became angry with "Beauvoir's desecration" of the book and took it back from her.

45. May 17, 1947, NA/OSU.

46. May 18, 1947, NA/OSU.

47. *America Day by Day*, p. 377.

25 | A BEAUTIFUL,
       CORNY LOVE STORY

1. The following information is based on interviews and conversations with SdB, D. V. Ehrenreich, HdB, J.-L. Bost, O. Bost, C. Lanzmann, S. le Bon de Beauvoir, J.-B. Pontalis, J. Pouillon, J. Gerassi and others. Also, the memoirs of SdB; the Hayman and Cohen-Solal biographies of Sartre; the *Lettres aux Castor*, Vol. II, pp. 338ff.; and the NA/OSU letters. All textual references to written materials will be cited specifically. Also, shortly before her death in 1986, SdB showed me a collection of letters dating from 1947–48 written by Sartre that she withheld from the volume she published, because of "details too sensitive for persons still alive." Although she did not permit me to quote from these letters, she allowed me to read some of them "to better understand what went on with Dolores from then [1947] until their relationship ended."

2. *Lettres au Castor*, Vol. II, p. 335, my translation.

3. Cohen-Solal, p. 323. The end of Sartre's involvement with Mrs. Ehrenreich is generally cited as June 1950.

4. In her letter to NA May 21 [1947], NA/OSU, she calls him "My beloved husband." From this date until the end of the correspondence several years later, she frequently addresses him as "husband," in both the greeting and the body of her letters. In a conversation July 16, 1982, without knowing anything at all about this ring, I told SdB that I thought it a striking piece of jewelry. She replied, "It's more than that. It's the ring Nelson Algren gave me. Despite everything, I have never taken it off. I never will."

5. SdB, Friday [May 23, 1947], NA/OSU.

6. SdB, Friday, June 20 [1947], NA/OSU.

7. This is one of the terms of endearment that NA used in his letters to SdB. I did not read the entire correspondence, but was permitted by SdB to read only a sampling she selected at random. They remain among her archives, and as of October 1988 her executor continues to insist that SdB's letters to NA (at OSU) will never be published and his to her will never be available for scholarly perusal.

8. SdB, Saturday [May 24, 1947], NA/OSU.

9. Sartre's output, Cohen-Solal points out (p. 280), "included lectures, essays, plays, articles, introductions, radio broadcasts, biographies, philosophical speculations, screenplays, songs, novels, reports. The themes ranged from esthetics, literature, ethics, politics, and philosophy to travel, art, and music." See also *Les Écrits de Sartre: Chronologie, bibliographie, commentée*, ed. Michel Contat and Michel Rybalka, pp. 130–221.

10. She did so because "I never trusted Jean Cau and he did not like me either."

11. She then added, "Well, we all know how wrong I was about that! I have to say that I now have the greatest admiration for Samuel Beckett, but at the same time I consider him one of the worst things to have happened to French writing. His influence is enormous, and there are a lot of less talented and totally untalented people out there who try to write like him and fail miserably. We will have no important fiction in this country until the influence of Beckett is ended."

12. Paule Allard worked for Gallimard and as an editorial consultant for *Les Temps Modernes*.

13. Samuel Beckett, conversation, April 13, 1972.

14. This is the version of the incident Samuel Beckett gave his bibliographers

Raymond Federman and John Fletcher, *Samuel Beckett: His Works and His Critics* (Berkeley: University of California Press, 1970), pp. 49–50, n.252.1. SdB confirmed that she allowed this version to stand because "it did not matter to me," until our April 29, 1983, conversation when she gave the explanation that follows here.

15. SdB, Saturday [May 24, 1947], NA/OSU.

16. SdB; SdB, Saturday [May 24, 1947], NA/OSU.

17. First mentioned in her letter of Friday [May 23, 1947], NA/OSU. She used "only this pen, for years, until it wore out."

18. SdB [June 2, 4, 6, 1947], NA/OSU. In the letter of June 2, she told him that she had already read William Faulkner's *Sanctuary* and Kuprin's *Yama* (quoted by NA in *The Man with the Golden Arm*), and that she would read Aldanov's *The Fifth Seal*.

19. SdB, n.d. [June 4, 1947], NA/OSU. *L'Affamée* was excerpted in *Les Temps Modernes* and published as a complete novel by Les Éditions Gallimard, 1948.

20. SdB, Thursday 12th June [1947], NA/OSU. Also described in *Force of Circumstance*, p. 135.

21. SdB, Tuesday, 24th February [June 24, 1947], NA/OSU.

22. SdB, Wednesday night [June 25, 1947], NA/OSU.

23. SdB, Wednesday [July 2, 1947], NA/OSU.

24. SdB, Tuesday 8th July [1947], NA/OSU. This trip to Corsica lasted only the weekend, because by July 12 she was back in Paris. It is not mentioned in any of her memoirs.

25. She describes her dislike of Nagel in *Force of Circumstance*, pp. 141–42. In her letters to Algren she usually refers to him as "an ugly little Frog-faced businessman" (see letter of 15 July [1947], NA/OSU). In conversation in early March 1985 she said she disliked Nagel because he "was always so strictly regimented and he wanted Sartre to be the same way. We thought him a pompous little grown-up." She described some incidents in which Nagel arranged publicity and Sartre either did not show at all or arrived very late, how Sartre never bothered to complete what Nagel considered to be necessary paperwork relating to the financial aspects of his books, and how she and Sartre often played tricks on the publisher, trying to elude him or deliberately thwart his in-

tentions. Without thinking, I blurted out something to the effect that theirs sounded like the behavior of two prankish children. She became very angry and scolded me for not understanding "how Sartre was," and brought our meeting to an abrupt end with the comment "You act here just like Nagel!"

26. SdB, Saturday 12th July [1947] and Tuesday 15 July [1947], NA/OSU.

27. SdB, Saturday 19 July [1947], NA/OSU.

28. *Force of Circumstance*, p. 142.

29. I base this observation on several of the letters NA wrote to SdB during this time, but she did not permit me to take notes or to quote from them. Her comments are from letters of 19 July [1947] and 22 July [1947].

30. In a 1986 conversation she asked me, "Well—what do you think? Was I trying to make him your 'Uncle Sam'?" I replied that she did seem to be making him into an archetypal American in her dream, and she replied, "No doubt about that."

31. Jean Delannoy's film, released in France in 1947.

32. SdB, Saturday 28th July [1947].

33. SdB, Thursday 31 July [1947]. She describes the telegram and her visit in *Force of Circumstance*, pp. 142ff. In a 1985 conversation she corrected the chronology: Dolores had actually left Paris a "month or so" before this, and her uneasiness during this time was not over Sartre, but about NA.

34. SdB, Thursday 31 July [1947], NA/OSU.

35. SdB, Sunday [Aug. 10, 1947], NA/OSU.

36. *Force of Circumstance*, p. 142.

37. SdB, Thursday 7th August [1947], NA/OSU. She was referring to the fact that she would be with him in one month to the day.

38. SdB, Wednesday 13th August [1947], NA/OSU.

39. SdB, Thursday 31 July [1947], NA/OSU.

40. The information in this paragraph is based on conversations with SdB and on her letters of Monday, 18 August [1947]; Wednesday, 20th August; Saturday 23rd August; and Sunday, August 3, all NA/OSU.

41. SdB confirmed this information in conversation, Sept. 6, 1984.

42. SdB, Thursday 7th Aug. [1947], NA/OSU.

26 | THE HIGH PRIESTESS
OF EXISTENTIALISM

1. SdB, Friday 26th [Sept. 1947], NA/OSU. He had given her (among others) James T. Farrell's *Studs Lonigan*, Ralph Ellison's *Invisible Man*, Willard Motley's *Knock on Any Door* and a collection of excerpts and short fiction by Henry James, the last a writer he greatly admired. "Not too many people know how much Algren was influenced by Henry James. He greatly admired James's fiction, especially *The Turn of the Screw* and *What Maisie Knew*. He always said he wished he could get into people's minds the way James did."—SdB.

2. SdB, Sunday [Sept. 28, 1947], NA/OSU.

3. The following information is from discussions with SdB Aug. 30, 1983, at the Algonquin Hotel, New York.

4. In 1983 she said this was probably "an unfair description" because of the way they parted when the affair was over.

5. SdB, Friday 3th October [1947], NA/OSU. All quotes are from this until otherwise noted.

6. SdB, Friday 26th [Sept. 1947], NA/OSU.

7. SdB, Friday 3th October [1947], NA/OSU. All comments are from this until noted otherwise.

8. SdB, Friday [Oct. 17, 1947], NA/OSU.

9. SdB discusses her political activity in *Force*, pp. 146ff., and in letters of Sept. 26 and 28 and Oct. 3, 7, 9, 14, 17, 21 and 23, all NA/OSU.

10. SdB, Sept. 26 [1947], NA/OSU.

11. SdB, Tuesday [Oct. 14, 1947], NA/OSU.

12. *Carrefour*, Paris, Oct. 29, 1947.

13. SdB, Thursday evening [Oct. 23, 1947], NA/OSU.

14. SdB, Tuesday night [Oct. 21, 1947] and Wednesday [Oct. 22], NA/OSU.

15. Sartre was persuaded by the other members of *Les Temps Modernes* to change his mind, and the broadcasts continued. SdB mentions recording several programs at the end of November in a letter to NA, Tuesday night [Nov. 25, 1947], NA/OSU.

16. I am grateful to Marjorie Van Halteren, who made these tapes available to me.

17. SdB, Thursday—Midnight [Oct. 9, 1947], NA/OSU. She also discusses this in *Force of Circumstance*, p. 148. There were actually 18 men present.

18. SdB, Tuesday Night [Oct. 21, 1947], NA/OSU. All quotes are from this until noted otherwise.

19. *Force of Circumstance*, pp. 148ff.

20. SdB. Also, S. le Bon de Beauvoir, Oct. 21, 1986, Paris, and M. Van Halteren interview with S. le Bon de Beauvoir, June 1987, Paris.

21. SdB, Friday [Oct. 17, 1947], NA/OSU.

22. *Force of Circumstance*, pp. 151–53. SdB also discussed this period during a related discussion concerning NA, May 7, 1983. Information is from this conversation until otherwise indicated.

23. In *Force of Circumstance*, p. 199, Beauvoir contradicts both her earlier account on pp. 151–53 and this comment as well when she writes: "In fact I was never treated as a target for sarcasm until after *The Second Sex*; before that, people were either indifferent or kind to me."

24. SdB, Tuesday [Oct. 14, 1947], NA/OSU. She refers to British Foreign Secretary Ernest Bevin, a strong supporter of the Marshall Plan.

25. Information in this paragraph is from SdB, Sunday [Sept. 28, 1947], Friday 3th October [1947], Thursday—Midnight [Oct. 9, 1947], and Tuesday [Oct. 14, 1947], NA/OSU.

26. SdB, Friday 3th Oct. [1947], NA/OSU.

27. SdB, Thursday—Midnight [Oct. 9, 1947], NA/OSU.

28. Much of the discussion that follows is taken from my article "Simone de Beauvoir: Politics, Language and Feminist Identity," in *Simone de Beauvoir: Witness to a Century, Yale French Studies*, No. 72, pp. 149–62. SdB never wrote anything exclusively devoted to the explication of a personal political credo, and, in fact, she usually denied in the strongest possible language any interest or involvement in politics *per se*. For her, political expression or action ultimately had to be grounded first in philosophy and/or feminist theory.

29. *Force of Circumstance*, p. 268.

30. *Ibid.*, p. 168. Emphasis mine.

31. Raymond Aron, "Mme. de Beauvoir et la pensée de droite," *Le Figaro littéraire*, Jan. 12, 1956.

32. SdB, Tuesday [Nov. 18, 1947], NA/OSU.

33. SdB.

34. SdB, Friday [Nov. 21, 1947] and Tuesday night [Nov. 25, 1947], NA/OSU. NA's article was his first "Chicago Letter," translated as "Du rire en bocaux:

Reportage de Chicago," *Les Temps Mo-*
dernes, Vol. 3, No. 28 (Jan. 1948).

35. SdB, Monday [Dec. 1, 1947], NA/
OSU.

27 | ' THE CROCODILE
IS THE FROG'S DESTINY

1. SdB, Tuesday [Nov. 11, 1947],
NA/OSU.

2. SdB, Thursday [Nov. 27], NA/OSU.

3. SdB, Saturday 6th December [1947],
Thursday 31 July [1947], Christmas night
[Dec. 24, 1947], NA/OSU.

4. SdB, Saturday 6th December [1947],
NA/OSU.

5. SdB, Tuesday [Nov. 11, 1947], NA/
OSU.

6. SdB, Tuesday [Nov. 18, 1947], NA/
OSU.

7. SdB, Thursday 11 [Dec. 1947].

8. SdB, Saturday night [Nov. 15, 1947]
and Saturday 6th December [1947], NA/
OSU.

9. SdB, Wednesday [Nov. 5, 1947],
NA/OSU.

10. SdB, Tuesday night [Nov. 25,
1947], Thursday [Nov. 27, 1947], Saturday 6th December [1947], and Christmas
night [Dec. 24, 1947].

11. She makes no comment about *Pale
Horse, Pale Rider*, but "did not like
Flowering Judas."—SdB, Saturday [March
6, 1948], NA/OSU. She was disappointed
with Erskine Caldwell's *Trouble in July*
because she felt she had already "read it
twenty times before—the same story of
Southern towns" that she liked in *Tobacco Road* and *God's Little Acre*. The
very idea of an epic poem such as *John
Brown's Body* bothered her, but she did
find "real poetry" in it.—SdB, Thursday
[Dec. 18, 1947].

12. In a letter of Tuesday [Jan. 20,
1948?], NA/OSU, SdB thanks NA for
the "lesson about Faulkner," telling him
she likes *Light in August* the best of all
his works, but the "tragic sense" in *Pylon*
seems to her "a little stereotypical."

13. R. W. Logan (ed.), *What the
Negro Wants* (Chapel Hill: University
of North Carolina Press, 1944), introd. by
W. T. Couch. SdB, Tuesday [Dec. 30,
1947], NA/OSU.

14. André Maurois, *Histoire des États-
Unis* (1947). SdB, Tuesday [Dec. 30,
1947], NA/OSU.

15. SdB, Tuesday [Dec. 30, 1947], Friday [Jan. 2, 1948].

16. SdB, Friday [Jan. 2, 1948], NA/

OSU. All quotations are from this until
noted otherwise. In a 1986 conversation
one month before her death, SdB said she
"believed" that she worked from this outline for the basic structure of the book,
and that the printed work "depended on
it in great part."

17. SdB, Friday [Jan. 9, 1948], NA/
OSU.

18. SdB had many homosexual or lesbian friends whom she genuinely liked,
but throughout her life she had a very
strong need to let the world know that
she was not one of them, and unfortunately the language with which she chose
to do so was often unjust and unkind. In
this case it was vocabulary that she shared
with Algren.

19. SdB, Friday [Jan. 8, 1948], Sunday
[Jan. 18, 1948], Tuesday [Jan. 20, 1948?],
Saturday [Feb. 28, 1948].

20. SdB, Friday 2th [April 1948], NA/
OSU.

21. SdB, Sunday [Jan. 18, 1948], NA/
OSU.

22. SdB, Saturday 14th February
[1948].

23. SdB, Tuesday [Feb. 17, 1948?],
NA/OSU.

24. SdB, Friday, [Jan. 9, 1948], NA/
OSU.

25. She refers to these meetings in
Force of Circumstance, p. 157. Information is from SdB, Sunday [March 14,
1948], Wednesday 17th [March 1948],
and Thursday [March 25, 1948], NA/
OSU. Cohen-Solal, pp. 300–301, says the
first meeting was a "press conference" and
gives the date as March 10, 1948; the second she calls "the first large meeting of
the RDR" and says it took place on
March 19, 1948, in the Salle Wagram.
Hayman, p. 259, agrees with her description and dating.

26. SdB, Thursday [Jan. 8, 1948],
Tuesday [Jan. 13, 1948], Saturday [Jan.
24, 1948], NA/OSU.

27. SdB, Friday [Feb. 6, 1948], NA/
OSU.

28. *Force of Circumstance*, pp. 164ff.

29. Shortly before her death in 1986,
SdB said that one of her saddest memories
was Algren's angry accusation during a
parting argument that the trip down the
Mississippi had meant nothing to her, and
she was "too angry and stubborn by that
time to contradict him. Besides, to what
end?"

30. SdB, Friday [Feb. 6, 1948], NA/
OSU.

31. Her account of this trip in *Force*

of Circumstance, pp. 153–55, closely parallels her two letters to NA Saturday [Jan. 31, 1948], and Friday [Feb. 6, 1948].

32. SdB, Thursday [April 8, 1948], NA/OSU. All quotations are from this letter until noted otherwise.

33. SdB, Monday [April 19, 1948], NA/OSU.

34. SdB, Sunday [April 4, 1948], NA/OSU. All quotes are from this until noted otherwise.

35. SdB, Thursday [April 15, 1948], NA/OSU.

36. She uses "cats" in the slang of the day, as in "hepcats."

37. NA later put SdB's habit of crushing bread into crumbs in his story "The Way to Médenine," first published in *Playboy* December 1972, reprinted as "Brave Bulls of Sidi Yahya" in *The Last Carousel* (New York: Putnam, 1973), pp. 97ff.

38. In 1983, on her last visit to the U.S., SdB remarked that a hot August day in New York reminded her of the weather in New Orleans. "I always wanted to go back there when the weather was cooler, because the heat was so blinding I was dizzy from it and did not appreciate my time there."

39. S. Gerassi.

40. SdB, Thursday night [July 15, 1948], NA/OSU. All quotes are from this until noted otherwise.

28 | A Book About Women

1. This chapter is the synthesis of nearly a decade of thinking and writing about *The Second Sex.* My aim is twofold: first, to trace the evolution of the book as it evolved in SdB's life; second, to introduce the work to readers who may not be as familiar with it as are the many scholars who have analyzed, explicated, lauded and/or reviled it. I have tried to fulfill the requirements of biography while still responding as much as possible to the needs of critical inquiry, but I have had to summarize much critical commentary because the necessities of biographical unity do not permit long digression from the life itself. Ever mindful of this dilemma, I have settled for trying to present the fullest possible overview. In the interest of brevity, I shall cite here only those works which I have quoted specifically, but I need to express my enormous debt to the scholars, writers and friends who have given their time and shown great patience in discussing this work with me. They will find my gratitude expressed in the acknowledgments.

2. C. Audry.

3. All this is not to say that SdB took the idea from Audry, or that Audry was directly responsible for SdB's desire to write about the contemporary condition of women. It is simply to show that as early as 1937 SdB was involved in conversations that dealt specifically with writing about the subject, even though she continued to insist for many years afterward that she had never personally experienced the second-class status that so frustrated Colette Audry.

4. SdB, *Force of Circumstance,* p. 195.

5. Madeleine Chapsal, "Une Interview de Simone de Beauvoir," *Les Ecrivains en personne,* pp. 17–37, reprinted in Francis and Gontier, *Ecrits,* p. 385.

6. *Force of Circumstance,* p. 196.

7. It was, and it has been since then, but in most of the more than 20 languages into which it has been translated it appears as a single book. Conservative estimates by her French publisher, Robert Gallimard, are that more than one million copies have been sold in French, and "between 2 and 3 million in all other languages." This book made SdB financially independent for the rest of her life.

8. The first phrase actually reached the U.S.: NA sent her an unidentified cartoon depicting her as such.

9. *Force of Circumstance,* p. 203. Still, although *The Second Sex* was published in 1949, she did not consider herself "dedicated primarily to the concerns of women" until almost 20 years later, when she said, "I began to call myself truly a Feminist and to lend myself to the goals and needs of the movement."—SdB.

10. "Talk of the Town," *New Yorker,* Vol. XXIII, No. 1 (Feb. 22, 1947), pp. 19–20.

11. SdB, Monday [July 26, 1948], NA/OSU, tells NA that she has asked "Giacometti's girl, a nice Swiss girl who left her parents to be with him" (Annette, whom he later married), to tell the story of her life, as she asks every woman she meets to do for the book.

12. SdB, *Prime of Life,* p. 572.

13. These descriptions were made by both French and American persons who were interviewed for this book. Many of them knew SdB in a professional sense, i.e., they were writers, photographers, editors who came into contact with her from the end of the war until the end of her

life. Others were involved at differing times and with differing degrees of intimacy with persons who knew Sartre and SdB, from something as casual as seeing them in cafés to being invited to dine by mutual friends. In some instances they were university professors who had drinks or dined with SdB once or twice during their summers or sabbaticals in France. In still other instances they were neighbors of SdB, her mother or her sister who exchanged frequent greetings or had occasional conversations with her. The main point is that, whatever their degree of intimacy with her, their opinions were surprisingly consistent.

14. Francis Jeanson, *Simone de Beauvoir ou l'entreprise de vivre*, p. 253.

15. SdB, *The Second Sex* trans. and ed. H. M. Parshley (New York: Bantam, 1961; hereafter *SS*), author's introd., p. xiii; my emphasis. There have been many criticisms of Parshley's translation (some will be discussed in later chapters), but in this instance he was faithful to the original French pronouns and verbs.

16. She also said she paid no attention to such developments as "Ecriture Feminine," and thought it "jousting at windmills" by those who sought to create a new, nonprejudicial language without categorization by gender. She herself had never considered trying to create a personal system or theory of linguistic revisionism. When she wrote what became the second volume of *The Second Sex*, she addressed specifically the many differing conditions and situations of women. Her responses are generally muted and compassionate, and her outrage is directed toward the injustices that a mainly Western patriarchal society dealt them.

17. SdB, Saturday [May 24, 1947], NA/OSU.

18. SdB, Saturday [6th June 1947], NA/OSU.

19. SdB, Thursday 7th August [1947], NA/OSU. She wrote from Sweden, where she was on holiday with Sartre, telling NA that she had worked very hard and well that week and, having finished this chapter, was ready to resume working on the "book about America again."

20. Chapsal, "Une Interview," *loc. cit.*, p. 385.

21. Christine Fauré, "The Twilight of the Goddesses, or The Intellectual Crisis of French Feminism," trans. Lillian S. Robinson, *Signs*, Vol. 7, No. 1 (Autumn 1981), p. 82. This article was originally published as "Le Crépuscule des déesses,

ou La Crise intellectuelle en France en milieu féministe," in *Les Temps Modernes* 414 (January 1981), pp. 1285–91.

22. C. B. Radford, Part I, p. 89, of "Simone de Beauvoir: Feminism's Friend or Foe?," in *Nottingham French Studies*, Vol. VI, No. 2 (Oct. 1967), pp. 87–102, and Vol. VII, No. 1 (May 1968), pp. 39–53. Radford's relatively early essays (1967–68) have not generated the spirited response (both pro and con) one would have expected. In Part I, Radford writes that Beauvoir has three continuing preoccupations, the Existential, the autobiographical and the political, and that these, in *The Second Sex*, "should show whether Simone de Beauvoir is guilty of painting women in her own colours or of directing women towards her own ideological goals. In this way, it should be possible to decide on the validity of her feminism" (p. 89). In Part II, Radford believes that Beauvoir's tendency "to call upon her own experiences and views" (p. 42) reveals "a narrowness of personal experience even in someone as inquisitive and energetic as Simone de Beauvoir, so the individual problems of the writer herself may assume an exaggerated importance in her discussions of femininity. Suspicions that *Le Deuxième Sexe* presents an image which is distorted by autobiographical influences may be strengthened by a brief glance at three facets of the essay: the bourgeois element, the interpretation of myths and, lastly, a comparison between what she says is generally true and what she shows is personally true, the distinction being particularly noticeable when she discusses such subjects as death, maternity, family, shame and guilt" (p. 46). Radford also wrote of "the likelihood that *Le Deuxième Sexe*, beneath the comprehensive title, is primarily a middle-class document . . ." (p. 46), but also wrote: "Her image of women may be distorted: it is nevertheless sincere. In all her work she is motivated by the honest conviction that her own solution is the best . . . it is this very sincerity that accounts for the exaggeration and even the violence of her work. Her severest critics could hardly deny that there are values in this outspoken vindication of the feminist cause . . ." (p. 52). The late Jacques Ehrmann takes a more positive response to Beauvoir's use of her own life to delineate the universal experiences of women: "Simone de Beauvoir is indeed speaking of herself, when she offers us the example of a woman who has rejected the conven-

tional paths trodden by womanhood, but this individual example may acquire the force of a principle. It is a principle which she submits to ceaseless examination, not only in her life, but in her books also. And when she defends the 'second sex,' she speaks of all women to all women. She speaks to them of a woman's rights, of her own right to choose her own life, to assume responsibility for her own destiny and to refuse what society would thrust upon her."—Jacques Ehrmann, "Simone de Beauvoir and the Related Destinies of Woman and Intellectual," *Yale French Studies*, No. 27 (Spring–Summer 1961), p. 32.

23. Fauré, *loc. cit.*, p. 83.

24. Prof. Margaret A. Simons points to this chapter specifically in her criticism of the Parshley translation. In *Yale French Studies*, No. 72, p. 170, she writes of "extensive unindicated deletions and the inaccurate and inconsistent translation of key philosophical terms. This important text is available in only one English translation [in which] over ten percent of the material in the original French edition has been deleted, including fully one-half of a chapter on history and the names of seventy-eight women. These unindicated deletions seriously undermine the integrity of Beauvoir's analysis of such important topics as the American and European nineteenth-century suffrage movements, and the development of socialist feminism in France." See also her article "The Silencing of Simone de Beauvoir; Guess what's Missing from *The Second Sex*," *Women's Studies International Forum*, No. 6 (1983): 559–64.

25. One of the feminist women SdB liked best and admired most was Kate Millet, but any discussion in which Millet or her work was mentioned usually ended with a slightly miffed SdB saying, "*Sexual Politics* is a very good book and people should pay more attention to it. But she should have given me credit for everything she took from me. She got it all, the form, the idea, everything, from me."

26. Elizabeth Hardwick, "The Subjection of Women," *Partisan Review*, Vol. 20, No. 3 (May–June, 1953), p. 321.

27. Keefe, *op. cit.*, pp. 110–11.

28. SdB, Some Day [Feb. 1952]; n.d. (late Jan. or Feb. 1 or 2, 1952), NA/OSU.

29. *Force of Circumstance*, pp. 177–78.

30. SdB, Tuesday 21th December [1948], and Wednesday [Jan. 5, 1949], NA/OSU. In a conversation September 1984, I asked her about these comments in the light of the account in *Force of Circumstance*, and she replied dryly, "Well, you couldn't expect me to tell *everything*, could you?" Later she said, "It's funny. *The Second Sex* was a serious book, on a serious subject that meant much to me when I wrote it, much more as the years passed, but at the same time I had such a cavalier attitude to so much of it. People always say I don't have a sense of humor, but truly I did find much to laugh about while I wrote it. I was very happy while I wrote that book."

31. SdB, *SS*, p. xxi; François Poulain de la Barre (1647–1725), *De l'égalité des deux sexes* (*On the Equality of Both Sexes*), 1673 (Paris: Librairie Arthème Fayard, 1984, published with the Concours du Centre National des Lettres, Paris). This work has not been translated into English. Elaine Marks and Isabelle de Courtivron (eds.), *New French Feminisms: An Anthology* (Amherst: Univ. of Massachusetts Press, 1980), say of this work (p. 14) that, "applying the Cartesian method and pre-sociological approach, [Poulain] opposes inferiority/superiority argument and discusses cultural conditioning as reason for sexual differentiation."

32. A book by Etienne Lamy, *La Femme de demain* (*The Woman of Tomorrow*), was published in 1901, went through more than 20 editions by the 1930s and was the best-selling work on French feminism before *The Second Sex*. In 1982 SdB said she had not read the book, nor did she remember ever hearing about it until she was "well along" in writing *The Second Sex*. She said she then "read it carefully, but I believe my own ideas were already so well formed that it had little value for me, and certainly no influence on my work." In 1986 I discovered that SdB's philosophy professor at the Sorbonne, Léon Brunschweig, was the husband of Cécile Brunschweig (1877–1946), the committed feminist who was responsible for the UFSF becoming the second-largest women's-rights group in France, and who was called by *La Française* "a woman of action of the first order." Cécile Brunschweig credited her husband for making her a feminist by insisting that women would achieve nothing until they had the right to vote. He himself became a vice-president of the Ligue d'Electeurs pour le Suffrage des Femmes, the men's auxiliary. (For further information, see Steven C. Hause and Anne R.

Kenney, *Women's Suffrage and Social Politics in the French Third Republic,* pp. 133 and 156.) When I spoke to SdB about this she was surprised, saying it was the first time she had ever heard of it. "I might have been kinder to him had I known this. Oh, no, certainly not. I knew nothing of the condition of women then. At that time, I believed I could do anything. I never thought about other women."

33. In *Force of Circumstance,* p. 177, she describes how reading this work "confirmed my notion of woman as *other;* it showed how the male remains the essential being, even within the matrilineal societies generally termed matriarchal." She also writes there that Leiris told her that Lévi-Strauss criticized her "for certain inaccuracies in the sections on primitive societies." Shortly before her death in 1986, at my request SdB telephoned Lévi-Strauss to ask him to discuss this with me. He declined to do so, saying (in SdB's words) "he made his peace with this work many years ago, and in reality had none of the strong criticisms that I, through Leiris, attributed to him. He said that he has no problems with this work now and would prefer not to reopen issues that were never important anyway."

34. The idea that psychology was something to distrust or at least to be wary of was a common theme in my discussions with SdB, from the first in 1981 to the last in 1986. She often said she was sorry she had not paid more attention to psychological interpretations of behavior during her writing life, but that in retrospect and with hindsight she had "protected the integrity" of her work and "its value as a system" by her "rigid adherence" to Existential philosophy. Of Lacan, whose views were raised to prominence by French feminists in the last years of her life, SdB said she had "tried" but did not really read either Lacan's writings or writings about him, believing him in the last years of her life to be "the enigma I barely knew when young and whom I never really cared to understand beyond what I used in *The Second Sex.*"

35. "Yes, Woolf is among the writers whose works I admire and sometimes reread, but only her feminist writings, because I don't agree with her novels. They don't have any center. There isn't any thesis."—SdB.

36. In many ways, she deserves credit for focusing the attention of later generations of gender scholars upon these heretofore neglected areas which have since become important sources for revising history to include the participation and contribution of women.

37. Marks and Courtivron, *op. cit.,* introd. pp. 6 and 7.

38. SdB's comment was made in response to my question concerning her statement in *Force of Circumstance,* p. 202, that "*The Second Sex* was possibly the book that has brought me the greatest satisfaction of all those I have written." She prefaced her remark above by saying, "I have to tell you the truth here because this book you plan to write will be the truthful account that says everything I either could not or did not want to say when I was writing the memoirs."

39. Portions entitled "La Femme et les mythes" were published in *Les Temps Modernes,* Vol. 3, Nos. 32 and 33 (May and June 1948) and Vol. 4, No. 34 (July 1948).

40. SdB, Tuesday [Aug. 3, 1948], NA/OSU.

41. One of the more interesting debates took place in *Saturday Review of Literature,* Vol. XXXVI, No. 8 (Feb. 21, 1953), pp. 26–31 and 41. Six persons were selected to review the book because "the encyclopaedic treatment of a problem as basic as that of the status of women is bound to provoke widely varying reactions in different readers, no one of whom would want to insist that his is the only appropriate reaction, or even the most appropriate reaction to the book as a whole." The reviewers were Dr. Karl A. Menninger, psychiatrist; Philip Wylie, writer; Ashley Montague, anthropologist; Phyllis McGinley, housewife and poet; Margaret Mead, anthropologist; and Olive R. Goldman, U.S. representative to the UN Commission on the Status of Women.

42. Mary Beard to Marjorie White, Feb. 9, 1953, The Arthur and Elizabeth Schlesinger Library on the History of Women in America, Radcliffe College. I am grateful to Prof. Nancy Cott, who called it to my attention. I showed this letter to SdB in 1983 and she said, "You cannot take this seriously. What do you expect from someone whose views were always opposed to mine?"

43. SdB, Thursday [Aug. 26, 1948?], NA/OSU.

44. SdB, Thursday [Dec. 6, 1951?]; Saturday [Dec. 15, 1951?]; Christmas [Dec. 25, 1951?], all NA/OSU.

45. SdB, Monday [Sept. 6, 1948], NA/OSU. On Thursday [Sept. 9, 1948], she

told NA that she worked "six to eight hours every day on the movie script and then on my book." On Sunday [Sept. 26, 1948] she wrote that she, Sartre and Bost were "at a fine seaside hotel working on a movie script for Bost." She said she did not like the work, but did it "for the money and out of friendship." She was referring to *Les Mains sales*, on which Bost worked with Sartre, but also perhaps to the script of Alexandre Astruc's *Le Rideau cramoisi* (1952), which he worked on for a long time.

46. SdB, Friday [Oct. 1, 1948], NA/OSU.

47. SdB, Monday [Oct. 4, 1948], NA/OSU.

48. SdB, Friday [Oct. 8, 1948], NA/OSU.

49. SdB, Wednesday [Oct. 20, 1948], NA/OSU. She wrote this letter from Nice, where she had gone for several days of pure holiday after the "working" holiday in Algiers.

50. SdB, Monday 8th [Nov. 1948], NA/OSU. All quotes are from this until noted otherwise.

51. SdB, Sunday [Nov. 28, 1948], NA/OSU. In a letter of Wednesday, 23 [March 1949], written when she was on holiday in Cagnes-sur-Mer, she told NA she was reading T. E. Lawrence's *Seven Pillars of Wisdom* and his letters and thought him "a strange, appealing man, and a fine writer." She urged NA to read them as well.

52. SdB, Tuesday [Jan. 18, 1949], NA/OSU.

53. SdB, Friday [Dec. 31, 1948], NA/OSU. She is referring to Alfred C. Kinsey et al., *Sexual Behavior in the Human Male* (1948); the other book is not identified. She retained this interest in the religion of the Church of Jesus Christ of Latter Day Saints throughout her life, and in the short-lived practice of polygamy as well. In 1984, when she made her last visit to the U.S., she regretted that she had never spent time in Utah and said she would have enjoyed seeing the Mormon monuments and culture in Salt Lake City.

54. SdB; the first two quotes are from Tuesday 21th December [1948], the last from Sunday [Nov. 28, 1948], NA/OSU. I did not see NA's portion of this correspondence, but, as SdB's letters continue to mention Stendhal, making brief references to what must have been Algren's longer comments, it seems that they must have discussed the novels in some depth.

55. SdB discusses Sartre's beneficence

throughout her correspondence with NA. As some of these persons are still alive and sensitive about Sartre's support, I cite my sources without specific mention.

56. SdB, Monday, [Nov. 22, 1948], NA/OSU. She discussed this in *Force of Circumstance*, p. 181.

57. SDB, Saturday [Dec. 11, 1948]. In a second letter, Dec. 20, 1948, Beauvoir wrote: "So we had this meeting last monday. 3,000 people in the hall and many of them could not go in because it was overcrowded. The cops were awful, they all stood for De Gaulle and they said everybody in the hall were pansies, pansies sold [out] to Russia and they hit badly some of the people who wanted to come in. Carlo Levi had come from Italy and Thorez from Germany and there were lots of foreigners and African and indo-chinese too. Camus spoke very eagerly and wildly but said rather stupid idealistic things; Sartre said good things but sternly. Rousset spoke too harshly and came away all sweaty, speaking too much against Russia and not enough against USA. Since Camus didn't want me to speak and I did not care for it, I did not. I only translated Wright's paper. It was a good paper, very striking and my translation was as always *wonderful* [her emphasis]. So *we* [her emphasis] were very much applauded. There was a little drama, because many foreigners spoke in a terribly broken french and were heard politely but no time was left for colonial people speaking, so they thought we despised them, having asked them to come and not letting them speak. And it is true, everybody spoke . . . saying we are all brothers, but the heads of this meeting, Rousset and his friends, in the bottom of their hearts don't think an African negro or an indo-chinese is as good as a white newspaper man. That was wrong and something else was wrong: the lies against Russia. Then everybody said what everybody in the hall wanted to hear, so there was much applause." SdB writes of this in *Force of Circumstance*, pp. 181ff.

58. SdB, Monday [Dec. 6, 1948] and Saturday [Dec. 11, 1948], NA/OSU.

59. SdB, Wednesday [Jan. 5, 1948], NA/OSU. She asked NA to "be nice to him [if he came to Chicago] even though he may seem cold, reserved and a little slow."

60. SdB, Friday [Jan. 21, 1949], NA/OSU.

61. SdB, 9th January [1949]. All quotes are from this until noted otherwise.

62. This comment is from my last con-

versation with SdB, March 9, 1986. I was supposed to leave Paris the next morning, but the airline was on strike and I telephoned her late that Sunday afternoon to tell her that I had spent the afternoon at the Musée Picasso, as she had suggested ("Terrible paintings, but the building is magnificent"), and that she might well find me on her doorstep the following day if my flight was canceled, because I had to vacate my apartment. She was in a jovial mood and began to talk about "turning points" in one's life when events sometimes seem to be "beyond control and it's either take charge of your life, regain control, or go crazy, or kill yourself, or die." In this mood, she told me the incident related here, ending with "You can read it all in the memoirs, but I had to make it serious there. When I think about it now, it was really very funny." She refers to *Force of Circumstance*, Chap. 4, pp. 174ff.

29 | ALL THE RIGHT ENEMIES

1. SdB, Wednesday night [Dec. 15, 1948], NA/OSU. She told him to buy only a one-way ticket, as the return would be cheaper if purchased in Paris. He was owed money from *Les Temp Modernes* for articles published there, and Gallimard, which had just translated his novel into French, also owed royalties. NA seemed worried about money, because in her letter of Tuesday, 21th December [1948], in reply to a delayed letter of his which had just reached her, she told him again not to worry about money in France. She said she would ask the publisher for his advance, and at any rate she would "take care of [him] in Paris."

2. Most of these dreams concern herself in bed with him, only to awake and find him gone; in several others she searches through the rooms of his Wabansia apartment but cannot find him; in only one, she comes upon him in bed with another woman and stands and watches. One of her major fears during this time concerns plane crashes, which she expressed repeatedly in letter after letter. Many of her worst nightmares began with the death of Marcel Cerdan, the French boxer killed on his way to fight the American Jake La Motta. Train wrecks became another irrational fear, and her letters to NA sometimes included news clippings of the more sensational ones. He asked her repeatedly why she was so fixated on irrational trag-

edy, and she replied that it was "better to die in wrecks and storms than in war" (SdB, Friday [December 1, 1950], NA/OSU), thus evading what was most likely a deeper reason concerning her feelings about him and the status of their relationship. From this time on, NA sent her collages of news articles, photos and other materials relating to tragedies, the more gruesome the better.

3. SdB, 11th April [1949], NA/OSU.

4. SdB allowed me to read this letter but asked me not to quote it. She agreed only that I could "give the sense of it." Her letter in reply is dated Sunday [Aug. 8, 1948], NA/OSU.

5. SdB's letters refer continually to Sartre's generosity, citing everyone from a painter whose wife wanted a new fur coat to young journalists and writers who needed help until their works were published. He did this in some instances anonymously, as in the case of Leduc, who believed it was Gallimard's advance against future royalties until Genet spitefully told her otherwise. Sartre also supported his mistresses, among them Wanda and Michelle Vian at that time (at his death there were at least six women who received annual incomes from his estate), and in one instance gave the equivalent of $1,000 to a couple who asked for money to buy a car, which, Beauvoir noted bitterly, "he cannot afford . . . himself." (SdB, Tuesday [Oct. 24, 1950], NA/OSU.

6. The question of SdB's contribution to Sartre's prolific output is one that has been questioned for years by distinguished scholars of the works of both. In my interviews in Paris with those who knew them well, the general consensus was that her contribution was much greater than either would acknowledge, that although she never did the actual writing, and her handwriting seldom actually appears on his mss, there were many instances in which he told her what he wished to write and she then presented him either a detailed written outline or else a verbal presentation of what the work should be. In both cases, her presentations were so detailed that all he needed to do was then set it down on paper. This was a question I asked SdB repeatedly throughout the years. One reply, of April 1983, can stand for all the rest: "Certainly I helped him. His work was more important than mine: he was a philosopher and people depended on him to show them a better way of being; I was a writer and my in-

fluence was not as great. People as close as Sartre and I, who had been together for so long, who thought the same things, believed the same things—we could not fail but to influence each other, and that is all I need to say about this. What did it matter who had the idea first or said it best? It was the one who wrote it down that counted."

7. SdB, Monday night 19 July [1948], NA/OSU.

8. She named only Bost and Koestler as lovers to NA. Bernard Wolfe, for example, she describes only as "my best friend in New York," Tuesday Night [Oct. 21, 1947]; Phillip Rahv is described throughout the correspondence in the most derogatory terms but never sexually.

9. NA's first marriage to Amanda Kontowicz lasted from 1937–46. She lived in Los Angeles and worked for several film studios in various capacities. They met again when she went to Hollywood for the filming of *The Man With the Golden Arm* in 1952, were remarried in 1953, and divorced the second time in 1955. In 1965 he married the actress Betty Bendyk, from whom he was divorced in 1969. He had no children by either woman. Long after SdB so angered NA by printing some of his letters to her in *The Mandarins* and after their bitter parting, she printed this letter in *Force of Circumstance*, p. 176. He never forgave her for it, and described her to anyone who dared to mention her name in his presence as a "bitter spinster with a vivid imagination." NA sent this letter in early November to Tunisia, when she was on holiday in Algeria, so it did not reach her until the end of December after she returned to Paris. Her reply to him is dated Wednesday [December 15, 1948].

10. She published this letter in *Force of Circumstance* (p. 176) in 1963, when their parting had turned acrimonious. NA reviewed the book's English translation in *Ramparts*, Vol. 4, no. 6 (October 1965), pp. 65–67, saying that it was "from announcing a severely edited autobiography as a confessional that the hypocrisy of *Force of Circumstance* derives . . . Her insistence upon aggrandizing a casual affection twenty years dead into a passion of classic dimension is employed to support her contention." This was his second review; he wrote an even more scathing one the first time in *Harper's*, May 1965, pp. 134–36, where his personal distress is, in the light of their relationship, clearly apparent. He zeroes in on her idea of con-

tingent love, and writes, "Anybody who can experience love contingently has a mind that has recently snapped." He describes the memoir in the language of castration and concludes even more painfully, "Will she ever quit talking?"

11. SdB, Wednesday [Nov. 17, 1948], NA/OSU.

12. SdB, Friday [Dec. 3, 1948], NA/OSU. For the rest of their affair, NA continued to tell SdB of the lovers he took when she was not with him. What he called them remains to be discovered when or if his letters to her are published; she called them such unkind names as "the little whore," "the Little Drug addict whore," "the Chicago woman," "the Japanese girl," "the little Bitch," "the Slut" and "the pig." The first four terms are found in her letters to NA, the last three are terms she used in conversations with DB. She sometimes used these terms to refer to characters in his fiction as well as to real women with whom he was involved. They refer to (among others, for it seems she used the terms indiscriminately for more than one woman) Janice Kingslow, the black actress who enjoyed some fame in Chicago after playing the title role in *Anna Lucasta*; Mari Sabosawa, the Nisei who later married James A. Michener; and an unidentified "Barbara." She was more discreet in her references to "Chris" (or "Chrissy") Rowland, who later married NA's friend Neil Rowland. SdB said it had made her "feel better to be sarcastic," but in 1985 she insisted that she was "definitely not jealous, only teasing. Men like Algren like to be teased this way. It makes them feel virile."

13. SdB, Wednesday [March 30, 1949], NA/OSU.

14. The text of Sartre's speech was printed in the publication of the RDR, *La Gauche-RDR*, November 1948. My translation.

15. SdB, Friday [Nov. 12, 1948], NA/OSU.

16. In the many interviews she gave before the 1980s, SdB dated her emergence as a feminist from the aftermath of the storm caused by the publication of *SS*; she amended this in conversations throughout the 1980s, saying that her feminism probably started with the beginning of her "political realism" at the time of her "brief foray into Sartre's politics and the RDR."

17. Cohen-Solal, p. 310.

18. NA, "Last Rounds in Small Cafés,"

loc. cit., p. 237. NA's remarks are from this until noted otherwise.

19. This is SdB's distinction, made during conversations in March 1985.

20. "We never gave him a key to Sartre's apartment; he always had to knock to be admitted. We never invited him to drink or dine; he always felt more for us than we for him."—SdB.

21. Bernard Frank worked for a brief time as director of literature for the review, meaning that he had the power to select or reject submissions. He was 21 at the time. He and Cau jousted for power, and Frank lost when Cau reviewed his novel *Les Rats* badly, and Frank departed. *Les Rats* (Paris: Editions de la Table Ronde, 1953; Flammarion, 1985) is a novel which depicts in part the time, circumstances and situation of Frank's collaboration with Sartre, SdB and the Family. SdB said she thought it "amusing, but dishonest in part. We were not like that." In the 1985 edition which Frank sent her, he inscribed it to her from her "elder son" (*cadet-aîné*). When asked if this was a role he played, she replied, "Well, the new ones [members of the Family] insisted on seeing us as mother and father, but we rebelled against this. Sartre especially—he insisted on being treated as one of them, equal to them in their youth. I knew I was getting old, so that did not mean so much to me as it did to him, but I was never anybody's mother, that is certain!"

22. SdB. She also said of Genet, "Later we got to like each other better, but we were never good friends."

23. SdB, Friday [Dec. 3, 1948], Sunday [Oct. 30, 1949], Wednesday [Nov. 9, 1949] and Friday night [Nov. 25, 1949?], NA/OSU.

24. Truman Capote, *Answered Prayers* (New York: Random House, 1987), p. 36. Capote also described Koestler as "never sober, an aggressive runt very free with his fists," and Camus as "reedy, diffident in a razory way, a man with crisp brown hair, eyes liquid with life, and a troubled, perpetually listening expression; an approachable person."

25. "I recognized at once that, like Beckett and those others chez Lindon [Editions de Minuit], something new was starting to happen in Duras's fiction. When I read it, I didn't like it all that much, but I was curious to find out about it."—SdB.

26. SdB, Wednesday 9th [Jan. 1952];

n.d. (late Jan. or Feb. 1 or 2, 1952), NA/OSU.

27. SdB, Friday [Nov. 9, 1951?], NA/OSU.

28. She described her daily schedule to NA as follows: "9–2 in the library, lunch with my mother or friends, and work at Sartre's from 5 to 8." (SdB, Friday 29th [Oct. 1948], NA/OSU.)

29. SdB, Sunday 29th [August 1948] and Saturday [Oct. 23, 1948], NA/OSU.

30. SdB, 11th April [1949], NA/OSU.

31. H. E. F. Donohue, *Conversations with Nelson Algren* (New York: Hill & Wang, 1964), pp. 182–83. In "Last Rounds in Small Cafés," *loc. cit.*, p. 210, NA wrote: "Madame lived in a large room four flights up an ancestral stair on the Rue de la Bûcherie. Only one avenue away, Notre Dame rose above the rooftops. All day long an Arabian lament grieved up to us from the dark café below."

32. NA, "Last Rounds," *loc. cit.*, p. 212.

33. J.-L. Bost, O. Bost.

34. NA, *Who Lost an American?* (New York: Macmillan, 1960), p. 94. He dedicated this book "For Simone de Beauvoir."

35. *Ibid.*, p. 96.

36. In the *Conversations*, H. E. F. Donohue asked NA, "Were there periods of time when the three of you, Miss de Beauvoir, Sartre, and you, were traveling together?" NA replied, "Oh, no, no, we never traveled together. I just traveled with her. She and Sartre haven't been together since, I guess, the twenties, something like that. They've lived separately since he was a professor at the Sorbonne. He was twenty-three, she was nineteen or something, but they'd been separated, at that time, for twenty years, I guess. Well, they saw each other every day, as far as that goes, but they lived separately and still do."

37. *Force of Circumstance*, p. 190.

38. *Ibid.*, pp. 196ff. All quotes are from this until otherwise indicated.

39. NA, *Who Lost an American?*, pp. 96ff.

40. *Ibid.*, p. 97. All quotes are from this until noted otherwise. Note that here he calls her Castor, which he never did during their relationship.

41. NA to SdB, undated note in her archives.

42. Donohue, *Conversations*, p. 266.

43. SdB.

44. Janet Flanner (Genêt) in *The New Yorker*, Feb. 4, 1950, p. 73.

45. *Force of Circumstance*, pp. 197–99.

46. Interview by John Gerassi, "Simone de Beauvoir: *The Second Sex*, 25 Years Later," *Society*, January–February 1976, p. 85.

47. *Force of Circumstance*, p. 197. In 1982 she recalled with zest and obvious satisfaction an article written by André Maurois, another writer she detested for his Gaullist positions, who returned the sentiments to her in kind. In *La Figaro Littéraire*, Oct. 21, 1965, p. 14, he wrote an article of grudging praise for *SS*, entitled "Simone de Beauvoir n'a pas encore gagné sa guerre" ("Simone de Beauvoir has not entirely won her war"). Maurois concluded that "after fifteen years it [the book] is not outdated. It remains strong, intelligent and pressing."

48. SdB. She recounts their travels in *Force of Circumstance*, pp. 191ff. NA gives an account of the African part of the trip in "Brave Bulls of Sidi Yahya," *The Last Carousel* (New York: Putnam, 1973), pp. 97ff. This article was first published in *Playboy*, December 1972, as "The Way to Médenine." SdB described the article in 1984 as "accurate in the facts, but the tone is very sarcastic toward me. He was bitter by then."

49. SdB, Tuesday night [Sept. 13, 1949], NA/OSU.

50. Both letters are NA/OSU.

30 | "Not Exactly Our Story, but . . ."

1. SdB, and *Force of Circumstance*, p. 201.

2. Ralph Ellison, letter to Richard Wright, Aug. 18, 1945. Quoted in Michel Fabre, *The World of Richard Wright* (Jackson: University of Mississippi Press, 1985), p. 160.

3. Fabre, *op. cit.*, p. 162.

4. *Force of Circumstance*, p. 209.

5. Quoted *ibid.*, p. 210. In 1983, SdB found this *cahier*, a small schoolchild's notebook, among her papers. She also found a collection of loose pages which she said belonged with it, and believed that there were "at least six or eight parts" to this abandoned text and that she "probably had them all." She said she would give what she had to Robert Gallimard, who would consult with Arlette Elkaïm-Sartre to see if it should be published in part or held until some fu-

ture time. As of SdB's death in April 1986, no decision had been made.

6. Jacques Ehrmann, in "Simone de Beauvoir and the Related Destinies," *loc. cit.*, p. 29, makes an accurate observation about this aspect of the novel: "When politics comes to the fore, when Simone de Beauvoir presents to us the central questions debated by French intellectuals in the post-war years, the book takes on conviction right away . . . *The Mandarins*, then, is less the novel it claims to be than a chronicle, an eye-witness account of the problems faced by the French Left after the Liberation. As a document, too—in view of the situation that confronted France in the immediate past—it has again come to possess a certain actuality."

7. SdB, Sunday [Oct. 23, 1940], NA/OSU.

8. SdB.

9. Among those who said this were J.-L. Bost and J. B. Pontalis.

10. NA, "Last Rounds," *loc. cit.*, p. 237.

11. She ordered two lamps, but only one worked. She had to call the electrician to install new wiring before she could use the second (SdB, Tuesday [Oct. 11, 1949], NA/OSU). NA tells an amusing anecdote about the proportions of scotch to water, in "Last Rounds," *loc. cit.*, p. 240.

12. *Force of Circumstance*, p. 276. She devotes pp. 274–88 to the novel, assigning it an important place within both her life and her canon, as she uses it to conclude the first half of this memoir.

13. *Flair*, Vol. 1, No. 3 (April 1950), pp. 76–77. All textual quotations until noted otherwise refer to this issue of the magazine.

14. SdB, Friday night [May 12, 1950], NA/OSU.

15. SdB, Tuesday [June 6, 1950?], NA/OSU.

16. SdB, Wednesday [Dec. 7, 1949], NA/OSU. She based the character Scriassine in *The Mandarins* on Koestler.

17. SdB, Saturday [Dec. 17, 1949], NA/OSU.

18. SdB, Sunday [Dec. 18, 1949], NA/OSU.

19. SdB, Wednesday [Dec. 21, 1949?], NA/OSU.

20. SdB, Tuesday [Nov. 15, 1949?], NA/OSU. Pagliero, the Italian actor she had liked so much in *Rome: Open City* (*Force of Circumstance*, p. 141), made the documentary *Saint-Germain-des-Prés*, which was narrated by Raymond Queneau.

SdB also described this event in conversation, May 7, 1983.

21. SdB, Tuesday [Oct. 18, 1949], NA/OSU.

22. SdB, Sunday [Oct. 30, 1949], NA/OSU; *ibid.*; Wednesday [Nov. 2, 1949]; Sunday [Nov. 6, 1949]; Sunday [Nov. 18, 1949]; Wednesday [Feb. 8, 1950].

23. SdB, Sunday [Feb. 5, 1950], NA/OSU. All comments are from this until noted otherwise.

24. SdB.

25. SdB.

26. SdB, Tuesday [Oct. 24, 1950], NA/OSU.

27. Mrs. Bradley, along with her husband, William, was probably the best-known literary agent in Paris for the first half of the 20th century. Her clients included James Joyce, F. Scott Fitzgerald and Ernest Hemingway, among others, and, for a time, Sartre, SdB and NA. For various reasons, the last three grew dissatisfied with her representation and left. SdB transferred the handling of her literary affairs to Ellen Wright when the latter began her own successful agency. Mrs. Wright represented Beauvoir for the rest of her life.

28. SdB, Tuesday [Oct. 24, 1950], NA/OSU.

29. SdB, Tuesday [Jan. 3, 1950], NA/OSU.

30. Sartre wanted to visit Egypt for several months beginning in the fall of 1950, and he wanted SdB to go with him. Cau was put in charge of all the arrangements, but the Egyptian government refused to grant the necessary permissions unless Sartre agreed to give a specified number of lectures on topics and in places they selected. He refused. SdB wrote to NA (Wednesday [Jan. 18, 1950], NA/OSU) that "Sartre was mad with anger. Suppose you and I had had to lecture to the Central American Indians?"

31. Chap. 6 of *The Mandarins* contains a slightly fictionalized account of the first part of their affair; pp. 422–23 include the episode of the sheet and the bed.

32. SdB told NA she was going to Africa on Saturday [Jan. 21, 1950]; he did not reply until Saturday [Feb. 18, 1950]; both NA/OSU. From that point on, her letters are filled with apologies for going with Sartre to visit some of the same places she had been to with him, and she begs him to believe that everything paled in comparison to when she was there with him.

33. In an earlier letter of Tuesday [Jan.

24, 1950], SdB reminded him not to tell Natasha that she had even been in the U.S. in 1948. Also, for some unexplained reason, she did not want Natasha to know that she and NA had become lovers before he went to Paris in 1949.

34. SdB, Wednesday [Feb. 22, 1950], NA/OSU.

35. SdB, Thursday [March 2, 1950], Saturday [March 4, 1950] and Thursday [Nov. 2, 1950], NA/OSU.

36. SdB, Saturday [March 4, 1950], NA/OSU.

37. *New York Herald Tribune Book News*, March 28, 1950, p. 1; SdB, 8th May [1950], NA/OSU.

38. SdB, Wednesday 3th May [1950]; 8th May [1950], NA/OSU.

39. SdB, Wednesday [May 17, 1950]; Sunday [May 21, 1950]; n.d. [week of May 28–June 3, 1950], NA/OSU.

40. SdB, Sunday [June 4, 1950?], NA/OSU.

41. *Force of Circumstance*, pp. 236ff.

42. *The Mandarins*, Chap. 10, pp. 671ff.

43. *The Mandarins*, p. 708.

44. *Ibid.*

45. SdB, n.d. [Sept. 30, 1950], NA/OSU.

46. SdB, Wednesday [Oct. 4, 1950], NA/OSU.

47. SdB, Friday [Dec. 8, 1950], NA/OSU.

48. He repeated the offer several times, and in a letter dated Sunday [Jan. 14, 1951], NA/OSU, she thanked him for his "offer of $100 to $200 to help us get settled in Mexico or Rio de Janeiro when we have to leave France."

49. SdB, Thursday [Dec. 14, 1950?], NA/OSU.

50. SdB, Friday [Dec. 22, 1950], NA/OSU.

51. SdB, Sunday [Dec. 31, 1950], NA/OSU.

52. SdB, Sunday [Jan. 7, 1951], NA/OSU.

53. *Force of Circumstance*, p. 244. This was "not a deliberate omission," she said in 1984; rather, she insisted that she had "quite forgotten about it" until it was pointed out to her in the Algren letters.

54. All these remarks were made during an interview Jan. 23, 1982. I have not changed the context, but I have removed them from a long, detailed conversation about all of her writing and have put them together here with ellipses to indicate where they have been extracted from other sections of the interview.

55. SdB was present throughout some of the most troubled years of the Wrights' marriage. He spent a year in Brazil, ostensibly to make a movie but really because he was passionately involved with a woman there. He went to Rome "making a fool of himself with a succession of Italian starlets," and returned to Paris flaunting a Haitian mistress to Ellen's distress and Sartre and Beauvoir's embarrassment. SdB writes of this in many of the letters to NA from 1950 to 1952.

56. SdB, Tuesday [March 13, 1951], NA/OSU.

57. As soon as the novel was published, readers chose to see the three main characters as Camus, herself and Sartre, which infuriated her, most especially because she had put parts of herself into each of the two male characters, especially Henri. "Why do people insist on doing this?" she demanded angrily. "Does everything I write have to come from my life? Can't people give me any credit for having an imagination?"—SdB to DB.

58. Many critics fault SdB for the sections set in the U.S. Terry Keefe (op. cit., p. 197) states the objection most succinctly when he argues that the three visits allow Anne's view of the U.S. to change from the liberator of France to the home of the atom bomb, but "this in itself is scarcely enough to justify devoting nearly a sixth of the whole book to Anne's 'aventure transatlantique.' And even if the affair with Brogan can be taken to be the crux of the matter, that does not altogether necessitate the fairly detailed descriptions of settings and of the long journey undertaken during Anne's second visit that so much resemble passages from Beauvoir's memoirs. Insofar as the centre of gravity of Les Mandarins is what is happening in Paris, one is bound to conclude that the sections taking place in America stand out rather awkwardly and are somewhat out of proportion, in spite of their oblique relevance to more crucial elements of the story."

59. SdB, Thursday [Dec. 6, 1951?], NA/OSU.

60. SdB, Christmas [Dec. 25, 1951], NA/OSU.

61. SdB, Monday 13th [Oct. 1952], NA/OSU. Her relationship with Blanche Knopf grew even more strained when Ellen Wright sold the American translation rights to the World Publishing Co.

62. SdB, 30th April [1954], NA/OSU.

63. SdB, 3rd January [1955]; n.d. [October or November 1954], NA/OSU.

64. Shay, "Author on the Make," p. 9. For several years, NA played a joke on the FBI: when he learned that he was being investigated for his left-wing political activities, he changed his listing in the 1954 Gary, Ind., telephone directory to "Simon de Beauvoir." Herbert Mitgang, "Annals of Government: Investigating Writers," New Yorker, Oct. 5, 1987, p. 77. Mitgang also notes that a memorandum in NA's FBI file notes that this was the only directory listing for his number, and that "Nelson Algren Abraham" —the name of his Army service record— used several aliases, including "Simon Beauvoir and Simon de Beauvoir."

65. NA's copy of The Mandarins is in NA/OSU.

31 | A $10 BOOK BY AN UNKNOWN FRENCH-WOMAN

1. SdB, Force of Circumstance, p. 262.

2. SdB, 13th July [1951], NA/OSU.

3. Natasha Moffatt had been in Paris that summer and agreed to transport illegally through customs $250 of SdB's money, which she then sent to NA to keep until SdB's arrival.—SdB, n.d. [July 2, 1951], NA/OSU.

4. This account is based on conversations with SdB, Aug. 30, 1984, in New York, and March 4 and 7, 1986, in Paris. Also, she wrote about it in a letter dated Thursday Evening [Tuesday, Oct. 30, 1951?], NA/OSU.

5. SdB, Wednesday [Oct. 31, 1951], NA/OSU.

6. Beauvoir quotes this letter in Force of Circumstance, p. 262. It was this, along with his other letters she used without his permission, that caused him to attack her repeatedly in print. He believed that she had been unfair to reveal his side of the correspondence without also citing her own. In a telephone conversation with DB, he accused Beauvoir of slanting their relationship to suit her own need to establish the primacy of her relationship with Sartre. When Beauvoir was asked about this in 1982 she said only, "I suppose he had some little reason to believe that."

7. SdB, Friday [Nov. 9, 1951?], NA/OSU.

8. Force of Circumstance, p. 263, and Friday [Nov. 9, 1951?], NA/OSU.

9. SdB, n.d. [July 2, 1951], NA/OSU. The essay, a hodgepodge of Existential

philosophy, faulty Freudian psychoanalysis and ill-considered views about pornography and her own contemporary society,
is almost as thoughtless as her joke. It is
one of her writings, especially since chronologically it comes so soon after *SS*, that
outrages feminist critics and scholars by
its inconsistency and contradiction. It is
of interest today only because she wrote
it. It was one of three that she published
as the book *Privileges* in 1955, the others
being the two occasional pieces *The
Thought of the Right Today* and *Merleau-
Ponty and Pseudo-Sartrism*. Throughout
her lifetime, her regard for these essays remained much higher than that of scholars
or critics of her writing. In 1982, when
she was asked where someone interested
in learning about the development of her
feminist philosophy (both as part of her
Existentialist position and separate from
it) should begin, she insisted that these
three offered the most appropriate place
to start and were examples of her most
significant philosophical and sociopolitical
commentary.

10. *Force of Circumstance*, p. 298.

11. This comment was made by SdB.
Information pertaining to the American
publication of *SS* is from interviews with
SdB, Ellen Wright and the late Mrs.
Jennie Bradley; also, conversations with
Mrs. Elsa Parshley Brown and Richard
Gilman. I am grateful to Mrs. Brown
for allowing me to use the correspondence
and documentation of her father, Prof.
H. M. Parshley. I have also consulted the
correspondence and publishing files of Al-
fred A. Knopf, Inc., which is now in the
Humanities Research Center of the Uni-
versity of Texas, Austin. I am grateful to
Mr. Alfred A. Knopf, Jr., for his permis-
sion to use his parents' papers.

12. Prof. Parshley became an international authority on *Hemiptera-Heteroptera*
and was the author of *Science and Good
Behavior* (1928) and editor of *A General
Catalogue of the Hemiptera*, as well as the
author of *The Science of Human Reproduction* (1933) and *A Survey of Biology*
(1940). He also published widely in the
American Mercury under the editorship of
H. L. Mencken, was a frequent reviewer
for the *New York Herald Tribune* and
many other periodicals, and was the author of more than 400 articles and scientific papers.

13. H. M. Parshley, "Report on *Le
Deuxième Sexe* by Simone de Beauvoir,
Vol. I," courtesy of Mrs. Elsa Parshley
Brown.

14. Alfred A. Knopf to H. M. Parshley,
Nov. 27, 1951. Original in Humanities Research Center, *loc. cit.*, copy in the Parshley papers of Mrs. Brown. I am grateful
to the HRC, Mr. Alfred A. Knopf, Jr.,
and Mrs. Brown for permission to quote.

15. Prof. Margaret Simons has long advocated the need for a new translation of
SS. She cites much that has since been discovered to be crucial that is missing from
the English-language translation. Since
many translations in other languages were
prepared from the English translation and
not from the original French, those who
have read the book in languages other
than French may not even realize how
much is missing. To support her argument, Simons gives details of the massive
cuts in Vol. I, particularly in the "History" section, where more than 50 biographies of women were removed, fully half
of the chapter was eliminated and the
names of more than 78 women are entirely missing. This causes frequent consternation among readers who are unable
to make the necessary cross-reference when
they find references to some of this same
material in other sections of the book.
Although his correspondence with the
Knopfs shows how valiantly Parshley tried
to immerse himself in Sartre, Hegel, Heidegger and others, philosophers still believe that he has either misconstrued or
misused much philosophical terminology
in Vol. II. In a paper entitled "A Tribute to *The Second Sex* and Simone de
Beauvoir," presented at *The Second Sex*
—Thirty Years Later: A Commemorative
Conference on Feminist Theory, New
York Institute for the Humanities, September 1979, Prof. Simons wrote: "Parshley translated 'la réalité humaine' as 'the
real nature of man,' which, as Beauvoir
has remarked to me, is exactly its opposite meaning." Simons is especially critical
of Parshley's reversal of *"pour-soi"* ("Being for-itself") and *"en-soi"* ("in-itself").
I am grateful to her for permission to
quote from this paper; another version of
it was published in *Ms.* magazine as "So
You Think You Read *The Second Sex?*"

16. Parshley to Blanche Knopf, Oct.
20, 1951. All quotations are from this until noted otherwise.

17. Parshley to SdB, May 18, 1951.

18. SdB, undated letter. All comments
are from this until noted otherwise.

19. The undated "Copy and Additions
to List of 'Passages marked in Vol. II of
de Beauvoir' " is among the Parshley papers, as is the "Memo to Mrs. Knopf"

dated Jan. 12, 1950, which covers Vol. I. Parshley notes that for him "summarize" means "reduce to a few sentences," and "condense" means "abbreviate somewhat." SdB's handwritten comments are next to each of Parshley's suggestions. Both memos bear the stamp of Mrs. Bradley's office, and Ellen Wright acted as go-between for SdB, who did not communicate with Parshley but addressed her letter to Blanche Knopf.

20. Blanche Knopf to Parshley, May 16, 1951. All quotes are from this until noted otherwise.

21. SdB's letter is characteristically undated, but it bears Parshley's handwritten comment "received June 21, 1951."

22. Parshley to Blanche Knopf, Oct. 20, 1951.

23. Blanche Knopf to Parshley, Oct. 19, 1951.

24. Ibid., Oct. 24, 1951.

25. Parshley to Blanche Knopf, Oct. 25, 1951.

26. Ibid., Nov. 3, 1951.

27. Blanche Knopf to Parshley, Nov. 10, 1952.

28. SdB, quoted in Blanche Knopf's letter to Parshley, Jan. 8, 1953.

29. Parshley wrote a convincing letter to Blanche Knopf which explained the many expenses connected with the book, and she authorized an additional $750 to be paid to him.

30. Harold Strauss to Parshley, Oct. 31, 1951.

31. Publicity circular courtesy Mrs. Elsa Parshley Brown.

32. Harold Strauss to Parshley, Feb. 12, 1953.

33. Alfred A. Knopf, Jr., to Parshley, Feb. 17, 1953.

34. Katherine Anne Porter to Parshley, Jan. 16, 1953.

35. Stevie Smith, "The Devil's Doorway," The Spectator, No. 6543 (Nov. 20, 1953), pp. 602–3.

36. Charles J. Rollo, "Cherchez la Femme," Atlantic Monthly, Vol. 191, No. 4 (April 1953), p. 86.

37. Dwight MacDonald, "The Lady Doth Protest," The Reporter, April 4, 1953, pp. 36–40.

38. William Phillips, "A French Lady on the Dark Continent: Simone de Beauvoir's Impressions of America," Commentary, July 1953, p. 25.

39. Elizabeth Hardwick, "The Subjection of Women," Partisan Review, Vol. 20, No. 3 (May–June 1953), pp. 321–31.

40. "A SR Panel Takes Aim at The Second Sex," Saturday Review of Literature, Feb. 21, 1953, pp. 26–31, 41. The other reviewers were poet Phyllis McGinley (representing the "housewife"), and Olive Remington Goldman, who was U.S. representative to the UN Commission on the Status of Women and also a translator of several plays from French into English.

41. Ruth Burt Robertson in The Library Journal, Vol. 78, No. 1 (Jan 1, 1953), p. 56.

42. "Lady with a Lance," Time, Vol. LXI, No. 8 (Feb. 23, 1953).

43. Brendan Gill, "No More Eve," New Yorker, Vol. XXIX, No. 2 (Feb. 28, 1953), pp. 97–99.

44. SdB, 21 June [1953], NA/OSU.

45. SdB discusses this in her letter of 21 June [1953] to Algren, NA/OSU. S. le Bon de Beauvoir has announced (fall, 1987) that she intends to publish these letters because they demonstrate how SdB's book affected the lives of so many women.

46. Both these remarks were made to me by so many people in so many differing circumstances during the six years in which I conducted interviews in France that I will not single out any individual to cite here.

47. SdB, June 21 [1953], NA/OSU.

32 | WHEN "THE DREAM I DREAMED" CAME TRUE

1. SdB, Wednesday 9th [Jan. 1952], NA/OSU.

2. In a number of instances (where the recepients wish to remain anonymous), SdB arranged for support to continue after her death.

3. In a long conversation about her general health, SdB also said that she was often horrified to discover how much time she allowed to elapse between routine gynecological examinations, but that she detested them so much she chose "to play roulette with my chances because I was always so healthy I felt invincible."

4. SdB. She described the progress of Lucienne Baudin's illness and subsequent death throughout the letters to NA of 1951. From January to July 1952 there are repeated references to herself as either aging or simply old.

5. This person wishes to remain anonymous.

6. SdB, n.d. [late Jan. or Feb. 1 or 2, 1952], NA/OSU.

7. All Claude Lanzmann's comments are from an interview Jan. 23, 1982, Paris.

8. SdB, 3rd August [1952], NA/OSU. See also *Force*, pp. 291ff. All comments are from this until noted otherwise.

9. SdB, 3rd October [1952] and Monday 13th [Oct. 1952], NA/OSU.

10. SdB writes of the beginning of her relationship with Lanzmann in *Force of Circumstance*, pp. 291–97. There she describes how their understanding evolved, especially with regard to her annual vacations with Sartre: "I didn't want to give them up; but a separation of two months would have been painful for both of us [Lanzmann and herself]. We agreed that Lanzmann would come every summer and spend ten days or so with myself and Sartre."

11. *Force of Circumstance*, pp. 297–98.

12. *Ibid.*, p. 298.

13. *Ibid.*, p. 296.

14. SdB, Monday 13th [Oct. 1952], NA/OSU.

15. SdB, n.d. [late Oct. or early Nov. 1952?], NA/OSU.

16. SdB, 9th December [1952], NA/OSU.

17. She called *The Nation* "an American left-wing magazine," and the June 28, 1952, issue is the one which appeared in the October–November 1952 issue of *Les Temps Modernes* as "La Chasse des sorcières aux États-Unis."

18. Sartre was also obsessed with the case of Henri Martin, a French sailor and Communist who was sentenced to five years in prison for his activities against the French in the Indochina war. André Marty and Charles Tillon were dismissed from the French Communist Party in December 1952 because of "nationalist deviations." The Slansky trial took place in Prague. SdB touches on these incidents in *Force of Circumstance*, pp. 301–3. Cohen-Solal, pp. 328–31, and Hayman, pp. 287–308, both give fairly detailed accounts of Sartre's political evolution during this time.

19. SdB, 9th December [1952], NA/OSU.

20. SdB, 2nd July [1952], NA/OSU.

21. *Force of Circumstance*, pp. 300–303. All quotations are from this until noted otherwise.

22. SdB, 15 February [1954], NA/OSU.

23. SdB, n.d. [1952], NA/OSU.

24. All of these terms, and many others, are to be found in her correspondence with NA. She also used them freely in her conversations, as many persons who were interviewed for this book confirmed.

25. *Force of Circumstance*, p. 314.

26. SdB, 5th October [1954], NA/OSU.

27. *Force of Circumstance*, p. 326.

28. SdB, 9th January [1955], NA/OSU. The photograph appears in *Paris-Match*, No. 298 (Dec. 11–18, 1954), p. 79.

29. *Force of Circumstance*, p. 328.

33 | "THE PLACE THAT GONCOURT BOUGHT"

1. SdB, 29th November [1954], NA/OSU.

2. This information came to light during my last meeting with SdB, March 9, 1986. While looking at photos she suddenly said, "Did I ever tell you that I once thought . . ." and then added this statement. She said she turned immediately to other topics because "I didn't even think about it. It was too ludicrous."

3. SdB, *Force of Circumstance*, p. 330.

4. She gives an incredibly garbled and simplistic account of what she thought and wrote in *ibid.*, pp. 330–32. All quotations are from these pages until noted otherwise.

5. Chapsal, "Une Interview," *loc. cit.*, pp. 380–96; This makes Terry Keefe's judgment of *Privileges* a valid one: "The significance . . . is that it constitutes a kind of still photograph of Beauvoir passing through a transitional stage in her development."—Keefe, *op. cit.*, p. 124.

6. SdB.

7. Catherine A. MacKinnon's editors' note to her article "Feminism, Marxism, Method and the State: An Agenda for Theory," *Signs* 7 (Spring 1982), pp. 515–44, reads: "Central to feminist theory and feminist method . . . is consciousness raising. Through this process, feminists confront the reality of women's condition by examining their experience and by taking this analysis as the starting point for individual and social change. By its nature, this method of inquiry challenges traditional notions of authority and objectivity, and opens a dialectical questioning of existing power structures, of our own experience, and of theory itself." Through her memoirs, SdB demonstrates the raising of her own unique consciousness, proving the validity of MacKinnon's thesis.

8. SdB, 1st September [1955], NA/OSU.

9. She had a small black-and-white set with terrible reception for many years un-

til Sylvie bought her a color set for one of her birthdays in the 1970s, and that was when she began "really to enjoy" watching it.—S. le Bon de Beauvoir, conversation with DB.

10. At the time of her death, it was full of mss, letters and other souvenir papers, all tossed in with old laundry lists, canceled checks, bits of string or ribbon and other residua of daily life. Unlike Sartre, SdB never gave or threw anything away, so her cellar "*cave*" was soon overflowing with paper. It provided her with a convenient excuse when scholars pestered her to study something she did not want them to see: "It's in my cellar," she would say, airily waving her hand, "it's simply impossible to find." *Cave* (pronounced "ka:v") is the French word for "cellar," but in our conversations SdB's way of joking about hers was to use the English pronunciation, or sometimes to combine the French and English words as I have done here.

11. SdB, *La Longue Marche: essai sur la Chine* (Paris: Gallimard, 1957); *The Long March* (New York: World Publishing, 1958). Her memoirs, written long after the trip, when she felt the need to cast her impressions in a particularly Marxist view indiscriminately supportive of the peasant revolution, are particularly slanted.

12. She made this comment about NA's personality in a 1983 conversation, to describe how she behaved toward him after 1952.

13. SdB. All quotations about China that follow are from her letters of 3rd November and 15th December [1955] and n.d. [autumn 1956], NA/OSU. In her memoirs she speaks of meeting Levi at a stopover in Moscow on their return from China; in her letters to NA she wrote, "Carlo Levi went with us," then proceeded to tell him how they all stopped in Moscow at the beginning as well as the end of the trip, and how Levi served in many instances as their guide to both countries.

14. SdB, 1st January [1957], NA/OSU.

15. Paul K. T. Sih, review of *The Long March* in *The Catholic World*, Vol. 187, No. 1,121 (August 1958), p. 393.

16. *L'Osservatore romano*, July 13, 1956. "Immoral Existentialism: A Decree of the Congregation of the Holy Office Has Put the Writings of Madame Simone de Beauvoir upon the Index of Banned Books." The story broke in France in *Le Monde*, July 14, 1956.

17. She gives a truncated, telescoped version of this call, as well as the period 1956–61, on pp. 505–6 of *Force of Circumstance*. The visit to Paris she writes about there actually did not take place until the end of 1960.

18. SdB, 12th July, 1956, NA/OSU. All quotes are from this until noted otherwise.

19. SdB, n.d. [autumn 1956], NA/OSU.

20. SdB, 1st January, 1957, NA/OSU. All quotes are from this until noted otherwise.

21. SdB, n.d. [Jan. 1957], NA/OSU.

34 | "MY LIFE . . . THIS CURIOUS OBJECT"

1. SdB, *All Said and Done*, pp. 9–10.

2. These dates are all for the original publication in France by Gallimard; English-language publications were respectively 1959, 1962, 1964 and 1974.

3. SdB, *Prime of Life*, p. 363.

4. As he explained it, "although we were together as a couple for seven years, we lived separately and pursued other interests and relationships for much of that time."

5. Beauvoir, Bost and others attested to this in interviews with DB.

6. SdB, *Force of Circumstance*, p. 397, and SdB, C. Lanzmann, J.-L. Bost, J.-B. Pontalis, J. Pouillon, F. Jeanson and others. Corydrane was a combination of aspirin and various amphetamines, available in drugstores over the counter until 1971, and advertised as an analgesic, an antipyretic and a tonic, but generally taken as a stimulant. Its popularity began with students but soon spread to various artists' groups and intellectual communities. The usual dose was no more than 3 or 4 per day; Sartre took between 10 and 20. Although Sartre's friends are divided on the specific amount of Orthodrine he took daily, they and SdB all described it as a "lethal amount" and said that he rotated his list of physicians so that none would suspect and perhaps deny his continuing requests for more.

7. When Zonina ran afoul of Soviet policies and could no longer work in an official capacity, Sartre paid her a regular stipend, which Arlette Elkaïm-Sartre continued after his death and until Zonina's. Both Sartre and SdB carried on an extensive and detailed correspondence with Zonina, much of which concerned politics and ideology. It remained with her daugh-

ter in Moscow after her death. In 1987 Robert Gallimard stated that he hoped to publish this correspondence, but no date had been established to do so. At that time, it appeared that the letters were dispersed among Zonina's daughter, Arlette Elkaïm-Sartre and the offices of Editions Gallimard, and scattered among other papers of both Sartre and SdB. Scholars on several continents agree that it will be of great value in contributing to the assessment of Sartre's thought from 1955 until his death.

8. *All Said and Done*, p. 111.

9. *Ibid.*, pp. 51, 52.

10. Cohen-Solal, p. 345.

11. Bienenfeld (now divorced) had returned to Paris and, to SdB's "chagrin," tried to return to the "supplicating pupil" relationship.

12. SdB, n.d. [Dec. 1960], NA/OSU. Ellen Wright (telephone conversations, Jan. 12, 1982 and March 6, 1985) claimed she had not read *The Mandarins* thoroughly enough to have remembered SdB's recreation of NA as Lewis Brogan.

13. Some of these, like the novelist Claude Courchay, became friends of lasting importance in her life. Moved by *Pyrrhus et Cinéas*, he wrote to her during the several years he was a seaman in the French Navy stationed on an aircraft carrier off the coast of Indochina during the war there; when he was mustered out in 1956 they met regularly in Paris and became friends. SdB became an intellectual mentor, interested in Courchay's writing, and helped him with a recommendation to publish his first novel. She became his first reader and most stringent critic of all the rest until her death.—Claude Courchay, interview, April 2, 1983, Philadelphia. In *Done*, p. 63, he is "the young man from Marseilles who introduced himself to me as a 'classic case of maladjustment' and who took very great risks to help the FLN during the war in Algeria . . ."

14. The first remark is from *All Said and Done*, p. 221; the second was made repeatedly during our years of interviews and conversations.

15. Loosely defined, Structuralism is a method of analyzing culture and society through linguistics. *Tel Quel* is an influential critical journal.

16. SdB, n.d. [late Oct. or early Nov. 1952?], NA/OSU; conversation with DB, Sept. 7, 1984.

17. SdB, 9th December [1952], NA/OSU; to DB, March 7, 1986.

18. SdB, Sunday [Oct. 15, 1950]; Friday [Dec. 22, 1950], NA/OSU.

19. In a 1965 interview, Pierre Verstraeten told Sartre that others had accused him of writing *The Critique* in a "clumsy, heavy-handed, interminable, involved, etc. . . . context," and asked what he thought of Lévi-Strauss's criticism that he had written "a book dealing with dialectics in an analytical discourse when with his dialectics he claimed to be going beyond or to be furnishing the basis for analytics." Sartre replied, "Lévi-Strauss does not know what dialectical thought is. Not only that—he is incapable of knowing."—Sartre, "The Writer and His Language," interview with Pierre Verstraeten, *Revue d'esthétique*, July–December 1965, reprinted in Sartre, *Situations IX* (Paris, 1972), and *Politics and Literature* (London: Calder & Boyars, 1973), p. 116.

20. Sartre, *Critique de la raison dialectique* (Paris: Gallimard, 1960); English ed., *The Critique of Dialectical Reason*, trans. Alan Sheridan-Smith (London: Verso, 1976).

21. Sartre, "The Writer and His Language," *loc. cit.*, p. 111.

22. Sartre, "Qu'est-ce que la littérature?," in his *Situations II* (Paris: Gallimard, 1948), p. 320 n.

23. Sartre, *The Family Idiot: Gustave Flaubert*, Vol. I, trans. Carol Cosman (Chicago: University of Chicago Press), 1981. Douglas Collins describes Sartre's thesis as having evolved from "his multifarious activities in literature, journalism, polemics, and political activism; namely, that his primary interest is applied philosophy." He explains it further: "For Sartre, the test of a system of ideas lies in its ability to perform in the real world, and this ability is best revealed in its capacity to reconstruct the life of an historical individual. A philosophical system is thus subordinate in interest to the biography it generates, because in the biography that system's success or failure is ultimately evaluated. Rather than being the bastardization of philosophy, biography is its legitimation."—Douglas Collins (ed.), *Sartre as Biographer* (Cambridge: Harvard University Press, 1980), p. 5.

24. The first quotation is from the Jan. 16, 1982, interview, the second is from "Tuesday," NA/OSU. In this letter, SdB also said she could not work "for a week, as Sartre asked that I read his manuscript about Genet," and during the intense effort required to edit it she caught a bad

cold, which she said "makes me a little angry because now I want eagerly to work, I need it."

25. In response to criticisms that Existentialism was incompatible with Marxism, Hazel Barnes wrote that Sartre "does not hedge. The only philosophy today . . . is Marxism. Existentialism is but a subordinate ideology, which, working from within, attempts to influence the future development of Marxism."—Sartre, *Search for a Method*, trans. Hazel Barnes (New York: Vintage, 1968), translator's introd., p. viii.

26. Sartre, *Critique of Dialectical Reason*, Vol. I, p. 48.

27. Also, when she attempts to reconstruct political events that led to Sartre's various positions and statements, she often confuses chronology, detail and situation. She explained her relative carelessness in these matters by saying she was much more concerned with her personal history than with public life and political events. How she told her story mattered as much to her as what he had to say mattered to Sartre.

28. Deirdre Bair, "My Life . . . This Curious Object: Simone de Beauvoir on Autobiography," in *The Female Autograph*, Domna C. Stanton, guest ed. (New York Literary Forum, 1984), p. 243.

29. SdB, *All Said and Done*, p. 179.

30. SdB, 2nd January [1959], NA/OSU. All quotes are from this until otherwise noted.

31. Bair, "My Life . . . ," *loc. cit.*, pp. 242–43.

32. When she wrote the memoirs, SdB relied only on her memory and a partial diary consisting mostly of occasional jottings, details of her dreams, and gossip about both friends and enemies. These notes have many misspelled names and erroneous details, from such minor items as the names of people she met to the size of various crowds at political and feminist meetings in France and elsewhere. The passing of time has given the memoirs the aura of historical fact, and they are frequently quoted by many scholars and writers who turn to them for an apt phrase or agreeable comment to support their own theses with a less-than-discerning eye. Historical record requires, in many instances, a more stringent, corrective attitude toward these volumes.

33. This phrase is mine, used with SdB to describe the examples given here as well as many others too frequent to note. At first she resented it as an aspersion on her veracity, but when I explained that I meant the term in a more positive sense,

as an example of how humans filter experience to their own personal needs, she accepted it as being "*in some cases only* [her emphasis] appropriate."

34. SdB, *Force of Circumstance*, p. 674.

35 | POLITICS AND FEMINISM

1. SdB, n.d. [autumn 1959?], NA/OSU. All quotes are from this until noted otherwise.

2. NA typed a rough draft of his response to SdB across the recto of her letter to him. The description of the boxing is SdB's.

3. The first two books are unidentified. SdB, 20th December, 1959, NA/OSU.

4. SdB, *Force of Circumstance*, p. 499. Until noted otherwise, all quotations are from pp. 498–99 of this book.

5. *Ibid.*, p. 503. She describes this trip on pp. 500–505. All quotes are from this until noted otherwise.

6. It was he who coined what became one of Sartre's temporarily favorite sayings: "It's not my fault if reality is Marxist." Quoted in *Les Ecrits de Sartre*, ed. Contat and Rybalka (Paris: Gallimard, 1970), p. 407, from the interview "L'Alibi," *Le Nouvel Observateur*, No. 1 (Nov. 19, 1964), pp. 1–6.

7. This had not yet happened on her first visit to Cuba, when interviews followed a more predictable line of questioning. She told Edith Depestre, a prominent journalist ("13 Preguntas a Simone de Beauvoir" [Thirteen Questions for Simone de Beauvoir], *Lunes de Revolución*, March 21, 1960, pp. 36–37, summarized in Francis and Grontier, *Les Ecrits*, pp. 189–90), that she had originally planned to spend much of her time in Cuba writing a screenplay on the subject of divorce for the filmmaker André Cayatte, but had become so passionately involved in the revolution that she was unable even to think of working on it. It was a convenient excuse: she accepted the commission before leaving Paris because of the large advance Cayatte payed her to work on it, but the subject bored her and she was delighted to abandon it with a semiclear conscience. She also said she liked French films very much, especially François Truffaut's *The Four Hundred Blows*. She declared all the New Wave filmmakers for the most part "talented," but "unfortunately, the stories they have to tell are often boring and without interest." Of the contemporary French novel, she said only that it was "at an impasse," and that

the New Novelists (here she cited Sarraute, Robbe-Grillet and Butor) were so preoccupied with excessive formalisms and theoretical conclusions that they forgot "to show us mankind in all his essential dimensions."

8. For a complete account of writings by and about the Cuban trip, see *Les Ecrits de Sartre*, pp. 343–52.

9. "Où en est la Révolution cubaine?," *France-Observateur*, April 7, 1960, pp. 12–14.

10. She describes his visit in *Force of Circumstance*, pp. 505–10. Until noted otherwise, all quotes are from this and from interviews and conversations with SdB throughout 1985.

11. NA, "Simone à Go Go," *Ramparts*, Vol. 4, No. 6 (October 1965), p. 66.

12. *Force of Circumstance*, p. 472.

13. Francis Jeanson, interview, Feb. 1, 1966, Claouy, France.

14. Anne Whitmarsh (*op. cit.*) is among the scholars who have recently addressed SdB's activity and influence. In her chapter "Possibilities for Action: II, The Practice," she concludes in case after case that "in practical terms Sartre did very little and Simone de Beauvoir even less." Whitmarsh agrees that SdB had "made the great refusal and remained a private rather than a public political person," and cites "social rather than political action [as] the sustained characteristic of Simone de Beauvoir's *engagement*."

15. Alice Schwartzer, *After "The Second Sex": Conversations with Simone de Beauvoir*, p. 11.

16. She discussed this in a series of conversations throughout our interviews concerning how *The Second Sex* changed her life as well as the lives of others.

17. *Force of Circumstance*, p. 510, and 1985 conversations.

18. SdB teases NA that "he should be ashamed" of this in her letter of 5 November [1960], NA/OSU.

19. *La Grande Peur d'aimer* and *Le Planning familial*.

20. *Force of Circumstance*, pp. 512–13.

21. Gisèle Halimi and SdB (preface), *Djamila Boupacha* (Paris: Gallimard, 1962), p. 1. Also by SdB: "Pour Djamila Boupacha," *Le Monde*, June 2, 1960, p. 6.

22. "Jeunesse et guerre d'Algérie," interview with K. S. Karol, in *Vérité-Liberté*, No. 3, July–August 1960; summarized in *Les Ecrits de Sartre*, p. 356.

23. *Force of Circumstance*, pp. 522–583.

24. SdB, Friday 25 [August 1960], 5 November [1960], 16 November [1960],

all NA/OSU. All quotes are from these letters until noted otherwise.

25. The remark is now believed to be apocryphal.

36 | NOVEMBER WAS A LONG SAD MONTH

1. SdB, 14th April [1961], NA/OSU. All quotes are from this until noted otherwise.

2. SdB, 16th Nov. [1960], NA/OSU. All quotes are from this until noted otherwise.

3. She writes of this in *Force of Circumstance*, p. 628.

4. André Gorz, telephone conversation, Jan. 13, 1982, Paris.

5. SdB, 14th April [1961], NA/OSU.

6. SdB, 16th Nov. [1960], NA/OSU. All quotes are from this until noted otherwise. She refers to *The Prime of Life*, originally published in France as *La Force de l'Age*, 1960.

7. Chapsal, "Une Interview," *loc. cit.*, p. 396.

8. SdB, 10th June, 1961, NA/OSU.

9. SdB, 14th April [1961], NA/OSU. She describes the dossier in *Force of Circumstance*, p. 598.

10. SdB, n.d. [late Feb. 1962], NA/OSU. SdB writes of many of these events in *Force of Circumstance*, pp. 612ff., but her chronology of many of them is confused.

11. SdB, n.d. [spring 1962], NA/OSU.

12. They spent part of December and all of January 1963 in Moscow and Leningrad and later the greater part of August, and the New Year 1964.

13. SdB, n.d. [spring 1963], NA/OSU.

14. SdB, n.d. [Sept. 1963], NA/OSU.

15. SdB, *A Very Easy Death* (New York: Warner Books, 1965), p. 13.

16. *Ibid.*, p. 119.

17. *Ibid.*, p. 109.

18. SdB, n.d. [Dec. 1963], NA/OSU.

19. I am grateful to Prof. Yolanda Astarita Patterson for providing me with a copy of this tape.

20. The first comment is from an interview with SdB, the second from *A Very Easy Death*, p. 122.

21. Charles Perrault, *Blue Beard and Other Fairy Tales*, trans. Richard Howard, introd. by SdB (trans. Peter Green) (New York: Macmillan, and London: Collier-Macmillan, 1964).

22. Violette Leduc, *La Batarde* (Paris: Gallimard, 1964), SdB's preface, pp. 7–23.

23. Her remarks were published in

"Que peut la littérature?, ouvrage collectif avec des interventions de Simone de Beauvoir, Yves Berger, Jean-Pierre Faye, Jean Ricardou, Jean-Paul Sartre et Jorge Semprun," *Clarté* 10/18, no. 249 (1965). SdB's contribution appears on pp. 73–92.

24. Since the decision of the Swedish Academy is private, there are only rumors to support this hypothesis, but the fact that they continue to be heard in Stockholm after more than 20 years gives them a certain tenuous validity.

25. This information was later conveyed to Sartre by officials at the Swedish Embassy in Paris, according to SdB.

26. Archives of the Swedish Academy, Stockholm.

27. The source of the first comment has asked not to be cited. Many of the persons I interviewed spoke of a "radio commentator," but none of my research has determined to whom this perhaps apocryphal comment should be attributed; Cohen-Solal (p. 444) attributes a similar remark to André Maurois, who said, "He wants to avoid making Simone jealous."

28. SdB mentions Sartre's improved health in the last known letter she wrote to NA, n.d. [November 1964?], NA/OSU.

29. Hayman, p. 404.

30. Cohen-Solal, p. 452.

31. John Gerassi, interview, Dec. 7, 1981, New York. Gerassi conducted more than 120 hours of taped conversation with Sartre.

32. SdB, *All Said and Done*, p. 150.

37 | THE FRIENDSHIPS OF WOMEN

1. Cited remark by SdB. Information in this chapter is from interviews and conversations with SdB, J.-L. Bost, C. Lanzmann, S. le Bon de Beauvoir and J.-B. Pontalis, and telephone conversations with O. Bost and Wanda Kosakievicz.

2. It was during this period that many of the persons who had long been associated with Sartre professionally or politically began to pull away toward other occupations and careers of their own. Their places were taken by a much younger group, in some cases barely out of their teens, mostly students or recent graduates who held strong leftist leanings. Sartre found their youth revitalizing and began to seek their company, to the dismay of his old (in both senses of the word) friends. The term "to baby-sit Sartre" springs from this group, originated by the

Americans among them and always said in English no matter what language they were speaking.

3. This was the version SdB told me at our first interview, Jan. 9, 1982. On March 26, 1982, when I reported to her what others had told me about her later relationship with Arlette, she said, "Well, now you know the truth I expect you will have to tell it."

4. NA, telephone conversation, April 18, 1981.

5. SdB. NA was very fond of cats, always kept several as pets and fed most of the neighborhood strays. He also decorated books and letters with amusing little drawings of cats. SdB said she tried "very much to like Algren's cats, but it was impossible."

6. Mary Guggenheim's letter and other third-party correspondence are in NA/OSU.

7. Some of these letters were in SdB's possession at the time of her death. She claimed that others had been misplaced or lost.

8. This information is from telephone conversations with Richard P. McDonough and Robert Ginna, May 21, 1981.

9. W. J. Weatherby, "The Life and Hard Times of Nelson Algren," *The Times*, May 10, 1981.

10. Whether or not NA would have sold the letters will never be known, because he died with them in his possession and his heirs later sold them to the Ohio State University Libraries.

11. HdB, letter to DB, Oct. 4, 1987.

12. SdB gives an account of their friendship in *Done*, pp. 69–76. She dedicated this volume "For Sylvie."

13. SdB, *All Said and Done*, p. 70.

14. *Ibid.*

15. In 1965 Leduc purchased a house in the little village of Faucon, Vaucluse, and left Paris forever. She corresponded sporadically with SdB after that, but they saw each other only once, when SdB drove through the village on her way to a holiday in Italy. Leduc died of cancer in 1972.

16. *All Said and Done*, pp. 87–98.

17. Although Sylvie never met Françoise de Beauvoir, she knew Sartre's mother, Mme. Mancy, very well. In 1967, when SdB and Sartre were participating in the Russell Tribunal in Stockholm, Sylvie spent four days with them. "When you go back to Paris, go see my mother and tell her I'm well," Sartre asked. In a 1986 conversation, Sylvie recalled what

happened next: "So I went, and I saw this little lady, living in the Hotel L'Aiglon on the Boulevard Raspail near Sartre's apartment. And she said to me, 'Is he dressing properly?'—she treated him like a little boy! I said yes, of course, and then she asked, 'He doesn't look too much like a pastor, does he?' Sometimes Castor and I would just go to L'Aiglon and drink port with Mme. Mancy, because she liked her port. 'I love that old woman,' Sartre used to tell us, 'so go see my mother.' And okay, fine, so we went. Both of them behaved so well to their mothers."

18. *All Said and Done*, pp. 75–76.

19. She has asked me not to identify her, but to add that "Simone de Beauvoir was angry because I had to gather up a coat, umbrella, tape recorder and purse, and all that took several minutes even though I moved as fast as I possibly could. The whole episode struck me as utterly comic once it was over, but I did not find it amusing at the time to be dismissed so rudely. I hadn't even asked her anything remotely personal."

20. S. le Bon de Beauvoir.

21. I wish to thank Professors Hazel Barnes, Blanche Weisen Cook, Dorothy Kaufmann, Isabel de Courtivron, Geneviève Fraisse, Marie-Claire Pasquier and Marcelle Marini, among many others, for conversations about the friendship of women. I found especially helpful Prof. Carolyn Heilbrun's 1985 unpublished lecture on biography by and about women at the New York University Biography Seminar. Among the many works of feminist scholarship I consulted, I wish to mention specifically the following: Elizabeth Abel, "(E) merging Identities: The Dynamics of Female Friendship in Contemporary Fiction by Women," *Signs*, Vol. 6, No. 3 (Spring 1981); Kathleen Barry, "Postcript," *Susan B. Anthony: A Biography of a Singular Feminist* (New York: New York University Press, 1988); Vera Brittain, *Testament of Friendship: The Story of Winifred Holtby* (London: Macmillan, 1947); Nancy Chodorow, *The Reproduction of Mothering* (Berkeley: University of California Press, 1978); Blanche Wiesen Cook, *Women and Support Networks* (New York: Out & Out Books, 1979); Karen Horney, "The Flight from Womanhood," *International Journal of Psychoanalysis*, Vol. VII (1926), and "Feminine Psychology," *New Ways in Psychoanalysis*, Vol. I (New York: Norton, 1939); Luce Irigaray, *Ce sexe qui n'en est pas un* (Paris: Éditions de Mi-

nuit, 1977); Joan Kelley, "The Social Relation of the Sexes: Methodological Implications of Women's History," in *Women, History and Theory* (Chicago: University of Chicago Press, 1984); Monique Plaza, " 'Phallomorphic Power' and the Psychology of 'Women: A Patriarchal Chain,' " *Questions Féministes* 1 (1978); Susan Quinn, *A Mind of Her Own: The Life of Karen Horney* (New York: Summit, 1987); Marilyn Yalom, "They Remember *Maman*: Attachment and Separation in Leduc, de Beauvoir, Sand and Cardinal," *Essays in Literature*, Spring 1981.

22. Schwartzer, *op. cit.*, pp. 108–9.

23. Vera Brittain, *op. cit.*, p. 2.

24. D. H. Lawrence, *Women in Love* (New York: Penguin, 1976), pp. 472–73.

25. Several days later, in another conversation, she said she wished she had reread the novel before she wrote her last two books of fiction, *Les Belles Images* and *The Woman Destroyed*, because "I could have refined slightly some of the relationships to make my intention more apparent to my reader."

26. Hazel Barnes, Feb. 27, 1987, conversation, Harvard University.

27. Cook, *op. cit.*, p. 20.

28. Abel, *op. cit.*, p. 416.

29. SdB, n.d. [Nov. 1964?] NA/OSU; to Helen P. Wenck (hereafter HPW), Dec. 1, 1964, and Feb. 8 and Aug. 17, 1965.

38 | "Something's Going to Happen"

1. This remark is representative of several on the same subject made by SdB during interviews in 1982; it is very similar to remarks she made to (among many others) Madeleine Chapsal ("Une Interview," *loc. cit.*, p. 396).

2. I have heard this expression used by too many women in several countries and cultures to credit any few of them here, and beg them all to know that they are included in the thinking that produced this passage.

3. Anna Boschetti, *The Intellectual Enterprise: Sartre and Les Temps Modernes*, trans. Richard C. McCleary (Evanston: Northwestern University Press, 1988), p. 185. Boschetti's note to this remark corroborates my earlier statements in this chapter, and reenforces her own contention by citing Beauvoir's attitude toward politics, that of leaving it "chiefly to Sartre, according to the traditional view that

politics is man's business." Chap. 9, no. 4, pp. 262–63.

4. This is a term used by A. Gortz, J.-B. Pontalis, F. Jeanson, J.-L. Bost and many others. They use it to mean SdB's conception of Sartre's writing and thinking and how she resisted it after he wrote the *Critique of Dialectical Reason*.

5. Jeanson, interview, March 1, 1986, Claouy, France. All his comments are from this interview unless noted otherwise.

6. *Le Monde*, April 18, 1964. See also "On the Idiot of the Family," interview with Michel Contat and Michel Rybalka, *Le Monde*, May 14, 1971, reprinted in Sartre, *Life Situations: Essays Written and Spoken*, trans. Paul Auster and Lynda Davis (New York: Pantheon, 1977), pp. 108–32.

7. SdB, *Adieux*, p. 7.

8. Editions Gallimard has announced plans to publish this correspondence sometime in the 1990s. Lena Zonina died Feb. 2, 1985, in Moscow, aged 62. She wrote a book based partly on her experiences as a translator and guide to French writers, *Thinkers of Our Time: Reflections on French Writers of the 1960's and 1970's*.

9. When she was asked to elaborate, to discuss something such as the personalities of the political leaders she met, she grew angry and said, "Everything worth knowing is in my book. Read that and you will know everything."

10. SdB's activities during the 1960s should be the focus of scholars who specialize in geopolitical studies and have both the time and the financial support to engage in a detailed and systematic project to recover information about the many aspects of her cooperation with women on feminist issues. Her work in these areas can only be touched upon here, but it seems clear that her later feminist stances, both in France and internationally, probably had some of their genesis in, for example, Brazil, the Soviet Union, Japan, Egypt and Israel.

11. SdB to HPW, Nov. 12, 1966.

12. *Ibid.*, Dec. 11, 1967.

13. *Ibid.*, April 22, 1968.

14. "We disagreed on politics, but that was not why I ended it. Sylvie didn't like him, so I saw no sense in continuing."— SdB. "It wasn't anything serious and it didn't last very long. She ended it when I told her what I thought of him."—S. le Bon de Beauvoir, Oct. 4, 1987.

15. I have based the subsequent analysis upon interviews with many who were either on the board or close to the review, but among the most important are those with SdB, Lanzmann, Bost, Pouillon, Pontalis, Jeanson and J. Gerassi. Also, conversations with Elisabeth de Fontenay, Henriette Asséo and André Gorz. Useful texts include Boschetti, *op. cit.*; Michel-Antoine Burnier, *Choice of Action*, trans. Bernard Murchland (New York: Vintage, 1969), and Alain D. Ranwez, *Jean-Paul Sartre's Les Temps Modernes: A Literary History, 1945–52* (Troy, N.Y.: Whitston Publishing, 1981), specifically Chap. II, "The Politics."

16. The first three comments are descriptions of the various editorial boards from Boschetti, pp. 224–26; the last is a phrase SdB used repeatedly to berate anything or anyone who did not meet her standards, and which some members of the board used behind her back in sarcastic imitation.

17. C. Lanzmann.

18. Boschetti, *op. cit.*, p. 226.

19. Or so it seemed to SdB, even though the popularity and influence of Structuralism dates to the mid-1950s, when Lévi-Strauss, Barthes and Foucault first began to publish.

20. Boschetti, p. 228 and n. 5, p. 268.

21. This is from Boschetti, p. 229 in the English ed. I read the original French and asked SdB to read it in 1986 so that we could discuss it together. She refused for "personal reasons." So I would only show her passages during our conversations and ask her to comment on them, mostly to confirm or deny because questions that required her interpretation usually made her angry. In this instance, she confirmed that the paragraph cited above accurately describes what Sartre was doing during this time, and she agreed that she was "puzzled by his actions, as I was frequently concerning his dealings with the review."

22. This is an expression used during separate interviews and conversations by SdB, Lanzmann and Bost. SdB was asked if they used it in common during conversations with one another. She was surprised to learn that they all three thought of the changing editorial boards in this manner, but said she could not recall any conversation in which any one of them used the expression before the other two.

23. The three members of the board who participated in a conversation with me at La Coupole in 1984 have asked not to be identified. They did not permit their conversation to be tape-recorded, nor was

I allowed to take notes. The following analysis is based on this conversation and interviews with SdB, Lanzmann and Bost. All unattributed quotes that follow are from the unnamed three.

24. Full citations for her remarks are to be found in *Les Ecrits*, as are summaries and in some cases, complete texts as well.

25. "Que peut la littérature?," *loc. cit.*, p. 82; my translation. In 1985 SdB said she wished she had used the word "people" instead of "man," and added, "But since I wrote it that way, you had better translate it as such. Someone will tell you, 'Aha! She was not yet feminist—look at her language.'"

26. When asked why, she alluded vaguely to Sartre's declining health and Arlette's increasing presence in his life.

27. SdB, *All Said and Done*, p. 270.

28. In *ibid.*, pp. 270ff., she omits all mention of Sylvie from this account and says it was Lanzmann who phoned and drove Sartre to the hospital. The version here is what she called "correction of something I misremembered, an oversight on my part," during a conversation of 1984.

29. SdB, *Les Belles Images* (Paris: Gallimard, 1966), p. 33; my translation. This novel was issued in English bearing the French title.

30. Sartre and Sagan became friends around this time, frequently lunching or dining together and joking about their shared birthdate, June 21. These comparisons with Sagan rankled SdB, who resented her personally and despised her writing.

31. A. S . Byatt, "Life-Lies," *New Statesman*, Jan. 5, 1968, p. 15.

32. *All Said and Done*, p. 140, and SdB.

33. André Billy, "Tristesse du vieillissement féminin," *Le Figaro*, Feb. 5, 1968.

34. SdB, *The Woman Destroyed* (London: Fontana/Collins, 1969), p. 220.

35. Because she was "offered a lot of money, which I needed because I had a lot of expenses that year."

36. Jacqueline Piatier, "La Femme rompue: Le Démon du bien," *Le Monde* (Hebdo), Jan. 25–31, 1968, p. 11.

37. A. M. Sheridan-Smith, "Obsessions," *London Magazine*, April 1969, p. 99.

38. Glendy Culligan in *Saturday Review of Literature*, Feb. 22, 1969, p. 45.

39. Evan S. Connell Jr., in *New York Times Book Review*, Feb. 23, 1969, p. 4.

Among the many who noted it also are John Weightman in *Washington Post Book World*, Feb. 2, 1969, p. 3, and Glendy Culligan, *loc. cit.*

40. Connell, *loc. cit.*

41. SdB to HPW, April 22, 1968.

39 | "WE HAVE LIVED THROUGH SOME EXHILARATING TIMES"

1. HPW, June 24 and Nov. 19, 1968.

2. This is an untranslatable French expression referring to the Autumn reopening of schools, theaters, law courts and other official institutions. In *Adieux*, p. 8, SdB wrote, "We had kept the habit of reckoning by school years," showing how she and Sartre retained the schoolteacher's way of measuring time throughout their lives.

3. SdB. In the interview with Pierre Viansson-Ponté (*Le Monde*, Jan. 10 and 11, 1978, and Francis and Gontier, *Les Ecrits*, p. 591), SdB addressed the criticism she received for this book and *Les Belles Images*: "Certain women have reproached me for not having written about positive heroines, for having shown many women as broken and unhappy; I made them that way because that's what I see today in the feminine condition, that's what I see, what I think, and I don't have any desire to show them as heroic militants or as utopians, something nonexistent in my eyes."

4. The events of May 1968 and the 12 years after until Sartre's 1980 death were topics that SdB talked about in every interview and conversation we had together from 1981 until her death in 1986. This was a subject she sometimes brought up when it had no connection to the topic under consideration. To me, it seemed that she needed to replay these events in her mind not only in search of catharsis (which she found by writing *Adieux*) but also because she had difficulty understanding what had happened to their relationship in his last decade of life and, as if by talking about it, might find peace in accepting the last strained years.

5. SdB, *All Said and Done*, p. 229.

6. In several interview sessions, I asked SdB if she had done any systematic reading of these authors, and she gave the same answer that she gave to a later question asking if she kept up with the burgeoning field of feminist scholarship: "I read what comes my way, what is easily

to hand, what people send to me. But I don't do it systematically, much of it I don't understand, don't like, don't find myself in sympathy with. I was really too old when all this started, and had too much of my own writing and too much reading I wanted to do to waste time on it." In regard to the first group of authors, I found that when I tried to discuss several specific works that we both had read, she had generally not read it thoroughly, did not remember it well and felt that it had no bearing on her own thinking and writing. In the case of feminist criticism, if she had read the book, she remembered it and could discuss it, but here again the important point is that she generally read only those books which the authors sent to her or that someone else gave to her. She seldom went out of her way to read anything else.

7. Hayman, p. 423.

8. *All Said and Done*, p. 456.

9. Daniel Cohn-Bendit, *The French Student Revolt* (New York, 1968), p. 58.

10. Selections from these documents and full citations are found in *Les Ecrits de Sartre*, pp. 461–66.

11. *All Said and Done*, pp. 458–59.

12. *Ibid.*, pp. 459–461; Cohen-Solal, p. 462. Marguerite Duras does not remember SdB's version of the event: 'Some of the writers grumbled, vexed at having come for nothing. 'I'm fed up with the star-system,' said Marguerite Duras."

13. Cohen-Solal, p. 462. She also notes (p. 463) that several months later "a minor event showed that his power of persuasion was also quite limited, and his influence much less real than it had seemed. 'Sartre, be clear, be brief: we have to discuss the adoption of a number of regulations.' " These were instructions students gave him before a speech on Feb. 10, 1969.

14. *All Said and Done*, pp. 462–63. In the French ed., p. 477, she wrote: "We did not vote in the referendum. . . . To choose between Poher and Pompidou didn't interest us. We didn't attach any importance to the change of personnel, which would do nothing to alter the way the system functioned." But in a letter to HPW, May 20, 1969, she wrote, "We are indeed happy here to be rid of De Gaulle. The Left isn't exactly flourishing, but if Poher had been elected, certain odious aspects of this regime would have disappeared."

15. SdB, *Adieux*, p. 102.

16. Deirdre Bair, interview with SdB,

"Women's Rights in Today's World," 1984 *Britannica Book of the Year*, p. 25.

17. *La Cause du Peuple*, May 1, 1970.

18. *Ibid.*, May 7, 1970.

19. *All Said and Done*, p. 478.

20. *Ibid.*, p. 467.

21. *Ibid.*, p. 468. All quotes until noted otherwise are from pp. 468–69.

22. This is how she joked about it in March 1986.

23. In *Adieux*, p. 9, SdB records delivery of the ms to Gallimard on Oct. 8, 1970.

24. This is the correct translation of her French title, but it was changed by her American publishers to *The Coming of Age* because they were afraid that her title was too blunt and depressing and would not sell many books.

25. "The Terrors of Old Age," *Newsweek*, Feb. 9, 1970, p. 54.

26. Nina Sutton, interview, "Simone de Beauvoir Faces up to Mortality," *The Guardian*, Feb. 16, 1970, p. 9, and Part II, "Sartre and the Second Sex," Feb. 19, 1970, p. 11. All quotations are from these until noted otherwise.

27. SdB, *Force of Circumstance*, pp. 659 and 144.

28. *Ibid.*, pp. 672–75. All quotes are from this until noted otherwise.

40 | WOMEN'S BATTLES

1. The first quotation is from a letter to DB, Sept. 16, 1980; the second is from a conversation, Jan. 9, 1981.

2. Portions of this chapter appeared in another form in "Simone de Beauvoir: Politics, Language and Feminist Identity," *Yale French Studies*, No. 72, pp. 149ff.

3. SdB, *All Said and Done*, p. 479.

4. At our first meeting, she told me she welcomed this biography because she had "long hoped for someone who will write about all my work, not just my feminism."

5. SdB, *Adieux*, p. 20 and p. 8.

6. John Gerassi, *"The Second Sex: 25 Years Later,"* *Society*, January–February 1976, pp. 84–85.

7. SdB, *All Said and Done*, pp. 483–84.

8. Mary Evans, *Simone de Beauvoir, A Feminist Mandarin* (London and New York: Tavistock, 1985), p. 74.

9. Jacques J. Zéphir argues that "it is by no means exaggerated to affirm that neo-feminism [i.e., the contemporary feminist movement] snatched SdB from her solitude, it allowed her to unite with

other women and gave a new dimension to her commitment." I quote from p. 9 of his unpublished paper, "Le Féminisme de Simone de Beauvoir: Son Evolution (1949–1981)," later incorporated into *Le Néo-féminisme de Simone de Beauvoir* (Paris: Denoël/Gontier, 1982).

10. Zéphir notes (*op. cit.*, pp. 15–16) that SdB's feminist writings since *SS* are not well known and adds: ". . . to my knowledge, there is neither book nor article which traces the evolution of Simone de Beauvoir's feminist writings . . . especially since 1970, the date of the birth of the M.L.F. [Mouvement de Libération des Femmes], the date after which Simone de Beauvoir began to work on behalf of these groups." Zéphir's point is well taken: many of SdB's actions, speeches and writings on behalf of women took place as early as her first trip to Cuba, notices of some appeared only in obscure provincial newspapers, and others can be found only in libraries whose holdings are inaccessible to most scholars.

11. SdB to HPW, March 22, 1971.

12. In 1984 she said that she "forgot" the young woman's name, and that "'friendship' for Sartre always meant more. Make of this what you will, but these liaisons cheered me because they meant he was in good—no, better—health."

13. Jeanson, *op. cit.*, p. 253. SdB's emphasis.

14. *1984 Britannica Book of the Year,* p. 23.

15. This was what some feminist critics, among them Christine Fauré, called a "metamorphosis in the meaning of politics," which aptly describes the period during the early '70s of crucial change in SdB's thought and work. ". . . [Recognition] of the failure of existing socialist models, and of the necessity if not to create, at least to understand the revolution in new terms, swung extra-parliamentary political thinking over to the side of the counterculture. . . . [The] women's liberation movement has profited from this metamorphosis in the meaning of politics more than other movements."— Christine Fauré, "Absent from History," *Signs* 7, Autumn 1981, pp. 82–83.

16. SdB to HPW, March 22, 1971.

17. Gerassi interview, *loc. cit.*

18. Jean Rabaut, *Histoire des féminismes français* (Paris: Stock, 1978), p. 355.

19. Stanley Hoffmann, *Decline and Renewal*, p. 127.

20. *All Said and Done*, p. 480.

21. *Ibid.*, pp. 483–84.

22. Mo Teitelbaum, "Women Against the System," London *Sunday Times Magazine*, April 29, 1973, pp. 28–31.

23. Francis and Gontier, *Les Écrits*, is a good starting place for a chronological listing of this activity, and a number of the major statements and interviews are included. However, many of the dates are wrong (the 1971 Manifesto of the 343, for example, is listed as 1970) and some of the information about sources is not correct (perhaps because of typological errors in dating). This book has never been translated into English. Unquestionably a major bibliographical study of Beauvoir's life and work, similar to Contat and Rybalka's for Sartre, should be undertaken.

24. SdB, "La Syrie et les prisonniers," *Le Monde*, Dec. 18, 1973, p. 2.

25. Viansson-Ponté interview, in Francis and Gontier, *op. cit.*

26. Catherine David, "Beauvoir elle-même," *Le Nouvel Observateur*, Jan. 22, 1979, p. 83.

27. Margaret A. Simons and Jessica Benjamin, "Simone de Beauvoir: An Interview."

28. Beauvoir's statement appeared in the February 1981 issue. The magazine was translated into English as *Feminist Issues* and appears regularly in the United States.

29. This is one of a number of mimeographed documents, including a letter to SdB dated Feb. 10, 1981, which were written and disseminated by five dissenters from the eight original editors of *Questions féministes*. They are signed by N. Bisseret, C. Guillaumin, N. Mathieu, M. Plaza and M. Wittig, calling themselves "Collectif Pour Un Front Lesbien." I am grateful to Prof. Margaret A. Simons for making them available to me.

30. The most thorough and reliable explanation of recent feminist history and conflict in France is by Dorothy Kaufmann [McCall], "Politics of Difference: The Women's Movement in France from May 1968 to Mitterrand," *Signs*.

31. The term usually appeared in print as the "MLF *deposé*" ("the legally registered MLF").

32. "La Différence internée," *Mensuelle des femmes en mouvements*, No. 2 (February 1978): and *Des femmes en mouvements hebdo*, No. 28 (May 16–23, 1980). I have used the Kaufmann [McCall] translation here.

33. Brigitte Gros, "Une Autre Époque," *Le Monde*, Jan. 27, 1978. Mme. Gros was then Sénateur des Yvelines [radicale], Maire de Melun.

34. Let me admit at once that this is an informal sampling which I conducted by asking the same questions of every French woman I met who was between the approximate ages of 16 and 25 during my research in the years 1981–87. I estimate that I asked my questions of approximately 350 women in Paris, Bordeaux, Strasbourg and in Normandy, Brittany, Dordogne and Provence. They included, among other occupations, university and lycée students, librarians, retail workers, household help and farmers. Their social and economic classes included all from former French royalty to blue-collar workers. My survey also depends heavily on scholars and writers who offered opinions of Simone de Beauvoir's posthumous reputation among younger women. These include (among many others) Henriette Asséo, Michelle Coquillat, Geneviève Fraisse, Françoise Gaill, Nancy Huston, Marcelle Marini, Nicole Mozet, Françoise Pasquier, Marie-Claire Pasquier and Yvette Roudy.

35. Nancy Huston.

36. *Le Nouvel Observateur*, No. 43 (Nov. 29–Dec. 5, 1985).

37. Jacques Ehrmann, "Simone de Beauvoir and the Related Destinies of Women and Intellectuals," *Yale French Studies*, No. 27 (1961), p. 30.

38. Gerassi interview, *loc. cit.*, pp. 84–85.

39. *1984 Britannica Book of the Year*, p. 25.

40. *Ibid.*, p. 27.

41. Viansson-Ponté interview, *loc. cit.*

42. Phyllis Rose, *Woman of Letters: A Life of Virginia Woolf* (Oxford: Oxford University Press, 1987), p. 257.

43. C. B. Radford, "Simone de Beauvoir: Feminism's Friend or Foe," Part I, p. 87, Part II, p. 51.

44. *1984 Britannica Book of the Year*, p. 28.

45. *Ibid.*

41 | BETWEEN DREAD
AND HOPE

1. This sentence is from the penultimate paragraph of SdB, *Adieux*, p. 127. During an interview discussing why she did not tell Sartre the truth about his illness, we read this portion of the then unpublished French ms together and she commented that were she to write a further volume of her memoirs she might try to use the sentence as a title, because it was the most accurate description of her life during those years.

2. J.-L. Bost.

3. SdB interviews and *Adieux*, pp. 17–19.

4. The first quotation is SdB from an interview; the second from *Adieux*, p. 19, as are all quotations that follow until noted otherwise.

5. SdB to HPW, Aug. 20, 1971.

6. *Adieux*, p. 22.

7. The first two quotes are from SdB interviews; the last is from *Adieux*, p. 33.

8. *Adieux*, p. 34. All quotes are from this until noted otherwise.

9. Hayman, *Sartre*, gives the most complete and accurate account of Sartre's illnesses in Chap. 26, "Fading Vision." After corroborating the testimony of those closest to Sartre during his last ten years and consulting various written testimonies, I have relied here for the most part on Hayman unless others are specifically cited.

10. Georges Michel, *Mes Années Sartre* (Paris: Hachette, 1981), p. 102.

11. *Adieux*, p. 52.

12. *Ibid.*, p. 53.

13. In 1984 I used this episode to inquire about the trio that Sylvie's presence in her life had created, and SdB spoke of the "double-edged guilt." I told her that I found it another example of the subtext within her writings, and she agreed that it was.

14. *Adieux*, p. 62.

15. *Ibid.*, p. 64.

16. *Ibid.*

17. This information is from conversations with SdB in 1982, 1984 and 1985. S. le Bon de Beauvoir, in an interview in October 1986, insisted that it was "unlikely" that Beauvoir expressed such concerns to me or anyone else, but J.-L. Bost and C. Lanzmann confirmed that Beauvoir "discussed it" (Bost) and "worried about it" (Lanzmann).

18. Originally published in *Libération*, they were issued in book form (Gallimard, 1974) as *On a raison de se révolter* (*We Are Right to Rebel*).

19. *Sartre par lui-même* (*Sartre by Himself*).

20. The first remark is SdB's recollection of what Sartre said and it is her emphasis; the second is from an interview.

21. Sartre eventually was instrumental in gaining French citizenship for Lévy

when he wrote a personal letter to Pres. Giscard d'Estaing, who granted his request.

22. Cohen-Solal, p. 495.

23. *Adieux*, p. 63.

24. *Ibid*. In interviews with DB, SdB often referred to Lévy sarcastically as "Schoenmann-Lévy."

25. *Adieux*, p. 63.

26. Cohen-Solal, p. 495.

27. It is difficult to arrive at any truth where Lévy is concerned because by the time Sartre died, in 1980, emotions were so inflamed that no one of the participants in the drama of his last years could consider any of the others with even minimal objectivity, and by 1987, when research for this book was mostly completed, the situation was not much changed.

28. Cohen-Solal, p. 497.

29. SdB, J. Pouillon, J.-L. Bost, C. Lanzmann and S. le Bon de Beauvoir all told me they heard Sartre say this. Cohen-Solal (p. 497) also attributes it to Robert Gallimard.

30. Cohen-Solal, p. 497.

31."Les femmes s'entênt," April–May, 1974; Collection "Idées," Editions Gallimard, Sept. 1975.

32. *Adieux*, p. 70.

33. Gustave Flaubert, *Correspondence*, Vol. 5, p. 69.

34. *Adieux*, p. 84.

35. These interviews were published as *After "The Second Sex": Conversations with Simone de Beauvoir*. In them, SdB discusses sex, morality, feminism, philosophy and all the other topics that concerned her over the years. Probably the most interesting point about them is that they show how little her thoughts and opinions changed in the years since she formed them and how consistent were her allegiances and beliefs.

36. *Adieux*, p. 71.

37. *Ibid.*, p. 306.

38. *Ibid.*, p. 304.

42 | The Last of the 1968 Demonstrations

1. The expression was common, so I cite no one in particular besides SdB. Olivier Todd used it in *Un Fils rebellé* (Paris: Grasset, 1981); also Cohen-Solal, p. 498.

2. Cohen-Solal, pp. 498–99.

3. *Libération*, Jan. 6, 1977.

4. SdB, *Adieux*, p. 109.

5. In *Adieux*, SdB wrote of the decision as if it had originated with Sartre; in any number of conversations from 1982 to 1986 she insisted that it was all Lévy's idea, and that her own "unclear language, written shortly after Sartre's death in great emotional pain and haste," was why it seemed otherwise.

6. Cohen-Solal, p. 510.

7. J.-L. Bost.

8. Cohen-Solal, p. 510.

9. J. Pouillon.

10. *Adieux*, p. 111.

11. Benny Lévy published his book, *Le Nom de l'homme: dialogue avec Sartre*, in 1984 (Paris: Verdier). It is a highly subjective reading of all Sartre's writings that is philosophical in its orientation. It was not widely reviewed, and the general tone of the reviews was more one of puzzlement than of either praise or negativity.

12. *Libération*, Jan. 6, 1977.

13. SdB and *Adieux*, p. 117.

14. *Adieux*, p. 117.

15. Cohen-Solal, p. 513. I met Benny Lévy at the University of Chicago on Oct. 3, 1981, during the symposium "Sartre and Biography." He agreed to be interviewed when I was next in Paris, but rebuffed all my subsequent attempts to meet with him, and thus I do not have his direct testimony for this book. Through an intermediary, he sent word that after Cohen-Solal he would not speak further about his association with Sartre. A capsule biography for the Chicago conference states that he teaches at the University of Paris VII (Jussieu), and that he was "closely associated with Sartre, especially as his close friend and confidant in Sartre's last years." His talk was entitled "The Ceremony of Birth" and was ostensibly a summation of more than three years of work "co-authoring a book with Sartre, *Pouvoir et Liberté* (*Power and Liberty*)." His précis reads as follows: "Primordial experience: neither psychological nor political, but opening out onto the psychological and onto the political, onto the thought of the project, *and* onto the thought of practical aggregates, of the individual and of the collective, tieing enigmatically one to the other. One utterance, obscurely luminous, for Sartre, bespeaks this experience: contingency. First or last word of biography? Thus, a womblike experience: The Mother, or what compels Sartre to think."

16. *Le Nouvel Observateur*, March 10, 1980. All quotes are from this until noted otherwise.

17. I have used Hayman's translation as it appears on p. 472 of his *Sartre*.

18. Cohen-Solal, p. 514.

19. *Ibid.*, p. 515.

20. Francine du Plessix Gray, review of *The War*, by Marguerite Duras, *New York Times Book Review*, May 4, 1986, p. 1.

21. In *Adieux*, she wrote that when Sartre asked this question she "said no, which was true." Others who attended that meeting remember that they spoke of little else.

22. *Adieux*, p. 121.

23. *Ibid.*, p. 123.

24. *Ibid.*

25. S. le Bon de Beauvoir, C. Lanzmann and H. and L. de Roulet.

26. *Adieux*, p. 126.

27. Michel, *Mes Années Sartre*, p. 41.

28. *Ibid.*, p. 42.

29. S. le Bon de Beauvoir, May 6, 1986. All quotes are from this until noted otherwise.

30. By disobeying the law, Arlette incurred a fine of more than 3 million old francs (approximately $6,000).

31. Lanzmann and Bost interviews.

32. S. le Bon de Beauvoir.

33. Sartre, *Cahiers pour une morale* (Paris: Gallimard, 1983).

43 | CLEANING UP LOOSE ENDS

1. HdB, *Souvenirs*, p. 270, and interviews and conversations of 1985–87; S. le Bon de Beauvoir, Oct. 4 and 21, 1987; SdB, May 7, 1983.

2. The following information is from interviews with SdB, S. le Bon de Beauvoir, J.-L. Bost, C. Lanzmann, HdB and *Souvenirs*, p. 272.

3. S. le Bon de Beauvoir, telephone conversation, April 17, 1986; interview, Oct. 4, 1986.

4. She is less discreet with those whom she called "gnats who irritated us" such as Olivier Todd, who returned her animosity. In *Adieux*, pp. 29–30, she takes him to task for trying to insinuate himself into Sartre's life as a son. In an interview May 7, 1983, she said, "We adored Nizan's daughter [Todd's ex-wife] and only suffered him because of Sartre's long history with the Nizan family." Todd retaliated in his memoir by saying that Sartre managed "to navigate amongst . . . his 'amours contingentes'" with lies. "'You lie to them all?' queried Todd. 'To

them all,' replied Sartre with a smile. 'Even to Castor?' '*Especially* to Castor.'"—quoted by Douglas Johnson in "La Grande Sartreuse," *London Review of Books*, 1981, No. 15, pp. 20–21.

5. Jean-Didier Wolfromm collects some of these statements in "Jean-Paul Sartre: la fin du voyage," *Magazine Littéraire*, No. 180 (Jan. 1982), p. 60.

6. Pascal Bruckner, "La Fin d'un philosophe," *Le Point*, Nov. 23–29, 1981.

7. Hazel E. Barnes also mentions some of these criticisms in "Beauvoir and Sartre: The Forms of Farewell," *Philosophy and Literature*, Vol. 9, No. 1 (April 1985), pp. 28–29.

8. Janick Jossin, "The Second Death of Sartre," *L'Express*, Dec. 4, 1981, p. 26.

9. Bertrand Poirot-Delpech, "Sartre tout compte fait," *Le Monde*, Nov. 28, 1981. He compares it to her book about her mother's death, which upset him by the seeming coldness and detachment of her prose. Obviously, he did not understand the reasons why (nor should he, a stranger to her, have been expected to) each book displayed so many afflictions in such graphic detail.

10. Ronald Hayman, "Multiple Truths," *Literary Review*, June 1982.

11. *Libération*, Dec. 3, 1981.

12. SdB to HPW, Jan. 2, 1980.

13. Whether this is true or not remains to be seen once her papers have been sorted by S. le Bon de Beauvoir. There is, for example, the charming manuscript of her first writing ("Cornichon" and "Marguerite"), the collection of sketches I call the Targ Ms and several other untitled fictional pages of varying lengths and subject matter that I have seen. There were also several deleted chapters of *L'Invitée* and what might have been an abandoned portion of *Les Belles Images*. There is no way to know what else exists that she may have forgotten, until all her papers have been catalogued.

14. SdB to HPW, Nov. 10, 1982.

15. *Ibid.*, Jan. 11, 1983.

16. *Ibid.*, March 25, 1983. The English title of *Cahiers* is mine; as of 1988, the book has not appeared in English translation.

17. Janick Jossin, "Arlette Elkaïm: 'Son attention au monde,'" *L'Express*, April 8–14, 1983, p. 47.

18. In the six years of cooperation she gave to this biography, no other question produced the anger and outrage that this one did.

19. On several occasions, our next

meeting began with a gruff Beauvoir waving a sheaf of her letters that she had supposedly "just found in the cellar among other things," all of which supported what became her most frequent and insistent response to the question of why she had not published them.

20. Prof. Yolanda Asterita Patterson was told by S. le Bon de Beauvoir in the fall of 1987 that she had found all these letters and would eventually publish them. In a letter to HPW, October 1988, S. le Bon de Beauvoir said that she was completing an edition which she hoped to publish in the near future. As of late summer 1989, they had not appeared.

21. The meeting took place April 28, 1981, at the Palais des Congrès, and the proceedings were later published as *Quel Président pour les femmes?: Réponses de François Mitterrand, préface de Gisèle Halimi* (Paris: Gallimard, 1981). Panelists included Martine Allain-Regnault (Antenne 2), Ménie Grégoire (RTL), Hélène Mathieu (*Marie-Claire*), Françoise Parturier (writer), Christine Ockrent (Europe no. 1), Josyane Savigneau (*Le Monde*).

22. *1984 Britannica Book of the Year*, p. 24. All her comments are from this until noted otherwise.

23. Ireland, Sen. David Norris; Poland, Malgorzata Niezabitowska; Mexico, Graciela Herrerro. All undated. I am grateful to Christopher Griffin, Ewa Zadrzynska and Robert V. Stone for information about Ireland, Poland and Mexico respectively.

44 | "WOMEN, YOU OWE EVERYTHING TO HER!"

1. The first three remarks are from a conversation with SdB in New York, Aug. 30, 1983; the last is from Peter Kemp, review of *The Southbank Show: Simone de Beauvoir* (London Weekend Thames TV program), *Times Literary Supplement*, Jan. 21, 1983.

2. S. le Bon de Beauvoir, May 6, 1983.

3. Portions of this chapter appeared previously in different form as "Simone de Beauvoir, in Paris and America," *New York Times Book Review*, May 6, 1984, pp. 12ff.

4. SdB called the Sonning Prize "a gift from the Danish government, from the University of Copenhagen. It is rather like the Nobel Prize. They even call it the 'Small Nobel,' the 'Danish Nobel.' Because it is a prize and a gift, there is no [French] tax on it."

5. Kate Millett, telephone conversation, Oct. 10, 1984.

6. Under the direction of filmmakers Malka Ribowska and Josée Dayan, who had earlier made a very successful film of Beauvoir's life that featured conversations between her, her sister, Lanzmann and others.

7. The degree to which this is true is a matter of speculation: whether she said it to avoid offending the many feminist writers, critics and scholars who had become her friends or whether it was the literal truth is open to debate, for on some occasions when she was called upon to discuss a matter pertaining to women she showed a remarkable knowledge of feminist writings in many countries and cultures.

8. As of 1989, it has not been translated into other languages or shown on television in other countries, but has been released in videocassettes and sometimes offered in art theaters in the original French. The film bears the following information: "TF 1 France, 1984, avec prod. A2. Avec participation Ministère de la Culture et Ministère Droits de la Femme. Distribué par INA (Archives INA/Casb). 4 emissions, 220 min. colour."

9. Juliette Faounda offers moving commentary for this part of the film, the only segment mentioned in all the reviews.

10. Marilyn August, "Simone de Beauvoir talks about *The Second Sex*," Gannett Westchester Newspapers, Nov. 4, 1984, Sect. E, p. 17.

11. SdB to HPW, Jan. 28, 1985.

12. *Ibid.*, 20, Dec. 1985.

13. She described her contribution as "only loans and then small ones."

14. Claude Lanzmann, *Shoah* (Paris: Librairie Arthème Fayard, 1985; New York: Pantheon, 1985).

15. *Mihloud*, Traduit de l'américain par Bruno Monthureux et Ghislaine Byramjee, préface de Simone de Beauvoir (Paris: Alinéa, 1986).

16. She said she hadn't worn a skirt for years: "I have one somewhere," she said, waving her hand in the direction of the sleeping loft. "They can bury me in it."

17. Portions of the following material appeared in another form under "Personal Recollections" in *Yale French Studies*, No. 72.

18. S. le Bon de Beauvoir, HdB.

Photo Credits

1, 2, 5, 6, 7, 8, 9, 12, 13, 18: courtesy of Hélène de Beauvoir.

3, 10: courtesy of M. Mantis de Bisschop.

4: courtesy of M. and Mme. Etienne Dauriac.

11: Photo "X," © Liliane Siegel, courtesy of Editions Gallimard, Paris.

14: courtesy of John Gerassi, Queens College, New York.

15, 24, 25, 26, 32, 40: courtesy of the Centre Audiovisuel Simone de Beauvoir, Paris.

16, 21: courtesy of Rowohlt Taschenbuch Verlag, West Germany.

17: © Papillon/Sygma, New York.

19: © Yves Manciet, Lyon.

20, 22, 23: courtesy of the Ohio State University Libraries.

27: V. Yegorov/Fotokhronika Tass, courtesy of Sovfoto, New York.

28: © Gisele Freund/Photo Researchers, New York.

29: Photo Jacques Robert © Editions Gallimard, Paris.

30: © 1971 by TIM courtesy of John Locke Studios, Inc., New York, and the New York Public Library Picture Collection.

31: © Jean Guyaux, Brussels.

33: © Roger-Viollet, Paris.

34: courtesy of the archives of Weidenfeld Publishers, London.

35: © Jacques Pavlovsky/Sygma, New York.

36: © Janine Niepce/Rapho, Paris.

37, 38: courtesy of Sylvie le Bon de Beauvoir.

39: © Le Tac/*Paris-Match*, courtesy of Scoop, Paris.

41: courtesy of L. H. Bair.

Index

Abel, Elizabeth, 513
Abetz, Otto, 260, 296, 642*n*
Abetz, Suzanne, 296
abortion rights, 543, 547, 548, 550, 552
Academy of Montparnasse 116
Adamov, Arthur, 275, 643*n*
Aden-Arabie (Nizan), 169
Adieux: A Farewell to Sartre (Beauvoir),
    517, 565, 583, 594–97, 601, 673*n*,
    678*n*
  Arlette's response to, 597, 599
  assessment of, 596–97
  as attempt at catharsis, 506, 594, 595
  critical response to, 595–96
  details of Sartre's illness in, 561, 562,
    583, 595–96
  as fifth volume of memoirs, 595
  interviews comprising second part of,
    573, 594, 596, 597
  Lévy affair in, 576, 577, 579, 582, 595
  shading of reality in, 582, 595
  writing of, 594
Adventures of the Dialectic
    (Merleau-Ponty), 452
Affamée, L' (Leduc), 348, 649*n*
Affinidades, 300
*After "The Second Sex": Conversations
    with Simone de Beauvoir*
    (Schwartzer), 573, 677*n*
Age d'homme, L' (Leiris), 284, 324
"Age of Discretion, The" (Beauvoir),
    526–27
"Air connu, L'" ("The Old Familiar
    Melody"), 134–35
Alain-Fournier (Henri-Alban Fournier),
    97, 103–5, 174
Alcott, Louisa May, 68–69, 623*n*
Aldanov, Mark A., 365, 649*n*
Algerian crisis, 463, 481, 485, 491, 513,
    520, 534

  Jeanson's attempt to involve Sartre
      and Beauvoir in, 477–78
  looting of Sartre's apartment in, 487
  meaning of "left" and "right" in, 452
  Métro incidents in, 487
  threats against Beauvoir and Sartre in,
      482, 483–84, 486, 487, 488
  torture in, 468, 478, 480, 487–88
Algiers:
  Beauvoir and Sartre's holiday in
      (1948), 392
  Beauvoir's lecture trip to (1946), 317
Algonquin Hotel, 607, 609
Algren, Nelson, 15, 333–37, 342, 348,
    363, 383, 384–85, 459, 497, 505,
    512, 513, 519, 540, 643*n*, 667*n*
  addressed as "husband," 344, 648*n*
  in *America Day by Day*, 334, 340, 348,
    349
  "anniversaries" of Beauvoir and, 371,
    399, 405, 421
  apartment of, 352
  background of, 335
  Beauvoir and Sartre's exile plans and,
    423–24, 661*n*
  Beauvoir joined in New York by (May
    1947), 340–41
  on Beauvoir's clothes, 646*n*
  Beauvoir's dreams about, 420, 444,
    657*n*
  Beauvoir's foreign junkets and, 475,
    476–77, 480, 481
  Beauvoir's pet name for, 336
  Beauvoir's travels with (1948), 371–
    378, 414, 454, 651*n*
  Beauvoir's visit to (Sept. 1947), 351,
    352–53, 355
  Beauvoir's visit to (1950), 415, 416,
    419–30, 421–23
  Beauvoir's visit to (1951), 429–30, 432

Algren, Nelson, *cont.*
  birth control and, 373, 374, 377
  bitterness and paranoia of, 457–58, 475
  books given or recommended to
    Beauvoir by, 365–66, 367–68, 374,
    380, 393, 650n, 651n
  breakup of Beauvoir and, 355, 408,
    411, 422–23, 428, 430–31, 432,
    440, 443, 499–501, 502–3, 658n
  "Castor" nickname and, 377, 659n
  cats owned by, 501, 670n
  Chicago shown to Beauvoir by, 335–
    336, 340
  correspondence of Beauvoir and, 333,
    336–38, 341, 344–45, 347–53, 356–
    359, 361, 364, 365–74, 378, 385,
    386, 388, 389, 391–99, 403, 404,
    410–11, 416–25, 427, 429, 430–31,
    439, 441–46, 448–49, 451, 455–58,
    463, 465, 468, 470, 471–72, 481–85,
    487–88, 490, 500, 501, 502, 647n–
    649n, 652n, 653n, 655n–59n, 661n,
    662n, 666n, 670n
  death of, 501–3, 605
  enraged by *Force of Circumstance*,
    500–501, 658n, 662n
  enraged by *The Mandarins*, 428, 457–
    458, 471, 472, 500, 658n
  Family and, 344, 401, 405, 406–7,
    409, 476
  FBI surveillance of, 446, 455, 662n
  finances of, 500, 657n
  first meeting of Beauvoir and, 333–35
  French not spoken by, 336, 406
  gifts sent to Paris by, 405, 472
  hostile public statements of, against
    Beauvoir, 500, 502, 658n, 662n
  "It's About Time" and, 415, 416
  Lanzmann affair and, 443–44
  literary career of, 335, 352, 353, 368,
    410, 419, 457, 471, 475, 500, 501–2,
    647n, 661n
  The Mandarins as story of Beauvoir
    and, 411, 419, 422–23, 425, 428,
    449, 457, 661n
  marriages and divorces of, 420, 428,
    429, 439, 440, 445, 446, 455, 658n
  marriage to Beauvoir wanted by,
    385–86, 398
  as mentor on all things American, 365,
    388, 545
  other lovers taken by, 398–99, 416,
    417, 658n
  Paris trip of (1949), 396, 399, 401,
    405–10, 657n
  Paris trip of (1960), 408, 455, 458, 471–
    472, 475–77, 479–80, 481, 482, 500
  passionate nature of Beauvoir's rela-
    tionship with, 333, 336
  pen given to Beauvoir by, 368
  relocation of Beauvoir to Chicago
    wanted by, 385–86, 429
  Rue de la Bûcherie apartment and,
    404–6, 659n
  Sartre-Beauvoir relationship and, 336,
    344–45, 353, 355–57, 370, 385, 386,
    396, 397, 400–401, 406, 419, 427,
    429, 430, 431, 475, 476–77, 479,
    500, 659n, 622n
  Sartre's meetings with, 406, 407,
    471–72
  The Second Sex and, 353, 364, 366,
    385–86, 388, 389, 395, 407–9, 410,
    439
  shyness of, 406
  silver ring given to Beauvoir by, 344,
    350, 368, 371, 444, 475, 500, 503,
    615, 648n
  as sounding board for Beauvoir, 445
  Wright's (Ellen) affair with, 463
  writings by, translated for *Les Temps
    Modernes*, 348, 363, 401, 648n,
    650n–51n, 657n
Allard, Paule, 346, 648n
Allen, Woody, 607
Alliance Française, 317, 326, 329, 339
*All Men Are Mortal (Tous les hommes
    sont mortels)* (Beauvoir), 297,
    307–10, 314, 318, 324, 638n, 643n
  as Beauvoir's favorite work, 307
  critical response to, 307, 309, 346
  film proposal for, 337, 338
  loneliness and alienation in, 307
  Regina's epilogue in, 312
  story line of, 308–9
  structure and form of, 310
  writing of, 283, 284, 305, 312
All Said and Done (Toute compte fait)
    (Beauvoir), 459, 518, 534, 595, 667n
  brutally frank account of Natasha in,
    505–6
  feminist activism and, 543, 544
  see also Beauvoir, Simone de,
    memoirs of
Alps, Beauvoir's trip in, 212
Altman, Georges, 358
Amado, Jorge, 481
Amado, Zelia, 481
American Day by Day (Beauvoir), 336,
    341, 363, 430, 438, 645n
  Algren written about in, 334, 340, 348,
    419

extracted in *Les Temps Modernes*, 334, 362, 385

women described in, 384, 646n–47n

writing of, 347, 348, 352, 353, 368, 380, 385–86, 456

American Academy of Arts and Letters, 335, 502

American Dilemma, An (Myrdal), 364, 368

American Federation of Labor, 400

Andersen, Hans Christian, 66, 352

Angelou, Maya, 609

"Anne" (Beauvoir), 195, 205, 624n–25n, 634n

anthropology:
    Sartre's theory and, 467
    in *The Second Sex*, 390, 655n
    shift toward, 521, 531–32, 553

Antibes, Beauvoir and Sartre's holiday in (1961), 485–86

anti-Communism, 361, 362, 446–47

anti-Semitism, 124, 236, 242, 278, 363, 636n–37n

Antoinette (Antoinette Fouque), 552, 553

Aragon, Louis, 464

Arc, L', 572

Arendt, Hannah, 332

Arland, Marcel, 282, 638n

Aron, Raymond, 187, 198, 305, 412, 572, 642n
    Beauvoir criticized for political ignorance by, 362–63
    Beauvoir's relationship with, 319, 363
    Sartre's rupture with, 313
    Les Temps Modernes and, 298–99
    The Victors left by, 319, 644n–45n

Artaud, Antonin, 643n

Associated Press, 611

Assouline, Pierre, 260, 638n

Astruc, Alexandre, 568, 656n

Audry, Colette, 185, 243, 345, 383
    on Beauvoir-Sartre relationship, 183, 514
    Beauvoir's friendship with, 182–83
    Beauvoir's visit in Grenoble with, 257–58
    book on women envisioned by, 325, 379–80, 652n
    on Olga trio, 194–95
    as political activist, 182–83, 184, 189, 220, 258, 325, 533

Awdykovicz, Estepha, *see* Gerassi, Stépha

baccalauréat, 88, 89–91, 94
    postponed during World War II, 237
    taken by Beauvoir, 90–91

Badinter, Elisabeth, 610, 617

Bakunin, Mikhail, 533

Ballad and the Source, The (Lehmann), 628n

Bandi, Heveshi, 166–67

Bank of the Meuse, 27, 34

Banville, Théodore de, 59

Barcelona, Beauvoir and Sartre's holiday in (1931), 175

Bardot, Brigitte, 269, 545

Bariona (Sartre), 259

Barnes, Hazel, 512, 596, 668n

Barnes Foundation, 331–32, 607

Barrès, Maurice, 97, 102

Barthes, Roland, 464, 473, 531, 573, 672n

Bartók, Béla, 461

Baruzi, Jean, 125

Basque nationalists, 550

Basque region, Beauvoir and Sartre's holiday in (1938), 209, 634n

Bataille, Georges, 284, 291

Batarde, La (Leduc), 492, 504–5

Baudelaire (Sartre), 466

Baudelaire, Charles, 100

Baudin, Lucienne, 441, 664n

BBC (British Broadcasting Corporation), 220, 279, 283, 295

Beach, Sylvia, 164, 198, 219

Beard, Mary, 391–92

Beauvoir, Ernest-Narcisse Bertrand de (grandfather), 23–24, 31, 33, 46, 50, 58, 61, 93, 106
    children's marriages and, 23–24, 27
    death and funeral of, 138, 139, 148
    personality and demeanor of, 23, 25–26, 622n

Beauvoir, Françoise de (née Brasseur) (mother), 27–32, 78, 79, 86, 106, 112, 216, 223, 220, 245, 255, 284, 300, 317, 367, 420, 449–50, 454, 509, 601, 636n, 670n, 671n
    Algren's gifts to, 405
    beauty of, 28, 29, 620n
    Champigneulle affair and, 98–99, 100, 105, 108, 113
    childbearing of, 32, 33, 620n
    childhood of, 28
    child rearing by, 36–38, 39, 41, 42, 44, 45, 48, 54–55, 58–59, 60, 62
    coolness and reserve of, 31, 41, 45, 72–73, 95
    correspondence of Simone and, 264, 265–67, 281, 282–83, 285, 294, 295, 638n–39n, 640n–41n
    daughters' clothing and, 82

Beauvoir, Françoise de, *cont.*
  daughters' marriage possibilities and,
    57, 134
  daughters' nighttime adventures and,
    118
  daughters' puberty and, 82, 85
  daughters' reading supervised by, 36,
    62, 65, 66–67, 69, 73, 90, 102, 491
  daughters' resentment toward, 39
  daughters' schooling and, 42–44, 45,
    48, 50, 52, 62, 65, 91–95, 100, 109,
    110, 139, 626n
  daughters' toys and, 41
  death of, 489–91, 492, 506, 584, 589,
    594, 596
  dowry of, 29, 30, 35–36, 50
  educated by husband, 31–32, 34, 35,
    36, 42, 65
  entertaining by, 40, 49, 52, 72, 81
  evening routine of, 34
  family background of, 22, 27–28
  family finances and, 112
  family papers burned by, 257, 638n
  father's financial failure and, 34–36,
    620n
  foreign languages learned by, 36
  Hélène's relationship with, 55, 95,
    108–9, 112–13
  household chores and, 58
  household economies of, 47, 51–52, 53,
    627n
  household responsibilities assumed by,
    29–30, 31, 32, 34
  husband's death and, 255, 256–57, 265
  husband's financial collapse and, 51–
    53, 54, 72
  husband's relationship with, 29, 30,
    31–32, 34, 36, 45, 49, 50, 54, 58,
    70, 112–13, 620n
  independent life lived by, 257, 489
  life style of, 40
  lovemaking of, 70, 74, 85–86, 172,
    620n
  meals prepared by, 37, 48, 627n
  monthly stipend given to, 263, 279, 441
  movies as passion of, 137, 138
  Paris apartments of, 29, 30, 31, 40–41,
    52–53, 257, 620n, 621n, 622n
  personality of, 30–31
  religious beliefs of, 31, 32, 36, 44, 50,
    62, 95
  Sartre and, 149–50, 177, 405, 630n
  schooling of, 28, 42, 620n
  Simone's childhood friends and, 77, 80,
    81, 114–15
  Simone's choice of career and, 91–93

  Simone's concept of aging and, 440,
    441
  Simone's dismissal from teaching and,
    279
  Simone's first book and, 206
  Simone's illness and, 203
  Simone's male university friends and,
    126, 129, 148
  Simone's Marseille teaching assignment
    and, 177
  Simone's memoirs and, 491
  Simone's move away from home and,
    140, 155
  Simone spoiled by, 37–38
  Simone's pubescent thoughts and, 75
  Simone's radio job and, 280
  Simone's relationship with, 45, 55–56,
    58, 59, 60, 62, 72–73, 95–96, 97,
    108, 112–14, 126, 137–38, 139,
    155, 197, 226, 283, 287, 317, 490–
    491, 644n
  Simone's Rouen teaching assignment
    and, 185–86
  Simone's weekly luncheons with, 317,
    359
  snubbed by Mme. Le Coin, 114, 133–
    134
  social conscience of, 74
  social conventions observed by, 21, 39
  temper and rages of, 49, 50, 58, 108,
    112–14
  Useless Mouths and, 268–69, 310
  wedding of, 27, 28–29
  World War I and, 46–47, 49, 50
  World War II and, 226–27, 238, 242,
    243, 256, 265
Beauvoir, Gaston Bertrand de (uncle),
    23, 24, 25, 26, 34, 46, 58, 84, 93,
    106
Beauvoir, Georges Bertrand de (father),
    73, 78, 79, 86, 90, 95, 96, 106, 159,
    216, 223, 245, 546, 589
  anti-Semitism of, 124, 242
  Champigneulle and, 83–84, 98, 99
  charming vs. silent moods of, 58
  childhood of, 23, 24–26
  child rearing by, 37–38, 41, 44, 45,
    54–55, 59–60
  clothes of, 236
  daughters exhorted to prepare for
    work by, 89
  daughters' nighttime adventures and,
    118
  daughters' schooling and, 42–43, 52,
    59, 65, 89, 90, 91, 92, 93, 100,
    108, 109, 110, 122, 139

death of, 255–57, 265, 490
entertaining by, 40, 49, 81
evening routine of, 34
family background of, 22–23
family finances handled by, 112
father-in-law's financial disaster and, 34–36
financial failure of, 47, 50–54, 57–58, 72, 82, 116, 157
foreign culture and people disdained by, 110
heart trouble of, 47, 50, 58
Hélène's relationship with, 61, 112
last job held by, 112
as lawyer, 26–27, 50
library of, 454
life style of, 40
lovemaking of, 70, 74, 85–86, 172, 620n
mistresses of, 112, 627n
as nonbeliever, 25, 26, 36, 44, 62
opulent tastes of, 31
Paris apartments of, 29, 30, 31, 40–41, 52–53, 620n, 621n, 622n
physical appearance of, 44
profession chosen by, 26–27
Sartre and, 149–50, 155, 630n
schooling of, 24, 25, 42, 136
Simone likened to man by, 104, 137
at Simone's birth, 33, 620n
Simone's choice of career and, 91–93, 97
Simone's earnings and, 112
Simone's first book and, 206, 207
Simone's intellectual precocity and, 38, 44, 56
Simone's job quest and, 167
Simone's male university friends and, 126, 129, 138
Simone's Marseille teaching assignment and, 177
Simone's move away from home and, 140
Simone spoiled by, 37–38
Simone's reading and, 65, 66
Simone's relationship with, 55–56, 59–62, 83–84, 91, 138, 155, 197, 256, 540
Simone's Rouen teaching assignment and, 185–86
Simone's unplanned trip to Meyrignac with, 122
study of, 40, 41, 49, 53
theatre and acting loved by, 26–27, 31, 59, 61
unable to provide dowry for daughters, 57, 89, 99

unable to remain employed, 51
wedding of, 27, 29
wife educated by, 31–32, 34, 35, 36, 42, 65
wife's relationship with, 29, 30, 31–32, 34, 36, 45, 49, 50, 54, 58, 70, 112–13, 620n
World War I and, 46–47, 48–49, 51
World War II and, 226–27, 238, 239, 242, 256
Beauvoir, Hélène Bertrand de (aunt), 23–24, 25, 46, 75, 93, 138, 619n
Beauvoir, Henriette-Hélène de (Hélène) (later Mme. de Roulet) (sister), 86, 90, 95, 107, 131, 139, 148, 155, 159, 185, 200, 216, 222, 238, 269, 272, 287, 300, 301, 310, 356, 369, 421, 441, 455, 469, 489, 490, 589, 601, 679n
and adoption of Sylvie, 592
Algren's death and, 502–3
as artist, 82, 109, 110, 116, 133, 146, 491, 492, 592, 614–15
bars and cafés frequented by, 111–12, 118
birth of, 38
books read by, 65–66, 69
career chosen by, 109
Champigneulle and, 84, 87, 98, 99
childhood of, 38–66, 70, 72, 73–74, 75
dowry lacked by, 57, 89
on family's poverty, 72
on father's death, 256
father's relationship with, 61, 112
Fernando Gerassi and, 164
first rebellion of, 108–9
friendships formed by, 81
games played by, 41, 42
household chores and, 58
jobs held by, 201, 209, 233
joint production of Simone and, 492
life style of, 491–92
living quarters of, 40, 53, 198, 263
marital ideal of, 60
marriage possibilities of, 134–35
mother's frugality and, 51–52
mother's relationship with, 55, 95, 108–9, 112–13
naming of, 621n
nighttime forays of, 140
personality of, 47
physical appearance of, 38, 48, 61
"Poupette" as nickname of, 38, 48, 621n
pubescent thoughts of, 75

Beauvoir, Henriette-Hélène de, *cont.*
"Purple Shrimp" as nickname of, 135,
628*n*–29*n*
religious upbringing of, 44, 50, 62
Roulet's first meeting with, 200–201
Sartre and, 141, 146, 149, 179, 201,
223, 233, 235
Sartre's death and, 586, 587
schooling of, 45, 50, 52, 59, 62, 64–65,
108
Simone's death and, 614–15, 616
Simone's illness and, 591, 592
Simone's male university friends and,
126, 129
Simone's Marseille teaching assignment
and, 177
Simone's relationship with, 39, 41–42,
54–55, 61, 63, 69, 77, 78, 79, 81,
85, 96, 97–98, 108–9, 111, 114,
164, 209, 491–92, 593
Sylvie's relationship with, 593
toys of, 41
wedding of, 237
World War I and, 46–47, 48, 49, 50
World War II and, 225, 226, 237
ZaZa and, 76, 77, 78, 108, 133, 152
Beauvoir, Jeanne de (later Mme.
Dauriac) (cousin), 61–62, 77, 81,
83, 96, 98, 134–35, 150, 277, 615,
623*n*
Beauvoir, Léontine Algaë-Mathilde
Bertrand de (née Wartelle) (grandmother), 23–24, 25, 26, 31, 33
Beauvoir, Marie-Elisabeth Bertrand de
(née de Champeaux) (great-
grandmother), 23
Beauvoir, Narcisse Bertrand de (great-
grandfather), 23
Beauvoir, Simone de:
acquaintances and friends of (1955–
65), 463–64
action as response to uncertainty in, 221
age-related infirmities of, 531
aging as viewed by, 160, 190–91, 302,
369, 440–41, 442, 445, 472, 528,
540–41, 625*n*
American politics and culture as
interest of, 545
animals detested by, 491–92
appetite of, 48, 627*n*
"approach to life" of, 180
arbitrary conclusion to arguments
found by, 86
authenticity as concern of, 123, 127
automobile accidents of, 431–32, 523,
673*n*

baccalauréat taken by, 90–91
Bair's decision to write about, 11–13
Bair's meetings with, 13–17
bars and cafés frequented by, 111–12,
118, 138, 169, 173, 177, 198, 263,
316, 317; *see also* Café de Flore
bicycling as pastime of, 239
birth control used by, 373, 374, 377
birth of, 33, 620*n*
books read by, 36, 38, 39, 41, 44, 59,
61, 63, 65–67, 68–70, 72–73, 78–79,
90, 96–97, 102–5, 107, 114–15, 121,
126–27, 131–32, 164, 173–74, 189,
220, 233–34, 321, 348, 365–66, 367–
368, 374, 388, 393–94, 491, 609,
623*n*, 624*n*, 625*n*, 649*n*, 650*n*,
651*n*, 656*n*, 673*n*–74*n*, 679*n*
breast cancer scare and, 441–42
cars owned by, 431, 442, 485
"Castor" as nickname of, 129, 377,
498, 628*n*, 659*n*
casual friendships difficult for, 110–11
casual physical affection difficult for,
120, 200
Catholicism rejected by, 62, 74, 95, 125
celebrity of, 284–88, 286, 408, 417,
442
changing literary landscape and, 346,
464, 473–74, 522, 669*n*
childhood of, 21–22, 33–87, 409
children not wanted by, 170, 509
Christ, devotion to, 65
collaboration with Nazis ascribed to,
241–42, 260, 295–96
in Combat, 293–94, 295
comic books as viewed by, 365
as confessional repository for women,
526, 527
confidence in women difficult for,
286–87
conversational manner of, 110–11
cooking as interest of, 263, 285, 483
criticism withstood by, 408, 409–10
daily routine of, 359–60, 368, 404,
444, 507, 659*n*
dancing classes taken by, 85
Daniel Secrétan as pseudonym of, 300–
301
death feared by, 207, 349, 441, 473,
481, 506, 540, 541, 594
death of, 17, 613–15
deaths experienced by, 73–74, 472–73,
594
depressive periods of, 107, 133, 168–69,
208, 212, 219, 350, 385, 443, 445,
469, 593–94, 626*n*

devotion of, to Christ, 65
diaries, journals, and notebooks kept by,
    106, 133, 171, 219–20, 222–23, 271,
    315, 322, 323, 562, 595, 628n, 634n,
    644n
in documentary film, 417, 660n
double standard denounced by, 86
dowry lacked by, 57, 82, 89, 99, 156
drinking habits of, 286, 338, 460, 461,
    472, 591, 594, 611, 612–13
drugs feared by, 319
drugs taken by, 341, 374, 392
drugstores and dime stores loved by,
    327–28, 607
emotional deprivation of, 70, 71
English language skills of, 78, 327,
    329, 336, 624n
exile considered by, 423–24, 661n
extreme and excessive behavior of, 117–
    119, 140, 177
family background of, 22–32
as feminist, 411, 453, 478–79, 531,
    542, 543–57, 559, 562, 571, 572–73,
    599, 602–4, 606, 618, 652n, 658n,
    663n, 672n, 674n–75n
finances of, 112, 159, 179–80, 226–27,
    263, 278–79, 282, 284, 279, 305,
    383, 390, 392, 441, 450, 453, 485,
    500, 652n
first plane flight of, 299, 317
fortieth birthday of, 368–69
forty-first birthday of, 395
forty-fourth birthday of, 440, 441
friendships of, with girls and women,
    75–81, 87, 96, 114–20, 123, 124,
    125, 132, 146–47, 182–83, 200, 227,
    286–87, 297–98, 314–15, 503–13
friendships of, with men, 124–30, 313–
    317, 323–24
funeral and burial of, 491, 615–17
games invented by, 41, 42, 46, 69
generosity of, 441, 504, 638n, 664n
gossip about, 280–81, 287, 360–61, 381
grace and athletic ability lacked by, 48
hands as fascination of, 185, 632n
handwriting of, 95, 427
homosexuality or lesbianism of
    friends, 651n
household chores and, 58
illnesses of, 133, 137, 203–4, 209, 588,
    591–92, 604, 605, 611, 612
indomitable disposition of, 62–63
insularity of thinking, 275–76
interviews given by, 310, 330, 333, 335,
    382, 453, 491, 492, 539–40, 551,
    554–55, 573, 610–11, 677n

Jo March character and, 69–70
lesbian identity ascribed to, 509, 510–
    511, 512
literary agents of, 418, 661n
literary theory of, 522–23
Maggie Tulliver character and, 70, 71
male colleagues' relationships with,
    136–37
marital ideal of, 60, 262
marriage as viewed by, 69, 105–6,
    134–35
modern literature discovered by, 98,
    102–3
movies frequented by, 137, 138, 156,
    157, 174, 214, 216, 217, 348, 377,
    454, 668n
music enjoyed by, 360, 413, 414, 508
naming of, 33
nineteenth birthday of, 113
order and discipline liked by, 47–48, 49
philosophy chosen as field of, 91–93
plane crashes and, tragedies as obses-
    sion of, 418, 420, 421, 422, 431,
    657n
professional friendships of, 123
psychology distrusted by, 191, 390, 392,
    426, 633n, 655n
puberty of, 74–75, 82, 85–86, 624n
as public speaker, 319, 326, 330, 331,
    363, 478, 480, 484, 538–39, 541–42,
    544, 645n–46n
publishers' rejections difficult for, 209
race relations as interest of, 388–89
radio job of, 279–80, 282, 284, 296,
    298, 305, 640n
record collection of, 453, 454, 594
religious upbringing of, 36, 44, 50, 65
repulsed by illness, 192, 441, 481, 506
schooling of, 21, 42–44, 45, 47, 48, 50,
    52, 58, 59, 62, 64–65, 77–78, 85,
    86, 88, 89–95, 96, 106
schoolmates' scorn for, 63
second-class status of women never
    experienced by, 368, 379, 383, 652n
second place in agrégation taken by,
    145–46
self-effacing about intellectual abilities,
    269–70, 639n
sexuality of, 117–19, 160, 171–73,
    191, 208, 272, 510–11
smoking habits of, 100, 317–18
social awkwardness of, 110, 162, 182,
    281
social events with prominent persons
    avoided by, 464–65
spoiled by parents, 37–38

Beauvoir, Simone de, *cont.*
  suicide fears and, 588
  superficial friendships of, 275
  Sylvie adopted by, 509, 592–93
  tearful outbursts of, in public places,
    169, 313–14, 350
  telephone hour of, 498–99
  television watched by, 454, 665n–66n
  temper tantrums of, 37, 38, 48, 92, 99,
    155
  tension-related ailments of, 168, 317–
    318, 644n
  toys of, 41
  typist of, 441
  unflattering appellations of, 317, 381
  unhappy adolescence of, 55, 57–58, 61,
    71, 626n
  as university student, 100, 110, 120,
    121–30, 131, 135, 138–39, 140–46,
    368–69, 628n
  unwilling to leave Paris, 140, 156, 492,
    592
  visitors given appointments by, 286, 297
  voice of, 142, 162, 182, 319, 358
  volunteer work done by, 109, 111
  walking as pastime of, 177, 209, 210,
    212, 239, 328–29, 330
  widening of solipsistic world of, 284–85,
    288
  younger people befriended by, 264
Beauvoir, Simone de, holidays and travels
    of, 37, 40
  in Algiers, 317, 392
  with Algren (1948), 371–78, 414, 454,
    651n
  in Antibes, 485–86
  automobile trips with Sylvie, 535, 561,
    563, 611
  in Basque region, 209, 634n
  Beauvoir sought out by women during,
    518–19
  in Brazil, 476, 478, 480, 481–82, 495
  in China, 455–56
  in Corsica, 349, 649n
  in Cuba, 474, 475, 476, 478, 480, 482,
    495, 668n
  in Czechoslovakia, 478, 489, 492, 520
  diary kept of, 518
  in Egypt, 420, 421, 478, 519, 526,
    661n
  in emerging socialist nations, 473, 474,
    476
  in Free Zone, 255, 257–58, 265–66
  genesis of Beauvoir's feminism in, 672n
  at La Grillère, 105, 146, 148–50, 204
  in Israel, 519, 526, 575–77, 677n

  in Japan, 478, 519
  with Lanzmann, 444, 448, 665n
  in London, 349–50, 649n
  in Massif Central, 277, 280, 281–82,
    641n
  at Meyrignac, 46, 65, 67, 105, 106,
    107, 121–22, 131, 146, 147, 148–50,
    277
  at Mme. Morel's Juan-les-Pins villa,
    215, 216
  in Morocco, 212
  in 1960s, 518–20, 526
  in North Africa, 179, 180, 420, 421,
    661n
  in Norway, 588
  in Portugal, 300–301
  at La Pouèze, 266–67, 270, 271, 277,
    282–84, 285, 294, 297, 304–5, 357,
    363, 366, 367–68, 424, 425
  in Ramateulle, 373, 374
  in Rome, 196, 410, 486, 488, 489,
    492, 535, 561–62, 563–64, 565, 568,
    573, 578, 594
  in Saint-Rémy-les-Chevreuse, 344–45
  skiing, 226, 288, 289, 311–12, 313,
    641n
  souvenirs of, 453–54
  in Soviet Union, 478, 488–89, 492,
    518, 526
  in Spain, 175–76, 179, 180, 181,
    300–301, 476
  in Sweden, 347, 351–52, 353, 519
  in Switzerland, 323
  in Tunis, 317
  in United States, *see* United States,
    Beauvoir's trips to
  in Yugoslavia, 476–77, 478, 520
Beauvoir, Simone de, homes of:
  appointments at, 507, 671n
  bomb warning and, 488
  cellar storage area of, 455, 502, 666n
  as child, 40–41, 52–53, 367, 469, 540,
    622n
  departure from family's apartment,
    140, 148, 150
  femme de charge period and, 263
  in grandmother's apartment, 140, 148,
    150, 155, 159, 161, 238, 243
  hideouts during Algerian War, 483–84,
    487, 488
  Lanzmann living with Beauvoir in,
    444, 460
  Leiris home's influence on, 285
  in Marseille, 176
  Paris hotel rooms, 197, 225, 239, 249,
    263, 271–72, 277, 285, 301

in Rouen, 181, 632n
Rue de la Bûcherie apartment, 404–6, 450, 453, 659n
Rue Schoelcher studio, 453–55, 495
Beauvoir, Simone de, memoirs of, 17, 91, 97, 98, 99, 104, 115, 120, 128, 137, 139, 141, 143, 146, 187, 270, 296, 321, 350, 391, 411, 442, 490, 493, 537, 641n, 657n
on Algerian crisis, 480
on Algren, 341, 372, 375, 472, 479, 500, 502, 647n, 658n
on All Men Are Mortal, 307
Beauvoir's first consideration of, 324–25
on Brazil trip, 481
on Camus, 289–90, 641n
on China trip, 455, 666n
on Comoedia affair, 259–60
and concern for privacy of others, 468–69
on correspondence with Sartre, 202
on dangerous behavior, 177
on dismissal from teaching post, 279
on Dolores, 302, 303–4
on father's death, 256
on Faulkner, 229
on feminist activism, 543, 544, 549
impetus for, 459–60, 466–67
inaccuracies in, 486, 668n
on L'Invitée, 230
on Korean War, 422, 424
on Lanzmann, 445
Leiris's influence on, 284, 324
McCarthy's criticism of, 290, 641n
on The Mandarins, 660n
on May '68 uprising, 531
on Mme. Morel and Jollivet, 161–62, 164
on Natasha, 248, 249, 505–6
on Olga trio, 192, 193
on other women writers, 625n
on political activism, 359, 447, 452, 486
on radio job, 280
on Ray, Evelyne, 462
real life vs. "reconstructed" life in, 469, 668n
on relationship with mother, 644n
on relationship with Sartre, 157, 158–59, 170, 171, 181, 244, 304, 351, 386, 415, 463, 631n
reread by Beauvoir, 594–95
response to, 506
Sartre as focus of, 447, 469, 486, 514, 595

on The Second Sex, 380, 382–83, 389, 410, 432, 655n
on sexual feelings, 172
on Spanish holiday, 175
on thesis project, 628n
on travels of 1960s, 518, 519
on World War II, 212, 238, 275, 294
writing of, 458, 459, 467, 468–70, 473–74, 484–85, 486, 668n
on ZaZa's death, 205
see also specific volumes
Beauvoir, Simone de, personality of, 47–48
changed by World War II, 212, 215
changed by year in Marseille, 180, 183
constant, rigid self-control and, 168, 169
interviewees' opinions on, 383, 652n–653n
introspection and, 133, 204, 628n
lack of sense of humor, 78, 365, 377, 654n
learning to live in present and, 180
obsessive behavior and, 48, 122–23
prudery and innocence in, 119–20, 125, 129, 160–61, 163, 199, 441–42
secrecy and evasion in, 95–96
self-absorption and, 146, 154, 212
self-preservation techniques and, 48, 209
voyeurism and, 90, 109, 110, 163, 199, 359, 383
Beauvoir, Simone de, philosophy of, 318, 324
and adherence to Being and Nothingness, 267, 270, 381, 452
disagreements with Sartre in, 270, 271
freedom notion in, 270, 305, 306, 321, 639n
immutability of, 452–53, 463
Kantian standard for, 271
in postwar period, 318, 320–22
readings and, 233–34, 240, 262, 271
responsibility notion in, 270, 271
self-effacement about abilities in, 269–70, 639n
Beauvoir, Simone de, physical appearance of, 13, 182, 330, 355, 357, 618
at age fifty-one, 541
Americans' views on, 331, 337–38
as child, 37, 48, 60–61, 78
clothing and, 82, 90, 96, 116, 123, 138, 142, 143, 161, 162, 176, 177, 181, 183, 213, 227, 264–65, 285–86, 292–93, 301–2, 331, 360, 407, 443, 613–14, 646n, 679n

Beauvoir, Simone de, physical appearance of, *cont.*
  and concern about Algren's Paris trip, 472
  "Existentialist uniform" and, 360
  father's rejection and, 61
  feigned indifference and, 82–83
  at first meeting with Lanzmann, 443
  hairstyles and, 91, 113, 176
  missing tooth and, 257–58, 301, 374
  nails and, 185, 472
  in postwar period, 301–2
  sloppiness of, 43, 82, 181
  Stépha and, 116, 123
  turban and, 113, 116, 264–65
  women's magazines and, 161, 213, 217, 631n
  during writing of *The Second Sex*, 395
Beauvoir, Simone de, political activism of, 354, 356–63, 366, 370–71, 394, 399–400, 412–13, 447, 451–53, 470, 472, 473, 474, 476–79, 481–82, 513, 518, 519–20, 528, 530, 532–39, 541–542, 544, 571–73, 656n, 669n
  Algerian War and, 452, 468, 477–78, 480, 482, 483–84, 485, 487–88
  apolitical phase and, 184–85, 212, 319, 453
  as feminist, 453, 478–79, 531, 542, 547–57, 559, 562, 571, 572–73, 602–4, 658n
  and lack of political credo, 362, 650n
  naivete and, 318, 644n
  not taken seriously, 358, 359, 362, 363
  Third World oppression and, 399–400
  and willingness to espouse unpopular causes, 547–48
Beauvoir, Simone de, romances and liaisons of, 340, 397–98
  with Algren, *see* Algren, Nelson
  with Bost, 208, 397, 427, 498, 658n
  first, 98–101; *see also* Champigneulle, Jacques
  with Guille, 172, 189
  with Koestler, 316, 361, 658n
  with Lanzmann, 442–45, 448, 451, 460, 468, 665n, 666n
  secrecy about, 302
  with Vitold, 301–2
  with younger men, 264
Beauvoir, Simone de, Sartre's relationship with, 137, 152, 154–67, 286, 294, 324, 325, 334, 341, 351, 459, 539, 573, 582, 585, 611, 673n
  Adieux as final salute to, 595
  Algren and, 336, 344–45, 353, 355–

357, 370, 385, 386, 396, 397, 400–401, 406, 419, 427, 429, 430, 431, 475, 476–77, 479, 500, 659n, 662n
Arlette and, 461–62, 496, 497, 499, 565
Audry's observations on, 193, 514
Beauvoir and Sartre changed by, 183
Beauvoir as "heavy" in, 211, 214, 235, 466, 559
Beauvoir family and, 155, 197, 630n
Beauvoir's acquiescence to Sartre in, 188, 193, 195, 269, 463
Beauvoir's adolescent ideal and, 60, 262
and Beauvoir's complicity in Sartre's sexual conquests, 163, 165, 171, 193, 202, 210–11, 214, 399
Beauvoir's dissatisfaction with, 210–11
Beauvoir's friendships with men independent of, 315–17
Beauvoir's jealousy in, 161–64
Beauvoir's most accurate assessment of, 370
and Beauvoir's preeminence in Sartre's life, 233, 342–43
Beauvoir's prudery and, 160–61
Beauvoir's self-absorption and, 154
Beauvoir's willingness to entertain questions about, 642n–43n
Beauvoir's women friends and, 189
cemented during sojourn in countryside (1947), 344
childbearing issue in, 170
contingency concept in, 158, 344, 353–354, 400, 631n, 658n
correspondence in, 153, 166, 169, 202, 203–4, 210, 215, 218–19, 221, 222–223, 224–25, 226, 227, 231, 233, 234–36, 238, 239–40, 244, 245, 246, 247, 311–12, 317, 340, 342, 598, 599–602, 630n, 636n, 678n–79n
and decline in mutual importance, 462, 470, 481, 513, 514–19, 529, 559
defining of roles in, 157–59, 214–15, 634n
and differences between Beauvoir and Sartre, 381
dislike for quirks and habits in, 181, 182
disparaged by Arlette, 597, 599, 601
Dolores and, 300, 301, 302–4, 309, 310, 313, 319, 322, 342–44, 414–15
equality in, 144
falling apart of, 298, 319, 322–23
feeling of "privilege" in, 515, 516
feminists' difficulty with, 514, 546
financial arrangement in, 179–80

first introduction and, 140–43
first lovemaking in, 149
formalities in, 272–73, 511
friends forming "family" around, *see*
    Family
Genet's description of, 631n
gossip sessions in, 198, 199
inequality of assistance in, 173, 174,
    203, 445
intellectual rapport in, 143–44, 514
and lack of common group of
    acquaintances, 463–65
lack of reality in, 155, 158
Lévy and, 559, 567, 570, 576, 577–82
lies in, 289
made public, 155, 156
marriage issue in, 155–56, 166, 169–
    171
memories of, difficult for Beauvoir,
    593–94
most tranquil year of, 260–61
Natasha as ideal completion of trio in,
    248–49
new levels of being and understanding
    added to, 287
Nobel Prize affair and, 495
Olga trio and, 186–87, 189–95, 196,
    199–200, 207, 210, 214, 215, 231,
    249, 309, 598, 633n
and outings with Nizans, 156–57
pact in, 157–59, 171, 182, 210, 215,
    344, 355, 477, 514–15, 631n
passion primarily verbal in, 154
periods of separation and, 146, 165,
    166–73, 176–78, 180, 187–89, 217–
    218, 221, 303, 317, 322, 326, 342–
    343, 344
political activism and, 319–20, 356,
    359, 362, 400, 451, 513, 572
private language in, 145
as professional couple, 287, 344, 363,
    385, 497
reading in, 173–74
and realizing of Beauvoir's potential,
    165–66
Roulet on, 201
Sartre as mentor in, 165, 173
Sartre's dependency in, 166, 414, 476–
    477, 519
Sartre's depression and, 191–92
Sartre's evasions and, 493, 495
Sartre's feelings of entrapment in, 188
Sartre's health problems and, 565,
    567–68, 572
Sartre's La Grillère visit and, 148–50,
    155, 168, 630n

Sartre's new philosophy and, 515, 516,
    517, 579–81, 583
Sartre's voracious sexual appetite and,
    202, 210–11, 287
sexuality in, 148, 171–73, 191, 215,
    302, 397
solipsistic world of, 284, 288
at Sorbonne, 127–28, 130, 138–39,
    140–46
Sylvie le Bon and, 517–18, 565, 676n
Sylvie's relationship with Beauvoir
    compared to, 507–8, 510, 512
total truthfulness and openness in, 158,
    159, 163, 164, 171
as union of two opposites, 154–55, 157
Wanda and, 201–2, 208, 210, 234–35,
    273
and women's demands on Beauvoir,
    518–19
as writing couple, 181, 273, 287, 318,
    319
Beauvoir, Simone de, teaching career of:
assistantship at Institut Sainte-Marie,
    112, 136
dismissal and, 277–79, 280, 281, 286,
    640n
haphazardness and mediocrity in, 186–
    187, 188, 195, 203, 213
Marseille assignment, 167, 168, 169,
    171, 175, 176–78, 180, 183, 186, 406
practice teaching, 136–37, 629n
Rouen assignment, 178, 179, 180–96
students' admiration and, 213
transfer to Paris, 195–96
and unwillingness to leave Paris, 140,
    156
during World War II, 224, 238, 242–
    243, 262–63, 277–79
Beauvoir, Simone de, writings of, 204–8,
    212–13, 297, 304–11, 346–47, 353
adherence to Sartre's philosophy in, 307
banned by Catholic Church, 456–57,
    666n
Beauvoir's views on most important of,
    269–70, 639n
catharsis attempted in, 506, 594, 595
conflict between individual and society
    in, 71
desperate, abandoned women in, 426
discovery of self in, 206–7, 634n
double narration technique in, 305,
    307–8
earliest stories, 67–68, 623n, 678n
on Existentialism, 270–71
fictional models for, 67, 107, 131–32,
    174, 184, 205, 229

Beauvoir, Simone de,
    writings of, *cont.*
    forces that determine women's lives in,
        204–6
    freedom concept in, 305, 306, 321
    friendship of two women in, 229
    on future of heterosexual relationships,
        415–16
    influence of Françoise vs. Georges on,
        56, 622n
    last work (*Mihloud*), 613
    literary criticism, 320–21
    literary prizes and, 285–86, 411, 427,
        428, 449, 572, 606, 679n
    loneliness and alienation in, 307
    manuscripts of, 636n
    as means of coping with personal prob-
        lems, 309, 321, 363, 380, 381, 385,
        386, 387, 415, 451, 459, 653n–54n
    names of characters in, 228, 634n
    prefaces and introductions, 487, 492,
        493, 505, 523, 550, 604, 612
    reason for tremendous output of, 298
    under Sartre's byline, 293–94, 567,
        641n
    Sartre's editorial assistance with, 174,
        271, 506
    Sartre's encouragement and, 166, 173,
        174, 178, 206, 228, 270
    Sartre's prodigious output and, 386–
        387
    in summers of 1927–29, 105, 107–8,
        131, 147, 626n, 629n–30n
    Sylvie as first reader of, 506
    travel writing, 281, 293, 300–301,
        455–56
    unpublished manuscripts, 597, 678n–
        679n
    during World War II, 228–34, 240,
        241–42, 262, 266–71, 273, 277,
        283, 284, 293–94
    ZaZa material in, 147, 175, 178, 205,
        228, 309, 449, 624n, 630n
    see also Beauvoir, Simone de, memoirs
        of; *specific works*
Beckett, Samuel, 254, 644n, 659n
    Bair's biography of, 11, 12, 13, 14, 16,
        637n
    Beauvoir's views on, 648n
    story submitted to Les Temps Modernes
        by, 346, 648n–49n
Beethoven, Ludwig van, 360
*Being and Nothingness (L'Etre et le
    néant)* (Sartre), 320, 402, 452, 461
    Beauvoir's adherence to, 267, 270, 381,
        452

critical response to, 274, 638n
    dedication of, 272
    manuscript of, 589
    sales of, 274, 639n–40n
    Sartre's move away from, 516, 580
    writing of, 233, 235, 240, 269, 623n
Belgium, 235, 478
    Beauvoir's lecture tours in, 484, 519
Bell, Pearl Kazin, 333
Belles Images, Les (Beauvoir), 523–26,
        622n, 671n, 673n, 678n
    critical response to, 524, 525, 526
    genesis of, 523–24
    plot of, 524–25
    as prescient novel, 525–26
    sales of, 525
Bendyk, Betty, 658n
Benjamin, Jessica, 551
Benson, Sidney, 505, 506
Berg, Alban, 360, 461
Berlin:
    opening of *The Flies* in, 372
    year spent by Sartre in, 187–88, 189,
        191
Bernard, Jacqueline, 293
Bertin, Célia, 629n
Bertrand, Mother, 28, 40, 620n
Bevin, Ernest, 361, 650n
Bibliothèque Cardinale, 44
Bibliothèque Nationale, 233, 240, 241,
        262, 325, 549, 600
Bibliothèque Rose series, 66
Bienenfeld, Bianca (later Mme. Lamblin),
        220, 223, 225, 226, 236, 237, 463,
        634n
    Beauvoir's relationship with, 214, 215,
        244, 349, 369, 667n
    Beauvoir's visit in Algiers with, 421
    Sartre's affair with, 208, 214, 215
    Sartre's correspondence with, 219, 598
Billy, André, 527
birth control, 480, 552, 604
    Beauvoir's need for information about,
        373, 374, 377
Bisschop, Magdeleine Mantis de (cousin),
        83, 84–85, 96, 110, 138, 615, 628n
    as Beauvoir's childhood playmate, 40,
        65, 67, 69, 74, 75, 77, 81, 96
    on Beauvoir's childhood tantrums, 37
    books read by, 65, 67, 624n
    Sartre's La Grillère visit and, 148, 149,
        150
    sexuality and, 74, 75, 491–92
    song written by cousins and, 134–35
Bisseret, Noelle, 551, 675n
Bjurstrom, Carl-Gustav, 494, 495

Black Boy (Wright), 374

Blanchot, Maurice, 271

Blood of Others, The (Le Sang des autres) (Beauvoir), 237, 297, 305–7, 309–10, 367, 634n, 636n
  Blomart's character and situation in, 305–6
  critical response to, 304–5, 306–7
  dual narration technique in, 305
  Existentialism and, 305, 306–7
  freedom concept in, 305, 306
  manuscript of, 305, 643n
  publication of, 638n
  writing of, 273, 277, 283, 284, 305

Blum, Maître, 418, 449

Bobigny abortion trial, 550

Bonafé, Alphonse, 357

Boschetti, Anna, 514, 671n–72n

Bost, Jacques-Laurent, 185, 192, 203, 258, 285, 311, 316, 323, 369, 396, 409, 410, 413, 442, 443, 445, 450, 460, 463, 472, 482, 483, 489, 560, 582, 585, 588, 594, 601, 612, 640n
  and adoption of Arlette, 496, 498
  and adoption of Sylvie, 592, 593
  Algren and, 406, 407, 471, 475, 476, 479, 482, 646n, 648n
  Beauvoir's friendship with, 243, 313, 511, 581, 598
  Beauvoir's illness and death and, 611, 614, 615
  Beauvoir's memoir writing and, 324, 458
  Beauvoir's skiing holiday with (1944), 289, 641n
  on bicycling trip in Free Zone (1942), 265–66
  Dolores and, 309, 322, 643n
  Duras's affair with, 403–4
  family relations of, 197–98, 264, 324
  financial support of, 263, 441
  Gerbert character and, 231
  Lévy's Israel article and, 576, 577, 579
  The Mandarins and, 427, 428
  memento of Sartre given to, 589
  Olga's relationship with, 199, 200, 208, 498, 598, 633n
  Resistance and, 250, 251
  Sartre's death and, 585, 586
  screenplays and, 392, 396, 656n
  The Second Sex title and, 389
  sexual intimacy of Beauvoir and, 208, 397, 427, 498, 658n
  Les Temps Modernes and, 521, 522
  wartime military service of, 220, 224–225, 237, 243
  as writer for *Combat*, 295, 313, 641n

Bost, Olga (née Kosakievicz), 13, 189–195, 196, 197, 203, 204, 212, 220, 223, 225, 236, 237, 243, 258, 263, 264, 292, 295, 311, 359, 410, 428, 445, 450, 463, 472, 489, 600, 612, 628n
  acting career of, 201–2, 267, 283, 286, 370
  Algren and, 401, 406–7, 476, 479
  background of, 186
  Beauvoir's relationship with, 186–87, 189, 190–91, 193, 199–200, 202, 208, 210, 214, 231, 303, 498–99, 509, 598–99
  husband's relationship with, 199, 200, 208, 498, 598, 633n
  Natasha compared to, 214, 215
  Natasha jealous of, 244, 249
  nickname for, 204
  Resistance and, 250
  Sartre's affair with, 187, 189–95, 199, 200, 208, 210, 214, 249, 303, 309
  Sartre's correspondence with, 219, 598–599, 601
  tuberculosis suffered by, 313, 349, 369, 403, 498
  Xavière character and, 207, 231
  Zuore's courtship of, 192–93

Bost, Pierre, 197, 279, 280

Bouches inutiles, Les (Beauvoir), *see Useless Mouths*

Boulanger, Marguerite, 77

Boupacha, Djamila, 480, 487

Bourla (Natasha's lover), 272, 278, 639n

Boyle, Kay, 446

Bradley, Jennie, 418, 434, 436, 439, 661n

Brasillach, Robert, 252, 637n

Brasserie Lipp, 314, 402

Brasseur, Aimé-Fidèle-Constant (great-grandfather), 27, 619n–20n

Brasseur, Françoise (mother), *see* Beauvoir, Françoise de

Brasseur, Gustave (grandfather), 27–28, 29, 38, 41, 106
  financial disaster of, 34–36, 620n
  granddaughters' weekly luncheons with, 36–37, 39, 81
  pessimism of, 622n
  Simone's earliest writings and, 68
  World War I and, 49, 51, 622n

Brasseur, Hubert (uncle), 28, 34, 35, 40

Brasseur, Lucie (née Moret) (grand-mother), 28, 30, 31, 33, 34, 35, 38, 220

Brasseur, Lucie, *cont.*
  Beauvoir living in home of, 140, 148,
    150, 155, 159, 161, 238, 243
  breakdown suffered by, 49, 51
  granddaughters' weekly luncheons with,
    36–37, 39, 81
  illness and death of, 239, 242
  World War II and, 238
Brasseur, Marie-Thérèse (aunt), 28, 34,
  35, 37, 40, 68, 81, 620n
"Brave Bulls of Sidi Yahya" (Algren),
  652n
Brazil, 484
  Beauvoir and Sartre's trip to (1960),
    476, 478, 480, 481–82, 495
Breton, André, 387
Brevoort Hotel, 333, 338, 340, 341
"Brigitte Bardot and the Lolita Syn-
  drome" (Beauvoir), 269, 545
Brontë, Emily, 163
Brooklyn Kid, The, 377
Bruckner, Pascal, 596
Brunetière, Ferdinand, 90
Brunschweig, Cécile, 654n
Brunschweig, Léon, 128, 628n
  feminism of, 654n–55n
Butor, Michel, 464, 669n
Byatt, A. S., 526

Café de Flore, 213, 217, 218, 220, 270,
  274, 280, 284, 287, 289, 314, 322,
  348, 402, 406
  Beauvoir's "court" moved from, 316
  Beauvoir's daily routine at, 273, 297
  as hangout of German propaganda
    staff, 241–42, 636n
  interruptions as problem at, 286, 297,
    316
Café des Arts, 632n
Café Raspail Vert, 503, 506
Cahiers pour une morale (Sartre), 589–
  590, 599, 678n
Caldwell, Erskine, 651n
California, Beauvoir's trip to (1947),
  337–38, 646n
Caligula (Camus), 311
Camus, Albert, 285, 289–93, 305, 313,
  319, 320, 355, 357, 427, 611, 659n
  Beauvoir's relationship with, 290, 291–
    293, 299–300, 311, 361–62, 394–95
  celebrity of, 291
  death of, 472, 473
  Dolores affair and, 300, 301
  Existentialism and, 292, 641n
  Koestler's fight with, 369–70
  The Mandarins and, 449, 662n

Nobel Prize won by, 493
  physical appearance of, 291
  political activism of, 370, 372, 394,
    656n
  private self hidden by, 291, 292
  Resistance activities of, 291, 292, 293,
    295, 641n
  romantic affairs of, 299–300
  rupture of Sartre's relationship with,
    289, 300, 361–62, 394, 642n
  Sartre's friendship with, 287, 289–92
  Les Temps Modernes and, 292, 298,
    299
  Useless Mouths and, 311
Camus, Francine, 299–300, 361
Candide (Voltaire), 270–71
Capote, Truman, 374, 403, 659n
Capra, Frank, 337
Carcassonne, Beauvoir and Sartre's trip to
  (1939), 216
Carnets de la drole de guerre, Les (*War
  Diaries: Notebooks from a Phoney
  War, 1939–40*) (Sartre), 155, 189,
  219, 222, 599, 600, 630n, 634n
Casarès, Maria, 299–300
Castro, Fidel, 464, 474, 476, 482, 550
Castro, Roland, 574
Catholic Church:
  Beauvoir's book banned by, 456–57,
    666n
  Beauvoir's religious upbringing and, 36,
    44, 50, 65
  Little Women and, 69
  rejected by Beauvoir, 62, 74, 95, 125
Catholic World, 456
Cau, Jean, 346, 401, 404, 406, 409, 430,
  442, 443, 464–65, 476, 648n, 659n
Cause du peuple, La, 536–39, 544, 547,
  562–63
  Friends of, 537, 538, 544
Cavalcade, 317
Cayatte, André, 668n
Cazalis, Anne-Marie, 404, 406, 476
Céline, Louis-Ferdinand (Louis
  Destouches), 205
Cerf (publishing house), 304
CET technical college, 550
Chamberlain, Neville, 212, 213
Champeaux, Guillaume de (ancestor), 22
Champeaux, Marie-Elisabeth de (great-
  grandmother), 23
Champigneulle, Charles, 83, 99
Champigneulle, Ernest, 83
Champigneulle, Jacques (cousin), 83–84,
  85, 86, 87, 98–101, 102–6, 108,
  109, 114, 123, 126

Beauvoir introduced to modern literature by, 98, 102–3
Beauvoir's journal entries on, 106
dispassionate nature of Beauvoir's relationship with, 103, 111
formal portrait photograph given to, 113
Françoise's outburst at home of, 113–14
marriage issue and, 105–6, 117, 119
Meaulnes character compared to, 103–5
novel based upon Beauvoir's unhappy situation with, 107
return to Paris of, 420
Champigneulle, Thérèse "Great-Aunt Titite," 38, 83
"Chantal" (Beauvoir), 195, 205, 624n, 633n
Chaplin, Charlie, 299, 465
Chapsal, Madeleine, 453, 486
Charterhouse of Parma, The (Stendhal), 393–94
Châtelet, François, 574
Chemins de la liberté, Les (The Roads to Freedom) (Sartre), 208
Chicago, Beauvoir's trips to:
  in April 1947, 333, 334–36, 340
  in Sept. 1947, 351, 352–53, 355
  in 1950, 415, 416, 419–20, 421–23
  in 1951, 429–30, 432
China, People's Republic of, 477, 489
  Beauvoir and Sartre's trip to (1955), 455–56
Chips Are Down, The (Les Jeux sont faits), 347–48, 350, 649n
Chodorow, Nancy, 631n
Choisir, 550, 553, 562, 563, 602
Christina T. (Sartre's lover), 482, 485
Chronicles of a Deception: From the Women's Liberation Movement to a Commercial Trademark, 552–53
Church of Jesus Christ of Latter Day Saints, 393, 656n
Cinémathèque on the Rue de Fleurus, 110, 111
Cité-Soir, 311
Cité Universitaire, 141–42, 143, 148, 185, 189
civil rights movement, U.S., 545
Cixous, Hélène, 552
Claudel, Paul, 102, 126, 291, 358, 387
Clavel, Maurice, 574
Cocteau, Jean, 97, 102, 284, 294, 349, 370, 402
  Mortimers and Eugènes of, 126–27, 128, 131
Cohen-Solal, Annie, 18, 258–59, 496,

570–71, 574, 576, 579, 581, 600, 639n–40n
Cohn-Bendit, Daniel, 532, 533
Colette, Sidonie-Gabrielle, 90, 241, 452, 625n
Collège de France, 452
Collège Stanislas, 42, 136
Collignon, André, 311
Collins, Douglas, 667n
Columbia University, 322, 328–29, 465
Combat, 253, 293, 295
Combat, 295, 298, 313, 641n
  Beauvoir's writings for, 293–94, 300–301, 641n
Comédie-Française, 61, 589
Coming of Age, The (Beauvoir), see Old Age
Comité National des Écrivains (CNE), 273–74, 275, 642n
Commission Femme et Culture, 603–4
Communist Party, French, 182, 243, 319, 329, 412, 446–47, 480, 665n
  in Resistance, 258
  Sartre attacked by, 258–59
  Sartre's rapprochement with, 447, 452
Comoedia, 59, 259–60, 279, 282, 296
Condemned of Altona, The (Sartre), 462
Congress of Industrial Organizations, 400
Connecticut College for Women, 326, 331
Conrad, Peter, 17–18
Conroy, Frank, 388
Considérant, Victor-Prosper, 453
Constant, Benjamin, 271
Contat, Michel, 568, 600, 641n
Contes de la Mère l'Oie (Perrault), 66, 492
contraception, see birth control
Cooper, Duff, 374
Cooper, James Fenimore, 44, 66
Coppée, François, 59
Coquillat, Michelle, 603
Cornell University, 501, 513, 519
Corsica, Beauvoir's holiday in (1947), 349, 649n
Corydrane, 460, 666n
Council of Europe, 491
counterculture, 547, 675n
La Coupole, 241, 517, 536, 560
Courchay, Claude, 507, 667n
Cours Adeline Désir, 21, 42–44, 45, 47, 50, 52, 122, 442, 450, 468, 621n–22n
  Beauvoir's friends at, 75–87, 96
  curriculum of, 64, 89–91
  Hélène graduated from, 108
  journal writing at, 106

Cours Adeline Désir, *cont.*
  Simone graduated from, 88, 89, 97,
    625n
  teachers at, 64–65, 622n
Couvent des Oiseaux, 28, 40
Cowles, Fleur, 415
Crapouillot, 220
Crimson (Harvard), 330
Critique of Dialectical Reason (*Critique
    de la raison dialectique*) (Sartre),
    451, 466, 467, 474, 513, 515, 516,
    667n, 672n
Cuba, 484, 531
  Beauvoir and Sartre's trip to (1960),
    474, 475, 476, 478, 480, 482, 495,
    668n
cummings, e. e., 368, 651n
Curtis School of Music, 327
Cyrano de Bergerac (Rostand), 59
Czechoslovakia, 212, 370
  Beauvoir and Sartre's trips to, 478,
    489, 492, 520
  "Prague Spring" in, 520
Czech Writers' Union, 489

Daniel, Jean, 576, 579, 581
Daniélou, Madame Charles, 94, 95
Darkness at Noon (Koestler), 361
Dauriac, Jeanne (cousin), *see* Beauvoir,
    Jeanne de
David (Cooper), 374
Davis, Angela, 545
Davis, Gary, 394
Davy (examination jury member), 145
Dayan, Josée, 610, 611, 679n
Days of Our Death, The (Rousset), 359
Debout, Simone, 251, 252
Deconstruction, 473
Dedijer, Vladimir, 520, 672n
dédoublement (doubling) concept, 365
Defoe, Daniel, 66
de Gaulle, Charles, 329, 363, 395, 656n,
    674n
  Algerian crisis and, 480, 482, 484
  Sartre's postwar activism against, 356,
    358, 361
  in World War II, 251, 253, 295
De la famille (Margerie), 620n
Delange, René, 259–60, 279
Delannoy, Jean, 277
Delphy, Christine, 550, 551, 552
Denmark, 519
Depression, Great, 184
Derrida, Jacques, 473, 531, 573
Desanti, Dominique, 251, 637n
Desanti, Jean-Toussaint, 251, 637n

Descartes, René, 262
Desire Caught by the Tail (*Désir
    attrapé par la queue*) (Picasso), 292
Deutsch, Helene, 434
Deuxième sexe, Le (Beauvoir), *see*
    Second Sex, The
Les Deux Magots, 322, 323, 348, 359,
    402, 417
Devil in the Flesh (*Le Diable au corps*),
    348
De Voto, Bernard, 365
Diana of the Crossways (Meredith), 131,
    173
Dirty Hands (*Les Mains sales*) (Sartre),
    370, 373, 392, 656n
Djamila Boupacha (Halimi), 487
Dome, 198, 203, 206, 208, 216, 241, 242
Donadio, Candida, 501–2
Dos Passos, John, 164, 199, 208, 229,
    366, 388
Dostoevsky, Feodor, 321
Drancy, 246, 636n
Drieu la Rochelle, Pierre-Eugène, 258,
    638n
Duclos, Charles-Pinot, 446
Dullin, Charles, 163, 195, 226, 231, 267
  duration of war predicted by, 220
  Les Mouches staged by, 272, 274
  Olga cast by, 201–2
Du Maurier, George, 374
Duras, Marguerite, 534, 554, 582, 659n,
    674n
  Bost's affair with, 403–4
Dusty Answer (Lehmann), 132, 173
Dutschke, Rudi, 532
Duval, Annie, 266

Ecole Normale Supérieure, 120, 124,
    129–30, 139, 141, 169, 191, 246,
    251, 503, 569
  see also Sorbonne
Ecrits de Simone de Beauvoir, Les, 597
"Ecriture Feminine," 551, 552, 653n
Editions de Minuit, 346
Editions Gallimard, 216, 260, 272, 286,
    292, 316, 427, 431, 434, 445, 448,
    449, 452, 485, 494, 572, 610, 648n,
    649n, 667n, 672n
  accusations of collaboration and, 260,
    642n
  L'Invitée and, 265, 277
  Leduc's stipend from, 394, 441, 644n,
    657n
  publishing parties of, 317, 348–49, 465,
    476
  Sartre's position at, 291

The Second Sex and, 404, 407, 416, 417
Les Temps Modernes and, 395
When Things of the Spirit Come First and, 206, 207–8
Editions Juillard, 395
Editions Tierce, 553, 604
Egoist, The (Meredith), 131
Egypt, Beauvoir and Sartre's trips to:
   in 1960, 420, 421, 661n
   in 1967, 478, 519, 526
Ehrenreich, Dolores Vanetti, 300, 301,
   313, 321, 323, 340, 371, 397, 454,
   644n, 649n
   All Men Are Mortal and, 309
   Beauvoir's feelings about, 302–4, 319,
   540
   Beauvoir's meetings with, 328, 329–30,
   645n
   Bost and, 309, 322, 643n
   as catalyst in Beauvoir-Sartre relation-
   ship, 342–44
   marriage demands of, 342, 343, 414
   Sartre's troubles with, 342–43, 345,
   372, 397, 414, 648n
   Les Temps Modernes issue dedicated
   to, 310
Ehrmann, Jacques, 554, 653n–54n, 660n
Eisenhower, Dwight D., 446
Elaine's (New York), 607
Elementary Structures of Kinship (Lévi-Strauss), 410
Eliot, George (Mary Ann Evans), 70–71,
   388, 624n
Elkaïm-Sartre, Arlette, 481, 482, 483,
   486, 507, 531, 536, 539, 540, 562,
   563, 564, 576, 579, 583, 595, 660n,
   666n, 667n
   acquiescence of, 461–62, 485
   Adieux attacked by, 597, 599
   adopted by Sartre, 496, 497, 499, 508,
   509, 518, 523–24, 592, 593
   Beauvoir-Sartre relationship publicly
   disparaged by, 597, 599, 601
   Beauvoir's relationship with, 499, 517,
   597, 598
   Cahiers pour une morale and, 589–90
   first interview given by, 599–600
   holidays and, 485, 508, 535
   Lévy and, 569–70, 571, 574, 577–78
   as literary executor, 598, 599–600, 601
   Sartre moved into new apartment by,
   566
   Sartre's affair with, 461–62, 479, 485,
   495–96, 559, 561
   Sartre's death and, 584, 585, 586
   Sartre's flat emptied by, 588–90, 678n

Sartre's refusal to discuss, 561
   on Sartre's rift with Beauvoir, 581–82
   Sylvie's relationship with, 508, 565, 568
Elle, 527
Ellis, Havelock, 432, 433, 437
Ellison, Ralph, 412, 650n
Emerson, Ralph Waldo, 623n
Equipe Social, 109, 111, 117
Etcherelli, Claire, 520, 593
Ethan Frome (Wharton), 365
Ethics of Ambiguity, The (*Pour une morale de l'ambiguité*) (Beauvoir),
   269, 297, 321–22, 324, 380, 638n,
   645n
Etoile, 254
Etre et le néant, L' (Sartre), see *Being and Nothingness*
Europe No. 1, 533
Evans, Mary, 544
Existentialism, 269, 311, 317, 347, 452,
   655n–63n
   All Men Are Mortal and, 309–10
   and Aron's remark about Husserl, 187
   Beauvoir's essays on, for *Les Temps Modernes*, 320–21
   Beauvoir's philosophical readings and,
   233–34, 240, 262, 271
   The Blood of Others and, 305, 306–7
   Camus and, 292, 641n
   clothing associated with, 360, 402
   as expression of youthful revolt, 402
   literary criticism and, 320–21
   Pyrrhus et Cinéas and, 270
   Sartre's formulation of, 187, 231–32,
   233–34
   Sartre's move away from, 466, 668n
   The Second Sex and, 380, 381, 382,
   385, 386, 390, 432, 433–34, 436, 549
   supplanted by new theories, 473, 520,
   521
   Useless Mouths and, 267–68
Existentialism and the Wisdom of Nations (*L'Existentialisme et la sagesse des nations*) (Beauvoir),
   362, 645n
Express, L', 596, 599–600

Fabius, Laurent, 616
Faguet, Emile, 90
"Famille Cornichon, La" (Beauvoir), 68,
   623n, 638n, 678n
"Famille Fenouillard, La" (Beauvoir), 68
Family, 305, 310, 313, 324, 362, 383,
   388, 413, 444, 449, 454, 463, 471,
   473, 483, 507, 532, 539, 547, 561,
   571, 593, 633n

Family, *cont.*
  adherence to "Sartrian ideal" in, 515
  Algren and, 344, 401, 405, 406–7, 409,
    476
  Arlette's adoption and, 497–98, 499
  Dolores and, 342, 343–44, 345, 414
  gossip in, 402, 403–4
  hangouts of, 316, 402–3
  in loco parentis roles in, 224–26,
    263–64, 272, 659n
  members of, 197, 198, 214, 316, 401–2,
    445
  as new social order, 197
  Nobel Prize and, 493, 494
  Sartre's lovers welcomed by, 462, 463
  solipsistic world of, 284, 288
  Sylvie and, 508
  in World War II, 224–26, 227, 237,
    247, 272, 273, 275, 278, 279, 284
  see also specific members
Family Idiot: Gustave Flaubert, The
    (Sartre), 466
  and Sartre's fascination with Flaubert,
    163, 516–17, 518
  writing of, 522, 532, 533, 534, 539,
    541, 562, 563, 569, 571
Farewell to Adolescence (Mauriac),
    107
Farrell, James T., 388, 650n
Farrow, Mia, 607
Faulkner, William, 199, 208, 393
  Algren contrasted with, 368
  Gallimard's reception for, 465
  L'Invitée influenced by, 229
  read by Beauvoir, 126, 164, 368, 649n,
    651n
Fauré, Christine, 386, 675n
Faux, Claude, 487
Federal Bureau of Investigation (FBI),
    446, 455, 662n
Feminine Mystique, The (Friedan),
    525–26, 546, 602
feminism, 463
  abortion rights and, 543, 547, 548,
    550, 552
  of Beauvoir, 411, 453, 478–79, 531,
    542, 543–57, 559, 562, 571, 572–73,
    599, 602–4, 606, 618, 652n, 658n,
    663n, 672n, 674n–75n
  Beauvoir's increasing radicalism and,
    556–57
  Beauvoir's unfulfilled book project and,
    549
  consciousness raising in, 665n
  contraception issue and, 552
  electoral politics, 555

exaltation of biological differences in,
    551
  legal registration of terms and, 552–53
  May '68 uprising and, 535–36, 555
  political groups aligned with, 548
  as refuge for Beauvoir during Sartre's
    illness, 572, 604
  rejection of Beauvoir's underpinnings
    in, 553–54
  The Second Sex and, 390–91, 478–79,
    554, 654n
  U.S. women's movement and, 525–26,
    545
  warring factions and, 550–52, 553–54
Femme de demain, La (Lamy), 654n
Femme rompue, La (Beauvoir), *see*
    Woman Destroyed, The
"Femme rompue, La" ("The Woman
    Destroyed") (Beauvoir), 526, 527
Fifth Seal, The (Aldanov), 365, 649n
Figaro, Le, 299, 311
Fitzgerald, F. Scott, 661n
Flair, 415–16, 417, 421
Flanner, Janet (Genêt), 409, 446
Flaubert, Gustave, 271, 572, 600
  Beauvoir's involvement with, 516–17
  Jollivet's interest in, 163
  Sartre's fascination with, 163, 516–17,
    518
  Sartre's volumes on, *see Family Idiot:*
    Gustave Flaubert, The
Flies, The (Les Mouches) (Sartre):
  Berlin production of, 372
  Paris productions of, 272, 274
    280, 282, 284, 289
  Useless Mouths and, 267
Florence family, 37, 621n
Flowering Judas (Porter), 651n
Foley, Martha, 377
Fontaine, 317
Force de l'age, La (Beauvoir), *see*
    Prime of Life, The
Force of Circumstance (La Force des
    choses) (Beauvoir), 459, 644n,
    647n, 660n, 665n
  on aging, 539, 540–41
  Algren's rage over, 500–501, 658n,
    662n
  blurring of facts in, 486
  critical response to, 658n
  Dolores affair in, 302, 303–4
  "I was gypped" phrase in, 469–70, 506
  reading from, at Beauvoir's funeral, 617
  Sartre's political activism in, 447, 486
  space dedicated to Sartre vs. Beauvoir
    in, 447, 469, 486, 595

Sylvie's response to, 506
see also Beauvoir, Simone de, memoirs of
Ford, John, 216
Forster, E. M., 229
Foucault, Michel, 562, 573, 672n
Fouque, Antoinette, 552, 553
"Four Days in Madrid" (Beauvoir), 300
Four Hundred Blows, The, 668n
Four Million, The (Henry), 365
France, Anatole, 90
France Libre, La, 298
France-Observateur, 474
France-Soir, 474, 477
Francis, Claude, 597, 632n
Frank, Bernard, 401, 659n
Franqui, Carlos, 474
"Freedom and Liberation" (Beauvoir), 648n
Free Zone:
    Beauvoir and Sartre's biking holiday in (1942), 265–66
    mission for Socialism and Liberty in, 255, 257–58
French Institute (Berlin), 187–88, 189
French Institute (Lisbon), 300
French Women's League, 430
Friedan, Betty, 501, 525–26, 546, 556, 602, 609
Friends of *La Cause du peuple*, 537, 538, 544
Front Libération National (FLN) (Algeria), 452, 477, 480, 488
Fuller, Margaret, 623n

Gaddis, William, 501–2
Gallimard, *see* Editions Gallimard
Gallimard, Gaston:
    accused of collaboration, 260, 642n
    Les Temps Modernes and, 299, 642n
Gallimard, Michel, 472
Gallimard, Robert, 589, 652n
    Beauvoir's unpublished writings and, 623n, 638n
    Nobel Prize affair and, 494
    Sartre's unpublished writings and, 598, 599, 660n, 667n
Gandhi, Indira, 555, 610
Gandillac, Maurice de, 127, 134, 138, 243
    Beauvoir's friendship with, 125, 126, 139
    on Beauvoir's intellectual abilities, 125, 269, 627n
    Catholic ideology of, 125, 126

Meyrignac visited by, 148
    on Sartre and Beauvoir's examination performance, 145–46
Gang from the Bois de Boulogne, 139
Garric, Robert, 109, 111, 117
Gauche Prolétarienne, 535, 537, 562–63, 570.
Gautier, Jean-Jacques, 311
Gavi, Philippe, 568, 574
Geismar, Alain, 536, 568, 569
Generation of Vipers (Wylie), 438
Genet, Jean, 294, 348–49, 431, 432, 562, 657n, 659n
    Beauvoir and Sartre avoided by, 402
    on Beauvoir-Sartre relationship, 631n
    Sartre's book on, 448, 466, 667n–68n
    on *Useless Mouths*, 268
Geneva Convention, 550
Gerassi, Chantal, 609
Gerassi, Fernando, 130, 175, 198, 331
    Beauvoir's prudery and, 119
    Beauvoir's visits in New York with, 327, 328, 329, 340, 377
    emigration of, to U.S., 237, 243
    Hélène's relationship with, 164
    politics and, 208–9, 217, 220
    wedding of, 133, 146
Gerassi, John, 198, 260, 327, 329, 496, 544, 606, 607, 609
Gerassi, Stépha (neé Estepha Awdyko-vicz), 129, 130, 132, 134, 146, 159, 164, 166, 198, 208–9, 331, 369, 627n
    on Algren-Beauvoir relationship, 377
    background of, 115
    Beauvoir's nighttime adventures and, 117–18, 119
    Beauvoir's prudery and, 119–20, 125
    Beauvoir's self-absorption and, 154
    Beauvoir's visits in New York with, 327, 328, 329–30, 340, 373, 374, 377, 421, 606
    birth control and, 373, 374, 377
    Dolores affair and, 328, 329–30
    emigration of, to U.S., 237, 243
    GéGé not introduced to, 123
    as Le Coins' governess, 115–16, 133–34
    wedding of, 133, 146
Germany, Nazi, 213, 214, 220, 224
    surrender of France to, 239
    Western Europe invaded by, 234, 235
    see also World War II
Giacometti, Alberto, 198, 246, 326, 406, 409, 454
    accident of, in *The Words*, 469
    Beauvoir's friendship with, 284, 314,

Giacometti, Alberto, *cont.*
    323–24, 366–67, 401, 643*n*–44*n*
    as model for Blomart, 367
    Sartre's relationship with, 324, 469
Giacometti, Annette, 323, 367, 401, 652*n*
Giacometti, Diego, 284
Gide, André, 257, 291
    read by Beauvoir, 97, 102, 217
    taught in Beauvoir's classes, 176–77,
        203, 213
Gill, Brendan, 439
Gilligan, Carol, 631*n*
Giscard d'Estaing, Valéry, 546, 572, 586,
    677*n*
Gobeil, Madeleine, 464, 492, 501, 505
God's Little Acre (Caldwell), 651*n*
Goldman, Olive Remington, 655*n*, 664*n*
Goldmann, Pierre, 574
Gontier, Fernande, 597, 632*n*
Gorz, André (André Horst), 463, 484,
    577, 581, 585
Gould, Florence, 296, 642*n*
Goytisolo, Juan, 445, 476
Graham, Nan, 606, 608
Grand Meaulnes, Le (Alain-Fournier),
    103–5
Grasset, 208, 209, 634*n*
Gray, Francine du Plessix, 582
Great Gatsby, The (Fitzgerald), 352
Gréco, Juliette, 345, 404, 406, 476
Greene, Graham, 393
Greer, Germaine, 609
Grenier, Jean, 270, 638*n*
La Grillère, 24, 77, 134–35, 204, 206,
    216, 220, 222, 225, 226, 492, 615
    Beauvoir's holidays at, 105, 146, 148–
        150, 204
    parties at, 84–85
    Sartre's visit to, 148–50, 155, 168, 630*n*
Gros, Brigitte, 553–54
Groupe du Lycée Buffon, 254
Groupe du Musée de l'Homme, 254, 285
Guardian (Manchester), 539–40
Guevara, Che, 474, 533, 668*n*
Guggenheim, Mary, 333–34, 340–41, 384,
    501
Guillaumin, Colette, 551, 675*n*
Guille, Pierre, 139, 185, 243, 349, 629*n*,
    631*n*
    Beauvoir and Sartre's holiday with
        (1932), 179, 180
    Beauvoir's affair with, 172, 189
    marriage and domesticity of, 198, 264
    Mme. Morel's liaison with, 160
Gulliver's Travels (Swift), 66, 102
Guyonnet, René, 446

Halimi, Gisèle, 480, 487, 553, 602
Hammersmith Art Theatre, 350
Hardwick, Elizabeth, 387–88, 438
Hardy, Thomas, 365
harkis, 487–88
Harper's Bazaar, 297, 333
Harvard University, 326, 330
Hayman, Ronald, 259, 496
Hayworth, Rita, 350
Hegel, G. W. F., 233, 240, 262, 271,
    357, 433
Heidegger, Martin, 233, 258, 262, 433
Hemingway, Ernest, 164, 229, 316, 661*n*
Hennequin, Claude, 550, 551
Henry, O. (William Sydney Porter), 365
Hindemith, Paul, 461
Histoire de la littérature française
    (Lanson), 59
"Historical Music," 279–80, 282, 284,
    296, 640*n*
History of the Conquest of Mexico, The
    (Prescott), 393
History of the United States (Maurois),
    368
Hitler, Adolf, 213, 216, 221, 237
Hoffmann, Stanley, 548
Holland, 234, 235, 478
Holy Willies, the, 124, 125, 127
Hook, Sidney, 400
Hôpital Cochin, 588, 591, 614
Hôpital Sainte-Anne, 191–92
Horst, André (André Gorz), 463, 484,
    577, 581, 585
Hotel Aubusson, 272, 277
Hotel du Danemark, 243, 249
Hotel du Pont-Royal, 403
Hotel L'Aiglon, 486, 671*n*
Hotel La Rochefoucauld (Rouen), 181,
    195
Hotel Lincoln, 327
Hotel Louisiane, 285, 301, 318
Hotel Mistral, 249, 263, 272
Hotel Pont-Royal, 316, 317
Hughes, Langston, 374
Hugo, Victor, 367
Huis Clos (No Exit) (Sartre), 293, 323
Humanité, L', 184
Hume, David, 128
Hungary, 461
Husserl, Edmund, 187, 508

Ibsen, Henrik, 97
"Idéalisme moral et réalisme politique"
    (Beauvoir), 645*n*
Illustration, L', 184
Imitation of Christ, The, 65, 69

"Immoral Existentialism," 456–57, 666n
"Indirect Language and the Voices of
    Silence" (Merleau-Ponty), 452
Indochina, 399, 520
    French war in, 513, 665n
    see also Vietnam War
Institut Adeline Désir, see Cours
    Adeline Désir
Institut Sainte-Marie, 120
    Beauvoir as assistant at, 112, 136
    Beauvoir as student at, 94–95, 96, 100
International Herald-Tribune, 545
International War Crimes Tribunal, see
    Russell Tribunal
Invisible Man (Ellison), 650n
Invitée, L' (She Came to Stay)
    (Beauvoir), 228–32, 273, 277, 286,
    287, 294, 296, 309–10, 391, 409,
    467, 531, 633n, 634n, 678n
    critical response to, 282, 284, 638n
    Elizabeth in, 228–29, 230, 636n
    Françoise in, 230, 523, 636n
    genesis of, 206–7
    Gerbert in, 231
    literary influences on, 229
    loneliness and alienation in, 307
    Olga trio and, 207, 231, 598
    Pierre in, 228, 229–30
    publication of, 265, 272, 281, 282,
        638n, 640n
    sales of, 284
    Sartre's philosophical formulations
        and, 231–32
    setting of, 231
    writing of, 212–13, 216, 223, 228,
        232, 233–34, 240, 241, 255
Ionesco, Eugène, 572
Ireland, Republic of, 604
Irving, Washington, 66
Israel, 478, 550
    Beauvoir, Sartre, and Lévy's trip to
        (1978), 575–77, 677n
    Beauvoir and Sartre's trip to (1967),
        519, 526
Italian Chronicles, The (Sismondi),
    267–68, 309
Italy, 283
    Beauvoir and Algren's holiday in
        (1949), 410
    Beauvoir and Sartre's holiday in
        (1946), 323
    see also Rome, Beauvoir and Sartre's
        summer holidays in
"It's About Time" (Beauvoir), 415–16

J'accuse, 537, 539, 550

Jacob, Max, 100
James, Henry, 365, 650n
Japan, Beauvoir and Sartre's trip to
    (1966), 478, 519
Jeanson, Francis:
    Algerian crisis and, 452, 477–78
    on Beauvoir's feminism, 383, 546
    on Beauvoir's friendships with women,
        511
    on "Sartrian ideal," 515
Jerusalem Prize, 572
Jeux sont faits, Les (The Chips Are
    Down), 347–48, 350, 649n
Jews:
    anti-Semitism and, 124, 236, 242, 278,
        363, 636n–37n
    measures against, in World War II,
        242, 296, 636n–37n, 642n
Jollivet, Simone, 195, 220, 226, 598, 601
    Beauvoir's meeting with, 163–64
    Sartre's affair with, 162–64
Jones, Gloria, 501
Jones, James, 476, 501
Jospin, Lionel, 616
Journals (Gide), 217
Joyce, James, 164, 198–99, 465, 661n

Kafka, Franz, 219, 271
Kahn-Weiler, 285
Kanapa, Jean, 226, 251, 412
Kant, Immanuel, 128, 187, 271
Kautsky, Karl, 220
Kaye, Danny, 377
Keefe, Terry, 388, 662n, 665n
Khrushchev, Nikita, 464, 488–89
Kingslow, Janice, 658n
Kinsey, Alfred C., 393, 432, 656n
Kipling, Rudyard, 44, 66
Knock on Any Door (Motley), 650n
Knopf, Alfred A., 416, 432, 433, 435
Knopf, Alfred A., Jr., 437
Knopf, Blanche, 416, 418, 432, 433, 435–
    436, 664n
Alfred A. Knopf, Inc., 421, 427, 434,
    436, 439
Koestler, Arthur, 316–17, 357, 406, 416,
    427, 449, 659n
    Beauvoir's affair with, 316, 361, 658n
    marital problems of, 389
    politics of, 361, 362, 370
    in quarrels with Sartre and Camus,
        361, 369–70
    as writer, 361, 374
Kontowicz, Amanda, 420, 429, 455, 471,
    658n
Korean War, 422, 423–24

Kosakievicz, Olga, *see* Bost, Olga
Kosakievicz, Wanda (Marie Ollivier),
    197, 219, 228, 236, 237, 243, 249,
    250, 264, 292, 311, 445, 531, 598,
    600
  acting career of, 280, 313, 323, 404,
    463
  Arlette's adoption and, 497, 498, 499
  background of, 186
  Beauvoir's memoirs criticized by, 476
  Beauvoir's relationship with, 210, 231,
    261, 262, 286, 303, 498
  financial support for, 223, 263, 584,
    657n
  living with Sartre, 272, 273
  marriage issue and, 234–35
  nickname for, 204
  Sartre introduced to, 201–2
  Sartre's affair with, 202, 208, 210,
    225, 227, 234–35, 272, 273, 289,
    303, 344, 345, 349, 404, 463, 479,
    481, 486
  Sartre's holidays with, 561, 564
Kronhausen, E. and P., 493
Kruks, Sonia, 639n
Kuprin, Aleksandr, 649n

Labiche, Eugène-Marin, 59
Lacan, Jacques, 284, 293, 390, 464, 473,
    531, 533, 655n
La Coste, Simone de la Chaume, 77, 78,
    624n
Lafourie, Serge, 479
Lagache, Daniel, 191
Lalande, Joseph-Jérome Le Français de,
    145
Lamblin, Bianca, *see* Bienenfeld, Bianca
Lamy, Etienne, 654n
Lang, Jack, 616
Lange, Monique, 445, 476
Lanson (historian), 59
Lanzmann, Claude, 450, 454, 463, 465,
    471, 476, 482, 483, 496, 511, 589,
    614, 636n, 673n, 679n
  and adoption of Sylvie, 592, 593
  Algerian crisis and, 487
  Beauvoir freed from age by, 445
  Beauvoir's affair with, 442–45, 448,
    451, 460, 468, 665n, 666n
  as Beauvoir's champion defender, 522
  Beauvoir's first meeting with, 442–43
  Beauvoir's funeral and, 615, 616, 617
  Beauvoir's travels with, 444, 448, 665n
  France-Soir articles and, 474, 477
  as only man with whom Beauvoir
    lived, 444, 460
  physical appearance of, 443
  in rapprochement with Communists,
    447
  Sartre-Lévy conversations and, 580–81,
    582
  Sartre's death and, 585–587, 588
  Sartre's relationship with, 444, 665n
  Shoah made by, 442, 612–13
  sister's depression and, 498
  Les Temps Modernes and, 442–43,
    498, 521, 522, 577, 611–12
Lapassade, Georges, 535
Larbaud, Valéry-Nicolas, 102
Larousse, 66
Lassithiotakis, Hélène, 566, 575
Lawrence, D. H., 229, 387, 393, 512
Lawrence, T. E., 266, 393, 639n, 656n
League for the Rights of Women, 550
le Bon de Beauvoir, Sylvie, 499, 506–13,
    517–18, 522, 523, 531, 533, 534,
    539, 541, 558, 559, 560, 566, 578,
    581, 582, 584, 604, 632n, 666n,
    673n, 676n
  adopted by Beauvoir, 509, 592–93
  age difference between Beauvoir and,
    507, 510, 511
  Arlette's relationship with, 508–9, 565,
    568
  background of, 503, 504
  at Beauvoir's funeral, 615, 616
  Beauvoir's illnesses and, 591, 605, 611,
    612, 613, 614, 615
  Beauvoir's travels with, 535, 561, 563,
    564, 565, 588, 602, 605–9, 611
  daily schedule of, 507
  emptying of Sartre's flat and, 588–89
  Françoise's death and, 506
  on Gobeil's relationship with Beauvoir,
    505
  Hélène's relationship with, 593
  Mme. Mancy met by, 670n–71n
  as philosophy teacher, 507, 508
  Sartre's death and, 585, 586, 587, 588
  Sartre's relationship with, 507–8, 517,
    535, 565
  speculation about Beauvoir's relation-
    ship with, 508–13, 593
  start of Beauvoir's friendship with,
    503–4
  unpublished writings and, 678n, 679n
  ZaZa compared to, 509–10
Le Boterf, Hervé, 639n–40n
Le Bris, Michel, 536
Le Coin, Elisabeth (ZaZa), 82, 94, 97,
    103, 110, 139, 150–53
  Beauvoir's fictional writings and, 147,

178, 205, 228, 309, 449, 624n, 630n
Beauvoir's friendship with, 75–81,
    86–87, 96, 114, 120, 133
Beauvoir's last letter from, 151
Beauvoir's summer visits with, 80,
    114–16, 130–31
birthday present given to, 81
bobbed haircut of, 76, 91, 113
books recommended by, 78–79
competitiveness between Beauvoir and,
    78, 79
dancing classes taken by, 85
death of, 151–53, 175, 205, 309, 449,
    540, 594, 596
disfigured by fire, 76–77
erratic behavior of, 76, 80
family situation of, 75–76, 79–80
marriage as future for, 80, 87, 114,
    126, 130, 132
Merleau-Ponty's relationship with, 125–
    126, 130–34, 146, 147, 151, 152–53
physical appearance of, 76, 77, 151
reticence of, 80–81
sent to Berlin, 132–33, 150, 151
Sylvie compared to, 509–10
Le Coin, Madame, 78, 82, 146, 147, 150,
    151
Beauvoir's hatred for, 81
Françoise snubbed by, 114, 133–34
marriage of, 79–80
marriage plans, for ZaZa, 80, 87,
    114, 126, 130
Merleau-Ponty's courtship opposed by,
    126, 130–34
relaxed liberalism of, 75–76
Stépha and, 115, 116, 133–34
Le Coin, Maurice, 76, 78, 79, 80, 94,
    115, 116
Merleau-Ponty's courtship opposed by,
    132, 151, 152
Le Core, José, 120, 146
le Dantec, Jean-Pierre, 536
Leduc, Violette, 315, 349, 370, 463, 670n
Beauvoir's relationship with, 297–98,
    314, 348, 369, 394, 401–2, 420–21,
    504–5, 644n
stipend paid to, 394, 441, 644n, 657n
as writer, 314, 348, 492, 504–5
Lefebvre, Henri, 533
"Legend of Truth, The" ("La Légende
    de la vérité") (Sartre), 168
Léger, Fernan, 454
Legion of Honor, 606
L'Eglise, Michelle, see Vian, Michelle
Lehmann, Rosamond, 132, 173, 174,
    628n

Leibniz, Gottfried, 128, 139, 141, 143,
    262, 629n
Leiris, Michel, 198, 274, 291, 292, 295,
    358, 390, 401, 406, 409, 533, 655n
Beauvoir's solipsistic world widened
    by, 284–85
La Cause du peuple and, 537, 538
memoirs of, 284, 324
Les Temps Modernes and, 298
Leiris, Zette, 286–87, 292, 295, 358,
    390, 401
Beauvoir's solipsistic world widened
    by, 284–85
Lemaître, Jules, 90
Le Pen, Jean-Marie, 614
Lesseps, Emmanuèle de, 550, 551
Le Sueur, Meridel, 388
"Letter from Chicago" (Algren), 363,
    650n–51n
Lettres Françaises, Les, 260
Levesque, Marie-Louise, 77
Levi, Carlo, 416, 656n
China trip and, 456, 666n
Lévinas, Emmanuel, 575
Lévi-Strauss, Claude, 136, 334, 390, 410,
    531, 573, 655n, 672n
Sartre's break with, 467–68, 667n
Lévy, Benny (Pierre Victor), 529, 536,
    559, 561, 567–80, 584
in Adieux, 576, 577, 579, 582, 595
Arlette and, 569–70, 571, 574, 577–78
Beauvoir's conflict with, 575, 576–77
daily duties of, 570–71
French citizenship acquired by, 569,
    676n–77n
hired as Sartre's secretary, 569–70
opinions about, 574
revolutionary politics of, 568–69, 570
rumored campaign against, 578
Sartre's furniture given to, 590
as Sartre's intellectual heir, 576, 580
Sartre's published conversations with,
    568, 574, 575, 578–81, 582–83, 597
Les Temps Modernes and, 575, 577
Lévy, Georgette, 120, 124
Lévy, Raoul, 251, 252, 253
Liberation, 293–94, 295, 338, 407, 641n
"Year Zero" and, 363
Libération, 253, 575, 597, 616
Liberty Films, 337
Library Journal, 438–39
Light in August (Faulkner), 651n
Lindon, Jerome, 346
Lindop, Grevel, 17–18
"Lisa" (Beauvoir), 192, 195, 205,
    633n–34n

"Literature and Metaphysics"
("Littérature et métaphysique")
(Beauvoir), 320–21, 644n, 645n,
648n
Little Women (Alcott), 68–69, 623n–
624n
London, Beauvoir and Sartre's trip to
(1947), 349–50, 649n
London Magazine, 527–28
Long March, The (Beauvoir), 455–56
Look, 446
Los Angeles, Beauvoir's trip to (1947),
337–38, 646n
Luxembourg, 235
Lycée Buffon, 254
Lycée Camille Sée, 224
Lycée Henri-Quatre, 142
Lycée Janson de Sailly, 136–37
Lycée Jeanne d'Arc, 178, 180, 181, 182,
184, 185, 186–87, 189, 195–96, 507,
632n
Lycée Molière, 195, 197, 202, 218, 221,
222, 224, 238
  Eastern European students at, 213–14
Lycée Pasteur, 249
Lycée Victor Duruy, 159, 165, 238

McCall's, 493
McCarthy, Mary, 332, 384, 640n
McCarthy, Patrick, 290, 292, 641n
McCullers, Carson, 365
MacDonald, Dwight, 332, 339, 438
MacDonald, Nancy, 339
McGinley, Phyllis, 655n, 664n
McLaughlin, Richard, 306–7
MacMillan, James F., 622n
Madagascar, 399
Madame Bovary (Flaubert), 163,
516–17
Madrid:
  Beauvoir and Sartre's holiday in
  (1931), 175–76
  Beauvoir's writing assignment in
  (1945), 300–301
Maheu, René, 127–29, 130, 137, 138,
139, 146, 160, 313, 320, 371, 372
  Beauvoir nicknamed "Castor" by, 127
  Beauvoir's rupture with, 172
  examination failed by, 145, 629n
  jealous of Sartre's relationship with
  Beauvoir, 145
  nature of Beauvoir's relationship with,
  129, 141, 142, 628n
  Sartre and Beauvoir introduced by,
  140–43
Mailer, Norman, 610

Mains sales, Les (*Dirty Hands*) (Sartre),
370, 373, 392 656n
"Malheurs de Marguerite, Les"
(Beauvoir), 67–68, 623n
Mallarmé, Stéphane, 100
Malraux, André, 257, 260, 291, 395
Malraux, Florence, 479
Mancy, Anne-Marie (née Schweitzer;
formerly Mme. Sartre), 180, 216,
219, 223, 226, 234, 367, 402, 534,
562
  Albert Schweitzer introduced to Sartre
  by, 464–65
  apartment shared by Sartre and, 322–
  323, 346, 414
  Beauvoir's concept of aging and, 440
  Beauvoir's relationship with, 217, 225
  bomb scare and, 483, 486
  Sartre pampered by, 198, 227
  Sartre's annual holiday with, 179, 185,
  197, 212
  Sartre's leave and, 225, 227
  Sylvie's meeting with, 670n–71n
Mancy, Monsieur, 180, 226, 227, 234,
562
  Beauvoir disdained by, 217, 225, 635n
  death of, 322
  Sartre's annual holiday with, 179, 185,
  197
Mandarins, The (*Les Mandarins*)
(Beauvoir), 237, 321, 424–28, 448,
449–50, 451, 452, 463, 523, 545,
636n, 639n, 644n, 667n
  Algren-Beauvoir affair recreated in,
  411, 419, 422–23, 425, 428, 449,
  457, 661n
  Algren enraged by, 428, 457–58, 471,
  472, 500, 658n
  American sections of, 662n
  banned by Catholic Church, 456–57,
  666n
  Beauvoir's feelings about, 270, 391,
  392, 424–25
  central plot of, 415, 425–26
  critical response to, 428, 450, 457,
  662n
  dedicated to Algren, 411, 428
  idea of human relationships in, 415,
  425
  lost manuscript pages of, 417
  objectives in, 412, 413
  postwar politics and, 412–13, 415,
  425–26, 660n
  Prix Goncourt awarded to, 427, 428,
  449, 453
  psychiatry in, 426

publication of, 427–28
readers' identification of characters in, 449, 662n
sales and earnings of, 453, 457
title of, 427
writing of, 392–93, 410–11, 427, 441, 443, 445, 447, 448
Manheim, Ralph, 648n
"Le Manifeste de 85," 554
"Manifesto of the 121," 480, 482
"Manifesto of the 343," 547, 550
Man with the Golden Arm, The (Algren), 335, 410, 419, 420, 471, 647n, 649n, 658n
Maoists, 534, 537, 539, 541, 548, 550, 562–63, 566, 568–69, 570, 574, 580
Mao Tse-tung, 456, 533, 536
Marcel, Gabriel, 208, 311, 320
"Marcelle" (Beauvoir), 195, 205, 633n
Marcellin, Raymond, 537
Margerie, Amédie de, 620n
"Marguerite" (Beauvoir), 195, 205, 634n, 678n
Marie-Claire, 161, 213, 217, 631n
Maritain, Jacques, 633n
Marseille:
  Beauvoir changed by year in, 180, 183
  Beauvoir's teaching assignment in, 167, 168, 169, 171, 175, 176–78, 180, 183, 186, 406
Martin, Henri, 665n
Martinique, 399
Marty, André, 446, 665n
Marx, Karl, 182, 533
Marxism, 252, 382, 426, 563, 666n, 668n
  Beauvoir's travel writing and, 301
  of Sartre, 466, 467, 473
Massif Central, Beauvoir's holiday in (1943), 277, 280, 281–82, 641n
Mathieu, Nicole-Claude, 551, 675n
Matthiesson, Peter, 501–2
Mauriac, Claude, 562
Mauriac, François, 107, 114–15, 284, 410
  Beauvoir and Merleau-Ponty's pilgrimage to country of, 126, 131
Maurois, André, 368, 660n
Mayer, Daniel, 257
May '68 uprising, 528, 530, 531, 532–36, 674n
  feminism arising from, 535–36, 555
  Sartre's statements in, 533, 534, 536
Mead, Margaret, 418, 438, 655n
Mégève, Beauvoir's skiing holidays in, 226, 311–12, 313
Melville, Herman, 259

Memoirs of a Dutiful Daughter (*Mémoires d'une jeune fille rangée*) (Beauvoir), 69, 76, 86, 459, 468, 504, 596, 646n
  Françoise's response to, 491
  ZaZa's death in, 151–52
  see also Beauvoir, Simone de, memoirs of
Mendès-France, Pierre, 452, 545
Menninger, Karl A., 438, 655n
Men Without Shadows (*Mort sans sépulture*) (Sartre), 349–50
Meredith, George, 131, 173, 174
Merleau-Ponty, Maurice, 122, 136, 138, 139, 198, 292, 319, 320, 357, 399, 406, 409, 637n
  Beauvoir's attack on, 452
  Beauvoir's friendship with, 124, 125–26, 129
  Beauvoir's pilgrimage to Bordeaux with, 126, 130–31
  death of, 485–86
  Resistance and, 251, 252–53, 255
  Les Temps Modernes and, 298, 313, 362, 395, 423, 452, 520
  ZaZa's relationship with, 125–26, 130–34, 146, 147, 151, 152–53
Merleau-Ponty, Monique, 151, 152
"Merleau-Ponty and Pseudo-Sartrism" (Beauvoir), 452, 663n
Mexico, 456, 604
  Beauvoir and Algren's trip to (1948), 371–74, 376–77, 414
  Sartre and Dolores's trip to (1949), 414
Meyrignac, 23, 24–25, 50, 42, 53, 54, 61, 62, 77, 93, 138, 206, 229, 441, 489, 615
  Beauvoir's holidays at, 46, 65, 67, 105, 106, 107, 121–22, 131, 146, 147, 148–50, 277
Michel, Georges, 564, 587–88
Mihloud, 613
Miller, Henry, 432
Millett, Kate, 606, 607, 608, 609, 654n
Mill on the Floss, The (Eliot), 70–71, 624n
Mills, C. Wright, 484
Mills College, 326
Ministry for the Rights of Women, 553, 555, 602–4
Ministry of Education, 167, 198, 224, 249, 278
Ministry of War, 47
Minuit (newspaper), 568
Miquel, Jean, 125

Miquel, Joseph, 125

Mitchell, Juliet, 609

Mitterrand, François, 606, 616
  feminism and, 553, 555, 599, 602–3,
    604
  in presidential elections, 546–47, 555,
    572, 602

Moby-Dick (Melville), 259

Moffatt, Ivan, 236–37, 505
  Beauvoir's visit in Los Angeles with,
    336–38, 646n, 647n
  wedding of, 313, 643n

Moffatt, Nathalie (Natasha) (née
    Sorokine), 226, 243, 244, 263, 323,
    349, 356, 634n
  Algren-Beauvoir affair hidden from,
    420, 661n
  background of, 214, 236
  Beauvoir's brutally frank account of,
    505–6
  Beauvoir's dismissal and, 277–78, 504
  Beauvoir's relationship with, 214,
    236–37, 249, 509
  Beauvoir's visit in Los Angeles with,
    337, 646n
  death of, 505, 506
  fictional characters modeled on, 237,
    449
  lovers of, 263, 264, 272, 278
  physical appearance of, 272, 506
  Resistance and, 250, 252, 286
  Sartre's relationship with, 214, 215,
    248–49
  wartime bicycle business of, 239, 241,
    257
  wedding of, 313, 643n

Monde, Le, 457, 535, 550, 666n

Monnier, Adrienne, 132, 164

"Monologue" (Beauvoir), 527

Montague, Ashley, 655n

Montaigne, Michel Eyquem de, 321

Montherlant, Henry-Marie-Joseph
    Millon de, 387, 435

Montparnasse Cemetery, 586–87, 615,
    616–17

Moravia, Alberto, 464

Moreau, Hégésippe, 59

Morel, Albert, 160

Morel, Jacqueline, 160, 220, 367

Morel, Madame, 185, 189, 202, 239,
    265, 349, 631n
  background of, 160
  Beauvoir's concept of aging and, 160,
    440
  Beauvoir's driving holidays with, 172,
    179, 180, 198

described in memoirs, 162
illness of, 367
Juan-les-Pins villa of, 160, 215, 216,
    485
Paris apartment of, as refuge for
    Beauvoir and Sartre, 358, 359–60
rumored liaisons of, 139, 160
social refinement of, 162

Morel, Madame, Loire Valley home of
    (La Pouèze), 160
  accommodations and life style at, 283,
    294, 304, 367
  Beauvoir and Sartre's holidays at,
    266–67, 270, 271, 277, 282–84, 285,
    294, 297, 304–5, 357, 363, 366,
    367–68, 424, 425
  as Beauvoir's wartime refuge, 220, 234,
    235, 237–38
  library at, 220, 267, 284, 366

Morel, Monsieur, 160, 367

Moret, Lucie (grandmother), see
    Brasseur, Lucie

Mormons, 393, 656n

Morocco, Beauvoir and Sartre's holiday
    in (1938), 212

Morrison, Toni, 609

Mort sans sépulture (Men Without
    Shadows) (Sartre), 349–50

Motley, Willard, 650n

Mots, Les (The Words) (Sartre), 235,
    451, 466, 469, 517, 573

Mouches, Les (Sartre), see Flies, The

Mouloudji, 406

Mouvement de Libération des Femmes
    (MLF), 543, 552–53

Mouvement du 22 Mars (M22M), 532,
    533

Muller, Henry, 209

Munich crisis (1938), 212

Mur, La (The Wall) (Sartre), 208, 227

Murphy, Muriel, 501–2

Musée Picasso, 657n

Musset, Alfred de, 367

"Must We Burn Sade?" (Beauvoir), 432,
    441, 452, 545, 622n–63n

Mutualité meetings, 493, 550, 572

Myrdal, Alva, 364, 365, 388

Myrdal, Gunnar, 364, 365, 368, 388

Nagel, Louis, 349–50, 362, 372, 443,
    649n

Nanterre, 532, 536

Napoleonic Code, 92

Nation, 446, 665n

National Book Award, 410, 421, 475

Nation and Family (Myrdal), 364

Nausea (*La Nausée*) (Sartre), 203, 208, 259, 629n
Navy, Yvon, 311
Naylor, Gloria, 609
Nazi-Soviet Pact, 243, 258
Neon Wilderness, The (Algren), 335
Netherlands, 234, 235, 478
Never Come Morning (Algren), 335, 337, 341, 648n
New Novel, 307, 346, 464, 522, 669n
New Orleans, Beauvoir and Algren's trip to (1948), 372, 373, 376, 652n
Newsweek, 539, 542
New Wave filmmakers, 668n
New York, Beauvoir's trips to, 421
    in 1947, 327–30, 333–34, 338–41
    in 1948, 371, 373, 374, 377–78
    in 1983, 606–8, 609
New York, Sartre's trips to:
    in 1945, 299, 300, 301, 303
    in 1945–46, 311–12, 313, 317, 319, 320, 321, 322
New Yorker, The, 307, 330, 333, 335, 382, 409, 607
New York Times, 327–28, 645n
Nietzsche, Friedrich Wilhelm, 163
Nixon, Richard M., 446
Nizan, Henriette, 130, 145, 185, 198, 629n, 631n
    Beauvoir and Sartre's outings with, 156–57
    on Beauvoir's entry into Sartre's group, 144
    on Beauvoir's physical appearance, 142–43
    resettled in America, 243
    spousal role accepted by, 157
Nizan, Paul, 127–28, 130, 160, 164, 184, 185, 198, 208, 629n
    Audry and, 182
    Beauvoir and Sartre's outings with, 156–57
    Communists' denunciations of, 243, 247
    death of, 243, 247
    literary career of, 169
    Sartre's friendship with, 142, 144, 156, 157, 258–59
    supplanted by Beauvoir, 144
Noailles, Marie-Laure de, 296, 642n
Nobel Prize, 670n
    refused by Sartre, 493–95, 500
No Exit (*Huis Clos*) (Sartre), 293, 323
Nom de l'homme: dialogue avec Sartre, Le (Lévy), 677n

North Africa:
    Beauvoir and Algren's holiday in (1949), 410
    Beauvoir and Sartre's holiday in (1932), 179, 180
    Beauvoir and Sartre's holiday in (1960), 420, 421, 661n
Norway, Beauvoir's holiday in (1980), 588
Not Without Laughter (Hughes), 374
Nouvelle Revue Française, 282, 298
Nouvelles Littéraires, Les, 311
Nouvelles Questions Féministes, 550–52, 675n
Nouvel Observateur, Le, 547, 576, 579, 581
Novick, Peter, 258
Number One (Dos Passos), 366

"Oeil pour oeil" (Beauvoir), 644n, 645n
Oeuvres complètes (Renard), 205
Offenbach, Jacques, 61, 143
Office of Cultural Relations, 326
Of Time and the River (Wolfe), 352
O'Hara, John, 388
Old Age (*La Vieillesse*) (Beauvoir), 528–529, 530, 533, 539–40, 542, 549, 674n
    Adieux as extension of, 595
    critical response to, 539
    research for, 531–32
Ollivier, Albert, 299
Ollivier, Marie, *see* Kosakievicz, Wanda
Opéra, 311
Ordeal of Richard Feverel, The (Meredith), 131
Ordre, L', 311
Organisation de l'Armée Secrète (OAS), 483
Orthodrine, 341, 460, 666n
Osservatore romano, L', 456–57, 666n
Other Kingdom, The (Rousset), 359
Other Voices, Other Rooms (Capote), 374
"Otto List," 260, 296, 642n
Ox-Bow Incident, The, 366

Padilla, Huberto, 550
Pagliero, 660n
Pale Horse, Pale Rider (Porter), 651n
Pantheon Books, 606, 608
Parain, Brice, 206, 207, 212, 213, 243, 265
Parallel Lives (Plutarch), 121
Pardaillon, 274, 581

Pardo, Geraldine (GéGé), 146, 185, 220, 222, 223, 225, 287, 311, 463, 615, 641n
  Beauvoir's prudery and, 119, 120
  marriage of, 164, 198, 209, 218
  nighttime adventures of, 118
  personality and demeanor of, 116–17
  Sartre's affair with, 202
  Stépha not introduced to, 123
Pardo, Monsieur, 218, 220
Paris Book Fair, 572
Paris-Match, 449
Paris Review, 493, 505
Paris-Soir, 218
Parshley, H. M., 432–37, 653n, 654n, 663n–64n
  death of, 439
  fee paid to, 436–37, 664n
  philosophical terms and, 433–34, 436, 663n
Partisan Review, 329, 332, 335, 339, 361
Pasquier, Françoise, 553, 604
Pathé-Cinéma, 277
Paulhan, Jean, 291, 298
Père Lachaise Cemetery, 256, 491, 586, 615, 638n
Péron, Alfred, 130, 254
Perrault, Charles, 36, 66, 492, 613, 623n
Pétain, Marshal Henri, 256
Peter Ibbetson (Du Maurier), 374
Petit Français illustré, Le, 66
Petits Camarades, 629n
Philadelphia, Beauvoir's trip to (1947), 331–33
Philippe, Gérard, 348
Phillips, William, 328, 332, 416, 438
Pia, Pascal, 293
Piatier, Jacqueline, 517, 527
Picabia, Gabrielle, 254
Picabia, Jeannine, 254
Picasso, Pablo, 284, 292, 299, 454, 589
Pilgrim's Progress, The (Bunyan), 69
Pingaud, Bernard, 586
Piovene, Guido, 464
Plaza, Monique, 551, 675n
Pléiade, 600
Plumed Serpent, The (Lawrence), 393
Poe, Edgar Allan, 352
Poincaré, Raymond, 46
Point, Le (Bruckner), 596
Poirot-Delpech, Bertrand, 596, 678n
Poland, 216, 220, 489, 604
Politics, 332
Pompidou, Georges, 674n
Pontalis, J. B., 310, 311, 357
Pontremoli, Michel, 125

Popular Astronomy, 102
Porter, Katherine Anne, 368, 651n
  on The Second Sex, 437–38
Portrait of a Man Unknown (Sarraute), 315
Portugal, Beauvoir's writing assignment in (1945), 300–301
Potomak, Le (Cocteau), 128, 131, 628n
Pouèze, La, see Morel, Madame, Loire Valley home of
Pouillon, Jean, 250, 251–52, 409, 463, 584
  Lévy and, 577, 578, 581
  Sartre's death and, 585, 586
Poulain de la Barre, François, 389, 654n
Poupée Modèle, La, 38, 66
Pour une morale de l'ambiguité (The Ethics of Ambiguity) (Beauvoir), 269, 297, 321–22, 324, 380, 638n, 645n
Powell, Rev. Adam Clayton, 329
Power and Liberty (Pouvoir et Liberté) (Sartre and Lévy), 677n
Power and the Glory, The (Greene), 393
Prescott, William H., 393
Prime of Life, The (La Force de l'age) (Beauvoir), 177, 295, 459, 469, 502, 639n, 641n
  on interviews with women, 382–83
  sales of, 485
  see also Beauvoir, Simone de, memoirs of
Privileges (Beauvoir), 269, 452–53, 545, 663n, 665n
Prix de la Pléiade, 291
Prix Fémina, 505
Prix Formentor, 476
Prix Goncourt, 285, 286, 411, 505, 572
  awarded to The Mandarins, 427, 428, 449, 453
Prix Renaudot, 285
Proust, Marcel, 102, 126, 600
Psyche et Po (Psychoanalysis and Politics), 552–53
psychoanalysis, 466, 467
psychology, 553
  distrusted by Beauvoir, 191, 390, 392, 426, 633n, 655n
  in The Second Sex, 390
Psychology of Sex, The (Ellis), 437
Pucciani, Oreste, 505
Puig, André, 563, 568, 569
Putain respecteuse, La (The Respectful Prostitute) (Sartre), 349–50
Pylon (Faulkner), 368
Pyrrhus et Cinéas (Beauvoir), 269, 270–271, 282, 638n, 639n, 667n

Quand prime le spiritual (Beauvoir), *see*
    *When Things of the Spirit Come
    First*
Queneau, Jeanine, 284, 286–87, 401
Queneau, Raymond, 198, 284, 291, 298,
    316, 401, 406, 427, 660*n*
Questions Féministes, 550–52, 675*n*
Quincy, Thomas de, 17–18

Radford, C. B., 386, 555–56, 653*n*
Radiguet, Raymond, 97, 102
Radiodiffusion Nationale, 279–80, 282,
    284, 296, 640*n*
Radio-Luxembourg, 533
Rahv, Phillip, 352, 658*n*
Ramadier, 357–58, 366
Ramateulle, Beauvoir and Sartre's holiday
    . in (1948), 373, 374
Randolph-Macon College, 326
Rassemblement Démocratique Révolu-
    tionnaire (RDR), 358–59, 394, 399,
    400, 412, 658*n*
Rassemblement du Peuple Français
    (RPF), 358
Rathenau, Emil, 220
Rats, Les (Frank), 659*n*
Ray, Evelyne, 462–63, 479, 481, 486, 498
Reagan, Ronald, 613, 646*n*
Renard, Jules, 205
Reprieve, The (Sartre), 293
Resistance, 273, 279, 281, 285, 294, 315,
    360, 417
    Beauvoir's articles for newspaper of,
        293–94, 300–301, 641*n*
    Beauvoir unaware of, 243–44
    The Blood of Others and, 283, 305–6,
        307
    Camus in, 291, 292, 293, 295, 641*n*
    literary, 274
    origins of, 253
    Sartre's attempts at involvement in,
        247–48, 249, 250–55, 257–58, 260–
        261, 262, 274–75, 276, 296, 637*n*–
        638*n*
    Sartre's knowledge of, 253–54
    see also Socialism and Liberty
Respectful Prostitute, The (*La Putain
    respecteuse*) (Sartre), 349–50
Revolución, 474
Revue d'en face, La, 551
Revue Française, La, 112, 282
Ribowska, Malka, 679*n*
Rideau cramoisi, Le, 656*n*
Rimbaud, Arthur, 100
RKO studios, 337, 338

Roads to Freedom, The (*Les Chemins
    de la liberté*) (Sartre), 208
Robbe-Grillet, Allain, 669*n*
Robinson Crusoe (Defoe), 66
Rollo, Charles J., 438
Rome, Beauvoir and Sartre's summer
    holidays in, 196, 410, 486, 488, 489,
    492, 535, 561–62, 563–64, 565, 568,
    573, 578, 594
Romola (Eliot), 388
Room of One's Own, A (Woolf), 390
Roosevelt, Eleanor, 421
Rosenberg, Ethel, 446
Rosenberg, Julius, 446
Rostand, Edmond, 59
Rotonde, Café, 111, 203, 241, 242
Roudy, Yvette, 553, 602–3, 604, 610, 616
Rouen:
    Audry's friendship with Beauvoir in,
        182–83
    Beauvoir and Sartre's trip to (1938),
        210
    Beauvoir's dislike of, 189
    Beauvoir's teaching assignment in, 178,
        179, 180–96
    L'Invitée set in, 231
    room taken by Beauvoir in, 181, 632*n*
    Sylvie's teaching post in, 507
Roulet, Hélène de (sister), *see* Beauvoir,
    Henriette-Hélène de
Roulet, Lionel de (brother-in-law), 185,
    210, 226, 233, 287, 300, 301, 310,
    369, 421, 489, 491, 586, 592, 614
    background of, 201
    Beauvoir sisters' first meeting with,
        200–201
    illness of, 209
    at Simone's funeral, 615, 616
    wedding of, 237
Rousseau, Jean-Jacques, 143
Rousset, David, 358–59, 361, 370, 394,
    399, 400, 656*n*
Route Napoléon, 212
Rowbotham, Sheila, 609
Roy, Claude, 534
Royal Air Force (RAF), 252, 281
Rubenstein, Arthur, 572
Russell, Lord Bertrand, 569–70, 575
Russell Tribunal, 478, 519, 520, 526,
    531, 546, 569–70, 670*n*
Russian Revolution, 50
Rybalka, Michel, 600, 641*n*

Sabosawa, Mari, 658*n*
Sade, Marquis de, 432, 441, 452, 545,
    662*n*–63*n*

Sagan, Françoise, 525, 539, 673n
Saint Genet (Sartre), 448, 466, 667n–
    668n
Saint-Germain-des-Prés, 198, 208, 213,
    217, 276, 316, 402, 432, 440, 443,
    522
    documentary about, 417, 660n
Saint-Rémy-les-Chevreause, Beauvoir and
    Sartre's holiday in (1947), 344–45
Salacrou, Armand, 284, 304, 311
Salacrou, Lucienne, 284
Salazar, Antonio, 301
Saler, Steve, 539
Sanctuary (Faulkner), 649n
Sang des autres, Le (Beauvoir), *see*
    Blood of Others, The
Sarraute, Nathalie, 464, 640n, 644n, 669n
    Beauvoir's relationship with, 297, 298,
        314–15
    Nizan's friendship with, 156, 157
Sartre, Jean-Paul, 18
    aging as concern of, 191
    Algerian crisis and, 452, 468, 477–78,
        480, 481, 482, 483–84, 486, 487, 491
    Algren's meetings with, 406, 407, 471–
        472
    ambition of, 141–42
    American Transcendentalists and, 623n
    anger and disillusion of, 461
    annual lectureship in Japan sought by,
        166–67
    anti-Communism of, 253
    antics of, as university student, 139
    apolitical period of, 184, 209
    appointed to CNE, 273, 275
    Arlette adopted by, 496, 497, 499, 508,
        509, 518, 523–24, 592, 593
    Aron's rupture with, 313
    Audry's friendship with, 182–83
    autobiography of, 235
    "baby-sitting" for, 499, 670n
    Beauvoir as chief spokesperson for
        philosophy of, 307
    Beauvoir buried beside, 615, 617
    Beauvoir encouraged to write by, 166,
        173, 174, 178, 206, 228, 270
    Beauvoir's dismissal and, 278–79
    Beauvoir's first book and, 206, 207–8,
        209
    Beauvoir's memoir writing and, 447,
        458, 460, 467–68, 469, 486, 514,
        595
    Beauvoir's notebook on health of, 562,
        595
    Beauvoir's passion for Lehmann hidden
        from, 628n
    Beauvoir's relationship with, *see*
        Beauvoir, Simone de, Sartre's
        relationship with
    Beauvoir's tape-recorded conversations
        with, 573, 594, 596, 597
    Beauvoir's U.S. lecture tour and, 330
    Beauvoir's writings under byline of,
        293–94, 567, 641n
    Beauvoir urged to analyze self by, 222–
        223
    Camus's friendship with, 287, 289–92
    Camus's rift with, 289, 300, 361–62,
        394, 642n
    celebrity of, 274, 280–81, 291, 385
    changes in theory of, 452, 466–67, 515,
        516, 517, 579–81, 582–83, 667n
    changing literary landscape and, 464,
        473
    childhood of, 157, 409
    clothes of, 181, 360, 402, 586
    collaboration with Nazis ascribed to,
        258–60, 275, 295–96, 360, 361
    colonialism and, 412
    in Combat, 293, 294, 295, 641n
    Communist Party's attacks on, 258–59
    competing ideologies and, 318, 573
    compulsory military service of, 146,
        156, 157, 159, 160–61, 165, 168, 172
    daily routine of, 345–46, 404, 444,
        570–71
    death of, 528, 583–86
    death threats against, 482, 483–84, 486,
        487
    demonstrations of affection or emotion
        awkward for, 272–73
    depressions of, 191–92, 562, 566, 567
    disciples of, 185
    drawing of Leibniz given to Beauvoir
        by, 139
    drinking habits of, 460, 461, 485, 558,
        563, 566, 575
    drugs taken by, 191–92, 319, 320, 341,
        392, 460, 466, 473, 485, 494, 666n
    eating habits of, 460
    enemies of, taken on as enemies of
        Beauvoir, 642n–43n
    English not spoken by, 464
    exile considered by, 423–24, 661n
    Existentialism formulated by, 187,
        231–32, 233–34
    finances of, 157, 168, 179–80, 263,
        279, 396, 569, 575, 583, 584
    first place in *agrégation* taken by,
        145–46
    Flaubert as obsession of, 163, 516–17,
        518

foreign women of no appeal to, 202
Françoise and, 149–50, 177, 405, 630n
freedom, concept of, 155, 157–58, 170, 269, 270, 632n, 639n
funeral and burial of, 562, 584, 586–88
generosity of, 179, 394, 396, 441, 656n, 657n
genius of, 143, 269, 516, 629n
Georges and, 149–50, 155, 630n
gossip about, 210–11, 360–61, 381
hallucinations and paranoia of, 494
hands as fascination of, 185, 632n
health problems of, 322, 323, 460, 473, 481, 485, 515, 528–29, 530–31, 534, 536, 540, 541, 542, 544, 558, 559–568, 570–71, 572, 573, 575, 604, 676n
hearing impairment of, 473
Hélène and, 141, 146, 149, 179, 201, 223, 233, 235, 586, 587
homes of, 141–42, 249, 272, 322–23, 414, 483, 486, 487, 495, 559, 560, 566, 588–90, 678n
as hypochondriac, 191
inheritance of, 168, 169, 175, 179
insularity of thinking, 275–76
introspective period of (1950s), 413, 414
L'Invitée and, 206, 207, 228, 229, 230
jealous of Beauvoir's friendships with women students, 200
Lanzmann's relationship with, 444, 665n
Laon teaching post of, 196, 197, 199
Leduc and, 394, 441, 657n
Le Havre teaching post of, 167, 176, 178, 185, 186, 187
Lévi-Strauss's break with, 467–68, 667n
Lévy's published conversations with, 568, 574, 575, 578–81, 582–83, 597
Lévy's relationship with, 559, 561, 567–571, 574–80
literary agents of, 661n
literary circles entered by, 198, 208
literary inheritance of, 496, 499
loss of, dreaded by Beauvoir, 541
The Mandarins and, 427, 428, 449, 450, 662n
Marxism of, 466, 467, 473
May '68 uprising and, 528, 532, 533, 534, 674n
mementos of, in Beauvoir's apartment, 454
Merleau-Ponty's death and, 485–86
music enjoyed by, 360, 413, 414, 508
mystery novels loved by, 393

Nagel and, 349–50, 649n
nervous manner of, 182
Nobel Prize refused by, 493–95, 500
people supported by, 263, 394, 396, 441, 499, 569, 584, 657n, 666n
as perennial adolescent, 235, 442
physical appearance of, 13, 130, 141, 181, 191, 235
Pierre Labrousse character as fictional equivalent of, 228, 230
political activism of, 354, 356–63, 366, 370–71, 372, 394, 399, 400, 412–13, 425, 446–47, 451–52, 472, 473, 474, 476–84, 486, 487, 513, 518, 519–20, 528, 531, 533, 534, 536–39, 548, 562–63, 568, 656n, 658n, 66on
as prisoner of war, 239–40, 244, 245–246, 247, 248
as public speaker, 319, 558
radio broadcasts of, 357–58, 360–61, 363, 366, 650n
in rapprochement with Communists, 447
released from prison camp, 244, 245–246, 258, 259, 260
Resistance and, 247–48, 249, 250–55, 257–58, 260–61, 262, 274–75, 276, 293, 294, 295, 296, 360, 637n–38n, 641n
restless and bored period of (1943), 273, 274–75, 276
Sarraute's relationship with, 298, 314–315
Schweitzer introduced to, 464–65
The Second Sex and, 325, 380
secretaries of, 487, 568, 569–70
shift in political thinking of, 399, 400
sixty-sixth birthday of, 560–61
smoking habits of, 558, 560, 566, 575
at Sorbonne, 127–28, 129–30, 133, 138–39, 140–46, 629n
superficial friendships of, 275
Sylvie's relationship with, 507–8, 517, 535, 565
teaching hated by, 187–88
Les Temps Modernes and, 292, 298–99, 310, 314–15, 318, 410, 442–43, 520, 521–22, 575, 577
transition to manhood difficult for, 188, 192
villification campaigns against, 358, 412–13, 423, 480–81
vision problems of, 473, 558, 564, 565, 566, 573
voice of, 182
voyeurism of, 291

Sartre, Jean-Paul, *cont.*
  wartime military service of, 216–17,
    218, 219, 235, 246–47
  wartime teaching post of, 249
  year spent in Berlin by, 187–88, 189, 191
  younger people befriended by, 264,
    670n
Sartre, Jean-Paul, holidays and travels of,
    535
  in Algiers, 392
  in Antibes, 485–86
  in Basque region, 209, 634n
  in Brazil, 476, 478, 481–82, 495
  canceled skiing trip (1944), 288, 289,
    641n
  in China, 455, 456
  in Cuba, 474, 476, 482, 495
  in Czechoslovakia, 478, 489, 492, 520
  in Egypt, 420, 421, 478, 519, 526,
    661n
  in emerging socialist nations, 473, 474,
    476
  in Free Zone, 255, 257–58, 265–66
  in Israel, 519, 526, 575–77, 677n
  in Japan, 478, 519
  with Lanzmann, 444, 448, 665n
  in London, 349–50, 649n
  in Mexico and Guatemala, 414
  at Mme. Morel's Juan-les-Pins villa,
    215, 216
  in Morocco, 212
  in 1960s, 518–20, 526
  in North Africa, 179, 180, 420, 421,
    661n
  at La Pouèze, 266–67, 270, 271, 277,
    282, 283, 294, 297, 304, 357, 363,
    366, 367, 424, 425
  in Ramateulle, 373, 374
  reliance on Beauvoir in, 414, 476–77,
    519
  in Rome, 196, 410, 486, 488, 489, 492,
    535, 561–62, 563–64, 565, 568, 573,
    578, 594
  in Saint-Rémy-les-Chevreuse, 344–45
  South American lecture tour, 372
  in Soviet Union, 461, 478, 488–89,
    492, 518, 526
  in Spain, 175–76, 179, 180, 181
  in Sweden, 347, 351, 519
  in Switzerland, 323
  in United States, 299, 300, 301, 303,
    311–12, 313, 317, 319, 320, 321, 322
  in Yugoslavia, 476–77, 478, 520
Sartre, Jean-Paul, romances and
    liaisons of:
  with American girl, 545, 675n

  with Arlette, 461–62, 479, 485, 495–
    496, 559, 561
  Arlette's adoption and, 497–98
  avoidance of conflict in, 515, 517, 561
  Beauvoir and Sartre's annual holidays
    and, 485
  Beauvoir as "heavy" in, 211, 214, 235,
    559
  Beauvoir's complicity and confidante
    role in, 163, 165, 171, 193, 202,
    210–11, 214, 399
  with Beauvoir's students, 202, 208,
    214–15
  with Bianca, 208, 214, 215
  in Brazil, 481, 482, 485
  dividing of time among, 404, 499, 507,
    566
  with Dolores, 300, 301, 302–4, 309,
    310, 313, 319, 321, 322, 328, 340,
    342–44, 345, 371, 372, 397, 414,
    644n, 648n
  with Evelyne Ray, 462–63, 479, 481,
    486
  with GéGé Pardo, 202
  with Hélène Lassithiotakis, 566, 575
  with intelligent women, Beauvoir's
    opposition to, 315
  with Lena Zonina, 461, 518
  with Michelle Vian, 316, 344, 345, 401,
    404, 461, 479, 481, 486, 497, 575,
    644n
  and mistresses' friendliness toward
    Beauvoir, 303
  with Mme. Morel, 139, 160
  with Natasha Moffatt, 214, 215, 248–
    249
  and near-celibate period during World
    War II, 262
  with Olga Bost, 187, 189–95, 199, 200,
    208, 210, 214, 249, 303, 309
  openness about, 302
  with Simone Jollivet, 162–64
  with Wanda Bost, 202, 208, 210, 225,
    227, 234–35, 272, 273, 289, 303, 344,
    345, 349, 404, 463, 479, 481, 486
Sartre, Jean-Paul, writings of, 155, 168,
    173, 174, 178, 191, 198, 209, 211,
    320, 361, 451, 573, 648n
  acclaim of, 208
  Beauvoir as primary critic and editor
    of, 203, 207, 228, 233, 251, 262,
    269, 372, 404, 448, 466, 474, 515,
    567, 578
  Beauvoir's competition with, 386–87
  in conceptualization of Beauvoir's
    memoirs, 466–67

Lévy's usurpation of Beauvoir's role in, 578
manuscripts of, 589
notes toward philosophical treatise on morals, 413, 600, 660n
prolific output of, 657n–58n
Sartre-Lévy articles, 576–77, 578–81, 582–83
Sartre's new theory of prose and, 466–467, 667n
screenplays, 277, 347–48, 350, 392, 396–97, 656n
unpublished manuscripts, 597–602
vision loss and, 564
during World War II, 219, 222, 227–228, 231–32, 233, 234, 235, 240, 246, 262, 267, 269, 630n
see also specific works
"Sartrian ideal," 515–16, 672n
"Sartrians," 574
Saturday Review of Literature, 438, 664n
Schlafly, Phyllis, 610
Schlesinger, Tess, 388
Schoenberg, Arnold, 360, 461
Schoenmann, Ralph, 569–70, 575
Schwartzer, Alice, 478, 510–11, 573
Schweitzer, Albert, 464–65
Scipion, Lisa, 401
Scipion, Robert, 401
Search for a Method, The (Sartre), 513
Second Sex, The (Le Deuxième Sexe) (Beauvoir), 11, 13, 270, 379–94, 411, 413, 416, 442, 447, 452, 467, 468, 504, 505, 518, 525, 528, 532, 540, 543, 544–45, 608, 623n, 639n, 645n, 646n, 647n
Algren and, 353, 364, 366, 385–86, 388, 389, 395, 407–9, 410, 439
American slant to, 388
Americans' letters in response to, 439, 664n
anthropology and psychology in, 390, 392, 655n
Audry's project for book on women and, 325, 379–80, 652n
authors discussed in, 387, 393–94
autobiographical basis for, 380, 381, 385, 386, 387, 451, 653n–54n
banned by Catholic Church, 456–57, 666n
Beauvoir's desire to make money from, 392
Beauvoir's separation from women in, 383–84
and comparisons of blacks to women, 388–89

critical response to, 383–84, 386, 387–388, 391–92, 409, 437–39, 653n–654n, 655n, 660n
and differences between American and French women, 382, 384
Existentialism and, 380, 381, 382, 385, 386, 390, 432, 433–34, 436, 549
feminism and, 390–91, 478–79, 554, 654n
film based on, 609, 610–11, 679n
focus of, 390–91
genesis of, 325, 361, 366, 367, 368, 380–83, 384–85
interviews with women and, 382–83, 384, 652n–53n
models for opinions about marriage in, 338, 389
otherness concept in, 389, 438–39, 549, 655n
outline for, 368, 651n
Parshley translation of, 432–37, 653n, 654n, 663n
philosophical terminology in, 433–34, 436, 663n
publication of, 404
research for, 364, 367, 374, 386, 387, 389–90
sales of, 407, 417, 438, 439, 457, 652n
scientific methodology in, 391–92
as "secret code" of emerging women's movement, 478–79
structure of, 387
supporters of, 417–18
title of, 389, 409
unpleasant incidents relating to, 395, 407–8, 409–10, 417, 658n
U.S. publication of, 432–39, 663n–664n
writing of, 325, 347, 363–64, 371–72, 380, 391, 392, 393, 395, 396, 399, 654n, 656n
Second Stage, The (Friedan), 556, 609
Ségur, Madame de, 36
Seiver, Edith, 331, 332
Seiver, George, 331, 332–33
Seiver, Lawrence M., 331, 332, 333
Semlier, Robert, 502
Sermadira, Louise, 29, 30, 33, 34, 36, 37, 38, 40, 48, 49, 51, 52, 68, 620n
Beauvoirs' employ left by, 53
son's death and, 73, 74
Seven Pillars of Wisdom (Lawrence), 266, 639n, 656n
Sèvres, elite training school at, 91–92, 93, 94, 280, 503, 626n
"Sexisme ordinaire" column, 550

Sexual Behavior in the Human Male
    (Kinsey), 393, 656*n*
Sexual Politics (Millett), 654*n*
Sexual Response in Women (Kronhausen
    and Kronhausen), 493
Shakespeare, William, 484
Shakespeare and Company Bookstore,
    198–99
She Came to Stay (Beauvoir) *see
    Invitée, L'*
Shoah, 442, 612–13
Siegel, Liliane Sendyk, 539
    Lévy and, 569, 570
    Sartre's declining health and, 560, 566,
        567–68
Silone, Darina, 464
Silone, Ignazio, 389, 416, 464
Simon, Claude, 464
"Simone's book," 68
Simons, Margaret A., 551, 663*n*
Sismondi, Jean, 267–68, 309
Skira, 323
Slansky, Rudolf, 446, 665*n*
Smith, Bonnie G., 622*n*–23*n*
Smith, Joseph, 393
Smith, Stevie, 438
Smith College, 326, 330, 432, 437
Social Contract, The (Rousseau), 143
socialism, 358, 546–47, 553, 602, 675*n*
Socialism and Liberty (Socialisme et
    Liberté), 250–53, 254–55
    actions of, 250–52
    Beauvoir and Sartre's trip to Free
        Zone for, 255, 257–58
    disintegration of, 258
    formation of, 250
    ideological squabbles in, 252
    leader of, 252–53
    manifestos of, 253, 255
Soir, Le, 310
Soldier's Pay (Faulkner), 164
Solzhenitsyn, Aleksandr, 488
Somebody in Boots (Algren), 335, 336
Sonning Prize for European Culture, 606,
    679*n*
Sontag, Susan, 610
Sorbonne, 92, 115, 116, 197, 226, 236
    Beauvoir as student at, 100, 110, 120,
        121–30, 131, 135, 138–39, 140–46,
        368–69, 628*n*
    Beauvoir's definition of success at, 123
    Beauvoir's friends at, 124–26, 127–30
    Beauvoir's obsessive behavior at, 122–23
    Beauvoir's social awkwardness at, 123,
        127
    Beauvoir's thesis project at, 139, 628*n*

day-long study sessions at, 141–43, 144
    examinations at, 138, 139, 140, 141–
        143, 144, 145–46, 629*n*
    May '68 uprising at, 532–35, 536
    program accelerated by Beauvoir at,
        121, 122, 131
    Sartre's circle at, 127–30, 133, 138–39,
        140–46, 629*n*
Sorokine, Nathalie (mother), 236, 277–
    278, 504
Sorokine, Nathalie (Natasha), *see*
    Moffatt, Nathalie
Sorokine, Porfiry, 236, 278
Soupault, Philippe, 323, 326
Sous la Botte, 251, 252
South America, Sartre and Camus's
    lecture tour in (1948), 372
Soviet Union, 220, 370, 399, 400, 513,
    550, 656*n*
    Beauvoir and Sartre's trips to, 461, 478,
        488–89, 492, 518, 526
    France's postwar stance toward, 356,
        357, 358
    Korean War and, 422, 423, 424
    Nazi pact with, 243, 248
Soviet Writers' Union, 488
Spain:
    Beauvoir and Algren's holiday in
        (1960), 476
    Beauvoir and Sartre's holiday in
        (1931), 175–76
    Beauvoir and Sartre's holiday in
        (1932), 179, 180, 181
Spanish Civil War, 208–9
Spanish Testament, The (Koestler), 361
Spearman, Neville, 471
Spinoza, Baruch, 271
Stagecoach, 216, 217
Stalag XII-D, 240
Stalin, Joseph, 329
Stalinism, 467
Stanford University, 614–15
State Department, U.S., 299
Stavisky, Serge, 184
Steinbeck, John, 348
Steiner, Jean-Françoise, 493
Stendhal (Marie-Henri Beyle), 387, 393–
    394, 656*n*
Stephens, James, 164
Stevens, George, 313, 337, 338, 647*n*
Strauss, Harold, 437
Streetcar Named Desire, A (Williams),
    377
"Strictly Personal" (Beauvoir), 297
Structuralism, 464, 467, 473, 522, 667*n*,
    672*n*

Structures de la parenté, Les (Lévi-Strauss), 390, 655*n*
Studs Lonigan (Farrell), 650*n*
"Suite" (Beckett), 346
Superman, 365
surrealism, 284, 291, 293–94
Sutton, Nina, 539–40
Sweden, 519
  Beauvoir and Sartre's holiday in
    (1947), 347, 351–52, 353
Sweet Briar College, 384
Switzerland, Beauvoir and Sartre's trip
    to (1946), 323
Synge, John, 164
Syria, 550

Tabou, 360
Targ, William, 626*n*
Tauchnitz, 66, 454
Tel Quel, 464, 667*n*
Temps Modernes, Les, 16, 297, 311, 313,
    316, 325, 337, 345, 355, 392, 394,
    409, 410, 413, 423, 445, 446, 473,
    479, 492, 493, 498, 516, 520–22,
    545, 572, 574, 581, 593, 598, 611–
    612, 615, 642*n*, 665*n*
  Algerian crisis and, 452, 477, 480, 482
  Algren's writings translated for, 348,
    363, 401, 648*n*, 650*n*–51*n*, 657*n*
  America Day by Day extracted in, 334,
    362, 385
  Beauvoir and Sartre's division of labor
    at, 514
  Beauvoir as only consistent element at,
    520–21
  Beauvoir's articles for, 318, 320–21,
    353, 363, 380, 430, 452, 644*n*, 646*n*,
    647*n*–48*n*
  Beauvoir's responsibilities at, 346, 347,
    362, 395, 404
  cover design for, 299
  day-to-day operations of, taken over by
    Merleau-Ponty, 362
  decline in influence of, 520, 521
  editorial board of, 298–99, 442–43,
    444, 520, 521–22, 672*n*
  first issue of, 298, 299, 310
  Gallimard's withdrawal from, 395
  issue dedicated "To Dolores," 310
  Lévy and, 575, 577, 583, 678*n*
  literary works submitted to, 346,
    648*n*–49*n*
  manifesto of, 298, 310
  Marxism and, 301
  Merleau-Ponty's departure from, 452

  radio broadcasts of, 357–58, 360–61,
    363, 366, 650*n*
  Sarraute and, 314–15
  Sartre and Camus's plans for, 292
  The Second Sex excerpted in, 381, 407
  "Le Sexisme ordinaire" column in, 550
  younger leadership at, 521–22, 672*n*
Tender Is the Night (Fitzgerald), 352
Terkel, Studs, 491
TF 1, 610
Thatcher, Margaret, 555
Théâtre des Carrefours, 310
Theatre Guild, 377
"third option," 357, 372
Third World, 399–400
Thomas, Dylan, 465
Thomas Aquinas, Saint, 91, 125
Thoreau, Henry David, 365, 623*n*
Thorez, Maurice, 446, 656*n*
"Thought of the Right Today, The"
    (Beauvoir), 452, 453, 545, 633*n*
Tillon, Charles, 446, 665*n*
Time, 352, 439
Times (London), 502
Tito, Marshal (Josip Broz), 476
Tobacco Road (Caldwell), 651*n*
Todd, Olivier, 678*n*
Töpffer, Rodolphe, 188
torture, in Algerian crisis, 468, 478, 480,
    487–88
Tous les hommes sont mortels (Beau-
    voir), *see All Men Are Mortal*
Tout, 537
Toute compte fait (Beauvoir), *see All
    Said and Done*
Transcendentalists, 623*n*
Treblinka (Steiner), 493
Tree, Iris, 337
Treich, Léon, 311
"Tribune des *Temps Modernes*, La,"
    357–58, 360–61, 363, 366, 650*n*
"trickle-down" theory, 646*n*
Trilling, Diana, 332
Triolet, Elsa, 464
"Les Troit Mousquetaires," 629*n*
Tropisms (Sarraute), 315
Trouble in July (Caldwell), 651*n*
Truffaut, François, 668*n*
Truman, Harry S., 446
Tunis, Beauvoir's lecture tour to (1946),
    317
Turn of the Screw, The (James), 650*n*
Twain, Mark (Samuel Clemens), 472
Twice a Year, 647*n*–48*n*

UNESCO, 505, 572

Ungaretti, Giuseppe, 464
United Nations (UN), 394
United States, 370, 399, 400, 424, 656n
  anti-Communist hysteria in, 446
  Beauvoir's attitude toward, 605
  Beauvoir's interest in politics and
    culture of, 545
  civil rights movement in, 545
  clothing in, 646n–47n
  education in, 331, 646n
  France's postwar stance toward, 356,
    357, 358
  Korean War and, 422, 423
  Sartre's first trip to (1945), 299, 300,
    301, 303
  Sartre's second trip to (1945–46), 311–
    312, 313, 317, 319, 320, 321, 322
  Vietnam and, 519–20, 513, 534
  women in, 339–40, 353, 382, 384,
    646n–47n
  women's movement in, 525–26, 545
United States, Beauvoir's trips to:
  in April 1947, 323, 326, 327–41, 360,
    382, 384, 645n–46n
  in Sept. 1947, 351, 352–53, 355
  in 1948, 371, 372, 373, 374–78, 651n
  in 1950, 415, 416, 419–20, 421–23
  in 1951, 429–30, 432
  in 1983, 602, 604, 605–9
  account of, see America Day by Day
  lectures at college campuses in, 326,
    330, 645n–46n
  visa problem and, 430
University of Pennsylvania, 326, 331
Useless Mouths (Les Bouches inutiles)
  (Beauvoir), 266–69, 297, 309–10,
    317, 320, 636n, 638n–39n, 643n
  assessment of, 268
  critical responses to, 311
  destruction of manuscript, 267
  Existentialism and, 267–68
  staging of, 301, 302, 310–11
  subject of, 267
utopianism, 546

Valéry, Paul, 102
Valley Forge, Beauvoir's visit to (1947),
  332–33
Vassar College, 326, 331, 384
Vatican, Beauvoir's book banned by,
  456–57, 666n
Venice, Beauvoir and Sartre's holiday in
  (1972), 564–65
Verne, Jules, 44, 66
Verny, Françoise, 610

Very Easy Death, A (Beauvoir), 490, 492,
  506, 596, 644n, 678n
Vian, Boris, 316, 324, 402, 406, 445,
  472–73, 644n
Vian, Michelle (née L'Eglise), 428, 445,
  448, 465, 472, 476, 537, 562, 612
  Algren and, 401, 406, 407, 648n
  Arlette's adoption and, 497
  English translations by, 345, 401, 648n
  financial support of, 584, 657n
  marital discord of, 402
  Sartre's affair with, 316, 344, 345, 401,
    404, 461, 479, 481, 486, 497, 575,
    644n
  Sartre's declining health and, 460, 531,
    566, 567–68, 575
Victor, Pierre, see Lévy, Benny
Victors, The (Sartre), 319, 644n–45n
Vieillesse, La (Beauvoir), see Old Age
Vienna Peace Congress (1953), 446
Vietnam War, 478, 513, 519–20, 534
  Russell Tribunal and, 478, 519, 520,
    526, 531, 546, 569–70, 670n
Ville, Marie, 202
Vitold, Michel, 301–2, 311
Voltaire (François-Marie Arouet), 270–71
Volonté, 300–301
Vonnegut, Kurt, 502
Voyage au bout de la nuit (Céline), 205
"Voyage de Monsieur Perrichon, Le," 65

Wahl (examination jury member), 145
Wahl, Jean, 418
Walberg, Patrick, 295
Walden (Thoreau), 365
Walker, Alice, 609
Wall, The (La Mur) (Sartre), 208
Wallace, Henry, 406
Walpole, Horace, 441
War Diaries: Notebooks from a Phoney
  War (Les Carnets de la drole de
  guerre) (Sartre), 155, 189, 219, 222,
  599, 600, 630n, 634n
Wartelle, Léontine Algaë-Mathilde
  (grandmother), 23–24, 25, 26, 31,
  33
Washington, George, 332–33
Wayne, John, 216
"Way to Médenine, The" (Algren), 652n
Weatherby, W. J., 502
Weil, Simone, 120, 122, 124
Weil-Hallé, Marie-Andrée L., 480
Wellesley College, 326
Wenck, Helen P., 520, 528, 545, 562,
  597, 611, 612, 624n
West, Anthony, 307, 309

Wharton, Edith, 365
What Maisie Knew (James), 650n
What the Negro Wants, 368
*When Things of the Spirit Come First
    (Quand prime le spirituel)* (Beau-
    voir), 107–8, 183, 228, 204–6
    "Anne" in, 195, 205, 624n–25n, 634n
    "Chantal" in, 195, 205, 624n, 633n
    "Lisa" in, 192, 195, 205, 633n–34n
    "Marcelle" in, 195, 205, 633n
    "Marguerite" in, 195, 205, 634n, 678n
    order of stories in, 633n–34n
    publisher sought for, 206, 207–8, 209,
        634n
    Sartre's praise for, 206
    subject matter of, 204–5
    title of, 633n
"Which President for Women?" forum,
    602, 679n
Whitmarsh, Anne, 669n
Wild Palms, The (Faulkner), 393
Wittig, Monique, 551, 675n
Wolfe, Bernard, 465, 658n
*Woman Destroyed, The (La Femme
    rompue)* (Beauvoir), 426, 498, 526–
    528, 530, 671n, 673n
    critical response to, 526, 527–28
    Hélène's illustrations for, 492
    women's response to, 526, 527
    writing of, 526
"Woman Destroyed, The" ("La Femme
    rompue") (Beauvoir), 526, 527
women:
    American, Beauvoir's views on, 339–
        340, 353, 382, 384, 646n–47n
    blacks compared to, 388–89
    concerns of, in first volume of memoirs,
        324
    earnings of, 112, 626n–27n
    education of, 88–89, 625n
    exhorted "to cultivate the man," 104,
        137, 626n
    French, suffrage of, 347, 353, 654n
    male colleagues' attitudes toward,
        136–37, 629n
    role in history of, 389, 390, 655n
    sexual equality and, 415–16
    see also feminism; *Second Sex, The*
Women in Love (Lawrence), 512, 671n
"Women Listen to Each Other," 572
Woolf, Virginia, 390, 555, 655n
Woolfert, Ira, 329
Words, The (Les Mots) (Sartre), 235,
    451, 466, 469, 517, 573
World War I, 46–51, 217, 220
    Beauvoirs' finances in, 47, 50–51

Georges's military service in, 47
shelling of Paris in, 48–49, 622n
World War II, 215–96, 316, 483
    anti-Jewish measures in, 242, 296,
        636n–37n, 642n
    Beauvoir and Sartre's correspondence
        in, 218–27, 231, 233, 234–36, 238,
        239–40, 244, 245, 246, 247, 636n
    Beauvoir and Sartre's trips to Free
        Zone in, 255, 257–58, 265–66
    Beauvoir changed by, 212, 215
    Beauvoir's attempt at understanding of,
        220–21
    Beauvoir's clandestine visit to Sartre
        in, 221–22
    Beauvoir's diaries in, 219–20, 222–23,
        634n
    Beauvoir's flight from Paris in, 235,
        237–38
    Beauvoir's happiness during, 260–61
    Beauvoir's lack of action in, 243–44,
        247–48
    Beauvoir's need to be with Sartre in,
        221
    Beauvoir's radio job in, 279–80, 282,
        284, 296, 640n
    Beauvoir's teaching assignments in,
        224, 238, 242–43, 262–63, 277–79
    Beauvoir's writings during, 228–34,
        240, 241–42, 262, 266–71, 273, 277,
        283, 284, 293–94
    black market in, 247, 256, 265
    collaboration ascribed to Beauvoir in,
        241–42, 260, 295–96
    collaboration ascribed to Sartre in,
        258–60, 275, 295–96, 360, 361
    daily life in, 218, 224, 238, 240–41,
        248, 249, 264, 293–94, 636n
    Dullin's prediction about duration of,
        220
    events leading to, 212, 213, 216
    fall of Paris in, 237
    Family in, 224–26, 227, 237, 247, 272,
        273, 275, 278, 279, 284
    food rationing and shortages in, 238,
        240, 256, 263, 264, 265, 636n
    invasion of Western Europe in, 234,
        235
    Liberation in, 293–94, 295, 338, 363,
        407, 641n
    literary censorship in, 296, 642n
    oaths required of teachers in, 242–43,
        247
    outbreak of, 218
    promise of future in, 262
    propaganda in, 224

World War II, *cont.*
   Resistance in, *see* Resistance;
      Socialism and Liberty
   Sartre as prisoner of war in, 239–40,
      244, 245–46, 247, 248
   Sartre's leaves in Paris during, 225,
      227, 233
   Sartre's military service in, 216–17,
      218, 219, 235, 246–47
   Sartre's release in, 244, 245–46, 258,
      259, 260
   Sartre's writings during, 219, 222,
      227–28, 231–32, 233, 234, 235, 240,
      246, 262, 267, 269, 630n
   surrender of France in, 239
   transportation difficulties in, 281, 289
Wright, Ellen, 370, 388–89, 463, 667n
   Algren's affair with, 463
   Beauvoir's visit in New York with, 329,
      338, 339, 340
   as literary agent, 389, 418, 661n
   marital problems of, 389, 425, 662n
Wright, Julia, 338
Wright, Richard, 370, 371, 374, 388–89,
      412, 413, 647n

   Beauvoir's visit in New York with, 329,
      338–39, 340
   exile plans and, 424
   marital problems of, 389, 425, 662n
   as speaker at RDF meeting, 394, 656n
Wyler, William, 337
Wylie, Philip, 438, 655n

Yale University, 326
Yama (Kuprin), 649n
Yugoslavia, Beauvoir and Sartre's trips
      to, 478
   in 1960, 476–77
   in 1968, 520
Yugoslavian Writers' Union, 476

Zadkine, Ossip, 275
Zazou, 316
Zeldin, Theodore, 620n, 621n
Zéphir, Jacques J., 674n–75n
Zonina, Lena, 461, 489, 518, 666n–67n,
      672n
Zuore, Marc, 185, 189, 192, 198, 199, 203

About the author

DEIRDRE BAIR won the National Book Award for her *Samuel Beckett* in 1981.
She has been a literary journalist as well as a university professor for twelve years.
For her work on Simone de Beauvoir, she was awarded fellowships from the
Guggenheim Foundation, the Rockefeller Foundation, and the Mary Ingraham
Bunting Institute of Radcliffe College.